ADVANCED

ACCOUNTING

ADVANCED ACCOUNTING

DEBRA C. JETER, PhD, CPA

Owen Graduate School of Management
Vanderbilt University

PAUL K. CHANEY, PhD, CPA, CMA

Owen Graduate School of Management
Vanderbilt University

John Wiley & Sons. Inc.

New York ■ Chichester ■ Weinheim ■ Toronto ■ Brisbane ■ Singapore

PUBLISHER	Susan Elbe
ACQUISITIONS EDITOR	Mark Bonadeo
MARKETING MANAGER	Ilse Wolfe
PRODUCTION SERVICES MANAGER	Jeanine Furino
TEXT DESIGNER	Lee Goldstein
COVER DESIGNER	Madelyn Lesure
COVER PHOTO	© David Muench Photography
PRODUCTION MANAGEMENT SERVICES	Ingrao Associates

This book was set in ITC New Baskerville by UG/GGS Information Services, Inc. and printed and bound by R.R. Donnelley & Sons. The cover was printed by Phoenix Color Corp.

This book is printed on acid-free paper.

Library of Congress Cataloging in Publication Data:
Jeter, Debra C. (Debra Coleman).
   Advanced accounting/Debra Jeter, Paul Chaney, Andrew Haried.—1st ed.
     p. cm.
   Previous ed. entered under Andrew Haried.
   Includes bibliographical references.
   ISBN 0-471-17397-5 (cloth alk. paper)
   1. Accounting.   I. Chaney, Paul K. (Paul Kent), 1953–   II. Haried, Andrew A.

HF5635.H256 2000
657'.046—dc21   99-058147

Printed in the United States of America

10 9 8 7 6 5 4 3 2

PREFACE

This book is designed for advanced courses dealing with financial accounting and reporting in the following topical areas: business combinations, consolidated financial statements, international accounting, foreign currency transactions, accounting for derivative instruments, translation of financial statements of foreign affiliates, segment reporting and interim reporting, partnerships, fund accounting and accounting for governmental units, and accounting for nongovernment nonbusiness organizations. The primary objective of this book is to provide a comprehensive treatment of selected topics in a clear and understandable manner. An important consideration in this revision was to provide maximum flexibility to the instructor in the selection and breadth of coverage for topics dealing with consolidated financial statements.

Like the previous edition, we assign certain topics to separate chapters or self-contained units that may be omitted or included as desired:

- Pooling of interests method of accounting for investments in subsidiaries
- Deferred income tax consequences relating to undistributed subsidiary income and unrealized intercompany profit, as well as to differences between the assigned values and tax bases of assets and liabilities of an acquired company (now in appendices to various chapters)
- Accounting for indirect ownership and reciprocal stockholdings
- The effects of alternative concepts of consolidation, such as the parent company and the entity concepts

All chapters have been updated where appropriate to reflect the most recent pronouncements of the Financial Accounting Standards Board and the Governmental Accounting Standards Board. In addition, all chapters have been thoroughly edited to assure accuracy, clarity, and consistency throughout the text.

In teaching consolidation concepts, a decision must be made about the recording method that should be emphasized in presenting consolidated workpaper procedures. The three major alternatives for recording investments in subsidiaries are the (1) cost method, (2) partial equity (or simple equity) method, and (3) complete equity (or sophisticated equity) method. A brief description of each method follows:

1. *Cost method.* The investment in subsidiary is carried at its cost, with no adjustments made to the investment account for subsidiary income or dividends. Dividends received by the parent company are recorded as an increase in cash and as dividend income.

2. *Partial Equity method.* The investment account is adjusted for the parent company's share of the subsidiary's reported earnings or losses, and dividends received from the subsidiary are deducted from the investment account. Generally, no other adjustments are made to the investment in subsidiary account.

3. *Complete Equity method.* This method is the same as the partial equity method except that additional adjustments are made to the investment in subsidiary account to reflect the effects of (a) elimination of unrealized intercompany profits, (b) amortization (depreciation) of the difference between cost and book value, and (c) the additional stockholders' equity transactions undertaken by the subsidiary that change the parent company's share of the subsidiary's stockholders' equity.

We have elected to present all three methods, using blue and gray tabs to distinguish among the three. The instructor has the flexibility to teach all three methods, or to instruct the students to ignore one or two. If the student is interested in learning all three methods, he or she may do so, even if the instructor only focuses on one or two. Also, we believe this feature makes the book an excellent reference for the student to keep after graduation, so that he or she can adapt to any method needed.

Our decision to include all three methods was influenced in part by surveys of practitioners and professors. In a survey of corporate controllers of *Fortune 500* companies who were asked to indicate the method used on their books for investments in subsidiaries that are consolidated, more than 71 percent indicated that they used the cost method. In contrast, in surveys of professors teaching advanced accounting courses, the most popular method was either the partial or complete equity method.

We next review some of the changes in the new edition, as well as the similarities to the previous edition.

What's New?

1. As mentioned previously, we integrate the complete equity method throughout the consolidation chapters rather than deferring it to Chapter 12, as in the previous edition. Surveys indicated that the majority of those participating preferred this approach (integration). We provide a more thorough discussion at the beginning of Chapter 4 (previously Chapter 3) on the three methods of accounting for investments, and the importance of the complete equity method for certain investments that are not consolidated, or in the parent-only statements.

2. We added learning objectives and end-of-chapter summaries to each chapter and a glossary of terms at the back of the book.

3. We added a new chapter (Chapter 12) on issues in international accounting.

4. We updated Chapter 13 to include a discussion of *SFAS No. 133.*

5. We introduced ''In the News'' boxes based on real-world examples throughout the text to enliven the reader's perspective on the material. We hope to include more in the next edition.

6. To distinguish among parent company entries, subsidiary entries, and workpaper entries, we presented parent entries in gray, subsidiary entries in white, and workpaper entries in blue.

7. We divided Chapter 1 (from the previous edition) into two chapters because there was a wealth of information here. Much of the information in the first chapter is now qualitative rather than quantitative, but lends itself to interesting classroom discussion. A number of ''In the News'' stories are included in the first chapter.

8. We moved the information on deferred taxes from Chapter 7 into various appendices throughout the earlier chapters. If the instructor wishes to address tax aspects in each chapter, the information is available. These might be deleted altogether, presented in one class period after Chapter 6 or 7, or integrated throughout the course, at the instructor's discretion.

9. We changed the ''analytical calculation'' of consolidated net income to a t-account approach that, we believe, is easier for the instructor to present and the student to comprehend, while accomplishing the same objective.

10. We updated sections for new FASB pronouncements and proposals, making it clear that proposals are not yet approved. For example, in Chapter 3, we include the following:

In October 1995, the FASB issued an Exposure Draft *broadening* the definition of control to include an indirect ability to control another entity's assets. In February 1999, the FASB issued a revised Exposure Draft, focusing on another entity's *policies and management* rather than its assets.

11. Chapters 18 through 20 on fund accounting have been updated for major changes resulting from new standards issued by the FASB and the GASB.

12. We continue, as in the previous edition, to introduce the chapter on ''consolidated statements after acquisition'' with the difference between cost and book value being allocated to land only. Surveys indicated that the majority of those participating preferred this approach (land only at this point). But we tried to *make the reason for this assumption clearer* by inserting the following statements in Chapter 4 (previously Chapter 3):

Throughout this chapter, any difference between the cost of the investment and the book value of the equity interest acquired is assumed to relate to the under- or overvaluation of subsidiary land and is, therefore, assigned to land in the second eliminating entry. Because land is subject to neither depreciation nor amortization, this serves to defer at least one complication to the next chapter. More realistic assumptions, and the resulting complications, will be dealt with fully in Chapter 5.

13. Throughout the consolidation chapters and particularly in Chapter 5, when the more realistic assumptions are made, we use a *Computation and Allocation Schedule* to indicate how the difference between purchase price and the book value of the underlying equity acquired is handled. The information in this schedule is useful in preparing the eliminating entries and also serves to satisfy the new disclosure requirements that have been proposed in place of the previous pro forma disclosures.

Among the features unchanged from the previous edition are the following:

1. The organization of the workpapers, using a format that separates accounts to the income statement, the statement of retained earnings, and the balance sheet

in distinct sections. Also, the placement of the workpapers near the relevant text is important to readers.

2. A section added to Chapter 5 (previously Chapter 4) treating the allocation of the difference between cost and book value to assets when they have a fair value less than book value and to liabilities when they have a fair value greater than book value.

3. A revised section treating intercompany sales of nondepreciable assets placed at the beginning of Chapter 7 (previously Chapter 6), and a section treating intercompany interest, rents, and service fees added to Chapter 7.

4. Discussion of the pooling of interests method of recording and consolidating stock acquisitions presented in a separate section in Chapter 11.

5. All illustrations are printed upright on the page and labeled clearly for convenient study and reference.

6. Entries made on consolidated statements workpapers are also presented in general journal form, and are shaded (now in blue) to distinguish them from book entries, to facilitate exposition and study.

Clearly there are more topics in this text than can be covered adequately in a one-semester or one-quarter course. We believe that it is generally better for both students and instructors to cover a selected number of topics in depth rather than to undertake a superficial coverage of a larger number of topics. Modules of material that an instructor may consider for exclusion in any one semester or quarter include the following:

- *Chapters 7 to 11.* An expanded analysis of problems in the preparation of consolidated financial statements.
- *Chapters 12 to 15.* International accounting, foreign currency transactions and translation, and segment and interim reporting.
- *Chapters 16 and 17.* Partnership accounting.
- *Chapters 18 through 20.* Fund accounting, accounting for governmental units, and accounting for nongovernment nonbusiness organizations (NNOs).

The text is also accompanied by a full range of teaching and learning supplements, most of which are available on the World Wide Web at the following address: http://www.wiley.com/college/jeter. Available supplements include:

- Web site
- Instructor's Manual and Solutions Manual
- Test Bank
- Checklist of Key Figures
- Study Guide
- PowerPoint
- Computer Worksheets

1. An instructor's manual that contains solutions (including computations) to all questions, exercises, and problems in a format suitable for the preparation of transparencies.

2. A comprehensive study guide that contains chapter synopses as well as exercises and problems, including solutions.

3. Two supplements designed to eliminate repetitive procedures in the preparation of solutions to problems requiring consolidated workpapers.

Computer Workpapers: Excel templates for each consolidated statements workpaper problem in the end-of-chapter material. This supplement makes it possible for the student to transfer a partially completed workpaper for any problem selected from the disk to a spreadsheet program that accepts spreadsheet files. After the student enters on the computer the appropriate adjusting and eliminating entries and the amount of noncontrolling interest in combined income, the consolidated statements workpaper is completed automatically and may be printed out.

For Manual Use: A set of partially completed workpapers with preprinted column and side headings and parent and subsidiary account balances.

4. A list of check figures.
5. A computerized test manual containing an expanded number and variety of examination question and problems for each chapter.

In closing, we thank the previous authors of this textbook (Andrew Haried, Leroy Imdieke, and Ralph Smith) for providing us with a great source of clear illustrations and excellent material in general. We also thank the following individuals for their assistance and suggestions in the preparation of this book: Sheila Reed, Travis Armayor, Fang Chen, Dmitriy Klimovskiy, Cindy Lampert, Jenny Meyers, Mike Ryan, Xia Sheng, Chip Wasson, Nancy Wang, Brad Yang, Hua Yu, Phillip Korb (UBaltimore); Vicki Rymer (UMaryland); Reg Rezac (Texas Woman's University); Dave Nichols (UMississippi); Tim Thompson (UCLA Extension); Hannah Wong (Rutgers University); J. Scott Whisenant (Georgetown University); Doug Heerema (Indiana University-Indianapolis); Christie Johnson (Montana State); Phillip Buchanan (George Mason University); Farah DeRouck (KPMG-Nashville, TN); Dan Stone (University of Illinois); Gordon Ndubizu (Drexel University); Kirk Philipich (Vanderbilt University); Robert Spencer; Betty Price; and for his support throughout the process, Debra's husband Norman Jeter.

Suggestions and comments from readers are appreciated.

Nashville, Tennessee
February 2000

Debra C. Jeter
Paul K. Chaney

BRIEF CONTENTS

CONTENTS

5 ALLOCATION, DEPRECIATION, AND AMORTIZATION OF THE DIFFERENCE BETWEEN COST AND BOOK VALUE   192

6 ELIMINATION OF UNREALIZED PROFIT ON INTERCOMPANY SALES OF INVENTORY   270

7 ELIMINATION OF UNREALIZED GAINS OR LOSSES ON INTERCOMPANY SALES OF PROPERTY AND EQUIPMENT   327

8 CHANGES IN OWNERSHIP INTEREST   384

9 INDIRECT OWNERSHIP AND RECIPROCAL STOCKHOLDINGS 419

10 INTERCOMPANY BOND HOLDINGS AND MISCELLANEOUS TOPICS—CONSOLIDATED FINANCIAL STATEMENTS 456

II ACCOUNTING IN THE INTERNATIONAL MARKETPLACE

III PARTNERSHIP ACCOUNTING

17 PARTNERSHIP LIQUIDATION 737

IV FUND AND NONPROFIT ACCOUNTING

18 INTRODUCTION TO FUND ACCOUNTING 767

19 INTRODUCTION TO ACCOUNTING FOR STATE AND LOCAL GOVERNMENTAL UNITS   **811**

20 ACCOUNTING FOR NONGOVERNMENT NONBUSINESS ORGANIZATIONS: COLLEGES AND UNIVERSITIES, HOSPITALS AND OTHER HEALTHCARE ORGANIZATIONS   **887**

1

INTRODUCTION TO BUSINESS COMBINATIONS

LEARNING OBJECTIVES

1. Describe historical trends in types of business combinations.
2. Identify the major reasons firms combine.
3. Identify the factors that managers should consider in exercising due diligence in business combinations.
4. Identify defensive tactics used to attempt to block business combinations.
5. Distinguish between an asset and a stock acquisition.
6. Indicate the factors used to determine the price and the method of payment for a business combination.
7. Calculate an estimate of the value of goodwill to be included in an offering price by discounting expected future excess earnings over some period of years.

When is big too big? "There is no theoretical limit to it," says Gary Weiss, a Merrill Lynch & Co. investment banker in London, in reference to the bid by France's Banque Nationale de Paris for two French rivals. Many believe it's only a matter of time before a merger creates a bank whose size rivals the gross domestic product of China, the seventh largest economy in the world.[1]

Beginning with the merger of Morgan Stanley and Dean Witter Discover and ending with the biggest acquisition to that date—WorldCom's bid for MCI, the year 1997 marked the third consecutive year of record mergers and acquisitions activity.[2] The pace accelerated still further in 1998 and 1999 with unprecedented merger activity in the banking industry, the auto industry, financial services, and telecommunications, among others. The fervor left experts wondering why and whether bigger was truly better, and consumers asking what the impact would be on service. A wave of stock swaps was undoubtedly sparked by record highs in the stock market, and stockholders reaped benefits from the mergers in many cases, at least in the short run. But regulators voiced concern about the dampening of competition, and consumers were quick to wonder where the real benefits lay.

---

[1] *WSJ*, "BNP Bid Raises Issue of How Large a Bank Can Get, or Should," by Matt Murray and Thomas Kamm, 3/11/98, p. A1.

[2] *WSJ Europe*, "U.S. Merger Activity Marks New Record," by Steven Lipin, 1/2/98, p. R9.

Growth is a major objective of many business organizations. Top management often lists growth or expansion as one of its primary goals. A company may grow slowly, gradually expanding its product lines, facilities, or services, or it may sky-rocket almost overnight. Some managers consider growth so important that they say their companies must "grow or die." In the past hundred years, many U.S. businesses have achieved their goal of expansion through business combinations. A *business combination* occurs when the operations of two or more companies are brought under common control.

NATURE OF THE COMBINATION

A business combination may be friendly or unfriendly. In a *friendly combination*, the boards of directors of the potential combining companies negotiate mutually agreeable terms of a proposed combination. The proposal is then submitted to the stockholders of the involved companies for approval. Normally, a two-thirds or three-fourths positive vote is required by corporate bylaws to bind all stockholders to the combination.

An *unfriendly (hostile) combination* results when the board of directors of a company targeted for acquisition resists the combination. A formal *tender offer* enables the acquiring firm to deal directly with individual shareholders. The tender offer, usually published in a newspaper, typically provides a price higher than the current market price for shares made available by a certain date. If a sufficient number of shares are not made available, the acquiring firm may reserve the right to withdraw the offer.

Because they are relatively quick and easily executed (often in about a month), tender offers are the preferred means of acquiring public companies. Thus, tender offer deals capture a large share of merger activity dollar value (around 14% in 1996, for example), but a much smaller percentage of numbers of mergers (only around 2% in 1996).

United Rentals Inc. launched a $560 million unsolicited tender offer for Rental Service Corp. Rental Service planned a board meeting by mid-April to consider the offer, and urged its shareholders not to respond before the meeting.[3]

Although tender offers are the preferred method for presenting hostile bids, most tender offers are friendly ones, done with the support of the target company's management. Nonetheless, hostile takeovers have become sufficiently common that a number of mechanisms have emerged to resist takeover.

Shortly after Warner-Lambert announced it had signed a merger agreement with American Home, Pfizer launched an $80 billion all-stock offer for Warner-Lambert, possibly the biggest hostile bid to date. The move is viewed as an effort by Pfizer to snag the cholesterol drug, Lipitor, and to create a giant in the pharmaceutical industry with a combined research and development (R&D) budget of $4 billion.[4]

---

[3] *WSJ*, "Rental Service's Board Plans to Meet by Mid-April to Mull Unsolicited Offer," by Paul Sherer, 4/6/99, p. A4.

[4] *WSJ*, "In Biggest Hostile Bid, Pfizer Offers $80 Billion For Warner-Lambert," by Steven Lipin, et al., 11/5/99, p. 1

Defense Tactics

Resistance often involves various moves by the target company, generally with colorful terms. Whether such defenses are ultimately beneficial to shareholders remains a controversial issue. Academic research examining the price reaction to defensive actions has produced mixed results, suggesting that the defenses are good for stockholders in some cases and bad in others. For example, when the defensive moves result in the bidder (or another bidder) offering an amount higher than initially offered, the stockholders benefit. But when an offer of $40 a share is avoided and the target firm remains independent with a price of $30, there is less evidence that the shareholders have benefited.

A certain amount of controversy surrounds the effectiveness, as well as the ultimate benefits, of the following defensive moves:

1. *Poison pill:* Issuing stock rights to existing shareholders enabling them to purchase additional shares at a price below market value, but exercisable only in the event of a potential takeover. This tactic has been effective in some instances, but bidders may take managers to court and eliminate the defense. In other instances the original shareholders benefit from the tactic. Chrysler Corp. announced that it was extending a poison pill plan until Feb. 23, 2008, under which the rights become exercisable if anyone announces a tender offer for 15% or more, or acquires 15%, of Chrysler's outstanding common shares.

IN THE NEWS

To fortify itself against a $2.8 billion takeover offer from United Video Satellite Group Inc., Gemstar International Group Ltd., Pasadena, California, adopted shareholder-rights, or "poison pill" measures that essentially prevented United Video from gaining control by buying a majority of Gemstar's shares on the open market.[5]

2. *Greenmail:* The purchase of any shares held by the would-be acquiring company at a price substantially in excess of their fair value. The purchased shares are then held as treasury stock or retired. This tactic is largely ineffective because it may result in an expensive excise tax; further, from an accounting perspective, the excess of the price paid over the market price is expensed.

3. *White knight or white squire:* Encouraging a third firm more acceptable to the target company management to acquire or merge with the target company.

4. *Pac-man defense:* Attempting an unfriendly takeover of the would-be acquiring company.

5. *Selling the crown jewels:* The sale of valuable assets to others to make the firm less attractive to the would-be acquirer. The negative aspect is that the firm, if it survives, is left without some important assets.

6. *Leveraged buyouts:* The purchase of a controlling interest in the target firm by its managers and third-party investors, who usually incur substantial debt in the process and subsequently take the firm private. The bonds issued often take the

---

[5] *WSJ*, "Gemstar Adopts 'Poison Pill' Measures in Face of United Video Satellite Offer," by David Kirkpatrick, 7/13/98, p. B2.

form of high-interest, high-risk "junk" bonds. Leveraged buyouts will be discussed in more detail in Chapter 2.

BUSINESS COMBINATIONS: WHY? WHY NOT?

A company may expand in several ways. Some firms concentrate on *internal* expansion. A firm may expand internally by engaging in product research and development. Hewlett-Packard is an example of a company that relied for many years on new product development to maintain and expand its market share. A firm may choose instead to emphasize marketing and promotional activities to obtain a greater share of a given market. Although such efforts usually do not expand the total market, they may redistribute that market by increasing the company's share of it.

For other firms *external* expansion is the goal; that is, they try to expand by acquiring one or more other firms. This form of expansion, aimed at producing relatively rapid growth, has exploded in frequency and magnitude in recent years. A company may achieve significant cost savings as a result of external expansion, perhaps by acquiring one of its major suppliers.

In addition to rapid expansion, the business combination method, or external expansion, has several other potential advantages over internal expansion:

1. *Operating synergies* may take a variety of forms. Whether the merger is *vertical* (a merger between a supplier and a customer) or *horizontal* (a merger between competitors), combination with an existing company provides management of the acquiring company with an established operating unit with its own experienced personnel, regular suppliers, productive facilities, and distribution channels. In the case of vertical mergers, synergies may result from the elimination of certain costs related to negotiation, bargaining, and coordination between the parties. In the case of a horizontal merger, potential synergies include the combination of sales forces, facilities, outlets, and so on, and the elimination of unnecessary duplication in costs. When a private company is acquired, a plus may be the potential to eliminate not only duplication in costs, but also unnecessary costs.

"Private-company expenses could be an upside. Anybody who looks at the earnings numbers but doesn't recognize that the entire extended family of the chairman has all sorts of perks, phone cards and cell phones and what have you, will be ignoring large expenses in the income statement that a new owner would not have on a recurring basis."[6]

Management of the acquiring company can draw upon the operating history and the related historical database of the acquired company for planning purposes. A history of profitable operations by the acquired company may, of course, greatly reduce the risk involved in the new undertaking. A careful examination of the acquired company's expenses may reveal both expected and unexpected

---

[6]*M&A*, "How Acquirers Can Be Blindsided By the Numbers," May/June 1997, p. 31.

costs that can be eliminated. On the more negative (or cautious) side, be aware that the term "synergies" is sometimes used loosely. If there are truly expenses that can be eliminated, services that can be combined, and excess capacity that can be reduced, the merger is more likely to prove successful than if it is based on growth and "so-called synergies," suggests Michael Jensen, a professor of finance at the Harvard Business School.

GAINS FROM BULKING UP[7]	
Industry	**Key Benefit of Consolidation**
Antenna Towers	Frees up capital and management time for wireless communications operators
Funeral Homes	Yields greater discounts on coffins, supplies and equipment
Health Clubs	Spreads regional marketing and advertising costs over more facilities
Landfill Sites	Lets operators cope with the new environment and regulatory demands
Physician Group Practices	Reduces overhead and costs of medical procedures

2. Combination may enable a company to compete more effectively in the *international marketplace*. For example, an acquiring firm may diversify its operations rather rapidly by entering new markets; alternatively it may need to ensure its sources of supply or market outlets. Entry into new markets may also be undertaken to obtain cost savings realized by smoothing cyclical operations. Diminishing savings from cost-cutting within individual companies makes combination more appealing. Also, the financial crisis in Asia is expected to accelerate the pace as American and European multinationals compete for a shrinking Asian market.

3. Business combinations are sometimes entered into to take advantage of *income tax* laws. The opportunity to file a consolidated tax return may allow profitable corporations' tax liability to be reduced by the losses of unprofitable affiliates. When an acquisition is financed using debt, the interest payments are tax deductible, creating a *financial synergy* or "tax gain." Many combinations in the past were planned to obtain the advantage of significant operating loss carryforwards that could be utilized by the acquiring company. However, the Tax Reform Act of 1986 limited the use of operating loss carryforwards in merged companies. Because tax laws vary from year to year and from country to country, it is difficult to do justice to the importance of tax effects within the scope of this chapter. Nonetheless it is important to note that tax implications are often a driving force in merger decisions.

4. *Diversification* resulting from a merger offers a number of advantages, including increased flexibility, an internal capital market, an increase in the firm's debt capacity, more protection from competitors over proprietary information, and sometimes a more effective utilization of the organization's resources. In debating the tradeoffs between diversification and focusing on one (or a few) specialties, there are no obvious answers.

---

[7]*Business Week*, "Buy 'Em Out, Then Build 'Em Up," by Eric Schine, 5/18/95, page 84.

In the first two days of 1998, articles appeared in the *Wall Street Journal* taking opposing views on the merits of specialization versus diversification. In one, we read that conglomerates were out, and being number one was in, with an example cited of Westinghouse's selling off its power and defense lines while expanding in broadcasting.[8] A day later, we read about a Soviet defense giant meeting with success in the building and fast food trades, after seeing the "inevitable" and deciding to diversify.[9]

5. *Divestitures* accounted for over 30% of the merger and acquisitions activity in each quarter from 1995 into mid-1998. Shedding divisions that are not part of a company's core business became common during this period. In some cases the divestitures may be viewed as "undoing" or "redoing" past acquisitions.

   A popular alternative to selling off a division is to "spin off" a unit. Examples include AT&T's spin-off of its equipment business to form Lucent Technologies Inc.; Sears Roebuck's spin-off of Allstate Corp. and Dean Witter Discover & Co.; and Cincinnati Bell's proposed spin-off of its billing and customer-management businesses to form Convergys Corp.

Dispositions are one response to a diversity of strategic trends—industry consolidations, trimming of peripheral operations, refocusing by major companies on fewer businesses, outsourcing, and so on. "This suggests that sell-offs will continue to be significant contributors to the supply of available properties in the m&a marketplace."[10]

Notwithstanding its apparent advantages, business combination may not always be the best means of expansion. An overriding emphasis on rapid growth may result in the pyramiding of one company on another without sufficient management control over the resulting conglomerate. Too often in such cases, management fails to maintain a sound enough financial equity base to sustain the company during periods of recession. Unsuccessful or incompatible combinations may lead to future divestitures.

In order to avoid large dilutions of equity, some companies have relied on the use of various debt and preferred stock instruments to finance expansion, only to find themselves unable to provide the required debt service during a period of decreasing economic activity. The junk bond market used to finance many of the mergers in the 1980s had essentially collapsed by the end of that decade.

Business combinations may destroy, rather than create, value in some instances. For example, if the merged firm's managers transfer resources to subsidize money-losing segments instead of shutting them down, the result will be a suboptimal allocation of capital. This situation may arise because of reluctance to eliminate jobs or to acknowledge a past mistake.

Some critics of the accounting methods used in the U.S. to account for business combinations argue that one of the methods does not hold executives accountable

---

[8] *WSJ*, "In the New Mergers, Conglomerates Are Out, Being No. 1 Is In: So Westinghouse Sells Off Power and Defense Lines, Expands in Broadcasting," by Bernard Wysocki, Jr., 1/1/98.

[9] *WSJ*, "A Soviet Defense Giant Saw the Inevitable and Decided to Diversify: So Now It Does Building, Fast Food Trade, Too, and They're Paying Off," by Neil King Jr., 1/2/98.

[10] *M&A*, "Paying the Market Price to Acquire," July/August 1997, p. 54.

for their actions if the price they pay is too high, thus encouraging firms to "pay too much." This method is illustrated in the following chapter. Although opinions are divided over the relative merits of the accounting alternatives, most will agree that the resulting financial statements should reflect the economics of the business combination. Furthermore, if and when the accounting standards and the resulting statements fail even partially at this objective, it is crucial that the users of financial data be able to identify the deficiencies. Thus we urge the reader to keep in mind that an important reason for learning and understanding the details of accounting for business combinations is to understand the economics of the business combination, which in turn requires understanding any possible deficiencies in the accounting presentation.

BUSINESS COMBINATIONS: HISTORICAL PERSPECTIVE

In the United States there have been three fairly distinct periods characterized by many business mergers, consolidations, and other forms of combinations: 1880–1904; 1905–1930; and 1945–present. During the first period, which ran from about 1880 through 1904, huge holding companies or trusts were created by investment bankers seeking to establish monopoly control over certain industries. This type of combination is generally called *horizontal integration* because it involves the combination of companies within the same industry. Examples of the trusts formed during this period are J. P. Morgan's U.S. Steel Corporation and other giant firms such as Standard Oil, American Sugar Refining Company, and the American Tobacco Company. By 1904 more than 300 such trusts had been formed, and they controlled more than 40% of the nation's industrial capital.

The second period of business combination activity, fostered by the federal government during World War I, continued through the 1920s. In an effort to bolster the war effort, the government encouraged business combinations to obtain greater standardization of materials and parts and to discourage price competition. After the war, it was difficult to reverse this trend, and business combinations continued. These combinations were efforts to obtain better integration of operations, reduce costs, and improve competitive positions rather than attempts to establish monopoly control over an industry. This type of combination is called *vertical integration* because it involves the combination of a company with its suppliers or customers. For example, Ford Motor Company expanded by acquiring a glass company, rubber plantations, a cement plant, steel mill, and other businesses that supplied its automobile manufacturing business. From 1925 to 1930, more than 1,200 combinations took place, and about 7,000 companies disappeared in the process.

The third period started after World War II and has exhibited rapid growth in merger activity since the mid-1960s, and even more rapid since the 1980s. The total dollar value of mergers and acquisitions grew from under $20 billion in 1967 to over $300 billion by 1995 and over $1,000 billion in 1998. Even allowing for changes in the value of the dollar over time, the acceleration is obvious. By 1996 the number of yearly mergers completed was nearly 7,000. Some observers have called this activity *merger mania*. Illustration 1-1 presents a rough graph of the level of merger activity from 1972 to 1997 in number of deals, and from 1979 to 1998 in dollar volume. Illustration 1-2 presents summary statistics on the level of activity for the year 1998 by industry sector for acquisitions with purchase prices valued in excess of $500 million.

ILLUSTRATION 1-1

Number of Mergers and Acquisitions Over $5 Million 1972 to 1997

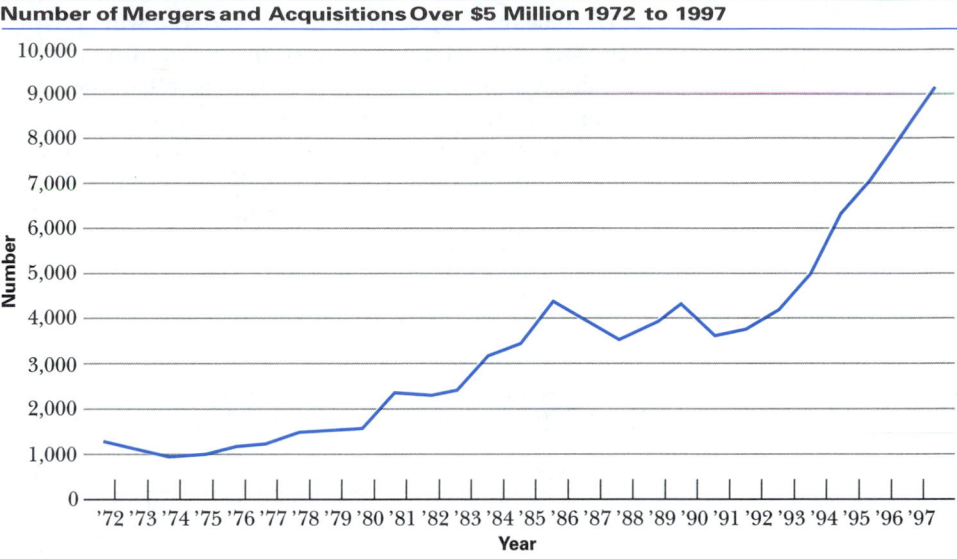

Adapted from Mergers and Acquisitions, March/April 1999, May/June 1989, and Almanac & Index 1982.

Value of Mergers and Acquisitions Over $5 Million 1979 to 1998

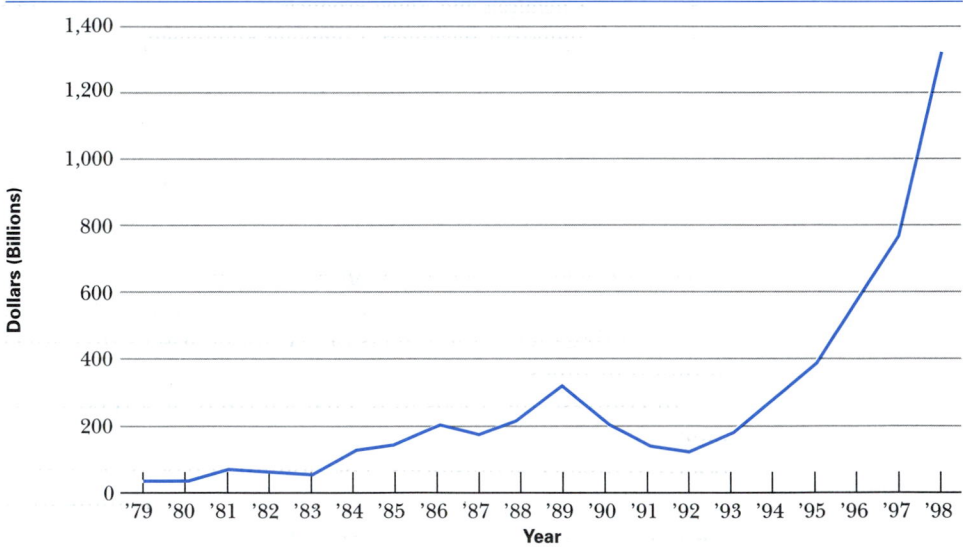

This most recent period can be further subdivided to focus on trends of particular decades or subperiods. For example, many of the mergers that occurred in the United States from the 1950s through the 1970s were ***conglomerate*** mergers. Here the primary motivation for combination was often to diversify business risk by combining companies in different industries having little, if any, production or market similarities, or possibly to create value by lowering the firm's cost of capital. One conjecture for the popularity of this type of merger during this time period was the strictness of regulators in limiting combinations of firms in the same industry. One conglomerate may acquire another, as Esmark did when it acquired Norton-Simon, and conglomerates may "spin off" or divest themselves of individual businesses. Management of the conglomerate hopes to smooth earnings over time

ILLUSTRATION 1-2

Ten Most Active Industries by Number of Transactions in 1998

Rank	Industry	Number of Deals	Value ($ millions)
1	Depository Institutions	269	4,596.8
2	Retailing	210	29,481.7
3	Wholesale Trade	206	2,895.9
4	Industrial Machinery, Computer Equipment	197	11,723.9
5	Holding and Other Investment Offices	161	11,300.1
6	Communications	161	9,251.5
7	Electrical and Electronic Equipment	149	9,665.0
8	Computer and Data Processing Services	149	2,626.3
9	Mining, Oil, and Gas Extraction	141	10,459.8
10	Food and Kindred Products	136	22,991.2

Ten Most Active Industries by Dollar Volume in 1998

Rank	Industry	Value ($ millions)	Number of Deals
1	Retailing	29,481.7	210
2	Food and Kindred Products	22,991.2	136
3	Chemicals and Allied Products	12,317.7	133
4	Industrial Machinery, Computer Equipment	11,723.9	197
5	Holding and Other Investment Offices	11,300.1	161
6	Mining, Oil, and Gas Extraction	10,459.8	141
7	Electrical and Electronic Equipment	9,665.0	149
8	Printing and Publishing	9,624.6	133
9	Communications	9,251.5	161
10	Insurance	7,862.4	87

Adapted from *Mergers & Acquisitions*, May/June 1989, p. 54.

by counterbalancing the effects of economic forces that affect different industries at different times.

In contrast, the 1980s were characterized by a relaxation in antitrust enforcement during the Reagan administration and by the emergence of high-yield junk bonds to finance acquisitions. The dominant type of acquisition during this period and into the 1990s has been **strategic acquisitions** claiming to benefit from **operating synergies**. These synergies may arise when the talents or strengths of one of the firms complement the products or needs of the other, or they may arise simply because the firms were former competitors. An argument can be made that the dominant form of acquisition shifted in the 1980s because many of the conglomerate mergers of the 1960s and 1970s proved unsuccessful; in fact, some of the takeovers of the 1980s were of a disciplinary nature, intended to break up conglomerates.

A temporary decline in activity near the end of the 1980s may be traced to the collapse of the junk bond market and to an economic recession. By the mid-1990s the credit markets had recovered, and the upsurge in mergers renewed to greater levels than ever before.

Deregulation undoubtedly played a role in the popularity of combinations in the 1990s. In industries that were once fragmented because concentration was forbidden, the pace of mergers has picked up significantly in the presence of deregulation. These industries include banking, telecommunications and broadcasting. Although recent years have witnessed few deals blocked due to antitrust enforcement, an example of a major transaction dropped in 1996 because of a planned FTC (Federal Trade Commission) challenge was in the drug store industry. The FTC challenged the impact of a proposed merger between Rite Aid Corp. and Revco D.S. Inc. on market power in several sectors of the East and Midwest. Nonetheless, subsequent deals in the industry saw both companies involved; Rite Aid acquired Thrifty PayLess Holdings Inc., and CVS Inc. purchased Revco in February 1997.

Still more recently, the Justice Department sued to block Primestar's acquisition of a satellite slot owned by MCI and News Corp. The Department claimed the deal would thwart competition by giving the companies the last direct competition to cable: a direct-broadcast satellite service using eighteen-inch dish receivers.[11] Other deals were dropped in the face of possible intervention, including a planned merger between CPA firms KPMG Peat Marwick and Ernst & Young in 1998, although other factors undoubtedly played a role as well. The intensity of merger activity in the 1990s, arising in part from the tolerant attitude of regulators, may ironically bring that attitude to an end. On May 13, 1998, the U.S. government announced its intent to appoint a panel of economic advisors to evaluate the impact of merger activity on the economy.

IN THE NEWS

The Justice Department said it will move to stop a merger between dairy concerns Suiza Foods Corp. and Broughton Foods Co. because the companies compete for school milk contracts in several Kentucky school districts. The department feared a merger would create a monopoly on bids to supply milk in some districts and reduce the number of bidders to two or three in other districts, thus affecting the pricing of milk contracts.[12]

Terminology and Types of Combinations

From an accounting perspective, the distinction that is most important at this stage is between an *asset acquisition* and a *stock acquisition.* In Chapter 2, we focus on the acquisition of the assets of the acquired company, where only the acquiring or new company survives. Thus the books of the acquired company are closed out, and its assets and liabilities are transferred to the books of the acquirer. In subsequent chapters, we will discuss the stock acquisition case where the acquired company and its books remain intact, and consolidated financial statements are prepared periodically. In such cases, the acquiring company debits an account "Investment in Subsidiary" rather than transferring the underlying assets and liabilities onto its own books.

Note that the distinction between an asset acquisition and a stock acquisition does not imply anything about the medium of exchange, or consideration used to consummate the acquisition. Thus a firm may gain control of another firm in a stock acquisition using cash, debt, stock, or some combination of the three as consideration. Alternatively, a firm may acquire the total assets of another firm using cash, debt, stock, or some combination of the three. There are three largely independent issues related to the consummation of, and accounting for, a combination: what is acquired (assets or stock), what is given up (the consideration for the combination), and how the combination is accounted for. These are shown in Figure 1-1.

---

[11] *WSJ,* "Antitrust Suit Filed to Block Primestar Purchase," by John Wilke, 5/14/98.

[12] *WSJ,* "U.S. to Oppose Merger of Suiza, Broughton Foods," by Carlos Tejada, 3/17/99, p. A13.

FIGURE 1-1

Overview of Business Combinations

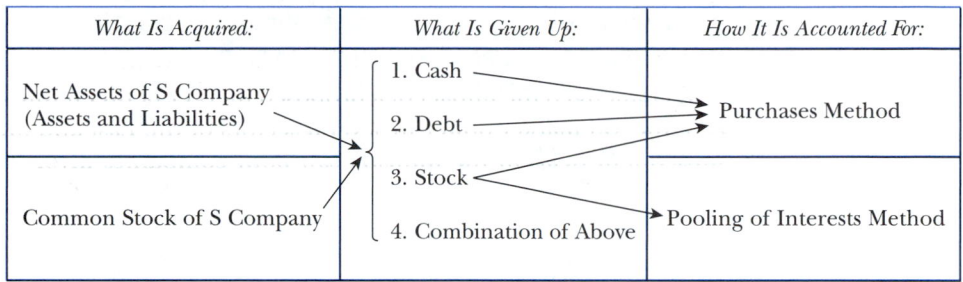

As illustrated in Figure 1-1, the three choices are independent of each other with one exception. In a pooling of interests, the middle column (what is given up) must be stock.[13] The methods of accounting (purchase and pooling) are described in the next chapter, and Appendix A of Chapter 2 discusses a proposal by the Financial Accounting Standards Board (FASB) to eliminate the pooling of interests method. If this proposal is approved, there will be only one accounting method (purchase) after the implementation date of the new standard.

In an asset acquisition, a firm must acquire 100% of the assets of the other firm. In a stock acquisition, a firm may obtain control by purchasing 50% or more of the voting common stock (or possibly even less). This introduces one of the most obvious advantages of the stock acquisition over the asset acquisition, a lower total cost in many cases. Also, in a stock acquisition, direct formal negotiations with the acquired firm's management may be avoided. Further, there may be advantages to maintaining the acquired firm as a separate legal entity. The possible advantages include liability limited to the assets of the individual corporation and greater flexibility in filing individual or consolidated tax returns. Finally, regulations pertaining to one of the firms do not automatically extend to the entire merged entity in a stock acquisition. A stock acquisition has its own complications, however, and the economics and specifics of a given situation will dictate the type of acquisition preferred.

Other terms related to mergers and acquisitions merit mention. For example, business combinations are sometimes classified by method of combination into three types—statutory mergers, statutory consolidations, and stock acquisitions. However, the distinction between these categories is largely a technicality, and the terms "mergers," "consolidations," and "acquisitions" are popularly used interchangeably.

A *statutory merger* results when one company acquires all the net assets of one or more other companies through an exchange of stock, payment of cash or other property, or the issue of debt instruments (or a combination of these methods). The acquiring company survives, whereas the acquired company (or companies) ceases to exist as a separate legal entity, although it may be continued as a separate division of the acquiring company. Thus, if A Company acquires B Company in a statutory merger, the combination is often expressed as

Statutory Merger

$$\boxed{\text{A Company}} \; + \; \boxed{\text{B Company}} \; = \; \boxed{\text{A Company}}$$

_____

[13]Up to 10% of the acquisition price in a pooling of interests may be non-stock.

The boards of directors of the companies involved normally negotiate the terms of a plan of merger, which must then be approved by the stockholders of each company involved. State laws or corporation bylaws dictate the percentage of positive votes required for approval of the plan.

A *statutory consolidation* results when a new corporation is formed to acquire two or more other corporations through an exchange of voting stock; the acquired corporations then cease to exist as separate legal entities. For example, if C Company is formed to consolidate A Company and B Company, the combination is generally expressed as

Statutory Consolidation

| A Company | + | B Company | = | C Company |

Stockholders of the acquired companies (A and B) become stockholders in the new entity (C). The combination of Chrysler Corp. and Daimler-Benz to form DaimlerChrysler is an example of this type of consolidation. The acquired companies in a statutory consolidation may be operated as separate divisions of the new corporation, just as they may under a statutory merger. Statutory consolidations require the same type of stockholder approval as do statutory mergers.

IN THE NEWS

Citicorp and Travelers named the new entity created by their pending merger Citigroup.[14]

A *stock acquisition* occurs when one corporation pays cash or issues stock or debt for all or part of the voting stock of another company, and the acquired company remains intact as a separate legal entity. When the acquiring company acquires a controlling interest in the voting stock of the acquired company (for example, if A Company acquires 50% of the voting stock of B Company), a parent-subsidiary relationship results. Consolidated financial statements (explained in later chapters) are prepared and the business combination is often expressed as

Consolidated Financial Statements

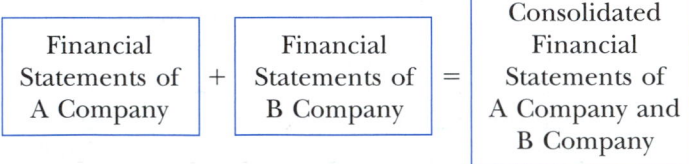

| Financial Statements of A Company | + | Financial Statements of B Company | = | Consolidated Financial Statements of A Company and B Company |

TAKEOVER PREMIUMS

A *takeover premium* is the term applied to the excess of the amount offered, or agreed upon, in an acquisition over the prior stock price of the acquired firm. It is not unusual for the takeover premium to be as high as 100% of the target firm's

---

[14] *WSJ*, "Dimon Is Named President of Citigroup," by Stephen Frank and Anita Raghavan, 5/7/98, p. A3.

market share price before the acquisition, and the average hovered around 40 to 50% into the late 1990s. In the face of the already high stock prices of this period, speculation is mixed as to the future of takeover premiums. Some experts claim the premiums are shrinking, leading to "takeunders" in some cases where companies are acquired below the listed stock prices.

IN THE NEWS

"Price tags [for acquisitions] vary widely depending on industry or market, the target's market position as proxied by share or product line, the uniqueness of the target, the buyer's objective, and, perhaps most obviously, the intensity of competition for the target."[15]

Possible reasons acquirers are willing to pay such high premiums are varied. One factor is that the acquirers' own stock prices may be at a level which makes it attractive to issue stock (rather than cash) to consummate the acquisition. Another factor is that credit throughout most of the 1990s has been fairly generous for mergers and acquisitions. In contrast to the junk bond market of the 1980s with interest rates ranging from mid to high teens, banks financed deals in the 1990s with interest rates in the single digits, and even junk bond rates have been below 12%.

Bidders may have private information about the target firm suggesting that it is worth more than its current market value, or has assets not reported on the balance sheet (such as in-process research and development). Alternatively, companies desperate to boost earnings may believe that growth by acquisitions is essential to survive in the global marketplace, and the competition necessitates the premiums. At the other end of the spectrum, a final possibility, which cannot be entirely ruled out, is that managers eager for growth are simply paying too much.

One research study presented evidence that higher premiums were offered for firms with high cash flows, relatively low growth opportunities, and high tax liabilities relative to their equity values.[16] Another study suggested that the bigger the ego of the acquiring firm's CEO, the higher the takeover premium, while still another suggested that any premium over 25% is extremely risky.[17] Some compensation analysts argue that the massive options payouts to executives combined with golden parachutes provide an unhealthy incentive for executives to negotiate mergers, citing Chrysler's merger with Daimler-Benz as an example.[18]

Takeover premiums have attracted so much attention that some strategists (e.g., Paine Webber's Edward Kerschner) have advised clients looking for investments to choose stocks that might get taken over. Cautious financial advisors point out that lofty stock prices are a double-edged sword for financial buyers because they mean high prices for both companies' stocks and costlier acquisitions. Also, when stock prices fluctuate, the agreed-upon purchase price may suddenly appear more or less attractive than it did at the time of agreement. For example, a proposed acquisition

---

[15] *M&A*, "Paying the Market Price to Acquire," July/August 1997, p. 52.

[16] The study entitled "Free Cash Flow and Stockholder Gains in Going Private Transactions" was conducted by Lehn and Poulsen (*Journal of Finance*, July 1989, pp. 771–787). Also see "The Case Against Mergers," by Phillip Zweig, *Business Week*, 10/30/95, pp. 122–130.

[17] "Acquisition Behavior, Strategic Resource Commitments and the Acquisition Game: A New Perspective on Performance and Risk in Acquiring Firms," by Mark Sirower, doctoral dissertation, Columbia University, 1994.

[18] *WSJ*, "Chrysler Executives May Reap Windfall," by Gregory White, 5/13/98, p. A3.

of Comsat Corp. by Lockheed Martin Corp. was announced in September 1998, with the acquisition valued at $2.6 billion, of which 49% was to be paid in cash and the rest in Lockheed stock. When Lockheed Martin's stock price subsequently faltered enough to suggest a 16% drop in the total value of the transaction, Comsat shareholders questioned whether the consideration for the transaction was fairly priced.[19]

Some statistics suggest that of "6000 acquisitions, only 900 return the cost of capital. It is easy to do deals. It is very difficult to make them succeed."[20]

AVOIDING THE PITFALLS BEFORE THE DEAL

To consider the potential impact on a firm's earnings realistically, the acquiring firm's managers and advisors must exercise *due diligence* in considering the information presented to them. Some of the factors to beware include:

1. Be cautious in interpreting any *percentages* presented by the selling company. For example, the seller may be operating below capacity (say at 60% of capacity), but the available capacity may be for a product that is unprofitable or that is concentrated at a specific location, while the desirable product line (which the acquirer wishes to expand) is already at capacity.

2. Don't neglect to include *assumed liabilities* in the assessment of the cost of the merger. The purchase price for a firm's assets is the sum of the cash or securities issued to consummate the merger *plus* any liabilities assumed. This is equivalent to viewing the purchase price for a firm's *net* assets (assets *minus* liabilities assumed) as the sum of the cash or securities issued to consummate the merger.

"International Paper Co., the world's largest forest-products company, said it agreed to acquire Union Camp Corp. for stock valued at $71 a share, or $5 billion, sending the shares of its smaller rival soaring 33%. In addition, International Paper said it will assume $1.6 billion of Union Camp debt. . . . International Paper said it considered the price a good deal because it is acquiring modern assets that would have cost the company twice as much to build itself."[21]

In addition to liabilities that are on the books of the acquired firm, be aware of the possibility of less obvious liabilities. Accounting standards require an acquiring firm to allocate the cost of an acquired firm to the assets acquired and liabilities assumed, whether or not shown in the financial statements of the acquired company.[22]

In some cases, the cost resulting from a plan to terminate or relocate employees of an acquired company should be recognized as an assumed liability. A task force assigned to examine the circumstances in which this recognition is

---

[19] *WSJ*, "Lockheed Bid for Comsat Hits Obstacles," by Anne Marie Squeo, 6/11/99, p. A3.

[20] *M&A*, "How Acquirers Can Be Blindsided by the Numbers," May/June 1997, p. 29.

[21] *WSJ*, "IP Agrees to Acquire Union Camp Corp.," by Jonathan Welsh, 11/25/98, p. A3.

[22] Accounting Principles Board, Opinion No. 16, *Business Combinations*, Paragraphs 87 and 88.

appropriate reached a consensus that a liability should be assumed if all the following criteria are met.[23]

    a. The plan of termination specifically identified the number of employees to be terminated (relocated), their job functions, and locations.

    b. Actions required by the plan will begin as soon as possible after the plan is finalized, and significant changes to the plan are unlikely.

    c. Qualified management begins the assessment and formulation of the plan as of the consummation date of the acquisition.

    d. Qualified management completes the assessment as soon as possible after the consummation date and communicates it in sufficient detail to affected employees, with finalization of the plan occurring no more than one year after the consummation date.

3. Watch out for the impact on earnings of the ***allocation of expenses*** and the effects of production increases, standard cost variances, LIFO liquidations, and by-product sales. For example, a firm that is planning to be acquired may grow inventory levels in order to allocate their fixed costs over more units, thus decreasing the cost of goods sold and increasing the bottom line. However, the inventory level that is acquired may be excessive and ultimately costly.

4. Note any ***nonrecurring items*** which may have artificially or temporarily boosted earnings. In addition to nonrecurring gains or revenues, look for recent ***changes in estimates***, ***accrual levels***, ***and methods***. While material changes in method are a required disclosure under GAAP, the rules on materiality are fuzzy, and changes in estimates and accruals are frequently not disclosed.

"While everything in the offering memorandum may very well be true, although not necessarily, the facts are designed to make the company look better than it would if an analyst were to dig into those facts."[24]

5. Be careful of ***CEO egos***. Striving to be number one may make business sense, but not everyone can hold that spot. Westinghouse CEO Michael H. Jordan has drawn both praise and criticism with his deal-of-the-month style. He states, "There are the big dogs, there are the ankle-biters, and then there are those caught in the middle," and he includes Westinghouse and Siemens in the midsize category. The midsize firms have to combine, he claims.[25]

DETERMINING PRICE AND METHOD OF PAYMENT IN BUSINESS COMBINATIONS

Whether an acquisition is structured as an asset acquisition or a stock acquisition, the acquiring firm must choose to finance the combination with cash, stock, or debt (or some combination). The cash-financed portion of acquisition prices dropped from 42.3% in 1994 to 13.4% in 1998, according to Securities Data Co., of Newark,

---

[23]Financial Accounting Standards Board, *EITF*95-3: "Recognition of Liabilities in Connection with a Purchase Business Combination." The guidance in this issue relates only to business combinations accounted for as purchases, not as poolings of interest (the methods addressed in Chapter 2 of this text).

[24]*M&A*, "How Acquirers Can Be Blindsided by the Numbers," May/June 1997, p. 29.

[25]*WSJ*, "In the New Mergers Conglomerates Are Out, Being No. 1 Is In," by Bernard Wysocki Jr., 1/1/98.

NJ. This represents the lowest share of cash in over ten years.[26] Note that the dollar volume of cash used in 1998 acquisitions was not down, but rather the percentage of cash included in the total purchase price.

The trend is readily explained by rising stock valuations. The higher the acquiring firm's stock valuation, the fewer shares are needed to pay for the acquisition. This means less dilution to existing shareholders, a frequent concern in the planning stages of a proposed acquisition. Another consideration is that the medium of exchange is linked in some cases to the method of accounting. Important differences between *purchase* and *pooling of interests* accounting methods are discussed in Chapter 2.

To qualify for pooling of interests accounting, a firm must use virtually all (at least 90%) stock to consummate the deal. Companies concerned that the pooling method might be eliminated in the near future may wish to merge before it is too late.[27] The FASB is considering other changes, however, that might make cash acquisitions more attractive, such as reporting income before goodwill amortization. If companies that pay cash are given more discretion over how they account for goodwill (the premium paid over the fair value of the acquired company's assets), cash acquisitions might increase.

When a business combination is effected through an open-market acquisition of stock, no particular problems arise in connection with determining price or method of payment. Price is determined by the normal functioning of the stock market, and payment is generally in cash, although some or all of the cash may have to be raised by the acquiring company through debt or equity issues. Effecting a combination may present some difficulty if there are not enough willing sellers at the open-market price to permit the acquiring company to buy a majority of the outstanding shares of the company being acquired. In that event, the acquiring company must either negotiate a price directly with individuals holding large blocks of shares or revert to an open tender offer.

When a business combination is effected by a stock swap, or exchange of securities, both price and method of payment problems arise. In this case, the price is expressed in terms of a **stock exchange ratio**, which is generally defined as the number of shares of the acquiring company to be exchanged for each share of the acquired company, and constitutes a **negotiated price**. It is important to understand that each constituent of the combination makes two kinds of contributions to the new entity—net assets and future earnings. The accountant often becomes deeply involved in the determination of the values of these contributions. Some of the issues and the problems that arise are discussed in the following section.

Net Asset and Future Earnings Contributions

Determination of an equitable price for each constituent company, and of the resulting exchange ratio, requires the valuation of each company's net assets, as well as their expected contribution to the future earnings of the new entity. The accountant is often called upon to aid in determining net asset value by assessing, for example, the expected collectibility of accounts receivable, current replacement

---

[26]*WSJ*, ''Mergers Reached This Year Are Using the Lowest Share of Cash in Ten Years,'' by Greg Ip, 4/16/98.

[27]The Financial Accounting Standards Board issued an Exposure Draft on September 7, 1999, proposing to eliminate the pooling method.

costs for inventories and some fixed assets, and the current value of long-term liabilities based on current interest rates. To estimate current replacement costs of real estate and other items of plant and equipment, the services of appraisal firms may be needed.

Estimation of the value of goodwill to be included in an offering price is subjective. A number of alternative methods are available, usually involving the discounting of expected future cash flows (or free cash flows), earnings, or excess earnings over some period of years. Generally, the use of free cash flows or earnings yields an estimate of the entire firm value (including goodwill), whereas the use of excess earnings yields an estimate of the goodwill component of total firm value. We next describe the steps in the excess earnings approach and then follow with an illustration.

Excess Earnings Approach to Estimating Goodwill

1. Identify a normal rate of return on assets for firms similar to the company being targeted. Statistical services are available to provide averages, or a normal rate may be estimated by examining annual reports of comparable firms. The rate may be estimated as a return on either total assets or on *net* identifiable assets (assets other than goodwill minus liabilities).

2. Apply the rate of return identified in step 1 to the level of identifiable assets (or net assets) of the target to approximate what the "normal" firm in this industry might generate with the same level of resources. We will refer to the product as "normal earnings."

3. Estimate the expected future earnings of the target. Past earnings are generally useful here, and provide a more objective measure than management's projections, although both should be considered. Exclude any nonrecurring gains or losses (extraordinary items, gains and losses from discontinued operations, etc.) from past earnings if they are used to estimate future earnings.

4. Subtract the normal earnings calculated in step 2 from the expected target earnings from step 3. The difference is "excess earnings." If the normal earnings are greater than the target's expected earnings, then no goodwill is implied under this approach.

5. To compute estimated goodwill from "excess earnings," we must assume an appropriate time period and a discount rate. The shorter the time period and the higher the discount rate, the more conservative the estimate. If the excess earnings are expected to last indefinitely, the present value of a perpetuity may be calculated simply by dividing the excess earnings by the discount rate. For finite time periods, use present-value tables or calculations to compute the present value of an annuity. Because of the assumptions needed in step 5, a range of goodwill estimates may be obtained simply by varying the assumed discount rate and/or the assumed discount period.

6. Add the estimated goodwill from step 5 to the fair value of the firm's net identifiable assets to arrive at a possible offering price.

Estimating Goodwill and Potential Offering Price Wanna Buy Company is considering acquiring Hot Stuff Inc. and is wondering how much it should offer. Wanna Buy makes the following computations and assumptions to help in the decision.

a. Hot Stuff's identifiable assets have a total fair value of $7,000,000. Hot Stuff has liabilities totaling $3,200,000. The assets include patents and copyrights with a fair value approximating book value, buildings with a fair value 50% higher than book value, and equipment with a fair value 25% lower than book value. The remaining lives of the assets are deemed to be approximately equal to those used by Hot Stuff.

b. Hot Stuff's pretax income for the year 2000 was $1,050,000, which is believed by Wanna Buy to be more indicative of future expectations than any of the preceding years. The net income of $1,050,000 included the following items, among others:

Amortization of patents and copyrights	$50,000
Amortization of goodwill on Hot Stuff's books	9,000
Depreciation on buildings	360,000
Depreciation on equipment	80,000
Extraordinary gain	250,000
Loss from discontinued operations	175,000
Pension expense	59,000

c. The normal rate of return on net assets for the industry is 14%.

d. Wanna Buy believes that any excess earnings will continue for seven years, and that a rate of return of 15% is required on the investment.

Based on the assumptions above and ignoring tax effects, we will first calculate an estimation of the implied goodwill, and then use that estimate to arrive at a reasonable offering price for Hot Stuff.

Normal earnings for similar firms: ($7,000,000 − $3,200,000) × 14% = $532,000

Expected earnings of target:

Pretax income of Hot Stuff		$1,050,000
Add: Amortization of goodwill	9,000	
Losses on discontinued operations	175,000	
Reduced depreciation on equipment	20,000	204,000
Subtotal		1,254,000
Subtract: Additional depreciation on building	180,000	
Extraordinary gain	250,000	430,000
Target's expected future earnings		824,000

Excess earnings of target: $824,000 − $532,000 = $292,000 per year

Present value of excess earnings (ordinary annuity) for seven years at 15% (see Table A4 in Appendix at the back of the text):

Estimated goodwill: $292,000 × 4.16042 = $1,214,843

Implied offering price = Fair value of assets − fair value of liabilities + estimated goodwill, or
= $7,000,000 − $3,200,000 + $1,214,843 = $5,014,843.

In the illustration above, in arriving at the target's expected future earnings, we ignored the items that are expected to continue after the acquisition, such as the amortization of the patents and copyrights and the pension expense. We backed out nonrecurring gains and losses on extraordinary items or discontinued operations. Also, the amortization of previously recorded goodwill is not expected to continue. We adjusted the prior reported earnings for the expected increase in depreciation on the building (50% higher than in the past), leading to a decrease in projected earnings. In contrast, we increased projected earnings for the decrease in equipment depreciation (25% lower than in the past).[28] In practice, more specific information should be available as to which components of earnings are expected to continue at the same level, which might be reduced because of economies

---

[28]These depreciation adjustments are made on the books under purchase accounting rules, as shown in subsequent chapters. Although they are not made on the books under pooling rules, it may be argued that the economic substance of the transactions (and thus the estimation of implied goodwill) is the same under purchase or pooling, even though goodwill is not recorded on the books under pooling rules.

or cost-cutting plans, and which might increase because of transition costs. The better the information, clearly the better the estimates of goodwill and offering price.

Where the constituent companies have used different accounting methods, the accountant will often need to reconstruct their financial statements on the basis of agreed-on accounting methods in order to obtain reasonably comparable data. Once comparable data have been obtained for a number of prior periods, they are analyzed further to project future contributions to earnings. The expected contributions to future earnings may vary widely among constituents, and the exchange ratio should reflect this fact. The whole process of valuation, of course, requires the careful exercise of professional judgment. Ultimately, however, the exchange ratio is determined by the bargaining ability of the individual parties to the combination.

Once the overall values of relative net asset and earnings contributions have been agreed on, the types of securities to be issued by the new entity in exchange for those of the combining companies must be determined. In some cases a single class of stock will be issued; in other cases equity may require the use of more than one class of security.

The concepts of earnings **dilution** and **accretion** are critical to the valuation of a merger. Does the merger increase or decrease expected earnings performance of the acquiring institution? From a financial and shareholder perspective, the price paid for a firm is hard to justify if earnings per share declines. When this happens, the acquisition is considered *dilutive.* Conversely, if the earnings per share increases as a result of the acquisition, it is referred to as an *accretive* acquisition.

DuPont Co. may have landed the biggest prize in biotechnology—but the purchase will come with some short-term pain in the form of depressed earnings next year. DuPont earned $2.54 a share in 1998, excluding its Conoco unit, which is being divested. Analysts are estimating earnings of $3.09 per share in 2000 *before* the dilution from the Pioneer acquisition.[29]

Many deals lower earnings per share initially but add significantly to value in later years. While initial dilution may not be a deal killer, however, many managers feel that they cannot afford to wait too long for a deal to begin to show a positive return. Opinions are divided, however, on what drives the market in relation to mergers and acquisitions, nor do research studies offer conclusive evidence on the subject. Bart Madden, a partner in a valuation advisory firm in Chicago, remarked, "I totally disagree that the market is EPS driven. From the perspective of the owner or manager of capital, what matters is cash in, cash out, not reported earnings."[30] He acknowledges, however, that CFOs, who "live in a world of accounting rules," are concerned about reported earnings.

"The deal [AmSouth Bancorp.'s acquisition of First American Corp.] is expected to be modestly accretive to the earnings per share of AmSouth in the year 2000 and more significantly additive to earnings in 2001."[31]

---

[29] *WSJ*, "DuPont May Get Edge Over Monsanto," by Susan Warren and Scott Kilman, 3/16/99, p. A2.

[30] *CFO*, "Say Goodbye to Pooling," by Ian Springsteel, February 1997.

[31] *WSJ*, "AmSouth to Purchase First American," by Steven Lipin and Rick Brooks, 6/1/99, p. A3.

SUMMARY

1. *Describe historical trends in types of business combinations.* Horizontal integration involving the combination of companies within the same industry was popular from 1880 to 1904. Vertical integration involving the combination of a company with its customers or suppliers became more prevalent from 1905 through 1930. The period beginning after World War II has been called merger mania. From the 1950s through the 1970s, conglomerate mergers between companies in different industries occurred in the face of antitrust regulation restricting combinations within a particular industry. A relaxation of antitrust regulation in the 1980s and the emergence of high-yield junk bonds led to a number of strategic acquisitions claiming to benefit from operating synergies. High stock prices in the 1990s created a wealth of mergers using stock as the medium of exchange.

2. *Identify the major reasons firms combine.* Firms combine to achieve growth goals or mandates, to obtain operating synergies, to compete more effectively in the international marketplace, to take advantage of tax laws in some cases, and to diversify or alternatively to eliminate competition.

3. *Identify the factors that managers should consider in exercising due diligence in business combinations.* Managers should be aware of unrecorded liabilities; take care in interpreting percentages quoted by the selling company; examine the impact on earnings from allocated expenses, changes in LIFO reserves and inventory levels, and by product sales; note any nonrecurring items, changes in estimates, accruals, or methods; and be careful of CEO egos.

4. *Identify defensive tactics used to attempt to block business combinations.* Defensive tactics employed by target companies to avoid potential takeover include poison pills, greenmail, white knights or white squires, pac-man defense, selling the crown jewels, and leveraged buyouts.

5. *Distinguish between an asset and a stock acquisition.* An asset acquisition involves the purchase of all of the acquired company's net assets, whereas a stock acquisition involves the attainment of control via purchase of a controlling interest in the stock of the acquired company.

6. *Indicate the factors used to determine the price and the method of payment for a business combination.* Factors to be considered include the effect the acquisition is expected to have on future earnings performance, referred to as dilution or accretion, and the value of the firm's identifiable net assets as well as the estimated value of its implied goodwill. The method of payment is affected by the liquidity position of the purchasing firm, the willingness of the sellers to accept alternative forms of financing (stock, debt, cash, or a combination), and tax and accounting issues.

7. *Calculate an estimate of the value of goodwill to be included in an offering price by discounting expected future excess earnings over some period of years.* Identify a normal rate of return for firms similar to the company being targeted. Apply the rate of return to the level of identifiable assets (or net assets) of the target to approximate what the "normal" firm in this industry might generate with the same level of resources (normal earnings). Estimate the expected future earnings of the target. Subtract the normal earnings from the expected target earnings. The difference is "excess earnings." Assume an appropriate time period and a discount rate to calculate the discounted value of the excess earnings, or the estimated goodwill.

QUESTIONS

1. Distinguish between internal and external expansion of a firm.

2. List four advantages of a business combination as compared to internal expansion.

3. What is the primary legal constraint on business combinations? Why does such a constraint exist?

4. Business combinations may be classified into three types based upon the relationships among the combining entities (e.g., combinations with suppliers, customers, competitors, etc.). Identify and define these types.

5. Distinguish among a statutory merger, a statutory consolidation, and a stock acquisition.

6. Define a tender offer and describe its use.

7. When stock is exchanged for stock in a business combination, how is the stock exchange ratio generally expressed?

8. Define some defensive measures used by target firms to avoid a takeover. Are these measures beneficial for shareholders?

9. Explain the potential advantages of a stock acquisition over an asset acquisition.

10. Explain the difference between an accretive and a dilutive acquisition.

11. What is the *primary* criterion that determines whether an acquisition might be accounted for using the pooling of interests method, assuming the other criteria are satisfied?

EXERCISES

EXERCISE 1-1 Estimating Goodwill and Potential Offering Price

Plantation Homes Company is considering the acquisition of Condominiums, Inc. To assess the amount it might be willing to pay, Plantation Homes makes the following computations and assumptions.

A. Condominiums, Inc. has identifiable assets with a total fair value of $15,000,000 and liabilities of $8,800,000. The assets include office equipment with a fair value approximating book value, buildings with a fair value 30% higher than book value, and land with a fair value 75% higher than book value. The remaining lives of the assets are deemed to be approximately equal to those used by Condominiums, Inc.

B. Condominiums, Inc.'s pretax incomes for the years 1998 through 2000 were $1,200,000, $1,500,000, and $950,000, respectively. Plantation Homes believes that an average of these earnings represents a fair estimate of annual earnings for the indefinite future. However, it *may* need to consider adjustments to the following items included in pretax earnings:

Depreciation on Buildings (each year)	960,000
Depreciation on Equipment (each year)	50,000
Extraordinary Loss (year 2000)	300,000
Sales Commissions (each year)	250,000

C. The normal rate of return on net assets for the industry is 15%.

Required:

A. Assume further that Plantation Homes feels that it must earn a 25% return on its investment, and that goodwill is determined by capitalizing excess earnings. Based on these assumptions, calculate a reasonable offering price for Condominiums, Inc. Indicate how much of the price consists of goodwill. Ignore tax effects.

B. Assume that Plantation Homes feels that it must earn a 15% return on its investment, but that average excess earnings are to be capitalized for three years only. Based on these assumptions, calculate a reasonable offering price for Condominiums, Inc. Indicate how much of the price consists of goodwill. Ignore tax effects.

EXERCISE 1-2 Estimating Goodwill and Valuation

Alpha Company is considering the purchase of Beta Company. Alpha has collected the following data about Beta:

	Beta Company Book Values	Estimated Market Values
Total Identifiable Assets	$585,000	$750,000
Total Liabilities	320,000	320,000
Owners' Equity	$265,000	—

Cumulative total net cash earnings for the past five years of $850,000 includes extraordinary cash gains of $67,000 and nonrecurring cash losses of $48,000.

Alpha Company expects a return on its investment of 15%. Assume that Alpha prefers to use cash earnings rather than accrual-based earnings to estimate its offering price, and that it estimates the total valuation of Beta to be equal to the present value of cash-based earnings (rather than excess earnings) discounted over five years. (Goodwill is then computed as the amount implied by the excess of the total valuation over the identifiable net assets valuation.)

Required:

A. Compute (a) an offering price based on the information above that Alpha might be willing to pay, and (b) the amount of goodwill included in that price.

B. Compute the amount of goodwill actually recorded, assuming the negotiations result in a final purchase price of $625,000 cash.

EXERCISE 1-3 **Estimated and Actual Goodwill**

Passion Company is trying to decide whether to acquire Desiree Inc. The following balance sheet for Desiree Inc. provides information about book values. Estimated market values are also listed, based upon Passion Company's appraisals.

	Desiree Inc. Book Values	Desiree Inc. Market Values
Current Assets	$260,000	$ 260,000
Property, Plant & Equipment (net)	650,000	740,000
Total Assets	$910,000	$1,000,000
Total Liabilities	$400,000	$ 400,000
Common Stock, $10 par value	160,000	
Retained Earnings	350,000	
Total Liabilities and Equities	$910,000	

Passion Company expects that Desiree will earn approximately $150,000 per year in net income over the next five years. This income is higher than the 12% annual return on gross tangible assets considered to be the industry "norm."

Required:

A. Compute an estimation of goodwill based on the information above that Passion might be willing to pay (include in its purchase price), under each of the following additional assumptions:

(1) Passion is willing to pay for *excess* earnings for an expected life of 5 years (undiscounted).

(2) Passion is willing to pay for *excess* earnings for an expected life of 5 years, which should be capitalized at the industry normal rate of return.

(3) Excess earnings are expected to last indefinitely, but Passion demands a higher rate of return of 20% because of the risk involved.

B. Comment on the relative merits of the three alternatives in part (A) above.

C. Determine the amount of goodwill to be recorded on the books if Passion pays $800,000 cash and assumes Desiree's liabilities.

METHODS OF ACCOUNTING FOR BUSINESS COMBINATIONS

LEARNING OBJECTIVES

1. Distinguish between the purchases and the pooling of interests methods of accounting for business combinations.
2. Explain how acquisition expenses are reported under each method.
3. Describe the issues of concern to the FASB that are currently under review, related to business combinations.
4. Describe the use of pro forma statements in business combinations.
5. Describe the valuation of assets, including goodwill, and liabilities acquired in a business combination accounted for by the purchase method.
6. Describe the valuation of assets and liabilities acquired in a business combination accounted for by the pooling of interests method.
7. Explain the equity allocation rule in terms of its relevance and the mechanics of implementation.
8. Identify the impact on the financial statements of the differences between pooling and purchase, and understand why some firms may prefer the pooling of interests.
9. Explain how contingent consideration affects the valuation of assets acquired in a business combination accounted for by the purchase method.
10. Describe a leveraged buyout and the technique of platforming.

INTRODUCTION TO THE METHODS OF ACCOUNTING FOR BUSINESS COMBINATIONS

"What's more important, economic substance or accounting appearance? Banks are voting for appearance, hands down."[1]

This statement refers to the preference of many companies to account for business combinations by an accounting method called pooling of interests. Although the two accounting methods for accommodating business combinations were devel-

_____

[1] *WSJ*, "A Modest Proposal to Stop 'Pooling,' " by Roger Lowenstein, 5/9/96.

oped in an effort to capture economic substance, this quote illustrates that many users believe the opposite has resulted. The Financial Accounting Standards Board (FASB) is among those concerned about the perceived flaws and deficiencies in the existing standards, particularly so in view of the tremendous popularity and growth of business combinations.

As discussed in Appendix A (later in this chapter), the FASB issued an Exposure Draft in September 1999 proposing revisions in the accounting for mergers and acquisitions. Among the issues being examined are the *likely elimination of the pooling of interests method* and the appropriate way to handle the amortization of goodwill for purchase acquisitions. The importance of these issues is discussed and illustrated in this chapter. Other concerns, which are addressed here or in subsequent chapters, include international comparability and a popular write-off technique involving in-process research and development.

Critics of the FASB's proposal to eliminate pooling argue that the change will prevent "good deals from being done." One such critic, Mark Nebergall of Software & Information Industry Association, questions why America, home to transparent standards, should emulate practices in countries whose standards are more opaque. Nebergall admits his concern is whether the change will stifle the market for mergers in his industry. According to another critic, Lehman Brothers' Bob Willens: "Companies that use purchase accounting see their stock price hammered."[2]

If the pooling of interests method is eliminated, then combining firms will use the purchase method for all acquisitions beyond some implementation date. In the interim, however, an upsurge may be expected in the number of acquiring firms structuring combinations to qualify for the pooling method. Thus, for the short-run at least, the advantages and disadvantages of the respective methods are of heightened importance. This chapter focuses on this issue. For Chapters 3 through 10, the purchase method is assumed. Chapter 11 addresses the pooling method once more in the context of stock (rather than asset) acquisitions, as well as alternative concepts for consolidated statements.

Companies that are considering a business combination generally decide early in their negotiations on the accounting method they will use to record the combination. The accounting method may significantly affect the reported financial position and results of operations of the combined entity in the current and future periods, as well as the form of payment (cash, other assets, stock, etc.).

Two methods of accounting—*purchase* and *pooling of interests*—are currently accepted in practice. Accounting standards do not permit a free choice between these two methods. Instead the standards clearly define the criteria necessary to qualify for accounting by the pooling method. All other combinations must be accounted for by the purchase method. However, the standards do not preclude the firms' managers from planning (before the deal) to structure the combination so as to qualify for one treatment or the other. It is not unusual for companies to take extraordinary steps to qualify for pooling accounting in order to avoid the large charges to income for goodwill amortization and additional depreciation. For example, as reported in the July 5, 1991, issue of the *Wall Street Journal*, in AT&T's

---

[2]*The Economist,* "Draining the Pool," 9/11/99, p. 82.

$7.5 billion acquisition of NCR Corporation, AT&T sold 6.3 million of NCR shares it held in order to undo the prior two years of treasury stock purchases by NCR, which would have blocked use of pooling. Without pooling, AT&T would have had to record $5.7 billion of goodwill and record amortization expense of more than $142 million yearly.

Also, some of the questionable aspects of a particular combination that might disqualify it for pooling treatment may be unraveled (referred to as "curing") on an ex post basis. Minute details of the pooling criteria have drawn the attention of the SEC, and additional interpretations from specific cases may shed insight into the likelihood of a particular combination qualifying for the pooling method. The criteria are described in Appendix B to this chapter.

Because First Bank System Inc. of Minneapolis announced its intent to buy back shares as part of a $10 billion bid for First Interstate Bancorp of Los Angeles, the SEC stopped the pooling deal; one of the twelve criteria was violated.

The SEC also disallowed as a pooling a $13.6 stock-swap in December 1996 between long-distance service provider WorldCom and MFS, a local telecommunications concern. The deal went through as a purchase. "To let the accounting drive the deal would have been crazy," said WorldCom's CFO Sullivan.[3]

Regardless of whether a business combination takes the form of an asset acquisition or a stock acquisition, the combination must be accounted for by one of these two methods, purchase or pooling. The two accounting methods are discussed, illustrated, and contrasted in the following sections. For those who prefer to see an illustration of the two methods before reading a more theoretical discussion, feel free to turn to the section entitled "Explanation and Illustration of Purchase Accounting" (and "Purchase Example") before reading the following discussion.

Do Firms Prefer Pooling? And If So, Why?

The majority of mergers in the United States do not satisfy the pooling criteria and hence are accounted for by the purchase method. However, in cases where the stock of one company is being exchanged for all the assets or most of the stock (90% or more) of the other, firms sometimes go to great lengths to satisfy the pooling criteria.

The FASB has expressed its opinion (in a proposed standard) that both methods should not continue to be allowed in the United States. Most other countries do not allow pooling of interests accounting. Among the few countries that allow an alternative to purchase accounting are Germany, where a "book value" form of the purchase method is allowed, and Canada, where the pooling method is allowed only when one of the combining companies cannot be identified as the acquirer.

Media stories have predicted the eventual demise of the pooling method, but the same stories often predict an increase in the number of poolings that will be attempted in the meantime. A recent flurry of proposed mergers desiring pooling treatment supports the latter prediction, including both Bank One's merger with First Chicago and Bank of America's with Nations Bank. Not surprisingly, the stan-

---

[3] *CFO*, "Say Goodbye to Pooling," by Ian Springsteel, February 1997.

dard setters are meeting considerable opposition from companies that want the pooling alternative left available to them.

One question of interest is: Why do firms care? The pooling of interests and purchase methods are simply accounting methods, and as such should in no way alter the underlying nature of the business combination or its economic consequences. However, the two methods do result in a substantial difference in the way the financial statements appear subsequent to the combination. In this section some of these differences are highlighted, and in a later section the differences will be illustrated in greater depth using data.

The essence of the pooling method is that neither of the two firms is considered dominant, and hence it is a bit of a misnomer to refer to one as the acquirer. Instead the preferred terminology is the issuer. The other firm might be more appropriately referred to as the nonissuing combining firm, but it is commonly referred to in practice as the acquired firm despite the technical inconsistency. The assets, liabilities, and retained earnings of the two companies are carried forward at their previous carrying amounts in a pooling of interests because no purchase or ''acquisition'' has occurred. Operating results of the two companies are combined for the entire period being presented, regardless of the date of acquisition, and previously issued statements (when presented) are restated as if the companies had always been combined.

ILLUSTRATION 2-1

Comparison of Purchase and Pooling of Interests

Purchase	Pooling of Interest
Balance Sheet	**Balance Sheet**
1. *Assets and liabilities* acquired are recorded at their *fair values*. Any excess of cost over the fair value of net assets acquired is *recorded* as *goodwill*.	*Assets and liabilities* acquired are recorded at their precombination *book values*. No excess of cost over book value exists, and *no new goodwill* is recorded.
2. The acquired company's *retained earnings* are *not recognized*, i.e., do not become a part of the acquiring company's retained earnings.	The acquired company's *retained earnings* are *added into* the acquiring company's retained earnings. Some adjustment may be required to maintain legal capital.
3. *Equity securities issued* as consideration are recorded at their (issuer's) fair *market value*.	*Equity shares issued* are recorded at the *book value of the acquired shares*.
Income Statement	**Income Statement**
4. The *excess of cost over book value* assigned to acquired assets is *depreciated* or *amortized* to reduce future earnings.	*No excess of cost over book value exists*; thus, there is *no additional depreciation or amortization* expense.
5. The acquired company's *earnings* are included with the acquiring firm's only *from the date of combination forward*.	The issuer and combiner companies' *earnings* are combined for the *full fiscal year in which the combination occurs*.
6. a. *Direct costs* incurred in the combination are included as part of the cost of the acquired company.	a. *Direct costs* incurred in the combination are expensed in the year in which incurred.
b. *Indirect costs* related to acquisitions are expensed in the year in which incurred.	b. *Indirect costs* are expensed (same as purchase).
c. *Security issuance costs* are deducted from the recorded value of the security.	c. *Security issuance costs* are expensed.

From an income statement perspective, the pooling method is often appealing because income statements subsequent to the pooling will not be burdened with goodwill amortization, additional depreciation expense, or other charges that arise when assets are revalued on the balance sheet. Under purchase accounting, assets are being acquired and hence are revalued, and additional future expenses result in cases where the purchase price is higher than the book value. Not only is net income adversely affected by these higher expenses under purchase accounting, but also return on assets (or return on equity) is weakened both in the numerator and the denominator. In comparison to pooling of interests, purchase accounting yields a lower net income divided by a larger base of assets and thus a substantially reduced return on assets in many cases.

An additional advantage of the pooling method is that the restatement of prior years' financial statements facilitates analysis of trends and comparisons over time. However, purchase accounting requires many of the same disclosures in the notes to the statements. From a balance sheet perspective, purchase accounting has the advantage of reflecting more current values for assets and liabilities of the acquired company. However, the retained earnings of the acquired company does not appear, whereas with the pooling method, the retained earnings of the combining company is often added to the retained earnings of the issuing company (exceptions will be addressed in a later section). See Illustration 2-1 for a comparison of the two methods.

As stated by Timothy Lucas, Research Director of the Financial Accounting Standards Board, "The existing U.S. accounting standards for business combinations have not worked very well, as evidenced by the amount of repair and maintenance that they have required over the years. Moreover, the recent heightened activity in mergers and acquisitions has highlighted what many see as flaws in the present standards, namely that the pooling and purchase methods can produce dramatically different accounting results for mergers and acquisitions that may be quite similar in most respects."[4]

Treatment of Acquisition Expenses Contrasted

Under *pooling of interests* rules, all types of acquisition expenses are expensed in the period incurred. These include direct, indirect, and security issuance costs. In contrast, under *purchase* accounting rules, each of the three categories of expenses is treated differently. The purchase price includes the ***direct expenses*** incurred in the combination, such as accounting and consulting fees. Thus these types of expenses are capitalized (charged to an asset account) under purchase accounting rules. ***Indirect***, ongoing costs, such as those incurred to maintain a mergers and acquisitions department, however, are charged to expense as incurred. Indirect costs also include managerial or secretarial time and overhead allocated to the merger, but which would have existed in its absence. Finally, ***security issuance costs*** are assigned to the valuation of the security in a purchase acquisition, thus reducing the additional contributed capital for stock issues or adjusting the premium or discount on bond issues. This comparison is summarized in Illustration 2-1, point number 6.

---

[4]*Financial Accounting Standards Board*, News Release, "FASB Issues Special Report on Business Combinations," 6/10/97, Norwalk, CT.

Acquisition Costs—An Illustration

Suppose that SMC Company acquires 100% of the net assets of Bee Company (net book value of $100,000) by issuing shares of common stock with a fair value of $120,000. With respect to the merger, SMC incurred $1,500 of accounting and consulting costs and $3,000 of stock issue costs. SMC maintains a mergers department that incurred a monthly cost of $2,000. The following illustrates how these direct and indirect merger costs and the security issue costs are recorded if the merger is accounted for as a purchase and as a pooling of interests. The reader may wish to return to this illustration after reading later sections of the chapter pertaining to recorded goodwill.

Pooling Accounting:

Accounting and Consulting Expense (Direct)	1,500	
Merger Department Expense (Indirect)	2,000	
Securities Issue Expense (Security Issue Costs)	3,000	
Cash		6,500

Purchase Accounting:

Goodwill (Direct)*	1,500	
Merger Department Expense (Indirect)	2,000	
Other Contributed Capital (Security Issue Costs)	3,000	
Cash		6,500

*This entry assumes that the company was acquired for an amount greater than the fair value of its identifiable net assets. In this case the direct costs are capitalized as part of the goodwill acquired in the merger. If the amount paid is less than the fair value of the net identifiable assets, the direct costs are debited to long-lived assets. This lessens the reduction in long-lived assets below their market value. The rules for bargain purchases are described later in this chapter.

Tyco International Ltd.'s shares fell about 25% over a three-week period in October 1999. The decline was attributed to concerns about its accounting practices, following a report by a Dallas money manager who suggested that investors were naively ignoring the company's practice of taking huge one-time charges following acquisitions. The company's all-stock acquisitions have been accounted for using pooling rules.[5]

PURCHASE VERSUS POOLING—AUTHORITATIVE POSITION

Prior to the issuance of *APB Opinion No. 16*, "Business Combinations," the pooling method was widely used and abused. It was largely in response to such abuses as partial pooling, retroactive pooling, and issuance of a second or third class of common stock to the new shareholders that the Accounting Principles Board issued *Opinion No. 16* in August 1970.

In *Opinion No. 16* the Board concluded:

> . . . that the purchase method and the pooling of interests method are both acceptable in accounting for business combinations, although not as alternatives in accounting for the same business combination. A business combination which meets specified conditions requires accounting by the pooling of interests method. A new basis of accounting is not permitted for a combination that meets the specified conditions, and the assets and liabilities of the combining companies are combined at their recorded amounts. All

---

[5] *WSJ*, "Tyco's Accounting Faces Renewed Criticism," by Mark Maremont, 11/1/99, p. A2.

other business combinations should be accounted for as an acquisition of one or more companies by a corporation.[6]

Thus, *Opinion No. 16* removes the purchase-pooling option. Only the interpretation of the facts of an actual or contemplated combination can determine which method is required.

Paragraphs 45–48 of *Opinion No. 16* spell out the specific conditions under which pooling is required. All of these conditions must be met. The main points are summarized as follows:

1. Independent ownership interests are combined to continue previously separate operations.
2. All or nearly all the common shares of one company are acquired in exchange for another firm's common shares, and all stockholders retain the same relative and unrestricted rights, in a single transaction that involves no planned or contingent realignment of rights in the near future.
3. An intention must exist to continue substantially all the operations and normal stockholder relationships of the combining companies.

Opinion No. 16 attempted to clearly define criteria, remove any choice of method (other than that provided by judicious planning of a combination's terms), and prohibit partial pooling. In *Opinion No. 16* the Board established 12 specific conditions; if *all* are met, use of the pooling method is required. These 12 conditions are presented in Appendix B. In simplified terms, the Board held that combinations effected by pure exchanges of common stock for common stock (with no contingency clauses, unusual extra agreements, convertible or otherwise complex securities) must be accounted for as poolings; all other combinations must be treated as purchases.

Advantages and disadvantages, both theoretical and practical, may be noted for both methods. Pooling is criticized on the ground that values given and received are ignored in a negotiated transaction. "Instant earnings" are alleged to result (a) from the early sale of newly pooled assets that are carried at their precombination (and often quite low) book values, and (b) from a reporting practice that requires that the surviving firm report earnings for the year of combination as if it had been combined during that entire year, even though the combination may have occurred well along in that year, or even after the fiscal year-end but before publication of the financial statements.

Pooling is defended, on the other hand, on the grounds that it is more objective than the purchase method (no appraisals of assets or stock values are necessary), that it properly continues generally accepted accounting principles rather than introducing extensive appraisal-based data, and that it avoids accounting for one part of the combined company on a fair value basis and the other part on a historical cost basis.

Those who endorse the purchase method believe that one company clearly acquires another in almost every business combination, and that control passes to the dominant corporation in a transaction bargained on the basis of current fair values given and received, regardless of the nature of the consideration. However,

---

[6] *Opinions of the Accounting Principles Board No. 16*, par. 8.

with the purchase method problems are alleged to exist with regard to objective determination of current values and the apparent inconsistency of accounting for only part of the combined company on an updated basis. Goodwill and the related amortization charges materially affect financial reports, even though they are subjective measures, being derived from current valuations (appraisals, etc.) of stock issued and assets received.

Opinion No. 16, issued in 1970, significantly reduced the proportion of business combinations accounted for as pooling of interests (as shown in Illustration 2-2) and generally improved business combination accounting and reporting. However, pooling remained a popular method for very large mergers, particularly in certain industries (banking and technology, among others), eventually drawing the scrutiny of both the SEC and the FASB. Thus, until the FASB's tentative decision to eliminate the method is made final, the basic controversy remains.

IN THE NEWS

One writer states, "If you can possibly account for a business combination as a pooling of interests, you pool. Compared to the alternative purchase method, poolings provide the party without the hangover."[7]

In a reply to this article, David Piller, CFA, VP and Portfolio Manager, Aegis Asset Management Inc., writes, "The purchase method creates inaccurate distortions of year-over-year and quarterly comparisons of EPS and cash flow

ILLUSTRATION 2-2

Percentage of Acquisitions Using Purchase versus Pooling of Interests

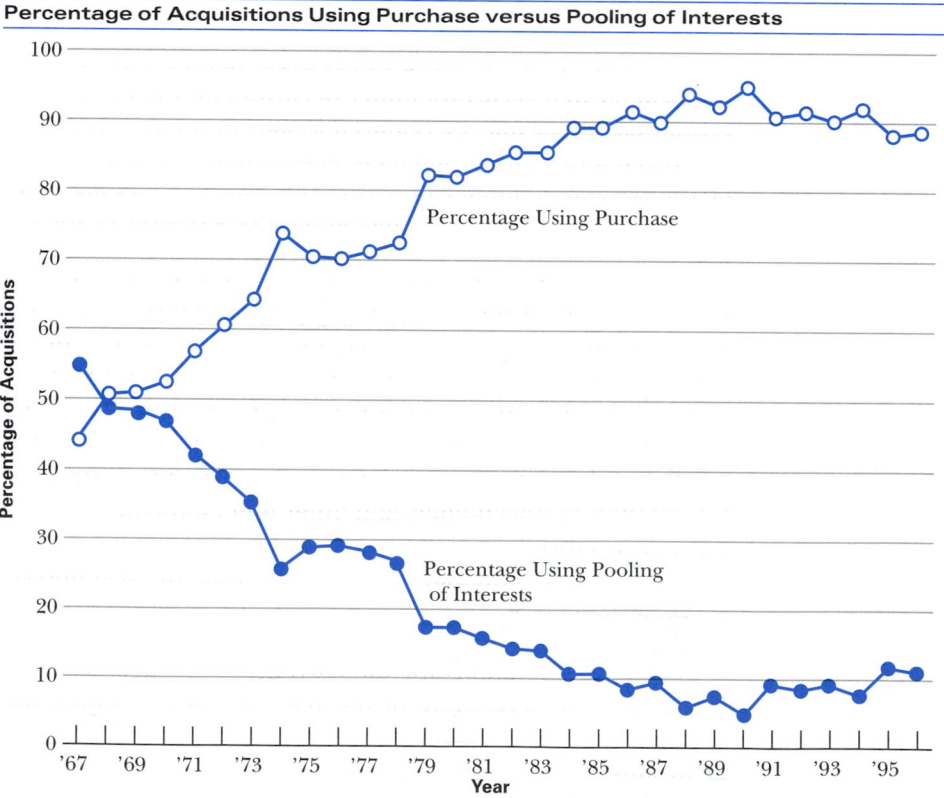

This graph is based on a sample of 600 firms using data from *Accounting Trends and Techniques*, 1966 through 1997 (New York: AICPA).

---

[7]*CFO*, "Say Goodbye to Pooling," February 1997, p. 79.

during the first year after the acquisition. . . . [T]here is a technique for getting a rough handle on the degree of addition or dilution relating to a purchase method acquisition by using the footnote in the annual report. . . . As a user of financial information, I make much greater use of cash flow than I do EPS."[8]

PRO FORMA STATEMENTS AND DISCLOSURE REQUIREMENT

Pro forma statements, sometimes called "as if" statements, are prepared to show the effect of planned or contemplated transactions by showing how they might have affected the historical financial statements if they had been consummated during the period covered by those statements. Pro forma statements serve two functions in relation to business combinations: (1) to provide information in the *planning* stages of the combination, and (2) to *disclose* relevant information subsequent to the combination.

First, pro forma statements are often prepared before the fact for combinations under consideration. When management is contemplating the purchase price offer, for example, a number of pro forma statements may be produced, using different assumed purchase prices and projecting one or more years into the future, or alternatively restating a past period as though the firms had been combined. After the boards of directors of the constituents have reached tentative agreement on a combination proposal, pro forma statements showing the effects of the proposal may be prepared for distribution to the stockholders of the constituents for their consideration prior to voting on the proposal. If the proposed combination involves the issue of new securities under Securities and Exchange Commission rules, pro forma statements may be required as part of the registration statement.

When a pro forma statement is prepared, the tentative or hypothetical nature of the statement should be clearly indicated, generally by describing it as "pro forma" in the heading and including a description of the character of the transactions given effect to. Further description of any other adjustments should be clearly indicated on the statement or in related notes. A pro forma balance sheet for an example of P Company's acquisition of S Company that might be prepared for use by the companies' stockholders is presented in Illustration 2-3. Details of this acquisition are presented in the next section of this chapter. The normal procedure is to show the audited balance sheet as of a given date, individual adjustments for the proposed transaction, and resulting account balances.

Second, pro forma presentation is a valuable method of disclosing relevant information to stockholders and other users subsequent to the combination. Some types of pro forma presentation are required by APB *Opinion No. 16.*

If a business combination occurred during the year and is accounted for by the *purchase* method, *notes* to financial statements should include on a pro forma basis:

1. Results of operations for the current year as though the companies had combined at the beginning of the year, unless the acquisition was at or near the beginning of the year.

2. Results of operations for the immediately preceding period as though the companies had combined at the beginning of that period if comparative financial statements are presented.

---

[8] *CFO,* Letters, "Don't Say Goodbye," May 1997.

ILLUSTRATION 2-3

P Company
Pro Forma Balance Sheet
Giving Effect to Proposed Issue of Common Stock for All the
Common Stock of S Company Under Purchase Accounting
January 1, 2000

Assets	Audited Balance Sheet	Adjustment	Pro Forma Balance Sheet
Cash and Receivables	$ 250,000	$ 170,000	$ 420,000
Inventories	260,000	140,000	400,000
Land	600,000	400,000	1,000,000
Buildings & Equipment	800,000	1,000,000	1,800,000
Accumulated Depreciation	(300,000)		(300,000)
Goodwill	—0—	230,000	230,000
Total Assets	$1,610,000		$3,550,000
Liabilities and Equity			
Current Liabilities	$ 110,000	150,000	260,000
Bonds Payable	—0—	350,000	350,000
Common Stock	750,000	450,000	1,200,000
Other Contributed Capital	400,000	990,000	1,390,000
Retained Earnings	350,000		350,000
Total Equities	$1,610,000		$3,550,000

Where a business combination has taken place during the period and is accounted for by the *pooling* method, financial statements and financial information of the separate companies presented for prior years should be restated on a combined basis beginning with the earliest year presented to furnish comparative information. (Note that for purchase only the *immediately preceding* period is restated in the notes to the statements.) Also, with pooling combinations, the *notes* to the financial statements include:

1. Disclosure that the statements of previously separate firms have been combined.
2. What operating results were of the separate firms for the partial period prior to the pooling of interests.

Thus, so long as two distinctly different methods of accounting for business combinations are allowed, the notes to the statements contain useful information to facilitate comparison between periods, as well as combinations accounted for by the two methods. If the FASB's proposal to eliminate pooling is finalized, the pro forma disclosure requirements may be eliminated as well.

EXPLANATION AND ILLUSTRATION OF PURCHASE ACCOUNTING

As the term implies, the purchase method treats the combination as the purchase of one or more companies by another. The acquiring company records the purchase at its cost, including direct acquisition expenses. If cash is given, the amount paid constitutes cost. If debt securities are given, the present value of future payments represents cost.

Assets acquired by issuing shares of stock of the acquiring corporation are recorded at the fair values of the stock given or the assets received, whichever is more clearly evident. If the stock is actively traded, its quoted market price, after making allowance for market fluctuations, additional quantities issued, issue costs, and so on, is normally better evidence of fair value than are appraisal values of the net assets of an acquired company. Thus, an adjusted market price of the shares issued normally is used. Where the issued stock is of a new or closely held company, however, the fair value of the assets received generally must be used. Recall that any security issuance costs, whether bonds or stocks, incurred to consummate the merger are deducted from the value assigned to the debt or equity under purchase accounting.

Once the total cost is determined, it must be allocated to the identifiable assets acquired (including intangibles other than goodwill) and liabilities assumed, all of which should be recorded at their fair values at the date of acquisition. Any excess of total cost over the sum of amounts assigned to identifiable assets and liabilities is recorded as goodwill. Under current generally accepted accounting principles (GAAP), goodwill must be amortized over its economic life but not in excess of 40 years.

Because of significant variation in how goodwill amortization is handled in different countries, this element has drawn a great deal of attention. The FASB has considered a variety of alternatives, including one proposal requiring companies to amortize goodwill over twenty years or less, with a rebuttable presumption that the useful life should not exceed *ten* years.[9] This suggestion came on the heels of a very different one that would have allowed companies to escape the periodic write-off for certain components of goodwill altogether, with the substitution of adjusting the goodwill value downward only when it was "impaired." In the Exposure Draft issued in September 1999, however, the FASB proposed a maximum life of 20 years with a review of goodwill for impairment within two years of the acquisition date if certain factors are present.

IN THE NEWS

"If the goodwill write-off gets wiped out, companies would more aggressively pursue acquisitions because earnings would not suffer dilution," said Daniel J. Donoghue, a member of the FASB's executive advisory council.[10]

Wiping out the write-off appears unlikely. The proposed alternative, however, is not yet a part of generally accepted accounting principles, and it is not clear what the final outcome will be. If FASB follows through on its proposal to reduce the maximum life from 40 years to 20, the yearly write-offs would hit earnings even harder than under present GAAP.

The FASB appears to be softening the blow by allowing, in its proposal, the goodwill amortization to be shown *net of tax as a separate line item within income before continuing operations*, with a subtotal prior to that line labeled "income before goodwill charges." See Appendix A of this chapter for more details regarding the proposal.

---

[9] *Financial Accounting Standards Board*, Financial Accounting Series "Status Report" No. 194-C, 2/25/99, p. 4.

[10] *WSJ*, "FASB May Change M&A Accounting to Favor Cash Over All-Stock Deals," by Elizabeth MacDonald, 4/27/98, p. A3.

Managers seeking to reduce the amount of goodwill amortization necessitated by the acquisition have found creative ways to avoid or reduce goodwill. This concern is driven by the impact goodwill amortization has on future reported net income and return on assets. One tactic involves identifying in-process research and development (R&D) in the acquired company. FASB standards require that R&D costs be expensed as incurred, and not capitalized. In an interpretation of the standard on R&D, FASB stated that some forms of R&D, including a specific research project in progress, which transferred in an acquisition, could also be expensed. Further, the amount to be expensed was to be determined not by the original cost of the actual R&D but rather by the amount paid by the acquiring company.

Adobe Systems Inc., in its acquisition of Ares Software Corp. in 1996, attributed 95% of the total acquisition cost ($14.7 million) to R&D and expensed it. IBM valued the R&D it acquired in its 1995 takeover of Lotus Development Corp. at $1.8 billion (over half the total acquisition cost).[11]

Near the end of 1996, the FASB initiated an examination of the rules governing R&D write-offs, and the SEC also expressed concern about the adequacy of disclosures related to acquired R&D valuation. In 1999, the FASB announced its decisions that in-process research and development would be addressed as a separate project from the business combinations project, and that separate statements would be issued. Later in the year, the FASB announced that the R&D project would be deferred until the business combinations project was completed. In the meantime, the importance of maintaining supporting documentation for any amounts assigned to R&D in a takeover is clear. Some experts believe that a change in the way in-process R&D is handled might slow the "torrid pace of mergers and acquisitions."[12]

When the net amount of the fair values of identifiable assets less liabilities *exceeds* the total cost of the acquired company, the acquisition is sometimes referred to as a *bargain*. When a bargain acquisition occurs, some of the acquired assets must be recorded at amounts below their market values under current GAAP. The rules for prioritizing these adjustments are listed later in the chapter. The appropriate accounting for bargain purchases is one of the issues being deliberated by the FASB, and could result in changes in the near future.

Purchase Example

Assume that on January 1, 2000, P Company, in a merger, *acquired the assets* and assumed the liabilities of S Company. P Company gave one of its $15 par value common shares to the former stockholders of S Company for every two shares

---

[11] *M&A*, "Maximizing R&D Write-offs to Reduce Goodwill," by Bryan Browning, September/October 1997.

[12] *WSJ*, "FASB Weighs Killing Merger Write-offs," 2/23/99, p. A2.

of the $5 par value common stock they held. Assume also that the business combination must be accounted for by the *purchase* method. Throughout this text, the company names P and S are frequently used to distinguish a parent company from a subsidiary. In an asset acquisition, these terms are inappropriate, as the books of the acquired firm are dissolved at the time of acquisition. Nonetheless the distinction is useful to avoid confusion between the acquirer and the acquired.

P Company common stock, which was selling at a range of $50 to $52 per share during an extended period prior to the combination, is considered to have a fair value per share of $48 after an appropriate reduction is made in its market value for additional shares issued and for issue costs. The total value of the stock issued is $1,440,000 (or $48 × 30,000 shares). Balance sheets for P and S Companies (along with relevant fair value data) on January 1, 2000, are presented in Illustration 2-4. Because the book value of the bonds is $400,000, bond discount in the amount of $50,000 ($400,000 − $350,000) must be recorded to reduce the bonds payable to their present value.

ILLUSTRATION 2-4

Balance Sheets of P and S Companies
January 1, 2000

	P Company	S Company	
	Book Value	Book Value	Fair Value
Cash and Receivables	$ 250,000	$ 180,000	$ 170,000
Inventories	260,000	100,000	140,000
Land	600,000	120,000	400,000
Buildings & Equipment	800,000	900,000	1,000,000
Accumulated Depreciation—			
Buildings & Equipment	(300,000)	(300,000)	
Total Assets	$1,610,000	$1,000,000	$1,710,000
Current Liabilities	$ 110,000	$ 110,000	$ 150,000
Bonds Payable, 9%, due 1/1/2010, interest payable semiannually on 6/30 and 12/31	—0—	400,000	350,000
Total Liabilities	$ 110,000	$ 510,000	$ 500,000
Stockholders' Equity			
Common Stock, $15 par value, 50,000 shares	750,000		
Common Stock, $5 par value, 60,000 shares		300,000	
Other Contributed Capital	400,000	50,000	
Retained Earnings	350,000	140,000	
Stockholders' Equity	1,500,000	490,000	
Total Liabilities and Stockholders' Equity	$1,610,000	$1,000,000	
Net Assets at Book Value (assets minus liabilities)	$1,500,000	$ 490,000	
Net Assets at Fair Value			$1,210,000

[Handwritten top margin: We wish to keep S company as a on-going business. We prefer to purchase its stock instead of its assets.]

To record the exchange of stock for the net assets of S Company, P Company will make the following entry:

[Handwritten: These journal entries aren't done in reality. S corp's liquidated. P purchase all the assets of S corp. This entry assumes market value]

Cash and Receivables	170,000	
Inventories	140,000	
Land	400,000	
Buildings & Equipment (Net)	1,000,000	
Discount on Bonds Payable	50,000	
Goodwill (1,440,000 − 1,210,000)	230,000	
Current Liabilities		150,000
Bonds Payable		400,000
Common Stock* (30,000 × $15)		450,000
Other Contributed Capital* (30,000 × [$48 − $15])		990,000

*The sum of common stock and other contributed capital is $1,440,000.

[Handwritten left margin: (purchase method) At par / Investments in S comp 1,440,000 / Common Stock 450,000 / Paid in Capital 990,000 / (Journal entry recorded in reality) / (S) The company is gone. This seldomly happens because you want the company to continue so we buy stock of the company.]

After the merger, S Company ceases to exist as a separate legal entity. Note that under the purchase method the cost of the net assets is measured by the fair value (30,000 shares × $48 = $1,440,000) of the shares given in exchange. Common stock is credited for the par value of the shares issued, with the remainder credited to other contributed capital. Individual assets acquired and liabilities assumed are recorded at their fair values. Plant assets are recorded at their fair values in their current depreciated state (without an initial balance in accumulated depreciation), the customary procedure for recording the purchase of new or used assets. Bonds payable are recorded at their fair value by recognizing a premium or a discount on the bonds. After all assets and liabilities have been recorded at their fair values, an excess of cost over fair value of $230,000 remains and is recorded as goodwill.

A balance sheet prepared after the acquisition of S Company is presented in Illustration 2-5.

If an acquisition takes place within a fiscal period, purchase accounting requires the inclusion of the acquired company's revenues and expenses in the purchaser's

ILLUSTRATION 2-5

Purchase Accounting
P Company
Balance Sheet
January 1, 2000

Cash and Receivables		$ 420,000
Inventories		400,000
Land		1,000,000
Buildings & Equipment	1,800,000	
Accumulatd Depreciation—Buildings & Equipment	(300,000)	1,500,000
Goodwill		230,000
Total Assets		$3,550,000
Current Liabilities		$ 260,000
Bonds Payable	$ 400,000	
Less: Bond Discount	50,000	350,000
Common Stock, $15 par value, 80,000 shares		
outstanding	1,200,000	
Other Contributed Capital	1,390,000	
Retained Earnings	350,000	
Stockholders' Equity		2,940,000
Total Liabilities and Equity		$3,550,000

income statement only from the date of acquisition forward. Income earned by the acquired company prior to the date of acquisition is considered to be included in the net assets acquired.

Income Tax Consequences in Business Combinations Accounted For by the Purchase Method

The fair values of specific assets acquired and liabilities assumed in a business combination may differ from the income tax bases of those items. *SFAS No. 109* requires that a deferred tax asset or liability be recognized for differences between the assigned values and tax bases of the assets and liabilities (except goodwill, unallocated "negative goodwill," and leveraged leases) recognized in a purchase business combination.[13] The treatment of income tax consequences is addressed in Appendix C to this chapter, including the tax consequences related to purchase method business combinations as well as reporting tax consequences in consolidated financial statements.

EXPLANATION AND ILLUSTRATION OF POOLING OF INTERESTS

The pooling of interests method interprets a business combination as a process in which two or more groups of stockholders unite their ownership interests by an exchange of common stock. No acquisition of one company (or companies) by another is recognized, because the combination is accomplished without disbursing assets of the constituents (a corporation's own stock is not considered an asset to that corporation). No owners of former firms are bought out. Instead, the owners, because they continue to be stockholders, retain proprietary rights, however small, in the larger surviving firm. Accordingly, both the net assets of the combining companies and the stockholder groups remain intact, but combined. Thus, fair values of assets and liabilities are ignored, except in the determination of an equitable exchange ratio of common stock, and the assets and liabilities assumed are carried forward to the new or surviving entity at their recorded (book) values. One exception occurs when fair values lower than book values should lead to a downward adjustment in the normal course of operations. For example, if an impairment of an asset's value has occurred, but has not been recorded on the acquirer's books, the acquirer would transfer the asset onto its books at the lower amount.

The stockholders' equity of the acquired company (in total) is combined with the stockholders' equity of the issuing company. (Recall the use of the terms "non-issuing combining" and "issuing" companies for pooling combinations in place of "acquired" and "acquiring" companies.) However, the allocation of the combining company's stockholders' equity among the specific equity accounts demands some attention. How much is allocated to common stock, to other contributed capital, and to retained earnings? The answer depends on the circumstances; in particular, the par value of the two firms' common stock and whether the total contributed capital of the nonissuing combiner is sufficient to cover the par value of the new shares issued (by the issuer).

If the par value of the shares issued in a pooling of interests exactly equals the

---

[13] *Statement of Financial Accounting Standards* No. 109, "Accounting for Income Taxes," FASB (Stamford, 1992), par. 30.

Pooling Method:

Assets

P-9/C

Liabilities

C/S → issuing company's

P-9/C

R/E

Purchase Method:

Investment

C/S — acquiring

P-9/e company's

FIGURE 2-1

Equity Allocation Rule—Pooling of Interests

If $\begin{pmatrix} \text{Par (or Stated)} \\ \text{Value Issued} \end{pmatrix}$	Exceeds	$\begin{pmatrix} \text{Total Par} \\ \text{(or Stated) Value of} \\ \text{Combining Firm} \end{pmatrix}$	Then	*Reduce* (in Order) 1. Combined Other Contributed Capital 2. Combined Retained Earnings
If $\begin{pmatrix} \text{Par (or Stated)} \\ \text{Value Issued} \end{pmatrix}$	Is Less Than	$\begin{pmatrix} \text{Total Par} \\ \text{(or Stated) Value of} \\ \text{Combining Firm} \end{pmatrix}$	Then	*Increase* 1. Combined Other Contributed Capital

par value of the existing shares on the books of the combining firm, then journal entries on the books of the issuing firm should reflect the addition of all other contributed capital and retained earnings from the nonissuing combining company onto the books of the issuing company. More often, however, these par values will not be equal. In such cases, Figure 2-1 illustrates the appropriate adjustments.

Perhaps the more tedious situation occurs when the par value of the shares issued exceeds the par value of the combining firm's shares. In this event, the allocation is based on the following *equity allocation rule*:

When the par (or stated) value of the shares issued by the issuing firm exceeds the total par or stated value of the combining company's stock, the excess should be deducted first from the **combined** *other contributed capital and then from* **combined** *retained earnings.*

To translate this rule into the journal entry needed to record the combination, note that the rule begins with an assumption that the two firms' retained earnings and other contributed capital are being combined, as in the case where par values are equal, and makes modifications from that starting point. For illustrative purposes, we apply the data from Illustration 2-4 to the pooling of interests method. In reality, a given combination will qualify for one treatment or the other (purchase or pooling).

Case A: P Company's "Other Contributed Capital" Is Reduced, and Retained Earnings Is Transferred Intact

Thirty thousand shares of P Company common stock (par value of $450,000) were exchanged for all the net assets of S Company. S Company has outstanding common stock with a par value of $300,000. Under pooling, the acquisition of net assets is recorded on P Company's books as follows:

At book value (pooling method)

Cash and Receivables	180,000	
Inventories	100,000	
Land	120,000	
Buildings	900,000	
Other Contributed Capital	100,000	
Accumulated Depreciation—Buildings & Equipment		300,000
Current Liabilities		110,000
Bonds Payable		400,000
Common Stock (30,000 × $15)		450,000
Retained Earnings		140,000

ILLUSTRATION 2-6

Pooling Accounting
P Company
Balance Sheet
January 1, 2000

Cash and Receivables		$ 430,000
Inventories		360,000
Land		720,000
Buildings	1,700,000	
Accumulated Depreciation—Buildings & Equipment	(600,000)	1,100,000
Total Assets		$2,610,000
Current Liabilities		$ 220,000
Bonds Payable		400,000
Common Stock, $15 par value, 80,000 shares		
outstanding	1,200,000	
Other Contributed Capital	300,000	
Retained Earnings	490,000	
Total Stockholders' Equity		1,990,000
Total Liabilities and Stockholders' Equity		$2,610,000

Notice that the entry records the assets and liabilities of S Company on P Company's books at their precombination book values. Common stock is recorded at its par value to comply with incorporation laws regarding legal capital. An adjustment in stockholders' equity is required because of the difference between the par value of the P Company stock issued, $450,000, and the par value of S Company stock acquired, $300,000. Where the amount of the par or stated value of the stock issued ($450,000) exceeds the total par or stated value of the combining company's stock ($300,000), the excess should be deducted first from the *combined* other contributed capital and then from *combined* retained earnings. Since the par value of the stock issued exceeds the par value of the stock acquired by $150,000, the excess serves to reduce S Company's other contributed capital ($50,000) to zero, and the remaining $100,000 reduces P Company's other contributed capital, as indicated in the foregoing entry. As a result, all of S Company's retained earnings of $140,000 will be combined with the retained earnings of P Company to constitute the surviving entity's retained earnings. A postcombination balance sheet for P Company is given in Illustration 2-6.

Case B: "Other Contributed Capital" Is Eliminated, and S Company's Retained Earnings Is Not Transferred Intact

Although the equity allocation rule is stated in terms of combined equity, journal entries are made on the books of P Company, and S Company's books are dissolved. Note that the combined other contributed capital of both companies would be reduced to zero before any reduction is made to combined retained earnings. For example, if the par value of the stock issued by P Company was $800,000, the entire other contributed capital of P Company would be eliminated and the following entry made. (The assets and liabilities would be recorded at book values on the books of P Company as in the previous entry. In the entries that follow, the net effect will be recorded as "net assets," so that attention can be directed toward the items that would be different, that is, the stockholders' equity structure.)

Net Assets	490,000	
Other Contributed Capital	400,000	
(reduces P Company's Other Contributed Capital to zero)		
Common Stock		800,000
Retained Earnings (140,000 − 50,000)		90,000

Par value of P Company stock issued	$800,000
Less: Par value of S Company stock retired	−300,000
Increase in par value	500,000
Reduce S Company other contributed capital	−50,000
Balance	450,000
Reduce P Company other contributed capital	−400,000
Balance	50,000
Reduce S Company retained earnings recorded	−50,000
Balance	—0—

The par value of the stock issued ($800,000) exceeds the par value of the stock acquired ($300,000) by $500,000, which serves to reduce S Company's other contributed capital by $50,000 (to zero), P Company's other contributed capital by $400,000 (also to zero), and S Company's retained earnings by $50,000. Thus only $90,000 of S Company's retained earnings ($140,000−50,000) is then combined with P Company's retained earnings to constitute the total retained earnings of the surviving company.

Case C: S Company's "Other Contributed Capital" Is Added in Part, and Retained Earnings Is Transferred Intact

In some cases, part of the combining company's other contributed capital will be combined with that of the issuing company. Assume, for example, that the par value of the stock issued was $330,000. The following entry would be made on P Company's books:

Net Assets	490,000	
Common Stock		330,000
Other Contributed Capital		20,000
(50,000 − 30,000)		
Retained Earnings		140,000

Par value of P Company stock issued	$330,000
Less: Par value of S Company stock retired	−300,000
Increase in par value	30,000
Reduce S Company other contributed capital recorded	−30,000
Balance	—0—

The par value of stock issued exceeds the par value of the stock acquired by $30,000, which serves to reduce the amount of S Company's other contributed capital by $30,000; the remaining $20,000 (of the original $50,000 other contributed capital from S Company) is thus added to the other contributed capital of P Company.

Case D: Additional "Other Contributed Capital" Is Added, and Retained Earnings Is Transferred Intact

Where the amount of the par or stated value of the combined entity is *less* than the total of the par or stated value of the combining entities, the difference is an addition to the combined other contributed capital. No portion of the difference is ever added to combined retained earnings. Retained earnings is transferred intact in such cases, but not in excess of the amount on the books of the combining company ($140,000 here). For example, if the par value of the stock issued was $275,000, the following entry on the books of P Company would be appropriate:

Net Assets	490,000	
Common Stock		275,000
Other Contributed Capital		
(50,000 + 25,000)		75,000
Retained Earnings		140,000

In summary, combined retained earnings may be equal to or less than the total of the precombination retained earnings of the constituents, but it can never be greater than that amount.

If the combination had taken place within one fiscal period (rather than on the first day of the period), the individual revenue and expense balances of S Company would also have been carried forward to be combined with those of P Company. Any corporation that applies the pooling method of accounting to a combination should report results of operations for the period in which the combination occurs as though the companies had been combined as of the beginning of the period.

Results of operations (using the pooling method) for that period, therefore, are the sum of the results of: (1) operations of the *separate* companies as if they had been combined from the beginning of the fiscal period to the date the combination is consummated; and (2) the *combined* operations from that date to the end of the period.

Under pooling accounting, all costs (direct and indirect costs, as well as security issuance costs) incurred to effect a business combination are deducted in determining the net income of the resulting combined company for the period in which the expenses are incurred. Thus, the costs of registering and issuing securities, and accounting and consulting fees, for example, are deducted as expenses in the period incurred. In contrast, recall that only *indirect* costs are expensed in a purchase combination.

FINANCIAL STATEMENT DIFFERENCES BETWEEN ACCOUNTING METHODS

The purchase and pooling of interests methods cannot be considered alternatives in accounting for a specific business combination. Two business combinations may be very similar; yet one may have to be accounted for as a purchase, and the other as a pooling. For either the participants or the users of financial data, it is important to understand the differences in financial statements that result from the use of the two methods. We alluded to these differences earlier in principle; we now illustrate them with data. Illustration 2-1 summarizes the differences.

Purchase accounting tends to report *higher asset values* than pooling because of the adjustment to market value and the recording of goodwill, but *lower earnings* because of the excess depreciation and amortization charges under purchase rules. A comparison of Illustrations 2-3 and 2-4 shows that total assets under the purchase method in the situation described exceed those under the pooling method by $940,000, of which $230,000 represents the intangible asset, goodwill (recorded only under the purchase method). The remaining $710,000 reflects the excess of the fair values of the assets of S Company over their precombination book values.

To the extent that this $710,000 relates to inventory or depreciable assets, future income charges will be greater under the purchase method, and reported net income less. Inventory effects are normally reflected in income during the first period subsequent to combination if the first-in, first-out (FIFO) inventory method is used by the surviving entity; under the last-in, first-out (LIFO) method, the effect is not reflected unless inventory quantities are reduced sufficiently in future periods. Depreciation charges will be greater under the purchase method over the remaining useful lives of the depreciable assets, and goodwill must be amortized to future periods. Thus, pooling generally reports greater future earnings and related earnings per share. In addition, long-term liabilities (bonds payable) under the purchase method are $50,000 less than under the pooling method. This $50,000 bond discount must also be amortized to future periods as increased interest expense. Note, however, that the direction of the effect on income is reversed for amortization of bond premium.

Illustration 2-7 shows the amount by which charges (expenses) for depreciation, amortization, and so on under purchase accounting rules exceed those under pooling of interests. Hence the income under the purchase method would be less than it would be under pooling of interests for the first period after the combination. Assume that the FIFO inventory method is used; the average remaining economic life of the buildings and equipment is 20 years; goodwill is amortized over the maximum period allowed, 40 years; and bond discount is amortized on a straight-line basis.

In addition, the future sale of any S Company assets combined will normally produce a greater gain (or smaller loss) under pooling of interests since the assets are carried at lower precombination book values. The stockholders' equity sections

ILLUSTRATION 2-7

Income Effects of Purchase versus Pooling

	Purchase	Pooling	Difference
Building & Equipment Depreciation (20 years)*	$ 75,000	$ 55,000	$20,000
Amortization of Goodwill (40 years)	5,750	—0—	5,750
Bond Discount Amortization (10 years, straight-line)	5,000	—0—	5,000
Inventory added to cost of sales	140,000	100,000	40,000
Total charges**	$225,750	$155,000	$70,750

*Building & Equipment Depreciation:
  Pooling: $(1,100,000 \div 20) = 55,000$
  Purchase: $(1,500,000 \div 20) = 75,000$
**Note: Higher charges translate into lower net income.

Net income using pooling of interests	$370,750
Less: higher charges under purchase	70,750
Net income using purchase	$300,000

of the balance sheets are considerably different under the two methods. The purchase method reports total stockholders' equity of $2,940,000 (Illustration 2-5), whereas the pooling method reports $1,990,000 (Illustration 2-6).

This combination of lower stockholders' equity and higher reported earnings under pooling tends to produce a doubling effect on *return on stockholders' equity*. For example, assume a reported net income of $370,750 (ignoring income taxes) under the pooling of interests method for the first full year after combination. Purchase net income would then be $300,000 or $370,750 − $70,750 (See Illustration 2-7). Computation of the return on stockholders' equity (beginning) would be:

Purchase method = $300,000 ÷ $2,940,000 = 10.2%

Pooling method = $370,750 ÷ $1,990,000 = 18.6%

Thus, pooling reports a significantly greater return on stockholders' equity in this example, *and the return under the purchase method would be further reduced if a shorter amortization period were used (as proposed by FASB).*

Bargain Purchase (Purchase Price Below Fair Value of Identifiable Net Assets)

When the price paid to acquire another firm is lower than the fair value of identifiable net assets (assets minus liabilities), the acquisition is referred to as a *bargain*. When a bargain acquisition occurs, some of the acquired assets must be recorded at an amount below their market values under purchase accounting rules. Although less common than purchases involving goodwill, bargain purchases do occur and require the application of specific rules to conform to generally accepted accounting principles. Note, however, that the FASB is deliberating this issue, however, and changes have been proposed, as discussed in Appendix A to this chapter.

IN THE NEWS

"GE Capital Corp. agreed to buy a Japanese leasing business with assets estimated at nearly $7 billion. . . . GE Capital, of Stamford, Conn., will get the assets at a 'big discount,' said an official familiar with the deal. . . . GE Capital insisted on buying only Japan Leasing's healthy assets."[14]

We first present the rules in effect at this writing, and we then summarize the proposed change. The current rules are listed below for allocating the reduction for bargain purchases. These rules reflect an effort to adjust those assets whose valuation is most subjective and leave intact the categories considered most reliable.

1. Current assets, long-term investments in marketable securities, and assumed liabilities are recorded at fair market value always.
2. Any previously recorded goodwill on the seller's books is eliminated (and no new goodwill recorded).
3. Long-lived assets (other than investments in marketable securities) are recorded at fair market value minus an adjustment for the bargain.

---

[14]*WSJ*, GE Capital to Buy $7 Billion in Japanese Assets," by Jathon Sapsford, 1/25/99, p. A13.

4. A deferred credit (negative goodwill) is recorded only in the event that all long-lived assets (other than investments) are reduced to zero, in which case the credit is amortized (to revenue) over a period not to exceed 40 years.

The excess of fair value over cost should be allocated to reduce long-lived assets (except investments in long-lived marketable securities) in proportion to their fair values in determining their assigned values. In determining how far to reduce long-lived assets, if needed, the standard setters decided to go all the way to zero before recording a deferred credit. This reluctance probably arose from the realization that a deferred credit would lead to revenue recognition as it is amortized over its estimated life. For example, if a balance sheet deferred credit of $400,000 is amortized over a 40-year life, each year the journal entry would be:

Negative Goodwill (deferred credit)	$10,000	
Amortization of negative goodwill (revenue)		$10,000

Note that the amortization of negative goodwill is recorded as a credit, or revenue-type account, the opposite of typical amortization expense. Thus each year's income is increased by the amortization of a deferred credit. Therefore, in some cases, the financial statements of "purchase" firms may look better than the financial statements of "pooling" firms. Note also that the FASB has proposed a change in the treatment of negative goodwill. If the proposed rules are approved, the deferred credit will be treated in the future as an extraordinary gain recognized in its entirety in the year of acquisition.

Example of a Bargain Purchase Assume that Payless Company pays $17,000 cash for all the net assets of Shoddy Company when Shoddy Company's balance sheet shows the following book values and fair values:

	Book Value	Fair Value
Current Assets	$ 5,000	$ 5,000
Buildings (net)	10,000	15,000
Land	3,000	5,000
Total Assets	$18,000	$25,000
Liabilities	$ 2,000	$ 2,000
Common Stock	9,000	
Retained Earnings	7,000	
Total Liabilities and Equity	$18,000	
Net Assets at book value	$16,000	
Net Assets at fair value		$23,000

Cost of the acquisition ($17,000) minus the fair value of net assets acquired ($23,000) produces a bargain, or an excess of fair value of net assets acquired over cost of $6,000. This $6,000 is allocated to reduce the values assigned to buildings and land in the ratio of their fair values as follows:

Buildings	$15,000/$20,000 × $6,000 =	$4,500
Land	$ 5,000/$20,000 × $6,000 =	1,500
Total		$6,000

The entry by Payless Company to record the acquisition is then:

Current Assets	5,000	
Buildings ($15,000 − $4,500)	10,500	
Land ($5,000 − $1,500)	3,500	
Liabilities		2,000
Cash		17,000

Note that the changes proposed by the FASB would not alter this illustration, but only the case where the bargain is so large that the recording of negative goodwill is still needed after lowering asset values to zero.

CONTINGENT CONSIDERATION IN A PURCHASE

Purchase agreements sometimes provide that the purchasing company will give additional consideration to the seller if certain specified future events or transactions occur. The contingency may require the payment of cash (or other assets) or the issuance of additional securities. During the contingency period, the purchaser has a contingent liability that should be properly disclosed in a footnote to the financial statements. If the specified future events or transactions occur, the purchaser must record the additional consideration given as an adjustment to the original purchase transaction. Accounting for the additional consideration depends on the nature of the contingency. The two general types of contingencies are (1) contingencies based on earnings and (2) contingencies based on security prices.

Contingency Based on Earnings

As discussed in Chapter 1, the expected contribution by the acquired company to the future earnings of the acquiring company is an important element in determining the price to be paid for the acquired company. Because future earnings are unknown, the purchase agreement may contain a provision that the purchaser will give additional consideration to the former stockholders of the acquired company if the combined company's earnings equal or exceed a specified amount over some specified period. In essence, the parties to the business combination agree that the total price to be paid for the acquired company will not be known until the end of the contingency period. Consequently, any additional consideration given must be considered as additional cost of the acquired company.

In some instances, the substance of the agreement with the shareholders may be to provide compensation for services, use of property, or profit sharing, rather than to alter the purchase price. The FASB appointed a task force to consider what criteria should be used to determine whether contingent consideration based on performance measures should be accounted for as (1) an adjustment to the purchase price, or (2) compensation expense for services, use of property, or profit sharing. The task force concluded that the distinction is a matter of judgment based on relevant facts and circumstances, and they suggested the following factors or indicators to consider.[15]

---

[15] *Financial Accounting Standards Board, EITF* 95-8, ''Accounting for Contingent Consideration Paid to the Shareholders of an Acquired Enterprise in a Purchase Business Combination.''

1. *Linkage of continuing employment and contingent consideration.* If the payments are automatically forfeited if employment terminates, for example, this indicates that the arrangement is for postcombination services. If, in contrast, the payments are not affected by employment termination, this indicates that the payments are probably an additional component of the purchase price.

2. *Duration of continuing employment.* If the term of required employment is equal to or longer than the contingent payment period, this would indicate that the payments are compensation.

3. *Level of compensation.* If the compensation for employment without the contingent payments is already at a reasonable level in comparison to other key employees in the combined firm, this would indicate that the payments are additional purchase price.

If the contingent payments are determined to be compensation, then they are simply expensed in the appropriate periods and no adjustment to the consideration (purchase price) is needed. On the other hand, assuming that the contingent payments are determined to be additional purchase price, let us consider how to account for them. If goodwill was recorded as part of the original purchase transaction, the fair value of any additional consideration given should be recorded as an addition to goodwill. In the event that an excess of the fair value of net assets acquired over cost was allocated to reduce the fair value of net assets recorded, the original purchase transaction must be reevaluated. The additional consideration given is assigned to noncurrent assets to raise them to their fair values, with any remaining additional consideration assigned to goodwill. The payment of the additional consideration is treated as a change in accounting estimate. The amount of additional consideration assigned to depreciable or amortizable assets is depreciated or amortized over the assets' remaining useful lives.

As an example, assume that P Company acquired all the net assets of S Company in exchange for P Company's common stock. P Company also agreed to issue additional shares of common stock with a fair value of $150,000 to the former stockholders of S Company if the average postcombination earnings over the next two years equal or exceed $800,000. Assume the contingency is met, P Company's stock has a par value of $5 per share and a market value of $25 per share at the end of the contingency period, and goodwill was recorded in the original purchase transaction. P Company will issue 6,000 additional shares ($150,000/$25) and make the following entry:

Goodwill	150,000	
Common Stock (6,000 × $5)		30,000
Other Contributed Capital		120,000

The goodwill recorded must be amortized by adding it to any goodwill recorded on the original purchase date and amortizing the total over its remaining useful life. The amortization period must end within 40 years from the original business combination date (within 20 years, if the FASB's proposal of September 1999 is approved).

If an excess of fair value over cost, in the amount of $50,000, was allocated to reduce the fair values assigned initially to equipment ($35,000) and land ($15,000) in the original purchase transaction, the issuance of the new shares to settle the contingency now reverses that effect. Thus, the new entry would be recorded as follows:

Equipment	35,000	
Land	15,000	
Goodwill	100,000	
Common Stock		30,000
Other Contributed Capital		120,000

The additional $35,000 cost assigned to equipment must be depreciated over the equipment's remaining useful life. The goodwill recorded must be amortized to expense as described earlier.

Contingency Based on Security Prices

In contrast to additional consideration given to satisfy a contingency based on earnings, which results in an adjustment to the total purchase price, a contingency based on security prices has no effect on the determination of cost to the acquiring company. That is, total cost is agreed on as part of the initial combination transaction. The unknown element is the future market value of the acquiring company's stock given in exchange and, consequently, the number of shares or amount of other consideration to be given. The stockholders of the acquired company may be concerned that the issuance of a significant number of additional shares by the acquiring company may decrease the market value of the shares. To allay this concern, the acquiring company may guarantee the market value of the shares given as of a specified future date. If the market value of the shares at the future date is less than the guaranteed value, the acquiring company will pay cash or issue additional shares in an amount equal to the difference between the then-current market value and the guaranteed value.

To illustrate, assume that P Company issues 50,000 shares of common stock with a par value of $5 per share and a market price of $30 per share for the net assets of S Company. P Company guarantees that the stock will have a market price of at least $30 per share one year later. At the original transaction date, P Company made the following entry:

Net Assets (50,000 × $30)	1,500,000	
Common Stock (50,000 × $5)		250,000
Other Contributed Capital		1,250,000

Assuming the market price of P Company's stock at the end of the contingency period is $25 per share, P Company must give additional consideration of $250,000 (50,000 × $5). Because the value assigned to the securities at the original transaction date was only an estimate, any additional consideration given should be recorded as an adjustment to other contributed capital. If the contingency is paid in cash, P Company will make the following entry:

Other Contributed Capital	250,000	
Cash		250,000

This adjustment will result in other contributed capital of $1,000,000, verified as follows:

Total purchase price agreed on	$1,500,000
Less: Cash paid	250,000
Payment in common stock	1,250,000
Less: Par value of stock issued	250,000
Other contributed capital	$1,000,000

If the contingency is satisfied by the issuance of additional shares of stock, P Company must issue 10,000 additional shares ($250,000/$25) to the former stockholders of S Company and will make the following entry:

Other Contributed Capital	50,000	
Common Stock (10,000 × $5)		50,000

This adjustment will result in other contributed capital of $1,200,000, verified as follows:

Total purchase price paid in stock	$1,500,000
Par value of stock issued (60,000 × $5)	300,000
Other contributed capital	$1,200,000

In some cases, consideration contingently issuable may depend on both future earnings and future security prices. In such cases, an additional cost of the acquired company should be recorded for the additional consideration contingent on earnings, and previously recorded consideration should be reduced to current value of the consideration contingent on security prices.

"The major change in contingent payment engineering during 1996 was the increase in the total value of the deals in which post-deal payoffs were used. The total advanced to $9.7 billion from $7.2 billion, suggesting a continuation of the mid-1990s trend in which earn-outs are increasingly appearing in large transactions. Earn-outs in many cases also are taking a greater share of individual purchase prices—sometimes a clear majority."[16]

Despite the trend mentioned in this quote, contingent payments based on earnings still appear in only a small fraction of deals, accounting for an even smaller percentage of total dollar value overall. While they may be helpful in getting past negotiating obstacles and possibly in reducing up-front payouts for buyers, they suffer from drawbacks in implementation. In particular, they are very difficult to administer and may trigger post-deal conflicts between buyers and sellers. Their primary niche is in the acquisition of private companies where management reten-

---

[16] *Mergers and Acquisitions*, "Dealwatch: Security Blankets," March/April 1997, pp. 33–34.

tion is a key issue. Other places where they are used include cross-border deals and deals where corporate sellers wish to maintain a share in future performance.

LEVERAGED BUYOUTS

A leveraged buyout (LBO) occurs when a group of employees (generally a management group) and third-party investors create a new company to acquire all the outstanding common shares of their employer company. The management group contributes whatever stock they hold to the new corporation and borrows sufficient funds to acquire the remainder of the common stock. The old corporation is then merged into the new corporation. The LBO term results because most of the capital of the new corporation comes from borrowed funds.

IN THE NEWS

Back in 1985, leveraged buyout firms were poring over spreadsheet databases looking for companies to buy and bust up. Now, many of those same firms, plus a whole new crop of others, are employing a strategy that's just as profitable and probably more productive: They're scouring the country for companies to buy out and build up. Using a technique known as "platform investing" or "leveraged buildup," buyout concerns are jump-starting the consolidation of dozens of highly fragmented, inefficient, mom-and-pop industries.[17]

The basic accounting question relates to the net asset values (fair or book) to be used by the new corporation. Accounting procedures generally follow the rules advocated by the Emerging Issues Task Force in *Consensus Position No. 88-16*. Essentially, the consensus position is that only the portion of the net assets acquired with the borrowed funds have actually been purchased and should, therefore, be recorded at their cost. The portion of the net assets of the new corporation provided by the management group is recorded at book values since there has been no change in ownership.

To illustrate, assume Old Company has 5,000 outstanding common shares, 500 of which are held by Old Company management. New Company, which is formed to merge Old Company into New Company, then borrows $31,500 to purchase the 4,500 shares held by nonmanagers. Management then contributes its 500 shares of Old Company to New Company, after which management owns 100% of New Company. Clearly, control of Old Company has changed hands. Based on the consensus position, the net assets (90%) purchased from Old Company shareholders for cash should be recorded at their cost. The net assets acquired from the 10% interest held by managers have not been confirmed through a purchase transaction and are, therefore, recorded at their book values. A summary of Old Company's net asset position just prior to the formation of New Company follows:

	Book Value	Fair Value
Plant assets	$ 9,000	$24,000
Other net assets	1,000	1,000
Total	$10,000	$25,000

[17]*Business Week*, "Buy 'Em Out, Then Build 'Em Up," by Eric Schine, 5/8/95, p. 84.

Book entries to record the transactions on New Company's books are:

Investment in Old Company .1($10,000)	1,000	
No Par Common Stock—New Company		1,000
To record the contribution of 500 shares of Old Company stock at book value.		
Cash	31,500	
Notes Payable		31,500
To record borrowings.		
Investment in Old Company	31,500	
Cash		31,500
To record the purchase of 4,500 shares of Old Company.		
Plant Assets*	22,500	
Other Net Assets	1,000	
Goodwill	9,000	
Investment in Old Company		32,500
To record the merger of Old Company into New Company.		

*[$9,000 + .9($24,000 − $9,000)]

Plant assets are recorded at book value plus 90% of the excess of fair value over book value. Other net assets are recorded at book value, which equals fair value. The $9,000 recorded as goodwill on the purchase from outside shareholders can be confirmed as follows:

Cost of shares	$31,500
Book value of net assets acquired .9($10,000)	9,000
Excess of cost over book value	22,500
Assigned to plant assets .9($24,000 − $9,000)	(13,500)
Assigned to goodwill	$ 9,000

After the merger, New Company's balance sheet will appear as follows:

NEW COMPANY
Balance Sheet
January 1, 1995

Plant Assets	$22,500
Other Assets	1,000
Goodwill	9,000
Total Assets	$32,500
Notes Payable	$31,500
Common Stock	1,000
Total Liabilities and Equity	$32,500

Note that the total liabilities and equity of New Company consist primarily of debt; thus the term *leveraged buyout*.

SUMMARY

1. *Distinguish between the purchase and the pooling of interests methods of accounting for business combinations.* Two methods of accounting—**purchase** and **pooling of interests**—are currently accepted in practice. Accounting standards do not permit a free choice between these two methods. Instead the standards clearly define the criteria necessary to qualify for accounting by the pooling method. All other combinations must be accounted for by the purchase method. Differences between the two methods are summarized in Illustration 2-1.

2. *Explain how acquisition expenses are reported under each method.* Under *pooling of interests* rules, all types of acquisition expenses are expensed in the period incurred, including direct, indirect, and security issuance costs. In contrast, under *purchase* accounting rules, each of the three categories of expenses is treated differently. The **direct expenses** incurred in the combination, such as accounting and consulting fees, are capitalized under purchase accounting rules. **Indirect**, ongoing costs, such as those incurred to maintain a mergers and acquisitions department, however, are charged to expense as incurred. Finally, **security issuance costs** are assigned to the valuation of the security in a purchase acquisition, thus reducing the additional contributed capital for stock issues or adjusting the premium or discount on bond issues.

3. *Describe the issues of concern to the FASB that are currently under review, related to business combinations.* Among the issues being examined are the likely elimination of the pooling of interests method and the appropriate way to handle the amortization of goodwill for purchase acquisitions. Other concerns include international comparability and a popular write-off technique involving in-process research and development.

4. *Describe the use of pro forma statements in business combinations.* Pro forma statements, sometimes called ''as if'' statements, are prepared to show the effect of planned or contemplated transactions by showing how they might have affected the historical financial statements if they had been consummated during the period covered by those statements. Pro forma statements serve two functions in relation to business combinations: (1) to provide information in the *planning* stages of the combination, and (2) to *disclose* relevant information subsequent to the combination.

5. *Describe the valuation of assets, including goodwill, and liabilities acquired in a business combination accounted for by the purchase method.* Assets and liabilities acquired are recorded at their fair values. Any excess of cost over the fair value of net assets acquired is recorded as goodwill.

6. *Describe the valuation of assets and liabilities acquired in a business combination accounted for by the pooling of interests method.* Assets and liabilities acquired are recorded at their precombination book values. No excess of cost over book value exists, and no new goodwill is recorded.

7. *Explain the equity allocation rule in terms of its relevance and the mechanics of implementation.* In a pooling of interests, the net assets acquired are recorded at their book values. The stock issued by the issuing company is recorded at the *issuer's* par value, and the balancing amount is allocated between other contributed capital and retained earnings based on the equity allocation rule. When the par (or stated) value of the shares issued by the issuing firm exceeds the total par or stated value of the combining company's stock, the excess should be deducted first from the combined other contributed capital and then from combined retained earnings.

8. *Identify the impact on the financial statements of the differences between pooling and purchase, and understand why some firms may prefer the pooling of interests.* Purchase accounting tends to report **higher asset values** than pooling because of the adjustment to market value and the recording of goodwill, but **lower earnings** because of the excess depreciation and amortization charges under purchase rules. This combination of higher assets and lower reported earnings under purchase accounting tends to produce a doubly undesirable effect on **return on assets**.

9. *Explain how contingent consideration affects the valuation of assets acquired in a business combination accounted for by the purchase method.* If certain specified future events or transactions occur, the purchaser must pay additional consideration. The purchaser records the additional consideration given as an adjustment to the original purchase transaction. Accounting for the additional consideration depends on the nature of the contingency.

10. *Describe a leveraged buyout and the technique of platforming.* A leveraged buyout (LBO) occurs when a group of employees (generally a management group) and third-party investors create a new

company to acquire all the outstanding common shares of their employer company. The term LBO is used because most of the capital of the new corporation comes from borrowed funds. Using a tech-nique known as platform investing or leveraged buildup, some buyout concerns are consolidating dozens of highly fragmented, inefficient, mom-and-pop industries.

APPENDIX A

A Summary of Proposed FASB Statement and Other Current Issues

BUSINESS COMBINATIONS AND INTANGIBLE ASSETS
SEPTEMBER 7, 1999

The FASB added a project on business combinations to its agenda in August 1996 to reconsider both APB *Opinion No. 16*, "Business Combinations," and APB *Opinion No. 17*, "Intangible Assets."

In a Special Report issued in April 1997, the FASB expressed concern that allowing both pooling and purchase methods impairs the comparability of financial statements. The Board addressed three possible alternatives for alleviating the problem: (a) adopt only one method for all combinations, (b) reduce the differences between pooling and purchase accounting outcomes, or (c) modify the pooling criteria specified in APB *Opinion No. 16*. The Board indicated that it did not favor the third alternative, modifying the criteria, and preferred instead to narrow the differences between the pooling and purchase methods.

In September 1999, the Board issued an Exposure Draft, *Business Combinations and Intangible Assets*. This proposal prohibits the use of the pooling of interests method. With regard to goodwill, it suggests the following:

- Every effort should be made to recognize all assets and liabilities acquired, including intangible assets, and to measure them at fair values.
- Any excess of purchase price over the fair market value of net assets acquired is recognized as an asset (goodwill).
- Goodwill should be amortized over its useful life, not to exceed 20 years, using straight-line amortization.
- Within two years of acquisition, goodwill should be reviewed for possible impairment if certain factors are present.
- Both goodwill amortization and any charges for impaired goodwill should be reported "net of taxes" and shown as a separate line item within income from continuing operations on the income statement. The subtotal immediately before this line item should be labeled "income before goodwill charges." The earnings per share presentation may include a per share amount both for this subtotal and for the goodwill charges.

With regard to *other* intangible assets, the proposed standard suggests that all reliably measurable intangible assets should be recognized separately as assets and generally amortized over their useful lives, not to exceed 20 years. However, if a particular intangible asset is expected to generate clearly identifiable cash flows for longer than 20 years and certain criteria are met (e.g., the asset is exchangeable or control over its future economic benefits is obtained through contractual or legal rights extending longer than 20 years), the asset should be amortized over its expected life of more than 20 years. Further, if a particular intangible asset satisfies the specified criteria and has an *indefinite* life, it would not be subject to amortization, but rather to annual review for impairment on a fair value basis.

The FASB also participated in the development of the G4+1 Position Paper, *Recommendations for Achieving Convergence on the Methods of Accounting for Business Combinations.* The G4+1 is an international group of standard setters made up of representatives from the standard-setting bodies in Australia, Canada, New Zealand, the United Kingdom, and the United States (and including representatives of the International Accounting Standards Committee as observers). This group's position also supported the use of a single method of accounting for combinations, and recommended the purchase method as the appropriate one to use.

In March 1999, the FASB announced its intention to address the accounting for purchased in-process R&D in a separate standard from the business combinations project. The FASB indicated at one point that it expected to issue a standard in the fourth quarter of 1999 changing the requirement from *expensing* the assessed value (of in-process R&D acquired in a purchase) to *capitalizing* it as an asset and amortizing it over its expected useful life.[18] Later in 1999, however, the Board announced that it would defer the consideration of in-process R&D to a later date. Another topic that the FASB is deliberating, also related to business combinations, is the handling of the excess of the market value of net assets acquired over the purchase price in a bargain purchase. Its proposal is to treat the bargain as an extraordinary gain in the period of the purchase. Any such changes, however, will be subject to the FASB's due process before final approval.

APPENDIX B

Criteria for Pooling of Interests

The 12 conditions that must be met for a pooling of interests are classified into three broad categories: attributes of the combining companies; conditions relating to the exchange; and absence of planned transactions. After detailing these criteria, this appendix summarizes the FASB's current position with regard to the pooling of interests method.

I. ATTRIBUTES OF THE COMBINING COMPANIES

(a) Each of the combining companies is autonomous and has not been a subsidiary or division of another corporation within two years before the plan of combination is initiated.

A pooling of interests is essentially a transaction between independent stockholder groups under which they unite substantially all their ownership interests by an exchange of common stock for common stock. The disposal of a subsidiary or division is a disposal of only a segment of a business and is therefore incompatible with the concept of pooling. An exception to this condition is made when a company must divest itself of a segment to comply with an order of a governmental authority or judicial body.

---

[18] *Financial Accounting Standards Board*, "Financial Accounting Series Status Report," No. 311, 3/30/99.

(b) Each of the combining companies is independent of the other combining companies. This condition means that at the dates the plan of combination is initiated and consummated, the combining companies hold as intercorporate investments no more than 10% in total of the outstanding voting common stock of any combining company.

This condition is included to prevent a company from circumventing the requirement that combining stockholders must unite substantially all their equity interests by buying out a large group of dissenting stockholders and then entering into a pooling of interests with the remaining stockholders. Such a procedure would materially alter the equity interests of the combining stockholders.

II. CONDITIONS RELATING TO THE EXCHANGE TO EFFECT THE COMBINATION

(a) The combination is effected in a single transaction or is completed in accordance with a specific plan within one year after the plan is initiated.

The essence of pooling is the exchange of equity securities without altering the equity interests of combining stockholders. Because the combining companies continue operations during the negotiation period, equity interests could change substantially over time. An arbitrary period of one year was selected as sufficient to negotiate the terms of the pooling.

(b) A corporation offers and issues only common stock with rights identical to those of the majority of its outstanding voting common stock in exchange for substantially all the voting common stock interest of another company at the date the plan of combination is consummated. Substantially all the voting common stock means 90% or more for this condition.

This condition contains the essence of the pooling concept. The 90% cut-off is an arbitrary one that was selected to prevent a relatively small group of dissenting stockholders from blocking the pooling. Thus, no more than 10% of the stock can be acquired with cash or other consideration.

(c) None of the combining companies changes the equity interest of the voting common stock in contemplation of effecting the combination either within two years before the plan of combination is initiated or between the dates the combination is initiated and consummated; changes in contemplation of effecting the combination may include distributions to stockholders and additional issuances, exchanges, and retirements of securities.

This condition was included to prevent the alteration of equity interests of the common stockholders. Extra dividend distributions, additional stock issues, and stock retirements all have the potential of changing equity interests.

(d) Each of the combining companies reacquires shares of voting common stock only for purposes other than business combinations, and no company reacquires more than a normal number of shares between the dates the plan of combination is initiated and consummated.

A pooling is an exchange of common stock for common stock without changing the equity interests of the combining stockholders. No corporate assets are distributed. If a company purchases its own shares, which are then used to consummate a business combination, the net effect is obviously a purchase rather than a pooling because corporate assets have been distributed and equity interests altered. Thus, treasury stock can be acquired only for normal purposes like providing stock for stock options and employee stock purchase plans.

(e) The ratio of the interest of an individual common stockholder to those of other common stockholders in a combining company remains the same as a result of the exchange of stock to effect the combination.

This condition was included specifically to prevent an altering of stockholder interests.

(f) The voting rights to which the common stock ownership interests in the resulting combined corporation are entitled are exercisable by the stockholders; the stockholders are neither deprived of nor restricted in exercising those rights for a period.

Limitations on or changes in voting rights would obviously alter stockholder interests.

(g) The combination is resolved at the date the plan is consummated, and no provisions of the plan relating to the issue of securities or other consideration are pending.

This condition was included to prevent the issuance of additional shares based on future earnings or stock market prices because such additional issuances would result in a change in stockholder interests.

III. ABSENCE OF PLANNED TRANSACTIONS

(a) The combined corporation does not agree directly or indirectly to retire or reacquire all or part of the common stock issued to effect the combination.

An agreement to retire or reacquire all or a part of the stock issued in a pooling is obviously inconsistent with the notion of combining the entire equity interests of common stockholders.

(b) The combined corporation does not enter into other financial arrangements for the benefit of the former stockholders of a combining company, such as a guaranty of loans secured by stock issued in the combination, which in effect negates the exchange of equity securities.

Arrangements of this type are also obviously inconsistent with the notion of combining entire equity interests.

 (c) The combined corporation does not intend or plan to dispose of a significant part of the assets of the combining companies within two years after the combination other than disposals in the ordinary course of business of the formerly separate companies and to eliminate duplicate facilities or excess capacity.

This condition is an attempt to prevent the recognition of "immediate" profits by pooling undervalued assets with the intention of selling them at their higher fair values shortly after the combination.

APPENDIX C

Deferred Taxes In Business Combinations

A common motivation for the selling firm in a business combination is to structure the deal so that any gain resulting is tax-free at the time of the combination. To the extent that the seller accepts common stock rather than cash or debt in exchange for the assets, the sellers may not have to pay taxes until a later date when the shares accepted are sold. In this situation, the purchasing firm inherits the book values of the assets purchased for *tax* purposes.

Whether the combination is accounted for by purchase or pooling of interests accounting depends on the criteria detailed in Appendix B. Appendix A summarizes the FASB's current position regarding possible future changes affecting the two methods. Any combination that does not satisfy the pooling criteria is accounted for as a purchase. Thus, a given combination may be accounted for as a purchase, even though some stock has been exchanged. When the purchaser has inherited the book values of the assets for tax purposes but has recorded market values under purchase accounting rules (as is frequently the case in a statutory merger or stock acquisition), a deferred tax liability needs to be recognized.

For example, suppose that Taxaware Company has net assets totaling $700,000 (market value), including fixed assets with a market value of $200,000 and a book value of $140,000. All other assets' book values approximate market values. Taxaware Company is acquired by Blinko in a combination that does not meet the pooling criteria; the combination does, however, qualify as a nontaxable exchange for Taxaware. Blinko issues common stock valued at $800,000 (par value $150,000). First, if we disregard tax effects, the entry to record the acquisition would be:

Assets	$700,000	
Goodwill	100,000	
Common Stock		$150,000
Additional Contributed Capital		650,000

Now consider tax effects, assuming a 30% tax rate. First, the excess of market value over book value of the fixed assets creates a deferred tax liability because the excess depreciation is not tax deductible. Thus, the deferred tax liability associated with the fixed assets equals 30% × $60,000 (the difference between market and book values), or $18,000. The entry to include goodwill is as follows:

Assets	700,000	
Goodwill	118,000	
Deferred Tax Liability (.3 × [200,000 − 140,000])		18,000
Common Stock		150,000
Additional Contributed Capital		650,000

While there are no official interpretations of whether goodwill should be "grossed up" on the balance sheet to allow for an additional deferred tax liability, it is not standard practice (and is not done in the entry above). If goodwill is grossed up, goodwill would be $168,571 (or $118,000/.7) and the deferred tax liability on goodwill would be $50,571 (or $168,571 × .3). This alternative results in higher recorded goodwill, which makes it unappealing to many.

(The letter A, B, or C indicated for a question, exercise, or problem means that the question, exercise, or problem relates to a chapter appendix.)

QUESTIONS

1. Discuss the basic differences between the purchase method and the pooling of interests method.

2. When a contingency is based on security prices and additional stock is issued, how should the additional stock issued be accounted for? Why?

3. Describe the treatment that must be applied to other contributed capital and retained earnings of constituents of a business combination under a pooling of interests (a) when the par value of the new company is more than the total of the par values of the constituents, and (b) when the par value of the new company is less than the total par values of the constituents.

4. What are pro forma financial statements? What is their purpose?

5B. In January 2002, Conglomerate Company acquired 90% of the outstanding common stock of Beatle Company in exchange for Conglomerate Company common stock as part of a business combination plan initiated in April 2001. Beatle Company was incorporated in February 2000 as a new venture. At the date the combination plan was initiated, Conglomerate Company owned 5% of Beatle Company stock, which it had acquired for cash during the preceding year. One of Beatle Company's major facilities is a chemical synthesis plant similar to one operated by Conglomerate Company. Conglomerate's directors see no need to maintain two such operations and plan to dispose of Beatle's plant soon after the combination. Considering only the facts given, is this combination eligible for the pooling of interests accounting treatment? Support your answer.

6. Prior to a merger, Overstate Company had a price to earnings (P/E) ratio of 30 and an earnings per share (EPS) of $3. This implied a stock price of $90 per share. Late in its accounting year, Overstate acquired a company, using the pooling of interests method to account for the acquisition. Overstate's EPS increased to $4 per share.
   (a) Why would Overstate's net income increase if the pooling of interests method is used (especially late in the year)?
   (b) If the market naively prices Overstate's EPS using P/E ratios, what is the implied value of Overstate Company subsequent to the merger? If multiples are used to price the stock, how should the company be valued?

7. Suppose that you were issuing stock to make an acquisition and that you could structure the deal such that either accounting method (pooling of interests or purchase) could be used. The acquisition's market value exceeds the book value of its net assets. In addition the company is expected to be profitable.
   (a) Discuss the advantages and disadvantages of each method.
   (b) Would you expect any differential impact on stock prices between the methods?

EXERCISES

EXERCISE 2-1 **Asset Purchase**

Preston Company acquired the assets (except for cash) and assumed the liabilities of Saville Company. Immediately prior to the acquisition, Saville Company's balance sheet was as follows:

	Book Value	Fair Value
Cash	$ 120,000	$ 120,000
Receivables (net)	192,000	228,000
Inventory	360,000	396,000
Plant and Equipment (net)	480,000	540,000
Land	420,000	660,000
Total Assets	$1,572,000	$1,944,000
Liabilities	$ 540,000	$ 594,000
Common Stock ($5 par value)	480,000	
Other Contributed Capital	132,000	
Retained Earnings	420,000	
Total Equities	$1,572,000	

Required:

A. Prepare the journal entries on the books of Preston Company to record the purchase of the assets and assumption of the liabilities of Saville Company if the amount paid was $1,560,000 in cash.

B. Repeat the requirement in (A) assuming the amount paid was $990,000.

EXERCISE 2-2 **Pooling and Purchase Methods**

The balance sheets of Petrello Company and Sanchez Company as of January 1, 2001, are presented below. On that date, after an extended period of negotiation, the two companies agreed to merge. To effect the merger, Petrello Company is to exchange its unissued common stock for all the outstanding shares of Sanchez Company in the ratio of ½ share of Petrello for each share of Sanchez. Market values of the shares were agreed on as Petrello, $48; Sanchez, $24. The fair values of Sanchez Company's assets and liabilities are equal to their book values with the exception of plant and equipment, which has an estimated fair value of $720,000.

	Petrello	Sanchez
Cash	$ 480,000	$ 200,000
Receivables	480,000	240,000
Inventories	2,000,000	240,000
Plant and Equipment (net)	3,840,000	800,000
Total Assets	$6,800,000	$1,480,000
Liabilities	$1,200,000	$ 320,000
Common Stock, $16 par value	3,440,000	800,000
Other Contributed Capital	400,000	—0—
Retained Earnings	1,760,000	360,000
Total Equities	$6,800,000	$1,480,000

Required:

Prepare a balance sheet for Petrello Company immediately after the merger under the assumption that:

A. The merger is treated as a purchase.

B. The merger is treated as a pooling of interests.

EXERCISE 2-3 **Asset Purchase, Cash and Stock**

Pretzel Company acquired the assets (except for cash) and assumed the liabilities of Salt Company on January 2, 2002. As compensation, Pretzel Company gave 30,000 shares of its common stock, 15,000 shares of its 10% preferred stock, and cash of $50,000 to the stockholders of Salt Company. On the acquisition date, Pretzel Company stock had the following characteristics:

Pretzel Company

Stock	Par Value	Fair Value
Common	$ 10	$ 25
Preferred	100	100

Immediately prior to the acquisition, Salt Company's balance sheet reported the following book values and fair values:

SALT COMPANY
Balance Sheet
January 2, 2002

	Book Value	Fair Value
Cash	$ 165,000	$ 165,000
Accounts Receivable (net of $11,000 allowance)	220,000	198,000
Inventory—LIFO cost	275,000	330,000
Land	396,000	550,000
Buildings and Equipment (net)	1,144,000	1,144,000
Total Assets	$2,200,000	$2,387,000
Curent Liabilities	$ 275,000	$ 275,000
Bonds Payable, 10%	450,000	495,000
Common Stock, $5 par value	770,000	
Other Contributed Capital	396,000	
Retained Earnings	219,000	
Total Liabilities and Stockholders' Equity	$2,110,000	

Required:

Prepare the journal entry on the books of Pretzel Company to record the acquisition of the assets and assumption of the liabilities of Salt Company.

EXERCISE 2-4 **Asset Purchase, Cash**

P Company acquired the assets and assumed the liabilities of S Company on January 1, 1999, for $510,000 when S Company's balance sheet was as follows:

S COMPANY
Balance Sheet
January 1, 1999

Cash	$ 96,000
Receivables	55,200
Inventory	110,400
Land	169,200
Plant and Equipment (net)	466,800
Total	$897,600
Accounts Payable	$ 44,400
Bonds Payable,10%, due 12/31/2004, par	480,000
Common Stock, $2 par value	120,000
Retained Earnings	253,200
Total	$897,600

Fair values of S Company's assets and liabilities were equal to their book values except for the following:

1. Inventory has a fair value of $126,000.
2. Land has a fair value of $198,000.
3. The bonds pay interest semiannually on June 30 and December 31. The current yield rate on bonds of similar risk is 8%.

Required:

Prepare the journal entry on P Company's books to record the acquisition of the assets and assumption of the liabilities of S Company.

EXERCISE 2-5 **Asset Purchase, Earnings Contingency**

Pritano Company acquired all the net assets of Succo Company on December 31, 1999, for $2,160,000 cash. The balance sheet of Succo Company immediately prior to the acquisition showed:

	Book Value	Fair Value
Current Assets	$ 960,000	$ 960,000
Plant and Equipment	1,080,000	1,440,000
Total	$2,040,000	$2,400,000
Liabilities	$ 180,000	$ 216,000
Common Stock	480,000	
Other Contributed Capital	600,000	
Retained Earnings	780,000	
Total	$2,040,000	

As part of the negotiations, Pritano agreed to pay the stockholders of Succo $360,000 cash if the postcombination earnings of Pritano averaged $2,160,000 or more per year over the next two years.

Required:

A. Prepare the journal entries on the books of Pritano to record the acquisition on December 31, 1999.

B. Assuming the earnings contingency is met, prepare the journal entry on Pritano's books needed to settle the contingency on December 31, 2001.

EXERCISE 2-6 **Asset Purchase, Stock Contingency**

On January 1, 1999, Platz Company acquired all the net assets of Satz Company by issuing 75,000 shares of its $10 par value common stock to the stockholders of Satz Company. During negotiations Platz Company agreed that their common stock would have at least its current value of $50 per share on January 1, 2000. The market price of Platz Company's common stock on January 1, 2000, was $40 per share.

Required:

Prepare the journal entry on Platz Company's books on January 1, 2000, assuming:

A. The contingency is settled in cash.

B. The contingency is settled by issuing additional shares of stock.

EXERCISE 2-7 **Leveraged Buyout**

Managers of Bayco own 500 of its 10,000 outstanding common shares. Draco is formed by the managers of Bayco to take over Bayco in a leveraged buyout. The managers contribute their shares in Bayco, and Draco then borrows $50,000 to purchase the remaining 9,500 outstanding shares of Bayco. Bayco is then merged into Draco. Data relevant to Bayco immediately prior to the leveraged buyout follow:

	Book Value	Fair Value
Current Assets	$ 3,000	$ 3,000
Plant Assets	12,000	25,000
Stockholders' Equity	$15,000	$28,000

Required:

Complete the following schedule showing the values to be reported in Draco's balance sheet immediately after the leveraged buyout.

Current Assets	$ _____
Plant Assets	_____
Goodwill	_____
Debt	_____
Stockholders' Equity	_____

EXERCISE 2-8 **Asset Acquisition, Pooling**

The stockholders of Porsche Company and Saab Company agree to combine their operations through a pooling of interests. On the date of the combination, the stockholders' equity of each company is as follows:

	Porsche	Saab
Current Assets	$ 400,000	$125,000
Plant Assets (net)	880,000	380,000
Total	$1,280,000	$505,000
Common Stock, $20 par value	$ 700,000	$300,000
Other Contributed Capital	250,000	75,000
Retained Earnings	330,000	130,000
Total	$1,280,000	$505,000

Required:

Prepare the journal entry on Porsche Company's books to record the acquisition of the net assets of Saab Company under each of the four assumptions as to the number of Porsche Company shares issued.

A. Porsche Company issues 12,000 shares.

B. Porsche Company issues 16,000 shares.

C. Porsche Company issues 19,500 shares.

D. Porsche Company issues 35,000 shares.

EXERCISE 2-9 **Multiple Choice, Various Pooling and Purchase**

Price Company issued 8,000 shares of its $20 par value common stock for the net assets of Sims Company in a business combination under which Sims Company will be merged into

Price Company. On the date of the combination, Price Company common stock had a fair value of $30 per share. Balance sheets for Price Company and Sims Company immediately prior to the combination were:

	Price	Sims
Current Assets	$ 438,000	$ 64,000
Plant and Equipment (net)	575,000	136,000
Total	$1,013,000	$200,000
Liabilities	$ 300,000	$ 50,000
Common Stock, $20 par value	550,000	80,000
Other Contributed Capital	72,500	20,000
Retained Earnings	90,500	50,000
Total	$1,013,000	$200,000

Required:

Select the letter of the best answer.

1. If the business combination is treated as a pooling of interests, the total other contributed capital immediately after the combination will be
   (a) $12,500.
   (b) $80,000.
   (c) $50,000.
   (d) $172,500.

2. If the business combination is treated as a pooling of interests, the total retained earnings of the pooled company immediately after the combination will be
   (a) $130,000.
   (b) $124,000.
   (c) $80,000.
   (d) $140,500.

3. If the business combination is treated as a purchase and Sims Company's net assets have a fair value of $228,800, Price Company's balance sheet immediately after the combination will include goodwill of
   (a) $10,200.
   (b) $12,800.
   (c) $11,200.
   (d) $18,800.

4. If the business combination is treated as a purchase and the fair value of Sims Company's current assets is $90,000, its plant and equipment is $242,000, and its liabilities are $56,000, Price Company's balance sheet immediately after the combination will include
   (a) Negative goodwill of $36,000.
   (b) Plant and equipment of $817,000.
   (c) Plant and equipment of $781,000.
   (d) Goodwill of $36,000.

EXERCISE 2-10 Pooling and Purchase

Effective December 31, 1999, Zintel Corporation proposes to issue additional shares of its common stock in exchange for all the assets and liabilities of Smith Corporation and Platz Corporation, after which Smith and Platz will distribute the Zintel stock to their stockholders in complete liquidation and dissolution. The plan of combination has been carefully developed so as to comply with the criteria for a pooling of interests. Balance sheets of each of the corporations immediately prior to merger on December 31, 1999, follow. The common stock exchange ratio was negotiated to be 1:1 for both Smith and Platz.

	Zintel	Smith	Platz
Current Assets	$1,600,000	$ 350,000	$ 12,000
Long-Term Assets (net)	5,700,000	1,890,000	98,000
Total	$7,300,000	$2,240,000	$110,000
Current Liabilities	$ 700,000	$ 110,000	$ 9,000
Long-Term Debt	1,100,000	430,000	61,000
Common Stock, $5 par value	2,500,000	700,000	20,000
Retained Earnings	3,000,000	1,000,000	20,000
Total ·	$7,300,000	$2,240,000	$110,000

Required:

A. Prepare journal entries on Zintel's books to record the combination.

B. Assume that the combination fails to meet the criteria for a pooling of interests because Platz had not been an autonomous entity for two years prior to the combination. The identifiable assets and liabilities of Smith and Platz are all reflected in the balance sheets (above), and their recorded amounts are equal to their current fair values except for long-term assets. The fair value of Smith's long-term assets exceed their book value by $20,000 and the fair value of Platz's long-term assets exceed their book value by $5,000. Zintel's common stock is traded actively and has a current market price of $15 per share. Prepare journal entries on Zintel's books to record the combination.
(*AICPA adapted.*)

EXERCISE 2-11 **Allocation of Purchase Price to Various Assets and Liabilities**

Company S has no long-term marketable securities. Assume the following scenarios:

Case A

Assume that P Company paid $130,000 cash for 100% of the net assets of S Company.

	S Company			
	Assets			
	Current Assets	Long-lived Assets	Liabilities	Net Assets
Book Value	$15,000	$85,000	$20,000	$80,000
Fair Value	20,000	130,000	30,000	120,000

Case B

Assume that P Company paid $110,000 cash for 100% of the net assets of S Company.

	S Company			
	Assets			
	Current Assets	Long-lived Assets	Liabilities	Net Assets
Book Value	$15,000	$85,000	$20,000	$80,000
Fair Value	30,000	80,000	20,000	90,000

Case C

Assume that P Company paid $15,000 cash for 100% of the net assets of S Company.

	S Company			
	Assets			
	Current Assets	*Long-lived Assets*	*Liabilities*	*Net Assets*
Book Value	$15,000	$85,000	$20,000	$80,000
Fair Value	20,000	40,000	40,000	20,000

Required:

Complete the following schedule by listing the amount that would be recorded on P's books.

	Assets			*Liabilities*
	Goodwill	*Current Assets*	*Long-lived Assets**	
Case A				
Case B				
Case C				

*Not including goodwill

EXERCISE 2-12   **Comparison of Earnings Effects of Purchase versus Pooling of Interests**

The Arthur Company is considering a merger with the Guinevere Corporation as of January 1, 2000. It has *not* been determined whether the transaction will meet the criteria for a pooling of interests. It has been determined, however, that the deal will be structured so as to qualify as a nontaxable exchange for tax purposes. If the deal goes through, the Arthur Company expects to issue 20,000 shares of its $5 par stock; the stock is currently trading at $22.25 per share.

The balance sheet of the Guinevere Corporation at the acquisition date is projected to appear as shown below. Also shown are Arthur's assessments of Guinevere's market values at January 1, 2000.

	Guinevere Book Values	*Guinevere Market Values*
Current Assets:		
Cash	$20,000	$20,000
Accounts Receivable	15,000	15,000
Inventory	30,000	30,000
Property, Plant & Equipment:		
Building (net)	$100,000	$250,000
Equipment (net)	60,000	120,000
Total Assets	$225,000	
Total Liabilities	$ 30,000	$ 30,000
Common Stock, $10 par value	80,000	
Retained Earnings	115,000	
Total Liabilities and Equities	$225,000	

Because Arthur Company's management is worried about the relative effects of purchase and pooling on future income statements, they have asked you to compare income before taxes for the year 2000 under purchase versus pooling of interests accounting.

Combined revenues for Arthur and Guinevere are estimated at $300,000 for 2000. Estimated expenses are $120,000, not including depreciation on Guinevere's property and equipment or any goodwill amortization related to the acquisition of Guinevere. Assume that the building has a remaining useful life of 20 years, and the equipment of 10 years. Assume that any goodwill is to be amortized over a 40-year period, and straight-line depreciation and amortization are used.

Required:

Compare income before taxes for the year 2000 under the purchase and pooling of interests methods. Show support for your calculations.

EXERCISE 2-13B **Multiple Choice, Criteria for Pooling**

Required:

Select the letter of the best answer.

1. The conditions required for a business combination to be accounted for as a pooling of interests have been divided into three groups. Which of the following is not one of those groups?
   (a) Conditions related to effecting the combination.
   (b) Attributes of combining companies.
   (c) Conditions related to originating the combination.
   (d) Absence of planned transactions.

2. In deciding whether a business combination meets the criteria for a pooling of interests, it is necessary to perform
   (a) A test of cash to total consideration given to acquire the shares of the combined company.
   (b) A relative-size test of the assets of the combining companies.
   (c) A test of the relative earnings of the combining companies.
   (d) A test of the number of shares exchanged in the combination.

3. Which one of the following would prevent a business combination plan from qualifying as a pooling of interests?
   (a) The combination plan cannot be consummated within one year after initiation.
   (b) One of the combining companies acquires its treasury stock for delivery under its employee stock option plan after initiation of the plan.
   (c) The other combining company was a subsidiary of a competitor company until 30 months before initiation of the combination plan.
   (d) The issuing company pays cash for the shares (a 1% interest) of a stockholder who objects to the combination plan.

4. In order to qualify for a pooling of interests, the issuing company must offer and issue only common stock for substantially all the outstanding voting stock of other combining companies. *Substantially* all means
   (a) 90% of the outstanding voting stock when the combination plan is consummated.
   (b) 90% of the outstanding voting stock less common shares and common share equivalents held by other combining companies.

(c) 90% of the outstanding voting stock not held by other combining companies.

(d) 90% of the outstanding voting stock when the combination plan is initiated.

5. Which of the following transactions related to a business combination would require that the combination be accounted for as a purchase?

(a) The combined company will dispose of numerous fixed assets representing duplicate facilities subsequent to the combination.

(b) The combined company is to retire a portion of the common stock exchanged to effect the combination within 12 months of the combination.

(c) The combination is to be completed within 12 months from the date the plan is initiated.

(d) 92% of one company's common stock is exchanged for only common stock in the other company.

EXERCISE 2-14B   **Evaluating the 90% Test for Pooling of Interests**

The Peter Pan Company has extended a formal offer to the shareholders of the Snow White Company. Peter Pan will exchange two shares of its common stock for each share of Snow White Company. On the consummation date, Peter Pan will own 96,000 of the 100,000 shares of Snow White. Although the percentage clearly exceeds the 90% threshold for pooling of interests, Peter Pan is concerned that not all the shares are eligible to be included in the test.

On the initiation date, Peter Pan and Snow White each already had holdings in the stock of the other company. Specifically, on that date, Peter Pan owned 3,000 shares of Snow White; and Snow White owned 5,000 shares of Peter Pan. In addition, Peter Pan acquired 2,800 shares of Snow White using cash after the initiation date, and Snow White acquired 2,500 shares of Peter Pan.

Required:

Apply the 90% test to the two companies described above. Is it possible that Peter Pan and Snow White can use the pooling method? If not, explain why not. Show support for your calculations.

EXERCISE 2-15B   **Evaluating the 90% Test for Pooling of Interests**

The Primavera Company and the Saskatchewan Company are contemplating a pooling of interests. Saskatchewan has 25,000 shares of common stock outstanding, and Primavera has 50,000 shares outstanding. Primavera proposes to issue three shares of its stock in exchange for five shares of Saskatchewan stock. Primavera already owned 500 shares of Saskatchewan on the initiation date, and Exodus Inc. (a 100%-owned subsidiary of Primavera) owned another 700 shares of Saskatchewan.

To complicate matters further, Primavera purchased 800 shares of Saskatchewan subsequent to the initiation date using cash. By the consummation date, Primavera has issued 13,800 shares in exchange for Saskatchewan stock in the planned exchange ratio.

Required:

Apply the 90% test to the two companies described above. Is it possible that Primavera and Saskatchewan can use the pooling method? If not, explain why not. Show support for your calculations.

EXERCISE 2-16C   **Acquisition Entry, Deferred Taxes**

Patel Company paid $600,000 cash for the net assets of Seely Company on January 1, 2001, in a statutory merger. Seely Company had the following assets, liabilities, and owners' equity at that time:

	Book Value Tax Basis	Fair Value	Excess
Cash	$ 20,000	$ 20,000	$—0—
Accounts Receivable	112,000	112,000	—0—
Inventory (LIFO)	82,000	134,000	52,000
Land	30,000	55,000	25,000
Plant Assets (net)	392,000	463,000	71,000
Total Assets	$636,000	$784,000	
Allowance for Uncollectible Accounts	$ 10,000	$ 10,000	$—0—
Accounts Payable	54,000	54,000	—0—
Bonds Payable	200,000	180,000	20,000
Common Stock, $1 par value	80,000		
Other Contributed Capital	132,000		
Retained Earnings	160,000		
Total Equities	$636,000		

Required:
Prepare the journal entry to record the assets acquired and liabilities assumed. Assume an income tax rate of 40%.

PROBLEMS

PROBLEM 2-1 **Consolidation, Pooling and Purchase**
Condensed balance sheets for Phillips Company and Solina Company on January 1, 2000, are as follows:

	Phillips	Solina
Current Assets	$180,000	$ 85,000
Plant and Equipment (net)	450,000	140,000
Total Assets	630,000	$225,000
Total Liabilities	$ 95,000	$ 35,000
Common Stock, $10 par value	350,000	160,000
Other Contributed Capital	125,000	53,000
Retained Earnings (Deficit)	60,000	(23,000)
Total Equities	$630,000	$225,000

On January 1, 2000, the stockholders of Phillips and Solina agreed to a consolidation whereby a new corporation, McGregor Company, would be formed to consolidate Phillips and Solina. McGregor Company issued 30,000 shares of its $20 par value common stock for the net assets of Phillips and Solina.

On the date of consolidation, the fair values of Phillip's and Solina's current assets and liabilities were equal to their book values. The fair value of plant and equipment for each company was: Phillips, $530,000; Solina, $150,000.

The investment banking house of Bradly and Bradly estimated that the fair value of McGregor Company's common stock was $35 per share. Phillips will incur $20,000 of direct acquisition costs and $6,000 in stock issue costs.

Required:
Prepare the journal entries to record the consolidation on the books of McGregor Company assuming that:

A. The consolidation is accounted for as a pooling of interests.

B. The consolidation is accounted for as a purchase.

PROBLEM 2-2 **Merger and Consolidation, Pooling and Purchase**

Stockholders of Acme Company, Baltic Company, and Colt Company are considering alternative arrangements for a business combination. Balance sheets and the fair values of each company's assets on October 1, 2001, were as follows:

	Acme	Baltic	Colt
Assets	$3,900,000	$7,500,000	$ 950,000
Liabilities	$2,030,000	$2,200,000	$ 260,000
Common Stock, $20 par value	2,000,000	1,800,000	540,000
Other Contributed Capital	—0—	600,000	190,000
Retained Earnings (Deficit)	(130,000)	2,900,000	(40,000)
Total Equities	$3,900,000	$7,500,000	$ 950,000
Fair Values of Assets	$4,200,000	$9,000,000	$1,300,000

Acme Company shares have a fair value of $50. A fair (market) price is not available for shares of the other companies because they are closely held. Fair values of liabilities equal book values.

Required:

Prepare a balance sheet for the business combination for each of the following assumptions:

A. Acme Company acquires all the assets and assumes all the liabilities of Baltic and Colt Companies by issuing in exchange 140,000 shares of its common stock to Baltic Company and 40,000 shares of its common stock to Colt Company. The combination is treated as a purchase.

B. Acme Company issues shares as in (A) above, but the combination is treated as a pooling of interests.

C. A new corporation, Santele Company, is formed to take over the assets and assume the liabilities of Acme, Baltic, and Colt. The new company issues no-par stock with a stated value of $20 per share as follows: to Acme Company, 120,000 shares; to Baltic Company, 150,000 shares; to Colt Company, 20,000 shares. The combination is treated as a pooling of interests.

PROBLEM 2-3 **Purchase of Net Assets Using Bonds**

On January 1, 2001, Perez Company acquired all the assets and assumed all the liabilities of Stalton Company and merged Stalton into Perez. In exchange for the net assets of Stalton, Perez gave its bonds payable with a maturity value of $600,000, a stated interest rate of 10%, interest payable semiannually on June 30 and December 31, a maturity date of January 1, 2011, and a yield rate of 12%.

Balance sheets for Perez and Stalton (as well as fair value data) on January 1, 2001, were as follows:

	Perez	Stalton	
	Book Value	Book Value	Fair Value
Cash	$ 250,000	$114,000	$114,000
Receivables	352,700	150,000	135,000
Inventories	848,300	232,000	310,000
Land	700,000	100,000	315,000
Buildings	950,000	410,000	54,900
Accumulated Depreciation—Buildings	(325,000)	(170,500)	
Equipment	262,750	136,450	39,450
Accumulated Depreciation—Equipment	(70,050)	(90,450)	
Total Assets	$2,968,700	$881,500	$968,350

	Perez	Stalton	
	Book Value	Book Value	Fair Value
Current Liabilities	$ 292,700	$95,300	$ 95,300
Bonds Payable, 8% due 1/1/2013,		300,000	260,000
Interest Payable 6/30 and 12/31			
Common Stock, $15 par value	1,200,000		
Common Stock, $5 par value		236,500	
Other Contributed Capital	950,000	170,000	
Retained Earnings	526,000	79,700	
Total Equities	$2,968,700	$881,500	

Required:

Prepare the journal entry on the books of Perez Company to record the acquisition of Stalton Company's assets and liabilities in exchange for the bonds.

PROBLEM 2-4 Pooling of Interests

Using the data in Problem 2-3, assume that Perez Company exchanged 44,000 shares of its unissued common stock for the net assets of Stalton Company (instead of issuing bonds) and that all conditions for pooling of interests accounting are met.

Required:

Prepare the journal entry to record the exchange of stock on the books of Perez Company. Recall that under generally accepted accounting principles, assets should be adjusted downward for permanent impairment, uncollectible accounts, and so on. In this problem, for example, even under the pooling method, Perez should not record accounts receivable in excess of their estimated fair value.

PROBLEM 2-5 Cash Acquisition, Earnings Contingency

Pham Company acquired the assets (except for cash) and assumed the liabilities of Senn Company on January 1, 2000, paying $720,000 cash. Senn Company's December 31, 1999, balance sheet, reflecting both book values and fair values, showed:

	Book Value	Fair Value
Accounts Receivable (net)	$ 72,000	$ 65,000
Inventory	86,000	99,000
Land	110,000	162,000
Buildings (net)	369,000	450,000
Equipment (net)	237,000	288,000
Total	$874,000	$1,064,000
Accounts Payable	$ 83,000	$ 83,000
Note Payable	180,000	180,000
Common Stock, $2 par value	153,000	
Other Contributed Capital	229,000	
Retained Earnings	229,000	
Total	$874,000	

As part of the negotiations, Pham Company agreed to pay the former stockholders of Senn Company $135,000 cash if the postcombination earnings of the combined company (Pham) reached certain levels during 2000 and 2001.

Required:

A. Record the journal entry on the books of Pham Company to record the acquisition on January 1, 2000.

B. Assuming the earnings contingency is met, prepare the journal entry on Pham Company's books to settle the contingency on January 2, 2002.

C. Repeat requirement (B) assuming the amount of the contingent payment was $80,000 rather than $135,000.

PROBLEM 2-6 **Leveraged Buyout**

The managers of Park Company own 1,000 of its 20,000 outstanding common shares. Step Company is formed by the managers of Park Company to take over Park Company in a leveraged buyout. The managers contribute their shares in Park Company and Step Company then borrows $90,000 to purchase the remaining 19,000 shares of Park Company for $80,000; the remaining $10,000 is used for working capital. Park Company is then merged into Step Company effective January 1, 2000. Data relevant to Park Company immediately prior to the leveraged buyout follow:

	Book Value	Fair Value
Current Assets	$12,000	$12,000
Plant Assets	35,000	70,000
Liabilities	(7,000)	(7,000)
Stockholders' Equity	$40,000	$75,000

Required:

A. Prepare journal entries on Step Company's books to reflect the effects of the leveraged buyout.

B. Prepare a balance sheet for Step Company immediately after the merger.

PROBLEM 2-7 **Asset Acquisition, Pro Forma**

Balance sheets for Salt Company and Pepper Company on December 31, 2000, follow:

	Salt	Pepper
Assets		
Cash	$ 95,000	$ 180,000
Receivables	117,000	230,000
Inventories	134,000	231,400
Plant Assets	690,000	1,236,500
Total Assets	$1,036,000	$1,877,900
Equities		
Accounts Payable	$ 180,000	$ 255,900
Mortgage Payable	152,500	180,000
Common Stock, $20 par value	340,000	900,000
Other Contributed Capital	179,500	270,000
Retained Earnings	184,000	272,000
Total Equities	$1,036,000	$1,877,900

Pepper Company tentatively plans to issue 30,000 shares of its $20 par value stock, which has a current market value of $37 per share net of commissions and other issue costs. Pepper Company then plans to acquire the assets and assume the liabilities of Salt Company for a cash payment of $800,000 and $300,000 in long-term 8% notes payable. Pepper Company's receivables include $60,000 owed by Salt Company. Pepper Company is willing to pay more than the book value of Salt Company assets because plant assets are undervalued by $215,000 and Salt Company has historically earned above-normal profits.

Required:

Prepare a pro forma balance sheet showing the effects of these planned transactions.

PROBLEM 2-8 **Purchase, Decision to Accept**

Spalding Company has offered to sell to Ping Company its assets at their book values plus $1,800,000 representing payment for goodwill. Operating data for 1999 for the two companies are as follows:

	Ping Company		Spalding Company	
Sales		$3,510,100		$2,365,800
Cost of Goods Sold		1,752,360		1,423,800
Gross Profit		1,757,740		942,000
Selling Expenses	$632,500		$292,100	
Other Expenses	172,600		150,000	
Total Expenses		805,100		442,100
Net Income		$ 952,640		$ 499,900

Ping Company's management estimates the following operating changes if Spalding Company is merged with Ping Company through a purchase:

A. After the merger, the sales volume of Ping Company will be 20% in excess of the present combined sales volume, and the sale price per unit will be decreased by 10%.

B. Fixed manufacturing expenses have been 35% of cost of goods sold for each company. After the merger the fixed manufacturing expenses of Ping Company will be increased by 70% of the current fixed manufacturing expenses of Spalding Company. The current variable manufacturing expenses of Ping Company, which is 70% of cost of goods sold, is expected to increase in proportion to the increase in sales volume.

C. Selling expenses of Ping Company are expected to be 85% of the present combined selling expenses of the two companies.

D. Other expenses of Ping Company are expected to increase by 85% as a result of the merger.

Any excess of the estimated net income of the merged company over the combined present net income of the two companies is to be capitalized at 20%. If this amount exceeds the price set by Spalding Company for goodwill, Ping Company will accept the offer.

Required:

Prepare a pro forma (or projected) income statement for Ping Company for 2000 assuming the merger takes place, and indicate whether Ping Company should accept the offer.

PROBLEM 2-9B **Various Pooling versus Purchase**

The boards of directors of Accent Corporation, Bent Company, Cent, Inc., and Decent Corporation are meeting jointly to discuss plans for a business combination. Each of the corporations has one class of common stock outstanding; Bent also has one class of preferred stock outstanding. Although terms have not been settled as yet, Accent will be the acquiring or issuing corporation. Because the directors want to conform to generally accepted accounting principles, they have asked you to attend the meeting as an adviser.

Required:

Consider each of the following questions independently and answer each in accordance with generally accepted accounting principles.

A. Assume that the combination will be consummated August 31, 2002. What is the philosophy underlying the accounting and how will the balance sheet accounts of each of the four corporations appear on Accent's consolidated balance sheet on September 1, 2002, if the combination is accounted for as a

(1) Pooling of interests? → book value

(2) Purchase? → maket value

B. Assume that the combination will be consummated August 31, 2002. How will the income statement accounts of each of the four corporations be accounted for in preparing Accent's consolidated income statement for the year ending December 31, 2002, if the combination is accounted for as a

(1) Pooling of interests? → no depreciation, amortization, net incomes greater

(2) Purchase? →

C. Some of the directors believe that the terms of the combination should be agreed on immediately and that the method of accounting to be used (whether pooling, purchase, or a mixture) may be chosen at some later date. Others believe that the terms of the combination and the method to be used are very closely related. Which position is correct?

D. Accent and Decent are comparable in size; Cent and Bent are much smaller. How do these facts affect the choice of accounting method? No. The size doesn't matter if other requirements for pooling meet

E. Bent was formerly a subsidiary of Tycoon Corporation, which has no other relationship to any of the four companies discussing combination. Eighteen months ago Tycoon voluntarily spun off Bent. What effect, if any, do these facts have on the choice of accounting method? disqualify for pooling

F. Accent holds 1,000 of Bent's 5,000 outstanding shares of preferred stock and 7,500 of Caper's 50,000 outstanding shares of common stock. All of Accent's holdings were acquired during the first three months of 2002. What effect, if any, do these facts have on the choice of accounting method? doesn't matter

G. It is almost certain that Mrs. Marshal Minor, Jr., who holds 5% of Decent's common stock, will object to the combination. Assume that Accent is able to acquire only 95% (rather than 100%) of Decent's stock, issuing Accent common stock in exchange. What accounting method is applicable?

H. Since the directors feel that one of Decent's major divisions will not be compatible with the operations of the combined company, they anticipate that it will be sold as soon as possible after the combination is consummated. They expect to have no trouble in finding a buyer. What effect, if any, do these facts have on the choice of accounting method?

(AICPA adapted.)

[Margin handwritten notes:]
Pooling of interest → two fairly equal value companies
disqualify — 90% rule doesn't work
still work 90% rule

PROBLEM 2-10B **Discussion Problem, Ethics**

Your client is Mega, Inc., a New York Stock Exchange company that has acquired several profitable businesses in recent years. It has subsidiaries in lines such as home computers, seismographic operations, agricultural chemicals, and solar energy. Its earnings have shown steady growth, and the stock market has valued the company with a high price-earnings ratio.

One month ago, you and Mega's treasurer discussed the proposed acquisition of Sellum, Inc., a southwestern real estate brokerage operation with subsidiaries that own and operate apartment houses. Because of the region's depressed real estate market and flat earnings, the stock of Sellum was trading at less than book value. The acquisition was to be made by a straightforward exchange of common stock for common stock using market prices. After reviewing the criteria for business combinations, the treasurer and you agreed that the accounting would follow the pooling of interests method.

But now the treasurer has suggested a complication. He tells you, "It looks like the deal for Sellum will go through. As I see it, if we intend to sell off some of the apartment house subsidiaries, or any of our other assets, we have to use the purchase method of accounting. Then we'll have a minimum of $20,000,000 negative goodwill to take into income over the next three years. We can discuss whether three is the right number of years later, but I just wanted to check and be sure that purchase accounting is okay before we close the deal." You say, "Yes, that's what the accounting standards say, provided it's a significant part of the assets and not a disposal in the ordinary course of business." The treasurer responds, "That's great; you can tell us later what is significant and that's the amount we intend to sell."

Your hesitations center around the thought that Mega may be able to "manipulate"

$20,000,000 or more into its future earnings stream by expressing an intention to sell off some properties. Six months earlier you were confronted with a similar situation. Another client had acquired a ladies' apparel manufacturing complex in a pooling of interests transaction with no intention (represented in writing) of selling off any assets. But 16 months after the acquisition, it had sold off a significant, unprofitable manufacturing subsidiary.

Required:

A. Discuss how the auditor can determine a client's "intent."

B. Discuss the form versus substance of a pooling of interests versus purchase transaction.

C. Was the right answer given to Mega? Discuss.

D. Discuss the question of what constitutes a "significant part of the assets."

E. If the purchase method is followed, what should be done if Mega does not sell off a significant amount of assets?

> (*Adapted from the Touche Ross Foundation Accounting and Auditing Case Studies.*)

PROBLEM 2-11C Acquisition Entry and Deferred Taxes

On January 1, 2002, Pruitt Company issued 30,000 shares of its $2 par value common stock for the net assets of Shah Company in a statutory merger accounted for as a purchase. Pruitt's common stock had a fair value of $28 per share at that time. A schedule of the Shah Company assets acquired and liabilities assumed at book values (which are equal to their tax bases) and fair values follows.

Item	Book Value Tax Basis	Fair Value	Excess
Receivables (net)	$125,000	$ 125,000	$—0—
Inventory	167,000	195,000	28,000
Land	86,500	120,000	33,500
Plant Assets (net)	467,000	567,000	100,000
Patents	95,000	200,000	105,000
Total	$940,500	$1,207,000	$266,500
Current Liabilities	$ 89,500	$ 89,500	$—0—
Bonds Payable	300,000	360,000	60,000
Common Stock	120,000		
Other Contributed Capital	164,000		
Retained Earnings	267,000		
Total	$940,000		

Additional Information:

1. Pruitt's income tax rate is 35%.

2. Shah's beginning inventory was all sold during 2002.

3. Useful lives for depreciation and amortization purposes are:

Plant assets	10 years
Patents	8 years
Bond premium	10 years
Goodwill	25 years

4. Pruitt uses the straight-line method for all depreciation and amortization purposes.

Required:

A. Prepare the entry on Pruitt Company's books to record the acquisition of the assets and assumption of the liabilities of Shah Company.

B. Assuming Pruitt Company had taxable income of $468,000 in 2002, prepare the income tax entry for 2002.

3

CONSOLIDATED FINANCIAL STATEMENTS—DATE OF ACQUISITION

LEARNING OBJECTIVES

1. Understand the concept of control as used in reference to consolidations.
2. Explain the role of a noncontrolling interest in business combinations.
3. Describe the reasons why a company acquires a subsidiary rather than its net assets.
4. Describe the valuation and classification of accounts in consolidated financial statements.
5. List the requirements for inclusion of a subsidiary in consolidated financial statements.
6. Discuss the limitations of consolidated financial statements.
7. Record the investment in the subsidiary on the parent's books at the date of acquisition.
8. Prepare the consolidated workpapers and eliminating entries at the date of acquisition.
9. Compute and allocate the difference between cost (purchase price) and book value of the acquired firm's equity.

IN THE NEWS

Corporate Family Solutions, co-founded by Captain Kangaroo, is merging with a Boston business in a $200 million-plus stock swap to create the nation's largest employer-sponsored child care company. Bright Horizons Inc. of Boston will own 57% of the stock in the new company, to be called Bright Horizons Family Solutions, which will manage 255 centers in 40 states and Washington, D.C.[1]

The decade of the 1990s has seen merger activity sweeping the service industries with unparalleled enthusiasm, if not always with equal success. A move to merge health-maintenance organizations, for example, is well under way and the consolidation of group physicians' practices is following. Small companies are often targeted, where the big investors are less interested, helping to keep the acquisition

---

[1]Associated Press, "Merger Would Create the Largest Employer-Sponsored Child Care Firm," by Karin Miller, 4/29/98.

price more affordable (e.g., five times cash flows, rather than six times cash flows). A technique called ''platform investing'' enables a buyer to start with one acquisition and to follow it with others until the company is large enough to take public. Examples of service-sector industries where this technique has proven successful include funeral homes, golf resorts, landfill sites, and antenna towers. Among the less-successful efforts to date are restaurants, service stations, and dry cleaners.[2]

Recall that business combinations may be negotiated either as *asset acquisitions* or as *stock acquisitions*. In Chapter 2 the procedural focus was on business combinations arising from *asset acquisitions*. In those situations the acquiring company survived, and the acquired company or companies ceased to exist as separate legal entities. The focus in this chapter is on accounting practices followed in *stock acquisitions*, that is, when one company **controls** the activities of another company through the direct or indirect ownership of some or all of its voting stock.

When this occurs, the acquiring company is generally referred to as the **parent** and the acquired company as a **subsidiary**. Those holding any remaining stock in a subsidiary are referred to as the **noncontrolling (minority) interest**. Any joint relationship is termed an **affiliation**, and the related companies are called **affiliated companies**. Each of the affiliated companies continues its separate legal existence, and the investing company carries its interest as an investment. The affiliated companies continue to account individually for their own assets and liabilities, with the parent company reflecting the investment on its books in a single account, Investment in Subsidiary. This account will ultimately be eliminated in the consolidating process to produce a set of consolidated financial statements. However, the investment account will be maintained in the ''parent'' records. Thus, an important distinction is noted between the *consolidated* statements and the *parent only* records or statements in the case of stock acquisitions.

A corporate affiliation may, of course, consist of more than two companies. A parent may obtain a controlling interest in the voting stock of several subsidiaries. If one or more of the subsidiaries owns a controlling interest in one or more other companies, a chain of ownership is forged by which the parent company controls, either directly or indirectly, the activities of the other companies. Many large American conglomerates have been formed by a variety of indirect ownerships.

DEFINITIONS OF SUBSIDIARY AND CONTROL

Although the term **subsidiary** takes on varied meanings in practice, in this text it refers to the situation wherein a parent company (and/or the parent's other subsidiaries) owns a controlling interest in the voting shares of another company, often more than 50% of the voting shares.[3] In October 1995, the FASB issued an Exposure

---

[2] *Business Week*, ''Buy 'Em Out, Then Build 'Em Up,'' by Eric Schine, 5/8/95, p. 85.

[3] The SEC distinguishes majority-owned, totally held, and wholly owned subsidiaries. The term **majority-owned** means a subsidiary more than 50% of whose outstanding voting shares are owned by its parent and/or the parent's other majority-owned subsidiaries. The term **totally held** means a subsidiary (1) substantially all of whose outstanding equity securities are owned by its parent and/or the parent's other totally held subsidiaries, and (2) which is not indebted to any person other than its parent and/or the parent's other totally held subsidiaries, in an amount that is material in relation to the particular subsidiary. The term **wholly owned** means a subsidiary all of whose outstanding voting shares are owned by its parent and/or the parent's other wholly owned subsidiaries.

Draft *broadening* the definition of control to include an indirect ability to control another entity's assets. In February 1999, the FASB issued a revised Exposure Draft, focusing on another entity's **policies and management** rather than its assets.

Specifically, the revised Exposure Draft defines control as the "ability of an entity to direct the policies and management that guide the ongoing activities of another entity so as to increase its benefits and limit its losses from that other entity's activities. For purposes of consolidated financial statements, control involves decision-making ability that is not shared with others." It stresses the need to prepare consolidated financial statements whenever *control* exists, even in the absence of a majority ownership. The Draft also provides a list of indicators of presumed control, and it notes that the proposed definition is similar to the explicit definitions adopted by the International Accounting Standards Committee.

The proposal by the FASB is expected to be opposed by some companies, particularly biotechnology and pharmaceutical conerns, whose financial strength could be hurt by the change. Accounting professionals have argued that some firms deliberately avoid consolidating results by owning less than 50% of the voting stock in an entity, even though they effectively control it by hiring and firing management.[4]

In this chapter we focus on situations where the control is evidenced by a majority ownership. The same procedures would apply, however, in the case where a smaller percentage ownership exists concurrently with evidence of effective control (for example, the parent owns 40% of the voting stock, and no other party has a significant interest). The Exposure Draft defines a subsidiary as an entity that is controlled by another entity. Other definitions and additional details from the Exposure Draft are summarized in Appendix A (later in this chapter).

Similarly, the Securities and Exchange Commission defines a subsidiary as an affiliate controlled by another entity, directly or indirectly, through one or more intermediaries. Control means the possession, direct or indirect, of the power to direct or cause the direction of the management and policies of another entity, whether through the ownership of voting shares, by contract, or otherwise.

REQUIREMENTS FOR THE INCLUSION OF SUBSIDIARIES IN THE CONSOLIDATED FINANCIAL STATEMENTS

The purpose of consolidated statements is to present for a single accounting entity the net resources and operating results of a group of companies under common control. Given this purpose and problems related to off-balance-sheet financing, the FASB has taken the position that essentially all controlled corporations should be consolidated. In addition, the FASB has reemphasized the basic position that parent-company-only financial statements are unacceptable for general purpose distribution; that is, the consolidated financial statements are the primary statements of the economic entity.

---

[4] *WSJ*, "FASB Seeks More Disclosure in Minor Stakes," by Elizabeth MacDonald, 3/3/99, p. C12.

Exceptions Under some circumstances, majority-owned subsidiaries should be excluded from the consolidated statements. Those circumstances include:

1. Ownership is temporary. Management of the parent company should intend a long-term relationship. A parent company should not consolidate a subsidiary it expects to dispose of.
2. Control does not rest with the majority owner. For example, a subsidiary in legal reorganization or bankruptcy should not be consolidated.
3. A foreign subsidiary is domiciled in a country with foreign exchange restrictions, controls, or other governmentally imposed uncertainties so severe that they cast significant doubt on the parent's ability to control the subsidiary.

Investments in majority-owned subsidiaries (greater than 50% ownership) that are not consolidated for one or more of the foregoing reasons are normally reported as investments using the cost method (with fair value adjustments, if needed) because the subsidiaries are neither controlled nor significantly influenced by the parent company.[5]

In general, the object of consolidation is to provide the most meaningful financial presentation possible in the circumstances. Considerable judgment must be exercised in accomplishing this objective. Typically the first note to the financial statements of any company is the statement of significant accounting policies required by *APB Opinion No. 22*. The consolidation policy followed should be disclosed as part of this note.

The FASB has an ongoing project on consolidations and related matters. Issues being examined by the Board are summarized in Appendix A to this chapter, as well as Appendix A to Chapter 2. The appendix to Chapter 2 discusses issues addressed in an exposure draft issued on September 7, 1999, ''Business Combinations and Intangible Assets,'' while the appendix to this chapter summarizes the exposure draft issued on February 23, 1999, ''Consolidated Financial Statements: Purpose and Policy.'' Among the changes being considered are the elimination of the pooling of interests method and, alternatively, ways to narrow the differences in the impact of pooling versus purchase accounting on the financial statements. The Board recognizes that allowing two methods impairs comparability and also that few other countries either require the amortization of goodwill or allow the pooling method. Consequently the Board is considering the elimination of the pooling method, as well as alternatives related to goodwill amortization. The discussions have not yet resulted in a final standard, however.

REASONS FOR SUBSIDIARY COMPANIES

There are several advantages to acquiring a controlling interest in the voting stock of another company rather than its assets or all its voting stock. For example:

1. Stock acquisition is relatively simple. Stock can be acquired by open market purchases or by cash tender offers to the subsidiary's stockholders. Such acqui-

---

[5] *Statement of Financial Accounting Standards No. 94*, ''Consolidation of All Majority-Owned Subsidiaries'' (Norwalk, CT: FASB, 1987).

The subsidiary may have good name, many customers, good contracts

sitions avoid the often lengthy and difficult negotiations that are required in an exchange of stock for stock in a complete takeover.

2. Control of the subsidiary's operations can be accomplished with a much smaller investment, since not all of the stock need be acquired.

3. The separate legal existence of the individual affiliates provides an element of protection of the parent's assets from attachment by creditors of the subsidiary. A parent may sometimes establish a subsidiary by forming a new corporation rather than simply adding a division to the existing company. The limited liability characteristic of the corporate form of business organization is often the primary reason for doing so.

CONSOLIDATED FINANCIAL STATEMENTS

The statements prepared for a parent company and its subsidiaries are called *consolidated financial statements*. They include the full complement of statements normally prepared for a separate entity and represent essentially the sum of the assets, liabilities, revenues, and expenses of the affiliates after eliminating the effect of any transactions among the affiliated companies. Accountants recognize that the unconsolidated financial statements of the parent company, the *legal entity*, are insufficient to present the financial position and results of operations of the *economic unit* controlled by the parent company.

Consider for a moment the unconsolidated financial statements of the parent company. When the parent acquires a controlling interest in the subsidiary, the parent makes an entry debiting *Investment in Subsidiary* and crediting either cash, debt, or stock (or some combination), depending upon the medium of exchange. Assume the acquisition relies on a cash purchase price of $5 million. The entry on the parent's books would be:

Investment in Subsidiary	$5,000,000	
Cash		$5,000,000

The parent's investment account represents the parent's investment in the different asset and liability accounts of the subsidiary and often includes a significant amount of goodwill. However, it is recorded in a single account entitled Investment. The subsidiary, in contrast, continues to keep its detailed books based on historical book values. These values are not as current as the market values assessed by the parent at the date of acquisition, but they are detailed as to classification. One way of looking at the process of consolidating is to consider the following table.

	Investment Account on the Parent's Books	Asset and Liability Accounts on the Susidiary's Books
Valuation	Market Value	Historical Value
Classification	One Account	Multiple Accounts

From the table above, we see that neither the parent's Investment account nor the subsidiary's detailed asset and liability accounts serves to provide *both* the valuation and classification desired in the consolidated financial statements. The process of preparing consolidated financial statements aims to achieve the desirable characteristics in the diagonal by showing the detailed asset and liability accounts on the consolidated balance sheet, but using the valuation established by the acquisition price (assuming purchase accounting applies). Further, this valuation provides the basis needed to measure earnings, reflecting all necessary charges.

The purpose of consolidated statements is to present, primarily for the benefit of the stockholders and creditors of the parent company, the results of operations and the financial position of a parent company and its subsidiaries essentially as if the group were a single company with one or more branches or divisions.[6] Consolidated statements ignore the legal aspects of the separate entities but focus instead on the economic entity under the "control" of management. The presumption is that most users of financial statements prefer to evaluate the economic entity rather than the legal entity. Thus, the preparation of consolidated statements is an example of focusing on substance rather than form.

Although consolidated statements for the economic entity are considered to be more appropriate for use by the stockholders and creditors of the parent company, they are not substitutes for the statements prepared by the separate subsidiaries. Creditors of the subsidiaries must look to the statements of the individual legal entities in assessing the degree of protection related to their claims. Likewise, noncontrolling stockholders need the statements of the individual companies to determine the degree of investment risk involved and the amounts available for dividends. Also, regulatory agencies are often concerned with the net resources and results of operations of the individual subsidiaries.

INVESTMENTS AT THE DATE OF ACQUISITION

The general principles used to record business combinations effected as asset acquisitions were discussed in Chapter 2. The principles to be followed varied depending on whether a purchases or pooling of interests approach was appropriate. The principles followed in accounting for stock acquisitions and in preparing consolidated financial statements also depend on whether the subsidiary stock acquisition is a purchase or a pooling of interests. *In this chapter and throughout Chapters 4 through 10, we will concentrate on accounting for the acquisition of another company's voting stock under the purchases method. The pooling of interests method will be discussed in Chapter 11.* Appendix B to this chapter presents issues related to deferred taxes at the date of acquisition.

Recording Investments at Cost (Parent's Books)

The basic guidelines for valuation discussed in Chapter 2 pertaining to business combinations apply equally to the acquisition of voting stock in another company. Under the purchase method, the stock investment is recorded at its cost as measured by the fair value of the consideration given or the consideration received, whichever is more clearly evident. Recall that the consideration given may consist of cash, other assets, debt securities, stock of the acquiring company, or a combination of these items. Only the direct costs of acquiring the stock should be included in the investment cost. Indirect costs relating to acquisitions (such as the costs of maintaining an acquisitions department) should be expensed as incurred.

---

[6]This position was expressed by the AICPA in *Accounting Research Bulletin No. 51* (and reconfirmed by the FASB in its *Statement of Financial Accounting Standards No. 94*).

If cash is used for the acquisition, the investment is recorded at its cash cost, including broker's fees and other direct costs of the investment. For example, assume that P Company acquires all 10,000 shares of the common stock of S Company for $25 per share and pays acquisition fees of $10,000. The entry to record the investment on P Company's books is:

Investment in S Company	260,000	
Cash (10,000)($25) + $10,000		260,000

If P Company acquired only 50% of the 10,000 shares at $25 per share and paid an acquisition fee of $8,000, the entry would be:

Investment in S Company	133,000	
Cash (5,000)($25) + $8,000		133,000

If P Company issues stock in the acquisition, the investment is recorded at the fair value of the stock issued, giving effect to any costs of registering the stock issue. Assume, for example, that P Company issues 20,000 of its $10 par value common shares with a fair value of $13 per share for the 10,000 shares of S Company, and that registration costs amount to $5,000, paid in cash. The entries to record the investment on P Company's books are:

Investment in S Company (20,000)($13)	260,000	
Common Stock (20,000)($10)		200,000
Other Contributed Capital (20,000)($3)		60,000
Other Contributed Capital	5,000	
Cash (registration costs)		5,000

If P Company paid an additional $10,000 as a finder's fee, the entry would be:

Investment in S Company (finder's fee)	10,000	
Cash		10,000

Note the difference in the effect of the finder's fee or other direct costs, and the registration costs related to the stock issue. The direct costs are considered part of the purchase price and increase the amount of the investment. In contrast, the registration costs serve to reduce the other contributed capital recorded in the transaction, which is consistent with the recording of stock issuances at an amount equal to the *net proceeds* received.

CONSOLIDATED BALANCE SHEETS: THE USE OF WORKPAPERS

Affiliated companies should prepare a full set of financial statements (balance sheet, or statement of position; income statement; statement of cash flows; and notes to the financial statements). As of the *date of acquisition* of one company by another, however, the most relevant statement is the consolidated balance sheet. Preparation of the other consolidated financial statements becomes important with the passage of time and is discussed in later chapters.

The consolidated balance sheet reports *the sum* of the assets and liabilities of a parent and its subsidiaries as if they constituted a single company. Assets and liabilities are summed in their entirety, regardless of whether the parent owns 100% or a smaller controlling interest. In the latter case, the noncontrolling interests are reflected as a component of owners' equity.

Since the parent and its subsidiaries are being treated as a single entity, eliminations must be made to cancel the effects of transactions among them. Intercompany receivables and payables, for example, must be eliminated to avoid double counting and to avoid giving the impression that the consolidated entity owes money to itself. Likewise, any intercompany profits in assets arising from subsequent transactions must be eliminated, since an entity cannot profit on transactions with itself. A *workpaper* is frequently used to summarize the effects of the various additions, eliminations, and so forth. Among the types of transactions that necessitate eliminating entries are the following:

Intercompany Accounts to Be Eliminated		
Parent's Accounts		*Subsidiary's Accounts*
Investment in subsidiary	Against	Equity accounts
Intercompany receivable (payable)	Against	Intercompany payable (receivable)
Advances to subsidiary (from subsidiary)	Against	Advances from parent (to parent)
Interest revenue (interest expense)	Against	Interest expense (interest revenue)
Dividend revenue[7] (dividends declared)	Against	Dividends declared (dividend revenue)
Management fee received from subsidiary	Against	Management fee paid to parent
Sales to subsidiary (purchases of inventory from subsidiary)	Against	Purchases of inventory from parent (sales to parent)

The process of eliminating these and other types of items (such as the profit or loss on intercompany sales of assets not realized in transactions with outsiders) will be discussed in detail in this and later chapters. This chapter will focus on balance sheet accounts, while later chapters will focus on both balance sheet and income statement accounts.

Investment Elimination

An important basic elimination in the preparation of consolidated statements is the elimination of the investment account and the related subsidiary's stockholders' equity. The investment account represents the investment by the parent company in the net assets of the subsidiary and is, therefore, reciprocal to the subsidiary company's stockholders' equity. Since the subsidiary company's assets and liabilities are combined with those of the parent company in the consolidated balance sheet, it is necessary to eliminate the investment account of the parent company against the related stockholders' equity of the subsidiary to avoid double counting of these net assets. In effect, when the parent company's share of the subsidiary company's

---

[7]The account used by the parent to record dividends received from the subsidiary will differ if the parent uses the equity method, described in Chapter 4, to account for its investment.

equity is eliminated against the investment account, the subsidiary company's net assets are substituted for the investment account in the consolidated balance sheet.

The process of combining the individual assets and liabilities of a parent company and its subsidiary at the date of acquisition is discussed next. To start the consolidating process, a useful first step is to prepare a ''Computation and Allocation of Difference Between Cost and Book Value'' schedule (CAD). Preparation of this schedule requires us to address two basic issues.

1. Determine the percentage of stock acquired in the subsidiary. (Is it a 100% acquisition, or a smaller percentage?)
2. Compare the purchase price (cost) to the book value of the equity acquired. If a difference between cost and book value exists (sometimes referred to as the *purchase differential*), we must then allocate that difference to adjust the underlying assets and/or liabilities of the acquired company.

The book value of the equity is the sum of all equity accounts (common stock, additional contributed capital, retained earnings, etc.), which equals the book value of the acquired firm's assets minus liabilities at the date of acquisition. If the acquisition is not a 100% acquisition, then the book value of the equity *acquired* is the total equity of the acquired company times the percentage acquired.

$$\text{Book value (BV) of acquired equity} = \begin{cases} \text{(Percentage acquired)(net assets of S Company), or} \\ \text{(Percentage acquired)(equity of S Company)} \end{cases}$$

Note that the comparison is purchase price (cost) to *book* value, rather than *market* value of the acquired entity. This comparison is appropriate because the subsidiary company's accounts are recorded at book value amounts, and the trial balance of the subsidiary company (along with the trial balance of the parent company) provides the starting point for the consolidation process. Thus, although market values are crucial in determining the numbers that are eventually reported in the consolidated financial statements, we use book values to establish a starting point. When the cost exceeds the book value, the difference will be distributed to adjust net assets upward. When the cost is less than the book value, the difference will be distributed to adjust net assets downward.

The two steps above lead to the following possible cases:

Case 1. The parent company's cost of its investment is *equal* to the book value of the subsidiary company's equity acquired, and
    (a) The parent company acquires 100% of the subsidiary company's stock; or
    (b) The parent company acquires less than 100% of the subsidiary company's stock.

Case 2. The parent company's cost of its investment *exceeds* the book value of the subsidiary company's equity acquired, and
    (a) The parent company acquires 100% of the subsidiary company's stock; or
    (b) The parent company acquires less than 100% of the subsidiary company's stock.

Case 3. The parent company's cost of its investment is *less* than the book value of the subsidiary company's equity acquired, and
    (a) The parent company acquires 100% of the subsidiary company's stock; or
    (b) The parent company acquires less than 100% of the subsidiary company's stock.

ILLUSTRATION 3-1

Balance Sheets for P Company and S Company
January 1, 2000

	P Company	S Company
Cash	$100,000	$ 20,000
Other Current Assets	140,000	50,000
Plant and Equipment (net)	120,000	40,000
Land	40,000	20,000
Total Assets	$400,000	$130,000
Liabilities	$ 60,000	$ 50,000
Common Stock, $10 par value	200,000	50,000
Other Contributed Capital	40,000	10,000
Retained Earnings	100,000	20,000
Total Liabilities and Equity	$400,000	$130,000

We next illustrate the alternatives above in the order listed, with the exception that we omit illustrations of Cases 2(a) and 3(a), which should be readily apparent after reading the others. Examples are based on the balance sheets as of January 1, 2000, for P Company and S Company as shown in Illustration 3-1.

It is important to distinguish between *actual entries* that are recorded in the books of one of the two companies and *workpaper-only entries*. The entries presented in the preceding section to record the Investment in S Company were actual entries, which would be recorded in the accounts of P Company. These types of entries would already be reflected in the trial balance, which constitutes the first column of the workpapers presented throughout this chapter (see, for example, Illustration 3-2 or 3-3).

The entries that we develop next, and which appear in the middle "elimination" columns of the workpapers, are *workpaper-only entries*. As such, they are never posted to the books or accounts of either company's general ledger. Consequently, the entries will need to be repeated each year in the consolidating process. In some cases a number of entries from prior years may be combined to simplify the process; but, in essence, the entries are being repeated each year. Throughout this book, workpaper-only entries will be presented *shaded in blue*. Parent company entries are shaded in *gray*, and subsidiary entries are presented in *white*.

Case 1(a): Parent Company's Cost of Investment Is Equal to Book Value of Subsidiary Company's Stock Acquired—Total Ownership (100% of Subsidiary Stock Acquired)

If the purchase price happens to be exactly equal to the book value of the equity acquired, the investment account (from the parent's trial balance) will eliminate cleanly against the equity accounts of the subsidiary. If we assume further that the market values of the assets acquired approximate their book values, then there is no need to adjust assets or liabilities from their recorded values, even under purchase accounting. The end result of the eliminating process is that the investment account is completely eliminated, as are the equity accounts of the subsidiary (since it is a 100% acquisition). In essence the investment account is replaced with the underlying assets and liabilities of the subsidiary.

To illustrate, assume that on January 1, 2000, P Company acquired all the outstanding stock (5,000 shares) of S Company for a cash payment of $80,000. P Company would record an actual journal entry as follows:

Investment in S Company	$80,000	
Cash		$80,000

Immediately after the acquisition, P Company has $20,000 in cash ($100,000 shown in Illustration 3-1, immediately prior to acquisition, minus $80,000 spent to acquire Company S) and $80,000 in an Investment in S Company account. These amounts appear in the first column of the workpaper presented in Illustration 3-2. The Computation and Allocation of Difference Between Cost and Book Value Schedule reveals no difference, as shown below.

Computation and Allocation of Difference Between Cost and Book Value

Cost of Investment (purchase price)	$80,000
Book Value of Equity Acquired	
($80,000 × 100%)	80,000
Difference Between Cost and Book Value	0

Note that the $80,000 equals the recorded value of S Company's stockholders' equity. Data for the preparation of formal consolidated statements are normally accumulated on a workpaper, on which any required adjusting and eliminating entries are made prior to combining remaining balances. *Adjusting entries* are those needed to correct any accounts of the affiliates that may be incorrect or to recognize the unrecorded effect of transactions that have been recorded by one party, but not by the other. Adjusting entries must be made ultimately on the books of one or more of the affiliates. *Eliminating entries* are made to cancel the effects of intercompany transactions and are made on the workpaper only. In all illustrations throughout this book, *letter notation* is used to identify related parts of adjusting entries, and *number notation* to identify related parts of eliminating entries. Note, however, that some of the eliminating entries will involve "adjustments" to accounts, particularly when there is a difference between cost and book values. Thus, it is technically more accurate to think of eliminating entries as eliminating/adjusting entries or as workpaper entries. These entries will be our focus throughout the next several chapters, and adjusting entries are used only rarely.

The workpaper entry to eliminate S Company's stockholders' equity against the investment account, in general journal form, is:

(1)	Common Stock—S Company	50,000	
	Other Contributed Capital—S Company	10,000	
	Retained Earnings—S Company	20,000	
	Investment in S Company		80,000

Remember, although it is expressed in general journal form, this is a *workpaper-only entry*. No entry is made on the books of either company. As mentioned previously, *all workpaper entries are shaded in blue* to distinguish them clearly from book entries.

A workpaper for the preparation of a consolidated balance sheet for P and S Companies on January 1, 2000, the date of acquisition, is presented in Illustration 3-2.

All the amounts we only on this worksheet, but not on the book yet.

Purchase Accounting

Cost Equals Book Value

Wholly Owned Subsidiary

Date of Acquisition

ILLUSTRATION 3-2

Consolidated Balance Sheet Workpaper

P Company and Subsidiary

January 1, 2000

	P Company	S Company	Eliminations Dr.	Eliminations Cr.	Consolidated Balances
Cash	20,000	20,000			40,000
Other Current Assets	140,000	50,000			190,000
Plant and Equipment	120,000	40,000			160,000
Land	40,000	20,000			60,000
Investment in S Company	80,000			(1) 80,000	*it's always zero*
Total Assets	$400,000	$130,000			$450,000
Liabilities	60,000	50,000			110,000
Common Stock					
P Company	200,000				200,000
S Company		50,000	(1) 50,000		
Other Contributed Capital					
P Company	40,000				40,000
S Company		10,000	(1) 10,000		
Retained Earnings					
P Company	100,000				100,000
S Company		20,000	(1) 20,000		
Total Liabilities and Equity	$400,000	$130,000	$80,000	$80,000	$450,000

(1) To eliminate investment in S Company.

Note the following on the workpaper:

1. The investment account and related subsidiary's stockholders' equity have been eliminated and the subsidiary company's net assets substituted for the investment account.

2. Consolidated assets and liabilities consist of the sum of the parent and subsidiary assets and liabilities in each classification.

3. Consolidated stockholders' equity is the same as the parent company's equity. This is as it should be, since the subsidiary company's stockholders' equity has been eliminated against the parent company's investment account. The consolidated balance sheet is that of the *economic* entity, and the only ownership interest is that represented by P Company's stockholders; that is, P Company owns all of S Company's stock.

Case 1(b): Parent Company's Cost of Investment Is Equal to Book Value of Subsidiary Company's Stock Acquired—Partial Ownership (Less Than 100% of Subsidiary Stock Acquired)

Next we introduce a noncontrolling interest. In this situation, the consolidated balance sheet will nonetheless reflect the combined assets and liabilities of parent and subsidiary *in their entirety*. To balance, the equity interests will then be separated into the noncontrolling interest's equity in net assets and the usual controlling interest equity accounts.

Assume that on January 1, 2000, P Company acquired 90% (4,500 shares) of the stock of S Company for $72,000. Since P Company owns less than 100% of S

Company's stock, consideration must be given to the existence of a noncontrolling interest (minority interest) in the net assets of S Company. A Computation and Allocation Schedule would appear as follows:

Computation and Allocation of Difference Between Cost and Book Value

Cost of Investment (purchase price)	$72,000
Book Value of Eqity Acquired	
($80,000 × 90%)	72,000
Difference Between Cost and Book Value	—0—

The workpaper investment elimination entry is:

(1)	Common Stock—S Company	45,000	
	(.9 × $50,000)		
	Other Contributed Capital—S Company	9,000	
	(.9 × $10,000)		
	Retained Earnings—S Company	18,000	
	(.9 × $20,000)		
	Investment in S Company		72,000

Only that percentage of S Company's equity acquired by P Company is eliminated against the investment account; the remainder of S Company's equity constitutes the noncontrolling interest. The purpose of the consolidated balance sheet is to report the net resources under the control of a single management, and the management of P Company effectively controls all S Company's resources. Thus, all S Company's assets and liabilities are combined with those of P Company on the

Purchase Accounting	ILLUSTRATION 3-3
Cost Equals Book Value	**Consolidated Balance Sheet Workpaper**
90% Owned Subsidiary	**P Company and Subsidiary**
Date of Acquisition	**January 1, 2000**

	P Company	S Company	Eliminations Dr.	Eliminations Cr.	Noncontrolling Interest	Consolidated Balances
Cash	$ 28,000	$ 20,000				$ 48,000
Other Current Assets	140,000	50,000				190,000
Plant and Equipment	120,000	40,000				160,000
Land	40,000	20,000				60,000
Investment in S Company	72,000			(1) 72,000		
Total Assets	$400,000	$130,000				$458,000
Liabilities	60,000	50,000				110,000
Common Stock						
P Company	200,000					200,000
S Company		50,000	(1) 45,000		5,000	
Other Contributed Capital						
P Company	40,000					40,000
S Company		10,000	(1) 9,000		1,000	
Retained Earnings						
P Company	100,000					100,000
S Company		20,000	(1) 18,000		2,000	
Noncontrolling Interest					8,000	8,000
Total Liabilities and Equity	$400,000	$130,000	$72,000	$72,000		$458,000

(1) To eliminate investment in S Company.

consolidated balance sheet, and the noncontrolling interest representing the non-controlling shareholders' interest in the net assets is a separate component of stock-holders' equity.

A workpaper for the preparation of a consolidated balance sheet at the date of acquisition in this situation is presented in Illustration 3-3. A separate column is added to the workpaper in this illustration between the eliminations columns and the consolidated balances to compute the noncontrolling interest in equity. The numbers in this column represent the percentage of each equity account of S Company *not* acquired by P Company, and the total noncontrolling interest is transferred to the consolidated balance sheet column.

In comparing Illustrations 3-2 and 3-3, it should be noted that: (1) consolidated assets are $8,000 greater in Illustration 3-3 since it took $8,000 less cash to acquire the investment, and (2) an $8,000 noncontrolling interest exists. Noncontrolling interest is accumulated on the consolidated workpaper in a separate column.

The proper classification of the noncontrolling interest has been a subject of debate. From the perspective of the controlling interest, it is similar to a liability. It is not, however, a liability because it does not require a future payment by the parent company or the consolidated entity. The shareholders who represent the noncontrolling interest are indeed stockholders, but only of the subsidiary company and not the parent. Some companies, in the past, presented this interest after lia-bilities and before stockholders' equity on the balance sheet to convey the "hybrid" nature of the noncontrolling interest. We believe that the noncontrolling interest is best presented as a part of stockholders' equity of the consolidated entity, but clearly labeled to distinguish it from the other equity accounts.[8]

Case 2(b): Parent Company's Cost of Investment Exceeds Book Value of Subsidiary Company's Stock Acquired—Partial Ownership (Less Than 100% of Subsidiary Stock Acquired)

Next, we continue to allow for a noncontrolling interest, and we introduce a dif-ference between the cost and the book value acquired. In Case 2, we illustrate the common situation where the purchase price is higher than the book value of equity acquired.

Assume that on January 1, 2000, P Company acquired 4,000 shares (80%) of the outstanding common stock of S Company for $74,000 cash, after which P Com-pany has $26,000 in cash and $74,000 in an Investment in S Company. Since the book value of the equity interest acquired by P Company is only $64,000 (80% × $80,000), cost exceeds the book value of equity acquired by $10,000. A Computation and Allocation Schedule for this situation begins as follows:

Computation and Allocation of Difference Between Cost and Book Value

Cost of Investment (purchase price)	$74,000
Book Value of Equity Acquired ($80,000 × 80%)	64,000
Difference Between Cost and Book Value	10,000

---

[8]The term "minority interest" may not reflect clearly the actual nature of some items. For example, a parent company may own 25% of its subsidiary's outstanding preferred stock. In this case, the use of the term "minority interest" to represent the 75% interest held by noncontrolling shareholders is not rep-resentative of the circumstances. Also, a parent may have control of a subsidiary with less than 50% of its common stock. We have elected to use the term "noncontrolling interest" throughout this text.

In this case, because there is a difference between cost and book value, we must not only *compute* the difference but also *allocate* that difference to the appropriate accounts. If we assume that the entire difference is attributable to land with a current market value higher than its historical recorded cost, we would complete the schedule as follows:

Computation and Allocation of Difference Between Cost and Book Value

Cost of Investment (purchase price)	$74,000
Book Value of Equity Acquired ($80,000 × 80%)	64,000
Difference Between Cost and Book Value	10,000
Adjust land upward (mark toward market)	(10,000)
Balance	—0—

The adjustment to land is a debit, and is shown in parentheses. The popular phrase "mark to market" may be used here, with the qualification that the purchase price may not always be great enough to mark the asset entirely to market. In no case would the asset be marked higher than its market value. The adjustment(s) are then added to the difference (treating debit adjustments as negative amounts) to yield a balance. The correct distribution of the difference between cost and book values depends upon the market values of the underlying assets and liabilities. If the difference is *more* than needed to adjust all net assets, then **the excess is goodwill**.

Many firms are concerned about the recording of large amounts of goodwill, because of the future charges to income that result as the goodwill is amortized. Firms looking for creative ways to avoid recording goodwill sometimes write off a portion of the purchase price as an immediate expense under the guise of in-process R&D. This issue is a controversial one, and is addressed in more detail in Chapter 5.

Writing off "purchased R&D" works to reduce rather than inflate profits. It does this by allowing firms to expense in one swoop the value of any R&D that is under way in an acquired firm at the date of acquisition. Many suspect that this accounting maneuver has become a "dustbin for anything that firms want to charge off."[9]

If the difference is not enough to adjust all net assets, then the allocation rules initially presented in Chapter 2 come into play once more. Recall that those rules reflect an effort to completely adjust those assets whose valuation is most objective and assign any deficiency to those assets whose valuation is deemed more subjective (intangible assets and other long-term assets other than marketable securities). We will illustrate these allocation issues again in Chapter 5.

Textbook problems (including those at the end of this chapter) will often make simplifying assumptions, such as "Assume that any difference between cost and book value is attributable solely to land," or "Assume that any difference between cost and book value is attributable to goodwill." This latter assumption is equivalent to stating that book values approximate fair market values. It is important, however, to be aware that more complex adjustments are often needed, and may include a variety of asset and liability accounts (as illustrated in detail in Chapter 5).

[9] *The Economist,* "Think of a Number," 9/11/99, p. 82.

Returning to the example above, in which a difference of $10,000 is attributed to land, a workpaper for a consolidated balance sheet at the date of acquisition in this situation is presented in Illustration 3-4.

The first workpaper investment elimination entry is:

(1)	Common Stock—S Company (.8 × $50,000)	40,000	
	Other Contributed Capital—S Company (.8 × $10,000)	8,000	
	Retained Earnings—S Company (.8 × $20,000)	16,000	
	Difference Between Cost and Book Value	10,000	
	Investment in S Company		74,000

Elimination entry (1) serves to eliminate the investment account against the equity accounts of the subsidiary and to recognize the difference between purchase price and the book values. A new account entitled Difference Between Cost and Book Value is created in this entry. This account is a temporary account, which will be immediately eliminated itself in the very next entry.

Elimination entry (2) (below) serves to allocate the Difference Between Cost and Book Value to the appropriate accounts, in this case land:

(2)	Land	10,000	
	Difference Between Cost and Book Value		10,000

Purchase Accounting	ILLUSTRATION 3-4
Cost Exceeds Book Value	Consolidated Balance Sheet Workpaper
80% Owned Subsidiary	P Company and Subsidiary
Date of Acquisition	January 1, 2000

	P Company	S Company	Eliminations Dr.	Eliminations Cr.	Noncontrolling Interest	Consolidated Balances
Cash	26,000	20,000				46,000
Other Current Assets	140,000	50,000				190,000
Plant and Equipment	120,000	40,000				160,000
Land	40,000	20,000	(2) 10,000			70,000
Investment in S Company	74,000			(1) 74,000		0
Difference Between Cost and Book Value			(1) 10,000	(2) 10,000		
Total Assets	$400,000	$130,000				$466,000
Liabilities	60,000	50,000				110,000
Common stock						
P Company	200,000					200,000
S Company		50,000	(1) 40,000		10,000	
Other Contributed Capital						
P Company	40,000					40,000
S Company		10,000	(1) 8,000		2,000	
Retained Earnings						
P Company	100,000					100,000
S Company		20,000	(1) 16,000		4,000	
Noncontrolling Interest					(16,000)	16,000
Total Liabilities and Equity	$400,000	$130,000	$84,000	$84,000		$466,000

(1) To eliminate investment in S Company.
(2) To distribute the difference between cost and book value.

forward to the balance sheet

Clearly entries (1) and (2) could be collapsed into one entry, and the account Difference Between Cost and Book Value avoided. It becomes useful, however, to separate the two entries in situations involving a number of accounts with more complex adjustments. As this account will be used in future chapters, it is helpful to become acquainted with it at this point.

Reasons an Acquiring Company May Pay More Than Book Value The parent company often pays an amount in excess of the book value of the subsidiary company's stock acquired. Although we have assumed here that it relates to the undervaluation of the subsidiary company's land, any one, or a combination, of the following conditions might exist:

1. The fair, or current, value of one or more specific tangible or intangible assets of the subsidiary company may exceed its recorded value because of appreciation. Sometimes the application of conservative accounting procedures under generally accepted accounting principles results in book values that are lower than fair values for assets. Examples are:
    a. The current expensing of some costs that may contain future benefits (for example, research and development expenditures),
    b. The use of accelerated depreciation methods,
    c. The use of the LIFO inventory method, and
    d. The general prohibition against recognizing unrealized gains.
2. The excess payment may indicate the existence of unrecorded goodwill of the subsidiary company as reflected by its above-normal earning capacity.
3. Liabilities, generally long-term ones, may be overvalued. For example, the subsidiary company may have 8% bonds payable outstanding when acquired by the parent company even though the market rate of interest is 12% at that time.
4. A variety of market factors may affect the price paid for the stock. The mere entry of another large buyer of stock into the market would generally have the effect of increasing the stock's market price. In essence, the parent company is willing to pay a premium for the right to acquire control and the related economic advantages it expects to obtain from integrated operations.

Banque Nationale de Paris (BNP) launched an unexpected bid for both French banks Societé Generale and Paribas, apparently seeking to thwart a planned merger between the two. A BNP official said the bids should offer a ''sizable premium for shareholders of both banks.''[10]

Case 3(b): Parent Company's Cost of Investment Is Less Than Book Value of Subsidiary Company's Stock Acquired—Partial Ownership (Less Than 100% of Subsidiary Stock Acquired)

Finally, we illustrate the less common situation where the purchase price is below the book value of the acquired equity, still assuming the existence of a noncontrolling interest.

Assume that on January 1, 2000, P Company acquired 4,000 shares (80%) of the outstanding common stock of S Company for $60,000, after which P Company

---

[10] *WSJ,* ''BNP Offer Could Block French Deal,'' by Thomas Kamm, 3/10/99, p. A14.

has $40,000 in cash and $60,000 in an Investment in S Company. Since the book value of S Company equity acquired is $64,000 ($80,000 × 80%), equity acquired exceeds cost by $4,000. Once more we assume that the difference between purchase price and book values is attributable to land, in this case an overvaluation. The Computation and Allocation of Difference Schedule would appear as follows:

Computation and Allocation of Difference Between Cost and Book Value

Cost of Investment (purchase price)	$60,000
Book Value of Equity Acquired ($80,000 × 80%)	64,000
Difference Between Cost and Book Value	(4,000)
Adjust land downward	4,000
Balance	—0—

In this instance the difference is negative and is shown in parentheses, and the adjustment is a credit to land. When the difference between cost and book value is negative (i.e., purchase price is below book values), it generally reflects one or a combination of the following:[11]

1. One or more of the subsidiary company's assets is overvalued,
2. One or more of the subsidiary company's liabilities is undervalued or unrecognized, or
3. The parent company simply made a bargain purchase.

As usual, the Computation and Allocation Schedule yields two eliminating/adjusting entries. The investment elimination entry is:

(1)	Common Stock—S Company (.8 × $50,000)	40,000	
	Other Contributed Capital—S Company (.8 × $10,000)	8,000	
	Retained Earnings—S Company (.8 × $20,000)	16,000	
	Investment in S Company		60,000
	Difference Between Cost and Book Value		4,000

Note that when the difference is negative, it appears in the journal entry as a credit in order to balance the entry. In the second workpaper entry, this account will be debited to eliminate it, and the appropriate underlying asset and/or liability accounts will be adjusted to reflect a net downward adjustment of net assets, in this case land. The second elimination entry is:

(2)	Difference Between Cost and Book Value	4,000	
	Land		4,000

A workpaper for a consolidated balance sheet at date of acquisition in this situation is presented in Illustration 3-5.

Subsidiary Treasury Stock Holdings

A subsidiary may hold some of its own shares as treasury stock at the time the parent company acquires its interest. Recall that treasury stock is a contra-equity account,

[11]Chapter 5 elaborates on these alternatives, with illustrations.

Purchase Accounting						
Book Value Exceeds Cost		**ILLUSTRATION 3-5**				
80% Owned Subsidiary		**Consolidated Balance Sheet Workpaper**				
Date of Acquisition		**P Company and Subsidiary**				
		January 1, 2000				

	P Company	S Company	Eliminations Dr.	Eliminations Cr.	Noncontrolling Interest	Consolidated Balances
Cash	40,000	20,000				60,000
Other Current Assets	140,000	50,000				190,000
Plant and Equipment	120,000	40,000				160,000
Land	40,000	20,000		(2) 4,000		56,000
Investment in S Company	60,000			(1) 60,000		
Difference Between Cost and Book Value			(2) 4,000	(1) 4,000		
Total Assets	$400,000	$130,000				$466,000
Liabilities	60,000	50,000				110,000
Common stock						
P Company	200,000					200,000
S Company		50,000	(1) 40,000		10,000	
Other Contributed Capital						
P Company	40,000					40,000
S Company		10,000	(1) 8,000		2,000	
Retained Earnings						
P Company	100,000					100,000
S Company		20,000	(1) 16,000		4,000	
Noncontrolling Interest					16,000	16,000
Total Liabilities and Equity	$400,000	$130,000	$68,000	$68,000		$466,000

(1) To eliminate investment in S Company.
(2) To distribute the difference between cost and book value.

which has a debit balance on the books of the subsidiary. The computation of the percentage interest acquired, as well as the total equity acquired, is based on shares outstanding and should, therefore, exclude treasury shares.

For example, assume that P Company acquired 18,000 shares of S Company common stock on January 1, 2000, for a payment of $320,000 when S Company's stockholders' equity section appeared as follows:

Common Stock, $10 par, 25,000 shares issued	$250,000
Other Contributed Capital	50,000
Retained Earnings	125,000
	425,000
Less: Treasury Stock at cost, 1,000 shares	20,000
Total Stockholders' Equity	$405,000

P Company's interest in S Company is 75% (18,000 shares/24,000 shares), and total equity acquired is 75% × $405,000, or $303,750, which results in a difference between cost and book value of $16,250 ($320,000 − $303,750).

Because the treasury stock account represents a contra stockholders' equity account, the parent company's share must be eliminated by a **credit** when the investment account and subsidiary company's equity accounts are eliminated on the workpaper. Thus, the workpaper eliminating entry is:

Common Stock—S Company (.75 × $250,000)	187,500	
Other Contributed Capital—S Company (.75 × $50,000)	37,500	
Retained Earnings—S Company (.75 × $125,000)	93,750	
Difference Between Cost and Book Value	16,250	
Investment in S Company		320,000
Treasury Stock—S Company (.75 × $20,000)		15,000

The remainder of the treasury stock ($5,000) represents a deduction in the non-controlling interest in net assets and is, therefore, carried over as a subtraction from the noncontrolling interest.

Other Intercompany Balance Sheet Eliminations

Up to this point we have discussed the elimination of the parent company's share of the subsidiary equity acquired against the related investment account. Balance sheet eliminations of a variety of intercompany receivables and payables are also often required. Intercompany accounts receivable, notes receivable, and interest receivable, for example, must be eliminated against the reciprocal accounts payable, notes payable, and interest payable. Cash advances among affiliated companies constitute receivables and payables and must be eliminated. Eliminations also must be made for all types of intercompany accruals for such items as rent and other services. The full amount of all intercompany receivables and payables is eliminated without regard to the percentage of control held by the parent company.

For example, to eliminate a $25,000 cash advance made by P Company and received by S Company, the following entry would be made:

Advance from P Company	$25,000	
Advance to S Company		$25,000

Similarly, to eliminate a $100,000 intercompany account receivable/payable, this entry would be made:

Accounts Payable (to S)	$100,000	
Accounts Receivable (from P)		$100,000

Adjusting Entries Prior to Eliminating Entries

At times, workpaper adjustments to accounting data may be needed before appropriate eliminating entries can be accomplished. The need for adjustments generally arises because of in-transit items where only one of the affiliates has recorded the effect of an intercompany transaction. For example, the parent company may have recorded a cash advance to one of its subsidiaries near year-end but the subsidiary has not yet recorded the receipt of the advance. Thus, the Advances to Subsidiary account on the parent company's books has no reciprocal account on the subsidiary company's books. An adjusting workpaper entry debiting Cash and crediting Advances from Parent is required so that the asset (cash) can be appropriately included in consolidated assets and a reciprocal account established that permits the elimination of intercompany advances. The workpaper eliminations columns may be used to enter these adjusting entries. Alternatively, it is possible simply to adjust the subsidiary company's statements prior to their entry on the workpaper.

A COMPREHENSIVE ILLUSTRATION—MORE THAN ONE SUBSIDIARY COMPANY

No particular problem exists where the parent company owns a direct controlling interest in more than one subsidiary company. The balance sheet of each affiliate is entered on the workpaper, any adjustments needed are prepared, and all related intercompany accounts, including those between subsidiary companies, are eliminated. The remaining balances are combined, and they constitute the consolidated balance sheet.

It is useful at this point to look at an illustrative workpaper and consolidated balance sheet for a parent company, P Company, and its two subsidiaries, S Company and T Company. Assume that on January 1, 2000, P Company acquired 90% and 80% of the outstanding common stock of S Company and T Company, respectively. Immediately after the stock acquisition, balance sheets of the affiliates were:

January 1, 2000

	P Company	S Company	T Company
Cash	$ 82,000	$ 36,000	$ 4,000
Accounts Receivable (net)	68,000	59,000	10,000
Inventories	76,000	64,000	15,000
Advances to T Company	20,000		
Investment in S Company	250,000		
Investment in T Company	115,000		
Plant and Equipment (net)	200,000	241,000	130,000
Land	24,000	10,000	6,000
Total Assets	$835,000	$410,000	$165,000
Accounts Payable	$ 85,000	$ 40,000	$ 25,000
Notes Payable	—0—	100,000	—0—
Common Stock, $10 par value	500,000	200,000	100,000
Retained Earnings	250,000	70,000	40,000
Total Liabilities and Equity	$835,000	$410,000	$165,000

Other information:

1. On the date of acquisition, P Company mailed a cash advance of $20,000 to T Company to improve T Company's working capital position. T Company had not yet received and, therefore, had not yet recorded the advance.

2. On the date of acquisition, P Company owed S Company $6,000 for purchases on open account, and S Company owed T Company $5,000 for such purchases. All these items had been sold by the purchasing companies prior to the date of acquisition.

3. The difference between cost and the book value of equity acquired relates to the undervaluation of subsidiary plant and equipment.

Since the Investments are carried in two separate accounts, it is best to prepare two separate Computation and Allocation Schedules, one for each investment, as follows:

Computation and Allocation of the Difference Between Cost and Book Value (Investment in S Company)

Cost of Investment (purchase price)	$250,000
Book Value of Equity Acquired ($270,000 × 90%)	243,000
Difference Between Cost and Book Value	7,000
Adjust plant and equipment upward	(7,000)
Balance	—0—

Computation and Allocation of the Difference Between Cost and Book Value (Investment in T Company)

Cost of Investment (purchase price)	$115,000
Book Value of Equity Acquired ($140,000 × 80%)	112,000
Difference Between Cost and Book Value	3,000
Adjust plant and equipment upward	(3,000)
Balance	—0—

A workpaper for the preparation of a consolidated balance sheet on January 1, 2000, for P, S, and T companies is presented in Illustration 3-6. Several items on the workpaper should be noted. The cash in transit from P Company to T Company was picked up through an adjusting entry; if it had not been, $20,000 cash would have been excluded from the consolidated balance sheet. The adjustment also provided a reciprocal account, Advance from P Company, that permitted the elimination of the intercompany transaction for advances. (The perceptive reader will

Purchase Accounting

Two Partially Owned Subsidiaries

Date of Acquisition

ILLUSTRATION 3-6

Consolidated Balance Sheet Workpaper

P Company and Subsidiaries

January 1, 2000

	P Company	S Company	T Company	Eliminations Dr.	Eliminations Cr.	Noncontrolling Interest	Consolidated Balances
Cash	82,000	36,000	4,000	(a) 20,000			142,000
Accounts Receivable (net)	68,000	59,000	10,000		(2) 11,000		126,000
Inventories	76,000	64,000	15,000				155,000
Advance to T Company	20,000				(1) 20,000		
Investment in S Company	250,000				(3) 250,000		
Investment in T Company	115,000				(4) 115,000		
Plant and Equipment (net)	200,000	241,000	130,000	(5) 7,000			
				(6) 3,000			581,000
Land	24,000	10,000	6,000				40,000
Difference Between Cost				(3) 7,000	(5) 7,000		
and Book Value				(4) 3,000	(6) 3,000		
Total Assets	835,000	410,000	165,000				1,044,000
Accounts Payable	85,000	40,000	25,000	(2) 11,000			139,000
Notes Payable		100,000					100,000
Common Stock							
P Company	500,000						500,000
S Company		200,000		(3) 180,000		20,000	
T Company			100,000	(4) 80,000		20,000	
Retained Earnings							
P Company	250,000						250,000
S Company		70,000		(3) 63,000		7,000	
T Company			40,000	(4) 32,000		8,000	
Advance from P Company				(1) 20,000	(a) 20,000		
Noncontrolling Interest						55,000	55,000
Total Liabilities and Equity	835,000	410,000	165,000	426,000	426,000		1,044,000

(a) To adjust for cash advance in transit from P Company to T Company.
(1) To eliminate intercompany advances.
(2) To eliminate intercompany accounts payable and receivable.
(3) To eliminate investment in S Company.
(4) To eliminate investment in T Company.
(5) To allocate the cost over book value for S Company to plant and equipment.
(6) To allocate the cost over book value for T Company to plant and equipment.

ILLUSTRATION 3-7

Consolidated Balance Sheet
P Company and Subsidiaries
January 1, 2000

Assets

Current Assets:		
Cash		$ 142,000
Accounts Receivable (net)		126,000
Inventories		155,000
Total Current Assets		423,000
Plant and Equipment (net)		581,000
Land		40,000
Total Assets		$1,044,000

Liabilities and Stockholders' Equity

Current Liabilities:		
Accounts Payable		$ 139,000
Notes Payable		100,000
Total Liabilities		239,000
Stockholders' Equity:		
Noncontrolling Interest in Consolidated Net Assets	$ 55,000	
Common Stock, $10 par value	500,000	
Retained Earnings	250,000	805,000
Total Liabilities and Stockholders' Equity		$1,044,000

have already noticed that the same net effect could have been accomplished by a combined adjusting and eliminating entry with a debit to Cash and a credit to Advance to T.)

The elimination of all intercompany accounts receivable and accounts payable, including those between subsidiary companies, was accomplished through one entry. There is no need to eliminate them individually. Notice also that the equity acquired in each subsidiary company was eliminated against each individual investment account.

The formal consolidated balance sheet is prepared from the detail in the consolidated balance sheet columns of the workpaper and is presented in Illustration 3-7. The balance sheet data are classified according to normal balance sheet arrangements. As discussed earlier, noncontrolling interest in consolidated net assets is classified in some cases as a liability, in others as a part of stockholders' equity, and in still others in a separate section. In the treatment illustrated here, the noncontrolling interest in consolidated net assets is reported as a component of stockholders' equity (preferably the first component of equity listed in the balance sheet).

LIMITATIONS OF CONSOLIDATED STATEMENTS

As noted earlier, consolidated statements may have limited usefulness for noncontrolling stockholders, subsidiary creditors, and regulatory agencies. Noncontrolling stockholders and regulatory agencies can find little information of value to them in the consolidated statements because they contain insufficient detail about the individual subsidiaries. Also, creditors of a specific company have claims only against the resources of that company unless the parent guarantees the claims.

In addition, financial analysts have criticized consolidated statements on several counts. For example, highly diversified companies operating across several industries, often the result of mergers and acquisitions, are difficult to analyze or compare. For instance, General Electric (GE) reports consolidated financial statements that include its credit corporation. The combining of a financial company with a manufacturing company makes interpreting the statements more difficult. In an attempt to make the statements more readable, GE reports three columns with each statement: one showing the total consolidated statements, a column for GE, and a column for the credit corporation. Consolidated operating results for such companies cannot be compared with industry standards, nor can one conglomerate be compared with another. Both the SEC and the FASB have developed requirements for segmental reporting in an effort to address these concerns. Determining what constitutes a segment is not easy, however, and the standards have met criticism and subsequent revision. Segmental reporting is discussed in Chapter 15.

Regardless of these limitations, however, consolidated statements continue to grow in importance. The vast majority of publicly held companies own one or more subsidiaries and report on a consolidated basis. Thus, consolidated statements have assumed the position of primary statements, and the separate statements of individual subsidiaries are considered supplementary.

 ## SUMMARY

1. *Understand the concept of control as used in reference to consolidations.* When one firm (referred to as the parent) effectively controls the activities of another firm (the subsidiary) through the direct or indirect ownership of some or all of its voting stock, consolidated financial statements are required. In a 1999 revised Exposure Draft, the FASB defined control as the ability of an entity to direct the policies and management that guide the ongoing activities of another entity so as to increase its benefits and limit its losses from that other entity's activities.

2. *Explain the role of a noncontrolling interest in business combinations.* The noncontrolling interest in a consolidated entity refers to the stock of the subsidiary firm, if any, which is not controlled by the parent. This interest appears as a component of equity in the consolidated balance sheet.

3. *Describe the reasons why a company acquires a subsidiary rather than its net assets.* A firm may acquire stock by open market purchases or by cash tender offers to the subsidiary's stockholders, thus avoiding the often lengthy and difficult negotiations that are required in a complete takeover. Control of the subsidiary's operations can be accomplished with a much smaller investment, since not all of the stock need be acquired. Also, the separate legal existence of the individual affiliates provides an element of protection

of the parent's assets from attachment by creditors of the subsidiary.

4. *Describe the valuation and classification of accounts in consolidated financial statements.* In the consolidated balance sheet, the assets and liabilities of the subsidiary are combined with those of the parent on an item-by-item basis. Under purchase accounting rules, those assets are reflected at their fair market values, as determined at the date of acquisition (and as subsequently depreciated or amortized), including goodwill, if any.

5. *List the requirements for inclusion of a subsidiary in consolidated financial statements.* Essentially all controlled corporations should be consolidated with the controlling entity. Exceptions include those situations where: ownership is temporary, the subsidiary is in legal reorganization or bankruptcy, or a foreign subsidiary operates in an environment that casts significant doubt about the parent's effective control.

6. *Discuss the limitations of consolidated financial statements.* Consolidated financial statements are of limited use to noncontrolling stockholders, to subsidiary creditors, and possibly to regulatory agencies (e.g., if only the subsidiary is regulated). Also, when highly diversified companies operate across several industries, the aggregation of dissimilar data makes analysis difficult.

7. *Record the investment in the subsidiary on the parent's books at the date of acquisition.* On the books of the parent company, the investment is recorded as a debit to Investment in Subsidiary and a credit to the appropriate account(s) based on the consideration used in the exchange (cash, debt, stock, or a combination). Under purchase accounting rules, any stock issued is recorded at its fair market value, and the investment is thus also recorded at the fair value of consideration paid (including direct acquisition costs, if any).

8. *Prepare the consolidated workpapers and eliminating entries at the date of acquisition.* The consolidated workpapers serve to sum the assets and liabilities of the parent and subsidiary, with adjustments made to assets and liabilities of the subsidiary to "mark" their values toward market values, based on the acquisition price. These adjustments are accomplished via "eliminating and adjusting" entries, which also serve to eliminate the investment account against the portion of the subsidiary's equity accounts owned by the parent. Thus, the consolidated balance sheet reflects only the equity of the controlling shareholders (in the parent firm) and the noncontrolling shareholders (in the subsidiary).

9. *Compute and allocate the difference between cost (purchase price) and book value of the acquired firm's equity.* The difference between cost and book value of the acquired firm's equity, sometimes referred to as the purchase differential, is the amount by which the subsidiary's assets and liabilities must be adjusted in total (including the recognition of goodwill, if any). The use of an account by this name facilitates this process in the eliminating entries, and the differential account itself is eliminated as well.

APPENDIX A

Summary of Proposed FASB Statement
(Consolidated Financial Statements: Purpose and Policy)
February 23, 1999

The proposed Statement would require a controlling entity to consolidate all entities that it controls (subsidiaries) unless control is temporary at the date the entity becomes a subsidiary. The new standard is expected to be issued in the second quarter of 2000, and would be applied by restatement to earlier periods presented in comparative statements.

"Business enterprises and not-for-profit organizations often carry out and finance a significant part of their economic activity through subsidiaries, joint ventures and complex strategic arrangements," says Ronald Bossio, senior project manager. "The Board believes that this Statement fills a significant need by providing a framework for assessing and determining whether a particular relationship between two entities involves control of one entity by the other entity."[12]

The following definitions, characteristics, and indicators were taken from the 1999 exposure draft.

- *Control* is defined as the ability of an entity to direct the policies and management that guide the ongoing activities of another entity so as to increase its benefits and limit its losses from that other entity's activities. For purposes of consolidated financial statements, control involves decision-making ability not shared with others.

---

[12]*Financial Accounting Standards Board*, News Release, "FASB Proposal Establishes When Entities Should Be Consolidated," 2/23/99.

- *Affiliate* is an entity that controls, is controlled by, or is under common control with, another entity, either directly or indirectly through one or more intermediaries.
- A *parent* is an entity that controls one or more subsidiaries.
- A *subsidiary* is an entity that is controlled by another entity.

The Board identifies a list of circumstances establishing the presumption of control, in the absence of evidence that demonstrates otherwise. Control is presumed (though rebuttable) if an entity (including its subsidiaries):

- Has a majority voting interest in the election of a corporation's governing body or a right to appoint a majority of the members of its governing body.
- Has a large minority voting interest in the election of a corporation's governing body and no other party or organized group of parties has a significant voting interest.
- Has a unilateral ability to (1) obtain a majority voting interest in the election of a corporation's governing body or (2) obtain a right to appoint a majority of the corporation's governing body through the present ownership of convertible securities or other rights currently exercisable at the option of the holder (and the expected benefit from exercise or conversion exceeds the expected cost).
- Is the only partner in a limited partnership and no other partner or organized group of partners has the current ability to dissolve the limited partnership or otherwise remove the general partner.

In a situation where a corporation is established without a governing body, the above indicators do not apply. Instead an assessment of all factors and circumstances surrounding the establishment of the corporation is substituted to establish presumed control. In these cases, some relevant factors to distinguish between a parent-subsidiary relationship and other relationships where control is *shared* (rather than resting with a single entity) include:

- Whether one or more entities provided significant funding;
- Whether an entity has or shares the decision-making powers and duties typical of a board of directors (especially those related to directing the use and access to the firm's assets and the selection and retention of its management);
- Whether an entity has the right to change the corporation's articles of incorporation; and
- Whether an entity has or shares significant risks and rewards of ownership.

The Board considered requiring both control and a specified level of ownership as two separate and necessary conditions for consolidation, but rejected this requirement, deciding instead that control alone is a sufficient and appropriate condition for requiring consolidated financial statements. Also, some respondents to the Preliminary Views issued prior to the original Exposure Draft questioned whether the policy should be extended to investment companies, venture capitalists, and other entities carrying investments at fair value. In the revised Exposure Draft, the Board admitted that difficult questions arise for special-purpose entities but concluded that there was no basis for providing an exemption to certain types of entities merely because difficulties may be encountered in assessing control.[13]

APPENDIX B

Deferred Taxes on the Date of Acquisition

If a purchase acquisition is tax-free to the seller, the tax bases of the acquired assets and liabilities are carried forward at historical book values. However, the assets and liabilities of the acquired company are recorded on the consolidated books at adjusted fair value. Under current guidelines, the tax effects of the difference between consolidated book values and the tax bases must be recorded as deferred tax liabilities or assets (*SFAS No. 109*).

Consider the following example. Suppose that Purchasing Company acquires 90% of Selling Company by issuing stock valued at $800,000. The only difference between book value and fair value relates to depreciable plant and equipment. Plant and equipment has a market value of $400,000 and a book value of $250,000. All other book values approximate market values. Assume that the combination qualifies as a nontaxable exchange. On the date of acquisition, Selling Company's book value of equity is $600,000, which includes $150,000 of common stock and $450,000 of retained earnings. Assume a 30% tax rate. Consider the following Computation and Allocation Schedule with and without considering deferred taxes.

Computation and Allocation of the Difference Between Cost and Book Value

	Without Deferred Taxes	*With Deferred Taxes*
Cost of Investment (Purchase Price)	$800,000	$800,000
Book Value of Equity Acquired ($600,000 × 90%)	540,000	540,000
Difference Between Cost and Book Value	260,000	260,000
Adjust plant and equipment upward		
(400,000 − 250,000)(90%)	(135,000)	(135,000)
Deferred tax liability on plant and equipment		
(400,000 − 250,000)(90%)(30%)		40,500
Goodwill	125,000	165,500

Notice that goodwill is increased when deferred taxes are computed on the timing difference related to the depreciable bases of plant and equipment. This occurs because the additional future depreciation from the write-up of plant and equipment is reported on the consolidated income statement but is nondeductible for tax purposes, creating a timing difference between book and tax. Recall that deferred taxes are classified in the balance sheet according to the item that gave rise to them. Since plant and equipment are long-term assets, the deferred tax liability would also be *long-term*.

---

[13]*FASB*, Proposed Statement, "Consolidated Financial Statements: Purpose and Policy," 2/23/99, par. 232.

The workpaper entry to eliminate the investment account is as follows:

(1)	Common Stock—Selling Company (.9 × $150,000)	135,000	
	Retained Earnings—Selling Company (.9 × $450,000)	405,000	
	Difference Between Cost and Book Value	260,000	
	Investment in S Company		800,000

The entry to allocate the difference between cost and book value is affected by the deferred tax amounts. The following entries show the allocation with and without deferred taxes.

		Without Deferred Taxes		*With Deferred Taxes*	
(2)	Plant and Equipment	135,000		135,000	
	Goodwill	125,000		165,500	
	Deferred tax liability (long-term)				40,500
	Difference Between Cost and Book Value		260,000		260,000

Of the two entries above, only the entry *with* deferred taxes is complete, according to *SFAS No. 109*. Thus a deferred tax liability or asset should be recorded for each adjustment in the Computation and Allocation Schedule that creates a timing difference. For instance, if inventory value is increased, a *current* deferred tax liability would be created.

One final point is worth noting about goodwill: while there are no official interpretations of whether goodwill itself should be ''grossed up'' on the balance sheet (with an additional deferred tax liability recorded), it is not common practice. If goodwill were grossed up in the previous example, goodwill would be $236,429 (or $165,500/.7) instead of $165,500, and the deferred tax liability on goodwill would be $70,928 (or $236,429 × .3). Clearly, this results in increased goodwill, which many preparers find unappealing.

(The letter A, B, or C indicated for a question, exercise, or problem refers to a related appendix.)

QUESTIONS

1. What are the advantages of acquiring the *majority* of the voting stock of another company rather than acquiring *all* its voting stock?

2. What is the justification for preparing consolidated financial statements when, in fact, it is apparent that the consolidated group is not a legal entity?

3. Why is it often necessary to prepare separate financial statements for each legal entity in a consolidated group even though consolidated statements provide a better economic picture of the combined activities?

4. What aspects of control must exist before a subsidiary is consolidated?

5. Why are consolidated workpapers used in preparing consolidated financial statements?

6. Define noncontrolling (minority) interest. List three methods of reporting the noncontrolling interest in a consolidated balance sheet.

7. Give several reasons why a parent company would be willing to pay more than book value for subsidiary stock acquired.

8. What effect do subsidiary treasury stock holdings have at the time the subsidiary is acquired? How should the treasury stock be treated on consolidated workpapers?

9. What effect does a noncontrolling interest have on the amount of intercompany receivables and payables eliminated on a consolidated balance sheet?

10B. Did the decision in *SFAS No. 109* to require that a deferred tax asset or liability be recognized for differences between the assigned values and tax bases of assets and liabilities recognized in purchase business combinations change the amount of consolidated net income reported in years subsequent to the business combination? Explain.

EXERCISES

EXERCISE 3-1 Workpaper Elimination Entries: Three Cases

Prepare in general journal form the workpaper entries to eliminate Prancer Company's investment in Saltez Company and to allocate any difference between cost and book value in the preparation of a consolidated balance sheet at the date of acquisition for each of the following independent cases:

			Saltez Company Equity Balances		
Case	Percent of Stock Owned	Investment Cost	Common Stock	Other Contributed Capital	Retained Earnings
a.	100%	$351,000	$160,000	$92,000	$43,000
b.	90	232,000	190,000	75,000	(29,000)
c.	80	159,000	180,000	40,000	(4,000)

Any difference between cost and book value of net assets acquired relates to subsidiary property plant and equipment.

EXERCISE 3-2 Stock Purchase Entries

On January 1, 2001, Polo Company purchased 100% of the common stock of Save Company by issuing 40,000 shares of its (Polo's) $10 par value common stock with a market price of $17.50 per share. Polo incurred cash expenses of $20,000 for registering and issuing the common stock. The combination did not qualify as a pooling of interests. The stockholders' equity sections of the two companies' balance sheets on December 31, 2000, were:

	Polo	Save
Common Stock, $10 par value	$350,000	$320,000
Other Contributed Capital	590,000	175,000
Retained Earnings	380,000	205,000

Required:

A. Prepare the journal entry(s) on the books of Polo Company to record the purchase of the common stock of Save Company and related expenses.

B. Prepare the elimination entry(s) required for the preparation of a consolidated balance sheet workpaper on the date of acquisition.

EXERCISE 3-3 Consolidated Balance Sheet, Stock Purchase

On January 2, 2001, Prunce Company acquired 90% of the outstanding common stock of Sun Company for $192,000 cash. Just before the acquisition, the balance sheets of the two companies were as follows:

	Prunce	Sun
Cash	$260,000	$ 64,000
Accounts Receivable (net)	142,000	23,000
Inventory	117,000	54,000
Plant and Equipment (net)	386,000	98,000
Land	63,000	32,000
Total Assets	$968,000	$271,000
Accounts Payable	$104,000	$ 47,000
Mortgage Payable	72,000	39,000
Common Stock, $2 par value	400,000	70,000
Other Contributed Capital	208,000	20,000
Retained Earnings	184,000	95,000
Total Equities	$968,000	$271,000

The fair values of Sun Company's assets and liabilities are equal to their book values with the exception of land.

Required:
A. Prepare a journal entry to record the purchase of Sun Company's common stock.
B. Prepare a consolidated balance sheet at the date of acquisition.

EXERCISE 3-4   **Purchase, Date of Acquisition**
On January 1, 2000, Peach Company issued 1,500 of its $20 par value common shares with a fair value of $60 per share in exchange for the 2,000 outstanding common shares of Swartz Company in a purchase transaction. Registration costs amounted to $1,700, paid in cash. Just prior to the acquisition, the balance sheets of the two companies were as follows:

	Peach Company	*Swartz Company*
Cash	$ 73,000	$ 13,000
Accounts Receivable (net)	95,000	19,000
Inventory	58,000	25,000
Plant and Equipment (net)	95,000	43,000
Land	26,000	22,000
Total Assets	$347,000	$122,000
Accounts Payable	$ 66,000	$ 18,000
Notes Payable	82,000	21,000
Common Stock, $20 par value	100,000	40,000
Other Contributed Capital	60,000	24,000
Retained Earnings	$ 39,000	19,000
Total Equities	$347,000	$122,000

Any difference between the cost of the investment and the book value of equity acquired relates to goodwill.

Required:
A. Prepare the journal entry on Peach Company's books to record the exchange of stock.
B. Prepare a Computation and Allocation Schedule for the difference between purchase price and book value.
C. Prepare a consolidated balance sheet at the date of acquisition.

EXERCISE 3-5   **Treasury Stock Held by Subsidiary**
Pool Company purchased 90% of the outstanding common stock of Spruce Company on December 31, 2001, for cash. At that time the balance sheet of Spruce Company was as follows:

Current Assets	$1,050,000
Plant and Equipment	990,000
Land	170,000
Total Assets	$2,210,000
Liabilities	$ 820,000
Common Stock, $20 par value	900,000
Other Contributed Capital	440,000
Retained Earnings	150,000
Total	2,310,000
Less Treasury Stock at Cost, 5,000 shares	100,000
Total Equities	$2,210,000

Required:

A. Prepare the elimination entry required for the preparation of a consolidated balance sheet workpaper on December 31, 2001, assuming:

(1) The purchase price of the stock was $1,400,000.

(2) The purchase price of the stock was $1,160,000.

Assume further that any difference between the cost of the investment and the book value of net assets acquired relates to subsidiary land.

B. Compute the amount of the noncontrolling interest that would appear on the December 31, 2001 consolidated balance sheet.

EXERCISE 3-6 **Elimination Entry, Consolidated Balance Sheet**

On December 31, 2000, Price Company purchased a controlling interest in Shipley Company. The balance sheet of Price Company and the consolidated balance sheet on December 31, 2000 were as follows:

	Price Company	*Consolidated*
Cash	$ 22,000	$ 37,900
Accounts Receivable	35,000	57,000
Inventory	127,000	161,600
Investment in Shipley Company	212,000	—0—
Plant and Equipment (net)	190,000	337,000
Land	120,000	218,400
Total	$706,000	$811,900
Accounts Payable	$ 42,000	$112,500
Note Payable	100,000	100,000
Noncontrolling Interest in Shipley Company	—0—	35,400
Common Stock	300,000	300,000
Other Contributed Capital	164,000	164,000
Retained Earnings	100,000	100,000
Total	$706,000	$811,900

On the date of acquisition, the stockholders' equity section of Shipley Company's balance sheet was as follows:

Common Stock	$ 90,000
Other Contributed Capital	90,000
Retained Earnings	56,000
Total	$236,000

Required:

A. Prepare the investment elimination entry made to prepare a consolidated balance sheet workpaper. Any difference between cost and book value relates to subsidiary land.

B. Prepare Shipley Company's balance sheet as it appeared on December 31, 2000.

EXERCISE 3-7 **Intercompany Receivables and Payables**

Polychromasia, Inc. had a number of receivables from subsidiaries at the balance sheet date, as well as several payables to subsidiaries. Of its five subsidiaries, four are consolidated in the financial statements (Green Company, Black Inc., White & Sons, and Silver Company). Only the Brown Company is not consolidated with Polychromasia and the other affiliates. The following list of receivables and payables shows balances at December 31, 2003.

Interest Receivable from the Brown Company	$50,000
Interest Payable to Black Inc.	75,000
Intercompany Payable to Silver Company	105,000
Long-Term Advance to Green Company	150,000

Long-Term Payable to Silver Company	450,000
Long-Term Receivable from Brown Company	500,000

Required:

A. Show the classification and amount(s) that should be reported in the consolidated balance sheet of Polychromasia, Inc. and Subsidiaries at December 31, 2003 as receivable from subsidiaries.

B. Show the classification and amount(s) that should be reported in the consolidated balance sheet of Polychromasia, Inc. and Subsidiaries at December 31, 2003 as payable to subsidiaries.

EXERCISE 3-8 **Stock Acquisition, Journal Entry by Parent**

Peep Inc. acquired 100% of the outstanding common stock of Shy Inc. for $2,500,000 cash and 15,000 shares of its common stock ($2 par value). The stock's market value was $40 on the acquisition date.

Required:

Prepare the journal entry to record the acquisition.

EXERCISE 3-9 **Acquisition Costs**

Assume the same information from Exercise 3-8. In addition, Peep Inc. incurred the following direct costs:

Accounting fees for the purchase	$15,000
Legal fees for registering the common stock	30,000
Other legal fees for the acquisition	45,000
Travel expenses to meet with Shy managers	5,000
SEC filing fees	2,000
	$97,000

Before the acquisition consummation date, $90,000 of the direct costs was charged to a deferred charges account pending the completion of the acquisition. The remaining $7,000 has not been accrued or paid.

Required:

Prepare the journal entry to record both the acquisition and the direct costs.

EXERCISE 3-10B **Deferred Tax Effects, Acquisition Entry and Eliminating Entries**

Patel Company paid $570,000 for 95% of the common stock of Seely Company on January 1, 2001. Seely Company had the following assets, liabilities, and owners' equity at that time:

	Book Value Tax Basis	Fair Value	Excess
Cash	$ 20,000	$ 20,000	$—0—
Accounts Receivable	112,000	112,000	—0—
Inventory (LIFO)	82,000	134,000	52,000
Land	30,000	55,000	25,000
Plant Assets (net)	392,000	463,000	71,000
Total Assets	$636,000	$784,000	
Allowance for Uncollectible Accounts	$ 10,000	$ 10,000	$—0—
Accounts Payable	54,000	54,000	—0—
Bonds Payable	200,000	180,000	20,000
Common Stock, $1 par value	80,000		
Other Contributed Capital	132,000		
Retained Earnings	160,000		
Total Equities	$636,000		

Required:

A. Prepare the stock acquisition entry on the books of Patel Company, taking into account tax effects. Assume an income tax rate of 40%.

B. Prepare eliminating entries for the preparation of a consolidated balance sheet workpaper on January 1, 2001.

EXERCISE 3-11B Deferred Tax Effects at Date of Acquisition

Profeet Company purchased the Starless Company in a nontaxable purchase combination consummated as a stock acquisition. Profeet issued 10,000 shares of $5 par value common stock, with a market value of $70, in exchange for all the stock of Starless. The following information about Starless Company is available on the combination date.

Starless Company

Book Value of Net Assets	$600,000
Deferred Tax Liability from using Modified Accelerated Cost Recover System (MACRS) depreciation for tax purposes	24,000

Other Items	Book Value	Fair Value
Fixed Assets	$410,000	$490,000
Long-Term Debt	450,000	500,000

The current and future tax rate is expected to be 40%.

Required:

Prepare the journal entry to record the acquisition, taking into account tax effects.

EXERCISE 3-12 Comparison of Asset Acquisition and Stock Acquisition (Comprehensive Exercise, Chapters 1–3)

Prime Company acquired the Sum Manufacturing Company (SMC) at a cost of $1,000,000 cash. The following information was available at the date of acquisition.

SMC Company Balance Sheet

	Book Value	Fair Value
Cash	$ 5,000	$ 10,000
Accounts Receivable, net (includes $30,000 from SMC)	95,000	90,000
Inventory	120,000	105,000
Land	400,000	375,000
Fixed Assets	1,500,000	800,000
Accumulated Depreciation	(800,000)	
Total Assets	$1,320,000	$1,380,000
Account Payable	$ 150,000	$ 150,000
Long-Term Debt	450,000	400,000
Total Liabilities	$600,000	$550,000
Common Stock	100,000	
Paid-in Capital	400,000	
Retained Earnings	220,000	
Total Stockholders' Equity	720,000	$ 830,000
Total Liabilities and Stockholders' Equity	$1,320,000	$1,380,000

Required:

A. Assume that Prime Company acquired all the *net assets* of Sum, and answer the following questions.

(1) Would the acquisition be accounted for using the purchase or the pooling of interests method?

(2) Is Prime Company or SMC Company the parent company, or neither?

(3) Which company is the subsidiary, if any?

    (4) Is SMC a legal entity after the acquisition is consummated?

    (5) Speculate as to why Prime might be willing to pay more than the fair value of SMC's net assets ($1,000,000 versus $830,000).

    (6) Prepare the entry that Prime Company would make to record the acquisition.

B. Assume the same information as in part A, except that Prime Company acquires all the outstanding common stock of SMC Company rather than acquiring all of SMC's assets and assuming all its liabilities. Answer the following questions.

    (1) Would the acquisition be accounted for using the purchase or the pooling of interests method?

    (2) Is Prime Company or SMC Company the parent company, or neither?

    (3) Which company is the subsidiary, if any?

    (4) Is SMC a legal entity after the acquisition is consummated?

    (5) Speculate as to why Prime might be willing to pay more than the fair value of SMC's equity ($1,000,000 versus $830,000).

    (6) Prepare the entry that Prime Company would make to record the acquisition.

    (7) Where is goodwill recorded?

PROBLEMS

PROBLEM 3-1 Consolidated Workpaper: Two Cases

The following two separate cases show the financial position of a parent company and its subsidiary company on November 30, 2001, just after the parent had purchased 90% of the subsidiary's stock:

	Case I		Case II	
	P Company	S Company	P Company	S Company
Current Assets	$ 880,000	$260,000	$ 780,000	$280,000
Investment in S Company	190,000		190,000	
Long-Term Assets	1,400,000	400,000	1,200,000	400,000
Other Assets	90,000	40,000	70,000	70,000
Total	$2,560,000	$700,000	$2,240,000	$750,000
Current Liabilities	$ 640,000	$270,000	$ 700,000	$260,000
Long-Term Liabilities	850,000	290,000	920,000	270,000
Common Stock	600,000	180,000	600,000	180,000
Retained Earnings	470,000	(40,000)	20,000	40,000
Total	$2,560,000	$700,000	$2,240,000	$750,000

Required:

Prepare a November 30, 2001, consolidated balance sheet workpaper for each of the foregoing cases. Any difference between the cost of the investment and the book value of equity acquired relates to subsidiary long-term assets.

PROBLEM 3-2 Consolidated Balance Sheet Workpaper

On January 1, 2001, Perry Company purchased 8,000 shares of Soho Company's common stock for $120,000. Immediately after the stock acquisition, the statements of financial position of Perry and Soho appeared as follows:

Assets	Perry	Soho
Cash	$ 39,000	$ 19,000
Accounts Receivable	53,000	31,000
Inventory	42,000	25,000
Investment in Soho Company	120,000	
Plant Assets	160,000	110,500
Accumulated Depreciation—Plant Assets	(52,000)	(19,500)
Total	$362,000	$166,000

Liabilities and Owners' Equity	Perry	Soho
Current Liabilities	$ 18,500	$ 26,000
Mortgage Notes Payable	40,000	
Common Stock, $10 par value	120,000	100,000
Premium on Common Stock	135,000	16,500
Retained Earnings	48,500	23,500
Total	$362,000	$166,000

Required:

A. Calculate the percentage of Soho acquired by Perry Company. Prepare a schedule to compute the difference between cost and book value of equity acquired. Any difference between the cost of the investment and the book value of equity acquired relates to subsidiary plant assets.

B. Prepare a consolidated balance sheet workpaper as of January 1, 2001.

PROBLEM 3-3 Intercompany Bond Holdings at Par, 90% Owned Subsidiary

Balance sheets for P Company and S Company on August 1, 2001, are as follows:

	P Company	S Company
Cash	$ 165,500	$106,000
Receivables	366,000	126,000
Inventory	261,000	108,000
Investment in Bonds	306,000	—0—
Investment in S Company Stock	586,500	—0—
Plant and Equipment (net)	573,000	320,000
Land	200,000	300,000
Total	$2,458,000	$960,000
Accounts Payable	$ 174,000	$ 58,000
Accrued Expenses	32,400	26,000
Bonds Payable, 8%	—0—	200,000
Common Stock	1,500,000	460,000
Other Contributed Capital	260,000	60,000
Retained Earnings	491,600	156,000
Total	$2,458,000	$960,000

Required:

Prepare a workpaper for a consolidated balance sheet for P Company and its subsidiary on August 1, 2001, taking into consideration the following:

1. P Company acquired 90% of the outstanding common stock of S Company on August 1, 2001, for a cash payment of $586,500.

2. Included in the Investment in Bonds account are $40,000 par value of S Company bonds payable that were purchased at par by P Company in 1992. The bonds pay interest on April 30 and October 31. S Company has appropriately accrued interest expense on August 1, 2001; P Company, however, inadvertently failed to accrue interest income on the S Company bonds.

3. Included in P Company receivables is a $35,000 cash advance to S Company that was mailed on August 1, 2001. S Company had not yet received the advance at the time of the preparation of its August 1, 2001, balance sheet.

4. Any difference between the cost of the investment and the book value of equity acquired relates to subsidiary land.

PROBLEM 3-4 Parent and Two Subsidiaries, Intercompany Notes

On January 2, 2001, Phillips Company purchased 80% of Sanchez Company and 90% of Thomas Company for $225,000 and $168,000, respectively. Immediately before the acquisitions, the balance sheets of the three companies were as follows:

	Phillips	Sanchez	Thomas
Cash	$400,000	$ 43,700	$ 20,000
Accounts Receivable	28,000	24,000	20,000
Note Receivable	—0—	10,000	—0—
Interest Receivable	—0—	300	—0—
Inventory	120,000	96,000	43,000
Equipment	60,000	40,000	30,000
Land	180,000	80,000	70,000
Total	$788,000	$294,000	$183,000
Accounts Payable	$ 28,000	$ 20,000	$ 18,000
Note Payable	—0—	—0—	10,000
Common Stock	300,000	120,000	75,000
Other Contributed Capital	300,000	90,000	40,000
Retained Earnings	160,000	64,000	40,000
Total	$788,000	$294,000	$183,000

The note receivable and interest receivable of Sanchez relate to a loan made to Thomas Company on October 1, 2000. Thomas failed to record the accrued interest expense on the note.

Required:
Prepare a consolidated balance sheet workpaper as of January 2, 2001. Any difference between cost and book value relates to subsidiary land.

PROBLEM 3-5 Determining Balance Sheet Prior to Consolidation

On January 1, 2001, Pat Company purchased 90% of the outstanding common stock of Solo Company for $236,000 cash. The balance sheet for Pat Company just before the acquisition of Solo Company stock, along with the consolidated balance sheet prepared at the date of acquisition, follows:

	Pat Company December 31, 2000	Consolidated January 1, 2001
Cash	$ 540,000	$ 352,000
Accounts Receivable	272,000	346,000
Advances to Solo Company	10,000	
Inventory	376,000	451,000
Plant and Equipment	622,000	820,000
Land	350,000	421,000
Total	$2,170,000	$2,390,000
Accounts Payable	$ 280,000	$ 386,000
Long-Term Liabilities	520,000	605,500
Noncontrolling Interest in Subsidiary		28,500
Common Stock	890,000	890,000
Other Contributed Capital	300,000	300,000
Retained Earnings	180,000	180,000
Total	$2,170,000	$2,390,000

One week before the acquisition, Pat Company had advanced $10,000 to Solo Company. Solo Company had not yet recorded the transaction on the date of acquisition. In addition, on the date of acquisition, Solo Company owed Pat Company $4,000 for purchases of merchandise on account. The merchandise had been sold to outside parties prior to the date of acquisition.

Required:
A. Determine the amount of cash that appeared on Solo Company's balance sheet immediately prior to the acquisition of its stock by Pat Company.

B. Determine the amount of total stockholders' equity on Solo Company's separate balance sheet at the date of acquisition.

C. Determine the amount of total assets appearing on Solo Company's separate balance sheet on the date of acquisition.

PROBLEM 3-6 **In-Transit Items**

On July 31, 2001, Ping Company purchased 90% of Santos Company's common stock for $2,010,000 cash. Immediately after the acquisition, the two companies' balance sheets were as follows:

	Ping	Santos
Cash	$ 320,000	$ 150,000
Accounts Receivable	600,000	300,000
Note Receivable	100,000	—0—
Inventory	1,840,000	400,000
Advance to Santos Company	60,000	—0—
Investment in Santos Company	2,010,000	—0—
Plant and Equipment (net)	3,000,000	1,500,000
Land	90,000	90,000
Total	$8,020,000	$2,440,000
Accounts Payable	$ 800,000	$ 140,000
Notes Payable	900,000	100,000
Common Stock	2,400,000	900,000
Other Contributed Capital	2,200,000	680,000
Retained Earnings	1,720,000	620,000
Total	$8,020,000	$2,440,000

Santos Company has not yet recorded the $60,000 cash advance from Ping Company. Ping Company's accounts receivable include $20,000 due from Santos Company. Santos Company's $100,000 note payable is payable to Ping Company. Neither company has recorded $7,000 of interest accrued on the note from January 1 to July 31. Any difference between cost and book value relates to land.

Required:

Prepare a consolidated balance sheet workpaper on July 31, 2001.

PROBLEM 3-7 **Purchase Using Cash and Using Stock**

Balance sheets for Prego Company and Sprague Company as of December 31, 2000, follow:

	Prego Company	Sprague Company
Cash	$ 700,000	$111,000
Accounts Receivable (net)	892,000	230,000
Inventory	544,000	60,000
Property and Equipment (net)	$1,927,000	$468,000
Land	120,000	94,000
Total Assets	$4,183,000	$963,000
Accounts Payable	$ 302,000	$152,000
Notes Payable	588,000	61,000
Long-Term Debt	350,000	90,000
Common Stock	1,800,000	500,000
Other Contributed Capital	543,000	80,000
Retained Earnings	600,000	80,000
Total Equities	$4,183,000	$963,000

The fair values of Sprague Company's assets and liabilities are equal to their book values.

Required:

Prepare a consolidated balance sheet as of January 1, 2001, under each of the following assumptions:

A. On January 1, 2001, Prego Company purchased 90% of the outstanding common stock of Sprague Company for $594,000.

B. On January 1, 2001, Prego Company exchanged 11,880 of its $20 par value common shares with a fair value of $50 per share for 90% of the outstanding common shares of Sprague Company. The transaction is a purchase.

PROBLEM 3-8 **Intercompany Items, Two Subsidiaries**

On February 1, 2001, Punto Company purchased 95% of the outstanding common stock of Sara Company and 85% of the outstanding common stock of Rob Company. Immediately before the two acquisitions, balance sheets of the three companies were as follows:

	Punto	*Sara*	*Rob*
Cash	$165,000	$ 45,000	$17,000
Accounts Receivable	35,000	35,000	26,000
Notes Receivable	18,000	—0—	—0—
Merchandise Inventory	106,000	35,500	14,000
Prepaid Insurance	13,500	2,500	500
Advances to Sara Company	10,000		
Advances to Rob Company	5,000		
Land	248,000	43,000	15,000
Buildings (net)	100,000	27,000	16,000
Equipment (net)	35,000	10,000	2,500
Total	$735,500	$198,000	$91,000
Accounts Payable	$ 25,500	$ 20,000	$10,500
Income Taxes Payable	30,000	10,000	—0—
Notes Payable	—0—	6,000	10,500
Bonds Payable	100,000	—0—	—0—
Common Stock, $10 par value	300,000	144,000	42,000
Other Contributed Capital	150,000	12,000	38,000
Retained Earnings (Deficit)	130,000	6,000	(10,000)
Total	$735,500	$198,000	$91,000

The following additional information is relevant.

1. One week before the acquisitions, Punto Company had advanced $10,000 to Sara Company and $5,000 to Rob Company. Sara Company recorded an increase to Accounts Payable for its advance, but Rob Company had not recorded the transaction.

2. On the date of acquisition, Punto Company owed Sara Company $12,000 for purchases on account, and Rob Company owed Punto Company $3,000 and Sara Company $6,000 for such purchases. The goods purchased had all been sold to outside parties prior to acquisition.

3. Punto Company exchanged 13,400 shares of its common stock with a fair value of $12 per share for 95% of the outstanding common stock of Sara Company. In addition, stock issue fees of $4,000 were paid in cash. The acquisition was accounted for as a purchase.

4. Punto Company paid $50,000 cash for the 85% interest in Rob Company.

5. Three thousand dollars of Sara Company's notes payable and $9,500 of Rob Company's notes payable were payable to Punto Company.

6. Any difference between cost and book value relates to subsidiary land.

Required:

A. Give the book entries to record the two acquisitions in the accounts of Punto Company.

B. Prepare a consolidated balance sheet workpaper immediately after acquisition.

C. Prepare a consolidated balance sheet at the date of acquisition for Punto Company and its subsidiaries.

PROBLEM 3-9 Intercompany Notes, 90% Acquisition

On January 1, 2002, Pope Company purchased 90% of Sun Company's common stock for $5,800,000 cash. Immediately after the acquisition, the two companies' balance sheets were as follows:

	Pope	Sun
Cash	$ 297,000	$ 165,000
Accounts Receivable	432,000	468,000
Notes Receivable	90,000	
Inventory	1,980,000	1,447,000
Investment in Sun Company	5,800,000	
Plant and Equipment (net)	5,730,000	3,740,000
Land	1,575,000	908,000
Total	$15,904,000	$6,728,000
Accounts Payable	$ 698,000	$ 247,000
Notes Payable	2,250,000	110,000
Common Stock ($15 par)	4,500,000	5,250,000
Other Contributed Capital	5,198,000	396,000
Treasury Stock Held		(1,200,000)
Retained Earnings	3,258,000	1,925,000
Total	$15,904,000	$6,728,000

Sun Company's notes payable include a $90,000 note payable to Pope Company. Any difference between cost and book value relates to subsidiary property and equipment.

Required:

A. Prepare a Computation and Allocation Schedule for the difference between cost (purchase price) and book value of equity acquired.

B. Prepare a consolidated balance sheet workpaper on January 1, 2002.

PROBLEM 3-10B Deferred Tax Effects

On January 1, 2002, Pruitt Company issued 25,500 shares of its common stock in exchange for 85% of the outstanding common stock of Shah Company. Pruitt's common stock had a fair value of $28 per share at that time ($2 per share par value). Pruitt Company uses the cost method to account for its investment in Shah Company and files a consolidated income tax return. A schedule of the Shah Company assets acquired and liabilities assumed at book values (which are equal to their tax bases) and at fair values follows:

Item:	Book Value/ Tax Basis	Fair Value	Excess
Receivables (net)	$125,000	$ 125,000	$ —0—
Inventory	167,000	195,000	28,000
Land	86,500	120,000	33,500
Plant Assets (net)	467,000	567,000	100,000
Patents	95,000	200,000	105,000
Total	$940,500	$1,207,000	$266,500
Current Liabilities	$ 89,500	$ 89,500	$ —0—
Bonds Payable	300,000	360,000	60,000
Common Stock	120,000		
Other Contributed Capital	164,000		
Retained Earnings	267,000		
Total	$940,500		

Additional Information:

1. Pruitt's income tax rate is 35%.
2. Shah's beginning inventory was all sold during 2002.
3. Useful lives for depreciation and amortization purposes are:

Plant Assets	10 years
Patents	8 years
Bond Premium	10 years
Goodwill	25 years

4. Pruitt uses the straight-line method for all depreciation and amortization purposes.

Required:

A. Prepare the stock acquisition entry on Pruitt Company's books.

B. Prepare the eliminating entries for a consolidated statements workpaper on January 1, 2002, immediately after acquisition.

*C. Assuming Shah Company earned $216,000 and declared a $90,000 dividend during 2002, prepare the eliminating entries for a consolidated statements workpaper on December 31, 2002.

*D. Assuming Shah Company earned $240,000 and declared a $100,000 dividend during 2003, prepare the eliminating entries for a consolidated statements workpaper on December 31, 2003.

*Note: Parts C and D may be deferred until Chapter 5.

4

CONSOLIDATED FINANCIAL STATEMENTS AFTER ACQUISITION

LEARNING OBJECTIVES

1. Describe the accounting treatment required under current GAAP for varying levels of influence or control by investors.

2. Prepare journal entries on the parent's books to account for an investment using the cost method, the partial equity method, and the complete equity method.

3. Understand the use of the workpaper in preparing consolidated financial statements.

4. Prepare a schedule for the computation and allocation of the difference between cost and book value.

5. Prepare the workpaper eliminating entries for the year of acquisition (and subsequent years) for the cost and equity methods.

6. Describe two alternative methods to account for interim acquisitions of subsidiary stock at the end of the first year.

7. Explain how the consolidated statement of cash flows differs from a single firm's statement of cash flows.

8. Understand how the reporting of an acquisition on the consolidated statement of cash flows differs when stock is issued rather than cash.

IN THE NEWS

SBC (a Texas Baby Bell) has proposed a takeover of Ameritech Corp. for over $55 billion, at a time when the company has not yet completed its $5 billion purchase of Southern New England Telecommunications Corp. and is just starting to realize cost savings from a $16.5 billion takeover of Pacific Telesis Group.[1]

Investments in voting stock of other companies may be consolidated, or they may be separately reported in the financial statements at cost, at fair value, or at equity. The method of reporting adopted depends on a number of factors including the size of the investment, the extent to which the investor exercises control over the activities of the investee, and the marketability of the securities. *Investor* refers to a

---

[1] *WSJ,* "A Driven Texan Seeks a Phone Empire," by Stephanie N. Mehta, 5/11/98, p. B1.

business entity that holds an investment in voting stock of another company. *Investee* refers to a corporation that issued voting stock held by an investor.

ACCOUNTING FOR INVESTMENTS BY THE COST, PARTIAL EQUITY, AND COMPLETE EQUITY METHODS

Generally speaking, there are three levels of influence or control by an investor over an investee, which determine the appropriate accounting treatment. There are no absolute percentages to distinguish among these levels, but there are guidelines. The three levels and the corresponding accounting treatment are summarized as follows:

Level	*Guideline Percentages*	*Usual Accounting Treatment*
No significant influence	Less than 20%	Investment carried at fair value at current year-end (trading or available for sale securities)—method traditionally referred to as *cost* method with an adjustment for market changes.
Significant influence (no control)	20 to 50%[2]	Investment measured under the *complete equity* method.
Effective control	Greater than 50%	Consolidated statements required (investment eliminated, combined financial statements): investment recorded under *cost, partial equity,* or *complete equity* method.

The focus in this chapter is on presenting financial statements for consolidated entities (i.e., those in the third category above). Nonetheless, the parent company must account for its investment income from the subsidiary in its own books by one of the methods used for accounting for investments. That investment income will subsequently be eliminated, as will the investment account itself, when the two sets of books are merged into one consolidated set of financial data. Thus, so long as the eliminating process is carried out accurately, the parent has a certain amount of discretion in choosing how it accounts for its investment. Nonetheless, to understand the effect of the earnings of the subsidiary on the consolidated entity, and on the noncontrolling interest, the reader needs to understand the mechanics that lead to the blending of two sets of books (income statement, retained earnings statement, and balance sheet) into one. Thus, we begin this chapter with a general discussion of accounting for investments, keeping in mind that our purpose is to prepare consolidated financial statements where appropriate.

In distinguishing among the three levels of influence/control, an investor is generally presumed not to have significant influence if the percentage owned is less than 20% of the investee's outstanding common stock. Exceptions are possible; for example, the investor might own only 18% but be the single largest investor, with the remaining 82% spread among a large number of very small investors, in

---

[2]Control may occur with less than 50%. The FASB issued a revised exposure draft on February 23, 1999, entitled "Consolidated Financial Statements: Purpose and Policy," in which control is defined as "the ability of an entity to direct the policies and management that guide the ongoing activities of another entity so as to increase its benefits and limit its losses from that other entity's activities." See Chapter 3, Appendix A, for further details.

which case the 18% would represent significant influence, and the equity method would be appropriate. In general, however, an investor owning less than 20% of the investee's stock accounts for the investment account at its fair value, under a method traditionally referred to as the "cost" method but with adjustments for changes in the fair value over time.

When a company owns a sufficient amount of another company's stock to have significant influence (usually at least 20%), but not enough to effectively control the other company (less than 50% in most cases), the equity method is required. Once the investor is deemed to have control over the other company, consolidated statements are required. Appendix A of Chapter 3 addresses situations where effective control may exist without a majority ownership. Such situations would also require consolidated statements.

In Chapter 3, we focused on the preparation of the consolidated balance sheet at the date of acquisition. With the passage of time, however, consolidating procedures are needed to prepare not only the consolidated balance sheet, but also a consolidated income statement, a consolidated statement of retained earnings, and a consolidated statement of cash flows. In this chapter we address the preparation of these statements subsequent to the date of acquisition.

When consolidated financial statements are appropriate (the investor has effective control over the investee), then the investment account, which is carried on the books of the parent company, will be eliminated in the consolidation process. Thus, it is not relevant to the consolidated statements whether the investor measures the investment account using the cost method or using the equity method, so long as the eliminating entries are properly prepared. When prepared correctly, the resulting financial statements will be *identical*, regardless of how the investment was carried in the books of the parent company (investor). At least three possible methods exist and are used in practice on the books of the parent company: the cost method, the partial equity method, and the complete equity method. Recognition of which of these methods is being used is important because the appropriate eliminating entries will vary depending on that choice. Further, because all three are used in practice, it is worthwhile to compare and contrast the three briefly at this point.

Of the three methods, only the complete equity method is acceptable for significant investments without majority ownership. Our focus, however, is on investments that will be consolidated (i.e., majority ownership). Nonetheless, from an internal decision-making standpoint, if the parent firm relies upon the unconsolidated statements for any purposes, this method might be considered superior to the other two in terms of approximating the operating effects of the investment. In contrast, the cost method is the simplest of the three to prepare on the books of the parent and is the most commonly used method in practice. The partial equity method might be viewed as a compromise, being somewhat easier to prepare on the books of the parent than the complete equity method but also providing a rough approximation of the operating effects of the investment. When decisions are based solely on the consolidated statements, the primary consideration is ease and cost of preparation; this may explain why many companies choose the simplest method (cost method).

Under all three methods, the investment account is initially recorded at its cost (assuming purchase accounting).[3] *The differences among the three methods then lie in subsequent*

---

[3]Pooling of interests will be addressed in Chapter 11.

entries. If the cost method is used, the investment account is adjusted only when additional shares of stock in the investee are purchased or sold (or in the event of a liquidating dividend).[4] Fair value adjustments may be made periodically, but these are generally accomplished using a separate account, Fair Value Adjustment, thus preserving historical cost in the investment account. (The fair value adjustment account has a debit balance when fair value is higher than historical cost, and a credit balance when fair value is lower than historical cost.)

Under the equity method, more frequent entries appear in the investment account on the books of the parent. Under the partial equity method, the investor adjusts the investment account upward for its share of the investee's earnings and downward for its share of the investee's dividends declared. Under the complete equity method, additional adjustments are made to the investment account for the effects of unrealized intercompany profits, the amortization of any difference between cost and book value, and stockholders' equity transactions undertaken by the subsidiary. *Remember, the cost method and various forms of the equity method are methods to record investments* **after acquisition,** *in contrast to the purchase and pooling of interests methods, which are methods used to record the* **initial acquisition of an** *investment.*

Because all three methods have advantages and disadvantages, and because individual preferences will vary as to which method(s) are most important to the student, book entries and workpaper eliminating entries assuming the use of each of the three methods are discussed and illustrated in separate sections throughout this text. In *some* portions of this chapter, however, partial equity and complete equity methods are indistinguishable given the assumptions of the example, in which case they are illustrated only once to conserve space.

First, though, we believe that every student should have a basic understanding of the differences among the three methods in accounting for the investment on the books of the parent. These are illustrated below, and are also summarized in Figure 4-1.

Cost Method on Books of Investor

To illustrate the accounting for an investment in a subsidiary accounted for by the *cost method,* assume that P Company acquired 90% of the outstanding voting stock of S Company at the beginning of Year 1 for $800,000. Income (loss) of S Company and dividends declared by S Company during the next three years are listed below. During the third year, the firm pays a liquidating dividend (i.e., the cumulative dividends declared exceeds the cumulative income earned).

Year	Income (Loss)	Dividends Declared	Cumulative Income Over (Under) Dividends
1	$90,000	$30,000	$60,000
2	(20,000)	30,000	10,000
3	10,000	30,000	(10,000)

[4] A liquidating dividend occurs when the investee has paid cumulative dividends in excess of cumulative earnings (since acquisition). Such excess dividends are treated as a return of capital and, upon their receipt, are recorded by the investor as a decrease in the investment account under the cost method.

Journal entries on the books of P Company to account for the investment in S Company during the three years follow:

Year 1—P's Books

Investment in S Company	800,000	
Cash		800,000
To record the initial investment.		
Cash	27,000	
Dividend Income		27,000
To record dividends received .9($30,000).		

Year 2—P's Books

Cash	27,000	
Dividend Income		27,000
To record dividends received .9($30,000).		

Year 3—P's Books

Cash	27,000	
Dividend Income		18,000
Investment in S Company		9,000
To record dividends received, $9,000 of which represents a return of investment.		

After these entries are posted, the investment account will appear as follows:

Investment in S Company (Cost Method)

Year 1 Cost	800,000		
		Year 3 Liquidating dividend	9,000
Year 3 Balance	791,000		

Year 1 entries record the initial investment and the receipt of dividends from S Company. In Year 2, although S Company incurred a $20,000 loss, there was a $60,000 excess of earnings over dividends in Year 1. Consequently, the dividends received are recognized as income by P Company. In Year 3, however, a *liquidating dividend* occurs. From the point of view of a parent company, a purchased subsidiary is deemed to have distributed a liquidating dividend when the cumulative amount of its dividends declared exceeds its cumulative reported earnings after its acquisition. Such excess dividends are treated as a return of capital, and are recorded as a reduction of the investment account rather than as dividend income. The liquidating dividend is 90% of the excess of dividends paid over cumulative earnings since acquisition (90% of $10,000).

Partial Equity Method on Books of Investor

Next, assume that P Company has elected to use the partial equity method to record the investment in S Company above. The entries for the first three years would appear as follows:

Year 1—P's Books

Investment in S Company	800,000	
Cash		800,000
To record the initial investment.		
Investment in S Company	81,000	
Equity in Subsidiary Income .9($90,000)		81,000
To record P's share of subsidiary income.		

Cash	27,000	
Investment in S Company		27,000
To record dividends received .9($30,000)		

Note: The entries to record equity in subsidiary income and dividends received may be combined into one entry, if desired.

Year 2—P's Books

Equity in Subsidiary Loss	18,000	
Investment in S Company		18,000
To record equity in subsidiary loss .9($20,000).		
Cash	27,000	
Investment in S Company		27,000
To record dividends received .9($30,000).		

Year 3—P's Books

Investment in S Company	9,000	
Equity in Subsidiary Income		9,000
To record equity in subsidiary income .9($10,000).		
Cash	27,000	
Investment in S Company		27,000
To record dividends received .9($30,000).		

After these entries are posted, the investment account will appear as follows:

Investment in S Company (Partial Equity Method)

Year 1 Cost	800,000		
Year 1 Equity in subsidiary income	81,000	Year 1 Share of dividends declared	27,000
Year 1 Balance	854,000		
		Year 2 Equity in subsidiary loss	18,000
		Year 2 Share of dividends declared	27,000
Year 2 Balance	809,000		
Year 3 Equity in subsidiary income	9,000	Year 3 Share of dividends declared	27,000
Year 3 Balance	791,000		

Complete Equity Method on Books of Investor

The complete equity method is usually required to report common stock investments in the 20% to 50% range, assuming the investor has the ability to exercise significant influence over the operating activities of the investee. In addition, a parent company may use the complete equity method to *account for* investments in subsidiaries that will be consolidated. This method is similar to the partial equity method up to a point, but it requires additional entries in most instances.

Continuing the illustration above, assume additionally that the $800,000 purchase price exceeded the book value of the underlying equity of S Company by $100,000; and that the difference was attributed entirely to goodwill. The amortization of goodwill, if spread over a life of 20 years, would result in a charge to earnings of $5,000 per year. This charge has the impact of lowering the equity in subsidiary income, or increasing the equity in subsidiary loss, recorded by the parent.

The entries for the first three years under the complete equity method are as follows:

Year 1—P's Books

Investment in S Company	800,000	
Cash		800,000
To record the initial investment.		
Investment in S Company	81,000	
Equity in Subsidiary Income .9($90,000)		81,000
To record equity in subsidiary income.		
Equity in Subsidiary Income	5,000	
Investment in S Company ($100,000/20 years)		5,000
To adjust equity in subsidiary income for the amortization of goodwill.		
Cash	27,000	
Investment in S Company		27,000
To record dividends received .9($30,000).		

Note: The entries to record equity in subsidiary income and dividends received may be combined into one entry, if desired.

[handwritten note in margin: It's frequently net off]

Year 2—P's Books

Equity in Subsidiary Loss	18,000	
Investment in S Company		18,000
To record equity in subsidiary loss .9($20,000).		
Equity in Subsidiary Loss ($100,000/20 years)	5,000	
Investment in S Company		5,000
To adjust equity in subsidiary loss for the amortization of goodwill.		
Cash	27,000	
Investment in S Company		27,000
To record dividends received .9($30,000).		

Year 3—P's Books

Investment in S Company	9,000	
Equity in Subsidiary Income		9,000
To record equity in subsidiary income .9($10,000).		
Equity in Subsidiary Income ($100,000/20 years)	5,000	
Investment in S Company		5,000
To adjust equity in subsidiary income for the amortization of goodwill.		
Cash	27,000	
Investment in S Company		27,000
To record dividends received .9($30,000).		

After these entries are posted, the investment account will appear as follows:

Investment in S Company (Complete Equity Method)

Year 1 Cost	800,000			
Year 1 Equity in subsidiary income	81,000	Year 1 Amortization of goodwill	5,000	
		Year 1 Share of dividends declared	27,000	
Year 1 Balance	849,000			
		Year 2 Equity in subsidiary loss	18,000	
		Year 2 Amortization of goodwill	5,000	
		Year 2 Share of dividends declared	27,000	
Year 2 Balance	799,000			
Year 3 Equity in subsidiary income	9,000	Year 3 Amortization of goodwill	5,000	
		Year 3 Share of dividends declared	27,000	
Year 3 Balance	776,000			

The additional entry to adjust the equity in subsidiary income for the amortization of goodwill in Year 1 may be viewed as reversing out a portion of the income recognized; the result is a net equity in subsidiary income for Year 1 of $76,000 ($81,000 minus $5,000). In Year 2, however, since the subsidiary showed a loss for the period, the amortization has the effect of increasing the loss from the amount initially recorded ($18,000) to a larger loss of $23,000.

A solid understanding of the entries made on the books of the investor (presented above) will help greatly in understanding the eliminating entries presented in the following sections. In some sense these entries may be viewed as "undoing" the above entries. It is important to realize, however, that the eliminating entries are not "parent-only" entries. In many cases an eliminating entry will affect certain accounts of the parent and others of the subsidiary. For example, the entry to eliminate the investment account (a parent company account) against the equity accounts of the subsidiary affects both parent and subsidiary accounts. Some accounts do not need eliminating because the effects on parent and subsidiary are offsetting. For example, in the entries above, we saw that the parent debited cash when dividends were received from the subsidiary. We know that cash on the books of the subsidiary is credited when dividends are paid. The net effect on cash of the consolidated entry is thus zero. No entry is made to the cash account in the consolidating process. See Figure 4-1 for a comparison of the three methods on the books of the parent.

FIGURE 4-1

Comparison of the Investment T-Accounts
(Cost versus Partial Equity versus Complete Equity Method)

Investment in S Company—Cost Method

Year 1 Acquisition cost	800,000		
Year 1 and 2 Balance	800,000		
		Year 3 Subsidiary liquidating dividend	9,000
Year 3 Balance	791,000		

Investment in S Company—Partial Equity Method

Year 1 Acquisition cost	800,000		
Year 1 Equity in subsidiary income	81,000	Year 1 Share of dividend declared	27,000
Year 1 Balance	854,000		
		Year 2 Equity in subsidiary loss	18,000
		Year 2 Share of dividend declared	27,000
Year 2 Balance	809,000		
Year 3 Equity in subsidiary income	9,000	Year 3 Share of dividend declared	27,000
Year 3 Balance	791,000		

Investment in S Company—Complete Equity Method

Year 1 Acquisition cost	800,000		
Year 1 Equity in subsidiary income	81,000	Year 1 Amortization of goodwill	5,000
		Year 1 Share of dividend declared	27,000
Year 1 Balance	849,000		
		Year 2 Equity in subsidiary loss	18,000
		Year 2 Amortization of goodwill	5,000
		Year 2 Share of dividend declared	27,000
Year 2 Balance	799,000		
Year 3 Equity in subsidiary income	9,000	Year 3 Amortization of goodwill	5,000
		Year 3 Share of dividend declared	27,000
Year 3 Balance	776,000		

CONSOLIDATED STATEMENTS AFTER ACQUISITION— COST METHOD

The preparation of consolidated financial statements after acquisition is not materially different in concept from preparing them at the acquisition date in the sense that reciprocal accounts are eliminated and remaining balances are combined. The process is more complex, however, because time has elapsed and business activity has taken place between the date of acquisition and the date of consolidated statement preparation. On the date of acquisition, the only relevant financial statement is the consolidated balance sheet; after acquisition, a complete set of consolidated financial statements—income statement, retained earnings statement, balance sheet, and statement of cash flows—must be prepared for the affiliated group of companies. Deferred tax issues are presented in Appendix B to this chapter.

Workpaper Format

Accounting workpapers are used to accumulate, classify, and arrange data for a variety of accounting purposes, including the preparation of financial reports and statements. Although workpaper style and technique vary among firms and individuals, we have adopted a three-section workpaper for illustrative purposes in this book. The format includes a separate section for each of three basic financial statements—income statement, retained earnings statement, and balance sheet. In some cases the input to the workpaper comes from the individual financial statements of the affiliates to be consolidated, in which case the three-section workpaper is particularly appropriate. At other times, however, input may be from affiliate trial balances, and the data must be arranged in financial statement form before the workpaper can be completed. Organizing the data provides a useful review for students, however, and emphasizes the linkages among these three financial statements. An alternative format to preparing the workpaper is provided in Appendix A in this chapter (using the information in Illustration 4-4).

The fourth statement, the statement of cash flows, is prepared from the information in the consolidated income statement and from two comparative consolidated balance sheets. It will be presented later in this chapter.

The discussion and illustrations that follow are based on trial balances at December 31, 2000, for P Company and S Company given in Illustration 4-1. Throughout this chapter, any difference between the cost of the investment and the book value of the equity interest acquired is assumed to relate to the under- or overvaluation of subsidiary land and is, therefore, assigned to land in the second eliminating entry. Because land is subject to neither depreciation nor amortization, this serves to defer at least one complication to the next chapter. More realistic assumptions, and the resulting complications, will be dealt with fully in Chapter 5.

Year of Acquisition—Cost Method

Assume that P Company purchased 80% of the outstanding shares of S Company common stock on January 1, 2000, for $165,000. The underlying book value of S

Company's net assets on that date was $190,000. P Company made the following entry:

P's Books

Investment in S Company	165,000	
Cash		165,000

On June 6, 2000, S Company paid a $10,000 dividend, and made the following **Cost** entry:

S's Books

Dividends Declared	10,000	
Cash		10,000

(Recall that the Dividends Declared account is a temporary account that is closed to retained earnings at year-end. An alternative is to debit retained earnings directly when dividends are declared.) Since P Company owns 80% of S Company's common stock, the receipt of the dividend was recorded by P Company as follows:

P's Books

Cash	8,000	
Dividend Income (80% × $10,000)		8,000

Note that the trial balance data in Illustration 4-1 reflect the effects of both the investment and dividend transactions.

ILLUSTRATION 4-1

P Company and S Company Trial Balances
December 31, 2000

	P Company		S Company	
	Dr.	*Cr.*	*Dr.*	*Cr.*
Cash	$ 79,000		$ 18,000	
Accounts Receivable (net)	64,000		28,000	
Inventory, 1/1	56,000		32,000	
Investment in S Company	165,000			
Property and Equipment (net)	180,000		165,000	
Land	35,000		17,000	
Accounts Payable		$ 35,000		$ 24,000
Other Liabilities		62,000		37,000
Common Stock, $10 par value		200,000		100,000
Other Contributed Capital		40,000		50,000
Retained Earnings, 1/1		210,000		40,000
Dividends Declared	20,000		10,000	
Sales		300,000		160,000
Dividend Income		8,000		
Purchases	186,000		95,000	
Expenses	70,000		46,000	
	$855,000	$855,000	$411,000	411,000
Inventory, 12/31	$ 67,000		$ 43,000	

(handwritten top margin: "worksheet not posted, entryorig not posted to anywhere", "the same")

Cost Method
80% Owned
Year of Acquisition

ILLUSTRATION 4-2
Consolidated Statements Workpaper—Cost Method
P Company and Subsidiary For the Year Ended December 31, 2000

Income Statement	P Company	S Company	Eliminations Dr.	Eliminations Cr.	Noncontrolling Interest	Consolidated Balances
Sales	300,000	160,000				460,000
Dividend Income	8,000		(3) 8,000			0
Total Revenue	308,000	160,000				460,000
Cost of Goods Sold:						
Inventory, 1/1	56,000	32,000				88,000
Purchases	186,000	95,000				281,000
	242,000	127,000				369,000
Inventory, 12/31	67,000	43,000				110,000
Cost of Goods Sold	175,000	84,000				259,000
Expenses	70,000	46,000				116,000
Total Cost and Expense	245,000	130,000				375,000
Net/Combined Income	63,000	30,000				85,000
Noncontrolling Interest in Income					6,000	(6,000)*
Net Income to Retained Earnings	63,000	30,000	8,000	—0—	6,000	79,000

(handwritten: 30,000 × 20% = 6,000)
(handwritten: = 8,000 + 30,000 × 80% = 79,000)

Retained Earnings Statement						
1/1 Retained Earnings						
P Company	210,000					210,000
S Company		40,000	(1) 32,000		8,000	
Net Income from above	63,000	30,000	8,000	—0—	6,000	79,000
Dividends Declared						
P Company	(20,000)					(20,000)
S Company		(10,000)		(3) 8,000	(2,000)	
12/31 Retained Earnings to Balance Sheet	253,000	60,000	40,000	8,000	12,000	269,000

(handwritten: 253,000 + (60,000 − 40,000) × 80% = 269,000)

Balance Sheet						
Cash	79,000	18,000				97,000
Accounts Receivable (net)	64,000	28,000				92,000
Inventory, 12/31	67,000	43,000				110,000
Investment in S Company	165,000			(1) 165,000		0
Difference Between Cost and Book Value			(1) 13,000	(2) 13,000		0
Property and Equipment (net)	180,000	165,000				345,000
Land	35,000	17,000	(2) 13,000			65,000
Total	590,000	271,000				709,000
Accounts Payable	35,000	24,000				59,000
Other Liabilities	62,000	37,000				99,000
Common Stock						
P Company	200,000					200,000
S Company		100,000	(1) 80,000		20,000	
Other Contributed Capital						
P Company	40,000					40,000
S Company		50,000	(1) 40,000		10,000	
Retained Earnings from above	253,000	60,000	40,000	8,000	12,000	269,000
Noncontrolling Interest in Net Assets					42,000	42,000
Total	590,000	271,000	186,000	186,000		709,000

(handwritten: (271,000 − 61,000) × 20% = 42,000)

*.2($30,000) = $6,000
(1) To eliminate the investment in S Company.
(2) To allocate the difference between cost and book value to land.
(3) To eliminate intercompany dividends.

Begin the consolidating process, as always, by preparing a Computation and Allocation Schedule, as follows:

Computation and Allocation of Difference Between Cost and Book Value

Cost of Investment (purchase price)		$165,000
Book Value of Equity Acquired		
S Common Stock (100,000)(.8)	80,000	
S Other Contributed Capital (50,000)(.8)	40,000	
S Retained Earnings (40,000)(.8)	32,000	
Total ($190,000)(.8)		152,000
Difference Between Cost and Book Value		13,000
Adjust land upward (mark toward market)		(13,000)
Balance		$ 0

Because the difference between purchase price and book value is established only at the date of acquisition, *this schedule will not change in future periods.* Thus, there will be $13,000 to distribute each year, although the makeup of that distribution may shift over time. Since it is attributed to land in this example, the distribution will not change unless the land is subsequently sold. That possibility will be explored in a later chapter.

A workpaper for the preparation of consolidated financial statements at December 31, 2000, the end of the year of acquisition, is presented in Illustration 4-2.

Data from the trial balances are arranged in statement form and entered on the workpaper. Consolidated financial statements should include only balances resulting from transactions with outsiders. Eliminating techniques are designed to accomplish this end. The consolidated income statement is essentially a combination of the revenue, expense, gain, and loss accounts of all consolidated affiliates after elimination of amounts representing the effect of transactions among the affiliates. The combined income of the affiliates is reduced by the noncontrolling interest's share (if any) of the net income of the subsidiaries. The remainder is the controlling interest in combined income, sometimes referred to as **consolidated net income**. It consists of parent company net income plus (minus) its share of the affiliate's income (loss) resulting from transactions with outside parties. The consolidated retained earnings statement consists of beginning consolidated retained earnings plus consolidated net income (or minus consolidated net loss), minus parent company dividends declared. The net balance represents consolidated retained earnings at the end of the period.

Workpaper Observations

Several observations should be noted concerning the workpaper presented in Illustration 4-2.

1. *Each section of the workpaper represents one of three consolidated financial statements:* Note that the *entire bottom line* of the income statement, which represents net income, is transferred to the Net Income line on the retained earnings statement. Similarly, the *entire bottom line* of the retained earnings statement, which represents ending retained earnings, is transferred to the Retained Earnings line on the balance sheet.

2. *Elimination of the investment account:* The elimination of the investment account at the end of the first year is the same one that would be made at the date of acquisition for the preparation of a consolidated balance sheet. One exception is that the parent's share of S Company's beginning retained earnings is eliminated in the *retained earnings section* of the workpaper, rather than in the balance sheet section. In subsequent years, the debit to Retained Earnings—S Company will always be for the parent's percentage of the subsidiary retained earnings at the *beginning of the current year.* Changes in retained earnings during the current year are always reflected in the retained earnings statement section of the workpaper. Also note that in subsequent years, there will be an additional entry preceding the elimination of the investment account, and this entry will arise from changes in the Retained Earnings account of the subsidiary from the date of acquisition to the beginning of the current year. This entry is not needed in year 1 because no such change has occurred yet.

It is useful to formulate eliminating entries in *general journal entry form,* even though they are not recorded in the general journal, to be sure that they balance before entering them in the workpaper. Be sure to number each entry as it is entered in the workpaper. This helps to keep the eliminating entries in balance as well. It may also be helpful to think of each entry by a shortened name, as indicated in quotation marks after the following entries.

(1)	Common Stock—S Company	80,000	
	Other Contributed Capital—S Company	40,000	
	1/1 Retained Earnings—S Company	32,000	
	Difference Between Cost and Book Value	13,000	
	Investment in S Company		165,000
	"The investment entry"		

3. *Allocation of the difference between cost and market value:* The second elimination entry is also identical to that which would have been made at the date of acquisition. It serves to distribute the difference between cost and book value of acquired equity to the appropriate account(s), in this case to land.

(2)	Land	13,000	
	Difference Between Cost and Book Value		13,000
	"The differential entry"		

4. *Intercompany dividends:* The elimination of intercompany dividends is made by a debit to Dividend Income and a credit to Dividends Declared. In placing this entry into the Eliminations columns of the workpaper, note that the Dividend Income debit appears in the *Income Statement* section, while the Dividends Declared credit appears in the *Retained Earnings Statement* section. It is commonly the case that an eliminating entry will affect more than one of the three statements, as here (and also in entry (1)).

(3)	Dividend Income	8,000	
	Dividends Declared—S Company		8,000
	"The dividend entry"		

This eliminating entry also serves to prevent the double counting of income, since the subsidiary's individual income and expense items are combined with the parent's in the determination of combined income.

5. *Noncontrolling interest in combined income:* There is one number on the workpaper that is calculated and then inserted directly into the income statement, and does not flow from the trial balance columns. That number is the ***noncontrolling interest in combined income.*** To facilitate the calculation of the noncontrolling and controlling interests in combined income, a t-account approach is helpful. In later chapters, the presence of intercompany profits and other complications will make the calculation more complex than it is at this point. It is, nonetheless, useful to form the habit of using the t-accounts now.

Cost

Noncontrolling Interest in Income

Internally generated income of S Company	$30,000
Any needed adjustments (see Chapter 5)	0
Adjusted income of subsidiary	30,000
Noncontrolling percentage owned	20%
Noncontrolling interest in income	6,000

The first t-account (above) calculates the distribution of net income to the non-controlling interest. This number can be inserted directly into the next-to-bottom line of the *Income Statement* section. When this amount is subtracted from the combined income of $85,000, the resulting amount of $79,000 represents the ***controlling interest in combined income.***

80%

The parent company t-account serves as a useful check of the controlling interest in combined income. The 80% controlling percentage in the adjusted income of subsidiary ($30,000 from t-account above) will appear in P Company's t-account as part of the controlling interest. For the parent company, the internally generated income represents the amount from the first column of the trial balance ($63,000) minus any income that came from the subsidiary (dividend income, in this case, of $8,000), or $55,000 income from P Company's independent operations.

Controlling Interest in Income

Internally generated income of P Company	$55,000
($63,000 income minus $8,000 dividend	
income from subsidiary)	
Any needed adjustments (see Chapter 5)	0
Percentage of subsidiary adjusted income	24,000
(80%)($30,000)	
Controlling interest in income	$79,000

6. *Consolidated retained earnings:* Consolidated retained earnings on December 31, 2000, of $269,000 can be determined as follows:

P Company's reported retained earnings, 1/1	$210,000
Plus: consolidated net income for 2000	79,000
Less: P Company's dividends declared during 2000	(20,000)
Consolidated retained earnings, 12/31	$269,000

The calculation above appears in the final column of the workpaper in the Retained Earnings Statement section. Alternatively, or as a check, consolidated retained earnings may be determined as:

P Company's reported retained earnings, 12/31	$253,000
Plus P Company's share of the increase in S Company's retained earnings from the date of acquisition to the end of 2000: .8($60,000 − $40,000)	16,000
Consolidated Retained Earnings, 12/31	$269,000

7. The eliminations columns in each section do not balance, since individual eliminations made involve more than one section. The total eliminations for all three sections, however, are in balance.

8. Noncontrolling interest in consolidated net assets ($42,000) can be determined directly by multiplying the noncontrolling interest percentage times the book value of the subsidiary's net assets. Thus, noncontrolling interest in consolidated net assets can be computed as .2($271,000 − $61,000) = $42,000. Alternatively, total noncontrolling interest of $42,000 can be verified by examining the following components:

Total Noncontrolling Interest	
6,000	A $6,000 (20% × $30,000) interest in the amount of S Company income that is included in combined income. The $6,000 is added to the noncontrolling interest and deducted from combined income in determining consolidated income.
8,000	An $8,000 share in the beginning balance of S Company's retained earnings. The other $32,000 was purchased by P Company and is, therefore, eliminated.
[2,000]	A $2,0000 (20% × $10,000) decrease for dividends distributed to the noncontrolling stockholders during the year. The other $8,000 in dividends represents parent company dividend income and is, therefore, eliminated.
30,000	A $20,000 and $10,000 interest, respectively, in the common stock and other contributed capital of S Company (representing the 20% initial interest). The remaining common stock and other contributed capital were purchased by P Company and are, therefore, eliminated.
42,000	Total Noncontrolling Interest

The sum of the noncontrolling interest column is transferred to the consolidated balance sheet as one amount since it reflects the noncontrolling stockholders' interest in the net assets of the consolidated group.

After Year of Acquisition—Cost Method

For illustrative purposes, assume continuation of the previous example with data updated to the following year. Trial balances for P Company and S Company at December 31, 2001, are given in Illustration 4-3. Because we are using the cost method, the Investment in S Company account still reflects the cost of the investment, $165,000. The beginning retained earnings balances for P and S Companies on January 1, 2001, are the same as the ending retained earnings balances on

ILLUSTRATION 4-3

P Company and S Company Trial Balances

December 31, 2001

	P Company		S Company	
	Dr.	Cr.	Dr.	Cr.
Cash	$74,000		$ 41,000	
Accounts Receivable (net)	71,000		33,000	
Inventory, 1/1	67,000		43,000	
Property and Equipment (net)	245,000		185,000	
Land	35,000		17,000	
Accounts Payable		$ 61,000		$ 30,000
Other Liabilities		70,000		45,000
Common Stock, $10 par value		200,000		100,000
Other Contributed Capital		40,000		50,000
Retained Earnings, 1/1		253,000		60,000
Dividends Declared	30,000		10,000	
Sales		350,000		190,000
Dividend Income		8,000		
Purchases	215,000		90,000	
Expenses	80,000		56,000	
	$982,000	$982,000	$475,000	$475,000
Inventory, 12/31	$ 82,000		$ 39,000	

December 31, 2000 (confirmed in Illustration 4-2, first two columns). Although the trial balance is dated December 31, 2001, the retained earnings balance is dated January 1, 2001, because the income statement and Dividends Declared accounts are still open.

A workpaper for the preparation of consolidated financial statements for P and S Companies for the year ended December 31, 2001, is presented in Illustration 4-4. Note that the detail comprising cost of goods sold is provided in Illustration 4-2 (beginning inventory plus purchases minus ending inventory). In Illustration 4-4 and subsequent illustrations in this chapter, the detail will be collapsed into one item, Cost of Goods Sold. In later chapters, however, we will use the detailed accounts when the focus is more directly upon inventory and the calculation of cost of goods sold (in the presence of intercompany profit, for instance).

The workpaper entries in years after the year of acquisition are essentially the same as those made for the year of acquisition (Illustration 4-2) with one major exception. Before the elimination of the investment account, a workpaper entry, (1) in Illustration 4-4, is made to the investment account and P Company's beginning retained earnings to recognize P Company's share of the cumulative undistributed income or loss of S Company from the *date of acquisition to the beginning of the current year* as follows:

(1) Investment in S Company		16,000	Cost
1/1 Retained Earnings—P Company			16,000
(Consolidated Retained Earnings)			
[80% × (60,000 − $40,000)]			

This entry may be viewed as either *the entry to convert from the cost method to the equity method or the entry to establish reciprocity.* The following two points explain these essentially complementary views of the entry.

Cost Method

80% Owned

Subsequent to Year

of Acquisition

ILLUSTRATION 4-4

Consolidated Statements Workpaper

P Company and Subsidiary

For the Year Ended December 31, 2001

Income Statement	P Company	S Company	Eliminations Dr.	Eliminations Cr.	Noncontrolling Interest	Consolidated Balances
Sales	350,000	190,000				540,000
Dividend Income	8,000		(4) 8,000			
Total Revenue	358,000	190,000				540,000
Cost of Goods Sold	200,000	94,000				294,000
Expenses	80,000	56,000				136,000
Total Cost and Expense	280,000	150,000				430,000
Net/Combined Income	78,000	40,000				110,000
Noncontrolling Interest in Income					8,000	(8,000)*
Net Income to Retained Earnings	78,000	40,000	8,000	—0—	8,000	102,000
Retained Earnings Statement						
1/1 Retained Earnings						
P Company	253,000			(1) 16,000		269,000
S Company		60,000	(2) 48,000		12,000	
Net Income from above	78,000	40,000	8,000	—0—	8,000	102,000
Dividends Declared						
P Company	(30,000)					(30,000)
S Company		(10,000)		(4) 8,000	(2,000)	
12/31 Retained Earnings to						
Balance Sheet	301,000	90,000	56,000	24,000	18,000	341,000
Balance Sheet						
Cash	74,000	41,000				115,000
Accounts Receivable (net)	71,000	33,000				104,000
Inventory, 12/31	82,000	39,000				121,000
Investment in S Company	165,000		(1) 16,000	(2) 181,000		
Difference Between Cost and Book Value			(2) 13,000	(3) 13,000		
Property and Equipment (net)	245,000	185,000				430,000
Land	35,000	17,000	(3) 13,000			65,000
Total	672,000	315,000				835,000
Accounts Payable	61,000	30,000				91,000
Other Liabilities	70,000	45,000				115,000
Common Stock						
P Company	200,000					200,000
S Company		100,000	(2) 80,000		20,000	
Other Contributed Capital						
P Company	40,000					40,000
S Company		50,000	(2) 40,000		10,000	
Retained Earnings from above	301,000	90,000	56,000	24,000	18,000	341,000
Noncontrolling Interest in Net Assets					48,000	48,000
Total	672,000	315,000	205,000	205,000		835,000

*.2($40,000) = $8,000

(1) To recognize P Company's share (80%) of S Company's undistributed income from date of acquisition to beginning of the current year. (Also referred to as "To establish reciprocity" or "To convert to equity method.")

(2) To eliminate the investment in S Company.

(3) To allocate the difference between cost and book value to land.

(4) To eliminate intercompany dividends.

1. The reciprocity entry adjusts P Company's beginning retained earnings balance on the workpaper to the appropriate beginning consolidated retained earnings amount. As indicated earlier, consolidated retained earnings on January 1, 2001, consists of P Company's reported retained earnings plus P Company's share of the undistributed earnings (income less dividends) of S Company from the date of stock acquisition to the beginning of 2001. Note that, after the reciprocity entry is made, the beginning (1/1/01) consolidated retained earnings of $269,000 (Illustration 4-4) equals the ending (12/31/00) consolidated retained earnings amount (Illustration 4-2).

2. If this entry is viewed as a conversion to the equity method, the following question might well arise: Why should we convert to the equity method, if all methods are acceptable and all yield the same final results? Recall that under the equity method, the parent records its equity in the subsidiary income in its income statement and thus ultimately in its retained earnings. If we consider the two accounts in the conversion entry, it is true that the investment is going to be eliminated to zero anyway; but the retained earnings account of the parent company, which must ultimately reflect the equity in subsidiary income, will not be eliminated. Instead it needs to be adjusted if the cost method is used.

Although it is true that the investment account must be eliminated after it is adjusted, the reciprocity (conversion) entry facilitates this elimination. After eliminating the parent company's share of the subsidiary's stockholders' equity accounts at the beginning of the year against the adjusted investment account, any remaining balance in the investment account now represents the difference between cost and book value. (In this example, the difference of $13,000 is attributed to land.)

The amount needed for the workpaper entry to establish reciprocity can be most accurately computed by multiplying the parent company's percentage of ownership times the increase or decrease in the subsidiary's retained earnings from the date of stock acquisition to the beginning of the current year. This approach adjusts for complications that might arise where the subsidiary may have made direct entries to its retained earnings for prior period adjustments.

This approach is also the most efficient because it provides a shortcut in lieu of making separate entries for each year's income and each year's dividend declarations. Recall that the workpaper entries are just that, workpaper only, and as such they do not get posted to the accounts of either the parent or subsidiary company. Hence entries that were made on a previous year's workpaper must be "caught up" in subsequent periods. If income and dividend entries were made separately for each year, imagine the number of entries in year 9 or year 20!

After the investment account is adjusted by workpaper entry (1), P Company's share of S Company's equity is eliminated against the **adjusted investment account** in entry (2) below:

(2)	Common Stock—S company	80,000
	Other Contributed Capital—S Company	40,000
	1/1 Retained Earnings—S Company	48,000
	Difference Between Cost and Book Value	13,000
	Investment in S Company ($165,000 + $16,000)	181,000

Cost

changed
unchanged
changed

Entry (3) distributes the difference between cost and book values, as follows:

| (3) | Land | 13,000 | |
| | Difference Between Cost and Book Value | | 13,000 |

Next, intercompany dividend income is eliminated as follows:

| (4) | Dividend Income | 8,000 | |
| | Dividends Declared—S Company | | 8,000 |

Consolidated balances are then determined in the same manner as in previous illustrations. Remember that the entry to establish reciprocity (convert to equity) is a cumulative one that recognizes the parent's share of the change in the subsid-

ILLUSTRATION 4-5

P Company and Subsidiary
Consolidated Statement of Income and Retained Earnings
For the Year Ended December 31, 2001

Sales	$540,000
Cost of Goods Sold	294,000
Gross Margin	246,000
Expenses	136,000
Combined Operating Income	110,000
Noncontrolling Interest in Income	8,000
Controlling Interest in Income	102,000
Retained Earnings, 1/1/01	269,000
Total	371,000
Dividends Declared	30,000
Retained Earnings, 12/31/01	$341,000

P Company and Subsidiary
Consolidated Balance Sheet
December 31, 2001

Assets

Current Assets:		
Cash		$115,000
Accounts Receivable (net)		104,000
Inventories		121,000
Total Current Assets		340,000
Property and Equipment (net)		430,000
Land		65,000
Total Assets		$835,000

Liabilities and Stockholders' Equity

Accounts Payable		$ 91,000
Other Liabilities		115,000
Total Liabilities		206,000
Stockholders' Equity:		
Noncontrolling Interest in Net Assets	48,000	
Common Stock, $10 par value	200,000	
Other Conributed Capital	40,000	
Retained Earnings	341,000	629,000
Total Liabilities and Stockholders' Equity		$835,000

iary's retained earnings from the date of acquisition to the beginning of the current year. Thus, for example, the reciprocity entry for the *third year* in the December 31, 2002, workpaper is as follows:

Investment in S Company	40,000	
1/1 Retained Earnings—P Company		40,000
.8($90,000 − $40,000)		
"*The reciprocity/conversion entry*"		

An example of a consolidated statement of income and retained earnings and a consolidated balance sheet (based on Illustration 4-4) is presented in Illustration 4-5. Notice that ***all (100%) of S Company's revenues and expenses*** are included in the consolidated income statement. The noncontrolling interest's share of the subsidiary's income is then deducted as a separate item in determining consolidated net income. Likewise, ***all of S Company's assets and liabilities*** are included with those of P Company in the consolidated balance sheet. The noncontrolling interest's share of the net assets is then included as a separate item within the stockholders' equity section of the consolidated balance sheet.

RECORDING INVESTMENTS IN SUBSIDIARIES—EQUITY METHOD (PARTIAL OR COMPLETE)

Companies may elect to use the equity method to record their investments in subsidiaries to estimate the operating effects of their investments for internal decision-making purposes. As with the cost method, the investment is recorded initially at its cost under the equity method. Subsequent to acquisition, the major differences between the cost and equity methods pertain to the period in which subsidiary income is formally recorded on the books of the parent company and the amount of income recognized. Under the assumptions of this chapter, partial and complete equity methods are indistinguishable. Thus, the differences between the two do not become important until Chapter 5. In Chapter 5, we will explore alternative assumptions regarding the disposition of the difference between purchase price and book value, which will necessitate amortization or depreciation adjustments. In subsequent chapters, we will explore other complications that may arise under the complete equity method.

Equity

One frequent complication occurs when the parent and subsidiary have different year-ends. The SEC allows the parent to use a different year-end for its subsidiary provided the subsidiary data are not more than 93 days old. The parent simply combines the data for the subsidiary's twelve months with its own, just as though the year-ends were the same. The SEC requirement has become broadly accepted in practice. In some cases, firms find it desirable for the subsidiary's year to end earlier to facilitate the adjusting, closing, and consolidating procedures in a timely fashion. However, the preference is to use the "best available data," weighing the tradeoffs between reliability and timeliness. Thus, in some cases, the best alternative may be to combine the subsidiary's interim data with the parent's year-end data.

As illustrated in previous sections of this chapter, no income from the subsidiary is recorded by the parent company under the cost method until it is distributed as dividends. When distributed, the parent records its share of the dividends as dividend income. Under the equity method, income is recorded in the books of the parent company in the same accounting period that it is reported by the subsidiary company, whether or not such income is distributed to the parent company.

Assume that P Company purchased 80% of the outstanding shares of S Company common stock on January 1, 2000, for $165,000. The underlying book value of S Company's net assets (100%) on that date was $190,000. P Company made the following entry:

P's Books		
Investment in S Company	165,000	
Cash		165,000

P Company would record income in the first year based not on dividends received, but on its share of the subsidiary's income. Under the partial equity method, this amount will be based on income *reported* by the subsidiary. Under the complete equity method, the subsidiary's reported income will be adjusted under certain circumstances, as illustrated at the beginning of this chapter. Throughout the remainder of this chapter, however, we assume that those adjustments will not be needed. Hence adjusted income will equal reported income. The "adjustments" concept will be introduced very briefly in this chapter and developed in later chapters.

Assuming a current period income of $30,000 reported by S Company, P Company would make the following entry on its books:

P's Books		
Investment in S Company	24,000	
Equity in subsidiary income .8($30,000)		24,000

Dividends received from the subsidiary (parent's share assumed to be $8,000) are then *credited* to the Investment account, as follows:

P's Books		
Cash (or Dividends Receivable)	8,000	
Investment in S Company		8,000

Consequently, the parent company's share of the ***cumulative undistributed income (income less dividends)*** of the subsidiary is accumulated over time as an addition to the investment account. In this example, the parent's share of undistributed income for the year was $16,000 (i.e., the same amount as the reciprocity entry for firms using the cost method!).

Investment Carried at Equity—Year of Acquisition

In this section we illustrate the consolidated workpaper used to prepare consolidated financial statements under the equity method. Keep in mind that workpapers are just that, a means to an end, with the real goal being the preparation of correct financial statements. Regardless of whether the parent's books are kept using the cost method or one of the equity methods, the consolidated financial statements should be identical. The eliminating entries needed to achieve the correct balances, however, are not identical.

Assume that at the end of the first year, the trial balances of P and S Company

ILLUSTRATION 4-6

P Company and S Company Trial Balances
December 31, 2000

	P Company Dr.	P Company Cr.	S Company Dr.	S Company Cr.
Cash	$ 79,000		$ 18,000	
Accounts Receivable (net)	64,000		28,000	
Inventory, 1/1	56,000		32,000	
Inventory in S company	181,000			
Property and Equipment (net)	180,000		165,000	
Land	35,000		17,000	
Accounts Payable		$ 35,000		$ 24,000
Other Liabilities		62,000		37,000
Common Stock, $10 par value		200,000		100,000
Other Contributed Capital		40,000		50,000
Retained Earnings, 1/1		210,000		40,000
Dividends Declared	20,000		10,000	
Sales		300,000		160,000
Equity in Subsidiary Income		24,000		
Purchases	186,000		95,000	
Expenses	70,000		46,000	
	$871,000	$871,000	$411,000	$411,000
Inventory, 12/31	$ 67,000		$ 43,000	

appear as shown in Illustration 4-6. Begin the consolidating process, as always, by preparing a Computation and Allocation Schedule, as follows:

Computation and Allocation of Difference Between Cost and Book Value

Cost of Investment (Purchase Price)	$165,000
Book Value of Equity Acquired ($190,000 × 80%)	152,000
Difference Between Cost and Book Value	13,000
Adjust land upward (mark toward market)	(13,000)
Balance	—0—

Because the difference between purchase price and book value is established only at the date of acquisition, this schedule will not change in future periods.   **Equity**

Note that the trial balance data in Illustration 4-6 reflect the effects of the investment, equity in subsidiary income, and dividend transactions presented above. These balances are next arranged into *income statement, retained earnings statement,* and *balance sheet statement* sections as they are entered into the first two columns of the consolidated workpaper presented in Illustration 4-7.

When the investment account is carried on the equity basis, it is necessary first to make a workpaper entry reversing the effects of the parent company's entries to the investment account for subsidiary income and dividends during the current year.

To eliminate the account "equity in subsidiary income" from the consolidated income statement, the following workpaper entry, presented in general journal form, is made:

(1)	Equity in Subsidiary Income	24,000	
	Investment in S Company		24,000

			ILLUSTRATION 4-7			
Equity Method						
80% Owned			**Consolidated Statements Workpaper**			
Year of Acquisition			**P Company and Subsidiary**			
			For the Year Ended December 31, 2000			

Income Statement	P Company	S Company	Eliminations Dr.	Eliminations Cr.	Noncontrolling Interest	Consolidated Balances
Sales	300,000	160,000				460,000
Equity in Subsidiary Income	24,000		(1) 24,000			
Total Revenue	324,000	160,000				460,000
Cost of Goods Sold	175,000	84,000				259,000
Expenses	70,000	46,000				116,000
Total Cost and Expense	245,000	130,000				375,000
Net/Combined Income	79,000	30,000				85,000
Noncontrolling Interest in Income					6,000	(6,000)*
Net Income to Retained Earnings	79,000	30,000	24,000	—0—	6,000	79,000
Retained Earnings Statement						
1/1 Retained Earnings						
P Company	210,000					210,000
S Company		40,000	(3) 32,000		8,000	
Net Income from above	79,000	30,000	24,000	—0—	6,000	79,000
Dividends Declared						
P Company	(20,000)					(20,000)
S Company		(10,000)		(2) 8,000	(2,000)	
12/31 Retained Earnings to Balance Sheet	269,000	60,000	56,000	8,000	12,000	269,000
Balance Sheet						
Cash	79,000	18,000				97,000
Accounts Receivable (net)	64,000	28,000				92,000
Inventory, 12/31	67,000	43,000				110,000
Investment in S Company	181,000		(2) 8,000	(1) 24,000		
				(3) 165,000		
Difference Between Cost and Book Value			(3) 13,000	(4) 13,000		
Property and Equipment (net)	180,000	165,000				345,000
Land	35,000	17,000	(4) 13,000			65,000
Total	606,000	271,000				709,000
Accounts Payable	35,000	24,000				59,000
Other Liabilities	62,000	37,000				99,000
Common Stock						
P Company	200,000					200,000
S Company		100,000	(3) 80,000		20,000	
Other Contributed Capital						
P Company	40,000					40,000
S Company		50,000	(3) 40,000		10,000	
Retained Earnings from above	269,000	60,000	56,000	8,000	12,000	269,000
Noncontrolling Interest in Net Assets					42,000	42,000
Total	606,000	271,000	210,000	210,000		709,000

*20% × $30,000 = $6,000

(1) To reverse the effect of parent company entry during the year for subsidiary income.
(2) To reverse the effect of parent company entry during the year for subsidiary dividends.
(3) To eliminate the investment in S Company.
(4) To allocate the excess of cost over book value to land.

Next, to eliminate intercompany dividends under the equity method, this workpaper entry is made:

(2)	Investment in S Company	8,000	
	Dividends Declared		8,000

Alternatively, these two entries may be collapsed into one entry, as follows:

(1)–(2)	Equity in Subsidiary Income	24,000	
	Investment in S Company		16,000
	Dividends Declared		8,000

This reversal has two effects. First, it eliminates the equity in subsidiary income and dividends recorded by P Company. Second, it returns the investment account to its balance as of the beginning of the year. This is necessary because it is the parent company's share of the subsidiary's retained earnings at the *beginning of the year* that is eliminated in the investment elimination entry. A third eliminating entry must then be made to eliminate the Investment account against subsidiary equity, and the fourth entry distributes the difference between cost and book value of equity acquired, as follows:

(3)	Common Stock—S Company	80,000		
	Other Contributed Capital—S Company	40,000		
	1/1 Retained Earnings—S Company	32,000		
	Difference Between Cost and Book Value	13,000		
	Investment in S Company ($181,000 − $16,000)		165,000	**Equity**

(4)	Land	13,000	
	Difference Between Cost and Book Value		13,000

The next few paragraphs relate to basic workpaper concepts that do not differ between the cost and equity methods. Thus, for those who have already read the section of the chapter on the cost method, this will serve as a review.

To complete the worksheet, the account balances are extended from left to right. Two lines merit attention. First, the *entire bottom line* of the income statement, which represents net income, is transferred to the Net Income line on the retained earnings statement. Similarly, the *entire bottom line* of the retained earnings statement, which represents ending retained earnings, is transferred to the retained earnings line on the balance sheet. Throughout this and future chapters on consolidation, we will see that any eliminating entries to the account Retained Earnings will be entered in the Beginning Balance on the retained earnings statements (not on the balance sheet, ending balance). Because the Current Year Income and Dividends Declared accounts are still open, current year changes in Retained Earnings will be adjusted through those accounts (or in the retained earnings section of the workpaper).

There is one number on the workpaper that is calculated and then inserted directly into the income statement, and does not flow from the trial balance columns. That number is the *noncontrolling interest in combined income*. To facilitate the calculation of the noncontrolling and controlling interests in combined income, a t-account approach is helpful. In later chapters, the presence of intercompany profits and other complications will make the calculation more complex than it is at this point. It is, nonetheless, useful to form the habit of using the t-accounts now.

The first t-account (below) calculates the distribution of net income to the noncontrolling interest. This number can be inserted directly into the next-to-bottom line of the Income Statement section. When this amount is subtracted from the combined income of $85,000, the resulting amount of $79,000 represents the *controlling interest in combined income* (often referred to as *consolidated net income*). It is interesting to note that this is the very same amount that the parent reported in its trial balance originally. In future chapters, we will see that this is the case only if the parent uses the complete equity method. For example, if profit or loss on intercompany sales between parent and subsidiary must be eliminated at the balance sheet date, an adjustment will be required to reconcile the two numbers under the partial equity method. Similarly, if any difference between cost and book value is attributed to depreciable assets or to goodwill, rather than to land, an adjustment will also be needed under the partial equity method. Hence it is useful to check the calculation of the controlling interest in combined income.

Noncontrolling Interest in Income

Internally generated income	$30,000
Any needed adjustments (see Chapter 5)	0
Adjusted income of subsidiary	30,000
Noncontrolling percentage owned	20%
Noncontrolling interest in income	6,000

The next t-account serves as such a check of the controlling interest in combined income. The 80% controlling percentage in the adjusted income of subsidiary ($30,000 from t-account above) will appear in P Company's t-account as part of the controlling interest. For the parent company, the internally generated income represents the amount from the first column of the trial balance ($79,000) minus any income which came from the subsidiary (equity in subsidiary income, in this case, of $24,000), or $55,000 income from P Company's independent operations.

$$80\%$$

Controlling Interest in Income

Internally generated income	$55,000
($79,000 income minus $24,000	
equity in subsidiary income)	
Any needed adjustments (see Chapter 5)	0
Percentage of subsidiary adjusted	
income (80%)($30,000)	24,000
Controlling interest in income	$79,000

Consolidated retained earnings on December 31, 2000, of $269,000 can be determined as follows:

P Company's reported retained earnings, 1/1	$210,000
Plus consolidated net income for 2000	79,000
Less P Company's dividends declared during 2000	(20,000)
Consolidated Retained Earnings, 12/31	$269,000

The calculation above appears in the final column of the workpaper in the Retained Earnings Statement section. Alternatively, or as a check, consolidated retained earnings may be determined as:

why not 269,000 + .8(60,000-60,000) = 285,000

P Company's reported retained earnings, 12/31	$253,000
Plus P Company's share of the increase in S Company's retained earnings from the date of acquisition to the end of 2000, .8($60,000 − $40,000)	16,000
Consolidated retained earnings, 12/31	$269,000

Equity

Note that the eliminations columns in each section do not balance, since individual eliminations often involve more than one section. The total eliminations for all three sections, however, are in balance.

Noncontrolling interest in consolidated net assets can be determined by multiplying the noncontrolling interest percentage times the book value of the subsidiary's net assets. Thus, noncontrolling interest in consolidated net assets can be computed as .2($271,000 − $61,000) = $42,000.

Comparison of Illustrations 4-2 and 4-7 brings out an important observation. *The consolidated column of the workpaper is the same under the cost and equity methods. Thus, the decision to use the cost or equity method to record investments in subsidiaries that will be consolidated has no impact on the consolidated financial statements. Only the elimination process is affected.*

Note once more that P Company's reported net income of $79,000 (Illustration 4-7) and consolidated net income are identical. Likewise, P Company's December 31, 2000, retained earnings equal consolidated retained earnings at that date. In later chapters we will see that this will always be true under the complete equity method, but not under the partial equity method. We obtain this result here because P Company has recorded its share of S Company's earnings, and because of the absence of complicating assumptions.

Investment Carried at Equity—After Year of Acquisition

To illustrate the preparation of a consolidated workpaper for years after the year of acquisition under the equity method, assume the data given in Illustration 4-8, and the use of the equity method rather than the cost method. After P Company has recorded its share of S Company's income ($32,000) and dividends declared ($8,000), the Investment in S Company account appears as follows:

Investment in S Company

12/31/00	Balance	181,000	Dividends	8,000
	Subsidiary income	32,000		
12/31/01	Balance	205,000		

The preparation of the Computation and Allocation Schedule is the same as it was in the year of acquisition; that is, it does not need to be prepared again. The elimination process also follows the same procedures as in the year of acquisition (with current year amounts). A consolidated statements workpaper in this case is presented in Illustration 4-9. We next review the workpaper entries in general journal entry form. Note that although the Computation and Allocation Schedule does not change, the third eliminating entry (to eliminate the Investment account against the equity accounts of the subsidiary) will change to reflect the Retained Earnings

ILLUSTRATION 4-8

P Company and S Company Trial Balances
(Year after Acquisition)
December 31, 2001

	P Company		S Company	
	Dr.	Cr.	Dr.	Cr.
Cash	$ 74,000		$ 41,000	
Accounts Receivable (net)	71,000		33,000	
Inventory, 1/1	67,000		43,000	
Investment in S Company	205,000			
Property and Equipment (net)	245,000		185,000	
Land	35,000		17,000	
Accounts Payable		$ 61,000		$ 30,000
Other Liabilities		70,000		45,000
Common Stock		200,000		100,000
Other Contributed Capital		40,000		50,000
Retained Earnings, 1/1		269,000		60,000
Dividends Declared	30,000		10,000	
Sales		350,000		190,000
Equity in Subsidiary Income		32,000		
Purchases	215,000		90,000	
Expenses	80,000		56,000	
	$1,022,000	$1,022,000	$475,000	$475,000
Inventory, 12/31	$ 82,000		$ 39,000	

Equity

balance of the subsidiary at the *beginning of the current year* and the corresponding change in the Investment account.

As in the year of acquisition, the Equity in Subsidiary account must be eliminated against the Investment in Subsidiary account. The amount of this entry is obtained from the trial balance column for P Company, and it equals the parent's percentage (80%) of S Company's reported net income ($40,000):

(1)	Equity in Subsidiary Income	32,000	
	Investment in S Company		32,000

Next, to eliminate intercompany dividends under the equity method, this workpaper entry is made:

(2)	Investment in S Company	8,000	
	Dividends Declared		8,000

Alternatively, these two entries may be collapsed into one entry, as follows:

(1)–(2)	Equity in Subsidiary Income	32,000	
	Investment in S Company		24,000
	Dividends Declared		8,000

As in the year of acquisition, these entries eliminate the equity in subsidiary income and dividends recorded by P Company, and return the investment account to its balance as of the beginning of the year. This is necessary because it is the parent company's share of the subsidiary's retained earnings at the *beginning of the year*

Equity Method			ILLUSTRATION 4-9			
80% Owned Subsidiary			**Consolidated Statements Workpaper**			
Subsequent to Year			**P Company and Subsidiary**			
of Acquisition			**For the Year Ended December 31, 2001**			

	P	S	Eliminations		Noncontrolling	Consolidated
Income Statement	Company	Company	Dr.	Cr.	Interest	Balances
Sales	350,000	190,000				540,000
Equity in Subsidiary Income	32,000		(1) 32,000			
Total Revenue	382,000	190,000				540,000
Cost of Goods Sold	200,000	94,000				294,000
Expenses	80,000	56,000				136,000
Total Cost and Expense	280,000	150,000				430,000
Net/Combined Income	102,000	40,000				110,000
Noncontrolling Interest in Income					8,000	(8,000)*
Net Income to Retained Earnings	102,000	40,000	32,000	—0—	8,000	102,000
Retained Earnings Statement						
1/1 Retained Earnings						
P Company	269,000					269,000
S Company		60,000	(3) 48,000		12,000	
Net Income from above	102,000	40,000	32,000	—0—	8,000	102,000
Dividends Declared						
P Company	(30,000)					(30,000)
S Company		(10,000)		(2) 8,000	(2,000)	
12/31 Retained Earnings to						
Balance Sheet	341,000	90,000	80,000	8,000	18,000	341,000
Balance Sheet						
Cash	74,000	41,000				115,000
Accounts Receivable (net)	71,000	33,000				104,000
Inventory, 12/31	82,000	39,000				121,000
Investment in S Company	205,000		(2) 8,000	(1) 32,000		
				(3) 181,000		
Difference Between Cost and Book Value			(3) 13,000	(4) 13,000		
Property and Equipment (net)	245,000	185,000				430,000
Land	35,000	17,000	(4) 13,000			65,000
Total	712,000	315,000				835,000
Accounts Payable	61,000	30,000				91,000
Other Liabilities	70,000	45,000				115,000
Common Stock						
P Company	200,000					200,000
S Company		100,000	(3) 80,000		20,000	
Other Contributed Capital						
P Company	40,000					40,000
S Company		50,000	(3) 40,000		10,000	
Retained Earnings from above	341,000	90,000	80,000	8,000	18,000	341,000
Noncontrolling Interest in Net Assets					48,000	48,000
Total	712,000	315,000	234,000	234,000		835,000

Equity

*20% × $40,000 = $8,000
(1) To reverse the effect of parent company entry during the year for subsidiary income.
(2) To reverse the effect of parent company entry during the year for subsidiary dividends.
(3) To eliminate the investment in S Company.
(4) To allocate the excess of cost over book value to land.

that is eliminated in the investment elimination entry. A third eliminating entry must then be made to eliminate the Investment account against subsidiary equity, and the fourth entry distributes the difference between cost and book value of equity acquired, as follows:

(3)	Common Stock—S Company	80,000	
	Other Contributed Capital—S Company	40,000	
	1/1 Retained Earnings—S Company	48,000 *— changed*	
	Difference Between Cost and Book Value	13,000	
	Investment in S Company ($205,000 − $24,000)		181,000 *(changed)*
(4)	Land	13,000	
	Difference Between Cost and Book Value		13,000

Equity   The only differences in the affiliates' account data as compared to the cost method workpaper appear in P Company's statements. The Investment account in P Company's balance sheet shows a balance of $205,000 rather than $165,000, and equity in subsidiary income of $32,000, rather than dividend income of $8,000, is listed in P Company's income statement. In addition, P Company's beginning and ending retained earnings are $16,000 and $40,000 larger, respectively, which reflects the effect of recording its share (80%) of S Company's income in 2000 and 2001 rather than recording only its share of dividends distributed by S Company.

Also, observe that the consolidated columns in Illustrations 4-4 and 4-9 are the same; regardless of the method used (cost or equity), the consolidated results are unaffected.

Investment Carried at Complete Equity

Under the assumptions of the preceding illustration, the complete equity method and the partial equity method are identical, not only in the end result but also in the steps to consolidate. Under other assumptions, however, the two may differ in the steps (though not in the end result). Recall that the complete equity method is quite similar to the partial equity method, but involves additional entries to the investment account on the books of the parent. These additional adjustments are made to the investment account for the amortization of a difference between cost and book value, the effects of unrealized intercompany profits, and stockholders' equity transactions undertaken by the subsidiary. In the absence of these types of transactions, the complete equity method is identical to the partial equity method, both on the books of the parent and in the workpaper eliminating entries, as in the preceding illustration.

Let us assume that no unrealized intercompany profits are involved (neither the parent nor the subsidiary made sales to the other party), and the subsidiary did not participate in any stockholders' equity transactions. In this situation we need only consider the possible amortization of a difference between cost and book value, in addition to the concepts presented in the preceding illustration. In that illustration, we assumed that any difference between purchase price and the book value of equity acquired related to the valuation of subsidiary land. Under generally accepted accounting principles, we do not amortize or depreciate (or appreciate) land over time. In Chapter 5, we will explore alternative assumptions regarding the disposition of the difference between purchase price and book value, which will necessitate amortization or depreciation adjustments. In subsequent chapters, we will explore other complications that may result in differences between the partial and complete equity methods.

Summary of Workpaper Eliminating Entries

Basic workpaper consolidating (eliminating/adjusting) entries depend on whether (1) the cost method or equity method is used to record the investment on the books of the parent company, and (2) the workpaper is being prepared at the end of the year of acquisition or at the end of periods after the year of acquisition. Workpaper eliminating entries for the alternatives are summarized in Illustration 4-10.

ILLUSTRATION 4-10
Summary of Basic Workpaper Eliminating Entries

Cost Method	Partial Equity Method	Complete Equity Method
End of Year of Acquisition		

Dividend Income
    Dividends Declared—S
	Equity in Subsidiary Income
	    Dividends Declared—S
	        Investment in S Company
		Equity in Subsidiary Income
		    Dividends Declared—S
		        Investment in S Company

To eliminate intercompany dividend income.	To eliminate equity in subsidiary reported income and dividends and return the investment account to its cost at date of acquisition.	To eliminate equity in subsidiary adjusted income and dividends and return the investment account to its cost at date of acquisition (adjustments are addressed in Chapter 5).

Capital Stock—S
Other Contributed Capital—S
Retained Earnings—S
Difference Between Cost and
    Book Value
        Investment in S Company
	Same as Cost Method	**Same as Cost Method**

To eliminate P Company's share of S Company's stockholders' equity against the investment account.		
End of Periods Subsequent to Year of Acquisition		
Investment in S Company **Retained Earnings—P**	**No Entry Needed**	**No Entry Needed**
To recognize P company's share of S Company's undistributed income from the date of acquisition to beginning of the current year (convert to equity or establish reciprocity).		

Dividend Income
    Dividends Declared—S
	Equity in Subsidiary Income
	    Dividends Declared—S
	        Investment in S Company
		Equity in Subsidiary Income
		    Dividends Declared—S
		        Investment in S Company

To eliminate intercompany dividend income.	To eliminate equity in subsidiary reported income and dividends and return the investment account to its balance as of beginning of the current year.	To eliminate equity in subsidiary adjusted income and dividends and return the investment account to its balance as of beginning of the current year (adjustments are addressed in Chapter 5).

Capital Stock—S
Other Contributed Capital—S
Retained Earnings—S
Difference Between Cost and
    Book Value
        Investment in Company
	Same as Cost Method	**Same as Cost Method**

To eliminate P Company's share of S Company's stockholders' equity against the investment account, using balances retained earnings at beginning of current year.		

ELIMINATION OF INTERCOMPANY REVENUE AND EXPENSE ITEMS

Discussion and illustrations to this point have emphasized the procedures used to eliminate the parent company's interest in subsidiary equity against the investment account at the end of the year of stock acquisition and for subsequent periods. Before proceeding with a discussion of some special topics relating to consolidated statements in succeeding chapters, it should be noted that several types of intercompany revenue and expense items must be eliminated in the preparation of a consolidated income statement.

Affiliates often engage in numerous sale/purchase transactions with other affiliates, such as the sale of merchandise or equipment by a subsidiary to its parent, or vice versa. Procedures used to eliminate these intercompany sales (purchases) as well as any unrealized profit remaining in inventories are discussed and illustrated in Chapters 6 and 7. Eliminating workpaper entries are also needed for such intercompany revenue and expense items as interest, rent, and professional services. For example, the workpaper entry to eliminate intercompany interest revenue and expense takes the following form:

Interest Revenue	8,000	
Interest Expense		8,000

INTERIM ACQUISITIONS OF SUBSIDIARY STOCK

Discussion and illustrations to this point have been limited to situations in which the parent company acquired its interest in a subsidiary at the beginning of the subsidiary's fiscal period. That condition is unrealistic because many stock acquisitions are made during the subsidiary's fiscal period. Thus, the proper treatment in consolidated financial statements of the subsidiary's revenue and expense items for the partial period *before* acquisition must be considered.

For example, suppose that P Company acquires 90% of the outstanding common stock of S Company on April 1, 2000. Both companies close their books on December 31. Consider S's income statement in Illustration 4-11. In this illustration, the revenues and expenses for S Company are presented in total and also separately for the periods before and after the acquisition. S Company earns $36,000 of income for the entire year. P Company is entitled to 90% of the income earned since April (90% of $27,000 or $24,300). As mentioned earlier, *under purchase accounting, revenues and expenses of the acquired company are included with those of the acquiring company only from the date of acquisition forward*. In essence, the amounts to be combined with the parent in the year of acquisition are shown in the third column of Illustration 4-11. However, the totals from column 1 are often shown as the starting point for two reasons: (1) the revenue and expense accounts in the books of the subsidiary are likely to reflect the entire year, and (2) users may be interested in preacquisition information.

Therefore two acceptable alternatives for presenting the subsidiary's revenue and expense items in the consolidated income statement in the year of acquisition are allowed under current generally accepted accounting principles. Although the

ILLUSTRATION 4-11

S Company
Income Statement and Allocation to Various Interests
For the Year Ended December 31, 2000

Income Statement	*(1)* *Entire Year*	*(2)* *January to April*	*(3)* *April to December*
Sales	160,000	40,000	120,000
Dividend Income			
Total Revenue	160,000	40,000	120,000
Cost of Goods Sold	80,000	20,000	60,000
Other Expenses	44,000	11,000	33,000
Total Cost and Expense	124,000	31,000	93,000
Net Income	36,000	9,000	27,000
Portion of Income Purchased (90%) by P Company		8,100	
Noncontrolling Interest in Income Before the Purchase (10%)		900	
Noncontrolling Interest in Income (10%) after Purchase			2,700 } 3,600
Net Income to Consolidated Income (Controlling Interest in Income after Purchase)			24,300

Note: P acquires S Company on April 1, 2000.

authoritative standard[5] expresses a preference for one of the two, this preference is not a requirement; thus, we present both. Both alternatives result in the same consolidated income; the difference lies in the detail included in the statement.

One alternative, the *full-year reporting alternative*, is to include the subsidiary's revenues and expenses in the consolidated income statement for the entire year (as though S has been acquired at the beginning of the year). These revenues and expenses are shown in the first column of Illustration 4-11. Then a deduction is needed at the bottom of the consolidated income statement for the applicable preacquisition earnings and noncontrolling interest in income. There will be two amounts deducted, subsidiary income purchased (90% of $9,000 income earned prior to acquisition, or $8,100) and noncontrolling interest in income for the entire year ($900 before acquisition plus $2,700 after acquisition, or $3,600). These adjustments reduce S's net income from $36,000 to $24,300, the amount of income earned since acquisition by the controlling interest. The amounts used in calculating the controlling interest are reflected in Illustration 4-11 as boxed items.

This alternative, which is preferred, is particularly practical when the subsidiary does not close its books on the date of acquisition. Since closing procedures normally occur only at the end of the fiscal year, this is usually the case with an interim acquisition. Hence the revenue and expense accounts of the subsidiary are accumulated throughout the year, and their totals in the trial balance include both the partial period preceding the acquisition and the partial period following the acquisition.

The second alternative, *the partial-year reporting alternative*, includes presentation of the subsidiary's revenue and expenses from the date of acquisition only. To accomplish this, the subsidiary closes the books on the date of acquisition (i.e., preacquisition income is closed to retained earnings). In Illustration 4-11, the third column shows the revenues and expenses to be reported under this alternative. Both alternatives are presented below.

---

[5] *Accounting Research Bulletin No. 51*, "Consolidated Financial Statements" (New York: AICPA, 1959), par. 11.

Interim Acquisition Under the Cost Method—Full-Year Reporting Alternative

Assume that P Company acquired 90% of the outstanding common stock of S Company on April 1, 2000, for a cash payment of $290,000. The difference between cost and book value relates to the undervaluation of S Company land. Trial balances at December 31, 2000, for P and S companies are as follows:

	P Company Dr.	P Company Cr.	S Company Dr.	S Company Cr.
Current Assets	$ 146,000		$ 71,000	
Investment in S Company	290,000			
Plant and Equipment (net)	326,000		200,000	
Land	120,000		90,000	
Liabilities		$ 100,000		$ 65,000
Common Stock		500,000		200,000
Retained Earnings, 1/1		214,000		80,000
Dividends Declared, 11/1	50,000		20,000	
Sales		600,000		160,000
Dividend Income		18,000		
Cost of Goods Sold	380,000		80,000	
Other Expense	120,000		44,000	
	$1,432,000	$1,432,000	$505,000	$505,000

As always, the first step is to prepare a Computation and Allocation Schedule. For an interim acquisition, this schedule will include one or two additional amounts in the calculation of equity acquired: one for the income purchased, and one for dividends declared (if any) by the subsidiary during the current year prior to acquisition.

Computation and Allocation of Difference Between Cost and Book Value

Cost of Investment (purchase price)			$290,000
Book Value of Equity Acquired:			
Common Stock	$200,000(90%)	180,000	
Retained Earnings 1/1	80,000(90%)	72,000	
Income Purchased (1/1–4/1)	9,000(90%)	8,100	
Dividends Declared (1/1–4/1)	(0)(90%)	(0)	260,100
Difference Between Cost and Book Value			29,900
Adjust land upward (mark toward market)			(29,900)
Balance			0

Note that the new amount(s) included in the Computation and Allocation Schedule relate to income and dividends of the subsidiary for the period from the beginning of the current year (1/1) to the date of acquisition (4/1). In essence these are amounts that would have been included in retained earnings of the subsidiary if closing procedures (to zero out the temporary accounts) had been performed on April 1 (as in the partial-year alternative we present next). April 1, however, is not the usual date for closing entries. Note, also, that dividends declared by the subsidiary for the period from 1/1 to 4/1 are listed as zero in our example because the subsidiary's dividends were not declared until 11/1. A workpaper for

Cost Method			ILLUSTRATION 4-12			
Interim Purchase of Stock			**Consolidated Statements Workpaper**			
90% Owned Subsidiary			**P Company and Subsidiary**			
Alternative One—Full-Year Reporting			**For the Year Ended December 31, 2000**			

Income Statement	*P Company*	*S Company*	Eliminations *Dr.*	Eliminations *Cr.*	*Noncontrolling Interest*	*Consolidated Balances*
Sales	600,000	160,000				760,000
Dividend Income	18,000		(3) 18,000			
Total Revenue	618,000	160,000				760,000
Cost of Goods Sold	380,000	80,000				460,000
Other Expenses	120,000	44,000				164,000
Total Cost and Expense	500,000	124,000				624,000
Net/Combined Income	118,000	36,000				136,000
Subsidiary Income Purchased			(1) 8,100			(8,100)
Noncontrolling Interest in Income					3,600	(3,600)*
Net Income to Retained Earnings	118,000	36,000	26,100	—0—	3,600	124,300
1/1 Retained Earnings						
P Company	214,000					214,000
S Company		80,000	(1) 72,000		8,000	
Net Income from above	118,000	36,000	26,100	—0—	3,600	124,300
Dividends Declared						
P Company	(50,000)					(50,000)
S Company		(20,000)		(3) 18,000	(2,000)	
12/31 Retained Earnings to						
Balance Sheet	282,000	96,000	98,100	18,000	9,600	288,300
Balance Sheet						
Current Assets	146,000	71,000				217,000
Investment in S Company	290,000			(1) 290,000		
Difference Between Cost and Book Value			(1) 29,900	(2) 29,900		
Property and Equipment (net)	326,000	200,000				526,000
Land	120,000	90,000	(2) 29,900			239,900
Total	882,000	361,000				982,900
Liabilities	100,000	65,000				165,000
Common Stock						
P Company	500,000					500,000
S Company		200,000	(1) 180,000		20,000	
Retained Earnings from above	282,000	96,000	98,100	18,000	9,600	288,300
Noncontrolling Interest in Net Assets					29,600	29,600
Total	882,000	361,000	337,900	337,900		982,900

*.1($36,000) = $3,600
(1) To eliminate the investment in S Company.
(2) To allocate the difference between cost and book value to land.
(3) To eliminate intercompany dividends.

the preparation of consolidated statements on December 31, 2000, is presented in Illustration 4-12.

S Company's entire income statement account balances are included on the workpaper, and P Company's share of S Company's net income earned before acquisition is deducted as "subsidiary income purchased." Thus, the workpaper eliminating entry for the investment account, in general journal form, is:

(1)	Common Stock—S Company	180,000	
	1/1 Retained Earnings—S Company	72,000	
	Subsidiary Income Purchased	8,100	
	Difference Between Cost and Book Value	29,900	
	Investment in S Company		290,000
(2)	Land	29,900	
	Difference Between Cost and Book Value		29,900

There is no need for a reciprocity/conversion entry in Year 1 because the retained earnings account has not changed on the books of the subsidiary since acquisition. Also note that if there were any dividends declared by the subsidiary between 1/1 and 4/1, they would have appeared in entry (1) above as a credit to eliminate 90% of the dividends during that period.

In the computation of subsidiary income purchased, it is assumed that S Company's income of $36,000 was earned evenly throughout the year. Because one-fourth of the year had expired by April 1, the date of acquisition, net income purchased is computed as $36,000 \times 1/4 \times .9 = \$8,100$. If S Company earns its income unevenly throughout the year, because of the seasonal nature of its business, for example, this should be taken into consideration in estimating the amount of net income earned before April 1. In the event the subsidiary incurs a net loss for the year, a "subsidiary loss purchased" is credited in the elimination entry and added to combined income in determining consolidated net income. Similarly, the noncontrolling interest in a net loss of a subsidiary is shown as a deduction in the noncontrolling interest column and an addition to combined income.

Noncontrolling interest in combined income is represented by the December 31, 2000, noncontrolling interest percentage times the reported subsidiary income ($10\% \times \$36,000$), or $3,600, plus the $8,100 net income that was purchased from the former stockholders by the parent company on April 1, 2000. Note, however, that only $3,600 should be reflected as a part of noncontrolling interest in consolidated net assets on the balance sheet, since the $8,100 portion earned to April 1 was sold by the former shareholders to the parent company. The $3,600 is included in the noncontrolling interest column of the income statement section of the workpaper from which it is appropriately carried forward to the retained earnings section and eventually to the balance sheet section.

In subsequent years, the establishment of reciprocity is based on the parent company's share of the change in subsidiary retained earnings from the date of acquisition, April 1, 2000, to the beginning of the appropriate year. S Company's retained earnings on the acquisition date, April 1, 2000, were $89,000, consisting of the 1/1/00 balance of $80,000 plus the $9,000 income earned from January 1 to April 1, 2000. If retained earnings on December 31, 2001, are $96,000, the December 31, 2001, workpaper entry to establish reciprocity, for example, is:

Cost

| Investment in S Company | 6,300 | |
| 1/1 Retained Earnings—P Company .9($96,000 − $89,000) | | 6,300 |

Consolidated net income and consolidated retained earnings can be verified as follows:

Consolidated Income

P Company income from its independent operations ($118,000 − $18,000 dividend income from S Company)	$100,000
P Company's share of S Company's income since acquisition (.9 × $27,000)	24,300
Consolidated Net Income	$124,300

Consolidated Retained Earnings

P Company's reported retained earnings	$282,000
P Company's share of the *undistributed* income of S Company since date of acquisition [($27,000 − $20,000) × .9]	6,300
Consolidated Retained Earnings	$288,300

Interim Acquisition Under the Cost Method—Partial-Year Reporting Alternative

Another method of prorating income is to include in the consolidated income statement only the subsidiary's revenue and expenses after the date of acquisition. Thus, assuming the interim purchase situation discussed earlier, in which the purchase of stock took place on April 1, only three-fourths of S Company's sales, cost of goods sold, and other expense is included in the consolidated income statement as if S Company's books had been closed on April 1, 2000. These are the amounts shown in column 3 of Illustration 4-11.

If the books are actually closed on April 1, 2000, this alternative is facilitated. The following entry should be made on S's books:

S's Books		
Income Summary	9,000	
Retained Earnings		9,000

If this occurs, the balance in the retained earnings account on the books of the subsidiary (after closing entries on 4/1) is: $80,000 (balance at 1/1) + $9,000 (income for first three months of the year, column 2 of Illustration 4-11), or $89,000.

Computation and Allocation of Difference Between Cost and Book Value

Cost of Investment (purchase price)		$290,000	Cost
Book Value of Equity Acquired:			
Common Stock	$200,000		
Retained Earnings ($80,000 + $9,000)	89,000		
Total	$289,000 × .9	260,100	
Difference Between Cost and Book Value		$29,900	
Adjust land upward (mark toward market)		($29,900)	
Balance		0	

A workpaper for the preparation of consolidated financial statements on December 31, 2000, is presented in Illustration 4-13.

The workpaper entry to eliminate the investment account is:

(1)	Common Stock—S Company	180,000	
	Retained Earnings—S Company (.9 × $89,000)	80,100	
	Difference Between Cost and Book Value	29,900	
	Investment in S Company		290,000

Cost Method			**ILLUSTRATION 4-13**			
Interim Purchase of Stock			**Consolidated Statements Workpaper**			
90% Owned Subsidiary			**P Company and Subsidiary**			
Alternative Two—Partial-Year Reporting			**For the Year Ended December 31, 2000**			

			Eliminations			
Income Statement	*P Company*	*S Company*	*Dr.*	*Cr.*	*Noncontrolling Interest*	*Consolidated Balances*
Sales	600,000	120,000				720,000
Dividend Income	18,000		(3) 18,000			
Total Revenue	618,000	120,000				720,000
Cost of Goods Sold	380,000	60,000				440,000
Other Expenses	120,000	33,000				153,000
Total Cost and Expense	500,000	93,000				593,000
Net/Combined Income	118,000	27,000				127,000
Noncontrolling Interest in Income					2,700	(2,700)*
Net Income to Retained Earnings	118,000	27,000	18,000	—0—	2,700	124,300
Retained Earnings Statement						
Retained Earnings						
P Company	214,000					214,000
S Company		89,000	(1) 80,100		8,900	
Net Income from above	118,000	27,000	18,000	—0—	2,700	124,300
Dividends Declared						
P Company	(50,000)					(50,000)
S Company		(20,000)		(3) 18,000	(2,000)	
12/31 Retained Earnings to						
Balance Sheet	282,000	96,000	98,100	18,000	9,600	288,300
Balance Sheet						
Current Assets	146,000	71,000				217,000
Investment in S Company	290,000			(1) 290,000		
Difference Between Cost and Book Value			(1) 29,900	(2) 29,900		
Property and Equipment (net)	326,000	200,000				526,000
Land	120,000	90,000	(2) 29,900			239,900
Total	882,000	361,000				982,900
Liabilities	100,000	65,000				165,000
Common Stock						
P Company	500,000					500,000
S Company		200,000	(1) 180,000		20,000	
Retained Earnings from above	282,000	96,000	98,100	18,000	9,600	288,300
Noncontrolling Interest in Net Assets					29,600	29,600
Total	882,000	361,000	337,900	337,900		982,900

*.1($27,000) = $2,700
(1) To eliminate the investment in S Company.
(2) To allocate the difference between cost and book value to land.
(3) To eliminate intercompany dividends.

Note that S Company's beginning retained earnings is $9,000 greater than it is in Illustration 4-12, reflecting the effect of the closing to retained earnings of income earned during the first three months. Noncontrolling interest in net income included in combined income is 10% of $27,000, or $2,700, and the noncontrolling interest's share of beginning retained earnings of S Company is $900 greater. Note, however, that consolidated net income, consolidated retained earnings, and the consolidated balance sheet are identical to those in Illustration 4-12. Only the detail included in the consolidated income statement is different.

Interim Acquisition Under the Equity Method—Full-Year Reporting Alternative

The preceding discussion assumed that the parent company recorded its investment using the cost method. If the equity method had been used, P Company would have recognized (in actual entries posted to the general ledger) its share of subsidiary income earned *after* acquisition. On the books of the parent company, dividends would be treated as usual as a reduction in the investment account. Thus, still using the example introduced in Illustration 4-11, P Company would make the following dividend and earnings entries relative to its investment in S Company for the year 2000:

P's Books		
Investment in S Company	24,300	
Equity in Subsidiary Income .9($27,000)		24,300
To record equity in subsidiary income.		
Cash	18,000	
Investment in S Company		18,000
To record dividends received .9($20,000).		

For an interim acquisition assuming the use of the full-year reporting alternative, the Computation and Allocation Schedule will include one or two additional amounts in the calculation of equity acquired: one for the income purchased, and one for dividends declared (if any) by the subsidiary during the current year prior to acquisition.

Computation and Allocation of Difference Between Cost and Book Value

Cost of Investment (purchase price)			$290,000	
Book Value of Equity Acquired:				
Common Stock	$200,000(90%)	180,000		
Retained Earnings 1/1	80,000(90%)	72,000		
Income Purchased (1/1–4/1)	9,000(90%)	8,100		
Dividends Declared (1/1–4/1)	(0)(90%)	(0)	260,100	
Difference Between Cost and Book Value			29,900	
Adjust land upward (mark toward market)			(29,900)	
Balance			0	

Equity

The new amount(s) included in the Computation and Allocation Schedule are for income and dividends of the subsidiary for the period from the beginning of the current year (1/1) to the date of acquisition (4/1). These are amounts that would have been included in retained earnings of the subsidiary if closing procedures had been performed on April 1 (not a normal date for closing entries, which usually are made at year-end). Note, also, that dividends declared by the subsidiary for the period from 1/1 to 4/1 are listed as zero because the subsidiary's dividends were not declared until 11/1 in our example.

A workpaper for the preparation of consolidated statements on December 31,

Equity Method	ILLUSTRATION 4-14
Interim Purchase of Stock	**Consolidated Statements Workpaper**
90% Owned Subsidiary	**P Company and Subsidiary**
Alternative One—Full-Year Reporting	**For the Year Ended December 31, 2000**

Income Statement	P Company	S Company	Eliminations Dr.	Eliminations Cr.	Noncontrolling Interest	Consolidated Balances
Sales	600,000	160,000				760,000
Equity in Subsidiary Income	24,300		(1) 24,300			
Total Revenue	624,300	160,000				760,000
Cost of Goods Sold	380,000	80,000				460,000
Other Expenses	120,000	44,000				164,000
Total Cost and Expense	500,000	124,000				624,000
Net/Combined Income	124,300	36,000				136,000
Subsidiary Income Purchased			(3) 8,100			(8,100)
Noncontrolling Interest in Income					3,600	(3,600)*
Net Income to Retained Earnings	124,300	36,000	32,400	—0—	3,600	124,300
1/1 Retained Earnings						
P Company	214,000					214,000
S Company		80,000	(3) 72,000		8,000	
Net Income from above	124,300	36,000	32,400	—0—	3,600	124,300
Dividends Declared						
P Company	(50,000)					(50,000)
S Company		(20,000)		(2) 18,000	(2,000)	
12/31 Retained Earnings to						
Balance Sheet	288,300	96,000	104,400	18,000	9,600	288,300
Balance Sheet						
Current Assets	146,000	71,000				217,000
Investment in S Company	296,300		(2) 18,000	(1) 24,300		
				(3) 290,000		
Difference Between Cost and Book Value			(3) 29,900	(4) 29,900		
Property and Equipment (net)	326,000	200,000				526,000
Land	120,000	90,000	(4) 29,900			239,900
Total	888,300	361,000				982,900
Liabilities	100,000	65,000				165,000
Common Stock						
P Company	500,000					500,000
S Company		200,000	(3) 180,000		20,000	
Retained Earnings from above	288,300	96,000	104,400	18,000	9,600	288,300
Noncontrolling Interest in Net Assets					29,600	29,600
Total	888,300	361,000	362,200	362,200		982,900

*.1($36,000) = $3,600
(1) To reverse the effect of parent company entry during the year for subsidiary income.
(2) To reverse the effect of parent company entry during the year for subsidiary dividends.
(3) To eliminate the investment in S Company.
(4) To allocate the excess of cost over book value to land.

2000, is presented in Illustration 4-14. S Company's entire income statement account balances are included in the workpaper and P Company's share of S Company's net income earned before acquisition is deducted as "subsidiary income purchased." Workpaper eliminating entries at the end of 2000 under the equity method would be:

(1)	Equity in Subsidiary Income	24,300	
	Investment in S Company		24,300
(2)	Investment in S Company	18,000	
	Dividends Declared—S Company		18,000
	To adjust investment account to beginning of year balance and to eliminate equity in subsidiary income and intercompany dividends.		
(3)	Common Stock—S Company	180,000	
	1/1 Retained Earnings—S Company	72,000	
	Subsidiary Income Purchased .9($9,000)	8,100	
	Difference Between Cost and Book Value	29,900	
	Investment in S Company		290,000
	To eliminate investment account.		
(4)	Land	29,900	
	Difference Between Cost and Book Value		29,900

Interim Acquisition Under the Equity Method—Partial-Year Reporting Alternative

If the partial year reporting alternative is used in conjunction with the equity method, P Company would recognize its share of S Company's income after acquisition in its general ledger accounts (as always with the equity method). S Company would, however, close its revenue and expense accounts at 4/1 into retained earnings. The 12/31 trial balance includes only the period from 4/1 to 12/31, or three-fourths of S Company's revenue and expense items for the year. These amounts are reflected in the third column of Illustration 4-11. This is the portion to itemize in the consolidated income statement under the partial-year reporting alternative as well. Thus, there is no need to subtract any "purchased income" at the bottom of the consolidated income statement.

Computation and Allocation of Difference Between Cost and Book Value

Cost of Investment (purchase price)		$290,000
Book Value of Equity Acquired:		
Common Stock	$200,000	
Retained Earnings ($80,000 + $9,000)	89,000	
Total	$289,000 × .9	260,000
Difference Between Cost and Book Value		$29,900
Adjust land upward (mark toward market)		($29,900)
Balance		0

A workpaper for the preparation of consolidated financial statements on December 31, 2000, is presented in Illustration 4-15. Workpaper elimination entries are then as follows:

(1)	Equity in Subsidiary Income	24,300		**Equity**
	Investment in S Company		24,300	
(2)	Investment in S Company	18,000		
	Dividends Declared—S Company		18,000	
(3)	Common Stock—S Company	180,000		
	4/1 Retained Earnings—S Company .9($89,000)	80,100		
	Difference Between Cost and Book Value	29,900		
	Investment in S Company		290,000	
(4)	Land	29,900		
	Difference Between Cost and Book Value		29,900	

Equity Method						
Interim Purchase of Stock			**ILLUSTRATION 4-15**			
90% Owned Subsidiary			**Consolidated Statements Workpaper**			
Alternative Two—Partial-Year Reporting			**P Company and Subsidiary**			
			For the Year Ended December 31, 2000			

Income Statement	*P Company*	*S Company*	Eliminations *Dr.*	Eliminations *Cr.*	*Noncontrolling Interest*	*Consolidated Balances*
Sales	600,000	120,000				720,000
Equity in Subsidiary Income	24,300		(1) 24,300			
Total Revenue	624,300	120,000				720,000
Cost of Goods Sold	380,000	60,000				440,000
Other Expenses	120,000	33,000				153,000
Total Cost and Expense	500,000	93,000				593,000
Net/Combined Income	124,300	27,000				127,000
Noncontrolling Interest in Income					2,700	(2,700)*
Net Income to Retained Earnings	124,300	27,000	24,300	—0—	2,700	124,300

Retained Earnings Statement						
Retained Earnings						
P Company	214,000					214,000
S Company		89,000	(3) 80,100		8,900	
Net Income from above	124,300	27,000	24,300	—0—	2,700	124,300
Dividends Declared						
P Company	(50,000)					(50,000)
S Company		(20,000)		(2) 18,000	(2,000)	
12/31 Retained Earnings to						
Balance Sheet	288,300	96,000	104,400	18,000	9,600	288,300

Balance Sheet						
Current Assets	146,000	71,000				217,000
Investment in S Company	296,300		(2) 18,000	(1) 24,300		
				(3) 290,000		
Difference Between Cost and Book Value			(3) 29,900	(4) 29,900		
Property and Equipment (net)	326,000	200,000				526,000
Land	120,000	90,000	(4) 29,900			239,900
Total	888,300	361,000				982,900
Liabilities	100,000	65,000				165,000
Common Stock						
P Company	500,000					500,000
S Company		200,000	(3) 180,000		20,000	
Retained Earnings from above	288,300	96,000	104,400	18,000	9,600	288,300
Noncontrolling Interest in Net Assets					29,600	29,600
Total	888,300	361,000	362,200	362,200		982,900

*.10($27,000) = $2,700
(1) To reverse the effect of parent company entry during the year for subsidiary income.
(2) To reverse the effect of parent company entry during the year for subsidiary dividends.
(3) To eliminate the investment in S Company.
(4) To allocate the excess of cost over book value to land.

To verify the amount of income reported, prepare t-accounts for the noncontrolling and controlling interests as follows:

Noncontrolling Income

Internally generated income of S Company (after acquisition)	$27,000
Any needed adjustments (Chapter 5)	0
Adjusted income of subsidiary	27,000
Noncontrolling percentage owned	10%
Noncontrolling interest in income	2,700
	90%

Controlling Interest in Income

Internally generated income of P Company (entire year: $124,300 − $24,300)	$100,000
Any needed adjustments (Chapter 5)	0
Percentage of subsidiary adjusted income (90%) ($27,000)	24,300
Controlling interest in income	$124,300

CONSOLIDATED STATEMENT OF CASH FLOWS

The procedures followed in the preparation of a statement of cash flows are discussed in most intermediate accounting texts. When the company is reporting on a consolidated basis, the statement of cash flows must also be presented on a consolidated basis. The starting point for the consolidated cash flow statement is the consolidated income statement and comparative consolidated balance sheets (beginning and end of current year). Thus the preparation of the consolidated statement of cash flows will be the same, regardless of how the parent accounts for its investment (cost method, partial equity method, or complete equity method). This is true because the final product (the consolidated financial statements) is always the same if the consolidating procedures are done correctly.

We will first discuss years subsequent to the year of acquisition, and then the preparation of the consolidated statement of cash flows in the year of acquisition. In years subsequent to the year of acquisition, a consolidated balance sheet should be available for both the beginning and end of the current year. The consolidated statement of cash flows reflects all cash outlays and inflows of the consolidated entity except those between parent and subsidiary. Therefore, we are interested in explaining 100% of the changes in balance sheet accounts of parent and subsidiary (not just the portion of the subsidiary controlled by the parent). Because the consolidated balance sheet reflects 100% of the assets and liabilities of both parent and subsidiary, the preparation of a consolidated statement of cash flows is quite similar in most respects to that of a single (unconsolidated) firm. At least three aspects of the statement do, however, differ (or require modification). They are:

1. *Noncontrolling interest in combined income:* Accounting standards require the disclosure of cash flows from operating activities for the reporting period. Like the

consolidated balance sheet and the consolidated income statement, the consolidated statement of cash flows presents *combined* information for the parent and its subsidiaries (i.e. combined cash flows). Cash flows from operating activities may be presented by either the direct or the indirect method. Under the indirect method, we begin with net income for the period and add back (or deduct) any items recognized in determining that net income that did not result in an outflow (or inflow) of cash. These adjustments normally include such items as depreciation and amortization. Assuming that the starting amount (net income) reflects only the *controlling interest* in net income (usually the "bottom line" on the consolidated income statement), an additional adjustment for a consolidated statement of cash flows is the **add-back of the noncontrolling interest in combined income** (or deduction of the noncontrolling interest's share of a loss). If the statement starts with the combined interests in net income, then the noncontrolling interest is included and need not be added back.

2. *Subsidiary dividends paid:* Because we are interested in reflecting 100% of cash outlays and inflows between the consolidated entity and outsiders, any subsidiary dividends **paid to the noncontrolling stockholders** must be included with dividends paid by the parent company when calculating cash outflow from financing activities. The dividends paid by the subsidiary to the parent do not involve cash flows to or from outsiders and thus are not reported on the consolidated statement of cash flows.

3. *Parent company acquisition of additional subsidiary shares:* The cost of the acquisition of additional shares in a subsidiary by the parent company may or may not constitute a cash outflow from investing activities. If the acquisition is an open market purchase, it does represent such an outflow. If it is an acquisition directly from the subsidiary, however, it represents an intercompany cash transfer that does not affect the total cash balance of the consolidated group.

Illustration of Preparation of a Consolidated Statement of Cash Flows: After Acquisition

As an illustration of the preparation of a consolidated statement of cash flows, a consolidated income statement and comparative consolidated balance sheets for P Company and its 90% owned subsidiary, S Company, along with other information, are presented in Illustration 4-16.

Other information:

1. Depreciation expense of $24,000 and amortization of goodwill of $2,000 are included in operating expenses.

2. Manufacturing equipment was acquired during 2001 for cash of $185,000.

3. Investments include a 30% common stock investment in Zorn Company on which $6,000 of equity in investee income was recognized. No dividends were received during the year.

4. Noncontrolling interest in combined income was $4,000. However, $2,000 was distributed to noncontrolling stockholders as dividends during the year. Thus noncontrolling interest in net assets on the balance sheet increased by only $2,000.

ILLUSTRATION 4-16

P Company and Subsidiary
Consolidated Income Statement
For the Year Ended December 31, 2001

Sales	$540,000
Cost of Goods Sold	294,000
Gross Profit	246,000
Operating Expenses	136,000
Income from Operations	110,000
Equity in Income of Zorn Company	6,000
Combined Income	116,000
Noncontrolling Interest in Combined Income	4,000
Consolidated Net Income	$112,000

P Company and S Company
Comparative Consolidated Balance Sheets

	December 31	
Assets	*2000*	*2001*
Cash	$ 60,000	$ 97,000
Accounts Receivable (net)	92,000	120,000
Inventories	110,000	101,000
Plant and Equipment (net)	245,000	406,000
Investments	152,000	158,000
Goodwill	20,000	18,000
Total Assets	$679,000	$900,000
Liabilities and Equity		
Accounts Payable	$ 60,000	$ 93,000
Accrued Expenses Payable	99,000	89,000
Total Liabilities	159,000	182,000
Stockholders' Equity:		
Noncontrolling Interest in Net Assets	20,000	22,000
Common Stock, $2 par value	200,000	220,000
Other Contributed Capital	40,000	140,000
Retained Earnings	260,000	336,000
Total Stockholders' Equity	520,000	718,000
Total Liabilities and Equity	$679,000	$900,000

---

5. Ten thousand shares of common stock were issued by P Company on the open market for cash at $12 per share.

6. Dividend payments totaled $38,000, of which $36,000 were to P Company stockholders (thereby reducing consolidated retained earnings), and $2,000 were to S Company noncontrolling stockholders.

A consolidated statement of cash flows, using the indirect method of presenting cash flows from operating activities, is shown in Illustration 4-17.

If the direct method is used to report cash from operations on the consolidated statement of cash flows, the statement would be identical to Illustration 4-17 with one exception. The "cash flows from operating activities" would be replaced with the following:

Cash flows from operating activities:		
Cash received from customers (1)		$512,000
Less cash paid for:		
Purchases of merchandise (2)	$252,000	
Operating expenses (3)	120,000	372,000
Net cash flow from operating activities		$140,000

(1)	Beginning accounts receivable	$ 92,000
	Sales	540,000
	Ending accounts receivable	(120,000)
	Cash received from customers	($512,000)

(2)	Cost of goods sold	$294,000
	Beginning inventory	(110,000)
	Ending inventory	101,000
	Accrual basis purchases	285,000
	Beginning accounts payable	60,000
	Ending accounts payable	(93,000)
	Cash basis purchases	$252,000

(3)	Operating expenses	$136,000
	Amortization and depreciation expense	(26,000)
	Beginning accrued expenses	99,000
	Ending accrued expenses	(89,000)
	Cash paid for operating expenses	$120,000

ILLUSTRATION 4-17

P Company and Subsidiary
Consolidated Statement of Cash Flows
For the Year Ended December 31, 2001

Cash flows from operating activities:		
Consolidated net income		$112,000
Noncontrolling interest in combined income		*4,000*
Combined Income		$116,000
Adjustments to convert net income to net cash flow from operating activities:		
Depreciation expense		24,000
Amortization expense		2,000
Increase in accounts receivable		(28,000)
Decrease in inventories		9,000
Increase in accounts payable		33,000
Decrease in accrued expenses payable		(10,000)
Equity in income of Zorn Company		(6,000)
Net cash flow from operating activities		140,000
Cash flows from investing activities:		
Payments for purchase of plant assets		(185,000)
Cash flows from financing activities:		
Proceeds from the issuance of common stock	$120,000	
Cash dividends declared and paid	(38,000)	
Net cash flow from financing activities		82,000
Increase in cash		$ 37,000
Cash Balance, beginning		60,000
Cash Balance, ending		$ 97,000

Illustration of Preparation of a Consolidated Statement of Cash Flows: Year of Acquisition

The preparation of the consolidated statement of cash flows in the year of acquisition is complicated slightly because the comparative balance sheets at the beginning and end of the current year are dissimilar. Specifically, the balance sheet at the *end* of the year of acquisition reflects consolidated balances, while the beginning of the year reflects parent-only balances. Thus the net change in cash that investors wish to interpret is the change from the parent's beginning-of-year balance to the combined (consolidated) end-of-year cash balance. To accomplish this reconciliation, two realizations are important.

1. Any cash spent or received in the acquisition itself should be reflected in the *Investing* activities section of the consolidated statement of cash flows. For example, if the parent paid total cash of $1,000,000 to acquire a subsidiary, which brought $300,000 to the consolidated entity, the net decrease would appear as a $700,000 outlay. On the other hand, if the parent issued only stock or debt (no cash) to acquire the same subsidiary, the net increase would appear as a $300,000 cash inflow. The issuance of stock or debt would appear in the notes to the financial statements as a significant non-cash investing and financing activity.

2. To explain the change in cash successfully, the assets and liabilities of the subsidiary *at the date of acquisition* must be added to those of the parent at the beginning of the current year. For example, assume that P Company had $1,500,000 in long-term notes payable at the beginning of the year, S Company had $500,000 in long-term notes payable at the date of acquisition, and the consolidated entity had $3,000,000 in long-term notes payable at the end of the year. To explain the net change, the *Financing* section of the statement of cash flows might reflect a cash inflow of $1,000,000 from borrowing activities.

To illustrate the preparation of a consolidated statement of cash flows in the year of acquisition, consider the information in Illustration 4-18. In this problem, S Company acquires 80% of P Company on April 1, 2001 for $200,000 cash. In this illustration the last six columns are the familiar columns used to prepare the consolidated balance sheet and income statement at the end of 2001. However, two additional columns have been added: one showing the beginning of year balances (January 1, 2001) for the balance sheet accounts for P Company and one showing the balances on the date of acquisition (April 1, 2001) for S Company. The information in these columns is needed to prepare the consolidated statement of cash flows for 2001, but does not affect any of the extensions or calculations needed to complete the worksheet in Illustration 4-18. Other information used in the example includes the following:

1. Total consolidated depreciation expense is $30,000.
2. The companies issued $205,000 of debt.
3. The companies purchased $95,000 of property, plant, and equipment.
4. The excess of cost over book value is attributable to land ($200,000 − .8($160,000 + $80,000) = $8,000).
5. The partial-year alternative is used for presenting subsidiary income and expense accounts.

ILLUSTRATION 4-18

Cost Method
Interim Purchase of Stock
80% Owned Subsidiary
Partial-Year Reporting

Consolidated Statement of Cash Flows
For the Year Ended December 31, 2001

Income Statement	P Company	S Company	P Company 1/1 to 12/31	S Company 4/1 to 12/31	Eliminations Dr.	Eliminations Cr.	Noncontrolling Interest	Consolidated Balances
Sales			350,000	200,000				550,000
Dividend income .8($12,000)			9,600		(3) 9,600			
Total Revenue			359,600	200,000				550,000
Cost of Goods Sold			200,000	95,000				295,000
Other Expenses			80,000	65,000				145,000
Total Cost and Expense			280,000	160,000				440,000
Net/Combined Income			79,600	40,000				110,000
Noncontrolling Interest in Income							8,000	(8,000)*
Net Income to Retained Earnings			79,600	40,000	9,600	—0—	8,000	102,000
Retained Earnings								
P Company, 1/1			90,000					90,000
S Company, 4/1				80,000	(1) 64,000		16,000	
Net Income from above			79,600	40,000	9,600	—0—	8,000	102,000
Dividends Declared								
P Company			(30,000)					(30,000)
S Company				(12,000)		(3) 9,600	(2,400)	
12/31 Retained Earnings to Balance Sheet			139,600	108,000	73,600	9,600	21,600	162,000

Balance Sheet	At 1/1/2001	At 4/1/2001	At 12/31/01	At 12/31/01	Eliminations Dr.	Eliminations Cr.	Noncontrolling Interest	Consolidated Balances
Cash	80,000	28,000	75,000	40,000				115,000
Accounts Receivable	65,000	38,000	70,000	53,000				123,000
Inventory	70,000	53,000	86,600	40,000				126,600
Investment in S Company			200,000			(1) 200,000		
Difference Between Cost and Book Value					(1) 8,000	(2) 8,000		
Property and Equipment (net)	180,000	175,000	245,000	175,000				420,000
Land	35,000	27,000	35,000	27,000	(2) 8,000			70,000
Total	430,000	321,000	711,600	335,000				854,600
Accounts Payable	35,000	34,000	60,000	22,000				82,000
Other Liabilities	65,000	47,000	272,000	45,000				317,000
Common Stock								
P Company	240,000		240,000					240,000
S Company		160,000		160,000	(1) 128,000		32,000	
Retained Earnings	90,000	80,000	139,600	108,000	73,600	9,600	21,600	162,000
Noncontrolling Interest in Net Assets							53,600	53,600
Total	430,000	321,000	711,600	335,000	217,600	217,600	53,600	854,600

*.2($40,000) = $8,000
(1) To eliminate the investment in S Company.
(2) To allocate the difference between cost and book value to land.
(3) To eliminate intercompany dividends.

ILLUSTRATION 4-19

P Company (and S Company at 12/31/01 only)
Comparative Balance Sheets
Year of Acquisition

	December 31	
Assets	*2000*	*2001*
Cash	$ 80,000	$115,000
Accounts Receivable (net)	65,000	123,000
Inventories	70,000	126,600
Plant and Equipment (net)	180,000	420,000
Land	35,000	70,000
Total Assets	$430,000	$854,600
Liabilities and Equity		
Accounts Payable	$ 35,000	$ 82,000
Other Liabilities	65,000	317,000
Total Liabilities	100,000	399,000
Stockholders' Equity:		
Noncontrolling Interest in Net Assets		53,000
Common Stock, $2 par value	240,000	240,000
Retained Earnings	90,000	162,000
Total Stockholders' Equity	330,000	455,000
Total Liabilities and Equity	$430,000	$854,000

The comparative consolidated balance sheet, prepared from Illustration 4-18, is shown in Illustration 4-19. Notice that the beginning of the year balance sheet amounts are the same as P Company's beginning of the year balance sheet (or the first column in the workpaper in Illustration 4-18). Therefore, the change in cash in the consolidated statement of cash flows is an increase of $35,000, calculated as the $115,000 ending consolidated balance less the $80,000 beginning balance.

Now consider the two points made above. How is the $200,000 cash acquisition reported on the statement of cash flows? The acquisition is listed in the investing activities section and represents the net assets acquired. But since S Company had $28,000 cash on hand on the date of acquisition, the net effect on cash from the acquisition is the $200,000 paid less the $28,000 acquired or $172,000. Hence, on the statement of cash flows, the acquisition is listed as a $172,000 cash outflow. The consolidated statement of cash flows is shown in Illustration 4-20.

Second, all calculations of changes in balance sheet accounts require that assets and liabilities acquired from S Company be added to the beginning P Company balances. For instance, on the comparative balance sheets shown in Illustration 4-19, accounts receivable has a beginning balance of $65,000 and an ending balance of $123,000. Because accounts receivable of $38,000 were acquired on April 1, 2001, the change in receivables is the ending consolidated amount of $123,000 less the beginning balance of $65,000 and the amount purchased in the acquisition of $38,000. (See Illustration 4-18.) This gives the correct increase in accounts receivable of $20,000. As a result, in published annual reports, the changes in the working capital accounts from the previous year's balance sheet do not reconcile to the amounts shown on the statement of cash flows in the year of acquisition. Similar reasoning is used for all the remaining changes in balance sheet accounts, such as property, plant, and equipment.

ILLUSTRATION 4-20

P Company and Subsidiary
Consolidated Statement of Cash Flows
For the Year Ended December 31, 2001

Cash flows from operating activities:		
Consolidated net income	$102,000	
Noncontrolling interest in combined income (.2*$40,000)	*8,000*	
Combined Income	$110,000	
Adjustments to convert net income to net cash flow from operating activities:		
Depreciation expense	30,000	
Increase in accounts receivable ($123,000 − 65,000 − 38,000)	(20,000)	
Increase in inventories ($126,600 − 70,000 − 53,000)	(3,600)	
Increase in accounts payable ($82,000 − 35,000 − 34,000)	13,000	
Net cash flow from operating activities		$129,400
Cash flows from investing activities:		
Payments for purchase of plant assets	(95,000)	
Cash paid (net) for acquisition of S ($200,000 less cash acquired of $28,000)	(172,000)	
Net cash flow from investing activities		($267,000)
Cash flows from financing activities:		
Proceeds from the issuance of debt	$205,000	
Cash dividends declared and paid by P Company	(30,000)	
Cash dividends declared and paid by S Company to noncontrolling shareholders (.2)($12,000)	(2,400)	
Net cash flow from financing activities		$172,600
Increase in cash		35,000
Cash Balance, beginning		80,000
Cash Balance, ending		$115,000

Another point about the consolidated statement of cash flows concerns the $12,000 dividends paid by S Company. Since P Company purchased 80% of S Company, $9,600 of the dividends must be eliminated. However, the $2,400 remaining dividends paid by S Company to the noncontrolling shareholders must be subtracted as a financing item. We have shown this separately on the cash flow statement in Illustration 4-20 even though in practice the dividend amounts paid by P Company and S Company are often combined.

Finally, the preparation of the consolidated statement of cash flows is the same regardless of whether the parent uses the cost method, partial equity method, or complete equity method to account for its investment in any subsidiaries that are consolidated. This is true because the preparation is based on the consolidated income statement and consolidated balance sheets, and these are identical under the three methods.

SUMMARY

1. *Describe the accounting treatment required under current GAAP for varying levels of influence or control by investors.* With few exceptions, all *subsidiaries* (invest-

ments in which the investor has a controlling interest) must be consolidated and may not be reported as separate investments in the consolidated financial statements. The parent may use any of at least three methods (cost, partial equity, or complete equity) to account for investments during the year that are going to be consolidated, provided the consolidating process is carried out properly. The equity method *must* be used to account for investments in investees in which the investor has significant influence but not control (usually 20%–50%). For investments in investees where the investor does not have significant influence (normally less than 20%), the investment should be reported at its fair value.

2. *Prepare journal entries on the parent's books to account for an investment using the cost method, the partial equity method, and the complete equity method.* The most important difference between the cost and equity methods pertains to the period in which the parent recognizes subsidiary income on its books. If the cost method is in use, the parent recognizes its share of subsidiary income only when dividends are declared by the subsidiary. If the partial equity method is in use, the investor will recognize its share of the subsidiary's income when reported by the subsidiary, regardless of whether dividends have been distributed. A debit to cash and a credit to the investment account record the receipt of dividends under the partial equity method. The complete equity method differs from the partial equity method only in that the share of subsidiary income to be recognized is adjusted in certain cases from the amount reported by the subsidiary (for example, for the amortization of goodwill implied in the purchase).

3. *Understand the use of the workpaper in preparing consolidated financial statements.* Accounting workpapers are helpful in accumulating, classifying, and arranging data for the preparation of consolidated financial statements. The three-section workpaper format used in this text includes a separate section for each of three basic financial statements—income statement, retained earnings statement, and balance sheet. In some cases the input to the workpaper comes from the individual financial statements of the affiliates to be consolidated, in which case the three-section workpaper is particularly appropriate. At other times, however, input may be from affiliate trial balances, and the data must be arranged in financial statement form before the workpaper can be completed.

4. *Prepare a schedule for the computation and allocation of the difference between cost and book value.* The schedule begins with the cost (or purchase price) and subtracts the book value of the equity acquired (the subsidiary's equity at the date of acquisition times the percentage acquired by the parent). This difference is then allocated to adjust the assets and/or liabilities

of the subsidiary for differences between their book values and fair values. Any remaining excess is labeled as goodwill. Special rules apply for bargain purchases.

5. *Prepare the workpaper eliminating entries for the year of acquisition (and subsequent years) for the cost and equity methods.* Under the cost method, dividends declared by the subsidiary are eliminated against dividend income recorded by the parent. The investment account is eliminated against the equity accounts of the subsidiary, with the difference between cost and book value recorded in a separate account by that name. The difference is then allocated to adjust underlying assets and/or liabilities, and to record goodwill in some cases. Under the equity method, the dividends declared by the subsidiary are eliminated against the investment account, as is the equity in subsidiary income. The investment account is eliminated in the same way as under the cost method. In subsequent years, the cost method requires an initial entry to establish reciprocity or convert to equity. This entry, which is not needed under the equity method, debits the investment account and credits retained earnings of the parent (for the change in retained earnings of the subsidiary from the date of acquisition to the beginning of the current year multiplied by the parent's percentage).

6. *Describe two alternative methods to account for interim acquisitions of subsidiary stock at the end of the first year.* If an investment in the common stock of a subsidiary is made during the year rather than on the first day, there are two methods available to treat the preacquisition revenue and expense items of the subsidiary. The first method includes the subsidiary in consolidation as though it had been acquired at the beginning of the year, and then makes a deduction at the bottom of the consolidated income statement for the preacquisition subsidiary earnings. The second method includes in the consolidated income statement only the subsidiary revenue and expense amounts for the period after acquisition. The first method is preferred.

7. *Explain how the consolidated statement of cash flows differs from a single firm's statement of cash flows.* In the preparation of a consolidated statement of cash flows, the noncontrolling interest in income is added to the controlling interest just as depreciation and amortization expenses are added, since noncontrolling interest in income is deducted in arriving at consolidated net income (and does not require cash). Subsidiary dividend payments to noncontrolling shareholders represent a *Financing* outflow of cash. Subsidiary dividend payments to the parent company represent an intercompany transfer and thus are not

reflected on the consolidated statement of cash flows. The cost of acquiring additional subsidiary shares of common stock is an *Investing* outflow of cash if the purchase is made from outsiders, but not if made directly from the subsidiary.

8. *Understand how the reporting of an acquisition on the consolidated statement of cash flows differs when stock*

is issued rather than cash. Any cash spent or received in the acquisition itself should be reflected in the *Investing* activities section of the consolidated statement of cash flows. The issuance of stock or debt would appear in the *Notes to the Financial Statements* as a significant non-cash investing and financing activity.

APPENDIX A

Alternative Workpaper Format

A variety of workpaper formats may be used in the preparation of consolidated financial statements. They may be classified generally into two categories, the three-division workpaper format used in this text, and the trial balance format. In the three-divisional format the account balances of the individual firms are first arranged into financial statement format. In contrast, in the trial balance format, columns are provided for the trial balances, the elimination entries, and normally, each financial statement to be prepared, except for the statement of cash flows.

The consolidated balances derived in a workpaper are the same regardless of the format selected. The statement preparer with a sound understanding of consolidation principles should be able to adapt quite easily to alternative workpaper formats. However, the reader may want to develop a familiarity with the trial balance format, since this format may be used by some companies.

To illustrate the trial balance workpaper format, and at the same time to verify that the results are the same as they would be if the three-divisional format were used, the same facts used in the preparation of Illustration 4-4 are assumed in Illustration 4-21.

The steps in the preparation of the workpaper are: (1) The trial balances of the individual affiliates are entered in the first two columns. In this case, the debit account balances are separated from the credit account balances. Or the accounts can be listed as they appear in the ledger. A debit column and a credit column may be provided for each firm or one column may be used and the credit balances identified by parentheses. (2) The account balances are analyzed, and the required adjustments and eliminations are entered in the next two vertical columns. (3) The net adjusted balances are extended to the appropriate columns. Separate columns are provided to accumulate the account balances needed for the preparation of the consolidated income statement, retained earnings statement, and balance sheet. In addition, an optional column is provided for the identification of the noncontrolling interest. (4) Once the accounts are extended, the combined income is computed from the income statement column and allocated between the noncontrolling and controlling interests. (5) The consolidated retained earnings balance and total noncontrolling interest can now be computed. The amounts are extended to the final column and should balance the liabilities and equities with the total assets. The reader will observe that these procedures are similar to the preparation of an eight-column worksheet developed to facilitate the preparation of financial statements for an individual firm.

A comparison of the elimination entries in Illustration 4-21 with those of Illustration 4-4 will reveal that the entries are the same, regardless of the form of workpaper used to accumulate the consolidated balances.

Cost Method

ILLUSTRATION 4-21

80% Owned Subsidiary — **Consolidated Statements Workpaper Based on Illustration 4-4**

Trial Balance Format

P Company and Subsidiary

For the Year Ended December 31, 2001

Debits	P Company	S Company	Eliminations Dr.	Eliminations Cr.	Consolidated Income Statement	Consolidated Retained Earnings Statement	Noncontrolling Interest	Consolidated Balance Sheet
Cash	74,000	41,000						115,000
Accounts Receivable	71,000	33,000						104,000
Inventory 1/1	67,000	43,000			110,000			
Investment in S Company	165,000		(1) 16,000	(2) 181,000				—0—
Difference Between Cost and Book Value			(2) 13,000	(3) 13,000				
Other Assets	280,000	202,000	(3) 13,000					495,000
Dividends Declared								
P Company	30,000					(30,000)		
S Company		10,000		(4) 8,000			(2,000)	
Purchases	215,000	90,000			305,000			
Other Expense	80,000	56,000			136,000			
Total	982,000	475,000						
Inventory 12/31 (Asset)	82,000	39,000						121,000
Total Assets								835,000
Credits								
Liabilities	131,000	75,000						206,000
Capital Stock								
P Company	240,000							240,000
S Company		150,000	(2) 120,000				30,000	
1/1 Retained Earnings								
P Company	253,000			(1) 16,000		269,000		
S Company		60,000	(2) 48,000				12,000	
Sales	350,000	190,000			(540,000)			
Dividend Income	8,000		(4) 8,000		—0—			
Totals	982,000	475,000						
Inventory 12/31 (COGS)	82,000	39,000			(121,000)			
			218,000	218,000				
Combined Income					110,000			
Noncontrolling Interest in Income [.8($40,000)]					(8,000)		8,000	
Consolidated Net Income					102,000	102,000		
Consolidated Retained Earnings						341,000		341,000
Noncontrolling Interest in Net Assets							48,000	48,000
Total Liabilities and Equity								835,000

(1) To establish reciprocity as of 1/1/2001 [($60,000 − $40,000) × .80].
(2) To eliminate investment account.
(3) To allocate the difference between cost and book value to land.
(4) To eliminate intercompany dividends.

APPENDIX B

Deferred Tax Consequences When Affiliates File Separate Income Tax Returns—Undistributed Income

When a parent company owns at least 80% of a domestic subsidiary, the companies generally elect to file a consolidated income tax return. If they do not elect to file a joint return or own less than 80%, the companies file separate tax returns. In these cases, the parent includes the amount of dividends received from the investment on its own tax return. In the main body of this text, we have assumed that the affiliates (80% or more ownership levels) file a consolidated income tax return. Deferred tax issues are discussed in appendices.

What happens when the companies do not file consolidated tax returns and file separate tax returns? Deferred tax consequences can arise since differences usually exist between the time income is reported in the consolidated financial statements and the time such income is included in the taxable income of the separate affiliates. Two major topics require attention in addressing the treatment of deferred income tax consequences when the affiliates each file separate income tax returns:

1. Undistributed subsidiary income (Appendix B of Chapter 4).
2. Elimination of unrealized intercompany profit (discussed in the appendices to Chapters 6 and 7).

CONSOLIDATED TAX RETURNS—AFFILIATED COMPANIES (80% OR MORE OWNERSHIP LEVELS)

When affiliated companies elect to file one consolidated return, the tax expense amount is computed on the consolidated workpapers rather than on the individual books of the parent and subsidiary. The amount of tax expense attributed to each company is computed from combined income and allocated back to each company's books.

When consolidated income tax returns are filed, temporary differences generally do not arise in the preparation of consolidated financial statements. For example, unrealized intercompany profit is generally treated the same way in calculating both consolidated taxable income and combined income on the consolidated income statement. Thus, no timing differences arise because of the elimination of unrealized intercompany profit.

SEPARATE TAX RETURNS—DEFERRED TAX CONSEQUENCES ARISING BECAUSE OF UNDISTRIBUTED SUBSIDIARY INCOME

When separate tax returns are filed, the parent company will include dividends received from the subsidiary in its taxable income, while the parent company's share of the subsidiary reported income is included in *consolidated net income*. Thus the difference between the subsidiary's income and dividends paid represents a temporary difference because eventually this undistributed amount will be realized through future dividends or upon sale of the subsidiary. Deferred taxes must be recorded on the books of the parent in the amount of undistributed income to the *consolidated entity.* Whether the deferred taxes are recorded by the parent company or are only recorded in the workpaper consolidated entries depends on how the parent accounts for its investment in the subsidiary—cost versus equity. Both methods are illustrated in the following sections of this appendix.

The measurement of the deferred tax consequences of the undistributed income of a subsidiary depends on assumptions as to the nature of the transaction(s) that result in the future taxation of the undistributed income. If the parent company's equity in the undistributed income is expected to be realized in the form of a taxable dividend, the deferred tax amount is computed considering all available tax credits and exclusions. Federal income tax rules permit a portion of the dividends received from a domestic subsidiary to be excluded from taxable income. Under current federal income tax rules, the following amount of dividends can be excluded from taxable income for a given level of ownership:

Ownership Percentage in Subsidiary	Amount of Dividends Excluded from Taxable Income
80% or more	100% of Dividends Excluded
20% up to 80%	80% of Dividends Excluded
Less than 20%	70% of Dividends Excluded

Thus, when the undistributed income of the subsidiary is expected to be received in the form of future dividend distributions, the dividends-received exclusion must be considered. On the other hand, if the undistributed earnings of the subsidiary is not expected to be realized until the subsidiary is sold, the dividends-received exclusion is not used in computing deferred taxes. In this case, the capital gains tax rate is used to compute deferred taxes.

APB (Accounting Principles Board) Opinion No. 23 allowed firms to demonstrate that undistributed subsidiary earnings are permanently reinvested and no timing differences are created. This indefinite reversal rule was eliminated by *SFAS No. 109*, which requires deferred taxes to be recorded for undistributed income.

THE COST METHOD—SEPARATE TAX RETURNS

Assume that the parent uses the cost method to account for the investment and that both the parent and the subsidiary file separate tax returns. This means each company records a tax provision based on the items reported on its individual books. Tax consequences relating to undistributed income are not recorded on the books of the parent company when the investment in the subsidiary is recorded using the cost method. This is because dividends are recognized as income on the parent's income statement and tax return. Therefore, no timing differences occur. However, for consolidated purposes, equity income is recognized on the income statement, while dividends are included on the tax return, creating a timing difference for consolidated purposes. Thus, *workpaper* entries are necessary each year to report the income tax consequences of past and current undistributed income.

Cost

To illustrate, assume that P Company owns 75% of the voting stock of S Company. The stock was acquired on January 1, 2001, when S Company's retained earnings amounted to $150,000. In the year of acquisition (2001), S Company reported net income of $90,000 and paid dividends of $30,000. Since P Company is filing a separate tax return, P Company reports $22,500 of dividend income (75% of S Company's dividends of $30,000) as income on its tax return. However, on the consolidated income statement, 75% of S Company's income, or $67,500, is reported as income. Assume that the undistributed income of $45,000 (75% of $90,000 less $30,000) is expected to be paid as a future dividend and is expected to be included on the tax return in some future years. Because the $45,000 will become future income, deferred taxes must be computed using this amount after considering the dividend exclusion rules (80% of dividends are excluded for 75% ownership).[6] The tax rate is assumed to be 40%, and the capital gains rate is assumed to be 25% in this example. The following workpaper entry is needed at the end of 2001:

Workpaper Entry—Cost Method—Year of Acquisition (2001) *Undistributed Income Expected to Be Received as Future Dividend*		
Tax Expense*	3,600	
Deferred Tax Liability		3,600

*Undistributed Income Expected to Be Received as Future Dividend

P Company's share of		
Undistributed income expected to be		
received as a future dividend	$45,000	(75% of $60,000)
Percent of future dividends that are taxed	20%	
Future dividends that will be taxed	$ 9,000	
Income tax rate	40%	
Deferred tax liability	$ 3,600	

At the end of the next year (2002), suppose that S Company's ending retained earnings is $320,000. Total undistributed earnings since acquisition are $170,000, or $320,000 less $150,000. P Company's share of undistributed earnings is $127,500 (or 75% of $170,000), including $45,000 from year 2001 and $82,500 from year 2002. Therefore, the amount of total deferred tax liability at the end of the second year can be computed as follows:

Undistributed Income Expected to Be Received as Future Dividends

	Year 2001	Year 2002	Total
P Company's share of undistributed Income			
expected to be received as dividends	$45,000	$82,500	$127,500
Percent of future dividends that are taxed	20%	20%	20%
Future dividends that will be taxed	$ 9,000	$16,500	$ 25,500
Tax rate	40%	40%	40%
Deferred tax liability	$ 3,600	$ 6,600	$ 10,200

---

[6]Note that P Company pays taxes of $1,800 on the $22,500 of dividends received from S Company (40% × 20% not excluded × $22,500). Therefore, combining the taxes paid on the dividend income of $1,800 and the tax expense of $3,600 recognized on the undistributed income totals a tax amount of $5,400. This equals the amount of taxes that would be owed if the entire amount of S Company's income was paid in dividends during the year ($90,000 × 75% × 20% × 40%).

The workpaper entry for the subsequent year is as follows:

Workpaper Entry—Cost Method—Year Subsequent to Acquisition (2002)		
Undistributed Income Expected to Be Received as Future Dividend		
Beginning Retained Earnings—P Company (prior year deferred taxes)	3,600	
Tax Expense (current year deferred taxes)	6,600	
Deferred Tax Liability		10,200

The debit to the beginning balance of P Company's retained earnings for each subsequent year reflects the sum of the debits from the *prior year's* deferred tax workpaper entry to tax expense and beginning retained earnings, if any. This is the estimated tax on P Company's share of the undistributed income of S Company from the date of acquisition to the beginning of the current year. If tax rates change, the adjustment to the deferred tax liability flows through the current deferred tax expense. Thus, the debit to beginning retained earnings is still the same as the credit made to the deferred tax liability in the prior year's workpaper.

UNDISTRIBUTED INCOME IS EXPECTED TO BE REALIZED WHEN THE SUBSIDIARY IS SOLD

If the undistributed income is not expected to be received as a future dividend but is expected to be realized when the investment is sold, the undistributed income is taxed at the capital gains rate as shown below:

Cost

Undistributed Income Expected to Be Received as Future Capital Gain			
	Year 2001	*Year 2002*	*Total*
P Company's Share of Undistributed Income expected to be realized in the future as a capital gain	$45,000	$82,500	$127,500
Capital gains tax rate	25%	25%	25%
Deferred tax liability	$11,250	$20,625	$ 31,875

Note that the 80% dividend exclusion is ignored. In addition, the appropriate tax rate to use is the capital gains tax rate.

The workpaper entries at the end of 2001 and 2002 to report the income tax consequences are as follows:

Workpaper Entry—Cost Method—Year of Acquisition and Year Subsequent to Acquisition (2001 and 2002)		
Undistributed Income Expected to Be Received as Gain Upon Sale of Subsidiary		
Year 2001		
Tax Expense	11,250	
Deferred Tax Liability		11,250
Year 2002		
Beginning Retained Earnings 1/1—P Company (prior year)	11,250	
Income Tax Expense (current year)	20,625	
Deferred Tax Liability		31,875

A similar workpaper entry is needed every year.

THE PARTIAL AND COMPLETE EQUITY METHODS— SEPARATE TAX RETURNS

If the equity method is used to account for the investment, there is a timing difference between book and tax on the books of the parent. Equity income is reported on the parent's income statement while dividends are included on the tax return. Therefore, deferred taxes on the parent's books must reflect the amount of undistributed income in the subsidiary. Generally, the parent will only make deferred tax entries if less than 80% of the subsidiary is owned since there is a 100% dividend exclusion for higher ownership percentages (regardless of whether the undistributed income is expected to be realized as a dividend or as a capital gain).

Partial

Consider the following example. P Company owns 75% of the voting stock of S Company. The stock was acquired on January 1, 2001, when S Company's retained earnings amounted to $150,000. In the year of acquisition (2001), S Company reported net income of $90,000 and paid dividends of $30,000. Since P Company is filing a separate tax return, P Company's income earned from the investment reported on the tax return is not the equity income but the amount of dividends received, $22,500 (75% of S Company's dividends of $30,000). However, on the consolidated income statement, 75% of S Company's income, or $67,500, is reported as equity income. Assume that the undistributed income of $45,000 (75% of $90,000 less $30,000) is expected to be paid as a future dividend and will be included on the tax return in some future years. Because the $45,000 is reported as current period equity income and is expected to be included on future tax returns when received either as a dividend or a capital gain, deferred taxes on this timing difference must be computed. If expected as a future dividend, the timing difference is computed after considering any dividend exclusion rules (80% excluded for 75% ownership). The current tax rate is assumed to be 40% and the capital gains tax rate to be 25%.

The entries on P Company's books for equity income and the receipt of dividends are as follows:

P Company Books—Partial and Complete Equity Methods		
Investment in S Company	67,500	
Equity in S Company Income		67,500
To record 75% of S Company income ($90,000).		
Cash	22,500	
Investment in S Company		22,500
To record the receipt of 75% of S Company's dividends paid ($30,000).		

Complete

Because P Company prepares its own tax return, the undistributed earnings of $45,000 (the $67,500 income less the dividends of $22,500) represents a timing difference. The following entry assumes that the undistributed income is expected to be received as a future dividend and only 20% is taxable (80% dividend exclusion). This entry adjusts tax expense and the deferred tax liability on P Company's books:

P Company Books—Partial and Complete Equity Methods *Undistributed Income Expected to Be Received as a Future Dividend*		
Tax expense (45,000 × .2 × .4)	3,600	
Deferred Tax Liability		3,600

Note that this entry is an adjustment of P Company's tax expense and not the equity income account. Because of this, no special workpaper entries are needed for deferred taxes if the equity method is used to account for the investment.

If the undistributed income is expected to be realized as a capital gain when the subsidiary is sold, the following entry would be made on P Company's books:

P Company Books—Partial and Complete Equity Methods		
Undistributed Income Expected to Be Received as a Capital Gain		
Tax Expense (45,000 × .25)	11,250	
Deferred Tax Liability		11,250

Partial

In this case, the 80% dividend exclusion is ignored. Because the entry is made on the books of P Company, again no workpaper entry is needed for deferred taxes in this instance under the equity method.

Complete

(The letter A, B, or C indicated for a question, exercise, or problem refers to a related appendix.)

QUESTIONS

1. How should nonconsolidated subsidiaries be reported in consolidated financial statements?

2. How are liquidating dividends treated on the books of an investor, assuming the investor uses the cost method? Assuming the investor uses the equity method?

3. How are dividends declared and paid by a subsidiary during the year eliminated in the consolidated workpapers under each method of accounting for investments?

4. How is the income reported by the subsidiary reflected on the books of the investor under each of the methods of accounting for investments?

5. Define: consolidated net income; consolidated retained earnings.

6. At the date of an 80% acquisition, a subsidiary had common stock of $100,000 and retained earnings of $16,250. Seven years later, at December 31, 2000, the subsidiary's retained earnings had increased to $461,430. What adjustment will be made on the consolidated workpaper at December 31, 2001, to recognize the parent's share of the cumulative undistributed profits (losses) of its subsidiary? Under which method(s) is this adjustment needed? Why?

7. On a consolidated workpaper for a parent and its partially owned subsidiary, the noncontrolling interest column accumulates the noncontrolling interests' share of several account balances. What are these accounts?

8. If a parent company elects to use the partial equity method rather than the cost method to record its investments in subsidiaries, what effect will this choice have on the consolidated financial state-

ments? if the parent company elects the complete equity method?

9. Describe two methods for treating the preacquisition revenue and expense items of a subsidiary purchased during a fiscal period.

10. A principal limitation of consolidated financial statements is their lack of separate financial information about the assets, liabilities, revenues, and expenses of the individual companies included in the consolidation. Identify some problems that the reader of consolidated financial statements would encounter as a result of this limitation.

11. In the preparation of a consolidated statement of cash flows, what adjustments are necessary because of the existence of a noncontrolling interest?

(AICPA adapted.)

12B. Is the recognition of a deferred tax asset or deferred tax liability when allocating the difference between cost and book value affected by whether or not the affiliates file a consolidated income tax return?

13B. What assumptions must be made about the realization of undistributed subsidiary income when the affiliates file separate income tax returns? Why?

14B. The FASB elected to require that deferred tax effects relating to unrealized intercompany profits be calculated based on the income tax paid by the selling affiliate rather than on the future tax benefit to the purchasing affiliate. Describe circumstances where the amounts calculated under these approaches would be different.

15B. Identify two types of timing differences that may arise in the consolidated financial statements when the affiliates file separate income tax returns.

EXERCISES

EXERCISE 4-1   Parent Company Entries, Liquidating Dividend

Percy Company purchased 80% of the outstanding voting shares of Song Company at the beginning of 1999 for $387,000. At the time of purchase, Song Company's total stockholders' equity amounted to $475,000. Income and dividend distributions for Song Company from 1999 through 2001 are as follows:

	1999	*2000*	*2001*
Net Income (Loss)	$63,500	$52,500	($55,000)
Dividend Distribution	25,000	50,000	35,000

Required:

Prepare journal entries on the books of Percy Company from the date of purchase through 2001 to account for its investment in Song Company under each of the following assumptions:

A. Percy Company uses the cost method to record its investment.

B. Percy Company uses the partial equity method to record its investment.

C. Percy Company uses the complete equity method to record its investment. The difference between cost and the book value of equity acquired was attributed solely to goodwill, with an expected life of ten years.

EXERCISE 4-2   Workpaper Eliminating Entries, Cost Method

Park Company purchased 90% of the stock of Salt Company on January 1, 1995, for $465,000, an amount equal to $15,000 in excess of the book value of equity acquired. This excess payment relates to an undervaluation of Salt Company's land. On the date of purchase, Salt Company's retained earnings balance was $50,000. The remainder of the stockholders' equity consists of no-par common stock. During 1999, Salt Company declared dividends in the amount of $10,000, and reported net income of $40,000. The retained earnings balance of Salt Company on December 31, 1998, was $160,000. Park Company uses the cost method to record its investment.

Required:

Prepare in general journal form the workpaper entries that would be made in the preparation of a consolidated statements workpaper on December 31, 1999.

EXERCISE 4-3   Workpaper Eliminating Entries, Equity Method

At the beginning of 1992, Presidio Company purchased 95% of the common stock of Succo Company for $494,000. On that date, Succo Company's stockholders' equity consisted of the following:

Common Stock	$300,000
Other Contributed Capital	100,000
Retained Earnings	120,000
Total	$520,000

During 2000, Succo Company reported net income of $40,000 and distributed dividends in the amount of $19,000. Succo Company's retained earnings balance at the end of 1999 amounted to $160,000. Presidio Company uses the equity method.

Required:

Prepare in general journal form the workpaper entries necessary in the compilation of consolidated financial statements on December 31, 2000. Explain why the partial and complete equity methods would result in the same entries in this instance.

EXERCISE 4-4 Workpaper Eliminating Entries, Losses by Subsidiary

Poco Company purchased 85% of the outstanding common stock of Serena Company on December 31, 1995, for $310,000 cash. On that date, Serena Company's stockholders' equity consisted of the following:

Common Stock	$240,000
Other Contributed Capital	55,000
Retained Earnings	50,000
	$345,000

During 1998, Serena Company distributed a dividend in the amount of $12,000 and at year-end reported a net loss of $10,000. During the time that Poco Company has held its investment in Serena Company, Serena Company's retained earnings balance has decreased $29,500 to a net balance of $20,500 after closing on December 31, 1998. Serena Company did not declare or distribute any dividends in 1996 or 1997. The difference between cost and book value relates to subsidiary land.

Required:

A. Assume that Poco Company uses the equity method. Prepare in general journal form the entries needed in the preparation of a consolidated statements workpaper on December 31, 1998. Explain why the partial and complete equity methods would result in the same entries in this instance.

B. Assume that Poco Company uses the cost method. Prepare in general journal form the entries needed in the preparation of a consolidated statements workpaper on December 31, 1998.

EXERCISE 4-5 Eliminating Entries, Noncontrolling Interest

On January 1, 1999, Plate Company purchased a 90% interest in the common stock of Set Company for $650,000, an amount $20,000 in excess of the book value of equity acquired. The excess relates to the understatement of Set Company's land holdings.

Excerpts from the consolidated retained earnings section of the consolidated statements workpaper for the year ended December 31, 1999, follow:

	Set Company	Consolidated Balances
1/1/99 Retained Earnings	$190,000	$880,000
Net Income from above	132,000	420,000
Dividends Declared	(50,000)	(88,000)
12/31/99 Retained Earnings to the balance sheet	$272,000	$1,212,000

Set Company's stockholders' equity is composed of common stock and retained earnings only.

Required:

A. Prepare the eliminating entries required for the preparation of a consolidated statements workpaper on December 31, 1999, assuming the use of the cost method.

B. Prepare the eliminating entries required for the preparation of a consolidated statements workpaper on December 31, 1999, assuming the use of the equity method.

C. Determine the total noncontrolling interest that will be reported on the consolidated balance sheet on December 31, 1999. How does the noncontrolling interest differ between the cost method and the equity method?

EXERCISE 4-6   Parent Entries and Eliminating Entries, Equity Method, Year of Acquisition

On January 1, 1999, Pert Company purchased 85% of the outstanding common stock of Sales Company for $350,000. On that date, Sales Company's stockholders' equity consisted of common stock, $100,000; other contributed capital, $40,000; and retained earnings, $140,000. Pert Company paid more than the book value of net assets acquired because the recorded cost of Sales Company's land was significantly less than its fair value.

During 1999 Sales Company earned $148,000 and declared and paid a $50,000 dividend. Pert Company uses the equity method to record its investment in Sales Company.

Required:

A. Prepare the investment-related entries on Pert Company's books for 1999.

B. Prepare the workpaper eliminating entries for a workpaper on December 31, 1999.

EXERCISE 4-7   Equity Method, Year Subsequent to Acquisition

Continue the situation in Exercise 4-6 and assume that during 2000 Sales Company earned $190,000 and declared and paid a $50,000 dividend.

Required:

A. Prepare the investment-related entries on Pert Company's books for 2000.

B. Prepare the workpaper eliminating entries for a workpaper on December 31, 2000.

EXERCISE 4-8   Interim Purchase of Stock, Full-Year Reporting Alternative, Cost Method

On May 1, 1997, Peters Company purchased 80% of the common stock of Smith Company for $50,000. Additional data concerning these two companies for the years 1997 and 1998 are:

	1997		1998	
	Peters	*Smith*	*Peters*	*Smith*
Common Stock	$100,000	$25,000	$100,000	$25,000
Other Contributed Capital	40,000	10,000	40,000	10,000
Retained Earnings (1/1)	80,000	10,000	120,000	53,000
Net Income (loss)	64,000	45,000	37,500	(5,000)
Cash Dividends (11/30)	15,000	2,000	5,000	—0—

Any difference between cost and book value relates to Smith Company's land. Peters Company uses the cost method to record its investment.

Required:

A. Prepare the workpaper entries that would be made on a consolidated statements workpaper for the years ended December 31, 1997 and 1998 for Peters Company and its subsidiary, assuming that Smith Company's income is earned evenly throughout the year. (Use the full-year reporting alternative.)

B. Calculate consolidated net income and consolidated retained earnings for 1997 and 1998.

EXERCISE 4-9   Interim Purchase, Partial-Year Reporting Alternative, Cost Method

Using the data presented in Exercise 4-8, prepare workpaper elimination entries for 1997 assuming use of the partial-year reporting alternative.

EXERCISE 4-10   Interim Purchase, Equity Method

On October 1, 2000, Para Company purchased 90% of the outstanding common stock of Star Company for $210,000. Additional data concerning Star Company for 2000 follows:

Common Stock	$70,000
Other Contributed Capital	30,000

Retained Earnings, 1/1	70,000
Net Income	60,000
Dividends Declared and Paid (12/15)	10,000

Any difference between cost and book value relates to Star Company land. Para Company uses the equity method to record its investment in Star Company.

Required:

A. Prepare on Para Company's books journal entries to record the investment related activities for 2000.

B. Prepare workpaper eliminating entries for a workpaper on December 31, 2000. Star Company's net income is earned evenly throughout the year. (Use the partial-year reporting alternative.)

C. Repeat part B, but use the full-year reporting alternative.

EXERCISE 4-11   Cash Flow from Operations

A consolidated income statement and selected comparative consolidated balance sheet data for Palano Company and subsidiary follow:

PALANO COMPANY AND SUBSIDIARY
Consolidated Income Statement
For the Year Ended December 31, 2000

Sales		$701,000
Cost of Sales		263,000
Gross Profit		438,000
Operating Expenses:		
Depreciation expense	$ 76,000	
Selling expenses	122,000	
Administrative expenses	85,000	283,000
Combined Income		155,000
Less Noncontrolling Interest		38,750
Consolidated Net Income		$116,250

	December 31	
	1999	2000
Accounts Receivable	$229,000	$318,000
Inventory	194,000	234,000
Prepaid Selling Expenses	26,000	30,000
Accounts Payable	99,000	79,000
Accrued Selling Expenses	96,000	84,000
Accrued Administrative Expenses	56,000	39,000

Required:

Prepare the cash flow from operating activities section of a consolidated statement of cash flows assuming use of the:

A. Direct method.

B. Indirect method.

EXERCISE 4-12   Allocation of Difference Between Cost and Book Value, Parent Company Entries, Three Methods

On January 1, 2002, Plutonium Corporation acquired 80% of the outstanding stock of the Sulfurst Inc. for $268,000 cash. The following balance sheet shows Sulfurst Inc.'s book values immediately prior to acquisition, as well as the appraised values of its assets and liabilities by Plutonium's experts:

	Sulfurst Inc.'s Book Values	*Sulfurst Inc.'s Market Values*
Current Assets	$90,000	$90,000
Property, Plant & Equipment:		
Land	80,000	100,000
Building & Machinery (net)	170,000	170,000
Total Assets	$340,000	
Total Liabilities	$100,000	$100,000
Common Stock, $5 par value	100,000	
Additional Paid-in-Capital	20,000	
Retained Earnings	120,000	
Total Liabilities and Equities	$340,000	

Required:

A. Prepare a Computation and Allocation Schedule for the Difference Between Cost and Book Value.

B. Prepare the entry to be made on the books of Plutonium Corporation to record its investment in Sulfurst Inc.

Assume that during the first two years after acquisition of Sulfurst Inc., Sulfurst reports the following changes in its retained earnings:

Retained Earnings, January 1, 2002	$120,000
Net Income, 2002	40,000
Less: Dividends, 2002	(24,000)
Net Income, 2003	45,000
Less: Dividends, 2003	(21,600)
Retained Earnings, December 31, 2003	$159,400

C. Prepare journal entries under each of the following methods to record the information above on the books of Plutonium Corporation for the years 2002 and 2003, assuming that any goodwill is to be amortized over a 40-year life.

(1) Plutonium uses the cost method to account for its investment in Sulfurst.

(2) Plutonium uses the partial equity method to account for its investment in Sulfurst.

(3) Plutonium uses the complete equity method to account for its investment in Sulfurst.

EXERCISE 4-13 Subsidiary Loss

The following accounts appeared in the separate financial statements at the end of 2006 for Pressing Inc. and its wholly owned subsidiary, Stressing Inc. Stressing was acquired in 2001.

	Pressing Inc.	*Stressing Inc.*
Investment in Subsidiary	660,000	
Dividends Receivable	5,000	
Dividends Payable	20,000	$5,000
Common Stock	300,000	20,000
Additional Paid-in-Capital	500,000	380,000
Retained Earnings, 12/31/06	500,000	260,000
Dividends Declared	(75,000)	(24,000)
Equity in Net Loss of Subsidiary	$(55,000)	
Retained earnings at 1/1/06	380,000	

Required:

1. How can you determine whether Pressing is using the cost or equity method to account for its investment in Stressing?
2. Compute controlling interest in combined income.
3. How much income did Pressing Inc. earn from its own independent operations?
4. Compute consolidated retained earnings at 12/31/06.
5. What are consolidated dividends?
6. Compute retained earnings at 1/1/06 for Stressing Inc.
7. Was there any difference between cost and book value at acquisition? Prepare workpaper entries needed at the end of 2006.
8. If Pressing used the cost method instead of the equity method, how would Pressing Inc.'s retained earnings change at the end of 2006? Describe in words.
9. If Pressing uses the cost method instead of the equity method, what workpaper entries would be required at the end of 2006? Describe in words.

EXERCISE 4-14 **Cash Flow Statement, Year of Acquisition**

Badco Inc. purchased a 90% interest in Lazytoo Company for $600,000 cash on January 1, 2001. Any excess of cost over book value was attributed to goodwill with a 15-year life. To help pay for the acquisition, Badco issued $300,000, 20-year, 12% bonds at par value. Lazytoo's balance sheet on the date of acquisition was as follows:

Assets		Liabilities and Equity	
Cash	$ 10,000	Accrued Payables	$ 90,000
Inventory	140,000	Bonds Payable	100,000
Fixed Assets (net)	540,000	Common Stock ($10 par)	200,000
		Retained Earnings	300,000
Total Assets	$690,000	Total Liabilities and Equity	$690,000

Consolidated net income for 2001 was $149,000, net of the noncontrolling interest of $8,000. Badco declared and paid dividends of $10,000 and Lazytoo declared and paid dividends of $5,000. There were no purchases or sales of property, plant, and equipment during the year.

At the end of 2001, the following information was also available:

	Badco Company 12/31/00		Consolidated 12/31/01	
	Debits	Credits	Debits	Credits
Cash	$ 390,000		$ 63,500	
Inventory	190,000		454,000	
Fixed Assets	750,000		1,230,000	
Goodwill			140,000	
Accrued Payables		150,000		111,000
Bonds Payable		200,000		600,000
Noncontrolling Interest				57,500
Common Stock ($10 par)		200,000		200,000
Additional Paid-in-Capital		550,000		550,000
Retained Earnings		230,000		369,000
Total	$1,330,000	$1,330,000	$1,887,500	$1,887,500

Required:
Prepare a consolidated statement of cash flows using the indirect method for Badco and its subsidiary for the year ended December 31, 2001.

EXERCISE 4-15B **Entries for Deferred Taxes from Undistributed Income, Cost and Equity**

On January 1, 1999, Plenty Company purchased a 70% interest in the common stock of Set Company for $650,000, an amount $20,000 in excess of the book value of equity acquired. The excess relates to the understatement of Set Company's land holdings.

Excerpts from both company's financial statements for the year ended December 31, 1999, follow:

	Set Company	Plenty Company
1/1/99 Retained Earnings	190,000	880,000
Income from Independent Operations	132,000	420,000
Dividends Declared	(50,000)	(88,000)

Set Company's stockholders' equity is composed of common stock and retained earnings only. Both companies file separate tax returns and the expected tax rate is 40%. The capital gains tax rate is 20% and there is an 80% dividend exclusion rate.

Required:

A. Prepare the entry(s) needed at the end of 1999 to report the income tax consequences of undistributed income assuming the use of the cost method, under each of the following assumptions. Indicate whether the entry is recorded on the books of Set, Plenty, or workpaper only.

  (1) Plenty expects the undistributed income will be realized in the form of future dividends.

  (2) Plenty expects the undistributed income will be realized only when the stock is sold, in the form of capital gains.

B. Prepare the entry(s) needed at the end of 1999 to report the income tax consequences of undistributed income assuming the use of the partial equity method, under each of the following assumptions. Indicate whether the entry is recorded on the books of Set, Plenty, or workpaper only.

  (1) Plenty expects the undistributed income will be realized in the form of future dividends.

  (2) Plenty expects the undistributed income will be realized only when the stock is sold, in the form of capital gains.

C. Prepare the entry(s) needed at the end of 1999 to report the income tax consequences of undistributed income assuming the use of the complete equity method, under each of the following assumptions. Indicate whether the entry is recorded on the books of Set, Plenty, or workpaper only.

  (1) Plenty expects the undistributed income will be realized in the form of future dividends.

  (2) Plenty expects the undistributed income will be realized only when the stock is sold, in the form of capital gains.

PROBLEMS

PROBLEM 4-1 **Parent Company Entries, Three Methods**

On January 1, 1997, Perelli Company purchased 90,000 of the 100,000 outstanding shares of common stock of Singer Company as a long-term investment. The purchase price of $4,972,000 was paid in cash. At the purchase date, the balance sheet of Singer Company included the following:

Current Assets	$2,926,550
Long-Term Assets	3,894,530
Other Assets	759,690
Current Liabilities	1,557,542

Common Stock, $20 par value	2,000,000
Other Contributed Capital	1,891,400
Retained Earnings	1,621,000

Additional data on Singer Company for the four years following the purchase are:

	1997	1998	1999	2000
Net income (loss)	$1,997,800	$476,000	$(179,600)	$(323,800)
Cash dividends paid, 12/30	500,000	500,000	500,000	500,000

Required:
Prepare journal entries under each of the following methods to record the purchase and all investment-related subsequent events on the books of Perelli Company for the four years, assuming that any excess of purchase price over equity acquired was attributable solely to *goodwill* (with a useful life of 15 years):

A. Perelli uses the cost method to account for its investment in Singer.

B. Perelli uses the partial equity method to account for its investment in Singer.

C. Perelli uses the complete equity method to account for its investment in Singer.

PROBLEM 4-2 Determine Method, Consolidated Workpaper, Wholly Owned Subsidiary

Parry Corporation acquired a 100% interest in Sent Company on January 1, 1999, paying $140,000. Financial statement data for the two companies for the year ended December 31, 1999 follow:

Income Statement	Parry	Sent
Sales	$476,000	$154,500
Cost of Goods Sold	285,600	121,000
Other Expense	45,500	29,500
Dividend Income	3,500	—0—
Retained Earnings Statement		
Balance, 1/1	76,000	19,500
Net Income	148,400	4,000
Dividends Declared	17,500	3,500
Balance Sheet		
Cash	84,400	29,000
Accounts Receivable	76,000	56,500
Inventory	49,500	36,500
Investment in Sent Company	140,000	—0—
Land	4,000	12,000
Accounts Payable	27,000	14,000
Common Stock	120,000	100,000
Retained Earnings	206,900	20,000

Required:

A. What method is being used by Parry to account for its investment in Sent Company? How can you tell?

B. Prepare a workpaper for the preparation of consolidated financial statements on December 31, 1999. Any difference between the cost of the investment and the book value of equity acquired relates to subsidiary land.

PROBLEM 4-3 Consolidated Workpaper, Wholly Owned Subsidiary

Perkins Company acquired 100% of Schultz Company on January 1, 2000, for $161,500. On December 31, 2000, the companies prepared the following trial balances:

	Perkins	Schultz
Cash	$ 25,000	$ 30,000
Inventory	105,000	97,500
Investment in Schultz Company	222,000	—0—
Land	111,000	97,000
Cost of Goods Sold	225,000	59,500
Other Expense	40,000	40,000
Dividends Declared	15,000	10,000
Total Debits	$743,000	$334,000
Accounts Payable	$ 72,500	$ 17,500
Capital Stock	160,000	75,000
Other Contributed Capital	35,000	17,500
Retained Earnings, 1/1	25,000	54,000
Sales	380,000	170,000
Equity in Subsidiary Income	70,500	—0—
Total Credits	$743,000	$334,000

Required:

A. What method is being used by Perkins to account for its investment in Schultz Company? How can you tell?

B. Prepare a workpaper for the preparation of consolidated financial statements on December 31, 2000. Any difference between the cost of the investment and the book value of equity acquired relates to subsidiary land.

PROBLEM 4-4 Consolidated Workpaper, Partially Owned Subsidiary, Cost Method

Place Company purchased 92% of the common stock of Shaw, Inc. on January 1, 2000, for $400,000. Trial balances at the end of 2000 for the companies were:

	Place	Shaw
Cash	$ 80,350	$ 87,000
Accounts and Notes Receivable	200,000	210,000
Inventory, 1/1	70,000	50,000
Investment in Shaw, Inc.	400,000	—0—
Plant Assets	300,000	200,000
Dividends Declared	35,000	22,000
Purchases	240,000	150,000
Selling Expenses	28,000	20,000
Other Expenses	15,000	13,000
	$1,368,350	$752,000
Accounts and Notes Payable	$ 99,110	$ 38,000
Other Liabilities	45,000	15,000
Common Stock, $10 par	150,000	100,000
Other Conributed Capital	279,000	149,000
Retained Earnings, 1/1	225,000	170,000
Sales	550,000	280,000
Dividend Income	20,240	—0—
	$1,368,350	$752,000

Inventory balances on December 31, 2000, were $25,000 for Place and $15,000 for Shaw, Inc. Shaw's accounts and notes payable contain a $15,000 note payable to Place.

Required:

Prepare a workpaper for the preparation of consolidated financial statements on December 31, 2000. The difference between cost and book value of equity acquired relates to subsidiary land, which is included in plant assets.

PROBLEM 4-5 Consolidated Workpaper, Partially Owned Subsidiary—Subsequent Years

On January 1, 1995, Perez Company purchased 90% of the capital stock of Sanchez Company for $85,000. Sanchez Company had capital stock of $70,000 and retained earnings of $12,000 at that time. On December 31, 1999, the trial balances of the two companies were:

	Perez	Sanchez
Cash	$ 13,000	$ 14,000
Accounts Receivable	22,000	36,000
Inventory, 1/1	14,000	8,000
Advance to Sanchez Company	8,000	—0—
Investment in Sanchez Company	85,000	—0—
Plant and Equipment	50,000	44,000
Land	17,800	6,000
Dividends Declared	10,000	12,000
Purchases	84,000	20,000
Other Expenses	10,000	16,000
Total Debits	$313,800	$156,000
Accounts Payable	$ 6,000	$ 6,000
Other Liabilities	37,000	—0—
Advance from Perez Company	—0—	8,000
Capital Stock	100,000	70,000
Retained Earnings	50,000	30,000
Sales	110,000	42,000
Dividend Income	10,800	—0—
Total Credits	$313,800	$156,000
Inventory, 12/31	$ 40,000	$ 15,000

Any difference between cost and book value relates to subsidiary land.

Required:

A. What method is being used by Perez to account for its investment in Sanchez Company? How can you tell?

B. Prepare a workpaper for the preparation of consolidated financial statements on 12/31/99.

PROBLEM 4-6 Consolidated Workpaper, Partially Owned Subsidiary—Subsequent Years

On January 1, 1996, Plank Company purchased 80% of the outstanding capital stock of Scoba Company for $53,000. At that time, Scoba's stockholders' equity consisted of capital stock, $55,000; other contributed capital, $5,000; and retained earnings, $4,000. On December 31, 2000, the two companies' trial balances were as follows:

	Plank	Scoba
Cash	$ 42,000	$ 22,000
Accounts Receivable	21,000	17,000
Inventory	15,000	8,000
Investment in Scoba Company	61,000	
Land	52,000	48,000
Dividends Declared	10,000	8,000
Cost of Goods Sold	85,400	20,000
Other Expense	10,000	12,000
	$296,400	$135,000

	Plank	Scoba
Accounts Payable	$ 12,000	$ 6,000
Other Liabilities	5,000	4,000
Capital Stock	100,000	55,000
Other Contributed Capital	20,000	5,000
Retained Earnings, 1/1	40,000	15,000
Sales	105,000	50,000
Equity in Subsidiary Income	14,400	—0—
	$296,400	$135,000

The accounts payable of Scoba Company include $3,000 payable to Plank Company.

Required:

A. What method is being used by Plank to account for its investment in Scoba Company? How can you tell?

B. Prepare a consolidated statements workpaper at December 31, 2000. Any difference between cost and book value relates to subsidiary land.

PROBLEM 4-7 **Consolidated Workpaper, Partially Owned Subsidiary—Subsequent Years, Cost Method**
Price Company purchased 90% of the outstanding common stock of Score Company on January 1, 1995, for $450,000. At that time, Score Company had stockholders' equity consisting of common stock, $200,000; other contributed capital, $160,000; and retained earnings, $90,000. On December 31, 1999, trial balances for Price Company and Score Company were as follows:

	Price	Score
Cash	$ 109,000	$ 78,000
Accounts Receivable	166,000	94,000
Note Receivable	75,000	—0—
Inventory	309,000	158,000
Investment in Score Company	450,000	—0—
Plant and Equipment	940,000	420,000
Land	160,000	70,000
Dividends Declared	70,000	50,000
Cost of Goods Sold	822,000	242,000
Operating Expenses	250,500	124,000
Total Debits	$3,351,500	$1,236,000
Accounts Payable	$ 132,000	$ 46,000
Notes Payable	300,000	120,000
Common Stock	500,000	200,000
Other Contributed Capital	260,000	160,000
Retained Earnings, 1/1	687,000	210,000
Sales	1,420,000	500,000
Dividend and Interest Income	52,500	—0—
Total Credits	$3,351,500	$1,236,000

Price Company's note receivable is receivable from Score Company. Interest of $7,500 was paid by Score to Price during 1999. Any difference between cost and book value relates to Score Company land.

Required:
Prepare a consolidated statements workpaper on December 31, 1999.

PROBLEM 4-8 Consolidated Workpapers, Two Consecutive Years, Cost Method

On January 1, 2000, Parker Company purchased 95% of the outstanding common stock of Sid Company for $160,000. At that time, Sid's stockholders' equity consisted of common stock, $120,000; other contributed capital, $10,000; and retained earnings, $23,000. On December 31, 2000, the two companies' trial balances were as follows:

	Parker	Sid
Cash	$ 62,000	$ 30,000
Accounts Receivable	32,000	29,000
Inventory	30,000	16,000
Investment in Sid Company	160,000	—0—
Plant and Equipment	105,000	82,000
Land	29,000	34,000
Dividends Declared	20,000	20,000
Cost of Goods Sold	130,000	40,000
Operating Expenses	20,000	14,000
Total Debits	$588,000	$265,000
Accounts Payable	$ 19,000	$ 12,000
Other Liabilities	10,000	20,000
Common Stock	180,000	120,000
Other Contributed Capital	60,000	10,000
Retained Earnings, 1/1	40,000	23,000
Sales	260,000	80,000
Dividend Income	19,000	—0—
Total Credits	$588,000	$265,000

Required:

A. Prepare a consolidated statements workpaper on December 31, 2000.

B. Prepare a consolidated statements workpaper on December 31, 2001, assuming trial balances for Parker and Sid on that date were:

	Parker	Sid
Cash	$ 67,000	$ 16,000
Accounts Receivable	56,000	32,000
Inventory	38,000	48,500
Investment in Sid Company	160,000	—0—
Plant and Equipment	124,000	80,000
Land	29,000	34,000
Dividends Declared	20,000	20,000
Cost of Goods Sold	155,000	52,000
Operating Expenses	30,000	18,000
Total Debits	$679,000	$300,500
Accounts Payable	$ 16,000	$ 7,000
Other Liabilities	15,000	14,500
Common Stock	180,000	120,000
Other Contributed Capital	60,000	10,000
Retained Earnings, 1/1	149,000	29,000
Sales	240,000	120,000
Dividend Income	19,000	—0—
Total Credits	$679,000	$300,500

PROBLEM 4-9 Consolidated Workpaper, Treasury Stock, Cost Method

December 31, 1999, trial balances for Pledge Company and its subsidiary Stom Company follow:

	Pledge	Stom
Cash and Marketable Securities	$ 184,600	$ 72,000
Receivables (net)	182,000	180,000
Inventory	214,000	212,000
Investment in Stom Company	300,000	—0—
Plant and Equipment (net)	309,000	301,000
Land	85,000	75,000
Cost of Goods Sold	460,000	185,000
Operating Expenses	225,000	65,000
Dividends Declared	50,000	30,000
Treasury Stock (10,000 shares at cost)	—0—	20,000
Total Debits	$2,009,600	$1,140,000
Accounts Payable	$ 96,000	$ 79,000
Accrued Expenses	31,000	18,000
Notes Payable	100,000	200,000
Common Stock, $1 par value	300,000	100,000
Other Contributed Capital	150,000	80,000
Retained Earnings, 1/1	422,000	320,000
Sales	880,000	340,000
Dividend and Interest Income	30,600	3,000
Total Credits	$2,009,600	$1,140,000

Pledge Company purchased 72,000 shares of Stom Company's common stock on January 1, 1994, for $300,000. On that date, Stom Company's stockholders' equity was as follows:

Common Stock, $1 par value	$100,000
Other Contributed Capital	80,000
Retained Earnings	160,000
Treasury Stock (10,000 shares at cost)	(20,000)
Total	$320,000

Other information:

1. Receivables of Pledge Company include a $55,000, 12% note receivable from Stom Company.

2. Interest amounting to $6,600 has been accrued by each company on the note payable from Stom to Pledge. Stom Company has not yet paid this interest.

3. The difference between cost and book value relates to subsidiary land.

Required:

Prepare a consolidated statements workpaper for the year ended December 31, 1999.

PROBLEM 4-10   **Consolidated Workpaper, Equity Method**

Poco Company purchased 80% of Solo Company's common stock on January 1, 2000, for $250,000. On December 31, 2000, the companies prepared the following trial balances:

	Poco	Solo
Cash	$161,500	$125,000
Inventory	210,000	195,000
Investment in Solo Company	402,000	—0—
Land	75,000	150,000
Cost of Goods Sold	410,000	125,000
Other Expense	100,000	80,000
Dividends Declared	30,000	15,000
Total Debits	$1,388,500	$690,000

	Poco	Solo
Accounts Payable	$154,500	$ 35,000
Common Stock	200,000	150,000
Other Contributed Capital	60,000	35,000
Retained Earnings, 1/1	50,000	60,000
Sales	760,000	410,000
Equity in Subsidiary Income	164,000	—0—
Total Credits	$1,388,500	$690,000

Required:

Prepare a consolidated statements workpaper on December 31, 2000. Any difference between cost and book value relates to subsidiary land.

PROBLEM 4-11 Consolidated Workpaper, Equity Method

(Note that this is the same problem as Problem 4-7, but assuming the use of the equity method.)

Price Company purchased 90% of the outstanding common stock of Score Company on January 1, 1995, for $450,000. At that time, Score Company had stockholders' equity consisting of common stock, $200,000; other contributed capital, $160,000; and retained earnings, $90,000. On December 31, 1999, trial balances for Price Company and Score Company were as follows:

	Price	Score
Cash	$ 109,000	$ 78,000
Accounts Receivable	166,000	94,000
Note Receivable	75,000	—0—
Inventory	309,000	158,000
Investment in Score Company	633,600	—0—
Plant and Equipment	940,000	420,000
Land	160,000	70,000
Dividends Declared	70,000	50,000
Cost of Goods Sold	822,000	242,000
Operating Expenses	250,500	124,000
Total Debits	$3,535,100	$1,236,000

	Price	Score
Accounts Payable	$ 132,000	$ 46,000
Notes Payable	300,000	120,000
Common Stock	500,000	200,000
Other Contributed Capital	260,000	160,000
Retained Earnings, 1/1	795,000	210,000
Sales	1,420,000	500,000
Equity in Subsidiary Income	120,600	—0—
Interest Income	7,500	—0—
Total Credits	$3,535,100	$1,236,000

Price Company's note receivable is receivable from Score Company. Interest of $7,500 was paid by Score to Price during 1999. Any difference between cost and book value relates to Score Company land.

Required:

Prepare a consolidated statements workpaper on December 31, 1999.

PROBLEM 4-12 **Equity Method, Two Consecutive Years**

On January 1, 2000, Parker Company purchased 90% of the outstanding common stock of Sid Company for $180,000. At that time, Sid's stockholders' equity consisted of common stock, $120,000; other contributed capital, $20,000; and retained earnings, $25,000. Assume that any difference between cost and book value of equity is attributable to land. On December 31, 2000, the two companies' trial balances were as follows:

	Parker	Sid
Cash	$ 65,000	$ 35,000
Accounts Receivable	40,000	30,000
Inventory	25,000	15,000
Investment in Sid Company	184,500	—0—
Plant and Equipment	110,000	85,000
Land	48,500	45,000
Dividends Declared	20,000	15,000
Cost of Goods Sold	150,000	60,000
Operating Expenses	35,000	15,000
Total Debits	$678,000	$300,000
Accounts Payable	$ 20,000	$ 15,000
Other Liabilities	15,000	25,000
Common Stock, par value $10	200,000	120,000
Other Contributed Capital	70,000	20,000
Retained Earnings, 1/1	55,000	25,000
Sales	300,000	95,000
Equity in Subsidiary Income	18,000	—0—
Total Credits	$678,000	$300,000

Required:

A. Prepare a consolidated statements workpaper on December 31, 2000.

B. Prepare a consolidated statements workpaper on December 31, 2001, assuming trial balances for Parker and Sid on that date were:

	Parker	Sid
Cash	$ 70,000	$ 20,000
Accounts Receivable	60,000	35,000
Inventory	40,000	30,000
Investment in Sid Company	193,500	—0—
Plant and Equipment	125,000	90,000
Land	48,500	45,000
Dividends Declared	20,000	15,000
Cost of Goods Sold	160,000	65,000
Operating Expenses	35,000	20,000
Total Debits	$752,000	$320,000
Accounts Payable	$ 16,500	$ 16,000
Other Liabilities	15,000	24,000
Common Stock, par value $10	200,000	120,000
Other Contributed Capital	70,000	20,000
Retained Earnings, 1/1	168,000	30,000
Sales	260,000	110,000
Equity in Subsidiary Income	22,500	—0—
Total Credits	$752,000	$320,000

PROBLEM 4-13 **Consolidated Workpaper, Treasury Stock, Equity Method**
(Note that this problem is the same as Problem 4-9, but assuming the use of the equity method.)

December 31, 1999, trial balances for Pledge Company and its subsidiary Stom Company follow:

	Pledge	Stom
Cash and Marketable Securities	$ 184,600	$ 72,000
Receivables (net)	182,000	180,000
Inventory	214,000	212,000
Investment in Stom Company	478,400	—0—
Plant and Equipment (net)	309,000	301,000
Land	85,000	75,000
Cost of Goods Sold	460,000	185,000
Operating Expenses	225,000	65,000
Dividends Declared	50,000	30,000
Treasury Stock (10,000 shares at cost)	—0—	20,000
Total Debits	$2,188,000	$1,140,000
Accounts Payable	$ 96,000	$ 79,000
Accrued Expenses	31,000	18,000
Notes Payable	100,000	200,000
Common Stock, $1 par value	300,000	100,000
Other Contributed Capital	150,000	80,000
Retained Earnings, 1/1	550,000	320,000
Sales	880,000	340,000
Equity in Subsidiary Income	74,400	—0—
Interest Income	6,600	3,000
Total Credits	$2,188,000	$1,140,000

Pledge Company purchased 72,000 shares of Stom Company's common stock on January 1, 1994, for $300,000. On that date, Stom Company's stockholders' equity was as follows:

Common Stock, $1 par value	$100,000
Other Contributed Capital	80,000
Retained Earnings	160,000
Treasury Stock (10,000 shares at cost)	(20,000)
Total	$320,000

Other information:
1. Receivables of Pledge Company include a $55,000, 12% note receivable from Stom Company.
2. Interest amounting to $6,600 has been accrued by each company on the note payable from Stom to Pledge. Stom Company has not yet paid this interest.
3. The difference between cost and book value relates to subsidiary land.

Required:
Prepare a consolidated statements workpaper for the year ended December 31, 1999.

PROBLEM 4-14 **Interim Purchase, Full-Year Reporting Alternative, Cost Method**
Punca Company purchased 85% of the common stock of Surrano Company on July 1, 2000, for a cash payment of $590,000. December 31, 2000, trial balances for Punca and Surrano were:

	Punca	Surrano
Current Assets	$ 150,000	$ 180,000
Treasury Stock at Cost, 500 shares	—0—	48,000
Investment in Surrano Company	590,000	—0—
Property and Equipment	1,250,000	750,000
Cost of Goods Sold	1,540,000	759,000
Other Expenses	415,000	250,000
Dividends Declared	—0—	50,000
Total	$3,945,000	$2,037,000
Accounts and Notes Payable	$ 277,500	$ 150,000
Dividends Payable	—0—	50,000
Capital Stock, $5 par value	270,000	40,000
Other Contributed Capital	900,000	250,000
Retained Earnings, 1/1	355,000	241,000
Sales	2,100,000	1,300,000
Dividend Income	42,500	6,000
Total	$3,945,000	$2,037,000

Surrano Company declared a $50,000 cash dividend on December 20, 2000, payable on January 10, 2001, to stockholders of record on December 31, 2000. Punca Company recognized the dividend on its declaration date. Any difference between cost and book value relates to subsidiary land, included in property and equipment.

Required:
Prepare a consolidated statements workpaper at December 31, 2000, assuming that revenue and expense accounts of Surrano Company for the entire year are included with those of Punca Company (full-year reporting alternative).

PROBLEM 4-15 **Interim Purchase, Partial-Year Reporting Alternative, Cost Method**
Using the data given in Problem 4-14, prepare a workpaper for the preparation of consolidated financial statements at December 31, 2000, assuming that Surrano Company's revenue and expense accounts are included in the consolidated income statement from the date of acquisition only (partial-year reporting alternative). (Round to the nearest dollar.)

PROBLEM 4-16 **Interim Purchase, Full-Year Reporting Alternative, Equity Method**
Pillow Company purchased 90% of the common stock of Satin Company on May 1, 1999, for a cash payment of $474,000. December 31, 1999, trial balances for Pillow and Satin were:

	Pillow	Satin
Current Assets	$ 390,600	$ 179,200
Treasury Stock at Cost, 500 shares		32,000
Investment in Satin Company	510,000	—0—
Property and Equipment	1,334,000	562,000
Cost of Goods Sold	1,261,000	584,000
Other Expenses	484,000	242,000
Dividends Declared	—0—	60,000
Total	$3,979,600	$1,659,200
Accounts and Notes Payable	$ 270,240	$ 124,000
Dividends Payable		60,000
Capital Stock, $10 par value	1,000,000	200,000
Other Contributed Capital	364,000	90,000
Retained Earnings	315,360	209,200
Sales	1,940,000	976,000
Equity in Subsidiary Income	90,000	—0—
Total	$3,979,600	$1,659,200

Satin Company declared a $60,000 cash dividend on December 20, 1999, payable on January 10, 2000, to stockholders of record on December 31, 1995. Pillow Company recognized the dividend on its declaration date. Any difference between cost and book value relates to subsidiary land, included in property and equipment.

Required:

Prepare a consolidated statements workpaper at December 31, 1999, assuming that revenue and expense accounts of Satin Company for the entire year are included with those of Pillow Company. (Assume the full-year reporting alternative.)

PROBLEM 4-17 **Interim Purchase, Partial-Year Reporting Alternative, Equity Method**

Using the data given in Problem 4-16, prepare a workpaper for the preparation of consolidated financial statements at December 31, 1999, assuming that Satin Company's revenue and expense accounts are included in the consolidated income statement from the date of acquisition only. (Assume the partial-year reporting alternative.) (Round to the nearest dollar.)

PROBLEM 4-18 **Consolidated Statement of Cash Flows, Indirect Method**

A consolidated income statement for 2001 and comparative consolidated balance sheets for 2000 and 2001 for P Company and its 80% owned subsidiary follow:

P COMPANY
Consolidated Income Statement
For the Year Ended December 31, 2001

Sales	$1,900,000
Cost of Goods Sold	1,000,000
Gross Margin	900,000
Expenses	300,000
Operating Income Before Tax	600,000
Dividend Income	50,000
Income Before Tax	550,000
Income Taxes	220,000
Income After Taxes	330,000
Less: Noncontrolling Interest	66,000
Consolidated Net Income	$ 264,000

P COMPANY
Consolidated Balance Sheets
December 31, 2000 and 2001

Assets	*2001*	*2000*
Cash	$ 250,000	$ 300,000
Accounts Receivable	360,000	250,000
Inventories	210,000	190,000
Equipment (net)	975,000	500,000
Long-Term Investments	800,000	800,000
Goodwill	150,000	175,000
Total Assets	$2,745,000	$2,215,000

Liabilities and Equity		
Accounts Payable	$ 268,000	$ 500,000
Accrued Payable	260,000	200,000
Bonds Payable	200,000	—0—
Premium on Bonds Payable	40,000	—0—
Noncontrolling Interest	148,000	90,000
Common Stock, $1 par value	600,000	450,000
Other Contributed Capital	275,000	225,000
Retained Earnings	954,000	750,000
Total Equities	$2,745,000	$2,215,000

Other information:

1. Equipment depreciation and goodwill amortization were $70,000 and $25,000, respectively.

2. Equipment was purchased during the year for cash, $545,000.

3. Dividends paid during 2001:
   (a) Declared and paid by S Company, $40,000.
   (b) Declared and paid by P Company, $60,000.

4. The bonds payable were issued on December 30, 2001, for $240,000.

5. Common stock issued during 2001, 150,000 shares.

Required:

Prepare a consolidated statement of cash flows for the year ended December 31, 2001, using the indirect method.

PROBLEM 4-19 **Consolidated Statement of Cash Flows, Direct Method**

The consolidated income statement for the year ended December 31, 1999, and comparative balance sheets for 1998 and 1999 for Parks Company and its 90% owned subsidiary SCR, Inc. are as follows:

PARKS COMPANY AND SUBSIDIARY
Consolidated Income Statement
For the Year Ended December 31, 1999

Sales		$239,000
Cost of Goods Sold		104,000
Gross Margin		135,000
Depreciation and Amortization Expense	$27,000	
Other Operating Expenses	72,000	99,000
Income from Operations		36,000
Investment Income		4,500
Combined Net Income		40,500
Noncontrolling Interest in Net Income		3,000
Consolidated Net Income		$ 37,500

PARKS COMPANY AND SUBSIDIARY
Consolidated Balance Sheets
December 31, 1998 and 1999

	1999	*1998*
Cash	$ 36,700	$ 16,000
Receivables	55,000	90,000
Inventory	126,000	92,000
Property, Plant & Equipment (net of depreciation)	232,500	225,000
Long-term Investment	39,000	39,000
Goodwill	58,500	60,000
Total Assets	$547,700	$522,000
Accounts Payable	$ 67,500	$ 88,500
Accrued Expenses	30,000	41,000
Bonds Payable, due July 1, 2013	100,000	150,000
Total Liabilities	197,500	279,500

	1999	1998
Noncontrolling Interest	32,200	30,000
Common Stock	187,500	100,000
Retained Earnings	130,500	112,500
Total Stockholders' Equity	318,000	212,500
Total Equities	$547,700	$522,000

SCR Inc. declared and paid an $8,000 dividend during 1999.

Required:

Prepare a consolidated statement of cash flows using the direct method.

5

ALLOCATION, DEPRECIATION, AND AMORTIZATION OF THE DIFFERENCE BETWEEN COST AND BOOK VALUE

LEARNING OBJECTIVES

1. Calculate the difference between cost and book value and allocate to the subsidiary's assets and liabilities.

2. Explain how any excess of fair value over acquisition cost of net assets is allocated to reduce the subsidiary's assets and liabilities in the case of bargain purchases.

3. Explain how goodwill is measured.

4. Describe how the allocation process differs if less than 100% of the subsidiary is acquired.

5. Record the entries needed on the parent's books to account for the investment under the three methods: the cost, the partial equity, and the complete equity methods.

6. Prepare workpapers for the year of acquisition and the year(s) subsequent to the acquisition, assuming that the parent accounts for the investment using the cost, the partial equity, and the complete equity methods.

7. Understand the allocation of the difference between cost and book value to long-term debt components.

8. Explain how to allocate the difference between cost and book value when some assets have fair values below book values.

9. Distinguish between recording the subsidiary depreciable assets at net versus gross fair values.

10. Understand the concept of push down accounting.

Technology billionaire Paul Allen, in his latest move to assemble a cable empire, agreed to pay $2.5 billion in cash for Charter Communications Inc. and assume $2 billion of the cable system's debt. The record price further escalates the premiums communications companies are willing to pay to gather up pieces of the cable industry.[1]

---

[1] *WSJ*, "Allen to Pay Record Sum for Cable Firm," by Eben Shapiro, 7/31/98, p. A3.

When a company pays a large premium to consummate an acquisition, the allocation of that premium to the accounts in the balance sheet becomes a crucial issue under purchase accounting rules. As they mature, the balance sheet accounts will impact the income statement via amortization, depreciation, cost of goods sold, and so on, affecting the patterns and trend in reported earnings for years to come. These effects on earnings provide incentives for firms to use creative means to avoid depressing future earnings. One such method is to charge large amounts to in-process research and development expense.

The Securities and Exchange Commission is cracking down on the popular write-offs for "in-process research and development." Regulators, who believe this trendy accounting is being improperly used to manipulate earnings, are trying to stay on top of an acquisition boom in which sheer speculation about a company can affect the buyer's bottom line. . . . Targeted companies are recoiling at the SEC initiative because it has forced earnings restatements. For example, when Envoy Corp. disclosed that the SEC was reviewing its accounting for three acquisitions, Envoy's stock price fell that day to $26.50 from $36. Three months later Envoy announced that it had lowered its previous R&D write-offs to $14.6 million from $68 million, resulting in restatements for three years. The following month the company agreed to be purchased by Quintiles Transnational Corp. in a stock swap valued at about $1.4 billion.[2]

In the preceding chapter, it was assumed that any difference between acquisition cost and the book value of the equity interest acquired was entirely attributable to the under- or overvaluation of land, a nonamortizable asset, on the books of the subsidiary. This chapter focuses on a more complex and realistic allocation of the difference to various assets and liabilities in the consolidated balance sheet and the amortization and depreciation of the difference in the consolidated income statement. In the following pages, we first provide examples of the allocation of the difference between cost and book value *on the acquisition date*. We next extend the examples to deal with the *subsequent* amortization of the difference.

ALLOCATION OF DIFFERENCE BETWEEN COST AND BOOK VALUE TO ASSETS AND LIABILITIES OF SUBSIDIARY: ACQUISITION DATE

When consolidated financial statements are prepared, asset and liability values must be adjusted by allocating the difference between cost and book value to specific recorded or unrecorded tangible and intangible assets and liabilities. In the case of a *wholly owned* subsidiary, the following two steps are taken.

> *Step One:* The difference between the purchase price and book value is used first to adjust the individual assets and liabilities to their fair values on the date of acquisition.
>
> *Step Two:* If, after adjusting identifiable assets and liabilities to fair values, a residual amount of difference remains, it is treated as follows:
>   1. When cost exceeds the aggregate fair values of identifiable assets less liabilities, the residual amount will be *positive* (a debit balance). A positive residual difference is evidence of an unspecified intangible and is accounted for as goodwill.

[2] *WSJ*, "High-Tech Firms Upset Over SEC Crackdown," by Michael Schroeder, 2/1/99, p. B4.

> **2.** When the purchase price (acquisition cost) is below the aggregate fair value of identifiable assets less liabilities, the residual amount will be negative (a credit balance). A negative residual difference is evidence of a bargain purchase, with the difference between acquisition cost and fair value designating the amount of the bargain.[3] When a bargain acquisition occurs, some of the acquired assets must be reduced below their fair values (as reflected after step 1).

The rules are reviewed below for allocating the reduction in the case of a bargain purchase. These rules, which were initially introduced in Chapter 2, reflect an effort to adjust those assets whose valuation is most subjective and leave intact the categories considered most reliable. A true bargain is not likely to occur except in situations where nonquantitative factors play a role; for example, a closely held company wishes to sell quickly because of the health of a family member. Also, recall from Chapter 2, Appendix A, that the FASB is considering the appropriate accounting for bargain purchases, with changes possible. No changes have been approved, however. Thus, the rules under current GAAP are presented below.

Bargain Rules:
1. Current assets, long-term investments in marketable securities, and assumed liabilities are recorded at fair market value always.
2. Any previously recorded goodwill on the seller's books is eliminated (and no new goodwill recorded).
3. Long-lived assets (other than investments in marketable securities) are recorded at fair market value minus an adjustment for the bargain.
4. A deferred credit (negative goodwill) is recorded only in the event that all long-lived assets (other than investments) are reduced to zero,[4] in which case the credit is amortized (to revenue) over a period not to exceed 40 years.

When needed, the reduction of noncurrent assets (except investments in long-term marketable securities) is made in proportion to their fair values in determining their assigned values.[5] This allocation is illustrated later in this chapter. The FASB is considering eliminating any deferred credit for negative goodwill and recognizing instead an extraordinary gain.

Acquisitions leading to the recording of goodwill have been far more common in recent years than bargain acquisitions. The impact of goodwill on future earnings has drawn a great deal of attention. Under current rules, managers must consider the impact of goodwill amortization in their decision-making process. In some instances creative alternatives have been found to avoid recording goodwill.

One such alternative, which has been alluded to earlier, is to expense as Research and Development (R&D) a portion of the excess of purchase price over fair value acquired. Two decades ago the FASB required that R&D incurred in the

---

[3]Note that the following situation is possible and, technically, would be a bargain purchase: FV > Cost > BV. Because the fair value is higher than purchase price, the bargain purchase rules apply, even though the purchase price is higher than the book value of the underlying equity. In practice this situation is less likely to be referred to as a ''bargain'' than the situation where BV > FV > Cost. Nonetheless, it is the comparison between FV and Cost that determines a bargain, regardless of the level of BV (book value).

[4]If the subsidiary is not wholly owned, long-lived assets (other than investments) would be reduced to the noncontrolling interest (rather than to zero) before recognizing a deferred credit.

[5]*APB Opinion No. 16* (par. 91).

regular course of business be expensed and subsequently interpreted the standard to allow the expensing of certain types of R&D transferred in corporate acquisitions. The Board went on to state that the R&D expense, or write-off, amount would be based on the amount paid by the acquiring firm rather than its historical cost to the acquired firm. By allocating large amounts to R&D in the period of the acquisition, firms take a large one-time hit to earnings but avoid future repeated charges. This practice has become increasingly popular in recent years among high-technology firms, drawing the attention of the SEC and causing the firms to complain that they are being singled out for scrutiny. The FASB announced a decision to delay its project on in-process R&D until after the business combinations project is completed.

The SEC isn't inclined to sympathize. Agency officials say they are now enforcing more aggressively rules in place since 1975. "As the number of companies claiming larger [in-process R&D] write-offs increased in early 1998, we began to dig deeper into the company's appraisal assumptions," says SEC Chief Accountant Lynn Turner. At issue is the size of write-offs that companies take for the premiums they pay when acquiring other companies, particularly high-tech concerns. . . . Buyers of technology have capitalized on a rule that lets them take a large one-time write-off for the value of as-yet-undeveloped products they pick up. The buyers thus avoid incurring repeated small charges that can depress earnings for years.[6]

In March 1999 the FASB indicated its intention to require that in-process R&D acquired after some implementation date should be recorded as an asset and amortized over the period of expected benefit. In July 1999, however, the Board decided that it was not feasible to address purchased in-process R&D costs separately from other R&D costs. See Appendix A to Chapter 2.

Case 1: Acquisition Cost in Excess of Fair Value of Identifiable Net Assets of a Subsidiary

To illustrate the allocation of the difference between cost and book value to individual assets and liabilities of a subsidiary, assume that on January 1, 2001, S Company has capital stock and retained earnings of $1,500,000 and $500,000, respectively, and identifiable assets and liabilities as presented in Illustration 5-1.

ILLUSTRATION 5-1

Identifiable Assets and Liabilities of S Company—January 1, 2001

	Fair Value	Book Value	Difference Between Fair Value and Book Value
Inventory	$ 350,000	$ 300,000	$ 50,000
Other Current Assets	450,000	450,000	—0—
Equipment (net)	600,000	300,000	300,000
Land	400,000	250,000	150,000
Other Noncurrent Assets	1,000,000	1,000,000	—0—
Liabilities	(300,000)	(300,000)	—0—
Identifiable Net Assets	$2,500,000	$2,000,000	$500,000

[6] *WSJ*, "High-Tech Firms Upset Over SEC Crackdown," by Michael Schroeder, 2/1/99, p. B4.

Adjustment of Assets and Liabilities: Wholly Owned Subsidiaries Assume further that P Company acquires a 100% interest in S Company on January 1, 2001, for $2,750,000. The Computation and Allocation Schedule would appear as follows:

Computation and Allocation of Difference Between Cost and Book Value

Cost of Investment (purchase price)	$2,750,000
Book Value of Equity Acquired	
($2,000,000 × 100%)	2,000,000
Difference Between Cost and Book Value	750,000
Adjust inventory upward (assume FIFO)	(50,000)
Adjust equipment upward (with remaining life of 10 years)	(300,000)
Adjust land upward	(150,000)
Balance	250,000
Record goodwill (amortized over 20-year estimated life)	(250,000)
Balance	$ 0

The consolidated statements workpaper entry to eliminate the investment balance on January 1, 2001, will result in a debit to the difference between cost and book value in the amount of $750,000 as follows:

Capital Stock—S Company	1,500,000	
Retained Earnings—S Company	500,000	
Difference Between Cost and Book Value	750,000	
Investment in S Company		2,750,000

Referring to the Computation and Allocation Schedule, the workpaper entry to allocate the difference between cost and book value to specific consolidated assets takes the following form:

Inventory	50,000	
Equipment (net)	300,000	
Land	150,000	
Goodwill	250,000	
Difference Between Cost and Book Value		750,000

The amount of the difference between cost and book value that is not allocated to specific identifiable assets and liabilities of the subsidiary is recognized as goodwill. As defined earlier, goodwill is the excess of acquisition cost over the parent company's equity in the *fair value* of the identifiable net assets of the subsidiary on the acquisition date [$2,750,000 − 100%($2,500,000) = $250,000].

Adjustment of Assets and Liabilities: Less Than Wholly Owned Subsidiaries When P Company exchanges $2,750,000 for a 100% interest in S Company, the implication is that the fair value of the net assets, including unspecified intangible assets, of S Company is $2,750,000. As illustrated above, if the recorded book value of those net assets is $2,000,000, adjustments totaling $750,000 are made to specific assets and liabilities, including goodwill, in the consolidated financial statements, serving to recognize the total implied fair value of the subsidiary assets and liabilities.

Assume now that rather than acquiring a 100% interest for $2,750,000, P Company pays $2,200,000 for an 80% interest in S Company. The fair value of the net assets, including unspecified intangible assets, of S Company implied by this trans-

ILLUSTRATION 5–2

Computation and Allocation of the Difference Between Cost and Book Value

Cost of Investment (Purchase Price)		$2,200,000
Book Value of Equity Acquired (.8)(2,000,000)		1,600,000
Difference Between Cost and Book Value		$ 600,000
Less Increase to Fair Value (by proportion owned)		
Inventory (.80 × $50,000), FIFO Method	$(40,000)	
Equipment—net (.80 × $300,000), 10-year life	(240,000)	
Land (.80 × $150,000)	(120,000)	(400,000)
Balance (Excess of Cost Over Fair Value)		$ 200,000
Goodwill, estimated 20-year life		(200,000)
Balance		$0

action is still $2,750,000 ($2,200,000/.80), and the implication remains that the net assets, including unspecified intangible assets, of S Company are understated by $750,000. In the case of a less than wholly owned subsidiary, however, current practice restricts the write-up of the net assets of S Company in the consolidated financial statements to the **amount actually paid by P Company in excess of the book value of the interest it acquires**, or $600,000 [$2,200,000 − .80($2,000,000) = $600,000].

Thus, consolidated net assets are *written up only by an amount equal to the parent company's share* of the difference on the date of acquisition between the implied fair value and the book value of the subsidiary company's net assets (.80 × $750,000 = $600,000). As before, any remaining amount is allocated to goodwill.

> In the event of a bargain purchase in the case where a noncontrolling interest exists, the bargain purchase rules are modified only slightly, as follows:
> 1. Any previously recorded goodwill on the seller's books is eliminated except for the noncontrolling interest, which remains on the books.
> 2. A deferred credit (negative goodwill) is recorded only in the event that all long-lived assets (other than investments) are reduced to the noncontrolling interest (rather than to zero), in which case the credit is amortized (to income) over a period not to exceed 40 years.

To illustrate the existence of a noncontrolling interest in the context of, first, a *positive* difference between cost and book value and, later, a *negative* difference, refer again to Illustration 5-1.

Assume first that P Company acquires an 80% interest in S Company for $2,200,000. The Computation and Allocation Schedule is prepared in Illustration 5-2. In this case, goodwill is equal to the excess of acquisition cost over the parent company's equity in the fair value of the identifiable net assets of the subsidiary [$2,200,000 − .80($2,500,000) = $200,000]. The following entries to eliminate the investment and to allocate the difference between cost and book value are workpaper-only entries:

Retained Earnings—S Company (.80)($500,000)	400,000	
Capital Stock—S Company (.80)($1,500,000)	1,200,000	
Difference Between Cost and Book Value	600,000	
Investment in S Company		2,200,000

Referring to the Computation and Allocation Schedule, the workpaper entry to allocate the difference between cost and book value is:

Inventory	40,000
Equipment (net)	240,000
Land	120,000
Goodwill	200,000
Difference Between Cost and Book Value	600,000

Case 2: Acquisition Cost Less Than Fair Value of Identifiable Net Assets of a Subsidiary

Less than Wholly Owned Subsidiaries Refer to Illustration 5-1 and assume that P Company acquires an 80% interest in S Company for $1,900,000. The difference between cost and **book value** is $300,000 [$1,900,000 − .80($2,000,000)]. However, the parent company's interest in the **fair value** of the identifiable net assets of the subsidiary [.80($2,500,000) = $2,000,000] exceeds acquisition cost by $100,000. The Computation and Allocation Schedule is started as usual, but a negative balance requires a subsequent reduction to the adjusted values of long-lived assets.

Computation and Allocation of Difference Between Cost and Book Value of Equity

Cost of Investment (Purchase Price)		$1,900,000
Book Value of Equity Acquired		
($2,000,000 × 80%)		1,600,000
Difference Between Cost and Book Value		300,000
Increase to fair value (by proportion owned):		
Inventory (.80 × $50,000)	(40,000)	
Equipment (.80 × $300,000)	(240,000)	
Land (.80 × $150,000)	(120,000)	(400,000)
Balance (Excess of Fair Value over Cost)		(100,000)
Decrease (in proportion to fair values):		
Equipment (6/20 × $100,000)		30,000
Land (4/20 × $100,000)		20,000
Other Noncurrent Assets (10/20 × $100,000)		50,000
Balance		$ 0

Note that the reduction of the assets below their adjusted values is recorded in proportion to their *fair values,* not book values. For example, the total fair value of equipment, land, and other noncurrent assets equals $2,000,000. Since the fair value of equipment is $600,000, the value of equipment is reduced by ($600,000/$2,000,000) or 6/20 times $100,000. Note, also, that the reduction does *not* affect current assets (e.g., inventory) and that it does affect *all* long-lived assets regardless of whether the asset required an initial adjustment (e.g., other noncurrent assets). Note, finally, that the amounts in parentheses in the Computation and Allocation Schedule require debits in the workpaper entry (to increase assets/decrease liabilities).

The amounts of the entries to the various asset accounts are obtained by netting any increase and/or decrease recorded in the Computation and Allocation Schedule as follows:

Account	Increase	Decrease	Net Increase (Decrease)
Inventory	$ 40,000	0	$ 40,000
Equipment	240,000	30,000	210,000
Land	120,000	20,000	100,000
Other Noncurrent	0	50,000	(50,000)
Total	$400,000	$100,000	$300,000

The workpaper entries to eliminate the investment account and to allocate the difference between cost and book value may be summarized in general journal form as follows:

Retained Earnings—S Company	400,000	
Capital Stock—S Company	1,200,000	
Difference Between Cost and Book Value	300,000	
Investment in S Company		1,900,000
Inventory	40,000	
Equipment (net)	210,000	
Land	100,000	
Other Noncurrent Assets		50,000
Difference Between Cost and Book Value		300,000

[handwritten margin note: If purchase price is lower than book value, same procedure as above mentioned]

Cost Less Than Book Value and Less Than Fair Value of Identifiable Net Assets

It is possible for acquisition cost to be less than the parent company's interest in the book value as well as in the fair value of the net assets of the subsidiary. In that case, the difference between cost and book value initially will be credited in the investment elimination workpaper entry. The analysis of the allocation of this credit balance, however, takes the same form as that just illustrated; that is, we begin by adjusting assets upward first and then determine the necessary decreases subsequently. For example, refer to Illustration 5-1 and assume that P Company acquired an 80% interest in S Company on January 1, 2001, for $1,500,000. (See Illustration 5-3.)

ILLUSTRATION 5–3

Final Allocation of Difference Between Cost and Book Value
Book Value of Interest Acquired Exceeds Cost

Cost of Investment (purchase price)	$1,500,000
Book Value of Equity (.8)($2,000,000)	1,600,000
Difference Between Cost and Book Value	(100,000)

Initial Assignment (Increase to fair value):	*(fair value − book value)(percent purchased)*
Inventory	$ (40,000) = (350,000 − 300,000).8
Equipment (net)	(240,000) = (600,000 − 300,000).8
Land	(120,000) = (400,000 − 250,000).8
Other Noncurrent Assets	—0— = (1,000,000 − 1,000,000).8
Excess of Fair Value Over Cost	(500,000)

Decrease (by proportion of fair value):		*Fair Values*	*Total Fair Value*	*Proportion of Fair Value*
Equipment (6/20)(500,000)	150,000	600,000	2,000,000	6/20
Land (4/20)(500,000)	100,000	400,000	2,000,000	4/20
Other Noncurrent Assets (10/20)(500,000)	250,000	1,000,000	2,000,000	10/20
		2,000,000		
Balance	0			

	Initial Allocation Increase	*Proportional Decrease*	*Net Amount Allocated*
Inventory	$ 40,000		$ 40,000
Equipment (net)	240,000	150,000	90,000
Land	120,000	100,000	20,000
Other Noncurrent Assets	—0—	250,000	(250,000)
Net Adjustment Needed			(100,000)

Computation and Allocation of Difference Between Cost and Book Value of Equity

Cost of Investment (Purchase Price)		$1,500,000
Book Value of Equity Acquired		
($2,000,000 × 80%)		1,600,000
Difference Between Cost and Book Value		(100,000)
Increase to fair value (by proportion owned):		
Inventory (.80 × $50,000)	(40,000)	
Equipment (.80 × $300,000)	(240,000)	
Land (.80 × $150,000)	(120,000)	(400,000)
Balance (Excess of Fair Value over Cost)		(500,000)
Decrease (in proportion to fair values):		
Equipment (6/20 × $500,000)		150,000
Land (4/20 × $500,000)		100,000
Other Noncurrent Assets (10/20 × $500,000)		250,000
Balance		0

Netting the increases against the decreases in the various accounts yields the amounts needed in the journal entry, as shown below:

Account	Increase	Decrease	Net Increase (Decrease)
Inventory	$ 40,000	0	$ 40,000
Equipment	240,000	150,000	90,000
Land	120,000	100,000	20,000
Other Noncurrent	0	250,000	(250,000)
Total	$400,000	$500,000	($100,000)

The workpaper entries to eliminate the investment account and to allocate the difference between cost and book value are presented below in general journal form:

Capital Stock—S Company	1,200,000	
Retained Earnings—S Company	400,000	
Difference Between Cost and Book Value		100,000
Investment in S Company		1,500,000
Difference Between Cost and Book Value	100,000	
Inventory	40,000	
Equipment (net)	90,000	
Land	20,000	
Other Noncurrent Assets		250,000

EFFECT OF ALLOCATION, AMORTIZATION, AND DEPRECIATION OF DIFFERENCE BETWEEN COST AND BOOK VALUE ON CONSOLIDATED NET INCOME: SUBSEQUENT TO ACQUISITION

Depreciation and amortization in the consolidated income statement should be based on the values allocated to depreciable and amortizable assets in the consolidated balance sheet. When any portion of the difference between cost and book value is allocated to such assets, recorded income must be adjusted in determining consolidated net income in current and future periods. *This adjustment is needed to reflect the difference between the amount of amortization and depreciation recorded by the subsidiary and the appropriate amount based on consolidated carrying values.*

To illustrate, assume that on January 1, 2001, P Company acquires an 80% interest in S Company for $2,200,000, at which time S Company has net assets of $2,000,000 as presented in Illustration 5-1. As previously shown in Illustration 5-2, the difference between cost and book value in the amount of $600,000 is allocated as follows:

Inventory	$ 40,000
Equipment (net)	240,000
Land	120,000
Goodwill	200,000
Difference Between Cost and Book Value	$600,000

A comparison of the recorded and consolidated carrying values of the assets and liabilities of S Company on January 1, 2001, is presented in Illustration 5-4.

ILLUSTRATION 5–4

Comparison of Consolidated and Recorded Carrying Values of Net Assets of S Company
January 1, 2001

	Carrying Value in S Company's Books (Illustration 5–1)	Allocation of Difference Between Cost and Book Value	Consolidated Carrying Value
Inventory	$ 300,000	$ 40,000	$ 340,000
Equipment (net)	300,000	240,000	540,000
Land	250,000	120,000	370,000
Goodwill (excess of cost over fair values)	—0—	200,000	200,000
Other Assets and Liabilities (net)	1,150,000	—0—	1,150,000
Net Assets	$2,000,000	$600,000	$2,600,000

Assume now that all the inventory is sold during 2001, that the equipment has a remaining life of 10 years from January 1, 2001, and that management determines that the goodwill should be amortized over 20 years. Adjustments in the computation of consolidated net income that result from the allocation, amortization, and depreciation of the difference between cost and book value are summarized in Illustration 5-5.

As a result of the sale of the inventory in 2001, S Company will include $300,000 in cost of goods sold, whereas from a consolidated point of view the cost of goods sold should be $340,000 (inventory from Illustration 5-4). Hence, recorded cost of goods sold must be increased by $40,000 in determining consolidated net income in 2001. This adjustment is necessary only in the year(s) the inventory is sold.

ILLUSTRATION 5–5

Adjustments in Determination of Consolidated Net Income
Resulting from Allocation, Amortization, and Depreciation
of Difference Between Cost and Book Value

	Difference Between Cost and Book Value	Annual Adjustment in Determining Consolidated Net Income		
		2001	2002–2010	2011–2020
Inventory	$ 40,000	$40,000	$ —0—	$ —0—
Equipment (net)	240,000	24,000	24,000	—0—
Land	120,000	—0—	—0—	—0—
Goodwill	200,000	10,000	10,000	10,000
Total	$600,000	$74,000	$34,000	$10,000

Note: Inventory is expensed in 2001 assuming the FIFO method, equipment is depreciated over 10 years, and the assumed useful life of the goodwill is 20 years.

S Company will record on its books $30,000 ($300,000/10 years) in depreciation of the equipment each year. Consolidated annual depreciation, however, should be $54,000 ($540,000/10 years). Accordingly, depreciation expense must be increased each year by $24,000 in determining consolidated net income. Note that this amount may be computed directly from the Computation and Allocation Schedule simply by dividing the adjustment to Equipment ($240,000) by the remaining life (10 years).

Similarly, amortization of the goodwill arising in the acquisition is not recorded by S Company. From a consolidated point of view, however, $10,000 should be amortized each year. Thus, recorded amortization expense must be increased by $10,000 each year for the estimated useful life of the goodwill of 20 years in determining consolidated net income. The allocation of a portion of the difference between cost and book value to land does not require an adjustment to recorded income in determining consolidated net income, since land is not a depreciable (or amortizable) asset.

The workpaper entries needed to ensure that all balance sheet and income statement accounts reflect the correct consolidated balances differ depending on which method the parent company uses to account for its investment: complete equity, partial equity, or cost. The correct consolidated balances will not differ, only the means of arriving at them. Thus, after the workpaper entries are made, the resulting balances should be identical under the three methods.

Much of the consolidating process is the same for all three methods, but im-

FIGURE 5–1
Cost Method
Three-Year Summary

Entries on P's Books

	Year 2001		Year 2002		Year 2003	
Investment in S	2,200,000					
Cash		2,200,000				
Cash	16,000		48,000		60,000	
Dividend Income		16,000		48,000		60,000

Entries on the Workpaper

	Year 2001		Year 2002		Year 2003	
Dividend Income	16,000		48,000		60,000	
Dividends Declared		16,000		48,000		60,000
Investment in S			84,000		148,000	
Beginning Retained Earnings—P				84,000		148,000
Beginning Retained Earnings—S	400,000		484,000		548,000	
Common Stock—S	1,200,000		1,200,000		1,200,000	
Difference Between Cost and Book Value	600,000		600,000		600,000	
Investment in S		2,200,000		2,284,000		2,348,000
Cost of Goods Sold	40,000					
Beginning Retained Earnings			40,000		40,000	
Equipment	240,000		240,000		240,000	
Land	120,000		120,000		120,000	
Goodwill	200,000		200,000		200,000	
Difference Between Cost and Book Value		600,000		600,000		600,000
Beginning Retained Earnings—P	—		24,000		48,000	
Depreciation Expense	24,000		24,000		24,000	
Equipment (net)		24,000		48,000		72,000
Beginning Retained Earnings—P	—		10,000		20,000	
Amortization Expense—Goodwill	10,000		10,000		10,000	
Goodwill		10,000		20,000		30,000

portant differences exist. Each of the following stand-alone sections presents the entire process. For those who are interested in focusing on only one or two of the three methods, the other sections may be omitted without loss of continuity. First, though, it is worth nothing that there are only three basic accounts that are reported differently in the books of the parent. A brief review of the entries made by the parent under the three methods (see opening of Chapter 3) reveals two of these accounts: the investment account itself and the income recognized from the subsidiary (dividend income or equity in subsidiary income). Since the amount of income recognized from the subsidiary is added into retained earnings of the parent each year, it follows that the third important account that differs among these methods is retained earnings of the parent.

Under all three methods, the workpaper entries will separate current year effects from the effects of the previous years because the current year income statement accounts are open and need to be reported separately and correctly. Hence workpaper entries to retained earnings will always adjust the balance at the *beginning* of the current year (or the date of acquisition, if it is the first year) under the cost and partial equity methods. Under the complete equity method, beginning retained earnings of the parent is the same as beginning consolidated retained earnings and hence needs no adjustment. Figures 5-1 through 5-3 present three years of entries

FIGURE 5–2
Partial Equity Method
Three-Year Summary

Entries on P's Books

	Year 2001		Year 2002		Year 2003	
Investment in S	2,200,000					
Cash		2,200,000				
Cash	16,000		48,000		60,000	
Investment in S		16,000		48,000		60,000
Investment in S	100,000		112,000		160,000	
Equity in S Income		100,000		112,000		160,000

Entries on the Workpaper

	Year 2001		Year 2002		Year 2003	
Investment in S	16,000		48,000		60,000	
Dividends Declared		16,000		48,000		60,000
Equity in S Income	100,000		112,000		160,000	
Investment in S		100,000		112,000		160,000
Beginning Retained Earnings—S	400,000		484,000		548,000	
Common Stock—S	1,200,000		1,200,000		1,200,000	
Difference Between Cost and Book Value	600,000		600,000		600,000	
Investment in S		2,200,000		2,284,000		2,348,000
Cost of Goods Sold	40,000					
Beginning Retained Earnings			40,000		40,000	
Equipment	240,000		240,000		240,000	
Land	120,000		120,000		120,000	
Goodwill	200,000		200,000		200,000	
Difference Between Cost and Book Value		600,000		600,000		600,000
Beginning Retained Earnings—P	—		24,000		48,000	
Depreciation Expense	24,000		24,000		24,000	
Equipment (net)		24,000		48,000		72,000
Beginning Retained Earnings—P	—		10,000		20,000	
Amortization Expense—Goodwill	10,000		10,000		10,000	
Goodwill		10,000		20,000		30,000

FIGURE 5–3
Complete Equity Method
Three-Year Summary

Entries on P's Books

	Year 2001		Year 2002		Year 2003	
Investment in S	2,200,000					
Cash		2,200,000				
Cash	16,000		48,000		60,000	
Investment in S		16,000		48,000		60,000
Investment in S	100,000		112,000		160,000	
Equity in S Income		100,000		112,000		160,000
Equity in S	74,000		34,000		34,000	
Investment in S		74,000		34,000		34,000

Entries on the Workpaper

	Year 2001		Year 2002		Year 2003	
Investment in S	16,000		48,000		60,000	
Dividends Declared		16,000		48,000		60,000
Equity in S Income	26,000		78,000		126,000	
Investment in S		26,000		78,000		126,000
Beginning Retained Earnings—S	400,000		484,000		548,000	
Common Stock—S	1,200,000		1,200,000		1,200,000	
Difference Between Cost and Book Value	600,000		600,000		600,000	
Investment in S		2,200,000		2,284,000		2,348,000
Cost of Goods Sold	40,000					
Investment in S			40,000		40,000	
Equipment	240,000		240,000		240,000	
Land	120,000		120,000		120,000	
Goodwill	200,000		200,000		200,000	
Difference Between Cost and Book Value		600,000		600,000		600,000
Investment in S	—		24,000		48,000	
Depreciation Expense	24,000		24,000		24,000	
Equipment (net)		24,000		48,000		72,000
Investment in S	—		10,000		20,000	
Amortization Expense—Goodwill	10,000		10,000		10,000	
Goodwill		10,000		20,000		30,000

for a parent company and for a consolidating workpaper under all three methods. In the following sections, we explain these entries in detail.

CONSOLIDATED STATEMENTS WORKPAPER—INVESTMENT RECORDED USING COST METHOD

In the preparation of consolidated financial statements, the recorded balances of individual assets, liabilities, and expense accounts must be adjusted to reflect the allocation, depreciation, and amortization of the difference between cost and book value. These adjustments are accomplished through the use of *workpaper entries* in the preparation of the consolidated statements workpaper.

To illustrate, assume the following:

Cost

1. P Company acquires an 80% interest in S Company on January 1, 2001, for $2,200,000, at which time S Company has capital stock of $1,500,000 and re-

tained earnings of $500,000. P Company uses the cost method to record its investment in S Company.

2. The allocation, amortization, and depreciation of the difference between cost and book value in the amount of $600,000 [$2,200,000 − .80($2,000,000)], as previously presented in Illustration 5-5, includes $40,000 to Inventory, $240,000 to Equipment (10 year life), $120,000 to Land, and $200,000 to Goodwill (20 year life).

3. In 2001, S Company reported net income of $125,000 and declared and paid dividends of $20,000.

4. In 2002, S Company reported net income of $140,000 and declared and paid dividends of $60,000.

5. In 2003, S Company reported net income of $200,000 and declared and paid dividends of $75,000.

Year of Acquisition

Entries on Books of P Company—2001 (Year of Acquisition) Entries recorded on the books of P Company under the cost method to reflect the purchase of its interest in S Company and the receipt of dividends in 2001 are as follows:

Investment in S Company	2,200,000	
Cash		2,200,000
To record purchase of an 80% interest in S Company.		
Cash	16,000	
Dividend Income		16,000
To record receipt of dividends from S Company (.80 × $20,000).		

Workpaper Entries—2001 (Year of Acquisition) The consolidated statements workpaper for the year ended December 31, 2001, is presented in Illustration 5-6. An analysis of the workpaper elimination entries in Illustration 5-6 is presented here:

(1)	Dividend Income	16,000	
	Dividends Declared		16,000
	To eliminate intercompany dividends.		

(2)	Beginning Retained Earnings—S Company (.80 × $500,000)	400,000	
	Capital Stock—S Company (.80 × $1,500,000)	1,200,000	
	Difference Between Cost and Book Value	600,000	
	Investment in S Company		2,200,000
	To eliminate the investment account against the equity accounts of S Company using equity balances at the *beginning of the current year*.		

It's sold in 2001

(3a)	Cost of Goods Sold (Beginning Inventory)	40,000	
	Equipment (net) (10-year remaining life)	240,000	
	Land	120,000	
	Goodwill (20-year useful life)	200,000	
	Difference Between Cost and Book Value		600,000
	To allocate the amount of difference between cost and book value at date of acquisition to specific assets and liabilities (see Illustration 5-2).		

By the end of the first year, under a FIFO (first-in, first-out) cost flow assumption, the inventory that necessitated the $40,000 adjustment would have been sold. Recall that at the date of acquisition, this adjustment was to Inventory. At the end

Cost

Cost Method

80% Owned Subsidiary

Year of Acquisition

ILLUSTRATION 5–6

Consolidated Statements Workpaper

P Company and Subsidiary

For Year Ended December 31, 2001

Income Statement	P Company	S Company	Eliminations Dr.	Eliminations Cr.	Noncontrolling Interest	Consolidated Balances
Sales	3,100,000	2,200,000				5,300,000
Dividend Income	16,000		(1) 16,000			
Total Revenue	3,116,000	2,200,000				5,300,000
Cost of Goods Sold	1,700,000	1,360,000	(3a) 40,000			3,100,000
Depreciation—Equipment	120,000	30,000	(3b) 24,000			174,000
Amortization of Goodwill			(3c) 10,000			10,000
Other Expenses	998,000	685,000				1,683,000
Total Cost and Expense	2,818,000	2,075,000				4,967,000
Net/Combined Income	298,000	125,000				333,000
Noncontrolling Interest in Income					25,000	(25,000)*
Net Income to Retained Earnings	298,000	125,000	90,000	—0—	25,000	308,000
Retained Earnings Statement						
1/1 Retained Earnings						
P Company	1,650,000					1,650,000
S Company		500,000	(2) 400,000		100,000	
Net Income from above	298,000	125,000	90,000	—0—	25,000	308,000
Dividends Declared						
P Company	(150,000)					(150,000)
S Company		(20,000)		(1) 16,000	(4,000)	
12/31 Retained Earnings to Balance Sheet	1,798,000	605,000	490,000	16,000	121,000	1,808,000
Balance Sheet						
Investment in S Company	2,200,000			(2) 2,200,000		
Difference Between Cost and Book Value			(2) 600,000	(3a) 600,000		
Land	1,250,000	250,000	(3a) 120,000			1,620,000
Equipment (net)	1,080,000	270,000	(3a) 240,000	(3b) 24,000		1,566,000
Other Assets (net)	2,402,000	1,885,000				4,287,000
Goodwill (Excess of Cost over Fair Value)			(3a) 200,000	(3c) 10,000		190,000
Total Assets	6,932,000	2,405,000				7,663,000
Liabilities	2,134,000	300,000				2,434,000
Capital Stock						
P Company	3,000,000					3,000,000
S Company		1,500,000	(2) 1,200,000		300,000	
Retained Earnings from above	1,798,000	605,000	490,000	16,000	121,000	1,808,000
Noncontrolling Interest in Net Assets					421,000	421,000
Total Liabilities and Equity	6,932,000	2,405,000	2,850,000	2,850,000		7,663,000

*.20 × $125,000 = $25,000.

(1) To eliminate intercompany dividends

(2) To eliminate investment account.

(3a) To allocate differences between cost and book value.

(3b) To depreciate the difference between cost and book value allocated to equipment (240,000/10)

(3c) To amortize the amount of goodwill recognized in the acquisition (200,000/20 yrs).

of the first year, however, the entry is to Cost of Goods Sold (or to Beginning Inventory, as a subcomponent of the Cost of Goods Sold). Since S Company will not have included the additional $40,000 allocated to inventory in its reported Cost of Goods Sold (COGS), consolidated Cost of Goods Sold must be increased by this workpaper entry. If the inventory were still on hand on December 31, 2001 (for example, if a LIFO flow were assumed), the $40,000 would be allocated to ending inventory in the balance sheet rather than to Cost of Goods Sold.

This entry to Cost of Goods Sold is appropriate only in the year of acquisition. In subsequent years, consolidated COGS will have been reflected in the 2001 consolidated net income and hence consolidated retained earnings at the end of 2001. Thus, the adjustment ($40,000 debit) in future years will be to Beginning Retained Earnings—P Company.

(3b)	Depreciation Expense ($240,000/10 years)	24,000	
	Equipment (net)[7]		24,000
	To depreciate the amount of difference between cost and book value allocated to equipment (see Illustration 5-5).		

As previously noted, depreciation in the consolidated income statement should be based on the value assigned to the equipment in the consolidated balance sheet. Since the depreciation recorded by S Company is based on the book value of the equipment on its records, consolidated depreciation must be increased by a workpaper entry.

(3c)	Amortization of Goodwill ($200,000/20 years)	10,000	
	Goodwill		10,000
	To amortize the amount of goodwill recognized in the acquisition (see Illustration 5-5).		

The amount of the difference between cost and book value not allocated to specific identifiable assets or liabilities is treated in the consolidated financial statements as goodwill and must be amortized (the straight-line method is recommended) over an appropriate period not to exceed 40 years.[8] Again, since it is not recognized on the records of S Company, no amortization of this asset is included in its income statement. Accordingly, a workpaper entry is necessary to recognize the annual charge to expense in the consolidated income statement.

It is possible, of course, to combine the workpaper entries relating to the allocation, amortization, and depreciation of the difference between cost and book value into one entry. In Illustration 5-6, for example, workpaper entries (3a), (3b), and (3c) could be presented in one combined entry as follows:

Cost

(3)	Cost of Goods Sold (Beginning Inventory)	40,000	
	Depreciation Expense	24,000	
	Amortization of Goodwill	10,000	
	Equipment (net) ($240,000 − $24,000)	216,000	
	Land	120,000	
	Goodwill ($200,000 − $10,000)	190,000	
	Difference Between Cost and Book Value		600,000

---

[7]The credit to this entry could alternatively be accumulated depreciation.

[8]Although goodwill must be amortized under current GAAP over a maximum life of 40 years (*APB Opinion No. 17*), the FASB has proposed shortening the maximum life to 20 years, as discussed in Appendix A to Chapter 2.

In Illustration 5-6, the calculation of noncontrolling interest is not affected by the amortization/depreciation of the differences between cost and book value. Since the differences between cost and book value represent a cost incurred by the parent company in the purchase of the subsidiary stock, its amortization is charged in its entirety to the parent company (controlling stockholders) under current generally accepted accounting principles (GAAP).

Year Subsequent to Acquisition

Entries on Books of P Company—2002 (Year Subsequent to Acquisition) In 2002, P Company will record dividend income as follows:

Cash	48,000	
Dividend Income		48,000
To record receipt of dividends from S Company (.8 × $60,000).		

Under the cost method, the parent company makes no entry for the reported income of the subsidiary.

Workpaper Entries—2002 (Year Subsequent to Acquisition) The consolidated statements workpaper for the year ended December 31, 2002 is presented in Illustration 5-7. Workpaper elimination entries in Illustration 5-7 are presented in general journal form as follows:

(1)	Investment in S Company	84,000	
	Beginning Retained Earnings—P Company		84,000
	To convert to equity/establish reciprocity as of 1/1/02		
	[($605,000 − $500,000) × .80)].		

This entry represents the change in retained earnings of S Company from the date of acquisition to the beginning of the current year. This also converts retained earnings to the value that would have been recorded if the partial equity method had been used.

(2)	Dividend Income	48,000	
	Dividends Declared		48,000
	To eliminate the intercompany dividends.		

(3)	Beginning Retained Earnings—S Company		
	(.80 × $605,000)	484,000	
	Capital Stock—S Company (.80 × $1,500,000)	1,200,000	
	Difference Between Cost and Book Value	600,000	
	Investment in S Company ($2,200,000 + $84,000)		2,284,000
	To eliminate the investment account against the equity accounts of S Company		
	using equity balances at the **beginning** of the current year.		

In the investment elimination entry, the amount debited or credited to the Difference Between Cost and Book Value may be treated as a plug figure to balance the entry and is equal to the amount of the difference between cost and book value on the date of acquisition. The amount does not change subsequent to acquisition and may be obtained from the Computation and Allocation Schedule (Illustration 5-2).

Cost Method			ILLUSTRATION 5–7			
80% Owned Subsidiary			Consolidated Statements Workpaper			
Subsequent to			P Company and Subsidiary			
Year of Acquisition			For Year Ended December 31, 2002			

	P	S	Eliminations		Noncontrolling	Consolidated
Income Statement	Company	Company	Dr.	Cr.	Interest	Balances
Sales	3,534,000	2,020,000				5,554,000
Dividend Income	48,000		(2) 48,000			
Total Revenue	3,582,000	2,020,000				5,554,000
Cost of Goods Sold	2,040,000	1,200,000				3,240,000
Depreciation—Equipment	120,000	30,000	(4b) 24,000			174,000
Amortization of Goodwill			(4c) 10,000			10,000
Other Expenses	993,000	650,000				1,643,000
Total Cost and Expense	3,153,000	1,880,000				5,067,000
Net/Combined Income	429,000	140,000				487,000
Noncontrolling Interest in Income					28,000	(28,000)*
Net Income to Retained Earnings	429,000	140,000	82,000	—0—	28,000	459,000
Retained Earnings Statement						
1/1 Retained Earnings						
P Company	1,798,000		(4a) 40,000 (4b) 24,000 (4c) 10,000	(1) 84,000		1,808,000
S Company		605,000	(3) 484,000		121,000	
Net Income from above	429,000	140,000	82,000	—0—	28,000	459,000
Dividends Declared						
P Company	(150,000)					(150,000)
S Company		(60,000)		(2) 48,000	(12,000)	
12/31 Retained Earnings to Balance Sheet	2,077,000	685,000	640,000	132,000	137,000	2,117,000
Balance Sheet						
Investment in S Company	2,200,000		(1) 84,000	(3) 2,284,000		
Difference Between Cost and Book Value			(3) 600,000	(4a) 600,000		
Land	2,000,000	250,000	(4a) 120,000			2,370,000
Equipment (net)	960,000	240,000	(4a) 240,000	(4b) 48,000		1,392,000
Other Assets (net)	2,137,000	2,200,000				4,337,000
Goodwill (Excess of Cost over Fair Value)			(4a) 200,000	(4c) 20,000		180,000
Total Assets	7,297,000	2,690,000				8,279,000
Liabilities	2,220,000	505,000				2,725,000
Capital Stock						
P Company	3,000,000					3,000,000
S Company		1,500,000	(3) 1,200,000		300,000	
Retained Earnings from above	2,077,000	685,000	640,000	132,000	137,000	2,117,000
Noncontrolling Interest in Net Assets					437,000	437,000
Total Liabilities and Equity	7,297,000	2,690,000	3,084,000	3,084,000		8,279,000

*.20 × $140,000 = $28,000.

(1) To establish reciprocity/convert to equity as of 1/1/02 [.80 × ($605,000 − $500,000)].

(2) To eliminate intercompany dividends.

(3) To eliminate investment account.

(4a) To allocate the difference between cost and book value at the date of acquisition to specific assets and liabilities.

(4b) To depreciate the amount of the difference between cost and book value allocated to equipment for the current and previous year(s).

(4c) To amortize goodwill for the current and previous year(s).

Handwritten annotations:
- Retained Earnings Statement: $1,798,000 − 48,000 + 140,000 × 80\% − 34,000 = 439,000$
- same as is on page 206
- Balance Sheet: $2,077,000 + (685,000 − 500,000) \times 80\% − 74,000 − 34,000 = 2,117,000$
- $(2,690,000 − 505,000) \times 20\% = 437,000$

Workpaper entry (4) is presented next, first in a combined single entry and then (alternatively) in its components. The authors find the second approach (components) easier to understand, though less space efficient.

(4)	Beginning Retained Earnings—P Company		
	(Beginning Consolidated Retained Earnings)		
	(40,000 + 24,000 + 10,000)	74,000	
	Depreciation Expense ($240,000/10)	24,000	
	Amotization Expense Goodwill ($200,000/20)	10,000	
	Equipment (net) ($240,000 − $24,000 − $24,000)	192,000	
	Land	120,000	
	Goodwill ($200,000 − $10,000 − $10,000)	180,000	
	Difference Between Cost and Book Value		600,000
	To allocate, amortize, and depreciate the difference between cost and book value.		

Beginning consolidated retained earnings must be adjusted each year for the cumulative amount of depreciation, amortization, and other deductions that have been made from consolidated net income because of the amortization and depreciation of the difference between cost and book value in the consolidated statements workpapers of prior years. By reducing previously reported consolidated net income, these workpaper adjustments also reduce previously reported consolidated retained earnings. The reduction of beginning consolidated retained earnings is accomplished by a debit to the beginning retained earnings of the parent company in the consolidated statements workpaper. The $74,000 debit to beginning retained earnings is equal to the $40,000 charged to cost of goods sold plus the $24,000 charged to depreciation expense plus the $10,000 charged to amortization of goodwill in the 2001 consolidated statements workpaper [see entry (3) in Illustration 5-6; see also Illustration 5-5]. Where part of the difference between cost and book value is allocated to depreciable or amortizable assets, the workpaper adjustment to the beginning retained earnings of the parent company will become progressively larger each year.

To separate the above entry into its more digestible components, begin with the allocation of the difference between cost and book value and then proceed to record excess depreciation and amortization, as follows:

(4a)	Beginning Retained Earnings—P Company		
	(previous year's cost of goods sold)	40,000	
	Equipment (net)	240,000	
	Land	120,000	
	Goodwill	200,000	
	Difference Between Cost and Book Value		600,000
	To allocate the amount of difference between cost and book value at date of acquisition to specific assets and liabilities (see Illustration 5-2).		

Entry (4a) is identical to that recorded in the preceding year, with the exception that the entry to Cost of Goods Sold is appropriate only in the year of acquisition. Thus, the adjustment in year 2 (and future years) is to Beginning Retained Earnings.

(4b)	Depreciation Expense (current year)	24,000	
	Beginning Retained Earnings—P Company		
	(previous year's depreciation expense)	24,000	
	Equipment (net)		48,000
	To depreciate the amount of difference between cost and book value allocated to equipment.		

This entry differs from the first year entry in that the excess depreciation from the year 2001 is now reflected in Beginning Retained Earnings—P Company. Although the adjustment to Equipment (net) was already made in the prior year workpaper for one year's depreciation adjustment, it was not posted to the books of S Company and hence must be made again. If the following year (2003) were being presented, the debit to Depreciation Expense would remain at 24,000, but the debit to Beginning Retained Earnings would be 48,000 to reflect two prior years of excess depreciation (and the credit to Net Equipment would total 72,000).

(4c)	Amortization of Goodwill (current year)	10,000	
	Beginning Retained Earnings—P Company		
	(previous year's amortization)	10,000	
	Goodwill		20,000
	To amortize goodwill for the current year and previous year(s).		

Cost

Once again this entry differs from the first year in that the amortization from the year 2001 is now reflected in Beginning Retained Earnings—P Company. As with excess depreciation, the adjustment to Goodwill was already made in the prior year's workpaper for one year's amortization expense, but it was not posted to the books of either company and hence must be made again. Clearly, if entries (4a) through (4c) are recorded separately, the combined entry (4) is not needed.

The amounts charged to expense each year were calculated in Illustration 5-5. Since inventory was sold in 2001, no part of the difference between cost and book value is allocated to inventory in the years after its sale. The amounts allocated to assets and liabilities are the unamortized amounts at the end of the year. Thus, the amounts allocated to amortizable or depreciable assets and liabilities in the balance sheet will become progressively smaller each year.

In the third year after acquisition (December 31, 2003) consolidated statements workpaper, for example, the workpaper elimination entry will be as follows (if combined into one entry):

Beginning Retained Earnings—P Company		
(Beginning Consolidated Retained Earnings)		
($74,000 + $34,000)	108,000	
Depreciation Expense ($240,000/10)	24,000	
Amortization Expense—Goodwill ($200,000/20)	10,000	
Equipment (net) ($240,000 − $24,000 − $24,000 − $24,000)	168,000	
Land	120,000	
Goodwill ($200,000 − $10,000 − $10,000 − $10,000)	170,000	
Difference Between Cost and Book Value		600,000

The debit to the beginning retained earnings of the parent company in 2003 ($74,000 + $34,000 = $108,000) is equal to the amount by which consolidated net income and consolidated retained earnings have been reduced because of the allocation, amortization, and depreciation of the difference between cost and book value in the 2001 ($40,000 + $24,000 + $10,000 = $74,000) and 2002 ($24,000 + $10,000 = $34,000) consolidated statements workpapers [see illustration 5-5; also see entries (3a), (3b), and (3c) in Illustration 5-6 and entries (4b) and (4c) in Illustration 5-7]. This entry can also be simplified by breaking it into its components.

Figure 5-1 on page 202 presents the entries in their separate components for all three years side by side for the cost method.

COST METHOD ANALYSIS OF CONTROLLING AND NON-CONTROLLING INTERESTS IN COMBINED INCOME AND RETAINED EARNINGS

In the preceding chapter, a t-account approach to the calculation of consolidated net income (or the controlling interest in combined income as well as the noncontrolling interest in combined income) was presented. This approach must now be refined to accommodate the effect of the allocation, amortization, and depreciation of the difference between cost and book value.

Consolidated net income is the parent company's income from its independent operations plus (minus) its share of reported subsidiary income (loss) plus or minus adjustments for the period relating to the amortization of the difference between cost and book value.

The calculation of *controlling and noncontrolling interests in combined income* for the year ended December 31, 2002, presented in Illustration 5-8 is based on Illustration 5-7. This, of course, is the same amount of consolidated net income as that calculated in the consolidated financial statements workpaper.

Consolidated retained earnings is the parent company's cost basis retained earnings plus (minus) the parent company's share of the increase (decrease) in reported subsidiary retained earnings from the date of acquisition to the current date plus or minus the cumulative effect of adjustments to date relating to the amortization of the difference between cost and book value.

The calculation of *consolidated retained earnings* on December 31, 2002, presented in Illustration 5-9 is based on Illustration 5-7. This is the same amount of consolidated retained earnings as that shown in the consolidated statements work-

ILLUSTRATION 5–8

Calculation of the Noncontrolling Interest in Combined Income—Cost Method
For Year Ended December 31, 2002

Noncontrolling Interest in Combined Income

	Net income reported by S Company	140,000
	Subsidiary Income included in Combined Income	140,000
	Noncontrolling Ownership percentage interest	20%
	Noncontrolling Interest in Combined Income	28,000

80%

Controlling Interest in Income

	P Company's net income from its independent operations ($429,000 reported net income less $48,000 dividend income from S Company included therein)	$381,000
	P Company's share of the reported income of S Company (.8 × $140,000)	112,000
Additional depreciation and amortization of the difference between cost and book value related to:		
Depreciation Expense ($240,000/10) 24,000		
Goodwill Amortization ($200,000/10) 10,000		
	Consolidated Net Income	$459,000

ILLUSTRATION 5–9

**Analytical Calculation of Consolidated Retained Earnings—Cost Method
December 31, 2002**

P Company's retained earnings on December 31, 2002			$2,077,000
P Company's share of the increase in S Company's retained earnings from date of acquisition to December 31, 2002 [.8 × ($685,000 − $500,000)]			148,000
Less cumulative effect to December 31, 2002, of the amortization of the difference between cost and book value:			

	2001	*2002*	
Inventory (to cost of goods sold)	$40,000	$—0—	
Depreciation from equipment	24,000	24,000	
Amortization of goodwill	10,000	10,000	
	74,000	34,000	(108,000)
Consolidated Retained Earnings on December 31, 2002			$2,117,000

paper presented in Illustration 5-7, and may be used as a means of checking the balance.

Alternatively, consolidated retained earnings can be computed by adding beginning consolidated retained earnings to consolidated net income and subtracting dividends declared by Company P.

Beginning Consolidated Retained Earnings	$1,808,000
Plus: Consolidated Net Income	459,000
Less: Dividends Declared by P Company	(150,000)
Ending Consolidated Retained Earnings	$2,117,000

CONSOLIDATED STATEMENTS WORKPAPER—INVESTMENT RECORDED USING PARTIAL EQUITY METHOD

In the preparation of consolidated financial statements, the recorded balances of individual assets, liabilities, and expense accounts must be adjusted to reflect the allocation, depreciation, and amortization of the difference between cost and book value.

Although the equity methods (partial and complete) reflect the effects of certain transactions more fully than the cost method on the books of the parent, the adjustments have not been made to individual underlying asset or income statement accounts. For example, under the partial equity method, the parent records its equity in subsidiary income in its books, but it does not record the underlying revenue and expense accounts that combine to form that total. Also, under this method, the parent does not record excess depreciation or amortization of goodwill arising in the acquisition in its investment account. These adjustments must be accomplished through the use of *workpaper entries* in the preparation of the consolidated statements workpaper.

To illustrate, assume the following:

1. P Company acquires an 80% interest in S Company on January 1, 2001, for $2,200,000, at which time S Company has capital stock of $1,500,000 and retained earnings of $500,000. P Company uses the partial equity method to record its investment in S Company.

2. The allocation, amortization, and depreciation of the difference between cost and book value in the amount of $600,000 [$2,200,000 − .80($2,000,000)] is as previously presented in Illustration 5-5 includes $40,000 to Inventory, $240,000 to Equipment (10 year life), $120,000 to Land, and $200,000 to Goodwill (20 year life).

3. In 2001, S Company reported net income of $125,000 and declared and paid dividends of $20,000.

4. In 2002, S Company reported net income of $140,000 and declared and paid dividends of $60,000.

5. In 2003, S Company reported net income of $200,000 and declared and paid dividends of $75,000.

Entries on Books of P Company—2001 (Year of Acquisition) Entries recorded on the books of P Company under the partial equity method are as follows:

(1)	Investment in S Company	2,200,000	
	Cash		2,200,000
	To record purchase of 80% interest in S Company.		
(2)	Cash	16,000	
	Investment in S Company		16,000
	To record dividends received (.80 × $20,000).		
(3)	Investment in S Company	100,000	
	Equity in Subsidiary Income		100,000
	To record equity in subsidiary income (.80 × $125,000).		

Entries on Books of P Company—2002 (Year Subsequent to Acquisition)

(4)	Cash	48,000	
	Investment in S Company		48,000
	To record dividends received (.80 × $60,000).		
(5)	Investment in S Company	112,000	
	Equity in Subsidiary Income		112,000
	To record equity in subsidiary income (.80 × $140,000).		

After these entries are posted, the Investment account will appear as follows:

Investment in S Company

(1) Cost	2,200,000	(2) Dividends	16,000
(3) Subsidiary Income	100,000		
12/31/01 Balance	2,284,000		
(5) Subsidiary Income	112,000	(4) Dividends	48,000
12/31/02 Balance	2,348,000		

Workpaper Entries—2001 (Year of Acquisition) A consolidated statements workpaper under the partial equity method for the year ended December 31, 2001, is presented in Illustration 5-10. Workpaper entries in Illustration 5-10 are presented in general journal form as follows:

(1)	Beginning Retained Earnings—S Company		
	(.80 × $500,000)	400,000	
	Capital Stock—S Company (.80 × $1,500,000)	1,200,000	
	Difference Between Cost and Book Value	600,000	
	Investment in S Company		2,200,000
	To eliminate investment account against the equity accounts of S Company at the date of acquisition.		

Partial

(2a)	Cost of Goods Sold (Beginning Inventory)	40,000	
	Equipment (net)	240,000	
	Land	120,000	
	Goodwill	200,000	
	Difference Between Cost and Book Value		600,000
	To allocate the amount of difference between cost and book value at date of acquisition to specific assets and liabilities (see Illustration 5-2).		

By the end of the first year, under a FIFO (first-in, first-out) cost flow assumption, the inventory which necessitated the $40,000 adjustment would have been sold. Recall that at the date of acquisition, this adjustment was to Inventory. At the end of the first year, however, the entry is to Cost of Goods Sold (or to Beginning Inventory, as a subcomponent of the Cost of Goods Sold). Since S Company will not have included the additional $40,000 allocated to inventory in its reported Cost of Goods Sold (COGS), consolidated Cost of Goods Sold must be increased by this workpaper entry. If the inventory were still on hand on December 31, 2001 (for example, if a LIFO flow were assumed), the $40,000 would be allocated to ending inventory in the balance sheet rather than to COGS.

This entry to COGS is appropriate only in the year of acquisition. In subsequent years, consolidated COGS will have been reflected in the 2001 consolidated net income and hence consolidated retained earnings at the end of 2001. Thus, the adjustment ($40,000 debit) in future years will be to Beginning Retained Earnings—P Company.

(2b)	Depreciation Expense	24,000	
	Equipment (net) or accumulated depreciation		24,000
	To depreciate the amount of difference between cost and book value allocated to equipment ($240,000/10 years; see Illustration 5-5).		

As previously noted, depreciation in the consolidated income statement should be based on the value assigned to the equipment in the consolidated balance sheet. Since the depreciation recorded by S Company is based on the book value of the equipment in its records, consolidated depreciation must be increased by a workpaper entry.

(2c)	Amortization of Goodwill	10,000	
	Goodwill		10,000
	To amortize the amount of goodwill recognized in the acquisition ($200,000/20 years; see Illustration 5-5).		

The amount of the difference between cost and book value not allocated to specific identifiable assets or liabilities is treated in the consolidated financial statements as

Partial Equity Method
80% Owned Subsidiary
Year of Acquisition

ILLUSTRATION 5–10
Consolidated Statements Workpaper
P Company and Subsidiary
For Year Ended December 31, 2001

Partial

Income Statement	P Company	S Company	Eliminations Dr.	Eliminations Cr.	Noncontrolling Interest	Consolidated Balances
Sales	3,100,000	2,200,000				5,300,000
Equity in Subsidiary Income	100,000		(3a) 100,000			
Total Revenue	3,200,000	2,200,000				5,300,000
Cost of Goods Sold	1,700,000	1,360,000	(2a) 40,000			3,100,000
Depreciation—Equipment	120,000	30,000	(2b) 24,000			174,000
Amortization of Goodwill			(2c) 10,000			10,000
Other Expenses	998,000	685,000				1,683,000
Total Cost and Expense	2,818,000	2,075,000				4,967,000
Net/Combined Income	382,000	125,000				333,000
Noncontrolling Interest in Income					25,000	(25,000)*
Net Income to Retained Earnings	382,000	125,000	174,000	—0—	25,000	308,000

Retained Earnings Statement — handwritten: $382 + 125 \times 80\% - 100 - 40 - 14 - 10 = 308$

Retained Earnings Statement	P Company	S Company	Eliminations Dr.	Eliminations Cr.	Noncontrolling Interest	Consolidated Balances
1/1 Retained Earnings						
P Company	1,650,000					1,650,000
S Company		500,000	(1) 400,000		100,000	
Net Income from above	382,000	125,000	174,000	—0—	25,000	308,000
Dividends Declared						
P Company	(150,000)					(150,000)
S Company		(20,000)		(3b) 16,000	(4,000)	
12/31 Retained Earnings to Balance Sheet	1,882,000	605,000	574,000	16,000	121,000	1,808,000

Balance Sheet — handwritten: $1,882 - 74 (40 + 14 + 10) = 1808$

Balance Sheet	P Company	S Company	Eliminations Dr.	Eliminations Cr.	Noncontrolling Interest	Consolidated Balances
Investment in S Company	2,284,000		(3b) 16,000	(1) 2,200,000 (3a) 100,000		
Difference Between Cost and Book Value			(1) 600,000	(2a) 600,000		
Land	1,250,000	250,000	(2a) 120,000			1,620,000
Equipment (net)	1,080,000	270,000	(2a) 240,000	(2b) 24,000		1,566,000
Other Assets (net)	2,402,000	1,885,000				4,287,000
Goodwill (Excess of Cost over Fair Value)			(2a) 200,000	(2c) 10,000		190,000
Total Assets	7,016,000	2,405,000				7,663,000
Liabilities	2,134,000	300,000				2,434,000
Capital Stock						
P Company	3,000,000					3,000,000
S Company		1,500,000	(1) 1,200,000		300,000	
Retained Earnings from above	1,882,000	605,000	574,000	16,000	121,000	1,808,000
Noncontrolling Interest in Net Assets					421,000	421,000
Total Liabilities and Equity	7,016,000	2,405,000	2,950,000	2,950,000		7,663,000

Handwritten notes near Difference Between Cost and Book Value: $= 2,200,000 + (605,00 - 500,00) \times 80\% = 2,284,000$

Handwritten note near Liabilities: $(1,500,000 + 605,000) \times 20\% = 421,000$

*.20 × $125,000 = $25,000.
(1) To eliminate investment account against the equity accounts of S Company at the date of acquisition.
(2a) To allocate the difference between cost and book value at the date of acquisition to specific assets and liabilities.
(2b) To depreciate the amount of the difference between cost and book value assigned to equipment ($240,000/10 years).
(2c) To amortize the amount of goodwill recognized in the acquisition ($200,000/20 years).
(3a) To reverse the effect of subsidiary income recognized on the books of the parent.
(3b) To reverse the effects of dividends declared by the subsidiary and received by the parent.

goodwill and must be amortized (the straight-line method is recommended) over an appropriate period not to exceed 40 years.[9] Again, since it is not recognized in the records of S Company, no amortization of this asset is included in its income statement. Accordingly, a workpaper entry is necessary to recognize the annual charge to expense in the consolidated income statement.

It is possible, of course, to combine the workpaper entries relating to the allocation, amortization, and depreciation of the difference between cost and book value into one entry. In Illustration 5-10, for example, workpaper entries (2a), (2b), and (2c) could be presented in one combined entry as follows:

(2)	Cost of Goods Sold (Beginning Inventory)	40,000	
	Depreciation Expense	24,000	
	Amortization of Goodwill	10,000	
	Equipment (net) ($240,000 − $24,000)	216,000	
	Land	120,000	
	Goodwill ($200,000 − $10,000)	190,000	
	Difference Between Cost and Book Value		600,000
	This combined entry is not needed if entries (2a) through (2c) are made individually.		

Next, the workpaper entries to reverse the effect of parent company entries during the year for subsidiary dividends and income may be separated to record the reversal of dividends in one entry and the reversal of income in another, as follows (and as shown in Illustration 5-10):

(3a)	Equity in Subsidiary Income	100,000	
	Investment in S Company		100,000
	To reverse the effect of subsidiary income recognized in the books of the parent.		

(3b)	Investment in S Company	16,000	
	Dividends Declared		16,000
	To reverse the effect of dividends declared by the subsidiary and received by the parent.		

Alternatively, the effects of entries (3a) and (3b) may be combined into one entry, as shown below:

(3)	Equity in Subsidiary Income	100,000	
	Dividends Declared		16,000
	Investment in S Company		84,000
	To reverse the effect of parent company entries during the year for subsidiary dividends and income; not needed if entries (3a) and (3b) are made individually.		

The calculation of noncontrolling interest in Illustration 5-10 is not affected by the amortization/depreciation of the differences between cost and book value. Since the differences between cost and book value represent a cost incurred by the parent company in the purchase of the subsidiary stock, its amortization is charged in its entirety to the parent company (controlling stockholders) under current generally accepted accounting principles (GAAP).

---

[9]Although the maximum life for goodwill amortization is 40 years under current GAAP (*APB Opinion No. 17*), the FASB has proposed shortening the maximum period to 20 years, as discussed in Appendix A to Chapter 2.

Workpaper Entries—2002 (Year Subsequent to Acquisition)

Next, a consolidated statements workpaper under the partial equity method for the year ended December 31, 2002, is presented in Illustration 5-11. Workpaper entries in Illustration 5-11 are presented in general journal form as follows:

(1)	Beginning Retained Earnings—S Company	
	(.80 × $605,000)	484,000
	Capital Stock—S Company (.80 × $1,500,000)	1,200,000
	Difference Between Cost and Book Value	600,000
	Investment in S Company	2,284,000
	To eliminate investment account against the equity accounts of S Company using equity balances at the *beginning* of the current year.	

For those who have read the cost method discussion, note that _under the partial equity method, there is no need to establish reciprocity._ That feature was unique to the cost method, and in fact may be viewed as a sort of conversion to the equity method. In the investment elimination entry, the amount debited or credited to the Difference Between Cost and Book Value may be treated as a plug figure to balance the entry and is equal to the amount of the difference between cost and book value on the date of acquisition. The amount does not change subsequent to acquisition and may be obtained from the Computation and Allocation Schedule (Illustration 5-2).

Workpaper entry (2) is presented next, first in a combined single entry and then (alternatively) in its components. The authors find the second approach (components) easier to understand, though less compact.

Partial

(2)	Beginning Retained Earnings—P Company	
	(Beginning Consolidated Retained Earnings)	74,000
	Depreciation Expense ($240,000/10)	24,000
	Amortization Expense—Goodwill ($200,000/20 years)	10,000
	Equipment (net) ($240,000 − $24,000 − $24,000)	192,000
	Land	120,000
	Goodwill ($200,000 − $10,000 − $10,000)	180,000
	Difference Between Cost and Book Value	600,000
	To allocate, amortize, and depreciate the difference between cost and book value.	

To separate the above entry into its more digestible components, begin with the allocation of the difference between cost and book value and then proceed to record excess depreciation and amortization, as follows:

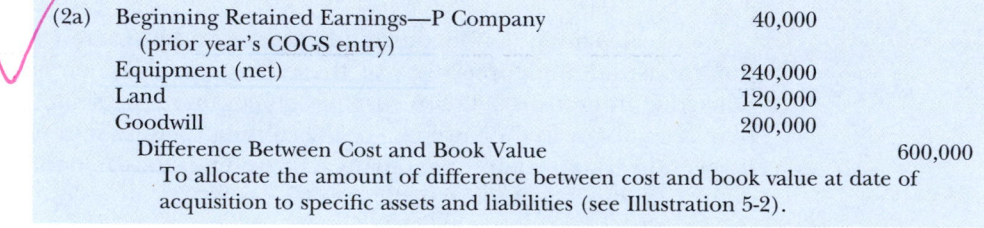

(2a)	Beginning Retained Earnings—P Company	40,000
	(prior year's COGS entry)	
	Equipment (net)	240,000
	Land	120,000
	Goodwill	200,000
	Difference Between Cost and Book Value	600,000
	To allocate the amount of difference between cost and book value at date of acquisition to specific assets and liabilities (see Illustration 5-2).	

Entry (2a) is identical to that recorded in the preceding year, with the exception that the entry to Cost of Goods Sold is appropriate only in the year of acquisition. Thus, the adjustment in year 2 (and future years) is to Beginning Retained Earnings.

ILLUSTRATION 5–11

Consolidated Statements Workpaper

P Company and Subsidiary

For Year Ended December 31, 2002

Income Statement	P Company	S Company	Eliminations Dr.	Eliminations Cr.	Noncontrolling Interest	Consolidated Balances
Sales	3,534,000	2,020,000				5,554,000
Equity in Subsidiary Income	112,000		(3) 112,000			
Total Revenue	3,646,000	2,020,000				5,554,000
Cost of Goods Sold	2,040,000	1,200,000				3,240,000
Depreciation—Equipment	120,000	30,000	(2b) 24,000			174,000
Amortization of Goodwill			(2c) 10,000			10,000
Other Expenses	993,000	650,000				1,643,000
Total Cost and Expense	3,153,000	1,880,000				5,067,000
Net/Combined Income	493,000	140,000				487,000
Noncontrolling Interest in Income					28,000	(28,000)*
Net Income to Retained Earnings	493,000	140,000	146,000	—0—	28,000	459,000

Retained Earnings Statement

Handwritten: 493 + 140 × 80% − 112 − 34 = 459

Retained Earnings Statement	P Company	S Company	Eliminations Dr.	Eliminations Cr.	Noncontrolling Interest	Consolidated Balances
1/1 Retained Earnings P Company	1,882,000		(2a) 40,000			1,808,000
			(2b) 24,000			
			(2c) 10,000			
S Company		605,000	(1) 484,000		121,000	
Net Income from above	493,000	140,000	146,000	—0—	28,000	459,000
Dividends Declared P Company	(150,000)					(150,000)
S Company		(60,000)		(3) 48,000	(12,000)	
12/31 Retained Earnings to Balance Sheet	2,225,000	685,000	704,000	48,000	137,000	2,117,000

Balance Sheet

Handwritten: 2,225 − 74 − 34 = 2,117

Balance Sheet	P Company	S Company	Eliminations Dr.	Eliminations Cr.	Noncontrolling Interest	Consolidated Balances
Investment in S Company	2,348,000			(3) 64,000		
				(1) 2,284,000		
Difference Between Cost and Book Value			(1) 600,000	(2a) 600,000		
Land	2,000,000	250,000	(2a) 120,000			2,370,000
Equipment (net)	960,000	240,000	(2a) 240,000	(2b) 48,000		1,392,000
Other Assets (net)	2,137,000	2,200,000				4,337,000
Goodwill (Excess of Cost over Fair Value)			(2a) 200,000	(2c) 20,000		180,000
Total Assets	7,445,000	2,690,000				8,279,000
Liabilities	2,220,000	505,000				2,725,000
Capital Stock P Company	3,000,000					3,000,000
S Company		1,500,000	(1) 1,200,000		300,000	
Retained Earnings from above	2,225,000	685,000	704,000	48,000	137,000	2,117,000
Noncontrolling Interest in Net Assets					437,000	437,000
Total Liabilities and Equity	7,445,000	2,690,000	3,064,000	3,064,000		8,279,000

Handwritten near Difference Between Cost: 2,05,000 + (685,000 − 505,000) × .8 = 2,348,000

Handwritten near Liabilities: (685,000 − 505,000) × 20% = 437,000

Handwritten label: Partial

*.20 × $140,000 = $28,000.
(1) To eliminate the investment account.
(2a) To allocate the difference between cost and book value at the date of acquisition to specific assets and liabilities.
(2b) To depreciate the amount of the difference between cost and book value assigned to equipment ($240,000/10 years).
(2c) To amortize the amount of goodwill recognized in the acquisition ($200,000/20 years)
(3) To reverse the effect of parent company entries during the year for subsidiary dividends and income.

(2b)	Depreciation Expense (current year)	24,000	
	Beginning Retained Earnings—P Company (prior year's depreciation expense)	24,000	
	Equipment (net)		48,000
	To depreciate the amount of difference between cost and book value allocated to equipment.		

This entry differs from the first year entry in that the excess depreciation from the year 2001 is now reflected in Beginning Retained Earnings—P Company. Although the adjustment to Equipment was already made in the prior year's workpaper for one year's depreciation adjustment, it was not posted to the books of S Company and hence must be made again. If the following year (2003) were being presented, the debit to Depreciation Expense would remain at 24,000, but the debit to Beginning Retained Earnings would be 48,000 to reflect two prior years of excess depreciation (and the credit to Equipment would total 72,000).

(2c)	Amortization of Goodwill (current year)	10,000	
	Beginning Retained Earnings—P Company (previous year's amortization)	10,000	
	Goodwill		20,000
	To amortize goodwill for the current year and previous year(s).		

Once again this entry differs from the first year in that the amortization from the year 2001 is now reflected in Beginning Retained Earnings—P Company. As with excess depreciation, the adjustment to Goodwill was already made in the prior year's workpaper for one year's amortization expense, but it was not posted to the books of S Company and hence must be made again. Clearly, if entries (2a) through (2c) are recorded separately, the combined entry (2) is not needed.

(3)	Equity in Subsidiary Income	112,000	
	Dividends Declared		48,000
	Investment in S Company		64,000
	To reverse the effect of parent company entries during the year 2002 for subsidiary dividends and income.		

Observe that the consolidated balances in Illustration 5-11 are the same as those in Illustration 5-7 (cost method workpaper). A comparison of the workpaper entries to eliminate the investment account and to allocate, amortize, and depreciate the difference between cost and book value are the same regardless of whether the investment is recorded using the cost method or the partial equity method. Only the entries for intercompany dividends and income and for reciprocity differ.

Figure 5-2 on page 203 presents the entries in their separate components for all three years (2001 through 2003) side by side for the partial equity method.

PARTIAL EQUITY METHOD ANALYSIS OF CONTROLLING AND NONCONTROLLING INTERESTS IN COMBINED NET INCOME AND RETAINED EARNINGS

The t-account calculation of consolidated net income (or the controlling interest in combined income) does not differ between the cost and partial equity methods. As stated earlier, *consolidated net income is the parent company's income from its independent operations plus (minus) its share of reported subsidiary income (loss) plus or minus adjustments for the period relating to the amortization of the difference between cost and book value.*

ILLUSTRATION 5–12

T-account Calculation of Controlling and Noncontrolling Interest in Combined Income
For Year Ended December 31, 2002

Noncontrolling Interest in Combined Income

Net income reported by S Company	140,000
Subsidiary Income included in Combined Income	140,000
Noncontrolling Ownership percentage interest	20%
Noncontrolling Interest in Combined Income	28,000

80%

Controlling Interest in Income

only against P, not S

	P Company's net income from its independent operations ($493,000 reported net income less $112,000 equity in subsidiary income included therein)	$381,000
	P Company's share of the reported income of S Company (.8 × $140,000)	112,000
Additional depreciation and amortization of the difference between cost and book value related to:		
Depreciation Expense ($240,000/10) 24,000		
Goodwill Amortization ($200,000/20) 10,000		
	Consolidated Net Income	$459,000

The calculation of consolidated net income for the year ended December 31, 2002, presented in Illustration 5-12 is based on Illustration 5-11. This, of course, is the same amount of consolidated net income as that calculated in the consolidated statements workpaper presented in Illustration 5-11.

When the parent company uses the partial equity method to account for its investment, the parent company's share of subsidiary income since acquisition is already included in the parent company's reported retained earnings. Consequently, *consolidated retained earnings is calculated as the parent company's recorded partial equity basis retained earnings plus or minus the cumulative effect of the adjustments to date relating to the amortization of the difference between cost and book value.*

The analytical calculation of consolidated retained earnings on December 31, 2002, presented in Illustration 5-13 is based on Illustration 5-11. This, too, is the

Partial

ILLUSTRATION 5–13

Analytical Calculation of Consolidated Retained Earnings
December 31, 2002

P Company's retained earnings on December 31, 2002			$2,225,000
Less cumulative effect to December 31, 2002, of the amortization of the difference between cost and book value:			

	2001	2002	
Inventory (to cost of goods sold)	$40,000	$—0—	
Depreciation from equipment	24,000	24,000	
Amortization of goodwill	10,000	10,000	
	74,000	34,000	(108,000)
Consolidated Retained Earnings on December 31, 2002			$2,117,000

same amount of consolidated retained earnings as that shown in the consolidated statements workpaper presented in Illustration 5-11.

Alternatively, consolidated retained earnings can be computed by adding beginning consolidated retained earnings to consolidated net income and subtracting dividends declared by Company P.

Beginning Consolidated Retained Earnings	$1,808,000
Plus: Consolidated Net Income	459,000
Less: Dividends Declared by P Company	(150,000)
Ending Consolidated Retained Earnings	$2,117,000

CONSOLIDATED STATEMENTS WORKPAPER—INVESTMENT RECORDED USING COMPLETE EQUITY METHOD

In the preparation of consolidated financial statements, the recorded balances of individual assets, liabilities, and expense accounts must be adjusted to reflect the allocation, depreciation, and amortization of the difference between cost and book value.

When the parent accounts for its investment using the complete equity method, the parent records excess depreciation and/or amortization of goodwill arising in the acquisition in its investment account. The income statement effects are recorded as adjustments to the amount recognized as "equity in subsidiary income" each year. Even under this method, however, adjustments are needed to record the effects in the proper accounts for the consolidated entity. For example, the account "equity in subsidiary income" will be eliminated in the consolidated financial statements, and the effects need to be shown directly in "depreciation expense" and/ or "amortization expense." Similarly, the investment account will be eliminated, and the adjustments for any differences between cost and book value need to be shown directly in the appropriate asset (inventory, land, equipment, goodwill, etc.) and/or liability accounts. These adjustments must be accomplished through the use of *workpaper entries* in the preparation of the consolidated statements workpaper.

To illustrate, assume the following:

1. P Company acquires an 80% interest in S Company on January 1, 2001, for $2,200,000, at which time S Company has capital stock of $1,500,000 and retained earnings of $500,000. P Company uses the complete equity method to record its investment in S Company.

2. The allocation, amortization, and depreciation of the difference between cost and book value in the amount of $600,000 [$2,200,000 − .80($2,000,000)] is as previously presented in Illustration 5-5, includes $40,000 to Inventory, $240,000 to Equipment (10 year life), $120,000 to Land, and $200,000 to Goodwill (20 year life).

3. In 2001, S Company reported net income of $125,000 and declared and paid dividends of $20,000.

4. In 2002, S Company reported net income of $140,000 and declared and paid dividends of $60,000.

5. In 2003, S Company reported net income of $200,000 and declared and paid dividends of $75,000.

Complete

Entries on Books of P Company—2001 (Year of Acquisition) and 2002 (Subsequent Year)

Entries recorded on the books of P Company under the complete equity method are as follows:

2001—Year of Acquisition

(1)	Investment in S Company	2,200,000	
	Cash		2,200,000
	To record purchase of 80% interest in S Company.		
(2)	Cash	16,000	
	Investment in S Company		16,000
	To record dividends received (.80 × $20,000).		
(3)	Investment in S Company	100,000	
	Equity in Subsidiary Income		100,000
	To record equity in subsidiary income (.80 × $125,000).		
(4)	Equity in Subsidiary Income	74,000	
	Investment in S Company		74,000
	To adjust equity in subsidiary income for excess depreciation ($24,000), the amortization of goodwill ($10,000), and the higher value placed on inventory and thus on cost of goods sold ($40,000). See Illustration 5-5.		

Complete

[handwritten: mostly combined]

Entries (3) and (4) could be collapsed into one combined entry of $26,000 ($100,000 minus $74,000).

2002—Year Subsequent to Acquisition

(1)	Cash	48,000	
	Investment in S Company		48,000
	To record dividends received (.80 × $60,000).		
(2)	Investment in S Company	112,000	
	Equity in Subsidiary Income		112,000
	To record equity in subsidiary income (.80 × $140,000).		
(3)	Equity in Subsidiary Income	34,000	
	Investment in S Company		34,000
	To adjust equity in subsidiary income for excess depreciation ($24,000) and goodwill amortization ($10,000).		

Again, entries (2) and (3) could be collapsed into one combined entry of $78,000 ($112,000 minus $34,000). Note also that the inventory adjustment was needed only in the first year under a first-in, first-out (FIFO) cost flow assumption.

After these entries are posted, the Investment account will appear as follows:

Investment in S Company

(1) Cost	2,200,000	(2) Dividends	16,000
(3) Subsidiary Income	100,000	(4) Excess Depreciation, Amortization, and Cost of Goods Sold	74,000
12/31/01 Balance	2,210,000		
(2) Subsidiary Income	112,000	(1) Dividends	48,000
		(3) Excess Depreciation and Amortization	34,000
12/31/02 Balance	2,240,000		

Workpaper Entries—2001 (Year of Acquisition) A consolidated statements workpaper under the complete equity method for the year ended December 31, 2001,

Complete Equity Method
80% Owned Subsidiary
Year of Acquisition

handwritten: 2 600 + 60,000 = 74,000

ILLUSTRATION 5–14
Consolidated Statements Workpaper
P Company and Subsidiary
For Year Ended December 31, 2001

Complete

Income Statement	P Company	S Company	Eliminations Dr.		Eliminations Cr.		Noncontrolling Interest	Consolidated Balances
Sales	3,100,000	2,200,000						5,300,000
Equity in Subsidiary Income	26,000		(3a)	100,000	(3c)	74,000		
Total Revenue	3,126,000	2,200,000						5,300,000
Cost of Goods Sold	1,700,000	1,360,000	(2a)	40,000				3,100,000
Depreciation—Equipment	120,000	30,000	(2b)	24,000				174,000
Amortization of Goodwill			(2c)	10,000				10,000
Other Expenses	998,000	685,000						1,683,000
Total Cost and Expense	2,818,000	2,075,000						4,967,000
Net/Combined Income	308,000	125,000						333,000
Noncontrolling Interest in Income							25,000	(25,000)*
Net Income to Retained Earnings	308,000	125,000		174,000		74,000	25,000	308,000

Retained Earnings Statement *handwritten:* 308,000 − 100,000 + 74,000 + 125,000 × 80% − 74,000 = 308,000

	P Company	S Company	Eliminations Dr.		Eliminations Cr.		Noncontrolling Interest	Consolidated Balances
1/1 Retained Earnings								
P Company	1,650,000							1,650,000
S Company		500,000	(1)	400,000			100,000	
Net Income from above	308,000	125,000		174,000		74,000	25,000	308,000
Dividends Declared								
P Company	(150,000)							(150,000)
S Company		(20,000)			(3b)	16,000	(4,000)	
12/31 Retained Earnings to Balance Sheet	1,808,000	605,000		574,000		90,000	121,000	1,808,000

Balance Sheet *handwritten:* 1,808,000 −

	P Company	S Company	Eliminations Dr.		Eliminations Cr.		Noncontrolling Interest	Consolidated Balances
Investment in S Company	2,210,000		(3b)	16,000	(1)	2,200,000		
			(3c)	74,000	(3a)	100,000		
Difference Between Cost and Book Value			(1)	600,000	(2a)	600,000		
Land	1,250,000	250,000	(2a)	120,000				1,620,000
Equipment (net)	1,080,000	270,000	(2a)	240,000	(2b)	24,000		1,566,000
Other Assets (net)	2,402,000	1,885,000						4,287,000
Goodwill (Excess of Cost over Fair Value)			(2a)	200,000	(2c)	10,000		190,000
Total Assets	6,942,000	2,405,000						7,663,000
Liabilities	2,134,000	300,000						2,434,000
Capital Stock								
P Company	3,000,000							3,000,000
S Company		1,500,000	(1)	1,200,000			300,000	
Retained Earnings from above	1,808,000	605,000		574,000		90,000	121,000	1,808,000
Noncontrolling Interest in Net Assets							421,000	421,000
Total Liabilities and Equity	6,942,000	2,405,000		3,024,000		3,024,000		7,663,000

handwritten annotations near Investment: = 2,200,000 + (605,000 + 90,000 ...) 80% − 74,000 = 2,240,000

handwritten near Liabilities/Capital: (2,405,000 − 300,000) × 20% = 421,000

*.20 × $125,000 = $25,000.
(1) To eliminate the investment account.
(2a) To allocate differences between cost and book value.
(2b) To depreciate the difference between cost and book value assigned to equipment (240,000/10).
(2c) To amortize the amount of goodwill recognized in the acquisition (200,000/20 yrs).
(3a) To eliminate equity in subsidiary income.
(3b) To eliminate intercompany dividends.
(3c) To reverse the adjustments to subsidiary income recognized by the parent.

is presented in Illustration 5-14. Workpaper entries in Illustration 5-14 are presented in general journal form as follows:

(1)	Beginning Retained Earnings—S Company		
	(.80 × $500,000)	400,000	
	Capital Stock—S Company		
	(.80 × $1,500,000)	1,200,000	
	Difference Between Cost and Book Value	600,000	
	Investment in S Company		2,200,000
	To eliminate investment account against the equity accounts of S Company at the date of acqusition.		

(2a)	Cost of Goods Sold (Beginning Inventory)	40,000	
	Equipment (net)	240,000	
	Land	120,000	
	Goodwill	200,000	
	Difference Between Cost and Book Value		600,000
	To allocate the amount of difference between cost and book value at date of acquisition to specific assets and liabilities (see Illustration 5-2).		

By the end of the first year, under a FIFO (first-in, first-out) cost flow assumption, the inventory which necessitated the $40,000 adjustment would have been sold. Recall that at the date of acquisition, this adjustment was to Inventory. At the end of the first year, however, the entry is to Cost of Goods Sold (or to Beginning Inventory, as a subcomponent of the Cost of Goods Sold). Since S Company will not have included the additional $40,000 allocated to inventory in its reported Cost of Goods Sold (COGS), consolidated Cost of Goods Sold must be increased by this workpaper entry. If the inventory were still on hand on December 31, 2001 (for example, if a LIFO flow were assumed), the $40,000 would be allocated to ending inventory in the balance sheet rather than to COGS.

This entry to COGS is appropriate only in the year of acquisition. In subsequent years, consolidated COGS will have been reflected in the 2001 consolidated net income and hence consolidated retained earnings at the end of 2001. On the books of P Company, the adjustment is reflected in equity in subsidiary income (and thus in ending retained earnings) and in the investment account. Because the investment account must be eliminated in the consolidating process, the entry to COGS is replaced in future years by an entry ($40,000 debit) to Investment in S Company; this workpaper entry serves to facilitate the elimination of the investment account by reversing an adjustment made by the parent.

Complete

(2b)	Depreciation Expense	24,000	
	Equipment (net)		24,000
	To depreciate the amount of difference between cost and book value allocated to equipment ($240,000/10 years; see Illustration 5-5).		

As previously noted, depreciation in the consolidated income statement should be based on the value assigned to the equipment in the consolidated balance sheet. Since the depreciation recorded by S Company is based on the book value of the equipment on its records, consolidated depreciation must be increased by a workpaper entry.

(2c)	Amortization of Goodwill	10,000	
	Goodwill		10,000
	To amortize the amount of goodwill recognized in the acquisition ($200,000/20 years; see Illustration 5-5).		

The amount of the difference between cost and book value not allocated to specific identifiable assets or liabilities is treated in the consolidated financial statements as goodwill and must be amortized (the straight-line method is recommended) over an appropriate period not to exceed 40 years.[10] Again, since it is not recognized in the records of S Company, no amortization of this asset is included in its income statement. Accordingly, a workpaper entry is necessary to recognize the annual charge to expense in the consolidated income statement.

It is possible, of course, to combine the workpaper entries relating to the allocation, amortization, and depreciation of the difference between cost and book value into one entry. For example, workpaper entries (2a), (2b), and (2c) could be presented in one combined entry as follows:

(2)	Cost of Goods Sold (Beginning Inventory)	40,000	
	Depreciation Expense	24,000	
	Amortization of Goodwill	10,000	
	Equipment (net) ($240,000 − $24,000)	216,000	
	Land	120,000	
	Goodwill ($200,000 − $10,000)	190,000	
	Difference Between Cost and Book Value		600,000
	This combined entry is not needed if entries (2a) through (2c) are made individually.		

Next we reverse the effect of parent company entries during the year for subsidiary dividends and income. Here also entries may be combined or separated to record the reversal of dividends in one entry, the reversal of reported income in a second entry, and the reversal of adjustments to subsidiary income in a third.

Complete

(3a)	Investment in S Company	16,000	
	Dividends Declared		16,000
	To reverse the effect of dividends declared by the subsidiary and received by the parent.		

(3b)	Equity in Subsidiary Income	100,000	
	Investment in S Company		100,000
	To reverse the effect of subsidiary reported income recognized in the books of the parent.		

(3c)	Investment in S Company	74,000	
	Equity in Subsidiary Income		74,000
	To reverse the adjustments to subsidiary income recognized by the parent ($40,000 cost of goods sold, $24,000 depreciation, and $10,000 goodwill amortization).		

[10]Although goodwill must be amortized under current GAAP over a maximum life of 40 years (*APB Opinion No. 17*), the FASB has proposed shortening the maximum life to 20 years, as discussed in Appendix A to Chapter 2.

Alternatively, the effects of entries (3a) through (3c) may be combined into one entry, as shown below:

(3)	Equity in Subsidiary Income	26,000	
	Dividends Declared		16,000
	Investment in S Company		10,000
	To reverse the effect of parent company entries during the year for subsidiary dividends and income.		

The calculation of noncontrolling interest in Illustration 5-14 is not affected by the amortization/depreciation of the differences between cost and book value. Since the differences between cost and book value represent a cost incurred by the parent company in the purchase of the subsidiary stock, its amortization is charged in its entirety to the parent company (controlling stockholders) under current generally accepted accounting principles (GAAP).

Entries on Workpapers—2002 (Year Subsequent to Acquisition) Next, a consolidated statements workpaper under the complete equity method for the year ended December 31, 2002, is presented in Illustration 5-15. Workpaper entries in Illustration 5-15 are presented in general journal form as follows:

(1)	Beginning Retained Earnings—S Company		
	(.80 × $605,000)	484,000	
	Capital Stock—S Company (.80 × $1,500,000)	1,200,000	
	Difference Between Cost and Book Value	600,000	
	Investment in S Company		2,284,000
	To eliminate investment account against the equity accounts of S Company using equity balances at the *beginning* of the current year.		

(2)	Investment in S Company	74,000	
	[adjustments from prior year for depreciation ($24,000), amortization ($10,000), and COGS ($40,000)]		
	Depreciation Expense ($240,000/10 years)	24,000	
	Amortization Expense—Goodwill ($200,000/20 years)	10,000	
	Equipment (net) ($240,000 − $24,000 − $24,000)	192,000	
	Land	120,00	
	Goodwill ($200,000 − $10,000 − $10,000)	180,000	
	Difference Between Cost and Book Value		600,000
	To allocate, amortize, and depreciate the difference between cost and book value.		

To separate the above entry into its more digestible components, begin with the allocation of the difference between cost and book value and then proceed to record excess depreciation and amortization, as follows:

(2a)	Investment in S Company (replaces COGS from 2001)	40,000	
	Equipment (net)	240,000	
	Land	120,000	
	Goodwill	200,000	
	Difference Between Cost and Book Value		600,000
	To allocate the amount of difference between cost and book value at date of acquisition to specific assets and liabilities (see Illustration 5-2).		

Complete Equity Method

80% Owned Subsidiary

Subsequent to Year of Acquisition

Complete

ILLUSTRATION 5–15

Consolidated Statements Workpaper

P Company and Subsidiary

For Year Ended December 31, 2002

Income Statement	P Company	S Company	Eliminations Dr.	Eliminations Cr.	Noncontrolling Interest	Consolidated Balances
Sales	3,534,000	2,020,000				5,554,000
Equity in Subsidiary Income	78,000		(3) 78,000			
Total Revenue	3,612,000	2,020,000				5,554,000
Cost of Goods Sold	2,040,000	1,200,000				3,240,000
Depreciation—Equipment	120,000	30,000	(2b) 24,000			174,000
Amortization of Goodwill			(2c) 10,000			10,000
Other Expenses	993,000	650,000				1,643,000
Total Cost and Expense	3,153,000	1,880,000				5,067,000
Net/Combined Income	459,000	140,000				487,000
Noncontrolling Interest in Income					28,000	(28,000)*
Net Income to Retained Earnings	459,000	140,000	112,000	—0—	28,000	459,000
Retained Earnings Statement						
1/1 Retained Earnings						
P Company	1,808,000					1,808,000
S Company		605,000	(1) 484,000		121,000	
Net Income from above	459,000	140,000	112,000	—0—	28,000	459,000
Dividends Declared						
P Company	(150,000)					(150,000)
S Company		(60,000)		(3) 48,000	(12,000)	
12/31 Retained Earnings to Balance Sheet	2,117,000	685,000	596,000	48,000	137,000	2,117,000
Balance Sheet						
Investment in S Company	2,240,000		(2a) 40,000 (2b) 24,000 (2c) 10,000	(3) 30,000 (1) 2,284,000		
Difference Between Cost and Book Value			(1) 600,000	(2) 600,000		
Land	2,000,000	250,000	(2a) 120,000			2,370,000
Equipment (net)	960,000	240,000	(2a) 240,000	(2b) 48,000		1,392,000
Other Assets (net)	2,137,000	2,200,000				4,337,000
Goodwill (Excess of Cost over Fair Value)			(2a) 200,000	(2c) 20,000		180,000
Total Assets	7,337,000	2,690,000				8,279,000
Liabilities	2,220,000	505,000				2,725,000
Capital Stock						
P Company	3,000,000					3,000,000
S Company		1,500,000	(2) 1,200,000		300,000	
Retained Earnings from above	2,117,000	685,000	596,000	48,000	137,000	2,117,000
Noncontrolling Interest in Net Assets					437,000	437,000
Total Liabilities and Equity	7,337,000	2,690,000	3,030,000	3,030,000		8,279,000

*.20 × $140,000 = $28,000.

(1) To eliminate the investment account.

(2a) To allocate the amount of difference between cost and book value at date of acquisition to specific assets and liabilities.

(2b) To depreciate the amount of difference between cost and book value allocated to equipment.

(2c) To amortize goodwill for the current year and previous year(s).

(3) To reverse the effect of parent company entries during the year for subsidiary dividends and income.

Entry (2a) is identical to that recorded in the preceding year, with the exception that the entry to Cost of Goods Sold is appropriate only in the year of acquisition. Consolidated COGS (after the $40,000 adjustment) will have been reflected in the 2001 consolidated net income and hence consolidated retained earnings at the end of 2001. On the books of P Company, the adjustment was reflected in equity in subsidiary income in 2001 (and thus in ending retained earnings) and in the investment account. Because the investment account must be eliminated in the consolidating process, the entry to COGS is replaced here and in future years by an entry ($40,000 debit) to Investment in S Company.

    This component of the entry captures one of the basic differences between the complete equity method and the other two methods. Only under the complete equity method does the parent's beginning retained earnings exactly match the amount reported as consolidated retained earnings at the end of the previous year. Hence fewer workpaper adjustments to Beginning Retained Earnings—P Company are needed under the complete equity method. The $40,000 adjustment in year 2 (and future years) related to inventory valuation is made to Investment in S Company, serving to facilitate the elimination of the investment account (by reversing an adjustment made by the parent).

(2b)	Depreciation Expense (current year)	24,000	
	Investment in S Company (prior year depreciation)	24,000	
	Equipment (net)		48,000
	To depreciate the amount of difference between cost and book value allocated to equipment.		

    This entry differs from the first year in that the excess depreciation from the year 2001 is now reflected in a lowered balance in the Investment account, and this entry serves to reverse that adjustment (again to facilitate eliminating the Investment account). Although the adjustment to Equipment was already made in the prior year's workpaper for one year's depreciation adjustment, it was not posted to the books of S Company and hence must be made again. If the following year (2003) were being presented, the debit to Depreciation Expense would remain at $24,000, but the debit to Investment in S Company would be $48,000 to reflect two prior years of excess depreciation (and the credit to Equipment would total $72,000).

    The next workpaper entry records the amortization of goodwill needed in the year 2002.

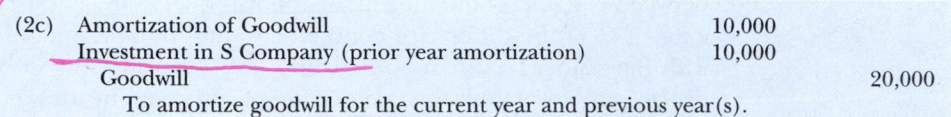

(2c)	Amortization of Goodwill	10,000	
	Investment in S Company (prior year amortization)	10,000	
	Goodwill		20,000
	To amortize goodwill for the current year and previous year(s).		

Once again this entry differs from the first year in that the amortization from the year 2001 is now reflected in Investment in S Company. As with excess depreciation, the adjustment to Goodwill was already made in the prior year's workpaper for one year's amortization expense, but it was not posted to the books of S Company and hence must be made again. To see how this entry would be handled in the year 2003, refer to Figure 5-3. Clearly, if entries (2a) through (2c) are recorded separately, the combined entry (2) is not needed.

Complete

(3)	Equity in Subsidiary Income	78,000	
	Dividends Declared		48,000
	Investment in S Company		30,000
	To reverse the effect of parent company entries during the year 2002 for subsidiary dividends and income.		

Observe that the consolidated balances in Illustration 5-15 are the same as those in Illustration 5-7 (cost method workpaper) and in Illustration 5-11 (partial equity workpaper). Figure 5-3 on page 204 presents the entries in their separate components for all three years side by side for the complete equity method.

COMPLETE EQUITY METHOD ANALYSIS OF CONTROLLING INTEREST IN COMBINED NET INCOME AND RETAINED EARNINGS

When the parent uses the complete equity method, its reported income equals consolidated net income. As with the other methods, the amount of consolidated income is *the parent company's income from its independent operations plus (minus) its share of adjusted subsidiary income (loss) plus or minus adjustments for the period relating to the amortization of the difference between cost and book value.*

The amount of consolidated net income for the year ended December 31, 2002, is $459,000. Observe that this amount is reported both in the farthest left-hand column of Illustration 5-15 (P Company income) and again in the farthest right-hand column (consolidated net income).

Similarly, the amount of consolidated retained earnings ($2,117,000) at the end of 2002 is the same as the ending retained earnings reported by P Company. Again compare the amount in the retained earnings section in the farthest left-hand column of Illustration 5-15 (P Company) to the amount in the farthest right-hand column (consolidated retained earnings). The amounts agree because P Company recognizes all adjustments in the income statement account "equity in subsidiary income" and thus in retained earnings.

ADDITIONAL CONSIDERATIONS RELATING TO TREATMENT OF DIFFERENCE BETWEEN COST AND BOOK VALUE

We present additional considerations relating to the treatment of the difference between cost and book value in the following sections. These considerations include allocation of the difference between cost and book value to liabilities and to assets with fair values less than book values; the separate disclosure of accumulated depreciation; premature disposals of long-lived assets by the subsidiary; and depreciable assets used in manufacturing.

Allocation of Difference Between Cost and Book Value to Debt

Adjustment of Contingent Liabilities and Reserves Often an acquiring firm reassesses the adequacy of the acquired firm's accounting for contingent liabilities, purchase commitments, reserves, and so forth prior to its allocation of any difference between cost and book values. If the accounting for these items falls into a gray area of GAAP, the purchaser may decide to allocate some of the difference between cost and book value to adjust or create liability accounts. For example, suppose that the purchaser assesses a contingent liability of the acquired firm's to be both probable and reasonably estimable, whereas the acquired firm had previously disclosed it only in a note because it was deemed reasonably possible (but not probable). By adjusting liabilities upward, the difference to be allocated to assets (and potentially to goodwill) is increased.

Interestingly, while many firms have been criticized for manipulating earnings to avoid recording goodwill, the Walt Disney Company, in its acquisition of Capital Cities/ABC, was accused by some sources of managing earnings via liabilities to record *excessive* goodwill. The *increase in recorded liabilities* in such a case could be viewed as providing a sort of cushion or management tool for future earnings manipulation.

IN THE NEWS

''How did Disney's accountants justify the creation of that huge reserve—justify adding some $2.5 billion in liabilities to its balance sheet? Especially liabilities that, 40 days before, hadn't existed on Cap Cities/ABC's balance sheet? Basically, by asserting that Cap Cities/ABC's accounting had ignored the impact of timing on anticipated cash flows from future programming that the network had agreed, at least in part, to finance. . . . The reason Disney went out on a limb to create its undisclosed reserve is clear enough: flexibility. It meant that as its new television arm ran up various programming costs after the merger, Disney had the option of merely writing those amounts off against those accrued liabilities instead of running them through its income statement—where they would have crimped reported profits.''[11]

Allocation of Difference Between Cost and Book Value to Long-Term Debt Notes payable, long-term debt, and other obligations of an acquired company should be valued for consolidation purposes at their fair values. Quoted market prices, if available, are the best evidence of the fair value of the debt. If quoted market prices are unavailable, then management's best estimate of the fair value may be based on fair values of debt with similar characteristics or on valuation techniques such as the present value of estimated future cash flows.[12] The present value should be determined using appropriate market rates of interest at the date of acquisition.

Assume, for example, that S Company has outstanding $500,000 in 6%, 30-year bonds that were issued at par on January 1, 1976, and that interest on the bonds is paid annually. Assume further that on January 1, 2001, when P Company acquires a 100% interest in S Company, the yield rate on bonds with similar risk is 10%. The present value of S Company's bonds payable determined at the effective yield rate on the acquisition date for five periods (the time until maturity) is calculated as follows:

(1) Interest Payments $30,000 × 3.79079 =	$113,724
(2) Principal Payment $500,000 × .62092 =	310,460
Present Value of Future Cash Payments Discounted at 10%	$424,184

(1) The present value of an annuity of one for five periods discounted at 10% is 3.79079.
(2) The present value of an amount of one received five periods hence discounted at 10% is 0.62092.

---

[11] *Barron's*, ''Disney's Real Magic,'' by Abraham Briloff, 3/23/98, pp. 17–20.

[12] *Financial Accounting Standards Board*, EITF 98-1, states, ''If a present value technique is used, the estimated future cash flows should not ignore relevant provisions of the debt agreement (for example, the right of the issuer to prepay).''

From the point of view of the consolidated entity, bonds payable are overstated on January 1, 2001, by $75,816 ($500,000 − $424,184), and a corresponding amount of the total difference between cost and book value on the date of acquisition must be allocated to "unamortized discount on bonds payable." In years after acquisition, interest expense reported by the subsidiary will be understated for consolidation purposes. Thus, workpaper entries must be made to amortize the discount in a manner that will reflect consolidated interest expense as a constant rate on the carrying value of the liability to the consolidated entity. An amortization schedule for this purpose is presented in Illustration 5-16. Consolidated statements workpaper entries necessary in the first five years subsequent to P Company's acquisition of S Company are summarized below:

Cost and Partial Equity Methods

December 31	2001 Debit	2001 Credit	2002 Debit	2002 Credit	2003 Debit	2003 Credit	2004 Debit	2004 Credit	2005 Debit	2005 Credit
Unamortized Discount on Bonds Payable	75,816		75,816		75,816		75,816		75,816	
Difference Between Cost and Book Value		75,816		75,816		75,816		75,816		75,816
Beginning Retained Earnings—P Company (Consolidated Retained Earnings)	—0—		12,418		26,078		41,104		57,633	
Interest Expense	12,418		13,660		15,026		16,529		18,183	
Unamortized Discount on Bonds Payable		12,418		26,078		41,104		57,633		75,816

Complete Equity Method

December 31	2001 Debit	2001 Credit	2002 Debit	2002 Credit	2003 Debit	2003 Credit	2004 Debit	2004 Credit	2005 Debit	2005 Credit
Unamortized Discount on Bonds Payable	75,816		75,816		75,816		75,816		75,816	
Difference Between Cost and Book Value		75,816		75,816		75,816		75,816		75,816
Investment in S Company	—0—		12,418		26,078		41,104		57,633	
Interest Expense	12,418		13,660		15,026		16,529		18,183	
Unamortized Discount on Bonds Payable		12,418		26,078		41,104		57,633		75,816

At maturity the bonds will be redeemed at par value ($500,000), which also will be the carrying value to the consolidated entity. In all subsequent years $75,816 of the difference between cost and book value will be debited to the beginning retained earnings of the parent company in the consolidated statements workpaper in order to reduce beginning consolidated retained earnings for the cumulative amount of additional interest expense recognized in the consolidated financial statements in prior years. If the complete equity method is used, the debit will be to the Investment account, as the parent should have already reflected the adjustment to earnings in its equity in subsidiary income and hence in its retained earnings.

The preceding example was based on the assumption that P Company owned a 100% interest in S Company. If P Company owned an 80% interest rather than

ILLUSTRATION 5–16

Bond Discount Amortization Schedule

Date	Interest Expense Recorded by S	Consolidated Interest Expense	Discount Amortization	Consolidated Carrying Value
1/1/01	$—0—	$—0—	$—0—	$424,184
12/31/01	30,000 (1)	42,418 (2)	12,418 (3)	436,602
12/31/02	30,000 (4)	43,660	13,660	450,262
12/31/03	30,000	45,026	15,026	465,288
12/31/04	30,000	46,529	16,529	481,817
12/31/05	30,000	48,183	18,183	500,000
	150,000	225,816	75,816	

(1) .10 × $424,184 = $42,418.
(2) $42,418 − $30,000 = $12,418.
(3) $424,184 + $12,418 = $436,602.
(4) .10 × $436,602 = $43,660.

a 100% interest in S Company, the amount of the difference between cost and book value allocated to unamortized discount on bonds payable on the date of acquisition would be $60,653 [.80 × ($500,000 − $424,184)] and the discount amortization would be 80% of the amounts shown in column 4 of Illustration 5-16.

Allocation of Difference to Assets (Liabilities) with Fair Values Less (Greater) Than Book Values

Sometimes the fair value of an asset on the date of acquisition is less than the amount recorded on the books of the subsidiary. In this case the allocation of the parent company's share of the difference between the fair value and the book value of the asset will result in a reduction of the asset. If the asset is depreciable, this difference will be amortized over the life of the asset as a reduction of depreciation expense. Likewise, the fair value of the long-term debt may be greater rather than less than its recorded value on the date of acquisition. In this case, entries are necessary to allocate the parent company's share of the difference between the fair value and book value of the debt to unamortized bond premium and to amortize it over the remaining life of the debt as a reduction of interest expense.

To illustrate, assume that P Company paid $2,240,000 for 80% of the outstanding stock of S Company when S Company had identifiable net assets with a fair value of $2,600,000 and a book value of $2,150,000. The fair values and book values of identifiable assets and liabilities are presented in Illustration 5-17. The Computation and Allocation Schedule is presented next:

ILLUSTRATION 5–17

Allocation of Difference Between Cost and Book Value

	Fair Value	Book Value	Difference Between Fair Value and Book Value (100%)
Securities	550,000	400,000	150,000
Equipment (net)	1,250,000	1,500,000	(250,000)
Land	1,225,000	550,000	675,000
Bonds Payable	(725,000)	(600,000)	(125,000)
Other Assets and Liabilities	300,000	300,000	—0—
Total	2,600,000	2,150,000	450,000

Computation and Allocation of Difference Between Cost and Book Value of Equity

Cost of Investment (purchase price)		$2,240,000
Book Value of Equity Acquired ($2,150,000 × 80%)		1,720,000
Difference Between Cost and Book Value		520,000
Increase securities (.80 × $150,000)	(120,000)	
Decrease equipment (.80 × $250,000), 4-year life	200,000	
Increase land (.80 × $675,000)	(540,000)	
Increase bonds payable (.80 × $125,000)	100,000	(360,000)
Balance (Excess of Cost Over Fair Value)		160,000
Record goodwill, 10-year life		(160,000)
Balance		$ 0

Assume that the $100,000 allocated to bond premium is amortized over five years using the straight-line method,[13] that equipment has a remaining life of four years, and that the goodwill is amortized over 10 years.

End of First Year After Acquisition (Workpaper Entries) At the end of the first year the workpaper entries are:

(1)	Securities	120,000	
	Land	540,000	
	Goodwill	160,000	
	Equipment (net)		200,000
	Unamortized Premium on Bonds Payable		100,000
	Difference Between Cost and Book Value		520,000
	To allocate the difference between cost and book value on the date of acquisition.		

Note that the assets accounts increased are recorded by debits and those decreased by credits (Equipment), while a credit records an increase in a liability (increase in Unamortized Premium on Bonds Payable).

(2)	Amortization of Goodwill	16,000	
	Goodwill		16,000
	To amortize goodwill ($160,000/10 years).		

(3)	Equipment (net)	50,000	
	Depreciation Expense		50,000
	To adjust depreciation expense downward ($200,000/4 years).		

(4)	Unamortized Premium on Bonds Payable	20,000	
	Interest Expense		20,000
	To amortize premium on bonds payable ($100,000/5 years).		

---

[13]The straight-line method is illustrated here as a matter of expediency. Where differences between the straight-line method and the effective interest rate method of amortization are material, the effective interest rate method as shown in Illustration 5-16 should be used.

End of Second Year After Acquisition (Workpaper Entries) At the end of the second year the workpaper entries are:

(1)		
Securities	120,000	
Land	540,000	
Goodwill	160,000	
Equipment (net)		200,000
Unamortized Premium on Bonds Payable		100,000
Difference Between Cost and Book Value		520,000

To allocate the difference between cost and book value on the date of acquisition (this entry is repeated in subsequent years because the year of acquisition entry was recorded only on a workpaper).

Cost and Partial Equity Methods			*Complete Equity Method*		
(2) Amortization of Goodwill	16,000		Amortization of Goodwill	16,000	
Beginning Retained					
Earnings—P Company	16,000		Investment in S Company	16,000	
Goodwill		32,000	Goodwill		32,000

To amortize goodwill for the current and prior year ($160,000/10 years).

Cost and Partial Equity Methods			*Complete Equity Method*		
(3) Equipment (net)	100,000		Equipment (net)	100,000	
Beginning Retained					
Earnings—P Company		50,000	Investment in S Company		50,000
Depreciation Expense		50,000	Depreciation Expense		50,000

To adjust depreciation downward for the current and prior year ($200,000/4 years).

Cost and Partial Equity Methods			*Complete Equity Method*		
(4) Unamortized Premium on			Unamortized Premium		
Bond Payable	40,000		on Bond Payable	40,000	
Beginning Retained			Investment in S		
Earnings—P Company		20,000	Company		20,000
Interest Expense		20,000	Interest Expense		20,000

To amortize premium on bond payable for current and prior year ($100,000/5 years).

In the second year, under the cost or partial equity method, adjustments to the beginning retained earnings of the parent company are necessary so that consolidated retained earnings at the beginning of the second year will be equal to the consolidated retained earnings reported at the end of the first year. The debits and credits are equal to the adjustments to consolidated net income that resulted from the reduction of depreciation expense ($50,000), the reduction in interest expense ($20,000), and the increase in amortization expense ($16,000) in the prior year's workpaper. Under the complete equity method, no such adjustment to retained earnings is needed since the parent's retained earnings accurately reflects the consolidated retained earnings each year. Instead entries are needed to the Investment account to facilitate the elimination of that account (by reversing the adjustments reflected therein).

Reporting Accumulated Depreciation in Consolidated Financial Statements as a Separate Balance

In previous illustrations we have assumed that any particular classification of depreciable assets will be presented in the consolidated financial statements as a single balance net of accumulated depreciation. When accumulated depreciation is reported as a separate balance in the consolidated financial statements, the workpaper entry to allocate and depreciate the difference between cost and book value must be slightly modified. To illustrate, assume that P Company acquires a 90% interest in S Company on January 1, 2001, and that the difference between cost and book value in the amount of $180,000 is entirely attributable to equipment with an original life of nine years and a remaining life on January 1, 2001, of six years. Pertinent information regarding the equipment is presented in Illustration 5-18.

In Illustration 5-18, the $1,200,000 fair value of the equipment (gross) is the replacement cost of the equipment if purchased *new* and is referred to as *replacement cost new*. The $400,000 in accumulated depreciation in the fair value column is the proportional amount of replacement cost new necessary to bring the net fair market value to $800,000, which is the fair market value of the subsidiary's *used* equipment. The $800,000 fair value of the used equipment is sometimes referred to in appraisal reports as the equipment's *sound value*.

If the equipment is to be presented in the consolidated financial statements as one balance net of accumulated depreciation, workpaper elimination entries to allocate and depreciate the difference between cost and book value are similar to those presented in Illustrations 5-6 and 5-7, and are summarized in Illustration 5-19 for three years. However, when equipment and accumulated depreciation are reported as separate balances in the consolidated financial statements, the workpaper elimination entries must be modified as presented in Illustration 5-20. The amount debited to Equipment (gross) minus the amount credited to Accumulated Depreciation in each of the workpaper entries in Illustration 5-20 is the same as the amount debited to Equipment (net) in the workpaper entries in Illustration 5-19, where equipment is presented in the consolidated financial statements net of accumulated depreciation.

To allocate the $180,000 difference assigned to Net Equipment between Equipment (gross) and Accumulated Depreciation, we need to know the replacement

---

ILLUSTRATION 5–18

Determination of Amount of Difference Between Cost and Book Value
Allocation to Equipment and to Accumulated Depreciation
January 1, 2001

	Fair Value	Book Value	Difference Between Fair Value and Book Value	P Company's 90% Interest Therein
Equipment (gross)	$1,200,000	$900,000	$300,000	$270,000
Accumulated Depreciation	400,000	300,000	100,000	90,000
Equipment (net)	$ 800,000	$600,000	$200,000	$180,000
Annual Depreciation (original life nine years, remaining life six years)		$100,000		$ 30,000

ILLUSTRATION 5–19

Summary of Workpaper Entries
Equipment Presented Net of Accumulated Depreciation

	1/1/01		12/31/01		12/31/02		12/31/03	
Cost or Partial Equity Method	*Debit*	*Credit*	*Debit*	*Credit*	*Debit*	*Credit*	*Debit*	*Credit*
Equipment (net)	180,000		180,000		180,000		180,000	
Difference Between Cost and Book Value		180,000		180,000		180,000		180,000
Depreciation Expense	—0—		30,000		30,000		30,000	
Beginning Retained Earnings—Parent Company	—0—		—0—		30,000		60,000	
Equipment (net)		—0—		30,000		60,000		90,000
Complete Equity Method								
Equipment (net)	180,000		180,000		180,000		180,000	
Difference Between Cost and Book Value		180,000		180,000		180,000		180,000
Depreciation Expense	—0—		30,000		30,000		30,000	
Investment in S Company	—0—		—0—		30,000		60,000	
Equipment (net)		—0—		30,000		60,000		90,000

ILLUSTRATION 5–20

Summary of Workpaper Entries
Accumulated Depreciation Presented as Separate Balance

	1/1/01		12/31/01		12/31/02		12/31/03	
Cost or Partial Equity Method	*Debit*	*Credit*	*Debit*	*Credit*	*Debit*	*Credit*	*Debit*	*Credit*
Equipment (net)	270,000		270,000		270,000		270,000	
Accumulated Depreciation		90,000		90,000		90,000		90,000
Difference Between Cost and Book Value		180,000		180,000		180,000		180,000
Depreciation Expense	—0—		30,000		30,000		30,000	
Beginning Retained Earnings—Parent Company	—0—		—0—		30,000		60,000	
Accumulated Depreciation		—0—		30,000		60,000		90,000
Complete Equity Method								
Equipment (net)	270,000		270,000		270,000		270,000	
Accumulated Depreciation		90,000		90,000		90,000		90,000
Difference Between Cost and Book Value		180,000		180,000		180,000		180,000
Depreciation Expense	—0—		30,000		30,000		30,000	
Investment in S Company	—0—		—0—		30,000		60,000	
Accumulated Depreciation		—0—		30,000		60,000		90,000

cost new and the sound (used) value of the equipment as shown in the appraisal report. Alternatively, these amounts may be inferred. If, for example, the equipment is one-third depreciated on January 1, 2001, the $180,000 difference between P Company's interest in the sound value and the book value of the equipment implies that the difference can be "grossed up" by dividing by 2/3 as follows:

Let
    Amount of Difference Allocated to Equipment (Gross) = X
    Amount of Difference Allocated to Accumulated Depreciation = (1/3)X
    Total Difference Allocated to Equipment (Net) = (2/3)X

$$X - (1/3)X = 180,000$$
$$(2/3)X = 180,000$$
$$X = 180,000 \div (2/3) = \$270,000 \text{ (Amount Allocated to Equipment)}$$
$$(1/3)X = (1/3)(270,000) = \$90,000 \text{ (Amount Allocated to Accumulated Depreciation)}$$

Disposal of Depreciable Assets by Subsidiary

Assume that on January 1, 2003, two years after its acquisition by P Company, S Company sells all the equipment referred to in Illustration 5-18 for $480,000. On January 1, 2003 (the date of the sale), the carrying value of the equipment on the books of the subsidiary is $400,000, but $520,000 from the consolidated point of view. These values are presented in Illustration 5-21. S Company reports a gain of $80,000 on the disposal of the equipment in its books:

S Company's Books		
Cash	480,000	
Accumulated Depreciation	500,000	
Gain on Sale		80,000
Equipment		900,000

From the point of view of the consolidated entity, however, there is a loss of $40,000. Recall the usual workpaper entry to allocate the difference between cost and book value includes:

Equipment	270,000	
Difference Between Cost and Book Value		180,000
Accumulated Depreciation		90,000

The workpaper entry necessary to adjust the amounts in the December 31, 2003, consolidated financial statements is as follows (shown first for the cost or partial equity methods, and second for the complete equity method):

Cost or Partial Equity Method		
Beginning Retained Earnings—Parent Company	60,000	
(depreciation expense adjustment for years 2001 and 2002)		
Gain on Disposal of Equipment (eliminates gain already recorded)	80,000	
Loss on Disposal of Equipment (creates loss account)	40,000	
Difference Between Cost and Book Value		180,000

ILLUSTRATION 5–21

Calculation of Recorded and Consolidated Gain or Loss

Disposal of Equipment

	S Company	Unamoritized Difference	Consolidated
Cost	$900,000	$270,000	$1,170,000
Accumulated Depreciation	500,000	150,000*	650,000
Undepreciated Base	400,000	120,000	520,000
Proceeds	(480,000)		(480,000)
(Gain) Loss on Sale	$(80,000)	$120,000	$ 40,000

*$150,000 equals $90,000 allocated at acquisition plus $30,000 from year 2001, plus $30,000 from year 2002.

Complete Equity Method

Investment in S Company	60,000	
(depreciation expense adjustment for years 2001 and 2002)		
Gain on Disposal of Equipment (eliminates gain already recorded)	80,000	
Loss on Disposal of Equipment (creates loss account)	40,000	
Difference Between Cost and Book Value		180,000

In the year of sale, any gain or loss recognized by the subsidiary on the disposal of an asset to which any of the difference between cost and book value has been allocated must be adjusted in the consolidated statements workpaper. The entry above serves to eliminate the gain recorded by the subsidiary and record the correct loss (or gain) to the consolidated entity. It also debits Beginning Retained Earnings—P Company (or Investment in S Company if the complete equity method is used) to "catch up" the effects to the consolidated entity of two prior years of depreciation expense adjustments.

Depreciable Assets Used in Manufacturing

When the difference between cost and book value is allocated to depreciable assets used in manufacturing, workpaper entries necessary to reflect additional depreciation may be more complex, because the current and previous years' additional depreciation may need to be allocated among work in process, finished goods on hand at the end of the year, and cost of goods sold. In practice, such refinements are often ignored on the basis of materiality, and all the current year's additional depreciation is charged to cost of goods sold.

PUSH DOWN ACCOUNTING

Push-down accounting is the establishment of a new accounting and reporting basis for a subsidiary company in its separate financial statements based on the purchase price paid by the parent company to acquire a controlling interest in the outstanding voting stock of the subsidiary company. This accounting method is required for the subsidiary in some instances such as in the banking industry, an industry overwhelmed by the frequency and extent of merger activity in recent years.

The valuation implied by the price of the stock to the parent company is "pushed down" to the subsidiary and used to restate its assets (including goodwill) and liabilities in its separate financial statements. If all the voting stock is purchased, the assets and liabilities of the subsidiary company are restated so that the excess of the restated amounts of the assets (including goodwill) over the restated amounts of the liabilities equals the purchase price of the stock. Push down accounting is based on the notion that the basis of accounting for purchased assets and liabilities should be the same regardless of whether the acquired company continues to exist as a separate subsidiary or is merged into the parent company's operations. Thus, under push down accounting, the parent company's cost of acquiring a subsidiary is used to establish a new accounting basis for the assets and liabilities of the subsidiary in the subsidiary's separate financial statements. Because push down accounting has not been addressed in authoritative pronouncements of the FASB or its predecessors, practice has been inconsistent. Some acquired companies have used a new pushed down basis, and others, in essentially the same circumstances, have used preacquisition book values.

Arguments For and Against Push Down Accounting

Proponents of push down accounting believe that a new basis of accounting should be required following a purchase transaction that results in a significant change in the ownership of a company's outstanding voting stock. In essence, they view the transaction as if the new owners had purchased an existing business and established a new company to continue that business. Consequently, they believe that the parent company's basis should be imputed to the subsidiary because the new basis provides more relevant information for users of the subsidiary's separate financial statements. In addition, *APB Opinion No. 16* requires that a business purchased in a business combination be stated in consolidated statements at the basis established in the purchase transaction. To provide symmetry, the separate financial statements of the subsidiary should be presented in the same manner.

Those who oppose push down accounting believe that, under the historical cost concept, a change in ownership of an entity does not justify a new accounting basis in its financial statements. Because the subsidiary did not purchase assets or assume liabilities as a result of the transaction, the recognition of a new accounting basis based on a change in ownership, rather than on a transaction on the part of the subsidiary, represents a breach in the historical cost concept in accounting. They argue further that implementation problems might arise. For example, noncontrolling stockholders may not have meaningful comparative financial statements. In addition, restatement of the financial statements may create problems in determining or maintaining compliance with various financial restrictions under debt agreements.

Push down accounting is an issue only if the subsidiary is required to issue separate financial statements for any reason, for example, because of the existence of noncontrolling interests or financial arrangements with nonaffiliates. Three important factors that should be considered in determining the appropriateness of push down accounting are:

1. Whether the subsidiary has outstanding debt held by the public.
2. Whether the subsidiary has outstanding a senior class of capital stock not acquired by the parent company.
3. The level at which a major change in ownership of an entity should be deemed to have occurred, for example, 100%, 90%, 51%.

Public holders of the acquired company's debt need comparative data to assess the value and risk of their investments. These public holders generally have some expressed (or implied) rights in the subsidiary that may be adversely affected by a new basis of accounting. Similarly, holders of preferred stock, particularly if the stock includes a participation feature, may have their rights significantly altered by a new basis of accounting.

Views on the percentage level of ownership change needed to apply a new basis of accounting vary. Some believe that the purchase of substantially all the voting stock (90% or more) should be the threshold level; others believe that the percentage level of ownership change should be that needed for control, usually, more than 50%. A related problem involves the amounts to be allocated to the individual assets and liabilities, noncontrolling interest, and goodwill in the separate statements of the subsidiary. Some believe that values should be allocated on the basis of the fair value of the subsidiary as a whole imputed from the transaction. Thus, if 80% of the voting stock is acquired for $32 million, the fair value of the net assets should be imputed to be $40 million ($32 million/.80), and values allocated on that basis. Others believe that values would be allocated on the basis of the proportional interest acquired. They believe that new values should be reflected on the books of the subsidiary only to the extent of the price paid in the transaction. Thus, if 80% of a company is acquired for $32 million, the basis of the subsidiary's net assets should be adjusted by the difference between the price paid and the book value of an 80% interest. This latter approach will result in the assignment of the same values to assets and liabilities on the books of the subsidiary as that previously illustrated in the workpaper entry to allocate the difference between cost and book value in the consolidated statements workpaper.

Status of Push Down Accounting

The Task Force on Consolidation Problems, Accounting Standards Division of the AICPA, released an issues paper entitled "Push Down Accounting" in 1979. The paper discussed the issues related to push down accounting and cited related literature. The paper also presented the conclusions of the Accounting Standards Executive Committee on the issues discussed in the paper. The majority of the Committee recommended the use of push down accounting where there had been at least a 90% change in ownership.

In 1983, the SEC released *Staff Accounting Bulletin (SAB) No. 54,* which discusses the staff's position on the appropriateness of applying push down accounting in the separate financial statements of subsidiaries acquired in purchase transactions. The SEC believes that purchase transactions that result in an entity becoming substantially wholly owned (as defined in Regulation S-X) should establish a new basis of accounting for the purchased assets and liabilities. When the form of ownership is within the control of the parent company, the basis of accounting for purchased assets and liabilities should be the same regardless of whether the entity continues to exist or is merged into the parent company's operations. ***As a general rule, the SEC requires push down accounting when the ownership change is greater than 95% and objects to push down accounting when the ownership change is less than 80%.*** In addition, the SEC staff in *SAB No. 54* express the view that the existence of outstanding public debt, preferred stock, or a significant noncontrolling interest in a subsidiary might have an impact on the parent company's ability to control the form of ownership.

In these circumstances, the staff encourages, but does not insist on, the application of push down accounting.

In December 1991, the FASB issued a Discussion Memorandum entitled *An Analysis of Issues Related to New Basis Accounting*. The discussion memorandum was published to solicit views on which, if any, transactions or events should result in changing the carrying amount of an entity's individual assets, including goodwill, and liabilities to amounts representing their current fair values. Transactions and events discussed include stock purchases, as well as significant borrowing transactions, reorganizations and restructurings, and formations and sales of interests in joint ventures.

Push Down Accounting Illustration

To illustrate the application of push down accounting, we use data presented earlier in this chapter, with some modifications, as follows:

1. P Company acquired an 80% interest in S Company on January 1, 2001, for $2,200,000, at which time S Company had capital stock of $1,500,000 and retained earnings of $500,000.
2. The difference between cost and book value ($600,000) is allocated as presented in Illustration 5-22.

In this example, we assume that values are allocated on the basis of the fair value of the subsidiary as a whole, imputed from the transaction.

3. In 2001, S Company reported net income of $32,500.

Note that the net income of S Company ($32,500) is $92,500 less than the amount of income reported in Illustration 5-6 because the effect of the amortization of the difference between cost and book value is recorded on the books of S Company under push down accounting. This difference of $92,500 consists of:

Increase in Cost of Goods Sold	$50,000
Increase in Depreciation Expense ($300,000/10 years)	30,000
Amortization of Goodwill ($250,000/20 years)	12,500
	$92,500

ILLUSTRATION 5–22

Allocation of Difference Between Cost and Book Value

	Cost Basis	Implied (100%) Push Down Basis
Inventory (FIFO basis)	$ 40,000	$ 50,000
Equipment (10-year life)	240,000	300,000
Land	120,000	150,000
Goodwill (20-year life)	200,000	250,000
Total	$600,000	$750,000

4. S Company declared a dividend of $20,000 on November 15, payable on December 1, 2001.

5. P Company uses the cost method to record its investment in S Company.

S Company Book Entries—2001 On January 1, 2001, the date of acquisition, S Company would make the following entry to record the effect of the pushed down values implied by the purchase of 80% of its stock by P Company:

Inventory, 1/1	50,000	
Equipment	300,000	
Land	150,000	
Goodwill	250,000	
Revaluation Capital		750,000

Assume the following: (1) all beginning inventory was sold during the year; (2) equipment has a remaining useful life of 10 years from 1/1/2001; and (3) goodwill is amortized over 20 years. Given these assumptions, the $50,000 excess cost allocated to beginning inventory would be included in cost of goods sold when the goods were sold. Similarly, depreciation expense recorded on S Company's books would be $30,000 greater than if the increase in equipment value had not been recorded. In addition, an entry would be made on S Company's books to record amortization of goodwill, $12,500.

A workpaper for the preparation of consolidated financial statements on December 31, 2001, under push down accounting is presented in Illustration 5-23. Workpaper elimination entries in general journal form are as follows:

(1)	Dividend Income	16,000	
	Dividends Declared—S Company		16,000
(2)	Capital Stock—S Company	1,200,000	
	Retained Earnings 1/1—S Company	400,000	
	Revaluation Capital—S Company	600,000	
	Investment in S Company		2,200,000

A comparison of Illustration 5-23 with Illustration 5-6 shows that combined income is smaller, as is the noncontrolling interest in combined income, when push down accounting is used. Consolidated net income and consolidated retained earnings are the same. Thus, when values are assigned on the basis of fair values of the subsidiary as a whole imputed from the transaction, the use of push down accounting has no effect on these consolidated balances. Note, however, that both consolidated net assets and the noncontrolling interest in consolidated net assets are $131,500 greater in Illustration 5-23, reflecting the decision to push down the full value of S Company implied by the amount paid by P Company for its 80% interest. This amount can be verified as follows:

The noncontrolling interest's share of revaluation capital .20($750,000)	$150,000
Less: amortization and depreciation thereon .20($92,500)	18,500
Balance	$131,500

Note also that no workpaper entries were necessary in Illustration 5-23 to allocate, amortize, or depreciate the difference between cost and book value since these adjustments have already been made on S Company's books.

Cost Method			ILLUSTRATION 5–23			
80% Owned Subsidiary			**Consolidated Statements Workpaper**			
Push Down Basis			**P Company and Subsidiary**			
			For Year Ended December 31, 2001			

| | P | S | Eliminations | | Noncontrolling | Consolidated |
Income Statement	Company	Company	Dr.	Cr.	Interest	Balances
Sales	3,100,000	2,200,000				5,300,000
Dividend Income	16,000		(1) 16,000			
Total Revenue	3,116,000	2,200,000				5,300,000
Cost of Goods Sold	1,700,000	1,410,000				3,110,000
Depreciation—Equipment	120,000	60,000				180,000
Amortization of Goodwill		12,500				12,500
Other Expenses	998,000	685,000				1,683,000
Total Cost and Expense	2,818,000	2,167,500				4,985,500
Net/Combined Income	298,000	32,500				314,500
Noncontrolling Interest in						
Income					6,500	(6,500)*
Net Income to Retained						
Earnings	298,000	32,500	16,000	—0—	6,500	308,000
Retained Earnings Statement						
1/1 Retained Earnings						
P Company	1,650,000					1,650,000
S Company		500,000	(2) 400,000		100,000	
Net Income from above	298,000	32,500	16,000	—0—	6,500	308,000
Dividends Declared						
P Company	(150,000)					(150,000)
S Company		(20,000)		(1) 16,000	(4,000)	
12/31 Retained Earnings to						
the Balance Sheet	1,798,000	685,000	416,000	16,000	102,500	1,808,000
Balance Sheet						
Investment in S Company	2,200,000			(2) 2,200,000		
Land	1,250,000	400,000				1,650,000
Equipment (net)	1,080,000	540,000				1,620,000
Other Assets (net)	2,402,000	1,885,000				4,287,000
Goodwill		237,500				237,500
Total	6,932,000	3,062,500				7,794,500
Liabilities	2,134,000	300,000				2,434,000
Capital Stock						
P Company	3,000,000					3,000,000
S Company		1,500,000	(2) 1,200,000		300,000	
Revaluation Capital		750,000	(2) 600,000		150,000	
Retained Earnings from						
above	1,798,000	512,500	416,000	16,000	102,500	1,808,000
Noncontrolling Interest in						
Net Assets					552,500	552,500
Total	6,932,000	3,062,500	2,216,000	2,216,000		7,794,500

*.20 × $132,500 = $6,500.
(1) To eliminate intercompany dividends.
(2) To eliminate investment account.

SUMMARY

1. *Calculate the difference between cost and book value and allocate to the subsidiary's assets and liabilities.* The difference between the purchase price and book value is used first to adjust the individual assets and liabilities to their fair values on the date of acquisition. If cost exceeds the aggregate fair values of identifiable assets less liabilities, the residual amount will be *positive* (a debit balance). A positive residual difference is evidence of an unspecified intangible and is accounted for as goodwill.

2. *Explain how any excess of fair value over acquisition cost of net assets is allocated to reduce the subsidiary's assets and liabilities in the case of bargain purchases.* When the purchase price (acquisition cost) is below the aggregate fair value of identifiable assets less liabilities, the residual amount will be negative (a credit balance). A negative residual difference is evidence of a bargain purchase, with the difference between acquisition cost and fair value designating the amount of the bargain. When a bargain acquisition occurs, some of the acquired assets must be reduced below their fair values. Specifically, long-lived assets (other than investments in marketable securities) are recorded at fair market value minus an adjustment for the bargain. The FASB is considering the appropriate accounting for bargain purchases, with one possibility being to recognize a portion of the bargain in some instances as an extraordinary gain.

3. *Explain how goodwill is measured.* Goodwill is measured as the excess of purchase price over the fair value of the net assets acquired.

4. *Describe how the allocation process differs if less than 100% of the subsidiary is acquired.* Consolidated net assets are written up only by an amount equal to **the parent company's share** of the difference on the date of acquisition between the implied fair value and the book value of the subsidiary company's net assets (rather than the entire difference between fair value and book value).

5. *Record the entries needed on the parent's books to account for the investment under the three methods: the cost, the partial equity, and the complete equity methods.* The most important difference between the cost and equity methods pertains to the period in which the parent recognizes subsidiary income on its books. If the cost method is in use, the parent recognizes its share of subsidiary income only when dividends are declared by the subsidiary. If the partial equity method is in use, the investor recognizes its share of the subsidiary's income when reported by the

subsidiary. A debit to cash and a credit to the investment account record the receipt of dividends under the partial equity method. The complete equity method differs from the partial equity method in that the share of subsidiary income recognized by the parent is adjusted from the amount reported by the subsidiary. Such adjustments include the amount of excess depreciation and goodwill amortization implied by the difference between purchase price and book values of the underlying assets acquired.

6. *Prepare workpapers for the year of acquisition and the year(s) subsequent to the acquisition, assuming that the parent accounts for the investment using the cost, the partial equity, and the complete equity methods.* Under the cost method, dividends declared by the subsidiary are eliminated against dividend income recorded by the parent. The investment account is eliminated against the equity accounts of the subsidiary, with the difference between cost and book value recorded in a separate account by that name. The difference is then allocated to adjust underlying assets and/or liabilities, and to record goodwill in some cases. Additional entries are made to record excess depreciation on assets written up (or to decrease depreciation if written down) and to amortize goodwill. Under the equity method, the dividends declared by the subsidiary are eliminated against the investment account, as is the equity in subsidiary income. The investment account is eliminated in the same way as under the cost method. In subsequent years, the cost method requires an initial entry to establish reciprocity or convert to equity. This entry, which is not needed under the equity method, debits the investment account and credits retained earnings of the parent (for the change in retained earnings of the subsidiary from the date of acquisition to the beginning of the current year multiplied by the parent's percentage). Only under the complete equity method does the parent's beginning retained earnings exactly match the amount reported as consolidated retained earnings at the end of the previous year. Hence fewer workpaper adjustments to beginning retained earnings of the parent are needed under the complete equity method than under the two other methods.

7. *Understand the allocation of the difference between cost and book value to long-term debt components.* Notes payable, long-term debt, and other obligations of an acquired company should be valued for consolida-

tion purposes at their fair values. Quoted market prices, if available, are the best evidence of the fair value of the debt. If quoted market prices are unavailable, then management's best estimate of the fair value may be based on fair values of debt with similar characteristics or on valuation techniques such as the present value of estimated future cash flows. The present value should be determined using appropriate market rates of interest at the date of acquisition.

8. *Explain how to allocate the difference between cost and book value when some assets have fair values below book values.* In this case the allocation of the parent company's share of the difference between the fair value and the book value of the asset will result in a reduction of the asset. If the asset is depreciable, this difference will be amortized over the life of the asset as a reduction of depreciation expense.

9. *Distinguish between recording the subsidiary depreciable assets at net versus gross fair values.* When the assets

are recorded net, no accumulated depreciation account is used initially. When they are recorded gross, an accumulated depreciation account is needed. To allocate the difference assigned to depreciable assets between the asset account (gross) and the accumulated depreciation account, we must know the replacement cost new and the sound (used) value of the asset as shown in the appraisal report. Alternatively, these amounts may be inferred.

10. *Understand the concept of push down accounting.* Push down accounting is the establishment of a new accounting and reporting basis for a subsidiary company in its separate financial statements based on the purchase price paid by the parent company to acquire a controlling interest in the outstanding voting stock of the subsidiary company. This accounting method is required for the subsidiary in some instances, usually when the ownership level is over 95% for publicly held companies.

QUESTIONS

1. Distinguish among the following concepts:
  (a) Difference between cost and book value.
  (b) Excess of cost over fair value.
  (c) Excess of fair value over cost.
  (d) Deferred excess of fair value over cost.

2. In what account is "the difference between cost and book value" recorded on the books of the investor? In what account is the "excess of cost over fair value" recorded?

3. How do you determine the amount of "the difference between cost and book value" to be allocated to a specific asset of a less than wholly owned subsidiary?

4. The parent company's share of the fair value of the net assets of a subsidiary may exceed acquisition cost. How must this excess be treated in the preparation of consolidated financial statements?

5. Why are marketable securities excluded from the noncurrent assets to which any excess of fair value over cost is to be allocated?

6. P Company acquired a 100% interest in S Company. On the date of acquisition the fair value of the assets and liabilities of S Company was equal to their book value except for land that had a fair value of $1,500,000 and a book value of $300,000. At what amount should the land of S Company be included in the consolidated balance sheet? At what amount should the land of S Company be included in the

consolidated balance sheet if P Company acquired an 80% interest in S Company rather than a 100% interest?

7. Corporation A purchased the net assets of Corporation B for $80,000. On the date of A's purchase, Corporation B had no long-term investments in marketable securities and $10,000 (book and fair value) of liabilities. The fair values of Corporation B's assets, when acquired, were:

Current Assets	$ 40,000
Noncurrent Assets	60,000
Total	$100,000

How should the $10,000 difference between the fair value of the net assets acquired ($90,000) and the cost ($80,000) be accounted for by Corporation A?
  (a) The $10,000 difference should be credited to retained earnings.
  (b) The noncurrent assets should be recorded at $50,000.
  (c) The current assets should be recorded at $36,000, and the noncurrent assets should be recorded at $54,000.
  (d) A deferred credit of $10,000 should be set up and then amortized to income over a period not to exceed 40 years.

8. Assume that Corporation A paid $110,000 for Corporation B's net assets and that all other information given in Question 7 remains the same. What is the minimum annual difference between financial accounting income and tax income because of this purchase?

(a) Zero.
(b) $500.
(c) $2,000.
(d) Cannot be determined from the information given.

9. Meredith Company and Kyle Company were combined in a purchase transaction. Meredith was able to acquire Kyle at a bargain price. The sum of the market or appraised values of identifiable assets acquired less the fair value of liabilities assumed exceeded the cost to Meredith. After reducing

noncurrent assets to zero, there was still some "negative goodwill." Proper accounting treatment by Meredith is to report the amount as

(a) An extraordinary item.
(b) Part of current income in the year of combination.
(c) A deferred credit and amortize it.
(d) Paid in capital.

10. How does the recording in the consolidated statements workpaper of the increase in depreciation that results from the allocation of a portion of the difference between cost and book value to depreciable property affect the calculation of noncontrolling interest in combined income?

EXERCISES

EXERCISE 5-1 Allocation of Cost

On January 1, 2000, Pam Company purchased an 85% interest in Shaw Company for $540,000. On this date, Shaw Company had common stock of $400,000 and retained earnings of $140,000. An examination of Shaw Company's assets and liabilities revealed that their book value was equal to their fair value except for marketable securities and equipment:

	Book Value	Fair Value
Marketable Securities	$ 20,000	$ 45,000
Equipment (net)	120,000	140,000

Required:

A. Prepare a Computation and Allocation Schedule for the difference between cost and book value of equity acquired.

B. Determine the amounts at which the above assets (plus goodwill, if any) will appear on the consolidated balance sheet on January 1, 2000.

EXERCISE 5-2 End of the Year of Acquisition Workpaper Entries

On January 1, 2002, Payne Corporation purchased a 75% interest in Salmon Company for $585,000. A summary of Salmon Company's balance sheet on that date revealed the following:

	Book Value	Fair Value
Equipment	$525,000	$705,000
Other Assets	150,000	150,000
	$675,000	$855,000
Liabilities	$ 75,000	$ 75,000
Common Stock	225,000	
Retained Earnings	375,000	
	$675,000	

The equipment had an original life of 15 years and has a remaining useful life of 10 years. Any goodwill will be amortized over the maximum period allowable.

Required:

For the December 31, 2002, consolidated financial statements workpaper, prepare the workpaper entry(s) to allocate, amortize, and depreciate the difference between cost and book value assuming:

A. Equipment is presented net of accumulated depreciation.

B. Accumulated depreciation is presented on a separate row in the workpaper and in the consolidated statement of financial position.

EXERCISE 5-3 **Allocation of Cost**

Pace Company purchased 20,000 of the 25,000 shares of Saddler Corporation for $525,000. On January 3, 2001, the acquisition date, Saddler Corporation's capital stock and retained earnings account balances were $500,000 and $100,000, respectively.

The following values were determined for Saddler Corporation on the date of purchase:

	Book Value	Fair Value
Inventory	$ 50,000	$ 70,000
Other Current Assets	200,000	200,000
Marketable Securities	100,000	125,000
Plant and Equipment	300,000	330,000

Required:

A. Prepare the entry on the books of Pace Company to record its investment in Saddler Corporation.

B. Prepare a Computation and Allocation Schedule for the difference between the cost and book value in the consolidated statements workpaper.

EXERCISE 5-4 **Allocation of Cost and Workpaper Entries at Date of Acquisition**

On January 1, 2002, Porter Company purchased an 80% interest in Salem Company for $260,000. On this date, Salem Company had common stock of $207,000 and retained earnings of $130,500.

An examination of Salem Company's balance sheet revealed the following comparisons between book and fair values:

	Book Value	Fair Value
Inventory	$ 30,000	$ 35,000
Other Current Assets	50,000	55,000
Equipment	300,000	350,000
Land	200,000	200,000

Required:

A. Determine the amounts that should be allocated to Salem Company's assets on the consolidated financial statements workpaper on January 1, 2002.

B. Prepare the January 1, 2002, consolidated financial statements workpaper entries to eliminate the investment account and to allocate the difference between cost and book value.

EXERCISE 5-5 **T-account Calculation of Controlling Interest in Combined Net Income**

On January 1, 2001, P Company purchased an 80% interest in S Company for $600,000, at which time S Company had retained earnings of $300,000 and capital stock of $350,000. Any difference between cost and book value was entirely attributable to a patent with a remaining useful life of 10 years.

Assume that P and S Companies reported net incomes from their independent operations of $200,000 and $100,000, respectively.

Required:

Prepare a t-account calculation of the controlling interest in combined net income for the year ended December 31, 2001.

EXERCISE 5-6 **Workpaper Entries**

Park Company acquires an 85% interest in Sunland Company on January 2, 2002. The resulting difference between cost and book value in the amount of $120,000 is entirely attributable to equipment with an original life of 15 years and a remaining useful life, on January 2, 2002, of 10 years.

Required:

Prepare the December 31 consolidated financial statements workpaper entries for 2002 and 2003 to allocate and depreciate the difference between cost and book value, recording accumulated depreciation as a separate balance.

EXERCISE 5-7 **Workpaper Entries**

On January 1, 2001, Packard Company purchased an 80% interest in Sage Company for $600,000. On this date Sage Company had common stock of $150,000 and retained earnings of $400,000. Sage Company's equipment on the date of Packard Company's purchase had a book value of $400,000 and a fair value of $600,000. All equipment had an estimated useful life of 10 years on January 2, 1996.

Required:

Prepare the December 31 consolidated financial statements workpaper entries for 2001 and 2002 to allocate and depreciate the difference between cost and book value, recording accumulated depreciation as a separate balance.

EXERCISE 5-8 **Workpaper Entries and Gain on Sale of Land**

Padilla Company purchased 80% of the common stock of Sanoma Company in the open market on January 1, 2000, paying $31,000 more than the book value of the interest acquired. The difference between cost and book value is attributable to land.

Required:

A. What workpaper entry is required each year until the land is disposed of?

B. Assume that the land is sold on 1/1/03 and that Sanoma Company recognizes a $50,000 gain on its books. What amount of gain will be reflected in combined income on the 2003 consolidated income statement?

C. In all years subsequent to the disposal of the land, what workpaper entry will be necessary?

EXERCISE 5-9 **Allocation of Cost and Workpaper Entries**

On January 1, 2000, Point Corporation acquired an 80% interest in Sharp Company for $2,000,000. At that time Sharp Company had capital stock of $1,500,000 and retained earnings of $700,000. The book values of Sharp Company's assets and liabilities were equal to their fair values except for land and bonds payable. The land had a fair value of $100,000 and a book value of $80,000. The outstanding bonds were issued at par value on January 1, 1995, pay 10% annually, and mature on January 1, 2005. The bond principal is $500,000 and the current yield rate on similar bonds is 8%.

Required:

A. Prepare a Computation and Allocation Schedule for the difference between cost and book value in the consolidated statements workpaper on the acquisition date.

B. Prepare the workpaper entries necessary on December 31, 2000, to allocate, amortize, and depreciate the difference between cost and book value.

EXERCISE 5-10 **Allocation of Cost and Workpaper Entries**

On January 2, 2000, Page Corporation acquired a 90% interest in Salcedo Company for $3,500,000. At that time Salcedo Company had capital stock of $2,250,000 and retained earnings of $1,250,000. The book values of Salcedo Company's assets and liabilities were equal to their fair values except for land and bonds payable. The land had a fair value of $200,000 and a book value of $120,000. The outstanding bonds were issued on January 1, 1995, at 9% and mature on January 1, 2005. The bonds' principal is $500,000 and the current yield rate on similar bonds is 6%.

Required:

A. Assuming interest is paid annually, prepare a Computation and Allocation Schedule for the difference between cost and book value in the consolidated statements workpaper on the acquisition date.

B. Prepare the workpaper entries necessary on December 31, 2000, to allocate, amortize, and depreciate the difference between cost and book value.

EXERCISE 5-11   Workpaper Entries for Three Years

On January 1, 2000, Piper Company acquired an 80% interest in Sand Company for $2,276,000. At that time the capital stock and retained earnings of Sand Company were $1,800,000 and $700,000, respectively. Differences between the fair value and the book value of the identifiable assets of Sand Company were as follows:

	Fair Value in Excess of Book Value
Inventory	$45,000
Equipment (net)	50,000

The book values of all other assets and liabilities of Sand Company were equal to their fair values on January 1, 2000. The equipment had a remaining useful life of eight years, and the management of Piper Company decided that the goodwill should be amortized over a 20-year period. Inventory is accounted for on a FIFO basis. Sand Company's reported net income and declared dividends for 2000 through 2002 are shown here:

	2000	*2001*	*2002*
Net Income	$100,000	$150,000	$80,000
Dividends	20,000	30,000	15,000

Required:

Prepare the eliminating/adjusting entries needed on the consolidated workpaper for the years ended 2000, 2001 and 2002. (It is not necessary to prepare the workpaper.)

1. Assume the use of the cost method.

2. Assume the use of the partial equity method.

3. Assume the use of the complete equity method.

EXERCISE 5-12   Workpaper Entries and Consolidated Retained Earnings, Cost Method

A 90% interest in Saxton Corporation was purchased by Palm Inc. on January 2, 2001. The capital stock balance of Saxton Corporation was $3,000,000 on this date, and the balance in retained earnings was $1,000,000. The cost of the investment to Palm Inc. was $3,750,000.

The balance sheet information available for Saxton Corporation on the acquisition date revealed these values:

	Book Value	*Fair Value*
Inventory (FIFO)	$ 700,000	$ 800,000
Equipment (net)	2,000,000	2,000,000
Land	1,600,000	2,000,000

The equipment was determined to have a 15-year useful life when purchased at the beginning of 1996. Saxton Corporation reported net income in 2001 of $250,000 and $300,000 in 2002. No dividends were declared in either of those years.

Required:

A. Prepare the workpaper entries, assuming that the cost method is used to account for the investment, to establish reciprocity, to eliminate the investment account, and to allocate, amortize, and depreciate the difference between cost and book value in the 2002 consolidated statements workpaper.

B. Calculate the consolidated retained earnings for the year ended December 31, 2002, assuming that the balance in Palm Inc.'s ending retained earnings on that date was $2,000,000.

EXERCISE 5-13   Push Down Accounting

Pascal Corporation purchased 90% of the stock of Salzer Company for $2,070,000 on January 1, 2002. On this date, the fair value of the assets and liabilities of Salzer Company was equal to their book value except for the inventory and equipment accounts. The inventory had a fair value of $725,000 and a book value of $600,000. The equipment had a book value of $900,000 and a fair value of $1,075,000.

The balances in Salzer Company's capital stock and retained earnings accounts on the date of acquisition were $1,200,000 and $600,000, respectively.

Required:

In general journal form, prepare the entries on Salzer Company's books to record the effect of the pushed down values implied by the purchase of its stock by Pascal Company assuming that:

A. Values are allocated on the basis of the fair value of Salzer Company as a whole imputed from the transaction.

B. Values are allocated on the basis of the proportional interest acquired by Pascal Company.

EXERCISE 5-14   Workpaper Entries and Consolidated Retained Earnings, Partial Equity Method

A 90% interest in Saxton Corporation was purchased by Palm Inc. on January 2, 2001. The capital stock balance of Saxton Corporation was $3,000,000 on this date, and the balance in retained earnings was $1,000,000. The cost of the investment to Palm Inc. was $3,750,000.

The balance sheet information available for Saxton Corporation on the acquisition date revealed these values:

	Book Value	Fair Value
Inventory (FIFO)	$ 700,000	$ 800,000
Equipment (net)	2,000,000	2,000,000
Land	1,600,000	2,000,000

The equipment was determined to have a 15-year useful life when purchased at the beginning of 1996. Saxton Corporation reported net income in 2001 of $250,000 and $300,000 in 2002. No dividends were declared in either of those years.

Required:

A. Prepare the workpaper entries, assuming that the partial equity method is used to account for the investment, to eliminate the investment account, and to allocate, amortize, and depreciate the difference between cost and book value in the 2002 consolidated statements workpaper.

B. Calculate the consolidated retained earnings for the year ended December 31, 2002, assuming that the balance in Palm Inc.'s ending retained earnings on that date was $2,495,000.

EXERCISE 5-15   Workpaper Entries and Consolidated Retained Earnings, Complete Equity Method

A 90% interest in Saxton Corporation was purchased by Palm Inc. on January 2, 2001. The capital stock balance of Saxton Corporation was $3,000,000 on this date, and the balance in retained earnings was $1,000,000. The cost of the investment to Palm Inc. was $3,750,000.

The balance sheet information available for Saxton Corporation on the acquisition date revealed these values:

	Book Value	Fair Value
Inventory (FIFO)	$ 700,000	$ 800,000
Equipment (net)	2,000,000	2,000,000
Land	1,600,000	2,000,000

The equipment was determined to have a 15-year useful life when purchased at the beginning of 1996. Saxton Corporation reported net income in 2001 of $250,000 and $300,000 in 2002. No dividends were declared in either of those years.

Required:

A. Prepare the workpaper entries, assuming that the complete equity method is used to account for the investment, to eliminate the investment account, and to allocate, amortize, and depreciate the difference between cost and book value in the 2002 consolidated statements workpaper.

B. Calculate the consolidated retained earnings for the year ended December 31, 2002, assuming that the balance in Palm Inc.'s ending retained earnings on that date was $2,435,000.

PROBLEMS

PROBLEM 5-1 **Workpaper Entries and Consolidated Net Income for Two Years, Cost Method**
On January 1, 2001, Palmero Company purchased an 80% interest in Santos Company for $2,800,000, at which time Santos Company had retained earnings of $1,000,000 and capital stock of $500,000. On the date of acquisition, the fair value of the assets and liabilities of Santos Company was equal to their book value, except for property and equipment (net), which had a fair value of $1,500,000 and a book value of $600,000. The property and equipment had an estimated remaining life of 10 years. Palmero Company amortizes the goodwill over 20 years. Palmero Company reported net income from independent operations of $400,000 in 2001 and $425,000 in 2002. Santos Company reported net income of $300,000 in 2001 and $400,000 in 2002. Neither company declared dividends in 2001 or 2002. Palmero uses the cost method to account for its investment in Santos.

Required:

A. Prepare in general journal form the entries necessary in the consolidated statements workpapers for the years ended December 31, 2001 and 2002.

B. Prepare a schedule or t-account showing the calculation of the controlling interest in combined net income for the years ended December 31, 2001 and December 31, 2002.

PROBLEM 5-2 **Workpaper Entries and Consolidated Net Income for Two Years, Partial Equity Method**
On January 1, 2001, Paxton Company purchased a 70% interest in Sagon Company for $1,300,000, at which time Sagon Company had retained earnings of $500,000 and capital stock of $1,000,000. On January 1, 2001, the fair value of the assets and liabilities of Sagon Company was equal to their book value except for bonds payable. Sagon Company had outstanding a $1,000,000 issue of 6% bonds that were issued at par and that mature on January 1, 2006. Interest on the bonds is payable annually, and the yield rate on similar bonds on January 1, 2001, is 10%. Paxton Company amortizes the goodwill over 16 years. Paxton Company reported net income from independent operations of $300,000 in 2001 and $250,000 in 2002. Sagon Company reported net income of $100,000 in 2001 and $120,000 in 2002. Neither company paid or declared dividends in 2001 or 2002. Palmero uses the partial equity method to account for its investment in Santos.

Required:

A. Prepare in general journal form the entries necessary in the consolidated statements workpapers for the years ended December 31, 2001, and December 31, 2002.

B. Prepare in good form a schedule or t-account showing the calculation of the controlling interest in combined net income for the years ended December 31, 2001, and December 31, 2002.

PROBLEM 5-3 **Workpaper Entries and Consolidated Net Income, Complete Equity Method**

Perke Corporation purchased 80% of the stock of Superstition Company for $1,970,000 on January 1, 2002. On this date, the fair value of the assets and liabilities of Superstition Company was equal to their book value except for the inventory and equipment accounts. The inventory had a fair value of $725,000 and a book value of $600,000. Sixty percent of Superstition Company's inventory was sold in 2002; the remainder was sold in 2003. The equipment had a book value of $900,000 and a fair value of $1,075,000. The remaining useful life of the equipment is seven years.

The balances in Superstition Company's capital stock and retained earnings accounts on the date of acquisition were $1,200,000 and $600,000, respectively. Any goodwill is amortized over the maximum time allowable. Perke uses the complete equity method to account for its investment in Superstition. The following financial data are from Superstition Company's records.

	2002	2003
Net Income	$750,000	$900,000
Dividends Declared	150,000	225,000

Required:

A. In general journal form, prepare the entries on Perke Company's books to account for its investment in Superstition Company for 2002 and 2003.

B. Prepare the eliminating entries necessary for the consolidated statements workpapers in 2002 and 2003.

C. Assuming Perke Corporation's net income for 2002 was $1,000,000, calculate the controlling interest in combined net income for 2002.

PROBLEM 5-4 **Eliminating Entries and Workpapers for Various Years**

On January 1, 2000, Porter Company purchased an 80% interest in the capital stock of Salem Company for $850,000. At that time, Salem Company had capital stock of $550,000 and retained earnings of $80,000. Differences between the fair value and the book value of the identifiable assets of Salem Company were as follows:

	Fair Value in Excess of Book Value
Equipment	$130,000
Land	65,000
Inventory	40,000

The book values of all other assets and liabilities of Salem Company were equal to their fair values on January 1, 2000. The equipment had a remaining life of five years on January 1, 2000, the inventory was sold in 2000, and goodwill is amortized over 40 years.

Salem Company's net income and dividends declared in 2000 and 2001 were as follows:

Year 2000 Net Income of $100,000; Dividends Declared of $25,000

Year 2001 Net Income of $110,000; Dividends Declared of $35,000

Required:

A. Prepare a Computation and Allocation Schedule for the difference between cost and book value of equity acquired.

B. Present the eliminating/adjusting entries needed on the consolidated workpaper for the year ended December 31, 2000. (It is not necessary to prepare the workpaper.)
  (1) Assume the use of the cost method.
  (2) Assume the use of the partial equity method.
  (3) Assume the use of the complete equity method.

C. Present the eliminating/adjusting entries needed on the consolidated workpaper for the year ended December 31, 2001. (It is not necessary to prepare the workpaper.)
  (1) Assume the use of the cost method.
  (2) Assume the use of the partial equity method.
  (3) Assume the use of the complete equity method.

Use the following financial data for 2002 for requirements D through G.

	Porter Company	Salem Company
Sales	$1,100,000	$ 450,000
Dividend Income	48,000	—
Total Revenue	1,148,000	450,000
Cost of Goods Sold	900,000	200,000
Depreciation Expense	40,000	30,000
Other Expenses	60,000	50,000
Total Cost and Expense	1,000,000	280,000
Net Income	$ 148,000	$ 170,000
1/1 Retained Earnings	$500,000	$230,000
Net Income	148,000	170,000
Dividends Declared	(90,000)	(60,000)
12/31 Retained Earnings	$ 558,000	$ 340,000
Cash	$ 70,000	$ 65,000
Accounts Receivable	260,000	190,000
Inventory	240,000	175,000
Investment in Salem Company	850,000	
Land	—0—	320,000
Plant and Equipment	360,000	280,000
Total Assets	$1,780,000	$1,030,000
Accounts Payable	$ 132,000	$ 110,000
Notes Payable	90,000	30,000
Capital Stock	1,000,000	550,000
Retained Earnings	558,000	340,000
Total Liabilities and Equity	$1,780,000	$1,030,000

Required:

D. Prepare a consolidated financial statements workpaper for the year ended December 31, 2002. (Hint: You can infer the method being used by the parent from the information in its trial balance.)

E. Prepare a consolidated statement of financial position and a consolidated income statement for the year ended December 31, 2002.

F. Describe the effect on the consolidated balances if Salem Company uses the LIFO cost flow assumption in pricing its inventory and there has been no decrease in ending inventory quantities since 2000.

G. Prepare an analytical calculation of consolidated retained earnings for the year ended December 31, 2002.

PROBLEM 5-5 **Workpaper Entries and Consolidated Financial Statements**

On January 1, 2001, Palmer Company acquired a 90% interest in Stevens Company at a cost of $1,000,000. At the purchase date, Stevens Company's stockholders' equity consisted of the following:

Common Stock	$500,000
Retained Earnings	190,000

An examination of Stevens Company's assets and liabilities revealed the following at the date of acquisition:

	Book Value	Fair Value
Cash	$ 90,726	$ 90,726
Accounts Receivable	200,000	200,000
Inventories	160,000	210,000
Equipment	300,000	390,000
Accumulated Depreciation—equipment	(100,000)	(130,000)
Land	190,000	290,000
Bonds Payable	(205,556)	(150,000)
Other	54,830	54,830
Total	$690,000	$955,556

Additional Information—Date of Acquisition:

Stevens Company's equipment had an original life of 15 years and a remaining useful life of 10 years. All the inventory was sold in 2001. The goodwill, if any, is amortized over 20 years. Stevens Company purchased its bonds payable on the open market on January 10, 2001, for $150,000 and recognized a gain of $55,556.

Financial statement data for 2003 are presented here:

	Palmer Company	Stevens Company
Sales	$ 620,000	$340,000
Cost of Sales	430,000	240,000
Gross Margin	190,000	100,000
Depreciation Expense	30,000	20,000
Other Expenses	60,000	35,000
Income from Operations	100,000	45,000
Dividend Income	31,500	0
Net Income	$ 131,500	$ 45,000
1/1 Retained Earnings	$ 297,600	$210,000
Net Income	131,500	45,000
	429,100	255,000
Dividends	(120,000)	(35,000)
12/31 Retained Earnings	$ 309,100	$220,000
Cash	$ 201,200	$151,000
Accounts Receivable	221,000	173,000
Inventories	100,400	81,000
Investment in Stevens Company	1,000,000	
Equipment	450,000	300,000
Accumulated Depreciation—equipment	(300,000)	(140,000)
Land	360,000	290,000
Total Assets	$2,032,600	$855,000

	Palmer Company	Stevens Company
Accounts Payable	323,500	$135,000
Bonds Payable	400,000	
Common Stock	1,000,000	500,000
Retained Earnings	309,100	220,000
Total Liabilities and Equity	$2,032,600	$855,000

Required:

A. What method is Palmer using to account for its investment in Stevens? How can you tell?

B. Prepare in general journal form the workpaper entry to allocate, amortize, and depreciate the difference between cost and book value in the December 31, 2001, consolidated statements workpaper.

C. Prepare a consolidated financial statements workpaper for the year ended December 31, 2003.

D. Prepare in good form a schedule or t-account showing the calculation of the controlling interest in combined net income for the year ended December 31, 2003.

PROBLEM 5-6 **Workpaper Entries for Two Years and Sale of Equipment in Year Two**
On January 1, 2001, Perini Company purchased an 85% interest in Silvas Company for $400,000. On this date, Silvas Company had common stock of $90,000 and retained earnings of $210,000. An examination of Silvas Company's assets and liabilities revealed that their book value was equal to their fair value except for the equipment:

	Book Value	Fair Value
Equipment	$360,000	
Accumulated Depreciation	(120,000)	
	$240,000	$300,000

The equipment had an expected remaining life of six years and no salvage value. Straight-line depreciation is used. Perini Company had decided to amortize any goodwill over a period of 10 years.

During 2001 and 2002, Perini Company reported net income from its own operations of $80,000 and paid dividends of $50,000 in each year. Silvas Company had income of $40,000 each year and paid dividends of $30,000 on each December 31.

Accumulated depreciation is presented on a separate row in the workpaper and in the consolidated financial statements.

Required:

A. Prepare eliminating entries for consolidated financial statements workpaper for the year ended December 31, 2001, assuming:
   (1) The cost method is used to account for the investment.
   (2) The partial equity method is used to account for the investment.

B. On January 1, 2002, Silvas Company sold all its equipment for $220,000. Prepare the eliminating entries for the consolidated financial statements workpaper for the year ended December 31, 2002, assuming:
   (1) The cost method is used to account for the investment.
   (2) The partial equity method is used to account for the investment.

PROBLEM 5-7 **Workpaper Entries and Sale of Equipment in Year Three, Complete Equity Method**
On January 1, 2001, Pueblo Corporation purchased a 75% interest in Sanchez Company for $900,000. A summary of Sanchez Company's balance sheet at date of purchase follows:

	Book Value	Fair Value
Equipment	$720,000	
Accumulated Depreciation	(240,000)	
Equipment (net)	480,000	$660,000
Other Assets	450,000	$450,000
	$930,000	
Liabilities	$255,000	$255,000
Common Stock	300,000	
Retained Earnings	375,000	
	$930,000	

The equipment had an original life of 15 years and remaining useful life of 10 years. Any goodwill will be amortized over the maximum period allowable.

During 2001 Pueblo Corporation reported income of $237,000 and paid dividends of $150,000. Sanchez Company reported net income of $123,000 and paid dividends of $120,000. Pueblo uses the complete equity method to account for its investment in Sanchez.

Required:
A. Prepare the elimination entries for the consolidated financial statements workpaper on December 31, 2001. Accumulated depreciation is presented on a separate row in the workpaper and in the consolidated financial statements.
B. Assume that Sanchez Company disposed of all its equipment on January 1, 2003, for $450,000.
   (1) What amount of gain (loss) will Sanchez Company report?
   (2) What is the consolidated gain (loss)?
   (3) Prepare the workpaper entry necessary to allocate the amount of the difference between cost and book value that was originally allocated to the equipment that has now been sold to outsiders.
   (4) What workpaper entry will be necessary to allocate this difference between cost and book value in future years?

PROBLEM 5-8   Eliminating Entries and Consolidated Net Income

Patten Corporation acquired an 85% interest in Savage Company for $3,100,000 on January 1, 2001. On this date, the balances in Savage Company's capital stock and retained earnings accounts were $2,000,000 and $700,000, respectively.

An examination of Savage Company's books on this date revealed the following:

	Book Value	Fair Value
Current Assets	$650,000	650,000
Inventory	560,000	610,000
Marketable Securities	430,000	430,000
Plant and Equipment	1,200,000	1,600,000
Land	400,000	900,000
Liabilities	540,000	540,000

The remaining useful life of the plant and equipment is 10 years, and all the inventory was sold in 2001. The net income from Patten Corporation's own operations was $950,000 in 2001 and $675,000 in 2002. Savage Company's net income for the respective years was $110,000 and $180,000. No dividends were declared.

Required:
A. Prepare a Computation and Allocation Schedule for the difference between purchase price and book value of equity.

B. Prepare the consolidated statements workpaper eliminating entries for 2001 and 2002 in general journal form, under each of the following assumptions:
   (1) The cost method is used to account for the investment.
   (2) The partial equity method is used to account for the investment.
   (3) The complete equity method is used to account for the investment.

C. Calculate the controlling interest in combined net income for 2001 and 2002.

PROBLEM 5-9 **Workpaper Entries and Consolidated Net Income for Year of Acquisition**

On January 1, 2001, Pump Company acquired all the outstanding common stock of Sound Company for $556,000 in cash. Financial data relating to Sound Company on January 1, 2001, are presented here:

	Balance Sheet	
	Book Value	*Fair Value*
Cash	$104,550	$ 104,550
Receivables	123,000	112,310
Inventories	220,000	268,000
Buildings	331,000	375,000
Accumulated Depreciation—buildings	(264,800)	(300,000)
Equipment	145,000	130,000
Accumulated Depreciation—equipment	(108,750)	(97,500)
Land	150,000	420,000
Total Assets	$700,000	$1,012,360

	Book Value	*Fair Value*
Current Liabilities	$106,000	$ 106,000
Bonds Payable, 8% due 1/1/2019		
Interest Payable on 6/30 and 12/31	300,000	
Common Stock	200,000	
Premium on Common Stock	80,000	
Retained Earnings	14,000	
Total Liabilities and Equities	$700,000	

Sound Company would expect to pay 10% interest to borrow long-term funds on the date of acquisition. During 2001, Sound Company wrote its receivables down by $10,690 and recorded a corresponding loss. Sound Company accounts for its inventories at lower of FIFO cost or market. Its buildings and equipment had a remaining estimated useful life on January 1, 2001, of 10 years and 2½ years, respectively. Sound Company reported net income of $80,000 and declared no dividends in 2001.

Required:

A. Prepare in general journal form the December 31, 2001, workpaper entries necessary to eliminate the investment account and to allocate, amortize, and depreciate the difference between cost and book value.

B. Assume that Pump Company's net income from independent operations in 2001 amounts to $500,000. Calculate the controlling interest in combined net income for 2001.

PROBLEM 5-10 **Workpaper Entries for Year of Acquisition**

Pearson Company purchased a 100% interest in Sanders Company and a 90% interest in Taylor Company on January 2, 2001, for $800,000 and $1,300,000, respectively. The account balances and fair values of the acquired companies on the acquisition date were as follows:

	Sanders		Taylor	
	Book Value	*Fair Value*	*Book Value*	*Fair Value*
Current Assets	$ 200,000	$200,000	$ 350,000	$350,000
Inventory	400,000	400,000	500,000	575,000
Plant and Equipment (net)	300,000	350,000	600,000	600,000
Land	600,000	600,000	550,000	625,000
Total	$1,500,000		$2,000,000	
Current Liabilities	$ 500,000	$500,000	$ 300,000	$300,000
Bonds Payable	300,000	300,000	600,000	600,000
Capital Stock	500,000		800,000	
Retained Earnings	200,000		300,000	
Total	$1,500,000		$2,000,000	

Sanders Company's equipment has a remaining useful life of 10 years. Two-thirds of Taylor Company's inventory was sold in 2001 and the rest was sold in the following year. Any goodwill is amortized over 20 years. In 2001, Sanders Company reported net income of $500,000 and declared dividends of $100,000. Taylor Company's net income and declared dividends for 2001 were $800,000 and $200,000, respectively. Assume the use of the cost method.

Required:

A. Prepare in general journal form the entries on the books of Pearson Company to account for its investments in 2001.

B. Prepare the elimination entries necessary in the consolidated statements workpaper for the year ended December 31, 2001.

PROBLEM 5-11 **Eliminating Entries and Workpapers for Various Years, Partial Equity Method**
(Note that this is the same problem as Problem 5-4, but assuming the use of the partial equity method.)

On January 1, 2000, Porter Company purchased an 80% interest in the capital stock of Salem Company for $850,000. At that time, Salem Company had capital stock of $550,000 and retained earnings of $80,000. Porter Company uses the partial equity method to record its investment in Salem Company. Differences between the fair value and the book value of the identifiable assets of Salem Company were as follows:

Analyze investment account

	Fair Value in Excess of Book Value
Equipment	$130,000
Land	65,000
Inventory	40,000

The book values of all other assets and liabilities of Salem Company were equal to their fair values on January 1, 2000. The equipment had a remaining life of five years on January 1, 2000, the inventory was sold in 2000, and goodwill is amortized over 40 years.

Salem Company's net income and dividends declared in 2000 and 2001 were as follows:

Year 2000 Net Income of $100,000; Dividends Declared of $25,000

Year 2001 Net Income of $110,000; Dividends Declared of $35,000

Required:

A. Present the eliminating/adjusting entries needed on the consolidated workpaper for the year ended December 31, 2000. (It is not necessary to prepare the workpaper.)

B. Present the eliminating/adjusting entries needed on the consolidated workpaper for the year ended December 31, 2001. (It is not necessary to prepare the workpaper.)

Use the following financial data for 2002 for requirements C through G.

	Porter Company	Salem Company
Sales	$1,100,000	$ 450,000
Equity in Subsidiary Income	136,000	—
Total Revenue	1,236,000	450,000
Cost of Goods Sold	900,000	200,000
Depreciation Expense	40,000	30,000
Other Expenses	60,000	50,000
Total Cost and Expense	1,000,000	280,000
Net Income	$ 236,000	$ 170,000
1/1 Retained Earnings	$ 620,000	$ 230,000
Net Income	236,000	170,000
Dividends Declared	(90,000)	(60,000)
12/31 Retained Earnings	$ 766,000	$ 340,000
Cash	$ 70,000	$ 65,000
Accounts Receivable	260,000	190,000
Inventory	240,000	175,000
Investment in Salem Company	1,058,000	
Land	—0—	320,000
Plant and Equipment	360,000	280,000
Total Assets	$1,988,000	$1,030,000
Accounts Payable	$ 132,000	$ 110,000
Notes Payable	90,000	30,000
Capital Stock	1,000,000	550,000
Retained Earnings	766,000	340,000
Total Liabilities and Equity	$1,988,000	$1,030,000

Required:

C. Prepare a t-account calculation of the controlling and noncontrolling interests in combined income for the year ended December 31, 2002.

D. Prepare a consolidated financial statements workpaper for the year ended December 31, 2002.

E. Prepare a consolidated statement of financial position and a consolidated income statement for the year ended December 31, 2002.

F. Describe the effect on the consolidated balances if Salem Company uses the LIFO cost flow assumption in pricing its inventory and there has been no decrease in ending inventory quantities since 2000.

G. Prepare an analytical calculation of consolidated retained earnings for the year ended December 31, 2002.

Note: If you completed Problem 5-4, a comparison of the consolidated balances in this problem with those you obtained in Problem 5-4 will demonstrate that the method (cost or partial equity) used by the parent company to record its investment in a consolidated subsidiary has no effect on the consolidated balances.

PROBLEM 5-12 **Workpaper Entries and Consolidated Financial Statements, Partial Equity Method**
(Note that this is the same problem as Problem 5-5, but assuming the use of the partial equity method.)

On January 1, 2001, Palmer Company acquired a 90% interest in Stevens Company at a cost of $1,000,000. At the purchase date, Stevens Company's stockholders' equity consisted of the following:

Common Stock	$500,000
Retained Earnings	190,000

An examination of Stevens Company's assets and liabilities revealed the following at the date of acquisition:

	Book Value	Fair Value
Cash	$ 90,726	$ 90,726
Accounts Receivable	200,000	200,000
Inventories	160,000	210,000
Equipment	300,000	390,000
Accumulated Depreciation—equipment	(100,000)	(130,000)
Land	190,000	290,000
Bonds Payable	(205,556)	(150,000)
Other	54,830	54,830
Total	$690,000	$955,556

Additional Information—Date of Acquisition:

Stevens Company's equipment had an original life of 15 years and a remaining useful life of 10 years. All the inventory was sold in 2001. The goodwill, if any, is amortized over 20 years. Stevens Company purchased its bonds payable on the open market on January 10, 2001, for $150,000 and recognized a gain of $55,556. Palmer Company uses the partial equity method to record its investment in Stevens Company.

Financial statement data for 2003 are presented here:

	Palmer Company	Stevens Company
Sales	$ 620,000	$340,000
Cost of Sales	430,000	240,000
Gross Margin	190,000	100,000
Depreciation Expense	30,000	20,000
Other Expenses	60,000	35,000
Income from Operations	100,000	45,000
Equity in Subsidiary Income	40,500	0
Net Income	$ 140,500	$ 45,000
1/1 Retained Earnings	$ 315,600	$210,000
Net Income	140,500	45,000
	456,100	255,000
Dividends	(120,000)	(35,000)
12/31 Retained Earnings	$ 336,100	$220,000
Cash	$ 201,200	$151,000
Accounts Receivable	221,000	173,000
Inventories	100,400	81,000
Investment in Stevens Company	1,027,000	
Equipment	450,000	300,000
Accumulated Depreciation—equipment	(300,000)	(140,000)
Land	360,000	290,000
Total Assets	$2,059,600	$855,000

	Palmer Company	Stevens Company
Accounts Payable	$ 323,500	$135,000
Bonds Payable	400,000	
Common Stock	1,000,000	500,000
Retained Earnings	336,100	220,000
Total Liabilities and Equity	$2,059,600	$855,000

Required:

A. Prepare in general journal form the workpaper entry to allocate, amortize, and depreciate the difference between cost and book value in the December 31, 2001, consolidated statements workpaper.

B. Prepare a consolidated financial statements workpaper for the year ended December 31, 2003.

C. Prepare in good form a schedule or t-account showing the calculation of the controlling interest in combined net income for the year ended December 31, 2003.

If you completed Problem 5-5, a comparison of the consolidated balances in this problem with those you obtained in Problem 5-5 will demonstrate that the method (cost or partial equity) used by the parent company to record its investment in a consolidated subsidiary has no effect on the consolidated balances.

PROBLEM 5-13 **Push Down Accounting**

On January 2, 2001, Press Company purchased on the open market 90% of the outstanding common stock of Sensor Company for $800,000 cash. Balance sheets for Press Company and Sensor Company on January 1, 2001, just before the stock acquisition by Press Company, were:

	Press Company	Sensor Company
Cash	$1,065,000	$ 38,000
Receivables	422,500	76,000
Inventory	216,500	124,000
Building (net)	465,000	322,000
Equipment (net)	229,000	185,000
Land	188,000	100,000
Patents	167,500	88,000
Total Assets	$2,753,500	$933,000
Liabilities	667,000	$249,000
Common Stock	700,000	300,000
Other Contributed Capital	846,000	164,000
Retained Earnings	540,500	220,000
Total Equities	$2,753,500	$933,000

The full implied value of Sensor Company is to be pushed down and recorded in Sensor Company's books. The excess of the implied fair value over the book value of net assets acquired is allocated as follows: to equipment, 30%; to land, 20%; to patents, 50%.

Required:

A. Prepare the entry on Sensor Company's books on January 2, 2001, to record the values implied by the 90% stock purchase by Press Company.

B. Prepare a consolidated balance sheet workpaper on January 1, 2001.

PROBLEM 5-14 **Push Down Accounting**

On January 1, 1999, Push Company purchased an 80% interest in the capital stock of WayDown Company for $820,000. At that time, WayDown Company had capital stock of $500,000 and retained earnings of $100,000. Differences between the fair value and the book value of identifiable assets of WayDown Company were as follows:

	Fair Value in Excess of Book Value
Equipment	$125,000
Land	62,500
Inventory	37,500

The book values of all other assets and liabilities of WayDown Company were equal to their fair values on January 1, 1999. The equipment had a remaining life of five years on January 1, 1999, the inventory was sold in 1999, and goodwill is amortized over 40 years. WayDown Company revalued its assets on January 2, 1999. New values were allocated on the basis of the fair value of WayDown Company as a whole imputed from the transaction.

Financial data for 2001 are presented here:

	Push Company	WayDown Company
Sales	$1,050,000	400,000
Dividend Income	40,000	0
Total Revenue	1,090,000	400,000
Cost of Goods Sold	850,000	180,000
Depreciation Expense	35,000	50,000
Other expenses	65,000	50,000
Total Cost and Expense	950,000	280,000
Net Income	$ 140,000	$ 120,000
1/1 Retained Earnings	$ 480,000	$ 102,500
Net Income	140,000	120,000
Dividends Declared	(100,000)	(50,000)
12/31 Retained Earnings	$ 520,000	$ 172,500
Cash	$ 80,000	$ 50,000
Accounts Receivable	250,000	170,000
Inventory	230,000	150,000
Investment in WayDown	820,000	
Goodwill	—0—	185,000
Land	—0—	362,500
Plant and Equipment	350,000	300,000
Total Assets	$1,730,000	$1,217,500
Accounts Payable	$ 160,000	$ 100,000
Notes Payable	50,000	20,000
Capital Stock	1,000,000	500,000
Revaluation Capital		425,000
Retained Earnings	520,000	172,500
Total Liabilities and Equity	$1,730,000	$1,217,500

Required:

A. In general journal form, prepare the entry made by WayDown Company on January 2, 1999, to record the effect of the pushed down values implied by the purchase of its stock by Push Company assuming that values were allocated on the basis of the fair value of WayDown Company as a whole imputed from the transaction.

B. Prepare a consolidated financial statements workpaper for the year ended December 31, 2001.

C. What effect does the decision to apply the full push down approach have on the following times (compared to the case where push down acounting is not used):

    (1) Consolidated net income?

    (2) Consolidated retained earnings?

    (3) Consolidated net assets?

    (4) Noncontrolling interest in consolidated net assets?

PROBLEM 5-15   **Push Down Accounting**

On January 1, 1999, Push Company purchased an 80% interest in the capital stock of Down Company for $820,000. At that time, Down Company had capital stock of $500,000 and retained earnings of $100,000. Differences between the fair value and the book value of identifiable assets of Down Company were as follows:

	Fair Value in Excess of Book Value
Equipment	$125,000
Land	62,500
Inventory	37,500

The book values of all other assets and liabilities of Down Company were equal to their fair values on January 1, 1999. The equipment had a remaining life of five years on January 1, 1999, the inventory was sold in 1999, and goodwill is amortized over 40 years. Down Company revalued its assets on January 2, 1999. New values were allocated on the basis of the proportional interest acquired by Push Company.

Financial data for 2001 are presented here:

	Push Company	Down Company
Sales	$1,050,000	$ 400,000
Dividend Income	40,000	0
Total Revenue	1,090,000	400,000
Cost of Goods Sold	850,000	180,000
Depreciation Expense	35,000	45,000
Other Expenses	65,000	49,000
Total Cost and Expense	950,000	274,000
Net Income	$ 140,000	$ 126,000
1/1 Retained Earnings	$ 480,000	$ 122,000
Net Income	140,000	126,000
Dividends Declared	(100,000)	(50,000)
12/31 Retained Earnings	$ 520,000	$ 198,000
Cash	$ 80,000	$ 50,000
Accounts Receivable	250,000	170,000
Inventory	230,000	150,000
Investment in Down Company	820,000	
Land	—0—	350,000
Goodwill	—0—	148,000
Plant and Equipment	350,000	290,000
Total Assets	$1,730,000	$1,158,000

	Push Company	Down Company
Accounts Payable	$ 160,000	$ 100,000
Notes Payable	50,000	20,000
Capital Stock	1,000,000	500,000
Revaluation Capital		340,000
Retained Earnings	520,000	198,000
Total Liabilities and Equity	$1,730,000	$1,158,000

Required:

A. In general journal form, prepare the entry made by Down Company on January 2, 1999, to record the effect of the pushed down values implied by the purchase of its stock by Push Company assuming that values were allocated on the basis of the proportional interest acquired by Push Company.

B. Prepare a consolidated financial statements workpaper for the year ended December 31, 2001.

C. How would the consolidated balances in the workpaper prepared in requirement B compare with those prepared in the consolidated statements without proportional pushdown.

PROBLEM 5-16 **Eliminating Entries and Workpapers for Various Years, Complete Equity Method**
(Note that this is the same problem as Problems 5-4 and 5-11, but assuming the use of the complete equity method.)

On January 1, 2000, Porter Company purchased an 80% interest in the capital stock of Salem Company for $850,000. At that time, Salem Company had capital stock of $550,000 and retained earnings of $80,000. Porter Company uses the partial equity method to record its investment in Salem Company. Differences between the fair value and the book value of the identifiable assets of Salem Company were as follows:

	Fair Value in Excess of Book Value
Equipment	$130,000
Land	65,000
Inventory	40,000

The book values of all other assets and liabilities of Salem Company were equal to their fair values on January 1, 2000. The equipment had a remaining life of five years on January 1, 2000, the inventory was sold in 2000, and goodwill is amortized over 40 years.

Salem Company's net income and dividends declared in 2000 and 2001 were as follows:

Year 2000 Net Income of $100,000; Dividends Declared of $25,000

Year 2001 Net Income of $110,000; Dividends Declared of $35,000

Required:

A. Present the eliminating/adjusting entries needed on the consolidated workpaper for the year ended December 31, 2000. (It is not necessary to prepare the workpaper.)

B. Present the eliminating/adjusting entries needed on the consolidated workpaper for the year ended December 31, 2001. (It is not necessary to prepare the workpaper.)

Use the following financial data for 2002 for requirements C through G.

	Porter Company	Salem Company
Sales	$1,100,000	$ 450,000
Equity in Subsidiary Income	111,250	—
Total Revenue	1,211,250	450,000
Cost of Goods Sold	900,000	200,000
Depreciation Expense	40,000	30,000
Other expenses	60,000	50,000
Total Cost and Expense	1,000,000	280,000
Net Income	$ 211,250	$ 170,000
1/1 Retained Earnings	$ 538,500	$ 230,000
Net Income	211,250	170,000
Dividend Declared	(90,000)	(60,000)
12/31 Retained Earnings	$ 659,750	$ 340,000
Cash	$ 70,000	$ 65,000
Accounts Receivable	260,000	190,000
Inventory	240,000	175,000
Investment in Salem Company	951,750	
Land	—0—	320,000
Plant and Equipment	360,000	280,000
Total Assets	$1,881,750	$1,030,000
Accounts Payable	$ 132,000	$ 110,000
Notes Payable	90,000	30,000
Capital Stock	1,000,000	550,000
Retained Earnings	659,750	340,000
Total Liabilities and Equity	$1,881,750	$1,030,000

Required:

C. Prepare a t-account calculation of the controlling and noncontrolling interests in combined income for the year ended December 31, 2002.

D. Prepare a consolidated financial statements workpaper for the year ended December 31, 2002.

E. Prepare a consolidated statement of financial position and a consolidated income statement for the year ended December 31, 2002.

F. Describe the effect on the consolidated balances if Salem Company uses the LIFO cost flow assumption in pricing its inventory and there has been no decrease in ending inventory quantities since 2000.

G. Prepare an analytical calculation of consolidated retained earnings for the year ended December 31, 2002.

Note: If you completed Problems 5-4 and 5-11, a comparison of the consolidated balances in this problem with those you obtained in Problems 5-4 and 5-11 will demonstrate that the method (cost or partial equity) used by the parent company to record its investment in a consolidated subsidiary has no effect on the consolidated balances.

PROBLEM 5-17 **Workpaper Entries and Consolidated Financial Statements, Complete Equity Method**
(Note that this is the same problem as Problems 5-5 and 5-12, but assuming the use of the complete equity method.)

On January 1, 2001, Palmer Company acquired a 90% interest in Stevens Company at a cost of $1,000,000. At the purchase date, Stevens Company's stockholders' equity consisted of the following:

Common Stock	$500,000
Retained Earnings	190,000

An examination of Stevens Company's assets and liabilities revealed the following at the date of acquisition:

	Book Value	Fair Value
Cash	$ 90,726	$ 90,726
Accounts Receivable	200,000	200,000
Inventories	160,000	210,000
Equipment	300,000	390,000
Accumulated Depreciation—equipment	(100,000)	(130,000)
Land	190,000	290,000
Bonds Payable	(205,556)	(150,000)
Other	54,830	54,830
Total	$690,000	$955,556

Additional Information—Date of Acquisition:
Stevens Company's equipment had an original life of 15 years and a remaining useful life of 10 years. All the inventory was sold in 2001. The goodwill, if any, is amortized over 20 years. Stevens Company purchased its bonds payable on the open market on January 10, 2001, for $150,000 and recognized a gain of $55,556. Palmer Company uses the complete equity method to record its investment in Stevens Company.

Financial statement data for 2003 are presented here:

	Palmer Company	Stevens Company
Sales	$ 620,000	$340,000
Cost of Sales	430,000	240,000
Gross Margin	190,000	100,000
Depreciation Expense	30,000	20,000
Other Expenses	60,000	35,000
Income from Operations	100,000	45,000
Equity in Subsidiary Income	28,100	0
Net Income	128,100	$ 45,000
1/1 Retained Earnings	$ 195,800	$210,000
Net Income	128,100	45,000
	323,900	255,000
Dividends	(120,000)	(35,000)
12/31 Retained Earnings	$ 203,900	$220,000
Cash	$ 201,200	$151,000
Accounts Receivable	221,000	173,000
Inventories	100,400	81,000
Investment in Stevens Company	894,800	
Equipment	450,000	300,000
Accumulated Depreciation—equipment	(300,000)	(140,000)
Land	360,000	290,000
Total Assets	$1,927,400	$855,000

	Palmer Company	Stevens Company
Accounts Payable	$ 323,500	$135,000
Bonds Payable	400,000	
Common Stock	1,000,000	500,000
Retained Earnings	203,900	220,000
Total Liabilities and Equity	$1,927,400	$855,000

Required:

E. Prepare in general journal form the workpaper entry to allocate, amortize, and depreciate the difference between cost and book value in the December 31, 2001, consolidated statements workpaper.

F. Prepare a consolidated financial statements workpaper for the year ended December 31, 2003.

G. Prepare in good form a schedule or t-account showing the calculation of the controlling interest in combined net income for the year ended December 31, 2003.

Note: If you completed Problems 5-5 and 5-12, a comparison of the consolidated balances in this problem with those you obtained in Problems 5-5 and 5-12 will demonstrate that the method (cost, partial equity, or complete equity) used by the parent company to record its investment in a consolidated subsidiary has no effect on the consolidated balances.

PROBLEM 5-18 **Impact on Future Profits and In-Process R&D**

The Mcquire Company is considering acquiring 100% of the Sosa Company. The management of Mcquire fears that the acquisition price may be too high, and that the goodwill charges might eliminate all potential future growth in profits. Condensed financial statements for Sosa Company for the current year are as follows:

Income Statement	2005
Revenues	$100,000
Cost of Goods Sold	40,000
Gross Margin	60,000
Operating Expenses	35,000
Pretax Income	25,000
Income Tax Expense	10,000
Net Income	15,000

Balance Sheet	Year Ended 12/31/04	Year Ended 12/31/05
Cash	$ 4,000	$ 4,000
Receivables	10,000	14,000
Inventory	31,000	27,000
Fixed Assets (net)	50,000	55,000
Total Assets	$95,000	$100,000
Current Liabilities	$15,000	$ 17,000
Long-Term Liabilities	25,000	18,000
Common Stock	20,000	20,000
Retained Earnings	35,000	45,000
Total Liabilities and Equity	$95,000	$100,000

You believe that Sosa might be currently acquired at a price resulting in a price to earnings (P/E) ratio of 8 to 12 times. Also, the fair market value of Sosa's net assets is approximately

$105,000, and the difference between fair value and book value is due solely to depreciable assets with a remaining useful life of 10 years. Sosa Company is heavily involved in research and development of new baseball bats that enable the batter to hit the ball further. You estimate that $30,000 of the acquisition price might be classified as in-process R&D and thus expensed in the year of acquisition. Sosa's net income is expected to grow an average of 10% per year for the next 10 years and remain constant thereafter. Your company's policy is to amortize goodwill over 20 years.

Required:
A. If the acquisition occurs on January 1, 2006, determine the decrease in income that would be included in combined income for the following 20 years assuming:
   (1) P/E ratio = 10.
   (2) P/E ratio = 12.
B. If the FASB changes the current rules and requires that in-process R&D be capitalized and amortized over 20 years, how would this change your answer to requirement A?

PROBLEM 5-19 **Deferred Tax Effects**
On January 1, 2002, Pruitt Company issued 25,500 shares of its common stock in exchange for 85% of the outstanding common stock of Shah Company. Pruitt's common stock had a fair value of $28 per share at that time (par value of $2 per share). Pruitt Company uses the cost method to account for its investment in Shah Company and files a consolidated income tax return. A schedule of the Shah Company assets acquired and liabilities assumed at book values (which are equal to their tax bases) and fair values follows:

Item:	Book Value/ Tax Basis	Fair Value	Excess
Receivables (net)	$125,000	$ 125,000	$ —0—
Inventory	167,000	195,000	28,000
Land	86,500	120,000	33,500
Plant Assets (net)	467,000	567,000	100,000
Patents	95,000	200,000	105,000
Total	$940,500	$1,207,000	$266,500
Current Liabilities	$ 89,500	$ 89,500	$ —0—
Bonds Payable	300,000	360,000	60,000
Common Stock	120,000		
Other Contributed Capital	164,000		
Retained Earnings	267,000		
Total	$940,000		

Additional Information:
1. Pruitt's income tax rate is 35%.
2. Shah's beginning inventory was all sold during 2002.
3. Useful lives for depreciation and amortization purposes are:

Plant assets	10 years	Bond Premium	10 years
Patents	8 years	Goodwill	25 years

4. Pruitt uses the straight-line method for all depreciation and amortization purposes.

Required:
A. Prepare the stock acquisition entry on Pruitt Company's books.
B. Assuming Shah Company earned $216,000 and declared a $90,000 dividend during 2002, prepare the eliminating entries for a consolidated statements workpaper on December 31, 2002.
C. Assuming Shah Company earned $240,000 and declared a $100,000 dividend during 2003, prepare the eliminating entries for a consolidated statements workpaper on December 31, 2003.

6

ELIMINATION OF UNREALIZED PROFIT ON INTERCOMPANY SALES OF INVENTORY

LEARNING OBJECTIVES

1. Describe the financial reporting objectives for intercompany sales of inventory.

2. Determine the amount of intercompany profit, if any, to be eliminated from the consolidated statements.

3. Understand the concept of eliminating 100% (rather than only the parent's share) of intercompany profit not realized in transactions with outsiders, and know the authoritative position.

4. Distinguish between upstream and downstream sales of inventory.

5. Compute the noncontrolling interest in combined income for upstream and downstream sales, when not all the inventory has been sold to outsiders.

6. Prepare consolidated workpapers for firms with upstream and downstream sales using the cost, partial equity, and complete equity methods.

7. Discuss the treatment of intercompany profit earned prior to the parent-subsidiary affiliation.

IN THE NEWS

"To boost its baking business, which is facing stiff competition from Diageo PLC's Pillsbury unit for a shrinking home-baking market, General Mills is folding its Gold Medal flours division, which includes Bisquick, under the Betty Crocker umbrella. Current Gold Medal President Jon Finley will head a new convenience-foods division that will include General Mills's yogurt business, recently launched refrigerated bakery snacks, and other snack ventures including the Chex line acquired two years ago."[1]

Affiliated companies may make intercompany sales of inventory or other assets. The term "affiliated group" is used to refer to a parent and all subsidiaries for which consolidated financial statements are prepared; alternatively, this group may be referred to as the consolidated entity.[2] Sales from a parent company to one or more

---

[1] *WSJ*, "General Mills Plans to Consolidate Units, Boost Betty Crocker," 5/26/98, p. A4.

[2] Note that this definition of an affiliated group is broader than the definition imposed by the Tax Code (Section 1504(a)). A parent must own at least 80% of the voting power of all stock classes and 80% of the fair value of its subsidiaries' outstanding stock to qualify as an affiliated group for tax purposes.

of its subsidiaries are referred to as *downstream sales.* Sales from subsidiaries to the parent company are referred to as *upstream sales.* Sales from one subsidiary to another subsidiary are referred to as *horizontal sales.*

Ordinarily, the selling affiliate will record a profit or loss on such sales. From the point of view of the consolidated entity, however, such profit or loss should not be reported until the inventory or other assets acquired by the purchasing affiliate have been used during the course of operations or sold to parties outside the affiliated group (third parties). Profit (loss) that has not been realized from the point of view of the consolidated entity through subsequent sales to third parties is defined as *unrealized intercompany profit (loss)* and must be eliminated in the preparation of consolidated financial statements. The elimination of unrealized profit resulting from intercompany sales of inventory is examined in this chapter. The elimination of unrealized profit resulting from intercompany sales of property and equipment will be examined in the next chapter.

EFFECTS OF INTERCOMPANY SALES OF MERCHANDISE ON THE DETERMINATION OF CONSOLIDATED BALANCES

The workpaper procedures illustrated in this chapter are designed to accomplish the following financial reporting objectives in the consolidated financial statements:

- Consolidated sales include only *sales with parties outside the affiliated group.*
- Consolidated cost of sales includes only *the cost to the affiliated group* of goods that have been sold to parties outside the affiliated group.
- Consolidated inventory on the balance sheet is recorded at its *cost to the affiliated group.*

Stated another way, the objective of eliminating the effects of intercompany sales of merchandise is to present consolidated balances for sales, cost of sales, and inventory as if the intercompany sale had *never* occurred. As a result, the recognition of income or loss on the intercompany transaction, including its allocation between the noncontrolling and controlling interests, is deferred until the profit or loss is confirmed by sales of the merchandise to nonaffiliates.

Thoughtful consideration of these financial reporting objectives will indicate that they are logical and noncontroversial. However, the workpaper procedures for accomplishing these objectives are not self-evident. Thus the workpaper procedures for accomplishing these objectives are the central topic of this chapter. These procedures include workpaper entries to adjust the recorded amounts of sales, cost of sales (or components thereof), and ending inventory to amounts based on the objectives stated above. In addition, the procedures are designed to equate beginning consolidated retained earnings with the amount reported as ending consolidated retained earnings in the previous reporting period for firms using the cost or partial equity methods and to allocate combined income to the noncontrolling interest based on its share of adjusted subsidiary income that is included in combined income.

In order to concentrate on intercompany profit eliminations and adjustments, reporting complications relating to accounting for the difference between cost and book value are avoided in the initial illustrations by assuming that all acquisitions are made at the book value of the acquired interest in net assets and that the book value of the subsidiary company's net assets equals their fair value on the date the parent company's interest is acquired. (This assumption is later relaxed.) It is also assumed that the affiliates file consolidated income tax returns. If the affiliates file separate tax returns, deferred tax issues arise. These are addressed in the appendix to this chapter.

Determination of Consolidated Sales, Cost of Sales, and Inventory Balances Assuming Downstream Sales

The basic workpaper eliminating entries required because of intercompany sales of merchandise are illustrated using the following simplifying assumptions:

1. P Company sells all goods it buys or manufactures to its wholly owned subsidiary, S Company, at 125% of cost.
2. During the first year of this arrangement, goods that cost P Company $200,000 are sold to S Company for $250,000 *(downstream sale)*.
3. During the same year, S Company sold all the goods purchased by it from P Company to third parties for $270,000.

Sales, cost of sales, and inventory balances reported by the affiliated companies are presented in Illustration 6-1. Recall that the cost of sales is computed as:

$$\begin{array}{l} \text{Beginning inventory} \\ + \text{ Net purchases}^3 \\ \hline \text{Total available for sale} \\ - \text{ Ending inventory} \\ \hline \text{Cost of sales} \end{array}$$

Depending upon the accounting system used, a given company may have a single account in its general ledger entitled "cost of sales" or "cost of goods sold"

ILLUSTRATION 6-1

Partial Consolidated Statements Workpaper
Elimination of Intercompany Sale of Inventory
No Unrealized Profit (All Inventory Sold to Third Parties)

difference

Income Statement	P Company	S Company	Eliminations Dr.	Eliminations Cr.	Consolidated Balances	%
Sales	250,000	270,000	(1) 250,000		270,000	100.0%
Cost of Sales	200,000	250,000		(1) 250,000	200,000	74.1%
Gross Profit	50,000	20,000			70,000	25.9%
Balance Sheet						
Inventory	—0—	—0—			—0—	

(1)   To eliminate intercompany sales.

---

[3]For a manufacturing concern, "purchases" is replaced by the total cost of goods manufactured, which includes labor and overhead in addition to the raw materials used. Nonetheless, when a company purchases manufactured items from an affiliate, the purchasing affiliate would record those items as "purchases" at the amount charged by the selling affiliate.

ILLUSTRATION 6-2

The Impact on Gross Profit Percentages If Intercompany Sales Are Not Eliminated

| | Without Eliminating Intercompany Sales | | | |
Account	Company P	Company S	Total	%
Sales	$250,000	$270,000	$520,000	100.0%
Cost of Sales	200,000	250,000	450,000	86.5%
Gross Profit	50,000	20,000	70,000	13.5%

and a single line on its workpaper or, alternatively, separate accounts for the various components. In this chapter, we assume that the trial balance lists each component separately, and we present the workpaper entries accordingly. Using this approach, the cost of sales line on the income statement is replaced with lines for Beginning Inventory—Income Statement; Purchases; Ending Inventory—Income Statement; and Cost of Sales. Note that under this assumption, Ending Inventory—Income Statement requires an entry distinct from that to the balance sheet account Inventory. The account "Ending Inventory—Income Statement" has a normal credit balance because it is subtracted in computing Cost of Sales. We list in parentheses those entries that might be replaced by the use of the single account "cost of sales."

The workpaper entry in the year of the sale to eliminate intercompany sales of merchandise takes the following form:

(1)	Sales	250,000	
	Purchases (Cost of Sales)		250,000
	To eliminate intercompany sales.		

No unrealized intercompany profit exists, since all goods sold by P Company to S Company have been resold to third parties. After the elimination of intercompany sales, consolidated sales of $270,000 equals the amount of sales by the affiliated group (S Company) to third parties, and consolidated cost of sales of $200,000 equals the cost to the affiliated group (P Company) of manufacturing the goods sold.

Failure to eliminate intercompany sales would result in an overstatement of sales and of cost of sales in the consolidated financial statements. If the intercompany sales were not eliminated, the gross profit would be calculated as shown in Illustration 6-2. Compare this to the gross profit computed in Illustration 6-1, with the proper eliminating entry. If the intercompany sales were not eliminated, the consolidated gross profit would be correct but the gross profit percentage would not. Whereas the gross profit percentage should be 25.9% ($70,000/$270,000), failure to eliminate the intercompany sales would show the gross percentage as only 13.5% ($70,000/$520,000). Since both sales and cost of sales would be overstated by the same amounts, consolidated net income is not affected by the failure to eliminate intercompany sales. However, a number of financial ratios based on sales revenues would be distorted if the elimination were not made.

Assume now that S Company sells 60% of the goods purchased from P Company to third parties prior to the end of the current year. Sales, cost of sales, and inventory balances reported by each of the affiliated companies are presented in Illustration 6-3. Entry (1) to eliminate sales and purchases is the same as explained before. However, intercompany profit in the amount of $20,000 [$100,000 − ($100,000/

ILLUSTRATION 6-3

Partial Consolidated Statements Workpaper*
Elimination of Downstream Intercompany Sale of Inventory
Unrealized Profit in Ending Inventory
(First Year of Intercompany Sales)

| | P | S | Eliminations | | Consolidated |
Income Statement	Company	Company	Dr.	Cr.	Balances
Sales	250,000	162,000	(1) 250,000		162,000
Beginning Inventory	0	0			0
Purchases	200,000	250,000		(1) 250,000	200,000
	200,000	250,000			200,000
Ending Inventory	0	100,000	(2) 20,000		80,000
Cost of Sales	200,000	150,000			120,000
Gross Profit	50,000	12,000			42,000
		62,000		20,000 →	
Balance Sheet					
Inventory (40% remains)	—0—	100,000		(2) 20,000	80,000

*These entries are the same for firms using the cost, partial equity, and complete equity methods.
(1) To eliminate intercompany sales.
(2) To eliminate unrealized intercompany profit in ending inventory.

1.25)] resides in the ending inventory balance of S Company. This profit has not yet been realized by the consolidated entity through sales to outsiders (third parties). When, at the end of the accounting period, some of the merchandise remains in the inventory of the purchasing affiliate, the intercompany profit recognized thereon must be excluded from consolidated net income and from the inventory balance in the consolidated balance sheet. The workpaper entry to accomplish this elimination and to reduce Inventory on both the Income Statement and the Balance Sheet is as follows:

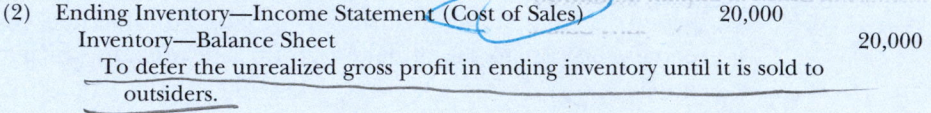

(2)	Ending Inventory—Income Statement (Cost of Sales)	20,000	
	Inventory—Balance Sheet		20,000
	To defer the unrealized gross profit in ending inventory until it is sold to outsiders.		

The form of the entry eliminating intercompany sales, entry (1), implicitly assumes that there is no unrealized intercompany profit. Accordingly, either that entry must be adjusted, or this second entry must be made to remove the unrealized intercompany profit from the ending inventory and to reduce the excessive credit to cost of sales.

The first and second eliminating entries could be combined and one entry prepared as follows, if a single account is used for "cost of sales":

Sales	250,000	
Cost of Sales		230,000
Inventory—Balance Sheet		20,000

As a practical matter, two entries are conventionally prepared as shown in Illustration 6-3. In either case, after adjustment, consolidated sales of $162,000 equals the amount of sales of the affiliated group to third parties. Consolidated cost of sales of $120,000 equals the cost to the affiliated group of the goods sold (.60 × $200,000), and the consolidated inventory balance of $80,000 equals the cost to the affiliated group of the goods held by S Company at the end of the year (.4 × $200,000).

The above entries for intercompany sales and unrealized profit in ending inventory are the same regardless of whether the parent uses the cost, partial equity, or complete equity method. However, as shown next, the entries for intercompany profit in beginning inventory differ slightly.

Year Two Eliminating Entries—Downstream Sales

Assume now that in the next period P Company sells merchandise to S Company in the amount of $500,000 (cost $400,000) and that S Company sells all its beginning inventory ($100,000 cost to S; $80,000 cost to consolidated entity) and one-half its current purchases from P Company ($250,000 cost to S; $200,000 cost to consolidated entity) to third parties for $378,000. Sales, cost of sales, and inventory balances reported by the affiliated companies are presented in Illustration 6-4. This illustration assumes that either the cost or the partial equity method is used.

Unrealized intercompany profit in the amount of $50,000 [$250,000 − ($250,000/1.25)] resides in the ending inventory of S Company. Workpaper eliminating entries (1) and (2) are similar to those discussed in the preceding example. Assuming a first-in, first-out (FIFO) inventory cost flow, intercompany profit in inventories excluded from consolidated net income in one period will be realized by sales to third parties in the next period. The form of the workpaper entry to recognize profit in the buying affiliate's beginning inventory that is realized during the current period depends on the method of accounting for the investment on the books of the parent.

ILLUSTRATION 6-4

Partial Consolidated Statements Workpaper—Cost or Partial Equity Method
Elimination of Downstream Intercompany Sale of Inventory
Unrealized Profit in Ending Inventory
(Second Year of Intercompany Sales)

Income Statement	P Company	S Company	Eliminations Dr.	Eliminations Cr.	Consolidated Balances
Sales	500,000	378,000	(1) 500,000		378,000
Beginning Inventory	0	100,000		(3) 20,000	80,000
Purchases	400,000	500,000		(1) 500,000	400,000
	400,000	600,000			480,000
Ending Inventory	0	250,000	(2) 50,000		200,000
Cost of Sales	400,000	350,000			280,000
Gross Profit	100,000	28,000	550,000	520,000	98,000
Retained Earnings					
Beginning Retained Earnings P Company	XXXX (a)		(3) 20,000		XXXX
Balance Sheet					
Inventory	—0—	250,000		(2) 50,000	200,000

(a) Includes $20,000 of gross profit on intercompany sales from the previous year (not yet sold to third parties).
(1) To eliminate intercompany sales.
(2) To eliminate unrealized intercompany profit in ending inventory.
(3) To recognize intercompany profit in beginning inventory realized during the period.

If the parent uses the *cost* or *partial equity* method of recording its investment in the subsidiary, the entry takes the following form (as shown in Illustration 6-4):

Cost or Partial Equity Method

(3)	Beginning Retained Earnings—P Company[4]	20,000	
	Beginning Inventory—Income Statement (Cost of Sales)		20,000
	To realize the gross profit in beginning inventory deferred in the prior period.		

The credit to beginning inventory *(Cost of Sales)* in entry (3) is necessary in order to recognize in consolidated income the amount of profit in the beginning inventory that has been confirmed by sales to third parties during the current period. S Company charged cost of sales for its cost of $100,000, whereas the cost to the affiliated group of the beginning inventory of S Company is only $80,000. Accordingly, cost of sales must be decreased by $20,000, which increases consolidated net income by $20,000. The adjustment to Beginning Inventory this period is in the same amount as that to Ending Inventory last period.

For firms using the cost or partial equity method to account for its investment in the subsidiary, the rationale for the debit of $20,000 to beginning retained earnings of P Company is as follows. In the previous year, P Company recorded $50,000 in profit on intercompany sales and transferred it to its Retained Earnings account as part of the normal accounting process. Since, at the beginning of the year, 40% of that amount has not been realized by sales to third parties, it must be eliminated from the beginning retained earnings of P Company to correctly reflect the beginning consolidated retained earnings.

The debit to beginning retained earnings may also be viewed in the following manner. In determining consolidated net income in the prior year, $20,000 was deducted from the reported income and thus from the retained earnings of the affiliated group by a workpaper entry (which, like all workpaper entries, was not posted to the ledger accounts). In order for beginning retained earnings to match the prior year's ending retained earnings (to the consolidated entity), this $20,000 adjustment must be made to beginning retained earnings. This entry is similar to those made in the previous chapter, in which one year's adjustment to an income statement account (such as Depreciation Expense or Amortization Expense) necessitated an adjustment in subsequent years to beginning retained earnings.

For firms using the *complete equity* method, the debit to beginning retained earnings is not needed, assuming the parent correctly adjusted for all intercompany profits/losses in its "revenue from subsidiary" account in the preceding year. Under the complete equity method, consolidated retained earnings is identical to the parent's reported retained earnings and thus no adjustment is needed. The debit to retained earnings is replaced by a debit to Investment in Subsidiary, which serves simply to facilitate the elimination of this account on the workpaper (as shown in Illustration 6-5):

Complete Equity Method

(3)	Investment in Subsidiary	$20,000	
	Beginning Inventory—Income Statement (Cost of Sales)		$20,000
	To realize the gross profit in beginning inventory deferred in the prior period.		

---

[4]If the parent firm uses the complete equity method, this debit is replaced by a debit to the Investment in Subsidiary account (see below).

ILLUSTRATION 6-5

Partial Consolidated Statements Workpaper—Complete Equity Method
Elimination of Downstream Intercompany Sale of Inventory
Unrealized Profit in Ending Inventory
(Second Year of Intercompany Sales)

Income Statement	P Company	S Company	Eliminations Dr.	Eliminations Cr.	Consolidated Balances
Sales	500,000	378,000	(1) 500,000		378,000
Beginning Inventory	0	100,000		(3) 20,000	80,000
Purchases	400,000	500,000		(1) 500,000	400,000
	400,000	600,000			480,000
Ending Inventory	0	250,000	(2) 50,000		200,000
Cost of Sales	400,000	350,000			280,000
Gross Profit	100,000	28,000	550,000	520,000	98,000

Balance Sheet					
Inventory	—0—	250,000		(2) 50,000	200,000
Investment in Subsidiary	XXX		(3) 20,000		

(1) To eliminate intercompany sales.
(2) To eliminate unrealized intercompany profit in ending inventory.
(3) To recognize intercompany profit in beginning inventory realized during the period.

Consolidated sales of $378,000 are equal to the amount of sales of the affiliated group to third parties. Consolidated cost of sales of $280,000 equals the cost to the affiliated group of the goods sold and is calculated as follows:

Cost of goods transferred to S Company in prior year and sold this year (40% × $200,000)	$80,000
Cost of goods transferred to S Company in current year and sold this year (50% × $400,000)	200,000
Cost of sales to third parties during current year	$280,000

Consolidated inventory of $200,000 equals the cost to the affiliated group (P Company) of the goods on hand at the end of the year (.50 × $400,000).

Over two consecutive periods, assuming a FIFO flow of inventory costs and no new deferrals, differences between the summed net income recorded on the books of the individual affiliates and consolidated net income offset each other, as do the effects of the differences on beginning retained earnings.

If an inventory cost flow assumption other than FIFO is used, unrealized intercompany profit in beginning inventory balances may continue to be included in the ending inventory. In that case, to the extent that unrealized intercompany profit from the beginning of the year remains unrealized, the effects on consolidated net income from the credit to Beginning Inventory—Income Statement (Cost of Sales) in entry (3) and the debit to Ending Inventory—Income Statement (Cost of Sales) in entry (2) offset each other. Thus, as a matter of workpaper procedure, there is no need to be concerned in formulating entry (3) as to whether FIFO or LIFO is used, as long as any unrealized gross profit in ending inventory is appropriately deferred.

Determination of Amount of Intercompany Profit

The proposed merger of Lockheed Martin Corp. and Northrop Grumman Corp. would couple the Northrop Grumman radars and electronic countermeasures for use on surveillance and battle-command airplanes with actual planes (already made by Lockheed). Northrop acquired much of this business by purchasing the former Westinghouse Electric Corp.'s defense electronics business.[5]

In the preceding examples, the amount of intercompany profit subject to elimination was calculated on the basis of the selling affiliate's *gross profit rate* stated as a percentage of cost. This is the concept that is normally applied in practice. An alternative would be to determine intercompany profit on the basis of the selling affiliate's profit after deducting selling and administrative expense. The effect of this approach, as compared with the gross profit (rate) method, would be to reduce the amount of profit subject to elimination and increase consolidated inventory balances by the amount of the selling and administrative expense associated with the goods still held by the affiliated group. Support for the gross profit method is based on the proposition that consolidated inventory balances should include manufacturing or acquisition costs only and that generally accepted accounting standards normally preclude the capitalization of selling and administrative costs.

Recall that gross profit may be stated either as a percentage of sales or as a percentage of cost. When it is stated as a percentage of cost, it is often referred to as "markup." To calculate the amount of intercompany gross profit to be eliminated from ending inventory, be careful to distinguish between percentages stated in terms of sales versus cost of sales. For example, if ending inventory (obtained from an affiliate) of $12,000 reflects a markup of 20% of cost of sales, the gross profit to be eliminated would be calculated as:

Sales	$12,000
Cost of Sales ($12,000/120%)	10,000
Gross Profit	$ 2,000

In contrast, if ending inventory of $12,000 reflects a gross profit of 20% of sales, the gross profit to be eliminated would be $2,400, or 20% of $12,000.

Inventory Pricing Adjustments

When inventory adjustments (write-downs) have been made on the books of one of the affiliated firms due to market fluctuations, the workpaper entries are modified accordingly. To illustrate, assume the following:

1. P Company sells S Company goods costing $200,000 for $250,000 (*downstream sale*);

2. At the end of the year, all these goods remain in the ending inventory of S Company and are written down from $250,000 to $215,000 on that company's books;

---

[5] *WSJ,* "Lockheed-Northrop Deal Faces Hurdles," by John R. Wilke, Thomas E. Ricks, and Frederic Biddle, 3/10/98.

3. The write-down on the books of S Company results from the application of the lower-of-cost-or-market rule in pricing its ending inventory; and

4. The related loss is included in the cost of sales of S Company, or may be disclosed separately if considered material.

What amount of intercompany profit is subject to elimination in the preparation of consolidated financial statements? Since the gross profit of $50,000 recognized by P Company is offset by the reduction of gross profit of $35,000 recognized by S Company, only the remaining $15,000 is still subject to elimination in the preparation of consolidated financial statements. The deduction of the amount of the current year's write-down of intercompany inventory from the amount of intercompany profit otherwise subject to elimination also results in the presentation of intercompany inventory at cost to the affiliated group ($215,000 − $15,000 = $200,000). In summary, the amount of intercompany profit subject to elimination should be reduced to the extent that the related goods have been written down by the purchasing affiliate.

Determination of Proportion of Intercompany Profit to Be Eliminated

It is clear that unrealized intercompany profit should not be included in consolidated net income or assets. However, two alternative views of the amount of intercompany profit that should be considered as "unrealized" exist. The elimination methods associated with these two points of view are generally referred to as *100% (total) elimination* and *partial elimination*. Current GAAP *require* 100% elimination of intercompany profit *in the preparation of consolidated financial statements.* Because not all users or authorities agree as to the appropriateness of this standard, we briefly discuss the relative merits of the alternatives next.

Proponents of 100% elimination regard *all* the intercompany profit associated with assets remaining in the affiliated group to be unrealized. Proponents of partial elimination regard only the parent company's share of the profit recognized by the *selling affiliate* to be unrealized. Stated another way, they regard the noncontrolling interests' share of the *selling affiliate's* profit on intercompany sales to be realized.

Under 100% elimination, the entire amount of unconfirmed intercompany profit is eliminated from combined income and the related asset balance. Under partial elimination, only the parent company's share of the unconfirmed intercompany profit recognized by the *selling affiliate* is eliminated.

This standard specifying 100% elimination was originally promulgated in paragraph 14 of *ARB No. 51* as follows:

> The amount of intercompany profit or loss to be eliminated . . . is not affected by the existence of a minority [noncontrolling] interest. The complete elimination of the intercompany profit or loss is consistent with the underlying assumption that consolidated statements represent the financial position and operating results of a single business enterprise.

Because generally accepted accounting standards currently require total elimination of intercompany profit in the preparation of consolidated financial statements, all illustrations of consolidating workpapers in this text are based on 100% elimination of intercompany profit. The reader needs to be aware, however, that there is support in the accounting literature for partial elimination of intercompany profit. The concepts underlying each of the approaches and their effects on consolidated balances are discussed in Chapter 11.

Determination of the Noncontrolling Interest in Combined Income—Upstream or Horizontal Sales

Subsidiary as Intercompany Seller In the preceding examples, the selling affiliate was the parent company (downstream sale). Accordingly, even though 100% of the unrealized intercompany profit was eliminated, no modification in the calculation of the noncontrolling interest in combined income or consolidated net assets was necessary. Had the selling affiliate been a less than wholly owned subsidiary (upstream sale), however, the controlling and the noncontrolling interests would have needed to be adjusted to reflect their interest in the amount of unrealized intercompany profit eliminated.

Intercompany sales of inventory necessitate adjustments to the calculation of the distribution of income to the controlling and noncontrolling interests. Whether the adjustments directly affect the noncontrolling interest (or only the controlling interest) depends on *who is the intercompany seller selling affiliate*. If the intercompany seller is the subsidiary, it is the subsidiary's income that needs adjustment, hence directly affecting the noncontrolling interest, as shown in Illustration 6-6.

In essence, the amount of the noncontrolling interest in combined income that is deducted to arrive at consolidated net income is based on the amount of reported subsidiary income (loss) that has been realized in transactions with third parties. This deduction is, as usual, made on the consolidated statements workpaper (final column) to be presented later in this chapter.

The general and succinct formats for the calculation of the noncontrolling interest in combined income in the case of an *upstream sale* are presented in Illustration 6-6.

The reader is reminded, however, that this modification of the calculation of the noncontrolling interest is applicable only when the subsidiary is the **selling affiliate** (upstream or horizontal sales). Where the parent company is the selling

ILLUSTRATION 6-6

Calculation of Noncontrolling Interest in Combined Income—Upstream Sales

General Format:

Noncontrolling Interest in Combined Income with Upstream Sales

Unrealized intercompany profit recorded by the subsidiary in the current period	XXXX	Net income reported by subsidiary Intercompany profit recognized by the subsidiary in the prior period(s) that is realized by sales to third parties during the current period	$XXXXX XXXX
		Subsidiary income included in combined income Noncontrolling ownership percentage interest Noncontrolling interest in combined income	$ XXXX % $ XXXX

Succinct Format:

Noncontrolling Interest in Combined Income with Upstream Sales

Unrealized profit in ending inventory	XXXX	Net income reported by subsidiary Realized profit from beginning inventory	$XXXXX XXXX
		Subsidiary income included in combined income Noncontrolling ownership percentage interest Noncontrolling interest in combined income	$ XXXX % $ XXXX

affiliate (*downstream sale*), the amount of subsidiary income included in combined income is not affected by the elimination of unrealized intercompany profit and no adjustment is necessary in the calculation of the noncontrolling interest in combined income. (See Illustration 6-11 for the effects of both upstream and downstream sales on income distribution.)

Conceptual Issue: Justification for Proportional versus No Allocation of Intercompany Profit—Upstream Sales

Although 100% elimination of intercompany profit is required in the preparation of consolidated financial statements, the adjustment in the calculation of the noncontrolling interest described before is *discretionary* under current GAAP. In other words, should the elimination of intercompany profit on upstream sales (100% as it is) affect only the controlling interest or both the controlling and noncontrolling interests? The authoritative position is stated in paragraph 14 of *ARB No. 51* as follows: "The elimination of intercompany profit or loss *may be* allocated proportionately between the majority [controlling] and minority [noncontrolling] interests [emphasis added]." Thus, the adjustments to the calculation of the noncontrolling interest (with corresponding effects on the controlling interest in combined net income) *may* be made but are not *required* under generally accepted accounting standards.

The objective of eliminating the effects of intercompany transactions from consolidated balances is to report the corresponding consolidated financial position and results of operations as if those transactions had never occurred. Given this objective, in our opinion, where the amounts are material, the allocation of intercompany profit and loss eliminations proportionately between the controlling and noncontrolling interests is preferred for fair presentation. Therefore, this is the procedure used in this text.

COST METHOD: CONSOLIDATED STATEMENTS WORKPAPER— UPSTREAM SALES

IN THE NEWS

"In a move to build a complete suite of products for fiber-optic networks, Ciena Corp. has agreed to acquire two closely held telecommunications-equipment makers for more than $980 million. Ciena, which makes gear that boosts the capacity of fiber-optic networks, itself was a takeover target last summer in a deal that ultimately fell through. The acquisitions of Lightera and Omnia should help Ciena establish itself as a full-service provider. Omnia makes gear aimed at helping local telephone companies mix voice and data traffic on fiber networks, while Lightera makes fiber-network switches that help long distance carriers."[6]

To illustrate consolidation procedures when the parent company records its investment using the cost method, assume the following:

1. P Company acquired an 80% interest in S Company on January 1, 2001, for $1,360,000, at which time S Company had capital stock of $1,000,000 and retained earnings of $700,000.

2. In 2001, S Company reported net income of $125,000 and declared dividends of $20,000.

3. In 2002, S Company reported net income of $140,000 and declared dividends of $60,000.

4. P Company uses the cost method to account for its investment in S Company.

---

[6] *WSJ*, "Ciena to Acquire 2 Telecom Firms For $980 Million," by Stephanie Mehta, 3/15/99.

5. The purchase price equals 80% of both the book values and fair values of S Company's net assets on the date of acquisition.

6. S Company sells merchandise to P Company as follows (upstream sales):

Year	Total Sales of S Company to P Company	Intercompany Merchandise in 12/31 Inventory of P Company	Unrealized Intercompany Profit (25% of Selling Price)
2001	$700,000	$400,000	$100,000
2002	1,000,000	500,000	125,000

Cost

Consolidated statements workpapers for the years ended December 31, 2001, and December 31, 2002, are presented in Illustrations 6-7 and 6-8, respectively. Entries *on the books* of P Company as well as *workpaper entries* necessary in the consolidated statements workpapers for the years ended December 31, 2001, and December 31, 2002, are summarized in general journal form below. The workpaper entries and the determination of the noncontrolling interest are explained in more detail as needed.

Entries on Books of P Company—Cost Method
2001—Year of Acquisition

(1)	Investment in S Company	1,360,000	
	Cash		1,360,000
	To record purchase of S Company stock.		
(2)	Cash	16,000	
	Dividend Income		16,000
	To record receipt of dividends from S Company (.8 × $20,000).		

Consolidated Statements Workpaper Entries—December 31, 2001 (Year of Acquisition)

(1)	Sales	700,000	
	Purchases *(COGS)*		700,000
	To eliminate intercompany sales.		

(2)	12/31 Inventory—Income Statement (Cost of Sales)	100,000	
	Inventory—Balance Sheet		100,000
	To defer (eliminate) unrealized intercompany profit in ending inventory.		

(3)	Dividend Income	16,000	
	Dividends Declared		16,000
	To eliminate intercompany dividends.		

(4)	Beginning Retained Earnings—S Company	560,000	
	Capital Stock—S Company	800,000	
	Investment in S Company		1,360,000
	To eliminate investment account.		

Since the selling affiliate is a partially owned subsidiary, unrealized intercompany profit is subtracted from reported subsidiary income when calculating the noncontrolling interest in combined income as follows:

$$.20 \times (\$125,000 - \$100,000) = \$5,000$$

[handwritten annotations:] if upstream sales; S's actual income; if downstream sales; .12 × 125,000 = 25,000

Cost Method			**ILLUSTRATION 6-7**			
80% Owned Subsidiary			**Consolidated Statements Workpaper**			
Upstream Sale of Inventory			**P Company and Subsidiary**			
Year of Acquisition			**For the Year Ended December 31, 2001**			

| | P | S | Eliminations | | Noncontrolling | Consolidated |
Income Statement	Company	Company	Dr.	Cr.	Interest	Balances
Sales	3,104,000	2,200,000	(1) 700,000			4,604,000
Dividend Income	16,000		(3) 16,000			
Total Revenue	3,120,000	2,200,000				4,604,000
Inventory 1/1	500,000	300,000				800,000
Purchases	1,680,000	1,370,000		(1) 700,000		2,350,000
	2,180,000	1,670,000				3,150,000
Inventory 12/31	480,000	310,000	(2) 100,000			690,000
Cost of Goods Sold	1,700,000	1,360,000				2,460,000
Other Expenses	1,124,000	715,000				1,839,000
Total Expense	2,824,000	2,075,000				4,299,000
Net/Combined Income	296,000	125,000				305,000
Noncontrolling Interest in Income					5,000	(5,000)*
Net Income to Retained Earnings	296,000	125,000	816,000	700,000	5,000	300,000
Retained Earnings Statement						
1/1 Retained Earnings						
P Company	1,650,000					1,650,000
S Company		700,000	(4) 560,000		140,000	
Net Income from above	296,000	125,000	816,000	700,000	5,000	300,000
Dividends Declared						
P Company	(150,000)					(150,000)
S Company		(20,000)		(3) 16,000	(4,000)	
12/31 Retained Earnings to Balance Sheet	1,796,000	805,000	1,376,000	716,000	141,000	1,800,000
Balance Sheet						
Inventory	480,000	310,000		(2) 100,000		690,000
Investment in S Company	1,360,000			(4) 1,360,000		
Other Assets (net)	5,090,000	2,310,000				7,400,000
Total	6,930,000	2,620,000				8,090,000
Liabilities	2,134,000	815,000				2,949,000
Capital Stock						
P Company	3,000,000					3,000,000
S Company		1,000,000	(4) 800,000		200,000	
Retained Earnings from above	1,796,000	805,000	1,376,000	716,000	141,000	1,800,000
Noncontrolling Interest in Net Assets					341,000	341,000
Total Liabilities and Equity	6,930,000	2,620,000	2,176,000	2,176,000		8,090,000

*.2($125,000 − $100,000) = $5,000.
(1) To eliminate intercompany sales.
(2) To eliminate unrealized intercompany profit in ending inventory.
(3) To eliminate intercompany dividends.
(4) To eliminate the investment account.

Cost Method
80% Owned Subsidiary
Upstream Sale of Inventory
Year Subsequent to Acquisition

ILLUSTRATION 6-8
Consolidated Statements Workpaper
P Company and Subsidiary
For the Year Ended December 31, 2002

Income Statement	P Company	S Company	Eliminations Dr.	Eliminations Cr.	Noncontrolling Interest	Consolidated Balances
Sales	3,546,000	2,020,000	(2) 1,000,000			4,566,000
Dividend Income	48,000		(5) 48,000			
Total Revenue	3,594,000	2,020,000				4,566,000
Inventory 1/1	480,000	310,000		(4) 100,000		690,000
Purchases	2,070,000	1,250,000		(2) 1,000,000		2,320,000
	2,550,000	1,560,000				3,010,000
Inventory 12/31	510,000	360,000	(3) 125,000			745,000
Cost of Goods Sold	2,040,000	1,200,000				2,265,000
Other Expenses	1,100,000	680,000				1,780,000
Total Expense	3,140,000	1,880,000				4,045,000
Net/Combined Income	454,000	140,000				521,000
Noncontrolling Interest in Income					23,000	(23,000)*
Net Income to Retained Earnings	454,000	140,000	1,173,000	1,100,000	23,000	498,000
Retained Earnings Statement						
1/1 Retained Earnings						
P Company	1,796,000		(4) 80,000	(1) 84,000		1,800,000
S Company		805,000	(4) 20,000		141,000	
			(6) 644,000			
Net Income from above	454,000	140,000	1,173,000	1,100,000	23,000	498,000
Dividends Declared						
P Company	(150,000)					(150,000)
S Company		(60,000)		(5) 48,000	(12,000)	
12/31 Retained Earnings to Balance Sheet	2,100,000	885,000	1,917,000	1,232,000	152,000	2,148,000
Balance Sheet						
Inventory	510,000	360,000		(3) 125,000		745,000
Investment in S Company	1,360,000		(1) 84,000	(6) 1,444,000		
Other Assets (net)	5,450,000	2,330,000				7,780,000
Total	7,320,000	2,690,000				8,525,000
Liabilities	2,220,000	805,000				3,025,000
Capital Stock						
P Company	3,000,000					3,000,000
S Company		1,000,000	(6) 800,000		200,000	
Retained Earnings from above	2,100,000	885,000	1,917,000	1,232,000	152,000	2,148,000
Noncontrolling Interest in Net Assets					352,000	352,000
Total Liabilities and Equity	7,320,000	2,690,000	2,801,000	2,801,000		8,525,000

*.2($140,000 − $125,000 + $100,000) = $23,000.
(1) To convert to equity/establish reciprocity as of 1/1/02 [.8 × ($805,000 − $700,000)].
(2) To eliminate intercompany sales.
(3) To eliminate unrealized intercompany profit in ending inventory.
(4) To recognize profit realized during year and to reduce the controlling and noncontrolling interests for their shares of unrealized intercompany profit at beginning of year.
(5) To eliminate intercompany dividends.
(6) To eliminate investment account.

Handwritten annotations:

$(142,000 + 100,000 - 125,000) \times 20\% = 23,000$

$(142,000 + 100,000 - 125,000) \times 20\% = 23,000$

$(454,000 - 150,000) + 80\% \times (1,173,000 + 100,000 - 125,000) = 1,838,000$

$2,100,000 + (885,000 - 15,000) \times 80\% - 125,000 \times 80\% = 2,148,000$

$(2,690,000 - 805,000 - 125,000) \times 20\% = 352,000$

$(1,000,000 + 885,000 - 125,000) \times 20\% = 352,000$

If it's upstream sales, do this way, otherwise same as P 228.

If the sale of merchandise had been *downstream* rather than *upstream*, the amount of subsidiary income included in combined income would not be affected by the elimination of unrealized intercompany profit and no adjustment would be necessary in the calculation of the noncontrolling interest in combined income.

Entry on Books of P Company—Cost Method **2002—Year Subsequent to Acquisition**		
Cash	48,000	
Dividend Income		48,000
To record receipt of dividends from S Company (.80 × $60,000).		

Consolidated Statements Workpaper Entries—December 31, 2002 (Year Subsequent to Acquisition)—Cost Method

(1)	Investment in S Company	84,000	
	Beginning Retained Earnings—P Company		84,000
	To convert to the equity method or to establish reciprocity [.80 × ($805,000 − $700,000)]		

(2)	Sales	1,000,000	
	Purchases (Cost of Sales)		1,000,000
	To eliminate intercompany sales.		

(3)	12/31 Inventory—Income Statement (Cost of Sales)	125,000	
	Inventory—Balance Sheet		125,000
	To eliminate unrealized intercompany profit in ending inventory.		

(4)	Beginning Retained Earnings—P Company (.80 × $100,000)	80,000	
	Beginning Retained Earnings—S Company (.20 × $100,000)	20,000	
	1/1 Inventory—Income Statement (Cost of Sales)		100,000
	To recognize intercompany profit in beginning inventory realized during the year and to reduce the controlling and noncontrolling interests for their shares of unrealized intercompany profit at beginning of year.		

(5)	Dividend Income	48,000	
	Dividends Declared—S Company		48,000
	To eliminate intercompany dividends (.80 × $60,000).		

(6)	Beginning Retained Earnings—S Company (.80 × $805,000)	644,000	
	Capital Stock—S Company (.80 × $1,000,000)	800,000	
	Investment in S Company ($1,360,000 + $84,000)		1,444,000
	To eliminate investment account.		

The unrealized profit in the current year's beginning inventory is the same as the unrealized profit in the prior year's ending inventory. Since the sale is *upstream*, the unrealized profit at the end of the prior year was apportioned between the controlling and noncontrolling interests by reducing the noncontrolling interest in combined income in the consolidated statements workpaper in the previous year.

ILLUSTRATION 6-9

Calculation of Realized Assets of Company S
December 31, 2002

	12/31/02	Unrealized Intercompany Profits in Ending Inventory	Realized 12/31/02
Total Assets—S Company	$2,690,000	125,000	$2,565,000
Total Liabilities—S Company	805,000		805,000
Capital Stock—S Company	1,000,000		1,000,000
Retained Earnings	885,000	125,000	760,000
Total Liabilities and Equity	$2,690,000		$2,565,000

Thus, the retained earnings effects in entry (4) are split between P Company's (80%) and S Company's (20%) beginning retained earnings accounts.

As a matter of workpaper procedure, adjustments to the controlling interest (consolidated retained earnings) are made by debiting (decreasing) or crediting (increasing) the beginning retained earnings row of the parent company. Adjustments to the noncontrolling interest are made by debiting (decreasing) or crediting (increasing) the beginning retained earnings row of the subsidiary company. The noncontrolling interest in the beginning retained earnings of S Company in the amount of $141,000 is equal to the noncontrolling interest's share of the reported retained earnings of S Company (.20 × $805,000 = $161,000) *reduced* by its share of the unrealized intercompany profit included therein (.20 × $100,000 = $20,000).

The net effect of the adjustments to the noncontrolling interest in the income statement and retained earnings statement sections of the consolidated statements workpaper that are necessary in the case of ***upstream sales*** is to adjust the amount of the noncontrolling interest in consolidated net assets. The amount of the noncontrolling interest reported in the consolidated balance sheet is based on the net assets of the subsidiary that have been realized in transactions with third parties.

In Illustration 6-8, for example, the noncontrolling interest in consolidated net assets on December 31, 2002, may be calculated as follows. First, as shown in Illustration 6-9, the reported assets are adjusted for the unrealized intercompany profit

ILLUSTRATION 6-10

Calculation of the Noncontrolling Interest
in Consolidated Net Assets
December 31, 2002

Method One:

Total Realized Assets—S Company (see Illustration 6-9)	$2,565,000
Less: Total Liabilities—S Company	(805,000)
Realized Net Assets—S Company	1,760,000
Noncontrolling percentage	20%
Noncontrolling interest in consolidated net assets	$ 352,000

Method Two:

Capital Stock—S Company	$1,000,000
Realized Retained Earnings—S Company (see Illustration 6-9)	760,000
Realized Net Assets—S Company	$1,760,000
Noncontrolling percentage	20%
Noncontrolling interest in consolidated net assets	$ 352,000

at the end of the year on upstream sales. Then, the noncontrolling interest in realized net assets can be computed either of two ways as shown in Illustration 6-10.

COST METHOD—ANALYSIS OF CONSOLIDATED NET INCOME AND CONSOLIDATED RETAINED EARNINGS

In Chapter 5, the calculations of consolidated net income and consolidated retained earnings were refined to accommodate the effect of the amortization of the difference between cost and book value. These analyses must now be further refined to accommodate the effect of unrealized intercompany profit.

The noncontrolling interest in combined income is calculated after subtracting end-of-year unrealized intercompany profit and adding intercompany profit realized during the current year to the net income reported by the subsidiary, as presented in Illustration 6-11. If the sale of merchandise had been downstream rather than upstream, the amount of subsidiary income included in combined income would not be affected by the workpaper entries related to unrealized intercompany profit, and no adjustment would be necessary in the calculation of the noncontrolling interest in combined income.

Cost

Consolidated Net Income

Consolidated net income is the parent company's income from its independent operations that has been realized in transactions with third parties plus (minus) its share of subsidiary income (loss) that has been realized in transactions with third parties plus or minus adjustments for the period relating to the amortization of the difference between cost and book value.

Using the data from Illustration 6-8, the calculation of the controlling and noncontrolling interests in combined net income for the year ended December 31, 2002, is presented in t-account form in Illustration 6-11.

ILLUSTRATION 6-11

Calculation of the Controlling and Noncontrolling Interest in Combined Income—Cost Method
For the Year Ended December 31, 2002

Noncontrolling Interest in Combined Income

Unrealized profit on upstream sales in ending inventory	125,000	Net income reported by S Company	$140,000
		Realized profit (upstream sales) from beginning inventory	100,000
		Subsidiary income included in combined income	$115,000
		Noncontrolling ownership percentage interest	20%
		Noncontrolling interest in combined income	$ 23,000

80%

Controlling Interest in Income

		Net income internally generated by P Company ($454,000 less $48,000 dividend income)	$406,000
Unrealized profit on downstream sales to S Company (ending inventory)	0	Realized profit (downstream sales) from begin. inventory	0
Amortization of the difference between cost and book value	0	P Company's percentage of S Company's income realized from third parties, .80($115,000)	92,000
		Consolidated Income	$498,000

Consolidated Retained Earnings

Consolidated retained earnings is the parent company's cost basis retained earnings that has been realized in transactions with third parties plus (minus) the parent company's share of the increase (decrease) in subsidiary retained earnings that has been realized in transactions with third parties from the date of acquisition to the current date plus or minus the cumulative effect of adjustments to date relating to the amortization of the difference between cost and book value.

On the basis of Illustration 6-8, a t-account calculation of consolidated retained earnings on December 31, 2002, is shown in Illustration 6-12. Notice that the retained earnings calculation reflects cumulative rather than only current-year data, in contrast to the distribution of current income (Illustration 6-11). There is no need, however, to include the realized profit in beginning inventory from January 1, 2002, or the unrealized profit in ending inventory at December 31, 2001, in the retained earnings calculation as they would cancel out.

Comprehensive Example: Upstream and Downstream Sales—Cost Method

To illustrate all aspects of the t-account calculations of consolidated net income and consolidated retained earnings, assume that:

1. Pepper Company acquired 80% of the voting stock of Salt Company on January 1, 2001, when Salt Company's retained earnings amounted to $150,000.

2. The difference between cost and book value on the date of acquisition was allocated as follows:

Land	$50,000
Equipment (10-year life)	20,000
Goodwill (40-year life)	40,000

3. Salt Company reported retained earnings of $260,000 on January 1, 2004, and $320,000 on December 31, 2004.

4. Salt Company reported net income of $90,000 and declared dividends of $30,000 in 2004.

5. Pepper Company reported net income in 2004 in the amount of $724,000 and retained earnings on December 31, 2004, of $3,500,000.

ILLUSTRATION 6-12

Calculation of Consolidated Retained Earnings
For the Year Ended December 31, 2002

Consolidated Retained Earnings

P Company's share of unrealized profit on upstream sales from S Company (in P's ending inventory), .8($125,000)	100,000	P Company's Retained Earnings on 12/31/02	$2,100,000
Unrealized profit on downstream sales to S Company (in S's ending inventory)	0	P Company's share of the increase in S Company's Retained Earnings since acquisition ($885,000 − $700,000).80	148,000
Cumulative amount of amortization and depreciation of the difference between cost and book value	0		
		Consolidated Retained Earnings	$2,148,000

ILLUSTRATION 6-13

Calculation of the Controlling and Noncontrolling Interest in Combined Income
For the Year Ended December 31, 2004

Noncontrolling Interest in Combined Income

Unrealized profit on *upstream* sales in ending inventory	5,000	Net income reported by Salt Company	$90,000
		Realized profit (*upstream* sales) from beginning inventory	10,000
		Subsidiary income included in combined income	$95,000
		Noncontrolling ownership percentage interest	20%
		Noncontrolling interest in combined income	$ 19,000

80%

Controlling Interest in Income

Unrealized profit on *downstream* sales to Salt Company (ending inventory)	20,000	Net income internally generated by Pepper Company ($724,000 less $24,000 dividends from Salt)	$700,000
Depreciation ($20,000/10)	2,000	Realized profit (*downstream* sales) from begin. inventory	15,000
Amortization goodwill ($40,000/40)	1,000	Pepper Company's percentage of Salt Company's income realized from third parties, .80($95,000)	76,000
		Consolidated Income	$768,000

6. There were no intercompany sales prior to 2003 and unrealized profits on January 1 and on December 31, 2004, resulting from intercompany sales are as summarized below:

	Unrealized Intercompany Profit on	
Resulting From	*1/1/04*	*12/31/04*
Sales by Salt Company to Pepper Company	$10,000	$ 5,000
Sales by Pepper Company to Salt Company	15,000	20,000

T-account calculations of consolidated net income for the year ended December 31, 2004, and consolidated retained earnings on December 31, 2004 are presented in Illustrations 6-13 and 6-14 respectively.

ILLUSTRATION 6-14

Calculation of Consolidated Retained Earnings—Cost Method
For the Year Ended December 31, 2004

Consolidated Retained Earnings

P Company's share of unrealized profit on *upstream* sales from S Company (in P's ending inventory), .8($5,000)	4,000	P Company's Retained Earnings on 12/31/04	$3,500,000
Unrealized profit on *downstream* sales to S Company (in S's ending inventory)	20,000	P Company's share of the increase in S Company's Retained Earnings since acquisition ($320,000 − $150,000).80	136,000
Cumulative amount of amortization and depreciation of the difference between cost and book value	12,000		
		Consolidated Retained Earnings	$3,600,000

Cost

CONSOLIDATED STATEMENTS WORKPAPER—PARTIAL EQUITY METHOD

The balances reported by the parent company in income, retained earnings, and the investment account differ depending on the method used by the parent company to record its investment. As demonstrated in Chapters 4 and 5, however, the method used by the parent company to record its investment has no effect on the consolidated balances. To illustrate consolidation procedures when the parent company records its investment using the partial equity method, assume the following:

Partial

1. P Company acquired an 80% interest in S Company on January 1, 2001, for $1,360,000, at which time S Company had capital stock of $1,000,000 and retained earnings of $700,000.

2. In 2001, S Company reported net income of $125,000 and declared dividends of $20,000.

3. In 2002, S Company reported net income of $140,000 and declared dividends of $60,000.

4. P Company uses the partial equity method to account for its investment in S Company.

5. The purchase price equals 80% of both the book values and fair values of S Company's net assets on the date of acquisition.

6. S Company sells merchandise to P Company as follows (upstream sales):

	Total Sales of S Company to P Company	Intercompany Merchandise in 12/31 Inventory of P Company	Unrealized Intercompany Profit (25% of Selling price)
2001	$ 700,000	$400,000	$100,000
2002	1,000,000	500,000	125,000

Entries on Books of P Company—Partial Equity Method

Entries recorded on the books of P Company under the partial equity method are as follows:

2001—Year of Acquisition—Partial Equity

(1)	Investment in S Company	1,360,000	
	Cash		1,360,000
	To record purchase of 80% interest in S Company.		
(2)	Cash	16,000	
	Investment in S Company		16,000
	To record dividends received (.80 × $20,000).		
(3)	Investment in S Company	100,000	
	Equity in Subsidiary Income		100,000
	To record equity in subsidiary income (.80 × $125,000).		

2002—Year Subsequent to Acquisition—Partial Equity

(4)	Cash	48,000	
	Investment in S Company		48,000
	To record dividends received (.80 × $60,000).		
(5)	Investment in S Company	112,000	
	Equity in Subsidiary Income		112,000
	To record equity in subsidiary income (.80 × $140,000).		

After these entries are posted, the investment account will appear as follows:

Investment in S Company

(1)	Cost	1,360,000	(2)	Dividends	16,000
(3)	Subsidiary Income	100,000			
	12/31/01 Balance	1,444,000			
(5)	Subsidiary Income	112,000	(4)	Dividends	48,000
	12/31/02 Balance	1,508,000			

Workpaper Entries—2002—Partial Equity Consolidated workpapers under the partial equity method for the years ended December 31, 2001 and 2002, are presented in Illustrations 6-15 and 6-16. Workpaper entries in Illustration 6-16 (the year subsequent to acquisition) are presented in general journal form as follows:

(1)	Equity in Subsidiary Income	112,000	
	Dividends Declared		48,000
	Investment in S Company		64,000
	To reverse the effect of parent company entries during the year for subsidiary dividends and income.		
(2)	Sales	1,000,000	
	Purchases (Cost of Sales)		1,000,000
	To eliminate intercompany sales.		
(3)	12/31 Inventory—Income Statement (Cost of Sales)	125,000	
	Inventory—Balance Sheet		125,000
	To eliminate unrealized intercompany profit in ending inventory.		
(4)	Beginning Retained Earnings—P Company	80,000	
	(.80 × $100,000)		
	Beginning Retained Earnings—S Company	20,000	
	(.20 × $100,000)		
	1/1 Inventory—Income Statement (Cost of Sales)		100,000
	To recognize intercompany profit in beginning inventory realized during the year and to reduce controlling and noncontrolling interest for their share of unrealized intercompany profit at beginning of year.		

Entries (2), (3), and (4) are the same as the corresponding entries in Illustration 6-8 (investment recorded using cost method).

Partial Equity Method
80% Owned Subsidiary
Upstream Sale of Inventory
Year of Acquisition

ILLUSTRATION 6-15
Consolidated Statements Workpaper
P Company and Subsidiary
For the Year Ended December 31, 2001

Income Statement	P Company	S Company	Eliminations Dr.	Eliminations Cr.	Noncontrolling Interest	Consolidated Balances
Sales	3,104,000	2,200,000	(2) 700,000			4,604,000
Equity in Subsidiary Income	100,000		(1) 100,000			
Total Revenue	3,204,000	2,200,000				4,604,000
Inventory 1/1	500,000	300,000				800,000
Purchases	1,680,000	1,370,000		(2) 700,000		2,350,000
	2,180,000	1,670,000				3,150,000
Inventory 12/31	480,000	310,000	(3) 100,000			690,000
Cost of Goods Sold	1,700,000	1,360,000				2,460,000
Other Expenses	1,124,000	715,000				1,839,000
Total Cost and Expense	2,824,000	2,075,000				4,299,000
Net/Combined Income	380,000	125,000				305,000
Noncontrolling Interest in Income					5,000	(5,000)*
Net Income to Retained Earnings	380,000	125,000	900,000	700,000	5,000	300,000

Handwritten: $(125,000 - 100,000) \times 20\% = 5,000$

Retained Earnings Statement

Handwritten: $(380,000 - 100,000) + (125,000 - 100,000) \times 80\% = 270,000$

	P Company	S Company	Eliminations Dr.	Eliminations Cr.	Noncontrolling Interest	Consolidated Balances
1/1 Retained Earnings						
P Company	1,650,000					1,650,000
S Company		700,000	(4) 560,000		140,000	
Net Income from above	380,000	125,000	900,000	700,000	5,000	300,000
Dividends Declared						
P Company	(150,000)					(150,000)
S Company		(20,000)		(1) 16,000	(4,000)	
12/31 Retained Earnings to Balance Sheet	1,880,000	805,000	1,460,000	716,000	141,000	1,800,000

Balance Sheet

Handwritten: $1,880,000 + (805,000 - 100,000) \times 80\% - 100,000 \times 80\% = 1,800,000$

	P Company	S Company	Eliminations Dr.	Eliminations Cr.	Noncontrolling Interest	Consolidated Balances
Inventory	480,000	310,000		(3) 100,000		690,000
Investment in S Company	1,444,000			(1) 84,000		
				(4) 1,360,000		
Other Assets (net)	5,090,000	2,310,000				7,400,000
Total	7,014,000	2,620,000				8,090,000
Liabilities	2,134,000	815,000				2,949,000
Capital Stock						
P Company	3,000,000					3,000,000
S Company		1,000,000	(4) 800,000		200,000	
Retained Earnings from above	1,880,000	805,000	1,460,000	716,000	141,000	1,800,000
Noncontrolling Interest in Net Assets					341,000	341,000
Total Liabilities and Equity	7,014,000	2,620,000	2,260,000	2,260,000		8,090,000

Handwritten near Investment: $= 1,360,000 + (805,000 - 700,000) \times 80\% = 1,444,000$

Handwritten near Liabilities: $(2,620,000 - 815,000 - 100,000) \times 20\% = 341,000$

*.20($125,000 − $100,000) = $5,000.
(1) To reverse the effect of parent company entries during the year for subsidiary dividends and income.
(2) To eliminate intercompany sales.
(3) To eliminate unrealized intercompany profit in ending inventory.
(4) To eliminate investment account.

Partial Equity Method		ILLUSTRATION 6-16				
80% Owned Subsidiary		Consolidated Statements Workpaper				
Upstream Sale of Inventory		P Company and Subsidiary				
Year Subsequent to Acquisition		For the Year Ended December 31, 2002				

	P	S	Eliminations		Noncontrolling	Consolidated
Income Statement	*Company*	*Company*	*Dr.*	*Cr.*	*Interest*	*Balances*
Sales	3,546,000	2,020,000	(2) 1,000,000			4,566,000
Equity in Subsidiary Income	112,000			(1) 112,000		
Total Revenue	3,658,000	2,020,000				4,566,000
Inventory 1/1	480,000	310,000		(4) 100,000		690,000
Purchases	2,070,000	1,250,000		(2) 1,000,000		2,320,000
	2,550,000	1,560,000				3,010,000
Inventory 12/31	510,000	360,000	(3) 125,000			745,000
Cost of Goods Sold	2,040,000	1,200,000				2,265,000
Other Expenses	1,100,000	680,000				1,780,000
Total Cost and Expense	3,140,000	1,880,000				4,045,000
Net/Combined Income	518,000	140,000				521,000
Noncontrolling Interest in Income					23,000	(23,000)*
Net Income to Retained Earnings	518,000	140,000	1,237,000	1,100,000	23,000	498,000
Retained Earnings Statement						
1/1 Retained Earnings						
P Company	1,880,000		(4) 80,000			1,800,000
S Company		805,000	(4) 20,000		141,000	
			(5) 644,000			
Net Income from above	518,000	140,000	1,237,000	1,100,000	23,000	498,000
Dividends Declared						
P Company	(150,000)					(150,000)
S Company		(60,000)		(1) 48,000	(12,000)	
12/31 Retained Earnings to						
Balance Sheet	2,248,000	885,000	1,981,000	1,148,000	152,000	2,148,000
Balance Sheet						
Inventory	510,000	360,000		(3) 125,000		745,000
Investment in S Company	1,508,000			(1) 64,000		
				(5) 1,444,000		
Other Assets (net)	5,450,000	2,330,000				7,780,000
Total	7,468,000	2,690,000				8,525,000
Liabilities	2,220,000	805,000				3,025,000
Capital Stock						
P Company	3,000,000					3,000,000
S Company		1,000,000	(5) 800,000		200,000	
Retained Earnings from above	2,248,000	885,000	1,981,000	1,148,000	152,000	2,148,000
Noncontrolling Interest in Net						
Assets					352,000	352,000
Total Liabilities and Equity	7,468,000	2,690,000	2,781,000	2,781,000		8,525,000

*.20($140,000 − $125,000 + $100,000) = $23,000.

(1) To reverse the effect of parent company entries during the year for subsidiary dividends and income.
(2) To eliminate intercompany sales.
(3) To eliminate unrealized intercompany profit in ending inventory.
(4) To recognize profit realized during year and to reduce the controlling and noncontrolling interests for their shares of unrealized intercompany profit at beginning of year.
(5) To eliminate investment account.

(5)	Beginning Retained Earnings—S Company	644,000	
	(.80 × $805,000)		
	Capital Stock—S Company (.80 × $1,000,000)	800,000	
	Investment in S Company ($1,508,000 − $64,000)		1,444,000
	To eliminate investment account.		

This entry is the same as entry (6) in Illustration 6-8 (investment recorded using cost method).

Observe that the consolidated balances in Illustration 6-16 are the same as those in Illustration 6-8 (cost method workpaper). However, when the parent company records its investment using the partial equity method, entry (1) in Illustration 6-16 replaces the cost method entries to establish reciprocity and to eliminate dividend income [entries (1) and (5) in Illustration 6-8]. Most importantly, a comparison of entries (2), (3), and (4) in Illustration 6-16 with entries (2), (3), and (4) in Illustration 6-8 demonstrates that the workpaper entries to eliminate intercompany sales and unrealized intercompany profit are the same regardless of whether the investment is recorded using the cost method or the partial equity method.

PARTIAL EQUITY METHOD—ANALYSIS OF CONSOLIDATED NET INCOME AND CONSOLIDATED RETAINED EARNINGS

The t-account calculation of consolidated net income is independent of the method used by the parent company to record its investment. As stated earlier, *consolidated net income is the parent company's income from its independent operations that has been realized in transactions with third parties plus (minus) its share of reported subsidiary income (loss) that has been realized in transactions with third parties plus or minus adjustments for the period relating to the amortization of the difference between cost and book value.*

ILLUSTRATION 6-17

Calculation of the Controlling and Noncontrolling Interest in Combined Income—Partial Equity Method
For the Year Ended December 31, 2002

Noncontrolling Interest in Combined Income

Unrealized profit on *upstream* sales in ending inventory	125,000	Net income reported by S Company	$140,000
		Realized profit (*upstream* sales) from beginning inventory	100,000
		Subsidiary income included in combined income	$115,000
		Noncontrolling ownership percentage interest	20%
		Noncontrolling interest in combined income	$ 23,000

80%

Partial

Controlling Interest in Income

		Net income internally generated by P Company ($518,000 less $112,000 equity income)	$406,000
Unrealized profit on *downstream* sales to S Company (ending inventory)	0	Realized profit (*downstream* sales) from begin. inventory	0
Amortization of the difference between cost and book value	0	P Company's percentage of S Company's income realized from third parties, .80($115,000)	92,000
		Consolidated Income	$498,000

ILLUSTRATION 6-18

Calculation of Consolidated Retained Earnings—Partial Equity Method
For the Year Ended December 31, 2002

Consolidated Retained Earnings

P Company's share of unrealized profit on *upstream* sales from S Company (in P's ending inventory), .8($125,000)	100,000	P Company's Retained Earnings on 12/31/02	$2,248,000
Unrealized profit on *downstream* sales to S Company (in S's ending inventory)	0		
Cumulative amount of amortization and depreciation of the difference between cost and book value	0		
		Consolidated Retained Earnings	$2,148,000

Partial

On the basis of Illustration 6-16, the t-account calculation of consolidated net income for the year ended December 31, 2002, is demonstrated in Illustration 6-17.

When the parent company uses the partial equity method to record its investment, the parent company's share of subsidiary income since acquisition is already included in the parent company's reported retained earnings. Consequently, *consolidated retained earnings is calculated as the parent company's recorded partial equity basis retained earnings that has been realized in transactions with third parties plus or minus the cumulative effect of the adjustments to date relating to the amortization of the difference between cost and book value.*

On the basis of Illustration 6-16, the t-account calculation of consolidated retained earnings on December 31, 2002, is shown in Illustration 6-18. There is no need to include adjustments for 12/31/01 ending inventory or 1/1/02 beginning inventory as they cancel out.

CONSOLIDATED STATEMENTS WORKPAPER— COMPLETE EQUITY METHOD

The balances reported by the parent company in income, in retained earnings, and in the investment account differ depending on the method used by the parent company to record its investment. As illustrated in Chapters 4 and 5, however, the method used by the parent company to record its investment has no effect on the consolidated balances. To illustrate consolidation procedures when the parent company records its investment using the complete equity method, assume the following:

1. P Company acquired an 80% interest in S Company on January 1, 2001, for $1,360,000, at which time S Company had capital stock of $1,000,000 and retained earnings of $700,000.

2. In 2001, S Company reported net income of $125,000 and declared dividends of $20,000.

3. In 2002, S Company reported net income of $140,000 and declared dividends of $60,000.

Complete

4. P Company uses the complete equity method to account for its investment in S Company.

5. The purchase price equals 80% of both the book values and fair values of S Company's net assets on the date of acquisition.

6. S Company sells merchandise to P Company as follows (upstream sales):

	Total Sales of S Company to P Company	Intercompany Merchandise in 12/31 Inventory of P Company	Unrealized Intercompany Profit (25% of Selling price)
2001	$ 700,000	$400,000	$100,000
2002	1,000,000	500,000	125,000

Entries on Books of P Company—Complete Equity Method

Entries recorded on the books of P Company under the complete equity method are as follows:

Complete

2001—Year of Acquisition—Complete Equity Method
(1)	Investment in S Company	1,360,000	
	Cash		1,360,000
	To record purchase of 80% interest in S Company.		
(2)	Cash	16,000	
	Investment in S Company		16,000
	To record dividends received (.80 × $20,000).		
(3)	Investment in S Company	100,000	
	Equity in Subsidiary Income		100,000
	To record equity in subsidiary income (.80 × $125,000).		
(4)	Equity in Subsidiary Income	80,000	
	Investment in S Company		80,000
	To adjust equity in subsidiary income for P Company's share of unrealized intercompany profit (.80 × $100,000) in ending inventory.		

Entries (3) and (4) can be collapsed into one entry.

2002—Year Subsequent to Acquisition—Complete Equity Method
(5)	Cash	48,000	
	Investment in S Company		48,000
	To record dividends received (.80 × $60,000).		
(6)	Investment in S Company	112,000	
	Equity in Subsidiary Income		112,000
	To record equity in subsidiary income (.80 × $140,000).		
(7)	Investment in S Company	80,000	
	Equity in Subsidiary Income		80,000
	To adjust equity in subsidiary income for realized intercompany profit in beginning inventory (.80 × $100,000).		
(8)	Equity in Subsidiary Income	100,000	
	Investment in S Company		100,000
	To adjust equity in subsidiary income for unrealized intercompany profit in ending inventory (.80 × $125,000).		

Complete Equity Method			ILLUSTRATION 6-19			
80% Owned Subsidiary			**Consolidated Statements Workpaper**			
Upstream Sale of Inventory			**P Company and Subsidiary**			
Year of Acquisition			**For the Year Ended December 31, 2001**			

Income Statement	P Company	S Company	Eliminations Dr.	Eliminations Cr.	Noncontrolling Interest	Consolidated Balances
Sales	3,104,000	2,200,000	(2) 700,000			4,604,000
Equity in Subsidiary Income	20,000		(1) 20,000			
Total Revenue	3,124,000	2,200,000				4,604,000
Inventory 1/1	500,000	300,000				800,000
Purchases	1,680,000	1,370,000		(2) 700,000		2,350,000
	2,180,000	1,670,000				3,150,000
Inventory 12/31	480,000	310,000	(3) 100,000			690,000
Cost of Goods Sold	1,700,000	1,360,000				2,460,000
Other Expenses	1,124,000	715,000				1,839,000
Total Cost and Expense	2,824,000	2,075,000				4,299,000
Net/Combined Income	300,000	125,000				305,000
Noncontrolling Interest in Income					5,000	(5,000)*
Net Income to Retained Earnings	300,000	125,000	820,000	700,000	5,000	300,000
Retained Earnings Statement						
1/1 Retained Earnings						
P Company	1,650,000					1,650,000
S Company		700,000	(4) 560,000		140,000	
Net Income from above	300,000	125,000	820,000	700,000	5,000	300,000
Dividends Declared						
P Company	(150,000)					(150,000)
S Company		(20,000)		(1) 16,000	(4,000)	
12/31 Retained Earnings to Balance Sheet	1,800,000	805,000	1,380,000	716,000	141,000	1,800,000
Balance Sheet						
Inventory	480,000	310,000		(3) 100,000		690,000
Investment in S Company	1,364,000			(1) 4,000		
				(4) 1,360,000		
Other Assets (net)	5,090,000	2,310,000				7,400,000
Total	6,934,000	2,690,000				8,090,000
Liabilities	2,134,000	815,000				2,949,000
Capital Stock						
P Company	3,000,000					3,000,000
S Company		1,000,000	(4) 800,000		200,000	
Retained Earnings from above	1,800,000	805,000	1,380,000	716,000	141,000	1,800,000
Noncontrolling Interest in Net Assets					341,000	341,000
Total Liabilities and Equity	6,934,000	2,690,000	2,180,000	2,180,000		8,090,000

*.20($125,000 − $100,000) = $5,000.
(1) To reverse the effect of parent company entries during the year for subsidiary dividends and income.
(2) To eliminate intercompany sales.
(3) To eliminate unrealized intercompany profit in ending inventory.
(4) To eliminate the investment account.

Complete Equity Method	ILLUSTRATION 6-20
80% Owned Subsidiary	Consolidated Statements Workpaper
Upstream Sale of Inventory	P Company and Subsidiary
Year Subsequent to Acquisition	For the Year Ended December 31, 2002

Income Statement	P Company	S Company	Eliminations Dr.	Eliminations Cr.	Noncontrolling Interest	Consolidated Balances
Sales	3,546,000	2,020,000	(2) 1,000,000			4,566,000
Equity in Subsidiary Income	92,000		(1) 92,000			
Total Revenue	3,638,000	2,020,000				4,566,000
Inventory 1/1	480,000	310,000		(4) 100,000		690,000
Purchases	2,070,000	1,250,000		(2) 1,000,000		2,320,000
	2,550,000	1,560,000				3,010,000
Inventory 12/31	510,000	360,000	(3) 125,000			745,000
Cost of Goods Sold	2,040,000	1,200,000				2,265,000
Other Expenses	1,100,000	680,000				1,780,000
Total Cost and Expense	3,140,000	1,880,000				4,045,000
Net/Combined Income	498,000	140,000				521,000
Noncontrolling Interest in Income					23,000	(23,000)*
Net Income to Retained Earnings	498,000	140,000	1,217,000	1,100,000	23,000	498,000

Handwritten: $(140,000 - 125,000 + 100,000) \times 20\% = 23,000$

Retained Earnings Statement

	P Company	S Company	Eliminations Dr.	Eliminations Cr.	Noncontrolling Interest	Consolidated Balances
1/1 Retained Earnings						
P Company	1,800,000					1,800,000
S Company		805,000	(4) 20,000		141,000	
			(5) 644,000			
Net Income from above	498,000	140,000	1,217,000	1,100,000	23,000	498,000
Dividends Declared						
P Company	(150,000)					(150,000)
S Company		(60,000)		(1) 48,000	(12,000)	
12/31 Retained Earnings to Balance Sheet	2,148,000	885,000	1,881,000	1,148,000	152,000	2,148,000

Balance Sheet

	P Company	S Company	Eliminations Dr.	Eliminations Cr.	Noncontrolling Interest	Consolidated Balances
Inventory	510,000	360,000		(3) 125,000		745,000
Investment in S Company	1,408,000		(4) 80,000	(1) 44,000		
				(5) 1,444,000		
Other Assets (net)	5,450,000	2,330,000				7,780,000
Total	7,368,000	2,690,000				8,525,000
Liabilities	2,220,000	805,000				3,025,000
Capital Stock						
P Company	3,000,000					3,000,000
S Company		1,000,000	(5) 800,000		200,000	
Retained Earnings from above	2,148,000	885,000	1,881,000	1,148,000	152,000	2,148,000
Noncontrolling Interest in Net Assets					352,000	352,000
Total Liabilities and Equity	7,368,000	2,690,000	2,761,000	2,761,000		8,525,000

Handwritten notes: $1,360,000 + (885,000 - 100,000) \times 80\%$; $(125,000 \times 80\% = 1,408,000)$; $(2,690,000 - 805,000 - 125,000) \times 20\% = 352,000$

*.20($140,000 − $125,000 + $100,000) = $23,000.
(1) To reverse the effect of parent company entries during the year for subsidiary dividends and income.
(2) To eliminate intercompany sales.
(3) To eliminate unrealized intercompany profit in ending inventory.
(4) To recognize profit realized during year and to reduce the controlling and noncontrolling interests for their shares of unrealized intercompany profit at beginning of year.
(5) To eliminate investment account.

After these entries are posted, the investment account will appear as follows:

Investment in S Company

(1)	Cost	1,360,000	(2)	Dividends	16,000
(3)	Subsidiary Income	100,000	(4)	Profit in Ending Inventory (80%)	80,000
12/31/01 Balance		1,364,000			
(6)	Subsidiary Income	112,000	(5)	Dividends	48,000
(7)	Profit in Beginning Inventory (80%)	80,000	(8)	Profit in Ending Inventory (80%)	100,000
12/31/02 Balance		1,408,000			

Complete

Workpaper Entries—2002—Complete Equity Method Consolidated workpapers under the complete equity method for the years ended December 31, 2001 and 2002, are presented in Illustrations 6-19 and 6-20. Workpaper entries in Illustration 6-20 (the year subsequent to acquisition) are presented in general journal form as follows:

(1)	Equity in Subsidiary Income ($112,000 + $80,000 − $100,000)	92,000	
	Dividends Declared		48,000
	Investment in S Company		44,000
	To reverse the effect of parent company entries during the year for subsidiary dividends and income (adjusted for parent's share of gross profit realized/ unrealized as needed).		

(2)	Sales	1,000,000	
	Purchases (Cost of Sales)		1,000,000
	To eliminate intercompany sales.		

(3)	12/31 Inventory—Income Statement (Cost of Sales)	125,000	
	Inventory—Balance Sheet		125,000
	To eliminate unrealized intercompany profit in ending inventory.		

(4)	Investment in S Company (.80 × $100,000)	80,000	
	Beginning Retained Earnings—S Company (.20 × $100,000)	20,000	
	1/1 Inventory—Income Statement (Cost of Sales)		100,000
	To recognize intercompany profit in beginning inventory realized during the year in the proper accounts for presentation on the consolidated financial statements; that is, even though the parent has adjusted its equity in subsidiary income, the effect must be shown in the cost of sales account (as the equity in subsidiary income is eliminated).		

Entries (2), (3), and (4) are the same as the corresponding entries in Illustration 6-8 (investment recorded using cost method) with one exception. The exception is that the debit to Investment in S Company in entry (4) above replaces the debit to Beginning Retained Earnings—P Company under the cost or partial equity methods. The difference is that under the complete equity method, P Company had appropriately adjusted the investment account for its share of unrealized gross profit in inventory at the end of 2001. But now the entire investment account must be eliminated.

(5) Beginning Retained Earnings—S Company	644,000	
(.80 × $805,000)		
Capital Stock—S Company (.80 × $1,000,000)	800,000	
Investment in S Company		1,444,000
To eliminate the investment account.		

This entry is the same as entry (5) in Illustration 6-16 (partial equity method) or entry (6) in Illustration 6-8 (cost method).

Observe that the consolidated balances in Illustration 6-20 are also the same as those in Illustration 6-8 (cost method workpaper) or in Illustration 6-16 (partial equity workpaper). However, when the parent company records its investment using the complete equity method, entry (1) in Illustration 6-20 replaces the cost method entries to establish reciprocity and to eliminate dividend income [entries (1) and (5) in Illustration 6-8]. Most importantly, a comparison of entries (2), (3), and (4) in Illustration 6-20 with entries (2), (3), and (4) in Illustration 6-8 or in Illustration 6-16 demonstrates that the workpaper entries to eliminate intercompany sales and unrealized intercompany profit differ in only one respect. That is, the parent company's retained earnings account needs no adjustment under the complete equity method. Any adjusting/eliminating entries made to that account under the other two methods are replaced by an entry to the Investment account under the complete equity method.

COMPLETE EQUITY METHOD—ANALYSIS OF CONSOLIDATED NET INCOME AND CONSOLIDATED RETAINED EARNINGS

Under the complete equity method, no formal calculation of consolidated net income is needed. The parent company has already made adjustments for realized/unrealized gross profit depending upon whether or not such profit has been confirmed through transactions with outsiders. Thus, *consolidated net income equals the parent company's recorded income.*

Nonetheless, this amount may be verified as the sum of the following components: *the parent company's net income from its independent operations that has been realized in transactions with third parties plus (minus) its share of reported subsidiary income (loss) that has been realized in transactions with third parties plus or minus adjustments for the period relating to the amortization of the difference between cost and book value.* See Illustration 6-17.

When the parent company uses the complete equity method to record its investment, the parent company's share of subsidiary income (including any needed adjustments for intercompany profits) since acquisition is already included in the parent company's reported retained earnings. Consequently, *consolidated retained earnings is equal to the parent company's recorded complete equity basis retained earnings.*

SUMMARY OF WORKPAPER ENTRIES RELATING TO INTERCOMPANY SALES OF INVENTORY

Consolidated statement workpaper eliminating entries for intercompany sales of inventory are summarized in Illustration 6-21. The entries are the same whether the parent company uses the cost method or the partial equity method to record its investment. However, the form of the workpaper entry for unrealized profit in

ILLUSTRATION 6-21
Intercompany Profit—Inventories
Summary of Workpaper Elimination Entries

	Selling Affiliate Is the Parent (Downstream Sales)			Selling Affiliate Is a Subsidiary (Upstream Sales)		
To eliminate intercompany sales:						
All Methods	Sales	X		Sales	X	
	Purchases (Cost of Sales)		X	Purchases (Cost of Sales)		X
To eliminate intercompany profit in ending inventory:						
All Methods	Ending Inventory (Cost of Sales)	X		Ending Inventory (Cost of Sales)	X	
	Inventory *(Balance Sheet)*		X	Inventory *(Balance Sheet)*		X
To recognize intercompany profit in beginning inventory realized during the year:						
Cost or Partial	Beginning Retained Earnings—P	X		Beginning Retained Earnings—P	X	
Equity Methods	Beginning Inventory—*Income*			Beginning Retained Earnings—S	X	
	Statement (Cost of Sales)		X	Beginning Inventory—*Income*		
				Statement (Cost of Sales)		X
Complete Equity	Investment in S Company	X		Investment in S Company	X	
Method	Beginning Inventory—*Income*			Beginning Retained Earnings—S	X	
	Statement (Cost of Sales)		X	Beginning Inventory—*Income*		
				Statement (Cost of Sales)		X

beginning inventories differs between upstream and downstream sales and between the complete equity method and the other two.

INTERCOMPANY PROFIT PRIOR TO PARENT-SUBSIDIARY AFFILIATION

Generally accepted accounting standards are silent as to the appropriate treatment of unrealized profit on assets that result from sales between companies prior to affiliation (preaffiliation profit). The question is whether preaffiliation profit should be eliminated in consolidation. In our opinion, workpaper entries eliminating preaffiliation profit are inappropriate.

If the selling company is the new subsidiary, the profit recognized by it prior to its acquisition is implicitly considered in determining the book value of the interest acquired by the parent company. Accordingly, such profit is automatically eliminated from consolidated retained earnings in the investment elimination entry. A second elimination would therefore result in a double reduction of the amount of preaffiliation profit from consolidated retained earnings on the date of acquisition. When the assets are sold to third parties in subsequent years, consolidated net income would be increased by a corresponding amount, thus restoring the amount of the second reduction to consolidated retained earnings. The net result is to make an unwarranted reduction of consolidated retained earnings on the date of acquisition in order to report preacquisition profit in consolidated net income in years subsequent to affiliation that has already been reported by the subsidiary prior to affiliation. In our opinion such effects lack both conceptual and practical merit.

If the selling company is the parent, the preaffiliation profit will ultimately be included in consolidated retained earnings in any case. However, a reduction of such profit from consolidated retained earnings on the date of affiliation simply results in the inclusion of the profit in the consolidated net income of subsequent years. Again, the effect of the elimination would be to report the profit twice, once before affiliation and once after affiliation. Support for the elimination of preaffiliation profit is based primarily on the application of conservatism to the valuation of consolidated assets on the date of acquisition.

SUMMARY

1. *Describe the financial reporting objectives for intercompany sales of inventory.* Intercompany sales of inventory are eliminated, and adjustments made, to report sales revenue, cost of sales, and inventory balances as if the intercompany sale had not occurred. Thus, consolidated sales reflects only sales with ''outsiders,'' consolidated cost of sales reflects the cost to the consolidated entity, and consolidated inventory is reported at its cost to the consolidated entity (affiliated group).

2. *Determine the amount of intercompany profit, if any, to be eliminated from the consolidated statements.* Intercompany sales (and selling prices) do affect the allocation of profits to the controlling and noncontrolling interests, once the profit is realized through sales to outsiders. Thus, intercompany profit needs to be eliminated *only if* assets are still on the books of the consolidated entity (one of the members of the affiliated group). In such cases, the amount of profit to be eliminated may be calculated using the selling affiliate's gross profit rate, which may be stated as a percentage of either sales or costs. (The amount of profit to be eliminated is the same, regardless of how the percentage is stated.)

3. *Understand the concept of eliminating 100% (rather than only the parent's share) of intercompany profit not realized in transactions with outsiders, and know the authoritative position.* Proponents of 100% elimination regard *all* the intercompany profit associated with assets remaining in the affiliated group to be unrealized. Proponents of partial elimination regard only the parent company's share of the profit recognized by the selling affiliate to be unrealized. Stated another way, they regard the noncontrolling interests' share of the selling affiliate's profit on intercompany sales to be realized. Current GAAP require 100% elimination of intercompany profit in the preparation of consolidated financial statements.

4. *Distinguish between upstream and downstream sales of inventory.* Sales from a parent company to one or more of its subsidiaries are referred to as **downstream**

sales. Sales from subsidiaries to the parent company are referred to as **upstream sales.**

5. *Compute the non-controlling interest in combined income for upstream and downstream sales, when not all the inventory has been sold to outsiders.* For downstream sales, no modification to the calculation of the noncontrolling interest in combined income is needed (it is simply the noncontrolling percentage interest times the subsidiary's reported income). For upstream or horizontal sales, however, the noncontrolling interest in income must be adjusted. The reported income of the subsidiary (the selling affiliate) is *reduced* by the amount of gross profit remaining in ending inventory of the purchasing affiliate before multiplying by the noncontrolling percentage interest; *it is increased for gross profit realized from beginning inventory.*

6. *Prepare consolidated workpapers for firms with upstream and downstream sales using the cost, partial equity, and complete equity methods.* In the consolidated workpapers, eliminating and adjusting entries serve to eliminate intercompany sales and adjust both beginning and ending inventories for the effects of any gross profit included from intercompany sales. The noncontrolling interest in combined income reflects the adjustment described in the preceding learning objective for upstream (or horizontal) sales. The final column of the workpapers is identical, regardless of whether the parent uses the cost, partial equity, or complete equity method for consolidated investments.

7. *Discuss the treatment of intercompany profit earned prior to the parent-subsidiary affiliation.* Generally accepted accounting standards are silent as to the appropriate treatment of unrealized profit on assets that result from sales between companies prior to affiliation (preaffiliation profit). The question is whether preaffiliation profit should be eliminated in consolidation. In our opinion, workpaper entries eliminating preaffiliation profit are inappropriate for purchase acquisitions.

APPENDIX

Deferred Taxes and Intercompany Sales of Inventory

DEFERRED TAX CONSEQUENCES ARISING BECAUSE OF UNREALIZED INTERCOMPANY PROFIT

If the affiliated companies file consolidated income tax returns, profits from intercompany transactions are included in taxable income in the same years that they are included in the consolidated income statement. In that case, the amount at which the asset is reported in the consolidated financial statements and its tax basis are the same, and it is not necessary to consider deferred tax consequences.

However, when the affiliates file separate income tax returns, the tax basis for an asset sold between affiliates is based on the price paid by the purchasing affiliate. Thus, the tax basis of the asset will differ from the amount reported for that asset in the consolidated financial statements. Assuming that the selling affiliate recognized a profit on the intercompany sale, the amount of this difference is equal to the *unrealized* profit associated with that asset on the balance sheet date. This difference is a temporary difference that will result in deductible amounts on the tax return of the *purchasing affiliate* in a future year(s) when the profit is considered realized in the consolidated financial statements through the sale or depreciation of the asset.

However, under *SFAS No. 109*, "Accounting for Income Taxes," the measurement of the tax benefit for temporary differences related to unrealized profit on intercompany sales is not subject to the basic principles that apply to other temporary differences that will result in deductible amounts in future years. Rather, the provisions of *ARB No. 51*, "Consolidated Financial Statements," relating to income taxes paid on intercompany profit, are applied.

This standard requires deferral of income taxes *paid by the seller* on intercompany profits on assets remaining within the consolidated group. In effect, the taxes paid by the selling affiliate on these profits are treated as prepaid taxes in the consolidated financial statements, and the tax expense is reported in the consolidated financial statements in the same period that the profit is reported as realized. By adopting these provisions, deferred tax effects are based on the income taxes paid by the selling affiliate rather than on the future tax benefit to the purchasing affiliate. The amounts calculated under these two approaches would be different, for example, if the affiliates had different marginal tax rates or were in different tax jurisdictions, or when expected future tax rates differ from the tax rate used to determine the tax paid or accrued by the selling affiliate.

The balances reported by the parent company in income, retained earnings, and the investment account differ depending on the method used by the parent company to record its investment. As illustrated in previous chapters, however, the method used by the parent company to record its investment has no effect on the consolidated balances. Workpaper entries to record deferred tax consequences of unrealized intercompany profit and undistributed subsidiary income are also the same when the parent company records its investment using the partial equity method or the cost method to record its investment. Hence, these methods are illustrated jointly in the following section. The complete equity method differs slightly, however, as illustrated in the final section of this appendix.

INTERCOMPANY SALES OF INVENTORY—COST AND PARTIAL EQUITY METHOD

To illustrate the treatment in the consolidated financial statements of deferred income taxes relating to intercompany sales of inventory assume that:

1. S Company is a 70% owned subsidiary of P Company.
2. The companies file separate income tax returns and the marginal income tax rates for both companies are 40%.
3. On December 31, 2001, there is $500,000 of unrealized intercompany profit in the ending inventory of the purchasing affiliate.
4. S Company reports net income of $900,000 in 2001 and $600,000 in 2002.

Workpaper eliminating entries relating to the unrealized profit included in inventory of the purchasing affiliate differ depending on whether the selling affiliate is the parent company (downstream sale) or the subsidiary (upstream or horizontal sale). Entries in the December 31, 2001, and December 31, 2002, consolidated statements workpapers under each of these conditions are illustrated below:

Consolidated Statements Workpaper Entries—Cost and Partial Equity Methods—December 31, 2001

Downstream Sales			Upstream Sales		
12/31 Inventory—			12/31 Inventory—		
(Income Statement)	500,000		(Income Statement)	500,000	
Inventory		500,000	Inventory		500,000
To eliminate unrealized profit in ending inventory.					
Deferred Tax Asset	200,000		Deferred Tax Asset	200,000	
Tax Expense		200,000	Tax Expense		200,000
To defer income tax paid or accrued by the selling affiliate on unrealized intercompany profit (.4 × $500,000 = $200,000).					

Although the workpaper entries are the same, the computation of noncontrolling interest in combined income is affected by upstream sales. The *after-tax* unrealized intercompany profit of $300,000 [($500,000 - $200,000) or (.60 × $500,000)] must be subtracted from reported subsidiary income in computing subsidiary income included in combined income. For example, if the sale is upstream and S Company reports net income of $900,000 in 2001, the noncontrolling interest in combined income is $180,000 [.30 × ($900,000 − (.60 × $500,000))]. Alternatively, the following schedule illustrates the previous points.

Upstream Sales

	S Company (000s)	
	With Intercompany Profit	Without Intercompany Profit
Income from Independent Operations	$1,000	$1,000
Unrealized Profit in Ending Inventory	500	
Pretax Income	$1,500	$1,000
Tax Expense (40%)	600	400
Net Income	900	600

	S Company (000s)	
	With Intercompany Profit	*Without Intercompany Profit*
Less: After-tax unrealized profit in inventory		
Unrealized profit	500	
Tax on unrealized profit (40%)	200	
Subsidiary Income in Combined Income		(300) $600	$600
Noncontrolling Interest percentage	30%	30%
Noncontrolling Interest in Combined Income	$180	$180

Partial

If the sale is downstream, the amount of subsidiary income included in combined income is not affected by the elimination of unrealized intercompany profit and no adjustment is necessary in the calculation of the noncontrolling interest in combined income.

Assume that in the next year, the inventory is sold.

Cost

Consolidated Statements Workpaper Entries—Cost and Partial Equity Methods—December 31, 2002

Downstream Sales		*Upstream Sales*	
1/1 Retained Earnings—		1/1 Retained Earnings—	
P Company	500,000	P Company	
		(.7 × $500,000)	350,000
		1/1 Retained Earnings—	
		S Company	
		(.3 × $500,000)	150,000
1/1 Inventory		1/1 Inventory	
(Income Statement)	500,000	(Income Statement)	500,000

To recognize intercompany profit realized during the year and to reduce the controlling and the noncontrolling interests for their share of unrealized intercompany profit at the beginning of the year.

Tax Expense	200,000	Tax Expense	200,000
		1/1 Retained Earnings—	
		P Company	
1/1 Retained Earnings—		(.7 × $200,000)	140,000
P Company	200,000	1/1 Retained Earnings—	
		S Company	
		(.3 × $200,000)	60,000

To recognize income tax expense on intercompany profit considered realized during the year and to adjust the controlling and noncontrolling interests for the tax consequence of unrealized intercompany profit eliminated in the previous entry.

Note that since the inventory is now sold to outsiders, there are no longer any deferred tax items recorded on the consolidated balance sheet.

In the case of upstream sales, the net after-tax adjustment to the noncontrolling interest at the *beginning of the year* is $90,000 ($150,000 − $60,000), which is the same amount by which the noncontrolling interest in combined income was reduced for after-tax unrealized intercompany profit at the end of the prior year (2001) [.3 × ($500,000 − $200,000) = $90,000].

Partial

Cost

If the sale is upstream, the noncontrolling interest in combined income for 2002 is calculated after adding the after-tax amount of intercompany profit that is included in combined income in the current year (.60 × $500,000 = $300,000). For example, if the sale is upstream and S Company reports net income of $600,000 in 2002, the noncontrolling interest in combined income is $270,000 [.30 × ($600,000 + $300,000)]. If the sale is downstream, no adjustment is necessary in the calculation of the noncontrolling interest in combined income. These concepts are illustrated fully in the next section.

UNDISTRIBUTED SUBSIDIARY INCOME—THE IMPACT OF UNREALIZED INTERCOMPANY PROFIT ON THE CALCULATION OF DEFERRED TAXES

Cost and Partial Equity Methods

The workpaper entries needed to report the tax consequences of past and current undistributed earnings of a subsidiary were described in Appendix B in Chapter 4. Workpaper entries are necessary under the cost method when there is undistributed subsidiary income and the affiliates file separate income tax returns. Now that we have discussed the effects of unrealized intercompany profits, it is important to note that the calculation of the tax consequences of undistributed income is based on the undistributed income of the subsidiary that has been *included in combined income.* Thus, before calculating the deferred tax consequences relating to undistributed subsidiary income, the amount of undistributed income of the subsidiary must be adjusted for the *after-tax amount of* unrealized intercompany profit *recorded by the subsidiary* that has been recognized in the determination of combined income.

To illustrate, assume that:

1. P Company acquired 75% of the voting stock of S Company when S Company's retained earnings amounted to $150,000.

ILLUSTRATION 6-22

Undistributed Income of S Company
That Has Been Included in Combined Income

S Company	From Acquisition to 1/1/2002	For Calendar Year 2002	From Acquisition to 12/31/2002
Retained earnings 1/1/2002	$260,000		
Retained earnings 12/31/2002			$320,000
Retained earnings date of acquisition	(150,000)		(150,000)
Increase in retained earnings	110,000		170,000
Net income 2002		$90,000	
Dividends 2002		(30,000)	
After-tax unrealized profit on 1/1/2002 (.6 × $10,000)	(6,000)	6,000	
After-tax unrealized profit on 12/31/2002 (.6 × $5,000)		(3,000)	(3,000)
Undistributed income that has been included in combined income	$104,000	$63,000	$167,000

Partial

2. S Company reported retained earnings of $260,000 on January 1, 2002, and $320,000 on December 31, 2002.

3. S Company reported net income of $90,000 and declared dividends of $30,000 in 2002.

4. P Company reported net income from independent operations in 2002 in the amount of $700,000 and retained earnings on December 31, 2002, of $3,500,000.

5. The affiliates file separate income tax returns.

6. Undistributed income is expected to be received in the form of future dividends.

Cost

7. The dividends received deduction is 80%, and past, current, and future expected marginal income tax rates are 40%.

8. There were no intercompany sales prior to 2001, and unrealized profits on January 1 and on December 31, 2002, resulting from intercompany sales are as summarized below:

	Unrealized Intercompany Profit on	
Resulting From	*1/1/02*	*12/31/02*
Sales by S Company to P Company	$10,000	$ 5,000
Sales by P Company to S Company	15,000	20,000

The calculation of the amounts of the undistributed income of S Company that is included in combined income is presented in Illustration 6-22. Illustration 6-23 shows the calculation of the noncontrolling and controlling interests in combined income for 2002.

ILLUSTRATION 6-23

Calculation of the Noncontrolling Interest and Controlling Interest in Combined Income
For the Year Ended December 31, 2002

Noncontrolling Interest in Combined Income

After-tax unrealized profit on upstream sales in ending inventory (.6 × $5,000)	3,000	Net income reported by S Company	$ 90,000
		After-tax realized profit (upstream sales) from beginning inventory (.6 × $10,000)	6,000
		Subsidiary income included in combined income	$ 93,000
		Noncontrolling ownership percentage interest	25%
		Noncontrolling interest in combined income	$ 23,250

75%

Controlling Interest in Income

		Net income internally generated by P Company	$700,000
After-tax unrealized profit on downstream sales to S Company (ending inventory) (.6 × $20,000)	12,000	After-tax realized profit (downstream sales) from begin. Inventory (.6 × $15,000)	9,000
Amortization of the difference between cost and book value	0	P Company's percentage of S Company's income realized from third parties, .75($93,000)	69,750
Deferred taxes on undistributed income of S Company ($93,000 − $30,000)(.75)(.20)(.40)	3,780		
		Controlling Interest in Income (Consolidated Income)	$762,970

Complete Equity Method—Intercompany Sales of Inventory

When the parent uses the complete equity method to account for the investment, the parent accounts for deferred taxes related to undistributed *adjusted* subsidiary income on its own books. This occurs because there is a difference between taxable income (dividends received from the subsidiary) and equity income (reported on the income statement) on the books of the parent, necessitating parent company entries for deferred taxes.

To illustrate the treatment in the consolidated financial statements of deferred income taxes relating to intercompany sales of inventory, assume that:

1. S Company is a 70% owned subsidiary of P Company.
2. The companies file separate income tax returns and the marginal income tax rates for both companies are 40%.
3. On December 31, 2001, there is $500,000 of unrealized intercompany profit in the ending inventory of the purchasing affiliate.
4. S Company reports net income of $900,000 in 2001 and $600,000 in 2002.

On the books of the parent, the following entries are made to account for the effects of intercompany sales of inventory.

Equity in Subsidiary Income	500,000	
Investment in S Company		500,000
To adjust equity in subsidiary income for unrealized intercompany profit in ending inventory.		

Deferred Tax Asset	200,000	
Tax Expense		200,000

Workpaper eliminating entries relating to the unrealized profit included in inventory of the purchasing affiliate differ in subsequent years, depending on whether the selling affiliate is the parent company (downstream sale) or the subsidiary (upstream or horizontal sale). Entries in the December 31, 2001, and December 31, 2002, consolidated statements workpapers under each of these conditions are illustrated below:

Consolidated Statements Workpaper Entries—Complete Equity Method
December 31, 2001

Downstream Sales			*Upstream Sales*		
Ending Inventory—			Ending Inventory—		
(Income Statement)	500,000		(Income Statement)	500,000	
Investment in S		500,000	Investment in S		500,000
To eliminate unrealized profit in ending inventory.					

In the year 2002, the inventory is sold. The entry on the books of the parent to reflect the reversal of the deferred tax asset is as follows:

Tax Expense	200,000	
Deferred Tax Asset		200,000

Then the following entry is made on the workpaper:

Consolidated Statements Workpaper Entries—Complete Equity Method
December 31, 2002

	Downstream Sales			Upstream Sales	
Investment in S	500,000		Investment in S		
			(.7 × $500,000)	350,000	
			1/1 Retained Earnings—		
			S Company		
			(.3 × $500,000)	150,000	
1/1 Inventory			1/1 Inventory		
(Income Statement)		500,000	(Income Statement)		500,000

To recognize intercompany profit realized during the year and to reduce the controlling and the noncontrolling interests for their share of unrealized intercompany profit at the beginning of the year.

Note that since the inventory is now sold to outsiders, there are no longer any deferred tax items recorded on the consolidated balance sheet.

In the case of upstream sales, the net after-tax adjustment to the noncontrolling interest at the **beginning of the year** is $90,000 ($150,000 − $60,000), the same amount by which the noncontrolling interest in combined income was reduced for after-tax unrealized intercompany profit at the end of the prior year (2001) [.3 × ($500,000 − $200,000) = $90,000].

If the sale is upstream, the noncontrolling interest in combined income is calculated after adding the after-tax amount of intercompany profit that is included in combined income in the current year (.60 × $500,000 = $300,000). For example, if the sale is upstream and S Company reports net income of $600,000 in 2002, the noncontrolling interest in combined income is $270,000 [.30 × ($600,000 + $300,000)]. If the sale is downstream, no adjustment is necessary in the calculation of the noncontrolling interest in combined income.

(The letter A indicated for a question, exercise, or problem refers to the appendix.)

QUESTIONS

1. Does the elimination of the effects of intercompany sales of merchandise always affect the amount of reported consolidated net income? Explain.

2. Why is the gross profit on intercompany sales, rather than profit after deducting selling and administrative expenses, ordinarily eliminated from consolidated inventory balances?

3. P Company sells inventory costing $100,000 to its subsidiary, S Company, for $150,000. At the end of the current year, one-half of the goods remains in S Company's inventory. Applying the lower of cost or market rule, S Company writes down this inventory to $60,000. What amount of intercompany profit should be eliminated on the consolidated statements workpaper?

4. Are the adjustments to the noncontrolling interest for the effects of intercompany profit eliminations

illustrated in this text necessary for fair presentation in accordance with generally accepted accounting principles? Explain.

5. Why are adjustments made to the calculation of the noncontrolling interest for the effects of intercompany profit eliminations and not for the amortization, depreciation, and allocation of the difference between cost and book value?

6. What procedure is used in the consolidated statements workpaper to adjust the noncontrolling interest in consolidated net assets at the beginning of the year for the effects of intercompany profits?

7. What is the essential procedural difference between workpaper eliminating entries for unrealized intercompany profit made when the selling affiliate is a less than wholly owned subsidiary and those made when the selling affiliate is the parent company or a wholly owned subsidiary?

8. Define consolidated net income using the t-account or analytical approach.

9. Why is it important to distinguish between upstream and downstream sales in the analysis of intercompany profit eliminations?

10. In what period and in what manner should profits relating to the intercompany sale of merchandise be recognized in the consolidated financial statements?

11A. The FASB elected to require that deferred tax effects relating to unrealized intercompany profits be calculated based on the income tax paid by the selling affiliate rather than on the future tax benefit to the purchasing affiliate. Describe circumstances where the amounts calculated under these approaches would be different.

12A. Must unrealized profit on intercompany transactions be considered when calculating the tax consequences of undistributed subsidiary income? Explain.

EXERCISES

EXERCISE 6-1 Downstream Sales

P Company owns 80% of the outstanding stock of S Company. During 2001, S Company reported net income of $525,000 and declared no dividends. At the end of the year, S Company's inventory included $487,500 in unrealized profit on purchases from P Company. Intercompany sales for 2001 totaled $2,700,000.

Required:

Prepare in general journal form all consolidated financial statement workpaper entries necessary at the end of the year to eliminate the effects of the 2001 intercompany sales.

EXERCISE 6-2 Noncontrolling Interest, Downstream Sales

Refer to Exercise 6-1. Calculate the amount of the noncontrolling interest to be deducted from combined income in arriving at 2001 consolidated net income.

EXERCISE 6-3 Noncontrolling Interest, Upstream Sales

Peabody Company owns 90% of the outstanding capital stock of Sloane Company. During 2001 and 2002 Sloane Company sold merchandise to Peabody Company at a markup of 25% of selling price. The selling price of the merchandise sold during the two years was $20,800 and $25,000, respectively. At the end of each year, Peabody Company had in its inventory one-fourth of the goods purchased that year from Sloane Company. Sloane Company reported net income of $30,000 in 2001 and $35,000 in 2002.

Required:

Determine the amount of the noncontrolling interest in combined income to be reported for 2001 and 2002.

EXERCISE 6-4 Controlling Interest, Downstream Sales

On January 1, 2001, Pearce Company purchased an 80% interest in the capital stock of Searl Company for $2,460,000. At that time, Searl Company had capital stock of $1,500,000 and retained earnings of $300,000. The difference between cost and the book value of the 80% interest acquired was attributed to specific assets of Searl Company as follows:

$300,000	to equipment of Searl Company with a five-year remaining life.
150,000	to land held by Searl Company.
90,000	to inventory of Searl Company. Searl uses the FIFO assumption in pricing its inventory.
480,000	that could not be assigned to specific assets or liabilities of Searl Company (amortized over 40 years).
$1,020,000	Total

downstream sale →

At year-end 2001 and 2002, Searl had in its inventory merchandise that it had purchased from Pearce at a 25% markup on cost during each year in the following amounts:

2001	$ 90,000 ÷ 1.25 = 72,000 → profit 18,000
2002	$105,000

During 2001, Pearce reported net income from independent operations (including sales to affiliates) of $1,500,000, while Searle reported net income of $600,000. In 2002, Pearce's net income from independent operations (including sales to affiliates) was $1,800,000 and Searl's was $750,000.

Required:

Calculate the controlling interest in combined net income for 2001 and 2002.

EXERCISE 6-5 Controlling Interest, Upstream Sales

Refer to Exercise 6-4. Using the same figures, assume that the merchandise mentioned was included in Pearce's inventory, having been purchased from Searl.

Required:

Calculate the controlling interest in combined net income for 2001 and 2002.

EXERCISE 6-6 Controlling Interest, Upstream Sales

Payne Company owns all the outstanding common stock of Sierra Company and 80% of the outstanding common stock of Santa Fe Company. The amount of intercompany profit included in the inventories of Payne Company on December 31, 2001, and December 31, 2002, is indicated here:

	Intercompany Profit on Goods Purchased From		
	Sierra Company	*Santa Fe Company*	*Total*
Inventory, 12/31/01	$3,800	$4,600	$8,400
Inventory, 12/31/02	4,800	2,300	7,100

The three companies reported net income from their independent operations (including sales to affiliates) for the year ended December 31, 2002, as follows:

Payne Company	$280,000
Sierra Company	172,000
Santa Fe Company	120,000

Required:

Calculate the controlling interest in combined net income for the year ended December 31, 2002.

EXERCISE 6-7 Workpaper Entries, Downstream Sales

Perkins Company owns 85% of Sheraton Company. Perkins Company sells merchandise to Sheraton Company at 20% above cost. During 2001 and 2002, such sales amounted to $450,000 and $486,000, respectively. At the end of each year, Sheraton Company had in its inventory one-third of the amount of goods purchased from Perkins during that year.

Required:

Prepare the workpaper entries necessary to eliminate the effects of the intercompany sales for 2001 and 2002.

EXERCISE 6-8 Workpaper Entries, Upstream Sales

Refer to Exercise 6-7. Using the same figures, assume that the sales were upstream instead of downstream.

Required:

Prepare the workpaper entries necessary to eliminate the effects of the intercompany sales for 2001 and 2002.

EXERCISE 6-9 Upstream and Downstream Sales

Peat Company owns a 90% interest in Seaton Company. The consolidated income statement drafted by the controller of Peat Company appeared as follows:

Peat Company and Subsidiary
Consolidated Income Statement
For Year Ended December 31, 2002

Sales		$14,000,000
Cost of Sales	$9,200,000	
Operating Expense	1,800,000	11,000,000
Combined Income		3,000,000
Less Noncontrolling Interest in Combined Income		200,000
Consolidated Net Income		$ 2,800,000

During your audit you discover that intercompany sales transactions were not reflected in the controller's draft of the consolidated income statement. Information relating to intercompany sales and unrealized intercompany profit is as follows:

	Cost	Selling Price	Unsold at Year-End
2001 Sales—Seaton to Peat	$1,500,000	$1,800,000	1/3
2002 Sales—Peat to Seaton	900,000	1,400,000	2/5

Required:

Prepare a corrected consolidated income statement for Peat Company and Seaton Company for the year ended December 31, 2002.

EXERCISE 6-10A Deferred Taxes and Intercompany Sales of Inventory (Upstream)

Pasco Company owns 75% of Shank Company. Pasco Company sells merchandise to Shank Company at 20% above cost. During 2001 and 2002, such sales amounted to $450,000 and $486,000, respectively. At the end of each year, Shank Company had in its inventory one-third of the amount of goods purchased from Pasco during that year. Marginal income tax rates for both companies are 40%.

Required:

Assume that the companies file separate income tax returns. Prepare the workpaper entries necessary to eliminate the effects of the intercompany sales for 2001 and 2002.

EXERCISE 6-11A Deferred Taxes and Intercompany Sales of Inventory (Downstream)

Refer to Exercise 6-10A. Using the same figures, assume that the sales were upstream instead of downstream.

Required:

Assume that the companies file separate income tax returns. Prepare the workpaper entries necessary to eliminate the effects of the intercompany sales for 2001 and 2002.

PROBLEMS

PROBLEM 6-1 Upstream Sales

Peel Company owns 90% of the common stock of Seacore Company. Seacore Company sells merchandise to Peel Company at 20% above cost. During 2001 and 2002, such sales amounted to $436,000 and $532,000, respectively. At the end of each year, Peel Company had in its inventory one-fourth of the goods purchased from Seacore Company during that year.

Peel Company reported $300,000 in net income from its independent operations in 2001 and 2002. Seacore Company reported net income of $130,000 in each year and did not declare any dividends in any year. There were no intercompany sales prior to 2001.

Required:

A. Prepare in general journal form all entries necessary on the consolidated financial statements workpaper to eliminate the effects of the intercompany sales for each of the years 2001 and 2002.

B. Calculate the amount of noncontrolling interest to be deducted from combined income in the consolidated income statement for 2002.

C. Calculate consolidated net income (controlling interest in combined income) for 2002.

PROBLEM 6-2 **Upstream Sales**

Shell Company, an 85% owned subsidiary of Plaster Company, sells merchandise to Plaster Company at a markup of 20% of selling price. During 2001 and 2002, intercompany sales amounted to $442,500 and $386,250, respectively. At the end of 2001, Plaster had one-half of the goods that it purchased that year from Shell in its ending inventory. Plaster's 1996 ending inventory contained one-fifth of that year's purchases from Shell. There were no intercompany sales prior to 2001.

Plaster had net income in 2001 of $750,000 from its own operations and in 2002 its independent income was $780,000. Shell reported net income of $322,500 and $335,400 for 2001 and 2002, respectively.

Required:

A. Prepare in general journal form all entries necessary on the consolidated financial statement workpapers to eliminate the effects of the intercompany sales for each of the years 2001 and 2002.

B. Calculate the amount of noncontrolling interest to be deducted from combined income in the consolidated income statement for 2002.

C. Calculate consolidated net income (controlling interest in combined income) for 2002.

PROBLEM 6-3 **Downstream Sales**

Peer Company owns 80% of the common stock of Seacrest Company. Peer Company sells merchandise to Seacrest Company at 25% above its cost. During 2001 and 2002 such sales amounted to $265,000 and $475,000, respectively. The 2001 and 2002 ending inventories of Seacrest Company included goods purchased from Peer Company for $125,000 and $170,000, respectively.

Peer Company reported net income from its independent operations (including sales to affiliates) of $450,000 in 2001 and $480,000 in 2002. Seacrest reported net income of $225,000 in 2001 and $275,000 in 2002 and did not declare dividends in either year. There were no intercompany sales prior to 2001.

Required:

A. Prepare in general journal form all entries necessary in the consolidated financial statements workpapers to eliminate the effects of the intercompany sales for each of the years 2001 and 2002.

B. Calculate the amount of noncontrolling interest to be deducted from combined income in the consolidated income statements for 2001 and 2002.

C. Calculate consolidated net income (controlling interest in combined income) for 2002.

PROBLEM 6-4 **Upstream and Downstream Sales**

Pace Company owns 85% of the outstanding common stock of Sand Company and all the outstanding common stock of Star Company. During 2002, the affiliates engaged in intercompany sales as follows:

Sales of Merchandise	
Pace to Sand	$ 40,000
Sand to Pace	60,000
Sand to Star	75,000
Star to Pace	50,000
	$225,000

The following amounts of intercompany profits were included in the December 31, 2001, and December 31, 2002, inventories of the individual companies:

	Intercompany Profit in December 31, 2001, Inventory of			
Selling Company	Pace	Sand	Star	Total
Pace Company		$7,000		$ 7,000
Sand Company	$ 5,000		$3,000	8,000
Star Company	8,000			8,000
Total	$13,000	$7,000	$3,000	$23,000

	Intercompany Profit in December 31, 2002, Inventory of			
Selling Company	Pace	Sand	Star	Total
Pace Company		$2,000		$ 2,000
Sand Company	$ 6,000		$9,000	15,000
Star Company	4,000			4,000
Total	$10,000	$2,000	$9,000	$21,000

Income from each company's independent operations (including sales to affiliates) for the year ended December 31, 2002, is presented here:

Pace Company	$200,000
Sand Company	150,000
Star Company	125,000

Required:

A. Prepare in general journal form the workpaper entries necessary to eliminate intercompany sales and intercompany profit in the December 31, 2002, consolidated financial statements workpaper.

B. Calculate the balance to be reported in the consolidated income statement for the following line items:
   Combined income
   Noncontrolling interest in combined income
   Consolidated net income (controlling interest)

PROBLEM 6-5 **Intercompany Downstream Sales, Cost Method**

Pruitt Corporation owns 90% of the common stock of Sedbrook Company. The stock was purchased for $625,500 on January 1, 2001, when Sedbrook Company's retained earnings were $95,000. Preclosing trial balances for the two companies at December 31, 2005, are presented here:

	Pruitt Corporation	Sedbrook Company
Cash	$ 90,800	$ 96,000
Accounts Receivable (net)	243,300	135,000
Inventory 1/1	165,000	132,000
Investment in Sedbrook Co.	625,500	
Other Assets	550,000	480,000
Dividends Declared	110,000	35,000
Purchases	935,000	420,000
Other Expenses	198,000	165,000
Total	$2,917,600	$1,463,000
Accounts Payable	$ 77,000	$ 36,000
Other Liabilities	120,700	47,000
Common Stock	880,000	600,000
Retained Earnings (1/1)	598,400	144,000
Sales	1,210,000	636,000
Dividend Income	31,500	—
Total	$2,917,600	$1,463,000
Ending Inventory	$ 220,000	$ 144,000

The January 1, 2005, inventory of Sedbrook Company includes $25,000 of profit recorded by Pruitt Corporation on 2004 sales. During 2005, Pruitt Corporation made intercompany sales of $250,000 with a markup of 20% on cost. The ending inventory of Sedbrook Company includes goods purchased in 2005 from Pruitt for $60,000.

Required:
A. Prepare the consolidated statements workpaper for the year ended December 31, 2005.
B. Calculate consolidated retained earnings on December 31, 2005, using the analytical or t-account approach.

PROBLEM 6-6 Trial Balance Workpaper—Cost Method
Using the information in Problem 6-5, prepare a consolidated statements workpaper using the trial balance format.

PROBLEM 6-7 Upstream Workpaper—Cost Method
Paque Corporation owns 90% of the common stock of Segal Company. The stock was purchased for $810,000 on January 1, 1997, when Segal Company's retained earnings were $150,000.

Financial data for 2001 are presented here:

	Paque Corporation	Segal Company
Sales	$1,650,000	$ 795,000
Dividend Income	54,000	
Total Revenue	1,704,000	795,000
Cost of Goods Sold:		
Beginning Inventory	225,000	165,000
Purchases	1,275,000	525,000
Cost of Goods Available	1,500,000	690,000
Less: Ending Inventory	210,000	172,500
Cost of Goods Sold	1,290,000	517,500
Other Expenses	310,500	206,250
Total Cost and Expense	1,600,500	723,750
Net Income	$ 103,500	$ 71,250

	Paque Corporation	Segal Company
1/1 Retained Earnings	811,500	180,000
Net Income	103,500	71,250
Dividends Declared	(150,000)	(60,000)
12/31 Retained Earnings	$ 765,000	$ 191,250
Cash	$ 93,000	$ 75,000
Accounts Receivable	319,500	168,750
Inventory	210,000	172,500
Investment in Segal Company	810,000	
Other Assets	750,000	630,000
Total Assets	$2,182,500	$1,046,250
Accounts Payable	$ 105,000	$ 45,000
Other Current Liabilities	112,500	60,000
Capital Stock	1,200,000	750,000
Retained Earnings	765,000	191,250
Total Liabilities and Equity	$2,182,500	$1,046,250

The January 1, 2001, inventory of Paque Corporation includes $45,000 of profit recorded by Segal Company on 2000 sales. During 2001, Segal Company made intercompany sales of $300,000 with a markup of 20% of selling price. The ending inventory of Paque Corporation includes goods purchased in 2001 from Segal Company for $75,000.

Required:

A. Prepare the consolidated statements workpaper for the year ended December 31, 2001.

B. Prepare a t-account calculation of consolidated net income for the year ended December 31, 2001.

PROBLEM 6-8 **Upstream Eliminating Entries and Consolidated Net Income, Comprehensive Problem**
On January 2, 1999, Patten Company purchased a 90% interest in Sterling Company for $1,400,000. At that time Sterling Company had capital stock outstanding of $800,000 and retained earnings of $425,000. The difference between cost and book value was allocated to the following assets:

Inventory	$ 37,500
Plant and Equipment (net)	180,000
Goodwill	80,000

The inventory was sold in 1999.

The plant and equipment had a remaining useful life of 12 years on January 2, 1999. Patten Company amortizes goodwill over 40 years.

During 1999 Sterling sold merchandise with a cost of $950,000 to Patten at a 20% markup above cost. At December 31, 1999, Patten still had merchandise in its inventory that it purchased from Sterling for $576,000.

In 1999, Sterling Company reported net income of $410,000 and declared no dividends.

Required:

A. Prepare in general journal form all entries necessary on the consolidated financial statements workpaper to eliminate the effects of the intercompany sales, to eliminate the investment account, and allocate the difference between cost and book value.

B. Assume that Patten Company reports net income of $2,000,000 from its independent operations. Calculate consolidated net income.

C. Calculate noncontrolling interest in combined income.

PROBLEM 6-9 Upstream and Downstream Workpaper, Comprehensive Problem
On January 1, 1999, Perry Company purchased 80% of Selby Company for $990,000. At that time Selby had capital stock outstanding of $350,000 and retained earnings of $375,000.

The fair value of Selby Company's assets and liabilities is equal to their book value except for the following:

	Fair Value	Book Value
Inventory	$210,000	$160,000
Plant and Equipment (10-year life)	780,000	630,000

One-half of the inventory was sold in 1999; the remainder was sold in 2000. Any goodwill is to be amortized over a 40-year period.

At the end of 1999, Perry Company had in its ending inventory $60,000 of merchandise it had purchased from Selby Company during the year. Selby Company sold the merchandise at 25% above cost. During 2000, Perry Company sold merchandise to Selby Company for $310,000 at a markup of 20% of the selling price. At December 31, 2000, Selby still had merchandise that it purchased from Perry Company for $82,000 in its inventory.

Financial data for 2000 are presented here:

	Perry Company	Selby Company
Sales	$1,400,000	$ 800,000
Dividend Income	20,000	—
Total Revenue	1,420,000	800,000
Cost of Goods Sold:		
Beginning Inventory	230,000	145,000
Purchases	900,000	380,000
Cost of Goods Available	1,130,000	525,000
Less: Ending Inventory	450,000	200,000
Cost of Goods Sold	680,000	325,000
Other Expenses	250,000	195,000
Total Cost and Expense	930,000	520,000
Net Income	$ 490,000	$ 280,000
1/1 Retained Earnings	$1,500,000	$ 480,000
Net Income	490,000	280,000
Dividends Declared	(50,000)	(25,000)
12/31 Retained Earnings	$1,940,000	$ 735,000
Cash	$ 95,000	$ 70,000
Accounts Receivable (net)	302,000	90,000
Inventory	450,000	200,000
Investment in Selby Company	990,000	
Plant and Equipment (net)	850,000	585,000
Other Assets (net)	390,000	230,000
Total Assets	$3,077,000	$1,175,000
Accounts Payable	$ 75,000	$ 30,000
Other Liabilities	102,000	60,000
Common Stock	960,000	350,000
Retained Earnings	1,940,000	735,000
Total Liabilities and Equity	$3,077,000	$1,175,000

Required:

A. Prepare the consolidated statements workpaper for the year ended December 31, 2000.

B. Calculate consolidated retained earnings on December 31, 2000, using the analytical or t-account approach.

PROBLEM 6-10 **Controlling and Noncontrolling Interest**

Penn Company owns a 90% interest in Salvador Company and an 80% interest in Sencal Company. Profit remaining in ending inventories from intercompany sales for 2001 and 2002 is indicated below.

| | Intercompany Profit in Ending Inventory of: | | | |
| | 2001 | | 2002 | |
Selling Company	Salvador	Sencal	Salvador	Sencal
Penn	$8,000	$4,000	$5,000	$ 9,000
Salvador		6,000		10,000
Sencal	5,000		2,000	

Salvador Company reported net income of $50,000 in 2001 and $45,000 in 2002, whereas Sencal Company's net income was $60,000 and $75,000 in 2001 and 2002, respectively.

Penn Company's net income from its own operations (including sales to affiliates) for 2001 and 2002 was $600,000 and $400,000, respectively.

Required:

A. Determine noncontrolling interest in combined income for 2001 and 2002.

B. Calculate the controlling interest in combined income for 2001 and 2002.

PROBLEM 6-11 **Downstream Workpaper—Partial Equity Method**

Pruitt Corporation owns 90% of the common stock of Sedbrook Company. The stock was purchased for $540,000 on January 1, 1997, when Sedbrook Company's retained earnings were $100,000. Preclosing trial balances for the two companies at December 31, 2001, are presented here:

	Pruitt Corporation	Sedbrook Company
Cash	$ 83,000	$ 80,000
Accounts Receivable (net)	213,000	112,500
Inventory 1/1	150,000	110,000
Investment in Sedbrook Co.	578,250	
Other Assets	500,000	400,000
Dividends Declared	100,000	30,000
Purchases	850,000	350,000
Other Expenses	180,000	137,500
	$2,654,250	$1,220,000
Accounts Payable	$ 70,000	$ 30,000
Other Liabilities	75,000	40,000
Common Stock	800,000	500,000
Retained Earnings	562,000	120,000
Sales	1,100,000	530,000
Equity in Subsidiary Income	47,250	
	$2,654,250	$1,220,000
Ending Inventory	$ 200,000	$ 120,000

The January 1, 2001, inventory of Sedbrook Company includes $30,000 of profit recorded by Pruitt Corporation on 2000 sales. During 2001, Pruitt Corporation made intercompany sales of $200,000 with a markup of 25% on cost. The ending inventory of Sedbrook Company includes goods purchased in 2001 from Pruitt for $50,000. Pruitt Corporation uses the partial equity method to record its investment in Sedbrook Company.

Required:

A. Prepare the consolidated statements workpaper for the year ended December 31, 2001.

B. Calculate consolidated retained earnings on December 31, 2001, using the analytical or t-account approach.

PROBLEM 6-12 **Downstream Trial Balance Workpaper**

Using the information in Problem 6-11, prepare a consolidated statements workpaper using the trial balance format.

PROBLEM 6-13 **Upstream Workpaper—Partial Equity Method**

(Note that this is the same problem as Problem 6-7, but assuming the use of the partial equity method.)

Paque Corporation owns 90% of the common stock of Segal Company. The stock was purchased for $810,000 on January 1, 1997, when Segal Company's retained earnings were $150,000.

Financial data for 2001 are presented here:

	Paque Corporation	*Segal Company*
Sales	$1,650,000	$ 795,000
Equity in Subsidiary Income	64,125	
Total Revenue	1,714,125	795,000
Cost of Goods Sold:		
Beginning Inventory	225,000	165,000
Purchases	1,275,000	525,000
Cost of Goods Available	1,500,000	690,000
Less: Ending Inventory	210,000	172,500
Cost of Goods Sold	1,290,000	517,500
Other Expenses	310,500	206,250
Total Cost and Expense	1,600,500	723,750
Net Income	$ 113,625	$ 71,250
1/1 Retained Earnings	838,500	180,000
Net Income	113,625	71,250
Dividends Declared	(150,000)	(60,000)
12/31 Retained Earnings	$ 802,125	$ 191,250
Cash	$ 93,000	$ 75,000
Accounts Receivable	319,500	168,750
Inventory	210,000	172,500
Investment in Segal Company	847,125	
Other Assets	750,000	630,000
Total Assets	$2,219,625	$1,046,250
Accounts Payable	$ 105,000	$ 45,000
Other Current Liabilities	112,500	60,000
Capital Stock	1,200,000	750,000
Retained Earnings	802,125	191,250
Total Liabilities and Equity	$2,219,625	$1,046,250

The January 1, 2001, inventory of Paque Corporation includes $45,000 of profit recorded by Segal Company on 2000 sales. During 2001, Segal Company made intercompany sales of $300,000 with a markup of 20% of selling price. The ending inventory of Paque Corporation includes goods purchased in 2001 from Segal Company for $75,000. Paque Corporation uses the partial equity method to record its investment in Segal Company.

Required:

A. Prepare the consolidated statements workpaper for the year ended December 31, 2001.

B. Calculate consolidated retained earnings on December 31, 2001, using the analytical or t-account approach.

C. If you completed Problem 6-7, compare the consolidated balances obtained in requirement A with those obtained in Problem 6-7.

PROBLEM 6-14   **Upstream and Downstream Workpaper—Partial Equity Method**

On January 1, 2000, Perry Company purchased 80% of Selby Company for $960,000. At that time Selby had capital stock outstanding of $400,000 and retained earnings of $400,000.

The fair value of Selby Company's assets and liabilities is equal to their book value except for the following:

	Fair Value	Book Value
Inventory	$230,000	$155,000
Plant and Equipment (10-year life)	800,000	600,000

One-half of the inventory was sold in 2000; the remainder was sold in 2001. Any goodwill is to be amortized over a 40-year period.

At the end of 2000, Perry Company had in its ending inventory $54,000 of merchandise it had purchased from Selby Company during the year. Selby Company sold the merchandise at 20% above cost. During 2001, Perry Company sold merchandise to Selby Company for $300,000 at a markup of 20% of the selling price. At December 31, 2001, Selby still had merchandise that it purchased from Perry Company for $78,000 in its inventory.

Financial data for 2001 are presented here:

	Perry Company	Selby Company
Sales	$1,385,000	$ 720,000
Equity in Subsidiary Income	208,000	
Total Revenue	1,593,000	720,000
Cost of Goods sold:		
Beginning Inventory	210,000	155,000
Purchases	875,000	360,000
Cost of Goods Available	1,085,000	515,000
Less: Ending Inventory	400,000	225,000
Cost of Goods Sold	685,000	290,000
Other Expenses	225,000	170,000
Total Cost and Expense	910,000	460,000
Net Income	$ 683,000	$ 260,000
1/1 Retained Earnings	$1,472,700	$ 450,000
Net Income	683,000	260,000
Dividends Declared	(40,000)	(30,000)
12/31 Retained Earnings	$2,115,700	$ 680,000

	Perry Company	Selby Company
Cash	$ 90,000	$ 65,000
Accounts Receivable (net)	297,000	85,000
Inventory	400,000	225,000
Investment in Selby Company	1,184,000	
Plant and Equipment (net)	880,000	540,000
Other Assets (net)	384,000	230,000
Total Assets	$3,235,000	$1,145,000
Accounts Payable	$ 24,300	$ 25,000
Other Liabilities	95,000	40,000
Common Stock	1,000,000	400,000
Retained Earnings	2,115,700	680,000
Total Liabilities and Equity	$3,235,000	$1,145,000

Required:

A. Prepare the consolidated statements workpaper for the year ended December 31, 2001.

B. Calculate consolidated retained earnings on December 31, 2001, using the analytical or t-account approach.

 **PROBLEM 6-15** **Upstream and Downstream Sales, Journal Entries and Controlling and Noncontrolling Interests**

On January 1, 1999, Paul Company purchased 80% of the voting stock of Simon Company for $1,360,000 when Simon Company had retained earnings and capital stock in the amounts of $450,000 and $1,000,000, respectively. The difference between cost and book value is amortized over 25 years. Simon Company's retained earnings amount to $780,000 on January 1, 2002, and $960,000 on December 31, 2002. In 2002, Simon Company reported net income of $270,000 and declared dividends of $90,000. Paul Company reported net income from independent operations in 2002 in the amount of $700,000 and retained earnings on December 31, 2002, of $1,500,000. During 2002, intercompany sales of merchandise from Paul to Simon amounted to $70,000 and from Simon to Paul were $50,000. Unrealized profits on January 1 and on December 31, 2002, resulting from intercompany sales are as summarized here:

	Unrealized Intercompany Profit on	
Resulting From	*1/1/02*	*12/31/02*
Sales by Simon Company to Paul Company	$20,000	$10,000
Sales by Paul Company to Simon Company	30,000	5,000

There were no intercompany sales prior to 2001.

Required:

A. Prepare in general journal form the entries necessary in the December 31, 2002, consolidated statements workpaper to eliminate the effects of the intercompany sales.

B. Calculate consolidated net income for the year ended December 31, 2002.

C. Calculate consolidated retained earnings on December 31, 2002.

D. Calculate noncontrolling interest in combined income for the year ended December 31, 2002.

PROBLEM 6-16 Complete Equity with Downstream Sales

(Note that this is the same problem as Problem 6-11, but assuming the use of the complete equity method.)

Pruitt Corporation owns 90% of the common stock of Sedbrook Company. The stock was purchased for $540,000 on January 1, 1997, when Sedbrook Company's retained earnings were $100,000. Preclosing trial balances for the two companies at December 31, 2001, are presented here:

	Pruitt Corporation	Sedbrook Company
Cash	$ 83,000	$ 80,000
Accounts Receivable (net)	213,000	112,500
Inventory 1/1	150,000	110,000
Investment in Sedbrook Co.	568,250	
Other Assets	500,000	400,000
Dividends Declared	100,000	30,000
Purchases	850,000	350,000
Other Expenses	180,000	137,500
	$2,644,250	$1,220,000
Accounts Payable	$ 70,000	$ 30,000
Other Liabilities	75,000	40,000
Common Stock	800,000	500,000
Retained Earnings, 1/1	532,000	120,000
Sales	1,100,000	530,000
Equity in Subsidiary Income	67,250	
	$2,644,250	$1,220,000
Ending Inventory	$ 200,000	$ 120,000

The January 1, 2001, inventory of Sedbrook Company includes $30,000 of profit recorded by Pruitt Corporation on 2000 sales. During 2001, Pruitt Corporation made intercompany sales of $200,000 with a markup of 25% on cost. The ending inventory of Sedbrook Company includes goods purchased in 2001 from Pruitt for $50,000. Pruitt Corporation uses the complete equity method to record its investment in Sedbrook Company.

Required:

A. Prepare the consolidated statements workpaper for the year ended December 31, 2001.

B. Calculate consolidated retained earnings on December 31, 2001, using the analytical or t-account approach.

C. If you completed Problem 6-11, compare the consolidated balances obtained in requirement A with those obtained in that problem.

PROBLEM 6-17 Complete Equity with Upstream Sales

(Note that this is the same problem as Problem 6-7 and Problem 6-13, but assuming the use of the complete equity method.)

Paque Corporation owns 90% of the common stock of Segal Company. The stock was purchased for $810,000 on January 1, 1997, when Segal Company's retained earnings were $150,000.

Financial data for 2001 are presented here:

	Paque Corporation	Segal Company
Sales	$1,650,000	$ 795,000
Equity in Subsidiary Income	91,125	
Total Revenue	1,741,125	795,000
Cost of Goods Sold:		
Beginning Inventory	225,000	165,000
Purchases	1,275,000	525,000
Cost of Goods Available	1,500,000	690,000
Less: Ending Inventory	210,000	172,500
Cost of Goods Sold	1,290,000	517,500
Other Expenses	310,500	206,250
Total Cost and Expense	1,600,500	723,750
Net Income	$ 140,625	$ 71,250
1/1 Retained Earnings	798,000	180,000
Net Income	140,625	71,250
Dividends Declared	(150,000)	(60,000)
12/31 Retained Earnings	$ 788,625	$ 191,250
Cash	$ 93,000	$ 75,000
Accounts Receivable	319,500	168,750
Inventory	210,000	172,500
Investment in Segal Company	833,625	
Other Assets	750,000	630,000
Total Assets	$2,206,125	$1,046,250
Accounts Payable	105,000	45,000
Other Current Liabilities	112,500	60,000
Capital Stock	1,200,000	750,000
Retained Earnings	788,625	191,250
Total Liabilities and Equity	$2,206,125	$1,046,250

The January 1, 2001, inventory of Paque Corporation includes $45,000 of profit recorded by Segal Company on 2000 sales. During 2001, Segal Company made intercompany sales of $300,000 with a markup of 20% of selling price. The ending inventory of Paque Corporation includes goods purchased in 2001 from Segal Company for $75,000. Paque Corporation uses the complete equity method to record its investment in Segal Company.

Required:

A. Prepare the consolidated statements workpaper for the year ended December 31, 2001.

B. Calculate consolidated retained earnings on December 31, 2001, using the analytical or t-account approach.

C. If you completed Problem 6-7 or Problem 6-13, compare the consolidated balances obtained in requirement A with those obtained in those problems.

PROBLEM 6-18 Comprehensive Complete Equity Problem, Cost Greater Than Fair Value with Intercompany Sales of Inventory

(Note that this is the same problem as Problem 6-14, but assuming the use of the complete equity method.)

On January 1, 2000, Perry Company purchased 80% of Selby Company for $960,000. At that time Selby had capital stock outstanding of $400,000 and retained earnings of $400,000.

The fair value of Selby Company's assets and liabilities is equal to their book value except for the following:

	Fair Value	Book Value
Inventory	$230,000	$155,000
Plant and Equipment (10-year life)	800,000	600,000

One-half of the inventory was sold in 2000; the remainder was sold in 2001. Any goodwill is to be amortized over a 40-year period.

At the end of 2000, Perry Company had in its ending inventory $54,000 of merchandise it had purchased from Selby Company during the year. Selby Company sold the merchandise at 20% above cost. During 2001, Perry Company sold merchandise to Selby Company for $300,000 at a markup of 20% of the selling price. At December 31, 2001, Selby still had merchandise that it purchased from Perry Company for $78,000 in its inventory.

Financial data for 2001 are presented here:

	Perry Company	Selby Company
Sales	$1,385,000	$ 720,000
Equity in Subsidiary Income	151,100	
Total Revenue	1,536,100	720,000
Cost of Goods Sold:		
Beginning Inventory	210,000	155,000
Purchases	875,000	360,000
Cost of Goods Available	1,085,000	515,000
Less: Ending Inventory	400,000	225,000
Cost of Goods Sold	685,000	290,000
Other Expenses	225,000	170,000
Total Cost and Expense	910,000	460,000
Net Income	$ 626,100	$ 260,000
1/1 Retained Earnings	1,417,000	450,000
Net Income	626,100	260,000
Dividends Declared	(40,000)	(30,000)
12/31 Retained Earnings	$2,003,100	$ 680,000
Cash	$ 90,000	$ 65,000
Accounts Receivable	297,000	85,000
Inventory	400,000	225,000
Investment in Selby Company	1,071,400	
Plant and Equipment (net)	880,000	540,000
Other Assets	384,000	230,000
Total Assets	$3,122,400	$1,145,000
Accounts Payable	24,300	25,000
Other Current Liabilities	95,000	40,000
Common Stock	1,000,000	400,000
Retained Earnings	2,003,100	680,000
Total Liabilities and Equity	$3,122,400	$1,145,000

Required:

A. Prepare the consolidated statements workpaper for the year ended December 31, 2001.

B. Calculate consolidated retained earnings on December 31, 2001, using the analytical or t-account approach.

C. If you completed Problem 6-14, compare the consolidated balances obtained in requirement A with those obtained in those problems.

PROBLEM 6-19A **Deferred Taxes and Intercompany Sales of Inventory**

Pearson Company owns 80% of the common stock of Sedbrook Company. Pearson Company sells merchandise to Sedbrook Company at 25% above its cost. During 2001 and 2002, such sales amounted to $265,000 and $475,000, respectively. The 2001 and 2002 ending inventories of Sedbrook Company included goods purchased from Pearson Company for $150,000 and $195,000, respectively.

Pearson Company reported net income from its independent operations (including sales to affiliates) of $450,000 in 2001 and $480,000 in 2002. Sedbrook reported net income of $225,000 in 2001 and $275,000 in 2002 and did not declare dividends in either year. There were no intercompany sales prior to 2001. The affiliated companies file separate income tax returns and have marginal income tax rates of 30%. Ignore the income tax consequences of undistributed subsidiary income.

Required:

A. Prepare in general journal form all entries necessary in the consolidated financial statements workpapers to eliminate the effects of the intercompany sales for each of the years 2001 and 2002.

B. Calculate the amount of noncontrolling interest to be deducted from combined income in the consolidated income statements for 2001 and 2002.

C. Calculate consolidated net income for 2002.

PROBLEM 6-20A **Deferred Taxes, Intercompany Sales of Inventory, Cost Method**

Peck Corporation owns 70% of the common stock of Seacrest Company. The stock was purchased for $420,000 on January 1, 1997, when Seacrest Company's retained earnings were $100,000. Preclosing trial balances for the two companies at December 31, 2001, are presented here:

	Peck Corporation	Seacrest Company
Cash	$ 35,000	$ 100,000
Accounts Receivable (net)	211,000	107,750
Inventory—1/1	150,000	110,000
Investment in Seacrest Company	420,000	
Other Assets	500,000	400,000
Dividends Declared	100,000	10,000
Purchases	850,000	350,000
Other Expenses	180,000	114,000
Income Tax Expense	27,000	28,250
Total	$2,473,000	$1,220,000
Accounts Payable	$ 70,000	$ 30,000
Other Liabilities	55,000	35,000
Deferred Tax Liability	20,000	5,000
Common Stock	680,000	500,000
Retained Earnings	541,000	120,000
Sales	1,100,000	530,000
Dividend Income	7,000	
Total	$2,473,000	$1,220,000
Inventory—12/31	$ 140,000	$ 115,000

The January 1, 2001, inventory of Peck Corporation includes $10,000 of profit recorded by Seacrest Company on 2000 sales. During 2001, Seacrest Company made intercompany sales of $100,000 with a markup of 25% on cost. The ending inventory of Peck Corporation includes goods purchased in 2001 from Seacrest Company for $40,000.

The affiliates file separate tax returns, and the prior, current, and expected future marginal income tax rates for both companies are 40%. Dividends received from Seacrest Company are subject to an 80% dividends received exclusion.

Required:

A. Prepare a consolidated statements workpaper for the year ended December 31, 2001.

B. Calculate consolidated net income for the year ended December 31, 2001, and consolidated retained earnings on December 31, 2001, using the analytical or t-account approach.

PROBLEM 6-21A **Deferred Taxes, Intercompany Sales of Inventory, Partial Equity Method**

Petra Corporation owns 70% of the common stock of Swain Company. The stock was purchased for $420,000 on January 1, 1997, when Swain Company's retained earnings were $100,000. Preclosing trial balances for the two companies at December 31, 2001, are presented here:

	Petra Corporation	Swain Company
Cash	$ 35,000	$ 100,000
Accounts Receivable (net)	211,000	107,750
Inventory—1/1	150,000	110,000
Investment in Swain Company	456,925	
Other Assets	500,000	400,000
Dividends Declared	100,000	10,000
Purchases	850,000	350,000
Other Expenses	180,000	114,000
Income Tax Expense	27,000	28,250
	$2,509,925	$1,220,000
Accounts Payable	$ 70,000	$ 30,000
Other Liabilities	55,000	35,000
Deferred Tax Liability	20,000	5,000
Common Stock	680,000	500,000
Retained Earnings	555,000	120,000
Sales	1,100,000	530,000
Equity in Subsidiary Income	29,925	
	$2,509,925	$1,220,000
Inventory—12/31	$ 140,000	$ 115,000

The January 1, 2001, inventory of Petra Corporation includes $10,000 of profit recorded by Swain Company on 2000 sales. During 2001, Swain Company made intercompany sales of $100,000 with a markup of 25% on cost. The ending inventory of Petra Corporation includes goods purchased in 2001 from Swain Company for $40,000.

The affiliates file separate tax returns, and the marginal income tax rate for both companies is 40%. Dividends received from Swain Company are subject to an 80% dividends received exclusion.

Required:

A. Prepare a consolidated statements workpaper for the year ended December 31, 2001.

B. Calculate consolidated net income for the year ended December 31, 2001, and consolidated retained earnings on December 31, 2001, using the analytical or t-account approach.

7

ELIMINATION OF UNREALIZED GAINS OR LOSSES ON INTERCOMPANY SALES OF PROPERTY AND EQUIPMENT

LEARNING OBJECTIVES

1. Understand the financial reporting objectives in accounting for intercompany sales of *nondepreciable* assets on the consolidated financial statements.

2. Explain the additional financial reporting objectives in accounting for intercompany sales of *depreciable* assets on the consolidated financial statements.

3. Explain when gains or losses on intercompany sales of depreciable assets should be recognized on a consolidated basis.

4. Explain the term "realized through usage."

5. Describe the differences between upstream and downstream sales in determining combined income and the controlling interest in combined income.

6. Compare the eliminating entries when the selling affiliate is a subsidiary (less than wholly owned) versus when the selling affiliate is the parent company.

7. Compute the noncontrolling interest in combined income when the selling affiliate is a subsidiary.

8. Compute consolidated net income considering the effects of intercompany sales of depreciable assets.

9. Describe the eliminating entry needed to adjust the consolidated financial statements when the purchasing affiliate sells a depreciable asset that was acquired from another affiliate.

10. Explain the basic principles used to record or eliminate intercompany interest, rent, and service fees.

"Exxon Corp. agreed to buy Mobil Corp. for stock valued at about $75.4 billion, or $94.72 a share, creating a mammoth energy company in the largest corporate purchase in history. The formation of what would be by far the largest global energy company in the world signals a seismic shift in an industry beset by painfully low commodity prices. . . . Trimming business overlap could save $1.5 billion, while sharing exploration, procurement budgets and technology could save another $780 million.[1]"

Affiliated companies often recognize gains or losses on intercompany sales of property or equipment. They also may recognize revenue or expense in connection with intercompany loans, intercompany service fees, or intercompany operating leases. As with intercompany sales of inventory discussed in Chapter 6, workpaper entries are also necessary in these situations in order to present related balances in the consolidated financial statements as if the intercompany transactions had never occurred.

In this chapter, the effects on the preparation of consolidated financial statements of intercompany transactions involving property and equipment, loans, services, and operating leases are described and illustrated.

Certain complications (specifically, those related to accounting for the difference between acquisition cost and book value) are avoided in all illustrations by assuming: (1) all acquisitions are made at the book value of the acquired interest in net assets, and (2) the book value of the subsidiary net assets equals their fair value on the date the parent company's interest is acquired. It is further assumed that the affiliates file consolidated income tax returns.

INTERCOMPANY SALES OF LAND (NONDEPRECIABLE PROPERTY)

When there have been intercompany sales of *nondepreciable* property, workpaper entries are necessary to accomplish the following financial reporting objectives in the consolidated financial statements.

- To include gains or losses on the sale of nondepreciable property in combined income only at the time such property is **sold to parties outside the affiliated group** and in an amount equal to the difference between the cost of the property to the affiliated group and the proceeds received from outsiders.
- To present nondepreciable property in the consolidated balance sheet at **its cost to the affiliated group.**

Workpaper procedures to accomplish these objectives are presented here. In addition, for firms using the cost or partial equity methods to account for the investments in subsidiaries, the workpaper entries serve to equate beginning consolidated retained earnings with the amount of consolidated retained earnings reported at the end of the prior reporting period.

Assume that S Company (an 80% owned subsidiary) sells land to P Company for $500,000 that cost S Company $300,000 (an upstream sale of land). Entries made on the books of each affiliate to record this intercompany sale are presented below.

---

[1] *WSJ*, "Exxon Agrees to Buy Mobil for $75 Billion," by Christopher Cooper and Steve Liesman, 12/2/98, p. A3.

Entry on Books of S Company		
Cash	500,000	
Land		300,000
Gain on Sale of Land		200,000

Entry on Books of P Company		
Land	500,000	
Cash		500,000

Additional Entry for Complete Equity Method Only: P Company Books

Equity in Subsidiary Income	160,000	
Investment in S Company		160,000

If P Company uses the complete equity method to account for its investment in S Company, the additional entry shown above is needed on the books of P Company to reduce its income from subsidiary by its share (80%) of the intercompany gain. Under this method, the amount of income reported on the books of the parent is its share of the subsidiary's reported income that has been realized in transactions with third parties.

In the year of the intercompany sale, a workpaper entry is necessary to eliminate the $200,000 gain reported by S Company and to reduce the land balance from the $500,000 recorded on the books of P Company to its $300,000 cost to the affiliated group. Both objectives are accomplished in one workpaper entry as follows:

Workpaper Entry in Year of Intercompany Sale

Gain on Sale of Land	200,000	
Land		200,000

If S Company reported $900,000 in income, the noncontrolling interest in combined income is $140,000 [.20 × ($900,000 − $200,000) = $140,000]. The noncontrolling interest in combined income is based on the amount of income of S Company that was realized in transactions with third parties ($900,000 in reported income less $200,000 unrealized gain on sale of land). Stated another way, the noncontrolling interest in combined income is based on the amount of income from the subsidiary included in combined income (after all workpaper adjustments). Since $200,000 of subsidiary income is excluded from combined income, the noncontrolling interest in combined income is reduced by $40,000 (.2 × $200,000).

In subsequent years, so long as P Company owns the land, it will be reported in the statements of P Company at the intercompany selling price of $500,000. However, in the consolidated balance sheet, the land should continue to be reported at its cost to the affiliated group of $300,000. Since in the year of the sale combined income was reduced by $200,000, the controlling interest in net income and consolidated retained earnings were reduced by $160,000 (.8 × $200,000) in that year. The workpaper entry necessary in all subsequent years, until the land is disposed of by P Company, is as follows:

Workpaper Entry in Subsequent Years

Cost or Partial Equity			Complete Equity		
Beginning Retained Earnings—P Company	160,000		Investment in S Company	160,000	
Beginning Retained Earnings—S Company	40,000		Beginning Retained Earnings—S Company	40,000	
Land		200,000	Land		200,000

Because the subsidiary is the intercompany seller, the $200,000 of unrealized profit is allocated between the controlling interest ($160,000 = .8 × $200,000) and the noncontrolling interest ($40,000 = .2 × $200,000) based on their percentage interests in the selling affiliate. As in Chapter 6, the workpaper procedure to adjust the controlling interest (consolidated retained earnings) is to debit the beginning retained earnings of the parent company (or investment account, if P Company uses the complete equity method). The workpaper procedure to adjust the noncontrolling interest is to debit the beginning retained earnings of the subsidiary. If the intercompany seller had been the parent (downstream sale), the entire $200,000 would go to the controlling interest, resulting in a $200,000 debit to the beginning retained earnings of the parent company.

If and when the land is sold by P Company to a nonaffiliate, P company will use the $500,000 carrying value of the land on its books to calculate any gain or loss. For example, if P Company sells the land it purchased for $500,000 from S Company to an outside party for $550,000, P company will record a gain on the sale of $50,000 ($550,000 − $500,000). However, the cost of the land to the affiliated group is $300,000, and the gain to the affiliated group confirmed by its sale for $550,000 to a nonaffiliate is $250,000 ($550,000 − $300,000). The workpaper entry to adjust the $50,000 gain reported by P Company to the $250,000 gain realized on the sale by the affiliated group is as follows:

Cost or Partial Equity			Complete Equity		
Beginning Retained Earnings—P Company	160,000		Investment in S Company	160,000	
Beginning Retained Earnings—S Company	40,000		Beginning Retained Earnings—S Company	40,000	
Gain on Sale of Land		200,000	Gain on Sale of Land		200,000

The debits are the same as if the sale to outsiders had not occurred. In the year of the sale of the land to outsiders, it is still necessary to adjust *beginning* consolidated retained earnings (or the investment account, under the complete equity method). This entry under the cost and partial equity methods serves to equate *beginning* consolidated retained earnings in the year of sale with the consolidated retained earnings reported at the end of the prior year. Under the complete equity method, as previously stated, the retained earnings of the parent company always equals the correct consolidated retained earnings; thus no adjustment is needed. Instead a debit to the investment account facilitates the elimination of the investment account.[2]

In the year of the sale of the land to outsiders, combined income is increased by $200,000, and consolidated net income, consolidated retained earnings, and noncontrolling interest in combined income are increased accordingly.

To the consolidated entity, the sales price (to third parties) of $550,000 exceeds the cost (to the consolidated entity) of $300,000, resulting in a gain of $250,000 to be included in consolidated income in the year of the sale to a third party.

---

[2]The investment account is reduced on the parent's books at the same time that the unrealized income is deducted from the parent's income under the complete equity method. Thus, the usual workpaper entry to eliminate the investment account against the underlying subsidiary equity accounts eliminates an amount greater than the actual beginning investment account balance. That entry, combined with the entry above, however, will eliminate the investment to exactly zero.

At the end of the year of the sale to outsiders, the amount of cumulative profit on the sale of the land recorded on the books of the affiliates and the amount of profit on the sale of the land recognized in the consolidated financial statements are equal, as shown below.

Cumulative Profit Recorded on the Individual Books of Affiliates

S Company on sale to P Company	$200,000	(year sold to affiliate)
P Company on sale to nonaffiliate	50,000	(year sold to third party)
Total	$250,000	

Profit Reported in Consolidated Income Statement in Year of Sale

Reported by P Company	$ 50,000	(year sold to third party)
Workpaper adjustment	200,000	(year sold to third party)
Reported in combined income	$250,000	

Retained earnings is thus correct in future years without adjustment, and no further workpaper entries relating to the intercompany sale of land are necessary in subsequent periods.

INTERCOMPANY SALES OF DEPRECIABLE PROPERTY (MACHINERY, EQUIPMENT, AND BUILDINGS)

Realization Through Usage

A firm may sell property or equipment to an affiliate for a price that differs from its book value. In the year of the sale, the amount of intercompany gain (loss) recorded by the selling affiliate must be eliminated in consolidation. After the sale, the purchasing affiliate will calculate depreciation on the basis of its cost, which is the intercompany selling price. The depreciation recorded by the purchasing affiliate will, therefore, be excessive (deficient) from a consolidated point of view and will also require adjustment.

From the view of the consolidated entity, the intercompany gain (loss) is considered to be realized from the use of the property or equipment in the generation of revenue. Because such use is measured by depreciation, the recognition of the realization of intercompany profit (loss) is accomplished through depreciation adjustments.

To contrast the intercompany sale of a depreciable asset to the intercompany sale of land, consider the following. Parental Guidance Company sells property with a book value of $2,000 to its fully owned subsidiary, Subservient Recipient Company for $5,000. Assume first that the property is nondepreciable land. When will the $3,000 gain be recognized in the consolidated financial statements?

The answer is: not until it is sold to outsiders. If the property is sold immediately by Subservient Recipient Company for $5,000, the $3,000 gain will be recognized immediately by the consolidated entity. If, on the other hand, it isn't sold until year 4, the gain will not be realized to the consolidated entity until year 4. Now suppose instead that the property (with a book value of $2,000) is depreciable equipment, with a remaining life of three years. Again it is sold to Subservient Recipient Company for $5,000. When will the $3,000 gain be recognized in the consolidated financial statements?

The answer might at first seem to be: not until it is sold to outsiders. But consider the combined effect on consolidated income of the intercompany sale and the depreciation adjustments needed on the consolidated workpaper. On the books of Subservient Recipient Company, depreciation expense is based on a purchase price of $5,000 (straight-line depreciation over three years). But to the consolidated entity, depreciation expense should be based on the book value of $2,000 (also over three years). The difference is $1,000 per year (equal to the $3,000 gain on the intercompany sale spread over three years). Thus, as the depreciation expense is adjusted downward, consolidated income is increased to realize a portion of the gain each year. The depreciation adjustment in such a case is often referred to as gain or revenue *realization through usage.*

When there have been intercompany sales of depreciable property, workpaper entries are necessary to accomplish the following financial reporting objectives in the consolidated financial statements.

- To report as gains or losses in the consolidated income statement only those that result from the sale of depreciable property *to parties outside the affiliated group.*
- To present property in the consolidated balance sheet at *its cost to the affiliated group.*
- To present accumulated depreciation in the consolidated balance sheet based on the *cost to the affiliated group* of the related assets.
- To present depreciation expense in the consolidated income statement based on the *cost to the affiliated group* of the related assets.

Workpaper procedures to accomplish these objectives are presented next. For firms using the cost or partial equity method, an additional objective is to equate beginning consolidated retained earnings with the amount of consolidated retained earnings reported at the end of the prior reporting. For firms using the complete equity method, this final objective is not necessary because the parent's retained earnings already reflects all adjustments accurately.

Illustration of Basic Workpaper Elimination Entries—Downstream Sales

The basic workpaper eliminating entries required because of intercompany sales of depreciable property are illustrated using the following simplifying assumptions. We first illustrate a downstream sale of depreciable property; the parent is the intercompany seller. Upstream sales are illustrated later in the chapter.

1. On January 1, 2002, P Company sells to S Company, a 90% owned subsidiary, equipment with a book value of $750,000 (original cost $1,350,000 and accumulated depreciation of $600,000) for $900,000.
2. On the date of the sale, the equipment has an estimated remaining useful life of three years, has no residual value, and is depreciated using the straight-line method.
3. No other equipment is owned by S Company or P Company.

The entries on the books of P Company and S Company to record the intercompany sale are summarized in general journal form below.

P Company Books		
Cash	900,000	
Accumulated Depreciation	600,000	
Equipment		1,350,000
Gain on Sale of Equipment		150,000

S Company Books		
Equipment	900,000	
Cash		900,000
Depreciation Expense	300,000	
Accumulated Depreciation		300,000

Workpaper Entries—Year of the Intercompany Sale

Balances on December 31, 2002, of the accounts of the affiliated companies affected by these transactions are presented in Illustration 7-1. Workpaper entries in the year of the sale are presented below in general journal form.

(1) Equipment ($1,350,000 − $900,000)	450,000	
Gain on Sale of Equipment	150,000	
Accumulated Depreciation		600,000

To eliminate the intercompany gain and restore equipment to its original cost to the consolidated entity (along with its accumulated depreciation at the point of the intercompany sale).

P Company recorded a gain of $150,000 on the intercompany sale and S Company recorded the equipment at $900,000. From the point of view of the consolidated entity, however, no gain should be reported on the intercompany sale, and equipment should be reported at cost to the affiliated group. The effect of this entry is to decrease combined net income by $150,000. It also restores equipment and accumulated depreciation to their amounts prior to the intercompany sale. Without this entry, equipment would be reported in the consolidated balance sheet

ILLUSTRATION 7-1

Partial Consolidated Statements Workpaper
Elimination of Intercompany Sale of Equipment
Year of Intercompany Sale
December 31, 2002

	P *Company*	*S* *Company*	Eliminations *Dr.*	Eliminations *Cr.*	*Consolidated Balances*
Income Statement					
Gain on Sale of Equipment	(150,000)		(1) 150,000		
Depreciation Expense		300,000		(2) 50,000	250,000
Balance Sheet					
Equipment		900,000	(1) 450,000		1,350,000
Accumulated Depreciation		(300,000)	(2) 50,000	(1) 600,000	(850,000)

(1) To eliminate the intercompany gain and restore equipment to its original cost to the consolidated entity.
(2) To adjust depreciation expense to the correct amount to the consolidated entity.

at its intercompany selling price of $900,000 instead of its historical cost of $1,350,000. Further, without the entry, accumulated depreciation on the equipment would commence from the point of the intercompany sale instead of from the original acquisition by the consolidated entity.

(2) Accumulated Depreciation	50,000	
Depreciation Expense		50,000
To adjust depreciation expense to the correct amount to the consolidated entity, thus realizing a portion of the gain through usage.		

The purchasing affiliate (S Company) will record depreciation in the amount of $300,000 ($900,000/3 years) each year. From the point of view of the consolidated entity, only $250,000 ($750,000/3 years) in depreciation on the equipment should be recognized. The effect of entry (2) is to increase combined net income by $50,000 and thus treat an equivalent amount of intercompany profit as realized through the use of the equipment.

The net effect of entries (1) and (2) is to reduce combined income by $100,000 (the original $150,000 of intercompany gain recorded by P Company for the sale less the $50,000 of intercompany gain that is considered realized during the year through the utilization of the equipment by S Company).

Workpaper Entries—Years Subsequent to the Year of the Intercompany Sale

Balances of the affected accounts of the affiliated companies on December 31, 2003, are presented in Illustration 7-2. In years subsequent to the year of the intercompany sale, the basic workpaper elimination entries related to the intercompany sale are presented below. As indicated, some entries differ slightly depending on whether the firm accounts for its investment using the cost, partial equity, or complete equity method. In the context of this chapter, the cost and partial equity

ILLUSTRATION 7-2

Partial Consolidated Statements Workpaper
Elimination of Unrealized Profit on Intercompany Sale of Equipment
Year Subsequent to Intercompany Sale
December 31, 2003

	P Company	S Company	Eliminations Dr.	Eliminations Cr.	Consolidated Balances
Income Statement					
Depreciation Expense		300,000		(2) 50,000	250,000
Retained Earnings Statement					
1/1 Retained Earnings					
P Company (Consolidated)	2,000,000		(1) 150,000	(2) 50,000	1,900,000
Balance Sheet					
Equipment		900,000	(1) 450,000		1,350,000
Accumulated Depreciation		(600,000)	(2) 100,000	(1) 600,000	(1,100,000)

(1) To eliminate the intercompany gain and restore equipment to its original cost to the consolidated entity.
(2) To adjust depreciation expense to the correct amount to the consolidated entity.

entries are the same, while the complete equity entries differ with one respect; that is, entries to Beginning Retained Earnings—P Company are replaced by entries to Investment in S Company under the complete equity method.

Cost or Partial Equity			Complete Equity		
(1) Equipment	450,000		Equipment	450,000	
Beginning Retained Earnings—P Company	150,000		Investment in S Company	150,000	
Accumulated Depreciation		600,000	Accumulated Depreciation		600,000

To eliminate the prior period intercompany gain and restore equipment to its original cost to the consolidated entity (along with its accumulated depreciation at the point of the intercompany sale).

In entry (1), the first entry from the prior year (2002) is repeated, with the debit to gain now replaced by a debit to the beginning retained earnings of the parent under the cost or partial equity methods. The debit to the equipment account and the credit to the accumulated depreciation account are for the same amount each year. This entry is necessary again (with any income statement accounts, e.g., gain, replaced by beginning retained earnings in subsequent years) because workpaper entries are not posted. If P Company uses the complete equity method, the debit to Beginning Retained Earnings—P Company is not needed, as the prior year income was adjusted for all unrealized amounts. The debit in this workpaper entry is replaced by a debit to the investment account to facilitate its elimination. Later in this chapter, both methods are illustrated in their entirety.

Cost or Partial Equity			Complete Equity		
(2) Accumulated Depreciation	100,000		Accumulated Depreciation	100,000	
Depreciation Expense (current year)		50,000	Depreciation Expense (current year)		50,000
Beginning Retained Earnings—P Company (prior year)		50,000	Investment in S Company		50,000

To adjust depreciation for the current and prior year on equipment sold to affiliate.

The explanation for entry (2) is the same as the preceding year with two modifications. Accumulated depreciation is adjusted for two years now, and the income statement account "depreciation expense" from the first year is now replaced by a credit to beginning retained earnings of P Company (or by a credit to Investment, for firms using the complete equity method).

As a result of these entries, consolidated depreciation expense ($250,000), consolidated equipment ($1,350,000), and consolidated accumulated depreciation ($1,100,000) are all based on the cost of the equipment to the affiliated companies. The net effect of these workpaper entries is to increase combined income by $50,000, which is the amount of gain recorded on the intercompany sale that is considered realized from a consolidated point of view through the utilization of the equipment during the current year.

The entries in the December 31, 2004, consolidated statements workpaper to eliminate the effects of the intercompany sale are as follows:

Cost or Partial Equity			Complete Equity		
(1) Equipment	450,000		Equipment	450,000	
Beginning Retained			Investment in S		
Earnings—P Company	150,000		Company	150,000	
Accumulated			Accumulated		
Depreciation		600,000	Depreciation		600,000

To reduce consolidated retained earnings for gain on intercompany sale and to restore equipment to its original cost to the consolidated entity (along with its accumulated depreciation at the point of the intercompany sale).

Cost or Partial Equity			Complete Equity		
(2) Accumulated Depreciation			Accumulated		
($50,000 × 3 year)	150,000		Depreciation	150,000	
Depreciation			Depreciation		
Expense			Expense		
(current year)		50,000	(current year)		50,000
Beginning Retained			Investment in		
Earnings—P Company			S Company		
(prior years)		100,000	(prior years)		100,000

To reverse amount of excess depreciation recorded during current year and to recognize amounts of intercompany gain realized in current and prior periods through usage (two prior years of depreciation expense since sale).

Over the life of the equipment, the amount of gain recognized in the consolidated income statement will be the same as the amount of gain recorded by the selling affiliate, and no further adjustments will be necessary in the consolidated statements workpaper. The recognition of the gain on the sale of the equipment on the books of the selling affiliate and in the consolidated income statement may be compared as follows:

	On Books of Selling Affiliate	In Consolidated Income Statement
Gain on Sale of Equipment—2002	$150,000	
Reduction of Depreciation Expense:		
2002		$50,000
2003		50,000
2004		50,000
	$150,000	$150,000

Determination of Noncontrolling Interest

Subsidiary as Intercompany Seller (Upstream Sale) In the preceding example, the selling affiliate was the parent company (downstream sale). Accordingly, even though 100% of the unrealized intercompany gain was eliminated, no modification in the calculation of the noncontrolling interest in combined income or consolidated net assets was necessary. Had the selling affiliate been a less than wholly owned subsidiary (upstream sale), however, workpaper modifications in the determination of the noncontrolling interest would have been necessary if the controlling and noncontrolling interests were to be adjusted in proportion to their interest in the amount of unrealized intercompany profit eliminated.

Intercompany sales of property, plant, and equipment, as in the case of intercompany inventory sales, necessitate adjustments to the calculation of the distribution of income to the controlling and noncontrolling interests. Whether the adjustments directly affect the noncontrolling interest (or only the controlling interest) depends on *who is the intercompany seller.* If the intercompany seller is the subsidiary, it is the subsidiary's income that needs adjustment, hence directly affecting the noncontrolling interest, as shown in Illustration 7-3.

Procedurally, the steps needed differ slightly between the year of the intercompany sale and subsequent years. To calculate the noncontrolling interest in combined income, begin as always with the subsidiary's reported income. In the year of the intercompany upstream sale (subsidiary is the intercompany seller), adjust

ILLUSTRATION 7-3

Calculation of the Noncontrolling Interest in Combined Income
Upstream Sales of Equipment

Noncontrolling Interest in Combined Income—Year of Sale—2002

Unrealized gain on upstream sales of equipment	150,000	Net income reported by S Company	$300,000
		Depreciation adjustment (gain realized through usage)	50,000
		Subsidiary Income included in Combined Income	$200,000
		Noncontrolling Ownership percentage interest	10%
		Noncontrolling Interest in Combined Income	$20,000

Noncontrolling Interest in Combined Income— Year Subsequent to Sale—2003

		Net income reported by S Company	$175,000
		Depreciation adjustment (gain realized through usage)	50,000
		Subsidiary Income included in Combined Income	$225,000
		Noncontrolling Ownership percentage interest	10%
		Noncontrolling Interest in Combined Income	$22,500

Noncontrolling Interest in Combined Income— Year Subsequent to Sale—2004

		Net income reported by S Company	$200,000
		Depreciation adjustment (gain realized through usage)	50,000
		Subsidiary Income included in Combined Income	$250,000
		Noncontrolling Ownership percentage interest	10%
		Noncontrolling Interest in Combined Income	$25,000

the subsidiary's reported income by subtracting the unrealized gain on the intercompany sale (or adding an unrealized loss, as appropriate). Next, add the portion of the intercompany gain (loss) that is considered *realized through usage* (i.e., the depreciation adjustment for the year of the sale). This is shown in Illustration 7-3 for the year 2002 in t-account form.

The calculations are the same in subsequent years except that the intercompany gain (or loss) does not need to be subtracted (or added) since it is not included in the subsidiary's reported income in those years. Realization through usage, however, occurs as long as the property is being used by the intercompany buyer (the parent, in the case of an upstream sale). Note, however, that the *adjustment for realization through usage* appears on the t-account to compute the *noncontrolling interest* in the case of upstream sales.

For example, assume that S Company is 90% owned, was the selling affiliate in the previous illustration, and reports $300,000 in income (including the $150,000 intercompany gain) in the year 2002, $175,000 of income in 2003, and $200,000 in 2004. The calculation of the noncontrolling interest in combined income in each of the respective years is presented in Illustration 7-3.

The adjustments shown in illustration 7-3 are needed only if we assume the subsidiary is the intercompany seller. With this assumption, adjustments are also needed to the workpaper eliminating/adjusting entries presented in the previous section of this chapter. Specifically, the workpaper entries to Beginning Retained Earnings—P Company in the preceding example for firms using the cost or partial equity method are replaced by entries to *both* Beginning Retained Earnings—P Company (controlling interest percentage) and Beginning Retained Earnings—S Company (noncontrolling interest percentage). No other changes are needed. If P Company uses the complete equity method, any debits or credits to Beginning Retained Earnings—P Company are not needed, as prior years' income is adjusted on the books of the parent for unrealized gains and for any amount realized through usage. Thus any debits or credits to beginning retained earnings of the parent in workpaper entries are replaced by debits or credits to the investment account, once more facilitating its elimination.

If S Company were the selling affiliate, entry (1) in Illustration 7-2 for 2003 would be modified as follows in order to adjust the controlling and the noncontrolling interests in net assets at the beginning of the year:

Upstream Sale

	Cost or Partial Equity			Complete Equity		
(1)	Equipment	450,000		Equipment	450,000	
	Beginning Retained			Investment in S		
	Earnings—P Company	135,000		Company	135,000	
	Beginning Retained			Beginning Retained		
	Earnings—S Company			Earnings—S Company		
	(noncontrolling			(noncontrolling		
	interest)			interest)		
	.10 × $150,000	15,000		.10 × $150,000	15,000	
	Accumulated			Accumulated		
	Depreciation		600,000	Depreciation		600,000

To reduce the controlling and noncontrolling interests for their respective shares of the unrealized intercompany gain at the date of the intercompany sale, and restore equipment and accumulated depreciation to original amounts to the consolidated entity.

As explained in the discussion of unrealized intercompany profit in inventory, as a matter of workpaper procedure, the noncontrolling interest in net assets is adjusted for intercompany gains (losses) by debiting (decrease in noncontrolling interest) or crediting (increase in noncontrolling interest) the beginning retained earnings of the subsidiary company.

To reduce repetition and conserve space, we do not present the three methods (cost, partial equity, and complete equity) in standalone sections in Chapters 7 through 10 to the same extent as in earlier chapters. In Chapters 7 and 10, the cost and partial equity methods are quite similar (under the assumptions in our presentation), while the complete equity method is different. In Chapters 8 and 9, in contrast, the partial and complete equity methods are similar, while the cost method is different. Thus, in the following section, we combine the presentation of the cost and partial equity methods. Worksheets are presented separately.

CONSOLIDATED STATEMENTS WORKPAPER—COST AND PARTIAL EQUITY METHODS

Subsidiary Is Intercompany Seller (Upstream Sale)

Assume that P Company acquires an 85% interest in S Company for $1,190,000 in 2000, when the retained earnings and capital stock of S Company amount to $400,000 and $1,000,000, respectively. The retained earnings of S Company on January 1, 2002, are $666,000. On January 1, 2002, S Company sells P Company equipment with a book value of $500,000 (original cost of $800,000 and accumulated depreciation of $300,000) for $600,000. On January 1, 2002, the equipment has an estimated remaining useful life of five years and is depreciated using the straight-line method. S Company will record a gain of $100,000 on the sale of the equipment, and each year P Company will record depreciation that is $20,000 [($600,000 − $500,000)/5 years] greater than depreciation based on the cost of the equipment to the consolidated group. Consolidated statements workpapers for the years ended December 31, 2002, and December 31, 2003, are presented in Illustrations 7-4A and 7-5A, respectively, assuming the use of the *cost* method by P Company to account for its investment in S Company. Consolidated statements workpapers for the years ended December 31, 2002, and December 31, 2003, are presented in Illustrations 7-4B and 7-5B, respectively, assuming the use of the *partial equity* method by P Company to account for its investment in S Company.

The balances reported by the parent company in income, in retained earnings, and in the investment account differ depending on the method used by the parent company to record its investment. As illustrated in prior chapters, however, the method used by the parent company to record its investment has no effect on the *consolidated* balances.

Also as illustrated in earlier chapters, when the parent company records its investment using the partial equity method, a workpaper entry to reverse the effect of parent company entries during the year for subsidiary dividends and income replaces the cost method entries to establish reciprocity (convert to equity) and to eliminate dividend income. However, as demonstrated in Chapters 5 and 6, the workpaper entries to allocate and amortize the difference between cost and book value, to eliminate intercompany sales, and to eliminate unrealized intercompany profit are the same regardless of whether the investment is recorded using the cost method or the partial equity method. The workpapers entries to eliminate the effects of intercompany sales of equipment are also the same when the parent uses the partial equity or the cost method. Therefore, to conserve space and avoid excessive repetition, we discuss the workpaper entries for the cost and partial equity methods together in the following section. When the investment is recorded using the complete equity method, however, the workpaper entries differ slightly, as illustrated in the next section.

Cost

Consolidated Statements Workpaper Entries—December 31, 2002 (Year of Intercompany Sale)

Workpaper entries in Illustrations 7-4A and 7-4B are presented in general journal form as follows:

(1) Investment in S Company	226,100	
Beginning Retained Earnings—P Company		226,100
To convert to equity/establish reciprocity [.85 × ($666,000 − $400,000) = $226,100].		

Entry (1) above is needed only for firms using the cost method to account for their investments in the subsidiary. This distinction is particularly easy to remember if the entry is thought of as the entry to convert to equity. If the parent is already using the equity method, there is no need to convert to equity. Thus, in illustration 7-4B, entry (1) above is replaced with an entry eliminating the equity in subsidiary income of $122,400 (85% × $144,000) against the investment account. Unless noted, the following workpaper entries are the same whether the parent uses the cost method or the partial equity method.

(2) Gain on Sale of Equipment	100,000	
Property and Equipment ($800,000 − 600,000)	200,000	
Accumulated Depreciation		300,000
To eliminate the unrealized gain recorded on intercompany sale of equipment ($100,000) and restore equipment to its original cost (and accumulated depreciation to its balance at the date of the intercompany sale).		

(3) Accumulated Depreciation	20,000	
Depreciation Expense		20,000
To adjust depreciation on equipment sold to affiliate, thus realizing a portion of the gain through usage ($100,000/5 years = $20,000).		

Partial

(4) Beginning Retained Earnings—S Company	566,100	
Capital Stock—S Company	850,000	
Investment in S Company ($1,190,000 + $226,100)		1,416,100
To eliminate investment account against underlying equity accounts of S Company.		

Since the selling affiliate is a partially owned subsidiary (upstream sale), the calculation of the noncontrolling interest in combined income is modified by subtracting the amount of the gain recognized by the subsidiary and adding the amount of the gain considered to be realized (through depreciation) to the reported net income of the subsidiary [.15 × ($144,000 − $100,000 + $20,000) = $9,600].

Noncontrolling Interest in Income

		Internally generated income of S Company	$144,000
Unrealized gain on intercompany (upstream) sale	100,000	Gain realized through usage (depreciation adjustment)	20,000
		Adjusted income of subsidiary	$64,000
		Noncontrolling percentage	× 15%
		Noncontrolling interest in income	$9,600

Note that the $9,600 appears in Illustration 7-4A as the noncontrolling interest in income.

If the sale of the equipment had been *downstream* rather than *upstream*, the amount of subsidiary income included in combined income would not be affected by the workpaper entries related to unrealized intercompany gain and no adjustment would be necessary in the calculation of the noncontrolling interest in combined income. Instead the *controlling* interest would be affected as indicated in bold type in the following t-account:

Controlling Interest in Income (Consolidated Net Income)

		Internally generated income of P Company	$300,000
Unrealized gain on intercompany (downstream) sale	**XX**	**Realization of gain through usage (depreciation adjustment)**	**XX**
		Other needed adjustments (see chapters 5–6)	XX
		Percentage of subsidiary adjusted income, or (ownership percentage) (subsidiary income) .85($64,000)	$54,400
		Controlling interest in income	$354,400

Consolidated Statements Workpaper Entries—December 31, 2003 (Year Subsequent to Intercompany Sale)

Workpaper entries in Illustrations 7-5A and 7-5B are presented in general journal form for the year subsequent to the intercompany sale as follows:

(1)	Investment in S Company	348,500	
	Beginning Retained Earnings—P Company		348,500
	To convert to equity/establish reciprocity [.85 × ($810,000 − $400,000)].		

↓ *beginning retained earnings*

As in the previous year, entry (1) above is needed only for firms using the cost method to account for their investments in the subsidiary. If the parent is already using the equity method, there is no need to convert to equity. In Illustration 7-5B, entry (1) is replaced by an entry once again eliminating equity in subsidiary income against the investment account.

Cost Method

85% Owned Subsidiary

Upstream Sale of Equipment

ILLUSTRATION 7-4A

Consolidated Statements Workpaper

P Company and Subsidiary

For the Year Ended December 31, 2002

Income Statement	P Company	S Company	Eliminations Dr.	Eliminations Cr.	Noncontrolling Interest	Consolidated Balances
Sales	3,500,000	2,000,000				5,500,000
Gain on Sale of Equipment		100,000	(2) 100,000			
Total Revenue	3,500,000	2,100,000				5,500,000
Cost of Sales	1,800,000	1,130,000				2,930,000
Depreciation Expense	380,000	330,000		(3) 20,000		690,000
Income Tax Expense	200,000	96,000				296,000
Other Expense	820,000	400,000				1,220,000
Total Cost and Expense	3,200,000	1,956,000				5,136,000
Net/Combined Income	300,000	144,000				364,000
Noncontrolling Interest in Income					9,600	(9,600)*
Net Income to Retained Earnings	300,000	144,000	100,000	20,000	9,600	354,400
Retained Earnings Statement						
1/1 Retained Earnings						
P Company	1,500,000			(1) 226,100		1,726,100
S Company		666,000	(4) 566,100		99,900	
Net Income from above	300,000	144,000	100,000	20,000	9,600	354,400
12/31 Retained Earnings to Balance Sheet	1,800,000	810,000	666,100	246,100	109,500	2,080,500
Balance Sheet						
Current Assets	1,000,000	570,000				1,570,000
Investment in S Company	1,190,000		(1) 226,100	(4) 1,416,100		
Land	1,000,000	200,000				1,200,000
Property and Equipment	3,800,000	2,700,000	(2) 200,000			6,700,000
(Accumulated Depreciation)	(1,520,000)	(960,000)	(3) 20,000	(2) 300,000		(2,760,000)
Total Assets	5,470,000	2,510,000				6,710,000
Liabilities	670,000	700,000				1,370,000
Capital Stock						
P Company	3,000,000					3,000,000
S Company		1,000,000	(4) 850,000		150,000	
Retained Earnings from above	1,800,000	810,000	666,100	246,100	109,500	2,080,500
Noncontrolling Interest in Net Assets					259,500	259,500
Total Liabilities and Equity	5,470,000	2,510,000	1,962,200	1,962,200		6,710,000

*.15 × ($144,000 − $100,000 + $20,000) = $9,600.
(1) To convert to equity/establish reciprocity [.85 × ($666,000 − $400,000) = $226,100].
(2) To eliminate the unrealized gain recorded on intercompany sale of equipment ($100,000) and restore equipment to its original cost (and accumulated depreciation to its balance at the date of the intercompany sale).
(3) To adjust depreciation on equipment sold to affiliate, thus realizing a portion of the gain through usage ($100,000/5 years = $20,000).
(4) To eliminate investment account against underlying equity accounts of S Company.

Handwritten annotations:
$($144,000 − $100,000 + $20,000$) \times 15\% = 9,600$
$30,000 + (144,000 - 100,000 + 20,000) \times 0.85 = 354,400$
$1,800,000 + .85 \times (810,000 - 100,000) .85 \times (100,000 - 10,000) = 2,080,500$
$(810,000 - 100,000 - 100,000 + 20,000) \times 0.15 = 259,500$

Partial Equity Method		ILLUSTRATION 7-4B			
85% Owned Subsidiary		**Consolidated Statements Workpaper**			
Upstream Sale of Equipment		**P Company and Subsidiary**			
Year of Sale		**For the Year Ended December 31, 2002**			

Income Statement	*P Company*	*S Company*	*Eliminations* Dr.	*Eliminations* Cr.	*Noncontrolling Interest*	*Consolidated Balances*
Sales	3,500,000	2,000,000				5,500,000
Equity in Subsidiary Income	122,400		(1) 122,400			
Gain on Sale of Equipment		100,000	(2) 100,000			
Total Revenue	3,622,400	2,100,000				5,500,000
Cost of Sales	1,800,000	1,130,000				2,930,000
Depreciation Expense	380,000	330,000		(3) 20,000		690,000
Income Tax Expense	200,000	96,000				296,000
Other Expense	820,000	400,000				1,220,000
Total Cost and Expense	3,200,000	1,956,000				5,136,000
Net/Combined Income	422,400	144,000				364,000
Noncontrolling Interest in Income					9,600	(9,600)*
Net Income to Retained Earnings	422,400	144,000	222,400	20,000	9,600	354,400
Retained Earnings Statement						
1/1 Retained Earnings						
P Company	1,726,100					1,726,100
S Company		666,000	(4) 566,100		99,900	
Net Income from above	422,400	144,000	222,400	20,000	9,600	354,400
12/31 Retained Earnings to Balance Sheet	2,148,500	810,000	788,500	20,000	109,500	2,080,500
Balance Sheet						
Current Assets	1,000,000	570,000				1,570,000
Investment in S Company**	1,538,500			(1) 122,400		
				(4) 1,416,100		
Land	1,000,000	200,000				1,200,000
Property and Equipment	3,800,000	2,700,000	(2) 200,000			6,700,000
(Accumulated Depreciation)	(1,520,000)	(960,000)	(3) 20,000	(2) 300,000		(2,760,000)
Total Assets	5,818,500	2,510,000				6,710,000
Liabilities	670,000	700,000				1,370,000
Capital Stock						
P Company	3,000,000					3,000,000
S Company		1,000,000	(4) 850,000		150,000	
Retained Earnings from above	2,148,500	810,000	788,500	20,000	109,500	2,080,500
Noncontrolling Interest in Net Assets					259,500	259,500
Total Liabilities and Equity	5,818,500	2,510,000	1,858,500	1,858,500		6,710,000

*.15 × ($144,000 − $100,000 + $20,000) = $9,600.
**The investment account equals $1,190,000 + 85% of the increase in S Company's Retained Earnings from the date of acquisition to the beginning of the year ($666,000 − 400,000) plus the current period's equity in subsidiary income ($122,400).
(1) To eliminate equity in subsidiary income and intercompany dividends, if any.
(2) To eliminate the unrealized gain recorded on intercompany sale of equipment and restore equipment to its original cost (and accumulated depreciation to its balance at the date of the intercompany sale).
(3) To adjust depreciation on equipment sold to affiliate, thus realizing a portion of gain through usage ($100,000/5 years = $20,000).
(4) To eliminate investment account against the underlying equity accounts of S Company.

Partial

(2)	Beginning Retained Earnings—P Company (100,000 × .85)	85,000	
	Beginning Retained Earnings—S Company (100,000 × .15)	15,000	
	Property and Equipment (800,000 − 600,000)	200,000	
	Accumulated Depreciation		300,000

To reduce the controlling and noncontrolling interests for their shares of unrealized intercompany gain ($100,000), and to restore equipment and accumulated depreciation to their original balances at the date of the intercompany sale.

Partial

(3)	Accumulated Depreciation	40,000	
	Depreciation Expense (current year)		20,000
	Beginning Retained Earnings—P Company (20,000 × .85)		17,000
	Beginning Retained Earnings—S Company (20,000 × .15)		3,000

To reverse amount of excess depreciation recorded during current year and prior year and to recognize intercompany gain realized through usage.

Cost

(4)	Beginning Retained Earnings—S Company	688,500	
	Capital Stock—S Company	850,000	
	Investment in S Company ($1,190,000 + $348,500)		1,538,500

To eliminate investment account against the underlying equity accounts of S Company.

The noncontrolling interest in combined income is calculated after adding the portion of the gain considered realized during the year to the net income reported by the subsidiary [.15 × ($162,000 + $20,000) = $27,300].

Noncontrolling Interest in Income (year subsequent to sale)

Internally generated income of S Company	$162,000
Gain realized through usage (depreciation adjustment)	20,000
Adjusted income of subsidiary	$182,000
Noncontrolling percentage	× 15%
Noncontrolling interest in income	$27,300

The net effect of the adjustments to the noncontrolling interest in the income statement and retained earnings sections of the consolidated statements workpaper for upstream sales also serve to adjust the noncontrolling interest in consolidated net assets. The amount of the noncontrolling interest reported in the consolidated balance sheet is based on the net assets of the subsidiary that have been realized in transactions with third parties. For example, the amount of the noncontrolling interest in consolidated net assets shown in Illustrations 7-5A and 7-5B is calculated in Illustration 7-6.

			Eliminations		Noncontrolling	Consolidated
Cost Method			**ILLUSTRATION 7-5A**			
85% Owned Subsidiary			**Consolidated Statements Workpaper**			
Upstream Sale of Equipment			**P Company and Subsidiary**			
Year Subsequent to Sale			**For the Year Ended December 31, 2003**			

	P	S	Eliminations		Noncontrolling	Consolidated
Income Statement	*Company*	*Company*	*Dr.*	*Cr.*	*Interest*	*Balances*
Sales	4,000,000	2,200,000				6,200,000
Cost of Sales	2,100,000	1,180,000				3,280,000
Depreciation Expense	380,000	330,000		(3) 20,000		690,000
Income Tax Expense	272,000	108,000				380,000
Other Expense	840,000	420,000				1,260,000
Total Cost and Expense	3,592,000	2,038,000				5,610,000
Net/Combined Income	408,000	162,000				590,000
Noncontrolling Interest in Income					27,300	(27,300)*
Net Income to Retained Earnings	408,000	162,000	—0—	20,000	27,300	562,700
Retained Earnings Statement						
1/1 Retained Earnings						
P Company	1,800,000		(2) 85,000	(1) 348,500		2,080,500
				(3) 17,000		
S Company		810,000	(2) 15,000	(3) 3,000	109,500	
			(4) 688,500			
Net Income from above	408,000	162,000	—0—	20,000	27,300	562,700
12/31 Retained Earnings to Balance Sheet	2,208,000	972,000	788,500	388,500	136,800	2,643,200
Balance Sheet						
Current Assets	1,190,000	790,000				1,980,000
Investment in S Company	1,190,000		(1) 348,500	(4) 1,538,500		
Land	1,600,000	200,000				1,800,000
Property and Equipment	3,800,000	2,700,000	(2) 200,000			6,700,000
(Accumulated Depreciation)	(1,900,000)	(1,290,000)	(3) 40,000	(2) 300,000		(3,450,000)
Total Assets	5,880,000	2,400,000				7,030,000
Liabilities	672,000	428,000				1,100,000
Capital Stock						
P Company	3,000,000					3,000,000
S Company		1,000,000	(4) 850,000		150,000	
Retained Earnings from above	2,208,000	972,000	788,500	388,500	136,800	2,643,200
Noncontrolling Interest in Net Assets					286,800	286,800
Total Liabilities and Equity	5,880,000	2,400,000	2,227,000	2,227,000		7,030,000

Cost

*.15 × ($162,000 + $20,000) = $27,300.
(1) To convert to equity/establish reciprocity as of 1/1/03 [.85 × ($810,000 − $400,000)].
(2) To reduce controlling and noncontrolling interests for their shares of unrealized intercompany gain and to restore equipment and accumulated depreciation to their original balances.
(3) To reverse amount of excess depreciation recorded during current year and prior year and to recognize intercompany gain realized through usage.
(4) To eliminate investment account.

Partial Equity Method						
ILLUSTRATION 7-5B						

85% Owned Subsidiary	**Consolidated Statements Workpaper**
Upstream Sale of Equipment	**P Company and Subsidiary**
Year Subsequent to Sale	**For the Year Ended December 31, 2003**

Income Statement	P Company	S Company	Eliminations Dr.	Eliminations Cr.	Noncontrolling Interest	Consolidated Balances
Sales	4,000,000	2,200,000				6,200,000
Equity Income	137,700		(1) 137,700			
Total Revenue	4,137,700	2,200,000				6,200,000
Cost of Sales	2,100,000	1,180,000				3,280,000
Depreciation Expense	380,000	330,000		(3) 20,000		690,000
Income Tax Expense	272,000	108,000				380,000
Other Expense	840,000	420,000				1,260,000
Total Cost and Expense	3,592,000	2,038,000				5,610,000
Net/Combined Income	545,700	162,000				590,000
Noncontrolling Interest in Income					27,300	(27,300)*
Net Income to Retained Earnings	545,700	162,000	137,700	20,000	27,300	562,700
Retained Earnings Statement						
1/1 Retained Earnings						
P Company	2,148,500		(2) 85,000	(3) 17,000		2,080,500
S Company		810,000	(2) 15,000	(3) 3,000	109,500	
			(4) 688,500			
Net Income from above	545,700	162,000	137,700	20,000	27,300	562,700
12/31 Retained Earnings to Balance Sheet	2,694,200	972,000	926,200	40,000	136,800	2,643,200
Balance Sheet						
Current Assets	1,190,000	790,000				1,980,000
Investment in S Company	1,676,200			(1) 137,700		
				(4) 1,538,500		
Land	1,600,000	200,000				1,800,000
Property and Equipment	3,800,000	2,700,000	(2) 200,000			6,700,000
(Accumulated Depreciation)	(1,900,000)	(1,290,000)	(3) 40,000	(2) 300,000		(3,450,000)
Total Assets	6,366,200	2,400,000				7,030,000
Liabilities	672,000	428,000				1,100,000
Capital Stock						
P Company	3,000,000					3,000,000
S Company		1,000,000	(4) 850,000		150,000	
Retained Earnings from above	2,694,200	972,000	926,200	40,000	136,800	2,643,200
Noncontrolling Interest in Net Assets					286,800	286,800
Total Liabilities and Equity	6,366,200	2,400,000	2,016,200	2,016,200		7,030,000

*.15 × ($162,000 + $20,000) = $27,300.
(1) To eliminate equity in subsidiary income and intercompany dividends, if any.
(2) To reduce controlling and noncontrolling interests for their shares of unrealized intercompany gain and to restore equipment and accumulated depreciation to their original balances.
(3) To reverse amount of excess depreciation recorded during current and prior year and to recognize intercompany gain realized through usage.
(4) To eliminate investment account.

ILLUSTRATION 7-6

Calculation of the Noncontrolling Interest in Consolidated Net Assets

Capital Stock—S Company		$1,000,000
Realized Retained Earnings—S Company		
Reported Retained Earnings	$972,000	
Unrealized Intercompany Profit on 12/31/03		
($100,000 − $20,000 − $20,000)	(60,000)	912,000
Realized Net Assets—S Company		$1,912,000
Noncontrolling Ownership Percentage		15%
Noncontrolling Interest in Consolidated Net		
Assets (.15 × $1,912,000)		$ 286,800

Disposal of Property and Equipment by Purchasing Affiliate

Assume that on January 1, 2004, P Company sells the equipment it purchased from S Company to a party outside the affiliated group for $400,000. The recorded and consolidated book values of the equipment on January 1, 2004, are calculated in Illustration 7-7. P Company will record a $40,000 gain on the sale of the equipment to the party outside the affiliated group, calculated as:

Selling price	$400,000
Book value (on P Company's books)	360,000
Gain on sale (recorded by P Company)	40,000

Partial

The following entry is made on the books of P Company to record the sale:

P Company Books (Cost or Partial Equity Method)

Cash	400,000	
Accumulated Depreciation	240,000	
Property and Equipment		600,000
Gain on Sale of Equipment		40,000

However, the consolidated book value of the equipment on the date of the sale by P Company is only $300,000, and from the point of view of the consolidated entity a $100,000 gain on the sale (selling price of $400,000 minus book value to consol-

ILLUSTRATION 7-7

Calculation of Book Value of Equipment on January 1, 2004

On Books of P Company

Cost (to P Company)	$600,000
Accumulated Depreciation [($600,000/5) × 2]	240,000
Recorded Book Value—January 1, 2004	$360,000

Consolidated

Cost (original cost to S Company)	$800,000
Accumulated Depreciation [$300,000 +	
([($800,000 − $300,000)/5] × 2)]	500,000
Consolidated Book Value—January 1, 2004	$300,000

ILLUSTRATION 7-8

Reconciliation of Income Recorded on Books with Income Reported on Consolidated Financial Statements

Amount of profit recorded by affiliates	
2002—Gain on sale from S Company to P Company	$100,000
2004—Gain on sale by P Company to nonaffiliate	40,000
Additional depreciation expense recorded by affiliates:	
2002	(20,000)
2003	(20,000)
Net amount of profit recorded by affiliates	$100,000
Amount of profit realized in the consolidated income statement	
Selling price to the consolidated entity	$400,000
Book value to the consolidated entity	300,000
Net amount of profit to the consolidated entity	$100,000

idated entity of $300,000) should be recognized. The entry on the December 31, 2004, consolidated statements workpaper necessary to achieve this result follows:

Beginning Retained Earnings—P Company		
(.85 × $60,000)	51,000	
Beginning Retained Earnings—S Company		
(.15 × $60,000)	9,000	
Gain on Sale of Equipment		60,000

    To adjust reported gain on the sale of equipment by P Company to third party from $40,000 recorded by P Company to $100,000 to be reported on the consolidated statement.

Cost

Partial

The above entry also serves to adjust the controlling and noncontrolling interests for their share of unrealized intercompany gain at beginning of year ($100,000 original gain minus $40,000 realized through usage [$20,000 in 2002 and $20,000 in 2003] = $60,000).

    Note that the entry does not include any adjustment to equipment or accumulated depreciation after the disposal, as these accounts are accurately reflected at zero. Also, it is not necessary to calculate the $60,000 adjustment to the controlling and noncontrolling interests directly in the above entry as it will always equal the gain adjustment. From a consolidated point of view, the amount of gain recorded by the selling affiliate will always be understated (or the amount of loss recorded will always be overstated) by an amount that is equal to the unrealized intercompany gain associated with the equipment on the date of its premature disposal.

    After December 31, 2004, no more book or workpaper entries relating to this equipment will be required, because by that date the amount of gain recorded by the affiliates is equal to the amount of gain considered realized in the consolidated financial statements. The equality of the recorded and consolidated amounts is confirmed in Illustration 7-8.

CALCULATION OF CONSOLIDATED NET INCOME AND CONSOLIDATED RETAINED EARNINGS

In Chapter 6, the t-account calculation of consolidated net income was refined to accommodate the effect of unrealized intercompany profit in inventory. We now refine it further to include unrealized gain or loss on intercompany sales of equipment.

Consolidated Net Income

After modification for the effects of unrealized intercompany profit, consolidated net income was calculated in Chapter 6 as the parent company's income from its independent operations that has been realized in transactions with third parties plus (minus) its share of subsidiary income (loss) that has been realized in transactions with third parties plus or minus adjustments for the period relating to the amortization of the difference between cost and book value.

On the basis of Illustration 7-4A, the t-account calculation of consolidated net income for the year ended December 31, 2002, is demonstrated in Illustration 7-9. The amount of consolidated net income calculated in Illustration 7-9 is the same as that shown in the consolidated statements workpaper in Illustration 7-4A.

On the basis of Illustration 7-5A, the t-account calculation of consolidated net income for the year ended December 31, 2003, is presented in Illustration 7-10. The amount of consolidated net income calculated in Illustration 7-10 is, of course,

ILLUSTRATION 7-9
Calculation of Controlling and Noncontrolling Interests in Net Income
For Year Ended December 31, 2002
Year of Intercompany Sale of Equipment

Noncontrolling Interest in Combined Income—Year 2002

		Internally generated income of S Company	$144,000
Unrealized profit on upstream sales in ending inventory	0	Gain realized through usage (depreciation adjustment)	20,000
Unrealized gain on 2002 intercompany sale of equipment (upstream sales)	100,000	Realized profit (upstream sales) from beginning inventory	0
		Subsidiary Income included in Combined Income	$ 64,000
		Noncontrolling Ownership percentage interest	15%
		Noncontrolling Interest in Combined Income	$ 9,600

85%

Controlling Interest in Income—Year 2002

Unrealized gain on intercompany sale (downstream sales)	0	Net income internally generated by P Company	$300,000
		Gain realized through usage (depreciation adjustment)	0
Unrealized profit on downstream sales to S Company (ending inventory)	0	Realized profit (downstream sales) from beginning inventory	0
		P Company's percentage of S Company's income realized from third parties, .85($64,000)	54,400
Amortization of excess depreciation	0		
Amortization of goodwill	0		
		Consolidated Income (controlling interest in income)	$354,400

ILLUSTRATION 7-10

Calculation of Controlling and Noncontrolling Interests in Net Income
For Year Ended December 31, 2003
Year Subsequent to the Year of Intercompany Sale of Equipment

Noncontrolling Interest in Combined Income—Year 2003

Unrealized profit on upstream sales in ending inventory	0	Internally generated income of S Company	$162,000
		Gain realized through usage (depreciation adjustment)	20,000
Unrealized gain on 2003 intercompany sale of equipment (upstream sales)	0	Realized profit (upstream sales) from beginning inventory	0
		Subsidiary Income included in Combined Income	$182,000
		Noncontrolling Ownership percentage interest	15%
		Noncontrolling Interest in Combined Income	$ 27,300

85%

Controlling Interest in Income—Year 2003

Unrealized gain on 2003 intercompany sales of equipment (downstream sales)	0	Net income internally generated by P Company	$408,000
		Gain realized through usage (depreciation adjustment)	0
Unrealized profit on downstream sales to S Company (ending inventory)	0	Realized profit (downstream sales) from beginning inventory	0
		P Company's percentage of S Company's income realized from third parties, .85($182,000)	154,700
Amortization of excess depreciation	0		
Amortization of goodwill	0		
		Consolidated Income (controlling interest in income)	$562,700

the same as that shown in the consolidated statements workpaper in Illustration 7-5A.

Consolidated Retained Earnings

Consolidated retained earnings were calculated in Chapter 6 as the parent company's cost method retained earnings that have been realized in transactions with third parties plus (minus) the parent company's share of the increase (decrease) in subsidiary retained earnings that has been realized in transactions with third parties from the date of acquisition to the current date plus or minus the cumulative effect of adjustments to date relating to the amortization of the difference between cost and book value.

On the basis of Illustration 7-5A, the t-account calculation of consolidated retained earnings on December 31, 2003, is demonstrated in Illustration 7-11.

As mentioned earlier, the workpaper entries to eliminate the effects of intercompany sales of equipment are the same when the parent uses the partial equity or the cost method, but differ slightly when the investment is recorded using the complete equity method. Therefore, we illustrate the complete equity method next.

ILLUSTRATION 7-11

Calculation of Consolidated Retained Earnings
December 31, 2003

Consolidated Retained Earnings

Inventory	P Company's Share of unrealized profit on upstream sales from S Company (in P's ending inventory)	0	P Company's Retained Earnings on 12/31/03	$2,208,000
	Unrealized profit on downstream sales to S Company (in S's ending inventory)	0	P Company's share of the increase in S Company's Retained Earnings since acquisition ($972,000 − $400,000).85	486,200
Equipment	P Company's share of unrealized gain on upstream sales of equipment from S Company (100,000 − 20,000 − 20,000).85	51,000		
	Unrealized gain on downstream sales of equipment to S Company	0		
	Cumulative amount of amortization and depreciation of the difference between cost and book value	0		
			Consolidated Retained Earnings	$2,643,200

CONSOLIDATED STATEMENTS WORKPAPER— COMPLETE EQUITY METHOD

Subsidiary Is Intercompany Seller (Upstream Sale)

Assume that P Company acquires an 85% interest in S Company for $1,190,000 in 2000, when the retained earnings and capital stock of S Company amount to $400,000 and $1,000,000, respectively. The retained earnings of S Company on January 1, 2002, are $666,000. On January 1, 2002, S Company sells P Company equipment with a book value of $500,000 (original cost of $800,000 and accumulated depreciation of $300,000) for $600,000. On January 1, 2002, the equipment has an estimated remaining useful life of five years and is depreciated using the straight-line method. S Company will record a gain of $100,000 on the sale of the equipment, and each year P Company will record depreciation that is $20,000 [($600,000 − $500,000)/5 years] greater than depreciation based on the cost of the equipment to the consolidated group.

Complete

Under the complete equity method, P Company makes additional entries to adjust its equity in subsidiary income for amounts unrealized (and subsequently realized) in intercompany transactions. In this example, in 2002, P Company would make the following entries:

P Company Books (Complete Equity)		
Investment in S Company	122,400	
Equity in Subsidiary Income		122,400
To record the parent's 85% share of subsidiary reported net income in 2002.		

| Equity in Subsidiary Income | 85,000 | |
| Investment in S Company | | 85,000 |

To adjust subsidiary income downward for the unrealized gain on the intercompany sale of equipment (100,000 × 85%).

| Investment in S Company | 17,000 | |
| Equity in Subsidiary Income | | 17,000 |

To adjust subsidiary income upward for the portion of the gain realized through usage (20,000 × 85%, or 85,000/5 years).

Consolidated statements workpapers for the years ended December 31, 2002, and December 31, 2003, are presented in Illustrations 7-12 and 7-13, respectively.

Consolidated Statements Workpaper Entries—December 31, 2002

Complete

Workpaper entries in Illustration 7-12 are presented in general journal form as follows:

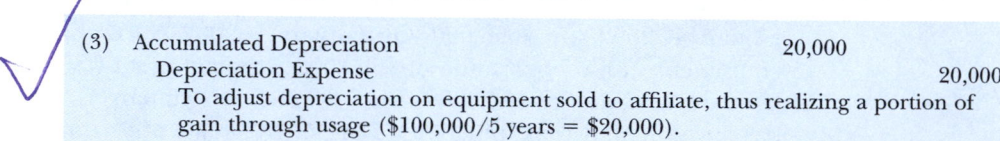

(1) Equity in Subsidiary Income ($122,400 − $85,000 + $17,000)   54,400
       Dividends Declared—S Company   0
       Investment in S Company   54,400
          To eliminate equity in subsidiary income and intercompany dividends, if any.

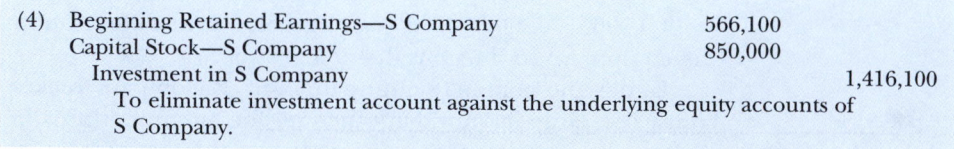

(2) Gain on Sale of Equipment   100,000
       Property and Equipment   200,000
         Accumulated Depreciation   300,000
          To eliminate the unrealized gain recorded on intercompany sale of equipment
          and restore equipment to its original cost (and accumulated depreciation to its
          balance at the date of the intercompany sale).

(3) Accumulated Depreciation   20,000
       Depreciation Expense   20,000
          To adjust depreciation on equipment sold to affiliate, thus realizing a portion of
          gain through usage ($100,000/5 years = $20,000).

(4) Beginning Retained Earnings—S Company   566,100
       Capital Stock—S Company   850,000
         Investment in S Company   1,416,100
          To eliminate investment account against the underlying equity accounts of
          S Company.

Since the selling affiliate is a partially owned subsidiary (upstream sale), the calculation of the noncontrolling interest in combined income is modified by subtracting the amount of the gain recognized by the subsidiary and adding the amount of the gain considered to be realized (through depreciation) to the reported net income of the subsidiary [.15 × ($144,000 − $100,000 + $20,000) = $9,600].

Complete Equity Method	ILLUSTRATION 7-12
85% Owned Subsidiary	**Consolidated Statements Workpaper**
Upstream Sale of Equipment	**P Company and Subsidiary**
Year of Sale	**For the Year Ended December 31, 2002**

Income Statement	P Company	S Company	Eliminations Dr.	Eliminations Cr.	Noncontrolling Interest	Consolidated Balances
Sales	3,500,000	2,000,000				5,500,000
Equity in Subsidiary Income	(54,400)		(1) 54,400			
Gain on Sale of Equipment		100,000	(2) 100,000			
Total Revenue	3,554,400	2,100,000				5,500,000
Cost of Sales	1,800,000	1,130,000				2,930,000
Depreciation Expense	380,000	330,000		(3) 20,000		690,000
Income Tax Expense	200,000	96,000				296,000
Other Expense	820,000	400,000				1,220,000
Total Cost and Expense	3,200,000	1,956,000				5,136,000
Net/Combined Income	354,400	144,000				364,000
Noncontrolling Interest in Income					9,600	(9,600)*
Net Income to Retained Earnings	354,400	144,000	154,400	20,000	9,600	354,400
Retained Earnings Statement						
1/1 Retained Earnings						
P Company	1,726,100					1,726,100
S Company		666,000	(4) 566,100		99,900	
Net Income from above	354,400	144,000	154,400	20,000	9,600	354,400
12/31 Retained Earnings to Balance Sheet	2,080,500	810,000	720,500	20,000	109,500	2,080,500
Balance Sheet						
Current Assets	1,000,000	570,000				1,570,000
Investment in S Company**	1,470,500			(1) 54,400		
				(4) 1,416,100		
Land	1,000,000	200,000				1,200,000
Property and Equipment	3,800,000	2,700,000	(2) 200,000			6,700,000
(Accumulated Depreciation)	(1,520,000)	(960,000)	(3) 20,000	(2) 300,000		(2,760,000)
Total Assets	5,750,500	2,510,000				6,710,000
Liabilities	670,000	700,000				1,370,000
Capital Stock						
P Company	3,000,000					3,000,000
S Company		1,000,000	(4) 850,000		150,000	
Retained Earnings from above	2,080,500	810,000	720,500	20,000	109,500	2,080,500
Noncontrolling Interest in Net Assets					259,500	259,500
Total Liabilities and Equity	5,750,500	2,510,000	1,790,500	1,790,500		6,710,000

*.15 × ($144,000 − $100,000 + $20,000) = $9,600.

**The investment account equals $1,190,000 + 85% of the increase in S Company's Retained Earnings from the date of acquisition to the beginning of the year ($666,000 − 400,000) plus the current period's equity in subsidiary income ($54,400).

(1) To eliminate equity in subsidiary income and intercompany dividends, if any.

(2) To eliminate the unrealized gain recorded on intercompany sale of equipment and restore equipment to its original cost (and accumulated depreciation to its balance at the date of the intercompany sale).

(3) To adjust depreciation on equipment sold to affiliate, thus realizing a portion of the gain through usage ($100,000/5 years = $20,000).

(4) To eliminate investment account against the underlying equity accounts of S Company.

Noncontrolling Interest in Income

		Internally generated income of S Company	$144,000
Unrealized gain on intercompany sale	$100,000	Gain realized through usage (depreciation adjustment)	20,000
		Adjusted income of subsidiary	$ 64,000
		Noncontrolling percentage	× 15%
		Noncontrolling interest in income	$9,600

Complete

If the sale of the equipment had been downstream rather than upstream, the amount of subsidiary income included in combined income would not be affected by the workpaper entries related to unrealized intercompany gain and no adjustment would be necessary in the calculation of the *noncontrolling interest* in combined income.

Consolidated Statements Workpaper Entries—December 31, 2003

In the year 2003, P Company would again make an entry to adjust its equity in subsidiary income for the portion of the gain on the intercompany sale that is realized through usage. This entry may be recorded separately from the one to record P's share of subsidiary *reported* income, as shown below, or the two could be collapsed into one entry for $154,700 ($137,700 + $17,000).

P Company Books (Complete Equity Method)

Investment in S Company	137,700	
Equity in Subsidiary Income		137,700

To record the parent's 85% share of subsidiary reported net income in 2003.

Investment in S Company	17,000	
Equity in Subsidiary Income		17,000

To adjust subsidiary income upward for the portion of the gain realized through usage (20,000 × 85%, or 85,000/5 years).

Workpaper entries in Illustration 7-13 are presented in general journal form as follows:

(1)
Equity in Subsidiary Income	154,700	
Dividends Declared—S Company		0
Investment in S Company		154,700

To eliminate equity in subsidiary income and intercompany dividends, if any.

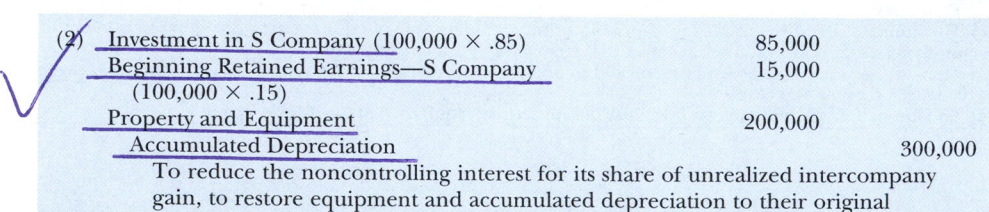

(2)
Investment in S Company (100,000 × .85)	85,000	
Beginning Retained Earnings—S Company (100,000 × .15)	15,000	
Property and Equipment	200,000	
Accumulated Depreciation		300,000

To reduce the noncontrolling interest for its share of unrealized intercompany gain, to restore equipment and accumulated depreciation to their original balances at the date of the intercompany sale, and to facilitate the elimination of the investment account.

Consider the debit to the investment account in entry (2), recalling that the investment account is reduced on the parent's books when the unrealized income is deducted from the parent's equity in subsidiary income under the complete equity method. Thus, the usual workpaper entry to eliminate the investment account against the underlying subsidiary equity accounts [entry (4) below] eliminates an amount greater than the actual beginning investment account balance. That entry, combined with entries (2) and (3), however, will eliminate the investment to exactly zero.

Complete

(3)	Accumulated Depreciation	40,000	
	Depreciation Expense		20,000
	Investment in S Company (20,000 × .85)		17,000
	Beginning Retained Earnings—S Company		
	(20,000 × .15)		3,000

To adjust depreciation recorded in current year and prior year, thus recognizing intercompany gain realized through usage (prior year adjustment for controlling interest to Investment account).

(4)	Beginning Retained Earnings—S Company	688,500	
	Capital Stock—S Company	850,000	
	Investment in S Company		1,538,500

To eliminate investment account against underlying equity accounts of S Company.

The noncontrolling interest in combined income is calculated after adding the portion of the gain considered realized during the year to the net income reported by the subsidiary [.15 × ($162,000 + $20,000) = $27,300].

Noncontrolling Interest in Income

Internally generated income of S Company	$162,000
Gain realized through usage (depreciation adjustment)	20,000
Adjusted income of subsidiary	$182,000
Noncontrolling percentage	× 15%
Noncontrolling interest in income	$27,300

Disposal of Property and Equipment by Purchasing Affiliate

Assume that on January 1, 2004, P Company sells the equipment it purchased from S Company to a party outside the affiliated group for $400,000. The recorded and consolidated book values of the equipment on January 1, 2004, are calculated in Illustration 7-14. P Company will record a $40,000 gain on the sale of the equipment to the party outside the affiliated group, calculated as:

Selling price	$400,000
Book value (on P Company's books)	360,000
Gain on sale (recorded by P Company)	40,000

Complete Equity Method			ILLUSTRATION 7-13			
85% Owned Subsidiary			**Consolidated Statements Workpaper**			
Upstream Sale of Equipment			**P Company and Subsidiary**			
Year Subsequent to Sale			**For the Year Ended December 31, 2003**			

	P	S	Eliminations		Noncontrolling	Consolidated
Income Statement	Company	Company	Dr.	Cr.	Interest	Balances
Sales	4,000,000	2,200,000				6,200,000
Equity Income	154,700		(1) 154,700			
Total Revenue	4,154,700	2,200,000				6,200,000
Cost of Sales	2,100,000	1,180,000				3,280,000
Depreciation Expense	380,000	330,000		(3) 20,000		690,000
Income Tax Expense	272,000	108,000				380,000
Other Expense	840,000	420,000				1,260,000
Total Cost and Expense	3,592,000	2,038,000				5,610,000
Net/Combined Income	562,700	162,000				590,000
Noncontrolling Interest in Income					27,300	(27,300)*
Net Income to Retained Earnings	562,700	162,000	154,700	20,000	27,300	562,700
Retained Earnings Statement						
1/1 Retained Earnings						
P Company	2,080,500					2,080,500
S Company		810,000	(2) 15,000 (3)	3,000	109,500	
			(4) 688,500			
Net Income from above	562,700	162,000	154,700	20,000	27,300	562,700
12/31 Retained Earnings to Balance Sheet	2,643,200	972,000	858,200	23,000	136,800	2,643,200
Balance Sheet						
Current Assets	1,190,000	790,000				1,980,000
Investment in S Company	1,625,200		(2) 85,000 (1)	154,700		
			(3)	17,000		
			(4)	1,538,500		
Land	1,600,000	200,000				1,800,000
Property and Equipment	3,800,000	2,700,000	(2) 200,000			6,700,000
(Accumulated Depreciation)	(1,900,000)	(1,290,000)	(3) 40,000 (2)	300,000		(3,450,000)
Total Assets	6,315,200	2,400,000				7,030,000
Liabilities	672,000	428,000				1,100,000
Capital Stock						
P Company	3,000,000					3,000,000
S Company		1,000,000	(4) 850,000		150,000	
Retained Earnings from above	2,643,200	972,000	858,200	23,000	136,800	2,643,200
Noncontrolling Interest in Net Assets					286,800	286,800
Total Liabilities and Equity	6,315,200	2,400,000	2,033,200	2,033,200		7,030,000

*.15 × ($162,000 + $20,000) = $27,300.
(1) To eliminate equity in subsidiary income and intercompany dividends, if any.
(2) To reduce controlling and noncontrolling interests for their shares of unrealized intercompany gain and to restore equipment and accumulated depreciation to their original balances.
(3) To reverse amount of excess depreciation recorded during current and prior year and to recognize intercompany gain realized through usage.
(4) To eliminate investment account.

ILLUSTRATION 7-14

Calculation of Book Value of Equipment on January 1, 2004

On Books of P Company

Cost (to P Company)	$600,000
Accumulated Depreciation [($600,000/5) × 2]	240,000
Recorded Book Value—January 1, 2004	$360,000

Consolidated

Cost (original cost to S Company)	$800,000
Accumulated Depreciation [$300,000 + (([$800,000 − $300,000)/5] × 2)]	500,000
Consolidated Book Value—January 1, 2004	$300,000

The following entry is made on the books of P Company to record the sale:

P Company Books—Complete Equity Method

Cash	400,000	
Accumulated Depreciation	240,000	
Property and Equipment		600,000
Gain on Sale of Equipment		40,000

Complete

In addition P Company would make an entry to adjust its equity in subsidiary income for the amount of the intercompany gain realized in the current period (85% of: the original $100,000 gain minus the depreciation adjustments of $40,000 for 2002–2003; or $51,000). This entry is made for 85% of the realized gain as the original intercompany transaction was an upstream sale, and thus the controlling interest in the realized gain is 85%.

Investment in S Company	51,000	
Equity in Subsidiary Income		51,000

However, the consolidated book value of the equipment on the date of the sale by P Company is only $300,000, and from the point of view of the consolidated entity a $100,000 gain on the sale (selling price of $400,000 minus book value to consolidated entity of $300,000) should be recognized. The entry on the December 31, 2004, consolidated statements workpaper necessary to achieve this result follows:

Investment in S Company		
(.85 × $60,000)	51,000	
Beginning Retained Earnings—S Company		
(.15 × $60,000)	9,000	
Gain on Sale of Equipment (100,000 gain to consolidated		
entity − 40,000 gain recorded by P Company)		60,000
To adjust reported gain on the sale of equipment by P Company to third party from		
$40,000 to $100,000.		

The above entry also serves to adjust the noncontrolling interest for its share of unrealized intercompany gain at beginning of year ($100,000 original gain minus $40,000 realized through usage [$20,000 in 2002 and $20,000 in 2003] = $60,000 × 15%), and to facilitate the elimination of the investment account (by debiting it for the controlling share $60,000 × 85%).

Note that the entry does not include any adjustment to equipment or accumulated depreciation after the disposal, as these accounts are accurately reflected at zero. Also, it is not necessary to calculate the $60,000 adjustment to the controlling and noncontrolling interests directly in the above entry as it will always equal the gain adjustment. From a consolidated point of view, the amount of gain recorded by the selling affiliate will always be understated (or the amount of loss recorded will always be overstated) by an amount that is equal to the unrealized intercompany profit associated with the equipment on the date of its premature disposal.

After December 31, 2004, no more book or workpaper entries relating to this equipment will be required. Under the complete equity method, entries are needed up through December 31, 2004, even though profit is accurately reflected in the books of P Company. Because the adjustments are reflected in P's books in the account Equity in Subsidiary Income and that account is eliminated in the consolidating process, it is still necessary to adjust the underlying accounts (gain, depreciation expense, etc.) until the asset is sold to outsiders and appropriately removed from the books entirely.

CALCULATION OF CONSOLIDATED NET INCOME AND CONSOLIDATED RETAINED EARNINGS: COMPLETE EQUITY METHOD

For firms using the complete equity method, consolidated net income will always equal the net income reported by the parent. Thus it is not necessary to reconcile the two. It is, nonetheless, useful to know how to check the amount of the controlling and noncontrolling interests in combined income using the t-account approach presented in Illustrations 7-9 and 7-10. Similarly, consolidated retained earnings will equal the retained earnings reported by the parent at any point, assuming the parent has correctly adjusted for any and all unrealized (and subsequently realized) intercompany profit. This amount may be verified using the t-account approach presented in Illustration 7-11.

SUMMARY OF WORKPAPER ENTRIES RELATING TO INTERCOMPANY SALES OF EQUIPMENT

Consolidated statements workpaper eliminating entries for intercompany sales of equipment are summarized in Illustration 7-15. The entries are the same whether the parent company uses the cost method or the partial equity method to record its investment. However, the form of the workpaper entry to adjust for unrealized intercompany profit at the beginning of the year differs as between upstream and downstream sales and between the complete equity method and the other two.

Complete

ILLUSTRATION 7-15

Intercompany Gain on Sale of Equipment
Summary of Workpaper Elimination Entries

Selling Affiliate Is the Parent (or Wholly Owned Subsidiary) (Downstream Sales)	Selling Affiliate Is a Subsidiary (Less than Wholly Owned Subsidiary) (Upstream Sales)

Entries in Year of Intercompany Sale (Cost, Partial Equity, and Complete Equity):

Gain on Sale
 Equipment
  Accumulated Depreciation
   To eliminate unrealized gain on intercompany sale in year of sale and to restore equipment to its original cost and accumulated depreciation to its balance at the date of the intercompany sale.

Accumulated Depreciation
 Depreciation Expense
  To reverse amount (if any) of excess depreciation recorded during current year, thus recognizing an equivalent amount of intercompany profit as realized.

Gain on Sale
 Equipment
  Accumulated Depreciation
   To eliminate unrealized gain on intercompany sale in year of sale and to restore equipment to its original cost and accumulated depreciation to its balance at the date of the intercompany sale.

Accumulated Depreciation
 Depreciation Expense
  To reverse amount (if any) of excess depreciation recorded during current year, thus recognizing an equivalent amount of intercompany profit as realized.

Entries in Years Subsequent to the Year of Intercompany Sale (Downstream):

Cost and Partial Equity	Complete Equity

Beginning Retained Earnings— P Company
 Equipment
  Accumulated Depreciation
   To reduce consolidated retained earnings for the intercompany gain, to restore accumulated depreciation and equipment to their original balances at the date of the intercompany sale.

Investment in S Company
 Equipment
  Accumulated Depreciation
   To facilitate elimination of the investment account and to restore accumulated depreciation and equipment to their original balances at the date of the intercompany sale.

Accumulated Depreciation
 Depreciation Expense
  Beginning Retained Earnings— P Company
   To reverse amount of excess depreciation recorded during current year and prior year, thus recognizing intercompany gain realized through usage.

Accumulated Depreciation
 Depreciation Expense
  Investment in S Company
   To reverse amount of excess depreciation recorded during current year and prior year, thus recognizing intercompany gain realized through usage.

(Upstream):

Cost and Partial Equity	Complete Equity

Beginning Retained Earnings—P
Beginning Retained Earnings—S
 Equipment
  Accumulated Depreciation
   To reduce the controlling and noncontrolling interests for their respective shares of the intercompany gain, to restore accumulated depreciation and equipment to their original balances at the date of the intercompany sale.

Investment in S Company
Beginning Retained Earnings—S
 Equipment
  Accumulated Depreciation
   To reduce the noncontrolling interest for its share of the intercompany gain, to facilitate the elimination of the investment account and restore accumulated depreciation and equipment to their original balances at the date of the intercompany sale.

Accumulated Depreciation
 Depreciation Expense
  Beginning Retained Earnings— P Company
  Beginning Retained Earnings— S Company
   To reverse amount of excess depreciation recorded during current year and prior year, thus recognizing intercompany gain realized through usage.

Accumulated Depreciation
 Depreciation Expense
  Investment in S Company
  Beginning Retained Earnings— S Company
   To reverse amount of excess depreciation recorded during current year and prior year, thus recognizing intercompany gain realized through usage.

INTERCOMPANY INTEREST, RENTS, AND SERVICE FEES

Income and expenses relating to interest, fees, and rents should be reported in the consolidated income statement only when they arise from transactions with parties outside the affiliated group. In addition, as discussed in Chapter 3, only receivables and payables that are receivable from or payable to parties outside the affiliated group should be reported in the consolidated balance sheet.

Intercompany Interest

When interest is charged on intercompany loans, the intercompany interest income on the lending affiliate's books is equal to the intercompany interest expense on the borrowing affiliate's books. The workpaper entry to eliminate intercompany interest is:

Interest Income	XXX	
Interest Expense		XXX

Since equal amounts of revenue and expense are removed from combined income, the net amount of combined income is not affected by this entry. When intercompany loans or interest remain unpaid on the balance sheet date, additional entries are necessary to eliminate related intercompany payables and receivables as follows:

Notes Payable	XXX	
Notes Receivable		XXX
Interest Payable	XXX	
Interest Receivable		XXX

Intercompany Rents

When there is an intercompany operating lease, intercompany rent income on the books of the lessor will equal intercompany rent expense on the books of the lessee. The workpaper entry to eliminate intercompany rent is:

Rent Income	XXX	
Rent Expense		XXX

Since equal amounts of revenue and expense are removed from combined income, the net amount of combined income is not affected by this entry.

Intercompany Service Fees

When one affiliate charges fees to another, the form of the eliminating entry is determined by how the transaction is recorded by the affiliates. If the affiliate that provides the service treats the fee as revenue and the affiliate that receives the service treats the fee as an expense, the necessary workpaper entry is simply a debit to service fee revenue and a credit to service fee expense. On the other hand, the affiliate that receives the service may treat the amount it is charged for the service as a capital addition. For example, fees for architectural services to an affiliate may be treated by the purchasing affiliate as part of the cost of a building. In this case, architectural fees should be debited for the amount recorded as revenue on the intercompany transaction, appropriate expense accounts (as recorded on the selling affiliates books) should be credited for the cost to the selling affiliate of providing the services, and the building should be credited for the difference between the revenue recorded and the cost of providing the service. Additional workpaper entries will also be necessary in subsequent years to report balances for the building, accumulated depreciation, and depreciation expense at amounts based on the cost of the building to the affiliated group.

For example, assume that P Company bills its subsidiary, S Company, $400,000 for architectural services. The cost to P Company of providing the services is $250,000. S Company charges the services to the cost of a building that it opens at the beginning of the next year with an estimated useful life of 15 years. Workpaper entries to eliminate the effects of the intercompany service fee are as follows:

In the Year the Services Are Rendered

Cost and Partial Equity			Complete Equity		
Architectural Fees	400,000		Architectural Fees	400,000	
Salary Expense		200,000	Salary Expense		200,000
Travel Expense		15,000	Travel Expense		15,000
Other Expense		35,000	Other Expense		35,000
Building		150,000	Building		150,000

In the Year the Building Is Opened

Cost and Partial Equity			Complete Equity		
Beginning Retained Earnings—P Company	150,000		Investment in S Company	150,000	
Building		150,000	Building		150,000
Accumulated Depreciation	10,000		Accumulated Depreciation	10,000	
Depreciation Expense		10,000	Depreciation Expense		10,000

In the Fifth Year After the Building Is Opened

Cost and Partial Equity			Complete Equity		
Beginning Retained Earnings—P Company	110,000		Investment in S Company	110,000	
Accumulated Depreciation	40,000		Accumulated Depreciation	40,000	
Building		150,000	Building		150,000
Accumulated Depreciation	10,000		Accumulated Depreciation	10,000	
Depreciation Expense		10,000	Depreciation Expense		10,000

Thus eliminating entries relating to intercompany transactions depend on how these transactions are recorded on the books of the affiliates. In all cases, however, the financial reporting objectives identified in previous sections of this chapter and in Chapter 6 apply. In the preceding example, the reporting objectives were:

- To include in revenue only the amounts that result from *transactions with parties outside the affiliated group.*
- To present property in the consolidated balance sheet at *its cost to the affiliated group.*

- To present accumulated depreciation in the consolidated balance sheet based on the ***cost to the affiliated group*** of the related assets.
- To present depreciation expense in the consolidated income statement based on the ***cost to the affiliated group*** of the related assets.

In order to apply the objectives identified in this chapter and in Chapter 6 to a situation that is not illustrated in this text, the student may wish to work out the workpaper entries necessary in a situation like the following. S Company is in the business of selling equipment that it manufactures. S Company treats equipment manufactured as finished goods inventory. S Company sells some equipment that it manufactured to its parent company at a profit. The equipment is capitalized and depreciated on the books of the parent company.

 SUMMARY

1. *Understand the financial reporting objectives in accounting for intercompany sales of **nondepreciable** assets on the consolidated financial statements.* The consolidated financial statements should include gains or losses only when the property is sold to outsiders (parties outside the affiliated group) for the difference between the cost to the consolidated entity and the proceeds from outsiders. Until it is sold to outsiders, the property should be presented in the consolidated balance sheet at its cost to the affiliated group.

2. *Explain the additional financial reporting objectives in accounting for intercompany sales of **depreciable** assets on the consolidated financial statements.* Accumulated depreciation should be presented in the consolidated balance sheet based on the cost of the asset to the affiliated group, and depreciation expense should be presented in the consolidated income statement also based on the cost to the affiliated group.

3. *Explain when gains or losses on intercompany sales of depreciable assets should be recognized on a consolidated basis.* Gains or losses on intercompany sales of depreciable assets are recognized either when the asset is sold to outsiders, or gradually over time as it is depreciated.

4. *Explain the term "realized through usage."* After an intercompany sale, the purchasing affiliate will calculate depreciation on the basis of its cost, which is the intercompany selling price. The depreciation recorded by the purchasing affiliate will, therefore, be excessive (deficient) from a consolidated point of view and will also require adjustment. From the view of the consolidated entity, the intercompany gain (loss) is considered to be realized from the use

of the property or equipment in the generation of revenue.

5. *Describe the differences between upstream and downstream sales in determining combined income and the controlling interest in combined income.* There is no difference between upstream and downstream sales in determining combined income. However, the controlling interest is affected differently. For downstream sales, the elimination of intercompany gains as well as the subsequent depreciation adjustments affect only the controlling interest. For upstream sales, the adjustments are made to the subsidiary income, and thus affect both the noncontrolling and controlling interests in the proportion of subsidiary ownership.

6. *Compare the eliminating entries when the selling affiliate is a subsidiary (less than wholly owned) versus when the selling affiliate is the parent company.* Because of the differences explained in the preceding item (#5), the eliminating entries are similarly affected. Specifically, the entries in subsequent years for downstream sales that reflect prior years' income or expense adjustments [entries to Retained Earnings—Parent (under the cost or partial equity method) or Investment in Subsidiary (under the complete equity method)] are replaced by eliminating entries for upstream sales to both Retained Earnings—Subsidiary and Retained Earnings—Parent under the cost or partial equity method or to both Retained Earnings—Subsidiary and Investment in Subsidiary under the complete equity method.

7. *Compute the noncontrolling interest in combined income when the selling affiliate is a subsidiary.* The noncon-

trolling interest in combined income is computed as the noncontrolling interest percentage of the internally generated income of the subsidiary minus the unrealized gain on upstream sales (year of sale only) plus the amount of the gain realized through usage (depreciation adjustment).

8. *Compute consolidated net income considering the effects of intercompany sales of depreciable assets.* The controlling interest in combined income is computed as the internally generated income of the parent minus the unrealized gain on downstream sales (year of sale only) plus the amount of the gain realized through usage (depreciation adjustment) plus the parent's percentage of the subsidiary income adjusted for upstream sales minus any other adjustments needed (such as excess depreciation and goodwill amortization, described in earlier chapters).

9. *Describe the eliminating entry needed to adjust the consolidated financial statements when the purchasing affiliate sells a depreciable asset that was acquired from another affiliate.* The entry does not include any adjustment to equipment or accumulated depreciation after the disposal, as these accounts are accurately reflected at zero. The entry merely adjusts the gain or loss reported by the purchasing affiliate from the amount it recorded to the correct amount from the perspective of the consolidated entity (based on original cost and depreciation), and adjusts the controlling and noncontrolling interests for the unrealized intercompany profit associated with the equipment on the date of its premature disposal (which equals the over- or understatement of the gain or loss).

10. *Explain the basic principles used to record or eliminate intercompany interest, rent, and service fees.* Income and expenses relating to interest, fees, and rents should be reported in the consolidated income statement only when they arise from transactions with parties outside the affiliated group. In addition, only receivables and payables that are receivable from or payable to parties outside the affiliated group should be reported in the consolidated balance sheet.

APPENDIX

Deferred Tax Consequences Related to Intercompany Sales of Equipment

To keep the focus of this appendix on deferred tax consequences rather than alternative methods of accounting for investments, we present the discussion only once. The balances reported by the parent company in income, retained earnings, and the investment account differ depending on the method used by the parent company to record its investment. As illustrated in previous chapters, however, the method used by the parent company to record its investment has no effect on the consolidated balances.

As has also been illustrated in previous chapters, when the parent company records its investment using the equity method, a workpaper entry to reverse the effect of parent company entries during the year for subsidiary dividends and income replaces the cost method entries to establish reciprocity and to eliminate dividend income. However, workpaper entries to allocate and amortize the difference between cost and book value, to eliminate intercompany sales, and to eliminate unrealized intercompany profit are the same regardless of whether the investment is recorded using the cost method or the partial equity method. Workpaper entries to record deferred tax consequences of unrealized intercompany profit and undistributed subsidiary income are also the same when the parent company records its investment using the partial equity method or the cost method. The principal difference between the workpaper entries for these methods and for the complete equity method is that entries to Retained Earnings—P Company are generally replaced by entries to the Investment in S Company, as indicated by an asterisk in the following analysis.

To illustrate the treatment in the consolidated financial statements of deferred income taxes relating to intercompany sales of equipment, assume that P Company owns a 70% interest in S Company and that on January 1, 2001, S Company sells P

Company equipment with a book value of $500,000 (original cost of $800,000 and accumulated depreciation of $300,000) for $600,000. On January 1, 2001, the equipment has a remaining useful life of five years and is depreciated using the straight-line method. The marginal income tax rates for both companies are 40% and separate income tax returns are filed.

S Company will record a gain of $100,000 on the sale of the equipment and each year P Company will record depreciation that is $20,000 greater than depreciation based on the cost of the equipment to the selling affiliate. Workpaper eliminating entries in the December 31, 2001, and December 31, 2002, consolidated statements workpapers relating to the unrealized profit on the intercompany sale of the equipment are illustrated below:

Consolidated Statements Workpaper Entries—December 31, 2001

(1)   Gain on Sale of Equipment   100,000
          Property and Equipment   100,000
              To eliminate unrealized profit recorded on intercompany sale of equipment
(2)   Accumulated Depreciation   20,000
          Depreciation Expense   20,000
              To reverse the amount of excess depreciation recorded during the current year.
(3)   Deferred Tax Asset   32,000
          Income Tax Expense   32,000
              To defer the net amount of income tax paid or accrued by the affiliates on the
              amount of unrealized intercompany profit in equipment at the end of the year
              [.4 × ($100,000 − $20,000)].
(4)   Property and Equipment   300,000
          Accumulated Depreciation   300,000
              To restate property and equipment at original cost to the selling affiliate.

Since the selling affiliate is a partially owned subsidiary (upstream sale), the calculation of the noncontrolling interest in combined income requires that the *after-tax* amount of gain recorded by the subsidiary (.60 × $100,000 = $60,000) be subtracted from the reported net income of the subsidiary and that the *after-tax* amount of the gain considered to be realized through depreciation (.6 × $20,000 = $12,000) be added to the reported net income of the subsidiary before multiplying by the noncontrolling interest percentage. Assuming that S Company reported net income of $144,000 in 2001, the noncontrolling interest in combined income is $28,800 [.30 × ($144,000 − $60,000 + $12,000)].

If the sale of equipment is downstream, no adjustments to the reported net income of the subsidiary are necessary in the calculation of the noncontrolling interest in combined income.

Consolidated Statements Workpaper Entries—December 31, 2002

(1)   1/1 Retained Earnings—P Company*
          [.70 × ($100,000 − $20,000)]   56,000
      1/1 Retained Earnings—S Company
          [.30 × ($100,000 − $20,000)]   24,000
      Accumulated Depreciation   20,000
          Equipment   100,000
              To reduce the controlling and the noncontrolling interests for their respective
              shares of unrealized intercompany profit at the beginning of the year, to reduce
              accumulated depreciation by the amount of excess depreciation accumulated to
              the beginning of the year, and to reduce the carrying value of equipment to its
              book value on the date of the intercompany sale.

| (2) | Accumulated Depreciation | 20,000 | |
| | Depreciation Expense | | 20,000 |

To reverse the amount of excess depreciation recorded during the current year.

(3)	Deferred Tax Asset	24,000	
	Income Tax Expense	8,000	
	1/1 Retained Earnings—P Company*		22,400
	1/1 Retained Earnings—S Company		9,600

To recognize deferred taxes for taxes paid in prior years on the amount of intercompany profit still considered unrealized at the **end of the year** [.40 × ($100,000 − $20,000 − $20,000) = $24,000], to recognize income tax expense on intercompany profit considered to be realized during the current year (.40 × $20,000 = $8,000), to adjust consolidated retained earnings for the controlling interest's share of the tax consequence of unrealized profit at the beginning of the year (.70 × $32,000 = $22,400), and to adjust the noncontrolling interest for its share of the tax consequence of unrealized profit at the beginning of the year (.30 × $32,000 = $9,600).

| (4) | Property and Equipment | 300,000 | |
| | Accumulated Depreciation | | 300,000 |

To restate property and equipment to original cost to the selling affiliate.

*Entry to R/E—P Company is replaced by an entry to Investment in S Company under the complete equity method.

The noncontrolling interest in combined income is calculated after adding the *after-tax* profit considered realized during the year (.6 × $20,000 = $12,000) to the reported net income of the subsidiary. If S Company reported net income of $162,000 in 2002, the noncontrolling interest in combined income is $52,200 [.30 × ($162,000 + $12,000)].

IMPACT OF UNREALIZED INTERCOMPANY PROFIT ON THE CALCULATION OF DEFERRED TAX CONSEQUENCES RELATED TO UNDISTRIBUTED SUBSIDIARY INCOME

Earlier we emphasized that the calculation of the tax consequences of undistributed income is based on the undistributed income of the subsidiary that has been *included in combined income.* Thus, before calculating the deferred tax consequences relating to undistributed subsidiary income, the amount of undistributed income must be adjusted for the *after-tax* amount of unrealized intercompany profit *recorded by the subsidiary* that has been recognized in the determination of combined income.

To illustrate, assume that

1. P Company acquired 70% of the voting stock of S Company when S Company's retained earnings amounted to $150,000.
2. On January 1, 2001, S Company recorded a $100,000 gain on the sale to P Company of equipment with a remaining life of five years.
3. On January 1, 2002, P Company recorded a $60,000 gain on the sale to S Company of equipment with a remaining life of six years.
4. S Company reported retained earnings of $260,000 on January 1, 2002, and $320,000 on December 31, 2002.

5. S Company reported net income of $90,000 and declared dividends of $30,000 in 2002.

6. P Company reported net income from independent operations in 2002 in the amount of $700,000 and retained earnings on December 31, 2002, of $3,500,000.

7. The affiliates file separate income tax returns.

8. Undistributed income is expected to be received in the form of future dividends.

9. The dividends received deduction is 80%, and the past, current, and expected future marginal income tax rates are 40%.

The calculation of the amounts of the undistributed income of S Company that have been included in combined income is presented in Illustration 7-16.

The following entry is needed in the December 31, 2002, consolidated statements workpaper to report the income tax consequences of past and current undistributed subsidiary income:

1/1 Retained Earnings—P Company (1)*	3,472	
Income Tax Expense (balancing amount) (2)	4,032	
Deferred Income Tax Liability (3)		7,504

(1)$62,000 × 70% × 20% × 40% = $3,472
(2)$7,504 − $3,472 = $4,032
(3)$134,000 × 70% × 20% × 40% = $7,504
*Entry to Retained Earnings—P Company is replaced by an entry in the same amount to the Investment in S Company account under the complete equity method.

Note that the calculation of the deferred income tax liability on undistributed subsidiary income is not affected by unrealized intercompany profit recorded by the parent company on sales to the subsidiary (downstream sales). The calculation is also not affected by the allocation, depreciation, or amortization of any difference between cost and book value.

ILLUSTRATION 7-16

Undistributed Income of S Company
That Has Been Included in Combined Income

S Company	From Acquisition to 1/1/02	For Calendar Year 2002	From Acquisition to 12/31/02
Retained earnings 1/1/02	$ 260,000		
Retained earnings 12/31/02			$ 320,000
Retained earnings date of acquisition	(150,000)		(150,000)
Increase in retained earnings	110,000		170,000
Net income 2002		$ 90,000	
Dividends 2002		(30,000)	
After-tax unrealized profit on 1/1/02 [.6 × ($100,000 − $20,000)]	(48,000)		
After-tax profit realized in 2002 (.6 × $20,000)		12,000	
After-tax unrealized profit on 12/31/02 [.6 × $100,00 − $20,000 − $20,000)]			(36,000)
Undistributed income that has been included in combined income	$ 62,000	$ 72,000	$ 134,000

CALCULATIONS OF CONSOLIDATED NET INCOME AND CONSOLIDATED RETAINED EARNINGS

When the affiliated companies file separate income tax returns, the calculations of consolidated net income and consolidated retained earnings must be modified to incorporate income tax consequences. When calculating the amounts of net income or retained earnings that have been realized in transactions with third parties, adjustments must now be made for the *after-tax amounts* of unrealized intercompany profit. In addition, consolidated net income is reduced by the income tax consequence of undistributed income for the current year and consolidated retained earnings is reduced by the income tax consequence of undistributed income from the date of acquisition to the date of the calculation.

The calculation of consolidated net income in Illustration 7-17 and the calculation of consolidated retained earnings in Illustration 7-18 are based on the same assumptions as those used in the preparation of Illustration 7-16.

ILLUSTRATION 7-17

Calculation of Controlling and Noncontrolling Interests in Income
For Year Ended December 31, 2002
Deferred Tax Considerations

Noncontrolling Interest in Combined Income—Year 2002

		Internally generated income of S Company	$ 90,000
Unrealized profit on upstream sales in ending inventory (after-tax)	0	After-tax gain realized through usage (depreciation adjustment) .60($20,000)	12,000
Unrealized gain on 2002 intercompany sale of equipment—upstream sales (after-tax)	0	Realized profit (upstream sales) from beginning inventory (after-tax)	0
		Subsidiary Income included in Combined Income	$102,000
		Noncontrolling Ownership percentage interest	30%
		Noncontrolling Interest in Combined Income	$ 30,600

70%

Controlling Interest in Income—Year 2002

After-tax unrealized gain on 2002 intercompany sales of equipment (downstream sales) .6($60,000)	36,000	Net income internally generated by P Company	$700,000
		After-tax gain realized through usage (depreciation adjustment) .6($10,000)	6,000
Unrealized profit on downstream sales to S Company (ending inventory) (after-tax)	0	Realized profit (downstream sales) from beginning inventory (after-tax)	0
		P Company's percentage of S Company's income realized from third parties, .70($102,000)	71,400
Amortization of excess depreciation	0		
Amortization of goodwill	0		
Deferred taxes on S Company's undistributed income for 2002 [($102,000 − 30,000)(.7)(.2)(.4)]	4,032		
		Consolidated Income (controlling interest in income)	$737,368

ILLUSTRATION 7-18

Calculation of Consolidated Retained Earnings
December 31, 2002

P Company's retained earnings on 12/31/02			$3,500,000
Less the after-tax amount of P Company's retained earnings that have not been realized in transactions with third parties [.6 × ($60,000 − $10,000)]			(30,000)
P Company's retained earnings that have been realized in transactions with third parties			3,470,000
Increase in retained earnings of S Company from date of acquisition to 12/31/02 ($320,000 − $150,000)		$ 170,000	
Less after-tax unrealized profit included in S Company's retained earnings on 12/31/02 [.6 × ($100,000 − $20,000 − $20,000)]		(36,000)	
Increase in reported retained earnings of S Company since acquisition that has been realized in transactions with third parties		$ 134,000	
P Company's share thereof (.70 × $134,000)			93,800
Less income tax consequence of undistributed income of S Company that has been included in combined income from date of acquisition to 12/31/02 ($134,000 × .70 × .20 × .40)			(7,504)
Less cumulative amortization of the difference between cost and book value			—0—
Consolidated retained earnings 12/31/02			$3,556,296

(The letter A indicated for an exercise or problem refers to the appendix.)

QUESTIONS

1. From a consolidated point of view, when should profit be recognized on intercompany sales of depreciable assets? Nondepreciable assets?

2. In what circumstances might a consolidated gain be recognized on the sale of assets to a nonaffiliate when the selling affiliate recognizes a loss?

3. What is the essential procedural difference between workpaper eliminating entries for unrealized intercompany profit when the selling affiliate is a less than wholly owned subsidiary and such entries when the selling affiliate is the parent company or a wholly owned subsidiary?

4. Define consolidated net income using the t-account approach.

5. Why is it important to distinguish between upstream and downstream sales in the analysis of intercompany profit eliminations?

6. In what period and in what manner should profits relating to the intercompany sale of depreciable property and equipment be recognized in the consolidated financial statements?

7. Define consolidated retained earnings using the analytical approach.

EXERCISES

EXERCISE 7-1   **Controlling Interest in Income**

On January 1, 2001, Sherwood Company, an 80% owned subsidiary of Paradise Company, sold to Paradise Company equipment with a book value of $600,000 for $840,000. The equipment had an estimated remaining useful life of eight years on the date of the intercompany sale.

Paradise Company reported net income from its independent operations of $550,000, and Sherwood Company reported net income of $300,000 in the years of 2001 and 2002.

Required:

Calculate the controlling interest in combined net income for the years ended December 31, 2001, and December 31, 2002.

EXERCISE 7-2 **Controlling Interest in Income**

On January 1, 2001, Polar Company, which owns an 80% interest in Superior Company, sold Superior Company equipment with a book value of $400,000 for $560,000. The equipment had an estimated remaining useful life of eight years on the date of the intercompany sale.

Polar Company reported net income from its independent operations (including sales to affiliates) of $400,000, and Superior Company reported net income of $200,000 from its independent operations in 2001 and 2002.

Required:

Calculate the controlling interest in combined net income for the years ended December 31, 2001, and December 31, 2002.

EXERCISE 7-3 **Workpaper Entries—Intercompany Sale of Equipment**

Pearson Company owns 90% of the outstanding common stock of Spring Company. On January 1, 2001, Spring Company sold equipment to Pearson Company for $200,000. Spring Company had purchased the equipment for $300,000 on January 1, 1996, and had depreciated it using a 10% straight-line rate. The management of Pearson Company estimated that the equipment had a remaining useful life of five years on January 1, 2001. In 2002, Pearson Company reported $150,000 and Spring Company reported $100,000 in net income from their independent operations (including sales to affiliates).

Required:

A. Prepare in general journal form the workpaper entries relating to the intercompany sale of equipment that are necessary in the December 31, 2001, and December 31, 2002, consolidated financial statements workpapers.

B. Calculate consolidated net income (controlling interest in combined income) for 2002.

EXERCISE 7-4 **Entries—Intercompany Sale of Land**

Procter Company owns 90% of the outstanding stock of Silex Company. On January 1, 2001, Silex Company sold land to Procter Company for $350,000. Silex had originally purchased the land on June 30, 1997, for $200,000.

Procter Company plans to construct a building on the land bought from Silex in which it will house new production machinery. The estimated useful life of the building and the new machinery is 15 years.

Required:

A. Prepare the entries on the books of Procter related to the intercompany sale of land for the years ended December 31, 2001, and December 31, 2002.

B. Prepare in general journal form the workpaper entries necessary because of the intercompany sale of land in:

(1) The consolidated financial statements workpaper for the year ended December 31, 2001.

(2) The consolidated financial statements workpaper for the year ended December 31, 2002.

EXERCISE 7-5 **Upstream and Downstream Sale**

Patterson Company owns 80% of the outstanding common stock of Stevens Company. On June 30, 2000, land costing $500,000 is sold by one affiliate to the other for $800,000.

Required:

Prepare in general journal form the workpaper entries necessary because of the intercompany sale of land in the consolidated financial statements workpaper for the year ended December 31, 2001, assuming that:

A. Patterson Company purchased the land from Stevens Company.

B. Stevens Company purchased the land from Patterson Company.

EXERCISE 7-6 **Calculating Gain on Sale**

P Company owns 90% of the outstanding common stock of S Company. On January 1, 2001, S Company sold land to P Company for $600,000. S Company originally purchased the land for $400,000.

On January 1, 2002, P Company sold the land purchased from S Company to a company outside the affiliated group for $700,000.

Required:

A. Calculate the amount of gain on the sale of the land that is recognized on the books of P Company in 2002.

B. Calculate the amount of gain on the sale of the land that should be recognized in the consolidated financial statements in 2002.

C. Prepare in general journal form the workpaper entries necessary because of the intercompany sale of land in the consolidated financial statements workpaper for the year ended December 31, 2002.

EXERCISE 7-7 **Entries—Intercompany Sale of Inventory and Equipment**

On January 1, 2000, Price Company acquired an 80% interest in the common stock of Smith Company on the open market for $750,000, the book value at that date.

On January 1, 2001, Price Company purchased new equipment for $14,500 from Smith Company. The equipment cost $9,000 and had an estimated life of five years as of January 1, 2001.

During 2002, Price Company had merchandise sales to Smith Company of $100,000; the merchandise was priced at 25% above Price Company's cost. Smith Company still owes Price Company $17,500 on open account and has 20% of this merchandise in inventory at December 31, 2002. At the beginning of 2002, Smith Company had in inventory $25,000 of merchandise purchased in the previous period from Price Company.

Required:

A. Prepare all workpaper entries necessary to eliminate the effects of the intercompany sales on the consolidated financial statements for the year ended December 31, 2002.

B. Assume that Smith Company reports net income of $40,000 for the year ended December 31, 2002. Calculate the amount of noncontrolling interest to be deducted from combined income in the consolidated income statement for the year ended December 31, 2002.

EXERCISE 7-8 **Controlling Interest in Income**

On January 1, 2001, P Company acquired a 90% interest in S Company. During 2002, S Company sold merchandise to P Company at 25% above cost in the amount (selling price) of $225,000. At the end of the year, P Company had in its inventory one-third of the amount of goods purchased from S Company.

On January 1, 2002, P Company sold equipment that had a book value of $80,000 to S Company for $120,000. The equipment had an estimated remaining life of four years.

S Company reported net income of $120,000, and P Company reported net income of $300,000 from their independent operations (including sales to affiliates) for the year ended December 31, 2002.

Required:

Calculate controlling interest in combined net income for the year ended December 31, 2002.

EXERCISE 7-9 **Workpaper Entries—Sales of Services**

P Company owns 80% of the outstanding stock of S Company. The 2001 sales of S Company included revenue of $390,000 consisting of consulting services billed to P Company at cost plus 30%. P Company was billed the full $390,000; of this amount $260,000 was charged to selling expenses and $130,000 was charged to administrative expense.

Required:
Prepare in general journal form the workpaper entry necessary to eliminate the effects of intercompany sales of services in the consolidated financial statements workpaper for the year ended December 31, 2001.

EXERCISE 7-10 **Workpaper Entries—Intercompany Fees**
During 2000, Pier One Company billed its 80% owned subsidiary, Scale Company, $700,000 for architectural services. The cost to Pier One Company of providing the services was $400,000 for salaries and $150,000 for other operating expenses. Scale Company charged the architecture fees to the cost of a building that it opened on January 1, 2001. The building had an estimated useful life of 30 years.

Required:
Prepare in general journal form the workpaper entries relating to the intercompany fees that are necessary in the consolidated statements workpapers for the years ended December 31, 2000, 2001, and 2002.

EXERCISE 7-11 **Workpaper Entries—Upstream and Downstream Sales**
Pinta Company, a forklift manufacturer, owns 80% of the voting stock of Standard Company. On January 1, 2001, Pinta Company sold forklifts to Standard Company for $400,000. The forklifts, which represented inventory to Pinta Company, had a cost to Pinta Company of $310,000. The management of Standard Company estimated that the forklifts had a useful life of nine years from the date of purchase. Standard Company uses the straight-line method to depreciate its capital assets.

In 2001, Pinta Company reported $700,000 in net income from its independent operations (including sales to affiliates), and Standard Company reported $250,000 in net income from its operations.

Required:
A. Prepare in general journal form the workpaper entries necessary because of the intercompany sales in:
  (1) The consolidated financial statements workpaper for the year ended December 31, 2001.
  (2) The consolidated financial statements workpaper for the year ended December 31, 2002.
B. Calculate consolidated net income for the year ended December 31, 2001.

EXERCISE 7-12 **Workpaper Entries—Sale of Equipment**
Pomeroy Corporation owns an 80% interest in Sherer Company and a 90% interest in Tampa Company. On January 2, 2001, Tampa Company sold equipment with a book value of $600,000 to Sherer Company for $780,000. This equipment has a remaining useful life of three years. Sherer Company reported $100,000 and Tampa Company reported $150,000 in net income (including sales to affiliates) in 2001.

Required:
Prepare the 2001 and 2002 consolidated statements workpaper entries to eliminate the effects of this sale of equipment.

EXERCISE 7-13A **Deferred Tax Consequences**
On January 1, 2001, Pillar Company acquires a 75% interest in Samatros Company. On that date Pillar Company sells Samatros Company equipment with a book value of $600,000 (original cost of $900,000 and accumulated depreciation of $300,000) for $700,000. On January 1, 2001, the equipment has an estimated remaining useful life of five years and is depreciated using the straight-line method.

The companies file separate income tax returns, and they have marginal income tax rates of 30%.

Required:

A. Prepare the entries to eliminate the effects of the intercompany sale of equipment in the consolidated statements workpapers for the years ended December 31, 2001, and December 31, 2002.

B. Assume that the intercompany sale is upstream rather than downstream. Prepare the entries to eliminate the effects of the intercompany sale of equipment in the consolidated statements workpapers for the years ended December 31, 2001, and December 31, 2002.

PROBLEMS

PROBLEM 7-1 **Workpaper Journal Entries and Income Statement Balances**

Powell Company owns 80% of the outstanding common stock of Sullivan Company. On June 30, 2001, Sullivan Company sold equipment to Powell Company for $500,000. The equipment cost Sullivan Company $780,000 and had accumulated depreciation of $400,000 on the date of the sale. The management of Powell Company estimated that the equipment had a remaining useful life of four years from June 30, 2001. In 2002, Powell Company reported $300,000 and Sullivan Company reported $200,000 in net income from their independent operations (including sales to affiliates).

Required:

A. Prepare in general journal form the workpaper entries necessary because of the intercompany sale of equipment in:

(1) The consolidated financial statements workpaper for the year ended December 31, 2001.

(2) The consolidated financial statements workpaper for the year ended December 31, 2002.

B. Calculate the balances to be reported in the consolidated income statement for the year ended December 31, 2002, for the following items:

(1) Combined income.

(2) Noncontrolling interest in combined income.

(3) Consolidated net income (controlling interest).

PROBLEM 7-2 **Workpaper Journal Entries**

Pico Company, a truck manufacturer, owns 90% of the voting stock of Seward Company. On January 1, 2001, Pico Company sold trucks to Seward Company for $350,000. The trucks, which represented inventory to Pico Company, had a cost to Pico Company of $260,000. The management of Seward Company estimated that the trucks had a useful life of six years from the date of purchase. Seward Company uses the straight-line method to depreciate its capital assets.

In 2001, Pico Company reported $600,000 in net income from its independent operations (including sales to affiliates), and Seward Company reported $200,000 in net income from its operations.

Required:

A. Prepare in general journal form the workpaper entries necessary because of the intercompany sales in:

(1) The consolidated financial statements workpaper for the year ended December 31, 2001.

(2) The consolidated financial statements workpaper for the year ended December 31, 2002.

B. Calculate consolidated net income for the year ended December 31, 2001.

PROBLEM 7-3 **P Company Entries and Determining Gain or Loss on Sale**

On January 1, 2001, P Company purchased equipment from its 80% owned subsidiary for $600,000. The carrying value of the equipment on the books of S Company was $450,000. The equipment had a remaining useful life of six years on January 1, 2001. On January 1, 2002, P Company sold the equipment to an outside party for $550,000.

Required:

A. Prepare in general journal form the entries necessary in 2001 and 2002 on the books of P Company to account for the purchase and sale of the equipment.

B. Determine the consolidated gain or loss on the sale of the equipment and prepare in general journal form the entry necessary on the December 31, 2002, consolidated statements workpaper to properly reflect this gain or loss.

PROBLEM 7-4 **Workpaper— Cost Method**

Prout Company owns 80% of the common stock of Sexton Company. The stock was purchased for $1,600,000 on January 1, 1998, when Sexton Company's retained earnings were $800,000. On January 1, 2000, Prout Company sold fixed assets to Sexton Company for $360,000. These assets were originally purchased by Prout Company for $400,000 on January 1, 1990, at which time their estimated depreciable life was 25 years. The straight-line method of depreciation is used.

On December 31, 2001, the trial balances of the two companies were as shown here:

	Prout Company	Sexton Company
Current Assets	$ 568,000	$ 271,000
Fixed Assets	1,972,000	830,000
Other Assets	1,000,800	1,600,000
Investment in Sexton Company	1,600,000	
Dividends Declared	120,000	100,000
Cost of Goods Sold	942,000	795,000
Other Expenses (including depreciation)	145,000	90,000
Income Tax Expense	187,200	90,000
Total	$6,535,000	$3,776,000
Liabilities	$ 305,000	$ 136,000
Accumulated Depreciation	375,000	290,000
Sales	1,475,000	1,110,000
Dividend Income	80,000	
Common Stock	3,000,000	1,200,000
Retained Earnings 1/1	1,300,000	1,040,000
Total	$6,535,000	$3,776,000

Required:

A. Prepare a consolidated statements workpaper for the year ended December 31, 2001.

B. Assuming that on January 1, 2002, Sexton Company sells the fixed assets purchased from Prout Company to a party outside the affiliated group for $300,000:

(1) Prepare the entry that would have been entered on the books of Sexton Company to record the sale.

(2) Prepare entries for the December 31, 2002, consolidated statements workpaper necessitated by the sale of the assets.

(3) Prepare any workpaper entries that will be needed in the December 31, 2003, consolidated statements workpaper in regard to these fixed assets.

PROBLEM 7-5 **Trial Balance Workpaper—Cost Method**

Using the information presented in Problem 7-4, prepare a consolidated financial statements workpaper for the year ended December 31, 2001, using the trial balance format.

PROBLEM 7-6   **Workpaper—Cost Method**

Pitts Company owns 80% of the common stock of Shannon Company. The stock was purchased for $960,000 on January 1, 1999, when Shannon Company's retained earnings were $675,000. On January 1, 2001, Shannon Company sold fixed assets to Pitts Company for $960,000; Shannon Company had purchased these assets for $1,350,000 on January 1, 1991, at which time their estimated useful life was 25 years. The estimated remaining useful life to Pitts Company on 1/1/01 is 10 years. Both companies employ the straight-line method of depreciation.

    The financial data for 2002 are presented here:

	Pitts Company	Shannon Company
Sales	$1,950,000	$1,350,000
Dividend Income	60,000	
Total Revenue	2,010,000	1,350,000
Cost of Goods Sold	1,350,000	900,000
Other Expenses	225,000	150,000
Total Cost and Expense	1,575,000	1,050,000
Net Income	$ 435,000	$ 300,000
1/1 Retained Earnings	$1,215,000	$1,038,000
Net Income	435,000	300,000
Dividends Declared	(150,000)	(75,000)
12/31 Retained Earnings	$1,500,000	$1,263,000
Inventory	$ 498,000	$ 225,000
Investment in Shannon Company	960,000	
Fixed Assets	2,168,100	2,625,000
Accumulated Depreciation—Fixed Assets	(900,000)	(612,000)
Total Assets	$2,726,100	$2,238,000
Liabilities	$ 465,600	$ 450,000
Common Stock	760,500	525,000
Retained Earnings	1,500,000	1,263,000
Total Liabilities and Equity	$2,726,100	$2,238,000

Required:

A. Prepare a consolidated statements workpaper for the year ended December 31, 2002.

B. Calculate consolidated retained earnings on December 31, 2002, using an analytical or t-account approach.

PROBLEM 7-7   **Workpaper Cost Method, Comprehensive Problem**

Parsons Company acquired 90% of the outstanding common stock of Shea Company on June 30, 2001, for $426,000. On that date, Shea Company had retained earnings in the amount of $60,000, and the fair value of its recorded assets and liabilities was equal to their book value. The excess of cost over the fair value of the recorded net assets was attributed to an unrecorded manufacturing formula held by Shea Company, which had an expected remaining useful life of five years from June 30, 2001.

    Financial data for 2003 are presented here:

	Parsons Company	Shea Company
Sales	$2,555,500	$1,120,000
Dividend Income	54,000	
Total Revenue	2,609,500	1,120,000
Cost of Goods Sold	1,730,000	690,500
Expenses	654,500	251,000
Total Cost and Expense	2,384,500	941,500
Net Income	$ 225,000	$ 178,500

	Parsons Company	Shea Company
1/1 Retained Earnings	$ 595,000	$ 139,500
Net Income	225,000	178,500
Dividends Declared	(100,000)	(60,000)
12/31 Retained Earnings	$ 720,000	$ 258,000
Cash	$ 119,500	$ 132,500
Accounts Receivable	342,000	125,000
Inventory	362,000	201,000
Other Current Assets	40,500	13,000
Land	150,000	
Investment in Shea Company	426,000	
Property and Equipment	825,000	241,000
Accumulated Depreciation	(207,000)	(53,500)
Total Assets	$2,058,000	$ 659,000
Accounts Payable	$ 295,000	$ 32,000
Other Liabilities	43,000	19,000
Capital Stock	1,000,000	300,000
Additional Paid-in Capital		50,000
Retained Earnings	720,000	258,000
Total Liabilities and Equity	$2,058,000	$ 659,000

On December 31, 2001, Parsons Company sold equipment (with an original cost of $100,000 and accumulated depreciation of $50,000) to Shea Company for $97,500. This equipment has since been depreciated at an annual rate of 20% of the purchase price. During 2002 Shea Company sold land to Parsons Company at a profit of $15,000.

The inventory of Parsons Company on December 31, 2002, included goods purchased from Shea Company on which Shea Company recognized a profit of $7,500. During 2003, Shea Company sold goods to Parsons Company for $375,000, of which $60,000 was unpaid on December 31, 2003. The December 31, 2003, inventory of Parsons Company included goods acquired from Shea Company on which Shea Company recognized a profit of $10,500.

Required:

A. Prepare a consolidated financial statements workpaper for the year ended December 31, 2003.

B. Prepare a schedule to calculate consolidated retained earnings on December 31, 2003, using an analytical or t-account approach.

PROBLEM 7-8 **Workpaper—Cost Method, Comprehensive Problem**

On January 1, 2000, Phelps Company purchased an 85% interest in Sloane Company for $955,000 when the retained earnings of Sloane Company were $150,000. The difference between cost and book value was assigned as follows:

Inventory	$40,000
Land	30,000
Discount on Bonds Payable	40,000
Goodwill	80,000

One-half of the inventory was sold in 2000 and the remaining inventory was sold in 2001. The bonds mature in eight years; any goodwill is amortized over the maximum period allowable.

On December 31, 2000, Phelps Company's inventory contained $10,000 in unrealized intercompany profit. During 2001 Phelps Company sold merchandise with a cost of $200,000 to Sloane Company at a 30% markup on cost. Only $65,000 (selling price) of this merchandise remains in Sloane Company's 2001 ending inventory. As of December 31, 2001, Sloane Company owes Phelps Company $40,000 for merchandise purchased during 2001.

Equipment with a book value of $500,000 was sold by Sloane Company on January 2, 2001, to Phelps Company for $640,000. This equipment had an estimated useful life when purchased by Sloane Company on July 1, 1998, of 10 years.

Financial data for 2001 are presented here:

	Phelps Company	Sloane Company
Sales	$1,291,500	$ 560,000
Other Income		140,000
Dividend Income	42,500	
Total Revenue	1,334,000	700,000
Cost of Goods Sold	660,000	300,000
Depreciation Expense	138,000	20,000
Interest Expense	8,000	10,000
Other Expenses	174,000	140,000
Total Cost and Expense	980,000	470,000
Net Income	$ 354,000	$ 230,000
1/1 Retained Earnings	$ 350,500	$ 250,000
Net Income	354,000	230,000
Dividends Declared	(100,000)	(50,000)
12/31 Retained Earnings	$ 604,500	$ 430,000
Cash	$ 127,000	$ 70,000
Accounts Receivable	300,000	210,000
Inventory	270,000	175,000
Investment in Sloane Company	955,000	
Land	100,000	290,000
Plant and Equipment	800,000	800,000
Accumulated Depreciation	(200,000)	(200,000)
Total Assets	$2,352,000	$1,345,000
Accounts Payable	$ 167,500	$ 65,000
Bonds Payable	80,000	100,000
Capital Stock	1,500,000	750,000
Retained Earnings	604,500	430,000
Total Liabilities and Equity	$2,352,000	$1,345,000

Required:

Prepare a consolidated financial statements workpaper for the year ended December 31, 2001.

PROBLEM 7-9 **Workpaper with Intercompany Sales of Inventory and Land**

Pierce Company acquired a 90% interest in Sanders Company on January 1, 2001, for $1,480,000. At this time, Sanders Company's common stock and retained earnings balances were $1,000,000 and $500,000, respectively. An examination of the books of Sanders on the date of purchase revealed the following:

	Book Value	Fair Value
Current Assets	$300,000	$300,000
Marketable Securities	200,000	200,000
Inventory	175,000	225,000
Plant and Equipment (net)	650,000	800,000
Land	500,000	600,000

Sanders Company's equipment has a remaining life of 11 years. Eighty percent of the inventory was sold in 2001, the remainder in 2002.

During 2001, Pierce Company sold merchandise costing $400,000 to Sanders at a 25% markup on cost, and Sanders sold merchandise to Pierce Company for $100,000 (this price included $25,000 in profit). In 2002, Pierce Company sold merchandise to Sanders Company for $350,000, while Sanders Company sold merchandise to Pierce Company for $80,000. The 2001 markup percentages were also used on the 2002 sales.

The selling price of intercompany merchandise remaining in ending inventories for both years is summarized here:

Merchandise from Intercompany Sales in Ending Inventory of	2001	2002
Pierce Company	$40,000	$20,000
Sanders Company	50,000	30,000

In 2002, Sanders Company also sold a piece of land that had a book value of $250,000 to Pierce Company for $300,000. On December 31, 2002, Pierce Company holds a $60,000 receivable on the merchandise it sold to Sanders Company.

Adjusted trial balances for the year ended December 31, 2002 are shown here:

	Pierce	Sanders
Cash	$ 200,000	$ 150,000
Accounts Receivable	300,000	250,000
Marketable Securities	100,000	200,000
Inventory 12/31	300,000	250,000
Investment in Sanders Company	1,480,000	
Land	400,000	350,000
Plant and Equipment (net)	1,000,000	800,000
Cost of Goods Sold	600,000	400,000
Depreciation Expense	60,000	40,000
Other Expenses	400,000	260,000
Dividends Declared	120,000	70,000
Total	$4,960,000	$2,770,000
Accounts Payable	$ 241,000	$ 140,000
Notes Payable	350,000	100,000
Common Stock	1,900,000	1,000,000
1/1 Retained Earnings	706,000	580,000
Sales	1,700,000	900,000
Gain on Sale of Land		50,000
Dividend Income	63,000	
Total	$4,960,000	$2,770,000

Required:
Prepare a consolidated statements workpaper for the year ended December 31, 2002.

PROBLEM 7-10 **Workpaper—Partial Equity Method**
(Note that this is the same problem as Problem 7-4, but assuming the use of the partial equity method.)

Prout Company owns 80% of the common stock of Sexton Company. The stock was purchased for $1,600,000 on January 1, 1998, when Sexton Company's retained earnings were $800,000. On January 1, 2000, Prout Company sold fixed assets to Sexton Company for $360,000. These assets were originally purchased by Prout Company for $400,000 on January 1, 1990, at which time their estimated depreciable life was 25 years. The straight-line method of depreciation is used.

On December 31, 2001, the trial balances of the two companies were as shown here:

	Prout Company	Sexton Company
Current Assets	$ 568,000	$ 271,000
Fixed Assets	1,972,000	830,000
Other Assets	1,000,800	1,600,000
Investment in Sexton Company	1,820,000	
Dividends Declared	120,000	100,000
Cost of Goods Sold	942,000	795,000
Other Expenses (including depreciation)	145,000	90,000
Income Tax Expense	187,200	90,000
Total	$6,755,000	$3,776,000
Liabilities	$ 305,000	$ 136,000
Accumulated Depreciation	375,000	290,000
Sales	1,475,000	1,110,000
Equity in Subsidiary Income	108,000	
Common Stock	3,000,000	1,200,000
Retained Earnings 1/1	1,492,000	1,040,000
Total	$6,755,000	$3,776,000

Required:

A. Prepare a consolidated statements workpaper for the year ended December 31, 2001.

B. Assuming that on January 1, 2002, Sexton Company sells the fixed assets purchased from Prout Company to a party outside the affiliated group for $300,000:

   (1) Prepare the entry that would have been entered on the books of Sexton Company to record the sale.

   (2) Prepare entries for the December 31, 2002, consolidated statements workpaper necessitated by the sale of the assets.

   (3) Prepare any workpaper entries that will be needed in the December 31, 2003, consolidated statements workpaper in regard to these fixed assets.

PROBLEM 7-11   **Trial Balance—Workpaper—Partial Equity Method**

Using the information presented in Problem 7-10 prepare a consolidated financial statements workpaper for the year ended December 31, 2001, using the trial balance format.

PROBLEM 7-12   **Workpaper—Partial Equity Method**

Prather Company owns 80% of the common stock of Stone Company. The stock was purchased for $960,000 on January 1, 1999, when Stone Company's retained earnings were $675,000. On January 1, 2001, Stone Company sold fixed assets to Prather Company for $960,000; Stone Company had purchased these assets for $1,350,000 on January 1, 1991, at which time their estimated useful life was 25 years. The estimated remaining useful life to Prather Company on 1/1/01 is 10 years. Both companies employ the straight-line method of depreciation.

The financial data for 2002 are presented here:

	Prather Company	Stone Company
Sales	$1,950,000	$1,350,000
Equity in Subsidiary Income	240,000	
Total Revenue	2,190,000	1,350,000
Cost of Goods Sold	1,350,000	900,000
Other Expenses	225,000	150,000
Total Cost and Expense	1,575,000	1,050,000
Net Income	$ 615,000	$ 300,000
1/1 Retained Earnings	$1,505,400	$1,038,000
Net Income	615,000	300,000
Dividends Declared	(150,000)	(75,000)
12/31 Retained Earnings	$1,970,400	$1,263,000

	Prather Company	Stone Company
Inventory	$ 498,000	$ 225,000
Investment in Stone Company	1,430,400	
Fixed Assets	2,168,100	2,625,000
Accumulated Depreciation—Fixed Assets	(900,000)	(612,000)
Total Assets	$3,196,500	$2,238,000
Liabilities	$ 465,600	$ 450,000
Common Stock	760,500	525,000
Retained Earnings	1,970,400	1,263,000
Total Liabilities and Equity	$3,196,500	$2,238,000

Required:

A. Prepare a consolidated statements workpaper for the year ended December 31, 2002.

B. Calculate consolidated retained earnings on December 31, 2002, using an analytical or t-account approach.

PROBLEM 7-13   **Workpaper—Partial Equity Method, Comprehensive Problem**

Padilla Company acquired 90% of the outstanding common stock of Sanchez Company on June 30, 2001, for $426,000. On that date, Sanchez Company had retained earnings in the amount of $60,000, and the fair value of its recorded assets and liabilities was equal to their book value. The excess of cost over the fair value of the recorded net assets was attributed to an unrecorded manufacturing formula held by Sanchez Company, which had an expected remaining useful life of five years from June 30, 2001.

Financial data for 2003 are presented here:

	Padilla Company	Sanchez Company
Sales	$2,555,500	$1,120,000
Equity in Subsidiary Income	160,650	
Total Revenue	2,716,150	1,120,000
Cost of Goods Sold	1,730,000	690,500
Expenses	654,500	251,000
Total Cost and Expense	2,384,500	941,500
Net Income	$ 331,650	$ 178,500
1/1 Retained Earnings	666,550	139,500
Net Income	331,650	178,500
Dividends Declared	(100,000)	(60,000)
12/31 Retained Earnings	$ 898,200	$ 258,000
Cash	$ 119,500	$ 132,500
Accounts Receivable	342,000	125,000
Inventory	362,000	201,000
Other Current Assets	40,500	13,000
Land	150,000	
Investment in Sanchez Company	604,200	
Property and Equipment	825,000	241,000
Accumulated Depreciation	(207,000)	(53,500)
Total Assets	$2,236,200	$ 659,000
Accounts Payable	$ 295,000	$ 32,000
Other Liabilities	43,000	19,000
Capital Stock	1,000,000	300,000
Additional Paid-in Capital		50,000
Retained Earnings	898,200	258,000
Total Liabilities and Equity	$2,236,200	$ 659,000

On December 31, 2001, Padilla Company sold equipment (with an original cost of $100,000 and accumulated depreciation of $50,000) to Sanchez Company for $97,500. This equipment has since been depreciated at an annual rate of 20% of the purchase price. During 2002, Sanchez Company sold land to Padilla Company at a profit of $15,000.

The inventory of Padilla Company on December 31, 2002, included goods purchased from Sanchez Company on which Sanchez Company recognized a profit of $7,500. During 2003, Sanchez Company sold goods to Padilla Company for $375,000, of which $60,000 was unpaid on December 31, 2003. The December 31, 2003, inventory of Padilla Company included goods acquired from Sanchez Company on which Sanchez Company recognized a profit of $10,500.

Required:

A. Prepare a consolidated financial statements workpaper for the year ended December 31, 2003.

B. Prepare a schedule to calculate consolidated retained earnings on December 31, 2003, using an analytical or t-account approach.

PROBLEM 7-14 **Entries and Computation of Income and Retained Earnings**

Platt Company acquired an 80% interest in Sloane Company when the retained earnings of Sloane Company were $300,000. On January 1, 2001, Sloane Company recorded a $250,000 gain on the sale to Platt Company of equipment with a remaining life of five years. On January 1, 2002, Platt Company recorded a $180,000 gain on the sale to Sloane Company of equipment with a remaining life of six years. Sloane Company reported net income of $180,000 and declared dividends of 60,000 in 2002. It reported retained earnings of $520,000 on January 1, 2002, and $640,000 on December 31, 2002. Platt Company reported net income from independent operations of $400,000 in 2002 and retained earning of $1,800,000 on December 31, 2002.

Required:

A. Prepare in general journal form the entries necessary in the December 31, 2002, consolidated statements workpaper to eliminate the effects of the intercompany sales.

B. Calculate consolidated net income for the year ended December 31, 2002.

C. Calculate consolidated retained earnings on December 31, 2002.

D. Calculate noncontrolling interest in combined income for the year ended December 31, 2002.

PROBLEM 7-15 **Workpaper—Complete Equity Method**

(Note that this is the same problem as Problems 7-4 and 7-10, but assuming the use of the complete equity method.)

Prout Company owns 80% of the common stock of Sexton Company. The stock was purchased for $1,600,000 on January 1, 1998, when Sexton Company's retained earnings were $800,000. On January 1, 2000, Prout Company sold fixed assets to Sexton Company for $360,000. These assets were originally purchased by Prout Company for $400,000 on January 1, 1990, at which time their estimated depreciable life was 25 years. The straight-line method of depreciation is used.

On December 31, 2001, the trial balances of the two companies were as shown here:

	Prout Company	Sexton Company
Current Assets	$ 568,000	$ 271,000
Fixed Assets	1,972,000	830,000
Other Assets	1,000,800	1,600,000
Investment in Sexton Company	1,716,000	
Dividends Declared	120,000	100,000
Cost of Goods Sold	942,000	795,000
Other Expenses (including depreciation)	145,000	90,000
Income Tax Expense	187,200	90,000
Total	$6,651,000	$3,776,000

	Prout Company	Sexton Company
Liabilities	$ 305,000	$ 136,000
Accumulated Depreciation	375,000	290,000
Sales	1,475,000	1,110,000
Equity in Subsidiary Income	116,000	
Common Stock	3,000,000	1,200,000
Retained Earnings 1/1	1,380,000	1,040,000
Total	$6,651,000	$3,776,000

Required:

A. Prepare a consolidated statements workpaper for the year ended December 31, 2001.

B. Assuming that on January 1, 2002, Sexton Company sells the fixed assets purchased from Prout Company to a party outside the affiliated group for $300,000:

   (1) Prepare the entry that would have been entered on the books of Sexton Company to record the sale.

   (2) Prepare entries for the December 31, 2002, consolidated statements workpaper necessitated by the sale of the assets.

   (3) Prepare any workpaper entries that will be needed in the December 31, 2003, consolidated statements workpaper in regard to these fixed assets.

C. If you completed Problem 7-4, compare the consolidated balance obtained in requirement A to those obtained in Problem 7-4.

PROBLEM 7-16 **Workpaper—Complete Equity Method**

Prather Company owns 80% of the common stock of Stone Company. The stock was purchased for $960,000 on January 1, 1999, when Stone Company's retained earnings were $675,000. On January 1, 2001, Stone Company sold fixed assets to Prather Company for $960,000; Stone Company had purchased these assets for $1,350,000 on January 1, 1991, at which time their estimated useful life was 25 years. The estimated remaining useful life to Prather Company on 1/1/01 is 10 years. Both companies employ the straight-line method of depreciation.

    The financial data for 2002 are presented here:

	Prather Company	Stone Company
Sales	$1,950,000	$1,350,000
Equity in Subsidiary Income	252,000	
Total Revenue	2,202,000	1,350,000
Cost of Goods Sold	1,350,000	900,000
Other Expenses	225,000	150,000
Total Cost and Expense	1,575,000	1,050,000
Net Income	$ 627,000	$ 300,000
1/1 Retained Earnings	$1,397,400	$1,038,000
Net Income	627,000	300,000
Dividends Declared	(150,000)	(75,000)
12/31 Retained Earnings	$1,874,400	$1,263,000
Inventory	$ 498,000	$ 225,000
Investment in Stone Company	1,334,400	
Fixed Assets	2,168,100	2,625,000
Accumulated Depreciation—Fixed Assets	(900,000)	(612,000)
Total Assets	$3,100,500	$2,238,000
Liabilities	$ 465,600	$ 450,000
Common Stock	760,500	525,000
Retained Earnings	1,874,400	1,263,000
Total Liabilities and Equity	$3,100,500	$2,238,000

Required:

A. Prepare a consolidated statements workpaper for the year ended December 31, 2002.

B. Calculate consolidated retained earnings on December 31, 2002, using a t-account or analytical approach.

PROBLEM 7-17   Workpaper—Complete Equity Method, Comprehensive Problem

Padilla Company acquired 90% of the outstanding common stock of Sanchez Company on June 30, 2001, for $426,000. On that date, Sanchez Company had retained earnings in the amount of $60,000, and the fair value of its recorded assets and liabilities was equal to their book value. The excess of cost over the fair value of the recorded net assets was attributed to an unrecorded manufacturing formula held by Sanchez Company, which had an expected remaining useful life of five years from June 30, 2001.

Financial data for 2003 are presented here:

	Padilla Company	Sanchez Company
Sales	$2,555,500	$1,120,000
Equity in Subsidiary Income	156,050	
Total Revenue	2,711,550	1,120,000
Cost of Goods Sold	1,730,000	690,500
Expenses	654,500	251,000
Total Cost and Expense	2,384,500	941,500
Net Income	$ 327,050	$ 178,500
1/1 Retained Earnings	591,200	139,500
Net Income	327,050	178,500
Dividends Declared	(100,000)	(60,000)
12/31 Retained Earnings	$ 818,250	$ 258,000
Cash	$ 119,500	$ 132,500
Accounts Receivable	342,000	125,000
Inventory	362,000	201,000
Other Current Assets	40,500	13,000
Land	150,000	
Investment in Sanchez Company	524,250	
Property and Equipment	825,000	241,000
Accumulated Depreciation	(207,000)	(53,500)
Total Assets	$2,156,250	$ 659,000
Accounts Payable	$ 295,000	$ 32,000
Other Liabilities	43,000	19,000
Capital Stock	1,000,000	300,000
Additional Paid-in Capital		50,000
Retained Earnings	818,250	258,000
Total Liabilities and Equity	$2,156,250	$ 659,000

On December 31, 2001, Padilla Company sold equipment (with an original cost of $100,000 and accumulated depreciation of $50,000) to Sanchez Company for $97,500. This equipment has since been depreciated at an annual rate of 20% of the purchase price. During 2002, Sanchez Company sold land to Padilla Company at a profit of $15,000.

The inventory of Padilla Company on December 31, 2002, included goods purchased from Sanchez Company on which Sanchez Company recognized a profit of $7,500. During 2003, Sanchez Company sold goods to Padilla Company for $375,000, of which $60,000 was unpaid on December 31, 2003. The December 31, 2003, inventory of Padilla Company included goods acquired from Sanchez Company on which Sanchez Company recognized a profit of $10,500.

Required:

A. Prepare a consolidated financial statements workpaper for the year ended December 31, 2003.

B. Prepare a schedule to calculate consolidated retained earnings on December 31, 2003, using a t-account or analytical approach.

PROBLEM 7-18A **Deferred Tax Consequences of Intercompany Inventory and Equipment**

Peer Company acquired an 80% interest in Sells Company on January 1, 2001, for $1,600,000. On this date, the common stock and retained earnings balances were $1,500,000 and $500,000, respectively. During the year, Peer Company sold merchandise to Sells Company for $200,000. Only one-fourth of this merchandise was in Sells Company's 2001 ending inventory, and $10,000 of this amount is unrealized profit.

On January 2, 2001, Sells Company sold equipment with a book value of $300,000 to Peer Company for $400,000. The equipment has a remaining useful life of four years. Sells Company's net income for 2001 was $300,000, while Peer Company's was $800,000. Neither company declared dividends in 2001. The affiliated companies file separate income tax returns, the dividends received exclusion is 80%, and the prior, current, and expected future marginal income tax rates for both companies are 40%.

Required:

A. Prepare in general journal form all consolidated statements workpaper entries necessary for 2001.

B. Calculate consolidated net income for the year ended December 31, 2001.

C. Calculate the noncontrolling interest in combined income for the year ended December 31, 2001.

8

CHANGES IN OWNERSHIP INTEREST

LEARNING OBJECTIVES

1. Identify the types of transactions that change the parent company's ownership interest in a subsidiary.

2. Describe the eliminating entries needed when the parent acquires subsidiary shares through multiple open market purchases.

3. Explain how the parent determines the cost basis of subsidiary shares sold subsequent to acquisition.

4. Compute the controlling interest in income after the parent sells some shares of the subsidiary company.

5. Describe the effect on the eliminating process when the subsidiary issues new shares entirely to the parent, and the parent pays either more or less than the book value of the subsidiary shares.

6. Describe the impact on the parent's investment account when the subsidiary issues new shares and either the new shares are purchased ratably by the parent and noncontrolling shareholders or entirely by the noncontrolling shareholders.

7. Describe the impact on the consolidation process when the subsidiary acquires treasury stock from the noncontrolling shareholders.

IN THE NEWS

"AT&T's $40.9 billion acquisition of cable giant Tele-Communications Inc. (TCI) . . . is expected to close in mid-February. Currently, TCI holds roughly 28% of At Home's common shares, though if warrants and options outstanding of employees are exercised, AT&T could see that fall to about 21%. Both the voting and economic interest could be diluted further by a deal [for At Home] to buy Excite Inc. . . . But it's expected that after the TCI deal, AT&T will continue to have voting control of At Home."[1]

---

[1] *WSJ*, "AT&T May Sell Internet-Access Lines, Including WorldNet to At Home Corp," by Kara Swisher and Rebecca Blumenstein, 1/22/99, p. A3.

Two assumptions regarding the equity interest acquired have been followed in previous chapters dealing with consolidated financial statements. Although not expressly stated, those assumptions were:

1. The interest in the subsidiary was obtained through a single open-market transaction.
2. The percentage of ownership remained constant.

As illustrated in the *Wall Street Journal* excerpt above, these assumptions are not always valid. For example, control of a purchased subsidiary might not be obtained until two or more stock purchases have been made. Similarly, the percentage of ownership may change for several reasons, such as (1) additional shares of the subsidiary may be purchased on the open market; (2) some of the shares held by the parent company may be sold; (3) the subsidiary may engage in capital transactions with the parent company and/or outside parties that change the parent company's percentage of ownership. In this chapter, we focus on changes in the ownership interest with only two principal companies involved, one parent and one subsidiary. In the following chapter, we will introduce the accounting consequences when more than two firms are involved (indirect ownership interests).

A summary of transactions and the recommended accounting treatment for each follows:

Situation	*Accounting Treatment*
Parent Transactions With Third Parties	
1. Parent **buys** additional shares of subsidiary from third parties.	Purchase of additional investment with allocation of difference between cost and book value.
2. Parent **sells** subsidiary shares to third parties.	Sale of investment with recognition of gain or loss.
Subsidiary Transactions With and Without the Parent	
3. Subsidiary **issues** additional shares (including treasury shares):	
a. Parent **buys** no shares or less than its pro-rata number of shares. Percentage of ownership decreases.	Sale of investment with recognition of gain or loss.
b. Parent **buys** more than its pro-rata number of shares. Percentage of ownership increases.	Purchase of additional investment with allocation of difference between cost and book value.
4. Subsidiary **buys** treasury stock:	
a. Parent **sells** no shares or less than its pro-rata number of shares. Percentage of ownership increases.	Purchase of additional investment with allocation of difference between cost and book value.
b. Parent **sells** more than its pro-rata number of shares. Percentage of ownership decreases.	Sale of investment with recognition of gain or loss.

Justification for these recommended accounting treatments is based on the concept of economic substance over form. That is, a parent company can effectively increase its ownership interest in a subsidiary by either (1) buying additional subsidiary shares directly from third parties or (2) having a subsidiary purchase its (subsidiary's) shares from third parties. Similarly, the parent can effectively decrease its ownership interest by either (1) selling some of its subsidiary shares directly to third parties or (2) having a subsidiary sell additional shares (including treasury shares) to third parties. Since the economic substance is essentially the same from the parent company's point of view, the transactions should be accounted for in a consistent manner. Accounting for these changes in the parent company's percentage of ownership is discussed and illustrated in this chapter.

PARENT ACQUIRES SUBSIDIARY STOCK THROUGH SEVERAL OPEN MARKET PURCHASES—COST METHOD

Sometimes the controlling interest in a subsidiary is acquired through the initial stock purchase; at other times control is not achieved until two or more stock purchases have been made. When control is achieved on the first purchase, the date of acquisition is the purchase date. However, when more than one purchase is made before control is obtained, there are actually two or more acquisition dates.

Cost

Determination of the date of acquisition is important under purchase accounting because subsidiary retained earnings accumulated before that date constitute a portion of the equity acquired by the parent company, whereas the parent's share of subsidiary retained earnings accumulated after acquisition is properly included in consolidated retained earnings. If two or more purchases are made over a period of time, the retained earnings of the subsidiary at acquisition should be determined on a step-by-step basis. Interpretation No. 2 of *APB Opinion No. 17* suggests that the purchasing company should identify the cost of each investment, the fair value of the underlying assets acquired, and the difference between cost and book value for *each* step purchase.

To illustrate the consolidation of an investment acquired on a step-by-step basis, assume that S Company had 10,000 shares of $10 par value common stock outstanding during 2000–2003 and retained earnings as follows:

	S Company Retained Earnings
January 1, 2000	$ 40,000
January 1, 2001	70,000
January 1, 2002	120,000
January 1, 2003	185,000
December 31, 2003	265,000

P Company purchased for cash S Company common stock on the open market as follows:

Date	Shares Acquired	Cost
January 1, 2000	1,500 (15% of 10,000 shares)	$ 24,000
January 1, 2002	7,500 (75% of 10,000 shares)	188,000
Total	9,000 shares	$212,000

Cost

Some additional simplifying assumptions are made to concentrate attention on the new issues introduced and because the complexities avoided by the assumptions have been discussed in detail in previous chapters. The assumptions are:

1. Any difference between cost and book value of the purchases relates solely to the misvaluation of land owned by S Company and is, therefore, not subject to amortization.
2. S Company distributes no dividends during the periods under consideration.
3. P Company uses the cost method to record its investment in S Company.[2]

The initial purchase of the 15% interest in S Company is recorded at its cost of $24,000 and reported as an investment on P Company's balance sheets on December 31, 2000 and 2001. No income on the investment is recognized for either 2000 or 2001 because no dividends were distributed by S Company. The second purchase on January 1, 2002, is also recorded in the investment account at its cost of $188,000. Again, no income is recognized on the investment during 2002 because S Company declared no dividends.

Since P Company now has controlling ownership of S Company, the investment must be consolidated. In the preparation of a consolidated workpaper on December 31, 2002, it is necessary to compute the amount of S Company equity to eliminate, as well as the difference between cost and book value. On a step-by-step basis, the Computation and Allocation Schedule is as follows:

Computation and Allocation of Difference Between Cost and Book Value

	First Purchase (15%)		Second Purchase (75%)		Total
Cost (Purchase Price)		$24,000		$188,000	$212,000
Equity Acquired:					
Common Stock ($10 par)	$15,000		$75,000		$90,000
Retained Earnings	6,000 (1)		90,000 (2)		96,000
Total		21,000		165,000	186,000
Difference Between Cost and Book Value		$ 3,000		$ 23,000	$ 26,000
Adjust land					(26,000)
Balance					—0—

(1) 15% × $40,000.
(2) 75% × $120,000.

Because P Company has owned a percentage of S Company since January 1, 2000, a workpaper entry is needed on December 31, 2002 to convert to equity/establish reciprocity to the beginning of 2002 as follows:

Investment in S Company	12,000	
1/1 Retained Earnings—P Company*		12,000

* [.15 × ($120,000 − $40,000) or the change in retained earnings from 1/1/00 to 1/1/02].

---

[2]We will follow the cost illustration with an illustration assuming the use of the equity method. Also, income tax deferral on the parent company's share of the undistributed income of the subsidiary is ignored in this chapter.

S Company retained earnings increased from $40,000 on January 1, 2000, to $120,000 on January 1, 2002. During that time, P Company owned 15% of S Company; thus, the reciprocity entry is made for $12,000 [15% × ($120,000 − $40,000)]. This entry would not have been needed if the percentage had remained at 15% because no consolidation would be required. In essence, the consolidation is being retroactively applied to the time period when the parent owned only 15% of the subsidiary.

After reciprocity is established, the investment is eliminated by the following workpaper entry:

Common Stock—S Company (.90 × $100,000)	90,000	
1/1 Retained Earnings—S Company (.90 × $120,000)	108,000	
Difference Between Cost and Book Value	26,000	
Investment in S Company ($212,000 + $12,000)		224,000

The workpaper is then completed as illustrated in previous chapters.

In subsequent periods, reciprocity (equity conversion) is established by taking 90% of the increase (decrease) in S Company's retained earnings from January 1, 2002, to the beginning of the current year, and then adding the $12,000 initial adjustment (from 1/1/00 to 1/1/02, at 15%). For example, for the preparation of a consolidated statements workpaper on December 31, 2003, reciprocity (equity conversion) would be established as follows:

Amount from the December 31, 2002, workpaper	$12,000
Add: Change in Retained Earnings	
[.90 × ($185,000 − $120,000)]	58,500
Total	$70,500

The computation of noncontrolling interest in combined income and net assets is made by multiplying the *end-of-year* noncontrolling interest percentage times realized subsidiary income and subsidiary stockholders' equity amounts, respectively.

In the preceding example, the difference between cost and book value was assumed to relate to land. If the differences were allocable to depreciable or amortizable assets (and liabilities), the difference from each purchase should be separately analyzed and allocated to the appropriate assets and/or liabilities as usual. Amortization effects of each should be determined separately from the date of each purchase, although the amounts might be combined into a single workpaper amortization entry. Although this treatment is theoretically preferred, for expediency purposes and because the amounts are often immaterial, the difference between cost and book value on each purchase is often amortized as if each purchase had been made on the date control was achieved.

Cost

PARENT SELLS SUBSIDIARY STOCK INVESTMENT ON THE OPEN MARKET—COST METHOD

The sale of all, or a portion of, its investment by the parent company is treated in a manner similar to the sale of any other corporate asset. The asset received is recorded, the portion of the investment sold is written off, and gain or loss is recognized on the sale as the difference between the value of the asset received and the carrying value of the investment sold. Because the value of the asset received (e.g., cash) is generally easily measured, the amount of any gain or loss recognized hinges on the appropriate measurement of the carrying value of the investment sold. If only a portion of the investment is sold, federal tax law specifies that either specific identification or the first-in, first-out (FIFO) method must be used to determine the value of the shares sold. These methods are also acceptable for financial reporting purposes; we use specific identification for illustrative purposes.

Recall the information from the previous example illustrated as follows:

	First Purchase	*Second Purchase*	*Total*
Shares	1,500 (15%)	7,500 (75%)	9,000 (90%)
Cost	$24,000	$188,000	$212,000

Assume that P Company sold 1,500 shares of the 9,000 shares of S Company stock on July 1, 2003, for $70,000. To determine the cost of the 1,500 shares sold, the company could use either the specific identification or the FIFO method. In this example, the shares were specifically identified as 20% (1,500/7,500) of those from the second purchase group (purchased on January 1, 2002) representing a cost of investment sold of $37,600 (or 20% of $188,000). After the sale, P Company retains control with a 75% ((9,000-1,500)/10,000) interest as follows:

After Sale Amounts	*First Purchase*	*Second Purchase*	*Total*
Shares	1,500 (15%)	6,000 (60%)	7,500 (75%)
Cost	$24,000	$150,400	$174,400

To record the sale of the shares, P Company makes the following entry in its books on July 1, 2003.

P Company's Books			Cost
Cash	70,000		
Investment in S Company (20% × $188,000)		37,600	
Gain on Sale of Investments		32,400	

From a consolidated standpoint, the cost of the shares sold ($37,600) needs to be adjusted for 15% of the undistributed earnings since the date of acquisition. This is computed as follows:

Cost of Shares		$37,600
Plus: Undistributed Income:		
(A) Change in Retained Earnings from the date of acquisition (1/1/02) to the beginning of the year (1/1/03).		
($185,000 − $120,000)	$65,000	
Ownership Percentage	15%	9,750
(B) Earnings from beginning of current year to the date of sale (1/1/03 to 7/1/03).		
($80,000/2)	40,000	
Ownership Percentage	15%	6,000
Adjusted cost of shares sold		$53,350

Therefore, the correct consolidated gain on the sale is $16,650, computed by subtracting the adjusted cost of $53,350 from the selling price of $70,000. Since a gain of $32,400 is recorded on the parent's books, an adjustment is needed on the workpapers to reduce the gain to $16,650. The adjustments, totaling $15,750, needed on the consolidated workpaper are as follows:

(1)	Gain on Sale of Investments	9,750
	1/1 Retained Earnings—P Company	9,750
	(Consolidated Retained Earnings)	

(2)	Gain on Sale of Investments	6,000
	Subsidiary Income Sold	6,000

The first entry represents undistributed income to the beginning of the year of sale on the shares sold accruing to the 15% of shares sold [($185,000-$120,000).15]. This amount reduces the gain and increases retained earnings for the prior year's unrecorded earnings in P's retained earnings.

The second entry adjusts for the subsidiary income earned during the first six months of 2003 that was sold to the noncontrolling stockholders. From January 1, 2003, to July 1, 2003, S Company earned $40,000. Because 15% of Company S is sold, $6,000 (15% × $40,000) represents net income purchased by the noncontrolling stockholders. The $6,000 should be excluded from noncontrolling interest in combined income, since it was purchased by the noncontrolling stockholders rather than being earned by them.

A workpaper for the preparation of consolidated financial statements on December 31, 2003, is presented in Illustration 8-1. Data necessary to complete the workpaper, other than those previously provided, are assumed. Workpaper entries, in addition to those made to adjust the gain on sale, are:

(3)	Investment in S Company	60,750
	1/1 Retained Earnings—P Company	60,750

Entry (3) converts to equity (establishes reciprocity) by recognizing P Company's share of the increase in S Company's retained earnings from the date of purchase to the beginning of 2003 on the *shares still held at the end of 2003*, computed as follows:

From January 1, 2000, to January 1, 2002 .15($120,000 − $40,000)	$12,000
From January 1, 2002, to January 1, 2003 .75($185,000 − $120,000)	48,750
Total	$60,750

After conversion/reciprocity is established, the workpaper investment elimination entry is:

(4)	Common Stock—S Company .75($100,000)	75,000
	1/1 Retained Earnings—S Company .75($185,000)	138,750
	Difference Between Cost and Book Value	21,400
	Investment in S Company	235,150
	($212,000 − $37,600 + $60,750)	

The elimination of S Company's equity against the investment account is based on end-of-year equity owned, or 75%. The difference between cost and book value is $21,400, rather than the $26,000 original amount. This results because 20% of the $23,000 difference (or $4,600) on the second stock purchase was sold with the

Cost Method			ILLUSTRATION 8-1			
Sale of Part of Investment			Consolidated Statements Workpaper			
75% Owned Subsidiary			P Company and Subsidiary			
			For Year Ended December 31, 2003			

| | P | S | Eliminations | | Noncontrolling | Consolidated |
Income Statement	*Company*	*Company*	*Dr.*	*Cr.*	*Interest*	*Balances*
Net Income Before Gain on Sale of Investment	120,000	80,000				200,000
			(1) 9,750			
Gain on Sale of Investment	32,400		(2) 6,000			16,650
Net/Combined Income	152,400	80,000				216,650
Subsidiary Income Sold				(2) 6,000		6,000
Noncontrolling Interest in Income .25($80,000)					20,000	(20,000)
Net Income to Retained Earnings	152,400	80,000	15,750	6,000	20,000	202,650
Retained Earnings Statement						
1/1 Retained Earnings						
			(1) 9,750			
P Company	282,000		(3) 60,750			352,500
S Company		185,000	(4) 138,750		42,650	
Net Income from above	152,400	80,000	15,750	6,000	20,000	202,650
Dividends Declared 10/30						
P Company	(40,000)					(40,000)
12/31 Retained Earnings to Balance Sheet	394,400	265,000	154,500	76,500	66,250	515,150
Balance Sheet						
Current Assets	220,000	100,000				320,000
Investment in S Company	174,400		(3) 60,750	(4) 235,150		
Difference Between Cost and Book Value			(4) 21,400	(5) 21,400		
Other Assets	512,600	300,000				812,600
Land	90,000	40,000	(5) 21,400			151,400
Total Assets	997,000	440,000				1,284,000
Liabilities	102,600	75,000				177,600
Common Stock						
P Company	500,000					500,000
S Company		100,000	(4) 75,000		25,000	
Retained Earnings from above	394,400	265,000	154,500	76,500	66,250	515,150
Noncontrolling Interest in Net Assets					91,250	91,250
Total Liabilities and Equity	997,000	440,000	333,050	333,050		1,284,000

Cost

(1) To adjust gain on sale of investment for portion included in income in prior years.
(2) To adjust for current year's income sold to noncontrolling stockholders.
(3) To recognize P Company's share of S Company's undistributed income from date of acquisition to beginning of the current year.
(4) To eliminate investment in S Company.
(5) To allocate the difference between cost and book value.

stock. If the difference is allocated to depreciable assets, the future adjustments to depreciation expense are reduced accordingly. Several items on the workpaper should be specifically noted:

1. The gain on sale of investment recognized for consolidation purposes is $16,650, consisting of the $32,400 recorded gain less the portion of the gain recog-

nized in consolidated income in prior years ($9,750) and the portion of the current year's income to the date of sale associated with the shares sold ($6,000).

2. Noncontrolling interest in combined income is represented by the December 31, 2003, noncontrolling interest percentage times reported subsidiary income (25% × $80,000), or $20,000. Note, however, in Illustration 8-1 that $6,000 of subsidiary income appears in the consolidated income statement columns of the workpaper as "subsidiary income sold." The $6,000 represents the amount that was purchased by the noncontrolling stockholders from the parent. Thus, the noncontrolling interest in combined income reported in the formal consolidated income statement reflects a net amount of $14,000 ($20,000 − $6,000). Note, however, that the full $20,000 is included as a part of the noncontrolling interest on the balance sheet (the $14,000 noncontrolling interest share of combined income plus the $6,000 purchased by the noncontrolling stockholders). That is, the full $20,000 represents an appropriate claim by the noncontrolling stockholders against the consolidated net assets, although $14,000 represents assets earned during the period and $6,000 reflects assets purchased.

3. The controlling and noncontrolling interests in net income may be verified using t-accounts as follows:

Noncontrolling Interest in Income

Internally generated income of S Company	$80,000
Adjustments	—0—
Adjusted income of subsidiary	$80,000
Noncontrolling percentage, First 6 months (10% × $40,000) = 4,000	
Noncontrolling percentage, Second 6 months (25% × $40,000) = 10,000	
Noncontrolling interest in income	$14,000

Controlling Interest in Income

	Internally generated income of P Company, (Includes gain on sale of stock realized for consolidation purposes) $120,000 + $16,650	$136,650
Unrealized gain or profit on intercompany sale —0—	Any needed adjustments (see Chapters 5–7)	—0—
	Percentage of subsidiary adjusted income: Controlling percentage, First 6 months (90% × $40,000) = 36,000	
	Controlling percentage, Second 6 months (75% × $40,000) = 30,000	
	(Percentage)(subsidiary income)	$ 66,000
	Controlling interest in income	$202,650

In subsequent periods, the amount needed to convert to equity/establish reciprocity is the total of 15% of the increase in S Company's retained earnings from January 1, 2000 to January 1, 2002, plus (minus) 75% of the increase (decrease) in S Company's retained earnings thereafter. Thus, the entry needed to establish reciprocity for a workpaper on December 31, 2004, would be:

Investment in S Company	120,750	
1/1 Retained Earnings—P Company		120,750
[15% × ($120,000 − $40,000)] + [75% × ($265,000 −		
$120,000)]		

EQUITY METHOD—PURCHASES AND SALES OF SUBSIDIARY STOCK BY THE PARENT

As stated in the previous section (cost method), sometimes the controlling interest in a subsidiary is acquired through the initial stock purchase; at other times control is not achieved until two or more stock purchases are made. When control is achieved on the first purchase, the date of acquisition is the purchase date. However, when more than one purchase is made before control is obtained, there are actually two or more acquisition dates.

Determination of the date of acquisition is important under purchase accounting because subsidiary retained earnings accumulated before that date constitute a portion of the equity acquired by the parent company, whereas the parent's share of subsidiary retained earnings accumulated after acquisition is properly included in consolidated retained earnings. If two or more purchases are made over a period of time, the retained earnings of the subsidiary at acquisition should be determined on a step-by-step basis. Interpretation No. 2 of *APB Opinion No. 17* suggests that the purchasing company should identify the cost of each investment, the fair value of the underlying assets acquired, and the difference between cost and book value for *each* step purchase.

Recall that under the equity method, the parent company adjusts its investment in subsidiary account for its share of subsidiary income or loss and dividends distributed. Under the complete equity method (as compared to the partial equity method) additional adjustments are made on the books of the parent company to adjust for excess depreciation, amortization, elimination of unrealized intercompany profit, and so forth.

However, under the assumptions presented at the beginning of this chapter (no intercompany sales and the difference between cost and book value attributed to land), the complete and partial equity methods require the same procedures (and, as always, yield the same consolidated results). To illustrate the procedures followed for open-market purchases and sales of subsidiary stock under the equity method, the previous cost method example will be used. For convenience, the facts are repeated here:

1. S. Company had 10,000 shares of $10 par value common stock outstanding during 2000–2003 and retained earnings as follows:

	S Company *Retained Earnings*
January 1, 2000	$ 40,000
January 1, 2001	70,000
January 1, 2002	120,000
January 1, 2003	185,000
December 31, 2003	265,000

2. P Company purchased S Company common stock on the open market as follows:

Date	Shares Acquired	Cost
January 1, 2000	1,500 (15%)	$ 24,000
January 1, 2002	7,500 (75%)	188,000
Total	9,000 (90%)	$212,000

3. Any difference between cost and book value of net assets acquired relates to land.

4. S Company distributed no dividends during the periods under consideration. Since no dividends were declared, the change in retained earnings represents the net income for that year.[3]

5. P Company sold 1,500 shares of S Company stock on July 1, 2003, for $70,000. The shares were identified as 20% (1,500/7,500) of those purchased on January 1, 2002.

As with the cost method, the initial purchase of the 15% interest is recorded at its cost of $24,000 and reported as an investment on P Company's balance sheets on December 31, 2000 and 2001. The second purchase on January 1, 2002, is also recorded in the investment account at its cost of $188,000. Since P Company now has a 90% interest in S Company and intends to apply the equity method, the investment account must be restated to recognize P Company's share (15%) of the increase in S Company's retained earnings from January 1, 2000, to January 1, 2002. In essence, consolidation is being retroactively applied to the time period when the parent owned only 15% of the subsidiary.

Recall that investments of less than 20% are almost always accounted for using the cost (fair value) method on the books of the investor.[4] Therefore, when a firm with a smaller interest (requiring the cost/fair value method) gains a controlling interest and chooses to account for the investment subsequently under the equity method, the previous changes in retained earnings of the investee must be reflected in the investment account. Note that the entry to restate the investment account is a *real entry* made and posted on the books of P Company (not a workpaper entry). The entry on P Company's books is:

P Company's Books

Investment in S Company	12,000	
Retained Earnings [15% × ($120,000 − $40,000)]		12,000

    To restate the investment account from the cost/fair value method to the equity method, because of the increase in percentage ownership (i.e., 15% of the change in retained earnings).

P Company will recognize its share of S Company income for 2002 with the following entry:

P Company's Books

Investment in S Company	58,500	
Equity in Subsidiary Income [90% × ($185,000 − $120,000)]		58,500

---

[3]The impact of deferred taxes is ignored.

[4]Any differences between cost and fair value are assumed to be reflected in a contra or adjunct account Fair Value Adjustment. This account must be adjusted periodically prior to the issuance of financial statements and would be adjusted to zero if it were no longer needed (as under the equity method).

Recall (from item 4) that because there were no dividends declared by S Company, the change in retained earnings equals the amount of net income.

When a sale of subsidiary shares is made during a fiscal period, the parent's share of the subsidiary's income to the date of sale is normally recorded by a book entry if the information is available. Thus, assuming P Company received a six-month interim income statement from S Company reporting $40,000 of net income, the following entry will be made by P Company on June 30, 2003:

P Company's Books		
Investment in S Company	36,000	
Equity in Subsidiary Income (90% × $40,000)		36,000

After this entry, the Investment in S Company account will appear as follows:

Investment in S Company

1/1/00 Purchase (15%)	24,000
1/1/02 Purchase (75%)	188,000
1/1/02 Adjustment	12,000
12/31/02 Subsidiary Income	58,500
6/30/03 Subsidiary Income	36,000
Balance	318,500

To record the sale of the S Company shares on July 1, 2003, P Company will make the following entry:

P Company's Books		
Cash	70,000	
Investment in S Company*		53,350
Gain on Sale of Investment		16,650

Carrying value of the investment sold:

Cost of second purchase (75% interest)	$188,000
2002 subsidiary income (75% × $65,000)	48,570
2003 subsidiary income to date of sale (75% × $40,000)	30,000
Total	266,750
Portion of second purchase sold	20%
Carrying value of investment sold	$ 53,350

The $16,650 difference between selling price and carrying value is appropriately reported as a gain for consolidated purposes and, as always, agrees with the amount reported for consolidated purposes under the cost method (Illustration 8-1). Since the investment account was brought up to date as of the date of sale under the equity method, no workpaper adjustments to the gain are necessary.

After the sale of the 1,500 shares, P Company holds a 75% interest in S Company consisting of the 15% interest acquired in 2000 and the 60% unsold interest acquired in 2002. Thus, for the second six months of 2003 (and for subsequent periods), P Company will recognize 75% of the reported income and dividends received from S Company. The December 31, 2003, book entry by P Company is:

P Company's Books		
Investment in S Company	30,000	
Equity in Subsidiary Income (75% × $40,000)		30,000
To record equity income for the second 6 months of 2003.		

A December 31, 2003, workpaper, using the same basic information as under the cost basis (Illustration 8-1), is presented in Illustration 8-2. Notice, again, that con-

Equity Method			ILLUSTRATION 8–2			
Sale of Part of Investment			Consolidated Statements Workpaper			
75% Owned Subsidiary			P Company and Subsidiary			
			For Year Ended December 31, 2003			

| | P | S | Eliminations | | Noncontrolling | Consolidated |
Income Statement	Company	Company	Dr.	Cr.	Interest	Balances
Net Income Before Gain on Sale and						
Equity in Subsidiary Income	120,000	80,000				200,000
Equity in Subsidiary Income	66,000		(1) 66,000			
Gain on Sale of Investment	16,650					16,650
Net/Combined Income	202,650	80,000				216,650
Subsidiary Income Sold				(1) 6,000		6,000
Noncontrolling Interest in Income					20,000	(20,000)
Net Income to Retained Earnings	202,650	80,000	66,000	6,000	20,000	202,650
Retained Earnings Statement						
1/1 Retained Earnings						
P Company	352,500					352,500
S Company		185,000	(2) 138,750		46,250	
Net Income from above	202,650	80,000	66,000	6,000	20,000	202,650
Dividends Declared 10/30						
P Company	(40,000)					(40,000)
12/31 Retained Earnings to Balance						
Sheet	515,150	265,000	204,750	6,000	66,250	515,150
Balance Sheet						
Current Assets	220,000	100,000				320,000
Investment in S Company	295,150			(1) 60,000		
				(2) 235,150		
Difference Between Cost and Book Value			(2) 21,400	(3) 21,400		
Other Assets	512,600	300,000				812,600
Land	90,000	40,000	(3) 21,400			151,400
Total Assets	1,117,750	440,000				1,284,000
Liabilities	102,600	75,000				177,600
Common Stock						
P Company	500,000					500,000
S Company		100,000	(2) 75,000		25,000	
Retained Earnings from above	515,150	265,000	204,750	6,000	66,250	515,150
Noncontrolling Interest in Net Assets					91,250	91,250
Total Liabilities and Equity	1,117,750	440,000	322,550	322,550		1,284,000

(1) To reverse the effect of subsidiary income for the year.
(2) To eliminate investment in S Company.
(3) To allocate the difference between cost and book value.

solidated net income, consolidated retained earnings, and consolidated balance sheet totals are identical in Illustrations 8-1 and 8-2.

SUBSIDIARY ISSUES STOCK OR ENGAGES IN TREASURY STOCK TRANSACTIONS

A parent company's equity interest in a subsidiary also may change as the result of the issuance of additional shares of stock by the subsidiary, or the purchase by a subsidiary of some of its outstanding shares. The effect of these subsidiary stock transactions on the parent company depends on whether the parent is a party to the transactions, as well as on the price at which the subsidiary shares are sold or treasury stock is purchased.

Issuance of Additional Shares by a Subsidiary

Assume that the parent company already has a controlling interest in a subsidiary, and the subsidiary issues additional shares of its common stock. The newly issued shares may be purchased (1) entirely by the parent company, (2) partly by the parent company and partly by the noncontrolling stockholders, or (3) entirely by the noncontrolling stockholders.

When shares are purchased by the noncontrolling stockholders, the situation is analogous to a sale of shares by P Company. If the shares are purchased by the noncontrolling stockholders for more than book value, the effect is equivalent to a sale of a portion of its interest by P Company at a gain. Conversely, if the shares are purchased by the noncontrolling stockholders for less than book value, the effect is equivalent to a sale of a portion of its interest at a loss. To keep the focus on the relevant issues in the next section as we illustrate these possibilities and to conserve space, we combine the presentation of cost and equity methods. Gains and losses resulting from subsidiary stock issuance transactions that decrease the parent company's percentage of ownership are recorded on the parent's books the same way under both methods. The effects of subsidiary stock issuance transactions that change the parent's percentage of ownership are adjusted to the difference between cost and book value when the investment is eliminated on the consolidated workpaper, as illustrated in the following section. In either case, subsequent recognition of the parent's share of subsidiary income and dividends is based on the new percentage of ownership. Of course, no entries are needed to establish reciprocity/convert to equity when the equity method is being used. Otherwise the entries are the same as those presented for the cost method.

One Hundred Percent of New Shares Purchased by the Parent Company When shares are purchased by the parent company directly from the subsidiary, care must be exercised in the determination of equity acquired. This occurs because the number of subsidiary shares outstanding is increased and the proceeds from the stock issue flow increase the subsidiary's total stockholders' equity. This affects the difference between cost and book value acquired.

If the parent company holds less than a 100% interest and purchases the entire new issue of stock directly from the subsidiary, one of two situations must exist. Either (1) the preemptive right has previously been waived or (2) the noncontrolling stockholders have elected not to exercise their rights. The purchase of the entire new issue by the parent company will increase the parent company's percentage of ownership with an equal reduction in the noncontrolling interest's percentage of ownership. Since a subsidiary's stock transactions affect the balances in the subsidiary's stockholders' equity accounts, a special computational method is needed to determine the change in the parent's share of the subsidiary's equity. The change is determined by comparing the parent's share of the subsidiary's equity immediately before and immediately after the new purchase.

New Shares Issued Above Existing Book Value per Share To illustrate, assume that P Company purchased 14,000 shares (70%) of S Company's $10 par value common stock on January 1, 1993, for $216,000, which included a $20,000 excess of cost over book value; the excess cost was assigned to land. S Company's retained earnings on January 1, 1993, were $50,000. On January 1, 2001, P Company purchased 4,000 additional shares of S Company stock directly from S Company at its current market price of $22 per share ($88,000). This price is **greater** than the existing book value per share of S Company. Noncontrolling stockholders elected not to participate in the new issue. S Company's stockholders equity on January 1, 2001, was:

S Company's Stockholders' Equity and Book Value per Share

	Immediately Before the New Issue	New Issue	Immediately After the New Issue
Common Stock, $10 par value	$200,000	$40,000	$240,000
Other Contributed Capital	30,000	48,000	78,000
Retained Earnings	120,000	—0—	120,000
Total Stockholders' Equity	$350,000	$88,000	$438,000
Common Shares	20,000	4,000	24,000
Book Value per Share	$17.50	$22.00	$18.25

Note that after P Company buys the new shares, the book value per share of S Company goes from $17.50 to $18.25. There are 24,000 shares of S Company stock outstanding after the new issue, 18,000 of which are owned by P Company. Thus, P Company's percentage of ownership has increased to 75% (18,000 shares/24,000 shares). The computation of the book value of the equity interest acquired in the purchase of the new shares is as follows:

Book Value of P Company's Share of S Company's Stockholders' Equity

	Before New Purchase (70%)	After New Purchase (75%)	Book Value of Interest Acquired
Common Stock	(1) $140,000	(4) $180,000	$40,000
Other Contributed Capital	(2) 21,000	(5) 58,500	37,500
Retained Earnings	(3) 84,000	(6) 90,000	6,000
Total	$245,000	$328,500	$83,500
Book Value per Share	$17.5	$18.25	

(1) .7 × $200,000.
(2) .7 × $30,000.
(3) .7 × $120,000.
(4) .75 × $240,000.
(5) .75 × $78,000
(6) .75 × $120,000

The cost of the new shares was $88,000 and the book value of the interest acquired was $83,500, as determined above. This results in a difference between cost and book value of $4,500. The new Computation and Allocation Schedule after the issuance of the new shares is as follows:

Computation and Allocation of Difference Between Cost and Book Value

	First Purchase	Second Purchase	Total
Cost	$216,000	$88,000	$304,000
Equity Acquired:			
Common Stock	(1) 140,000	40,000*	180,000
Other Contributed Capital	(2) 21,000	37,500*	58,500
Retained Earnings	(3) 35,000	6,000*	41,000
Total	196,000	83,500	279,500
Difference Between Cost and Book Value	$ 20,000	$ 4,500	$ 24,500
Adjust land (mark toward market)			(24,500)
Balance			—0—

(1) 70% × $200,000.
(2) 70% × $ 30,000.
(3) 70% × $ 50,000.
*Book Value of Interest Acquired, from Previous Schedule (last column)

It should be noted that the $4,500 excess cost resulted because P Company purchased the additional shares from S Company at a price of $22 per share, which exceeded the $17.50 book value of S Company's shares ($350,000/20,000 shares). The noncontrolling shareholders' book value per share increased from $17.50 to $18.25 or 0.75 per share. Since they own 6,000 shares, the book value of their shares increased by $4,500 (or .75 × 6,000). This difference is allocated following the procedures described in Chapter 5. Here we assume it relates to subsidiary land.

Although the noncontrolling stockholders did not participate in the new issue and their percentage of ownership decreased (30% to 25%), the amount of their total book value interest in S Company's net assets increased by $4,500. It is not a coincidence that the increase in the noncontrolling interest equals the difference between cost and book value in the new purchase. The noncontrolling interest will increase if the cost of the new shares is greater than the book value of the interest acquired. Because the shares were purchased directly from the subsidiary, the $4,500 represents a transfer of interest from the controlling interest to the noncontrolling stockholders. This can be verified as follows:

Noncontrolling Interest in S Company

Before the new issue	.30 × $350,000 = $105,000
After the new issue	.25 × $438,000 = 109,500
Increase in noncontrolling interest	$ 4,500

Essentially, because the controlling stockholders paid more than the existing book value per share, the noncontrolling stockholders' book value must increase.

To record the purchase of the new shares, P Company will make the following entry:

P Company's Books

Investment in S Company	88,000	
Cash		88,000

If a workpaper were prepared immediately after the purchase of the new shares, the workpaper entries to establish reciprocity (convert to equity) and eliminate the investment account would be:

Investment in S Company	49,000	
1/1 Retained Earnings—P Company		49,000
[70% × ($120,000 − $50,000)]		
To establish reciprocity (convert to equity).*		
*Conversion entry not needed if equity method is used.		
Common Stock—S Company .75($240,000)	180,000	
Other Contributed Capital—S Company .75($78,000)	58,500	
Retained Earnings—S Company .75($120,000)	90,000	
Difference Between Cost and Book Value ($20,000 + $4,500)	24,500	
Investment in S Company		353,000
($216,000 + $88,000 + $49,000)		
To eliminate the investment account.		

Because this entry only reflects the change in Retained Earnings—S Company up to the *beginning of the year*, we use the percentage of ownership as of the beginning of the year (70%). In later years, reciprocity is established on the basis of a 70% interest to the date of purchase of the new shares plus a 75% interest thereafter. The elimination of S Company's stockholders' equity, however, is based on the level of ownership held after the purchase of the new shares (75%).

New Shares Issued At or Below the Existing Book Value per Share

In the previous example, the parent paid more than the existing book value per share of S Company. If the new shares are issued at a price *equal* to their book value, there is no difference between cost and book value. For example, if the shares are issued at their book value of $17.50, the computation is as follows:

P Company's Share of S Company's Net Assets

Before the new issue	.75 × $350,000 =	$245,000
After the new issue	.75[$350,000 + (4,000 × $17.50)] =	$315,000
Increase in P Company's share		70,000
Cost of the investment		
(4,000 × $17.50)		70,000
Difference		$—0—

Although the noncontrolling stockholders' percentage of ownership decreases from 30% to 25%, their share of the net assets of S Company remains unchanged, as shown here:

Noncontrolling Interest in S Company

Before the new issue	.30 × $350,000 =	$105,000
After the new issue	.25 × ($350,000 + $70,000) =	$105,000
Change in noncontrolling interest		$—0—

If the new shares are issued at a price *less* than their book value, total noncontrolling book value interest decreases, and the controlling book value interest increases. In this case an excess of book value over cost results (the difference between cost and book value is negative in the Computation and Allocation Schedule for the new purchase). For example, assume the new shares were issued at $14 per share. The excess of book value over cost is computed as follows:

Before the new issue	.70 × $350,000 =	$245,000
After the new issue	.75[$350,000 + (4,000 × $14)] =	$304,500
Increase in P Company's share (book value acquired)		59,500
Cost of the investment (4,000 × $14)		56,000
Excess of book value over cost		$ 3,500

The resulting decrease in the noncontrolling interest is verified as:

Noncontrolling Interest in S Company

Before the new issue	.30 × $350,000 =	$105,000
After the new issue	.25[$350,000 + (4,000 × $14)] =	$101,500
Decrease in noncontrolling interest		$ 3,500

In this case, the journal entry by P Company to record the purchase of the new shares is:

P Company's Books		
Investment in S Company	56,000	
Cash		56,000

In this case, the $3,500 excess of book value over cost is treated as a *reduction* in the difference between cost and book value assigned to land. Thus, the workpaper entries to establish reciprocity and eliminate the investment account in the preparation of a consolidated workpaper immediately after the purchase are:

Investment in S Company	49,000	
1/1 Retained Earnings—P Company		49,000
[70% × ($120,000 − $50,000)]		
To establish reciprocity/convert to equity*		
Common Stock—S Company .75($240,000)	180,000	
Other Contributed Capital—S Company .75($46,000)	34,500	
Retained Earnings—S Company .75($120,000)	90,000	
Difference Between Cost and Book Value		
($20,000 − $3,500)	16,500	
Investment in S Company		321,000
($216,000 + $56,000 + $49,000)		
To eliminate the investment account.		
*Entry not needed if equity method is used.		

As demonstrated in the preceding analyses, a difference between cost and book value results whenever the parent company purchases stock from the subsidiary for more or less than book value per share.

New Shares Purchased Ratably by Parent and Noncontrolling Stockholders In the previous example, noncontrolling stockholders elected not to exercise their right to purchase a ratable number of the new shares. If the noncontrolling stockholders had elected to exercise their rights, the percentage of stock owned by the parent and noncontrolling stockholders after the new issue would be the same as their respective interests prior to the new issue.

Assume, for example, that the shares are issued at $22 each, that P Company is permitted to purchase only its ratable share of the new issue, and that the remaining shares are purchased by the noncontrolling stockholders. Thus, P Company would purchase 2,800 of the 4,000 new shares and retain its 70% (16,800 shares/24,000 shares) interest in S Company. Comparison of cost with the book value of the interest acquired by P Company is as follows:

Cost of investment (2,800 × $22)		$61,600
Book value of equity interest acquired:		
P Company's share of S Company's net assets:		
Before the new purchase .7($350,000)	$245,000	
After the new purchase.7[$350,000 + (4,000 × $22)	306,600	
Increase in P Company's share of S Company		61,600
Difference		$—0—

Note that the book value of the interest acquired is equal to the cost of the shares to P Company; thus, no difference between cost and book value arises. This condition will always result if the shares are purchased ratably by the existing stockholders, regardless of whether the new shares are issued at a price below, equal to, or above their book value.

New Shares Purchased Entirely by Noncontrolling Stockholders Occasionally, in order to obtain an additional capital increment for the consolidated entity or to meet the requirements of employee stock options or stock purchase plans, the subsidiary may issue new shares entirely to noncontrolling stockholders. Since any shares purchased by the parent represent a transfer of funds within the affiliated group, purchases by the parent do not provide any additional capital to the group as a whole. As long as the number of new shares issued is not so large that it reduces the parent's percentage of ownership below that needed for control, new financing can be made available and control retained.

The issuance of all the new shares to noncontrolling stockholders does, of course, reduce the parent's percentage of ownership. Thus, the economic substance of the transaction is a sale of interest by P Company. However, the book value of the parent's interest in the subsidiary may increase, decrease, or remain unchanged depending on the relationship of the issue price to book value per share of stock.

To illustrate, assume the previous example except that the 4,000 new shares were issued entirely to noncontrolling stockholders at the current market price of $22 per share. The new issue results in a decrease in P Company's percentage of ownership from 70% to 58.33% (14,000 shares/24,000 shares). The change in the book value of P Company's interest in S Company is determined as before by an immediately "before" and "after" computation as follows:

P Company's Share of S Company's Net Assets

Before the new issue	70% × $350,000 =	$245,000
After the new issue	58.33% × [$350,000 + (4,000 × $22)] =	255,500
Increase		$ 10,500

Although P Company's ownership interest decreased from 70% to 58.33%, the book value of its interest in S Company after the new issue increased by $10,500. The $10,500 increase in P Company's book value interest is accompanied by a decline in the noncontrolling book value interest relative to the cost of the new shares. The total $88,000 cost of the new shares is allocated between the controlling and non-controlling interests in essence, even though the noncontrolling interest paid the entire amount as follows:

Cost of new shares to noncontrolling interest		
(4,000 × $22)		$88,000
Less equity in net assets acquired:		
Noncontrolling interest's share of net assets:		
Before the purchase .3($350,000)	$105,000	
After the purchase	182,500	
41.667% × ($350,000 + $88,000)		
Increase in noncontrolling interest		77,500
Increase in controlling interest		$10,500

Since the purchase of the shares by the noncontrolling stockholders decreased P Company's ownership percentage, the situation is analogous to a sale of shares by P Company. The transfer of the $10,500 interest in consolidated net assets from the noncontrolling stockholders to the controlling stockholders is recorded on the books of P Company as follows:

P Company's Books		
Investment in S Company	10,500	
Gain from Subsidiary Issuance of Shares		10,500

Because the shares were purchased by the noncontrolling stockholders for more than book value, P Company's percentage interest decreased, and P Company's interest in the consolidated net assets increased, the effect is the equivalent of a sale of a portion of its interest by P Company at a gain.

Note that, in this example, the new shares are purchased by the noncontrolling stockholders at a price in excess of book value, which results in an increase in P Company's share of consolidated net assets. If the new shares are issued at book value, there is no change in P Company's book value interest as shown here:

P Company's Share of S Company's Equity		
Before the new issue	70% × $350,000 =	$245,000
After the new issue	58.33% × [$350,000 + ($17.50 × 4,000)] =	245,000
Change in P Company's interest		$—0—

If the shares are issued below book value, P Company's book value interest decreases and a book entry debiting Loss from Subsidiary Issuance of Shares and crediting Investment in S Company is made. For example, assuming the issue of the entire 4,000 shares to noncontrolling stockholders at $14 per share, the computation and journal entry are:

P Company's Share of S Company's Equity		
Before the new issue	70% × $350,000 =	$245,000
After the new issue	58.33% × [$350,000 + ($14 × 4,000)] =	236,833
Decrease in P Company's interest		$ 8,167

P Company's Books		
Loss from Subsidiary Issuance of Shares	8,167	
Investment in S Company		8,167

SUBSIDIARY TREASURY STOCK TRANSACTIONS AFTER ACQUISITION

The parent company's percentage of ownership and total equity interest in its subsidiary may increase or decrease as a result of its subsidiary's dealings in its own shares. The reissue (sale) of treasury stock by the subsidiary creates no new problems. The accounting is analogous to that previously discussed in relation to the issuance of new shares of subsidiary stock. However, purchases of treasury stock by the subsidiary result in a decrease in total subsidiary stockholders' equity and require some additional discussion.

Although it is possible for a subsidiary to reacquire some of its own shares entirely from noncontrolling stockholders, entirely from the parent company, or in part from both, the latter two situations are relatively rare and, therefore, are not discussed here. Subsidiary treasury stock transactions are usually open-market purchases under which the shares are acquired from noncontrolling stockholders.

The purchase by a subsidiary of some of its shares from the noncontrolling stockholders results in an increase in the parent company's percentage interest in the subsidiary. The parent company's share of the subsidiary's net assets will remain unchanged, decrease, or increase, depending on whether the shares are purchased at a price equal to, below, or above book value.

Increases and decreases in the parent company's interest in the net assets of a subsidiary resulting from purchases of treasury stock by the subsidiary are treated in the same way whether the parent uses the equity or the cost method to account for its investment in the subsidiary. Increases are treated as additions to (and decreases as subtractions from) the difference between cost and book value when the workpaper investment elimination entry is made. The adjusted difference is then allocated following the procedures described in Chapter 5. If the equity method is used, there is, of course, no entry needed to establish reciprocity/convert to equity. Again, to keep the focus on the main issues, we combine our presentation of the equity and cost methods in the following illustrations.

Illustrations of the various possibilities are based on the following case: P Company owns 18,000 shares (75%) of the common stock of S Company on January 1, 2001, when S Company's stockholders' equity consists of the following:

S Company's Stockholders' Equity	
Common Stock, $10 par value	$240,000
Retained Earnings	144,000
Total	$384,000

Book Value per Common Share = $384,000/24,000 shares = $16 per share

The shares were purchased for $255,000 when S Company's stockholders' equity consisted of $240,000 of common stock and $60,000 of retained earnings. Thus, the difference between cost and book value was $30,000 [$255,000 − (75% × $300,000)]. The difference was assigned to undervalued subsidiary land.

On January 1, 2001, S Company purchased 1,500 shares of its common stock from noncontrolling stockholders. Thus, P Company's percentage of ownership increased from 75% to 80% (18,000 shares/22,500 shares). The treatment by P Company under three assumptions as to the purchase price of the treasury stock follows.

Treasury Shares Purchased at Book Value ($16 per Share)

Assuming the 1,500 shares are purchased by S Company at book value of $16 per share, there is no net effect on the dollar amount of P Company's share of S Company's equity. The decrease in P Company's share of S Company's net assets from the purchase of the treasury stock is exactly offset as a result of the increase in P Company's ownership percentage as shown here:

P Company's Share of S Company's Net Assets

Before the treasury stock purchase	.75($384,000) =	$288,000
After the treasury stock purchase	.8[$384,000 − (1,500 × $16)] =	288,000
Change in P Company's interest		$—0—

The workpaper entry needed under the cost method to establish reciprocity/convert to equity and eliminate the investment account for a workpaper prepared on December 31, 2001, is:

Investment in S Company	63,000	
1/1 Retained Earnings—P Company .75($144,000 − $60,000)		63,000

The above entry is not needed, of course, for firms using the equity method. Conversion/reciprocity is established based on the percentage of ownership prior to the treasury stock purchase (75%). Next, the investment account is eliminated as follows:

Common Stock—S Company .8($240,000)	192,000	
1/1 Retained Earnings—S Company .8($144,000)	115,200	
Difference Between Cost and Book Value	30,000	
Treasury Stock .8($240,000)		19,200
Investment in S Company ($255,000 + $63,000)		318,000

In subsequent periods, reciprocity is established on the basis of a 75% interest *to the date of treasury stock purchase* plus an 80% interest thereafter. For example, if S Company earned $50,000 during 2001 and declared no dividends, the amount needed to establish reciprocity for a workpaper on December 31, 2002, is as follows:

To January 1, 2001: .75($144,000 − $60,000)	$ 63,000
From January 1, 2001 to January 1, 2002: .8($194,000 − $144,000)	40,000
Total	$103,000

Treasury Shares Purchased at More or Less Than Book Value

Accounting standards provide that the purchase of treasury stock by a subsidiary for more or less than book value per share should be treated as though the parent company purchased additional shares of the subsidiary because the transaction results in an increase in the parent's percentage interest. If the shares are purchased at more than book value, the decrease in the parent company's interest in the net assets of the subsidiary will result in an increase in the difference between cost and book value when the investment is eliminated in the preparation of consolidated financial statements. Conversely, if the shares are purchased at less than book value, the increase in the parent company's interest will result in a decrease in the difference between cost and book value.

Treasury Shares Purchased for More Than Book Value ($25 per share)

Assume the 1,500 shares are purchased at $25 per share, which is more than its book value of $16 per share. The decrease in P Company's equity interest is computed as follows:

P Company's Share of S Company's Net Assets

Before the treasury stock purchase	.75($384,000) =	$288,000
After the treasury stock purchase	.8[$384,000 − (1,500 × $25)] =	277,200
Decrease in P Company's interest		$ 10,800

The price paid implies an undervaluation of subsidiary net assets, and the decrease in P Company's equity interest is added to the difference between cost and book value in the workpaper investment elimination entry as follows:

Common Stock—S Company .8($240,000)	192,000	
1/1 Retained Earnings—S Company .8($144,000)	115,200	
Difference Between Cost and Book Value	40,800	
($30,000 + $10,800)		
Treasury Stock—S Company .8($37,500)		30,000
Investment in S Company		318,000

The $10,800 increase in the difference between cost and book value is allocated following the procedures for treatment of the difference between cost and book value as described in Chapter 5.

Treasury Shares Purchased at Less Than Book Value ($10 per share)

Assume that the shares are purchased at $10 per share, which is less than its book value ($16 per share). The increase in P Company's equity interest is computed as follows:

P Company's Share of S Company's Net Assets

Before the treasury stock purchase	.75($384,000) =	$288,000
After the treasury stock purchase	.8[$384,000 − (1,500 × $10)] =	295,200
Increase in P Company's interest		$ 7,200

The price paid implies the overvaluation of subsidiary net assets, and the increase in P Company's equity interest is deducted from the original difference between cost and book value in the workpaper investment elimination entry as follows:

Common Stock—S Company	192,000	
1/1 Retained Earnings—S Company	115,200	
Difference Between Cost and Book Value ($30,000 − $7,200)	22,800	
Treasury Stock—S Company .8($15,000)		12,000
Investment in S Company		318,000

The $7,200 decrease in the difference between cost and book value is allocated following the procedures for the treatment of the difference between cost and book value as described in Chapter 5.

Reissuance of Treasury Shares by Subsidiary

As indicated earlier, the subsidiary may reissue some or all of its treasury shares entirely to the parent company, entirely to noncontrolling stockholders, or to both. In all these treasury stock reissuance cases, the accounting is analogous to that previously discussed in relation to the issuance of new shares of subsidiary stock. An immediately before-and-after computation of the parent's share of the net assets of the subsidiary is made to determine the amount of the increase or decrease in the parent company's equity interest in the subsidiary. If the parent company purchases all the treasury stock, its percentage of ownership increases and the purchase is treated as a purchase of additional investment with the appropriate allocation of any difference between cost and book value. If the treasury shares are purchased by noncontrolling stockholders, the parent's percentage of ownership decreases, and any change in the parent's equity interest is recorded as a nonoperating gain or loss.

 SUMMARY

1. *Identify the types of transactions that change the parent company's ownership interest in a subsidiary.* The parent may buy additional shares of the subsidiary from third parties; the parent may sell subsidiary shares to third parties; the subsidiary may issue additional shares, including treasury shares, either to the parent or to others, or both; the subsidiary may buy its own shares either from its parent or from others.

2. *Describe the eliminating entries needed when the parent acquires subsidiary shares through multiple open market purchases.* Multiple purchases necessitate a step-like approach. In the year of the second purchase, the entry to establish reciprocity (convert to equity) is made based on the initial percentage (for firms using the cost method). In subsequent periods this amount must be added into the reciprocity/conversion entry. The entry to eliminate the investment account against the underlying equity accounts of the subsidiary is based on the percentage of equity owned at the balance sheet date, while the credit to the investment account is the sum of the purchase prices paid at various times to acquire that equity plus the reciprocity/conversion entry. Thus the difference between cost and book value reflects the sum of the differences implied by each acquisition (cost minus equity acquired).

3. *Explain how the parent determines the cost basis of subsidiary shares sold subsequent to acquisition.* To determine the cost of the shares sold, the company may use either the specific identification or the FIFO method. The cost of the shares must then be adjusted for the parent's percentage of undistributed earnings since the date of acquisition.

4. *Compute the controlling interest in income after the parent*

sells some shares of the subsidiary company. The controlling interest in income is computed as the internally generated income of the parent (including any gain on sale of stock realized for consolidation purposes) plus or minus the usual adjustments for excess depreciation, and so on, plus the controlling percentage of the subsidiary adjusted income. The controlling percentage of the subsidiary adjusted income is layered in the year of sale so that the portion of the year's income prior to the sale reflects the initial percentage ownership and the portion subsequent to the sale reflects the new lower percentage ownership.

5. *Describe the effect on the eliminating process when the subsidiary issues new shares entirely to the parent, and the parent pays either more or less than the book value of the subsidiary shares.* The number of subsidiary shares outstanding is increased, and the proceeds from the stock issue flow increase the subsidiary's total stockholders' equity. This affects the difference between cost and book value acquired. The change in the parent's share of the subsidiary's equity is determined by comparing the parent's share of the subsidiary's equity immediately before and immediately after the new purchase. The noncontrolling interest will increase if the cost of the new shares is greater than the book value of the interest acquired and decrease if the cost is less than the book value. The change in interests represents a transfer between the controlling interest and the noncontrolling stockholders.

6. *Describe the impact on the parent's investment account when the subsidiary issues new shares and either the new shares are purchased ratably by the parent and noncontrolling shareholders or entirely by the noncontrolling*

shareholders. If the shares are purchased ratably by both, the percentage of stock owned by the parent and noncontrolling stockholders after the new issue would be the same as their respective interests prior to the new issue. If the shares are purchased entirely by the noncontrolling shareholders, the parent's percentage of ownership is reduced. Thus, the economic substance of the transaction is a sale of interest by P Company. However, the book value of the parent's interest in the subsidiary may increase, decrease, or remain unchanged depending on the relationship of the issue price to book value per share of stock. If the price is higher than book value, the parent's interest increases, equivalent to a sale at a gain. If the price is lower than book value, the parent's interest decreases, and a loss is recognized.

7. *Describe the impact on the consolidation process when the subsidiary acquires treasury stock from the noncontrolling shareholders.* Purchases of treasury stock by the subsidiary from the noncontrolling shareholders result in a decrease in total subsidiary stockholders' equity but an increase in the parent company's percentage interest in the subsidiary. The parent company's share of the subsidiary's net assets will remain unchanged, decrease, or increase, depending on whether the shares are purchased at a price equal to, below, or above book value. Conversion/reciprocity in the year of the acquisition is established (for firms using the cost method) based on the percentage of ownership prior to the treasury stock purchase.

QUESTIONS

1. Identify three types of transactions that result in a change in a parent company's ownership interest in its subsidiary.

2. Why is the date of acquisition of subsidiary stock important under the purchase method?

3. When a parent company has obtained control of a subsidiary through several purchases and subsequently sells a portion of its shares in the subsidiary, how is the carrying value of the shares sold determined?

4. A gain or loss on the sale of a portion of its investment by a parent company that records its investment using the cost method during a fiscal period consists of three elements. What are they?

5. ABC Corporation purchased 10,000 shares (80%) of EZ Company at $30 per share and sold them several years later for $35 per share. The consolidated income statement reports a loss on the sale of this investment. Explain.

6. Explain how a parent company that owns less than 100% of a subsidiary can purchase an entire new issue of common stock directly from the subsidiary.

7. When a subsidiary issues additional shares of stock to noncontrolling stockholders and such issuance results in an increase in the book value of the parent's share of the subsidiary's equity, what justification exists for treating this increase as a gain?

8. P Company holds an 80% interest in S Company. Determine the effect (that is, increase, decrease, no change, not determinable) on both the total book value of the noncontrolling interest and the noncontrolling interest's percentage of ownership in the net assets of S Company for each of the following situations:

A. P Company acquires additional shares directly from S Company at a price equal to the book value per share of the S Company stock immediately prior to the issuance.

B. S Company acquires its own shares on the open market. The cost of these shares is less than their book value.

C. Assume the same situation as in (B) except that the cost of the shares is greater than their book value.

D. P Company and a noncontrolling stockholder each acquire 100 shares directly from S Company at a price below the book value per share.

EXERCISES

EXERCISES 8-1 Multiple Stock Purchases—Journal Entries

Peck Company purchased Sanno Company common stock in a series of open-market cash purchases from 2000 through 2002 as follows:

Date	Shares Acquired	Cost
January 1, 2000	1,800	$ 46,000
January 1, 2001	4,500	95,000
January 1, 2002	9,900	262,000

Sanno Company had 18,000 shares of $20 par value common stock outstanding during the entire period. Retained earnings balances for Sanno Company on relevant dates were

January 1, 2000	$ 20,000
January 1, 2001	(30,000)
January 1, 2002	85,000
December 31, 2002	170,000

Dividends in the amount of $50,000 were distributed by Sanno Company only in 2002. Any difference between cost and book value is assigned to subsidiary land. Peck Company uses the cost method to account for its investment in Sanno Company.

Required:

A. Prepare the journal entries that Peck Company would record on its books during 2002 to account for its investment in Sanno Company.

B. Prepare the workpaper eliminating entries necessary to prepare a consolidated statements workpaper on December 31, 2002.

EXERCISE 8-2 **Parent Company Entries—Multiple Stock Purchase, Cost Method**

Papke Company acquired 85% of the common stock of Serbin Company in two separate cash transactions. The first purchase of 72,000 shares (60%) on January 1, 2001, cost $490,000. The second purchase, one year later, of 30,000 shares (25%) cost $220,000. Serbin Company's stockholders' equity was as follows:

	December 31 2001	December 31 2002
Common Stock, $5 par	$600,000	$600,000
Retained Earnings, 1/1	175,000	201,000
Net Income	46,000	60,000
Dividends Declared, 9/30	(20,000)	(25,000)
Retained Earnings, 12/31	201,000	236,000
Total Stockholders' Equity, 12/31	$801,000	$836,000

On April 1, 2002, after a significant rise in the market price of Serbin Company's stock, Papke Company sold 21,600 of its Serbin Company shares for $260,000. Serbin Company notified Papke Company that its net income for the first three months was $15,000. The shares sold were identified as those obtained in the first purchase. Any difference between cost and book value relates to subsidiary land. Papke uses the cost method to account for its investment in Serbin Company.

Required:

Prepare the journal entries Papke Company would record on its books during 2002 to account for its investment in Serbin Company.

EXERCISE 8-3 **Workpaper Entries—Multiple Stock Purchases**

Use the data provided in Exercise 8-2.

Required:

A. Prepare the workpaper eliminating entries needed for a consolidated statements workpaper on December 31, 2002.

B. Determine the amount of noncontrolling interest that would be reported on the consolidated balance sheet on December 31, 2002.

EXERCISE 8-4 **Parent Company Entries—Multiple Stock Purchases, Equity Method**
Use the data from Exercise 8-1, but assume use of either the complete or the partial equity method rather than the cost method.

Required:
A. Prepare the journal entries Peck Company will make on its books during 2001 and 2002 to account for its investment in Sanno Company.
B. Prepare workpaper eliminating entries necessary to prepare a consolidated statements workpaper on December 31, 2002.

EXERCISE 8-5 **Parent Company and Workpaper Entries—Equity Method**
Use the data presented in Exercise 8-2, but assume use of the complete or the partial equity method rather than the cost method.

Required:
A. Prepare the journal entries Papke Company will make on its books during 2001 and 2002 to account for its investment in Serbin Company.
B. Prepare the workpaper eliminating entries needed for a consolidated statements workpaper on December 31, 2002.

EXERCISE 8-6 **Parent Company and Workpaper Entries—New Shares Issued by Subsidiary**
On January 1, 2002, Pace Company purchased 250,000 shares of common stock directly from its subsidiary, Sime Company, for $1.50 per share. Noncontrolling stockholders elected not to participate in the new issue.

Pace Company acquired its initial 92.5% interest in Sime Company by purchasing on the open market 462,500 shares of Sime's common stock for $578,125 on January 1, 1998. Sime Company's stockholders' equity just before each of the two purchases was as follows:

	December 31 1997	December 31 2001
Common Stock $1 par	$500,000	$500,000
Other Contributed Capital	40,000	40,000
Retained Earnings	60,000	150,000
Total	$600,000	$690,000

During 2002 Sine Company reported $90,000 net income and declared a dividend in the amount of $30,000. Any difference between cost and book value relates to subsidiary land. Pace uses the cost method to account for its investment.

Required:
A. Prepare the journal entry on Pace Company's books to record the purchase of the additional shares on January 1, 2002.
B. Prepare the eliminating entries needed for the preparation of a consolidated statements workpaper on December 31, 2002.

EXERCISE 8-7 **Parent Company and Workpaper Entries—New Shares Issued by Subsidiary**
Use the same data provided in Exercise 8-6, with the exception that Pace Company purchased the additional shares from Sime Company on January 1, 2002, at a price of $1.30 per share rather than $1.50.

Required:

A. Prepare the journal entry on Pace Company's books to record the purchase of the additional shares on January 1, 2002.

B. Prepare the eliminating entries needed for the preparation of a consolidated statements workpaper on December 31, 2002.

EXERCISE 8-8 **Parent Company and Workpaper Entries—New Shares Issued by Subsidiary**
Padilla Company acquired 80% of the outstanding common stock of Skon Company on January 1, 2000, for $132,000. At the date of purchase, Skon Company had a balance in its $2 par value common stock account of $120,000 and retained earnings of $30,000.

On January 1, 2002, Skon Company issued 15,000 shares of its previously unissued stock to noncontrolling stockholders for $3.00 per share. On this date, Skon Company had a retained earnings balance of $50,500. The difference between cost and book value relates to subsidiary land. No dividends were paid in 2002.

Skon Company reported income of $10,000 in 2002.

Required:

A. Prepare the journal entry on Padilla's books to record the effect of the issuance assuming
   (1) Cost Method
   (2) Complete or Partial Equity Method

B. Prepare the eliminating entries needed for the preparation of a consolidated statements workpaper on December 31, 2002 assuming
   (1) Cost Method
   (2) Complete or Partial Equity Method

EXERCISE 8-9 **Treasury Stock Purchases by Subsidiary**
Pitt Company purchased 112,500 of the outstanding common shares of Simik Company on January 1, 1999, for $326,000 when Simik Company's stockholders' equity consisted of the following:

Common Stock $2 par value	$300,000
Retained Earnings	84,000
Total	$384,000

On January 1, 2002 Simik Company purchased 25,000 of its common shares from noncontrolling stockholders for $80,000. The shares will be held as treasury stock. Simik uses the cost method to account for treasury stock. Stockholders' equity for Pitt and Simik companies on the date of treasury stock purchase was:

	Pitt	Simik
Common Stock	$500,000	$300,000
Retained Earnings	230,000	60,000
Total	$730,000	$360,000

No dividends were declared in 2002. The difference between cost and book value relates to land.

Simik Company reported a loss of $10,000 in 2002.

Required:

A. Prepare the workpaper eliminating entries needed for the preparation of a consolidated statements workpaper on December 31, 2002 assuming the cost method is used.

B. Prepare the workpaper eliminating entries on the consolidated workpaper on December 31, 2002 assuming either the complete or partial equity method is used.

PROBLEMS

PROBLEM 8-1 **Multiple Stock Purchases**

Sarko Company had 300,000 shares of $10 par value common stock outstanding at all times, and retained earnings balances as indicated here:

January 1, 2001	$260,000
January 1, 2002	540,000
January 1, 2003	630,000
January 1, 2004	820,000

Pelzer Company acquired Sarko Company stock through open-market purchases as follows:

Date	Shares	Cost
1/1/01	30,000	$ 365,000
1/1/02	75,000	960,000
1/1/03	135,000	1,860,000

Sarko Company declared no dividends during this period. The fair values of Sarko Company's assets and liabilities were approximately equal to their book values throughout this period (2001 through 2003). Pelzer Company's policy is to amortize goodwill over an estimated economic life of 10 years from the date of each stock purchase. Pelzer Company uses the cost method.

Required:

A. Prepare a schedule to compare investment cost with the book value of equity acquired for each stock purchase.

B. Prepare elimination entries for the preparation of a consolidated statements workpaper on December 31, 2003.

PROBLEM 8-2 **Worksheet, Multiple Stock Purchases, Cost Method**

Trial balances for Phan Company and its subsidiary Sato Company on December 31, 2001, are as follows:

	Phan	Sato
Current Assets	$ 191,500	$ 138,000
Investment in Sato Company	600,500	
Other Assets	920,000	672,000
Dividends Declared	150,000	70,000
Cost of Goods Sold	1,100,000	325,000
Other Expenses	350,000	125,000
	$3,312,000	$1,330,000
Liabilities	$ 168,000	$ 80,000
Capital Stock, $10 par	700,000	400,000
1/1 Retained Earnings	581,000	250,000
Sales	1,800,000	600,000
Dividend Income	63,000	
	$3,312,000	$1,330,000

Phan Company acquired its investment in Sato Company through open-market purchases of stock as follows:

Date	Shares Purchased	Cost	Sato Company Retained Earnings Balance
1/1/99	9,000	$110,500	$ 46,000
1/1/00	12,500	210,000	165,000
1/1/01	14,500	280,000	250,000
Total	36,000	$600,500	

Any difference between cost and book value of the interest acquired relates to Sato Company land, which is included in Other Assets.

Sato Company issued 40,000 shares of stock on July 1, 1996, its date of incorporation. No other capital stock transactions were undertaken by Sato Company after that time.

No intercompany transactions had occurred between Phan Company and Sato Company before 2001. During 2001, however, Phan Company made sales of merchandise to Sato Company in the amount of $150,000. Phan Company sells merchandise to Sato Company at a markup of 25% above cost. One-fourth of the goods purchased from Phan were still in Sato's inventory on December 31, 2001. At the end of the year, Phan owed Sato $22,000 for goods purchased during the year.

Required:

Prepare a consolidated financial statements workpaper for Phan Company and its subsidiary Sato Company on December 31, 2001.

PROBLEM 8-3 **Workpaper—Multiple Stock Purchases, Cost Method**

The accounts of Pyle Company and its subsidiary, Stern Company, are summarized below as of December 31, 2001:

Debits	Pyle	Stern
Current Assets	$ 600,000	$ 320,000
Investment in Stern Company	480,000	
Other Assets	1,180,000	668,000
Dividends Declared, 11/1	80,000	60,000
	$2,340,000	$1,048,000

Credits	Pyle	Stern
Liabilities	$ 190,000	$ 90,000
Common Stock, $5 par	500,000	300,000
Other Contributed Capital	160,000	180,000
1/1 Retained Earnings	1,200,000	292,000
Net Income	290,000	186,000
	$2,340,000	$1,048,000

Pyle Company made the following open-market purchase and sale of Stern Company common stock: January 2, 1999, purchased 51,000 shares, cost $510,000; April 1, 2001, sold 3,000 shares, proceeds, $100,000.

The book value of Stern Company's net assets on January 2, 1999, $600,000, approximated the fair value of those net assets. Subsequent changes in book value of the net assets are entirely attributable to earnings of Stern Company. Stern Company earns its income evenly throughout the year.

Required:

Prepare a consolidated financial statements workpaper as of December 31, 2001. Begin the income statement section of the workpaper with "Net Income Before Dividend Income and

Gain on Sale of Investment," which is $172,000 and $186,000 for Pyle Company and Stern Company, respectively.

PROBLEM 8-4 **Workpaper—Multiple Stock Purchases, Cost Method**
Trial balances for Porter Company and its subsidiary, Spitz Company, as of December 31, 2001, follow:

Debits	Porter	Spitz
Cash	$ 90,000	$ 40,000
Accounts Receivable (net)	62,000	38,000
Inventory	106,000	64,000
Investment in Spitz Company	121,500	
Plant Assets	320,000	149,000
Land	69,000	46,000
Dividends Declared, 10/1	50,000	30,000
Total	$818,500	$367,000

Credits		
Liabilities	$102,000	$ 61,000
Common Stock, $2 per value	250,000	100,000
Other Contributed Capital	158,000	20,000
1/1 Retained Earnings	206,500	126,000
Income Summary	102,000	60,000
Total	$818,500	$367,000

Porter Company made the following open-market purchase and sale of Spitz Company common stock: January 1, 1997, purchased 45,000 shares for $135,000; May 1, 2001, sold 4,500 shares for $28,000.

The book value of Spitz Company's net assets on January 1, 1997, was $140,000; the excess of cost over net assets acquired relates to land. Subsequent changes in the book value of Spitz Company's net assets are entirely attributable to earnings retained in the business. Spitz Company earns its income evenly throughout the year. Porter Company uses the cost method to account for its investment.

Required:
Prepare a consolidated financial statements workpaper as of December 31, 2001. Begin the income statement section of the workpaper with "Net Income Before Dividend Income and Gain on Sale of Investment," which is $63,200 for Porter Company and $60,000 for Spitz Company.

PROBLEM 8-5 **Workpaper—Multiple Stock Purchases, Equity Method**
(Note that this is the same problem as Problem 8-3, but assuming use of the complete or the partial equity method.)

The accounts of Pyle Company and its subsidiary, Stern Company, are summarized below as of December 31, 2001:

Debits	Pyle	Stern
Current Assets	$ 600,000	$ 320,000
Investment in Stern Company	718,400	
Other Assets	1,180,000	668,000
Dividends Declared, 11/1	80,000	60,000
Total	$2,578,400	$1,048,000

Credits	Pyle	Stern
Liabilities	$ 190,000	90,000
Common Stock, $5 par value	500,000	300,000
Other Contributed Capital	160,000	180,000
1/1 Retained Earnings	1,346,200	292,000
Net Income	382,200	186,000
Total	$2,578,400	$1,048,000

Pyle Company made the following open-market purchase and sale of Stern Company common stock: January 2, 1999, purchased 51,000 shares, cost $510,000; April 1, 2001, sold 3,000 shares, proceeds, $100,000.

The book value of Stern Company's net assets on January 2, 1999, $600,000, approximated the fair value of those net assets. Subsequent changes in book value of the net assets are attributable to earnings of Stern Company. Stern Company earns its income evenly throughout the year.

Required:
Prepare a consolidated financial statements workpaper as of December 31, 2001. Begin the income statement section of the workpaper with "Income Before Equity in Subsidiary Income and Gain on Sale of Investment," which is $172,000 and $186,000 for Pyle Company and Stern Company, respectively.

PROBLEM 8-6 **Workpaper—Multiple Stock Purchases, Equity Method**
(Note that this is the same problem as Problem 8-4, but assuming use of the complete or the partial equity method.)

Trial balances for Porter Company and its subsidiary, Spitz Company, as of December 31, 2001, follow:

Debits	Porter	Spitz
Cash	$ 90,000	$ 40,000
Accounts Receivable (net)	62,000	38,000
Inventory	106,000	64,000
Investment in Spitz Company	231,660	
Plant Assets	320,000	149,000
Land	69,000	46,000
Dividends Declared, 10/1	50,000	30,000
Total	$928,660	$367,000

Credits	Porter	Spitz
Liabilities	$102,000	$ 61,000
Common Stock, $2 par value	250,000	100,000
Other Contributed Capital	158,000	20,000
1/1 Retained Earnings	301,900	126,000
Income Summary	116,760	60,000
Total	$928,660	$367,000

Porter Company made the following open-market purchase and sale of Spitz Company common stock: January 1, 1997, purchased 45,000 shares for $135,000; May 1, 2001, sold 4,500 shares for $28,000.

The book value of Spitz Company's net assets on January 1, 1997, was $140,000; the excess of cost over net assets acquired relates to land. Subsequent changes in the book value of Spitz

Company's net assets are entirely attributable to earnings retained in the business. Spitz Company earns its income evenly throughout the year.

Required:

Prepare a consolidated financial statements workpaper as of December 31, 2001. Begin the income statement section of the workpaper with "Net Income Before Equity in Subsidiary Income and Gain on Sale of Investment," which is $63,200 for Porter Company and $60,000 for Spitz Company.

PROBLEM 8-7 Multiple Stock Purchases

On January 1, 2001, Plum Company made an open-market purchase of 30,000 shares of Spivey Company common stock for $122,000. At that time, Spivey Company had common stock ($2 par) of $600,000 and retained earnings of $240,000. On July 1, 2001, an additional 210,000 shares were purchased on the open market by Plum Company at a cost of $790,000. On November 1, 2001, 3,000 of the shares purchased on January 1, 2001, were sold on the open market for $21,000.

During 2001, Plum Company earned $22,000 (excluding any gain or loss on the sale of the shares). Plum Company received income statements from Spivey Company reporting the following results.

January 1, 2001 to June 30, 2001	$ 60,000
January 1, 2001 to October 31, 2001	96,000
For the year ended December 31, 2001	130,000

Neither company declared dividends during the year. Plum Company's retained earnings were $460,000 on January 1, 2001.

Required:

A. Prepare the book entries Plum Company would make during 2001 to account for its investment in Spivey Company, assuming
   (1) The use of the cost method.
   (2) The use of either the complete or the partial equity method.

B. Prepare in general journal form the eliminating entries for a consolidated statements workpaper on December 31, 2001, assuming
   (1) The use of the cost method.
   (2) The use of either the complete or the partial equity method.

C. Compute consolidated net income for 2001.

PROBLEM 8-8 New Shares Purchased by Parent

Pryor Company acquired 51,000 shares of Spero Company's common stock on January 1, 2000, for $400,000 when Spero Company had common stock ($5 par) of $300,000 and retained earnings of $200,000.

On January 1, 2002, Spero Company issued 7,500 additional shares of its common stock for $8.50 per share. The new shares were purchased entirely by Pryor Company. Spero Company's retained earnings had increased to $360,000 by that date.

During 2002 Spero Company declared dividends of $40,000 and reported net income at year-end of $90,000. Pryor Company uses the cost method.

Required:

A. Prepare the journal entry on Pryor's books to record the purchase of the new shares.

B. Prepare in general journal form the workpaper entries needed for the preparation of a consolidated statements workpaper on December 31, 2002.

PROBLEM 8-9 **New Subsidiary Shares Issued to Outsider**

On January 1, 2000, Purdy Company acquired 84% of the capital stock of Sally Company for $840,000. On that date, Sally Company's stockholders' equity was:

Capital Stock, $20 par	$600,000
Other Contributed Capital	200,000
Retained Earnings	160,000
Total	$960,000

The difference between cost and book value relates to land owned by Sally Company.

On January 2, 2002, Sally Company issued 6,000 shares of its authorized capital stock, with a market value of $55 per share, to Marcy Smith in exchange for a patent. Sally Company's retained earnings balance on this date was $400,000; capital stock and other contributed capital balances had not changed during 2000 and 2001.

Required:

A. Prepare (1) the entry on Purdy's books to record the effect of the issuance, and (2) the elimination entries for the preparation of a consolidated balance sheet workpaper immediately after the new issue of shares assuming use of the cost method.

B. Assuming that the market value of the new shares issued was $34 per share, repeat requirement A above.

PROBLEM 8-10 **Treasury Stock—Equity Method**

Plat Company purchased on the open market 33,750 shares of the capital stock of Sova Company for $300,000 on January 2, 1999, when Sova Company had the following stockholder's equity:

Capital Stock, $5 par value	$225,000
Other Contributed Capial	85,000
Retained Earnings	40,000
Total	$350,000

The difference between cost and book value relates to Sova Company land.

On January 1, 2002, Sova Company purchased 7,500 of its own shares from a noncontrolling stockholder for cash of $95,000. The shares are to be held as treasury stock. Sova Company's retained earnings had increased to $100,000 by January 1, 2002; capital stock and other contributed capital balances had not changed since January 2, 1999. Sova Company uses the cost method to account for its treasury shares. Plat Company uses the equity method to account for its investment in Sova Company.

Required:

Prepare all determinable workpaper entries for the preparation of a consolidated statements workpaper on December 31, 2002.

PROBLEMS 8-11 **Open Market Purchases and Sales of Stock—Cost Method**

On January 2, 1996, Pullen Company purchased, on the open market, 135,000 shares of Souza Company common stock for $665,000. At that time, Souza Company had common stock ($2 par value) of $300,000 and retained earnings of $400,000. On May 1, 2001, Pullen

Company sold 13,500 of its Souza Company shares on the open market for $91,000. Changes in Souza Company retained earnings during 2001 follow:

Retained Earnings, 1/1/01	$500,000
Net Income for 2001 (earned evenly throughout the year)	270,000
Dividends Declared on 11/1/01 and paid on 12/16/01	(70,000)
Retained Earnings, 12/31/01	$700,000

Pullen Company, which uses the cost method to record its investment in Souza Company, reported net income for 2001 amounting to $352,500. Any difference between cost and book value relates to subsidiary land.

Required:

A. Prepare the book entries Pullen Company will make during 2001 to account for its investment in Souza Company.

B. Prepare, in general journal form, the eliminating entries needed to prepare a consolidated statements workpaper on December 31, 2001.

C. Prepare a schedule to calculate consolidated net income for 2001.

D. Prepare the workpaper entry to establish reciprocity for the 2002 consolidated statements workpaper.

9

INDIRECT OWNERSHIP AND RECIPROCAL STOCKHOLDINGS

LEARNING OBJECTIVES

1. Explain the term "indirect ownership."

2. Distinguish reciprocal stockholdings from indirect ownership.

3. Compute the controlling interest in combined income when there is an indirect ownership interest.

4. Describe the effect on the elimination process when the parent acquires a controlling interest in a subsidiary that already owns a controlling interest in another subsidiary.

5. Explain the term "connecting affiliates."

6. Compare the two general approaches for handling the effects of reciprocal stockholdings.

7. Describe the procedures used to record reciprocal holdings using the treasury stock method.

8. Explain why consolidated net income does not equal the parent's reported income under the complete equity method when the treasury stock method is used for reciprocal holdings, and how this affects the elimination process.

"AT&T Corp. is considering selling its Internet-access business to At Home Corp. . . . But people familiar with the negotiations cautioned that any deal was contingent on a much larger deal that is pending for AT&T, its $40.9 billion acquisition of cable giant Tele-Communications Inc. (TCI). When it acquires TCI, AT&T will assume TCI's 58% share in voting stock of At Home."[1]

In preceding chapters, we have dealt only with situations in which one company, the parent company, had a direct controlling interest in another company, the subsidiary. At times a parent may have an interest in a subsidiary that has an interest in a subsidiary of its own. For example, P Company may own 90% of S Company, which, in turn, owns 80% of R Company. Thus, P Company has a 90% direct interest

---

[1] *WSJ*, "AT&T May Sell Internet-Access Lines, Including WorldNet to At Home Corp.," by Kara Swisher and Rebecca Blumenstein, 1/22/99, p. A3.

in S Company and a 72% (90% × 80%) indirect interest in R Company. Consequently, consolidated net income should consist of P Company's income from independent operations plus 90% and 72% of S Company's and R Company's income from independent operations, respectively.

As another example, P Company may own 90% of S Company and 80% of R Company, and S Company may own a portion, say 10%, of R Company. Thus, P Company owns a direct interest in S Company of 90% and a combined direct and indirect interest in R Company of 89% [80% + (90% × 10%)]. With relationships of this type, it is often helpful to prepare an affiliation diagram identifying ownership relationships, with the direction of the arrow indicating the direction of ownership. The two situations described above may be diagrammed as follows:

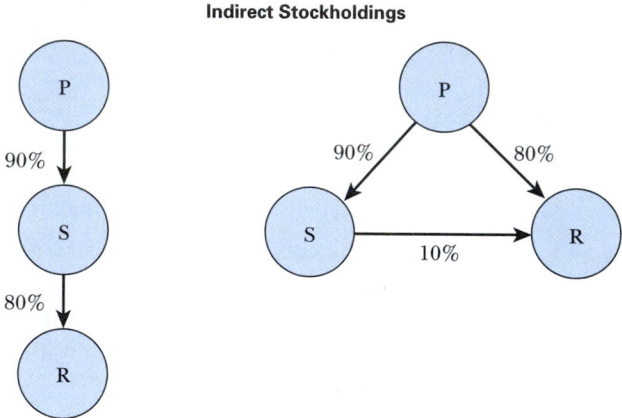

Occasionally two or more affiliates may have ownership interests in each other. For example, P Company may own 90% of S Company, which, in turn, owns 10% of P Company. Or P Company may own 90% of S Company, which owns 80% of R Company, which, in turn, owns 10% of S Company. Relationships of this type are generally termed *reciprocal stockholdings*. They may be diagrammed as follows:

Problems in preparing consolidated financial statements where there are indirect or reciprocal stockholdings are discussed in this chapter. Many indirect and reciprocal possibilities exist, and no attempt will be made to discuss them all. However, sufficient illustrations are presented to give the reader a basic understanding of the principles involved.

In an effort to expand its property-casualty business to the Western half of the United States, Nationwide Mutual Insurance Co. launched an unsolicited $1.44 billion tender offer for a Des Moines, Iowa, car and home insurer: Allied Group Inc. Nationwide also proposed a merger with Allied Mutual Insurance Co., the former parent of the larger, publicly traded Allied Group. Although Allied Mutual spun off Allied Group in a 1985 initial public offering, the two still share much of the same top management and Allied Mutual still holds a voting stake in the publicly held Allied Group.[2]

INDIRECT OWNERSHIP—COST METHOD

The preparation of consolidated financial statements for a group of affiliates where there is some type of indirect ownership involves two primary determinations—earnings and total stockholders' equity. After the investment and retained earnings accounts are properly adjusted to establish reciprocity, the consolidation procedures are essentially the same for indirect ownership as they are for direct ownership situations.

Three illustrations of indirect ownership affiliations are presented, with appropriate affiliation diagrams. Since the date of acquisition of individual investments is an important consideration, the diagrams indicate both the percentage of ownership and the date of acquisition. Illustrations are based on the following investment cost and stockholders' equity information:

	P Company	S Company
Cost of:		
P's investment in S Company (90%)	$295,000	
S's investment in R Company (80%)		$145,000

	P Company	S Company	R Company
Stockholders' equity:			
Common Stock	$500,000	$200,000	$100,000
Retained Earnings, 1/1/00	230,000	70,000	50,000
2000 Reported Income	100,000	50,000	20,000
2000 Dividends Declared	(30,000)	(20,000)	(10,000)
Retained Earnings, 12/31/00	300,000	100,000	60,000
2001 Reported Income	110,000	50,000	30,000
2001 Dividends Declared	(30,000)	(20,000)	(10,000)
Retained Earnings, 12/31/01	380,000	130,000	80,000
Stockholders' Equity, 12/31/01	$880,000	$330,000	$180,000

P Company's investment is acquired on 1/1/2000, while S Company's investment is acquired on 1/1/2001. The difference between cost and book value (computed

[2] *WSJ,* "Nationwide Makes an Unsolicited Offer Totaling $1.44 Billion for Allied Group," by Deborah Lohse, 5/19/98, p. A4.

below) relates to subsidiary land. The companies use the *cost method* to record their investments (the equity method is illustrated later in the chapter).

	P's Investment in S Company Acquired 1/1/00	S's Investment in R Company Acquired 1/1/01
Cost of Investment	$295,000	$145,000
Book Value of Net Assets Acquired (common stock and retained earnings):		
.9($200,000 + $70,000) on 1/1/2000	243,000	
.8($100,000 + $60,000) on 1/1/2001		128,000
Difference Between Cost and Book Value	$ 52,000	$ 17,000
Allocated to land	52,000	17,000
Balance	—0—	—0—

P Company's Interest in S Company Is Acquired Prior to S Company's Interest in R Company—Cost Method

Assume first that P Company purchased a 90% interest in S Company on January 1, 2000, and that S Company purchased an 80% interest in R Company on January 1, 2001. (This type of affiliation is often referred to as a *father–son–grandson* affiliation.) The appropriate diagram is:

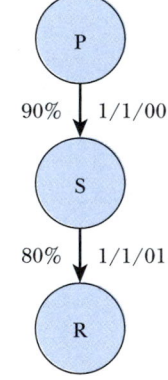

Father–Son–Grandson Affiliation

Notice that P Company has a 90% direct interest in S Company and a 72% (90% × 80%) indirect interest in R Company. Noncontrolling stockholders therefore have a 10% direct interest in S Company and a 28% [20% + (10% × 80%)] combined direct and indirect interest in R Company.

In accounting for their investments during 2001, S Company and P Company made the following book entries (assuming both companies use the *cost method* to account for their investment in subsidiaries):

S Company's Books		
Cash	8,000	
Dividend Income (80% × $10,000)		8,000

Thus, S Company's income from independent operations for 2001 is $42,000 ($50,000 − $8,000).

P Company's Books		
Cash	18,000	
Dividend Income (90% × $20,000)		18,000

Thus, P Company's income from independent operations for 2001 is $92,000 ($110,000 − $18,000).

Consolidated net income for 2001 is $151,400, which might be computed in *one of several ways* as follows:

1. P Company's share of its income from the independent operations of its subsidiaries is added to P Company's income from its own independent operations:

	P Company	S Company	R Company
Reported income	$110,000	$50,000	$30,000
Divided income (from affiliates)	18,000	8,000	
Income from independent operations	92,000	42,000	30,000
Percentage owned by P Company	100%	90%	72%
	92,000	37,800	21,600
Consolidated net income (or controlling interest in combined income)		$151,400	

2. Alternatively, P Company's share of the undistributed income of its subsidiaries is added to P Company's reported income:

	S Company	R Company
Reported income	$50,000	$30,000
Dividends declared	20,000	10,000
Undistributed income	30,000	20,000
Percentaged owned by P Company	90%	72%
	27,000	14,400
Undistributed income of affiliates accruing to P Company	41,400	
P Company's reported income	110,000	
Consolidated net income (or controlling interest in combined income)	$151,400	

3. Still another means of calculating the controlling interest in combined income (consolidated income) is to deduct the noncontrolling stockholders' interest in income from the combined income from independent operations of all affiliates:

Combined income from independent operations of all companies ($92,000 + $42,000 + $30,000)	$164,000
Less noncontrolling interest in the independent income of:	
S Company (10% × $42,000)	(4,200)
R Company (28% × $30,000)	(8,400)
Consolidated net income	$151,400

A ***partial*** workpaper for the preparation of consolidated financial statements on December 31, 2001, is presented in Illustration 9-1. Recall that this is the second year that P Company owns an investment in S Company, but this is the first year that S Company owns an investment in R Company. The remainder of the work-paper would be completed in the same manner as presented in previous chapters. Workpaper eliminating entries in general journal form are:

(1)	Investment in S Company	27,000	
	1/1 Retained Earnings—P Company		27,000
	To establish reciprocity (convert to equity) (change in retained earnings of S from 1/1/00 to 1/1/01 (90% × ($100,000 − $70,000))).		
(2)	Dividend Income	26,000	
	Dividends Declared—S Company		18,000
	Dividends Declared—R Company		8,000
	To eliminate intercompany dividends.		
(3)	Common Stock—R Company .8($100,000)	80,000	
	1/1 Retained Earnings—R Company .8($60,000)	48,000	
	Difference Between Cost and Book Value (Land)	17,000	
	Investment in R Company		145,000
	To eliminate S Company's investment in R Company.		
(4)	Common Stock—S Company .9($200,000)	180,000	
	1/1 Retained Earnings—S Company .9($100,000)	90,000	
	Difference Between Cost and Book Value (Land)	52,000	
	Investment in S Company ($295,000 + $27,000)		322,000
	To eliminate P Company's investment in S Company.		

In the entries above, there was no need to establish reciprocity for S Company's investment in R because S did not acquire that investment in the current year. In subsequent years, reciprocity must be established for *each* investment if the parent uses the cost method to account for its investments in subsidiaries. In doing so, it is important to recognize that establishing reciprocity should proceed "up the ladder"; that is, reciprocity should be established for P Company's investment in S Company after S Company has recognized in its beginning-of-the-year retained earnings its (S Company's) share of the change in the retained earnings of R Company. For example, in the preparation of a consolidated statements workpaper on December 31, 2002 (i.e., the second year that S owns an investment in R Company), the following reciprocity entry (equity conversion) would be made for S Company's investment in R Company:

Investment in R Company	16,000	
1/1 Retained Earnings—S Company		16,000
To establish reciprocity for S Company's investment in R Company (change in retained earnings of R Company from 1/1/01 to 1/1/02, or [80% × ($80,000 − $60,000)]).		

After this adjustment is made, reciprocity is established for P Company's investment in S Company:

Investment in S Company	68,400	
1/1 Retained Earnings—P Company		68,400
To establish reciprocity (convert to equity) for P Company's investment in S Company (change in retained earnings of S Company from 1/1/00 to 1/1/02 plus the amount of the reciprocity entry above, or [90% × ($130,000 − $70,000 + 16,000)]).		

Cost Method

Partially Owned Subsidiaries

Indirect Ownership

ILLUSTRATION 9–1

P Company and Subsidiaries

Partial Consolidated Statements Workpaper

For Year Ended December 31, 2001

Income Statement	P Company	S Company	R Company	Eliminations Dr.	Eliminations Cr.	Noncontrolling Interest	Consolidated Balances
Income Before Dividend Income	92,000	42,000	30,000				164,000
Dividend Income	18,000	8,000		(2) 26,000			
Noncontrolling Interest in Income						12,600	(12,600)*
Net Income to Retained Earnings	110,000	50,000	30,000	26,000	—0—	12,600	151,400
Retained Earnings Statement							
1/1 Retained Earnings							
P Company	300,000				(1) 27,000		327,000
S Company		100,000		(4) 90,000		10,000	
R Company			60,000	(3) 48,000		12,000	
Net Income from above	110,000	50,000	30,000	26,000	—0—	12,600	151,400
Dividends Declared							
P Company	(30,000)						(30,000)
S Company		(20,000)			(2) 18,000	(2,000)	
R Company			(10,000)		(2) 8,000	(2,000)	
12/31 Retained Earnings to the Balance Sheet	380,000	130,000	80,000	164,000	53,000	30,600	448,400
Balance Sheet							
Investment in S Company	295,000			(1) 27,000	(4) 322,000		
Investment in R Company		145,000			(3) 145,000		
Difference Between Cost and Book Value (Land)				(3) 17,000 (4) 52,000			69,000
Common Stock							
P Company	500,000						500,000
S Company		200,000		(4) 180,000		20,000	
R Company			100,000	(3) 80,000		20,000	
Retained Earnings from above	380,000	130,000	80,000	164,000	53,000	30,600	448,400
Noncontrolling Interest in Net Assets						70,600	70,600
				520,000	520,000		

*(10% × $42,000) + (28% × $30,000).
(1) To convert to equity (establish reciprocity) for P Company's investment in S Company 90% × ($100,000 − $70,000).
(2) To eliminate intercompany dividends.
(3) To eliminate S Company's investment in R Company.
(4) To eliminate P Company's investment in S Company.

Cost

The above entries would not be needed if P Company accounts for its investments in S and R Companies using the partial or complete equity method.[3] Note that reciprocity is established for P Company's share of the difference between the *adjusted retained earnings* of S Company on January 1, 2002 ($130,000 + $16,000 = $146,000), and S Company's retained earnings on the date of acquisition by P Company ($70,000). Adjusted retained earnings refers to the $130,000 retained earnings of S Company plus the $16,000 from the reciprocity entry.

---

[3]Entries are presented in a later section under the assumption that P Company accounts for its investments in subsidiaries using the equity method.

S Company's Interest in R Company Is Acquired Prior to P Company's Interest in S Company—Cost Method

As a second illustration, assume the same data as in the first case except that S Company purchased an 80% interest in R Company on January 1, 2000, and P Company purchased a 90% interest in S Company on January 1, 2001. The appropriate affiliation diagram is as follows:

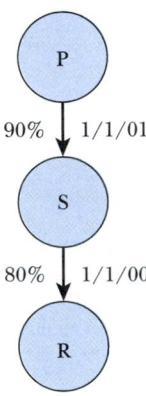

When one company (P Company) acquires a controlling interest in another company (S Company) that already owns a controlling interest in a third company (R Company), two important points must be considered. First, additional care must be exercised in determining the amount of subsidiary equity acquired by P Company, since S Company may have an equity interest in some prior years' undistributed income of R Company that is not included in S Company's retained earnings at the date of acquisition by P Company. Second, extra care must be used in determining the amount needed to establish reciprocity; that is, as explained earlier, reciprocity should be established for P Company's investment in S Company after reciprocity is established for S Company's investment in R Company.

The cost of each investment and stockholders' equity information for each company is repeated here for the reader's convenience:

	P Company	S Company	R Company
Cost of:			
P's Investment in S Company (90%)	$295,000		
S's Investment in R Company (80%)		$145,000	
Stockholders' Equity:			
Common Stock	$500,000	$200,000	$100,000
Retained Earnings, 1/1/00	230,000	70,000	50,000
2000 Reported Income	100,000	50,000	20,000
2000 Dividends Declared	(30,000)	(20,000)	(10,000)
Retained Earnings, 12/31/00	300,000	100,000	60,000
2001 Reported Income	110,000	50,000	30,000
2001 Dividends Declared	(30,000)	(20,000)	(10,000)
Retained Earnings, 12/31/01	380,000	130,000	80,000
Stockholders' Equity, 12/31/01	$880,000	$330,000	$180,000

The difference between cost and book value for each investment may be computed as follows:

	P's Investment in S Company Acquired 1/1/01	S's Investment in R Company Acquired 1/1/00
Cost of investment	$295,000	$145,000
Book value of net assets acquired (common stock and retained earnings):		
.9($200,000 + $108,000) on 1/1/2001	277,200	
.8($100,000 + $50,000) on 1/1/2000		120,000
Difference between cost and book value	$ 17,800	$ 25,000
Allocated to land	17,800	25,000
Balance	—0—	—0—

When S Company acquired its interest in R Company, the determination of equity acquired was straightforward. On January 1, 2000, R Company had stockholders' equity of $150,000 ($100,000 common stock + $50,000 retained earnings), of which S Company acquired an 80% interest, or $120,000. When P Company acquired its interest in S Company, however, the computation of equity acquired is more complex because S Company's share of R Company's undistributed income for 2000 is not reflected in S Company's retained earnings account. During 2000 R Company earned $20,000, distributed a dividend of $10,000, and, therefore, had $10,000 of undistributed income, 80% of which accrues to the benefit of S Company. On January 1, 2001, S Company's retained earnings actually consist of the $100,000 reflected on its books plus its $8,000 (80% × $10,000) share of the undistributed income of R Company, which has not been recorded on S Company's books. Thus, the equity acquired by P Company on January 1, 2001, is computed as follows:

90% × ($200,000 Capital stock
+ $108,000 Adjusted retained earnings) = $277,200

Eliminating entries for the preparation of a consolidated statements workpaper on December 31, 2001, follow. It is assumed that the difference between cost and book value relates to subsidiary land. The first entry presented below is needed only if the parent company uses the cost method to account for its investment in the subsidiary R Company.

(1)	Investment in R Company	8,000	
	1/1 Retained Earnings—S Company		8,000

To convert to equity/establish reciprocity (80% × $10,000, the change in retained earnings of R Company) for the investment by S Company in R Company.

As discussed earlier, a workpaper reciprocity (equity conversion) entry is made under the cost method to give recognition, in retained earnings as of the beginning of the year, to the investor's share of the undistributed earnings of its subsidiary from the date of acquisition to the beginning of the current year. Note that there is no reciprocity (equity conversion) entry for P Company's investment in S Company even under the cost method because the investment was acquired on January 1, 2001 (the beginning of the current year). As always, there is no need for reciprocity entries under the partial or complete equity methods.

(2)	Common Stock—R Company .8($100,000)	80,000	
	1/1 Retained Earnings—R Company .8($60,000)	48,000	
	Difference Between Cost and Book Value (Land)	25,000	
	Investment in R Company ($145,000 + $8,000)		153,000

To eliminate S Company's investment in R Company.

(3)	Common Stock—S Company .9($200,000)	180,000	
	1/1 Retained Earnings—S Company .9($108,000)	97,200	
	Difference Between Cost and Book Value (Land)	17,800	
	Investment in S Company		295,000
	To eliminate P Company's investment in S Company.		

After the reciprocity (conversion) entry is made, the investment accounts are eliminated, as usual, against the related subsidiary equity. Note that in the elimination of P Company's investment in S Company, 90% of S Company's *adjusted retained earnings* of $108,000 on January 1, 2001, is eliminated. These entries (2 and 3) are the same regardless of whether P Company uses the cost, partial equity, or complete equity method.

Next, intercompany dividends would be eliminated if P Company uses the cost method, as follows:

(4)	Dividend Income	26,000	
	Dividends Declared—S Company		18,000
	Dividends Declared—R Company		8,000
	To eliminate intercompany dividends.		

If P Company uses the partial or complete equity method to account for its investments, the entry to eliminate intercompany dividends would be replaced with entries to eliminate intercompany subsidiary income and dividends against the Investment accounts (as always). These entries are illustrated numerically in a later section.

The computation of noncontrolling interest in combined income must reflect an adjustment to S Company's income for its share of the undistributed income of R Company for 2001, as follows:

Noncontrolling interest in income of R Company		
(20% × $30,000)		$ 6,000
Noncontrolling interest in income of S Company:		
S Company's reported income	$50,000	
Add S Company's share of undistributed income of		
R Company during 2001 [80% × ($30,000 − $10,000)]	16,000	
S Company's adjusted net income	66,000	
Noncontrolling interest percentage	10%	6,600
Total noncontrolling interest in combined income		$12,600

Recall that when establishing reciprocity (converting to equity) in subsequent years, reciprocity should be established for S Company's investment in R Company *before* reciprocity is established for P Company's investment in S Company. For example, in the preparation of a consolidated statements workpaper on December 31, 2002 (the second year after P's acquisition of S Company, but the third year after S acquired R Company), the following reciprocity entry should be made for S Company's investment in R Company:

	Investment in R Company	24,000	
	1/1 Retained Earnings—S Company		24,000
	[80% × ($80,000 − $50,000)]		

After this adjustment is made, reciprocity (equity conversion) is established for P Company's investment in S Company:

Investment in S Company	41,400	
1/1 Retained Earnings—P Company		
[90% × ($130,000 + $24,000 − $108,000)]		41,400

Note that reciprocity is established for P Company's share of the difference between the *adjusted retained earnings* of S Company on January 1, 2002 ($154,000), and the *adjusted retained earnings* of S Company on the date of acquisition by P Company ($108,000, or $100,000 + 80% of $10,000). These adjustments are also reflected in the investment elimination entries on the 2002 workpaper as shown below. The differences between cost and book value remain the same:

Common Stock—R Company	80,000	
1/1 Retained Earnings—R Company .8($80,000)	64,000	
Difference Between Cost and Book Value	25,000	
Investment in R Company ($145,000 + 24,000)		169,000
To eliminate S Company's investment in R Company.		
Common Stock—S Company	180,000	
1/1 Retained Earnings—S Company .9($154,000)	138,600	
Difference Between Cost and Book Value	17,800	
Investment in S Company ($295,000 + $41,400)		336,400
To eliminate P Company's investment in S Company.		

Connecting Affiliates: Cost Method

As a third illustration of indirect holdings, assume that on January 1, 2000, P Company acquired 90% and 70% of the common stock of S Company and R Company for $295,000 and $145,000 respectively. One year later, on January 1, 2001, S Company acquired 20% of the common stock of R Company for $35,000. (These affiliations are sometimes referred to as *connecting affiliates*.) The relationships are diagrammed as follows:

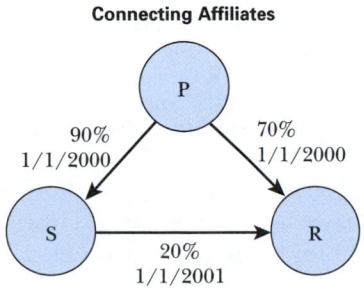

Connecting Affiliates

Notice that P Company has a 90% direct interest in S Company and an 88% combined direct and indirect interest in R Company [70% + (90% × 20%)]. Consequently, noncontrolling stockholders have a 10% interest in S Company and a 12% interest in R Company.

Stockholders' equity of the three companies is the same as in prior illustrations, as reveiwed here:

	P Company	S Company	R Company
Cost of:			
P's investment in S Company	$295,000		
P's investment in R Company	145,000		
S's investment in R Company		$ 35,000	
Stockholders' Equity:			
Common Stock	$500,000	$200,000	$100,000
Retained Earnings, 1/1/00	230,000	70,000	50,000
2000 Reported Income	100,000	50,000	20,000
2000 Dividends Declared	(30,000)	(20,000)	(10,000)
Retained Earnings, 12/31/00	300,000	100,000	60,000
2001 Reported Income	110,000	50,000	30,000
2001 Dividends Declared	(30,000)	(20,000)	(10,000)
Retained Earnings, 12/31/01	380,000	130,000	80,000
Stockholders' Equity, 12/31/01	$880,000	$330,000	$180,000

The difference between cost and book value, which relates to land, is computed next. The difference between cost and book value would, of course, be computed the same way if it relates to assets other than land. In such cases, however, additional adjustments would be needed at year-end for depreciation, cost of goods sold, or amortization effects (depending on the underlying assets that are undervalued).

	P Company's Investment in S Company	P Company's Investment in R Company	S Company's Investment in R Company
Investment Cost	$295,000	$145,000	$35,000
Equity Acquired			
90% × $270,000	243,000		
70% × $150,000		105,000	
20% × $160,000			32,000
Difference Between Cost and Book Value	$ 52,000	$ 40,000	$ 3,000

The companies record their investments using the cost method. Net income from independent operations for each company for 2001 is:

	P Company	S Company	R Company
Reported income	$110,000	$50,000	$30,000
Less intercompany dividends:			
P Company from S Company	(18,000)		
P Company from R Company	(7,000)		
S Company from R Company		(2,000)	
Income from independent operations	$ 85,000	$48,000	$30,000

A partial workpaper for the preparation of consolidated financial statements on December 31, 2001 is given in Illustration 9-2. Workpaper entries, in general journal form, are presented below:

(1) Investment in S Company   27,000
     1/1 Retained Earnings—P Company   27,000
       To convert to equity (establish reciprocity) [90% × ($100,000 − $70,000)].

(2) Investment in R Company   7,000
     1/1 Retained Earnings—P Company   7,000
       To convert to equity (establish reciprocity) [70% × ($60,000 − $50,000)].

(3)	Dividend Income	27,000	
	Dividends Declared—S Company		18,000
	Dividends Declared—R Company		9,000
	To eliminate intercompany dividends.		
(4)	Common Stock—R Company .2($100,000)	20,000	
	1/1 Retained Earnings—R Company .2($60,000)	12,000	
	Difference Between Cost and Book Value (Land)	3,000	
	Investment in R Company		35,000
	To eliminate S Company's investment in R Company.		
(5)	Common Stock—S Company .9($200,000)	180,000	
	1/1 Retained Earnings—S Company .9($100,000)	90,000	
	Difference Between Cost and Book Value (Land)	52,000	
	Investment in S Company ($295,000 + $27,000)		322,000
	To eliminate P Company's investment in S Company.		
(6)	Common Stock—R Company .7($100,000)	70,000	
	1/1 Retained Earnings—R Company .7($60,000)	42,000	
	Difference Between Cost and Book Value (Land)	40,000	
	Investment in R Company ($145,000 + $7,000)		152,000
	To eliminate P Company's investment in R Company.		

Consolidated net income of $154,600 can be verified as follows:

	P Company	S Company	R Company
Reported income	$110,000	$50,000	$30,000
Dividend income (from affiliates)	25,000	2,000	
Income from independent operations	85,000	48,000	30,000
Percentage owned by P Company	100%	90%	88%
	85,000	43,200	26,400
Consolidated net income (or controlling interest in combined incomes)		$154,600	

As an alternative, consolidated net income can be verified by adding P Company's share of the undistributed reported income of its subsidiaries to P Company's reported income:

	S Company	R Company
Reported income	$50,000	$30,000
Dividends declared	20,000	10,000
Undistributed income	30,000	20,000
S's share of R's undistributed income (20% of $20,000)	4,000	
Undistributed income accruing to S	34,000	
Percentage owned by P Company	90%	70%
	30,600	14,000
Undistributed income of affiliates accruing to P Company		44,660
P Company's reported income		110,000
Consolidated net income (or controlling interest in combined incomes)		$154,600

Cost Method

Partially Owned Subsidiaries

Indirect Ownership

ILLUSTRATION 9–2

P Company and Subsidiaries

Partial Consolidated Statements Workpaper

For Year Ended December 31, 2001

Income Statement	P Company	S Company	R Company	Eliminations Dr.	Eliminations Cr.	Noncontrolling Interest	Consolidated Balances
Income Before Dividend Income	85,000	48,000	30,000				163,000
Dividend Income	25,000	2,000		(3) 27,000			
Noncontrolling Interest in Income						8,400	(8,400)*
Net Income to Retained Earnings	110,000	50,000	30,000	27,000	—0—	8,400	154,600
Retained Earnings Statement							
1/1 Retained Earnings					(1) 27,000		
P Company	300,000				(2) 7,000		334,000
S Company		100,000		(5) 90,000		10,000	
				(4) 12,000			
R Company			60,000	(6) 42,000		6,000	
Net Income from above	110,000	50,000	30,000	27,000	—0—	8,400	154,600
Dividends Declared							
P Company	(30,000)						(30,000)
S Company		(20,000)			(3) 18,000	(2,000)	
R Company			(10,000)		(3) 9,000	(1,000)	
12/31 Retained Earnings to the							
Balance Sheet	380,000	130,000	80,000	171,000	61,000	21,400	458,600
Balance Sheet							
Investment in S Company	295,000			(1) 27,000	(5) 322,000		
Investment in R Company	145,000			(2) 7,000	(6) 152,000		
Investment in R Company		35,000			(4) 35,000		
Difference Between Cost and				(4) 3,000			95,000
				(5) 52,000			
Book Value (Land)				(6) 40,000			
Common Stock							
P Company	500,000						500,000
S Company		200,000		(5) 180,000		20,000	
				(4) 20,000			
R Company			100,000	(6) 70,000		10,000	
Retained Earnings from above	380,000	130,000	80,000	171,000	61,000	21,400	458,600
Noncontrolling Interest in Net							
Assets						51,400	51,400
				570,000	570,000		

*(12% × $30,000) + (10% × $48,000).
(1) To convert to equity (establish reciprocity) for P Company's investment in S Company.
(2) To convert to equity (establish reciprocity) for P Company's investment in R Company.
(3) To eliminate intercompany dividends.
(4) To eliminate S Company's investment in R Company.
(5) To eliminate P Company's investment in S Company.
(6) To eliminate P Company's investment in R Company.

Indirect Ownership—Several Levels

In some cases, a chain of ownership may exist in which the "primary" parent company actually has an indirect interest of less than 50% in one or more of the affiliates. Assume, for example, the following affiliation:

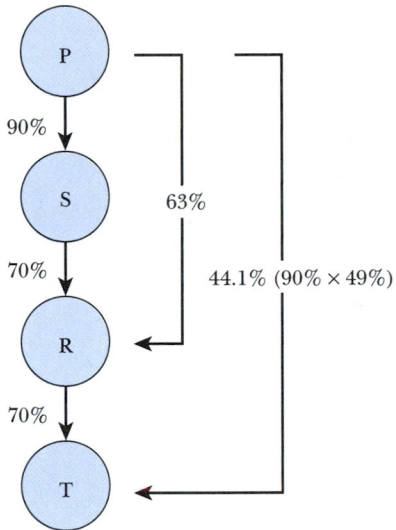

P Company has an indirect interest in T Company of only 44.1% (90% × 70% × 70%). Nonetheless, T Company is properly included in the consolidated group, because P Company effectively controls the operations of T Company through its ability to elect boards of directors of all three subsidiaries. Of course, only 44.1% of T Company's income will be included in consolidated net income. The remainder represents noncontrolling interest.

INDIRECT OWNERSHIP—EQUITY METHOD

If the equity method is used to record the investments, P Company should record its share of S Company's income *after* S Company has recorded its share of R Company's income. Workpaper elimination entries are then prepared following the procedures illustrated in previous chapters for the equity method. We have simplified the assumptions of the illustration so that the partial and complete equity methods require the same workpaper entries. Differences arise between the two equity methods when the difference between cost and book value is attributed to depreciable or amortizable assets rather than land, when intercompany profit or gain exists, and so on. These differences have been addressed in Chapters 5, 6, and 7 and are not repeated here.

Basic data under the equity method are given below. On January 1, 2000, P Company acquired 90% and 70% of the common stock of S Company and R Company for $295,000 and $145,000, respectively. One year later, on January 1, 2001, S

Company acquired 20% of the common stock of R Company for $35,000. Investment account balances and stockholders' equity amounts at various dates follow:

	P Company	S Company	R Company
Investment balances, 1/1/01:			
P's Investment in S Company (90%)	$322,000		
P's Investment in R Company (70%)	152,000		
S's Investment in R Company (20%)		$ 35,000	
Stockholders' Equity:			
Common Stock	$500,000	$200,000	$100,000
Retained Earnings, 1/1/00	230,000	70,000	50,000
2000 Reported Income	134,000	50,000	20,000
2000 Dividends Declared	(30,000)	(20,000)	(10,000)
Retained Earnings, 12/31/00	334,000	100,000	60,000
2001 Reported Income	154,600	54,000	30,000
2001 Dividends Declared	(30,000)	(20,000)	(10,000)
Retained Earnings, 12/31/01	458,600	134,000	80,000
Stockholders' Equity, 12/31/01	$958,600	$334,000	$180,000
Investment balances, 12/31/01:			
P's Investment in S Company (90%)	$352,600		
P's Investment in R Company (70%)	166,000		
S's Investment in R Company (20%)		$ 39,000	

Book entries for 2001 made by S Company and P Company on December 31, 2001 are:

S Company's Books

Cash	2,000	
Investment in R Company		2,000
To record S Company's share of dividends paid by R Company (20% of $10,000)		

Investment in R Company	6,000	
Equity in Subsidiary Income		6,000
To record S Company's share of income earned by R Company (20% of $30,000)		

P Company's Books

Cash	7,000	
Investment in R Company		7,000
To record P Company's share of dividends paid by R Company (70% of $10,000).		

Investment in R Company	21,000	
Equity in Subsidiary Income		21,000
To record P Company's share of income earned by R Company (70% of $30,000)		

Cash	18,000	
Investment in S Company		18,000
To record P Company's share of dividends paid by S Company (90% of $20,000)		

Investment in S Company	48,600	
Equity in Subsidiary Income		48,600
To record P Company's share of income earned by S Company (90% of $54,000)		

The eliminating entries are presented next for a consolidated statements workpaper on December 31, 2001 (the year after P Company acquired S and R Companies). These entries are also reflected in Illustration 9-3, which presents a partial consol-

Equity Method			ILLUSTRATION 9–3				
Partially Owned Subsidiaries			**P Company and Subsidiaries**				
Indirect Ownership			**Partial Consolidated Statements Workpaper**				
			For Year Ended December 31, 2001				

	P	S	R	Eliminations		Noncontrolling	Consolidated
Income Statement	*Company*	*Company*	*Company*	*Dr.*	*Cr.*	*Interest*	*Balances*
Income Before Equity Income	85,000	48,000	30,000				163,000
Equity in Subsidiary Income	69,600	6,000		(1) 6,000			
				(2) 21,000			
				(3) 48,600			
Noncontrolling Interest in Income						8,400	(8,400)*
Net Income to Retained Earnings	154,600	54,000	30,000	75,600	—0—	8,400	154,600
Retained Earnings Statement							
1/1 Retained Earnings							
P Company	334,000						334,000
S Company		100,000		(5) 90,000		10,000	
				(4) 12,000			
R Company			60,000	(6) 42,000		6,000	
Net Income from above	154,600	54,000	30,000	75,000	—0—	8,400	154,600
Dividends Declared							
P Company	(30,000)						(30,000)
S Company		(20,000)			(3) 18,000	(2,000)	
					(1) 2,000		
R Company			(10,000)		(2) 7,000	(1,000)	
12/31 Retained Earnings to the							
Balance Sheet	458,600	134,000	80,000	219,600	27,000	21,400	458,600
Balance Sheet							
Investment in S Company	352,600				(3) 30,600		
Investment in R Company	166,000				(5) 322,000		
					(2) 14,000		
					(6) 152,000		
Investment in R Company		39,000			(1) 4,000		
					(4) 35,000		
Difference Between Cost and				(4) 3,000			95,000
Book Value (Land)				(5) 52,000			
				(6) 40,000			
Common Stock							
P Company	500,000						500,000
S Company		200,000		(5) 180,000		20,000	
R Company			100,000	(4) 20,000		10,000	
				(6) 70,000			
Retained Earnings from above	458,600	134,000	80,000	219,600	27,000	21,400	458,600
Noncontrolling Interest in Net							
Assets						51,400	51,400
				584,600	584,600		

*(12% × $30,000) + (10% × $48,000).
(1) To eliminate intercompany income and dividends for S Company's investment in R Company.
(2) To eliminate intercompany income and dividends for P Company's investment in R Company.
(3) To eliminate intercompany income and dividends for P Company's investment in S Company.
(4) To eliminate S Company's investment in R Company.
(5) To eliminate P Company's investment in S Company.
(6) To eliminate P Company's investment in R Company.

idated statements workpaper for the year ended December 31, 2001, under the equity method.

Equity Income and Dividend Elimination Entries (Combined Approach)[4]

(1) Equity in Subsidiary Income (20% of $30,000)   6,000
          Dividends Declared—R (20% of $10,000)   2,000
          Investment in R Company   4,000
              To eliminate intercompany income and dividends for S Company's investment in
              R Company.

(2) Equity in Subsidiary Income (70% of $30,000)   21,000
          Dividends Declared—R Company (70% of $10,000)   7,000
          Investment in R Company   14,000
              To eliminate intercompany income and dividends for P Company's investment in
              R Company.

(3) Equity in Subsidiary Income (90% of $54,000)   48,600
          Dividends Declared—S Company (90% of $20,000)   18,000
          Investment in S Company   30,600
              To eliminate intercompany income and dividends for P Company's investment in
              S Company.

Investment Elimination Entries

(4) Common Stock—R Company .2($100,000)   20,000
     1/1 Retained Earnings—R Company .2($60,000)   12,000
     Difference Between Cost and Book Value (Land)   3,000
          Investment in R Company   35,000
              To eliminate S Company's investment in R Company.

(5) Common Stock—S Company .9($200,000)   180,000
     1/1 Retained Earnings—S Company .9($100,000)   90,000
     Difference Between Cost and Book Value (Land)   52,000
          Investment in S Company   322,000
              To eliminate P Company's investment in S Company.

(6) Common Stock—R Company .7($100,000)   70,000
     1/1 Retained Earnings—R Company .7($60,000)   42,000
     Difference Between Cost and Book Value (Land)   40,000
          Investment in R Company   152,000
              To eliminate P Company's investment in R Company.

RECIPROCAL STOCKHOLDINGS

Indirect ownership situations are relatively common; reciprocal stockholdings are not. Occasionally a subsidiary owns a small equity interest in its parent company, or subsidiaries of the same parent own equity interests in one another. Where these reciprocal stockholdings exist, the reciprocal effect is often immaterial. The infrequency of occurrence of reciprocal stockholdings, and the often relatively immaterial

---

[4]These entries may be recorded separately, one for income and another for dividends.

effect where they do exist, suggests that this topic may not require as much attention as others. Nevertheless, some familiarity with the problems created may be useful.

Two general approaches are used to treat the effect of reciprocal stockholdings—a mathematical approach and a treasury stock approach. The mathematical approach gives explicit recognition to the effect of the reciprocal stockholding, whereas the treasury stock approach simply treats the reciprocal stockholding as treasury stock on the consolidated balance sheet. For example, if S Company purchased an investment in its parent company for $10,000, this amount would be shown on the consolidated balance sheet as Treasury Stock (parent company stock held by a subsidiary).

Surveys of practice show that this treasury stock approach is the one most often used in practice. Because the treasury stock approach is generally used in practice, it is discussed and illustrated in the following section. The mathematical approach is presented in the appendix for those who may be interested in its application. Both methods are currently acceptable.

Treasury Stock Approach

Subsidiary stockholdings in the parent company are generally treated the same as treasury stock because the parent company is considered to have reacquired some of its own shares by using subsidiary resources. Under this approach, the reciprocal relationship is ignored, and the cost of the subsidiary's investment in the stock of the parent company is reclassified as treasury stock and is deducted from total stockholders' equity on the consolidated balance sheet. Dividends distributed to the subsidiary by the parent company are recognized by the subsidiary as dividend income.[5]

Cost Method. To illustrate, assume that P Company acquired 90% of the common stock of S Company on January 1, 2001. On the same date, S Company acquired 10% of the common stock of P Company. P Company records its investment in S Company using the cost method. An affiliation diagram, along with relevant investment cost, stockholders' equity, income, and dividend data follows:

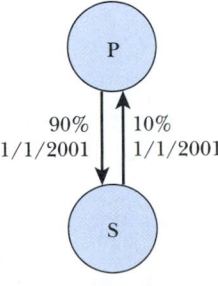

Cost

---

[5]If the subsidiary owned 20% or more of the common stock of the parent company, its investment in the parent would have to be adjusted to the equity method when reporting to parties outside the affiliated group. In the event the subsidiary elected to use the equity method on its books to account for its investment in the stock of its parent, a workpaper entry to return the investment account to its cost would be required so that the investment account could be deducted at its cost from stockholders' equity on the consolidated balance sheet.

	P Company	S Company
Cost of investment in S Company	$240,000	
Cost of investment in P Company		$ 70,000
Common Stock	$500,000	$200,000
Retained Earnings, 1/1/01	150,000	50,000
2001 Reported Income	105,000	60,000
2001 Dividends Declared	(20,000)	(10,000)
Retained Earnings, 12/31/01	235,000	100,000
2002 Reported Income	140,000	60,000
2002 Dividends Declared	(30,000)	(10,000)
Retained Earnings, 12/31/02	$345,000	$150,000

Because S Company's investment in P Company is treated as treasury stock, any difference between cost and book value acquired on the investment is irrelevant in

Cost Method	ILLUSTRATION 9–4
Reciprocal Stockholdings	P Company and Subsidiary
Treasury Stock Method	Partial Consolidated Statements Workpaper
	For Year Ended December 31, 2002

Income Statement	P Company	S Company	Eliminations Dr.	Eliminations Cr.	Noncontrolling Interest	Consolidated Balances
Income Before Dividend Income	131,000	57,000				188,000
Dividend Income	9,000	3,000	(2) 12,000			
Noncontrolling Interest in Income						
.1($60,000)					6,000	(6,000)
Net Income to Retained Earnings	140,000	60,000	12,000	—0—	6,000	182,000
Retained Earnings Statement						
1/1 Retained Earnings						
P Company	235,000			(1) 45,000		280,000
S Company		100,000	(3) 90,000		10,000	
Net Income from above	140,000	60,000	12,000	—0—	6,000	182,000
Dividends Declared						
P Company	(30,000)			(2) 3,000		(27,000)
S Company		(10,000)		(2) 9,000	(1,000)	
12/31 Retained Earnings to the						
Balance Sheet	345,000	150,000	102,000	57,000	15,000	435,000
Balance Sheet						
Investment in S Company	240,000		(1) 45,000	(3) 285,000		
Investment in P Company		70,000		(4) 70,000		
Difference Between Cost and			(3) 15,000			15,000
Book Value (Land)						69,000
Common Stock						
P Company	500,000					500,000
S Company		200,000	(3) 180,000		20,000	
Retained Earnings from above	345,000	150,000	102,000	57,000	15,000	435,000
Treasury Stock			(4) 70,000			(70,000)
Noncontrolling Interest in Net Assets					35,000	35,000
			342,000	342,000		

(1) To convert to equity (establish reciprocity)—P Company's investment in S Company .9($100,000 − $50,000).
(2) To eliminate intercompany dividends.
(3) To eliminate P Company's investment in S Company.
(4) To reclassify S Company's investment in P Company to Treasury Stock.

the preparation of consolidated financial statements. However, there is a $15,000 difference between cost and book value [$240,000 − .9($200,000 + $50,000)] relating to P Company's investment in S Company; we assume it relates to subsidiary land.

A *partial* consolidated statements workpaper is presented in Illustration 9-4. Several items related to the workpaper should be specifically noted:

1. Because the cost of S Company's investment in P Company is treated as treasury stock, there is no reciprocity entry for this investment.

2. In the computation of the amount needed to establish reciprocity for P Company's investment in S Company, the reciprocal nature of S Company's investment in P Company is ignored. Thus, the reciprocity amount is [90% × ($100,000 − $50,000)].

3. S Company's investment in P Company is reclassified as treasury stock. It will be deducted on the consolidated balance sheet just as though it were held by P Company, as shown in Illustration 9-4.

4. Noncontrolling interest in combined income is based on the noncontrolling stockholders' share of the *reported* income of S Company. That is, the noncontrolling stockholders' share of combined income includes their share of dividend income received from P Company. If the noncontrolling stockholders' share of this dividend income were excluded, total noncontrolling interest on the consolidated balance sheet would be less than the noncontrolling stockholders' share of the reported net assets of S Company. The authors believe that the noncontrolling interest on the consolidated balance sheet should reflect the noncontrolling stockholders' full share of the net assets of S Company that are included in the consolidated balance sheet, 10%($200,000 + $150,000), since the reciprocal relationship is ignored.

5. Only $27,000 of P Company dividends declared are deducted from consolidated retained earnings, since that is the amount that was distributed to outside stockholders. The other $3,000 is eliminated because it represents an interaffiliate dividend distribution.

The consolidated balance sheet, in condensed form, that results from the data in Illustration 9-4 is presented in Illustration 9-5. (The "liabilities" amount is an assumed amount.)

ILLUSTRATION 9-5

P Company and Subsidiary
Consolidated Balance Sheet
For the Year Ended December 31, 2002

Assets		$1,467,000
Liabilities		$ 567,000
Stockholder's Equity		
Common Stock	$500,000	
Retained Earnings	435,000	
Less P Company shares held by subsidiary (at cost)	(70,000)	
		865,000
Noncontrolling Interest		35,000
Total Liabilities and Stockholders' Equity		$1,467,000

Equity Method. Under the equity method, P Company recognizes its share of S Company's income, but ***ignores the reciprocal relationship.*** Thus, during 2002, P Company will recognize $51,300 [.9 × ($60,000 S Company reported income less $3,000 dividend income from P Company)] of subsidiary income and reduce the Investment in S Company for the $9,000 dividends received, through the following book entries:

P Company Books

Investment in S Company	51,300	
Equity in Subsidiary Income		51,300
Cash	9,000	
Investment in S Company		9,000

The amount of dividends paid by P Company to S Company is included in S Company's reported income and reduces P Company's retained earnings. Yet for consolidated purposes, this amount cannot be included as income. Therefore, consolidated income and P Company's net income will no longer be the same under the equity method when the treasury stock method is used for reciprocal holdings. To correct for this, an additional workpaper entry, similar to the reciprocity entry under the cost method, is needed to adjust P Company's beginning retained earnings to the amount of beginning consolidated retained earnings as follows:

Investment in S Company	1,800	
Beginning Retained Earnings—P Company		1,800
To adjust for the cumulative dividends of P Company paid to S Company from the date of acquisition (P's acquisition of S) to the beginning of the year (90% of $2,000).		

The remaining workpaper entries (on December 31, 2002) to eliminate intercompany equity in subsidiary income, dividend income, and the investment account are:

Equity in Subsidiary Income	51,300	
Dividends Declared—S Company		9,000
Investment in S Company		42,300
Dividend Income	3,000	
Dividends Declared—P Company		3,000
1/1 Retained Earnings—S Company (90% of $100,000)	90,000	
Common Stock—S Company (90% of $200,000)	180,000	
Difference Between Cost and Book Value (Land)	15,000	
Investment in S Company		285,000

The final entry (below) reclassifies S Company's investment in P Company to Treasury Stock as follows:

Treasury Stock	70,000	
Investment in P Company		70,000

These entries and their effects on the consolidated accounts are shown in the workpaper presented in Illustration 9-6.

Equity Method
Reciprocal Stockholdings
Treasury Stock Method

ILLUSTRATION 9–6
P Company and Subsidiary
Partial Consolidated Statements Workpaper
For Year Ended December 31, 2002

Income Statement	P Company	S Company	Eliminations Dr.	Eliminations Cr.	Noncontrolling Interest	Consolidated Balances
Income Before other Items	131,000	57,000				188,000
Dividend Income		3,000	(3) 3,000			
Equity in Subsidiary Income	51,300		(2) 51,300			
Noncontrolling Interest in Income .1($60,000)					6,000	(6,000)
Net Income to Retained Earnings	182,300	60,000	54,300	—0—	6,000	182,000
Retained Earnings Statement						
1/1 Retained Earnings						
P Company	278,200			(1) 1,800		280,000
S Company		100,000	(4) 90,000		10,000	
Net Income from above	182,300	60,000	54,300	—0—	6,000	182,000
Dividends Declared						
P Company	(30,000)			(3) 3,000		(27,000)
S Company		(10,000)		(2) 9,000	(1,000)	
12/31 Retained Earnings to the Balance Sheet	430,500	150,000	144,300	13,800	15,000	435,000
Balance Sheet						
Investment in S Company	325,500		(1) 1,800	(2) 42,300		
				(4) 285,000		
Investment in P Company		70,000		(5) 70,000		
Difference Between Cost and Book Value (Land)			(4) 15,000			15,000 69,000
Common Stock						
P Company	500,000					500,000
S Company		200,000	(4) 180,000		20,000	
Retained Earnings from above	430,500	150,000	144,300	13,800	15,000	435,000
Treasury Stock			(5) 70,000			(70,000)
Noncontrolling Interest in Net Assets					35,000	35,000
			411,100	411,100		

(1) To adjust P Company's retained earnings for dividends paid to S Company from the date of acquisition (of S Company by P Company) to the beginning of the year, (90% of $2,000).
(2) To eliminate intercompany income and dividends for P Company's investment in S Company.
(3) To eliminate intercompany dividends.
(4) To eliminate P Company's investment in S Company.
(5) To reclassify S Company's investment in P Company to Treasury Stock.

SUMMARY

1. *Explain the term "indirect ownership."* When a parent company has an interest in a subsidiary that has an interest in a subsidiary of its own, the parent has an indirect interest in the subsidiary's subsidiary. Indirect ownership also occurs when a parent has more than one subsidiary, one of which owns a portion of another subsidiary of the parent.

2. *Distinguish reciprocal stockholdings from indirect ownership.* Reciprocal stockholdings occur when two or more affiliates have ownership interests in each other.

3. *Compute the controlling interest in combined income when there is an indirect ownership interest.* The controlling interest in such cases may be computed in several

ways, including: (1) The parent's income from independent operations is added to *its share* of income from the independent operations of its subsidiaries; (2) The parent's share of the *undistributed* income of its subsidiaries is added to the parent's *reported* income; (3) The noncontrolling interest in income is deducted from the combined income from independent operations of all affiliates.

4. *Describe the effect on the elimination process when the parent acquires a controlling interest in a subsidiary that already owns a controlling interest in another subsidiary.* When one company (P Company) acquires a controlling interest in another company (S Company) that already owns a controlling interest in a third company (R Company), S Company may have an equity interest in some prior years' undistributed income of R Company that is not included in S Company's retained earnings at the date of acquisition by P Company. In determining the amount needed to establish reciprocity, reciprocity should be established for P Company's investment in S Company *after* reciprocity is established for S Company's investment in R Company.

5. *Explain the term "connecting affiliates."* This term is sometimes used when a parent company owns more than one subsidiary, and at least one of the subsidiaries owns stock in another of its parent's subsidiaries.

6. *Compare the two general approaches for handling the effects of reciprocal stockholdings.* The mathematical approach gives explicit recognition to the effect of the

reciprocal stockholding, whereas the treasury stock approach simply treats the reciprocal stockholding as treasury stock on the consolidated balance sheet. The treasury stock approach is the approach most often used in practice.

7. *Describe the procedures used to record reciprocal holdings using the treasury stock method.* (1) Because the cost of the subsidiary's (S Company) investment in the parent (P Company) is treated as treasury stock, there is no reciprocity entry for this investment. (2) In the computation of the amount needed to establish reciprocity for P Company's investment in S Company, the reciprocal nature of S Company's investment in P Company is ignored. (3) S Company's investment in P Company is reclassified as treasury stock. (4) Noncontrolling interest in combined income is based on the noncontrolling stockholders' share of the *reported* income of S Company.

8. *Explain why consolidated net income does not equal the parent's reported income under the complete equity method when the treasury stock method is used for reciprocal holdings, and how this affects the elimination process.* The amount of dividends paid to the subsidiary by the parent is included in the subsidiary's reported income and reduces the parent's retained earnings. For consolidated purposes, however, this amount cannot be considered income. Thus, an additional workpaper entry is needed under the equity method, similar to the reciprocity entry under the cost method, to adjust the parent's beginning retained earnings to beginning consolidated retained earnings.

APPENDIX

Mathematical Approach to Reciprocal Stockholdings

When reciprocal stockholdings exist and the mathematical approach is used (an alternative to the treasury stock method), the allocation of the total income of the affiliates between consolidated income and the noncontrolling interest must reflect the interdependency of the relationship. In the example that follows (the same as that presented earlier under the treasury stock approach), consolidated net income consists of P Company's income from its independent operations plus P Company's share of S Company's reciprocally determined income. Conversely, the noncontrolling stockholders' share of the total affiliated income is based on S Company's reciprocally determined income. The mathematical approach uses *simultaneous equations* to determine the allocation of total affiliated income.

To illustrate, assume that P Company acquired 90% of the common stock of S Company on January 1, 2001. On the same date, S Company acquired 10% of the common stock of P Company. P Company records its investment in S Company using the cost method. Investment cost, stockholders' equity, income, and dividend data are the same as previously presented. The difference between cost and book value on P Company's investment in S Company is again $15,000. Since the cost of S Company's investment in P Company was treated as consolidated treasury stock under the treasury stock approach, there was no reported difference between cost and book value on that investment. Under the mathematical approach, however, S Company's investment in P Company is treated as an intercompany investment that must be eliminated on the consolidated statements workpaper. When the investment is eliminated, a $5,000 difference between cost and book value will be reported, computed as follows:

Investment cost	$70,000
Book value of P Company's equity acquired:	
10%($500,000 capital stock + retained earnings)	65,000
Difference between cost and book value	$ 5,000

Consolidated net income and noncontrolling interest in combined income must be determined considering the reciprocal nature of the investments. The computation begins with the incomes from independent operations of P Company and S Company, which for 2001 are:

	P Company	S Company
Reported income	$105,000	$60,000
Less intercompany dividend income	9,000	2,000
Income from independent operations	$ 96,000	$58,000

Thus, the 2001 reciprocally based incomes of P Company and S Company, and the noncontrolling interest in combined incomes can be determined as follows:

Let P = P Company's reciprocally based income
S = S Company's reciprocally based income

The algebraic formulation is:

(1) $P = \$96,000 + .9S$
(2) $S = \$58,000 + .1P$

Substitute for S in equation (1) using the definition of S in equation (2):

$$P = 96,000 + .9(58,000 + .1P)$$
$$P = 96,000 + 52,200 + .09P$$
$$.91P = 148,200$$
$$(3) \quad P = 162,857$$

Substitute equation (3) into equation (2) to solve for S:

$$S = 58,000 + .1(162,857)$$
$$S = 58,000 + 16,286$$
$$(4) \quad S = 74,286$$

Cost Method

Reciprocal Stockholdings

Mathematical Approach

ILLUSTRATION 9–7

P Company and Subsidiary

Partial Consolidated Statements Workpaper

For Year Ended December 31, 2001

Income Statement	P Company	S Company	Eliminations Dr.	Eliminations Cr.	Noncontrolling Interest	Consolidated Balances
Income Before Dividend Income	96,000	58,000				154,000
Dividend Income	9,000	2,000	(2) 11,000			
Noncontrolling Interest in Income					7,429	(7,429)
Net Income to Retained Earnings	105,000	60,000	11,000	—0—	7,429	146,571
Retained Earnings Statement						
1/1 Retained Earnings						
P Company	150,000		(3) 15,000			135,000
S Company		50,000	(2) 45,000		5,000	
Net Income from above	105,000	60,000	11,000	—0—	7,429	146,571
Dividends Declared						
P Company	(20,000)			(1) 2,000		(18,000)
S Company		(10,000)		(1) 9,000	(1,000)	
12/31 Retained Earnings to the						
Balance Sheet	235,000	100,000	71,000	11,000	11,429	263,571
Balance Sheet						
Investment in S Company	240,000			(2) 240,000		
Investment in P Company		70,000		(3) 70,000		
Difference Between Cost and			⎰(2) 15,000			20,000
Book Value (Land)			⎱(3) 5,000			
Common Stock						
P Company	500,000		(3) 50,000			450,000
S Company		200,000	(2) 180,000		20,000	
Retained Earnings from above	235,000	100,000	71,000	11,000	11,429	263,571
Noncontrolling Interest in Net Assets					31,429	31,429
			321,000	321,000		

Cost

(1) To eliminate intercompany dividends.
(3) To eliminate P Company's investment in S Company.
(5) To reclassify S Company's investment in P Company.

Thus, P Company's reciprocal income is $162,857, S Company's reciprocal income is $74,286, and the noncontrolling interest in combined income is $7,429 (10% × $74,286). Consolidated net income is 90% of P Company's reciprocal income of $162,857, or $146,571. The remaining 10% of P Company's reciprocal income represents intercompany income on shares held by S Company. The combined income is, therefore, $154,000 ($146,571 + $7,429), which is equal to the actual income of both companies from their independent operations ($96,000 + $58,000). A partial consolidated statements workpaper for this case is presented in Illustration 9-7. Workpaper entries are presented also in general journal form for the convenience of the reader.

(1) Dividend Income	11,000	
Dividends Declared—P Company		2,000
Dividends Declared—S Company		9,000
To eliminate intercompany dividends.		

(2)	Common Stock—S Company	180,000	
	1/1 Retained Earnings—S Company	45,000	
	Difference Between Cost and Book Value (Land)	15,000	
	Investment in S Company		240,000
	To eliminate P Company's investment in S Company.		
(3)	Common Stock—P Company	50,000	
	1/1 Retained Earnings—P Company	15,000	
	Difference Between Cost and Book Value (Land)	5,000	
	Investment in P Company		70,000
	To eliminate S Company's investment in P Company.		

SUBSEQUENT YEARS

The previous example demonstrated the preparation of a consolidated workpaper at the end of the year of acquisition. In subsequent periods, an additional computation must be made, on a reciprocal basis, to determine the amount needed to establish reciprocity for each of the investments. For example, the computation of the amounts needed to establish reciprocity for a workpaper at the end of 2002 would be:

Let P = P Company's reciprocally based income, or

     = Increase in P Company's retained earnings since date of acquisition of P Company stock by S Company ($235,000 − $150,000 = $85,000) plus 90% of S Company's reciprocally based income.

Let S = S Company's reciprocally based income, or

     = Increase in S Company's retained earnings since date of acquisition of S Company stock by P Company ($100,000 − $50,000 = $50,000) plus 10% of P Company's reciprocally based income.

Then:

$$P = \$85,000 + .9S$$
$$S = 50,000 + .1P$$

$$S = 50,000 + .1(85,000 + .9S)$$
$$S = 50,000 + 8,500 + .09S$$
$$.91S = 58,500$$
$$S = 64,286$$

$$P = 85,000 + .9(64,286)$$
$$P = 85,000 + 57,857$$
$$P = 142,857$$

Based on these computations, the workpaper entries to convert to establish reciprocity in the preparation of a consolidated statements workpaper on December 31, 2002, are:

Investment in P Company	14,286	
1/1 Retained Earnings—S Company		14,286
To establish reciprocity for S Company's investment in P Company (10% × $142,857).		

Investment in S Company	57,857	
1/1 Retained Earnings—P Company		57,857
To establish reciprocity for P Company's investment in S Company (90% × $64,286).		

In all other respects, the workpaper at December 31, 2002, is completed as in previous illustrations.

(The letter A indicated for an exercise or problem refers to the appendix.)

QUESTIONS

1. Distinguish among direct, indirect, and reciprocal stockholder interests.
2. What is meant by "up-the-ladder" elimination?
3. X Company owns 70% of Y Company, and Y Company owns 60% of Z Company. Are consolidated financial statements for X, Y, and Z companies appropriate? Justify your answer.
4. A Company owns 90% of B Company, 80% of C Company, and 70% of E Company. B Company owns 75% of D Company, which in turn, owns 60% of

F Company. C Company owns 15% of E Company. E Company owns 5% of F Company. What percent of each company's income should be included in consolidated net income?
5. Describe two approaches to the treatment of reciprocal stockholdings in the preparation of consolidated financial statements.
6. How does the determination of noncontrolling interests differ in the two approaches to the treatment of reciprocal stockholdings?

EXERCISES

EXERCISE 9-1 Indirect Holdings

Alto Company purchased 80% of the outstanding common stock of Bat Company on January 1, 2001, and Bat Company purchased a 90% interest in the capital stock of Curt Company on January 1, 2002. Income from the independent operations of the three companies and dividends declared during 2001 and 2002 were:

	Alto	Bat	Curt
Income from Independent Operations			
2001	$300,000	$150,000	$105,000
2002	350,000	180,000	126,000
Dividends Declared			
2001	50,000	40,000	36,000
2002	90,000	45,000	46,000

Required:

A. Prepare entries on the books of Alto and Bat Companies during 2001 and 2002 to recognize the effect of dividends declared by affiliates. Assume that the investments are accounted for using
   (1) The cost method
   (2) The complete or the partial equity method
B. Prepare a schedule to compute the amount of consolidated net income for 2002.

EXERCISE 9-2 Indirect Holdings

On January 1, 2000, Prill Company purchased 90% of the outstanding common stock of Speer Company and 30% of the outstanding common stock of Rack Company. One year later, on January 1, 2001, Speer Company purchased 60% of the outstanding common stock of Rack Company. Income from independent operations and dividends declared during 2001 were:

	Prill	Speer	Rack
Income from Independent Operations	$150,000	$60,000	$40,000
Dividends Declared	60,000	20,000	15,000

Required:

A. Prepare an affiliation diagram.

B. Prepare entries on the books of Prill and Speer to recognize the effects of dividends declared by affiliates during 2001, assuming (1) the use of the cost method to record investments, and (2) the use of the complete or partial equity method to record the investments.

C. Prepare a schedule to compute the amount of consolidated net income for 2001.

EXERCISE 9-3 Consolidated Retained Earnings and Noncontrolling Interest

On January 1, 2001, Bill Company purchased 90% of the capital stock of Chris Company. On January 1, 2001, Allen Company purchased 80% of the capital stock of Bill Company. On January 1, 2002, Allen Company purchased 10% of the capital stock of Chris Company. The following data are relevant to the affiliates:

	Allen	Bill	Chris
Retained earnings, 1/1/00	$300,000	$180,000	$120,000
Income from independent operations:			
2000	190,000	70,000	70,000
2001	200,000	80,000	50,000
2002	230,000	90,000	80,000
Dividends declared:			
2000	60,000	30,000	25,000
2001	80,000	50,000	30,000
2002	85,000	40,000	30,000

Required:

A. Calculate consolidated retained earnings on December 31, 2001.

B. Calculate consolidated retained earnings on December 31, 2002.

C. Calculate noncontrolling interest in combined income for 2001 and 2002.

EXERCISE 9-4 Indirect Holdings—Multiple Types

A Company owns 80% of B Company, 70% of C Company, 90% of D Company, and 50% of E Company. In addition, D Company owns 20% of C Company, and B Company owns 90% of F Company. During 2002 the companies had the following incomes from their independent operations:

A Company	$140,000
B Company	90,000
C Company	100,000
D Company	60,000
E Company	70,000
F Company	40,000
Total	$500,000

Required:

A. Draw an affiliation diagram.

B. Calculate consolidated net income for 2002.

C. Calculate noncontrolling interest in combined income for 2002.

EXERCISE 9-5 **Indirect Holdings—Cost Method Entries**

The following investments were all made on January 1, 2002.

Acquiring Company	Acquired Company	% Interest Acquired	Cost
P	S	90%	$306,000
S	T	80%	154,880
T	U	70%	80,000

Stockholders' equity, earnings, and dividend data for the affiliated companies at the end of 2002 were:

	P	S	T	U
Capital stock	$250,000	$200,000	$100,000	$50,000
Retained earnings, 1/1	174,250	108,000	93,600	53,250
Reported net income	120,404	83,560	54,250	30,250
Dividends declared	20,000	15,000	10,000	10,000
Retained earnings, 12/31	274,654	176,560	137,850	73,500

Investments are recorded using the cost method.

Required:

Prepare the workpaper eliminating entries for the preparation of a consolidated statements workpaper on December 31, 2002. Assume that any difference between cost and book value pertains to subsidiary land.

EXERCISE 9-6 **Computing Reciprocity Under the Cost Method**

	Company S's Books				
Year	Beginning of Year Retained Earnings	Reported Net Income (loss)	Dividends Declared	End of Year Retained Earnings	Reciprocity Amount
2001	$100,000	$20,000	$ 6,000	$114,000	
2002	$114,000	$35,000	$20,000	$129,000	
2003	$129,000	($6,000)	$10,000	$113,000	
2004	$113,000	$25,000	$10,000	$128,000	
2005	$128,000				

Required:

Determine the dollar amount for the entry to establish reciprocity or to convert to the equity method for each year. Assume that 80% of S Company was acquired on 1/1/2001.

EXERCISE 9-7A **Mathematical Approach to Reciprocal Holdings**

P Company owns 80% of S Company, and S Company owns 10% of P Company. During 2002, the companies earned net income from their independent operations of:

P Company	$300,000
S Company	100,000

Required:

Using the mathematical approach of treating reciprocal stockholdings:

A. Compute consolidated net income.

B Compute noncontrolling interest in combined income.

EXERCISE 9-8A **Mathematical Approach to Reciprocal Holdings**

A Company owns 80% of B Company and 90% of G Company. B Company owns 20% of A Company. G Company owns 10% of B Company. The companies earned the following amounts from their independent operations during the current year:

A Company	$400,000
B Company	270,000
G Company	140,000
Total	$810,000

Required:

Using the mathematical approach of treating reciprocal stockholdings:

A. Compute the noncontrolling interest in the net income of B Company and G Company.

B. Compute consolidated net income.

C. Prepare a schedule to reconcile the amounts above with the total combined income of the three companies.

PROBLEMS

PROBLEM 9-1 **Indirect Holdings—Cost Method**

Adel Company made an open-market purchase of 85% of the common stock of Bell Company on January 1, 2001, at a cost of $188,000. On that date, Bell Company had common stock of $180,000 and retained earnings of $50,000. On January 1, 2002, Bell Company made an open-market purchase of 90% of the common stock of Camp Company for $96,000. Camp Company's equity on January 1, 2002, consisted of common stock of $80,000 and retained earnings of $25,000. Stockholders' equity accounts for the three companies on December 31, 2002, were:

	Adel Company	Bell Company	Camp Company
Common stock	$400,000	$180,000	$80,000
Retained earnings, 1/1	240,000	90,000	25,000
Net income before dividend income	90,000	40,000	27,000
Dividends declared	38,000	17,500	9,000

Any difference between cost and book value of equity acquired represents an over (under)-valuation of land. Investments are recorded using the cost method.

Required:

A. Prepare journal entries on the books of Adel Company and Bell Company to recognize subsidiary dividends for 2002.

B. Prepare eliminating entries in general journal form for the preparation of a consolidated statements workpaper on December 31, 2002.

C. Compute:
   (1) Noncontrolling interest in combined income.
   (2) Consolidated net income for 2002.

PROBLEM 9-2 Indirect Holdings

Blue Company purchased an 80% interest in Green Company on the open market for $128,750 on January 1, 2001. On that date, Green Company had capital stock of $100,000 and retained earnings of $50,000. One year later, on January 1, 2002, Dean Company purchased a 90% interest in Blue Company on the open market for $310,000. Relevant account balances for the three companies on December 31, 2002, were

	Dean	Blue	Green
Capital stock	$350,000	$200,000	$100,000
Retained earnings, 1/1	240,000	140,000	70,000
Net income from independent operations	74,000	36,000	25,000
Dividends declared	30,000	15,000	10,000

Any difference between cost and book value acquired is assignable to subsidiary land.

Required:

A. Prepare a schedule to compute the difference between cost and book value acquired for each investment.

B. Prepare in general journal form the eliminating entries necessary for the preparation of a consolidated statements workpaper on December 31, 2002.

C. Compute:

(1) Noncontrolling interest in combined income for 2002.

(2) Consolidated net income for 2002.

(3) Consolidated retained earnings at December 31, 2002.

PROBLEM 9-3 Indirect Holdings

On January 1, 2000, A Company purchased an 80% interest in the common stock of B Company for $400,000 and a 70% interest in the common stock of C Company for $175,000. One year later, on January 1, 2001, B Company purchased a 15% interest in the common stock of C Company for $49,500. Stockholders' equity for the three companies on January 1, 2000, was:

	A	B	C
Common stock	$ 800,000	$400,000	$200,000
Retained earnings	320,000	80,000	40,000
Total	$1,120,000	$480,000	$240,000

Each company had income from independent operations of $60,000 for each of 2000 and 2001. No dividends were declared by any of the companies. Any difference between cost and book value pertains to subsidiary land. Investments are recorded using the cost method.

Required:

Prepare a partial workpaper for the preparation of consolidated financial statements for A, B, and C Companies on December 31, 2001. Start your workpaper with "Income from Independent Operations" in the income statement section.

PROBLEM 9-4 Reciprocal Holdings—Cost Method Workpaper

Phung Company purchased 70% of the outstanding common stock of Soto Company on January 2, 2002. On that date Soto Company held a 10% interest in common stock of Phung

Company. Summary account data for Phung Company and Soto Company on December 31, 2002 are as follows:

Debits	Phung	Soto
Assets	$282,000	$121,250
Investment in Soto Company	68,000	
Investment in Phung Company		12,500
Cost of Goods Sold and Expenses	220,000	95,000
Dividends Declared	25,000	15,000
Total	$595,000	$243,750

Credits		
Liabilities	$ 43,000	$ 31,250
Common Stock, $10 par value	100,000	25,000
Retained Earnings	140,000	60,000
Sales	301,500	125,000
Dividend Income	10,500	2,500
Total	$595,000	$243,750

Required:
Prepare a consolidated statements workpaper on December 31, 2002, using the treasury stock approach for the reciprocal investment in Phung Company. Any difference between cost and book value relates to land.

PROBLEM 9-5 Indirect Holdings
B Company purchased an 80% interest in C Company on the open market for $125,000 on January 1, 2001. On that date, C Company had capital stock of $100,000 and retained earnings of $42,500. One year later, on January 1, 2002, A Company purchased a 90% interest in B Company on the open market for $330,000. Relevant account balances for the three companies on December 31, 2002 were:

	A	B	C
Capital stock	$350,000	$200,000	$100,000
Retained earnings, 1/1	240,000	130,000	55,000
Net income reported for 2002	87,500	43,000	25,000
Dividends declared during 2002	30,000	15,000	10,000

The difference between cost and book value is assignable to land.

Required:
A. Prepare a schedule to compute the difference between cost and book value for each investment.

B. (1) Assume that the investments are recorded using the cost method. Prepare in general journal form reciprocity and elimination entries for the preparation of a consolidated statements workpaper on December 31, 2002.
   (2) Assume that the investments are recorded using either the complete or partial equity method. Prepare in general journal form the elimination entries for the preparation of a consolidated statements workpaper on December 31, 2002.

C. Compute:
   (1) Noncontrolling interest in combined income for 2002.
   (2) Consolidated net income for 2002.
   (3) Consolidated retained earnings at December 31, 2002.

PROBLEM 9-6   **Indirect Holdings—Controlling and Noncontrolling Interest**

The following investments were all made on January 1, 2002:

Acquiring Company	Acquired Company	% Interest Acquired	Cost
Allen	Barry	85%	$310,000
Barry	Candy	80%	148,000
Candy	Dandy	70%	68,000

Stockholders' equity, earnings, and dividend data for the affiliated companies at the end of 2002 were:

	Allen	Barry	Candy	Dandy
Capital stock	$250,000	$200,000	$100,000	$50,000
Retained earnings, 1/1	174,250	108,000	93,600	53,250
2002 Net income reported	58,700	48,160	42,100	30,250
2002 Dividends declared	20,000	15,000	10,000	10,000
Retained earnings, 12/31	212,950	141,160	125,700	73,500

Required:

A. Compute controlling interest in consolidated net income for 2002.

B. Compute consolidated retained earnings at December 31, 2002.

C. Compute noncontrolling interest in combined income for 2002.

PROBLEM 9-7   **Complex Holdings—Balance Sheet Workpaper**

Condensed balance sheets for A Company, B Company, and C Company on December 31, 2001, are as follows:

	A Company	B Company	C Company
Current Assets	$ 693,600	$ 440,200	$ 420,600
Investment in B Company	1,135,000		
Investment in C Company	75,000	590,000	
Other Assets	1,441,400	680,200	785,000
Total Assets	$3,345,000	$1,710,400	$1,205,600
Liabilities	$ 988,800	$ 494,400	$ 413,800
Capital Stock	1,200,000	600,000	400,000
Other Contributed Capital	381,200	174,800	205,000
Retained Earnings	775,000	441,200	186,800
Total Equities	$3,345,000	$1,710,400	$1,205,600

B Company purchased an 80% interest in C Company for $590,000 on January 1, 1997, when C Company had stockholders' equity consisting of Capital Stock, $400,000; Other Contributed Capital, $205,000; and Retained Earnings, $82,400.

On January 1, 2001, A Company purchased an 85% interest in B Company for $1,135,000 and a 10% interest in C Company for $75,000. Stockholders' equity for B and C Companies on January 1, 2001 was:

	B Company	C Company
Capital Stock	$ 600,000	$400,000
Other Contributed Capital	174,800	205,000
Retained Earnings	480,000	124,600
Total	$1,254,800	$729,600

Required:
Prepare a workpaper for a consolidated balance sheet on December 31, 2001. Include a schedule to verify the difference between cost and book value, which is assignable to land (included in Other Assets).

PROBLEM 9-8 Reciprocal Holdings—Treasury Stock Approach
Pagone Company acquired 90% of the outstanding stock of Suter Company on January 2, 2001. On that date, Suter Company held a 15% interest in Pagone Company. Summary account data for Pagone Company and Suter Company on December 31, 2001, were:

Debits	*Pagone*	*Suter*
Assets	$284,750	$116,250
Investment in Suter Company	72,250	
Investment in Pagone Company		15,000
Cost of Sales and Expenses	220,000	95,000
Dividends Declared	25,000	15,000
Total	$602,000	$241,250

Credits		
Liabilities	$ 49,250	$ 27,500
Capital Stock, $10 par value	100,000	25,000
Retained Earnings	140,000	60,000
Sales	299,250	125,000
Dividend Income	13,500	3,750
Total	$602,000	$241,250

Required:
Prepare a consolidated statements workpaper on December 31, 2001, using the treasury stock approach for the reciprocal investment in Pagone Company.

PROBLEM 9-9 Calculating Consolidated Retained Earnings and Net Income
On January 1, 2000, B Company purchased 90% of the capital stock of C Company. On January 1, 2001, A Company purchased 80% of the capital stock of B Company. On January 1, 2002, A Company purchased 10% of the capital stock of C Company. The following data relate to the affiliated companies:

	A	*B*	*C*
Capital Stock	$200,000	$125,000	$50,000
Retained Earnings, 1/1/00	60,000	40,000	25,000
Reported Net Income			
2000	35,000	20,000	15,000
2001	45,000	25,000	10,000
2002	50,000	25,000	15,000
Dividends Declared and Paid			
2000	15,000	5,000	5,000
2001	20,000	10,000	5,000
2002	20,000	10,000	5,000

Required:
A. Calculate consolidated retained earnings on January 1, 2002.
B. Calculate consolidated retained earnings on January 1, 2003.
C. Calculate consolidated net income for 2002.

PROBLEM 9-10 Indirect Holdings—Equity Method

(This is the same problem as Problem 9-1, but assuming use of the complete or partial equity method.)

Adel Company made an open-market purchase of 85% of the common stock of Bell Company on January 1, 2001, at a cost of $188,000. On that date, Bell Company had common stock of $180,000 and retained earnings of $50,000. On January 1, 2002, Bell Company made an open-market purchase of 90% of the common stock of Camp Company for $96,000. Camp Company's equity on January 1, 2002, consisted of common stock of $80,000 and retained earnings of $25,000. Stockholders' equity accounts for the three companies on December 31, 2002, were:

	Adel Company	Bell Company	Camp Company
Common Stock	$400,000	$180,000	$80,000
Retained Earnings, 1/1	240,000	90,000	25,000
Net Income from Independent Operations	90,000	40,000	27,000
Dividends Declared	38,000	17,500	9,000

Any difference between cost and book value of equity acquired represents an over- (under)-valuation of land.

Required:

A. Prepare journal entries on the books of Bell Company and Adel Company to recognize subsidiary income and dividends received for 2002.

B. Prepare eliminating entries in general journal form for the preparation of a consolidated statements workpaper on December 31, 2002.

C. Compute:
   (1) Noncontrolling interest in combined income for 2002.
   (2) Consolidated net income for 2002.

PROBLEM 9-11 Reciprocal Holdings—Equity Method

(This is the same problem as Problem 9-4, but assuming use of the partial equity method.)
Phung Company purchased 70% of the outstanding common stock of Soto Company on January 2, 2002. On that date Soto Company held a 10% interest in common stock of Phung Company. Summary account data for Phung Company and Soto Company on December 31, 2002, follows:

Debits	Phung	Soto
Assets	$282,000	$121,250
Investment in Soto Company	78,500	
Investment in Phung Company		12,500
Cost of Goods Sold and Expenses	220,000	95,000
Dividends Declared	25,000	15,000
Total	$605,500	$243,750

Credits		
Liabilities	$ 43,000	$ 31,250
Common Stock, $10 par value	100,000	25,000
Retained Earnings	140,000	60,000
Sales	301,500	125,000
Dividend Income		2,500
Equity in Subsidiary Income	21,000	
Total	$605,500	$243,750

Required:

Prepare a consolidated statements workpaper on December 31, 2002, using the treasury stock approach for the reciprocal investment in Phung Company.

PROBLEM 9-12A **Mathematical Approach to Reciprocal Holdings**

On January 1, 1999, the date of incorporation of S Company, P Company purchased 32,000 shares of S Company capital stock at par value of $320,000. On January 1, 2000, S Company purchased 10,000 shares of P Company capital stock on the open market at $22 per share.

The capital stock of each company is $400,000, consisting of 40,000 shares with a par value of $10 per share. Retained earnings balances on January 1, 1999, and earnings and dividends declared for each company for 1999, 2000, and 2001 were:

	Par Company	Sub Company
Retained Earnings, 1/1/99	$160,000	$—0—
Net Income, 1999	60,000	40,000
Dividends Declared, 1999	(20,000)	(20,000)
Net Income, 2000	80,000	20,000
Net Income, 2001	100,000	40,000
Retained Earnings, 12/31/01	$380,000	$80,000

Required:

Assuming the use of the mathematical approach of treating reciprocal stockholdings, (1) prepare workpaper entries to establish reciprocity and eliminate the investment accounts for the preparation of consolidated financial statements on December 31, 2001; (2) prepare the workpaper entries to eliminate the investment account for the preparation of the consolidated financial statements on December 31, 2001, assuming either the partial or complete equity method is used.

10

INTERCOMPANY BOND HOLDINGS AND MISCELLANEOUS TOPICS—CONSOLIDATED FINANCIAL STATEMENTS

LEARNING OBJECTIVES

1. Describe the term "constructive retirement of debt."

2. Describe how the gain or loss on constructive retirement of intercompany bond holdings is allocated between the purchasing and issuing companies.

3. Explain the impact on the consolidated financial statements when a company issues a note to an affiliated company, which then discounts the note with an outside company.

4. Determine the effect on the consolidated financial statements when a subsidiary issues a stock dividend.

5. Understand the difference in how stock dividends and cash dividends issued by a subsidiary company affect the consolidated financial statements.

6. Determine the impact on the investment account when a subsidiary issues a stock dividend from preacquisition earnings and from postacquisition earnings.

7. Explain how the purchase price is allocated when the subsidiary has both common and preferred stock outstanding.

8. Determine the controlling interest in income when the parent company owns both common and preferred stock of the subsidiary.

"For the first time in four years, investors would have been better to ignore the asset-allocation advice of Wall Street's brightest minds and just buy bonds in the final months of 1997. As stock indexes swung wildly throughout the fourth quarter, bond prices marched higher, sending interest rates to their lowest levels since the 1960s. . . . Investors began to view fixed-income investments as a source of profits as well as a haven from the turbulence that dominated most other financial markets."[1]

---

[1] *WSJ*, "Most of Wall Street's Firms Missed Boat on Bond Move," by Suzanne McGee, 2/4/98, p. C1.

In this chapter, we discuss several areas related to the preparation of consolidated financial statements, including:

1. Intercompany bond holdings.
2. Intercompany notes receivable discounted.
3. Stock dividends issued by a subsidiary company.
4. Cash dividends from preacquisition earnings.
5. Preferred stock of a subsidiary.

All new aspects of consolidations introduced in this chapter are the same whether the parent uses the cost or partial equity method. As in prior chapters, the complete equity method differs from the other two in that the beginning retained earnings of the parent always equals the beginning consolidated retained earnings under the complete equity method.[2] Hence no entries are needed to the beginning retained earnings of the parent in the consolidating workpaper. There is, of course, no entry under this method (nor under the partial equity method) to establish reciprocity/convert to equity.

Reporting complications relating to accounting for the difference between the cost of a common stock investment and the book value interest acquired are avoided by assuming that all acquisitions of common stock are made at the book value of the acquired interest in net assets, and that the book values of the subsidiary's assets and liabilities are equal to their fair values on the date of acquisition. Also, deferred tax consequences are avoided by assuming the affiliates file consolidated tax returns. To conserve space, we present the entries for the cost and the complete equity methods only. The workpaper entries for the partial equity method would be identical to those for the cost method with one exception. As in previous chapters, a workpaper entry to reverse the effect of the parent company entries during the year for subsidiary income and dividends replaces the cost method entries to establish reciprocity/convert to equity and eliminate dividend income, if any.

INTERCOMPANY BOND HOLDINGS

An affiliate company may purchase bonds issued by another affiliate directly from the issuing company or from outsiders after the original issue. In either case, because the bonds are held within the affiliated group, the intercompany bond investment (a receivable) and the bonds payable (a liability), along with any related intercompany interest expense and interest revenue, must be eliminated. In other words, because the bonds are not held by external parties, they are viewed as being *constructively retired* in the consolidated financial statements. Constructively retired means that the bonds are considered retired from a consolidated entity point of view, but legally the bonds are still outstanding as far as the issuing company is concerned. Since this is viewed as an early retirement of debt, a gain or loss on the constructive retirement is computed and allocated to the affiliated companies. A brief review of accounting for bond transactions is presented in the next section before the preparation of a consolidated statements workpaper involving intercompany bond holdings is illustrated.

---

[2]As noted in Chapter 9, an exception occurs under the complete equity method when the treasury stock method is used for reciprocal holdings.

ACCOUNTING FOR BONDS—A REVIEW

To review accounting for bonds, assume that a company issued $100,000 par value bonds on January 2, 2001, for $90,000. The bonds mature 10 years later and pay 12% interest each December 31. The bonds were all acquired by one investor, and the fiscal year-end of both entities is December 31. The journal entries for the first year of operations, assuming straight-line amortization of the discount, are:[3]

Issuing Company
2001

Jan. 2	Cash	90,000	
	Discount on Bonds Payable	10,000	
	Bonds Payable		100,000
Dec. 31	Interest Expense	12,000	
	Cash		12,000
31	Interest Expense	1,000	
	Discount on Bonds Payable		1,000

Investor Company
2001

Jan. 2	Investment in Bonds	90,000	
	Cash		90,000
Dec. 31	Cash	12,000	
	Interest Revenue		12,000
31	Investment in Bonds	1,000	
	Interest Revenue		1,000

From the point of view of the issuing company, $90,000 was received, but the company must pay $100,000 to the bondholders when the bonds mature 10 years later. Instead of deferring the $10,000 discount to be reported as a reduction in income in the year that the bonds mature, one-tenth of the discount ($1,000) is amortized each year as an increase in interest expense. The increase in expense results in a reduction of $1,000 in net income each year, which also reduces the retained earnings balance. At the end of 10 years, the issuing company's retained earnings is reduced $120,000 for the cash interest paid and $10,000 for the discount amortization. In effect, the $10,000 discount is recognized as additional interest expense over the life of the bonds. From the investor's point of view, $90,000 is paid for the bonds, but if the bonds are held to maturity, $100,000 will be received. One-tenth of this $10,000 is added to interest revenue each period, which results in an increase in reported income. As a result of acquiring the bond investment at a discount, retained earnings is increased $1,000 each year for a cumulative total of $10,000 over the life of the bonds.

If, in the foregoing example, the bonds had been issued for $110,000, the issuing company receives $10,000 more on the date of issue than must be paid when the bonds mature, while the investor will receive $10,000 less than the purchase price when the bonds mature. The investor (issuing) company, rather than re-porting a reduction (increase) in income when the bonds mature, records one-tenth of the reduction (increase) each year as the premium on the bonds is

---

[3]For simplicity, it is assumed in this chapter that straight-line amortization is used. However, the reader is reminded that the interest method is required unless the straight-line method does not result in a material difference. *Opinion of the Accounting Principles Board No. 21*, "Interest on Receivables and Paya-bles" (New York: AICPA; 1971), par. 15.

amortized to interest revenue (expense) over the remaining life of the bonds. The effect is that the net income of the investor (issuing) company is $1,000 less (greater) each year as a result of amortizing the premium. The effect on income is, of course, also reflected in the reported retained earnings balance.

CONSTRUCTIVE GAIN OR LOSS ON INTERCOMPANY BOND HOLDINGS

The purchase of an affiliate's bonds does not alter the accounting in the books of the individual companies. As noted in the preceding section, the issuing company and the purchasing company recognize a gain or loss on the bond transaction indirectly as the related premium or discount is amortized to interest expense and interest revenue over the remaining life of the bonds. Thus, on the books of the individual companies, the bonds are accounted for as if the transactions were with independent parties. In the preparation of consolidated statements, however, the acquisition of an affiliate's outstanding bonds from outsiders is considered a *constructive retirement* of the bond obligation by the consolidated entity.[4] The generally accepted practice of accounting for the early extinguishment of debt is to report an extraordinary gain (loss) if the carrying value of the bonds is greater than (less than) the purchase price.[5] Thus, as with the intercompany sale of inventory or other assets, the constructive gain or loss is eventually recognized both on the books of the individual companies and the consolidated financial statements but in different periods.

Observe, however, that the constructive gain or loss on the bond retirement *is recognized in the consolidated income statement prior to the recognition of the gain or loss on the books of the individual companies*. In contrast (see Chapter 6), a gain or loss on the intercompany sale of inventory or other assets *is recognized currently on the books of the selling company, but the gain or loss is deferred for consolidation purposes* until the profit or loss is confirmed by an arm's-length transaction with an independent party. Thus, the objectives of the intercompany bond workpaper entries are essentially opposite the objectives of making workpaper entries for the intercompany sale of inventory or other assets. That is to say, in the period the bonds are purchased, workpaper entries are made to accelerate the recognition of the constructive gain or loss. After the bonds are purchased, workpaper entries are then needed to eliminate the portion of the constructive gain or loss recorded during the period on the books of the individual companies. In the case of the intercompany sale of inventory or other assets, workpaper entries are made in the year of the sale to eliminate or defer the profit or loss recorded on the books of the individual companies. In subsequent periods when the asset is sold to a third party and the profit or loss realized from a consolidated point of view, workpaper entries are made to recognize the profit or loss.

As noted in a preceding paragraph, the gain or loss on the bond retirement is computed as the difference between the carrying value (book value) of the liability

---

[4]When one affiliate purchases bonds directly from another affiliate, the purchase price of the bond investment will be equal to the issue price of the bonds. Therefore, there is no constructive gain or loss reported in the consolidated income statement. However, under the approach used in this text, if the issue price is greater than or less than par value, one company will be allocated a gain and the other allocated a loss of an equal amount.

[5]A gain or loss on the early extinguishments of debt is reported as an extraordinary item net of related income tax consequences. *Statement of Financial Accounting Standards No. 4*, "Reporting Gains or Losses from Extinguishments of Debt" (Stamford, CT: Financial Accounting Standards Board, March 1975), par. 8.

and the purchase price of the bonds. There is general agreement on the amount of the gain or loss to be reported, but not on how the gain or loss should be allocated between the affiliated companies involved in the bond transaction for purposes of calculating consolidated net income and the noncontrolling interest in combined income.

Allocation of Constructive Gain or Loss

Four methods for allocating the constructive gain or loss between the parent and subsidiary are supported in practice and in the accounting literature.

1. The constructive gain or loss is allocated entirely to the issuing company. Support for this method is based on the contention that the purchasing affiliate, as a member of the consolidated group operating under the control of common management, was simply acting as an agent for the issuing company. Thus, any gain or loss on the constructive retirement is allocated entirely to the issuing company.

2. The constructive gain or loss is allocated entirely to the purchasing company. Support for this method rests on the contention that the purchasing company initiated the transaction and should be assigned the full amount of the gain or loss.

3. The constructive gain or loss is allocated entirely to the parent company. Under this approach, it is maintained that the management of the parent company controls the financing decisions of the consolidated affiliates. Since management directed or permitted the purchase of the bonds, any gain or loss is allocated entirely to the parent company.

4. The constructive gain or loss is allocated between the purchasing and issuing companies. This method recognizes that a discount or premium will often be associated with both the issuance and purchase of the bonds on the open market. A gain or loss will be recognized over the remaining life of the bonds as each company amortizes the related discount or premium to interest expense and interest revenue. If the bonds are held to maturity, the full amount of the gain or loss will be recognized by the two entities.

The authors consider the fourth method to be the soundest conceptually. The method is consistent with the allocation of a gain or loss between the noncontrolling and controlling interest on other types of intercompany transactions. It also recognizes that if the purchasing company holds the bonds to maturity, the maturity value is paid by the issuing company. In such cases, each company realizes a gain or loss on the bond issuance or purchase that has been recognized on the books of the individual companies over the life of the bonds. Thus, if one of the companies is a partially owned subsidiary, the noncontrolling shareholders have an interest in the portion of the gain or loss allocated to and recorded by the subsidiary. It should be noted, however, that although consolidated net income each year may vary depending on the method used to allocate the gain or loss, *over the life of the issue, use of any of the methods results in the same total consolidated net income* and the same total noncontrolling interest in combined income.

Computing the Constructive Gain or Loss

On the date that bonds of an affiliate are purchased, a constructive gain or loss is computed and this total gain or loss is allocated between the issuing and purchasing companies. The portion of the gain or loss allocated to the issuing company is the difference between the book value (carrying value) of the bonds issued and their par value; the portion allocated to the purchasing company is the difference between the par value of the bonds and their cost. There is no constructive gain or loss to the issuing company if the bonds are issued at par value, nor is there a constructive gain or loss to the purchasing company if the bonds are purchased at par value. If the issue price and the purchase price of the bonds were not equal to par value, there are four possible combinations that can result when a constructive gain or loss to the consolidated entity is allocated between two affiliated companies. The combinations are shown below assuming two different book values of $110,000 and $90,000 and two different purchase prices of $115,000 and $85,000. The bonds have a par value of $100,000 in all situations.

	Issuing *Company*				*Purchasing* *Company*
1.	Book value $110,000	>	Par value $100,000	>	Purchase price $ 85,000
2.	Book value $ 90,000	<	Par value $100,000	<	Purchase price $115,000
3.	Book value $110,000	>	Par value $100,000	<	Purchase price $115,000
4.	Book value $ 90,000	<	Par value $100,000	>	Purchase price $ 85,000

The constructive gain or loss for combination 3 is illustrated below. To compute the gain or loss allocated to each affiliate, the par value is subtracted from the book value and then the purchase price is subtracted from the par value. If the number is positive, it is a gain; if it is negative, it is a loss.

Issuing company	{	Book value	$110,000	}	+$10,000	Constructive gain
	{	Par value	$100,000	}		
Purchasing company	{			}	−$15,000	Constructive loss
	{	Purchase price	$115,000	}		
		Net constructive gain (loss)			($5,000)	

There is a net constructive loss of $5,000 to the consolidated entity because the purchase price of the bonds on the open market exceeded the carrying value of the debt.

To illustrate another situation, assume that the $100,000 par value bonds with a book value of $90,000 were purchased by an affiliated company for $85,000 (combination 4 above).

Issuing company	{	Book value	$ 90,000	}	−$10,000	Constructive loss
	{	Par value	$100,000	}		
Purchasing company	{			}	+$15,000	Constructive gain
	{	Purchase price	$ 85,000	}		
		Net constructive gain (loss)			$5,000	

In this case there is a favorable settlement of debt (carrying value > purchase price) and a constructive gain of $5,000 is reported in the consolidated income statement, of which a $10,000 loss is allocated to the issuing company and a $15,000 gain is allocated to the purchasing company.

Constructive Gains and Losses

	Originally Issued At	
	Premium	*Discount*
Issuing Company	Constructive Gain	Constructive Loss
	Purchased At	
	Premium	*Discount*
Purchasing Company	Constructive Gain	Constructive Loss

In the year that the bonds are constructively retired, if either the issuing company or the purchasing company is a partially owned subsidiary, the noncontrolling interest in combined income is reduced (increased) by a loss (gain). In subsequent periods, the income of the subsidiary will be decreased or increased as the related discount or premium is amortized. The noncontrolling interest is also affected by this increase or decrease in income.

ACCOUNTING FOR INTERCOMPANY BONDS ILLUSTRATED

To illustrate entries that are necessary on the books of the affiliated companies and in the consolidated statements workpaper when one affiliate holds bonds of another affiliate, the following are assumed:

1. P Company acquired an 80% interest in S Company for $1,200,000 on January 2, 1992, when the retained earnings and common stock accounts of S Company were $500,000 and $1,000,000, respectively.
2. On December 31, 2001, P Company acquired $300,000 of S Company's par value bonds (60% of S Company's bonds) on the open market for $310,000 after the semiannual interest payment had been made. At the time of purchase there were $500,000 par value bonds outstanding with a book value of $480,000. The bonds mature in four years on December 31, 1999, and carry a nominal interest rate of 9%. Interest is paid semiannually on June 30 and December 31.
3. Both companies use the straight-line method to amortize bond discounts and premiums because the results obtained do not materially differ from those that would be obtained if the effective-interest method were used.
4. The fiscal year-end of both companies is December 31.

In this illustration, bonds of the subsidiary are purchased by the parent company. Book entries, as well as consolidated statements workpaper entries and procedures, would be similar if the parent company bonds were purchased by a subsidiary company except that the Investment in Bonds account is carried on the books of the subsidiary and the bond liability is carried on the parent company's books. Also note that in this example the parent purchased the bonds at a premium (on investment), while the subsidiary issued the bonds at a discount (on bonds payable). Clearly it is possible that the reverse might occur (purchase at a discount, issue at a premium) or that both the purchase and the issue might occur at a premium, or both at a discount.

BOOK ENTRY RELATED TO BOND INVESTMENT

P Company will prepare the following entry to record the bond investment:

Dec. 31	Investment in S Company Bonds	310,000	
	Cash		310,000

Note that the usual practice of recording a bond investment does not separate the discount or premium. Since the bonds were purchased on the open market, there is no entry made on the issuing company's books. In this illustration, the bonds were purchased on the last day of the fiscal period after the semiannual interest had been paid. Thus, there is no accrued interest to be recorded in the current period.

Consolidated Statements Workpaper—2001

The total gain or loss on the constructive retirement to be reported in the 2001 consolidated income statement and the constructive gain or loss allocated to each company is computed as follows:

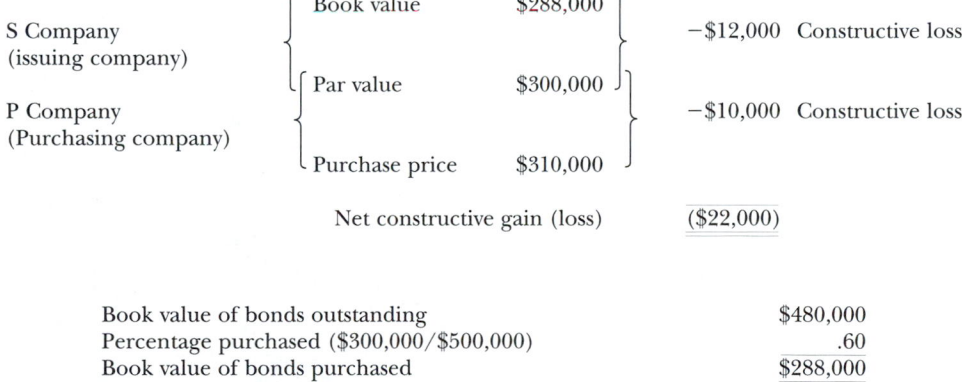

Book value of bonds outstanding		$480,000
Percentage purchased ($300,000/$500,000)		.60
Book value of bonds purchased		$288,000

If the purchase price were less than the book value of $288,000, a total constructive gain would result.

On the books of the individual companies, the constructive loss is not recorded in the year that the bonds are purchased on the open market. From a consolidated entity point of view, however, the purchase is a constructive retirement of debt. Thus, the constructive loss is recognized in the determination of combined income in the year of the purchase.

Workpaper entries necessary in the consolidated statements workpaper for the year ended December 31, 2001, are presented in general journal form below. The consolidated statements workpaper for 2001 is presented in Illustration 10-1.

Cost Method						
80% Owned Subsidiary						
Constructive Retirement of						
Subsidiary's Bonds—Year of Retirement						

ILLUSTRATION 10–1
Consolidated Statements Workpaper
P Company and Subsidiary
For the Year Ended December 31, 2001

Income Statement	P Company	S Company	Eliminations Dr.	Eliminations Cr.	Noncontrolling Interest	Consolidated Balances
Sales	3,104,000	2,200,000				5,304,000
Dividend Income	16,000		(5) 16,000			—0—
Total Revenue	3,120,000	2,200,000				5,304,000
Cost of Goods Sold	1,700,000	1,360,000				3,060,000
Interest Expense		50,000				50,000
Other Expense	1,124,000	665,000				1,789,000
Loss on Constructive Retirement of Bonds			(2) 10,000 (3) 12,000			22,000
Total Cost and Expense	2,824,000	2,075,000				4,921,000
Net/Combined Income	296,000	125,000				383,000
Noncontrolling Interest in Income*					22,600	(22,600)
Net Income to Retained Earnings	296,000	125,000	38,000	—	22,600	360,400
Retained Earnings Statement						
1/1 Retained Earnings						
P Company	1,650,000			(1) 160,000		1,810,000
S Company		700,000	(6) 560,000		140,000	
Net Income from above	296,000	125,000	38,000		22,600	360,400
Dividends Declared						
P Company	(150,000)					(150,000)
S Company		(20,000)		(5) 16,000	(4,000)	
12/31 Retained Earnings to Balance Sheet	1,796,000	805,000	598,000	176,000	158,600	2,020,400
Balance Sheet						
Investment in S Company Bonds	310,000			(2) 10,000 (4) 300,000		—0—
Investment in S Company Stock	1,200,000		(1) 160,000	(6) 1,360,000		—0—
Other Assets	5,420,000	2,620,000				8,040,000
Total Assets	6,930,000	2,620,000				8,040,000
9% Bonds Payable		500,000	(4) 300,000			200,000
Discount on Bonds Payable		(20,000)		(3) 12,000		(8,000)
Other Liabilities	2,134,000	335,000				2,469,000
Capital Stock						
P Company	3,000,000					3,000,000
S Company		1,000,000	(6) 800,000		200,000	
Retained Earnings from above	1,796,000	805,000	598,000	176,000	158,600	2,020,400
Noncontrolling Interest in Net Assets					358,600	358,600
Total Liabilities and Equity	6,930,000	2,620,000	1,858,000	1,858,000		8,040,000

*Noncontrolling interest in income computation: ($125,000 − $12,000) × .20 = $22,600.
(1) To establish reciprocity (convert to equity) as of 1/1/2001 [($700,000 − $500,000) × .80 = $160,000].
(2) To recognize constructive loss not recorded by P Company and adjust the bond investment to par value.
(3) To recognize the constructive loss not recorded by S Company and adjust the intercompany bonds payable to par value.
(4) To eliminate intercompany bond investment and liability.
(5) To eliminate intercompany dividends.
(6) To eliminate investment account.

Cost

Consolidated Statements Workpaper Entries—2001

(1)	Investment in S Company Stock	160,000	
	Beginning Retained Earnings—P Company		160,000
	To establish reciprocity.		

The amount of the reciprocity (conversion to equity) entry is computed as follows:

Retained earnings balance—January 1, 2001	$700,000
Retained earnings balance—date of acquisition	500,000
Increase in retained earnings	200,000
Percentage interest held by P Company	.80
Amount to establish reciprocity	$160,000

(2)	Loss on Constructive Retirement of Bonds	10,000	
	Investment in S Company Bonds		10,000
	To recognize the constructive loss not recorded by P Company and *adjust the bond investment to par value* (i.e., the premium paid by P Company over the par value).		

(3)	Loss on Constructive Retirement of Bonds	12,000	
	Discount on Bonds Payable		12,000
	To recognize the constructive loss not recorded by the subsidiary and *adjust the intercompany bonds to par value* (i.e., the difference between the carrying value to S Company and par value).		

Entries (2) and (3) recognize the constructive loss allocated to each company and adjust the bond investment and carrying value of the intercompany debt to par value in preparation for the elimination of the intercompany receivable and payable.

(4)	Bonds Payable	300,000	
	Investment in S Company Bonds		300,000
	To eliminate intercompany bond investment and liability.		
(5)	Dividend Income	16,000	
	Dividends Declared—S Company		16,000
	To eliminate intercompany dividends.		
(6)	Beginning Retained Earnings—S Company	560,000	
	Common Stock—S Company	800,000	
	Investment in S Company Stock		1,360,000
	To eliminate investment account.		

Entries (2), (3), and (4) could be combined into one entry as follows:

Loss on Constructive Retirement of Bonds	22,000	
Bonds Payable	300,000	
Discount on Bonds Payable		12,000
Investment in S Company Bonds		310,000

Complete Equity Method If the complete equity method is used, entry (1), the reciprocity entry, is not needed and the following entry replaces entry (5) above. The consolidated statements workpaper for 2001, assuming the use of the complete equity method, is presented in Illustration 10-2.

(1)	Equity in S Company Income	80,400	
	Dividends Declared		16,000
	Investment in S Company Stock		64,400
	To eliminate the intercompany income and dividends.		

Complete Equity Method			ILLUSTRATION 10-2				
80% Owned Subsidiary			**Consolidated Statements Workpaper**				
Constructive Retirement of			**P Company and Subsidiary**				
Subsidiary's Bonds—Year of Retirement			**For the Year Ended December 31, 2001**				

	P	S	Eliminations		Noncontrolling	Consolidated
Income Statement	*Company*	*Company*	*Dr.*	*Cr.*	*Interest*	*Balances*
Sales	3,104,000	2,200,000				5,304,000
Equity Income	80,400		(1) 80,400			—0—
Total Revenue	3,184,400	2,200,000				5,304,000
Cost of Goods Sold	1,700,000	1,360,000				3,060,000
Interest Expense		50,000				50,000
Other Expense	1,124,000	665,000				1,789,000
Loss on Constructive Retirement						
of Bonds			(2) 22,000			22,000
Total Cost and Expense	2,824,000	2,075,000				4,921,000
Net/Combined Income	360,400	125,000				383,000
Noncontrolling Interest in Income*					22,600	(22,600)
Net Income to Retained Earnings	360,400	125,000	102,400	—	22,600	360,400
Retained Earnings Statement						
1/1 Retained Earnings						
P Company	1,810,000					1,810,000
S Company		700,000	(4) 560,000		140,000	
Net Income from above	360,400	125,000	102,400		22,600	360,400
Dividends Declared						
P Company	(150,000)					(150,000)
S Company		(20,000)		(1) 16,000	(4,000)	
12/31 Retained Earnings to Balance						
Sheet	2,020,400	805,000	662,400	16,000	158,600	2,020,400
Balance Sheet						
Investment in S Company Bonds	310,000			(2) 10,000		—0—
				(3) 300,000		
Investment in S Company Stock	1,424,400			{(1) 64,400		—0—
				{(4) 1,360,000		
Other Assets	5,420,000	2,620,000				8,040,000
Total Assets	7,154,400	2,620,000				8,040,000
9% Bonds Payable		500,000	(3) 300,000			200,000
Discount on Bonds Payable		(20,000)		(2) 12,000		(8,000)
Other Liabilities	2,134,000	335,000				2,469,000
Capital Stock						
P Company	3,000,000					3,000,000
S Company		1,000,000	(4) 800,000		200,000	
Retained Earnings from above	2,020,400	805,000	662,400	16,000	158,600	2,020,400
Noncontrolling Interest in Net Assets					358,600	358,600
Total Liabilities and Equity	7,154,400	2,620,000	1,762,400	1,762,400		8,040,000

*Noncontrolling interest in income computation: ($125,000 − $12,000) × .20 = $22,600.
(1) To eliminate intercompany income and dividends.
(2) To recognize the constructive loss and adjust the bond investment and the intercompany bond to par value.
(3) To eliminate intercompany bond investment and liability.
(4) To eliminate investment account.

Since the bonds were purchased on the open market on the *last day of the fiscal period*, there is no intercompany interest reported in the 2001 income statement. Accordingly, no elimination of intercompany interest revenue and expense is required in the 2001 consolidated statements workpaper. Since the amount of net income reported by S Company that is included in combined income is reduced by the constructive loss allocated to S Company, noncontrolling interest in combined income is 20% of the income reported by S Company reduced by the constructive loss of $12,000 allocated to the subsidiary [.20 × ($125,000 − $12,000) = $22,600].

A careful review of Illustrations 10-1 and 10-2 will reveal these important points concerning the objectives of the bond elimination entries:

1. Since the bonds were purchased this year, the constructive loss is reported in full in the determination of combined income.

2. Interest expense is the amortized interest paid to outside parties during the fiscal period. In this illustration, the intercompany portion was purchased on December 31. Therefore, the bonds were held by outside parties for the full 12 months. Interest expense reported in the consolidated income statement is for the full year, which is equal to the cash interest paid of $45,000 plus discount amortization of $5,000. As shown in the next illustration, if the bonds are held by P Company during the period, interest expense, net of amortization, is eliminated. Thus, for a 12-month period, $30,000 in interest expense is eliminated, resulting in consolidated interest expense of $20,000 ($50,000 times the 40% held by outside parties).

3. The book value of the debt is the amount held by outside parties on the balance sheet date, which is $192,000 [($500,000 − $20,000) × .40]. The 60% held by the parent is eliminated by workpaper entries (2) and (4) in Illustration 10-1 and (1) and (2) in Illustration 10-2.

Consolidated net income and retained earnings for the year ended December 31, 2001, using the t-account approach, are computed as shown in Figure 10-1.

Year Subsequent to Acquisition of Bonds, Entries on the Books of Affiliated Companies—2002

During 2002, the two companies record on their individual books the following entries related to the bond transaction:

P Company's Books		
Entries on June 30 and December 31		
Cash	13,500	
Interest Revenue		13,500
To record receipt of interest ($300,000 × .09 × 6/12).		
Interest Revenue	1,250	
Investment in S Company Bonds		1,250
To amortize premium on outstanding bonds ($10,000 ÷ 8 periods).		

For the full year 2002, P Company received total cash of $27,000, recognized total interest revenue of $24,500, and recorded amortization of the premium on the bond of $2,500.

FIGURE 10-1

**T-Account Approach to Consolidated
Net Income and Related Earnings**

Consolidated Net Income—2001

	Reported net income of P Company		$ 296,000
	Less: Dividend income		(16,000)
	Net income from independent operations		280,000
	Less: Constructive loss not recorded by P Company in		
	the current year (premium amortization)		(10,000)
	P Company's contribution to combined income		270,000
	Reported net income of S Company	$125,000	
	Less: Constructive loss not recorded by S Company	(12,000)	
	S Company's contribution to combined income	113,000	
	Percentage interest in S Company	.80	90,400
	Consolidated net income		$ 360,400

Consolidated Retained Earnings—December 31, 2001

		Ending retained earnings—P Company, December 31,		
		2001		$1,796,000
Constructive loss on bond retirement not recorded by P Company	10,000			
		Retained earnings adjusted for unrecorded constructive		
		loss		1,786,000
		Ending retained earnings—S Company	$805,000	
		Less: Retained earnings—date of acquisition	(500,000)	
		Increase in recorded retained earnings	305,000	
		Less: Constructive loss on bond retirement not		
		recorded by S Company	(12,000)	
		Adjusted increase in recorded retained earnings	293,000	
		Percentage interest in S Company	.80	234,400
		Consolidated retained earnings on December 31, 2001		$2,020,400

Complete Equity Method—Additional Entries on the Books of P Company Subsequent to Acquisition of Debt

In the years subsequent to the acquisition of the subsidiary's debt, there are additional entries needed by P Company. The following entries would be made to the Investment in S Company Stock account in the year subsequent to acquisition:

Investment in S Company Stock	112,000	
Equity in S Company Income		112,000
To record equity income (80% of $140,000).		
Cash	48,000	
Investment in S Company Stock		48,000
To record dividends received (80% of $60,000).		
Investment in S Company Stock	4,900	
Equity in S Company Income		4,900
To eliminate the intercompany effect from the amortization of P Company's share of the constructive loss.		

This last entry ensures that P Company's income equals consolidated income. The $4,900 can be computed several ways. First, the total constructive loss is $22,000, of which P Company is allocated $19,600. Since the total loss will be recognized to income over the term of the bond through amortization and because the bond has four years remaining, one-fourth of the loss is amortized in each period ($19,600/4 = $4,900). Because this is an intercompany transaction, under the complete equity method, an additional $4,900 must be added to income to offset the additional expense. Recall that the entire $22,000 is recognized as a loss in the year of purchase. Alternatively, the $4,900 can be computed by comparing the amount of interest expense and interest revenue recognized by each company as follows:

Interest Expense (60% of S Company's $50,000 interest expense reported in 2002)	$30,000
Interest Revenue recognized by P Company (2002)	24,500
Excess Expense	5,500
Controlling interest's share of the total constructive loss ($19,600/$22,000) =	.8909
	4,900

S Company's Books

Entries on June 30 and December 31

Interest Expense	22,500	
Cash		22,500
To record payment of interest ($500,000 × .09 × 6/12).		
Interest Expense	2,500	
Discount on Bonds Payable		2,500
To amortize discount on outstanding bonds ($20,000 ÷ 8 periods).		

Thus, S Company paid $45,000 in cash interest and amortized $5,000 of the bond discount. Since 60% of the bonds ($300,000) were purchased by P Company, S Company paid $27,000 cash to P Company and amortized $3,000 of the related bond discount.

Recall in the prior year, a constructive loss of $22,000 was reported on the consolidated income statement. This amount is equal to the sum of the premium yet to be amortized by P Company ($10,000) and the discount yet to be amortized by S Company ($12,000). Therefore, as the companies amortize these amounts, they, in essence, recognize a portion of the total constructive loss throughout the term of the bond. For the full year (2002), $2,500 ($1,250 × 2) of the total constructive loss was recognized on the books of P Company as a result of amortizing the premium on the investment. S Company recognized $3,000 [($2,500 × 2) × .60] of its share of the loss through the amortization of the discount. To prevent double counting, these amortization amounts must be eliminated for consolidated purposes.

The account balances related to the intercompany bond holdings at the end of 2002 are:

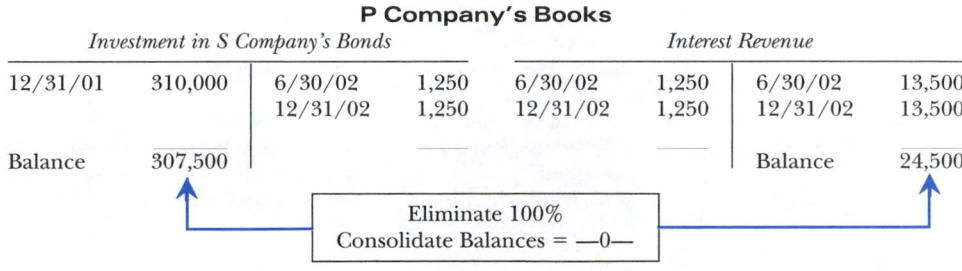

P Company's Books

Investment in S Company's Bonds				*Interest Revenue*		
12/31/01	310,000	6/30/02	1,250	6/30/02	1,250	6/30/02	13,500
		12/31/02	1,250	12/31/02	1,250	12/31/02	13,500
Balance	307,500					Balance	24,500

Eliminate 100%
Consolidate Balances = —0—

S Company's Books

9% Bonds Payable			*Discount on Bonds Payable*			
	12/31/01	500,000	12/31/01	20,000		
					6/30/02	2,500
					12/31/02	2,500
			Bal.	15,000		

Consolidated balance = $500,000 × .40 = $200,000	Consolidated balance = $15,000 × .40 = $6,000

Interest Expense			
2002			
6/30/02	22,500		
6/30/02	2,500		
12/31/02	22,500		
12/31/02	2,500		
Balance	50,000		

Consolidated balance = $50,000 × .40 = $20,000

> Rationale: For consolidated balances, 60% of the bonds held by the affiliated company must be eliminated. The remaining 40%, held by outside parties, is reported in the consolidated financial statement.

Consolidated Statements Workpaper Entries—December 31, 2002

Workpaper entries necessary in the consolidated statements workpaper for the year ended December 31, 2002, are presented in general journal form below. The consolidated statements workpaper for 2002 is presented in Illustration 10-3.

(1)	Investment in S Company Stock	244,000	
	Beginning Retained Earnings—P Company		244,000
	To establish reciprocity/convert to equity [($805,000 − $500,000) × .80 = $244,000].		
(2)	Beginning Retained Earnings—P Company	10,000	
	Investment in S Company Bonds		10,000
	To adjust beginning retained earnings for constructive loss (recorded in prior year as workpaper entry only; see 2001 entry (2)) and to adjust investment to par.		
(3)	Beginning Retained Earnings—P Company ($12,000 × .80)	9,600	
	Beginning Retained Earnings—S Company ($12,000 × .20)	2,400	
	Discount on Bonds Payable ($15,000 × .60)		12,000
	To adjust beginning retained earnings balances for unrecorded constructive loss at beginning of the year (recorded in 2001 as workpaper entry only; see 2001 entry (3)) and adjust intercompany bonds to par value.		

Cost Method

80% Owned Subsidiary

Constructive Retirement of

Subsidiary's Bonds—

One Year After Retirement

ILLUSTRATION 10-3

Consolidated Statements Workpaper

P Company and Subsidiary

For the Year Ended December 31, 2002

Income Statement	P Company	S Company	Eliminations Dr.		Eliminations Cr.		Noncontrolling Interest	Consolidated Balances
Sales	3,546,000	2,020,000						5,566,000
Dividend Income	48,000		(8)	48,000				—0—
Interest Income	24,500		(6)	27,000	(4)	2,500		—0—
Total Revenue	3,618,500	2,020,000						5,566,000
Cost of Goods Sold	2,040,000	1,200,000						3,240,000
					(5)	3,000		
Interest Expense		50,000			(6)	27,000		20,000
Other Expense	1,124,500	630,000						1,754,500
Total Cost and Expense	3,164,500	1,880,000						5,014,500
Net/Combined Income	454,000	140,000						551,500
Noncontrolling Interest in Income*							28,600	(28,600)
Net Income to Retained Earnings	454,000	140,000		75,000		32,500	28,600	522,900
Retained Earnings Statement								
1/1 Retained Earnings								
P Company	1,796,000		(2)	10,000				2,020,400
			(3)	9,600	(1)	244,000		
S Company			(3)	2,400				
		805,000	(9)	644,000			158,600	
Net Income from above	454,000	140,000		75,000		32,500	28,600	522,900
Dividends Declared								
P Company	(150,000)							(150,000)
S Company		(60,000)			(8)	48,000	(12,000)	
12/31 Retained Earnings to Balance Sheet	2,100,000	885,000		741,000		324,500	175,200	2,393,300
Balance Sheet								
			(2)	10,000				
Investment in S Company Bonds	307,500		(4)	2,500	(7)	300,000		—0—
Investment in S Company Stock	1,200,000		(1)	244,000	(9)	1,444,000		—0—
Other Assets	5,812,500	2,690,000						8,502,500
Total Assets	7,320,000	2,690,000						8,502,500
9% Bonds Payable		500,000	(7)	300,000				200,000
Discount on Bonds Payable		(15,000)	(5)	3,000	(3)	12,000		(6,000)
Other Liabilities	2,220,000	320,000						2,540,000
Capital Stock								
P Company	3,000,000							3,000,000
S Company		1,000,000	(9)	800,000			200,000	
Retained Earnings from above	2,100,000	885,000		741,000		324,500	175,200	2,393,300
Noncontrolling Interest in Net Assets							375,200	375,200
Total Liabilities and Equity	7,320,000	2,690,000		2,090,500		2,090,500		8,502,500

*Noncontrolling interest in income computation: ($140,000 + $3,000) × .20 = $28,600.
(1) To establish reciprocity (convert to equity) as of 1/1/2002 [($805,000 − $500,000) × .80 = $244,000].
(2) To adjust beginning retained earnings for unrecorded constructive loss recorded in prior years as workpaper entry only and adjust bond investment to par value.
(3) To adjust beginning retained earnings for unrecorded constructive loss at the beginning of year, adjust interest expense for the loss recorded this period, and adjust intercompany bond payable to par value.
(4) To reverse the amortization of premium on investment recorded by P Company during the year.
(5) To reverse the amortization of discount on bonds payable recorded by S Company during the year.
(6) To eliminate intercompany interest.
(7) To eliminate intercompany bond investment and bonds payable.
(8) To eliminate intercompany dividends.
(9) To eliminate investment account.

(4) Investment in S Company Bonds	2,500	
Interest Revenue ($1,250 + $1,250)		2,500
To reverse the amortization of premium on investment recorded by P Company during the current year (and not needed by consolidated entity since the constructive loss was recorded in its entirety in 2001).		
(5) Discount on Bonds Payable ($5,000 × .60)	3,000	
Interest Expense		3,000
To reverse amortization of discount on bonds payable recorded by S Company during current year (and not needed by consolidated entity since the constructive loss was recorded in its entirety in 2001).		

Recall that the individual companies record a portion of the loss ($5,500 in total) this year as amortization of the discount ($5,000 × .60 = $3,000) and premium ($2,500). Workpaper entries are necessary to add back this portion of the loss reported as a reduction in the current income of the individual companies because the entire loss was reported in the consolidated income statement in the year that the bonds were acquired by P Company. Failure to do so will result in reporting the constructive loss twice, once in the year of acquisition and again in subsequent periods when the companies record the loss. The credit to interest revenue for $2,500 [entry (4)] and the credit to interest expense for $3,000 [entry (5)] increase combined income by $5,500.

(6) Interest Revenue ($45,000 × .60) or ($13,500 + $13,500)	27,000	
Interest Expense		27,000
To eliminate intercompany interest.		
(7) Bonds Payable ($500,000 × .60)	300,000	
Investment in S Company Bonds		300,000
To eliminate intercompany bond investment and bonds payable.		
(8) Dividend Income	48,000	
Dividends Declared		48,000
To eliminate intercompany dividends.		
(9) Beginning Retained Earnings—S Company	644,000	
Common Stock—S Company	800,000	
Investment in S Company Stock		1,444,000
To eliminate the investment account.		

Workpaper entries (2) through (7) could be combined into one entry as follows:

Beginning Retained Earnings—P Company	19,600	
Beginning Retained Earnings—S Company	2,400	
Interest Revenue	24,500	
Bonds Payable	300,000	
Interest Expense		30,000
Discount on Bonds Payable		9,000
Investment in S Company Bonds		307,500

Noncontrolling interest in combined income is 20% of the income reported by S Company plus the portion of the loss recorded by S during 2002, but fully reported in the 2001 consolidated income statement, the year the bonds were constructively retired [.20 × ($140,000 + $3,000) = $28,600].

Consolidated Statements Workpaper Entries—2002

The Complete Equity Method

(1)	Investment in S Company Stock	19,600	
	Beginning Retained Earnings—S Company	2,400	
	($12,000 × .20)		
	Investment in S Company Bonds		10,000
	Discount on Bonds Payable ($15,000 × .60)		12,000
	To adjust beginning retained earnings balances for unrecorded constructive loss at beginning of the year (recorded in 2001 in workpaper entry only; see 2001 entry 3)) and adjust intercompany bonds to par value.		
(2)	Investment in S Company Bonds	2,500	
	Interest Revenue ($1,250 + $1,250)		2,500
	To reverse the amortization of premium on investment recorded by P Company during the current year (and not needed by consolidated entity since the constructive loss was recorded in its entirety in 2001).		
(3)	Discount on Bonds Payable ($5,000 × .60)	3,000	
	Interest Expense		3,000
	To reverse amortization of discount on bonds payable recorded by S Company during current year (and not needed by consolidated entity since the constructive loss was recorded in its entirety in 2001).		
(4)	Bonds Payable ($500,000 × .60)	300,000	
	Investment in S Company Bonds		300,000
	To eliminate intercompany bond investment and bonds payable.		
(5)	Interest Revenue ($45,000 × .60) or ($13,500 + $13,500)	27,000	
	Interest Expense		27,000
	To eliminate intercompany interest.		
(6)	Equity Income	116,900	
	Investment in P Company Stock		68,900
	Dividends Declared		48,000
	To eliminate intercompany dividends and income.		
(7)	Beginning Retained Earnings—S Company	644,000	
	Common Stock—S Company	800,000	
	Investment in S Company Stock		1,444,000
	To eliminate the investment account.		

Whether a single entry or a series of entries are made, the eliminating entries must accomplish the following under the cost (or complete equity) method (Illustration 10-4):

1. Under the *cost* or *partial equity method*, the parent company's beginning retained earnings is reduced by:
   a. 100% of the constructive loss allocated to P Company that has not been recorded in prior periods as a decrease in interest revenue via the periodic amortization of premium ($10,000).
   b. 80% of the constructive loss allocated to S Company that has not been recorded in prior periods as an increase in interest expense via the periodic discount amortization ($9,600).

   Under the *complete equity method*, the parent company's beginning retained earnings does not need to be adjusted for these amounts because each year adjustments are made to the parent company accounts Equity in Subsidiary Income (and hence to retained earnings of P Company) and Investment in S Company. Thus, replacing the entries to Beginning Retained Earnings—P Company

Complete Equity Method
80% Owned Subsidiary
Constructive Retirement of
Subsidiary's Bonds—
One Year After Retirement

ILLUSTRATION 10–4
Consolidated Statements Workpaper
P Company and Subsidiary
For the Year Ended December 31, 2002

Income Statement	P Company	S Company	Eliminations Dr.	Eliminations Cr.	Noncontrolling Interest	Consolidated Balances
Sales	3,546,000	2,020,000				5,566,000
Equity Income	116,900		(6) 116,900			—0—
Interest Income	24,500		(5) 27,000	(2) 2,500		—0—
Total Revenue	3,687,400	2,020,000				5,566,000
Cost of Goods Sold	2,040,000	1,200,000				3,240,000
				(3) 3,000		
Interest Expense		50,000		(5) 27,000		20,000
Other Expense	1,124,500	630,000				1,754,500
Total Cost and Expense	3,164,500	1,880,000				5,014,500
Net/Combined Income	522,900	140,000				551,500
Noncontrolling Interest in Income*					28,600	(28,600)
Net Income to Retained Earnings	522,900	140,000	143,900	32,500	28,600	522,900
Retained Earnings Statement						
1/1 Retained Earnings						
P Company	2,020,400					2,020,400
			(1) 2,400			
S Company		805,000	(7) 644,000		158,000	
Net Income from above	522,900	140,000	143,900	32,500	28,600	522,900
Dividends Declared						
P Company	(150,000)					(150,000)
S Company		(60,000)		(6) 48,000	(12,000)	
12/31 Retained Earnings to Balance Sheet	2,393,300	885,000	790,300	80,500	175,200	2,393,300
Balance Sheet						
			(2) 2,500	(1) 10,000		
Investment in S Company Bonds	307,500			(4) 300,000		—0—
Investment in S Company Stock	1,493,300		(1) 19,600	(6) 68,900		—0—
				(7) 1,444,000		
Other Assets	5,812,500	2,690,000				8,502,500
Total Assets	7,613,300	2,690,000				8,502,500
9% Bonds Payable		500,000	(4) 300,000			200,000
Discount on Bonds Payable		(15,000)	(3) 3,000	(1) 12,000		(6,000)
Other Liabilities	2,220,000	320,000				2,540,000
Capital Stock						
P Company	3,000,000					3,000,000
S Company		1,000,000	(7) 800,000		200,000	
Retained Earnings from above	2,393,300	885,000	790,300	80,500	175,200	2,393,300
Noncontrolling Interest in Net Assets					375,200	375,200
Total Liabilities and Equity	7,613,300	2,690,000	1,915,400	1,915,400		8,502,500

*Noncontrolling interest in income computation: ($140,000 + $3,000) × .20 = $28,600.
(1) To adjust the investment in S Company Stock account and beginning retained earnings of S Company for the constructive loss reported in the previous year.
(2) To reverse the amortization of premium on investment recorded by P Company during the current year.
(3) To reverse the amortization of discount on bonds payable recorded by S company during the current year.
(4) To eliminate intercompany bond investment and bonds payable.
(5) To eliminate intercompany interest.
(6) To eliminate intercompany dividends and income.
(7) To eliminate the investment account.

with entries to the investment account facilitates the elimination of the investment account under the complete equity method.

The sum of these two components is the controlling interest share of the constructive loss not recorded on the books of the affiliated companies as of the beginning of the current period. This sum is also equal to (a) 100% of the unamortized premium on the books of the parent ($10,000) plus (b) the parent's share of the unamortized discount related to the intercompany bonds on the subsidiary's books (.80 × $12,000 = $9,600) at the beginning of the year.

2. The beginning retained earnings balance of the subsidiary is reduced by the noncontrolling interest share of the constructive loss allocated to the subsidiary that has not been recorded in prior periods through periodic amortization of the discount related to the intercompany bonds.

3. The interest expense and interest revenue related to the intercompany bonds and reported by the respective companies are eliminated from the income statement.

4. The bond investment and the carrying value of the intercompany bonds are eliminated from the balance sheet.

Consolidated net income and retained earnings for the year ended December 31, 2002, using the t-account approach, are computed as shown in Figure 10-2.

Second Year Subsequent to the Debt Acquisition—2003

In subsequent years until the bonds mature, the companies will continue to recognize a portion of the loss each year as the discount and premium are amortized on their separate books. The consolidated statements workpaper entries are similar to those illustrated for 2002. Recall that the constructive loss occurred on the last day of 2001. Thus 2002 was the first year necessitating amortization reversals, and 2003 is the second. Workpaper entries in general journal form related to the intercompany bondholdings in the 2003 consolidated statements workpaper are as follows:

Consolidated Statement Workpapers Entries—2003

(1) Beginning Retained Earnings—P Company*   10,000
      Investment in S Company Bonds   10,000
        To adjust beginning retained earnings for constructive loss (recorded in 2001 as
        workpaper entry only; see 2001 entry (2)) and to adjust investment to par.

(2) Beginning Retained Earnings—P Company   9,600
      ($12,000 × .80)*
      Beginning Retained Earnings—S Company   2,400
      ($12,000 × .20)
      Discount on Bonds Payable ($15,000 × .60)   12,000
        To adjust beginning retained earnings balances for constructive loss (recorded in
        2001 as workpaper entry only; see 2001 entry (3)) and adjust intercompany bonds
        to par value.

(3) Investment in S Company Bonds   5,000
      Retained Earnings—P Company*   2,500
        (reverse amortization of premium from
          2002 workpaper entry)
      Interest Revneue ($1,250 + $1,250)   2,500
        To reverse the amortization of premium on investment recorded by P Company
        during the current year and prior year (and not needed by consolidated entity
        since the constructive loss was recorded in its entirety in 2001).

(4)	Discount on Bonds Payable ($5,000 × .60)	6,000	
	Retained Earnings—P Company*		3,000
	Interest Expense		3,000

To reverse amortization of discount on bonds payable recorded by S Company during current year and prior year (and not needed by consolidated entity since the constructive loss was recorded in its entirety in 2001).

(5)	Interest Revenue	27,000	
	Interest Expense		27,000

To eliminate intercompany interest.

(6)	Bonds Payable	300,000	
	Investment in S Company Bonds		300,000

To eliminate intercompany bond investment and bonds payable.

FIGURE 10–2

**T-Account Approach to Consolidated
Net Income and Retained Earnings**

Consolidated Net Income—2002

Reported net income of P Company			$ 454,000
Less: Dividend income			(48,000)
Net income from independent operations			406,000
Add: Constructive loss recorded by P Company in the current year (premium amortization)			2,500
P Company's contribution to combined income			408,500
Reported net income of S Company		$140,000	
Add: Constructive loss recorded by S Company in the current year (discount amortization)		3,000	
S Company's contribution to combined income		143,000	
Percentage interest in S Company		.80	114,400
Consolidated net income			$ 522,900

Consolidated Retained Earnings—December 31, 2002

Ending retained earnings—P Company, December 31, 2002			$2,100,000
Constructive loss on bond retirement not recorded by P Company ($10,000 − $2,500) 7,500			
Retained earnings adjusted for unrecorded constructive loss			2,092,500
Ending retained earnings—S Company		$ 885,000	
Less: Retained earnings—date of acquisition		(500,000)	
Increase in recorded retained earnings		1,385,000	
Less: Constructive loss on bond retirement not recorded by S Company ($12,000 − 3000)		(9,000)	
Adjusted increase in recorded retained earnings		1,376,000	
Percentage interest in S Company		.80	1,100,800
Consolidated retained earnings on December 31, 2002			$3,193,300

Under the complete equity method, the amounts in entries (1) through (4) recorded to P Company's beginning retained earnings would be assigned to the Investment in S Company Stock account. These accounts are marked with an asterisk.

Three-Year Comparision

Figures 10-3 and 10-4 show the entries on P Company's books, S Company's books, and the consolidated workpaper entries using both the cost method and the com-

FIGURE 10–3

Cost Method
Three-Year Summary

Entries on P Company's Books

	Year 2001 Dr	Year 2001 Cr	Year 2002 Dr	Year 2002 Cr	Year 2003 Dr	Year 2003 Cr
Investment in S Company Bond	310,000					
Cash		310,000				
Cash	16,000		48,000		60,000	
Dividend Income		16,000		48,000		60,000
Cash (on an annual basis)			27,000		27,000	
Investment in S Company Bond				2,500		2,500
Interest Income				24,500		24,500

Entries on S Company's Books

	Year 2001 Dr	Year 2001 Cr	Year 2002 Dr	Year 2002 Cr	Year 2003 Dr	Year 2003 Cr
Interest Expense			30,000		30,000	
Discount on Bond Payable				3,000		3,000
Cash				27,000		27,000

Entries on the Workpaper

	Year 2001 Dr	Year 2001 Cr	Year 2002 Dr	Year 2002 Cr	Year 2003 Dr	Year 2003 Cr
Investment in S	160,000		244,000		308,000	
Beginning Retained Earnings—P Company		160,000		244,000		308,000
Loss on Constructive Retirement of Bond	22,000					
Beginning Retained Earnings—P Company			19,600		19,600	
Beginning Retained Earnings—S Company			2,400		2,400	
Discount on Bond Payable		12,000		12,000		12,000
Investment in S Company Bond		10,000		10,000		10,000
Investment in S Company Bond			2,500		5,000	
Interest Income				2,500		2,500
Beginning Retained Earnings—P Company						2,500
Discount on Bond Payable			3,000		6,000	
Interest Expense				3,000		3,000
Beginning Retained Earnings—P Company						3,000
Interest Income			27,000		27,000	
Interest Expense				27,000		27,000
Bond Payable	300,000		300,000		300,000	
Investment in S Company Bond		300,000		300,000		300,000
Dividend Income	16,000		48,000		60,000	
Dividend Declared		16,000		48,000		60,000
Beginning Retained Earnings—S Company	560,000		644,000		708,000	
Common Stock—S Company	800,000		800,000		800,000	
Difference Between Cost and Book Value	0		0		0	
Investment in S Company		1,360,000		1,444,000		1,508,000

FIGURE 10–4

**Complete Equity Method,
Three-Year Summary**

Entries on P Company's Books

	Year 2001		Year 2002		Year 2003	
Investment in S Company Bond	310,000					
Cash		310,000				
Cash (For Interest)			27,000		27,000	
Investment in S Company Bonds				2,500		2,500
Interest Income				24,500		24,500
Cash (For Dividends)	16,000		48,000		60,000	
Investment in S Company Stock		16,000		48,000		60,000
Investment in S Company	100,000		112,000		160,000	
Equity in S Income		100,000		112,000		160,000
Equity in S Income	19,600					
Investment in S Company Stock		19,600				
Investment in S Company Stock			4,900		4,900	
Equity in S Income ($19,600/4)				4,900		2,900

Entries on S Company's Books

	Year 2001		Year 2002		Year 2003	
Interest Expense			30,000		30,000	
Discount on Bond Payable				3,000		3,000
Cash				27,000		27,000

Entries on the Workpaper

	Year 2001		Year 2002		Year 2003	
Equity in S Income	80,400		116,900		164,900	
Dividends Declared		16,000		48,000		60,000
Investment in S Company Stock		64,400		68,900		104,900
Beginning Retained Earnings—S Company	560,000		644,000		708,000	
Common Stock—S Company	800,000		800,000		800,000	
Difference Between Cost and Book Value	0		0		0	
Investment in S Company		1,360,000		1,444,000		1,508,000
Loss on Constructive Retirement of Bonds	22,000					
Investment in S Company Stock			19,600		19,600	
Beginning Retained Earnings—S Company			2,400		2,400	
Investment in S Company Bond		10,000		10,000		10,000
Discount on Bonds Payable		12,000		12,000		12,000
Interest Income			27,000		27,000	
Interest Expense				27,000		27,000
Bond Payable	300,000		300,000		300,000	
Investment in S Company Bond		300,000		300,000		300,000
Investment in S Company Bonds			2,500		5,000	
Interest Income				2,500		2,500
Investment in S Company Stock						2,500
Discount on Bonds Payable			3,000		6,000	
Interest Expense				3,000		3,000
Investment in S Company Stock						3,000

plete equity method. For the year 2003, S Company income is assumed to be $200,000 with $75,000 of dividends declared.

INTERIM PURCHASE OF INTERCOMPANY BONDS

In the preceding illustration, the intercompany bonds were initially purchased on December 31, the fiscal year-end of both affiliates. Had the bonds been held during 2001, P Company would have amortized a portion of the premium and S Company would have amortized a part of the discount that was related to the intercompany bonds. Thus, a part of the constructive loss would have been recorded in 2001 by the individual companies. Assuming that P Company amortized $500 and S Company amortized $600 during 2001, the original workpaper entries (2) and (3) (for constructive losses) are modified as follows:

(2)	Loss on Constructive Retirement Bonds	10,000	
	Interest Revenue		500
	Investment in S Company Bonds		9,500
(3)	Loss on Constructive Retirement of Bonds	12,000	
	Interest Expense		600
	Discount on Bonds Payable		11,400

The consolidated income statement will still show a total loss on the constructive retirement of $22,000. The credits to interest revenue and interest expense add back the portion of the loss that was recorded by the individual companies, but which is reported in total in 2001, the year the bonds were constructively retired. Failure to add back the $1,100 ($500 + $600) to the reported income of the individual companies will result in reporting this portion of the loss twice, as part of the $22,000 and again as a reduction in interest revenue and as an increase in interest expense, both of which have reduced reported income.

NOTES RECEIVABLE DISCOUNTED

Occasionally a company may issue a note to an affiliated company that may then discount the note with an outside party, or a company holding a note receivable from an outside party may discount the note with an affiliated company. The affiliate acquiring the note may discount the note again with an outside party. From a consolidation point of view, a receivable held by one of the affiliated companies should be reported in the consolidated balance sheet only if the note is due from an outside party. A contingent liability should be disclosed if a note has been discounted with an outside party and the endorsement was with recourse.

To illustrate the workpaper elimination entries required, assume that P Company issued a $100,000 note to its subsidiary, S Company, for cash. The two companies prepare the usual entries on their own books when the debt is issued, that is, P Company debits cash and establishes a note payable account and S Company credits cash and records a note receivable. Assume further that S Company discounted the note at a nonaffiliated bank before maturity. Ignoring interest for simplicity, one of two methods might be used by Company S to record the discounting of a note. These methods are:

S Company's Books			
Method 1:	Cash	100,000	
	Notes Receivable		100,000
Method 2:	Cash	100,000	
	Notes Receivable Discounted		100,000

If consolidated statements are prepared before the note matures, an elimination entry may be required, depending on the method used by S Company to record the discounting of the note. If Method 1 is used to record the discounted note, the credit to notes receivable would cancel the debit made to notes receivable when the note was received. The consolidated balance sheet would appropriately report the $100,000 note held by the bank and still reported on the books of P Company as a liability. If the second method was used, the notes receivable and the notes receivable discounted accounts would have to be eliminated, because the consolidated group is not contingently liable for the note, but is the primary maker of the note held by an outside party.

Now assume that P Company discounts with S Company a note that had originally been received from one of its customers. Now, P Company might record the transfer in one of two ways. Again, if the first method (above) is used, no elimination would be required, for the reasons discussed in the preceding paragraph. However, if the second method was used, both companies would report the same note receivable as an asset, and P Company would show a contingent liability for a note receivable discounted. In the consolidating workpaper, one note receivable must be eliminated, along with the note receivable discounted account, as shown below in the partial balance sheet section of a consolidated statements workpaper:

			Eliminations		
Debits	*P Company*	*S Company*	*Dr.*	*Cr.*	*Consolidated Balances*
Notes Receivable	100,000	100,000		(1) 100,000	100,000
				0	
Credits					
Notes Receivable Discounted	100,000		(1) 100,000		—0—

The consolidated balance sheet would report one receivable from an outside party. The note was discounted to an affiliated company and, therefore, there is no contingent liability to an outside party.

Next, assume that S Company discounted the customer's note with an outside firm. If both companies used Method 1 to record the two discounting transactions, no elimination entry would be required. If the second method was used, the accounts would appear as follows in the trial balances of the two companies:

Debits	*P Company*	*S Company*
Notes Receivable	100,000	100,000
Credits		
Notes Receivable Discounted	100,000	100,000

In this case, one of the notes receivable and one of the notes receivable discounted should be eliminated. The consolidated balance sheet would report:

Notes Receivable	$100,000	
Less: Notes Receivable Discounted	100,000	—0—

Alternatively, both notes receivable and both discount accounts could be eliminated and the contingent liability disclosed in a footnote to the consolidated statement.

In the foregoing examples the notes were always transferred from the parent to the subsidiary. The same analysis is appropriate if the notes were transferred from the subsidiary to the parent.

STOCK DIVIDENDS ISSUED BY A SUBSIDIARY COMPANY

A subsidiary may issue *stock dividends* in the same class of stock that is held by the parent company. The parent company records the receipt of the shares in a memorandum entry only, since a dividend in like stock is not considered income to the recipient. For consolidated purposes, the stock dividend does not alter the investor's proportionate interest in the subsidiary. On the books of the subsidiary, the declaration of a stock dividend is recorded as a transfer from the retained earnings account to one or more paid-in capital accounts. The amount transferred is dependent on whether the dividend is a large or small stock dividend. (Recall that a large stock dividend, one in which the number of shares issued is greater than 20–25% of the outstanding shares, reduces retained earnings by the par value of the stock issued, while a small stock dividend reduces retained earnings by the market value of the stock issued.) Also, stock dividends are assumed to be distributed from the earliest earnings accumulated in the retained earnings balance. Conversely, a cash dividend is considered to be a distribution of the most recent profits (usually current period income).

To illustrate the effects of a stock dividend on the preparation of the consolidated statements workpaper, assume that P Company purchased 4,000 shares of S Company's $100 par value common stock on January 2, 2001, for $560,000. At the time of purchase, S Company reported common stock and retained earnings balances of $500,000 and $200,000, respectively. If consolidated statements were prepared on January 2, 2001, the investment eliminating entry would be:

Capital Stock—S Company	400,000	
1/1 Retained Earnings—S Company	160,000	
Investment in S Company		560,000

Now assume that S Company reports net income of $50,000 and declares a 30% stock dividend (1,500 shares) on December 31, 2001. S Company would record the dividend as follows, assuming that the company capitalized the par value of the stock issued:

Stock Dividend Declared (or Retained Earnings)	150,000	
Capital Stock (1,500 shares × $100)		150,000

Note that this entry has no effect on the total stockholders' equity. Only the composition of the account balances change as shown here:

	S Company's Capital Account Balances		
Accounts	*Before the Stock Dividend*	*Stock Dividend*	*After the Stock Dividend*
Capital Stock	$500,000	150,000	$650,000
Retained Earnings	250,000*	(150,000)	100,000
Totals	$750,000	—0—	$750,000

*$200,000 + $50,000

If the dividend had been considered a small stock dividend, the totals in the schedule above would not change. To record a small stock dividend, the retained earnings account is normally reduced by an amount equal to the number of shares to be issued times the fair market value per share; capital stock and other paid-in capital accounts are increased by the same amount.

The only book entry made by P Company in 2001 is the following memorandum entry to record the receipt of the 1,200 shares from S Company, since no cash dividends were declared during the period.

> Memorandum entry—Received 1,200 shares (1,500 × .80) of S Company common stock based on the declaration of a 30% stock dividend.

A condensed consolidated statements workpaper for the year ended December 31, 2001, is presented in Illustration 10-5. In the year that the stock dividend is declared, one additional workpaper eliminating entry is made to eliminate the effects of the dividend on the parent's interest in the capital accounts of the subsidiary. This entry is necessary because the capital stock account has been increased by $150,000, but the stock dividend declared account has not been closed to retained earnings. In other words, the balance in the capital stock account is the ending balance and needs to be restored to the beginning of year balance before elimination of the investment account.

The workpaper entries in general journal form are as follows:

Workpaper Entries—Year Stock Dividends Are Declared

(1)	Capital Stock—S Company	120,000	
	Stock Dividends Declared—S Company		120,000
	To reverse effects of stock dividend ($150,000 × .80).		
(2)	1/1 Retained Earnings—S Company (.8 × $200,000)	160,000	
	Capital Stock—S Company (.8 × $500,000)	400,000	
	Investment in S Company		560,000
	To eliminate investment account.		

In the closing process the stock dividends declared account is closed to the retained earnings account. In subsequent periods, the two workpaper entries are combined as follows (this is the entry before the reciprocity entry):

1/1 Retained Earnings—S Company ($160,000 − $120,000)	40,000	
Capital Stock—S Company ($400,000 + $120,000)	520,000	
Investment in S Company		560,000
To eliminate investment account before reciprocity.		

Cost Method		ILLUSTRATION 10–5				
80% Owned Subsidiary		**Consolidated Statements Workpaper**				
Subsidiary Issued		**P Company and Subsidiary**				
Stock Dividend		**For the Year Ended December 31, 2001**				

Income Statement	*P Company*	*S Company*	Eliminations *Dr.*	Eliminations *Cr.*	*Noncontrolling Interest*	*Consolidated Balances*
Net/Combined Income	240,000	50,000				290,000
Noncontrolling Interest in Income						
($50,000 × .20)					10,000	(10,000)
Net Income to Retained Earnings	240,000	50,000			10,000	280,000
Retained Earnings Statement						
1/1 Retained Earnings						
P Company	460,000					460,000
S Company		200,000	(2) 160,000		40,000	
Net Income from above	240,000	50,000			10,000	280,000
Dividends Declared S Company—						
Stock Dividend		(150,000)		(1) 120,000	(30,000)	
12/31 Retained Earnings to Balance						
Sheet	700,000	100,000	160,000	120,000	20,000	740,000
Balance Sheet						
Investment in S Company	560,000			(2) 560,000		—0—
Fixed Assets	1,240,000	800,000				2,040,000
Total Assets	1,800,000	750,000				2,040,000
Total Liabilities	200,000	50,000				250,000
Capital Stock						
P Company	900,000					900,000
S Company		650,000	(1) 120,000			
			(2) 400,000		130,000	
Retained Earnings from above	700,000	100,000	160,000	120,000	20,000	740,000
Noncontrolling Interest in Net Assets					150,000	150,000
Total Liabilities and Equity	1,800,000	750,000	680,000	680,000		2,040,000

(1) To reverse effects of the stock dividend.
(2) To eliminate investment account.

The result is that the debit to capital stock is increased $120,000, and a corresponding decrease is made in the debit to the retained earnings balance.

In the consolidated workpapers the entry to establish reciprocity is based on the undistributed income earned by the subsidiary since the date of acquisition. A cash dividend declared by the subsidiary is generally considered to be a distribution of the most recent profits, which, of course, reduces undistributed profits of the subsidiary accumulated after the date the parent obtained control of the subsidiary. Conversely, the source of a stock dividend is the earliest earnings accumulated in the retained earnings balance.

In this illustration the procedures to compute the amount of the entry to establish reciprocity must be modified to recognize that the retained earnings balance at the date of acquisition has been reduced to $50,000 as a result of the stock dividend. The workpaper entries for the *second* year, December 31, 2002, are as follows:

(1) Investment in S Company	40,000	
Beginning Retained Earnings—P Company		40,000
To establish reciprocity as of 1/1/02 ($50,000 × .80).		
1/1 Retained earnings balance		
($200,000 − $150,000 + $50,000)		$100,000
Retained earnings balance—date of acquisition	$200,000	
Less: Stock dividend	150,000	
Adjusted retained earnings balance—date of acquisition	50,000	
Increase in retained earnings since date of acquisition		$ 50,000
(2) Beginning Retained Earnings—S Company ($100,000 × .80)	80,000	
Common Stock—S Company ($650,000 × .80)	520,000	
Investment in S Company ($560,000 + $40,000)		600,000
To eliminate investment account.		

A portion of the retained earnings section of the December 31, 2002 workpaper is presented here:

	P Company	S Company	Eliminations Dr.	Eliminations Cr.	Noncontrolling Interest	Consolidated Balances
1/1 Retained Earnings						
P Company	700,000			(1) 40,000		740,000
S Company		100,000	(2) 80,000		20,000	

Observe that these entries make the beginning retained earnings balances for the second year equal to the first year's ending retained earnings balances reported for the noncontrolling interest and the consolidated retained earnings on the December 31, 2001, workpaper (see Illustration 10-5).

The issuance of a stock dividend does not affect the computation of consolidated retained earnings. As proof, the consolidated retained earnings balance as of December 31, 2001, can be computed as follows:

P Company's retained earnings balance at December 31, 2001	$700,000
P Company's share of the change in the subsidiary's adjusted retained earnings since the date of acquisition ($50,000 × .80)	40,000
Consolidated retained earnings—December 31, 2001	$740,000

Stock Dividends Issued from Postacquisition Earnings

In the foregoing illustration, the retained earnings transferred to paid-in capital ($150,000) was less than the retained earnings balance ($200,000) at the date of acquisition. If the stock dividend had been more than $200,000, some of the post-acquisition earnings of the subsidiary would have been capitalized. For example, assume that S Company made the following entry to record the stock dividend:

Stock Dividends Declared (or Retained Earnings)	220,000	
Capital Stock		220,000

The entry capitalized $200,000 of the retained earnings that existed at the date of acquisition plus $20,000 of the net income reported after the date of acquisition.

The capitalization of the current earnings does not affect consolidated retained earnings, which is still $740,000 as determined in Illustration 10-5, but it does result in the inclusion of earnings in the consolidated retained earnings balance that have been capitalized and are not available for the payment of dividends. The amount of the subsidiary's postacquisition earnings that have been capitalized and included in the consolidated retained earnings should be disclosed in the consolidated financial statements. Some may contend that the portion of the retained earnings that has been capitalized should be reported as contributed capital in the consolidated balance sheet. In response to this contention, the Committee on Accounting Procedure of the American Institute of Certified Public Accountants made the following comment:

> Occasionally, subsidiary companies capitalize earned surplus [retained earnings] arising since acquisition, by means of a stock dividend or otherwise. This does not require a transfer to capital surplus on consolidation, inasmuch as the retained earnings in the consolidated financial statements should reflect the accumulated earnings of the consolidated group not distributed to the shareholders of, or capitalized by, the parent company.[6]

DIVIDENDS FROM PREACQUISITION EARNINGS

The nature of a liquidating dividend (dividend from preacquisition earnings) and the entries to record a liquidating dividend were discussed in Chapter 3. The objective of this section is to illustrate the effects of a liquidating dividend on the consolidated statements workpaper entries.

To illustrate the workpaper adjustment required when a liquidating dividend is involved, assume that P Company acquired an 80% interest in S Company on January 2, 2001, for $560,000. At the time of purchase, S Company had capital stock and retained earnings in the amounts of $500,000 and $200,000, respectively. During the first year that the investment was held, S Company reported net income of $200,000. On December 31, 2001, the subsidiary declared and paid a cash dividend of $250,000. In this case, $50,000 of the dividend is a distribution of earnings accumulated before the controlling interest was obtained in the subsidiary. As discussed in Chapter 3, there is general agreement that a liquidating dividend should be accounted for as a return of part of the original investment rather than income to the parent company.

Recall that the source of a cash dividend is considered to be the most recent earnings. Under the cost method the following entry is made on the books of P Company to recognize that $200,000 of the dividend is based on the current earnings and $50,000 is a distribution of preacquisition earnings:

P Company's Books		
Cash	200,000	
Dividend Income ($200,000 × .80)		160,000
Investment in S Company ($50,000 × .80)		40,000
To record receipt of a cash dividend from S Company		

[6]Committee on Accounting Procedure, American Institute of Certified Public Accountants, *Accounting Research and Terminology Bulletin*, Final Edition (New York: AICPA, 1961), *Bulletin No. 51*, par. 18.

This entry reduces the investment account balance to $520,000. In the year of the liquidating dividend, one additional workpaper entry must be made to reverse the effects of the liquidating dividend, since the dividend has been adjusted to the investment account, but the dividends declared are still shown as a separate amount in the trial balance of S Company. Although the consolidated statements workpaper is not presented, the December 31, 2001, eliminating entries are as follows:

(1) Dividend Income	160,000	
Dividends Declared—S Company		160,000
To eliminate intercompany dividends.		
(2) Investment in S Company	40,000	
Dividends Declared—S Company		40,000
To reverse the liquidating dividend.		
(3) Beginning Retained Earnings—S Company		
($200,000 × .80)	160,000	
Capital Stock—S Company ($500,000 × .80)	400,000	
Investment in S Company		560,000
To eliminate investment account.		

In the workpapers prepared in subsequent years, the amount of the entry made to establish reciprocity is based on the difference between the current year's beginning retained earnings balance and the retained earnings balance at the date of acquisition reduced by the $50,000 liquidating dividend. The investment elimination entry is a combination of entries (2) and (3) above. The December 31, 2002 (the second year) workpaper entry would be:

(1) Beginning Retained Earnings—S Company		
($150,000 × .80) or ($200,000-50,000) × .80	120,000	
Capital Stock—S Company ($500,000 × .80)	400,000	
Investment in S Company		520,000
To eliminate investment account.		

No entry is needed to establish reciprocity, because all the earnings of the subsidiary since acquisition ($200,000) have been distributed, and the parent's share is reported in the retained earnings balance of P Company.

SUBSIDIARY WITH BOTH PREFERRED AND COMMON STOCK OUTSTANDING

A subsidiary company may have both common and preferred stock outstanding. To justify consolidation, the parent must hold a controlling interest in the outstanding voting stock. At the same time, the parent may or may not hold shares of the preferred stock. In either case, in the preparation of consolidated financial statements, the shares of the preferred stock not held by the parent company are considered part of the noncontrolling interest.

Determining Equity Interest of Each Class of Stockholders

The existence of preferred stock creates special problems in the preparation of consolidated financial statements because each class of stockholders has an interest in the net assets of the firm. To determine the equity interest of each class of stockholders on a certain date, it is necessary to allocate the subsidiary's stockholders' equity between the preferred and common stock interests. In doing so, the provisions of the preferred stock issue, in particular the *call price*, sometimes called the *redemption price*, and dividend provisions, must be analyzed and provided for in making the allocation. After the date of acquiring the controlling interest, the operating results of the subsidiary must also be allocated to determine the interest of the two classes of stockholders in the changes in the retained earnings balance. The dividend preference of the preferred stock issue will determine the amounts allocated to each class of stockholders.

The effects that the various rights and priorities granted to the preferred stockholders have on the determination of the book value interests and the claim to earnings are discussed in other accounting texts. The procedures and the steps (indicated numerically) for determining such allocations for some of the more common alternatives are summarized in Illustration 10-6.

ILLUSTRATION 10–6

Allocation of Retained Earnings Balance and Net Income When Subsidiary Has Both Common and Preferred Stock Outstanding

	Accumulated Retained Earnings Balance		Allocation of Net Income	
	Preferred Stock*	*Common Stock*	*Preferred Stock*	*Common Stock*
Noncumulative/ nonparticipating	1. Zero.	2. Balance in retained earnings account.	1. Current year's dividend if one was declared.	2. Net income in excess of preferred dividend.
Cumulative/ nonparticipating	1. Dividends in arrears.	2. Balance after subtracting dividend in arrears.	1. Current year's dividend whether declared or not.	2. Net income in excess of preferred dividend.
Noncumulative/ fully participating	1. Allocated between preferred and common stock.		1. Current year's dividend if one was declared.	2. Current year's dividend if declared on common, but not to exceed the amount to match the percentage on preferred.
			3. Remaining net income is allocated between preferred and common stock.†	
Cumulative/fully participating‡	1. Dividends in arrears.		1. Current year's dividend whether declared or not.	2. Current year's dividend if declared on common, but not to exceed the amount to match the percentage on preferred.
	2. Balance after subtracting any dividend in arrears is allocated between preferred and common stock.†		3. Remaining net income is allocated between preferred and common stock.†	

*It is assumed that the call price of the preferred stock is equal to the stock's par value. If the call price is greater, the preferred stock interest in retained earnings is increased by the amount of the call premium and a corresponding reduction is made in the common stock interest.
†It is assumed that the allocation is based on the ratio of the par values of each class of stock.
‡It is assumed that a common stock dividend is lost if not declared in any one year to match the preference rate on the preferred stock. In other words, before the participation feature is effective, the common stockholders normally receive a dividend equal to the same percentage paid to the preferred stockholders. However, if an equal percentage is not declared on the common stock during the period, it is lost to the common stockholders and will not be paid in subsequent periods. Since the preferred stock is cumulative, a passed dividend on preferred stock is considered in arrears in the determination of dividend payments in future periods. Such a dividend agreement with the preferred stockholders could be detrimental to the interest of the common stockholders. Alternative agreements could be negotiated, and this is only one possibility.

Illustration 10-6 does not include the steps to be taken in the allocation of a deficit balance in the retained earnings account or a subsidiary reporting a net loss during an operating period. If the preferred stock is noncumulative, nonparticipating, and has a call price equal to par value, the full deficit in the retained earnings account or net loss is allocated totally to the common stock interest. If the preferred stock is cumulative and nonparticipating, a deficit balance in retained earnings is assigned to the common stock, unless there are dividends in arrears, in which case the amount of the preferred dividends in arrears increases the book value interest of the preferred stockholders and is added to the deficit assigned to the common equity. In the case of a net loss, the current year's dividends on the preferred stock are added to the preferred interest and added to the net loss (which reduces the common interest) to determine the interest of the common stockholders in current operations. In the case of deficit operations, the participating provision can be ignored.

Allocation of Difference Between Cost of Preferred Stock Investment and Book Value Interest Acquired

In the case of a common stock investment, the difference between the cost of the investment and the book value of the interest acquired is allocated to undervalued or overvalued assets and liabilities. However, because holders of cumulative/nonparticipating preferred stock do not have a residual interest in the firm's net assets, the excess paid for a preferred stock interest is generally not related to the market value of the firm's net assets. If the preferred stock is nonconvertible and nonparticipating, the market price is more closely associated with the preferred dividend return related to the market rate of return on investments of similar risk. In essence, the market factors that cause movements in the market value of the preferred stock are similar to the market factors that cause movements in the market value of the firm's bonds. Thus, the difference between the cost of preferred stock and the book value of the interest acquired is similar to a discount or premium on a bond issue. One of the major differences between preferred stock and debt is that a preferred stock issue does not normally have a maturity date.

Because the preferred stock does not normally have a maturity date, the period selected to amortize the difference would be arbitrary. One approach is to recognize the difference as a loss in the consolidated income statement in the year of the purchase. However, in our view, the acquisition of outstanding preferred stock by the consolidated entity reflects a constructive retirement of the stock and should be accounted for as an equity transaction. Thus, the difference between cost and the book value interest acquired (a debit difference) is accounted for as a reduction in consolidated other contributed capital, or if none exists, is recorded as a reduction in consolidated retained earnings. If the book value of the interest acquired is greater than the cost of the preferred stock, the credit difference is carried to other contributed capital.

Most preferred stock agreements contain the cumulative feature and are nonparticipating. For this reason, the preparation of consolidated financial statements when cumulative/nonparticipating preferred stock is outstanding is illustrated in the next section. The reader must recognize, however, that the illustration is only one of many possibilities, since the rights and priorities granted to the preferred stockholders may take numerous forms. When there is preferred stock outstanding, the stock agreement should be carefully reviewed to assess the rights and priorities of each class of stock. Allocations of the stockholders' equity and net income should be made in accordance with the agreement.

CONSOLIDATING A SUBSIDIARY WITH PREFERRED STOCK OUTSTANDING

To illustrate the accounting for a subsidiary and the consolidated statements work-paper procedures to be followed when the subsidiary has both preferred stock and common stock outstanding, the following information concerning the capital accounts of S Company as of January 2, 2001, is assumed:

8%, $100 par value preferred stock, cumulative, nonparticipating, dividends in arrears for 2000, call price is $103, 5,000 shares outstanding	$ 500,000
Common stock, $10 par value	1,000,000
Other contributed capital—excess on issue of common stock over par	305,000
Retained earnings	200,000
Total stockholders' equity	$2,005,000

On January 2, 2001, P Company acquired 80% of the outstanding common stock for $1,160,000 and 30% of the outstanding preferred stock for $180,000. The entry to record the purchase is:

P Company's Books		
Investment in S Company Preferred Stock	180,000	
Investment in S Company Common Stock	1,160,000	
Cash		1,340,000

During the year, S Company reported net income of $200,000 and declared no cash dividends.

The stockholders' equity accounts of S Company must be allocated to determine the book value interest in the net assets of the preferred and common stockholders. The allocation on the date of acquisition would be made as shown in Illustration 10-7.[7]

In this illustration, if the preferred shares were called, a payment of $111 ($103 call price + $8 dividend in arrears) must be made to acquire each share of stock. Accordingly, retained earnings of $55,000 (5,000 shares outstanding × $11 per share) is allocated to the preferred stockholders' interest. Thus, on the date of

---

[7]Another approach to determine the allocation of equity interest is:

Book value of net assets		$2,005,000
Less: Allocated to preferred stock		
Par value of preferred stock	$500,000	
Call premium (5,000 shares × $3)	15,000	
Dividends in arrears (5,000 shares × $8)	40,000	
Total allocated to preferred stock		555,000
Residual allocated to common stock		$1,450,000

ILLUSTRATION 10–7

Allocation of Difference Between Cost and Book Value

| | | Book Value Interest | |
| | Account Balance | Preferred Stock | Common Stock |
Account			
$100 par Preferred Stock—8%	$ 500,000	$500,000	—
$10 par Common Stock	1,000,000		$1,000,000
Other Contributed Capital—common stock	305,000		305,000
Retained Earnings	200,000	55,000*	145,000
Totals	$2,005,000	555,000**	1,450,000
Percentage Interest Acquired		30%	80%
Book Value Interest Acquired		166,500	1,160,000
Cost		180,000	1,160,000
Difference Between Cost and Book Value Interest		$ 13,500	$ —0—

*($103 call price + $8 dividends in arrears − $100 par value) × 5,000 shares = $11 × 5,000 = $55,000
**($103 call price × 5,000 shares) + ($8 dividends in arrears × 5,000 shares) = $555,000

acquisition the preferred stock interest in the net assets ($555,000) is equal to the call price of $515,000 plus the $40,000 dividends in arrears.

Consolidated Statements Workpaper—2001

Workpaper procedures are similar to those illustrated in earlier sections of this text. The only difference is that an additional workpaper entry must be made to eliminate the preferred stock investment account. The consolidating statements workpaper at December 31, 2001, is contained in Illustration 10-8. The balances are assumed except for the ones previously given. Note that the beginning retained earnings balance of S Company is allocated between the two classes of stock. Making the allocation in the workpaper is necessary because dividends in arrears are not recorded in the accounts of S Company. If P Company uses the cost method, dividends in arrears are not recorded as dividend income. However, if the complete equity method is used, dividends on cumulative preferred stock are recognized as income regardless of whether they are paid. Therefore, in 2001, under the complete equity method, P Company records equity income from the preferred stock investment of $12,000 (.3 × $40,000).

Consolidated Statements Workpaper Entries—2001

Cost Method or Partial Equity Method

(1)	Beginning Retained Earnings—S Company		
	($55,000 × .30)	16,500	
	Preferred Stock—S Company ($500,000 × .30)	150,000	
	Other Contributed Capital—P Company	13,500	
	Investment in S Company Preferred Stock		180,000
	To eliminate the preferred stock investment account.		

As discussed earlier, the $13,500 difference between the cost of the preferred stock investment and the book value interest acquired is not allocated to specific assets or liabilities, but rather is accounted for as an equity transaction and debited to other contributed capital (Illustration 10-8).

Cost Method			**ILLUSTRATION 10–8**			
80% Owned Subsidiary			**Condensed Consolidated Statements Workpaper**			
Subsidiary Has Preferred			**P Company and Subsidiary**			
Stock Outstanding			**For the Year Ended December 31, 2001**			

	P	S	Eliminations		Noncontrolling	Consolidated
Income Statement	Company	Company	Dr.	Cr.	Interest	Balances
Net/Combined Income	800,000	200,000				1,000,000
Noncontrolling Interest in Dividend						
Preferred Stock (in arrears)						
($40,000 × .70)					28,000	
Common Stock						
[($200,000 − $40,000) × .20]					32,000	(60,000)
Net Income to Retained Earnings	800,000	200,000	—0—	—0—	60,000	940,000
Retained Earnings Statement						
1/1 Retained Earnings						
P Company	1,450,000					1,450,000
S Company						
Preferred Stock		55,000	(1) 16,500		38,500	
Common Stock		145,000	(2) 116,000		29,000	
Net Income from above	800,000	200,000			60,000	940,000
Dividends Declared P Company	(500,000)					(500,000)
12/31 Retained Earnings to Balance						
Sheet	1,750,000	400,000	132,500	—0—	127,500	1,890,000
Balance Sheet						
Investment in S Company Preferred						
Stock	180,000			(1) 180,000		—0—
Investment in S Company Common						
Stock	1,160,000			(2) 1,160,000		—0—
Other Assets	5,410,000	2,805,000				8,215,000
Total Assets	6,750,000	2,805,000				8,215,000
Liabilities	1,600,000	600,000				2,200,000
Preferred Stock						
S Company		500,000	(1) 150,000		350,000	
Common Stock						
P Company	3,000,000					3,000,000
S Company		1,000,000	(2) 800,000		200,000	
Other Contributed Capital						
P Company	400,000		(1) 13,500			386,500
S Company		305,000	(2) 244,000		61,000	
Retained Earnings from above	1,750,000	400,000	132,500		127,500	1,890,000
Noncontrolling Interest in Net						
Assets*					738,500	738,500
Total Liabilities and Equity	6,750,000	2,805,000	1,340,000	1,340,000		8,215,000

*Noncontrolling interest in net assets can be verified as follows:
(1) To eliminate the preferred stock investment account.
(2) To eliminate the common stock investment account.

	$	Noncontrolling Percentage	Total
Total stockholders' equity	$2,205,000		
Allocated to the preferred:			
Par value	$500,000		
Call premium	15,000		
Dividends in arrears	80,000		
Book value of preferred stock	595,000	0.70	$416,500
Book value of common stock	$1,610,000	0.20	322,000
Noncontrolling interest—12/31			$738,500

Cost

(2) Beginning Retained Earnings—S Company ($145,000 × .80)	116,000	
Common Stock—S Company ($1,000,000 × .80)	800,000	
Other Contributed Capital—S Company ($305,000 × .80)	244,000	
Investment in S Company Common Stock		1,160,000
To eliminate the common stock investment account.		

In computing the noncontrolling interest in combined income, S Company's contribution to combined income is first allocated between the two classes of stock. Because of the cumulative feature of the preferred stock, $40,000 of S Company's net income is first allocated to the cumulative preferred stock even though no cash dividends were declared in this period. This of course reduces the amount of income available for distribution to the common stockholders. The residual net income of $160,000 is allocated to the common stockholders' interest since the preferred stock is nonparticipating. Noncontrolling interest in the combined income for 2001 is computed as follows:

	Contribution to Combined Income	Noncontrolling Percentage	Noncontrolling Interest
Reported net income of S Company	$200,000		
Income allocated to preferred stock	40,000	.70	$28,000
Income allocated to common stock	$160,000	.20	32,000
Noncontrolling interest in combined income			$60,000

Such an allocation is necessary whether or not P Company holds any of the preferred stock.

Note that the allocation of net income is unaffected by dividends in arrears on preferred stock at the beginning of the year. The allocation of net income reflects the increase in the book value interest of each class of stock due to operations of the current period only. Dividends in arrears at the beginning of the year are recognized as an allocation of the beginning retained earnings balance.

Consolidated net income for 2001 and consolidated retained earnings as of December 31, 2001, can be verified as shown in Illustration 10-9.

Complete Equity Method The consolidated workpapers assuming that P Company uses the complete equity method are reported in Illustration 10-10. Recall that the Investment in S Company Common Stock account is increased by equity income ($128,000) and decreased by dividends received (none were received in 2001). However, equity income on the cumulative preferred stock must still be recognized even though no dividends were declared in 2001. In this case, the equity income in preferred stock ($12,000) increases the Investment in S Company Preferred Stock account. Therefore, on the consolidated workpapers, this entry must be reversed (see entry (3) in Illustration 10-10).

Accounting Subsequent to the Year of Acquisition—2002

Now assume that S Company reported net income of $300,000 in 2002 and paid cash dividends of $120,000 to the preferred stockholders ($80,000 for the arrearages of 2000 and 2001 plus $40,000 for the current year) and $50,000 to the common stockholders.

Cost Method: Entries on the Books of P Company—2002 P Company would record receipt of the cash dividends as follows:

Cash	36,000	
Dividend Income		24,000
Investment in S Company Preferred Stock		12,000

      To record receipt of dividends on preferred stock investment ($12,000 represents dividends in arrears at the acquisition date). ($120,000 × .30 = $36,000).

Note that the distribution of $40,000 for preferred dividends in arrears at the date of acquisition is a liquidating dividend, and P Company's 30% thereof is accounted for as a reduction in the investment account.

Cash	40,000	
Dividend Income		40,000

      To record the receipt of dividends on the common stock investment ($50,000 × .80 = $40,000).

Complete Equity Method: Entries on the Books of P Company—2002 P Company would record the receipt of the cash dividends as follows:

Cash	36,000	
Equity Income—S Company Preferred Stock		12,000
Investment in S Company Preferred Stock		
(dividends in arrears recognized as revenue in 2001)		12,000
Investment in S Company Common Stock		
(dividends in arrears at date of acquisition, liquidating dividend)		12,000

      To record receipt of dividends on preferred stock investment ($120,000 × .30 = $36,000).

ILLUSTRATION 10–9

**T-Account Approach to Consolidated
Net Income and Retained Earnings**

Consolidated Net Income—2001

Net income from independent operations		$ 800,000
P Company's share of S Company's reported income:	$ 12,000	
Allocated to preferred stock interest: $40,000 × .30		
Allocated to common stock interest: $160,000 × .80 =	128,000	$ 140,000*
Consolidated net income		$ 940,000

Consolidated Retained Earnings—December 31, 2001

P Company's December 31, 2001, retained earnings balance		1,750,000
Undistributed net income earned since date of acquisition		
Preferred stock ($40,000 × .3) =	$ 12,000	
Common stock ($160,000 × .8) =	128,000	$ 140,000*
Consolidated retained earnings on December 31, 2001		$1,890,000

*Undistributed net income can be computed as follows when income statements of prior years are not available:

	Retained Earnings Allocation		
	Preferred Stock	*Common Stock*	*Total*
Retained earnings balance			
End of current year	$95,000	$305,000	$400,000
Date of acquisition	55,000	145,000	200,000
Increase in retained earnings	40,000	160,000	$200,000
Percentage interest	.30	.80	
Share of undistributed income	$12,000	$128,000	$140,000

Complete Equity Method			ILLUSTRATION 10–10			
80% Owned Subsidiary			**Condensed Consolidated Statements Workpaper**			
Subsidiary Has Preferred			**P Company and Subsidiary**			
Stock Outstanding			**For the Year Ended December 31, 2001**			

	P Company	*S* Company	Eliminations Dr.	Eliminations Cr.	Noncontrolling Interest	Consolidated Balances
Income Statement						
Income Before Equity Income	800,000	200,000				1,000,000
Equity Income in Common						
Stock	128,000		(4) 128,000			
Equity Income in Preferred						
Stock	12,000		(3) 12,000			
Net/Combined Income	940,000					
Noncontrolling Interest in						
Income						
Preferred Stock						
($40,000 × .70)					28,000	
Common Stock						
[($200,000 − $40,000) × .20]					32,000	(60,000)
Net Income to Retained						
Earnings	940,000	200,000	140,000	—0—	60,000	940,000
Retained Earnings Statement						
1/1 Retained Earnings						
P Company	1,450,000					1,450,000
S Company						
Preferred Stock		55,000	(1) 16,500		38,500	
Common Stock		145,000	(2) 116,000		29,000	
Net Income from above	940,000	200,000	140,000		60,000	940,000
Dividends Declared P Company	(500,000)					(500,000)
12/31 Retained Earnings to						
Balance Sheet	1,890,000	400,000	272,500	—0—	127,500	1,890,000
Balance Sheet						
Investment in S Company				(3) 12,000		
Preferred Stock	192,000			(1) 180,000		—0—
Investment in S Company				(2) 1,160,000		
Common Stock	1,288,000			(4) 128,000		—0—
Other Assets	5,410,000	2,805,000				8,215,000
Total Assets	6,890,000	2,805,000				8,215,000
Liabilities	1,600,000	600,000				2,200,000
Preferred Stock						
S Company		500,000	(1) 150,000		350,000	
Common Stock						
P Company	3,000,000					3,000,000
S Company		1,000,000	(2) 800,000		200,000	
Other Contributed Capital						
P Company	400,000		(1) 13,500			386,500
S Company		305,000	(2) 244,000		61,000	
Retained Earnings from above	1,890,000	400,000	272,500		127,500	1,890,000
Noncontrolling Interest in Net						
Assets					738,500	738,500
Total Liabilities and Equity	6,890,000	2,805,000	1,480,000	1,480,000		8,215,000

(1) To eliminate the preferred stock investment account.
(2) To eliminate the common stock investment account.
(3) To eliminate equity income in preferred stock.
(4) To eliminate equity income in common stock.

Complete

Note that the distribution of $40,000 for preferred dividends in arrears at the date of acquisition is a liquidating dividend, and P Company's 30% (or $12,000) is accounted for as a reduction in the Investment in S Company Common Stock account:

Investment in S Company Common Stock	208,000	
Equity Income in S Company Common Stock		208,000
To record equity in subsidiary income ($300,000 S Company income − $40,000 allocated to preferred stock) × .80.		

Consolidated Statements Workpaper—2002

Consolidated statements workpapers for December 31, 2002 are presented in Illustration 10-11 using the cost method and in Illustration 10-12 assuming the complete equity method. To facilitate making the eliminating entries, the beginning retained earnings balance of $400,000 of S Company is allocated between the two classes of stock as follows:

Retained earnings balance—1/1		$400,000
Allocated to preferred stock:		
Undistributed income assigned to preferred stock		
interest—2000 and 2001—$40,000 × 2 years =	$80,000	
Call premium ($3/share)	15,000	95,000
Residual assigned to common stock		$305,000

Consolidated Statements Workpaper Entries—2002

Cost Method The December 31, 2002, workpaper elimination entries in journal form (Illustration 10-11) are as follows:

(1)	Investment in S Company Preferred Stock	12,000	
	Investment in S Company Common Stock	128,000	
	Beginning Retained Earnings—P Company		140,000
	To establish reciprocity/convert to equity as of 1/1/02.		
	($95,000 − $55,000) × .3 = $12,000		
	($305,000 − $145,000) × .80 = $128,000		
(2)	Dividend Income	64,000	
	Dividends Declared—S Company (Preferred)		24,000
	Dividends Declared—S Company (Common)		40,000
	To eliminate intercompany dividends.		
(3)	Investment in S Company Preferred Stock	12,000	
	Dividends Declared—S Company ($40,000 × .3)		12,000
	To reverse the liquidating dividend (dividends in arrears at the date of acquisition).		
(4)	Beginning Retained Earnings—S Company	28,500	
	Preferred Stock—S Company	150,000	
	Other Contributed Capital—P Company	13,500	
	Investment in S Company Preferred Stock		192,000
	To eliminate preferred stock investment account.		
(5)	Beginning Retained Earnings—S Company	244,000	
	Common Stock—S Company	800,000	
	Other Contributed Capital—S Company	244,000	
	Investment in S Company Common Stock		1,288,000
	To eliminate common stock investment account.		

ILLUSTRATION 10–11

Cost Method						
80% Owned Subsidiary		**Consolidated Statements Workpaper**				
Subsidiary Has Preferred		**P Company and Subsidiary**				
Stock Outstanding		**For the Year Ended December 31, 2002**				

Income Statement	P Company	S Company	Eliminations Dr.	Eliminations Cr.	Noncontrolling Interest	Consolidated Balances
Net/Income Before Dividend Income	636,000	300,000				936,000
Dividend Income ($24,000 preferred + $40,000 common)	64,000		(2) 64,000			—0—
Net/Combined Income	700,000	300,000				936,000
Noncontrolling Interest in Income						
Preferred Stock ($40,000 × .70)					28,000	
Common Stock [($260,000 × .20)					52,000	(80,000)
Net Income to Retained Earnings	700,000	300,000	64,000	—0—	80,000	856,000
Retained Earnings Statement						
1/1 Retained Earnings						
P Company	1,750,000			(1) 140,000		1,890,000
S Company						
Preferred Stock		95,000	(4) 28,500		66,500	
Common Stock		305,000	(5) 244,000		61,000	
Net Income from above	700,000	300,000	64,000		80,000	856,000
Dividends Declared P Company						
P Company	(500,000)					(500,000)
S Company				(2) 24,000		
Preferred Stock		(120,000)		(3) 12,000	(84,000)	
Common Stock		(50,000)		(2) 40,000	(10,000)	
12/31 Retained Earnings to Balance Sheet	1,950,000	530,000	336,500	216,000	113,500	2,246,000
Balance Sheet						
Investment in S Company						
Preferred Stock			(1) 12,000			
($180,000 − $12,000)	168,000		(3) 12,000	(4) 192,000		—0—
Investment in S Company						
Common Stock	1,160,000		(1) 128,000	(5) 1,288,000		—0—
Other Assets	5,322,000	2,785,000				8,107,000
Total Assets	6,650,000	2,785,000				8,107,000
Liabilities	1,300,000	450,000				1,750,000
Preferred Stock						
S Company		500,000	(4) 150,000		350,000	
Common Stock						
P Company	3,000,000					3,000,000
S Company		1,000,000	(5) 800,000		200,000	
Other Contributed Capital						
P Company	400,000		(4) 13,500			386,500
S Company		305,000	(5) 244,000		61,000	
Retained Earnings from above	1,950,000	530,000	336,500	216,000	113,500	2,246,000
Noncontrolling Interest in Net Assets						724,500
					724,500	
Total Liabilities and Equity	6,650,000	2,785,000	1,696,000	1,696,000		8,107,000

Cost

(1) To establish reciprocity (convert to equity) as of 1/1/02
(2) To eliminate intercompany dividends.
(3) To reverse liquidating dividend.
(4) To eliminate preferred stock investment account.
(5) To eliminate common stock investment account.

ILLUSTRATION 10–12

Consolidated Statements Workpaper

P Company and Subsidiary

For the Year Ended December 31, 2002

Income Statement	P Company	S Company	Eliminations Dr.	Eliminations Cr.	Noncontrolling Interest	Consolidated Balances
Net/Income Before Dividend Income	636,000	300,000				936,000
Equity income in S Company Common Stock	208,000		(3) 208,000			
Equity income in S Company Preferred Stock	12,000		(1) 12,000			—0—
Net/Combined Income	856,000	300,000				936,000
Noncontrolling Interest in Income						
Preferred Stock ($40,000 × .70)					28,000	
Common Stock ($260,000 × .20)					52,000	(80,000)
Net Income to Retained Earnings	856,000	300,000	220,000	—	80,000	856,000
Retained Earnings Statement						
1/1 Retained Earnings						
P Company	1,890,000					1,890,000
S Company						
Preferred Stock		95,000	(2) 28,500		66,500	
Common Stock		305,000	(4) 244,000		61,000	
Net Income from above	856,000	300,000	220,000		80,000	856,000
Dividends Declared						
P Company	(500,000)					(500,000)
S Company						
Preferred Stock		(120,000)		(1) 36,000	(84,000)	
Common Stock		(50,000)		(3) 40,000	(10,000)	
12/31 Retained Earnings to Balance Sheet	2,246,000	530,000	492,500	76,000	113,500	2,246,000
Balance Sheet						
Investment in S Company Preferred Stock ($192,000 − $12,000)	180,000		(1) 12,000	(2) 192,000		—0—
Investment in S Company Common Stock	1,444,000		(1) 12,000	(3) 168,000 {(4) 1,228,000		—0—
Other Assets	5,322,000	2,785,000				8,107,000
Total Assets	6,946,000	2,785,000				8,107,000
Liabilities	1,300,000	450,000				1,750,000
Preferred Stock						
S Company		500,000	(2) 150,000		350,000	
Common Stock						
P Company	3,000,000					3,000,000
S Company		1,000,000	(4) 800,000		200,000	
Other Contributed Capital						
P Company	400,000		(2) 13,500			386,500
S Company		305,000	(4) 244,000		61,000	
Retained Earnings from above	2,246,000	530,000	492,500	76,000	113,500	2,246,000
Noncontrolling Interest in Net Assets					724,500	724,500
Total Liabilities and Equity	6,946,000	2,785,000	1,724,000	1,724,000		8,107,000

(1) To eliminate intercompany dividends of $36,000 (30% of $120,000), of which $12,000 represents a liquidating dividend (dividends in arrears on the date of acquisition of the preferred stock), $12,000 a reversal of the prior year's equity income previously recognized, and $12,000 of current year's dividends.

(2) To eliminate preferred stock investment account.

(3) To eliminate intercompany income and dividends.

(4) To eliminate common stock investment account.

Complete

At the end of the year, there are no dividends in arrears on the preferred stock. This means that all income allocated to the preferred stock interest since the date of acquisition has been distributed. Thus, at the end of the period, $15,000 of the ending retained earnings balance is allocated to the preferred stock for the call premium. The residual balance of $515,000 is allocated to the common stock interest.

Consolidated net income and retained earnings for the year ended December 31, 2002, using the t-account approach, are computed as follows:

Controlling Interest in Income

Internally generated income of P Company ($700,000 − $64,000 dividends)	$636,000
Other needed adjustments (see Chapters 5 and 6)	
Percentage of subsidiary adjusted income (%) ($subsidiary income):	
Assigned to preferred stock $40,000 × .30 =	$ 12,000
Assigned to common stock $260,000 × .80 =	208,000
Controlling interest in income	$856,000

Consolidated Retained Earnings P Company's interest in the undistributed net income at the end of 2002 is computed as follows:

Retained Earnings—S Company	Preferred Stock	Common Stock	Total
End of current year	$15,000	$515,000	$530,000
Date of acquisition	15,000*	145,000	160,000*
Undistributed income	—0—	370,000	$370,000
Percentage interest	.30	.80	
Share of undistributed income	$—0—	$296,000	$296,000

*Dividends in arrears of $40,000 were paid and accounted for as a liquidating dividend.

Consolidated Retained Earnings

P Company's ending retained earnings balance	$1,950,000
P Company's share of undistributed income of S Company earned since date of acquisition	
Preferred stock	—0—
Common stock	296,000
Consolidated retained earnings, December 31, 2002	$2,246,000

The entry to establish reciprocity/convert to equity in the December 31, 2003, consolidated statements workpaper is:

Investment in S Company Common Stock	296,000	
Beginning Retained Earnings—P Company		296,000

A reciprocity entry is not needed for the preferred stock interest because there is no undistributed income relating to the preferred stock at the end of 2002 (and, as usual, no reciprocity entry is needed under the partial or complete equity methods).

Complete Equity Method The December 31, 2002, workpaper elimination entries in journal form (Illustration 10-12) are as follows:

(1)	Investment in S Company Preferred Stock	12,000	
	(dividends in arrears recognized in prior year)		
	Investment in S Company Common Stock	12,000	
	(dividends in arrears on date of acquisition)		
	Equity Income—S Company Preferred Stock	12,000	
	(current period dividends)		
	Dividends Declared—S Company (Preferred)		36,000
	To eliminate intercompany dividends of $36,000 (30% of $120,000), of which $12,000 represents a liquidating dividend (dividends in arrears on the date of acquisition on the preferred stock), $12,000 a reversal of the prior year's equity income previously recognized, and $12,000 current year's dividends.		
(2)	Beginning Retained Earnings—S Company	28,500	
	Preferred Stock—S Company	150,000	
	Other Contributed Capital—P Company	13,500	
	Investment in S Company Preferred Stock		192,000
	To eliminate preferred stock investment account.		
(3)	Equity Income in S Company Common Stock	208,000	
	Dividends Declared—S Company Common Stock		40,000
	Investment in S Company Common Stock		168,000
	To eliminate intercompany income and dividends.		
(4)	Beginning Retained Earnings—S Company	244,000	
	Common Stock—S Company	800,000	
	Other Contributed Capital—S Company	244,000	
	Investment in S Company Common Stock		1,288,000
	To eliminate common stock investment account.		

 SUMMARY

1. *Describe the term "constructive retirement of debt."* An affiliate company may purchase bonds issued by another affiliate directly from the issuing company or from outsiders after the original issue. Because the bonds are held within the affiliated group, they are viewed as being **constructively retired** in the consolidated financial statements. The bonds, however, remain outstanding legally from the perspective of the issuing company.

2. *Describe how the gain or loss on constructive retirement of intercompany bond holdings is allocated between the purchasing and issuing companies.* Although the gain or loss may be allocated entirely to the issuing company, entirely to the purchasing company, or entirely to the parent company, the preferred method allocates it between the purchasing and issuing companies, thus allocating it between the controlling and noncontrolling interests. This method recognizes that a discount or premium is often associated with both the issuance and purchase of the bonds on the open market. The gain or loss is recognized over the life

of the bonds as each company amortizes the related discount or premium to interest expense and interest revenue.

3. *Explain the impact on the consolidated financial statements when a company issues a note to an affiliated company, which then discounts the note with an outside company.* A receivable held by one of the affiliated companies should be reported in the consolidated balance sheet only if the note is due from an outside party. A contingent liability should be disclosed if a note has been discounted with an outside party and the endorsement was with recourse.

4. *Determine the effect on the consolidated financial statements when a subsidiary issues a stock dividend.* The parent company records the receipt of the shares in a memorandum entry only, since a dividend in like stock is not considered income to the recipient. For consolidated purposes, the stock dividend does not alter the investor's proportionate interest in the subsidiary. Although the composition of the subsidiary's stockholders' equity accounts is changed, neither the total stockholders' equity nor the noncontrolling interest is altered.

5. *Understand the difference in how stock dividends and cash dividends issued by a subsidiary company affect the consolidated financial statements.* A cash dividend declared by the subsidiary is generally considered to be a distribution of the most recent profits, which reduces undistributed profits of the subsidiary accumulated after the date the parent obtained control of the subsidiary. Conversely, the source of a stock dividend is the earliest earnings accumulated in the retained earnings balance. Under the cost method, the amount of the entry to establish reciprocity must be modified to recognize that the retained earnings balance at the date of acquisition has been reduced as a result of the stock dividend.

6. *Determine the impact on the investment account when a subsidiary issues a stock dividend from preacquisition earnings and from postacquisition earnings.* The amount of the subsidiary's postacquisition earnings that have been capitalized and included in the consolidated retained earnings should be disclosed in the consolidated financial statements, but the parent's investment account is not affected. Stock dividends from preacquisition earnings do not affect the investment account or the computation of consolidated retained earnings.

7. *Explain how the purchase price is allocated when the subsidiary has both common and preferred stock outstanding.* In the preparation of consolidated financial statements, the shares of the preferred stock not held by the parent company are considered part of the noncontrolling interest. To determine the equity interest of each class of stockholders on a certain date, it is necessary to allocate the subsidiary's stockholders' equity between the preferred and common stock interests, referring to the provisions of the preferred stock issue and analyzing dividend provisions.

8. *Determine the controlling interest in income when the parent company owns both common and preferred stock of the subsidiary.* The controlling interest in income includes the internally generated income of the parent plus or minus other needed adjustments discussed in previous chapters plus the parent's share of the subsidiary's adjusted income. The parent's share of the subsidiary's income includes an amount assigned for its ownership of the subsidiary's common stock plus an amount assigned for its ownership of the subsidiary's preferred stock.

QUESTIONS

1. Define "constructive retirement of debt." How is the total constructive gain or loss computed?

2. The gain or loss on the constructive retirement of debt is recognized subsequently by the individual companies. Explain.

3. Allocating the gain or loss on constructive bond retirement between the purchasing and issuing companies is preferred conceptually. Describe how this allocation would be made.

4. Give the primary argument(s) in favor of assigning the *total* gain or loss on constructive bond retirement to the company that issued the bonds.

5. Under the allocation method followed in this text, how is the noncontrolling interest in combined income affected by intercompany bondholdings?

6. Investor Company purchased 70% of the $500,000 par value outstanding bonds of Investee Company, a 70% owned subsidiary. The bonds cost $338,000 and had a carrying value of $360,000 on the date of purchase.
   (a) What portion of the gain or loss resulting from the constructive bond retirement should be allocated to Investor Company?
   (b) What portion of the constructive gain or loss should be allocated to Investee Company?

7. An outside party issued a note to Affiliate X, who then sold the note to Affiliate Y. Y discounted the note at an unaffiliated bank, endorsing it with recourse. Which party is primarily liable and which party is contingently liable for the note?

8. Cash dividends are viewed as a distribution of the most recent earnings. How are stock dividends viewed?

9. Explain how the reciprocity calculation is modified in periods after the declaration of a stock dividend for firms using the cost method.

10. What journal entry, if any, would the parent company make to record the receipt of a stock dividend?

11. What effect does a stock dividend have on the consolidated statements workpaper in the year of declaration? In subsequent periods?

12. How does the existence of preferred stock affect the calculation of noncontrolling interest?

13. Explain how to account for the difference between cost and book value interest of an investment in preferred stock of a subsidiary.

14. What effect would cumulative preferred stock have on the allocation of a net loss to the common stockholders?

EXERCISES

EXERCISE 10-1 **Computing the Constructive Gain or Loss on Retirement of Debt**

Pacelli Company issued 10-year, 10% bonds with a par value of $1,000,000 on January 2, 2000, for $940,000. Interest is paid semiannually on June 30 and December 31. On December 31, 2001, $800,000 of the par value bonds were purchased by Salez Company for $820,000. Salez Company is an 80%-owned subsidiary of Pacelli Company. Both companies use the straight-line method to amortize bond discounts and premiums.

Salez Company declared cash dividends of $60,000 each year during the period 2001–2002.

Required:

A. Compute the total gain or loss on the constructive retirement of debt.

B. Allocate the total gain or loss between Pacelli Company and Salez Company.

C. Prepare the book entries related to the bonds made by the individual companies during 2002.

D. Assume that the two companies reported net income as follows:

	Pacelli Company	Salez Company
2001	$260,000	$140,000
2002	280,000	190,000

Compute consolidated net income and the noncontrolling interest in combined income for 2001 and 2002.

EXERCISE 10-2 **Intercompany Bond Workpaper Elimination Entries**

Refer to the data provided in Exercise 10-1.

Required:

Prepare in general journal form the intercompany bond elimination entries required in the preparation of the December 31, 2001, December 31, 2002, and December 31, 2003, consolidated statements workpapers.

EXERCISE 10-3 **Computing the Constructive Gain or Loss on Debt Retirement and Book Entries**

Weber Company issued five-year, 10% bonds on January 2, 2001, for 105. Par value is $850,000. Interest is paid semiannually on June 30 and December 31. Weber Company is a 90%-owned subsidiary of Fairfield Company. On December 31, 2001, Fairfield Company purchased $510,000 of Weber Company's par value bonds at 90 after the semiannual interest payment had been made. Weber Company declared dividends of $60,000 in 2001 and $80,000 in 2002. Both companies use the straight-line method to amortize bond discount and premium.

Required:

A. Compute the total gain or loss on the constructive retirement of the debt.

B. Allocate the total gain or loss between Weber Company and Fairfield Company.

C. Prepare the book entries related to the bonds made by the individual companies in 2002.

D. Assume that the two companies reported net income as follows:

	Fairfield Company	Weber Company
2001	$275,000	$190,000
2002	350,000	225,000

Compute consolidated net income and the noncontrolling interest in combined income for 2001 and 2002.

EXERCISE 10-4 Intercompany Bond Workpaper Elimination Entries

Use the information relating to Weber Company and Fairfield Company in Exercise 10-3.

Required:

Prepare in general journal form the intercompany bond elimination entries for the consolidated statements workpapers prepared on December 31, 2001, December 31, 2002, and December 31, 2003.

EXERCISE 10-5 Computing Carrying Value, Interest Revenue and Expense, Controlling and Noncontrolling Income

On January 2, 2001, Peoples, Inc. acquired an 80% interest in Schmidt Corporation for $900,000. Schmidt reported total stockholders' equity of $1,000,000 on this date. An examination of Schmidt's books revealed that book value was equal to fair value for all assets and liabilities except for inventory, which was undervalued by $60,000. All of the undervalued inventory was sold during 2001. Any goodwill will be amortized over 10 years.

Peoples also purchased 30% of the $500,000 par value outstanding bonds of Schmidt Corporation for $140,000 on January 2, 2001. The bonds mature in 10 years, carry an 11% annual interest rate payable on June 30 and December 31, and had a carrying value of $505,000 on the date of purchase. Both companies use the straight-line method to amortize bond discounts and premiums.

Peoples reported net income of $300,000 for 2001 and paid dividends of $130,000 during 2001. Schmidt Corporation reported net income of $320,000 for 2001 and paid dividends of $90,000 during the year.

Required:

Compute the following items at December 31, 2001:

1. Carrying value of the debt.
2. Interest revenue reported by Peoples, Inc.
3. Interest expense reported by Schmidt Corporation
4. Balance in the Investment in Schmidt Bonds account.
5. Consolidated net income for 2001 using the t-account approach.
6. Noncontrolling interest in combined income for 2001.

EXERCISE 10-6 Discounting a Note, Computing Proceeds, and Workpaper Eliminating Entry

Wyatt Corporation, an 80%-owned subsidiary, accepted a $60,000, 12%, 90-day note from a customer for services performed. On that same date, because Wyatt Corporation was in need of cash for operations, the subsidiary endorsed the note over to its parent company in exchange for $60,000. After holding the note for 30 days, the parent discounted the note with an independent bank. The discount rate was 13%. Both companies record discounted notes in a Discounted Notes Receivable account.

Required:

A. Compute the proceeds received by the parent company from discounting the note.
B. Prepare the workpaper entry, if any, needed to eliminate the note. If none is needed, explain why.

EXERCISE 10-7 Subsidiary Stock Dividend—Cost Method

Perez, Inc. owns 7,000 shares (70% interest) of Salata Company's $100 par value common stock. The stock was purchased for $1,250,000 on January 2, 2000, when Salata reported a common stock balance of $1,000,000, a retained earnings balance of $400,000, and other contributed capital balance of $100,000. Any difference between cost and book value interest acquired is attributable to the under- or overvalaution of land. During 2001, Salata reported net income of $80,000. Because the company was short of liquid assets, dividends have not been paid since 1996. During 2001, however, the company declared and issued a 15% stock dividend (market price of common stock on the date of issue, $160 per share). The retained earnings balance at the beginning of 2001 was $500,000.

Required:

A. Prepare the journal entries required in the books of Perez, Inc. during 2001.

B. Prepare in general journal form the workpaper entries necessary in the consolidated statements workpaper for the year ended December 31, 2001.

C. Prepare the workpaper entry to establish reciprocity to be made in the 2002 consolidated statements workpaper.

EXERCISE 10-8 Liquidating Dividend

On January 1, 2001, Pacelli Company acquired a 90% interest in Swartz Corporation for $720,000. On this date, Swartz Corporation reported common stock of $500,000 and retained earnings of $200,000. Any difference between cost and book value interest acquired is attributable to the under- or overvaluation of land.

Other information pertaining to Swartz Corporation follows:

2001 Net income	$65,000
2001 Cash dividends	90,000
2002 Net income	80,000
2002 Cash dividends	40,000

Pacelli Company uses the partial equity method to account for its investment in Swartz Corporation.

Required:

A. Prepare the general journal entries for 2001 and 2002 to record the receipt of the cash dividends.

B. Prepare all determinable workpaper entries that would be made in the preparation of the 2001 consolidated statements workpaper.

C. Prepare all determinable workpaper entries that would be made in the preparation of consolidated statements for 2003.

D. How would the entry in part A change if the cost method was used to account for the investment?

EXERCISE 10-9 Purchase Common and Preferred Stock

On January 2, 2001, Pasqual Corporation purchased 80% of the outstanding common stock and 30% of the outstanding cumulative, nonparticipating, preferred stock of Sung Company for $400,000 and $70,000, respectively. At this date, Sung Company reported account balances of $400,000 in common stock, $200,000 in preferred stock, and $100,000 in retained earnings. No other contributed capital accounts exist. The difference between cost and book value of the common stock is attributable to under- or overvalued land. Dividends on the 12% cumulative preferred stock (par $10) were not paid during 2000.

Other information:

	Pasqual Corporation	Sung Company
1/2/2001 Retained Earnings	$45,000	$100,000
2001 Reported Net Income	84,600	90,000
2001 Dividends Declared	25,000	50,000

Required:

A. Prepare the journal entries made by Pasqual Corporation in 2001 to account for the investments assuming (1) the cost method is used, (2) the partial equity method is used, and (3) the complete equity method is used.

B. Compute the noncontrolling interest in Sung Company's net income.

C. Prepare the 2001 workpaper entries related to the foregoing investments assuming (1) the cost method is used to account for the investment, (2) the partial equity method is used to account for the investment, and (3) the complete equity method is used to account for the investment.

EXERCISE 10-10 **Various Preferred Stock Characteristics—Workpaper Entries**

Sam's Company reported the following stockholders' equity account balances on December 31, 2001.

Preferred stock (12%, $100 par value, call price is $105)	$100,000
Common stock, $10 par value	500,000
Other contributed capital—premium on issue of common stock	160,000
Retained earnings	110,000
Total	$870,000

On December 31, 2001, Peterson, Inc. acquired 60% of Sam Company's common stock for $550,000 and 40% of its preferred stock for $55,000.

The difference between the cost of the common stock (preferred stock) and the book value interest acquired is allocated entirely to land (other contributed capital).

Required:

Prepare in general journal form the December 31, 2001, workpaper entries to eliminate the investment in common and preferred stock for each of the following independent cases:

Case 1: The preferred stock is noncumulative and nonparticipating.

Case 2: The preferred stock is cumulative and nonparticipating, and dividends were not paid in 2000 and 2001.

Case 3: The preferred stock is noncumulative and fully participating.

EXERCISE 10-11 **Various Preferred Stock Characteristics—Compute Consolidated Income**

On January 1, 2001, Perez Company acquired 80% of Serrano Company's $300,000 par value common stock for $200,000 and 40% of Serrano Company's 8%, $100,000 par value preferred stock for $86,000. During 2001, Serrano Company reported net income of $80,000 and declared cash dividends of $45,000. Perez Company reported net income (including dividends from subsidiary) of $200,000 in 2001.

Required:

In each of the following independent cases, compute consolidated net income for 2001.

Case 1: The preferred stock is noncumulative and nonparticipating.

Case 2: The preferred stock is cumulative and nonparticipating. Dividends were in arrears two years as of January 1, 2001.

Case 3: The preferred stock is noncumulative and fully participating.

Case 4: The preferred stock is cumulative and fully participating. Dividends were in arrears one year as of January 1, 2001.

PROBLEMS

PROBLEM 10-1 **Constructive Gain or Loss on Bonds**

On January 1, 1998, Pace Corporation issued $500,000 par value, 10-year, 15% bonds. Interest is payable each June 30 and December 31. On January 1, 2001, Supra Corporation, a 90%-

owned subsidiary, purchased on the open market all of the parent company bonds. Both companies have a December 31 year-end. For this problem, assume the following four independent cases.

	Issue Price by Pace Corporation on January 1, 1998	Purchase Price by Supra Corporation on January 1, 2001
Case 1	$512,000	$514,000
Case 2	488,000	486,000
Case 3	512,000	486,000
Case 4	488,000	514,000

Required:

A. For cases 1 and 2, compute the total constructive gain or loss and the portion allocated to each company.

B. For cases 1 and 2 prepare the journal entry or entries to be made by Pace Corporation and Supra Corporation on June 30, 2001. Both companies amortize discounts and premiums each interest payment date and use the straight-line method of amortization. Assume that Pace uses the partial equity method to account for its investment in Supra.

C. Complete the following schedules as of December 31, 2001, after the December 31 interest payment (receipt) and amortization of discount or premium have been recorded.

	Issue Price	
Pace Corporation	$512,000	$488,000
Bond Payable	_____	_____
Unamortized Premium (discount)	_____	_____
Carrying Value of Bonds	_____	_____
2001 Cash Payment for Interest	_____	_____
(Premium) Discount Amortization	_____	_____
2001 Bond Interest Expense	_____	_____
Increase (decrease) in Net Income from Amortization	_____	_____

	Purchase Price	
Supra Corporation	$514,000	$486,000
Investment in Pace Corp. Bonds	_____	_____
2001 Cash Receipts for Interest	_____	_____
(Premium) Discount Amortization	_____	_____
2001 Bond Interest Income	_____	_____
Increase (decrease) in Net Income from Amortization	_____	_____

	Case			
	1	2	3	4
Amount of constructive gain (loss) recognized by Pace Corporation	_____	_____	_____	_____
Amount of constructive gain (loss) recognized by Supra Corporation	_____	_____	_____	_____

D. For cases 1 and 2, prepare in general journal form the intercompany bond elimination entries required in the December 31, 2001, consolidated statements workpaper.

PROBLEM 10-2 **Constructive Gain or Loss on Bond Retirement with Workpaper—Cost Method**
Prezo Company purchased 80% of Satz Company's common stock for $880,000 on January 2, 2001. Condensed financial information for Prezo Company and Satz Company is given below.

Balance Sheet
December 31, 2001

	Prezo Co.	Satz Co.
Current Assets	$ 920,000	$ 580,000
Investment in Satz Company Common Stock	880,000	
Investment in Satz Company Bonds	227,143	
Other Assets	2,345,457	1,320,000
	$4,372,600	$1,900,000
Bonds Payable (10%)	$ 700,000	$ 400,000
Premium on Bonds Payable	20,000	9,000
Other Liabilities	1,434,600	141,000
Common Stock	1,600,000	800,000
Retained Earnings	618,000	550,000
	$4,372,600	$1,900,000

Retained Earnings Statement
For the Year Ended December 31, 2001

	Prezo Co.	Satz Co.
1/1 Balance	$ 480,000	$ 300,000
Net Income	388,000	400,000
Dividends	(250,000)	(150,000)
12/31 Balance	618,000	$ 550,000

Income Statement
For the Year Ended December 31, 2001

	Prezo Co.	Satz Co.
Sales	$2,680,000	$1,860,000
Dividend Income	120,000	
Other Income	266,000	120,000
Total Revenue	3,066,000	1,980,000
Expenses	2,678,000	1,580,000
Net Income	$ 388,000	$ 400,000

On July 1, 2001, Prezo Company purchased 60% of Satz Company's bonds for $225,000. The bonds mature on December 31, 2004. Interest of 10% per annum is paid on June 30 and December 31 each year. Both companies use the straight-line method to amortize bond discounts and premiums.

Required:
A. Compute the gain or loss on the constructive retirement of the bonds allocated to each of the affiliated companies.
B. Prepare a consolidated financial statements workpaper on December 31, 2001.

C. Prepare in good form a schedule showing the calculation of consolidated net income for the year ended December 31, 2001.

PROBLEM 10-3 **Workpaper, Cost Method—Constructive Gain or Loss with Stock Dividend**
On January 1, 2000, Pasta Company purchased an 80% interest in Salsa Company for $152,000. On this date, Salsa Company reported capital stock and retained earnings of $100,000 and $90,000, respectively. During 2000, Salsa Company reported net income of $30,000 and declared a cash dividend of $35,000. At the end of 2001, Salsa Company was facing a cash shortage. Rather than distributing a cash dividend to the common stockholders, the board of directors elected to issue a 30% stock dividend. Salsa Company's accountant recorded the stock dividend as follows:

Stock Dividend Declared	30,000	
Common Stock		30,000

On December 31, 2001, Pasta Company purchased on the open market bonds of Salsa Company with a par value of $100,000 for $94,000. Financial data for the two companies as of December 31, 2001, follows:

Income Statement	*Pasta Company*	*Salsa Company*
Sales	$370,000	$200,000
Other Revenues	15,000	2,000
	385,000	202,000
Cost of Goods Sold	180,000	110,000
Other Expenses	80,000	30,000
Net Income	$125,000	$ 62,000

Retained Earnings	*Pasta Company*	*Salsa Company*
1/1 Retained Earnings	$ 96,000	$ 85,000
Net Income	125,000	62,000
Less: Dividends Declared		
Stock Dividend Declared	(30,000)	(30,000)
12/31 Retained Earnings	$191,000	$117,000

Balance Sheet	*Pasta Company*	*Salsa Company*
Current Assets	$171,000	$169,000
Investment in Salsa Company Stock	148,000	
Investment in Salsa Company Bonds	94,000	
Other Assets	300,000	315,000
Totals	$713,000	$484,000
Accounts Payable	$ 72,000	$ 40,000
Long-Term Bonds payable	250,000	200,000 *
Discount on Bonds Payable	—	(3,000)
Common Stock ($10 par value)	200,000	130,000
Retained Earnings	191,000	$117,000
Totals	$713,000	$484,000

*8%, maturity date December 31, 2004.

Required:

A. Prepare a consolidated statements workpaper on December 31, 2001.

B. Prepare in general journal form the entry that would be made in the December 31, 2002, workpaper to establish reciprocity as of January 1, 2002.

PROBLEM 10-4 **Workpaper, Partial Equity Method—Constructive Gain or Loss on Bonds**
Condensed financial information for Prince Company and South Company follows:

Balance Sheet
December 31, 2001

	Prince Company	South Company
Current Assets	$ 826,000	$ 700,000
Investment in South Company Stock	1,120,000	
Investment in South Company Bonds	312,000	
Other Assets	1,252,000	1,400,000
Totals	$3,510,000	$2,100,000
Bonds Payable	$ 300,000	$ 500,000
Premium on Bonds Payable	20,000	40,000
Other Liabilities	380,000	160,000
Common Stock	2,000,000	1,000,000
Retained Earnings	810,000	400,000
Totals	$3,510,000	$2,100,000

Combined Statement of Income and Retained Earnings
For the Year Ended December 31, 2001

	Prince Company	South Company
Sales	$3,000,000	$2,000,000
Equity in Subsidiary Income	160,000	
Other Income	100,000	200,000
Total Revenues	3,260,000	2,200,000
Expenses	2,800,000	2,000,000
Net Income	460,000	200,000
1/1 Retained Earnings Balance	600,000	300,000
	1,060,000	500,000
Dividends	(250,000)	(100,000)
12/31 Retained Earnings Balance	$ 810,000	$ 400,000

Prince Company purchased 80% of South Company's common stock for $1,000,000 at the beginning of 2000 and uses the partial equity method to account for the investment. At the time of purchase, South Company reported a common stock balance of $1,000,000 and a retained earnings balance of $250,000.

On July 1, 2001, Prince Company purchased 60% of South Company's 10% bonds for $315,000. The bonds mature on December 31, 2003. Interest is paid on June 30 and December 31.

Required:

A. Prepare the entries made on the books of Prince Company during 2001 to record its interest in South Company and account for the bond investment.

B. Prepare a consolidated financial statements workpaper on December 31, 2001.

PROBLEM 10-5 **Workpaper, Cost Method—Preferred Stock**
On January 1, 1996, Pabst Company acquired 80% of Secor Company's common stock and 30% of Secor Company's 10% preferred stock. Pabst Company paid $680,000 for the com-

mon stock and $135,000 for the preferred stock. The preferred stock is cumulative and nonparticipating and has a call price of $104. On the date of acquisition, there were no dividends in arrears. On January 1, 1996, Secor Company reported the following account balances:

10% Preferred Stock ($100 par value)	$ 400,000
Common Stock ($10 par value)	500,000
Other Contributed Capital (Sale of common stock in excess	
of par value)	100,000
Retained Earnings	230,000
Total	$1,230,000

Condensed preclosing trial balances for the two companies at December 31, 2001 are presented below.

	Pabst Company	Secor Company
Income Statement		
Sales	$ 700,000	$ 450,000
Expenses	(580,000)	(350,000)
Net Income	$ 120,000	$ 100,000
Retained Earnings		
1/1 Balance	$ 507,000	$ 430,000
Net Income	120,000	100,000
Less: Dividends Declared	(100,000)	
12/31 Balance	$ 527,000	$ 530,000
Balance Sheet		
Current Assets	$1,618,000	$ 890,000
Investment in Secor Company Common Stock	680,000	
Investment in Secor Company Preferred Stock	135,000	
Other Assets	1,025,000	1,000,000
Totals	$3,458,000	$1,890,000
Liabilities	$ 931,000	$ 360,000
Preferred Stock	400,000	400,000
Common Stock	1,000,000	500,000
Other Contributed Capital	600,000	100,000
Retained Earnings	527,000	530,000
Totals	$3,458,000	$1,890,000

On December 31, 2001, dividends on the preferred stock were in arrears for 2000 and 2001.

Required:
Prepare a consolidated statements workpaper for the year ended December 31, 2001. Assume that any difference between cost and book value interest acquired is attributable to an undervaluation in the land of Secor Company in the case of common stock, and any difference between the cost of preferred stock and the book value interest acquired is assignable to other contributed capital.

PROBLEM 10-6   **Workpaper, Cost Method—Preferred Stock**

PAL Corporation acquired 40% of the outstanding preferred stock of Saltz, Inc. for $60,000 and 90% of that firm's outstanding common stock for $600,000 on January 1, 2000. On the date that the controlling interest was acquired, the stockholders' equity section of Saltz, Inc. was as follows.

Preferred stock—10%, cumulative, fully participating, liquidation value is equal to par value	$100,000
Common stock—$10 par value	400,000
Retained earnings	200,000
Total	$700,000

There were no dividends in arrears on January 1, 2000. For the fiscal year ended December 31, 2000, Saltz, Inc. reported net income of $130,000. No cash or stock dividends were declared by the company during 2000.

    The difference between cost and the book value of the equity interest acquired in the common stock relates to the land owned by Saltz, Inc. Condensed financial information for the two companies at December 31, 2001, are presented below.

Income Statement Date	Pal Corp.	Saltz Inc.
Sales	$ 890,000	$750,000
Interest, Dividends, and Other Revenues	91,000	50,000
Cost of Goods Sold	(500,000)	(400,000)
Selling, Administrative, and Other Expenses	(330,000)	(280,000)
Net income	$ 151,000	$120,000

Retained Earnings		
1/1 Balance	$ 560,000	$330,000
Net Income	151,000	120,000
Less: Dividends Declared		(90,000)
12/31 Balance	$ 711,000	$360,000

Balance Sheet		
Current Assets	$ 810,000	$380,000
Investment in Common Stock	600,000	
Investment in Preferred Stock	60,000	
Other Assets	1,276,000	600,000
Totals	$2,746,000	$980,000
Liabilities	$1,335,000	$120,000
Preferred Stock		100,000
Common Stock	700,000	400,000
Retained Earnings	711,000	360,000
Totals	$2,746,000	$980,000

Required:

A. Prepare a schedule to compute the difference between the cost of the common stock and the book value interest acquired.

B. Prepare consolidated statements workpapers for the year ended December 31, 2001.

PROBLEM 10-7   **Preferred Stock**

P Company owns 80% of S Company's common stock (cost $650,000) and 20% of its preferred stock (cost $50,000). Both interests were acquired on January 1, 1999. On the date of purchase, S Company's stockholders' equity consisted of the following accounts.

Preferred stock	$200,000	
Common stock	500,000	
Retained earnings	160,000	

The preferred stock is $25 par value, 9% cumulative, and nonparticipating. The call price is $27 per share. Dividends have been declared in all years except for 2000.

An examination of S Company's assets and liabilities revealed that their book values were equal to fair values except for the inventory and equipment.

	Book Value	Fair Value
Inventory	$120,000	$150,000
Equipment (net)	560,000	640,000

The equipment had a remaining life of five years at the date of the equity purchase, and the FIFO cost flow assumption is used in costing inventory. The goodwill, if any, is to be amortized over 40 years.

S Company sells inventory to P Company at 25% above cost. During 2000 and 2001, such sales amounted to $350,000 and $390,000, respectively. The 2000 and 2001 ending inventories of P Company included goods purchased from S Company for $77,500 and $54,000, respectively.

The companies file consolidated tax returns. Ignore deferred income taxes when assigning the difference between cost and book value.

Selected data for the 2001 December 31 fiscal year-end are given below:

	P Company	S Company
Net income (including dividend income and sales to affiliates)	$234,500	$100,000
1/1/01 Retained earnings	430,000	310,000
Dividends declared and paid	80,000	50,000

Required:

A. Prepare a schedule to compute the book value interest acquired for each equity investment.

B. Prepare a schedule to assign the difference between the cost of the common stock investment and the book value interest acquired.

C. Compute the following items:

   (1) Dividends received during 2001 by P Company from S Company for each equity interest held.

   (2) Noncontrolling interest in 2001 combined income.

   (3) Consolidated net income for 2001.

   (4) Consolidated retained earnings on January 1, 2001.

PROBLEM 10-8 Comprehensive Workpaper—Cost Method

Parson Industries purchased 80% of the common stock of Succo Company on January 1, 1994, for $300,000 when Succo Company's capital consisted of common stock of $200,000, preferred stock of $100,000, other contributed capital of $50,000, and retained earnings of $62,000.

The $100 par value preferred is 15%, cumulative and nonparticipating, and has a call price of $104 per share. Dividends on the preferred stock were not paid in 1993.

Trial balances for the parent and subsidiary for the December 31, 2001, year-end are presented below.

Income Statement	Parson Industries	Succo Company
Sales	$ 404,000	$300,000
Dividend Income	4,000	
Cost of Goods Sold	(200,000)	(160,000)
Operating Expenses	(36,400)	(50,000)
Income Taxes	(40,200)	(27,000)
Net Income	$ 131,400	$ 63,000

Retained Earnings		
1/1 Retained Earnings	$ 157,400	$107,000
Net Income	131,400	63,000
Less: Dividends Declared	(65,000)	(50,000)
12/31 Retained Earnings	$ 223,800	$120,000

Balance Sheet		
Cash and Receivables	$ 396,800	$205,000
Inventories	200,000	170,000
Land	300,000	120,000
Buildings and Equipment	697,000	245,000
Accumulated Depreciation	(100,000)	(70,000)
Investment in Succo Company	300,000	
Totals	$1,793,800	$670,000
Current Liabilities	$ 370,000	$100,000
Bonds Payable	400,000	100,000
Preferred Stock		100,000
Common Stock, $10 par value	600,000	200,000
Other Contributed Capital	200,000	50,000
Retained Earnings	223,800	120,000
Totals	$1,793,800	$670,000

Additional information:

1. At the beginning of 2001, dividends on the preferred stock were in arrears for 1999 and 2000.

2. Succo Company owed Parson Industries $10,000 for purchases of inventory on account.

3. At the date of acquisition, the portion of the difference between cost and the book value interest acquired that was attributed to tangible assets of Succo Company was allocated as follows:

Equipment (net)	$10,000
Inventories	5,000
Land	5,000

The amount not allocated to tangible assets was allocated to goodwill (excess of cost over fair value). The equipment had a remaining life of 20 years at the date of acquisition. Succo Company uses the FIFO cost flow assumption in pricing inventory. The amount not assignable to tangible assets is to be amortized over a period of 20 years.

4. The building and equipment account of Parson Industries includes $50,000 of equipment acquired from Succo Company on July 1, 2000. When sold to Parson Industries, the asset was carried on the books of Succo Company at a cost of $100,000 and accumulated depreciation of $20,000. The asset is being depreciated by Parson Industries over a remaining life of five years. Parson Industries uses the straight-line method of depreciation.

5. The 2000 and 2001 ending inventories of Succo Company included goods purchased from Parson Industries for $15,000 and $25,000, respectively. Parson Industries sells merchandise to Succo Company at 20% above cost. During 2001, such sales amounted to $100,000.

6. The affiliates file consolidated tax returns. Ignore deferred income taxes in the assignment of the difference between cost and book value.

Required:

A. Compute the book value interest acquired by Parson Industries at the date of acquisition and allocate the difference to undervalued assets of Succo Company.

B. Prepare a consolidated statements workpaper for the year ended December 31, 2001.

C. Prepare a schedule showing the calculation of controlling interest in consolidated net income for the year ended December 31, 2001.

PROBLEM 10-9 Comprehensive Workpaper—Complete Equity Method

Parson Industries purchased 80% of the common stock of Succo Company on January 1, 1994, for $300,000 when Succo Company's capital consisted of common stock of $200,000, preferred stock of $100,000, other contributed capital of $50,000, and retained earnings of $62,000.

The $100 par value preferred is 15%, cumulative and nonparticipating, and has a call price of $104 per share. Dividends on the preferred stock were not paid in 1993.

Trial balances for the parent and subsidiary for the December 31, 2001, year-end are presented below.

Income Statement	Parson Industries	Succo Company
Sales	$ 404,000	$300,000
Equity Income	29,153	
Cost of Goods Sold	(200,000)	(160,000)
Operating Expenses	(36,400)	(50,000)
Income Taxes	(40,200)	(27,000)
Net Income	$ 156,553	$ 63,000

Retained Earnings		
1/1 Retained Earnings	$ 176,040	$107,000
Net Income	156,553	63,000
Less: Dividends Declared	(65,000)	(50,000)
12/31 Retained Earnings	$ 267,593	$120,000

Balance Sheet		
Cash and Receivables	$ 396,800	$205,000
Inventories	200,000	170,000
Land	300,000	120,000
Buildings and Equipment	697,000	245,000
Accumulated Depreciation	(100,000)	(70,000)
Investment in Succo Company	343,793	
Totals	$1,837,593	$670,000
Current Liabilities	$ 370,000	$100,000
Bonds Payable	400,000	100,000
Preferred Stock		100,000
Common Stock, $10 par value	600,000	200,000
Other Contributed Capital	200,000	50,000
Retained Earnings	267,593	120,000
Totals	$1,837,593	$670,000

Additional information:

1. At the beginning of 2001, dividends on the preferred stock were in arrears for 1999 and 2000.

2. Succo Company owed Parson Industries $10,000 for purchases of inventory on account.

3. At the date of acquisition, the portion of the difference between cost and the book value interest acquired that was attributed to tangible assets of Succo Company was allocated as follows:

Equipment (net)	$10,000
Inventories	5,000
Land	5,000

The amount not allocated to tangible assets was allocated to goodwill (excess of cost over fair value). The equipment had a remaining life of 20 years at the date of acquisition. Succo Company uses the FIFO cost flow assumption in pricing inventory. The amount not assignable to tangible assets is to be amortized over a period of 20 years.

4. The building and equipment account of Parson Industries includes $50,000 of equipment acquired from Succo Company on July 1, 2000. When sold to Parson Industries, the asset was carried on the books of Succo Company at a cost of $100,000 and accumulated depreciation of $20,000. The asset is being depreciated by Parson Industries over a remaining life of five years. Parson Industries uses the straight-line method of depreciation.

5. The 2000 and 2001 ending inventories of Succo Company included goods purchased from Parson Industries for $15,000 and $25,000, respectively. Parson Industries sells merchandise to Succo Company at 20% above cost. During 2001, such sales amounted to $100,000.

6. The affiliates file consolidated tax returns. Ignore deferred income taxes in the assignment of the difference between cost and book value.

Required:

A. Compute the book value interest acquired by Parson Industries at the date of acquisition and allocate the difference to undervalued assets of Succo Company.

B. Prepare a consolidated statements workpaper for the year ended December 31, 2001.

C. Prepare a schedule showing the calculation of controlling interest in consolidated net income for the year ended December 31, 2001.

11

ALTERNATIVE CONCEPTS OF CONSOLIDATED FINANCIAL STATEMENTS

LEARNING OBJECTIVES

1. Explain why the FASB is considering the elimination of the pooling of interests method.

2. Distinguish the primary differences between the pooling of interests method and the purchases method.

3. Compare the book value method and the equity method in a pooling of interests.

4. Indicate the principal requirement for the use of the pooling of interests method to account for an acquisition.

5. Understand how the equity transfer rule is used in a pooling of interests.

6. Describe two alternative concepts of consolidated financial statements (other than purchase and pooling).

To most executives, the main reason to preserve pooling can be summed up in two words—stock price. "While it shouldn't matter that much if we book goodwill, or whether we write it off now or over time, to the markets it does," says Christopher Paisley, CFO of 3ComCorp., of Santa Clara, California, which used pooling with four out of six acquisitions in the past two years.[1]

POOLING OF INTERESTS IN A PARENT–SUBSIDIARY RELATIONSHIP

The preservation of the pooling of interests method is subject to considerable uncertainty. The FASB voted unanimously in April 1999 to eliminate the method. "We believe that the purchase method of accounting gives investors a better idea of the initial cost of a transaction and the investment's performance over time than does the pooling of interests method," said FASB Chairman Edmund L. Jenkins.[2]

---

[1] *CFO*, "Say Goodbye to Pooling," by Ian Springsteel, February 1997, p. 80.

[2] *Financial Accounting Standards Board*, "Financial Accounting Series Status Report," No. 313, May 18, 1999.

An exposure draft to this effect was issued in September 1999, with a final standard projected to be issued by the end of 2000. In 1998, when discussion was underway about the possible elimination of the method, a huge upsurge in pooling activity occurred. In the first two quarters of 1999, however, the number of poolings appeared to have slowed. If, as expected, the method is eliminated, it will fall under the general heading of "alternative concepts of consolidated financial statements." It is unlikely that the move will be met with unanimous approval. In fact, at the date of this writing, some businesses were appealing to Congress to intervene before the FASB reaches a final decision.

One consideration in the proposed elimination is the issue of international comparability. The pooling method is rarely used outside the United States.

The United States not only is out of step with other countries on the pooling versus purchase issue, but domestically we have a great deal of diversity in practice as well. Pooling of interests is the exception almost everywhere else in the world, and some countries ban the use of it altogether.[3]

A method similar to pooling, however, is approved in the standards of the International Accounting Standards Committee (IASC). This method, called a uniting of interests, requires (among other conditions) that the combining firms not differ significantly in size. There is no such condition for the pooling method as applied in the United States. The possibility of adding a size requirement was considered and rejected by the FASB in its deliberations. The change in standards laid out in the exposure draft is subject to the FASB's usual due process, and until the end of that process, no one can be sure whether a proposed standard will be revised, eliminated, or put into effect. Possibly in an attempt to soften the blow of the proposed change, the FASB also proposed changes in the amortization of goodwill for firms under the purchase method, and in the presentation of such amortization on the income statement. The proposed changes should make it easier for readers to discern what income would be without the inclusion of goodwill amortization. See Appendix A of Chapter 2 for further details on the exposure draft (Business Combinations and Intangible Assets).

But the seven-member Board [FASB] considered whether to continue to allow the pooling method in the small number of cases where two companies of equal size decide to merge, according to Edmund Jenkins, the chairman of the Board. The Board discussed whether rules could be written to prevent companies of unequal size from finding loopholes to use pooling, while allowing firms to pool when really appropriate.[4]

The American Accounting Association's Financial Accounting Standards Committee, in response to an FASB invitation to comment on the alternative methods of accounting for business combinations, stated its belief that purchase accounting "puts business combinations on a reporting basis that is consistent with the accounting for other capital investments while pooling does not."[5] The Committee

---

[3]Ibid.

[4]*New York Times,* "Accounting for Mergers May Change," by Melody Petersen, April 21, 1999, p. 3.

[5]*Accounting Horizons,* "Response to FASB on Methods of Accounting for Business Combinations," by AAA's Financial Accounting Standards Committee, September 1999, p. 299.

admitted, however, that it was unaware of any empirical research that directly addresses this issue. The Committee members provided two reasons for their belief that the purchase method provides relevant information for assessing the profitability of business combinations: (1) It informs investors and creditors of the current cost of the acquisition, and (2) In conjunction with the standard on asset impairment, it allows users to learn in a timely fashion when the benefits are insufficient to recover the premium paid at initiation of the deal.[6]

Because a number of large combinations in recent years have been accounted for by the pooling method, understanding the differences between this method and the purchase alternative will continue to be important for years to come. Thus, we present the pooling method for combinations consummated as a stock acquisition in the following sections of this chapter. Obviously, some or all of this presentation may be omitted, as desired.

IN THE NEWS

The chief executive of Tyco International Ltd., L. Dennis Kozlowski, announced the company's decision to quit doing all stock deals after it came under fire for its accounting methods. Kozlowski said the decision came in view of the depressed stock prices and the controversy over the pooling method. The shift in strategy suggests that Tyco may be "less likely to do the kind of megadeals that have been its hallmark in recent years, including the $11.9 billion purchase of electronic-parts maker AMO Inc. earlier this year."[7]

The pooling of interests method of accounting for a business combination achieved via an asset acquisition was discussed and illustrated in Chapter 2. Recall that in an asset acquisition, the assets and liabilities of the acquired company are recorded on the books of the acquiring company, and the acquired company (or companies) ceases to exist as a separate legal entity; that is, the acquired company is dissolved. But, as indicated in *APB Opinion No. 16*, dissolution of the acquired company is not a necessary condition for use of the pooling method.[8]

> Dissolution of a combining company is not a condition for applying the pooling of interests method of accounting for a business combination. One or more combining companies may be subsidiaries of the issuing corporation after the combination is consummated if the other conditions are met.[9]

One requirement of the pooling method is that the acquiring company issue common stock for substantially all (at least 90%) of the voting common stock of the acquired company. Thus, a ***stock acquisition*** accomplished through an exchange of voting stock for at least 90% of the voting stock of the acquired company must be accounted for as a pooling of interests if all other pooling requirements are met. This section will cover accounting and consolidation procedures followed for *stock acquisitions* treated as poolings of interests. Whether the combination is achieved through an asset acquisition or a stock acquisition, the issues and criticisms related to the pooling technique, discussed in earlier chapters, apply equally.

---

[6]Ibid.

[7]*WSJ*, "Tyco Puts Stock Deals Behind It," by Mark Maremont, 11/3/99, p. C1.

[8]We use the present tense throughout this discussion, since the pooling method is still a part of GAAP as of this writing.

[9]Opinion of the Accounting Principles Board No. 16, "Business Combinations" (New York: AICPA, 1970), par. 49.

"Critics say the accounting method, known as a pooling of interests, is not in the best interest of shareholders because it does not hold executives accountable for their actions if the total price paid—stock valued at $74 billion in Exxon's proposed merger with Mobil—is too high. Some analysts add that pooling restricts how the new combined company can run many parts of its business. For example, the new merged entity cannot sell more than 10 percent of its assets in the next two years without imperiling the accounting treatment, even if such sales make good business sense. If the oil companies were forced to use purchase accounting, analysts estimate that a $50 billion premium would be written off [as goodwill amortization] over twenty years, eating up 21 percent of the $11.7 billion that the two firms reported in combined profits in 1997."[10]

Accounting for a Pooled Subsidiary at Date of Acquisition

The discussion and illustrations in this section are based on the following preacquisition balance sheets for P Company and S Company on December 31, 1999:

	P Company	S Company	
Cash	$100,000	$ 20,000	
Other Current Assets	140,000	50,000	
Property and Equipment (net)	120,000	40,000	
Land	40,000	20,000	
Total Assets	$400,000	$130,000	
Liabilities	$ 60,000	$ 50,000	
Common Stock, $10 par value	200,000	50,000	
Other Contributed Capital	40,000	10,000	$80,000
Retained Earnings	100,000	20,000	
Total Equities	$400,000	$130,000	

Wholly Owned Subsidiary Three situations are possible in a pooling of interests. The par value of stock issued by P Company can exceed, be equal to, or be less than the par value of S Company's acquired stock. First, we consider the case when P Company's par value issued exceeds the total par value of S Company's stock acquired. To illustrate the pooling method for a wholly owned subsidiary, assume that, on January 1, 2000, P Company exchanged 6,000 shares of its common stock for all the shares (5,000) of the common stock of S Company. The exchange of stock is recorded by P Company by the following entry:

P Company's Books

Investment in S Company	80,000	
Common Stock (6,000 × $10)		60,000
Retained Earnings		20,000

Where a stock acquisition is treated as a pooling and a parent–subsidiary relationship is established, the acquired stock is recorded as an investment in subsidiary on the parent company's books at an amount ***equal to the book value*** of the equity (net assets) acquired. The debit to the investment account is equal to the subsidiary's stockholders' equity acquired, 100% in this case. The credit to common stock reflects the par value of P Company stock issued, which is $10,000 more than the par

---

[10]*New York Times,* "Big Oil: The Arithmetic," by Melody Petersen, December 2, 1998, p. 3.

value of S Company stock acquired in this example. To balance the entry, this excess should be deducted first from the combined other contributed capital and then from combined retained earnings. Since the par value of the stock issued exceeds the par value of the stock acquired by $10,000, the excess serves to reduce S Company's other contributed capital to zero, and the entire amount of S Company's retained earnings is carried forward. Upon first glance, it does not appear that S Company's other contributed capital has been reduced. Suppose instead, that the par value of P Company's stock issued equaled the par value of S Company's stock. The debit to the investment account would still equal the book value of S Company's net assets; however, the credits would now include $50,000 to common stock (at par), $20,000 to retained earnings, and $10,000 to other contributed capital. In essence, this entry moves S Company's equity accounts onto the books of P Company. Now refer back to the entry made earlier. Since P Company's par value exceeded S Company's par value by $10,000, no other contributed capital amounts were recorded in the entry (hence S Company's other contributed capital is reduced rather than transferred to P Company).

A workpaper for the preparation of a consolidated balance sheet on the date of acquisition is presented in Illustration 11-1.

The workpaper investment elimination entry is:

(1)	Common Stock—S Company	50,000	
	Other Contributed Capital—S Company	10,000	
	Retained Earnings—S Company	20,000	
	Investment in S Company		80,000

Pooling Accounting	**ILLUSTRATION 11–1**
Par Value Issued Exceeds	**Consolidated Balance Sheet Workpaper**
Par Value Acquired	**P Company and Subsidiary**
Wholly Owned Subsidiary	**January 1, 2000**
Date of Acquisition	

	P Company	S Company	Eliminations Dr.	Eliminations Cr.	Consolidated Balances
Cash	100,000	20,000			120,000
Other Current Assets	140,000	50,000			190,000
Plant and Equipment	120,000	40,000			160,000
Land	40,000	20,000			60,000
Investment in S Company	80,000			(1) 80,000	
Total Assets	480,000	130,000			530,000
Liabilities	60,000	50,000			110,000
Common Stock					
P Company	260,000				260,000
S Company		50,000	(1) 50,000		
Other Contributed Capital					
P Company	40,000				40,000
S Company		10,000	(1) 10,000		
Retained Earnings					
P Company	120,000				120,000
S Company		20,000	(1) 20,000		
Total Equities	480,000	130,000	80,000	80,000	530,000

(1) To eliminate investment in S Company.

In this entry, the investment account is eliminated against S Company's common stock, other contributed capital, and retained earnings. Note that this entry is not affected by the relative par values of the two companies. It is based strictly on S Company equity values.

In recording the exchange of stock, the excess of the par value of the shares issued over the par value of the shares acquired is deducted first from **combined** other contributed capital. If combined other contributed capital is reduced to zero, retained earnings is reduced. For example, if P Company exchanged 9,000 of its shares for all of those of S Company, the following analysis and acquisition entry would be made:

Par value of P Company stock issued (9,000 × $10)	$90,000
Par value of S Company stock acquired	50,000
Difference in par value	40,000
Reduce S Company other contributed capital	(10,000)
Reduce P Company other contributed capital	$30,000

P Company's Books

Investment in S Company	80,000	
Other Contributed Capital	30,000	
Common Stock (9,000 × $10)		90,000
Retained Earnings		20,000

Since S Company's $10,000 of other contributed capital was never on P Company's books, there is no need to debit other contributed capital for that amount, only for the $30,000 already on P Company's books.

After the appropriate eliminating entry [the same as entry (1) above] is prepared on the workpaper, consolidated stockholders' equity on the consolidated balance sheet would be reported as:

Consolidated Balance Sheet Equity

Common Stock, $10 par ($200,000 + $90,000)	$290,000
Other Contributed Capital ($40,000 − $30,000)	10,000
Retained Earnings ($100,000 + $20,000)	120,000
Total	$420,000

The point at which combined retained earnings would be reduced in this case is reached when the par value of the shares issued is more than $50,000 (the total other contributed capital of both S and P Companies) greater than the par value of the shares acquired. For example, if P Company exchanged 11,000 shares for all the shares of S Company, the analysis and acquisition entry would be:

Par value of P Company stock issued (11,000 × $10)	$110,000
Par value of S Company stock acquired	50,000
Difference in par value	60,000
Reduce S Company other contributed capital	(10,000)
Reduce P Company other contributed capital	(40,000)
Reduce S Company retained earnings recorded	$ 10,000

P Company's Books

Investment in S Company	80,000	
Other Contributed Capital	40,000	
Common Stock (11,000 × $10)		110,000
Retained Earnings ($20,000 − $10,000)		10,000

Only $10,000 of S Company's retained earnings is carried forward to be combined with P Company's retained earnings for a total consolidated retained earnings of $110,000. If the par value of the shares issued is *more* than $70,000 greater than the par value of the shares acquired, P Company's retained earnings would be reduced in the acquisition entry.

In the event that the par value of P Company stock issued is *less* than the par value of S Company stock acquired, other contributed capital is increased. Retained earnings cannot be credited for more than S Company's retained earnings balance ($20,000). Assume, for example, that P Company gave only 4,000 of its shares for all those of S Company. In this case, P Company would make the following analysis and acquisition entry:

Par value of P Company stock issued (4,000 × $10)	$40,000
Par value of S Company stock acquired	50,000
Difference in par value	(10,000)
Increase combined other contributed capital	$10,000

P Company's Books

Investment in S Company	80,000	
Common Stock (4,000 × $10)		40,000
Other Contributed Capital ($10,000 + $10,000)		20,000
Retained Earnings		20,000

Partially Owned Subsidiary Acquisition of less than 100% of the subsidiary's stock does not change the basic concept of pooling. The investment account is debited on the parent company's books for the percentage of S Company's book value of equity acquired; the common stock account is credited for the par value of the stock issued; and other equity accounts are adjusted based on the differences in par value (as discussed in the previous section).

Assume the earlier case except that P Company exchanges 5,000 of its shares of common stock for 95% (4,750 shares) of the common stock of S Company. P Company would make the following analysis and acquisition entry:

Par value of P Company stock issued (5,000 × $10)	$50,000
Par value of S Company stock acquired (4,750 × $10)	47,500
Difference in par value	2,500
Reduce S Company other contributed capital recorded	$(2,500)

P Company's Books

Investment in S Company ($80,000 × .95)	76,000	
Common Stock (5,000 × $10)		50,000
Other Contributed Capital [.95($10,000) − $2,500]		7,000
Retained Earnings ($20,000 × .95)		19,000

Since the par value of the stock given ($50,000) exceeds the par value of the stock acquired ($47,500), the $2,500 increase in par value serves to reduce P Company's interest to $7,000 ($9,500 - $2,500). P Company's share of S Company's reported retained earnings (95% × $20,000) is carried forward.

The noncontrolling interest in S Company is not affected by the difference in par value. The noncontrolling interest is 5% of S Company's book value of $80,000, or $4,000. A date of acquisition workpaper in this case is presented in Illustration 11-2.

Pooling Accounting						
Par Value Issued Exceeds						
Par Value Acquired						
95% Owned Subsidiary						
Date of Acquisition						

ILLUSTRATION 11–2

Consolidated Balance Sheet Workpaper

P Company and Subsidiary

January 1, 2000

	P Company	S Company	Eliminations Dr.	Eliminations Cr.	Noncontrolling Interest	Consolidated Balances
Cash	100,000	20,000				120,000
Other Current Assets	140,000	50,000				190,000
Plant and Equipment	120,000	40,000				160,000
Land	40,000	20,000				60,000
Investment in S Company	76,000			(1) 76,000		
Total Assets	476,000	130,000				530,000
Liabilities	60,000	50,000				110,000
Common Stock						
P Company	250,000					250,000
S Company		50,000	(1) 47,500		2,500	
Other Contributed Capital						
P Company	47,000					47,000
S Company		10,000	(1) 9,500		500	
Retained Earnings						
P Company	119,000					119,000
S Company		20,000	(1) 19,000		1,000	
Noncontrolling Interest					4,000	4,000
Total Equities	476,000	130,000	76,000	76,000		530,000

(1) To eliminate investment in S Company.

Elimination of 95% of S Company's equity against the investment account is accomplished by the following workpaper entry:

(1)	Common Stock—S Company	47,500	
	Other Contributed Capital—S Company	9,500	
	Retained Earnings—S Company	19,000	
	Investment in S Company		76,000

Note that the difference in par values once more has no effect on the elimination entry.

Accounting for a Pooled Subsidiary After Acquisition

Just as two methods—the cost method and the equity method—may be used to account for an investment *after* acquisition under the purchase approach, two methods—the book value method and the equity method—may be used to account for an investment *after* acquisition under the pooling approach.

The Book Value Method The book value method is used to record a pooled subsidiary on the books of the parent company. The method is applied in the same way as the cost method under the purchase approach, except that the investment is recorded initially at an amount equal to the book value of the subsidiary equity acquired, as illustrated earlier. Subsidiary earnings are not recorded until dividends are declared, at which time the parent company recognizes dividend income. Thus, the investment account remains at an amount equal to the initial book value of the subsidiary equity acquired unless the parent company acquires additional subsidiary shares or disposes of a part of its investment.

To illustrate, assume that, on January 1, 2000, P Company issued 8,100 of its $10 par value common shares for 90% (9,000 shares) of the outstanding common stock of S Company when S Company's stockholders' equity was as follows:

S Company Balance Sheet Equity

Common Stock, $10 par value	$100,000
Other Contributed Capital	50,000
Retained Earnings	40,000
Total	$190,000

P Company made the following analysis and book entry to record its investment in S Company:

Par value of P Company stock issued (8,100 × $10)	$81,000
Par value of S Company stock acquired (9,000 × $10)	90,000
Difference in par value	(9,000)
Increase combined other contributed capital	$ 9,000

P Company's Books

Investment in S Company .9($190,000)	171,000	
Common Stock (8,100 × $10)		81,000
Other Contributed Capital [.9($50,000) + $9,000]		54,000
Retained Earnings .9($40,000)		36,000

Because the par value of S Company's stock acquired ($90,000) exceeds the par value of P Company's stock issued ($81,000) by $9,000, the $9,000 is recorded as an increase in other contributed capital.

Assume further that during 2000, S Company reported earnings of $30,000 and declared a $15,000 dividend. Trial balances for P and S Companies on December 31, 2001 (the year subsequent to acquisition) are presented in Illustration 11-3, assuming that P Company uses the book value method to account for its investment in S Company. (Note that S Company's retained earnings on January 1, 2001 are $55,000, reflecting the $15,000 excess of earnings over dividends during 2000. Note also that S Company declared $10,000 of dividends in 2001 and P Company recognized dividend income of $9,000 in 2001.)

A workpaper for the preparation of consolidated financial statements on December 31, 2001 (the year subsequent to acquisition) is presented in Illustration 11-4. The method of preparing consolidated workpapers for years subsequent to acquisition under the book value method is similar to the purchase method but simpler. Because there was no recognition of a difference between purchase price and book value, there is no need to adjust depreciation or amortization expense in subsequent years. If the book value method is used, a workpaper entry is made, in each year subsequent to acquisition, to establish reciprocity or convert to equity. The dollar amount of this entry equals the parent's share of the undistributed earnings (change in retained earnings) of the subsidiary from the date of acquisition (*always* the beginning of the year of acquisition under pooling rules) to the beginning of the current year.

ILLUSTRATION 11-3

P Company and S Company Trial Balances
Book Value Method
December 31, 2001

	P Company		S Company	
	Dr.	Cr.	Dr.	Cr.
Cash	$ 261,500		$ 36,000	
Accounts Receivable (net)	68,000		32,000	
Inventory, 1/1	82,000		39,000	
Investment in S Company	171,000			
Property and Equipment (net)	220,000		185,000	
Other Assets	38,000		18,000	
Accounts Payable		$ 52,000		$ 30,000
Other Liabilities		70,000		45,000
Common Stock, $10 par value		281,000		100,000
Other Contributed Capital		94,000		50,000
Retained Earnings, 1/1		294,500		55,000
Dividends Declared	30,000		10,000	
Sales		350,000		190,000
Dividend Income		9,000		
Cost of Goods Sold	200,000		94,000	
Other Expenses	80,000		56,000	
	$1,150,500	$1,150,500	$470,000	$470,000

(1)	Investment in S Company		13,500	
	1/1 Retained Earnings—P Company			13,500
	.9($55,000 − $40,000)			

Next, intercompany dividends and the parent's share of the subsidiary's equity are eliminated:

(2)	Dividend Income		9,000	
	Dividends Declared—S Company			9,000
(3)	1/1 Retained Earnings—S Company		49,500	
	Common Stock—S Company		90,000	
	Other Contributed Capital—S Company		45,000	
	Investment in S Company			184,500

Note that entry (3) eliminates P's share (90%) of S Company's Retained Earnings at the beginning of the *current* year, not the year of acquisition.

Equity Method Under the partial or complete equity method, the investment is recorded initially at an amount equal to the book value of the subsidiary stockholders' equity acquired. Accounting after acquisition follows the same procedures as those used under the partial equity method with a purchase approach, with the parent company recording its share of subsidiary earnings as reported by the subsidiary and treating dividends received as reductions in the investment account. The complete equity method is the same as the partial equity method under the assumptions of this illustration. Since no difference between purchase cost and book value is recognized by the parent, there is no need to adjust reported income

Pooling Accounting						
Book Value Method						
90% Owned Subsidiary						
After Year of Acquisition						

ILLUSTRATION 11–4
Consolidated Statements Workpaper
P Company and Subsidiary
For the Year Ended December 31, 2001

Income Statement	P Company	S Company	Eliminations Dr.	Eliminations Cr.	Noncontrolling Interest	Consolidated Balances
Sales	350,000	190,000				540,000
Dividend Income	9,000		(2) 9,000			
Total Revenue	359,000	190,000				540,000
Cost of Goods Sold	200,000	94,000				294,000
Other Expense	80,000	56,000				136,000
Total Cost and Expense	280,000	150,000				430,000
Net/Combined Income	79,000	40,000				110,000
Noncontrolling Interest in Income					4,000	(4,000)*
Net Income to Retained Earnings	79,000	40,000	9,000	—0—	4,000	106,000
Retained Earnings Statement						
1/1 Retained Earnings						
P Company	294,500			(1) 13,500		308,000
S Company		55,000	(3) 49,500		5,500	
Net Income from above	79,000	40,000	9,000	—0—	4,000	106,000
Dividends Declared						
P Company	(30,000)					(30,000)
S Company		(10,000)		(2) 9,000	(1,000)	
12/31 Retained Earnings to Balance						
Sheet	343,500	85,000	58,500	22,500	8,500	384,000
Balance Sheet						
Cash	261,500	36,000				297,500
Accounts Receivable (net)	68,000	32,000				100,000
Inventory, 12/31	82,000	39,000				121,000
Investment in S Company	171,000		(1) 13,500	(3) 184,500		
Property and Equipment (net)	220,000	185,000				405,000
Other Assets	38,000	18,000				56,000
Total	840,500	310,000				979,500
Accounts Payable	52,000	30,000				82,000
Other Liabilities	70,000	45,000				115,000
Common Stock						
P Company	281,000					281,000
S Company		100,000	(3) 90,000		10,000	
Other Contributed Capital						
P Company	94,000					94,000
S Company		50,000	(3) 45,000		5,000	
Retained Earnings from above	343,500	85,000	58,500	22,500	8,500	384,400
Noncontrolling Interest in Net Assets					23,500	23,500
Total	840,500	310,000	207,000	207,000		979,500

*.1($40,000) = $4,000.
(1) To establish reciprocity/convert to equity as of 1/1/01 [($55,000 − $40,000) × .9].
(2) To eliminate intercompany dividends.
(3) To eliminate the investment in S Company.

for excess depreciation and/or amortization (as under purchase rules with the complete equity method). The complete equity method will differ from the partial equity method, however, if we allow the possibility of intercompany profit from sales of inventory or property that has not been realized. Workpaper entries for the elimination of unrealized profit under all three methods (cost/book value, partial equity, and complete equity) are the same whether the consolidation is accounted for as a purchase or as a pooling of interests.

The Investment in S Company account under the partial or complete equity method appears as follows:

Investment in S Company (Equity Method)

Year 2000 Cost	171,000		
Year 2000 Equity in subsidiary income	27,000	Year 2000 Share of dividends declared	13,500
Year 2000 Balance	184,500		
Year 2001 Equity in subsidiary income	36,000	Year 2001 Share of dividends declared	9,000
Year 2001 Balance	211,500		

The trial balances of both companies under the equity method are reported in Illustration 11-5. The workpaper to prepare the consolidated financial statements is shown in Illustration 11-6. On the workpaper, the following entries are made.

To eliminate the account "equity in subsidiary income" from the consolidated income statement, the workpaper entry is:

(1)	Equity in Subsidiary Income	36,000	
	Investment in S Company		36,000

ILLUSTRATION 11–5

P Company and S Company Trial Balances
Equity Method
December 31, 2001

	P Company		S Company	
	Dr.	Cr.	Dr.	Cr.
Cash	$ 261,500		$ 36,000	
Accounts Receivable (net)	68,000		32,000	
Inventory, 1/1	82,000		39,000	
Investment in S Company	211,500			
Property and Equipment (net)	220,000		185,000	
Other Assets	38,000		18,000	
Accounts Payable		$ 52,000		$ 30,000
Other Liabilities		70,000		45,000
Common Stock, $10 par value		281,000		100,000
Other Contributed Capital		94,000		50,000
Retained Earnings, 1/1		308,000		55,000
Dividends Declared	30,000		10,000	
Sales		350,000		190,000
Equity in Subsidiary Income		36,000		
Cost of Goods Sold	200,000		94,000	
Other Expenses	80,000		56,000	
	$1,191,000	$1,191,000	$470,000	$470,000

Pooling Accounting			ILLUSTRATION 11–6				
Equity Method			Consolidated Statements Workpaper—Equity Method				
90% Owned Subsidiary			P Company and Subsidiary				
After Year of Acquisition			For the Year Ended December 31, 2001				
			Eliminations		Noncontrolling	Consolidated
	P	*S*			Noncontrolling	Consolidated
Income Statement	*Company*	*Company*	*Dr.*	*Cr.*	*Interest*	*Balances*
Sales	350,000	190,000				540,000
Equity Income	36,000		(1) 36,000			
Total Revenue	386,000	190,000				540,000
Cost of Goods Sold	200,000	94,000				294,000
Other Expense	80,000	56,000				136,000
Total Cost and Expense	280,000	150,000				430,000
Net/Combined Income	106,000	40,000				110,000
Noncontrolling Interest in Income					4,000	(4,000)*
Net Income to Retained Earnings	106,000	40,000	36,000	—0—	4,000	106,000
Retained Earnings						
Statement						
1/1 Retained Earnings						
P Company	308,000					308,000
S Company		55,000	(3) 49,500		5,500	
Net Income from above	106,000	40,000	36,000	—0—	4,000	106,000
Dividends Declared						
P Company	(30,000)					(30,000)
S Company		(10,000)		(2) 9,000	(1,000)	
12/31 Retained Earnings to Balance						
Sheet	384,000	85,000	85,500	9,000	8,500	384,000
Balance Sheet						
Cash	261,500	36,000				297,500
Accounts Receivable (net)	68,000	32,000				100,000
Inventory, 12/31	82,000	39,000				121,000
Investment in S Company	211,500		(2) 9,000	(1) 36,000		
				(3) 184,500		
Property and Equipment (net)	220,000	185,000				405,000
Other Assets	38,000	18,000				56,000
Total	881,000	310,000				979,500
Accounts Payable	52,000	30,000				82,000
Other Liabilitites	70,000	45,000				115,000
Common Stock						
P Company	281,000					281,000
S Company		100,000	(3) 90,000		10,000	
Other Contributed Capital						
P Company	94,000					94,000
S Company		50,000	(3) 45,000		5,000	
Retained Earnings from above	384,000	85,000	85,500	9,000	8,500	384,000
Noncontrolling Interest in Net Assets					23,500	23,500
Total	881,000	310,000	229,500	229,500		979,500

*.1($40,000) = $4,000.
(1) To reverse the effect of parent company entry during the year for subsidiary income.
(2) To eliminate intercompany dividends.
(3) To eliminate the investment in S Company.

Next, to eliminate intercompany dividends under the equity method, this workpaper entry is made:

(2)	Investment in S Company	9,000	
	Dividends Declared		9,000

A third workpaper entry eliminates the Investment account against subsidiary equity accounts:

(3)	Common Stock—S Company	90,000	
	Other Contributed Capital—S Company	45,000	
	1/1 Retained Earnings—S Company	49,500	
	Investment in S Company		184,500

Interim Acquisition Under the Pooling Method

Under the pooling of interests method, the revenue and expense accounts of the subsidiary are combined with those of the parent company for the entire year in which the pooling takes place. As a result, the investment is recorded as if the pooling had taken place at the beginning of the year of acquisition. Because consolidated net income includes the parent's share of the subsidiary's net income for the entire year in which the acquisition occurs, a deduction for "net income purchased," which was required under the purchase method, is not needed. (See Chapter 4.)

Unrealized Profits on Intercompany Sales of Assets

The practice of recognizing in the consolidated financial statements only profits resulting from the sale of goods and services to parties outside the affiliated group is the same under pooling of interests as under purchase accounting. Therefore, workpaper entries for the elimination of unrealized profit are the same whether the consolidation is accounted for as a purchase or as a pooling of interests. (See Chapters 6 and 7.)

Acquisition of a Noncontrolling Interest

Accounting standards specifically provide that the acquisition of some or all of the shares held by noncontrolling stockholders of a subsidiary should be accounted for by the purchase method, rather than by the pooling of interests method. This requirement holds whether the shares are acquired by the parent company, the subsidiary itself, or another affiliate.[11] This provision is consistent with the basic notion that a pooling should take place in a single transaction, but it appears to be somewhat inconsistent with the prohibition of the use of the "part-purchase, part-pooling" approach discussed in Chapter 2.

ALTERNATIVE CONCEPTS OF CONSOLIDATED FINANCIAL STATEMENTS

In previous chapters, we have presented the principles currently followed in the preparation of consolidated financial statements. In its revised exposure draft, "Consolidated Financial Statements: Purpose and Policy," issued in February 1999, the FASB stated that it had considered and rejected the concept of proportionate consolidation for subsidiaries. This concept, although not used in current practice,

[11]Opinions of the Accounting Principles Board No. 16, op. cit., par. 43.

has been advocated by some as an alternative to full consolidation. Under proportionate consolidation, the consolidated statements would include only a portion, based on the parent's ownership interest, of the subsidiary's assets, liabilities, revenues, expenses, gains, and losses. In the exposure draft, the Board stated that because the consolidated entity has the power to direct the use of all the assets of a controlled entity, omitting a portion of those assets from the statements would not be representationally faithful. Similarly, omitting part of the revenues and expenses from the consolidated income statement would not be representationally faithful.[12]

Current practice essentially reflects a compromise between two general concepts of consolidation given various designations in the accounting literature. For our purposes, we will refer to them as the *parent company concept* and the *economic unit concept* (sometimes called the *entity concept*.) The concepts are described by the Financial Accounting Standards Board as follows:[13]

Parent Company Concept:

> The parent company concept emphasizes the interests of the parent's shareholders. As a result, the consolidated financial statements reflect those stockholder interests in the parent itself, plus their undivided interests in the net assets of the parent's subsidiaries. The consolidated balance sheet is essentially a modification of the parent's balance sheet with the assets and liabilities of all subsidiaries substituted for the parent's investment in subsidiaries. The stockholders' equity of the parent company is also the stockholders' equity of the consolidated entity. Similarly, the consolidated income statement is essentially a modification of the parent's income statement with the revenues, expenses, gains, and losses of subsidiaries substituted for the parent's income from investment in subsidiaries. These multi-line substitutions for single lines in the parent's balance sheet and income statement are intended to make the parent's financial statements more informative about the parent's total ownership holdings.

Economic Unit Concept:

> The economic unit concept emphasizes control of the whole by a single management. As a result, under this concept, consolidated financial statements are intended to provide information about a group of legal entities—a parent company and its subsidiaries—operating as a single unit. The assets, liabilities, revenues, expenses, gains, and losses of the various component entities are the assets, liabilities, revenues, expenses, gains, and losses of the consolidated entity. Unless all subsidiaries are wholly owned, the business enterprise's proprietary interest (assets less liabilities) is divided into the controlling interest (stockholders or other owners of the parent company) and one or more noncontrolling interests in subsidiaries. Both the controlling and the noncontrolling interests are part of the proprietary group of the consolidated entity, even though the noncontrolling stockholders' ownership interests relate only to the affiliates whose shares they own.

The parent company concept represents the view that the primary purpose of consolidated financial statements is to provide information relevant to the controlling stockholders. The parent company effectively controls the assets and operations of the subsidiary. Noncontrolling stockholders do not exercise any ownership control over the subsidiary company or the parent company. Thus, the parent company concept places emphasis on the needs of the controlling stockholders, and the noncontrolling interest is essentially relegated to the position of

---

[12]*FASB*, Revised Exposure Draft, "Consolidated Financial Statements: Purpose and Policy," 2/23/99, par. 187.

[13]*FASB* Discussion Memorandum, "Consolidated Policy and Procedures" (Norwalk, CT: FASB, September 10, 1991), pars. 63 and 64.

a claim against the consolidated entity. Thus, the noncontrolling, or minority, interest should be presented as a liability in the consolidated statement of financial position under the parent company concept or, as described in the next section, as a separate component before stockholders' equity.

The economic unit concept represents the view that the affiliated companies form a separate, identifiable economic entity. Meaningful evaluation by any interested party of the financial position and results of operations of the economic entity is possible only if the individual assets, liabilities, revenues, and expenses of the affiliated companies making up the economic entity are combined. Strictly interpreted, the economic unit concept denies the primacy of the interest of the parent company stockholders and treats both controlling and noncontrolling stockholders as contributors to the economic unit's capital. Thus, the noncontrolling, or minority, interest should be presented as a component of equity in the consolidated financial statement under the economic unit concept.

Differences between the concepts are relevant only to less than wholly owned subsidiaries; they center around conflicting views concerning answers to three basic questions:

1. What is the nature of a noncontrolling interest?
2. What income figure constitutes consolidated net income?
3. What values should be reported in the consolidated balance sheet?

A related issue concerns the percentage (total or partial) of unrealized intercompany profit to be eliminated in the determination of consolidated balances.

Noncontrolling Interest

Under the *economic unit* concept, a noncontrolling interest is a part of the ownership equity in the entire economic unit. Thus, a noncontrolling interest is of the same general nature and is accounted for in essentially the same way as the controlling interest (i.e., as a component of owners' equity). Under the *parent company* concept, the nature and classification of a noncontrolling interest are unclear. The parent company concept views the consolidated financial statements as those of the parent company. From that perspective, the noncontrolling interest is similar to a liability; but because the parent does not have a present obligation to pay cash or release other assets, it is not a liability based on the FASB's technical definition of a "liability." Nor is it a true component of owners' equity since the noncontrolling investors in a subsidiary do not have an ownership interest in the subsidiary's parent. Consequently, the parent company concept theoretically supports reporting the noncontrolling interest below liabilities but above stockholders' equity in the consolidated balance sheet.

Consolidated Net Income Under the *parent company* concept, consolidated net income consists of the realized combined income of the parent company and its subsidiaries after deducting noncontrolling interest in income; that is, the noncontrolling interest in income is deducted as an expense item in determining consolidated net income. This view emphasizes that the parent company stockholders are directly interested in their share of the results of operations as a measure of earnings in relation to their investment and dividend expectations.

Under the *economic unit* concept, consolidated net income consists of the total realized combined income of the parent company and its subsidiaries. The total combined income is then allocated proportionately to the noncontrolling interest and the controlling interest. Noncontrolling interest in income is considered an allocated portion of consolidated net income, rather than an element in the determination of consolidated net income. The concept emphasizes the view that the consolidated financial statements represent those of a single economic unit with several classes of stockholder interest. Thus, noncontrolling interest in net assets is considered a separate element of stockholders' equity, and the noncontrolling interest in net income reflects the share of consolidated net income allocated to the noncontrolling stockholders.

Consolidated Balance Sheet Values

As indicated in Chapter 5, in the case of less than wholly owned subsidiaries, the question arises whether to value the subsidiary assets and liabilities at the *total* fair value implied by the price paid for the controlling interest, or at their book value adjusted only for the excess of cost over book value paid by the parent company. For example, assume that P Company acquires a 60% interest in S Company for $960,000 when the book value of the net assets and of the stockholders' equity of S Company is $1,000,000. The implied fair value of the net assets of S Company is $1,600,000 ($960,000/.6), and the difference between the implied fair value and the book value is $600,000 ($1,600,000 − $1,000,000). For presentation in the consolidated financial statements, should the net assets of S Company be written up by $600,000 or by 60% of $600,000?

Application of the *parent company* concept in this situation restricts the write-up of the net assets of S Company to $360,000 (.6 × $600,000) on the theory that the write-up should be restricted to the amount actually paid by P Company in excess of the book value of the interest it acquires [$960,000 − (.6 × $1,000,000) = $360,000]. In other words, the value assigned to the net assets should not exceed cost to the parent company. Thus, the net assets of the subsidiary are included in the consolidated financial statements at their book value ($1,000,000) plus *the parent company's share* of the difference between fair value and book value (.6 × $600,000 = $360,000), or at a total of $1,360,000 on the date of acquisition. Noncontrolling interest is reported at its percentage interest in the *reported book value* of the net assets of S Company, or $400,000 (.4 × $1,000,000).

Application of the *economic unit* concept results in a write-up of the net assets of S Company in the consolidated statements workpaper by $600,000 to $1,600,000 on the theory that the consolidated financial statements should reflect 100% of the net asset values of the affiliated companies. On the date of acquisition, the net assets of the subsidiary are included in the consolidated financial statements at their book value ($1,000,000) plus *the entire difference* between their fair value and their book value ($600,000), or a total of $1,600,000. Noncontrolling interest is reported at its percentage interest in the *fair value* of the net assets of S Company, or $640,000 (.4 × $1,600,000).

Regardless of the concept followed, the controlling interest in the net assets of the subsidiary reported in the consolidated financial statements is the same and is equal to P Company's cost, as demonstrated here:

	Parent Company Concept	Economic Unit Concept
Net assets of S Company included in consolidation	$1,360,000	$1,600,000
Less noncontrolling interest	400,000	640,000
Controlling interest (cost)	$ 960,000	$ 960,000

Note that current standards are more consistent with the parent company concept with respect to write-up of net assets.

Elimination of Unrealized Intercompany Profit

As discussed in Chapter 6, there are two alternative points of view as to the amount of intercompany profit that should be considered unrealized in the determination of consolidated income. The elimination methods associated with these two points of view are generally referred to as *total* (100%) *elimination* and *partial elimination*.

Proponents of total elimination regard all the intercompany profit associated with assets remaining in the affiliated group to be unrealized. Proponents of partial elimination regard only the parent company's share of the profit recognized by the selling affiliate to be unrealized. Under total elimination, the entire amount of unconfirmed intercompany profit is eliminated from combined income and the related asset balance. Under partial elimination, only the parent company's share of the unconfirmed intercompany profit recognized by the selling affiliate is eliminated.

In the case of all downstream sales and in the case of upstream or horizontal sales *where the selling affiliate is a wholly owned subsidiary*, the amount of intercompany profit eliminated is the same under total elimination and partial elimination. In those cases, 100% of the intercompany profit is eliminated, since the parent company's interest in the profits of the selling affiliate (the parent company itself or its wholly owned subsidiary) is 100%. The two approaches give different results, however, in the case of upstream or horizontal sales *where the selling affiliate is a less than wholly owned subsidiary*.

Partial elimination is consistent with the *parent company* concept. Because the noncontrolling interest is viewed as a claim or liability of the consolidated entity under the parent company concept, any intercompany profit in an affiliate company's assets acquired from a partially owned subsidiary is considered to be realized to the extent of the noncontrolling stockholders' interest in the selling subsidiary. Thus, under the parent company view, the noncontrolling interest is deemed to be entitled to its share of the reported profit of the subsidiary regardless of whether the profit results from sales to affiliates or to third parties.

Total elimination is consistent with the *economic unit* concept. Note that current standards are more consistent with the economic unit concept with respect to the elimination of unrealized profit. Because the noncontrolling interest is considered to be a part of consolidated stockholders' equity under the economic unit concept, the noncontrolling stockholders are not considered to be outside parties. Thus, their share of intercompany profit in an affiliate company's assets acquired from a partially owned subsidiary is considered to be unrealized.

As an illustration of the difference between the parent company concept and the economic unit concept, assume that, on January 1, 2000, P Company acquired a 60% interest in S Company for $960,000 when the book value of the net assets of S Company was $1,000,000. P Company records its investment in S Company using the cost method. In addition, assume the following:

1. The book values and the fair values of individual assets and liabilities of S Company on the date of acquisition are the same, except for the fair value of a depreciable asset with a remaining life of 20 years, which is $600,000 greater than its book value.

2. Intercompany sales from S Company to P Company during 2000 amount to $1,000,000, on which S Company recognized a gross profit of $300,000, or 30%.

3. On December 31, 2000, P Company has on hand goods it purchased from S Company for $500,000.

4. Income tax consequences are ignored.

5. S Company declared and paid a $40,000 dividend in 2000.

6. S Company reported net income of $200,000 for 2000.

Entries on the books of P Company during 2000 are as follows:

P Company's Books		
Investment in S Company	960,000	
Cash		960,000
To record purchase of a 60% interest in S Company.		
Cash	24,000	
Dividend Income		24,000
To record receipt of dividends (.6 × $40,000).		

Book entries to account for the investment are not affected by the concepts (parent company or economic unit) used in the preparation of consolidated financial statements. The differences between the parent company concept and the economic unit concept are reflected by different workpaper elimination entries. The applications of the parent company concept and the economic unit concept in the preparation of consolidated financial statements workpapers are presented in Illustrations 11-7 and 11-8, respectively. The effects of the two methods on consolidated balances are compared in Illustration 11-9. The workpaper entries in Illustration 11-7 and 11- 8 are presented here in general journal form.

		Parent Company Concept (Illustration 11-7)		Economic Unit Concept (Illustration 11-8)	
(1)	Sales	1,000,000		1,000,000	
	Cost of Goods Sold		1,000,000		1,000,000
	To eliminate intercompany sales.				
(2)	Cost of Goods Sold	90,000		150,000	
	Inventory, 12/31		90,000		150,000
	To eliminate unrealized intercompany profit in ending inventory.				
(3)	Dividend Income	24,000		24,000	
	Dividends Declared		24,000		24,000
	To eliminate intercompany dividends.				
(4)	Capital Stock—S Company	420,000		420,000	
	Retained Earnings—S Company	180,000		180,000	
	Difference Between Cost and				
	Book Value	360,000		360,000	
	Investment in S Company		960,000		960,000
	To eliminate investment account.				
(5)	Property, Plant and Equipment	360,000		600,000	
	Difference Between Cost and				
	Book Value		360,000		360,000
	Noncontrolling Interest		—0—		240,000
	To allocate the difference between cost and book value (Parent Company), and to write up assets to their fair value (Economic Unit).				
(6)	Other Expenses	18,000		30,000	
	Property, Plant and Equipment				
	(net)		18,000		30,000
	To recognize depreciation on difference between book value and cost (Parent Company) or book value and implied fair value (Economic Unit).				

Parent Company Concept

Cost Method

60% Owned Subsidiary

ILLUSTRATION 11–7

Consolidated Statements Workpaper

P Company and Subsidiary

For the Year Ended December 31, 2000

Income Statement	P Company	S Company	Eliminations Dr.	Eliminations Cr.	Noncontrolling Interest	Consolidated Balances
Sales	3,400,000	2,000,000	(1) 1,000,000			4,400,000
Dividend Income	24,000		(3) 24,000			
Total Revenue	3,424,000	2,000,000				4,400,000
Cost of Goods Sold	2,380,000	1,400,000	(2) 90,000	(1) 1,000,000		2,870,000
Other Expenses	670,000	400,000	(6) 18,000			1,088,000
Total Cost and Expense	3,050,000	1,800,000				3,958,000
Net/Combined Income	374,000	200,000				442,000
Noncontrolling Interest in Income					80,000	(80,000)*
Net Income to Retained Earnings	374,000	200,000	1,132,000	1,000,000	80,000	362,000
Retained Earnings Statement						
1/1 Retained Earnings						
P Company	768,000					768,000
S Company		300,000	(4) 180,000		120,000	
Net Income from above	374,000	200,000	1,132,000	1,000,000	80,000	362,000
Dividends Declared						
P Company	—0—					
S Company		(40,000)		(3) 24,000	(16,000)	
12/31 Retained Earnings to Balance Sheet	1,142,000	460,000	1,312,000	1,024,000	184,000	1,130,000
Balance Sheet						
Inventory, 12/31	510,000	260,000		(2) 90,000		680,000
Investment in S Company	960,000			(4) 960,000		
Difference Between Cost and Book Value			(4) 360,000	(5) 360,000		
Property and Equipment (net)	2,000,000	1,000,000	(5) 360,000	(6) 18,000		3,342,000
Other Assets	172,000	60,000				232,000
Total	3,642,000	1,320,000				4,254,000
Liabilitites	500,000	160,000				660,000
Capital Stock						
P Company	2,000,000					2,000,000
S Company		700,000	(4) 420,000		280,000	
Retained Earnings from above	1,142,000	460,000	1,312,500	1,024,000	184,000	1,130,000
Noncontrolling Interest in Net Assets					464,000	464,000
Total	3,642,000	1,320,000	2,452,000	2,452,000		4,254,000

*.4($200,000) = $80,000.

(1) To eliminate intercompany sales.

(2) To eliminate/defer unrealized intercompany profit in ending inventory.

(3) To eliminate intercompany dividends.

(4) To eliminate the investment account.

(5) To allocate the difference between cost and book values to depreciable assets.

(6) To recognize depreciation on the difference between cost and book value.

Economic Unit Concept
Cost Method
60% Owned Subsidiary

ILLUSTRATION 11–8
Consolidated Statements Workpaper
P Company and Subsidiary
For the Year Ended December 31, 2000

Income Statement	P Company	S Company	Eliminations Dr.	Eliminations Cr.	Noncontrolling Interest	Consolidated Balances
Sales	3,400,000	2,000,000	(1) 1,000,000			4,400,000
Dividend Income	24,000		(3) 24,000			
Total Revenue	3,424,000	2,000,000				4,400,000
Cost of Goods Sold	2,380,000	1,400,000	(2) 150,000	(1) 1,000,000		2,930,000
Other Expense	670,000	400,000	(6) 30,000			1,100,000
Total Cost and Expense	3,050,000	1,800,000				4,030,000
Net/Combined Income	374,000	200,000				370,000
Noncontrolling Interest in Income					8,000	(8,000)*
Net Income to Retained Earnings	374,000	200,000	1,204,000	1,000,000	8,000	362,000
Retained Earnings Statement						
1/1 Retained Earnings						
P Company	768,000					768,000
S Company		300,000	(4) 180,000		120,000	
Net Income from above	374,000	200,000	1,204,000	1,000,000	8,000	362,000
Dividends Declared						
P Company	—0—					
S Company		(40,000)		(3) 24,000	(16,000)	
12/31 Retained Earnings to Balance Sheet	1,142,000	460,000	1,384,000	1,024,000	112,000	1,130,000
Balance Sheet						
Inventory, 12/31	510,000	260,000		(2) 150,000		620,000
Investment in S Company	960,000			(4) 960,000		
Difference Between Cost and Book Value			(4) 360,000	(5) 360,000		
Property and Equipment (net)	2,000,000	1,000,000	(5) 600,000	(6) 30,000		3,570,000
Other Assets	172,000	60,000				232,000
Total	3,642,000	1,320,000				4,422,000
Liabilities	500,000	160,000				660,000
Capital Stock						
P Company	2,000,000					2,000,000
S Company		700,000	(4) 420,000		280,000	
Retained Earnings from above	1,142,000	460,000	1,384,000	1,024,000	112,000	1,130,000
Noncontrolling Interest in Net Assets				(5) 240,000	392,000	632,000
Total	3,642,000	1,320,000	2,764,000	2,764,000		4,422,000

*.4($200,000 − 150,000 − 30,000) = $8,000
(1) To eliminate intercompany sales.
(2) To eliminate/defer unrealized intercompany profit in ending inventory.
(3) To eliminate intercompany dividends.
(4) To eliminate the investment account.
(5) To allocate the difference between cost and book values to depreciable assets.
(6) To recognize depreciation on the difference between cost and book value.

If the equity method is used, entry (3) would be replaced with the following entry for both the parent company concept and the economic unit concept:

Equity in Subsidiary Income	120,000	
Dividends Declared—S Company		24,000
Investment in S Company		96,000
To eliminate intercompany dividends and equity in subsidiary income.		

A comparison of the consolidated balances presented in Illustration 11-9 demonstrates that the concept followed in the preparation of consolidated financial statements has no effect on the controlling interest in combined net income. Application of the economic unit concept decreases the amount of combined income and the amount of noncontrolling interest in combined income by the same amount, $72,000. In a similar manner, application of the economic unit concept increases combined net assets and noncontrolling interest in combined net assets by the same amount, $168,000, on the consolidated balance sheet. Thus, the noncontrolling interest in combined net assets is unaffected. Note also that, because the controlling interest in combined net income is unaffected by the concept followed, consolidated retained earnings is also unaffected.

Current Practice

Current practice follows neither the parent company nor the economic unit concept entirely. The differences in practice relate primarily to the classification of noncontrolling interest and the total elimination of unrealized intercompany prof-

ILLUSTRATION 11–9

Comparison of Consolidated Financial Statements
Parent Company Concept versus Economic Unit Concept

		(000 Omitted)	
Consolidated Income Statement	*Parent Company Concept (Illustration 11–7)*	*Economic Unit Concept (Illustration 11–8)*	*Difference*
Sales	$4,400	$4,400	$ 0
Cost of Goods Sold	2,870	2,930	($ 60)
Gross Margin	$1,530	$1,470	$ 60
Other Expenses	1,088	1,100	($ 12)
Combined Income	$ 442	$ 370	$ 72
Less: Noncontrolling Interest	(80)	(8)	($ 72)
Net Income	$ 362	$ 362	$ 0
Consolidated Balance Sheet			
Inventory	$ 680	$ 620	$ 60
Property, Plant, and Equipment	3,342	3,570	($228)
Other Assets	232	232	0
Total Assets	$4,254	$4,422	($168)
Liabilities	$ 660	$ 660	$ 0
Noncontrolling Interest	464	632	($168)
Capital Stock	2,000	2,000	$ 0
Retained Earnings	1,130	1,130	$ 0
Total Equities	$4,254	$4,422	($168)

its in assets acquired from an affiliate. Current practice views noncontrolling interest in income neither as an expense nor as an allocation of consolidated net income, but as a special equity interest in the consolidated entity's combined income that must be recognized when all the earnings of a less than wholly owned subsidiary are combined with the earnings of the parent company. Noncontrolling interest in net assets is viewed neither as a liability nor as true stockholders' equity. Rather, it is viewed as a special interest in the combined net assets that must be recognized when all the assets and liabilities of a less than wholly owned subsidiary are combined with those of the parent company.

Current accounting standards require the total elimination of unrealized intercompany profit in assets acquired from affiliated companies, regardless of the percentage of ownership. This procedure is basically consistent with the economic unit concept view, as discussed earlier. The primary issue, however, in the elimination of intercompany profits is not whether the economic unit concept or parent company concept should prevail, but that of compliance with the cost principle in accounting that the reported value of assets should not exceed cost to the reporting entity. Total elimination of unrealized intercompany profits complies with this principle by reporting consolidated balances as if intercompany transactions between consolidated affiliates had never occurred.

Authors' View

We believe the economic unit concept more clearly meets the primary objective of consolidated financial statements, which is to present to the stockholders and creditors of the parent company the financial condition and results of operations of a parent company and its subsidiaries as if they were a single company. Both the parent company concept and current practice include, in the consolidated balance sheet, the parent company's share of the *fair value* of S Company's net assets, but the noncontrolling interest's share of the *book value* of those net assets. We believe that users view the consolidated financial statements as those of a single economic unit. Consequently, for consistency purposes, the entire fair value of the subsidiary's net assets, as well as the effects of the use of those net assets, should be included in the consolidated financial statements.

 ## SUMMARY

1. *Explain why the FASB is considering the elimination of the pooling of interests method.* The method is rarely used outside the United States, and critics believe that it fails to hold managers accountable for the total value of the price paid because the stock's market value is not recorded on the balance sheet.

2. *Distinguish the primary differences between the pooling of interests method and the purchase method.* The parent records its investment in the subsidiary initially at cost under the purchase method, but at the book value of the equity acquired under the pooling method. In the consolidation process, the investment account is essentially replaced with the underlying net assets of the subsidiary, recorded at their

fair values implied by the purchase price under purchase rules but at their previous book values under pooling rules. Thus, the pooling method recognizes no new goodwill, nor does it require excess depreciation or amortization.

3. *Compare the book value method and the equity method in a pooling of interests.* Under the book value method, subsidiary earnings are not recorded until dividends are declared, at which time the parent company recognizes dividend income. Thus, the investment account remains at an amount equal to the initial book value of the subsidiary equity acquired unless the parent company acquires additional subsidiary shares or disposes of a part of its investment. Under the equity

method, the parent company records its share of subsidiary earnings as reported by the subsidiary and treats dividends received as reductions in the investment account.

4. *Indicate the principal requirement for the use of the pooling of interests method to account for an acquisition.* The principal requirement of the pooling method is that the acquiring company issue common stock for substantially all (at least 90%) of the voting common stock of the acquired company.

5. *Understand how the equity transfer rule is used in a pooling of interests.* In total, the equity accounts of the parent must be increased by an amount equal to the book value of the subsidiary equity acquired. The equity transfer rule is used to allocate this amount among the parent's equity accounts when the par value of the parent's stock differs from the par value of the

subsidiary's stock. If the par value of the shares issued exceeds the par value of the shares acquired, the excess is deducted first from *combined* other contributed capital. If combined other contributed capital is reduced to zero, retained earnings is reduced.

6. *Describe two alternative concepts of consolidated financial statements (other than purchase and pooling).* Under the parent company concept, the consolidated financial statements reflect the stockholders' interests in the parent, plus their undivided interests in the net assets of the parent's subsidiaries. Thus the focus is on the interests of the parent's shareholders. In contrast, the economic unit concept emphasizes control of the whole by a single management. As a result, under this concept, consolidated financial statements are intended to provide information about a group of legal entities—a parent company and its subsidiaries—operating as a single unit.

QUESTIONS

1. Describe the accounting treatment of a difference between the par value of common stock issued and the par value of common stock acquired in a pooling of interests if:
   (a) The par value of the common stock issued exceeds the par value of the common stock acquired.
   (b) The par value of the common stock acquired exceeds the par value of the common stock issued.

2. In general terms, how does the balance in a parent company's retained earnings account differ after a subsidiary is acquired through a pooling of interests from the balance in the same account after a subsidiary is acquired through a purchase?

3. How are the preacquisition revenue and expense items of a subsidiary acquired during a fiscal period treated under the pooling of interests method?

4. Identify and briefly describe the alternatives for accounting for a subsidiary on the books of a parent company subsequent to acquisition under the pooling of interests method as explained in this chapter.

5. Describe the difference between the economic unit concept and parent company concept approaches to the reporting of subsidiary assets and liabilities in the consolidated financial statements on the date of acquisition.

6. What arguments might be used to support partial elimination as opposed to 100% elimination of intercompany profit in the preparation of consolidated financial statements?

7. What are the effects on the consolidated balance sheet if the partial elimination method, rather than the 100% elimination method, is used in the preparation of consolidated financial statements? Be specific.

8. Contrast the consolidated effects of the parent company concept and the economic unit concept in terms of:
   (a) The treatment of noncontrolling interests.
   (b) The elimination of intercompany profit.
   (c) The valuation of subsidiary net assets in the consolidated financial statements.
   (d) The definition of consolidated net income.

9. Under the economic unit concept, the net assets of the subsidiary are included in the consolidated financial statements at the total fair value that is implied by the price paid by the parent company for its controlling interest. What practical or conceptual problems do you see in this approach to valuation?

10. Compare the effects of partial elimination and 100% elimination of unrealized intercompany profit on the determination of:
   (a) Combined income.
   (b) Noncontrolling interest in combined income.
   (c) Consolidated net income.
   (d) Consolidated net assets.
   (e) Noncontrolling interest in consolidated net assets.
   (f) Controlling interest in consolidated net assets.

11. Discuss the arguments for and against elimination of the pooling of interests method.

EXERCISES

EXERCISE 11-1   Pooling Journal Entries

Page Company intends to issue common stock in exchange for the common stock of Sime Company. Four possibilities follow:

				Sime Company Equity Balances	
Case	Percent of Ownership	Page Shares Issued	Common Stock	Other Contributed Capital	Retained Earnings
a.	100%	6,000	$200,000	$110,000	$140,000
b.	100%	10,500	200,000	120,000	140,000
c.	90%	7,500	200,000	90,000	30,000
d.	95%	6,000	200,000	60,000	(35,000)

Page Company common stock is $40 par value; Page has total other contributed capital of $50,000.

Required:

Assuming the use of pooling of interests accounting, prepare in general journal form for each case (1) the investment acquisition entry, and (2) the workpaper entry to eliminate the investment account in the preparation of a consolidated balance sheet workpaper on the date of acquisition.

EXERCISE 11-2   Stock Exchange Entry and Workpaper

On February 1, 2001, Paag Company acquired 100% of the outstanding common stock of Santee Company in a pooling of interests. Paag Company exchanged 19,000 shares of its $10 par value common stock with a market value of $20 per share for all Santee Company's common stock. Immediately before the acquisition, the two companies had the following balance sheets:

	Paag Company	Santee Company
Current Assets	$ 386,500	$106,200
Property, Plant, and Equipment	704,000	108,000
Total Assets	$1,090,500	$214,200
Liabilities	$ 192,500	$ 36,000
Common Stock, $10 par	400,000	
Common Stock, $12 par		140,000
Other Contributed Capital	250,000	20,000
Retained Earnings	248,000	18,200
Total Equities	$1,090,500	$214,200

Required:

A. Prepare the entry on the books of Paag Company to record the exchange of shares.

B. Prepare a consolidated balance sheet workpaper immediately after the exchange of shares.

EXERCISE 11-3   Stock Exchange Entries

Pack and Sims companies had the following balance sheets just before a pooling of interests:

	Pack	Sims
Current Assets	$346,000	$122,000
Property, Plant, and Equipment	589,000	244,000
Total Assets	$935,000	$366,000

	Pack	Sims
Liabilities	$197,000	$ 82,000
Common Stock, $4 par	500,000	
Common Stock, $2 par		90,000
Other Contributed Capital	120,000	83,000
Retained Earnings	118,000	111,000
Total Equities	$935,000	$366,000

Pack Company will exchange shares of its authorized but unissued stock for the outstanding shares of Sims Company.

Required:

Record the exchange of shares on the books of Pack Company for each of the following cases:

Case	Pack Shares Issued	Sims Shares Acquired
a.	24,000	45,000
b.	22,500	45,000
c.	27,000	40,500
d.	50,000	40,500

EXERCISE 11-4 **Book Value versus Partial Equity Method**

On February 1, 2001, Pogue Company issued 55,000 shares of its $5 par value common stock for 90% of the outstanding common stock of Singh Company in a business combination meeting all criteria for a pooling of interests. Singh Company's general ledger accounts showed the following stockholders' equity amounts on that date:

Common stock, $10 par value	$200,000
Other contributed capital	110,000
Retained earnings, 1/1	80,000

During 2001 Singh Company reported net income of $250,000 and declared and paid a $70,000 cash dividend.

Required:

A. Prepare journal entries on the books of Pogue Company to record the investment-related events for 2001 assuming:

  (1) Pogue Company uses the book value method.

  (2) Pogue Company uses the partial equity method.

B. Prepare eliminating entries for the preparation of a consolidated statements workpaper on December 31, 2001, assuming:

  (1) Pogue Company uses the book value method.

  (2) Pogue Company uses the partial equity method.

EXERCISE 11-5 **Eliminating Entries—Book Value, Partial Equity Methods**

Assume the situation presented in Exercise 11-4, and that Singh Company reported net income of $240,000 and declared and paid an $80,000 cash dividend during 2002.

Required:

Prepare eliminating entries for the preparation of a consolidated statements workpaper on December 31, 2002, assuming:

A. Pogue Company uses the book value method.

B. Pogue Company uses the partial equity method.

EXERCISE 11-6 **Consolidated Financial Statements—Economic Unit and Parent Company Concepts**

Pippin Company acquired an 80% interest in the capital stock of Stein Company on January 1, 2001, for $360,000. The trial balances for each company on December 31, 2001, follow:

	Pippin Company	*Stein Company*
Current Assets	$ 210,000	$249,000
Investment in Stein Company	360,000	
Equipment (net)	290,500	141,000
Land	61,000	125,000
Dividends Declared		35,000
Cost of Goods Sold	188,000	125,000
Expenses	63,000	52,500
	$1,172,500	$727,500
Liabilities	$ 46,000	$ 37,500
Capital Stock	350,000	210,000
Retained Earnings, 1/1	298,500	140,000
Sales	450,000	340,000
Dividend Income	28,000	
	$1,172,500	$727,500

The entire difference between cost and book value is assigned to land.

Required:

Prepare a consolidated balance sheet as of December 31, 2001, and a consolidated income statement for the year then ended:

A. Using the economic unit concept.

B. Using the parent company concept.

EXERCISE 11-7 **Workpaper Entries—Economic Unit and Parent Company Concepts**

Paar Company purchased 90% of the outstanding common stock of Star Company for $446,500 on March 1, 2001. On that date, Star Company had stockholders' equity as follows:

Common Stock, $2 par value	$200,000
Other Contributed Capital	110,000
Retained Earnings	75,000
Total	$385,000

The book values of Star Company's assets and liabilities are equal to their fair values except for the following:

	Book Value	*Fair Value*
Equipment	$ 60,000	$ 85,000
Land	140,000	200,000

Ignore income tax consequences.

Required:

A. Prepare in general journal form the workpaper entries needed to eliminate the investment account in the preparation of a consolidated balance sheet workpaper on the date of acquisition:

(1) Following the economic unit concept.

(2) Following the parent company concept.

B. Compute the total noncontrolling interest that would be reported in the consolidated balance sheet:

(1) Following the economic unit concept.

(2) Following the parent company concept.

PROBLEMS

PROBLEM 11-1 **Stock Exchange Entry and Workpaper, Pooling**

On March 1, 2001, Perry Company acquired 36,000 of the 40,000 outstanding common shares of Sands Company (par $10) by issuing 35,000 shares of its own common stock (par $15). Before the acquisition, balance sheets of the two companies were as follows:

	Perry Company	Sands Company
Cash	$ 200,000	$72,000
Receivables	190,000	84,500
Inventories	270,000	175,000
Property, Plant, and Equipment	600,000	350,000
Patents	70,500	
Total	$1,330,500	$681,500
Current Liabilities	$ 47,000	$ 57,500
Long-Term Liabilities	207,500	100,000
Common Stock	600,000	400,000
Other Contributed Capital	172,000	85,000
Retained Earnings	304,000	39,000
Total	$1,330,500	$681,500

Required:

Assuming that the acquisition meets all the criteria for a pooling of interests:

A. Prepare the entry to record the stock exchange on the books of Perry Company.

B. Prepare a consolidated balance sheet workpaper immediately after the acquisition.

PROBLEM 11-2 **Stock Exchange Entry and Workpaper, Pooling**

On January 1, 2001, Phan Company acquired 171,000 of the outstanding common shares of Scali Company (par $2) by issuing 110,000 shares of its own common stock (par $5). The balance sheets of the two companies were as follows just before the acquisition:

	Phan Company	Scali Company
Cash	$ 195,000	$170,000
Other Current Assets	625,000	240,000
Long-Term Assets	1,580,000	410,000
Other Assets	140,000	
Total	$2,540,000	$820,000
Current Liabilities	$ 325,000	$ 85,000
Bonds Payable	400,000	
Common Stock	1,000,000	400,000
Treasury Stock at Par		(40,000)
Other Contributed Capital	320,000	120,000
Retained Earnings	495,000	255,000
Total	$2,540,000	$820,000

Required:

Assume that the acquisition meets all the criteria for a pooling of interests:

A. Give the entry to record the stock exchange in the accounts of Phan Company.

B. Prepare a consolidated balance sheet workpaper immediately after the acquisition.

PROBLEM 11-3 **Pooling Workpaper—Book Value Method**

On January 2, 1997, Paine Company exchanged 20,000 shares of its $10 par value common stock for 95% of the outstanding common stock of Sato Company in a business combination meeting all conditions for a pooling of interests. On that date, Sato Company's stockholders' equity consisted of common stock of $180,000 and retained earnings of $65,000. Trial balances for Paine Company and Sato Company on December 31, 2001, follow:

	Paine Company	Sato Company
Current Assets	$ 218,750	$132,000
Investment in Sato Company	232,750	—0—
Plant Assets	426,000	360,000
Dividends Declared	90,000	50,000
Cost of Goods Sold	321,000	220,000
Other Expenses	120,000	87,000
Total Debits	$1,408,500	$849,000
Liabilities	$ 102,000	$ 71,000
Common Stock	300,000	180,000
1/1 Retained Earnings	397,000	198,000
Sales	562,000	400,000
Dividend Income	47,500	—0—
Total Credits	$1,408,500	$849,000

Required:

Prepare a consolidated statements workpaper at December 31, 2001.

PROBLEM 11-4 **Pooling Workpaper—Equity Method**

(Note that this problem is the same as Problem 11-3, but assuming the use of the equity method.)

On January 2, 1997, Paine Company exchanged 20,000 shares of its $10 par value common stock for 95% of the outstanding common stock of Sato Company in a business combination meeting all conditions for a pooling of interests. On that date, Sato Company's stockholders' equity consisted of common stock of $180,000 and retained earnings of $65,000. Trial balances for Paine Company and Sato Company on December 31, 2001, follow:

	Paine Company	Sato Company
Current Assets	$ 218,750	$132,000
Investment in Sato Company	399,950	—0—
Plant Assets	426,000	360,000
Dividends Declared	90,000	50,000
Cost of Goods Sold	321,000	220,000
Other Expenses	120,000	87,000
Total Debits	$1,575,700	$849,000
Liabilities	$ 102,000	$ 71,000
Common Stock	300,000	180,000
1/1 Retained Earnings	523,350	198,000
Sales	562,000	400,000
Equity in Subsidiary Income	88,350	—0—
Total Credits	$1,575,700	$849,000

Required:

Prepare a consolidated statements workpaper at December 31, 2001.

PROBLEM 11-5 **Entity Concept—Noncontrolling Interest**

The following account balances were taken from the December 31, 2001 trial balance of Sun Company:

Common Stock—$5 par	$100,000
1/1 Retained Earnings	32,000
Sales	393,000
Cost of Sales	236,000
Expenses	105,500
Dividends Declared	12,500

Prime Company acquired 80% of the common stock of Sun Company on January 1, 2001, for $156,000. The difference between cost and book value was attributable to several small computers owned by Sun, which, anticipating a faster than experienced advance in computer technology, had depreciated the computers too rapidly. The computers had been acquired by Sun on January 1, 1998, and were being depreciated over a six-year estimated life by the straight-line method. Ignore income tax consequences.

Required:

Applying the entity concept, compute:

A. The noncontrolling interest in the net income of Sun Company for 2001.

B. The noncontrolling interest in the net assets of Sun Company on December 31, 2001.

PROBLEM 11-6 **100% versus Partial Elimination**

On January 1, 2001, P Company purchased 90% of the common stock of S Company. At that time the retained earnings of S Company were $120,000. Selected financial information for the affiliated companies on December 31, 2002, follows:

	December 31, 2002	
	P Company	S Company
Sales	$400,000	$200,000
Purchases	200,000	104,000
Expenses	16,000	8,000
Inventory, January 1	72,000	32,000
Inventory, December 31	96,000	48,000
Retained Earnings, January 1	365,900	172,000
Dividends Declared	40,000	10,000
Dividend Income	9,000	—0—

During 2002 P Company purchased merchandise from S Company for $60,000. S Company sells merchandise to P Company at cost plus 25% of cost. On December 31, 2002, merchandise purchased from S Company for $30,000 remains in the inventory of P Company. On January 1, 2002, P Company's inventory contained merchandise purchased from S Company for $10,000. The affiliated companies file a consolidated income tax return. There was no difference between cost and book value and no goodwill on the date of acquisition. P Company uses the cost method to record its investment in S Company.

Required:

A. Prepare the income statement and retained earnings statement sections of the consolidated financial statements workpaper for the year ended December 31, 2002, under each of the following assumptions:

(1) Intercompany profits are eliminated using the 100% elimination method.

(2) Intercompany profits are eliminated using the partial elimination method.

B. List and compare the balances obtained using each method in requirement A for:
  (1) Combined income.
  (2) Noncontrolling interest in combined income.
  (3) Consolidated net income.
  (4) Consolidated retained earnings—December 31, 2002.
  (5) Consolidated inventories—December 31, 2002.

PROBLEM 11-7 **Economic Unit versus Parent Company Concept—Complete Equity Method**

On January 1, 1999, Peak Company purchased an 80% interest in the capital stock of Stull Company for $450,000. At that time, Stull Company had capital stock of $250,000 and retained earnings of $50,000. The difference between implied fair value and book value of the total net assets of Stull was attributed to specific assets of Stull Company as follows:

To equipment with five-year remaining life on 1/1/99 (original life of 10 years)	$ 80,000
To land	100,000
To inventory (Stull Company uses the FIFO inventory method)	30,000
To goodwill (amortized over 20 years)	52,500
Total	$262,500

The adjusted trial balances of Peak Company and Stull Company follow:

December 31, 2001
Adjusted Trial Balances

	Peak Company	Stull Company
Cash	$ 40,000	$ 25,000
Accounts Receivable	85,000	85,000
12/31 Inventory	115,000	75,000
Investment in Stull Company	461,300	
Land		150,000
Property and Equipment (net)	175,000	125,000
Cost of Goods Sold	425,000	90,000
Other Expense	50,000	35,000
Dividends Declared	50,000	25,000
Total	$1,401,300	$610,000
Accounts Payable	$ 83,000	$ 50,000
Notes Payable	25,000	10,000
Capital Stock	500,000	250,000
1/1 Retained Earnings	226,200	100,000
Sales	522,000	200,000
Equity Income	45,100	
Total	$1,401,300	$610,000

Required:

A. Prepare in general journal form the entries required on the books of Peak Company during 2001 to account for its investment in Stull Company. Peak uses the complete equity method to account for the investment.

B. Prepare a consolidated financial statements workpaper for the year ended December 31, 2001 using the economic unit concept.

C. Repeat requirement B using the parent company concept; list and compare the consolidated balances with those in requirement B.

PROBLEM 11-8 Economic Unit versus Parent Company Concept—Cost Method

Pinney Company owns 80% of the common stock of Star Company. The stock was purchased for $240,000 on January 1, 1997, when Star Company's retained earnings were $50,000. Pre-closing trial balances for the two companies at December 31, 2001, are:

	Pinney Company	Star Company
Cash	$ 40,000	$ 25,000
Accounts Receivable (net)	106,500	56,250
Inventory, 1/1	85,000	55,000
Investment in Star Co.	240,000	
Other Assets	250,000	200,000
Dividends Declared	50,000	30,000
Purchases	425,000	175,000
Other Expenses	60,000	45,000
Income Tax Expense	43,500	23,750
	$1,300,000	$610,000
Accounts Payable	$ 28,000	$ 15,000
Other Liabilities	27,500	20,000
Common Stock	350,000	250,000
Retained Earnings	270,500	60,000
Sales	600,000	265,000
Dividend Income	24,000	
	$1,300,000	$610,000
Inventory, 12/31	$ 70,000	$ 57,500

The January 1, 2001 inventory of Pinney Company includes $20,000 of profit recorded by Star Company on 2000 sales. During 2001 Star Company made intercompany sales of $100,000 with a markup of 20% on cost. The ending inventory of Star Company includes goods purchased in 2001 from Star Company for $30,000.

The affiliates file a consolidated income tax return.

Required:

A. Prepare the entries made on the books of Pinney Company during 2001 to record its interest in Star Company.

B. Prepare a consolidated statements workpaper for the year ended December 31, 2001, using the parent company concept (partial elimination).

C. Repeat requirement B using the economic unit concept (100% elimination); list and compare the consolidated balances with those in requirement B.

12

INTERNATIONAL ACCOUNTING AND THE GLOBAL ECONOMY

LEARNING OBJECTIVES

1. Describe how the changing world environment is leading to an increased focus on international accounting standards.

2. Explain some differences in accounting methods as they are applied internationally.

3. List five major classifications of accounting models used in different geographical regions.

4. Describe the role of the International Accounting Standards Committee in establishing international accounting standards.

5. List the steps that a non-U.S. company must follow to list its shares on a U.S. stock market.

6. Explain the role of form *20-F* filed with the Securities and Exchange Commission.

7. Indicate the role of American Depository Receipts in the issuing of securities of non-U.S. companies in the United States.

"We're not going to embrace any standard that isn't as good as our own. We're the best capital market in the world."[1]

INCREASING INTEREST IN INTERNATIONAL ACCOUNTING STANDARDS

Accounting standards and practices differ across geographical regions and cultures. In a segmented world, where the investors, creditors, and other key constituents to a company were typically confined within the geographical boundaries of the country of operation, such cross-border differences in accounting treatments were not a major issue. There was sufficient uniformity of reporting practices among the companies and their target audiences in the financial and investor communities to make valuations relatively straightforward. However, this world of segmented mar-

---

[1]Arthur Levitt Jr., Chairman, SEC, Speech at New York University, September 28, 1998.

kets began to undergo significant structural change starting in the late 1980s. The tremendous spurt in cross-border financial activity and the resulting internationalization of equity caused a transformation in the investor profiles of companies, resulting in increased focus on the issue of international accounting diversity.

General Electric was ranked number one of the largest transnational firms with assets held in foreign countries. Eighty-three billion dollars of GE's 272 billion dollars of assets were held outside the United States. Four other U.S. firms ranked in the top six (Ford, Exxon, General Motors, and IBM). Royal Dutch Shell, a UK/Netherlands firm, ranked second with 82 billion dollars of foreign held assets. Exxon ranked first in total foreign sales.[2]

The internationalization of equity and a concomitant increased interest in the study of international accounting differences have been driven by various concerns. First, as segmentation among financial markets around the world began to vanish, it became easier for companies to go beyond their geographical boundaries to raise capital. According to an estimate by the Bank of International Settlements (BIS), the total value of cross-border equity raised increased 26% annually from 1990 to 1996, in comparison to an 8% annual growth rate in the previous decade. Most of the cross-border capital issuances involved an international offering either in the United States (U.S.) or the European (primarily London) markets. This initiative among companies to start looking abroad was accompanied by a distinct trend

FIGURE 12-1

Securities Sales by Foreign Issuers in U.S. Markets
Amount of Capital Raised and Number of Issuers

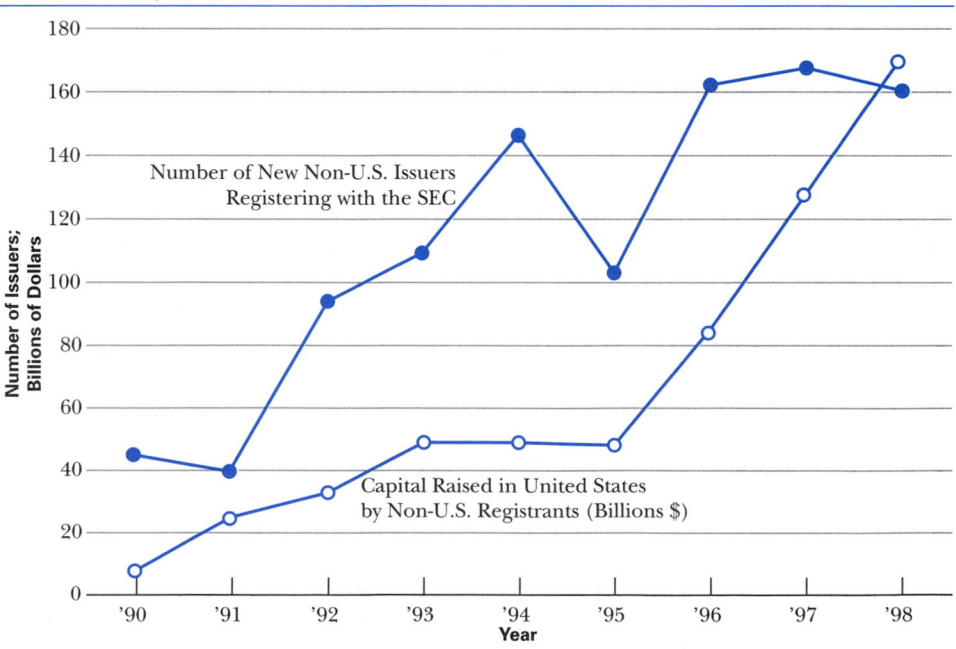

Adapted from the SEC Division of Corporation Finance, Statistical Report 1997, and SEC Annual Report 1998.

---

[2] *World Investment Report 1998: Trends and Determinants*, United Nations Conference on Trade and Development, Table II.1, p. 36.

FIGURE 12-2

Holdings of Non-U.S. Equities by U.S. Residents

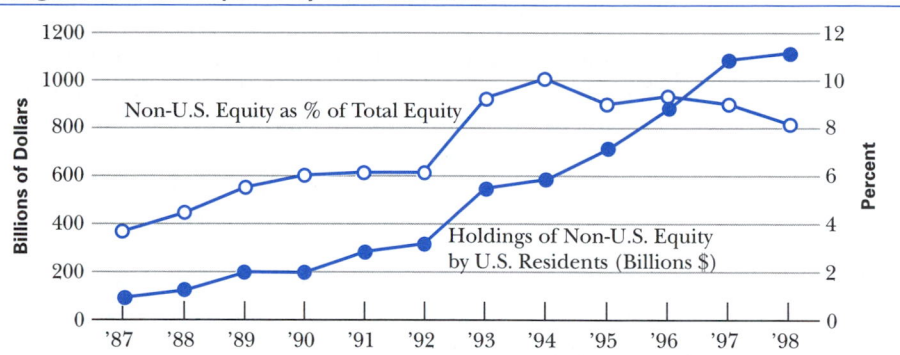

Source: "Flow of Funds Accounts," Board of Governors of the Federal Reserve System.

among investors, especially in the developed markets, to internationalize their portfolio holdings.

These trends are further illustrated in Figures 12-1 and 12-2. Figure 12-1 shows the dramatic increase both in the number of non-U.S. issuers registering with the SEC and in the dollar amount of capital raised in the United States by non-U.S. registrants in the 1990s. As seen in Figure 12-2, the holdings of non-U.S. equity by U.S. residents have also increased over this time period.

For example, the U.S. holdings of non-U.S. equity increased from 200 billion U.S. dollars in 1990 to 1.1 trillion within a period of eight years in the 1990s. This internationalization of equity resulted in the investor profile of companies around the world changing significantly and becoming more diverse in terms of nationality and financial reporting practices. This brought the issue of international differences in accounting practices into the forefront and set the stage for the beginnings of the development of uniform international accounting standards. Ideally, these standards would be used by companies worldwide and could be understood by international investors.

Further, a gradual shift in financing activities has occurred, moving from a primarily debt-financed world with an informal flow of information between the companies and their creditors to a largely equity-financed world demanding more formal financial communication. This shift toward equity financing, especially in the emerging markets, has placed greater importance on the need for transparent accounting standards acceptable worldwide.

In this chapter, we provide a discussion of some of the international accounting issues. We begin by introducing the movement toward harmonization of worldwide accounting standards. A brief analysis of the characteristics of some of the major accounting models in the world is presented next. We then provide a discussion of the recent initiatives to develop a unified set of accounting standards and the specific role of the International Accounting Standards Committees (IASC) in developing such standards.

HARMONIZATION OF WORLDWIDE ACCOUNTING STANDARDS

Financial accounting practices, required disclosures, and auditing requirements are not uniform across countries. Not only are there differences in broad principles but there are also many variations in the everyday application of these principles.

An extensive list of differences is not necessary here, but the following examples provide evidence of the wide variations that exist in accounting practices:

- In some countries, goodwill is not amortized until it is apparent that is has diminished in value. For example, prior to 1998, companies in England were able to write off goodwill against stockholders' equity rather than capitalizing and amortizing the amount.
- Outside the United States the pooling of interests method of recording a business combination is permitted in only a few countries.
- Some countries do not require comprehensive tax allocation.
- LIFO inventory costing is not permitted in some countries.
- In the United States, development costs are expensed, whereas in many countries this cost is capitalized.
- Reserves are more frequently recorded in other countries for such items as self-insurance or contingencies for expected future losses or expenses that are not allowable under U.S. GAAP.

Accounting reports of a foreign subsidiary or investee should be made to conform to U.S. generally accepted accounting standards before consolidation or the equity method is applied. An accountant working with the financial statements of a foreign company must therefore be familiar with the differences between accounting terminology and practices in the United States and those in the foreign country in which it is domiciled and be prepared to deal with them. Note that restatement into U.S. dollars does not necessarily imply conformity with U.S. GAAP.

With the growth of international trade, multinational firms, and a global financial marketplace, significant resources have been devoted to the "harmonization" of accounting principles and auditing standards. One approach to harmonization in international accounting standard setting focuses on the communication of information in a form that can be interpreted and understood internationally, rather than standardization of procedures to be used in all countries. Under this approach, international standards are drafted in broad terms and permit acceptable alternatives to be adopted by rule-makers in various developed countries. However, to a growing number of preparers and users of financial statements, harmonization means the narrowing of differences among generally accepted accounting procedures of different countries.

In the last decade the International Accounting Standards Committee (IASC) has emerged as the driving force behind the drive toward global harmonization of accounting practices. The IASC is an independent private-sector body working to achieve uniformity in the accounting principles that are used by businesses and other organizations for financial reporting around the world. The IASC was established in 1973 by the leading accountancy bodies of Australia, Canada, France, Germany, Japan, Mexico, the Netherlands, the United Kingdom and Ireland, and the United States. The objective of the IASC is to formulate and publish standards to be followed in the preparation of financial statements, promote worldwide acceptance of the standards, and work generally for improvements in international accounting. The IASC Board makes decisions on accounting issues, and these decisions are then reported in the form of *International Accounting Standards (IAS)*. The first international accounting standard was issued in January 1975; 39 standards had been issued as of June 1999. These international accounting standards (IAS) are listed in Illustration 12-1. Members of the IASC have agreed to make an effort to ensure that financial statements issued in their respective countries conform to

ILLUSTRATION 12–1

List of Current International Accounting Standards Issued by the IASC

Standard	Topic
IAS 1	Presentation of Financial Statements
IAS 2	Inventories
IAS 3	No longer effective. Replaced by IAS 27 and IAS 28.
IAS 4	Depreciation Accounting
IAS 5	No longer effective. Replaced by IAS 1.
IAS 6	No longer effective. Replaced by IAS 15.
IAS 7	Cash Flow Statements
IAS 8	Profit or Loss for the Period, Fundamental Errors and Changes in Accounting Policies
IAS 9	Research and Development Costs (will be superseded by IAS 38 effective 1/7/99)
IAS 10	Events After the Balance Sheet Date
IAS 11	Construction Contracts
IAS 12	Income Taxes
IAS 13	No longer effective. Replaced by IAS 1.
IAS 14	Segment Reporting
IAS 15	Information Reflecting the Effects of Changing Prices
IAS 16	Property, Plant and Equipment
IAS 17	Leases
IAS 18	Revenue
IAS 19	Employee Benefits
IAS 20	Accounting for Government Grants and Disclosure of Government Assistance
IAS 21	The Effects of Changes in Foreign Exchange Rates
IAS 22	Business Combinations
IAS 23	Borrowing Costs
IAS 24	Related Party Disclosures
IAS 25	Accounting for Investments
IAS 26	Accounting and Reporting by Retirement Benefit Plans
IAS 27	Consolidated Financial Statements and Accounting for Investments in Subsidiaries
IAS 28	Accounting for Investments in Associates
IAS 29	Financial Reporting in Hyperinflationary Economies
IAS 30	Disclosures in the Financial Statements of Banks and Similar Financial Institutions
IAS 31	Financial Reporting of Interests in Joint Ventures
IAS 32	Financial Instruments: Disclosures and Presentation
IAS 33	Earnings per Share
IAS 34	Interim Financial Reporting
IAS 35	Discontinuing Operations (1/1/99)
IAS 36	Impairment of Assets (1/7/99)
IAS 37	Provisions, Contingent Liabilities and Contingent Assets
IAS 38	Intangible Assets
IAS 39	Financial Instruments: Recognition and Measurement

Source: http://www.iasc.org.uk.

the standards issued by the IASC and that noncompliance with those standards be disclosed in the financial reports. The structure of the IASC is discussed in greater detail later in this chapter.

The Supreme Court of Justice in Panama ordered the "temporary suspension" of a resolution to adopt IAS as the official accounting model for businesses in Panama, after having approved the resolution earlier in 1999. The Court said that the authority to adopt IAS did not lie with the accounting board, but with the Ministry of Commerce and Industry. The ruling, however, does not affect similar requirements adopted by the Superintendent of Banks that all Panamanian banks should follow IAS beginning in the year 2000.[3]

It is now recognized that a global financial marketplace exists and that the use of different accounting standards works against the efficiency of international capital markets. With the emergence of significant global corporate operations and markets, the IASC is attempting to improve the quality of its standards.

COMPARATIVE ACCOUNTING MODELS

Various types of accounting practices are currently popular in different parts of the world. Differing accounting practices could result in the same economic event being reported differently depending on the environment in which it occurred. Consider the information summarized in Illustration 12-2 for Daimler-Benz (a German company, now Daimler-Chrysler), Novo Nordisk (a Danish Company), and Fantom Technologies (a Canadian company). In Illustration 12-2, national GAAP refers to the country's GAAP. For example, the ratios listed under national GAAP for Fantom Technologies are based on numbers calculated using Canadian GAAP.

In the ratio of U.S. GAAP net income to national GAAP net income, shown in Illustration 12-2, the variation is as much as 50%. (Daimler-Benz's net income computed using U.S. GAAP is only 50% of that reported using German rules.) The

ILLUSTRATION 12–2

Comparison of Ratios Based on Differing GAAP

Ratio	GAAP Used	Daimler-Benz (German) 1994/1995	Novo Nordisk (Danish) 1997	Fantom Technologies (Canadian) 1997
U.S. GAAP Net Income / National GAAP Net Income		0.506	0.863	0.977
Net Income / Total Assets	U.S. GAAP	0.01	0.069	0.116
	National GAAP	0.022	0.086	0.121
Long-Term Debt / Total Equity	U.S. GAAP	0.379	0.094	0.767*
	National GAAP	0.619	0.097	0.765*

*Uses total liabilities rather than long-term debt.

---

[3]"Late News from the IASC," International Accounting Standards Committee's (IASC) web site, www.iasc.org.uk, 8/31/99.

FIGURE 12-3

U.S. GAAP Earnings Adjustment Index

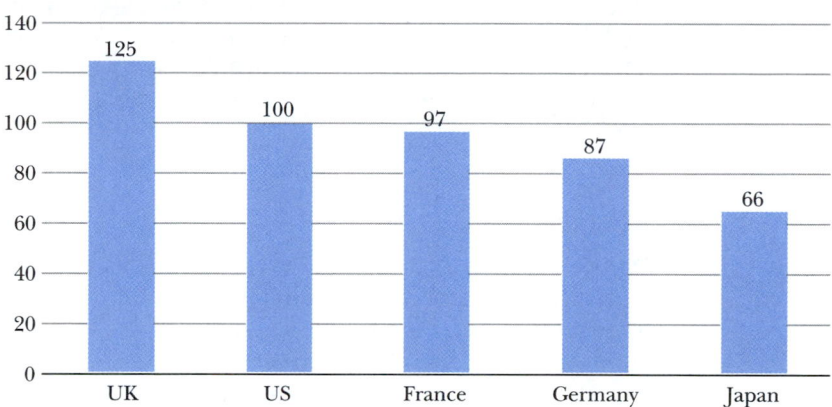

Source: Adapted from L. Radebaugh and S. Gray, *International Accounting and Multinational Enterprises*, 4th Edition, 1997, John Wiley & Sons, Inc.

possible reasons for such differences are discussed in later sections of this chapter. Similarly, the return on assets (net income to total assets) and the debt to equity ratios differ depending on the type of GAAP used. The ongoing globalization of the equity markets has resulted in a need for companies to address the concerns of their investors, who may be located in different countries and not conversant in local accounting practices. At the other end of the spectrum, the task of analysts following international companies has become more onerous, especially if different companies adopt differing accounting standards. For example, a U.S. analyst following a company reporting under a model different from U.S. GAAP should not only be able to recognize the differences between the company's methods and U.S. GAAP, but also be able to determine the impact of these differences on financial indicators like earnings, return on equity, leverage, and so on. The complexity of such tasks in some cases may provide disincentives for international analysts to follow the company's stock and, in others, may lead to inaccurate valuations of the company. Therefore a need exists for companies with global aspirations to be able to speak a common accounting language that is understood worldwide. Before examining the issues and the logistics surrounding the creation or administration of a unified accounting model around the world, it is useful for us to understand a bit more about the differences that exist among the various accounting systems in place today.

The information presented in Figure 12-3 suggests that U.S. GAAP is not as conservative as GAAP in most other countries. If U.S. GAAP is considered a benchmark (i.e., 100 = U.S. GAAP net income), the income of most non-U.S. companies stated using local GAAP would have to be adjusted downward to be comparable to U.S. firms. However, firms in the United Kingdom are generally *less* conservative than firms in the United States, based on this source.

IN THE NEWS

"Japan's Ministry of Finance (MOF) yesterday announced far-reaching reforms designed to raise Japanese corporate accounting standards and practices to world-class levels over the next two years. The reforms are likely to have a profound impact on the structure of 'Japan Inc.' and the way it operates, according to senior MOF officials. The reforms will render it no longer possible for Japanese firms to manipulate their financial results by concealing profits or losses in unconsolidated subsidiaries, or by using their own discretion in the way they value securities and other assets, an MOF spokesman said. This is seen as vital to securing investor confidence and to a sustained recovery in the Tokyo stock market. The accounting reforms are also designed to improve the transparency of corporate pension funds in Japan. This in turn is expected to uncover 'huge' funding deficits, and companies will be obligated to make good these deficits by injections of cash or securities."[4]

Format and Terminology Differences

Many annual reports for non-U.S. companies are already stated in terms of U.S. dollars. However, the user should be cautious. Some non-U.S. companies prepare statements in English still using their national GAAP, others report several columns of information denominated in their local currency with a column that is translated into U.S. dollars, and some prepare their statements in English conforming to U.S. GAAP. The first step in analyzing an international company is to determine which GAAP is being used. The consolidated financial statements for Glaxo Wellcome are reported in Illustrations 12-3 and 12-4. The statements for this UK firm are prepared in English and in accordance with UK GAAP.

Format Differences Various formats are allowed in presenting financial statements in different countries. Glaxo Wellcome's balance sheet is used here to illustrate some of the more common accounting differences between the United Kingdom and the United States. Recall that under U.S. GAAP, assets are listed on

---

ILLUSTRATION 12–3

Glaxo Wellcome
Consolidated Profit and Loss Account in Accordance with UK GAAP

	1998 £ Millions
Turnover	7,983
Cost of Sales	1,545
Selling, General and Administrative Expenditure	2,688
Research and Development Expenditure	1,163
Other Operating (Income)/Expense	(96)
Total Operating Costs	5,300
Trading Profit	2,683
Share of Profits/(Losses) of Joint Ventures and Associated Undertakings	22
Profit on Dissolution of Joint Venture	57
Profit Before Interest	2,762
Net Interest Payable	91
Profit on Ordinary Activities Before Taxation	2,671
Taxation	815
Profit on Ordinary Activities after Taxation	1,856
Minority Interests	20
Profit Attributable to Shareholders	1,836
Dividends	1,300
Retained Profit	536

---

[4]*Business Times* (Singapore), "Sweeping Tokyo Accounting Reforms to Fight Abuses," by Anthony Rowley, 4/10/99, pp. 1, 5.

ILLUSTRATION 12–4

Glaxo Wellcome
Consolidated Balance Sheet in Accordance with UK GAAP

	1998 £ Millions	1997 £ Millions
Goodwill	106	
Tangible Assets	3,633	3,583
Investments	98	52
Fixed Assets	3,837	3,635
Stocks	1,154	855
Debtors	2,470	2,285
Equity Investments	28	39
Liquid Investments	1,617	1,408
Cash at Bank	240	215
Current Assets	5,509	4,802
Loans and Overdrafts	1,317	1,104
Convertible Bonds		77
Other Creditors	2,828	2,705
Creditors: amounts due within one year	4,145	3,886
Net Current Assets	1,364	916
Total Assets Less Current Liabilities	5,201	4,551
Loans	1,804	1,841
Other Creditors	161	123
Creditors: amounts due after one year	1,965	1,964
Provisions for Liabilities and Charges	468	697
Net Assets	2,768	1,890
Called-up Share Capital	906	894
Share Premium Account	1,149	805
Goodwill Reserve		(4,840)
Other Reserves	647	4,984
Equity Shareholders' Funds	2,702	1,843
Equity Minority Interests	66	47
Capital Employed	2,768	1,890

the balance sheet in the order of decreasing liquidity, with current assets separated from fixed assets (or plant assets), investments, and intangible assets. Liabilities are separated into current and long-term categories and then added to the owners' equity accounts to arrive at "total liabilities and equity." Thus total assets equal total liabilities and equity, and those totals are reported. In contrast, Glaxo Wellcome's balance sheet follows a net approach. Assets and liabilities are combined in such a way as to compute both working capital (i.e., called "net current assets" on the report) and total *net* assets (i.e., stockholders' equity, also called "employed capital on the report").

Fixed assets are listed first in UK balance sheets, with current assets listed second, as illustrated in Glaxo Wellcome's balance sheet (Illustration 12-4). In addition, current assets are listed in the order of *increasing* liquidity (i.e., the most liquid assets are listed last). On the income statement (profit and loss statement), dividends are subtracted from profit to shareholders to arrive at "retained profit." In the United States, dividends are typically not shown on the income statement.

Terminology Differences If foreign financial statements are restated into English, the terminology is usually consistent with U.S. usage. However, in comparison to UK statements, there are several differences. Examine Glaxo Wellcome's income statement. Notice that revenues in the United Kingdom, for instance, are called turnover. The following table lists some of the terminology differences between the United Kingdom and the United States.

U.K. Terminology	U.S. Terminology
Income Statement Terms	
Turnover	Revenues or sales
Profit attributable to shareholders	Net income
Balance Sheet Terms	
Stock (in asset section)	Inventory
Debtors	Accounts receivable
Creditors	Payables
Called-up share capital	Common stock
Share premium account	Paid-in capital
Reserves	Retained earnings

INTERNATIONAL ACCOUNTING MODELS

Practitioners sometimes classify international accounting models into five major geographical classifications:

Type of Accounting Practice	Region
Anglo-Saxon	United States
Anglo-Saxon	United Kingdom
German	Germany, Switzerland
Latin	France, Italy, Brazil
Asia-Pacific	Japan, China

Most of the differences in accounting models can be traced back to the objectives of financial reporting in different regions of the world. For example, in the United States and the United Kingdom financial reporting is directed toward informing the credit and equity markets, whereas under the German and French models, preparation of accounts has historically been directed toward calculation of taxable income and subsequent profit distribution. An oft-quoted example, with at least some legitimate backing, is that German companies tend to report lower earnings, because reported earnings and taxable earnings are the same. This results in higher price to earnings (P/E) ratios for such companies in comparison to those for companies reporting under the market-oriented U.S. model. Similarly, the effect of accounting differences on the reported performance of companies can be staggering. When Daimler-Benz became the first German company to reconcile its accounts to U.S. GAAP in 1993, its DM 610 million profit turned into a loss of DM 1,900 million.

Accounting Standards in the United Kingdom

Accounting standards in the United Kingdom are referred to as Financial Reporting Standards (FRS). These are issued by the Accounting Standards Board (ASB), which is a subsidiary of an independent not-for-profit company that promotes consistent financial reporting practices. The ASB strongly supports international accounting standards (IAS) issued by the IASC and in most cases, compliance with an FRS achieves compliance with an IAS. For example, when the IASC issued its statement on the treatment of goodwill, the ASB changed its standards to comply with the IAS. At the time of this writing, the UK Department of Trade was considering allowing UK companies to follow IAS. Currently, UK companies must use UK GAAP, while foreign companies listing in the United Kingdom may use UK, U.S., or IAS GAAP. Other countries' GAAP may be allowed if a reconciliation is provided. One primary difference between UK accounting principles and U.S. standards relates to the revaluation of fixed assets. UK GAAP allows revaluation of fixed assets to an equity reserve account.

The Institute of Chartered Accountants of Scotland (ICAS) has announced its support for the "principle that UK listed companies should be allowed to use internationally accepted accounting standards in place of present UK standards. ICAS supports the use of IAS in the UK and internationally. Given the IASC's current restructuring proposals, however, it is necessary to see that the IASC establishes itself for the future as a robust, strongly constituted body, supported by the major international accounting standard setters, and that it continues to be capable of developing quality standards over the long term."[5]

Accounting Standards in Germany

In 1998, a new independent body, the German Accounting Standards Committee, was formed (Deutsches Rechnungslegungs Standards Committee, DRSC). This committee allows German companies with publicly traded securities to issue consolidated financial statements using either IAS or U.S. GAAP rather than German GAAP. German firms are usually financed by banks. This results in financial reporting oriented toward creditor protection. The tax laws are closely related to the financial rules, leading to a generally more conservative approach to reporting.

In Germany, the principal traditional purpose of accounts was to establish the basis for collecting tax, and therefore the basis of accounting was highly legalistic. Consequently, there was every incentive for companies to keep their reported level of profits down. This has resulted in the general belief that German accounts understate both profits and assets as a result of using accelerated depreciation and generous provisioning. However, it is not as simple as that. Many German companies have developed the practice of setting aside reserves in good years to provide a cushion in leaner times, thus smoothing out some of the normal cyclical fluctuations.[6]

Accounting Standards in Japan

Accounting in Japan is strongly influenced by legal and tax laws with little involvement by the private sector. Three primary laws are governed by the Ministry of Finance: the Commercial Code, the Securities and Exchange Law, and the Corporate Income Tax Law. The first law defines assets, liabilities, revenues, and ex-

---

[5]"ICAS Supports International Comparability of Accounting Standards," International Accounting Standards Committee's (IASC) web site, www.iasc.org.uk, 9/7/99.

[6]*Australian Financial Review*, "Accountants Gather Round Different Standards," by Steward Hamilton, 11/25/98, p. 10.

penses. The second law governs financial reporting, and the third law further defines other accounting measurement issues. Taxable income is very close to income measured under the Commercial Code with minor adjustments. Accounting standards are set by the Business Accounting Deliberation Council (BADC). Debt ratios in Japan tend to be significantly higher than in the United States. These higher debt ratios arise because of the close relationships between firms and banks. Japanese banks tend to be more willing to assist firms in poor economic times than banks in most countries. Because of these and other factors, Japanese firms place much emphasis on firm growth.

INTERNATIONAL REPORTING ISSUES

Next we consider some of the major "styles" of accounting practices used throughout the world. The accounting methods listed below cover the reporting practices of more than 80% of the publicly traded companies in the world. Our comparative analysis identifies specific accounting concepts and approaches adopted by firms in various geographical classifications, including similarities as well as differences. When reading a report, care must be exercised because of differences in methods or how certain methods are applied in different countries. The first footnote to the financial statements in most countries is a summary of significant accounting policies. It should be examined carefully to determine the methods used in the report. The following sections describe some of the differences in methods or application of methods as of the date of this writing. Be aware, however, that accounting standards are constantly changing.

Treatment of Goodwill

Methods and allowable lives for the amortization of goodwill vary significantly across various regions and often cause significant differences in reported earnings. At one extreme, U.S. GAAP requires amortization over a period not to exceed 40 years; at the other extreme, the Germanic code allows an immediate write-off of goodwill. Amortization is also required under the Japanese model, with a shorter time frame of five years. In the United Kingdom, the rules for goodwill changed in 1998 to conform to IASC rules. Prior to 1998, goodwill was charged off against an equity account (goodwill reserve). Currently, UK firms must capitalize goodwill and amortize it over a five-year period. A period up to 20 years can be used if justified. This is consistent with *IAS No. 22* (partially revised in 1998), which deals with business combinations and the amortization of goodwill. The treatment of goodwill impacts both earnings and net assets of companies reporting under different methods. The FASB has issued an exposure draft proposing significant changes in the handling of goodwill amortization in the United States. In particular, the amortization period is likely to be shortened, and the amortization *may* be reported net of tax and given a special line on the income statement under U.S. GAAP.

Inventories

There are usually fewer choices allowed in valuing inventory for companies in most countries than in the United States. For instance, LIFO has only been an acceptable method in Germany since the early 1990s, and is still not a common method internationally. The LIFO reserves of German companies are much smaller than those of companies in the United States that have been using LIFO in many cases since the 1970s. The IASC issued *IAS No. 2* on inventories recommending specific cost. If specific cost is not determinable, the benchmark is FIFO or weighted average. However, LIFO is an allowed alternative provided the firm *discloses* the lower of net realizable value and either the FIFO, weighted average, or current cost.

Research and Development

In the United States, research and development (R&D) costs are expensed as incurred. In acquisitions, in-process R&D is recognized as an expense (although the FASB plans to reconsider this issue also). Many U.S. firms involved in acquisitions use this standard to avoid having large amounts of goodwill recorded in the acquisition. Historically, most countries have allowed R&D expenditures to be capitalized. However, *IAS No. 38* on intangibles now requires R&D costs to be expensed. It also specifically requires that purchased R&D costs in an acquisition be capitalized and amortized over their useful life, but not more than five years. An exception, however, allows a 20-year period to be justified in some cases.

Business Combinations

The pooling of interests method has been very popular in the United States because it allows firms to acquire other companies and report consolidated assets and liabilities at book value, thereby avoiding any new goodwill. The FASB recently proposed eliminating the pooling of interests method. While the method is not a popular one outside of the United States, the IASC does allow the "uniting of interests" method, which is quite similar to the pooling of interests method. To qualify for the uniting of interests method, several conditions must be met. First, the combining firms must not differ significantly in size. Second, a substantial majority of the voting common shares of the combining firm(s) is exchanged. Third, the shareholders of each firm maintain substantially the same voting rights and interests in the combined entity.

Fixed Assets and Depreciation

In several countries, fixed assets are valued at depreciated historical cost (Germany, Japan, and the United States), while in certain regions automatic reevaluations of fixed assets are allowed (United Kingdom) and in still others (e.g., France) such reevaluations are allowed subject to governmental approval.

In a survey of foreign registrants that reported a material difference in reconciling to U.S. GAAP net income, 87 reported reconciling items that increased income, while 186 reported reconciling items that reduced income. Eight firms reported U.S. GAAP net income 100 percent greater than income based on domestic GAAP, while 33 firms reported U.S. GAAP net income 100 percent less.[7]

Other Differences

• Under U.S. GAAP, certain types of long-term leases are required to be accounted for as capital leases. Similar arrangements in other countries often are accounted for as operating leases.

---

[7]Survey of Financial Statement Reconciliations by Foreign Registrants, Division of Corportion Finance, Securities and Exchange Commission, May 1, 1993.

- In certain countries (United Kingdom and United States) it is quite common to see firms provide funding for a very high percentage, if not all, of their pension commitments. In Europe and Japan, such funded pensions are not very common.

The following table provides a brief description of differences in certain accounting issues among U.S. GAAP, International Accounting Standards (IAS), and various other countries.

	U.S. GAAP	International Accounting Standards	Other Countries
Consolidation Methods	Purchase and pooling of interests are allowed, but FASB has proposed eliminating the pooling method.	Purchase is required. Uniting of interests is unusual but allowed if there are no significant differences in firm size, and if an acquirer cannot be identified.	Pooling is not permitted in Japan and is used infrequently in other countries.
Property, Plant and Equipment	Recorded at historical cost and carried on the books at net book value.	The initial measurement is at original cost. An allowed alternative is to revalue assets to fair value.	In France and the UK, it is common to revalue assets to an equity reserve account.
Depreciation	Straight-line is the predominant method for financial purposes. Alternative methods are used for tax purposes.	The method must be applied on a systematic basis.	Taxation authorities determine depreciation methods in Japan and Latin America.
Research and Development	Both costs are expensed.	Research costs are expensed and some development costs may result in the recognition of an intangible asset.	In Japan, some research and development costs can be capitalized and are subject to amortization over a period less than 5 years. In the UK, some development costs are capitalized.
Treatment of Goodwill	Amortization, over a period not to exceed 40 years (changes have been proposed). Deductible for tax purposes in limited cases.	Goodwill must be amortized over its useful life, not to exceed 5 years unless longer (up to 20 years) can be justified. The 20-year ceiling is a rebuttable presumption rather than an absolute limit.	Most countries capitalize goodwill, but tend to amortize it over a shorter time period. Check to see if the country allows goodwill deductions for tax purposes.
Inventories	LIFO and FIFO are common.	The lower of cost or net realizable value is recommended. FIFO and weighted average are the primary methods, while LIFO is an acceptable alternative.	LIFO is not acceptable for tax purposes in the UK and Canada, so its use is limited.
Deferred Taxes	Deferred tax liabilities and assets are recorded on all taxable and deductible temporary differences. Valuation allowances for deferred tax assets are required in some cases.	Deferred tax liabilities on most taxable temporary differences and deferred tax assets on most deductible temporary differences (if probable). No deferred taxes on nontaxable goodwill.	The liability method is used in the UK and Germany, while in Japan deferred taxes are not recognized.

THE INTERNATIONAL ACCOUNTING STANDARDS COMMITTEE (IASC) AND THE INTERNATIONAL STANDARD-SETTING PROCESS

The preceding section illustrated the extent of diversity in existing accounting standards around the world. With the internationalization of the equity markets and an increase in cross-border equity offers and stock listings, the need for greater uniformity in accounting practices and reporting standards is clear. Since its formation in 1973, the IASC counts as its members 142 accounting organizations in 103 countries (including five associate members and four affiliate members). These organizations represent over 2,000,000 accountants worldwide. In addition to accountants, the IASC network encompasses the global business community, the financial sector, stock exchanges all over the world, securities regulatory bodies, national legal organizations, and the national governments of member countries. Since the IASC has embarked on developing a uniform standard for companies worldwide, it interacts regularly with national standard-setting bodies, as well as multilateral organizations like the European Commission, the United Nations (UN), and the World Bank.

Market regulators and accounting specialists the world over have repeatedly told investors that much of last year's market meltdown in East Asia stemmed from shoddy and disparate bookkeeping practices in the region. Even U.S. Federal Reserve Chairman Alan Greenspan told America's Congress last year that the turbulence in overseas markets wouldn't abate unless the regulators in those markets enforce better and clearer bookkeeping rules.[8]

Members of the IASC Board are appointed by the International Federation of Accountants (IFAC) in consultation with the membership of the IASC. The Board at present includes thirteen country members and four additional organizational members. Board members may serve for a renewable period of two and a half years. The Board also has three observer members who contribute to the debate but do not vote. The formulation of the International Accounting Standards (IAS) involves a three-staged process. A Steering Committee makes recommendations to the Board on the structure of the particular standard under debate, which is then published as an Exposure Draft containing a description of the proposed requirements for the standard, the arguments for and against each requirement, and an invitation for public comment. The public feedback is then considered, and appropriate modifications made prior to the design of the final form of the standard. An Exposure Draft is issued only when two-thirds of Board members have voted in favor of doing so, and a final standard requires three-quarters of Board votes for approval. The IASC standards are accepted as sufficient for listing companies in most major stock exchanges except the U.S. and Canadian markets, and they are allowed in the United States for foreign companies if a schedule is provided reconciling income under IAS to income based on U.S. GAAP.

Three Danish companies announced their intent to switch to IAS beginning in 1999: FLS Industries, GN Great Nordic, and Incentive.[9]

---

[8] *Asian WSJ*, "Accounting Rules are Less than Rigorous in Many Countries," by Elizabeth Macdonald, 5/3/99, p. s4.

[9] "Late News from the IASC," International Accounting Standards Committee's (IASC) web site, www.iasc.org.uk, 9/20/99.

Since the mission of the IASC is to formulate accounting standards used in the presentation of financial statements, a secondary objective is to promote their worldwide acceptance and observation. The efforts of the IASC met with significant success in Europe as the major continental economies (Germany, Italy, Belgium, etc.) abolished their national accounting practices in favor of a common practice based on the International Accounting Standards. In 1993, the International Organization of Securities Commissions (IOSCO) identified a core set of standards that should be a part of any future universal accounting model. Such a model could then be used across geographical regions by securities regulators as sufficient for cross-border listing by companies. In 1995, the IASC began a project to develop a core set of standards in twelve critical areas that the IOSCO identified as mandatory for consideration prior to recommending the IAS as a universal standard for cross-border offering and listing. This initiative is moving toward completion by the end of the millennium. However, its acceptability by IOSCO is dependent on its acceptance by the U.S. Securities and Exchange Commission (SEC). Though the SEC has been reasonably supportive of this cause, an eventual acceptance of the IASC for non-U.S. issuers listing in the U.S. markets could potentially create problems due to different requirements for listed domestic companies (U.S. GAAP) and non-U.S. companies (IAS).

Despite its lack of acceptance in the United States, the IASC has begun to make a significant impact on international finance. Many countries have abandoned their national accounting practice in favor of IAS. As mentioned previously, stock exchanges, especially in Europe and certain parts of Asia, have begun to accept IAS-based financial statements as sufficient for listing on their exchanges. The growing acceptance of IAS has influenced the standard-setting process both in the United States and in the United Kingdom. Conversely, FASB practices in many areas have influenced the IAS (e.g., *IAS No. 33* on earnings per share).

The SEC will deliberate on a decision of whether to accept the IASC-developed core accounting standards as sufficient for registration and public trading of securities of non-U.S. issuers on the U.S. equity markets. In addition to the accounting concerns discussed earlier, there are concerns about the interpretation and enforcement of the IAS guidelines by companies. One of the primary criticisms made by the SEC is that the IAS leaves too much room for interpretation and thus potentially for manipulation.

At the core of the standard-setting process in the United States is the Financial Accounting Standards Board (FASB), a private organization that is supported by the SEC for establishing standards that companies follow to obtain a listing on one of the U.S. stock exchanges. What role will the FASB play in the new standard-setting process under the IASC initiative? Unless the SEC and the FASB approve the standards for use in the U.S. markets, these rules are unlikely to have international legitimacy.

In a 1998 report of the FASB regarding the future of international accounting, the FASB described its vision of a successful international accounting system. The FASB stated its belief that the worldwide use of a single set of accounting standards is desirable and eventually attainable, but that the ideal outcome will result from "pursuing the overall objective of increasing international compatibility while maintaining the highest quality accounting standards in the United States."[10] Other key considerations mentioned in the report include the following:

---

[10] *FASB*, "International Accounting Standard Setting: A Vision for the Future," 1998.

- The FASB has a leadership role to play in the evolution of the international accounting system.
- The FASB is willing to commit the required resources needed to ensure high-quality standards while increasing the convergence and quality of standards used in different nations until the ideal outcome is achieved.
- The FASB will participate in establishing a quality international accounting standard-setting structure and process.
- The FASB recognizes that structural and procedural changes to the FASB may result, as well as potential changes in its national role.

The FASB identified eight basic functions as essential for an international standard setter to attain the needed quality level. The essential functions identified are as follows:

1. *Leadership.* The standard setter should work jointly with others, but should be able to lead rather than codify the status quo.
2. *Innovation.* The standard setter should be at the forefront of advanced thinking and research.
3. *Relevance.* The standard setter's process and structure should be designed to be proactive in meeting capital market demands.
4. *Responsiveness.* The standard setter should be able to move expeditiously to deal with new developments and demands.
5. *Objectivity.* The standard setter should serve the public interest, with minimal susceptibility to self-serving needs of private-interest groups.
6. *Acceptability and Credibility.* The quality of the standard setter should be recognized and respected.
7. *Understandability.* The standards should be broadly understood by constituents to facilitate consistent application and interpretation.
8. *Accountability.* The standard setter should be accountable to the public interest. Some form of oversight should exist to act as both a mechanism and a catalyst for needed change.

IN THE NEWS

Edmund Jenkins, the Chairman of the FASB, in an address to the 1999 Financial Executive Summit in Vancouver, BC, Canada, stated that there is a clear connection between the efficient and effective U.S. capital markets and the high quality of U.S. financial reporting standards. He further quoted other financial market leaders as follows:

Alan Greenspan, chairman of the U.S. Federal Reserve: "Transparent accounting plays an important role in maintaining the vibrancy of our financial markets."

Abbey Joseph Cohen, Goldman Sachs: "The quality of information we now receive from companies in the U.S. is about the best we have ever seen and dramatically exceeds that of almost any other nation."

Lawrence Summers, deputy secretary of the U.S. Treasury: "The single most important innovation shaping [the American capital] market was the idea of generally accepted accounting principles. We need something similar internationally."[11]

---

[11]Address on global financial reporting and the global financial market, by Edmund L. Jenkins, Chairman, Financial Accounting Standards Board, at the 1999 Financial Executive Summit, Vancouver, BC, Canada, May 28, 1999.

ILLUSTRATION 12-5

Stock Exchanges that Do and Do Not Allow Firms to Use IAS Financial Statements for Foreign Listings

Countries that **Allow*** IAS Financial Statements for Foreign Listings		Countries that **Do Not Allow** IAS Financial Statements for Foreign Listings	
Country	*Exchange*	*Country*	*Exchange*
Argentina	Buenos Aires Stock Exchange	Brazil	Rio De Janeiro Stock Exchange
Australia	Australian Stock Exchange	Canada	Toronto Stock Exchange
Austria	Vienna Stock Exchange	Chile	Santiago Stock Exchange
Bangladesh	Chittagong Stock Exchange	Indonesia	Jakarta Stock Exchange
Belgium	Brussels Stock Exchange	Iran	Tehran Stock Exchange
Canada	Montreal Stock Exchange	Israel	Tel Aviv Stock Exchange
Cayman Islands	Cayman Islands Stock Exchange	Jamaica	Jamaica Stock Exchange
Croatia	Zagreb Stock Exchange	Kazakhstan	Kazakhstan Stock Exchange
Cyprus	Cyprus Stock Exchange	Kyrgyz Republic	Kyrgyz Stock Exchange
Denmark	Copenhagen Stock Exchange	Mexico	Mexican Stock Exchange
Egypt	Cairo Stock Exchange	New Zealand	New Zealand Stock Exchange
Estonia	Tallinn Stock Exchange	Romania	Bucharest Stock Exchange
Europe	EASDAQ	Taiwan	Taiwan Stock Exchange
Finland	Helsinki Exchanges	Uzbekistan	Tashkent Republican Stock Exchange
France	Paris Stock Exchange		
Germany	Deutsche Börse		
Hong Kong	Stock Exchange of Hong Kong		
Hungary	Budapest Stock Exchange		
Italy	Rome Stock Exchange		
Iran	Tehran Stock Exchange		
Japan	Tokyo Stock Exchange		
Jordan	Amman Stock Exchange		
Korea	Korea Stock Exchange		
Latvia	Riga Stock Exchange		
Lithuania	National Stock Exchange of Lithuania		

*Continued on next page

In Illustration 12-5, we provide a list of countries that do and do not allow the use of IAS financial statements (statements prepared in conformity with IAS) for listing on foreign exchanges. In many cases, such as in the United States, companies on the "allowed" list must reconcile the income reported in their financial statements (whether based on IAS GAAP or their local GAAP) to the GAAP of the country in which they want to list. The specific requirements for listing, and the extent and nature of reconciliation required, vary widely from one exchange to another. In the following section of this chapter, we discuss the requirements for foreign companies to list on the U.S. stock exchanges.

ILLUSTRATION 12–5
(continued)

Countries that **Allow*** IAS Financial Statements for Foreign Listings		Countries that **Do Not Allow** IAS Financial Statements for Foreign Listings	
Country	Exchange	Country	Exchange
Luxembourg	Luxembourg Stock Exchange		
Macedonia	Macedonian Stock Exchange		
Malaysia	Kuala Lumpur Stock Exchange		
Malta	Malta Stock Exchange		
Netherlands	Amsterdam Stock Exchange		
New Zealand	New Zealand Stock Exchange		
Norway	Oslo Stock Exchange		
Pakistan	Karachi Stock Exchange		
Peru	Lima Stock Exchange		
Poland	Warsaw Stock Exchange		
Singapore	Stock Exchange of Singapore		
Slovakia	Bratislava Stock Exchange		
Slovenia	Ljubljana Stock Exchange		
South Africa	Johannesburg Stock Exchange		
Spain	Madrid Stock Exchange		
Sri Lanka	Colombo Stock Exchange		
Sweden	Stockholm Stock Exchange		
Switzerland	Swiss Stock Exchange		
Thailand	The Stock Exchange of Thailand		
Turkey	Istanbul Stock Exchange		
United Kingdom	London Stock Exchange		
United States	New York Stock Exchange, NASDAQ, American Stock Exchange		
Zimbabwe	Zimbabwe Stock Exchange		

*Although all the countries in this list allow IAS-based financial statements for foreign listings, additional requirements are unique to each country and its exchanges. For example, in the United States, firms that submit financial statements prepared under IAS GAAP must include a reconciliation to U.S. GAAP in order to be acceptable.

The FASB has issued the second edition of a special report comparing U.S. GAAP to IASC standards, entitled "The IASC–U.S. Comparison Project: A Report on the Similarities and Differences between IASC Standards and U.S. GAAP." The report provides information useful in comparing U.S. companies to companies reporting under IASC standards.[12]

Illustration 12-6 lists the total number of firms registered on various stock exchanges throughout the world as of May 1999. In addition, the proportion of domestic and foreign companies listed on these exchanges is provided. In the

[12]The report may be ordered from the FASB Order Dept. at (203) 847-0700, ext. 555, or fasbpubs@fasb.org, for $40.00 each.

ILLUSTRATION 12–6

Number of Domestic and Foreign Companies Listed on Major Stock Exchanges May 1999

Exchange	Total Number of Companies	Domestic Companies		Foreign Companies	
		Number	Percentage	Number	Percentage
NYSE	2,652	2,267	0.85	385	0.15
Nasdaq	4,894	4,477	0.91	418	0.09
AMEX	705	642	0.91	63	0.09
Toronto	1,412	1,363	0.97	49	0.03
Sao Paulo	492	491	0.998	1	0.002
Rio de Janeiro	531	530	0.998	1	0.002
Germany	3,872	775	0.19	3,117	0.81
London	2,863	2,361	0.82	502	0.18
Paris	1,121	946	0.84	175	0.16
Hong Kong	685	671	0.98	14	0.02
Tokyo	1,901	1,854	0.98	47	0.02
Australian	1,218	1,157	0.95	61	0.05

Source: Adapted from the web site of the Federation Internationale des Bourses de Valeurs (FIBV, International Federation of Stock Exchanges), www.fibv.com.

United States, the NYSE has approximately 85% of its firms from the United States and 15 percent from foreign countries. In contrast, the stock exchange in Germany reports 81 percent of its firms as foreign, while in Tokyo only 2 percent of the listed firms are foreign.

SEC REGISTRATION AND U.S. LISTING FOR NON-U.S. COMPANIES

In this section, we consider how international firms might be able to issue securities in the United States. A registration with the SEC under the 1934 Securities Act is mandatory for non-U.S. companies that intend to list on a U.S. stock market. Such a registration can be achieved for firms that intend to do only a listing by filing a form *20-F* with the SEC. However, if non-U.S. companies issue securities in the United States along with the U.S. listing, then the sale of these securities must be registered under the 1933 Securities Act, typically through the filing of an *F-1* statement. This registration must be declared effective subsequent to the actual listing or the offering of securities for sale in the event of an equity capital acquisition program. The informational requirements of a *20-F* and an *F-1* are reasonably similar. Foreign companies are required to comply with the SEC continuous reporting requirements in a manner very similar to that of U.S.-listed companies. Annual reporting requirements for U.S. companies involve filing a form *10-K*, and in the case of non-U.S. companies, involve filing a form *20-F* with the

SEC. Under the Securities Act of 1934, a non-U.S. company that registered with the SEC and listed its shares on a U.S. exchange would have to file *annual* reports on forms *20-F* and *interim* reports on forms *6-K* in order to keep the registration "current."

"The U.S. rejected a plan Wednesday that would have created an international accounting model for multinational companies to use when seeking to obtain a stock listing. The U.S. Financial Accounting Standards Board said the International Accounting Standards Committee's proposal wasn't adequate. The FASB said the plan didn't create a high-quality, independent standard setter that would be acceptable globally."[13]

20-F Statement

The *20-F* filing is similar to the *10-K* filing required of any publicly held domestic U.S. company, but the *20-F* allows the non-U.S. company to retain its local GAAP reporting, so long as it meets one of two alternative conditions for explaining any differences between the reported numbers and numbers derived under U.S. GAAP. The firm may either (1) reconcile net income and the shareholders' equity, thus showing earnings based on U.S. GAAP; or (2) fully disclose all financial information required of U.S. firms, including such detailed information as segmental disclosures.

The *20-F* is comprised of various subsections, each of which provides detailed information on the company and the securities issues in the United States. The key information provided in the *20-F* includes:

- A description of the firm's business model, its legal structure, regulatory framework, its management, shareholders, management discussion and analysis (MD&A) statement, and information on the structure of the company's outstanding securities and the markets on which those securities are traded.
- A detailed description of the securities that are being registered for U.S. public trading, including definitions of the rights of the shareholders.
- A description of the company's financial structure and the issuer's financial statements (audited, U.S. GAAP-reconciled, two-year comparative balance sheets and three-year comparative income statements).

F-1 Statement

A first-time offer of securities by any non-U.S. company that comes under the definition of a "foreign private issuer" requires filing an *F-1* statement as the principal registration statement. To qualify as a "foreign private issuer," a non-U.S. company must meet certain conditions of ownership, location of assets, and location of executive officers. The *F-1* forms are typically used only in a first-time offer by non-U.S. issuers, and on subsequent issuance, as long as the company has met certain periodic reporting requirements, a shorter *F-2* or *F-3* form may be used. Though the content and the structure of the registration statement of a non-U.S. issuer can vary from case to case depending on the nature of the offering, there are a few basic characteristics that are common across all types of statements.

---

[13]*Financial Times* (USA edition), "U.S. Board Says Plan for Global Accounting Standard Isn't Adequate," by Jim Kelly, 4/15/99, p. 1.

In a survey of 528 foreign registrants that filed either registration statements or annual reports with the SEC, 158 firms reported no material differences in reconciling to U.S. GAAP net income, 286 reported reconciling items, and 84 prepared their statements using U.S. GAAP. All Japanese companies (19 firms) prepared their statements using U.S. GAAP.[14]

The most important component of a registration statement is the offer prospectus. The prospectus contains all information deemed necessary by the SEC for investors to make an informed investing decision. In addition to the financial statements (reconciled to U.S. GAAP), the prospectus also contains detailed nonfinancial information about the company, such as a description of the business, regulatory structure, management structure, capital structure, shareholding patterns, and shareholder rights. The financial statements must either be presented in accordance with U.S. GAAP or include an audited reconciliation of the home country GAAP numbers to U.S. GAAP. Non-U.S. companies often choose the reconciliation alternative. In addition to the prospectus, the *F-1* statement has information about the articles of association of the company, the registrant's bylaws, and significant legal and contractual obligations of the company. Such information is available on request by any related party.

AMERICAN DEPOSITORY RECEIPTS (ADRs): AN OVERVIEW

With the globalization of the equity markets, a pattern has been established, both among investors and issuers, to go beyond their geographical boundaries to look for investments and sources of capital, respectively. The complexities in the mechanics of the resulting cross-border investing and capital raising may serve to explain, at least in part, the popularity of the Depository Receipt (DR). A DR can be defined as a derivative instrument usually representing a certain fixed number of publicly traded shares of a non-U.S. corporation. A DR that is traded in the United States is called an American Depository Receipt (ADR), while one that is traded globally (outside the United States) is called a Global Depository Receipt (GDR). It is emphasized here that an ADR is identical to a GDR in terms of its structure, operation, and legal perspective. ADRs may trade freely, subject to some conditions, like any U.S. security on one of the major exchanges like the New York Stock Exchange (NYSE), NASDAQ, or the American Stock Exchange (AMEX), or trade Over-the-Counter (OTC) in the "pink sheet" market. The ADR is treated similarly to a domestic security for the purposes of clearance, settlement, transfer, and ownership.

An intermediary known as the Depository Bank (DR bank) creates ADRs, usually with the consent of the issuing company. The major DR banks are the Bank of New York, J. P. Morgan, and Citibank, who together account for more than 85% of the existing ADR programs at the time of this writing. The DR bank is central to the creation and maintenance of the ADR market. The DR bank provides the interface between the non-U.S. company and the U.S. investors who buy its ADRs from one of the U.S. stock exchanges or from an OTC facilitator. The creation of an ADR involves the purchase of shares of a non-U.S. company from the home

---

[14] *Survey of Financial Statement Reconciliations by Foreign Registrants*, Division of Corporation Finance, Securities and Exchange Commission, May 1, 1993.

markets by the brokers of the DR bank and placement with its custodian. On completion of this step, the bank issues ADRs (denominated in U.S. dollars) in the United States equivalent to the shares that were deposited with the home market custodians. This results not only in the transfer of the trading location of the shares from a home country to the United States, but also in the creation of a dollar-denominated U.S. security that represents the shares of a non-U.S. company. In addition to this type of transfer, during the event of a new public offering, U.S. issuers can create ADRs that represent the newly issued shares, which then can be sold directly to the U.S. investors as a part of the offering.

Types of ADR Programs

ADRs may be classified as follows based on their characteristics:

Unsponsored ADRs: As discussed in the previous section, the DR banks, with consent from the issuer, create most of the ADR programs. However, it is possible for a DR bank to create a DR program without a formal agreement with the issuing non-U.S. company. Such ADR programs, called unsponsored ADRs, usually arise due to existence of a great demand for the company's securities in the U.S. market. However, unsponsored programs are becoming obsolete.

Sponsored ADRs: Sponsored programs account for over 98% of existing ADR programs in the United States. A sponsored program requires an exclusive agreement between the issuing company and its depository bank prior to the creation of the DR program. The bank agrees to issue ADRs to U.S. investors and to undertake ongoing tasks in providing information, as well as disbursements of various payouts (dividends, rights, etc.) that the company may make from time to time. Sponsored ADRs may be of four types, depending on whether the company registers the ADRs with the SEC and/or whether there is a capital campaign concomitant with the creation of the ADR program. It must be understood here that registration with the SEC is mandatory for a company that wants to list its ADRs on a U.S. stock exchange like the NYSE, NASDAQ, or AMEX. If a company chooses not to register with the SEC, it could still raise capital from private equity markets comprised of large institutional investors, and could thus trade the ADRs on the OTC markets. The following table is useful in understanding the various types of ADRs that exist in the markets today.

Types of Sponsored ADR Programs

	No SEC Registration	*SEC Registration*
Not Issuing Capital	Level I	Level II
Issuing Capital	Rule 144 A	Level III

Level I: This method is the simplest way for non-U.S. companies to access the U.S. markets. Under this method, depository banks create an ADR program based on the underlying shares that already trade on the home markets. There is *no* capital raised, and the ADRs are *not* listed on the U.S. markets. Companies must file an *F-6* with the SEC, which requires them to disclose some preliminary information about their operations and their finances. There is no need for a

U.S. GAAP reconciliation, and Level I issuers are exempt from continuous reporting with the SEC (as required by publicly traded U.S. companies). Level I programs are often used by non-U.S. companies as a method to familiarize themselves with U.S. equity markets and also to evaluate potential interest in their stock. As of year-end 1998, there were over 800 outstanding Level I programs. These issues are not traded publicly on U.S. exchanges. Until April 1998, Level I issues were traded on electronic bulletin boards that were part of the OTC market, but subsequent to an SEC rule change, trading in these issues is now confined to the "pink sheet" market.

Level II: These types of ADRs are similar to Level I since they do not involve raising new capital, but in contrast to Level I, Level II issues are registered with the U.S. SEC and listed on a major U.S. stock exchange. A U.S. SEC registration and an exchange listing require the company to file with the SEC an *F-6* registration of their ADRs and a *20-F* registration statement listing certain financial disclosures, including a reconciliation of the company's financial statements to U.S. GAAP. Level II ADRs have greater visibility because of their public listing.

Level III: Firms that want to raise capital from the public equity markets in the United States and also to list on a major U.S. stock exchange use the Level III ADRs. These programs comply with various rules and regulations of the SEC and with the requirements of the stock exchange on which they are traded. Level III ADRs are a part of a capital program and are accompanied by a full SEC registration. At the time of the equity offering, a non-U.S. company files a form *F-1* in order to register the shares underlying the Level III ADRs. Investors are informed of all material aspects of the firm and its business. Financial statements are prepared including a U.S. GAAP reconciliation, and firms agree to meet annual reporting requirements by filing form *20-F* and other annual financial disclosures.

Rule 144A: Public offerings in the United States by non-U.S. issuers require a registration of their securities under the Securities Act of 1934. However, there are exemptions from such registration requirements for private placements. Rule 144A ADRs are those ADRs that are placed privately among large institutional buyers with over 100 million dollars under management (known as QIB firms) with restrictions on the subsequent trading of these securities. Rule 144A ADRs are neither publicly traded nor listed on any U.S. stock exchanges and can be exchanged only among QIBs. Firms, especially those from emerging markets, have favored the use of this 144A market for raising capital from the private placement market since they can do so without the costly process of preparing a U.S. GAAP reconciliation and without reporting the detailed disclosures that are required for an SEC registration.

SUMMARY

1. *Describe how the changing world environment is leading to an increased focus on international accounting standards.* A dramatic rise in cross-border financial activity and the resulting internationalization of equity markets since the late 1980s have transformed the investor profiles of many companies. The movement has been away from a primarily debt-financed business world, in which a relatively informal flow of

information between companies and creditors sufficed, to a primarily equity-financed environment in which more financial communication is demanded.

2. *Explain some differences in accounting methods as they are applied internationally.* Some of the areas in which important differences arise include the accounting for goodwill, inventories, research and development expenditures, business combinations, fixed assets and depreciation, long-term leases, and pension plans. Differences in format and terminology used in financial statements are also common.

3. *List five major classifications of accounting models used in different geographical regions.* Accounting models are usually divided into five geographical classifications: Anglo-Saxon (United States), Anglo-Saxon (United Kingdom), German, Latin, and Asia-Pacific. Each area's accounting evolved according to the needs and objectives of financial reporting for that community. For instance, in Germany, there is a high correlation between tax and financial reporting, resulting in more conservative reporting; while in the United States, firms are financed primarily through equity markets, and hence the focus is on investor information.

4. *Describe the role of the International Accounting Standards Committee in establishing international accounting standards.* Since 1973, the IASC has issued 39 standards with the objective of providing guidance to companies in financial reporting. The IASC works with accounting standard-setting bodies in various countries in an attempt to gain widespread acceptance of its standards.

5. *List the steps that a non-U.S. company must follow to list its shares on a U.S. stock market.* A registration with the SEC under the 1934 Securities Act is mandatory for non-U.S. companies that intend to list on a U.S. stock market. Such a registration can be achieved for firms that intend to do only a listing by filing a form *20-F* with the SEC. However, if non-U.S. companies issue securities in the United States along with the U.S. listing, then the sale of these securities must be registered under the 1933 Securities Act, typically through the filing of an *F-1* statement. This registration must be declared effective subsequent to the actual listing or the offering of securities for sale in the event of an equity capital acquisition program.

6. *Explain the role of form 20-F filed with the Securities and Exchange Commission.* The *20-F* allows the non-U.S. company to retain its local GAAP reporting and still be able to list on a U.S. stock exchange, so long as it meets one of two alternative conditions for explaining any differences between the reported numbers and numbers derived under U.S. GAAP. The firm may either (1) reconcile net income and the shareholders equity, thus showing earnings based on U.S. GAAP; or (2) fully disclose all financial information required of U.S. firms, including such detailed information as segmental disclosures.

7. *Indicate the role of American Depository Receipts in the issuing of securities of non-U.S. companies in the United States.* A depository receipt (DR) is a derivative instrument usually representing a certain fixed number of publicly traded shares of a non-U.S. corporation. A DR that is traded in the United States is called an American Depository Receipt (ADR). ADRs may trade freely, subject to some conditions, like any U.S. security on one of the major exchanges like the New York Stock Exchange (NYSE), NASDAQ, or the American Stock Exchange (AMEX), or trade Over-the-Counter (OTC) in the "pink sheet" market. The ADR is treated similarly to a domestic security for the purposes of clearance, settlement, transfer, and ownership.

QUESTIONS

1. What is the rationale for the harmonization of international accounting standards?

2. Why is the SEC so reluctant to accept IAS in allowing firms to issue securities in the U.S. stock market?

3. Discuss the types of ADRs that non-U.S. companies might use to access the U.S. markets.

4. Describe the attitude of the FASB toward the IASC (International Accounting Standards Committee).

5. How does the FASB view its role in the development of an international accounting system?

6. List and briefly comment on each of the eight basic functions identified by the FASB in its 1998 report on the future of international accounting as essential for a high-quality international accounting standard setter.

EXERCISES

EXERCISE 12-1   Convert Balance Sheet to U.S Format
Examine Glaxo Wellcome's balance sheet in Illustration 12-4. Recast the balance sheet to conform to a traditional U.S. balance sheet format.

EXERCISE 12-2   **IASC Issues**

The International Accounting Standards Committee's (IASC) web address is www.iasc.org.uk. On this web page, there is a section labeled "news." List some of the recent issues affecting the IASC.

EXERCISE 12-3   **World-Wide Web Exercise**

The International Federation of Accountants' web address is www.ifac.org. On this page is a section labeled "articles and speeches." Choose one of the items on this page and write a brief description.

PROBLEMS

PROBLEM 12-1   **U.S. GAAP Reconciliation**

The International House of Doughnuts (IHOD) maintains its financial statements following non-U.S. GAAP. The income statement and balance sheet are as follows:

IHOD
Income Statement

	2001		2002	
Sales	2,000,000	FC	2,200,000	FC
Cost of Goods Sold	1,500,000		1,600,000	
Gross Margin	500,000		600,000	
Selling and Administration Expense	300,000		310,000	
Income Before Tax	200,000		290,000	
Tax Expense	60,000		87,000	
Net Income	140,000	FC	203,000	FC

IHOD
Balance Sheet

	2001		2002	
Cash	40,000	FC	44,000	FC
Accounts Receivable	300,000		330,000	
Inventory	320,000		319,000	
Current Assets	660,000		693,000	
Deferred Charges	40,000		65,000	
Gross Fixed Assets	700,000		750,000	
Less: Accumulated Depreciation	(400,000)		(420,000)	
Total Assets	1,000,000	FC	1,088,000	FC
Accounts Payable	200,000	FC	213,333	FC
Notes Payable	100,000		100,000	
Accrued Payables	80,000		88,000	
Current Liabilities	380,000		401,333	
Bonds Payable	200,000		200,000	
Common Stock	230,000		235,767	
Retained Earnings and Reserves	190,000		250,900	
Total Liabilities and Equity	1,000,000	FC	1,088,000	FC

FC denotes foreign currency.

IHOD wishes to issue securities in the United States and needs to prepare a reconciliation schedule to U.S. GAAP. The following differences with U.S. GAAP are noted. (All amounts are stated in FC.)

1. Goodwill, in the amount of 100,000 FC, acquired in an acquisition at the beginning of 2001 was written off to equity. Goodwill in the United States would have been amortized over 20 years.

2. Certain development costs (25,000 FC) were capitalized on the balance sheet in 2002. None of this amount has been amortized. In the United States, these costs would have been considered R&D expense.

3. Interest incurred on a bond issued strictly for the construction of a building was expensed in 2001 and 2002. The amount expensed was 20,000 FC in each year. The building was completed in 2003.

4. Deferred taxes have not been recorded (i.e., tax expense reflects the amount of taxes actually owed). Timing differences between tax and accounting were 250,000 FC and 300,000 FC in 2001 and 2002, respectively. Both timing differences resulted in taxable income being lower than accounting pretax income. Cumulative timing differences at the beginning of 2001 were 100,000 FC. The tax rate is 30%. These amounts reflect adjustments, if needed, for all above items.

Required:
Prepare a schedule to reconcile IHOD's net income to U.S. GAAP net income.

PROBLEM 12-2 Journal Entries to Reconcile to U.S. GAAP Net Income

Required:
Using the information in Problem 12-1, prepare the journal entries needed to convert the financial statements to U.S. GAAP for the year 2002. Assume that no entries have been made to convert the statements in 2001.

PROBLEM 12-3 Reconciliation to U.S. GAAP Stockholders' Equity

Required:
Using the information in Problem 12-1, prepare a schedule to reconcile stockholders' equity to U.S. GAAP.

PROBLEM 12-4 International Accounting Differences
Acme Limited presented its balance sheet using U.S. GAAP and also using non-U.S. GAAP as follows [stated in foreign currency (FC)]:

At December 31, 2002	U.S. GAAP	Non-U.S. GAAP
Cash	40,000 FC	40,000 FC
Accounts Receivable	300,000	300,000
Inventory	320,000	345,000
Current Assets	660,000	685,000
Deferred Charges and Goodwill	40,000	65,000
Gross Fixed Assets	700,000	750,000
Less: Accumulated Depreciation	(400,000)	(420,000)
Total Assets	1,000,000 FC	1,080,000 FC
Current Liabilities	350,000 FC	380,000 FC
Bonds Payable	200,000	200,000
Deferred Tax Liability	30,000	20,000
Common Stock	230,000	230,000
Retained Earnings and Reserves	190,000	250,000
Total Liabilities and Equity	1,000,000 FC	1,080,000 FC

Required:
For each difference between U.S. GAAP and non-U.S. GAAP, speculate as to likely reasons for the differing amounts on the balance sheet.

PROBLEM 12-5 International Reporting
UFO Inc. presented its balance sheet using non-U.S. GAAP. In order to assist the users of the financial statements, the company also provided its financial statements in U.S. dollars.

	Income Statement	
For the Year Ending 2002	*French Franc*	*U.S. Dollar*
Sales	4,000,000	800,000
Cost of Goods Sold	2,000,000	400,000
Gross Margin	2,000,000	400,000
Selling and Administrative Expenses	750,000	150,000
Income Before Tax	1,250,000	250,000
Tax Expense	375,000	75,000
Net Income	875,000	175,000

	Balance Sheet	
At December 31, 2002	*French Franc*	*U.S. Dollar*
Cash	200,000	40,000
Accounts Receivable	1,500,000	300,000
Inventory	1,725,000	345,000
Current Assets	3,425,000	685,000
Deferred Charges and Goodwill	325,000	65,000
Gross Fixed Assets	3,750,000	750,000
Less: Accumulated Depreciation	(2,100,000)	(420,000)
Total Assets	5,400,000	1,080,000
Current Liabilities	1,900,000	380,000
Bonds Payable	1,000,000	200,000
Deferred Tax Liability	100,000	20,000
Common Stock	1,150,000	230,000
Retained Earnings and Reserves	1,250,000	250,000
Total Liabilities and Equity	5,400,000	1,080,000

Note: These financial statements are prepared in accordance with French GAAP and have been converted into U.S. dollars. (In this problem, we assume the foreign currency exchange rate is constant. More realistic assumptions about exchange rates are addressed in Chapter 14.)

Required:
1. Does restatement into U.S. dollars necessarily imply conformity with U.S. GAAP? Why or why not?
2. Suppose that the following differences existed between French GAAP and U.S. GAAP (all amounts stated in U.S. dollars):
   (a) Over the past several years, a $45,000 reserve for self-insurance was included in current liabilities. This reserve is not allowed by U.S. GAAP. Current period additions to the reserve were $15,000 (included in cost of goods sold).
   (b) Fixed assets have been revalued. If fixed assets were recorded using historical costs, they would have been recorded at $675,000 gross with $395,000 of accumulated depreciation as of the end of 2002. Depreciation expense would have been $40,000 for

the year 2002 instead of $47,500 (depreciation expense is included in selling and administrative expenses).

(c) All other differences are considered immaterial.

Restate the balance sheet and the income statement to conform to U.S. GAAP.

PROBLEM 12-6 **Journal Entries to Convert Financial Statements to U.S. GAAP**

Required:

Using the information from Problem 12-5, prepare the journal entries needed to convert the financial statements to U.S. GAAP at the end of 2002.

13

ACCOUNTING FOR FOREIGN CURRENCY TRANSACTIONS

LEARNING OBJECTIVES

1. Distinguish between the terms "measured" and "denominated."
2. Describe a foreign currency transaction.
3. Understand some of the more common foreign currency transactions.
4. Identify three stages of concern to accountants for foreign currency transactions and explain the steps used to translate foreign currency transactions for each stage.
5. Explain the use of an economic hedge of a net investment in a foreign entity.
6. Describe a forward exchange contract.
7. Identify some of the common situations in which a forward exchange contract can be used as a hedge.
8. Describe a derivative instrument and understand how it may be used as a hedge.
9. Explain the accounting for the gains or losses on forecasted transactions.

IN THE NEWS

In a boost to its international expansion efforts, UtiliCorp United Inc. and a partner won the bidding for an Australian natural-gas company, agreeing to pay $1.2 billion. The transaction adds to UtiliCorp's nearly $2 billion spending spree in Australia and New Zealand, where it has been buying electricity and natural-gas distribution companies over the past five years. UtiliCorp became the first American company to acquire a utility in Australia in 1995 with its purchase of United Energy.[1]

Many companies in the United States engage in international activities such as exporting or importing goods, establishing a foreign branch, or holding an equity investment in a foreign company. Recording and reporting problems are encountered when transactions with a foreign company or the financial statements of a foreign branch or investee are measured in a currency other than U.S. currency. Transactions to be settled in a foreign currency must be translated—that is, expressed in dollars—before they can be aggregated with the domestic transactions of the U.S. firm. When a foreign branch or investee maintains its accounts and prepares its financial statements in terms of the currency of the country in which it is domiciled, the accounts must be translated from the foreign currency into

---

[1] *WSJ*, "UtiliCorp Wins Australian Firm for $1.2 Billion," by Kathryn Kranhold, 3/15/99, p. B13.

dollars before financial statements for the combined entity are prepared. Translation is necessary because useful financial reports cannot be prepared until all transactions and account balances are stated in a common unit of currency.

Because of the widespread involvement of U.S. companies in foreign activities, accountants must be familiar with the problems associated with accounting for those activities. The expansion of international business has been of particular concern to accountants because of developments in the worldwide monetary system. These developments, coupled with the existence of a number of acceptable methods of translating foreign financial statements and reporting gains or losses on foreign currency fluctuations, have drawn the attention of the FASB at various points in time.[2] This chapter includes a discussion of the nature and use of exchange rates in the translation process, as well as the accounting standards applied in the translation of transactions measured in a foreign currency. The translation of accounts maintained in terms of a foreign currency is discussed in the next chapter.

EXCHANGE RATES—MEANS OF TRANSLATION

Transactions that are to be settled in a foreign currency and financial statements of an affiliate maintained in terms of a foreign currency are translated (converted) into dollars by multiplying the number of units of the foreign currency by a direct exchange rate. Thus, *translation* is the process of expressing monetary amounts that are stated in terms of a foreign currency in the currency of the reporting entity by using an appropriate exchange rate. An *exchange rate* "is the ratio between a unit of one currency and the amount of another currency for which that unit can be exchanged at a particular time."

A *direct exchange quotation* is one in which the exchange rate is quoted in terms of how many units of the domestic currency can be converted into *one unit of foreign currency.* For example, a direct quotation of U.S. dollars for one British pound of 1.517 means that $1.517 could be exchanged for one British pound. To translate pounds into dollars, the number of pounds is multiplied by the direct exchange rate expressed in dollars per pound. Exchange rates are also stated in terms of converting *one unit of the domestic currency* into units of a foreign currency, which is called an *indirect quotation.* In the example above, one U.S. dollar could be converted into .6592 pounds (1.00/1.517). To translate pounds into dollars, the number of pounds could also be divided by the indirect exchange rate.

Exchange rates may be quoted for the immediate delivery of currencies exchanged (*spot rate*), or for future delivery (*forward* or *future rate*) of currencies exchanged. The forward rate is an exchange rate established at the time a forward exchange contract is negotiated. A *forward exchange contract* is a contract to exchange at a specified rate (the *forward rate*) currencies of different countries on a stipulated future date. Before the currencies are exchanged, the spot rate may move above or below the contracted forward exchange rate, but this has no effect on the forward rate established when the forward exchange contract was negotiated. In both the spot and forward markets, a foreign exchange trader provides a quotation

---

[2]The discussion in this chapter is based primarily on the accounting prescribed in *SFAS No. 52,* "Foreign Currency Translation" (Norwalk, CT: FASB, 1981), as modified in *SFAS No. 133,* "Accounting for Derivative Instruments and Hedging Activities" (Norwalk, CT: FASB, 1998).

for buying (the *bid rate*) and a quotation for selling (the *offer rate*) foreign currency. The trader's buying rate will be lower than the quoted selling rate, and the spread between the two rates is profit for the trader. Exchange rates are reported daily in terms of both direct and indirect quotations (see Illustration 13-1) in the financial section of many newspapers.

Before the 1970s, rates of exchange of free market countries were controlled to some extent by member countries of the International Monetary Fund. Most of the member countries agreed to establish exchange rates in terms of U.S. dollars and gold. Although the actual rate was free to fluctuate, the countries that established *official* or *fixed* rates agreed to maintain the actual rate within 1% (2% after 1971) of the official rate by buying or selling U.S. dollars or gold. Because of pressure on the dollar, the United States in 1971 suspended its commitment to convert dollars into gold at $35 per ounce. The relationship between major currencies is now determined largely by supply and demand factors, called *floating rates.* As a result, significant realignments have occurred between the currencies of various countries over a relatively short period of time.

ILLUSTRATION 13–1

Exchange Rates

CURRENCY TRADING

Thursday, September 23, 1999

EXCHANGE RATES

The New York foreign exchange mid-range rates below apply to trading among banks in amounts of $1 million and more, as quoted at 4 P.M. Eastern time by Reuters and other sources. Retail transactions provide fewer units of foreign currency per dollar. Rates for the 11 Euro currency countries are derived from the latest dollar-euro rate using the exchange ratios set 1/1/99.

Country	U.S. $ equiv. Thu	U.S. $ equiv. Wed	Currency per U.S. $ Thu	Currency per U.S. $ Wed
Argentina (Peso)	1.0002	1.0002	.9998	.9998
Australia (Dollar)	.6489	.6510	1.5410	1.5360
Austria (Schilling)	.07634	.07591	13.100	13.174
Bahrain (Dinar)	2.6525	2.6525	.3770	.3770
Belgium (Franc)	.0260	.0259	38.4045	38.6195
Brazil (Real)	.5249	.5249	1.9050	1.8890
Britain (Pound)	1.6459	1.6290	.6075	.6139
1-month forward	1.6461	1.6292	.6076	.6138
3-months forward	1.6296	6.073	.6136	.6465
6-months forward	1.6468	1.6300	.6072	.6135
Canada (Dollar)	.6788	.6801	1.4731	1.4704
1-month forward	.6793	.6805	1.4722	1.4694
3-months forward	.6801	.6813	1.4704	1.4677
6-months forward	.6817	.6829	1.4670	1.4643
Chile (Peso) (d)	.001891	.001896	528.85	527.55
China (Renminbi)	.1208	.1208	8.2776	8.2777
Colombia (Peso)	.0005010	.0005010	1996.00	1996.20
Czech. Rep. (Koruna)				
Commercial rate	.02899	.02895	34.500	34.543
Denmark (Krone)	.1413	.1406	7.0747	7.1145
Ecuador (Sucre)				
Floating rate	.00007246	.00007788	13800.00	12840.00
Finland (Markka)	.1767	.1757	5.6605	5.6922
France (Franc)	.1601	.1592	6.2448	6.2798
1-month forward	.1605	.1596	6.2302	6.2647
3-months forward	.1616	.1607	6.1867	6.2211
6-months forward	.1639	.1630	6.0996	6.1341
Germany (Mark)	.5371	.5340	1.8620	1.8725
1-month forward	.5383	.5353	1.8576	1.8680
3-months forward	.5421	.5391	1.8447	1.8550
6-months forward	.5498	.5467	1.8187	1.8290
Greece (Drachma)	.003211	.003198	311.45	312.67
Hong Kong (Dollar)	.1287	.1287	7.7670	7.7671
Hungary (Forint)	.004100	.004098	243.92	244.02
India (Rupee)	.02297	.02297	43.535	43.535
Indonesia (Rupiah)	.0001133	.0001187	8825.00	8425.00
Ireland (Punt)	1.3346	1.3266	.7493	.7538
Israel (Shekel)	.2342	.2345	4.2695	4.2645
Italy (Lira)	.0005427	.0005395	1842.75	1853.69

Country	U.S. $ equiv. Thu	U.S. $ equiv. Wed	Currency per U.S. $ Thu	Currency per U.S. $ Wed
Japan (Yen)	.009639	.009606	103.75	104.10
1-month forward	.009682	.009650	103.29	103.62
3-months forward	.009816	.009784	101.87	102.21
6-months forward	.010108	.010075	98.93	99.26
Jordan (Dinar)	1.4063	1.4063	.7111	.7111
Kuwait (Dinar)	3.2927	3.2949	.3037	.3035
Lebanon (Pound)	.0006634	.0006634	1507.50	1507.50
Malaysia (Ringgit)	.2632	.2632	3.8001	3.8000
Malta (Lira)	2.5013	2.4869	.3998	.4021
Mexico (Peso)				
Floating rate	.1070	.1077	9.3500	9.2820
Netherlands (Guilder)	.4768	.4740	2.0973	2.1097
New Zealand (Dollar)	.5215	.5232	1.9175	1.9113
Norway (Krone)	.1283	.1271	7.7937	7.8655
Pakistan (Rupee)	.01930	.01930	51.815	51.805
Peru (new Sol)	.2912	.2920	3.4345	3.4250
Philippines (Peso)	.02445	.02484	40.900	40.250
Poland (Zloty)	.2441	.2450	4.0965	4.0815
Portugal (Escudo)	.005241	.005210	190.80	191.94
Russia (Ruble) (a)	.03947	.03938	25.335	25.395
Saudi Arabia (Riyal)	.2666	.2666	3.7503	3.7503
Singapore (Dollar)	.5824	.5856	1.7170	1.7077
Slovak Rep. (Koruna)	.02421	.02399	41.299	41.687
South Africa (Rand)	.1653	.1647	6.0500	6.0700
South Korea (Won)	.0008278	.0008282	1208.00	1207.50
Spain (Peseta)	.006313	.006278	158.40	159.29
Sweden (Krona)	.1220	.1211	8.1993	8.2595
Switzerland (Franc)	.6558	.6507	1.5248	1.5369
1-month forward	.6582	.6530	1.5194	1.5313
3-months forward	.6653	.6602	1.5030	1.5148
6-months forward	.6796	.6743	1.4714	1.4830
Taiwan (Dollar)	.03147	.03147	31.780	31.780
Thailand (Baht)	.02414	.02471	41.425	40.475
Turkey (Lira)	.00000217	.00000216	461290.00	460540.00
United Arab (Dirham)	.2723	.2723	3.6729	3.6730
Uruguay (New Peso)				
Financial	.08521	.08529	11.736	11.725
Venezuela (Bolivar)	.001595	.001597	627.00	626.25
SDR	1.3822	1.3839	.7235	.7226
Euro	1.0504	1.0445	.9520	.9574

Special Drawing Rights (SDR) are based on exchange rates for the U.S., German, British, French, and Japanese currencies. Source: International Monetary Fund.

a-Russian Central Bank rate. Trading band lowered on 8/17/98. b-Government rate. d-Floating rate; trading band suspended on 9/2/99.

The Wall Street Journal daily foreign exchange data from 1996 forward may be purchased through the Readers' Reference Service (413) 592-3600.

Floating rates increase the risk to companies doing business with a foreign company.[3] After a rate change occurs, all transactions are conducted at the new rate until the next change occurs. Because the amount to be received or paid is affected by a change in exchange rates, there is a direct economic impact on a company's operations. For example, a payable to be settled in 100,000 yen has a dollar equivalent value of $434 when the direct exchange rate is $.00434. An increase in the value of the yen to $.00625 would result in an increase in the payable to $625.

The selection of an exchange rate to be used in the translation process is complicated by the fact that some countries maintain multiple exchange rates. The government of a country may maintain official rates that differ from the market-determined rate, depending on the nature of the transaction. For example, a government may establish a set exchange rate for "essential goods and services" and allow the exchange rate for nonessential goods and services to float.

IN THE NEWS

While PepsiCo and Coke are locked in a fierce duel in the United States, where Coke's market share is 44.6% and Pepsi's is around 31%, it's no contest abroad: Coke's international share of 53.9% towers over Pepsi's 14.6%, according to Beverage Marketing Corp., a New York consulting firm. "As Coke moves to near monopoly status in some markets, certain local regulatory authorities could well balk at Coke's dominance," cautions analyst Michael Branca. In several markets, including Brazil, high taxes on soft drinks hurt Coke's sales by making its products too costly. Coke has met with opposition from government regulators in Australia, Italy, and France as well.[4]

MEASURED VERSUS DENOMINATED

Transactions are normally *measured* and recorded in terms of the currency in which the reporting entity prepares its financial statements. This currency is usually the domestic currency of the country in which the company is domiciled and is called the *reporting currency.* In subsequent illustrations the U.S. dollar is assumed to be the reporting currency of U.S.-based firms. Assets and liabilities are *denominated* in a currency if their amounts are fixed in terms of that currency. Thus, a transaction between two U.S. companies requiring payment of a fixed number of dollars is both measured and denominated in dollars. In a transaction between a U.S. firm and a foreign company, the two parties usually negotiate whether the settlement is to be made in dollars or in the domestic currency of the foreign company. If the transaction is to be settled by the payment of a fixed amount of foreign currency, the U.S. firm measures the receivable or payable in dollars, but the transaction is denominated in the specified foreign currency. To the foreign company, the transaction is both measured and denominated in its domestic currency.

---

[3] The concepts of economic exposure and accounting exposure are not identical. A company's economic exposure may be broadly defined as the uncertainty associated with the effect of exchange rate changes on the expected cash flows of the reporting entity. Accounting exposure, in contrast, is directly related to accounts that are translated at the current exchange rate.

[4] *WSJ,* "Australia Blocks Coke's Bid to Purchase Brands of Cadbury Schweppes There," by Nikhil Deogun, 4/9/99, p. A3.

FOREIGN CURRENCY TRANSACTIONS

A transaction that requires settlement in a foreign currency is called a *foreign currency transaction.* A transaction with a foreign company that is to be settled in dollars is not a foreign currency transaction to a U.S. firm because the number of dollars to be received or paid to settle the account is fixed and remains unaffected by subsequent changes in the exchange rate. Thus, a transaction of a U.S. firm with a foreign entity to be settled in dollars is accounted for in the same manner as if the transaction had been with a U.S. company.

A foreign currency transaction will be settled in a foreign currency, and the U.S. firm is exposed to the risk of unfavorable changes in the exchange rate that may occur between the date the transaction is entered into and the date the account is settled. For example, assume that a U.S. firm purchased goods from a French firm and the U.S. firm is to settle the liability by the payment of 20,000 francs. The French firm would measure and record the transaction as normal because the billing is in its reporting currency. Because the billing is in a foreign currency (denominated in francs), the U.S. firm must translate the amount of the foreign currency payable into dollars before the transaction is entered in its accounts. An increase (decrease) in the direct exchange rate will increase (decrease) the number of dollars required to buy the fixed number of francs needed to settle the foreign currency liability.[5] In the case of a foreign currency receivable, a change in the exchange rate between dollars and the foreign currency in which the transaction is denominated increases or decreases the number of dollars that will be obtained when the foreign currency received to settle the receivable is converted into dollars. As will be shown later, the U.S. firm may *hedge,* that is, protect itself against an unfavorable change in the exchange rate.

Some of the more common foreign currency transactions are:

1. Importing or exporting goods or services on credit with the receivable or payable denominated in a foreign currency.
2. Borrowing from or lending to a foreign company with the amount payable or receivable denominated in a foreign currency.
3. Engaging in a transaction with the intention of hedging a net investment in a foreign entity.
4. Entering into a forward contract to buy or sell foreign currency.

Accounting for each of these types of transactions is discussed below.

Importing or Exporting of Goods or Services

Probably the most common form of foreign currency transaction is the exporting or importing of goods or services. In each unsettled foreign currency transaction,

---

[5]The direct exchange rate is often said to be increasing, or the foreign currency unit to be strengthening, if more dollars are needed to acquire the foreign currency units. If fewer dollars are needed, then the foreign currency is weakening or depreciating in relation to the dollar (the direct exchange rate is decreasing).

there are three stages of concern to the accountant. These stages and the appropriate exchange rate to use in translating accounts denominated in units of foreign currency (except for forward exchange contracts) are as follows:

1. *At the date the transaction is first recognized in conformity with GAAP.* Each asset, liability, revenue, expense, gain, or loss arising from the transaction is measured and recorded in dollars by multiplying the units of foreign currency by the current exchange rate. (The *current exchange rate* is the spot rate in effect on a given date.)

2. *At each balance sheet date that occurs between the transaction date and the settlement date.* Recorded balances that are denominated in a foreign currency are adjusted to reflect the current exchange rate in effect at the balance sheet date.

3. *At the settlement date.* In the case of a foreign currency payable, a U.S. firm must convert U.S. dollars into foreign currency units to settle the account, whereas foreign currency units received to settle a foreign currency receivable will be converted into dollars. Although translation is not required, a transaction gain or loss is recognized if the number of dollars paid or received upon conversion does not equal the carrying value of the related payable or receivable.

Application of these rules results in accounting for a change in the exchange rate that occurs during a reporting period as a change in estimate. In other words, using the current exchange rate to translate foreign currency receivables and payables at each measurement date *provides an estimate of the number of dollars to be received or to be paid to settle the amount.* Note that both gains and losses are adjusted to the receivable or payable, resulting in a form of current value accounting. The increase or decrease in the expected cash flow is generally reported as a foreign currency *transaction gain or loss*, sometimes referred to as an *exchange gain or loss*, in determining net income for the current period. Exceptions to this treatment of transaction gains and losses are:

1. Intercompany transactions that are of a long-term financing or capital nature between an investor and an investee that is consolidated, combined, or accounted for by the equity method.

2. Transactions that are designated as, and are effective as, economic hedges of a net investment in a foreign entity.

3. Transactions that are designated as, and are effective as, economic hedges of an identifiable foreign currency commitment.

Transaction gains and losses that result from the first two exceptions are reported as a component of stockholders' equity; gains and losses for exception number 3 are generally deferred and included in the measurement of the related foreign currency transaction.

Importing Transaction To illustrate an importing transaction, assume that on December 1, 2001, a U.S. firm purchased 100 units of inventory from a French firm for 500,000 euros to be paid on March 1, 2002. The firm's fiscal year-end is December 31. Assume further that the U.S. firm did not engage in any form of hedging activity. The spot rate for euros ($/euro) at various times is as follows:

Transaction date—December 1, 2001	$1.05
Balance sheet date—December 31, 2001	1.08
Settlement date—March 1, 2002	1.07

The U.S. firm would prepare the following journal entry on December 1, 2001:

Dec. 1	Purchases	525,000	
	Accounts Payable (500,000 euros × $1.05/euro)		525,000

At the balance sheet date, the payable denominated in foreign currency is adjusted using the exchange rate in effect at the balance sheet date. The entry is

Dec. 31	Transaction Loss	15,000	
	Accounts Payable		15,000

Commitment at 12/31 (500,000 euros × $1.08/euro)	$540,000
Recorded liability	525,000
Adjustment needed	$ 15,000
or	
[500,000 euros × ($1.08 − $1.05) = $15,000]	

If the exchange rate had declined below $1.05,[6] for example, to $1.03, the U.S. firm would have recognized a gain of $10,000 since it would have taken only $515,000 (500,000 euros × $1.03) to settle the $525,000 recorded liability.

Before the settlement date, the U.S. firm must buy euros in order to satisfy the liability. With a change in the exchange rate to $1.07, the firm must pay $535,000 ($5,000 less than the estimated commitment at 12/31) on March 1, 2002, to acquire the 500,000 euros. The journal entry to record the settlement is:

Mar. 1	Accounts Payable	540,000	
	Transaction Gain		5,000
	Cash		535,000

Over the three-month period, the decision to delay making payment cost the firm $10,000. This net amount was recognized as a loss of $15,000 in 2001 and a gain of $5,000 in 2002.

Note in the example above that at December 31, the balance sheet date, a transaction loss was recognized on the open account payable. Such a loss is considered unrealized because the account has not yet been settled or closed. When an account payable (or receivable) is settled or closed, a transaction gain or loss on the settlement is considered realized. The FASB reasoned that users of financial statements are best served by reporting the effects of exchange rate changes on a firm's financial position in the accounting period in which they occur, even though they are unrealized and may reverse or partially reverse in a subsequent period, as in the illustration above. This procedure is criticized, however, because under

---

[6]Throughout this chapter, we often state the exchange rate simply in dollars; thus a rate of $1.05 means $1.05 per unit of foreign currency (euro in this case).

GAAP, gains are not ordinarily reported until realized and because the recognition of unrealized gains and losses results in increased earnings volatility.

Exporting Transaction Now assume that the U.S. firm sold 100 units of inventory for 500,000 euros to a French firm. All other facts are the same as those for the importing transaction. The journal entries to record this exporting transaction on the books of the U.S. company are

December 1, 2001—Date of Transaction

Accounts Receivable (500,000 euros × $1.05)	525,000	
Sales		525,000

December 31, 2001—Balance Sheet Date

Accounts Receivable	15,000	
Transaction Gain		15,000
[(500,000 euros × $1.08 = $540,000) − $525,000]		

March 1, 2002—Settlement Date

Cash (500,000 euros × $1.07)	535,000	
Transaction Loss	5,000	
Accounts Receivable		540,000

A comparison of the entries to record the exporting transaction with those prepared to record an importing transaction reveals that a movement in the exchange rate has an opposite effect on the company's reported income. That is, the increase in the exchange rate from $1.05 to $1.08 resulted in a transaction gain in the case of a foreign currency receivable, whereas a transaction loss was reported in the case of a foreign currency payable. When the exchange rate decreased from $1.08 to $1.07, a transaction loss was reported on the exposed receivable, whereas a transaction gain was reported on the exposed payable. Thus, one tool available to management to hedge a potential loss on a foreign currency receivable is to enter into a transaction to establish a liability to be settled in the same foreign currency. Similarly, a liability to be settled in units of a foreign currency can be hedged by entering into a receivable transaction denominated in the same foreign currency. These relationships are summarized below.

	Balance Sheet		
	Exposed Account	*Effect on Balance Reported*	*Income Statement Effect*
Increase in direct exchange rate			
Importing transaction	Liability	Increase	Transaction loss
Exporting transaction	Receivable	Increase	Transaction gain
Decrease in direct exchange rate			
Importing transaction	Liability	Decrease	Transaction gain
Exporting transaction	Receivable	Decrease	Transaction loss

How should a transaction gain or loss be reported? In the previous examples, the dollar amount recorded in the Sales account and the Purchases account was determined by the exchange rate prevailing at the transaction date. Adjustments to the foreign currency denominated receivable or payable were recorded directly to transaction gain or loss. Under this approach, referred to as the *two-transaction approach,* the sale or purchase is viewed as a transaction separate and distinct from the financing arrangement. Thus, the transaction gain or loss does not result from an operating decision to buy or sell goods or services in a foreign market, but from a financial decision to delay the payment or receipt of foreign currency and not to hedge the exposed receivable or payable against possible unfavorable currency rate changes.

An alternative view that was rejected by the FASB considers the initial transaction and settlement to be one transaction. Supporters of this method contend that the initial transaction is incomplete and the amounts recorded are estimates until such time as the total sacrifice from the purchase (units of domestic currency paid) or the total benefits from the sale (units of domestic currency received) are known. Under this view, transaction gains or losses should be accounted for as an adjustment to the cost of the asset purchased or to the revenue recorded in a sales transaction. There is an obvious implementation problem with this method when the sale or purchase is recorded in one fiscal period and the receipt or payment occurs in another period.

Other Forms of Foreign Borrowing or Lending

In the preceding section, the exporting or importing of inventory was illustrated. Accounting for other types of foreign borrowing or lending transactions is similar; that is, the two-transaction approach is followed in which the cost of an asset acquired or revenue recognized is accounted for independently from the method of settlement. For example, if a fixed asset is acquired from a foreign company on credit, the cost of the asset is the number of foreign currency units that would be paid in a cash transaction multiplied by the exchange rate at the transaction date. The cost of the asset is not adjusted for subsequent changes in the exchange rate, but the liability is adjusted at each balance sheet date on the basis of the exchange rate in effect at that date. The adjustment to the liability is reported currently in income. The amount recorded for interest expense is the equivalent number of U.S. dollars needed to make the interest payment.

Economic Hedge of a Net Investment in a Foreign Entity

A U.S. firm that maintains an equity investment in a foreign company may enter into a foreign currency transaction in an effort to minimize or offset the effects of currency fluctuations on the net investment. A foreign currency transaction is considered a hedge of a net investment in a foreign entity if both of the following conditions are met:

1. The forward contract is designated as, and is effective as, a hedge of the net investment.
2. The foreign currency commitment is firm.

For example, assume that a U.S. firm holds an investment in the net assets of a French company that conducts its business primarily in francs. As will be shown in Chapter 14, the investor company applying the equity method to a less than 50%

owned investee will record its share of the effect of a change in the exchange rate on the net assets of the foreign investee. To hedge against the exposure to exchange rate changes, the U.S. firm may enter into an agreement to borrow francs from a French bank. Assume further that the loan is designated as, and is effective as, a hedge of the net investment in the French company. On subsequent balance sheet dates, both the net assets of the foreign company and the loan denominated in francs are adjusted to reflect the current exchange rate. A gain (loss) from the adjustment of the liability will offset a loss (gain) from the adjustment of the net investment in the foreign company, and a hedge results. Both adjustments are reported as a component of stockholders' equity rather than reported currently in income. However, if the adjustment to the loan balance exceeds the adjustment of the balance of the net investment, the excess is reported in the determination of net income as a transaction gain or loss. The gains or losses accumulated in a separate component of stockholders' equity remain there until part or all of the investment in the foreign company is sold.

Forward Exchange Contracts

A forward exchange contract (forward contract) is an agreement to exchange currencies of two different countries at a specified rate (the forward rate) on a stipulated future date. At the inception of the contract, the forward rate normally varies from the spot rate. *The difference between the two rates is referred to as a discount (premium) if the forward rate is less than (greater than) the spot rate,* as shown here.

	Exchange Rate	
Forward rate	$.175	
		.007 premium
Spot rate	.168	
		.006 discount
Forward rate	.162	

Although there are several reasons why the forward and spot rates may not be the same, the FASB considered the difference normally to reflect the interest rate differential between the two countries.

There are a number of business situations in which a firm may desire to acquire a forward exchange contract. Forward contracts may be classified as follows:

1. Hedges
   a. To hedge a foreign currency exposed receivable or payable position.
   b. To hedge a net investment in a foreign entity (see Illustration 13-2).
   c. To hedge an identifiable foreign currency commitment on an after-tax basis.
2. Speculation
   a. To speculate in foreign currency in anticipation of a gain.

The classification above is important because the accounting for a particular type of forward contract depends on the purpose for which it was obtained. The difference in accounting relates primarily to two questions.

1. How is a transaction gain or loss on the forward contract computed and when should the gain or loss be reported?
2. How is the discount or premium on a forward contract accounted for over the life of the contract?

Hedge of a Foreign Currency Exposed Asset or Exposed Liability Position It has been demonstrated that a U.S. firm buying goods on account from a foreign company or selling goods on credit to a foreign customer in a transaction denominated in a foreign currency is exposed to an added risk that the exchange rate will change unfavorably before the receivable or payable is settled. To eliminate or reduce this risk, the firm may enter into a forward contract to buy or sell foreign currency. For example, assume that a U.S. firm purchased inventory on account for 500,000 euros, payable in 90 days. If the exchange rate is $1.05 on the settlement date, the U.S. firm could acquire 500,000 euros for $525,000 to settle the account payable. However, if the exchange rate is $1.10, it would require $550,000 (500,000 euros × $1.10) to satisfy the firm's obligation. To eliminate the risk, the firm could acquire 500,000 euros when the goods were purchased, but by doing so, it would lose the use of the money for 90 days and the effect would be the same as that of a cash purchase.

Another approach that the firm can take is to shift the risk of a possible unfavorable rate change by negotiating a forward contract to buy a specific number of euros with dollars in 90 days at a specified exchange rate. Conversely, assume that the firm sold goods to a foreign customer for 500,000 euros to be received in 90 days. A decrease in the exchange rate of $.05 would reduce the value of the euros received upon settlement of the receivable balance by $25,000 (500,000 euros × $.05). To hedge this exposed asset position, the firm may negotiate a forward contract to sell the foreign currency for a fixed number of U.S. dollars on the date payment is received. In either case, by obtaining a forward contract, a firm is able to eliminate or reduce the risk of exchange rate fluctuations and fix the number of dollars that are to be received or paid at the settlement date.

Hedge of a Foreign Currency Exposed Liability To illustrate the accounting for a forward contract that is a hedge of an exposed liability position, we will use the same set of assumptions that was used in the section on exporting and importing of goods so that the reader can compare the effects on the operations of the firm from acquiring a forward contract. The assumptions were as follows:

1. On December 1, 2001, a U.S. firm purchased inventory for 500,000 euros payable on March 1, 2002.
2. Spot rates were as follows:

Date of purchase (12/1/01)	$1.05
Balance sheet date (12/31/01)	$1.08
Settlement date (3/1/02)	$1.07

3. The transaction is denominated in euros.

Now assume that on the date of purchase, the U.S. firm entered into a forward contract to buy 500,000 euros on March 1, 2002, for $1.055. It should be noted that in the series of journal entries that follow, the purchase transaction and the forward contract are accounted for as separate transactions. The entries to record the purchase transaction were discussed earlier and will not be elaborated on in the discussion that follows.

The entries to record the purchase and forward exchange contract are:

December 1, 2001—Transaction Date

(1)	Purchases	525,000	
	Accounts Payable (500,000 euros × $1.05)		525,000
	To record purchase of goods on account.		
(2)	Foreign Currency (FC) Receivable from Exchange		
	Dealer (500,000 euros × $1.05)	525,000	
	Premium on Forward Contract*	2,500	
	Dollars Payable to Exchange Dealer		
	(500,000 euros × $1.055)		527,500
	To record forward contract to buy 500,000 euros.		

*A premium is recorded because the forward rate ($1.055) is greater than the spot rate ($1.05). In the entry the total premium is a balancing amount, but it can be computed directly by multiplying the number of foreign currency units by the difference between the forward rate and the spot rate [($1.055 − $1.05) × 500,000 euros = $2,500].

At the date of the transaction, the U.S. firm records the forward contract by recognizing an obligation of $527,500 for the number of dollars to be paid (units of foreign currency to be purchased multiplied by forward rate) to the exchange dealer when the forward contract matures.[7] At the same time, the foreign currency contracted for in the forward contract is recorded. The 500,000 euros to be received are translated into $525,000 using the spot rate ($1.05) in effect at the date of the transaction. Note that the obligation is for a fixed amount of dollars ($527,500), and that it is based on the contracted forward rate, while the right to receive 500,000 euros reflects the units to be received at the current spot rate. In future periods the obligation is not adjusted since it represents a commitment to pay a fixed number of dollars and is unaffected by future changes in the exchange rate. However, because the currency to be received is a foreign currency, fluctuations in the exchange rate are recognized in the reporting period in which a change occurs. The premium is accounted for separately from any transaction gain or loss on the forward contract and is amortized to income over the life of the forward contract using the straight-line method of amortization.

December 31, 2001—Balance Sheet Date

(3)	Transaction Loss	15,000	
	Accounts Payable		15,000
	To record a loss on the liability denominated in euros [(500,000 euros ×		
	$1.08 = $540,000) − $525,000] or [500,000 euros × ($1.08 − $1.05)].		
(4)	FC Receivable from Exchange Dealer	15,000	
	Transaction Gain		15,000
	To record a gain on foreign currency to be received from exchange dealer		
	[(500,000 euros × $1.08 = $540,000) − $525,000].		

---

[7]In practice, a journal entry may not be made to record a forward contract when the contract was negotiated because it represents an executory contract. Although arguments can be made either for or against recording such contracts, in this chapter forward contracts are recorded because it is easier to analyze the subsequent adjustments required to report the effects of a forward contract on the firm's reported income.

[As will be discussed later, the transaction loss in entry (3) and the transaction gain in entry (4) are offset, producing no income statement effect since the exposed position is fully hedged.]

(5)	Amortization Expense	833	
	Premium on Forward Contract		833

To record amortization of premium on forward contract for one month [(1 month expired 3-month life of forward contract) × $2,500].

At December 31, the account payable is adjusted [entry (3)] to reflect the current spot rate since it is denominated in euros. Entries (4) and (5) recognize the two components of the forward contract. In entry (4) a gain or loss on the number of euros contracted for in the forward contract is recorded. Since the forward contract is for the same number of foreign currency units and is for the same period of time as the original purchase contract, the transaction loss on the exposed liability position is offset by the transaction gain on the foreign currency receivable from the exchange broker. In entry (5) the premium on the forward contract is amortized using the straight-line method.

March 1, 2002—Settlement Date

(6)	Accounts Payable	5,000	
	Transaction Gain		5,000

To record a gain from 12/31/01 to 3/1/02 on liability denominated in euros [(500,000 euros × $1.07 = $535,000) − $540,000].

(7)	Transaction Loss	5,000	
	FC Receivable from Exchange Dealer		5,000

To record a loss from 12/31/01 to 3/1/02 on euros to be received from exchange dealer.

(8)	Dollars Payable to Exchange Dealer	527,500	
	Investment in FC	535,000	
	FC Receivable from Exchange Dealer		535,000
	Cash		527,500

To record payment to exchange dealer and receipt of 500,000 euros (500,000 euros × $1.07 = $535,000).

(9)	Accounts Payable	535,000	
	Investment in FC		535,000

To record payment of liability upon transfer of 500,000 euros.

(10)	Amortization Expense	1,667	
	Premium on Forward Contract		1,667

To record amortization of premium on forward contract for two months [(2/3) × $2,500].

At the settlement date, the exposed liability position and the foreign currency receivable related to the forward contract are both adjusted to reflect the current spot rate [entries (6) and (7)]. Other entries are needed to record payment to the exchange dealer in exchange for the 500,000 euros [entry (8)], the delivery of the 500,000 euros to settle the liability related to the original inventory purchase [entry (9)], and amortization of the premium on the forward contract [entry (10)].

By obtaining the forward contract, the firm was able to establish at the transaction date the number of dollars ($527,500) that it would take to acquire the 500,000 euros needed to settle the account with the foreign firm. Note, however, that the cost of the inventory of $525,000 was established on December 1 [entry (1)]. The $2,500 difference between these two numbers is expensed over the life of the contract. If the forward contract had not been obtained, the firm would have had to pay $535,000 to settle the account and would have reported a net loss of $10,000 ($15,000 loss − $5,000 gain) on the exposed liability position. The net gain from entering into the forward contract, however, canceled out the net loss on the exposed liability position.

Hedge of a Foreign Currency Exposed Asset In the above example, the U.S. firm entered into a forward purchase contract to hedge an exposed liability position at a time when the forward rate was at a premium. Accounting for a forward contract entered into as a hedge of an exposed receivable position is based on similar analysis. However, because the U.S. firm will be receiving foreign currency in settlement of the exposed receivable balance, it would enter into a forward contract to sell foreign currency for U.S. dollars. In this case, the receivable from the dealer is denominated in a fixed number of dollars, the amount of which is based on the contracted forward rate, whereas the obligation to the dealer is denominated in a foreign currency, which is translated into dollars using the current spot rate. The difference between the receivable and liability is accounted for as a discount or premium on a forward contract.

Illustration 13-2 compares the entries to record a forward contract to either purchase or sell foreign currency at the transaction date, when the forward rate is at a premium or at a discount. On intervening balance sheet dates, the foreign currency receivable from or payable to the exchange dealer is adjusted to reflect the current spot rate resulting in a gain or loss being recorded in the period that the exchange rate changes. Note that the dollars payable or receivable are recorded at the forward rate and are not adjusted because they represent a fixed obligation or receivable. The discount or premium is amortized to income over the life of the forward contract using the straight-line method.

ILLUSTRATION 13–2

Recording a Forward Contract

Importing Transaction
Exposed payable for 500,000 euros.
Forward contract to buy 500,000 euros for $1.05 per euro.

	Spot Rate—$1.045		Spot Rate—$1.055	
FC Receivable from Exchange Dealer	522,500		527,500	
Premium on Forward Contract*	2,500		—0—	
Discount on Forward Contract**		—0—		2,500
Dollars Payable to Exchange Dealer		525,000		525,000

Exporting Transaction
Exposed receivable for 500,000 euros.
Forward contract to sell 500,000 euros for $1.05 per euro.

	Spot Rate—$1.045		Spot Rate—$1.055	
Dollars Receivable from Exchange Dealer	525,000		525,000	
Discount on Forward Contract**	—0—		2,500	
Premium on Forward Contract**		2,500		—0—
FC Payable to Exchange Dealer		522,500		527,500

*Forward rate > spot rate ($1.05 − $1.045) × 500,000 euros = $2,500.
**Forward rate < spot rate ($1.055 − $1.05) × 500,000 euros = $2,500.

Derivative Instruments After the issuance of *SFAS No. 52* on foreign currency translation, the FASB became aware that firms were using creative instruments with increasing frequency to accomplish their desired hedging, many of which were not included in the scope of *SFAS No. 52.* Consequently, the FASB issued another standard, *SFAS No. 133,* which expanded the scope of hedges that are eligible for the treatment illustrated in the preceding section to include hedges of forecasted foreign currency transactions.

A *derivative instrument* may be defined as a financial instrument that, by its terms at inception or upon occurrence of a specified event, provides the holder (or writer) with the right (or obligation) to participate in some or all of the price changes of another *underlying* value of measure but does not require the holder to own or deliver the underlying value of measure. Thus its value is *derived* from the underlying value of measure. The underlying value of measure may be one or more referenced financial instruments, commodities, or other assets, or other specific items to which a rate, an index of prices, or another market indicator is applied. Derivatives differ from traditional instruments (stocks and bonds, for example) in that the eventual dollar amount of the performance is dependent upon subsequent value changes, rather than upon a static measure, and the eventual outcome is necessarily favorable to one of the parties involved and unfavorable to the other. The cash payments involved are made at the end of the contract rather than at its inception for the most part, and the instruments have consequently been treated in the past in many cases as a type of "off-balance sheet" agreement.

In *SFAS No. 133,* the FASB identified the following as keystones for the accounting for derivative instruments:

- Derivative instruments represent rights or obligations that meet the definitions of assets or liabilities and should be reported in financial statements.
- Fair value is the most relevant measure for financial instruments and the only relevant measure for derivative instruments.
- Only items that are assets or liabilities should be reported as such in the balance sheet.
- Special accounting for items designated as being hedged should be provided only for qualifying items, as demonstrated by an assessment of the expectation of effective offsetting changes in fair values or cash flows during the term of the hedge for the risk being hedged.

Although over a thousand different types of derivative instruments have been created, they are sometimes separated into the following two broad categories:

1. Forward-based derivatives, such as forwards, futures, and swaps, in which either party can *potentially* have a favorable or unfavorable outcome, but not both simultaneously (e.g., both will not simultaneously have favorable outcomes).
2. Option-based derivatives, such as interest rate caps, option contracts, and interest rate floors, in which only *one* party can potentially have a favorable outcome and it agrees to a premium at inception for this potentiality; the other party is paid the premium, and can potentially have only an unfavorable outcome.

Derivative instruments are characterized by the following two attributes: (1) their market value is quite volatile and, with the exception of option-based derivatives, can change from positive to negative quite rapidly; and (2) the entity's exposure to risk is not adequately represented by the amount reported in the books (carrying value) because of the great potential for future losses (and gains). Thus, the FASB's task in establishing standards to account for these instruments is important but not an easy one.

Derivatives are recognized in the balance sheet at their fair value. Determination of that value is based upon the changes in the underlying value of measure (commodity, financial instrument, index, etc.) and assessment of the expected future cash flows. The result is a payable position for one of the involved parties and a receivable position for the other.

Hedge of a Forecasted Transaction   The FASB allows deferral of the income statement recognition of the gains and losses on forecasted transactions if certain criteria are met. Like other gains and losses that are excluded from the income statement, they must be included as components of "other comprehensive income" and reported in the stockholders' equity section of the balance sheet. The criteria for this treatment include the following:

- The forecasted transaction is specifically identifiable at the time of the designation as a single transaction or a group of individual transactions.
- The forecasted transaction is probable and it presents exposure to price changes that are expected to affect earnings and cause variability in cash flows.
- If the variable cash flows relate to a debt security classified as held-to-maturity, the risk being hedged is the risk of cash flow changes due to default or creditworthiness of the obligor, not due to changes in market interest rates.
- The forecasted transaction involves an exchange with an outside (unrelated) party. (When related parties are involved as well as an outside party, the transaction may be eligible, as elaborated upon in the following paragraph.)
- The forecasted transaction does not involve a business combination.

Hedges of forecasted foreign currency transactions may include some intercompany transactions. The hedging of foreign currency intercompany cash flows with foreign currency options is not uncommon. Because of its belief that the accounting for all derivative instruments should be the same, the FASB broadened the scope of hedges that are eligible for the treatment presented earlier in this chapter. If an *intercompany* foreign currency derivative is created, it can only be a hedging instrument in the *consolidated* financial statements *if* the other member enters an offsetting contract with an outside (unaffiliated) party to hedge its exposure; this restriction applies because the standards require that some component with foreign currency exposure must be a party to the hedging transaction. In the stand-alone statements of the subsidiary, however, the intercompany derivative could be designated as a hedge in the absence of third-party involvement.

We next present an illustration of the accounting for a forecasted transaction meeting the criteria identified by the FASB for deferral of the gains or losses.

Illustration   To illustrate the hedge of a forecasted foreign currency transaction with the use of an option, assume the following:

1. On December 1, 2001, a U.S. firm estimates that inventory will be sold to a company in the United Kingdom during January of 2002 for 500,000 euros.

2. Spot rates were as follows (dollars per euro):

December 1, 2001	$1.03
Balance sheet date (12/31/01)	$1.00
February 1, 2002	$0.98

3. The transaction is to be denominated in euros.

4. On December 1, 2001, the company purchases an option for $5,000 to hedge any changes that may occur in the euro. This option (called a ***put option***) allows the firm to sell 500,000 euros at $1.02 with an expiration date of February 1, 2002. The spot rate was $1.03 on this date so the option is "out of the money." At year-end (the balance sheet date), the value of the option in the options market had increased to $14,000, and the spot rate ($1.00) was lower than the exercise rate ($1.02). The option was thus "in the money."

The rationale for the use of the option is as follows. Because the inventory sale is expected to occur in the future (next January) and because the exchange rate may change unfavorably, the company buys an option to sell 500,000 euros at $1.02 or $510,000. When the sale of inventory occurs and the company receives the euros, the firm is subject to any exchange losses. However, because the firm now has an option to sell euros, the company can use the euros that it receives from the sale to deliver on the option. Therefore, if the exchange rate drops below the exercise rate ($1.02), the firm is covered (i.e., the firm exercises the option and sells the 500,000 euros for $510,000). If the exchange rate exceeds the exercise rate, the option will not be exercised.

The entries to record the purchase and forward exchange contract are as follows:

December 1, 2001—Transaction Date

(1)	Option to sell euros	5,000	
	Cash		5,000
	To record purchase of a put option (option to sell currency at a specified price).		

On the balance sheet date (December 31, 2001), the option is adjusted to its market value of $14,000. Note that because a market quotation is used, the value is not calculated using the 12/31/01 spot rate of $1.00. *SFAS No. 133* does not allow split accounting for foreign exchange options. This means that the intrinsic value of the option (the difference between the spot rate and the exercise price) and the part of the option value related to time (and not the intrinsic value) are not separated. Therefore, on December 31, 2001, the following entry is made:

December 31, 2001—Balance Sheet Date

(2)	Option to sell euros	9,000	
	Deferred gain on option (balance sheet equity)		9,000
	To record a gain on the change in option value ($14,000 − $5,000).		

The recognition of the gain is delayed because it qualifies under the criteria designated in *SFAS No. 133*; for example, the forecasted transaction is probable and it presents exposure to price changes that are expected to affect earnings and cause variability in cash flows. Amounts deferred from earnings are reported in other comprehensive income, and are reclassified into earnings in the period during which the hedged forecasted transaction "affects earnings" (for example, when a forecasted sale actually occurs).[8] Note that this deferral lessens the criticism alluded to earlier in this chapter (in the context of import transactions) of increased earnings volatility.

February 1, 2002—Option Expiration Date

(3)	Option to sell euros	6,000	
	Gain on option		6,000

To adjust the option value to its current realizable value of $20,000. The value of the option [($1.02 exercise price less $0.98 spot rate) × 500,000 euros] of $20,000 less the carrying value of the option ($14,000).

(4)	Deferred gain on option (balance sheet equity)	9,000	
	Gain on option		9,000

To transfer the deferred gain into income (realized gain) for the previous change in option value.

(5)	Cash	510,000	
	Option to sell euros		20,000
	Payable to option trader ($.98 × 500,000 euros)		490,000

To exercise the option and settle with the trader.

Disclosure Requirements Although a loss or gain on an exposed liability or receivable position is offset by a gain or loss on a forward contract entered into to hedge the exposed position, the two are accounted for separately, since they are considered independent transactions (i.e., the decision to buy or sell in a foreign market is separate from the decision to hedge the transaction). For reporting purposes, however, the gains or losses may be combined. The firm is required to disclose the aggregate transaction gain or loss included in the determination of net income for the period. A gain or loss on a forward contract is considered a transaction gain or loss. Firms are also required to disclose changes in the exchange rate that occur after the balance sheet date and their effect on unsettled foreign currency transactions, if significant, and the fair value of contractual obligations to deliver cash for which it is practicable to estimate that value.[9]

SFAS No. 133 specifies certain minimal disclosures for derivative instruments and nonderivative instruments designated as qualifying hedging instruments. The disclosures include the objectives of the instruments, the strategies for achieving those objectives, the context needed for understanding them, and the risk management policy. In addition, a description of transactions or items that are hedged must be disclosed for each of the following categories:

- Fair value hedges (includes hedges of the foreign currency exposure of unrecognized firm commitments as well as available-for-sale securities)
- Cash flow hedges (includes forecasted transactions)
- Foreign currency net investment hedges
- All other derivatives

---

[8] *SFAS No. 133,* par. 31, "Accounting for Derivative Instruments and Hedging Activities" (Norwalk, CT: FASB, 1998).

[9] *SFAS No. 107,* "Disclosure about Fair Value of Financial Instruments" (Norwalk, CT: FASB, 1991), par. 10.

All derivative instruments not designated as hedges must be identified as to their purpose, and qualitative disclosures about the use of derivatives are encouraged.

Finally, the amount of net gains or losses from cash flow hedges on derivative instruments that is included in "other comprehensive income" must be shown as a separate classification. The disclosures should include beginning and ending accumulated gains or losses from derivative instruments, the net change during the period from hedging activities, and the net amount reclassified to earnings.

Hedging an Identifiable Foreign Currency Commitment In the preceding discussion of the importing and exporting of goods, the purchase or sale of an asset was recorded on the transaction date. This date is considered the point at which title to the goods is transferred, which is consistent with the recording of a transaction with another domestic company. However, if the U.S. firm at a date earlier than the transaction date made a commitment to a foreign company to sell goods or buy goods, and the price was established in foreign currency at the commitment date, changes in the exchange rate between the commitment date and transaction date would be reflected in the cost or sales price of the asset. For example, assume that a U.S. firm made an agreement on June 1 to buy goods from a French company for 500,000 francs. At this date, the spot rate was $.20, but on the transaction date, when title to the goods transferred and a journal entry was recorded, the spot rate was $.22. The entry to record the purchase is

Purchases (500,000 francs × $.22)	110,000	
Accounts Payable		110,000

Thus, the change in the exchange rate that occurred between the commitment and the transaction date becomes a part of the cost of inventory, rather than being reported as a separate gain or loss item. The company, however, may still acquire a forward contract to hedge against unfavorable rate changes that may occur after the commitment date.

A forward contract is considered a hedge of an identifiable foreign currency commitment if the forward contract is designated as, and is effective as, a hedge of a foreign currency commitment, and the foreign currency commitment is firm. A gain or loss on a forward contract that meets both conditions is deferred and included in the measurement of the related foreign currency transaction when recorded.[10] Thus, the effect of this treatment is to account for the forward contract as an integral part of the importing or exporting transaction. For example, a gain or loss on a forward contract used to hedge a commitment to buy equipment that is to be paid for with foreign currency would be included in the cost of the equipment when it is recorded.

The forward contract, to be a hedge of an identifiable foreign currency commitment, need not be equal to the commitment, nor must there be a linkage between the contract dates. However, if the contract is intended as a hedge of a

---

[10]Losses on a forward contract "shall not be deferred, however, if it is estimated that deferral would lead to recognizing losses in later periods." For example, a loss on a forward contract shall not be deferred if future revenue from the sale or other disposition of an asset is estimated to be less than the sum of (a) the asset's cost, including the deferred loss on the related forward contract, and (b) reasonably predictable costs of sale or disposal (*Statement of Financial Accounting Standards No. 52,* par. 21).

particular foreign currency commitment, management must designate it as such. To the extent that the amount of the forward contract exceeds the amount of the commitment on an after-tax basis, the gain or loss pertaining to that part of the forward contract in excess of the after-tax commitment should not be deferred.[11] Likewise, if the life of the forward contract extends beyond the transaction date, a gain or loss pertaining to the extended period should not be deferred, but should be included in net income currently.

To illustrate the accounting for a forward contract acquired to hedge an identifiable foreign currency commitment, the following facts are assumed:

1. On March 1, 2001, a U.S. firm contracts to sell equipment to a foreign customer for 200,000 German marks. The equipment is expected to cost $60,000 to manufacture and is to be delivered and the account is to be settled on March 1, 2002.

2. On March 1, 2001, the U.S. firm enters into a forward contract to sell 200,000 German marks in 12 months at the forward rate of $.41.

3. Spot rates for German marks on selected dates are

Date	Exchange Rate
March 1, 2001	$.40
December 31, 2001	.395
March 1, 2002	.38

The journal entries to record the forward contract during 2001 are as follows:

March 1, 2001

(1)	Dollars Receivable from Exchange Dealer		
	(200,000 marks × $.41)	82,000	
	Deferred Transaction Adjustment		2,000
	FC Payable to Exchange Dealer (200,000 marks × $.40)		80,000
	To record the forward contract to sell 200,000 German marks.		

December 31, 2001

(2)	FC Payable to Exchange Dealer	1,000	
	Deferred Transaction Adjustment		1,000
	To record gain on foreign currency to be delivered to exchange dealer [$80,000 − (200,000 marks × $.395)].		

There are two major differences between accounting for a contract to hedge an identifiable foreign currency commitment and a contract to hedge a foreign currency exposed asset or liability position. First, the discount or premium on the forward contract "that relates to the commitment period may be included in the measurement of the basis of the related foreign currency transaction when recorded."[12] Second, the transaction gain (or loss if the spot rate was greater than $.40) is deferred rather than reported currently in income. As will be seen in a March 1, 2002, entry [see entry (7) below], these elements are included in the

---

[11]The amount of the gain or loss pertaining to the portion of the forward contract in excess of the commitment and related to the tax impact should be deferred and "included as an offset to the related tax effects in the period in which such tax effects are recognized" (*SFAS No. 52,* par. 21).

[12]Alternatively, a firm may amortize a premium or discount on the forward contract to income over the life of the contract.

determination of the dollar basis of the foreign currency transaction on the transaction date. Since both the discount or premium and transaction gains or losses are eventually closed into the same account, both are accumulated in one account, called Deferred Transaction Adjustment.

On March 1, 2002 (the transaction date), the journal entries are:

(3)	FC Payable to Exchange Dealer	3,000	
	Deferred Transaction Adjustment		3,000
	To record gain on forward contract from 12/31/01 to 3/1/02		
	[$79,000 − (200,000 marks × $.38)].		
(4)	Investment in FC	76,000	
	Sales (200,000 marks × $.38)		76,000
	To record sale of equipment to foreign customer.		
(5)	Cost of Goods Sold	60,000	
	Inventory		60,000
	To record cost of equipment sold.		
(6)	Cash	82,000	
	FC Payable to Exchange Dealer	76,000	
	Investment in FC		76,000
	Dollars Receivable from Exchange Dealer		82,000
	To record settlement of forward contract.		
(7)	Deferred Transaction Adjustment	6,000	
	Sales		6,000
	To close the deferred transaction adjustment account to revenue.		

Most of the entries on March 1, 2002 are self-explanatory. It should be emphasized that the transaction gain or loss on a forward contract acquired to hedge a specific commitment or an exposed asset or liability position is computed on the basis of changes in the spot rates that occurred during the current operating period. In this case the spot rate for German marks decreased from $.395 at the last balance sheet date to $.38 at the transaction date. The transaction gain of $3,000 plus the $1,000 gain from 2001, along with the $2,000 premium on the forward contract, are included as an adjustment to the sales account.

The effect of these transactions on the firm's profitability is as follows:

Sales ($76,000 + $6,000)	$82,000
Cost of goods sold	60,000
Gross profit	$22,000

The number of dollars to be received was locked in by the forward contract at $82,000 and the equipment was expected to cost $60,000. Thus, the forward contract permitted the U.S. firm to lock in an expected profit of $22,000 on the sales contract. If the forward contract had not been obtained, the profit on the contract would have been affected by the exchange rate in effect when payment was received from the German customer. An exchange rate of $.30 would have eliminated any gross profit on the contract (200,000 marks × $.30 = $60,000).

Forward Contracts Acquired to Speculate in the Movement of Foreign Currencies

A forward contract may be acquired for speculative purposes in anticipation of realizing a gain. For example, assume that on December 1, 2001, the spot rate for the British pound is $2.35 and that the 90-day futures rate is $2.36. Further assume that a company expecting the exchange rate to increase to, say, $2.43, enters into a contract on December 1 to acquire £100,000 on March 1, 2002. (A forward contract to sell foreign currency would be negotiated if the firm expected the future spot rate to be lower than the forward rate.) The firm's fiscal year ends on December 31, and on that date the futures rate for pounds to be purchased on March 1, 2002 is $2.37. The spot rate is $2.42 on March 1, 2002. The journal entries to record the transactions are:

December 1, 2001

(1) FC Receivable from the Exchange Dealer	236,000	
Dollars Payable to Exchange Dealer		236,000
To record the forward contract (£100,000 × $2.36).		

This entry recognizes that the U.S. firm has contracted to buy £100,000 in 90 days when the payment of $236,000 is made to the exchange dealer. Both the debit and credit related to a forward contract are measured by multiplying the £100,000 by the forward rate of $2.36. The FASB reasoned that the forward rate should be used because a firm speculating in foreign currency changes is exposed to the risk of movements in the forward rate. Since both accounts are based on the forward rate, there is no separate accounting for any discount or premium on the forward contract.

December 31, 2001

(2) FC Receivable from Exchange Dealer	1,000	
Transaction Gain		1,000
To record gain on foreign currency to be received from exchange dealer [(£100,000 × $2.37 = $237,000) − $236,000] or [£100,000 × ($2.37 − $2.36)].		

The foreign currency receivable is adjusted at the financial statement date since it is denominated in foreign currency units. The amount of the adjustment is computed by multiplying the units of foreign currency to be received by the difference between the forward rate available for the remaining life of the forward contract and the rate last used to value the contract. The transaction gain (or loss) is reported currently in income.

March 1, 2002

(3) FC Receivable from Exchange Dealer	5,000	
Transaction Gain		5,000
To record gain on foreign currency to be received from exchange dealer [(£100,000 × $2.42 = $242,000) − $237,000].		
(4) Dollars Payable to Exchange Dealer	236,000	
Investment in FC	242,000	
Cash		236,000
FC Receivable from Exchange Dealer		242,000
To record payment to exchange dealer and receipt of foreign currency.		
(5) Cash	242,000	
Investment in FC		242,000
To record conversion of pounds into cash.		

On March 1, the firm records any gain or loss as a result of changes in the exchange rate from the last valuation date to the date of the transaction. Upon payment of $236,000 to the exchange dealer, the firm will receive £100,000, which can be converted into $242,000. The total gain of $6,000 recognized over the life of the contract is the difference between the value of the foreign currency received ($242,000)

ILLUSTRATION 13–3

Summary of Accounting for Forward Contracts

Purpose of the Forward Contract	Basis for Valuation of Forward Contract at Balance Sheet Date	Reporting Transaction Gain or Loss	Accounting for Discount or Premium on Forward Contract
1. Hedge of net investment in a foreign entity.	Spot rate at balance sheet date.	Included with translation adjustments in a separate component of stockholders' equity.	Included with translation adjustments in a separate component of stockholders' equity.
2. Hedge of an exposed asset or liability position.	Spot rate at balance sheet date.	Reported currently in determination of income.	Amortized over the life of the forward contract as a component of net income.
3. Hedge of an identifiable foreign currency commitment.	Spot rate at balance sheet date.	Deferred and included in the measurement of the related foreign currency transaction.	Deferred and included in the measurement of related foreign currency transaction or amortized to income over life of contract.
4. Speculation.	Forward rate at balance sheet date available over remaining life of forward contract.	Reported currently in determination of income.	Not accounted for separately.

when the forward contract was exercised and the amount paid ($236,000) to the exchange dealer.

If the firm had entered into a forward contract to sell foreign currency, the accounting would be similar to that above, except the debit in entry (1) is for a fixed amount of dollars to be received; the credit records the obligation to buy foreign currency units for delivery to the exchange dealer. The estimated cost of units to be delivered will vary as the exchange rate fluctuates.

Accounting for forward contracts in accordance with the provisions of *SFAS No. 52* is summarized in Illustration 13-3.

 SUMMARY

1. *Distinguish between the terms "measured" and "denominated."* Transactions are normally **measured** and recorded in terms of the currency in which the reporting entity prepares its financial statements. Assets and liabilities are **denominated** in a currency if their amounts are fixed in terms of that currency.

2. *Describe a foreign currency transaction.* A foreign currency transaction is a transaction that requires settlement in a foreign currency, not in U.S. dollars (for a U.S. firm).

3. *Understand some of the more common foreign currency transactions.* Some common transactions include:

(1) importing or exporting goods or services on credit with the receivable or payable denominated in a foreign currency; (2) borrowing from or lending to a foreign company with the amount payable or receivable denominated in the foreign currency; (3) engaging in a transaction with the intention of hedging a net investment in a foreign entity; and (4) entering into a forward contract to by or sell foreign currency.

4. *Identify three stages of concern to accountants for foreign currency transactions and explain the steps used to translate foreign currency transactions for each stage.* At the initial

date the transaction is recognized (in conformity with GAAP), the account (balance sheet or income statement) arising from the transaction is measured and recorded in dollars by multiplying the foreign currency units by the current exchange rate. At each subsequent balance sheet date until settlement, recorded balances that are denominated in a foreign currency are adjusted to reflect the current exchange rate in effect at the balance sheet date. At the settlement date, the treatment depends on whether the balance to be settled is a foreign currency payable or receivable. If a foreign currency payable is being settled, a U.S. firm must convert U.S. dollars into foreign currency units to settle the account. At the settlement of a foreign currency receivable, the foreign currency units received are converted into dollars.

5. *Explain the use of an economic hedge of a net investment in a foreign entity.* A U.S. firm holding an investment in the net assets of a foreign company that conducts its business primarily in foreign currency units may hedge against the exposure to exchange rate changes by borrowing from a foreign lender, with the loan denominated in the same foreign currency units. Because both the net assets of the foreign company and the loan are adjusted to reflect the current exchange rate, a gain (loss) from the adjustment of the liability will offset a loss (gain) from the adjustment of the net investment.

6. *Describe a forward exchange contract.* A forward ex-

change contract (forward contract) is an agreement to exchange currencies of two different countries at a specified rate (the forward rate) on a stipulated future date. At the inception of the contract, the forward rate is usually different from the spot rate.

7. *Identify some of the common situations in which a forward exchange contract can be used as a hedge.* Hedges may be used to hedge a foreign currency exposed receivable or payable position, to hedge a net investment in a foreign subsidiary, or to hedge an identifiable foreign currency commitment on an after-tax basis.

8. *Describe a derivative instrument and understand how it may be used as a hedge.* A derivative is an executory contract between two parties to be executed at a later date, with the resulting future cash flows dependent on the change in some other underlying measure of value. The eventual dollar amount of the performance is determined by subsequent value changes, and the eventual outcome is necessarily favorable to one of the parties involved and unfavorable to the other.

9. *Explain the accounting for the gains or losses on forecasted transactions.* The FASB allows deferral of the income statement recognition of the gains and losses on forecasted transactions if certain criteria are met. Like other gains and losses that are excluded from the income statement, they are included as components of "other comprehensive income" and reported in the stockholders' equity section of the balance sheet.

QUESTIONS

1. Define currency exchange rates and distinguish between "direct" and "indirect" quotations.

2. Explain why a firm is exposed to an added risk when it enters into a transaction that is to be settled in a foreign currency.

3. Name the three stages of concern to the accountant in accounting for import–export transactions. Briefly explain the accounting for each stage.

4. How should a transaction gain or loss be reported that is related to an unsettled receivable recorded when the firm's inventory was exported?

5. A U.S. firm carried a receivable for 100,000 yen. Assuming that the direct exchange rate declined from $.009 at the date of the transaction to $.006 at the balance sheet date, compute the transaction gain or loss. What balance would be reported for the receivable in the firm's balance sheet?

6. Explain what is meant by the "two-transaction method" in recording exporting or importing transactions. What support is given for this method?

7. Describe a forward exchange contract.

8. Explain the effects on income from hedging a foreign currency exposed net asset position or net liability position.

9. What criteria must be satisfied for a foreign currency transaction to be considered a hedge of an identifiable foreign currency commitment?

10. The FASB classifies forward contracts as those acquired for the purpose of hedging and those acquired for the purpose of speculation. What main differences are there in accounting for these two classifications?

11. How are unrealized transaction gains and losses from hedging an identifiable foreign currency commitment reported?

12. What is a put option, and how might it be used to hedge a forecasted transaction?

13. Define a derivative instrument, and describe the keystones identified by the FASB for the accounting for such instruments.

14. Differentiate between forward-based derivatives and option-based derivatives.

15. List some of the criteria laid out by the FASB that are required for a gain or loss on forecasted transactions to be excluded from the income statement. If these criteria are satisfied, where are the gains or losses reported, and when (if ever) are they shown in the income statement? What is the rationale for this treatment?

EXERCISES

EXERCISE 13-1 Journal Entries

Selco, a U.S. Company, imports and exports tools, shop equipment, and industrial construction supplies. The company uses a periodic inventory system. During April the company entered into the following transactions. All rate quotations are direct exchange rates.

April	3	Purchased power tools from a wholesaler in Japan, on account, at an invoice cost of 1,600,000 yen. On this date the exchange rate for the yen was $.0072.
	5	Sold hand tools on credit that were manufactured in the U.S. to a retail outlet located in West Germany. The invoice price was $2,800. The exchange rate for marks was $.5829.
	9	Sold electric drills on account to a retailer in New Zealand. The invoice price was 16,800 U.S. dollars and the exchange rate for the New Zealand dollar was $.576.
	11	Purchased drill bits on account from a manufacturer located in Belgium. The billing was for 801,282 francs. The exchange rate for francs was $.0312.
	16	Paid 1,000,000 yen on account to the wholesaler for purchases made on April 3. The exchange rate on this date was $.0067.
	18	Settled the accounts payable with the Belgium manufacturer. The exchange rate was $.0368.
	22	Received full payment from the New Zealand retailer. The exchange rate was $.568.
	30	Completed payment on the April 3 purchase. The exchange rate was $.0078.

Required:
Prepare journal entries on the books of Selco to record the transactions listed above.

EXERCISE 13-2 Journal Entries

During December of the current year, Teletex Systems, Inc., a company based in Seattle, Washington, entered into the following transactions:

| Dec. | 10 | Sold seven office computers to a company located in Colombia for 8,541,000 pesos. On this date, the spot rate was 365 pesos per U.S. dollar. |
| | 12 | Purchased computer chips from a company domiciled in Taiwan. The contract was denominated in 500,000 Taiwan dollars. The direct exchange spot rate on this date was $.0391. |

Required:

A. Prepare journal entries to record the transactions above on the books of Teletex Systems, Inc. The company uses a periodic inventory system.

B. Prepare journal entries necessary to adjust the accounts as of December 31. Assume that on December 31 the direct exchange rates were as follows:

| Colombia peso | $.00268 |
| Taiwan dollar | $.0351 |

C. Prepare journal entries to record settlement of both open accounts on January 10. Assume that the direct exchange rates on the settlement dates were as follows:

Colombia peso	$.00320
Taiwan dollar	$.0398

D. Prepare journal entries to record the December 10 transaction, adjust the accounts on December 31, and record settlement of the account on January 10, assuming that the transaction was denominated in dollars rather than pesos. Assume the same exchange rates as those given.

EXERCISE 13-3 **Multiple Choice**

On December 1, 2001, Tuscano Corp. entered into a transaction to import raw materials from a foreign company. The account is to be settled on February 1 with the payment of 60,000 foreign currency units (FCU). On December 1, Tuscano also entered into a forward contract to hedge the exposed position resulting from the import transaction. The forward rate is $.71 per unit of foreign currency. Tuscano Corp. has a December 31 fiscal year-end. Spot rates on relevant dates were:

Date	Per Unit of Foreign Currency
December 1	$.69
December 31	.72
February 1	.73

Required:

Use the data given to select the best answer to each question.

1. The forward contract entered into on December 1 is an example of

   (a) A hedge of an exposed receivable position.
   (b) A hedge of a foreign currency commitment.
   (c) A contract entered into for speculation.
   (d) A hedge of an exposed payable position.

2. The entry to record the forward contract is

(a) Dollars Receivable	42,600	
Premium on Forward Contract		1,200
FCU Payable		41,400
(b) FCU Receivable	42,600	
Premium on Forward Contract		1,200
Dollars Receivable		41,400
(c) Dollars Receivable	42,600	
Discount on Forward Contract		1,200
FCU Payable		41,400
(d) FCU Receivable	41,400	
Premium on Forward Contract	1,200	
Dollars Payable		42,600
(e) None of the above.		

3. On December 31, what will be the adjusted balance in the Accounts Payable account and how much gain or loss was recorded as a result of the adjustment?

	Payable Balance	Gain or Loss Recorded
(a)	$43,200	$1,800 gain
(b)	40,800	2,400 loss
(c)	40,800	2,400 gain
(d)	43,200	1,800 loss

4. What amount of transaction gain or loss from the transaction should be included in the determination of the 2001 net income?

    (a) $2,400 loss.
    (b) $1,800 loss.
    (c) $—0— Because a gain or loss on the forward contract is offset by a loss or gain on the exposed position.
    (d) $2,400 gain.

5. Which of the following statements is *not* true?

    (a) Assuming the account payable is to be settled on February 1, Tuscano Corp. was able to reduce its cash outflow for the purchases as a result of entering into the forward contract.
    (b) During 2002, a transaction loss of $600 was recorded on the forward contract.
    (c) Tuscano Corp. paid $42,600 to complete the forward contract.
    (d) During 2002 a transaction loss of $600 was recorded on the exposed payable.

EXERCISE 13-4   Multiple Choice

Select the best answer for each of the following.

1. The discount or premium on a forward contract entered into as a hedge of an identifiable foreign currency commitment should be

    (a) Included in net income in the period that the forward contract is entered into.
    (b) Deferred and amortized over a period not to exceed 40 years.
    (c) Deferred and included in the measurement of the related foreign currency transaction when recorded.
    (d) Included as a separate item in the equity section of the balance sheet.

2. A forward contract is a hedge of an identifiable foreign currency commitment if

    (a) The forward contract is designated as, and is effective as, a hedge of a foreign currency commitment.
    (b) The foreign currency commitment is firm.
    (c) The amount of the forward contract is equal to the amount of the commitment.
    (d) Both (a) and (b).
    (e) Both (a) and (c).

3. The Carnival Company has a receivable from a foreign customer that is payable in the local currency of the foreign customer. The account receivable for 800,000 local currency units (LCU), has been translated into $280,000 on Carnival's December 31, 2001 balance sheet. On January 15, 2002, the receivable was collected in full when the exchange rate was 4 LCU to $1. What journal entry should Carnival make to record the collection of this receivable?

(a) Cash	200,000	
Accounts Receivable		200,000
(b) Cash	200,000	
Transaction Loss	80,000	
Accounts Receivable		280,000
(c) Cash	200,000	
Deferred Transaction Loss	80,000	
Accounts Receivable		280,000
(d) Cash	280,000	
Accounts Receivable		280,000

4. A foreign currency transaction to a company domiciled in the United States is a transaction in which the amount is

    (a) Measured in a foreign currency.
    (b) Denominated in U.S. dollars.
    (c) Denominated in a foreign currency.
    (d) Measured in U.S. dollars.

5. A direct exchange quotation is one in which the exchange rate is quoted
   (a) In terms of how many units of the domestic currency can be converted into one unit of foreign currency.
   (b) In terms of how many units of the foreign currency can be converted into one unit of the domestic currency.
   (c) For the future delivery of currencies exchanged.
   (d) For the immediate delivery of currencies exchanged.

EXERCISE 13-5 Multiple Choice

Select the best answer for each of the following.

1. A sale of goods by a U.S. company was denominated in a foreign currency. The sale resulted in a receivable that was fixed in terms of the amount of foreign currency that would be received. Exchange rates between the dollar and the currency in which the transaction was denominated changed so that a loss was incurred. This loss should be included as a(n)
   (a) Extraordinary item in the income statement.
   (b) Component of income from continuing operations.
   (c) Separate component of stockholders' equity.
   (d) Deferred item in the balance sheet.

2. A discount or premium on a forward contract is required to be amortized over the life of the forward contract if the contract is classified as a
   (a) Contract to speculate in the movement of exchange rates.
   (b) Hedge of a net investment in a foreign entity.
   (c) Hedge of an exposed asset or liability position.
   (d) Hedge of an identifiable foreign currency commitment.

3. On September 1, 2001, Change Corp. received an order for equipment from a foreign customer for 300,000 units of foreign currency when the U.S. dollar equivalent was $96,000. Change shipped the equipment on October 15, 2001, and billed the customer for 300,000 units of foreign currency when the U.S. dollar equivalent was $110,000. Change received the customer's remittance in full on November 16, 2001, and sold the 300,000 foreign currency units for $105,000. In its income statement for the year ended December 31, 2001, Change should report a foreign exchange loss of
   (a) $9,000
   (b) $5,000
   (c) $14,000
   (d) $—0—

4. McNeil, a U.S. corporation, bought inventory items from a supplier in Germany on November 5, 2001 for 100,000 marks, when the spot rate was $.4395. At McNeil's December 31, 2001 year-end, the spot rate was $.4345. On January 15, 2002, McNeil's bought 100,000 marks at the spot rate of $.4445 and paid the invoice. How much should McNeil report in its income statement for 2001 and 2002 as transaction gain or loss?

2001	*2002*
(a) $—0—	$ 500 loss
(b) $500 loss	$ —0—
(c) $500 loss	$1,000 gain
(d) $500 gain	$1,000 loss

5. During 2001 a U.S. firm sold inventory to a foreign customer. The transaction was denominated in the local currency of the buyer. The direct exchange rate decreased from the date of the transaction to the end of the fiscal period; the rate increased from the

end of the fiscal year to the date the account was settled in 2002. A transaction gain or loss should be recognized

2001	2002
(a) Loss	Loss
(b) Gain	Loss
(c) Loss	Gain
(d) Gain	Gain

(AICPA adapted)

EXERCISE 13-6 **Transaction Gain or Loss**

Agentel Corporation is a U.S.-based importing–exporting company. The company entered into the following transactions during the month of November.

Nov.	6	Purchased merchandise from AGT, a Swiss firm, for 600,000 francs.
	5	Sold merchandise to SLS, Inc., a firm located in Berlin, for $200,000.
	18	Sold merchandise to TNT, Ltd., a British firm, for 130,000 pounds.
	20	Purchased merchandise from SDS, Ltd., a British firm, for $160,000.

All the transactions were unsettled at December 31, Agentel's fiscal year-end. Spot rates are as follows:

		Currency	
Date	*Franc*	*Mark*	*Pound*
November 6	$.490	$.412	$1.520
November 15	.487	.409	1.509
November 18	.476	.414	1.506
November 20	.468	.405	1.498
December 31	.460	.398	1.482

Required:

A. Compute the amount that Agentel would report for each unsettled receivable and payable in its balance sheet prepared at December 31.

B. Compute the transaction gain or loss on each unsettled receivable and payable that would be reported in the income statement prepared for the year ended December 31.

EXERCISE 13-7 **Journal Entries, Income Effect, and Amount of Cash Received**

ASI recently completed the development and installation of an accounting information system for a company located in Munich, Germany. The company considered that all revenue realization criteria were satisfied and accordingly recorded on October 2, 2001, a receivable from the foreign company. The receivable is to be settled in 120 days on February 1 by the delivery of 300,000 German marks. To hedge against an unfavorable change in the foreign exchange rate, ASI acquired a forward contract to sell 300,000 German marks on February 1 for $.4730 per mark. The following exchange rates were quoted:

Date	*Spot Rate*	*Forward Rate* *(Delivery on 2/1)*
October 2	$.4737	$.4730
December 31	.4895	.4810
February 1	.4950	—

ASI is a calendar-year company.

Required:

A. Prepare the journal entries to record the transactions, adjust the accounts on December 31, and settle the receivable and forward contract on February 1.

B. **(1)** Based on the data given above, complete the following table.

	2001	2002
Revenue	_____	_____
Transaction gain (loss) related to the exposed receivable balance	_____	_____
Transaction gain (loss) related to the forward contract	_____	_____
Increase (decrease) in net income from amortization of the discount or premium related to the forward contract	_____	_____
Effect on net income	_____	_____

(2) What was the cumulative effect on net income (i.e., 2001 plus 2002)?

(3) How much cash was received when the account was settled?

EXERCISE 13-8 **Journal Entries**

Vanderbilt Clothing Company placed a clothing order with a company located in Taiwan. The order was placed on November 1, 2001, for delivery on May 1, 2002. Vanderbilt agreed to pay for the goods on May 1, 2002 with the delivery of 5,000,000 Taiwan dollars. To protect against fluctuations in the exchange rate, the company entered into a forward contract on November 1, 2001, to buy 5,000,000 Taiwan dollars on May 1, 2002, for $.02634 per unit.

Direct exchange rates per Taiwan dollar on specific dates are as follows:

Date	Spot Rate	Forward Rate— Maturity May 1
November 1, 2001	$.02631	$.02634
December 31, 2001	.02740	.02735
May 1, 2002	.02591	—

Required:

Prepare the journal entries to be made by Vanderbilt Clothing Company during 2001 and 2002 to account for the transactions described above.

EXERCISE 13-9 **Journal Entries—Forward Contract**

Sharon Myers, chief finance officer for Sitco Products, convinced the president of the company to enter into a 90-day forward contract to sell 900,000 German marks as a speculative venture. When the forward contract was acquired on November 1, 2001, the spot rate for the mark was $.5045 and the 90-day future rate was $.5085. At December 31, 2001, the end of the firm's fiscal year, the spot rate was $.4981 and the future rate for marks to be sold on January 30, 2002 was $.4996. On January 30, 2002, the spot rate was $.4826.

Required:

Prepare all necessary journal entries in regard to the forward contract.

EXERCISE 13-10 **Journal Entries—Forward Contract**

Use the data given in Exercise 13-9, except assume that on November 1, Sitco Products entered into a 90-day forward contract to buy 900,000 German marks on January 30 for $.5085 per mark.

Required:

Prepare all necessary journal entries in regard to the forward contract.

EXERCISE 13-11   **Equipment Purchase, Issuance of a Note**

Roland Brothers, Inc. purchased equipment from a British firm for £120,000 on April 1, 2001. To finance the purchase of the equipment, the president of the company signed a note for £120,000 with a British bank. The loan is denominated in pounds, matures on March 31, 2002, and bears interest at 12% per annum payable on June 30, September 30, December 31, and March 31. Spot rates for the British pound are as follows:

April 1, 2001	$1.574
June 30, 2001	1.560
September 30, 2001	1.526
December 31, 2001	1.498
March 31, 2002	1.538

Required:

Prepare journal entries to record the purchase of the equipment, the interest payments, the adjustment of the accounts on December 31 (the fiscal year-end), and the payment of the note at maturity.

EXERCISE 13-12   **Compute Amounts Related to Forward Contract**

On November 15, 2001, Solanski Inc. imported 500,000 barrels of oil from an oil company in Venezuela. Solanski agreed to pay 50,000,000 bolivars on January 15, 2002. To ensure that the dollar outlay for the purchase will not fluctuate, the company entered into a forward contract to buy 50,000,000 bolivars on January 15 at the forward rate of $.0269. Direct exchange rates on various dates were:

November 15	$.0239
December 31	.0224
January 15	.0291

Solanski Inc. is a calendar-year company.

Required:

Compute the following:

1. The dollars to be paid on January 15, 2002, to acquire the 50,000,000 bolivars from the exchange dealer.
2. The dollars that would have been paid to settle the account payable had Solanski not hedged the purchased contract with the forward contract.
3. The discount or premium on the forward contract.
4. The transaction gain or loss on the exposed liability related to the oil purchase in 2001 and 2002.
5. The transaction gain or loss on the forward contract in 2001 and 2002.
6. The total transaction gain or loss to be reported in 2001 and 2002.
7. The amount of the discount or premium on the forward contract amortized in 2001 and 2002.

PROBLEMS

PROBLEM 13-1   **Journal Entries—Exporting Transactions**

GAF manufactures electrical cells at its St. Louis facility. The company's fiscal year-end is September 30. It has adopted the perpetual inventory cost flow method to control inventory costs. The company entered into the following transactions during the month of September. All exchange rates are direct quotations.

Date		Transaction	Billing Amount	Rate of Exchange
2001				
Sept.	5	Exported 10 electrical cells to a company located in Argentina. Cost per unit, $950.	17,341 pesos	$1.1291
	9	Received raw materials ordered from a British company. The goods were shipped FOB destination and had not been recorded on the books of GAF, Inc.	12,200 pounds	1.6821
	14	Exported 12 electrical cells to a company domiciled in Paris. Cost per unit, $970.	160,274 francs	.1450
	30	End of fiscal year-end.		
		Peso		1.1091
		British pound		1.6911
		Franc		.1530
Oct.	5	Received full payment for the 10 units sold on September 5.		1.1190
	9	Paid British company in full for raw materials purchased September 9.		1.5948
	30	Received full payment for 12 units sold on September 14.		.1440

Required:

A. Prepare the journal entries required on the books of GAF to record the transactions and year-end adjustments. Round all computations to the nearest dollar.

B. Based on the two exporting transactions listed above, complete the following table.

	Transaction	
	Sept. 5	Sept. 14
September 30, 2001 year-end:		
1. Sales	_____	_____
2. Transaction gain (loss)	_____	_____
September 30, 2002 year-end:		
3. Sales	_____	_____
4. Transaction gain (loss)	_____	_____
5. Net effect on income for both years (Sum lines 1–4)	_____	_____
6. Cash received on settlement date	_____	_____

PROBLEM 13-2 **Foreign Trade Journal Entries**

Crystal Exporting Co. is a U.S. wholesaler engaged in foreign trade. The following transactions are representative of its business dealings. The company uses a periodic inventory system and is on a calendar-year basis. All exchange rates are direct quotations.

Dec.	1	Crystal Exporting purchased merchandise from Chang's Ltd., a Hong Kong manufacturer. The invoice was for 210,000 Hong Kong dollars, payable on April 1. On this same date, Crystal Exporting acquired a forward contract to buy 210,000 Hong Kong dollars on April 1 for $.1314.
Dec.	29	Crystal Exporting sold merchandise to Zintel Retailers for 120,000 Hong Kong dollars, receivable in 90 days. No hedging was involved.
April	1	Crystal Exporting received 120,000 Hong Kong dollars from Zintel Retailers.
	1	Crystal Exporting submitted full payment of 210,000 Hong Kong dollars to Chang's, Ltd., after obtaining the 210,000 Hong Kong dollars on its forward contract.

Spot rates for the Hong Kong dollar were as follows:

Dec. 1	$.1265
Dec. 29	.1240
Dec. 31	.1259
April 1	.1430

Required:

A. Prepare journal entries for the transactions including the necessary adjustments on December 31.

B. Explain the income statement treatment given to any transaction gains and losses recognized at December 31.

PROBLEM 13-3   **Foreign Trade Journal Entries and Income Effects**

On December 1, 2001, King Company exported equipment that had cost $210,000 to a Netherlands company for 1,000,000 guilders. The account is to be settled on January 31, 2002. King Company is a calendar-year company and uses a perpetual inventory system. Direct exchange rates were:

December 1	$.4441
December 31	.3690
January 31	.4421

Required:

A. Prepare journal entries to record the exporting transaction, adjust the accounts on December 31, and settle the account on January 31.

B. What effect did changes in the exchange rate have on income in 2001 and 2002?

C. Assume the facts given above, except that on December 1, King Company entered into a forward contract to sell 1,000,000 guilders on January 31 for $.4451 per guilder. Prepare the journal entries needed in 2001 and 2002 to record the forward contract and settle the accounts.

D. What is the combined effect on income in 2001 and 2002 from the exporting transaction and the forward contract?

PROBLEM 13-4   **Journal Entries—Exporting Transactions**

Centennial Exchange of St. Louis, Missouri, imports and exports grains. The company has a September 30 fiscal year-end. The periodic inventory system and the weighted-average cost flow method are used by the company to account for inventory cost. The company negotiated the following transactions during 2001.

Sept.	1	Sold 1,000,000 bushels of wheat to a Paris company for 16,500,000 francs. The account is to be settled on October 30.
Sept.	1	The management of Centennial was concerned that the franc would decline in value. They therefore entered into a forward contract to sell 16,500,000 francs on October 30 for $.1442 per franc.
Sept.	5	Sold 1,000,000 bushels of wheat to a Madrid company for $5,300,000. The account is to be settled on November 5.
Sept.	15	Purchased rice from an exporting company that operates in Japan. The contract provides for the payment of 20,000,000 yen on October 15.
Sept.	15	Entered into a forward contract to buy 20,000,000 yen on October 15 for $.006490 per yen.
Sept.	18	Sold 500 tons of soybean meal to Able & Born, Ltd., a Toronto company, for 48,000 Canadian dollars. The account is to be settled on December 17.

Oct. 15 Completed the forward contract to buy 20,000,000 yen and then submitted payment to pay for the rice purchased on September 15.

Oct. 30 Received 16,500,000 francs from the Paris customer and settled forward contract.

Nov. 5 Received payment in full for the wheat sold on September 5 to the Madrid company.

Dec. 17 Received payment from Able & Born, Ltd. for the September 18 sale.

Direct exchange quotations for specific dates are presented below:

	France— Franc	Spain— Peseta	Japan— Yen	Canada— Dollar
September 1	$.1480	$.00738	$.006427	$.8250
September 5	.1458	.00740	.006428	.8248
September 15	.1456	.00741	.006430	.8246
September 18	.1456	.00737	.006431	.8245
September 30	.1455	.00736	.006433	.8243
October 15	.1458	.00734	.006435	.8241
October 30	.1457	.00732	.006370	.8241
November 5	.1456	.00730	.006439	.8244
December 17	.1453	.00731	.006438	.8250

Required:
Prepare journal entries, including year-end adjustments, to record the above transactions.

PROBLEM 13-5 Various Hedging Cases

Apple Company was incorporated in Delaware in 1999. On November 2, 2001, the controller of the company entered into a forward contract to sell 50,000 British pounds for $1.5920 on March 1, 2002. The following exchange rates were quoted on the indicated dates:

November 2, 2001	Spot rate	$1.6021
December 31, 2001	Spot rate	1.5820
Future delivery on March 1		1.5800
March 1, 2002	Spot rate	1.6543

Apple Company's fiscal year-end is December 31.

Required:

A. Assume that the forward contract was entered into as a hedge against an exposed foreign currency receivable balance in the amount of £50,000. Prepare the journal entries that would be made by Apple Company on

(1) November 2—to record the sale of the goods on account for £50,000 and to record the forward contract.

(2) December 31—to adjust the accounts related to the exposed asset and forward contract at fiscal year-end.

(3) March 1—to adjust the accounts related to the exposed asset and forward contract and to record the settlement of the receivable and delivery of the pounds to the exchange dealer.

B. Assume that the controller indicated on November 2 that the forward contract was acquired as a hedge of a future foreign currency transaction that is a commitment of Apple to sell inventory for £50,000 on March 1. Apple Company follows the practice of including discounts and premiums and transaction gains or losses related to the forward contract in the dollar basis of the related transaction. Prepare the journal entries related to the forward contract and commitment to sell inventory that would be made by Apple Company on November 2, December 31, and March 1.

C. Assume that the contract was entered into to speculate in future exchange rate fluctuations. Prepare the journal entries that would be made by Apple Company on November 2, December 31, and March 1.

D. Compute the effect of the transactions in (A), (B), and (C) on the net income for the fiscal years ended December 31, 2001, and December 31, 2002. Indicate how the balance sheet accounts related to the forward contract would be reported in the December 31, 2001, balance sheet.

PROBLEM 13-6 **Hedge of a Foreign Currency Commitment**

Citron Company is a U.S.-based citrus grower. On October 1, 2001, the company entered into a contract to ship 25,000 boxes of grapefruit on January 28 to Japan. Payment of 50,100,000 yen is to be received on March 29, 2002. On October 1, Citron also entered into a forward contract to sell 50,100,000 yen on March 29 at the forward rate of $.007412. The forward contract is considered a hedge of the foreign currency commitment. The direct exchange rate and forward rate for the yen were as follows:

	October 1	December 31	January 29	March 29
Spot rate	$.007235	$.007879	$.007623	$.007640
Forward rate available for the remaining period of the forward contract	.007412	.007910	.007674	Not appl.

Required:

A. Prepare the necessary journal entries to record the following transactions and events:

Oct.	1	Entered into the contract to sell the grapefruit and negotiated the forward contract.
Dec.	31	Fiscal year-end of Citron Company.
Jan.	28	The grapefruit were shipped FOB shipping point. The grapefruit cost Citron $7.50 per box. Citron uses a perpetual inventory system.
Mar.	29	Received the payment and delivered the yen to the exchange broker to settle the forward contract.

B. Compute the increase or decrease in income for each fiscal year as a result of the transactions above.

C. Compute the increase or decrease in income each period that would have occurred if Citron had not entered into the forward contract.

PROBLEM 13-7 **Foreign Currency Risk**

During her first quarter review of the financial statements, Debra Bell, the CFO of HAL Computer Corporation, was distressed to notice the company's transaction loss had been steadily increasing each month. HAL is a publicly held manufacturer of "PC clone" personal computers. Like most manufacturers of its kind, HAL does not manufacture domestically but utilizes lower cost offshore suppliers for components and subcontractors for assembly. As it is HAL's policy to denominate foreign contracts in U.S. dollars whenever possible, the increase in transaction losses was particularly puzzling.

Subsequent conversations with HAL's controller, Tom Stewart, revealed all new contracts had been denominated in foreign currencies (primarily the South Korean won and Taiwanese dollar) in order to obtain more favorable purchase terms. Further, Mr. Stewart believed that the U.S. dollar would strengthen due to it being an election year. Since these contracts specify delivery and payment at various dates over the next 12 months, tremendous potential for exposure exists for the company if the dollar continues to decline against the major foreign currencies.

Required:

A. Mr. Stewart executed all new foreign contracts in foreign currencies in the belief it would help the company.

(1) Do you think he was justified in his actions given the company policy?

(2) On what basis did you decide if the controller was justified or not?

(3) Was the loss a factor in your decision? Is this appropriate?

B. A substantial amount of foreign denominated contracts already exist for goods and services not yet received.

(1) What actions may HAL take to minimize potential losses?

(2) What are the advantages and disadvantages of these actions?

(3) What implication does each of these scenarios have for financial statement disclosure?

C. Assume that you are Ms. Bell, and you are concerned about how the Board of Directors and the stockholders may react. Additionally, you are about to purchase a new home and are planning to sell some HAL stock for the down payment.

(1) After carefully considering all of your options, what action do you decide to take?

(2) Did concern over the Board, stockholders, or HAL's stock price enter into your decision? Why or why not?

PROBLEM 13-8 **Hedge of a Forecasted Sale Using a Foreign Currency Option**

A U.S. company estimated that, in the first two months of 2003, its export sales to a French company would generate 400,000 francs. On December 1, 2002, in an effort to protect against the weakening franc, the company purchased an option (out of the money) to sell 400,000 French francs at an exchange rate of $0.60 with an expiration date of February 25, 2003. The cost of the option was $6,000. The spot rates on the following dates were:

December 1, 2002	$0.62
December 31, 2002	$0.60
February 25, 2003	$0.57

The option's value in the options market on December 31, 2002, was $9,000. December 31 is also an interim reporting date. The option was exercised on February 25, 2003.

Required:

Prepare all journal entries needed on December 1, December 31, and February 25 to account for the option.

14

TRANSLATION OF FINANCIAL STATEMENTS OF FOREIGN AFFILIATES

LEARNING OBJECTIVES

1. Distinguish between the current exchange rate and the historical exchange rate.

2. Understand the objectives of financial statement translation.

3. Identify the functional currency of a foreign entity.

4. Compare the two methods used to convert the financial statements of a foreign entity into U.S. dollars.

5. Distinguish between the circumstances under which each of the two methods is appropriate under current GAAP.

6. Explain the factors involved in translating the statements of a foreign entity operating in a highly inflationary economy.

7. Translate the statements of a foreign entity when the functional currency is the local currency.

8. Translate the statements of a foreign entity when the functional currency is the U.S. dollar.

9. Understand the concept of comprehensive income in the context of foreign currency translation.

10. Identify the disclosure requirements for firms with foreign entities.

"Quarterly corporate earnings will be even more important than usual to a stock market looking for clues about how fast the economy is slowing down. But first, investors will have to separate the wheat from the chaff. The chaff is the dollar, which this year [1995] has gone through convulsions not seen in years. The story varies, however, depending on which countries a firm operates in and the degree to which the company hedges against currency swings."[1]

In the preceding chapter, the translation of various types of foreign currency transactions entered into by a U.S. company was described. A U.S. company also may be

---

[1] *WSJ*, "Dollar to Play a Central Role in Profit Data," by Michael Gonzalez, 4-17-95.

involved in foreign activities through the operations of a branch, a subsidiary, or an investee company in a foreign country. If the foreign entity maintains its books in a foreign currency, its accounts must be restated into dollars so that the accounts of the U.S. company and the foreign entity are stated in a common currency before the accounts are combined or consolidated or the equity method of accounting is applied. The concepts underlying the restatement of the accounts of a foreign entity are discussed in this chapter.

"The dollar hit a three-year low against the yen, after traders bid up the Japanese currency on news of Japan's unexpectedly strong GDP growth. The greenback dipped to 107.55 yen before recovering to 107.94 yen. Despite the dollar's steady decline, the United States shows no signs that it is ready to intervene."[2]

ACCOUNTING FOR OPERATIONS IN FOREIGN COUNTRIES

A U.S. firm may maintain branch offices or hold equity interests in companies that are domiciled in foreign countries. As a general rule, a foreign subsidiary is consolidated if the parent company owns, directly or indirectly, a controlling interest in the voting stock of the subsidiary. The exceptions to the general rule are as follows:

1. The intent to control is likely to be temporary.
2. Control does not actually rest with the parent company. For example, some governments restrict the withdrawal of assets from the country or impose exchange restrictions. Thus, a foreign entity may operate under conditions of foreign exchange restrictions, controls, or other government-imposed regulations that are of a type that raise significant doubt as to the parent company's ability to control the subsidiary.[3]

APB Opinion No. 18 extended the equity method of accounting to an investment in common stock of a foreign company in which the investor can exert significant influence (generally holds a 20 to 50% interest in the voting stock) over the investee, unless the investee operates under conditions of exchange restrictions, controls, or other uncertainties that would affect the ability to influence the policies of the foreign investee. In other words, the APB considered it misleading to include in operations the investor's equity interest in the investee's net income if the income might not be distributed because of government restrictions. Investments in common stock not accounted for using the equity method are reported at fair value or at cost.

Accounting for a foreign entity is further complicated when there are significant differences between accounting principles in the United States and those in the other country. For example, long-term leases are not capitalized and the pooling of interests method of accounting for a business combination is not used in France or Germany. When such differences in accounting concepts exist, it is difficult to compare the results of operations and the financial position of companies

---

[2] *WSJ,* "Dollar Intervention by U.S. Is Unlikely," by Michael Phillips, 9/10/99, p. A3.

[3] *Opinions of the Accounting Principles Board No. 18,* "The Equity Method of Accounting for Investments in Common Stock" (New York: AICPA, 1971), par. 17.

operating in different countries. To aid statement users in making comparisons, foreign statements that are not in conformity with generally accepted accounting standards in the United States must be adjusted to conform to U.S. standards before conversion into U.S. dollars.

TRANSLATING FINANCIAL STATEMENTS OF FOREIGN AFFILIATES

A foreign entity will generally measure and record its transactions in terms of the currency of the country in which it is located, called the *local currency.* A U.S. company maintaining a branch office in a foreign country or holding an equity interest in a foreign company must convert the account data expressed in a foreign currency into dollars before the financial statements can be combined or consolidated. Furthermore, if the equity method of accounting is used to account for an investment in a foreign investee company, the financial statements of the affiliate must be converted into dollars before the investor's share of the investee's reported net income or loss is properly determinable. The conversion from another currency into the currency of the parent company is frequently called "translation." Because the term is popularly used in this manner and because the FASB used the term "translation" in this way in the definitive standard *(SFAS No. 52)* on which much of this chapter is based, we too use the term to refer to the conversion process. Note, however, that the word has a dual meaning as used in the context of foreign currency conversion, and some users may prefer to restrict their use of the term to one of the following two definitions: (1) a generic term to apply to any restatement of foreign currency units into the currency of the parent (as used heretofore in this text) and (2) a specific term that applies only to one of the two methods of conversion described in the following sections (i.e., to the "current method" rather than to the "temporal method"). The FASB uses the term in both ways, as do we.

In the process of translation, all accounts of the foreign entity stated in units of foreign currency are converted into the reporting currency by multiplying the foreign currency amounts by an exchange rate. The development of translation procedures is complicated by the fact that the rate of exchange between two currencies is not stable. There has been considerable controversy as to which foreign currency accounts should be translated using the current exchange rate and which accounts should be converted using historical exchange rates. The *current exchange rate* is the spot rate in effect at the end of the accounting period (i.e., the balance sheet date). The *historical exchange rate* is the spot rate in effect on the date a transaction takes place. Another controversial area relates to how to report the adjustment that is needed to balance the accounts that results when there are changes in the exchange rate.

"This isn't a German or American thing," according to Robert Eaton, one of the co-chairmen of DaimlerChrysler. He and the other co-chairman, Juergen Schrempp, portrayed the combination as a "merger of equals" and kept dual headquarters in Stuttgart, Germany, and Auburn Hills, Michigan. They recognized the riskiness of their juncture, and did their own analysis of international mergers' success rates, finding that 70% failed to achieve the level of success that was anticipated.[4]

[4]Associated Press, "Management Shakeup Rocks DaimlerChrysler," by Justin Hyde, 9/25/99.

Translation Adjustment or Translation Gain or Loss

The translation of some accounts using the current exchange rate and others using the historical exchange rate will result in an inequality between the total of the debit account balances and the total of the credit account balances. This difference may be referred to as a **translation adjustment** or **translation gain or loss.** As will be shown in a later section of this chapter, the amount of the translation adjustment is affected by an entity's accounting exposure to changes in the exchange rate. In an accounting sense, an entity's exposure to exchange risk is related to the set of accounts translated at the current rate. Current accounting standards require that the translation adjustment (gain or loss) be reported currently in income *or* deferred as a component of stockholders' equity, depending on the method used to translate the accounts. The appropriate method is not a free choice, but rather is dictated by the circumstances as described in *SFAS No. 52*. If the adjustment is reported as a component of equity, it is not included in current earnings *but* is nonetheless a component of **comprehensive income.**

OBJECTIVES OF TRANSLATION—*SFAS NO. 52*

Functional Currency Concept

In *Statement of Financial Accounting Standards (SFAS) No. 52*, the board determined that the objectives of translation are to:[5]

1. Provide information that is generally compatible with the exposed economic effects of an exchange rate change on an enterprise's cash flows and equity [par. 4(a)].

2. Reflect in consolidated statements the financial results and relationships of the individual consolidated entities as measured in their *functional currencies* in conformity with U.S. generally accepted accounting principles [par. 4(b)].

With respect to the first objective, compatibility in terms of effect on equity is achieved if, for example, an entity is in an exposed asset position and the translation process results in an increase in stockholders' equity when there is a favorable change in the exchange rate. (An entity's exposed asset position is the excess of assets that are translated at the current exchange rate over liabilities that are translated at the current exchange rate.) An unfavorable change in the exchange rate should result in a reduction in stockholders' equity. Compatibility in terms of cash flow consequences is achieved if favorable (unfavorable) rate changes that are reasonably expected to affect cash flows are *reflected* as gains (losses) in determining net income for the period, and the effect of rate changes that have only remote and uncertain implications for realization are *excluded* from determining net income for the period.

In objective 2, the Board moved from a single-enterprise perspective of consolidation of a foreign entity to a multiple-enterprise perspective. The Board reasoned that foreign operations are often conducted in economic and currency environments that differ from those of the U.S. parent. Thus, a foreign entity is

---

[5] *Statement of Financial Accounting Standards No. 52*, ''Foreign Currency Translation'' (Norwalk, CT: FASB, 1981).

viewed as a separate business entity that generates its earnings in its local economic, legal, and political environment. The Board believes that the operating performance and financial condition of a foreign entity are best measured by expressing its accounts in the currency of the economic environment in which it primarily conducts its operations and generates and expends its cash, its *functional currency*. The determination of an entity's functional currency is discussed in a later section of this chapter. Also see Illustration 14-1 for a list of indicators to help in identifying the functional currency. Under the Board's view of a foreign entity, the translation of accounts expressed in the functional currency should retain the financial results and relationships that were created in the economic environment of the foreign operations rather than as if the operations had been conducted in the economic environment of the reporting currency.

TRANSLATION METHODS

To accomplish the objectives of translation, two translation methods are used depending on the functional currency of the foreign entity:

> *Current rate method.* When using the current rate method, all assets and liabilities are translated using the current exchange rate. Revenue and expense transactions are translated at the exchange rate prevailing on the date each underlying transaction occurred. Since separate translation of each transaction is usually impractical, an appropriate average rate can be used to approximate the results that would be obtained from translation of each transaction.

> *Temporal method.* Under this method, monetary assets and liabilities such as cash, receivables, and payables are translated at the current exchange rate. Assets and liabilities carried at historical cost are translated at historical exchange rates. Assets and liabilities carried at current values (such as inventory carried at market when applying the lower of cost or market rule) are translated at the current exchange rate. Thus, the temporal method places emphasis on whether an account is measured in terms of historical cost or current values.

Revenue and expense transactions, except those related to assets and liabilities translated at historical rates, are translated at exchange rates in effect on the dates the underlying transaction occurred. An appropriate average rate can be used to approximate the results that would be obtained from translation of each transaction. Revenues and expenses that relate to assets and liabilities translated at historical rates (such as depreciation expense, amortization expense, and the cost of sales) are translated at the historical rates used to translate the related assets and liabilities.

"You have to separate out the effect of the currency and ask yourself, How would the company have done in local currency?" says Terry Bivens, food, tobacco, and beverage analyst for Argus Research. "If you see a company that has done badly because of currency translations, but is going strong in local terms, then you're more reassured."[6]

---

[6] *WSJ*, "Dollar to Play a Central Role in Profit Data," by Michael Gonzalez, 4-17-95.

IDENTIFYING THE FUNCTIONAL CURRENCY

The functional currency may be (1) the currency of the country in which the foreign entity is located (the local currency), (2) the U.S. dollar, or (3) the currency of another foreign country. Often, the functional currency is the local currency of the country in which the entity is located and in which the accounting records are maintained. For example, a French subsidiary with operations that are relatively self-contained and integrated in France would have the French franc as its functional currency. In this example, the French subsidiary primarily generates and expends francs.

In other cases, the dollar may be identified as the functional currency when a foreign subsidiary is a direct extension or an integral component of the reporting U.S. parent company. For example, the dollar would ordinarily be the functional currency for a subsidiary domiciled in Mexico that is financed by a U.S. parent company, that acquires significant assets by expending dollars, and whose only business is to assemble components that are manufactured in the United States and are returned to the United States to be sold by the parent company. In this case, the dollar may be the functional currency even though transactions of the subsidiary are recorded in pesos in the subsidiary's books.

ILLUSTRATION 14–1

Functional Currency Indicators

Economic Indicator	Indicators Pointing to Local Currency as Functional Currency	Indicators Pointing to U.S. Dollar as Functional Currency
Cash flows	Primarily in the local currency and do not directly affect parent's cash flows.	Directly affect the parent's cash flows on a current basis and are readily available for remittance to the parent.
Sales prices	Are not primarily responsive in the short term to exchange rate changes; determined primarily by local conditions.	Are primarily responsive in the short term to exchange rate changes; determined primarily by worldwide competition.
Sales market	Active local market although there may be significant amounts of exports.	Sales are mostly in the United States, or sales contracts are denominated in dollars.
Expenses	Production costs and operating expenses are determined primarily by local conditions.	Production costs and operating expenses are obtained primarily from U.S. sources.
Financing	Primarily denominated in the local currency, and foreign entity's cash flow from operations is sufficient to service existing and normally expected obligations.	Primarily from parent or other dollar-denominated obligations, or parent company is expected to service the debt.
Intercompany transactions	Low volume of intercompany transactions and there is not an extensive interrelationship between operations of the foreign entity and those of the parent. However, foreign entity may rely on parent's or affiliates' competitive advantages such as patents and trademarks.	High volume of intercompany transactions; there is an extensive interrelationship between operations of the parent and those of the foreign entity, or the foreign entity is an investment or financing device for the parent.

Source: Statement of Financial Accounting Standards No. 52, par. 42.

In still other cases, the identification of the functional currency will not be as clear as in these two examples. For example, a Mexico City subsidiary might manufacture a component for a product, a significant number of which are sold in Mexico or to companies domiciled in other foreign countries, in addition to providing some units for the U.S. parent, or a foreign entity might conduct significant amounts of business in two or more currencies. In such situations the functional currency could be a currency other than the dollar, such as the local currency of the foreign entity or the currency of a third country. To provide some guidance in selecting the functional currency, the FASB identified six economic indicators for management to consider. These indicators are listed in Illustration 14-1. The order in which the indicators are listed does not suggest any priority; rather, the indicators are to be considered both individually and collectively. When the indicators are mixed and the functional currency cannot be clearly identified, *SFAS No. 52* indicates that management's judgment is required to assess the facts and circumstances in identifying the functional currency.

A foreign entity may operate and generate cash flows through more than one distinct and separable operation. Each of these operations may be identified as an entity and may have a different functional currency if conducted in different economic environments.

TRANSLATION OF FOREIGN CURRENCY FINANCIAL STATEMENTS

The method used to translate a foreign entity's financial statements and the disposition of the resulting translation adjustment depends on the determination of the functional currency. As indicated earlier, the functional currency of the foreign entity might be (1) the local currency of the foreign entity, (2) the U.S. dollar, or (3) the currency of a third country (i.e., a country other than the country in which the subsidiary is located or the United States). The translation process and the disposition of the translation adjustment for these three situations, assuming that the books are kept in the local currency of the foreign entity and that the accounting conforms to U.S. generally accepted accounting principles, are summarized in a flow chart in Illustration 14-2. As shown in Illustration 14-2, an exception is made when the foreign economy is highly inflationary. In this case, the functional currency (as defined here) is not used to determine the appropriate accounting. Also, if the books of the foreign entity are kept in dollars, translation is not necessary. Further, if the books of the foreign entity are not kept in accordance with U.S. generally accepted accounting principles, the accounts must be adjusted to conform before translating the account balances.

Note in Illustration 14-2 that the terms *remeasurement* and *translation* are used when the accounts stated in one currency are converted into another currency. The distinction between the two is as follows:

> *Remeasurement.* If a foreign entity does not maintain its records in its functional currency, the local currency accounts are remeasured into the functional currency using the temporal method. *Remeasurement* is the process of translating the accounts of a foreign entity into its functional currency when they are stated in another currency.

ILLUSTRATION 14-2

Summary of Translation Process and Disposition of Translation Gain or Loss

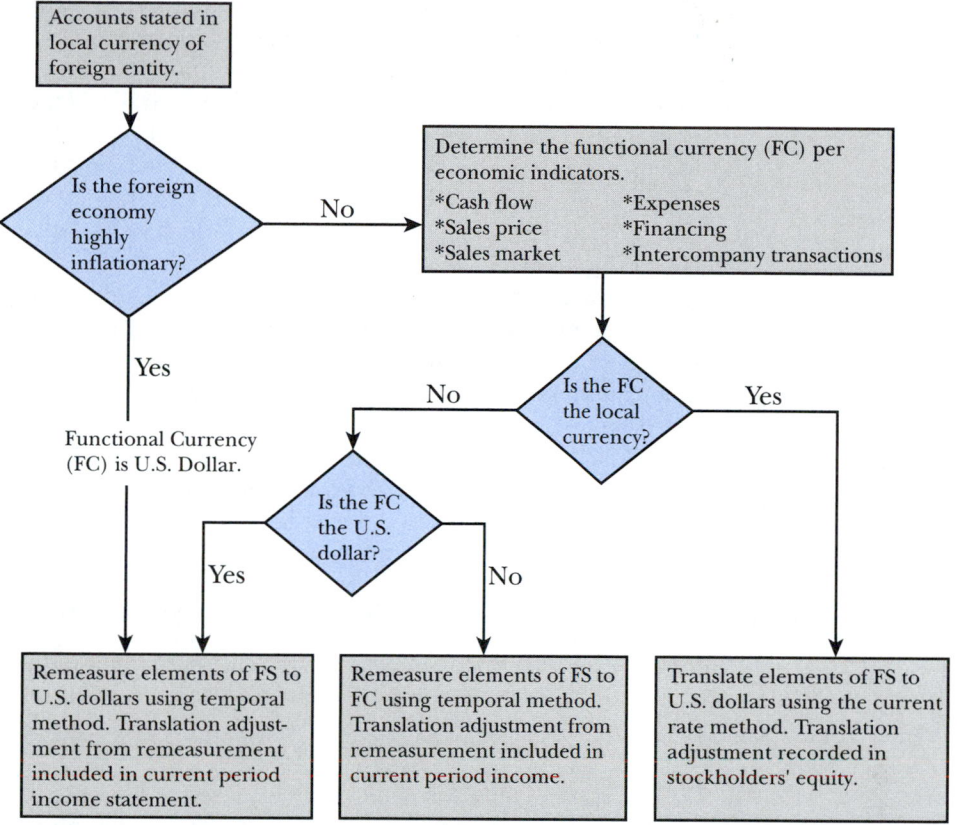

Source: Adapted from Dahli Gray, "Functional Currency Concept—Flexibility and Comparability Effects," *The Woman CPA*, January 1983, p. 22.

> *Translation.* Accounts measured in the functional currency are translated into the reporting currency using the current rate method.

As explained later, remeasurement is a change in the unit of measure, whereas translation retains the functional currency as the unit of measure and simply changes the form in which the accounts are stated. Recall that the term *translation* is used in two different ways: (1) as a generic term to apply to any restatement of foreign currency units into dollars and (2) more specifically to apply to the restatement of foreign currency units that are already measured in the functional currency into dollars (current rate method). Thus, "translation" may be used synonymously with the current method, while "remeasurement" is used synonymously with the temporal method. The first step in the translation process is to determine if the foreign entity is operating in a highly inflationary economy.

Foreign Entity Operates in a Highly Inflationary Economy

The relative rate of inflation between two countries is an important contributing factor to changes in exchange rates. Often, the currency of a country experiencing high inflation will weaken (i.e., one unit of that country's currency can be purchased with less domestic currency) substantially against the currency of a more stable economy. Thus, using the current rate method to translate inventories and fixed assets of foreign operations in highly inflationary economies often results in a substantial reduction in the translated amounts.

To illustrate, assume that a foreign subsidiary acquired land for 100,000 foreign currency units (FCU) when the exchange rate was $1 per FCU. In subsequent years, the foreign country experienced significant inflation and the exchange rate decreased to $.20 per FCU. If the current exchange rate is used, the land would translate to $20,000 (100,000 FCU × $.20) and a cumulative translation loss of $80,000 is reported.

It is the Board's belief that the currency of a country that has a highly inflationary economy has lost its utility as a store of value and cannot be a functional measuring unit. As a practical solution to the problem, the Board prescribed that the financial statements of a foreign entity operating in a highly inflationary economy shall be remeasured as if the functional currency were the reporting currency (U.S. dollar). For such entities this means that the foreign financial statements should be translated using the **temporal method.** According to the foregoing illustration, the land account would be translated to $100,000 (100,000 FCU × $1.00) using the historical exchange rate when the land was purchased.

Foreign Entity Operates in an Economy That Is Not Highly Inflationary

If the foreign entity does not operate in a highly inflationary economy, the functional currency must be identified. The translation process for the three possibilities follows:

1. *The local currency is the functional currency.* The accounts are translated into dollars using the current rate method. Since the functional currency is the local currency, the accounts are already measured in the functional currency, and remeasurement is unnecessary. The resulting translation adjustment is recorded as a separate component of stockholders' equity.

2. *The U.S. dollar is the functional currency.* When the foreign entity does not maintain its records in its functional currency, the accounts are remeasured into the functional currency, in this case dollars, using the temporal method. Since the U.S. dollar is the functional currency, remeasurement translates the accounts into dollars and no further translation is necessary. The resulting translation adjustment is reported in the current period's income statement.

3. *The functional currency is the currency of a third country.* The local currency accounts are first (a) remeasured in the functional currency (the currency of the third country) using the temporal approach, and then (b) the remeasured functional currency amounts are translated into dollars using the current rate approach. The translation gain or loss from using the temporal method is reported in income, while the adjustment resulting from use of the current rate approach is reported in a separate component of owners' equity.

The steps in the translation process may be diagrammed as shown in Illustration 14-3. Identification of the functional currency is the key step in the translation process as it determines the method to be used to translate the foreign currency accounts.

ILLUSTRATION 14-3

Diagram of Translation Process

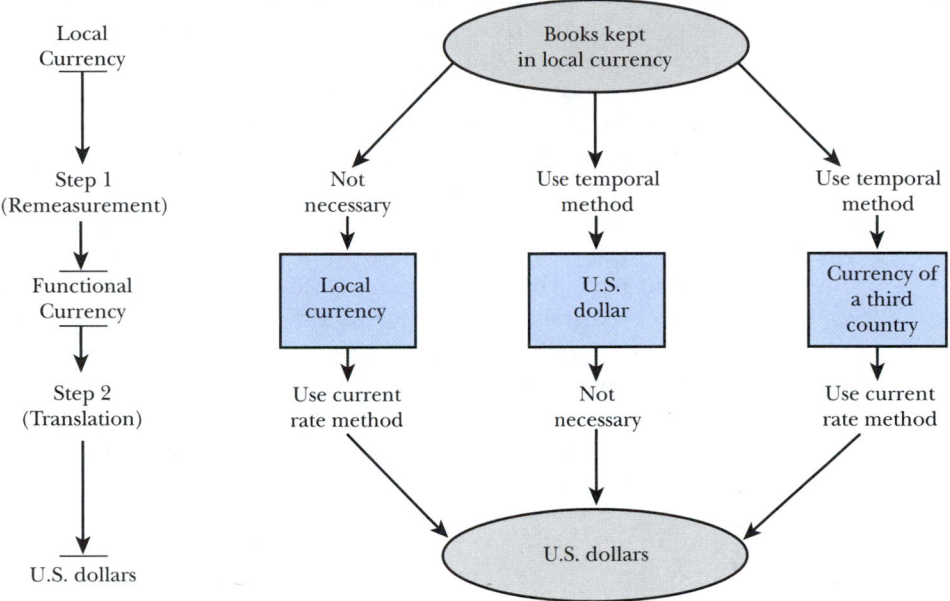

The approach outlined is consistent with the objective of preserving the financial results and relationships of an individual consolidated entity as measured in its functional currency. That is, when the local currency is identified as the functional currency, use of the current rate method retains the local currency as the unit of measure. A translation method preserves the financial results if a net income or loss reported in the functional currency statements is retained in the translated income statement. Maintaining relationships as measured in their functional currency is achieved when, for example, the current ratio is 2 : 1 when computed from the functional currency balance sheet and the ratio is also 2 : 1 when computed from the translated statements. The current rate method retains the financial results and relationships as measured in their functional currency by translating the assets and liabilities at one constant rate (the current rate) and the income statement items at one constant rate (the average rate).

Remeasurement using the temporal method when the functional currency is the U.S. dollar is consistent with a single-enterprise perspective of consolidation. In this case, the operations of the foreign entity are viewed as a direct extension or an integral component of the parent's domestic operations. That is, the parent and subsidiary are viewed as if they were a single company. The objective of translation is to change the unit of measure from that of the local currency to the reporting currency of the parent company, the functional currency. The translation process should then reflect all transactions of the subsidiary as if they were conducted or measured in one currency only, the parent's reporting currency. The use of historical exchange rates to translate accounts carried at historical cost preserves the original cost of the accounts in conformity with the historical cost concept. In effect, the accounts are restated as if dollars had been used to measure and record the assets and liabilities on the transaction dates.

When the functional currency is that of a third country, the accounts of the foreign entity maintained in its local currency are remeasured (translated) into the functional currency using the temporal method. The relationships as measured in the functional currency are retained by translating the functional currency balances into the reporting currency using the current rate method.

The reporting of the translation adjustment is also dependent on the selection of the functional currency. When the foreign entity's accounts are remeasured (temporal method) to the functional currency, either the U.S. dollar or the currency of a third country, the resulting adjustment is reported in the current period's income statement. When translating the accounts from the functional currency into dollars (current rate method), translation adjustments are accumulated and reported as a separate component of stockholders' equity. In the latter case, the Board regarded translation adjustments associated with a foreign investment as unrealized and considered their effect on cash flow to be uncertain and remote. As discussed earlier, one objective of translation is to provide information that is compatible with the expected economic effects of rate changes on cash flow. Compatibility is achieved when the effect of rate changes that have uncertain and remote implications for realization are excluded from income.

The cumulative translation adjustment is carried in the accounts until sale of the foreign entity. At that time, the amount attributable to that entity is removed from the separate component of equity and reported as part of the gain or loss on the sale.

TRANSLATION OF FOREIGN FINANCIAL STATEMENTS ILLUSTRATED

To illustrate the translation process, assume that on January 2, 2002, P Company, a U.S.-based company, acquired for 2,000,000 francs an 80% interest in SFr Company, a French company. SFr maintains its books in francs, and they are in conformity with GAAP in the United States. The translation process will be illustrated under two different assumptions: (1) the French franc is the functional currency, and (2) the U.S. dollar is the functional currency.

Exchange rates for the franc for the 2002 fiscal year are as follows:

Date	Spot Rate
January 2 (date of acquisition)	$.150
September 1	.160
December 31	.170
Average for the fourth quarter	.165
Average for the year	.156

In translating the income statement accounts, it is assumed that revenues were generated and expenses were incurred evenly during the year. It is also assumed that the company uses the FIFO cost flow assumption, and that the ending inventory was acquired during the last quarter.

Entries made on the books of P Company to account for the investment and the preparation of a consolidated statements workpaper based on the translated account balances are illustrated in the appendix to this chapter.

Functional Currency Is the Local Currency—Current Rate Method

Year-end financial statements at December 31 in francs for the subsidiary and the translation of the account balances into dollars using the current rate method are presented in Illustration 14-4. The translation rules are as follows:

1. All assets and liabilities are translated from the local currency into the reporting currency using the current exchange rate (i.e., the spot rate on the balance sheet date).

2. Paid-in capital accounts are translated using the historical rate, but the date to which the historical rate pertains depends on whether the acquisition was accounted for as a purchase or a pooling of interests. In a **_purchase transaction,_** the accounts are translated using the historical rate on the date the acquisition of the equity interest occurred. In the case of a **_pooling of interests,_** these accounts are translated using the historical rate(s) that existed on the date(s) that the foreign entity's capital transaction(s) occurred.

3. Components of the ending retained earnings are translated as follows:
   a. The beginning retained earnings balance is set equal to the ending balance of last year. In this case, since this is the first year of acquisition, the balance is set equal to the January 2 balance of $72,000 (480,000 francs × $.15).
   b. As a component of equity, dividends are translated into dollars using the exchange rate in effect when the dividend was declared.
   c. Net income or loss is carried forward from the translated income statement as discussed later.
   d. The cumulative translation adjustment is a balancing amount in the balance sheet. (The adjustment is discussed in more detail in the next section.)

4. Revenue and expense accounts (including cost of goods sold and depreciation), gains, and losses are translated using the exchange rate when the elements were recognized during the period. Because separate translation of numerous transactions is usually impractical, the use of an appropriate average to translate revenue and expense accounts is permitted.

An Analysis of the Translation Adjustment When some accounts in a trial balance are translated using one rate and other accounts are translated using a different rate, an inequality will result between the total of the debit account balances and the total of the credit account balances. For example, in Illustration 14-4 the 608,000 franc debit balance in the accounts receivable account is translated to $103,360 using the current exchange rate of $.17, and the 608,000 franc credit included in the sales account balance is translated to $94,848 (608,000 francs × $.156) using the average exchange rate for the period. On these transactions there is a translation adjustment credit of $8,512, since the accounts receivable could be converted into $103,360 at the balance sheet date, as opposed to $94,848 at the time of the sale. A translation adjustment will also result when items that are translated at the current rate are included in two successive trial balances and the exchange rate changes.

In Illustration 14-4 the translation adjustment is a balancing amount that reconciles the total debit balances with the total credit balances after the individual accounts have been translated and is reported as a component of stockholders' equity. The translation adjustment for the period results from an entity's accounting

Functional Currency	ILLUSTRATION 14–4
Is Local Currency	**SFr Company**
(Franc)—Current	**Workpaper to Translate Account**
Rate Method	**Balances of Foreign Subsidy**
	December 31, 2002

		Current Rate Method	
Combined Statement of Income and Retained Earnings	Adjusted Trial Balance (Francs)	Translation Rate	Adjusted Trial Balance (Dollars)
Sales	3,020,000	(A) $.156	471,120
Cost of Goods Sold	1,850,000	(A) .156	288,600
Depreciation Expense	100,000	(A) .156	15,600
Other Expenses	655,000	(A) .156	102,180
Income Tax Expense	82,000	(A) .156	12,792
Net Income	333,000		51,948
1/1 Retained Earnings	480,000	(1)	72,000
	813,000		123,948
Less: 9/1 Dividends Declared	300,000	(H) .16	48,000
12/13 Retained Earnings	513,000		75,948
Balance Sheet			
Cash	930,000	(C) .17	158,100
Accounts Receivable (net)	608,000	(C) .17	103,360
Inventories (FIFO cost)	830,000	(C) .17	141,000
Land	500,000	(C) .17	85,000
Buildings (net)	650,000	(C) .17	110,500
Equipment (net)	430,000	(C) .17	73,100
Total	3,948,000		671,160
Accounts Payable	640,000	(C) .17	108,800
Short-Term Notes Payable	635,000	(C) .17	107,950
Bonds Payable	900,000	(C) .17	153,000
Common Stock	960,000	(H) .15	144,000
Additional Paid-in Capital	300,000	(H) .15	45,000
Retained Earnings	513,000		75,948
Total	3,948,000		634,698
Cumulative Translation Adjustment—		(B/A)	
Credit Balance*			36,462
Total			671,160

*Include as a component of stockholders' equity
(1) Retained earnings in dollars on January 2.
(A) Average exchange rate used to approximate the rate on the date these elements were recognized.
(H) Historical exchange rate.
(C) Current exchange rate.
(B/A) Balancing amount.

exposure to exchange risk, which in an accounting sense is related to the set of accounts that are translated at the current rate. Fluctuations in the exchange rate have no effect on the translated amount of an account translated at a historical rate on two balance sheets.

The translation adjustment under the current rate method may be verified by a direct computation as in Illustration 14-5. Since all assets and liabilities are translated at the current rate under the current rate method, only net assets (assets minus liabilities) are exposed to currency fluctuations and thus result in a transla-

ILLUSTRATION 14–5

Verification of the Translation Adjustment
Current Rate Method
Functional Currency—Franc

	Francs	Translation Rate	Reporting Currency (Dollars)
1/1 Exposed net asset position	1,740,000 *	$.15	261,000
Adjustments for changes in net asset position during year			
Net income for year	333,000	.156	51,948
Dividends declared	(300,000)	.16	(48,000)
Net asset position translated using rate in effect at date of each transaction			264,948
12/31 Exposed net asset position	1,773,000	.17	301,410
Change in cumulative translation adjustment during year—net increase			36,462
1/1 Cumulative translation adjustment[†]			—0—
12/31 Cumulative translation adjustment			36,462

*A condensed balance sheet for SFr Company on January 2, 2002 was as follows:

	Francs		Francs
Monetary Assets	1,100,000	Monetary Liabilities	1,800,000
Nonmonetary Assets		Common Stock	960,000
Inventory	760,000	Additional Paid-in Capital	300,000
Fixed Assets	1,680,000	Retained Earnings	480,000
Total	3,540,000	Total	3,540,000

1/1 Net assets = 3,540,000 francs − 1,800,000 francs = 1,740,000 francs.
[†]The beginning balance is zero since this was the first year the investment was held.

tion gain or loss. This net investment view of the firm recognizes that functional currency assets produce revenues in a foreign currency and can be an effective hedge of liabilities that require payment in the same foreign currency. Thus, equal amounts of functional currency assets and liabilities hedge one another and only net assets are exposed to exchange risk. Most firms will be in a net asset position, which results in a transaction gain (loss), when the direct exchange rate increases (decreases). Note that the steps shown in Illustration 14-5 provided a check for the current period *change* in the cumulative translation adjustment. To reconcile with the amount reported in the stockholders' equity section of the balance sheet, it is necessary to add (subtract) the cumulative translation adjustment reported in the prior period. To the extent that the adjustment is sometimes a gain and sometimes a loss, the cumulative amount may remain near zero. On the other hand, a series of adjustments in the same direction may result in a relatively large credit (debit) balance. Credit balances may be viewed as net cumulative gains, while debt balances reflect net cumulative losses.

The first column in Illustration 14-5 reconciles the net asset position at the beginning of the year to the net asset position at the end of the year. Note that only the transactions that affected stockholders' equity will cause a change in the net asset position. The franc balances in column 1 are translated into dollars using different exchange rates as follows. The beginning exposed net asset position is translated using the exchange rate in effect at the beginning of the period. The increases and decreases in the net asset position are translated using the exchange rate at the date the transactions were assumed to occur. The ending exposed net asset position is translated using the current exchange rate.

"International operations constitute about 15% of our 1998 consolidated operating profit, excluding unusual impairment and other items. As currency exchange rates change, translation of the income statements of our international businesses into U.S. dollars affects year-over-year comparability of operating results. We do not generally hedge translation risks because cash flows from international operations are generally reinvested locally. We do not enter into hedges to minimize volatility of reported earnings because we do not believe it is justified by the exposure or the cost."[7]

Interpretation of Results In the preceding illustration, the current rate method was used to translate the foreign currency financial statements when the franc, as opposed to the dollar, was identified as the functional currency. As noted earlier, one of the objectives of translation is to retain in the translated statements the financial results and relationships of the financial statements as measured in the functional currency. With respect to financial results, a net income is reported in both the functional currency statements and the translated statements. A few selected financial ratios are computed here to show that the current rate method retains the financial relationships:

	Francs	*Dollars*
Current ratio	$\dfrac{2,368,000}{1,275,000} = 1.86$	$\dfrac{402,560}{216,750} = 1.86$
Debt to equity	$\dfrac{2,175,000}{1,773,000} = 1.23$	$\dfrac{369,750}{301,410} = 1.23$
Gross profit percentage	$\dfrac{1,170,000}{3,020,000} = 38.7\%$	$\dfrac{182,520}{471,120} = 38.7\%$
Net income to sales	$\dfrac{333,000}{3,020,000} = 11.0\%$	$\dfrac{51,948}{471,120} = 11.0\%$

Another objective of translation is to provide information that is generally compatible with the expected economic effects of a change in exchange rates. In the illustration, the exchange rate increased from $.15 to $.17 during the period, a favorable change for a U.S. parent company holding an investment in an exposed net asset position.

Translation of the foreign currency financial statements using the current rate approach resulted in a $36,462 increase in stockholders' equity.

Statement of Comprehensive Income, and Statement of Shareholders' Equity

Opinions remain divided as to the appropriateness of excluding currency translation adjustments from net income, as currently done under the "current" method. These adjustments represent one of several items of concern to the FASB because of their frequency of occurrence and relative importance, coupled with their exclusion from reported earnings. The FASB labeled such items as "other comprehensive income." In the early 1980s, the FASB defined comprehensive income as including *all* changes in equity during a period except those resulting from invest-

---

[7]Pepsi Company's annual report, 1998.

Functional Currency	ILLUSTRATION 14–6
Is Local Currency	**SFr Company**
(Franc)—Current	**Comprehensive Income Statement**
Rate Method	**For the Year Ended**
	December 31, 2002

Net Income	$51,948
Other comprehensive income:	
Currency translation adjustment	$36,462
Comprehensive income	$88,410

SFr Company
Statement of Shareholders' Equity
For the Year Ended December 31, 2002

	Common Stock	Additional Paid-in Capital	Retained Earnings	Accumulated Other Comprehensive Income	Total
Balance, 1/1/02	$144,000	$45,000	$72,000	0	$261,000
Comprehensive income:					
Net income			51,948		51,948
Other comprehensive income:					
Currency translation adjustment				36,462	36,462
Total comprehensive income					*88,410*
Dividends declared			(48,000)		(48,000)
Balance, 12/31/02	$144,000	$45,000	$75,948	$36,462	$301,410

ments by owners and distributions to owners. Thus, comprehensive income consists of net income plus other items such as unrealized gains (losses) on available-for-sale securities and certain pension costs related to minimum pension liability that are excluded from net income under current GAAP. More recently, the FASB added the requirement that a statement of comprehensive income must be included in a complete set of financial statements.

In Illustration 14-6, we show the statement of comprehensive income and the reconciliation of changes in all shareholders' equity accounts for the year 2002 for SFr Company in dollars. Of course, these amounts would be added to the parent's balances for preparation of a consolidated statement of comprehensive income (and a consolidated statement of shareholders' equity).

Functional Currency Is the U.S. Dollar—Temporal Method

The temporal method is used to remeasure the accounts of a foreign entity when the entity operates in a highly inflationary economy or its books are maintained in a currency other than its functional currency. The objective of the remeasurement process is to produce the same results as if the transactions of the foreign entity had been recorded initially in its functional currency. To accomplish this, the historical exchange rate is used to translate accounts carried at historical cost, while the current exchange rate is used to translate other accounts. The remeasurement process is as follows:

1. Monetary assets and liabilities (for example, cash, receivables, and most liabilities) that are expressed in the balance sheet at current values are translated using

the current rate. (An asset or a liability is monetary if it represents a claim to a fixed amount of dollars. All other assets and liabilities are nonmonetary.)

2. Nonmonetary assets and liabilities carried at past exchange prices (historical cost) are translated at historical exchange rates, which results in translating these amounts to the equivalent number of dollars on the date the transaction took place.

3. Nonmonetary assets and liabilities carried at current or future exchange prices (for example, marketable securities or inventory carried at replacement cost) are translated at the current exchange rate.

4. Paid-in capital accounts are translated using the historical exchange rate at the date of acquisition if a purchase transaction and at the date the original capital transaction(s) occurred if the acquisition is a pooling of interests.

5. The components that make up the ending retained earnings balance are translated as follows:
   a. The beginning balance is set equal to the ending balance of the last period.
   b. Dividends are translated at the rate existing on the date of the declaration.
   c. Net income or loss is carried forward from the translated income statement.

6. Revenues and expenses related to assets and liabilities translated at historical rates (primarily inventory cost and depreciation) are translated at the respective historical rates used to translate the related asset or liability.

7. Other revenue and expense accounts are translated in a manner that produces approximately the same results as if the individual transactions were translated at the rate in effect when the transaction occurred.

8. The translation gain or loss is reported in the income statement.

A list of some common nonmonetary items that should be remeasured using the historical rate is presented in Illustration 14-7. Remeasurement of the nonmonetary accounts using historical exchange rates normally requires that the foreign entity maintain detailed records identifying the purchase date and the exchange rate.

The December 31 trial balance of SFr Company in francs and the remeasurement of the accounts using the temporal method are shown in Illustration 14-8. The first step is to translate the individual accounts, except for the ending retained earnings balance of 513,000 francs, using the appropriate exchange rate. The ending retained earnings balance of $76,660 is computed as a balancing amount required to equate the firm's liabilities and stockholders' equity with the total assets. Next, the ending retained earnings is carried to the combined statement of income and retained earnings where the translation loss of $11,918 is the balancing amount in the combined statement.

An Analysis of the Translation Gain or Loss The translation loss in the temporal method of translation is derived by a direct calculation in Illustration 14-9. Procedurally, the approach is based on the same underlying concept as that used to verify the translation adjustment reported when the current rate method was used. That is, the translation loss is related to those accounts translated at the current exchange rate. However, in applying the temporal method, in general, monetary items only are translated at the current rate while most nonmonetary items are translated at historical rates. Accordingly, the dollar value of monetary items is affected by variations in the exchange rate, giving rise to a gain or loss. On the other hand, non-

---

ILLUSTRATION 14–7

Nonmonetary Items Remeasured Using the Historical Rate

Balance Sheet Items
- Equity securities carried at cost
- Inventories carried at cost
- Prepared expenses such as insurance, advertising, and rent
- Property, plant, and equipment
- Accumulated depreciation on property, plant, and equipment
- Patents, trademarks, licenses, and formulas
- Goodwill
- Other intangible assets
- Deferred charges and credits, except deferred income taxes and policy acquisition costs for life insurance companies
- Deferred income
- Common stock
- Preferred stock carried at issuance price

Income Statement Items
- Cost of goods sold
- Depreciation of property, plant, and equipment
- Amortization of intangible items such as goodwill, patents, licenses, etc.
- Amortization of policy acquisition costs for life insurance companies.

Source: Statement of Financial Accounting Standards No. 52, par. 48.

---

monetary items will not result in a gain or loss because each item is translated in successive balance sheets using its respective historical exchange rate. As a result, as long as these items are reported in the balance sheet, they will retain their original translated dollar amounts (less accumulated amortization), even though the exchange rate may have changed.

A translation loss results from application of the temporal method, as opposed to the credit translation adjustment calculated on the exposed assets using the current rate method, because SFr Company maintained a net monetary liability position throughout the year. An increasing exchange rate will produce a translation loss on an exposed net monetary liability position.

Comparison of the Two Methods

In translating the balance sheet, the differences and similarities between the temporal and current rate methods are highlighted in the following schedule:

	Balance Sheet Translation Rates	
	Current Rate Method	*Temporal Method*
Monetary asset	Current	Current
Nonmonetary asset carried at historical cost	Current	Historical
Nonmonetary asset carried at market value	Current	Current
Monetary liability	Current	Current
Nonmonetary liability	Current	Historical

The two methods differ primarily in terms of the appropriate rate to use for nonmonetary items carried at historical cost. In the income statement, a net income of $51,948 resulted when the franc was the functional currency (Illustration 14-4), whereas a net income of $52,660 was reported when the U.S. dollar was the functional currency (Illustration 14-8). There are two reasons for this difference. First,

ILLUSTRATION 14–8

SFr Company

Workpaper to Translate Account

Balances of Foreign Subsidiary

December 31, 2002

		Temporal Method	
Balance Sheet	Adjusted Trial Balance (Francs)	Exchange Rate	Adjusted Trial Balance (Dollars)
Cash	930,000	(C) .17	158,100
Accounts Receivable (net)	608,000	(C) .17	103,360
Inventories (FIFO cost)	830,000	Sch. 1	136,950
Land	500,000	(H) .15	75,000
Buildings (net)	650,000	(H) .15	97,500
Equipment (net)	430,000	(H) .15	64,500
Total	3,948,000		635,410
Accounts Payable	640,000	(C) .17	108,800
Short-Term Notes Payable	635,000	(C) .17	107,950
Bonds Payable	900,000	(C) .17	153,000
Common Stock	960,000	(H) .15	144,000
Additional Paid-in Capital	300,000	(H) .15	45,000
Retained Earnings	513,000	(B/A)	76,600 ⌐
Total	3,948,000		635,410

**Combined Statement of Income
and Retained Earnings**

Sales	3,020,000	(A) .156		⌐471,120
Cost of Goods Sold	1,850,000	Sch. 1		276,570	① Carry
Depreciation Expense	100,000	(H) .15	②	15,000	down
Other Expenses	655,000	(A) .156		102,180	retained
Income Tax Expense	82,000	(A) .156		12,792 ⌐	earnings
Translation					
(Remeasurement) Loss	—	(B/A)	④	11,918	
Net Income	333,000			⌐52,660	
1/2 Retained Earnings	480,000	(1)		72,000	
	813,000		③	124,660	
Less: 9/1 Dividends					
Declared	300,000	(H) .16		48,000	
12/31 Retained Earnings	513,000			76,660 ⌐	

(1) Retained earnings in dollars on January 2.
(A) Average exchange rate used to approximate the rate on the date these elements were recognized.
(H) Historical exchange rate.
(C) Current exchange rate.
(B/A) Balancing amount.

Schedule 1
Translation of cost of goods sold

	Francs	Exchange Rate	Dollars
Beginning inventory (assumed)	760,000	.15	114,000
Purchases (assumed)	1,920,000	.156	299,520
	2,680,000		413,520
Less: Ending inventory	830,000	.165	136,950
Cost of goods sold	1,850,000		276,570

Steps to determine translation (remeasurement) gain or loss using "plug" technique:
① Carry down retained earnings.
② Complete income statement down to translation gain or loss.
③ Beginning with ending retained earnings, work back to net income.

Ending retained earnings	+ Dividends −	Beginning retained earnings	Net = Income
$76,660	+ $48,000 −	$72,000	= $52,660

④ Compute translation gain or loss in dollars:
Translation gain (loss) = Net Income − (Sales − Expenses)
= $52,660 − ($471,120 − $406,542) = ($11,918)

ILLUSTRATION 14–9

Verification of the Translation (Remeasurement) Loss
Temporal Method
Functional Currency—U.S. Dollar

	Francs	Exchange Rate	Reporting Currency (U.S. Dollar)
1/1 Exposed net monetary liability position	700,000*	$.15	105,000
Adjustments for changes in net monetary position during the year:			
Less: Increase in cash and receivables from sales	(3,020,000)	.156	(471,120)
Add: Decrease in monetary assets or increase in monetary liabilities:			
Purchases	1,920,000	.156	299,520
Other expenses	655,000	.156	102,180
Income taxes	82,000	.156	12,792
Dividends declared	300,000	.16	48,000
Net monetary liability position translated using rate in effect at date of each transaction	—		96,372
12/31 Exposed net monetary liability position	637,000†	.17	108,290
Translation (remeasurement) gain (loss)			(11,918)

*The January 2, 2002, condensed balance sheet is given in Illustration 14–5.

	Francs
Monetary liabilities	1,800,000
Less: Monetary assets	1,100,000
Net monetary liability position	700,000

†See Illustration 14–8.

	Francs
Monetary liabilities (640,000 + 635,000 + 900,000)	2,175,000
Less: Monetary assets (930,000 + 608,000)	1,538,000
Net monetary liability position	637,000

when the foreign currency is strengthening against the dollar, cost of goods sold and depreciation expense are usually greater when the current rate method of translation is used. Second, a translation loss of $11,918 is reported in the dollar functional currency income statement, whereas a credit adjustment of $36,462 is reported in stockholders' equity in the franc functional currency statement.

FINANCIAL STATEMENT DISCLOSURE

Companies are required to disclose certain items, as follows:

1. The aggregate translation gain or loss included in the determination of net income for the period, including gains or losses related to forward contracts, should be disclosed in either the financial statements or notes thereto.

2. An analysis of the cumulative translation adjustment equity account should be provided in a separate statement or note or as part of a statement of changes in equity. The analysis should include:
   a. The beginning and ending cumulative translation adjustment amounts.
   b. The aggregate adjustment for the period resulting from the translation of foreign currency statements and gains and losses from certain hedging activities and intercompany long-term investment transactions.

    c. The amount of income taxes for the period allocated to the cumulative translation adjustment equity account.

    d. The amounts transferred from the cumulative translation adjustment equity account and included in the determination of net income for the period as a result of the sale of part or all of an investment in a foreign entity.

3. Exchange rate changes that occur after the balance sheet date and their effect on unsettled foreign currency transactions, if significant.

    U.S. companies must also comply with the provisions of the Foreign Corrupt Practices Act (FCPA). The FCPA was enacted in 1977 in response to disclosures by more than 400 U.S. corporations of questionable or improper payments made to foreign officials to elicit their support for business arrangements with the U.S. firms. An extensive investigation by the SEC revealed that in a significant number of cases, the foreign payments had been made to appear in the corporate records as a normal operating expense and that inadequate documentation precluded the verification of the purpose of the payment.

    The FCPA contains two major sections: an antibribery section and an accounting standards section. The antibribery provision makes it a criminal offense to offer a bribe to a foreign government official or foreign political official. The accounting standards section of the Act is intended to help prevent the concealment of foreign corrupt payments.

    In February 1978 the SEC issued *Accounting Series Release No. 242*, which emphasized the importance of the provisions of the Act and the need to comply with its requirements. In the release the SEC stated that although the Act imposed new requirements with respect to the maintenance of internal accounting controls and outlawed certain foreign corrupt practices, it did not alter the existing obligation to adequately disclose questionable and illegal corporate payments and practices. The SEC went on to state that "registrants have a continuing obligation to disclose all material information and all information necessary to prevent other disclosures made from being misleading with respect to such transactions."

HISTORICAL DEVELOPMENTS OF ACCOUNTING STANDARDS

    The expansion of international business has been of particular concern to accountants because of developments in the worldwide monetary system during the 1970s. These developments, coupled with the existence of a number of acceptable methods of translating foreign financial statements and reporting gains or losses on foreign currency fluctuations, led the FASB to place the topic on its agenda in 1973. The result was the issuance in October 1975 of *Statement of Financial Accounting Standards No. 8*, "Accounting for the Translation of Foreign Currency Transactions and Foreign Currency Financial Statements."

    One objective of *Statement No. 8* was to provide uniform accounting standards for the translation of foreign financial statements. A second objective was to fill the gap in authoritative literature on accounting for transactions with foreign companies. The *Statement* was not well received; it proved to be one of the most controversial statements issued by the FASB. Major criticism of the statement focused on the following points:

1. Reporting translation gains and losses in current income often resulted in unnecessary fluctuations in reported income.

2. Translation required by the statement sometimes resulted in reporting a loss when the economic effects of a rate change were expected to be favorable, and a gain when the economic effects were expected to be unfavorable.

3. Certain effective hedges of foreign exchange risk were ignored.

Concerned with the increasing criticism leveled against *Statement No. 8*, the Board added to its agenda a project to reconsider it in January 1979. As a result of this project, an exposure draft entitled ''Foreign Currency Translation'' was issued in August 1980. On the basis of more than 360 comment letters and views expressed in a public hearing, the Board issued a revised exposure draft. These series of developments culminated in the issuance of *SFAS No. 52*, which was discussed in this and the previous chapter. Although few would contend that the accounting as prescribed under *SFAS No. 52* is flawless, it has met with generally less criticism than *SFAS No. 8*.

As the European countries move to the use of the new currency called the ''euro,'' there should be fewer instances where it is necessary to use both remeasurement and translation for a single subsidiary (i.e., the approach used when the functional currency is the currency of a third country). By 2002, it is expected that at least 11 European nations will be using the euro—Austria, Belgium, Finland, France, Germany, Ireland, Italy, Luxembourg, the Netherlands, Portugal, and Spain.

To prepare for trade under the European Union (EU), U.S. companies must update their information systems, their internal and external financial reporting, and assess the impact of the *euro* on all business functions. CFOs, controllers, and CPAs will all play a role in helping businesses manage the complexities of currency conversion, as well as ensuring that reporting requirements are met and tax strategies are optimal.[8]

SUMMARY

1. *Distinguish between the current exchange rate and the historical exchange rate.* The current exchange rate is the spot rate in effect at the end of the accounting period (i.e., the balance sheet date). The historical exchange rate is the spot rate in effect on the date a transaction takes place.

2. *Understand the objectives of financial statement translation.* The objectives are to provide information that is compatible with the exposed economic effects of an exchange rate change on a firm's cash flows and equity, and to reflect in the consolidated statements the financial results and relationships of the individual entities as measured in their functional currencies in conformity with U.S. GAAP.

3. *Identify the functional currency of a foreign entity.* The functional currency is the currency of the primary economic environment in which the foreign entity conducts its operations and generates and expends its cash.

4. *Compare the two methods used to convert the financial statements of a foreign entity into U.S. dollars.* Under the **current method**, all assets and liabilities are translated using the current exchange rate on the balance sheet date. For income statement accounts (revenues and expenses), a weighted-average exchange rate is used to approximate the results that would be obtained from translation of each transaction. Under the **temporal method**, monetary assets and liabilities are translated at the current exchange rate. Assets and liabilities carried at historical cost are translated at historical exchange rates. Assets and liabilities carried at current values (such as inventory carried at market under the lower of cost or market rule) are translated at the current exchange rate. Revenues and expenses that relate to assets and liabilities translated at historical rates (such as depreciation expense, amortization expense, and the cost of sales) are translated at the historical rates used for the related assets and lia-

_____

[8]*Journal of Accountancy*, ''Are You Euro-Fluent?'' by Anette Estrada and Sander Wechsler, June 1999, p. 22.

bilities. Other revenues and expenses are converted using a weighted-average rate.

5. *Distinguish between the circumstances under which each of the two methods is appropriate under current GAAP.* The temporal method (also referred to as remeasurement) is appropriate when the functional currency is the U.S. dollar or when the foreign environment is highly inflationary. The current method (also referred to as translation) is appropriate when the foreign currency is the local currency. If the functional currency is the currency of a third country, it is necessary to remeasure the accounts *first* into the functional currency using the temporal method and *then* to translate the accounts into U.S. dollars (the reporting currency) using the current method.

6. *Explain the factors involved in translating the statements of a foreign entity operating in a highly inflationary economy.* The currency of a country experiencing high inflation will weaken substantially against the currency of a more stable economy. Thus, using the current rate method to translate inventories and fixed assets of foreign operations in highly inflationary economies often results in a substantial reduction in the translated amounts. Because the currency of the country has lost its utility as a store of value and cannot be a functional measuring unit, the Board prescribed that the financial statements be remeasured as if the functional currency were the reporting currency (U.S. dollar).

7. *Translate the statements of a foreign entity when the functional currency is the local currency.* The accounts are translated into dollars using the current rate method. The resulting translation adjustment is recorded as a separate component of stockholders' equity.

8. *Translate the statements of a foreign entity when the functional currency is the U.S. dollar.* When the foreign entity does not maintain its records in its functional currency, the accounts are remeasured into the functional currency (dollars) using the temporal method. The resulting translation adjustment is reported in the current period's income statement.

9. *Understand the concept of comprehensive income in the context of foreign currency translation.* The currency translation adjustment under the "current" method represents one of several items of concern to the FASB because of their frequency of occurrence and relative importance, coupled with their exclusion from reported earnings. These items are, however, included in comprehensive income, defined as *all* changes in equity during a period except those resulting from investments by owners and distributions to owners. A statement of comprehensive income must be included in a complete set of financial statements.

10. *Identify the disclosure requirements for firms with foreign entities.* Companies must disclose: (1) the aggregate transaction gain or loss included in earnings for the period, including gains or losses related to forward contracts; (2) an analysis of the cumulative translation adjustment equity account; and (3) the effect of any significant exchange rate changes that occur after the balance sheet date.

APPENDIX

Accounting for a Foreign Affiliate and Preparation of Consolidated Statements Workpaper Illustrated

To illustrate the accounting for a foreign affiliate and the preparation of a consolidated statements workpaper, the illustration of the 80% interest in SFr Company will be continued. Since SFr Company maintains its books in francs, the trial balance in dollars is based on the translated balances contained in Illustrations 14-4 and 14-8.

DATE OF ACQUISITION

The direct exchange rate for francs on January 2, 2002, was $.15. Thus it would have taken $300,000 (2,000,000 francs × $.15) to buy the 2,000,000 francs needed for the purchase price. The entry to record the acquisition is

Investment in SFr Company	300,000	
Cash		300,000

ILLUSTRATION 14–10

Allocation of Difference Between Cost and Book Value

	Francs	Translation Rate	Dollars
Cost	2,000,000	$.15	300,000
Book value interest acquired:			
(1,740,000 francs × .80)	1,392,000	.15	208,000
Difference between cost and book			
value interest acquired	608,000		91,200
Allocated to:			
Land	(308,000)*	.15	(46,200)
Buildings—10 year-remaining life	(300,000)*	.15	(45,000)
Unallocated balance	—0—		—0—

*Amounts are assumed.

On the date of acquisition, since the business combination must be accounted for using the purchase method of accounting (cash was used to acquire the voting stock), assets, liabilities, and stockholders' equity accounts are translated from francs into dollars using the spot rate of $.15. Any difference between cost and book value interest acquired is allocated to individual assets and liabilities of a foreign subsidiary using essentially the same approach as that illustrated in Chapter 5. On January 2, SFr Company reported common stock of 960,000 francs, additional paid-in capital of 300,000 francs, and retained earnings of 480,000 francs for a net asset balance of 1,740,000 francs. The difference between cost and book value in francs and dollars is allocated to land and buildings in Illustration 14-10. When an acquisition qualifies as a purchase transaction, all accounts of the subsidiary are translated at the date of acquisition using the then-current exchange rate whether the current rate method or the temporal method is used in the translation process. Thus, the computation of the difference and its allocation is the same for both methods.

ACCOUNTING FOR AN INVESTMENT IN A FOREIGN AFFILIATE— AFTER ACQUISITION

After the initial entry to record the purchase of the equity interest in SFr Company, P Company will make a book entry to record the declaration and receipt of cash dividends. P Company accounts for its investment by the cost method. In this case, SFr Company declared and paid a 300,000 franc dividend on September 1 when the direct exchange rate was $.16. The book entry to record the dividend receipt is:

Cash	38,400	
Dividend Income		38,400
300,000 francs × $.16 = $48,000 × .80 = $38,400		

Before consolidated financial statements are prepared, the subsidiary's financial statements must be translated into dollars using either the current rate method (Illustration 14-4) or the temporal method (Illustration 14-8). A workpaper to consolidate P Company and SFr Company is presented in Illustration 14-11 assuming that the current rate method was appropriate for translating the subsidiary's accounts (i.e., the functional currency of the subsidiary was its local currency). Workpaper entries in general journal form are given here (Illustration 14-11):

Consolidated Statements Workpaper Entries—December 31, 2002

(1)	Dividend Income	38,400	
	Dividends Declared—SFr Company		38,400
	To eliminate intercompany dividends.		
(2)	Beginning Retained Earnings—SFr Company	57,600	
	Common Stock—SFr Company	115,200	
	Additional Paid-in Capital—SFr Company	36,000	
	Difference Between Cost and Book Value	91,200	
	Investment in SFr Company		300,000
	To eliminate the investment account.		
(3)	Cumulative Translation Adjustment—SFr Company	29,170	
	Cumulative Translation Adjustment—P Company		29,170
	To recognize P Company's interest in the increase in stockholders' equity resulting from a change in exchange rates.		
(4)	Depreciation Expense	4,680	
	Land	52,360	
	Buildings	45,900	
	Cumulative Translation Adjustment—P Company		11,740
	Difference Between Cost and Book Value		91,200
	To allocate the difference between cost and book value and to recognize the related translation adjustment.		

The major differences between the foregoing entries for the current rate method and those prepared in Chapter 5 are as follows:

1. Using the current rate method to translate the accounts of the subsidiary resulted in a cumulative translation adjustment of $36,462. The $36,462 increases stockholders' equity and translated net assets of the subsidiary. Since this amount is not reported in the income statement, a workpaper entry [entry (3)] is made to recognize the parent's interest therein ($36,462 × .80 = $29,170). The remaining portion ($36,462 × .20 = $7,292) is extended to the noncontrolling interest column.

2. The difference between cost and book value at the date of acquisition was allocated to specific assets and translated into dollars using the exchange rate in effect on the purchase date. However, with a change in the exchange rate, the amortization expense in the income statement is translated using the average exchange rate, and the unamortized ending balances in the balance sheet are translated using the current exchange rate at the balance sheet date. As a result, there will be a translation adjustment related to the translation of these accounts. The amount of the adjustment balances the sum of the debits and the credits in entry (4), and can be verified as shown in Illustration 14-12.

Subsequent to the Year of Acquisition

In years after the year of acquisition, an entry to establish reciprocity is made based on the undistributed net income. In this case the entry for the next year is:

Investment in SFr Company	3,158	
Beginning Retained Earnings—P Company		3,158

Retained Earnings—12/31/2002	$75,948
Retained Earnings—Date of acquisition	72,000
Undistributed net income	$ 3,948
$3,948 × .80 = $3,158	

The other workpaper entries are similar to those illustrated before.

ILLUSTRATION 14–11

Cost Method						

Cost Method

80% Owned Foreign Subsidiary — **Consolidated Statements Workpaper**

Current Rate Method of Translation — **P Company and Foreign Subsidiary**

Year of Acquisition — **For Year Ended December 31, 2002**

	P Company	S Company	Eliminations Dr.	Eliminations Cr.	Noncontrolling Interest	Consolidated Balances
Income Statement						
Sales and Other Revenue	4,200,000	471,120				4,671,120
Dividend Income	38,400		(1) 38,400			—
Total Revenue	4,238,400	471,120				4,671,120
Cost of Goods Sold	2,720,000	288,600				3,008,600
Depreciation Expense	210,000	15,600	(4) 4,680			230,280
Other Expense	914,000	102,180				1,016,180
Income Tax Expense	100,000	12,792				112,792
Total Cost and Expense	3,944,000	419,172				4,367,852
Net/Combined Income	294,400	51,948				303,268
Noncontrolling Interest in Net Income ($51,948 × .20)					10,390	(10,390)
Net Income to Retained Earnings	294,400	51,948	43,080	—0—	10,390	292,878
Retained Earnings Statement						
1/1 Retained Earnings						
P Company	450,000					450,000
SFr Company		72,000	(2) 57,600		14,400	
Net Income from above	294,400	51,948	43,080		10,390	292,878
Dividends Declared						
P Company	(200,000)					(200,000)
SFr Company		(48,000)		(1) 38,400	(9,600)	
12/31 Retained Earnings to Balance Sheet	544,400	75,948	100,680	38,400	15,190	542,878
Balance Sheet						
Current Assets	1,324,400	402,560				1,726,960
Investment in SFr Company	300,000			(2) 300,000		—
Land	450,000	85,000	(4) 52,360			587,360
Buildings (net)	720,000	110,500	(4) 45,900			876,400
Equipment (net)	390,000	73,100				463,100
Difference Between Cost and Book Value	—		(2) 91,200	(4) 91,200		—
Total Assets	3,184,400	671,160				3,653,820
Current Liabilities	840,000	216,750				1,056,750
Bonds Payable	700,000	153,000				853,000
Common Stock						
P Company	800,000					800,000
SFr Company		144,000	(2) 115,200		28,800	
Additional Paid-in Capital						
P Company	300,000					300,000
SFr Company		45,000	(2) 36,000		9,000	
Cumulative Translation Adjustment						
P Company	—			{(3) 29,170 {(4) 11,740		40,910
SFr Company		36,462	(3) 29,170		7,292	
Retained Earnings from above	544,400	75,948	100,680	38,400	15,190	542,878
Noncontrolling Interest in Net Assets					60,282	60,282
Total Liabilities and Owners' Equity	3,184,400	671,160	470,510	470,510		3,653,820

(1) To eliminate intercompany dividends.
(2) To eliminate the investment account.
(3) To recognize interest in cumulative translation adjustment.
(4) To allocate difference between cost and book value.

ILLUSTRATION 14–12

Verification of Cumulative Translation Adjustment

	Francs	Translation Rate	Dollars
Undervalued net assets at beginning of year	608,000	$.15	91,200
Amortization this period	(30,000)	.156	(4,680)
Net asset position translated using rate in effect at date of transaction			86,520
Unamortized balance at end of year*	578,000	.17	98,260
Current year change in cumulative translation adjustment			11,740

	Francs		Dollars
*Land	308,000	.17	52,360
Buildings	270,000	.17	45,900
Total	578,000		98,260

CONSOLIDATION WHEN THE TEMPORAL METHOD OF TRANSLATION IS USED

In completing the remeasurement process using the temporal method, a consolidated statements workpaper would be similar to the one previously illustrated for the current rate method. The major differences between the workpapers are as follows:

1. Under the temporal method, the translation gain or loss is included in the subsidiary's income statement and becomes a part of its ending retained earnings balance. The controlling interest in the gain or loss is recognized as part of consolidated net income in the current period. In subsequent periods the gain or loss is included in consolidated retained earnings as part of the reciprocity entry. Thus, a separate entry is not needed to recognize the parent's share of the translation gain or loss such as was done in entry (3) when the current rate method of translation was used.

2. The unamortized portion of the difference assigned to land and buildings and the amortization for the current period retain their historical dollar values since such nonmonetary assets are translated using historical rates.

REMEASUREMENT AND TRANSLATION OF FOREIGN CURRENCY TRANSACTIONS

SFAS No. 52 defines a foreign currency transaction as one that is denominated in a currency other than the entity's functional currency. As discussed in Chapter 13, at the transaction date, the current exchange rate is used to measure and record a foreign currency transaction in the functional currency of the recording entity. At subsequent balance sheet dates, recorded balances that are denominated in a currency other than the functional currency are adjusted to the functional currency using the current exchange rate. Any transaction gain or loss resulting from this procedure is recognized currently in income. Although a thorough discussion and illustration of the effects on the financial statements of affiliated companies and on consolidated statements is beyond the scope of this text, two examples are presented to illustrate the procedures.

Assume that a French subsidiary has a $100,000 loan payable to a U.S. bank. The loan is denominated in dollars and the franc is the functional currency of the subsidiary. Thus, this is a foreign currency transaction to the subsidiary but not to the U.S. bank. The current exchange rate was $.20 on the transaction date and $.16 on the balance sheet date. The subsidiary would compute a gain or loss as follows at the balance sheet date:

	Francs
Transaction date	$100,000 ÷ .20 = 500,000
Balance sheet date	$100,000 ÷ .16 = 625,000
Transaction loss reported in income	125,000

The U.S. bank would not record a gain or loss on its books because the payable is denominated in dollars.

Before consolidation, the accounts of the subsidiary are translated into dollars (the reporting currency) using the current rate method. In this illustration the payable of 625,000 francs as measured in the functional currency is translated to $100,000 (625,000 francs × $.16) to reflect the dollar denominated amount of the loan. In the income statement, the transaction loss of 125,000 francs is translated using the average exchange rate. When the current rate method is used, the adjustment resulting from translating the accounts into dollars is made to stockholders' equity.

If, in the foregoing illustration, the loan were denominated in francs (the functional currency of the subsidiary), the translation would not be a foreign currency transaction to the subsidiary. The loan is a foreign currency transaction, however, to the U.S. bank. The bank will measure the 500,000 franc receivable into dollars at the transaction and balance sheet dates using the current rate. A transaction loss is computed at the balance sheet date as follows:

Transaction date	500,000 francs × $.20 = $100,000
Balance sheet date	500,000 francs × $.16 = $ 80,000
Transaction loss reported in income	$ 20,000

In the trial balance of the subsidiary, the payable is already measured in francs. Thus, a transaction gain or loss is not recognized currently in income. Note, however, that the payable is a component of the subsidiary's net asset position and will affect the translation gain or loss reported in the stockholders' equity section of the balance sheet when the payable is translated into U.S. dollars for consolidation purposes.

If the dollar is identified as the foreign entity's functional currency, then a dollar-denominated transaction is not a foreign currency transaction to either party. In the dollar trial balance of the subsidiary, the payable is restated to $100,000 at both the transaction date and the balance sheet date. Finally, if the functional currency is the dollar and the loan is denominated in francs, it is a foreign currency transaction to both parties, and the 500,000 franc loan is remeasured to $80,000 at the balance sheet date by both.

INTERCOMPANY RECEIVABLES AND PAYABLES

SFAS No. 52 requires that transaction gains and losses on intercompany receivables and payables be recognized in the period that the exchange rate changes. The procedures for doing so are similar to those discussed in the preceding section. However, a company is required to distinguish between transactions that are of a long-term investment nature and other transactions. Intercompany transactions for which settlement is not planned or intended in the foreseeable future are considered a part of the net investment in the foreign entity. Accordingly, transaction gains or losses on the receivable or payable, whether denominated in dollars or in the local currency of the foreign entity, are deferred and accumulated with the translation adjustment in a separate component of stockholders' equity. A transaction gain or loss attributable to other intercompany accounts is reported currently in the determination of net income because it is expected to affect functional currency cash flows.

ELIMINATION OF INTERCOMPANY PROFIT

Profits and losses attributable to intercompany sales or transfers are eliminated on the basis of the exchange rate at the date of each sale or transfer. Here again, the use of averages or reasonable approximations of specific rates in effect on the due date of each transaction is permitted. To illustrate, the following assumptions are made:

1. Exchange rates: date of sale, $.14; balance sheet date, $.17.
2. The intercompany sale and profit in dollars and francs is:

	Dollars	Francs
Sales price to foreign subsidiary	14,000	100,000
Cost to parent company	10,500	75,000
Intercompany profit	3,500	25,000

3. None of the inventory was sold by the subsidiary during the current period.
4. The franc is the functional currency of the foreign entity.

At year-end, the inventory balance of 100,000 francs is translated to $17,000 using the current rate at the balance sheet date. In the consolidated balance sheet, the intercompany profit of $3,500 is eliminated from the inventory, which results in a carrying value for the inventory of $13,500. As shown below, this process includes $750 in the inventory carrying value that is related to the effect of the exchange rate change on the intercompany profit element.

	Francs	Translation Rate	Dollars
Inventory cost	75,000	.17	12,750
Intercompany profit	25,000	(.17 − .14)	750
Carrying value of ending inventory	100,000		13,500

The Board reasoned that intercompany profit occurs at the date of sale and that is the amount that should be eliminated. The $750 results from a subsequent change in the exchange rate, an event considered independent from the sale.

LIQUIDATION OF A FOREIGN INVESTMENT

Upon the sale of part or all of an investment in a foreign entity, a pro-rata share of the amount included in the accumulated translation adjustment equity account associated with that foreign investment is removed and reported as part of the gain or loss from the disposition of the investment. For example, if a company disposed of 50% of its interest in a foreign entity, 50% of the related accumulated translation adjustment would be removed from stockholders' equity and recognized in measuring the gain or loss on the sale.

(The letter A indicated for an exercise or problem refers to the appendix.)

QUESTIONS

1. What requirements must be satisfied if a foreign subsidiary is to be consolidated?

2. What is meant by an entity's functional currency and what are the economic indicators identified by the FASB to provide guidance in selecting the functional currency?

3. The _____ is the functional currency of a foreign subsidiary with operations that are relatively self-contained and integrated within the country in which it is located. In such cases, the _____ method of translation would be used to translate the accounts into dollars.

4. The _____ is the functional currency of a foreign subsidiary that is a direct and integral component or extension of a U.S. parent company. In such cases, the _____ method of translation is used to translate (remeasure) the accounts into dollars.

5. Which method of translation is used to convert the financial statements when a foreign subsidiary operates in a highly inflationary economy?

6. Define remeasurement.

7. Under the current rate method, how are assets and liabilities that are stated in a foreign currency translated?

8. How does the method of accounting for a business combination (purchase or pooling of interests) affect the translation of a foreign affiliate's financial statements when the current rate method is used to translate the accounts?

9. What is the objective of the temporal method of translation?

10. Assuming that the temporal method is used, how are revenue and expense items in foreign currency financial statements converted?

11. A translation adjustment results from the process of translating financial statements of a foreign subsidiary from its functional currency into dollars. Where is the translation adjustment reported in the financial statements if the current rate method is used to translate the accounts?

EXERCISES

EXERCISE 14-1 Identifying the Exchange Rate

Accounts are listed below for a foreign subsidiary that maintains its books in its local currency. The equity interest in the subsidiary was acquired in a purchase transaction. In the space provided, indicate the exchange rate that would be used to translate the accounts into dollars assuming that the functional currency was identified (a) as the U.S. dollar and (b) as the foreign entity's local currency. Use the following letters to identify the exchange rate:

H—historical exchange rate
C—current exchange rate
A—average exchange rate for the current period

Account	Exchange Rate if the Functional Currency Is:	
	U.S. Dollar	Local Currency
Cash	_____	_____
Accounts receivable	_____	_____
Inventory carried at cost	_____	_____
Inventory carried at market	_____	_____
Prepaid rent	_____	_____
Property, plant, and equipment	_____	_____
Goodwill	_____	_____
Accounts payable	_____	_____
Bonds payable	_____	_____
Unamortized premium on bonds payable	_____	_____
Preferred stock carried at issuance price	_____	_____
Common stock	_____	_____
Sales	_____	_____
Cost of goods sold	_____	_____
Depreciation expense	_____	_____

EXERCISE 14-2 **Multiple Choice**

Select the best answer for each of the following items:

1. Golf Company acquired 80% of the outstanding stock of Ping Company, a foreign company, in an acquisition accounted for as a purchase transaction. In preparing consolidated statements, the paid-in capital of Ping Company should be translated into dollars at the

   (a) Current exchange rate in effect at the balance sheet date.
   (b) Exchange rate in effect at the date the capital transactions of the subsidiary took place.
   (c) Exchange rate in effect at the date Golf Company purchased the Ping Company stock.
   (d) Exchange rate effective when Ping Company was organized.

2. The account balances of a foreign entity are required by *SFAS No. 52* to be measured using that entity's functional currency. The functional currency of an entity is defined as

   (a) The currency in which the entity's transactions are recorded.
   (b) The currency of the primary economic environment in which the entity operates.
   (c) The U.S. dollar.
   (d) The local currency of the country in which the entity is physically located.

3. When translating foreign currency financial statements for an entity whose functional currency is the local currency of the country in which it is physically located, which of the following accounts is translated using current exchange rates?

	Bonds Payable	Inventories Carried at Market
(a)	No	No
(b)	Yes	No
(c)	No	Yes
(d)	Yes	Yes

4. A translation adjustment (or translation gain) that is a consequence of translation of a functional currency that is different from the reporting currency should be

   (a) Deferred and amortized over a period not to exceed 40 years.
   (b) Deferred until a subsequent year when a loss occurs and offset it against that loss.
   (c) Included as a separate item in the equity section of the balance sheet.
   (d) Included in net income in the period in which it occurs.

5. A wholly owned foreign subsidiary of Import Corporation has certain expense accounts for the year ended December 31, 2001, stated in local currency units (LCU) as follows:

	LCU
Amortization of patent (patent was acquired January 1, 1999)	40,000
Provision for doubtful accounts	40,000
Rent	120,000

The exchange rates at various dates are as follows:

	Dollar Equivalent of 1 LCU
December 31, 2001	$.20
Average for the year ended December 31, 2001	.24
January 1, 1999	.25

The subsidiary's operations were an extension of the parent company's operations. What total dollar amount should be included in Import's income statement to reflect the foregoing expenses for the year ended December 31, 2001?

(a) $48,000.

(b) $40,000.

(c) $48,400.

(d) $42,000.

(AICPA adapted)

EXERCISE 14-3 **Multiple Choice**

Select the best answer choice for each of the following items.

1. Perez Company's operations are unrelated to the operations of its subsidiary. Certain balance sheet accounts of the foreign subsidiary at December 31, 2001, have been translated into U.S. dollars as follows:

	Translated at:	
	Current Rates	*Historical Rates*
Accounts receivable, current	$200,000	$220,000
Accounts receivable, long-term	130,000	140,000
Prepaid insurance	50,000	55,000
Goodwill	100,000	110,000

If the accounting is in accordance with *SFAS No. 52*, what total should be included in Perez's balance sheet at December 31, 2001, for the foregoing items?

(a) $480,000.

(b) $490,000.

(c) $495,000.

(d) $580,000.

2. When the functional currency of a foreign operation is the U.S. dollar, translation gains and losses resulting from translating (remeasuring) foreign currency financial statements into U.S. dollars should be included as

(a) An extraordinary item in the income statement for the period in which the rate changes.

(b) An ordinary item in the income statement for losses but deferred for gains in accordance with the conservatism convention.

(c) An ordinary item in the income statement for the period in which the rate changes.

(d) A deferred item in the balance sheet.

3. Pal Company is translating account balances of its foreign subsidiary into dollars for its December 31, 2001, balance sheet and its 2001 income statement. The functional currency was identified as the local currency of the foreign subsidiary. The average exchange rate for 2001 should be used to translate

(a) Retained earnings at January 1, 2001.
(b) Equipment purchased in 2001.
(c) Sales for 2001.
(d) Cash at December 31, 2001.

4. One of the first steps in translating the financial statements of a foreign subsidiary is the identification of the functional currency of that entity. Which of the following indicates that the functional currency is the local currency of the foreign entity?

(a) There is a high volume of intercompany transactions.
(b) Financing is primarily denominated in the local currency.
(c) Sales are mostly in the United States, or sales contracts are denominated in dollars.
(d) Sales prices are primarily responsive in the short term to exchange rate changes.

5. When the foreign operations are conducted in a highly inflationary economy, at what translation rates should the goodwill and accounts receivable accounts in foreign statements be translated into U.S. dollars?

	Goodwill	Accounts Receivable
(a)	Current	Average for year
(b)	Historical	Current
(c)	Historical	Historical
(d)	Current	Current

(AICPA adapted)

EXERCISE 14-4 **Foreign Currency Translation—Current Rate Method**

On January 1, 2001, Trenten Systems, a U.S.-based company, purchased a controlling interest in Grant Management Consultants located in Zurich, Switzerland. The acquisition was treated as a purchase transaction. The 2001 financial statements stated in Swiss francs are given below.

GRANT MANAGEMENT CONSULTANTS
Comparative Balance Sheets
January 1 and December 31, 2001

	Jan. 1	Dec. 31
Cash and Receivables	20,000	55,000
Net Property, Plant, and Equipment	40,000	37,000
Totals	60,000	92,000
Accounts and Notes Payable	30,000	32,000
Common Stock	20,000	20,000
Retained Earnings	10,000	40,000
Totals	60,000	92,000

GRANT MANAGEMENT CONSULTANTS
Combined Income and Retained Earnings Statement
For the Year Ended December 31, 2001

Revenues	75,000
Operating Expenses including depreciation of 3,000 francs	30,000
Net income	45,000
Dividends Declared and Paid	15,000
Increase in Retained Earnings	30,000

Direct exchange rates for the Swiss franc are:

	Dollars per Franc
January 1, 2001	$.5987
December 31, 2001	.5321
Average for 2001	.5654
Dividend declaration and payment date	.5810

Required:

A. Translate the year-end balance sheet and income statement of the foreign subsidiary using the current rate method of translation.

B. Prepare a schedule to verify the translation adjustment.

EXERCISE 14-5 **Foreign Currency Remeasurement—Temporal Method**
Use the information provided in Exercise 14-4.

Required:

A. Convert (remeasure) the financial statements of the foreign subsidiary using the temporal method of translation.

B. Prepare a schedule to verify the translation gain or loss.

EXERCISE 14-6 **Local Currency Is a Foreign (Non-U.S.) Currency**
Refer to Exercise 14-4. Using the same information, assume that the German mark is identified as the functional currency of the subsidiary.

Required:

A. Remeasure the account balances that are expressed in Swiss francs in German marks. Direct exchange rates for the German mark are:

	Marks per Franc
Beginning of current year	1.3940
End of current year	1.2899
Average for current year	1.3445
Dividend payment date	1.2438

B. Translate the remeasured accounts that are now stated in German marks into dollars using the current rate method. Direct exchange rates for the German mark are:

	Dollars per Mark
Beginning of current year	$.4891
End of current year	.4630
Average for current year	.4751
Dividend payment date	.4740

EXERCISE 14-7 **Current Rate Method**
Dorsey Corporation purchased 90% of the common stock of Lansing Company on January 1, 1995. The cost of the investment was equal to the book value interest acquired. Dorsey Corporation accounted for the acquisition as a purchase transaction. Lansing Company operates two retail stores and an exporting business in London that specializes in buying and

selling British tweeds. The subsidiary provided the following financial statements in pounds to the parent company:

LANSING COMPANY
Combined Income and Retained Earnings Statement
For the Year Ended December 31, 2001

Sales	2,900,000
Cost of Goods Sold	(1,400,000)
Depreciation Expense	(300,000)
Other Expenses	(400,000)
Net Income	800,000
1/1 Retained Earnings	900,000
	1,700,000
Less: Dividends Declared and Paid, December 31	(325,000)
12/31 Retained Earnings	1,375,000

LANSING COMPANY
Balance Sheet
December 31, 2001

Cash and Receivables	1,275,000
Merchandise Inventory	490,000
Property, Plant, and Equipment	3,450,000
Total	5,215,000
Current Liablities	640,000
Long-Term Notes Payable	1,200,000
Capital Stock	2,000,000
Retained Earnings	1,375,000
Total	5,215,000

Lansing Company was incorporated on January 1, 1993, at which time all the property, plant, and equipment was purchased. The long-term notes were issued to partially finance the purchase of the fixed assets.

Direct exchange rates for the British pound are as follows:

January 1, 1993	$1.8996
January 1, 1995	1.8365
Average for the last quarter 2000	1.5300
January 1, 2001	1.4919
December 31, 2001	1.4730
Average for 2001	1.4788
Average for August–December 2001	1.4950

The January 1, 2001, retained earnings balance of Lansing in dollars was $1,593,408, and the cumulative translation adjustment was a debit balance of $939,898. The beginning inventory of £420,000 was acquired during the last quarter of 2000 and the ending inventory was acquired during the last five months of 2001. Sales were made and purchases and other expenses were incurred evenly during the year.

Required:
Translate the December 31, 2001, account balances of Lansing Company into dollars assuming that the pound is the functional currency of Lansing Company.

EXERCISE 14-8 **Temporal Method (Remeasurement)**
Refer to the data provided in Exercise 14-7 for Dorsey Corporation and Lansing Company.

Required:

Translate (remeasure) the account balances of Lansing into dollars assuming that the dollar is the functional currency of Lansing Company. The beginning retained earnings balance of Lansing Company in dollars was $1,791,324.

EXERCISE 14-9 **Translation Assuming Various Functional Currencies**

Slocome Travel owns a travel agency that operates in London. Account balances in pounds for the subsidiary are summarized below:

	2001	
	January 1	*December 31*
Cash and Receivables	32,000	35,000
Office Supplies	1,500	900
Land, Building, and Equipment	70,000	65,000
Accounts Payable	(15,500)	(6,900)
Long-Term Note Payable	(25,000)	(15,000)
Common Stock	(40,000)	(40,000)
Retained Earnings	(23,000)	(23,000)
Dividends—Declared and Paid on December 31	—	4,000
Revenues	—	(40,000)
Operating Expenses	—	20,000
Totals	—0—	—0—

Exchange rates for 2001 were as follows:

January 1	$1.5403
December 31	1.5961
Average for year	1.5532

The subsidiary did not make any purchases of office supplies or plant assets during the year. Revenues were earned and operating expenses, other than depreciation and supplies used, were incurred evenly throughout the year.

Required:

A. Prepare a schedule to compute the translation adjustment for the year, assuming the foreign entity's functional currency is the pound.

B. Prepare a schedule to compute the translation gain or loss, assuming the foreign entity's functional currency is the U.S. dollar.

C. Explain why your results differ under the two methods.

EXERCISE 14-10A **Consolidated Workpaper**

A U.S. company owns an 80% interest in a company located in Germany. During the year the parent company sold inventory that had cost $24,000 to the subsidiary on account for $30,000 when the exchange rate was $.5192. The subsidiary still held one-half of the inventory and had not paid the parent company for the purchase at the end of the fiscal period. The unsettled account is denominated in dollars. The exchange rate at the fiscal year-end was $.4994.

Required:

A. **(1)** Compute the amounts that would be reported for the inventory and accounts payable in the subsidiary's translated balance sheet. The entity's functional currency is the mark.

(2) Compute the subsidiary's transaction gain or loss on the accounts payable denominated in dollars.

(3) How is the transaction gain or loss reported in the foreign entity's financial statements?

B. Compute the amount of the intercompany profit to be eliminated in the consolidated statements workpaper prepared for the current year.

C. **(1)** Assuming that the transaction had been denominated in 50,204 German marks rather than dollars, compute the transaction gain or loss that would be reported by the parent company.

(2) How is the gain or loss reported in the consolidated financial statements?

(3) How would your answer differ if the loan to the foreign subsidiary was considered to be of a long-term investment nature?

PROBLEMS

PROBLEM 14-1   **Translation—Local Currency Is the Functional Currency**

On January 1, 2001, a U.S. company purchased 100% of the outstanding stock of Ventana Grains, a company located in Latz City, New Zealand. Ventana Grains was organized on January 1, 1987. All the property, plant, and equipment held on January 1, 2001, was acquired when the company was organized. The business combination was accounted for as a purchase transaction. The 2001 financial statements for Ventana Grains, prepared in its local currency, the New Zealand dollar, are given here.

VENTANA GRAINS
Comparative Balance Sheets
January 1 and December 31, 2001

	Jan. 1	Dec. 31
Cash and Receivables	500,000	880,000
Inventories	600,000	500,000
Land	400,000	400,000
Buildings (net)	650,000	605,000
Equipment (net)	465,000	470,000
Totals	2,615,000	2,855,000
Short-Term Accounts and Notes	295,000	210,000
Long-Term Notes (600,000 issued September 1, 1997, 80,000 issued July 1, 2001)	600,000	680,000
Common Stock	800,000	800,000
Additional Paid-in Capital	200,000	200,000
Retained Earnings	720,000	965,000
Total	2,615,000	2,855,000

VENTANA GRAINS
Combined Income and Retained Earnings Statement
For the Year Ended December 31, 2001

Revenues		3,225,000
Cost of Goods Sold:		
Beginning Inventory	600,000	
Purchases	2,100,000	
Goods Available for Sale	2,700,000	
Less: Ending Inventory	500,000	
Cost of Goods Sold		2,200,000
Gross Profit on Sales		1,025,000
Depreciation Expense	140,000	
Other Expenses	540,000	680,000
Net Income		345,000
Jan. 1 Retained Earnings		720,000
Total		1,065,000
Less: Dividends Paid		100,000
Dec. 31 Retained Earnings		965,000

The account balances are computed in conformity with U.S. generally accepted accounting standards.

Other information is as follows:

1. Direct exchange rates for the New Zealand dollar on various dates were:

Date	Exchange Rate
January 1, 1987	$.8011
September 1, 1997	.5813
January 1, 2001	.7924
July 1, 2001	.7412
December 31, 2001	.7298
Average for 2001	.7480
Average for the last four months of 2001	.7476

2. Ventana Grains purchased additional equipment for 100,000 New Zealand dollars on July 1, 2001, by issuing a note for 80,000 New Zealand dollars and paying the balance in cash.

3. Sales were made and purchases and "Other Expenses" were incurred evenly throughout the year.

4. Depreciation for the period in New Zealand dollars was computed as follows:

Building	45,000
Equipment—Purchased before 1/1/2001	85,000
Equipment—Purchased July 1, 2001	10,000

5. The inventory is valued on a FIFO basis. The beginning inventory was acquired when the exchange rate was $.7480. The ending inventory was acquired during the last four months of 2001.

6. Dividends of 50,000 New Zealand dollars were paid on July 1 and December 31.

Required:

A. Translate the financial statements into dollars assuming that the local currency of the foreign subsidiary was identified as its functional currency.

B. Prepare a schedule to verify the translation adjustment determined in requirement A. Describe how the translation adjustment would be reported in the financial statements.

PROBLEM 14-2 Remeasurement—U.S. Dollar Is the Functional Currency

Refer to the information given in Problem 14-1.

Required:

A. Remeasure the financial statements into dollars assuming that the U.S. dollar was identified as the functional currency of the foreign subsidiary.

B. Prepare a schedule to verify the translation gain or loss determined in requirement A. Describe how the translation gain or loss would be reported in the financial statements.

PROBLEM 14-3 Translation—Local Currency Is the Functional Currency

(This problem is a continuation of the illustration presented in the chapter.)

On January 2, 2001, P Company, a U.S.-based company, acquired for 2,000,000 francs an 80% interest in SFr Company, a French company. On January 2, 2001, SFr Company reported a retained earnings balance of 480,000 francs. SFr's books are maintained in francs and are in conformity with U.S. generally accepted accounting principles. Trial balances of the two companies as of December 31, 2002, are presented here:

Debits	P Company (Dollars)	SFr Company (Francs)
Cash	500,200	962,500
Accounts Receivable	516,400	660,000
Inventories (FIFO cost)	627,800	1,037,500
Investment in SFr Company	300,000	—
Land	450,000	500,000
Buildings (net)	610,000	550,000
Equipment (net)	290,000	405,000
Dividends declared	200,000	375,000
Cost of Goods Sold	2,720,000	2,312,500
Depreciation Expense	210,000	125,000
Other Expense	914,000	818,750
Income Tax Expense	100,000	102,500
Totals	7,438,400	7,848,750

Credits		
Accounts Payable	540,000	800,000
Short-term Notes Payable	300,000	650,750
Bonds Payable	700,000	850,000
Common Stock	800,000	960,000
Additional Paid-in Capital	300,000	300,000
Retained Earnings, 1/1	544,400	513,000
Sales	4,200,000	3,775,000
Dividend Income	54,000	—
Totals	7,438,400	7,848,750

Other information related to the subsidiary follows:

1. Beginning inventory of 830,000 francs was acquired when the exchange rate was $.165.
2. Purchases made uniformly throughout 2002 were 2,520,000 francs.
3. The franc is identified as the subsidiary's functional currency.
4. The subsidiary's beginning (1/1/02) retained earnings and cumulative translation adjustment (credit) in dollars were $75,948 and $36,462, respectively.
5. All plant assets were acquired before the parent obtained a controlling interest in the subsidiary.
6. Sales are made and all expenses are incurred uniformly throughout the year.
7. The ending inventory was acquired during the last quarter.
8. The subsidiary declared and paid dividends of 375,000 francs on September 2.
9. The following direct exchange rate quotations were available:

Date of subsidiary acquisition	$.15
Average for 2001	.156
January 1, 2002	.17
September 2, 2002	.18
December 31, 2002	.19
Average for the 4th quarter, 2002	.185
Average for 2002	.176

Required:

A. Prepare a translated balance sheet and combined statement of income and retained earnings for the subsidiary.

B. Prepare a schedule to verify the translation adjustment.

C. Compute the following ratios based on the franc and the U.S. dollar financial statements.

(1) Current ratio.
(2) Debt to equity.
(3) Gross profit percentage.
(4) Net income to sales.

PROBLEM 14-4 **Remeasurement—U.S. Dollar Is the Functional Currency**
Use the information provided in Problem 14-3 for P Company and SFr Company.

Required:
A. Convert the accounts of the foreign subsidiary, assuming that the U.S. dollar is the functional currency of both companies. For this problem assume that the subsidiary's beginning (1/1/02) retained earnings balance in the translated balance sheet is $76,660.
B. Prepare a schedule to verify the translation gain or loss, assuming a 637,000 franc net exposed liability position at the beginning of the year.

PROBLEM 14-5 **Temporal Method**
Pasquale Company is a manufacturer of oil drilling equipment located in Canada. The company is 90% owned by a U.S. parent company. The accounting department of Pasquale Company accumulated the following 2001 information for the company's auditor.

Equipment
1. The equipment account contained the following items:

Description	Cost (Can. $)	Useful Life	Acquisition Date	Exchange Rate on Acquisition Date
Drill press	30,000	5 years	July 15, 1997	$.8430
Stamping press	80,000	4 years	January 2, 1999	.7360
Fork lift	42,000	6 years	September 1, 2000	.6998

2. Pasquale Company depreciates assets by the straight-line method and assumes a zero residual value.

3. Its policy is to take a full year's depreciation on all depreciable assets acquired before July 1 and no depreciation on all depreciable assets required after July 1.

Inventory
1. The beginning inventory of 60,000 Canadian dollars was acquired during the last quarter of 2000.
2. Inventory purchases of 400,000 Canadian dollars were made uniformly during the year.
3. The ending inventory of 60,000 Canadian dollars was acquired during November and December, 2001.

Marketable Securities
1. Marketable securities, carried at cost, were acquired for 30,000 Canadian dollars when the direct exchange rate was $.9320.

Direct Exchange Rates
Average for the last quarter of 2000, $.7322
January 1, 2001, $.7080
Average for November and December, 2001, $.6845
Average for 2001, $.7140
December 31, 2001, $.6960

Required:

A. Compute the account balances that would be reported for equipment, inventory, and marketable securities in the December 31, 2001, balance sheet expressed in U.S. dollars, assuming that the temporal method was used to translate the accounts.

B. Compute the depreciation expense and cost of goods sold for 2001 in U.S. dollars, assuming that the temporal method was used to translate the accounts.

C. Repeat requirements A and B, assuming that the current rate method was used to translate the accounts.

D. Contrast the effects on income from using the current rate method and the temporal method to translate cost of goods sold and depreciation expense. Explain why net income is increased or decreased when the accounts were translated using the current rate method.

PROBLEM 14-6A   **Cost Method Workpaper—Current Rate Method**

For this problem, refer to the information provided in Problem 14-3 for P Company and SFr Company. Ignore deferred income taxes in the assignment of the difference between cost and book value.

Required:

A. If you have not already done so, prepare a workpaper to translate the trial balance of the subsidiary into dollars using the current rate method.

B. Prepare the journal entries made on the books of P Company during 2002 to account for its investment in SFr Company. P Company uses the cost method to record its investment in SFr Company. At the date of acquisition, the 608,000 franc difference between cost and book value interest acquired was allocated as follows:

Asset	Francs	Translation Rate	Dollars
Land	308,000	$.15	46,200
Building	300,000	.15	45,000
Total	608,000		91,200

The building is depreciated over a 10-year remaining life using the straight-line method of amortization.

C. Prepare a consolidated statements workpaper at December 31, 2002.

PROBLEM 14-7A   **Cost Method Workpaper—Temporal Method**

P Company holds an 80% interest in SFr Company, a French company. A trial balance for P Company and SFr Company at December 31, 2002, and other data are given in Problems 14-3 and 14-4. Ignore deferred income taxes in the assignment of the difference between cost and book value.

Required:

A. If you have not already done so (Problem 14-4), prepare a workpaper to translate the trial balance of the subsidiary into dollars using the temporal method of translation. The subsidiary's beginning retained earnings balance in the translated balance sheet is $76,660.

B. Prepare the journal entries made on the books of P Company during 2002 to account for the investment in SFr Company. P Company uses the cost method to record its investment in SFr Company. At the date of acquisition, the 608,000 franc difference between cost and book value interest acquired was allocated as follows:

Asset	Francs	Translation Rate	Dollars
Land	308,000	$.15	46,200
Building	300,000	.15	45,000
Total	608,000		91,200

The building is depreciated over a 10-year remaining life using the straight-line method of amortization.

C. Prepare a consolidated statements workpaper at December 31, 2002.

PROBLEM 14-8A Cost Method Workpaper—Local Currency Is the Functional Currency

Babbit, Inc., a multinational corporation based in the United States, owns an 80% interest in Nakima Company, which is located in Sydney, Australia. The acquisition, which was made on January 1, 2001, was accounted for using the purchase method of accounting. The difference between cost of 648,500 Australian dollars and the book value of the 80% interest acquired was attributed to specific assets of Nakima Company as follows:

	80% of Difference (Australian Dollars)
Equipment that has a 5-year remaining life	59,100
Land	43,250
Inventories—Nakima uses the FIFO cost flow assumption in pricing its inventory	21,750
Amount that could not be assigned to specific assets or liabilities (amortize over 10 years)	120,000
Total difference in Australian dollars	244,100

Ignore deferred income taxes in the assignment of the difference between cost and book value. The adjusted trial balances for the two companies on December 31, 2001 are presented here:

Debits	Babbit Inc. (U.S. Dollars)	Nakima Company (Australian Dollars)
Cash	65,885	95,250
Accounts Receivable	150,116	106,250
12/31 Inventory	115,000	83,250
Investment in Nakima Company	514,585	—0—
Land	59,400	187,500
Buildings and Equipment	200,000	250,000
Cost of Goods Sold	425,000	121,500
Other Expenses	75,000	51,750
Dividends Declared	50,000	31,250
Totals	1,654,986	926,750

Credits		
Accumulated Depreciation	125,000	93,750
Accounts Payable	14,750	62,500
Notes Payable	25,000	15,000
Capital Stock	600,000	340,500
1/1 Retained Earnings	325,000	165,000
Sales	545,475	250,000
Dividend Income	19,761	—0—
Totals	1,654,986	926,750

Other Information

1. Sales, purchases, and other expenses were incurred evenly during the year.
2. Dividends of 15,625 Australian dollars were paid on April 30 and October 31.
3. The accounts are presented in conformity with U.S. generally accepted accounting principles.
4. Direct rates of exchange.

1/1/01	$.7935
4/30/01	.7899
10/31/01	.7910
12/31/01	.7575
Average for 2001	.7962

5. The Australian dollar is identified as the functional currency of Nakima Company.

Required:

A. Prepare a workpaper to translate the trial balance of the subsidiary into U.S. dollars.

B. Prepare a schedule to verify the translation adjustment.

C. Prepare journal entries on the books of the parent company to record the purchase of the 80% interest in the subsidiary and to apply the cost method of accounting.

D. Prepare a consolidated statements workpaper at December 31, 2001. Journal entries made in requirement C that are not reflected in the trial balance of Babbit, Inc. are to be made as adjusting entries in the elimination columns of the workpaper.

PROBLEM 14-9 **Local Currency Is the Functional Currency, Equity Method for Investment**

On January 2, 2001, P Company, a U.S.-based company, acquired for 2,000,000 francs an 80% interest in SFr Company, a French company. On January 2, 2001, SFr Company reported a retained earnings balance of 480,000 francs. SFr's books are maintained in francs and are in conformity with U.S. generally accepted accounting principles. Trial balances of the two companies as of December 31, 2002, are presented here:

Debits	P Company (Dollars)	SFr Company (Francs)
Cash	500,200	962,500
Accounts Receivable	516,400	660,000
Inventories (FIFO cost)	627,800	1,037,500
Investment in SFr Company	297,806	—
Land	450,000	500,000
Buildings (net)	610,000	550,000
Equipment (net)	290,000	405,000
Dividends Declared	200,000	375,000
Cost of Goods Sold	2,720,000	2,312,500
Depreciation Expense	210,000	125,000
Other Expense	914,000	818,750
Income Tax Expense	100,000	102,500
Totals	$7,436,206	7,848,750

Credits		
Accounts Payable	540,000	800,000
Short-Term Notes Payable	300,000	650,750
Bonds Payable	700,000	850,000
Common Stock	800,000	960,000
Additional Paid-in Capital	300,000	300,000
Retained Earnings, 1/1	542,878	513,000
Sales	4,200,000	3,775,000
Equity Income	53,328	—
Totals	$7,436,206	7,848,750

Other information related to the subsidiary follows:

1. Beginning inventory of 830,000 francs was acquired when the exchange rate was $.165.
2. Purchases made uniformly throughout 2002 were 2,520,000 francs.
3. The franc is identified as the subsidiary's functional currency.
4. The subsidiary's beginning (1/1/02) retained earnings and cumulative translation adjustment (credit) in dollars were $75,948 and $36,462, respectively.
5. All plant assets were acquired before the parent obtained a controlling interest in the subsidiary.
6. Sales are made and all expenses are incurred uniformly throughout the year.
7. The ending inventory was acquired during the last quarter.
8. The subsidiary declared and paid dividends of 375,000 francs on September 2.
9. The following direct exchange rate quotations were available:

Date of subsidiary acquisition	$.15
Average for 2001	.156
January 1, 2002	.17
September 2, 2002	.18
December 31, 2002	.19
Average for the fourth quarter, 2002	.185
Average for 2001	.176

Required:
A. Prepare a translated balance sheet and combined statement of income and retained earnings for the subsidiary.
B. Prepare a schedule to verify the translation adjustment.
C. Compute the following ratios based on the franc and the U.S. dollar financial statements:
   (1) Current ratio.
   (2) Debt to equity.
   (3) Gross profit percentage.
   (4) Net income to sales.

PROBLEM 14-10 **U.S. Dollar Is the Functional Currency, Equity Method for Investment**
Use the information provided in Problem 14-9 for P Company and SFr Company.

Required:
A. Convert the accounts of the foreign subsidiary, assuming that the U.S. dollar is the functional currency of both companies. For this problem assume that the subsidiary's beginning (1/1/02) retained earnings balance in the translated balance sheet is $76,660.
B. Prepare a schedule to verify the translation gain or loss, assuming a 637,000 franc net exposed liability position at the beginning of the year.

PROBLEM 14-11A **Complete Equity Workpaper—Current Rate Method**
For this problem, refer to the information provided in Problem 14-9 for P Company and SFr Company. Ignore deferred income taxes in the allocation of the difference between cost and book value.

Required:
A. If you have not already done so, prepare a workpaper to translate the trial balance of the subsidiary into dollars using the current rate method.
B. Prepare the journal entries made on the books of P Company during 2002 to account for its investment in SFr Company. P Company uses the complete equity method to record

its investment in SFr Company. At the date of acquisition, the 608,000 franc difference between cost and book value interest acquired was allocated as follows:

Asset	Francs	Translation Rate	Dollars
Land	308,000	$.15	46,200
Building	300,000	.15	45,000
Total	608,000		91,200

The building is depreciated over a 10-year remaining life using the straight-line method of amortization.

C. Prepare a consolidated statements workpaper at December 31, 2002.

PROBLEM 14-12A **Complete Equity Workpaper—Temporal Method**

P Company holds an 80% interest in SFr Company, a French company. A trial balance for P Company and SFr Company at December 31, 2002, and other data are given in Problems 14-9 and 14-10. The following numbers should change, however, from the amounts stated in Problem 14-9: In the P Company trial balance as of December 31, 2002, Investment in SFr Company is 307,256; Retained Earnings, 1/1 is 543,628; and Equity Income is 62,028. Ignore deferred income taxes in the allocation of the difference between cost and book value.

Required:

A. If you have not already done so (Problem 14-10), prepare a workpaper to translate the trial balance of the subsidiary into dollars using the temporal method of translation. The subsidiary's beginning retained earnings balance in the translated balance sheet is $76,660.

B. Prepare the journal entries made on the books of P Company during 2002 to account for the investment in SFr Company. P Company uses the complete equity method to record its investment in SFr Company. At the date of acquisition, the 608,000 franc difference between cost and book value interest acquired was allocated as follows:

Asset	Francs	Translation Rate	Dollars
Land	308,000	$.15	46,200
Building	300,000	.15	45,000
Total	608,000		91,200

The building is depreciated over a 10-year remaining life using the straight-line method of amortization.

C. Prepare a consolidated statements workpaper at December 31, 2002.

15

REPORTING FOR SEGMENTS AND FOR INTERIM FINANCIAL PERIODS

LEARNING OBJECTIVES

1. Understand the need for disaggregated financial data.
2. Describe the basic requirements of public companies in reporting segmental data.
3. Determine an operating segment.
4. Define a reportable segment.
5. Describe how common costs are handled in segmental reporting.
6. Identify the information to be presented for each reportable segment.
7. Explain when and what types of geographic data must be reported.
8. Explain when information about major customers must be reported.
9. Compare the international accounting standards for segmental reporting with the U.S. requirements.
10. Describe current requirements for companies to report interim information.
11. Indicate some problems with interim reporting and the authoritative position on the issue.

Most analysts consider segment performance data followed by the three financial statements as the most useful data for their investment decisions. Though incomplete, the segment data does provide significant additional insights into the past operating performance of the company and its segments and insight into possible future performance.[1]

In previous chapters we have dealt with the process of aggregating the financial data relating to the activities of an affiliated group of companies. Investors and lenders holding equity or creditor interests are aware of the importance of consolidated statements in reporting the financial position and results of operations of a group of companies under common control. At the same time, investors, creditors,

---

[1] *Strategic Finance*, "What Financial Analysts Want," by Marc Epstein and Krishna Palepu, April 1999, p. 49.

and other users of financial statements also need disaggregated data that provide information about the various segments of an enterprise or affiliated group of companies.

NEED FOR DISAGGREGATED FINANCIAL DATA

Research studies conducted by various organizations such as the Financial Executives Research Foundation, the Financial Analysts Federation, and the National Association of Accountants concluded that financial statement users want information to aid them in evaluating prospective investments. If return on investment is computed on the basis of expected cash flows, the evaluation of risk requires an assessment of the uncertainty surrounding both the timing and the amount of these expected cash flows. Major uncertainty results from (1) factors unique to individual companies, (2) factors related to the industries and geographical areas in which those companies operate, and (3) related national and international economic and political factors.

Users need financial statement information to determine conditions, trends, and ratios that assist in predicting cash flows of firms. These factors are often compared with those of other firms, as well as with industrywide data, and general national and international economic information is considered in making an overall evaluation of the risk involved. When a firm engages in activities in several industries or geographic areas, analysis and the process used to predict future cash flows become more complex. Different industries or geographic areas may have different rates of profitability, opportunities for growth, and types of risk. Thus, most users agree that, although consolidated financial information is important, it is more useful if supplemented with disaggregated information to assist in analyzing the uncertainties surrounding the timing and amounts of expected cash flows.

STANDARDS OF FINANCIAL ACCOUNTING AND REPORTING

Recognizing the importance of "segment" data and the necessity of establishing standards for disclosure, the Financial Accounting Standards Board issued *Statement of Financial Accounting Standards (SFAS) No. 14*, "Financial Reporting for Segments of a Business Enterprise." *SFAS No. 14* was subsequently amended by *SFAS No. 21*, and later superseded by *SFAS No. 131*, "Disclosures about Segments of an Enterprise and Related information." Segmental disclosures have limitations as well as strengths. The primary benefit is the unveiling of information that has been merged and possibly buried in the consolidated data. For example, specific information about a declining or growing product line or unstable geographic area may be useful in projecting future cash flows or in assessing risk. The arguments *against* segmental disclosures include the following:

- Segmental information may be misleading or meaningless due to inherent accounting classification and allocation problems, to lack of user knowledge, or to variation in the measurement techniques applied by different companies.

- Disclosures to competing firms, labor unions, and so on could have adverse effects and could discourage management from taking on desirable but risky projects in order to avoid the disclosures.
- Users are already bombarded with an excessive amount of accounting detail, and segmental disclosures merely add to the burden.

Nonetheless, most people believe the advantages outweigh the disadvantages. In addition, the increased pace of merger activity and the increase in foreign operations have led to greater importance being attached to segmental disclosures. Thus, the FASB issued *SFAS No. 131*, requiring all public companies to report information about the countries in which they earn revenues and hold assets, about major customers, and about revenues for each product and service, even when *some* of the information is not used by the firm in its operating decisions.

"Get ready. Your disclosure will be cracking up. Cracking up and breaking open into new segment reporting, that is. As of year-end 1998 and for quarterly periods beginning thereafter, public companies have to start new segment reporting. Companies also have to restate their financials going back three years."[2]

In general, **SFAS No. 131** *implemented a management approach, focusing on the way in which management organizes segments internally to make operating decisions and to assess performance.* The objective of this approach is to facilitate consistency between internal and external reporting. Information may be segmented by product or service, by geographic area, by customer type, or by legal entity. For each operating segment, firms must report segmental profit or loss, certain items of revenue and expense, segmental assets, and other items.

Although there was concern that segment reporting would "give away the farm," many analysts and other users believed the previous rules, under *SFAS No. 14*, did not work well because the information reported didn't reflect management's internal accounting. Companies presented segmental information that didn't "relate to reality," leading to bad communications. The new rule should be a win-win for management and analysts, says one expert, making it easier for investor relations officials to talk to analysts and to communicate internally. "They might even learn a few new things about their companies."[3]

SFAS No. 131 does not limit segmental reporting to financial data only. It also requires a discussion of the firm's rationale or method for categorizing its operations into segments, as well as any difference in measurement techniques between periods being reported or between the segment and the entire entity. The standard became effective for years beginning after December 15, 1997. If statements are presented for more than one period, the required information must be presented

---

[2] *Investor Relations Business*, "Cracking Up: Segment Reporting Disclosure Is Coming," by Matthew Greco, June 22, 1998, p. 1.

[3] Ibid.

for each period. The information required should be a disaggregation of *consolidated financial information* where the firm has consolidated subsidiaries, and a disaggregation of the individual firm data if it has no consolidated subsidiaries.

We next define some terms that have been given specific connotations for purposes of segmental reporting. The terms and their definitions are as follows:

a. *Operating segment.* A component of an enterprise that may earn revenues and incur expenses, about which separate financial information is evaluated regularly by the chief operating decision maker in deciding how to allocate resources and in assessing performance.

b. *Reportable segment.* A segment considered to be significant to an enterprise's operations; specifically, one that has passed one of three 10% tests or has been identified as being reportable through other criteria (aggregation, for example).

c. *Chief operating decision maker.* A person whose general function (not specific title) is to allocate resources to, and assess the performance of, the segments of an enterprise.

d. *Segment revenue.* The revenue from sales to unaffiliated customers and from intersegment sales or transfers.

e. *Segment operating profit or loss.* All of a segment's revenue minus all operating expenses, including any allocated revenues or expenses (e.g., common costs).

f. *Common costs.* Operating expenses incurred by the enterprise for the benefit of more than one segment.

g. *Segment assets.* Those tangible and intangible assets directly associated with, or used by, a segment, including any allocated portion of assets used jointly by more than one segment. If portions of assets are allocated internally and used by the chief operating decision maker, then those amounts should be allocated on a reasonable basis and disclosed for external reporting purposes as well.

h. *Corporate assets.* Assets maintained for general corporate purposes and not used in the operations of any segment.

i. *General corporate expense.* An expense incurred for the benefit of the corporation as a whole, which cannot be reasonably allocated to any segment.

j. *Transfer pricing.* The pricing of products or services between operating segments or geographic areas.

Two of the most difficult tasks in applying the segment disclosure requirements are those of determining (1) an appropriate basis for the allocation of common costs and (2) appropriate operating segments.

Common Cost Allocation

The emphasis here is on *operating* expenses, as general corporate expenses are not allocated. Common costs should be allocated to a segment for external reporting purposes only if they are included in the segment's profit or loss calculations that are used internally by the chief operating decision maker (as defined above).

Although judgment must be used, prior research contains recommendations concerning common cost allocation methods. Probably the most extensive study on appropriate allocation methods was conducted by the Cost Accounting Standards Board, and its recommendations were issued in *Cost Accounting Standard No.*

403. Although *Standard No. 403* concerns the problem of allocating common home office expenses to segments of an organization involved in defense contracts, the general guidelines developed should be useful in applying the allocation provisions of *SFAS No. 14.* In essence, *Cost Accounting Standard No. 403* suggests that, where possible, joint costs should be accumulated into logical and relatively homogeneous expense pools. The pools are then allocated to segments on the basis of beneficial or casual relationships as measured by activity or output of the segments.

For example, common data-processing expenses might be allocated on the basis of machine time or number of reports, joint personnel administration expenses on the basis of number of personnel or total labor hours, and joint centralized warehouse expenses on the basis of square footage, value of materials, or volume of transactions. Any remaining expenses that cannot be logically included in any of the homogeneous expense pools are allocated proportionately under a three-factor formula based on payroll costs, revenue, and assets of the segments. That is, the percentage of the residual expenses to be allocated to any segment is the arithmetical average of the following three percentages:

1. The segment's payroll dollars to the total payroll dollars of all segments.
2. The segment's operating revenue to the total operating revenue of all segments.
3. The average net book value of the sum of the segment's tangible capital assets plus inventories to the total average net book value of such assets of all segments.

Determining Operating Segments

SFAS No. 131 provides that *operating segments* of the firm are to be determined using a modified management approach. An operating segment is a component that exhibits all of the following characteristics:

- It engages in business activities that may earn revenues and incur expenses (including transactions with other components of the entity).
- The entity's chief operating decision maker (may be one individual or a group of executives) regularly reviews the component's operating results to assess its performance and make decisions about resources to be allocated to it.
- Discrete financial information is available.

"Many companies boast in their annual reports about the myriad businesses they participate in—then, in their financials [under the old rules] reported as though they operated in a single industry. Patricia McConnell, accounting analyst for Bear, Stearns & Co., says, 'I don't think there's any more important information about a company than its businesses broken down into segments. Dividing the information along the same lines that management looks at is a fairly reasonable request—and should prevent companies from claiming they're in only one line of business.' "[4]

Disclosures are required for each operating segment, subject to the quantitative thresholds and aggregation criteria presented next. Because the aggregation can occur before performing the quantitative tests, we present those criteria first.

[4]*Institutional Investor,* "Dilutions of Grandeur," by Mary Lowengard, January 1998, p. 34.

Aggregation Criteria An entity is permitted (but not required) to aggregate operating segments that have similar economic characteristics if the segments are also similar in **all** the following areas:

- The nature of their products or services.
- The nature of the production processes.
- The types or class of customers.
- The methods used to distribute products or provide services.
- The nature of the regulatory environment (banking, for example).[5]

Quantitative Thresholds Each operating segment that is significant to the enterprise as a whole must be identified as a *reportable* segment. A segment is considered to be significant if it meets **one or more** of the following tests, the tests being applied separately for each fiscal year for which financial statements are prepared:

- Its combined external and internal revenue is **10% or more** of the combined external and internal revenue of all reportable segments.
- The absolute amount of its reported profit or loss is **10% or more** of the *greater* absolute amount of:
  - The combined reported profit of all operating segments not reporting a loss
  - The combined reported loss of all operating segments that reported a loss
- Its assets are **10% or more** of the combined assets of all operating segments.

Entities are permitted to present operating segments separately that fall below the quantitative thresholds, or such operating segments may be combined with other segments not meeting the quantitative thresholds if the segments share a *majority* of the aggregation criteria.

An example of the application of these tests for Papco, Inc. is presented in Illustration 15-1. In this example the information of Papco is segmented by its products. The results of the tests should be evaluated from the standpoint of **comparability**. Thus, a segment that has been significant in the past and is expected to be significant in the future should be treated as a reportable segment even though it fails to meet a test in the current year. Further, if the structure of the organization changes so that the reportable segments are redefined, the information presented from prior periods should be **restated** so that it is comparable with the current structure (if practical). In such cases, the firm should explicitly disclose the fact that the earlier periods have been restated and why. Also, if a particular segment that was previously not considered significant becomes significant in the current period, then segmental data should be presented for that segment for the prior periods as well as the current one.

Seventy-Five Percent Combined Revenue Test

In addition to the tests described above, the reportable segments taken together must represent a substantial portion of the firm's total operations. To determine whether a substantial portion of a firm's operations are explained by its segment information, *the combined revenue from sales to unaffiliated customers of all reportable segments must constitute at least 75% of the combined revenue from sales to unaffiliated customers of all operating segments.* If the 75% test is not satisfied, additional segments

---

[5]See par. 17 of *SFAS No. 131* for more details on the regulatory environment.

ILLUSTRATION 15-1
Significance Tests
Year Ended December 31, 2003
(Thousands of Dollars)
Papco, Inc.

			Segments			
Revenue Test	*Lumber*	*Paper*	*Printing*	*Furniture*	*Leather*	*Combined*
Sales to Unaffiliated Customers	$16,000	$ 3,000	$2,000	$1,500	$1,000	$23,500
Intersegment Sales	5,000	2,000	500	500	—0—	8,000
Total Revenue	$21,000	$ 5,000	$2,500	$2,000	$1,000	$31,500
Percentage of Total Revenue	67%	16%	8%	6%	3%	100%

The lumber and paper segments are reportable segments under the revenue test because their total revenues are at least 10% of combined total revenue of $31,500, whereas the other segments are not reportable segments under this test.

Operating Profit Test						
Operating Profit (Loss)	$ 2,500	$ 600	$ (300)	$ 150	$ (100)	$ 2,850
Percentage of $3,250*	77%	18%	9%	5%	3%	

The lumber and paper segments are reportable segments under the operating profit test because the absolute amounts of their operating profit or loss are each *at least **10%** of the greater of* (1) the combined profit of all segments that did not incur a loss* ($2,500 + $600 + $150 = $3,250), or (2) the combined loss of all segments that incurred a loss ($300 + $100 = $400). The other segments are not reportable segments under this test.

Assets Test						
Segment Assets	$25,000	$12,000	$8,000	$3,000	$4,000	$52,000
Percentage of Total Assets	48%	23%	15%	6%	8%	100%

The lumber, paper, and printing segments are reportable segments because their assets are at least 10% of combined identifiable assets of $52,000. The furniture and leather segments are not reportable segments under this test.

Reportable Segments (still subject to the 75% Combined Revenue Test)
1) Lumber (met all three tests above)
2) Paper (met all three tests above)
3) Printing (met the asset test above)

75% Combined Revenue Test						
Sales to Unaffiliated Customers	$16,000	$ 3,000	$2,000	$1,500	$1,000	$23,500
Percentage of Total Sales	68.1%	12.8%	8.5%	6.4%	4.3%	100.0%
Combined Percentage		89.4%				

The three reportable segments have combined revenue in excess of 75% of total unaffiliated revenue; therefore, no additional segments need be identified. The furniture and leather segments would be combined when reported.

must be identified until the test is met. The test is applied separately for each fiscal period for which financial statements are prepared.

Application of this 75% test to the situation presented in Illustration 15-1 produces the following:

$$\frac{\text{Combined sales to } unaffiliated \text{ customers by the lumber, paper, and printing segments}}{\text{Combined sales to unaffiliated customers by all segments}} = \frac{(\$16,000 + \$3,000 + \$2,000)}{\$23,500} = 89\%$$

Thus, the 75% test is met, and the lumber, paper, and printing segments will be reported individually and the furniture and leather segments combined into one unit. If the 75% test had not been met, one or more of the segments that did not qualify as reportable segments under the previous tests would have to be included as reportable segments.

Information to Be Presented The following types of information must be presented for each of a firm's reportable segments, and in the aggregate for the segments that are not separately reported.

- *General information.* SFAS No. 131 requires an explanation of how management identified its reportable segments, as well as whether any segments have been aggregated. A description is also required of the types of products or services from which each segment obtains its revenues.
- *Information about segment operating profit or loss.* Rather than specifying a strict definition of profit or loss for segmental purposes, the standard designates that a management approach focusing on internal decision making be used to determine the measurement of segmental profit or loss. Thus, the following items are disclosed only *if* they are included in the measures reviewed by the chief operating decision maker: revenues from external customers, revenues from other segments, interest revenue and expense, depreciation, depletion and amortization expense, income tax expense, equity income from investments, extraordinary items, other unusual items, and other significant noncash items. The absence of specific rules in calculating segment profit or loss leaves room for possible departures from GAAP as applied at the consolidated level. For example, pension expense may not be allocated to segments if not reviewed by the decision maker for that segment. The possibility of departures from GAAP for segmental disclosures is addressed further in a later section of this chapter, in comparison to recommended international standards.
- *Information about segment assets.* Firms are required to disclose those assets that are evaluated by the chief operating decision maker for the segment, including the following information *if* such information is reviewed by the officer: expenditures for most long-lived assets and the carrying basis of "influential" investments, or those measured using the equity method.
- *Information about the bases for measurement.* Differences in measurement between segments and the consolidated entity must be disclosed for: income before tax, discontinued operations, extraordinary items, and the cumulative effect of any changes in accounting principle; and for segment profit or loss. Similarly, differences in measurement between segment assets and the consolidated assets must be disclosed, if any. For example, information on how jointly used assets are allocated to segments may be needed to understand the segment information. The basis should be disclosed for any transactions between segments, and any asymmetrical allocations to segments should be explained. Finally, any changes from the measurement methods used in prior periods must be disclosed, and their effects on segment profit or loss.
- *Reconciliation of segment amounts and consolidated amounts for revenue, profit or loss, assets, and other significant items.* Differences occur for a variety of reasons, including the following: Some segments not meeting the quantitative thresholds are

presented as "all other." Some items are not allocated to segments if there is no reasonable basis for doing so, or because the information is not used by the chief operating decision maker. Transactions between segments may give rise to "intersegment" revenue, profit, or loss amounts that are eliminated from the consolidated totals. Because the focus in segmental reporting is a management approach, it may result in different accounting methods from those used for external reporting for the consolidated entity. A reconciliation of such items must be presented in sufficient detail to explain the differences. It should include:

- Revenue to revenue reported in the consolidated income statement.
- Operating profit or loss to pretax income from continuing operations in the consolidated income statement.
- Segment assets to consolidated total assets.

Illustration 15-5, presented later in this chapter, illustrates a reconciliation of the above items.

- *Interim disclosures.* Unlike the previous standard on segmental reporting, *SFAS No. 131* requires that segmental disclosures be included in interim reports. The extent of the disclosures depends on whether the firm presents a complete set of financial statements for the interim period, or condensed financial statements. If the firm presents a complete set of statements, the interim disclosures are the same as presented above for reportable segments. If condensed statements are presented for interim periods, they should include the following for each reportable segment: revenues, including intersegment sales; profit or loss; disclosures of any changes in measurement bases for segmentation or components of profit or loss since the most recent annual report; any material changes in assets since the most recent annual report; and a reconciliation of income from continuing operations for the consolidated entity and for the total of the reportable segments.

- *Enterprisewide Disclosures.* Because of the choice allowed in designating reportable segments, a given firm may report its segmental information based on products or services, geographic areas, and so on. Thus other information about the bases not chosen is not provided as part of the above disclosures. *SFAS No. 131* requires that such information be presented if practicable. If not practicable, the reason for not including the disclosures should be stated. These additional disclosures are made on an enterprisewide basis rather than a segmental basis, and are required even if a firm has only a single reportable segment. They include:

  —*Product or service disclosures:* revenues from external customers for each **product or service** or group of products or services, on the same basis as the general-purpose financial statements. This disclosure is not required if the reportable segments are structured around products or services.

  —*Geographic area disclosures:* revenues from external customers and long-lived assets for the firm's country of domicile and for all other countries in total, also on the same basis as the general-purpose financial statements; *and* revenues from external customers and long-lived assets for *each foreign country or group of foreign countries*, if material, along with the basis for allocating revenues (location of customer, where shipped, etc.). These disclosures are generally not required if the company's reportable segments have been organized around **geographic area**.

  —*Major customer disclosures:* information about **major customers** for each customer representing **10% or more** of total enterprise revenues, including the amount of revenues and the segment(s) to which the revenue is traceable. A group of customers under common control is treated as a single customer, as are the various agencies of a government.

Methods of Presentation Information about the reportable segments of a firm may be included in its financial statements in any of the following ways:

- Within the body of the financial statements, with appropriate explanatory disclosures in the footnotes to the financial statements.
- Entirely in the footnotes to the financial statements.
- In a separate schedule that is included as an integral part of the financial statements.

ILLUSTRATION 15-2

Papco Inc.
Consolidated Income Statement
(Thousands of Dollars)

	Year Ended December 31	
	2003	*2002*
Sales	$23,500	$22,100
Cost of Goods Sold	16,400	15,300
Selling, General, and Administrative Expense	4,530	4,380
Interest Expense	600	570
Total Cost and Expense	21,530	20,250
Operating Income	1,970	1,850
Equity in Income of B Company	150	120
Income Before Income Taxes	2,120	1,970
Income Taxes	1,020	980
Net Income	$ 1,100	$ 990

Papco Inc.
Consolidated Balance Sheet
(Thousands of Dollars)

	December 31	
	2003	*2002*
Cash	$ 1,870	$ 1,785
Receivables	2,640	2,860
Inventories	6,400	6,345
Investment in B Company	700	600
Plant and Equipment (net of accumulated depreciation of $17,500 in 2003 and $16,200 in 2002)	41,500	40,400
Other Assets	690	970
Total Assets	$53,800	$52,960
Current Liabilities	$ 2,400	$ 2,320
Bonds Payable	12,000	12,000
Common Stock, $50 par value	30,000	30,000
Additional Paid-in Capital	3,000	3,000
Retained Earnings	6,400	5,640
Total Liabilities and Stockholders' Equity	$53,800	$52,960

Financial information such as revenue, operating profit or loss, and identifiable assets must be presented in dollar amounts; related percentages may be shown if desired.

As an illustration of segment reporting, assume the segment data presented in Illustration 15-1. In addition, assume that the consolidated income statements and balance sheets for 2002 and 2003 for Papco, Inc. are as shown in Illustration 15-2. Disclosure of segmental information organized by products/services might take the form of the supporting schedules and footnotes as shown in Illustration 15-3. This illustration also serves to reconcile the segmental data to the totals for the consolidated entity.

Geographic Areas

As mentioned in the preceding section, *SFAS No. 131* requires enterprises to report revenues from external customers and long-lived assets attributable to their domestic operations and foreign operations. Foreign operations are defined as those located outside the United States (or other "home country") that produce revenue from sales to unaffiliated customers or from intra-enterprise sales or transfers between countries or geographic areas. Foreign operations do *not*, however, include unconsolidated subsidiaries and investees. If operations are conducted in two or more foreign countries or geographic areas, information must be presented separately for each significant foreign country or geographic area and in the aggregate for all other foreign operations. Where the operations in some foreign countries

ILLUSTRATION 15-3

Papco Inc.
Segmental Disclosures by Product/Service
(Thousands of Dollars)

Year Ended December 31, 2003	Lumber	Paper	Printing	Other	Total
Revenues from external customers	$16,000	$ 3,000	$2,000	$2,500	$23,500
Intersegment revenues	5,000	2,000	500	500	8,000
Depreciation and amortization	640	290	190	100	1,220
Interest expense	200	100	80	100	480
Segment operating profit	2,500	600	(300)	50	2,850
Segment assets	25,000	12,000	8,000	7,000	52,000
Capital expenditures	1,540	420	30	210	2,200

Year Ended December 31, 2002	Lumber	Paper	Printing	Other	Total
Revenues from external customers	$15,200	$ 2,800	$2,100	$2,000	$22,100
Intersegment revenues	4,800	1,700	300	460	7,260
Depreciation and amortization	600	290	175	125	1,190
Interest expense	190	90	75	90	445
Segment operating profit	2,460	580	(430)	70	2,680
Segment assets	24,460	11,500	7,900	7,520	51,380
Capital expenditures	1,280	360	20	240	1,900

Note A—Product and Service Segments.
    The Company operates in three main areas of product/service: lumber products, paper products, and printing. More detailed information about specific products and services is included in the "Business Operations" section of this report.
    Intersegment sales are made at the same prices as sales to nonaffiliates.

ILLUSTRATION 15-4

Papco Inc.
Enterprisewide Disclosures
(Thousands of Dollars)

Geographic Information

Revenue	Year Ended December 31 2003	2002
United States	$18,000	$17,500
Foreign Countries		
Canada	4,000	3,500
Mexico	1,500	1,100
Total Revenue from Foreign Countries	5,500	4,600
Total Consolidated Revenue	$23,500	$22,100

Long-Lived Assets	2003	2002
United States	$28,827	$28,180
Foreign Countries		
Canada	9,375	9,193
Mexico	4,688	4,597
Total Assets in Foreign Countries	14,063	13,790
Total Consolidated Assets	$42,890	$41,970

Major Customers

We do not provide information on major customers because no single external customer represented 10% or more of total revenues.

are grouped into geographic areas, the groupings should be made on the basis of a consideration of (1) proximity, (2) economic affinity, (3) similarities of business environments, and (4) the nature, scale, and degree of interrelationship of the operations in the various countries.

To illustrate, foreign operations information for Papco, Inc. might be presented as shown in Illustration 15-4, assuming that the company conducts operations in the United States, Canada, and Mexico.

Information About Major Customers

To provide information about the potential effects of dependency on one or more major customers, if *10% or more* of the revenue of a firm is derived from sales to any *single customer,* that fact and the amount of revenue from each such customer must be disclosed, as stated previously. Also, if *10% or more* of the revenue is derived from sales to the *federal government, a state government, a local government, or a foreign government,* that fact and the amount of revenue must be disclosed. Disclosure should include the amount of sales to each customer and the reportable segment making the sales. Customers' names, however, need not be disclosed. These disclosures are required even if the firm has only one reportable segment.

Reconciliation

A reconciliation of major segmental data presented in earlier illustrations and the consolidated data in the income statement for Papco, Inc. is presented in Illustration 15-5.

ILLUSTRATION 15-5

Papco Inc.
Reconciliation of Major Segment Information
(Thousands of Dollars)

	Year Ended December 31	
Revenue	*2003*	*2002*
Total revenue for reportable segments	$28,500	$26,900
Revenue for other segments aggregated	3,000	2,460
Elimination of intersegment revenue	8,000	7,260
Total consolidated revenue	$23,500	$22,100
Profit and Loss		
Total profit and loss for reportable segments	$ 2,800	$ 2,610
Other profit and loss	50	70
Elimination of intersegment profits	(680)	(630)
Unallocated amounts relating to corporate headquarters:		
Interest expense	(120)	(125)
Depreciation	(80)	(75)
Equity in income of B Company	150	120
Income before taxes	$ 2,120	$ 1,970
Assets		
Total assets for reportable segments	$45,000	$43,860
Other assets	7,000	7,520
Corporate investment in B Company	700	600
General corporate assets	1,100	980
Total consolidated assets	$53,800	$52,960
Other Significant Items		
Segment depreciation and amortization	$ 1,120	$ 1,065
Other depreciation and amortization	100	125
Adjustment for depreciation on corporate assets	80	75
Total consolidated depreciation and amortization	$ 1,300	$ 1,265
Segment interest expense	$ 380	$ 355
Other interest expense	100	90
Adjustment for interest on corporate borrowing	120	125
Total consolidated interest expense	$ 600	$ 570
Segment capital expenditures	$ 1,990	$ 1,660
Other capital expenditures	210	240
Adjustment for acquisition of corporate assets	200	150
Total consolidated capital expenditures	$ 2,400	$ 2,050

INTERNATIONAL ACCOUNTING STANDARDS COMMITTEE (IASC) POSITION ON SEGMENT REPORTING

Segmenting consolidated financial information (along product and service lines and along geographic lines) has proved highly relevant for assessing the profitability, risks, and prospects of a diversified or multinational enterprise. Investors, financial analysts, and credit grantors say segment information is indispensable.[6]

---

[6]*Accountancy*, ''Segment Reporting Strengthened,'' by Paul Pacter, April 1997, p. 66.

The International Accounting Standards Committee has required segment information since around 1982. A new international accounting standard (IAS) on segment reporting took effect in 1998, *IAS No. 14* (Revised), "Reporting Financial Information by Segmentation." With its issuance, segment reporting was no longer required for large nonpublic companies, but only for those with publicly traded equity or debt securities. The new standard provided more guidance than the one it replaced for identifying segments, requiring a company to look to its organizational structure and internal reporting system to identify reportable segments. Certain differences between *IAS No. 14* (Revised) and the U.S. standard (*SFAS No. 131*) are discussed below.

The objectives of the two standards are not identical. Whereas the U.S. standard focuses on the data reported and used internally by a chief operating decision maker, the IASC states its objective as providing insight into how the diversity of products and services and geographic operations affects an enterprise's overall risks and returns. The differences between the two standards include segment definition, measurement differences, uniformity across companies, and asymmetry allowed/disallowed in measurement.

The IASC's reportable segments must earn a majority of their revenue from outside customers, whereas U.S. segments include vertically integrated revenues, even with zero external revenue, if reported internally. The U.S. allows mixed segmentation (some segments by product, others by geographic area) if that's how it is reported internally. The IASC does not; it requires separate product and geographic segmentation.

For its primary operating segments, Wal-Mart reports two line-of-business segments, Wal-Mart Stores and Sam's, and one geographical segment, international, based on the three company divisions reporting to the chief decision-maker.[7]

Early adopters of *SFAS No. 131* tended to report fewer segments than adopters of the international standard, with most U.S. adopters reporting only three or four, with a maximum of 10 (consistent with the guidelines in *SFAS No. 131*). In contrast, Hoechst reported 11 segments under *IAS No. 14R*.

The IASC segment data must follow the same accounting policies as used in the general-purpose financial statements (for the consolidated entity). The U.S. standard allows the segment data to follow the internal policies, even if such policies do not conform to GAAP and thus differ from those used for the consolidated entity. The IASC requires a standardized measure of segment operating profit or loss (before interest and tax) to improve comparability among companies. The U.S. standard allows more flexibility, with early adopters reporting measures ranging from operating income before interest and taxes to net income before taxes. Other differences among early adopters of the U.S. standard included whether such items as acquired in-process R&D charges, severance costs, goodwill amortization, and certain actuarial costs were allocated between segments. Finally, the IASC requires symmetry in measuring segment results and segment assets. *SFAS No. 131* does not, though it requires that any asymmetrical measures be disclosed. The Securities and Exchange Commission has stated its support of the IASC approach for cross-border offerings.

---

[7] *Accountancy*, "A New Era of Segment Reporting," by S. Gray, D. Street, and N. Nichols, April 1999, pp. 76–78.

''For projects on the same subject running in a similar time-frame [*SFAS No. 131 and IAS No. 14R*], and in the context of the demand for international harmonization, one might hope that the measurement and disclosure rules would be identical. Not so! Companies that use International Accounting Standards and that also have SEC reporting obligations need to focus on these differences and ensure that full account is taken in their filing documents.''[8]

INTERIM FINANCIAL REPORTING

In a dynamic business environment, financial information must be available on a timely basis if sound investment decisions are to be made. Although businesses have historically considered the fiscal year to be the primary reporting period, interim financial statements have been presented frequently to provide information concerning financial status and progress for time periods of less than one year. The normal time period for interim reporting is a quarter of a year (such reports are generally called quarterly reports), but other periods such as a month might be used. These interim statements are generally prepared for the most recent interim period, as well as on a cumulative or year-to-date basis; they may consist of statements of financial position, income, and cash flows. The primary focus, however, has been on the presentation of interim income information, and some companies present only interim income statements.

Publicly owned companies are generally required to file some type of quarterly report as part of the agreement with the stock exchanges that list their stock. In addition, the SEC requires public companies to file Form 10-Q with the Commission within 45 days after the end of each of the first three quarters of the fiscal year. The financial information disclosure portion of Form 10-Q requires that condensed financial statements include (1) comparative income statements for the quarter and year-to-date for the current and preceding year, (2) comparative statements of financial position at the end of the most recent quarter for the current and preceding year, and (3) comparative statements of cash flows for the current and preceding year. Most public companies also issue these reports required by the SEC to their stockholders and to other interested parties.

Problems in Interim Reporting

Although the SEC established disclosure requirements for the financial information included in Form 10-Q, the development of accounting practices to be followed in preparing interim financial reports for external reporting purposes was left to the accounting profession. No official guide or pronouncement on the practices to be used was issued until the Accounting Principles Board issued *Opinion No. 28*, ''Interim Financial Reporting,'' in May 1973. Thus, before *APB Opinion No. 28* was issued, the form and content of interim reports and the accounting practices to be used in their preparation were left to the discretion of the reporting companies. In addition, interim reports are essentially unaudited reports. As a result, several problems evolved in the preparation of interim reports.

---

[8]*Accountancy*, ''Segment Reporting: IAS vs. US GAAP,'' by Robert Dove and Ago Vilu, May 20, 1999, pp. 64–65.

The seasonal nature of operations in many industries can cause wide fluctuations in revenues, expenses, and net income from one interim period to another. The relatively short time period available to determine interim results and the added cost of determining accurate figures for accruals, deferrals, and inventories encouraged the use of a variety of estimation techniques, some of which proved to be highly inaccurate. In fact, many firms used a wider variety of accounting practices and estimation procedures for interim reports than they did for year-end reports. In addition, two essentially conflicting views of the nature of interim periods exist among accountants. Some accountants hold that each interim period should **stand alone** as a basic accounting period; they conclude, therefore, that the results of operations for each interim period should be determined in the same manner as if the interim period were an annual period. Under this **discrete** view of an interim period, deferrals, accruals, and estimations at the end of each interim period are determined by following essentially the same principles and judgments that apply to annual periods.

Other accountants view each interim period as essentially an **integral** part of the annual period. Under this view, deferrals, accruals, and estimations at the end of each interim period are affected by judgments made at the interim date as to results of operations for the balance of the annual period. Thus, an expense item that might be considered as falling wholly within an annual accounting period could be allocated among interim periods on the basis of estimated time, sales volume, productive activity, or some other basis.

As a result of the problems just described, some companies issued interim financial statements reporting significant quarterly and year-to-date income for the first three quarters, but full-year statements that reported substantial net losses. The SEC filed complaints against several companies for failure to make adequate adjustments for accruals and deferrals of revenue and expenses on an interim basis and for failing to make appropriate adjustments on an interim basis for amortization, depreciation, and inventory obsolescence. In response to SEC complaints and general pressure from the financial and investing community, the APB issued *APB Opinion No. 28* in May 1973.

APB Opinion No. 28

In *Opinion No. 28*, the Board indicated that its basic objective was "to clarify the application of accounting principles and reporting practices to interim financial information, including interim financial statements and summarized interim financial data of publicly traded companies issued for external reporting purposes." The Board also concluded that "**each interim period should be viewed primarily as an integral part of an annual period**." The Board also took the position that financial statements for each interim period should be based on the same accounting practices that are used for the preparation of annual financial statements. The *Opinion* presents guidelines for the presentation of revenue, costs associated with revenue, all other costs and expenses, and income tax provisions.

Revenue Revenue from products sold or services performed should be recognized as earned during an interim period on the same basis as that used for the full year. In addition, business with material seasonal variations should disclose the seasonal nature of their activities.

Costs Associated with Revenue Costs and expenses that are associated directly with or allocated to the products sold or to the services rendered for annual reporting purposes should be similarly treated for interim reporting purposes. However, the following are acceptable alternatives for inventory costing:

1. Estimated gross profit rates may be used by some companies to determine the cost of goods sold during interim periods, or they may use methods other than those used for year-end inventories. Companies using these methods should disclose the method used in the interim report and any significant adjustments that result from reconciliations with the annual physical inventory.

2. Companies using the LIFO method may encounter a liquidation of base period inventories at an interim date that is expected to be replaced by the end of the annual period. In these cases, cost of goods sold should be charged with the expected replacement cost of the liquidated LIFO base.

3. Inventory losses from market declines should be recognized in the interim period in which the decline occurs. Subsequent recoveries of these losses in interim periods should be recognized as gains to the extent of losses previously recognized in interim periods of the same fiscal period. However, market declines that are expected to be temporary within the fiscal year need not be recognized.

To illustrate, assume that Drex Company, which uses the FIFO inventory method, had 18,000 units in inventory at the beginning of the year at a FIFO cost per unit of $6. No purchases were made during the year. Information concerning quarterly sales and end-of-quarter replacement cost follows:

Quarter	Sales in Units	End-of-Quarter Units on Hand	End-of-Quarter Replacement Cost
1	3,000	15,000	$6.30
2	3,500	11,500	5.80
3	2,500	9,000	6.10
4	5,000	4,000	5.50
Total	14,000		

Assuming that the market decline in the second quarter was not expected to be temporary, cost of sales for the four quarters would be:

Quarter	Computation of Cost of Goods Sold		Cost of Goods Sold Quarter	Cost of Goods Sold Cumulative
1	Sold 3,000 units @ $6		$18,000	$18,000
2	Sold 3,500 units @ $6	$21,000		
	Plus write-down of ending inventory of 11,500 units to market [11,500 × ($6.00 − $5.80)]	+2,300	23,300	41,300
3	Sold 2,500 units @ $5.80	14,500		
	Less write-down recovery on ending inventory of 9,000 units [9,000 × ($6.00 − $5.80)]	(1,800)	12,700	54,000
4	Sold 5,000 units @ $6	30,000		
	Plus write-down of ending inventory of 4,000 units to market [(4,000 × ($6.00 − $5.50)]	+2,000	32,000	86,000

Because each interim period is considered an integral part of an annual period, the cumulative cost of goods sold ($86,000) should equal the amount that would be computed if the lower-of-cost-or-market method were applied on an annual basis. Thus, we can verify as follows:

Units Sold During Year		FIFO Cost/Unit	Amount
14,000	×	$6.00	$84,000
Add: Write-down of ending inventory to the			
lower of cost or market (4,000 × $.50)			2,000
Total cost of goods sold for the year			$86,000

This procedure also has the effect of determining the cumulative cost of goods sold at the end of any quarter within the year.

4. Companies that use standard cost for determining inventory and product cost should generally follow the procedures in reporting variances that are used for the fiscal year. Purchase price and volume variances that are expected to be absorbed by the end of the annual period should ordinarily be deferred at interim reporting dates. Unplanned purchase price and volume variances, however, should be reported at the end of the interim period by the procedures used at the end of the fiscal year.

All Other Costs and Expenses The Board concluded that, in accounting for costs and expenses that are not allocated to products sold or to services rendered, the following standards should apply:

1. Costs and expenses other than product costs should be charged to income in interim periods as incurred, or be allocated among interim periods based on an estimate of time expired, benefit received or activity associated with the periods. Procedures adopted for assigning specific cost and expense items to an interim period should be consistent with the bases followed by the company in reporting results of operations at annual reporting dates. However, when a specific cost or expense item charged to expense for annual reporting purposes benefits more than one interim period, the cost or expense item may be allocated to those interim periods.

2. Some costs and expenses incurred in an interim period cannot be readily identified with the activities or benefits of other interim periods and should be charged to the interim period in which incurred. Disclosure should be made as to the nature and amount of such costs unless items of a comparable nature are included in both the current interim period and in the corresponding interim period of the preceding year.

3. Arbitrary assignment of the amount of such costs to an interim period should not be made.

4. Gains and losses that arise in any interim period similar to those that would not be deferred at year-end should not be deferred to later interim periods within the same fiscal year.[9]

---

[9] *Opinion of the Accounting Principles Board No. 28,* "Interim Financial Reporting" (New York: AICPA, May 1973), par. 15.

In a research study investigating restructuring charges, Chaney, Hogan, and Jeter find that for a sample of 177 restructuring charge observations reported between 1987 and 1993, 8.3% were reported in the first quarter of the fiscal year, 10.2% in the second quarter, 25.5% in the third quarter, and 56% in the fourth quarter.[10]

Provision for Income Taxes Accounting for income taxes in interim financial statements can be very complex for a company with such items as operating loss carrybacks or carryforwards, extraordinary gains and losses, capital gains and losses, and other similar items. Our treatment here will cover the basic issue of interim provision of income taxes. The reader is referred to *FASB Interpretation No. 18*, "Accounting for Income Taxes in Interim Periods," which discusses complicating issues in detail and presents numerous examples of appropriate treatment.

The basic technique for computing income tax provisions for interim financial statements is described in *APB Opinion Nos. 28, 23,* and *24,* and in *SFAS No. 109.* At the end of each interim period the company should make its best estimate of the effective tax rate expected to be applicable for the full fiscal year. The rate so determined should be used in providing for income taxes on a current year-to-date basis. The effective rate should reflect anticipated tax credits, foreign tax rates, percentage depletion, and other available tax planning alternatives. However, in arriving at this effective tax rate no effect should be included for the tax related to significant unusual or extraordinary items that will be separately reported or reported net of their related tax effect in reports for the interim period or for the fiscal year.

To illustrate the basic procedures, assume that during 2002 Drex Company had actual first-quarter earnings of $150,000 and expected to have full-year earnings of about $500,000. On the basis of its full-year earnings projection, Drex Company estimated that its combined state and federal tax rate would be 30%. Assume further that Drex Company estimated that it would have permanent differences between accounting income and taxable income during the year of $20,000 for amortization of goodwill, and a dividend exclusion of $50,000. On the basis of this information, Drex Company would compute its estimated effective income tax rate for the year as follows:

Estimated income before taxes	$500,000
Add: Goodwill amortization	20,000
Less: Dividends exclusion	(50,000)
Estimated taxable income	$470,000
Estimated combined income tax payable ($470,000 × 30%)	$141,000
Estimated effective combined tax rate ($141,000/$500,000)	28.2%

This estimated rate is used to determine the income tax provision for the first quarter. Drex Company would, therefore, make the following entry:

Income Tax Expense ($150,000 × 28.2%)	42,300	
Income Tax Payable		42,300

---

[10] *Journal of Accounting and Economics,* "The Effect of Reporting Restructuring Charges on Analysts' Forecast Revisions and Errors," by Paul Chaney, Chris Hogan, and Debra Jeter, vol. 27, June 1999, pp. 261–284.

Now assume that during the second quarter of 2002 Drex Company had actual earnings of $170,000, and that estimated total income for the year is $600,000. Estimated permanent differences remain the same as projected during the first quarter. Using this new information, Drex Company would again compute an estimated combined federal and state tax rate for the year.

Estimated income before taxes	$600,000
Less: Net permanent differences ($50,000 − $20,000)	(30,000)
Estimated taxable income	$570,000
Estimated combined income tax payable ($570,000 × 30%)	$171,000
Estimated effective combined tax rate ($171,000/$600,000)	28.5%

The new estimated tax rate is used to compute the estimated year-to-date income tax provision, and the provision required for the second quarter as indicated here:

Cumulative income for the first two quarters ($150,000 + $170,000)	$320,000
Estimated effective tax rate	28.5%
Cumulative tax provision needed	91,200
Less: Tax provided in first quarter	42,300
Tax provision for second quarter	$ 48,900

Drex Company would make the following tax provision entry for the second quarter:

Income Tax Expense	48,900	
Income Tax Payable		48,900

Note that the new estimated effective tax rate is *not* applied retroactively; that is, the first-quarter results are not restated. Tax expense reported in the second-quarter interim income statement would be $48,900, and the year-to-date tax expense and tax payable would be reported in the year-to-date income statement and statement of financial position at $91,200. The procedures for the third-quarter would duplicate those followed for the second quarter, taking new information and estimates into consideration. It should also be noted that the treatment provided in *APB Opinion No. 28*, and just illustrated, is entirely consistent with the normal treatment afforded a change in estimate under the provisions of *APB Opinion No. 20*, "Accounting Changes"; that is, changes in estimates are treated currently and prospectively, not retroactively.

The preceding illustration assumed that there were no temporary differences. If temporary differences existed, they would have no effect on the computation of the combined effective tax rate, but would affect the tax expense and the tax liability recorded. For example, if there were an excess of tax depreciation over book depreciation during the first quarter amounting to $40,000, the first-quarter tax entry would be modified as follows:

Income Tax Expense	42,300	
Income Tax Payable [.282($150,000 − $40,000)]		31,020
Deferred Income Tax Liability (.282 × $40,000)		11,280

Interim Operating Losses When an interim operating loss gives rise to an expected income tax benefit, an asset is created to recognize the benefit. For example, if the loss for the interim or year-to-date period is expected to be offset by operating profit later in the same fiscal period, a tax benefit is traceable to the interim or year-to-date loss. *SFAS No. 109*, however, requires that the asset be reduced by a valuation allowance if it is "more likely than not" that some or all of the benefit may not be recognized. Clearly this criterion is one of the more subjective the FASB has required, and its implementation is thus subject to managerial discretion (and auditor review).

Accounting Changes in Interim Periods

Change in Estimate A change in estimate should be accounted for in the interim period in which the change is made. No restatement of previously reported interim information should be made, but the effect on earnings of a change in estimate made in a current interim period should be reported in the current and subsequent interim periods, if material in relation to any period presented, and should continue to be reported as long as necessary to avoid misleading comparisons.

Changes in Principle Changes in principle are of two types: those that require retroactive restatement and those that require a cumulative effect adjustment in the income statement of the period of change. These changes should be accounted for in interim financial statements in accordance with the provisions of *APB Opinion No. 20*, "Accounting Changes," with the following exception:

If a cumulative effect type accounting change is made during the first interim period of an enterprise's fiscal year, the cumulative effect of the change on retained earnings at the beginning of that fiscal year shall be included in net income of the first interim period (and in last-twelve-months-to-date financial reports that include that first interim period).

The cumulative effect should always be reported in the first quarter of the fiscal period. If the change did not occur in that quarter, all quarters of the current period should be restated using the new method, and the cumulative effect shown as if it had occurred in the first period. Whenever financial information that includes those prechange interim periods is presented, it shall be presented on the restated basis.

Minimum Disclosures in Interim Reports

Because the amount of financial information disclosed in interim reports varies widely, the APB established minimum disclosure standards relating to the following:

a. Sales or gross revenues, provision for income taxes, extraordinary items (including related income tax effects), cumulative effect of a change in accounting principles or practices, and net income.
b. Basic and diluted earnings-per-share data for each period presented determined in accordance with the provisions of *SFAS No. 128*.
c. Seasonal revenue, costs, or expenses.
d. Significant changes in estimates or provisions for income taxes.
e. Disposal of a segment of a business and extraordinary, unusual, or infrequently occurring items.
f. Contingent items.
g. Changes in accounting principles or estimates.
h. Significant changes in financial position.

Overall, the APB and FASB have made a significant effort to improve the quality of interim financial reports. However, considerable controversy still exists and appears to center around the APB's assumption that an interim period should be accounted for as an integral part of the annual period.

International Issues in Interim Reporting

Some companies are still reporting only the minimum amount of information in their interim reports, despite publication of the Accounting Standards Boards' guidance in November 1996. For example, clothing manufacturer Albion, in its interim statement for the half-year ended March 31, 1998, reported only a one-page sheet of the minimum information required by the London Stock Exchange's Listing Rules. It did not say that the interim reports were prepared in a basis consistent with the policies used in the last reported annual period, though presumably this was the case. The ASB guidance statement recommends that interim reports use the same measurement and recognition bases and accounting methods as used in the annual reports, and that this should be stated in the interim report.[11]

International harmonization of accounting standards has been slow in reaching the area of interim reporting. The IASC issued an exposure draft, E57, "Interim Financial Reporting," recommending the use of a discrete approach to interim reporting. The Institute of Management Accountants' (IMA) Financial Reporting Committee reviewed the exposure draft and expressed an opinion disagreeing with this approach, and stating its preference for the integral approach used in the United States.

"The Committee does agree that determination of what needs to be included in the notes to the interim financial statements about unusual events should be based on the stand-alone interim data. However, as users of financial statements, the Committee would find the 'accordion effect' associated with the discrete approach both disruptive and confusing . . . the Committee believes the most useful and practical approach to dealing with interim accounting is the integral approach."[12]

 SUMMARY

1. *Understand the need for disaggregated financial data.* To aid in evaluating prospective investments and particularly the risk of those investments, financial statement users must assess the uncertainty surrounding both the timing and the amounts of expected cash flows. Major uncertainty results from factors unique to individual companies, factors related to the industries and geographical areas in which those companies operate, and related national and international economic and political factors. When a firm engages in activities in several industries or geographic areas, analysis and the prediction of future cash flows become somewhat more complicated because different segments may have different rates of profitability, growth opportunities, and types of risk.

---

[11] *Accountancy*, "Gradual Acceptance of ASB Guidelines," vol. 122, September 1998, p. 78.

[12] *Management Accounting*, "Interim Reporting," vol. 79, February 1998, p. 59.

2. *Describe the basic requirements of public companies in reporting segmental data.* In *SFAS No. 131*, the FASB requires all public companies to report information about the countries in which they earn revenues and hold assets, about major customers, and about revenues for each product and service, even when *some* of the information is not used by the firm in its operating decisions. In general, *SFAS No. 131* implemented a management approach, focusing on the way in which management organizes segments internally to make operating decisions and to assess performance.

3. *Determine an operating segment.* An operating segment is a component of an enterprise that may earn revenues and incur expenses, about which the chief operating decision maker regularly evaluates separate financial information in deciding how to allocate resources and in assessing performance. Discrete financial information is available about the segment.

4. *Define a reportable segment.* A reportable segment is a segment considered to be significant to an enterprise's operations; specifically, one that has passed one of three 10% tests or has been identified as being reportable through other criteria (aggregation, for example). The three 10% tests relate to combined external and internal revenues, reported profit or loss, and assets.

5. *Describe how common costs are handled in segmental reporting.* Common costs should be allocated to a segment for external reporting purposes only if they are included in the segment's profit or loss calculations that are used internally by the chief operating decision maker. The emphasis here is on operating expenses, as general corporate expenses are not allocated.

6. *Identify the information to be presented for each reportable segment.* The information presented includes: general information; information about segment operating profit or loss; information about segment assets; information about the bases for measurement; a reconciliation of segment amounts to the consolidated amounts for revenue, profit or loss, assets, and other significant items; interim disclosures; and enterprisewide disclosures regarding products or services, geographic areas, and major customers.

7. *Explain when and what types of geographic data must be reported.* Geographic disclosures are required on an enterprisewide basis unless the company's reportable segments have been organized around geographic area. When required, firms must report revenues from external customers and long-lived assets attributable to their domestic operations and foreign operations. If operations are conducted in two or more foreign countries or geographic areas, information must be presented separately for each significant foreign country or geographic area and in the aggregate for all other foreign operations.

8. *Explain when information about major customers must be reported.* If 10% or more of the revenue of a firm is derived from sales to any single customer, that fact and the amount of revenue from each such customer must be disclosed. Also, if 10% or more of the revenue is derived from sales to the federal government, a state government, a local government, or a foreign government, that fact and the amount of revenue must be disclosed. These disclosures are required even if the firm has only one reportable segment.

9. *Compare the international accounting standards for segmental reporting with the U.S. requirements.* Whereas the U.S. standard focuses on the data reported and used internally by a chief operating decision maker, the IASC states its objective as providing insight into how the diversity of products and services and geographic operations affects an enterprise's overall risks and returns. The differences between the two standards include segment definition, measurement differences, uniformity across companies, and asymmetry allowed/disallowed in measurement.

10. *Describe current requirements for companies to report interim information.* Publicly owned companies are generally required to file some type of quarterly report as part of the agreement with the stock exchanges that list their stock. In addition, the SEC requires public companies to file Form 10-Q with the Commission within 45 days after the end of each of the first three quarters of the fiscal year.

11. *Indicate some problems with interim reporting and the authoritative position on the issue.* The seasonal nature of operations in many industries can cause wide fluctuations in revenues, expenses, and net income from one interim period to another. The relatively short time period available to determine interim results and the added cost of determining accurate figures for accruals, deferrals, and inventories encouraged the use of a variety of estimation techniques, some of which proved to be highly inaccurate. Two conflicting views of the nature of interim periods are: each period is *discrete* and should *stand alone* as a basic accounting period; or each interim period is an *integral* part of the annual period. In *APB Opinion No. 28*, the Board supported the integral view.

QUESTIONS

1. For what types of companies would segmented financial reports have the most significance? Why?

2. Why do financial statement users (financial analysts, for example) need information about segments of a firm?

3. Define the following:
   (a) Operating segment.
   (b) Reportable segment.

4. Describe the guidelines to be used in determining (a) what constitutes an operating segment, and (b) whether a specific operating segment is a significant segment.

5. List the three major types of enterprisewide information disclosures required by *SFAS No. 131*, and explain how the firm's designation of reportable segments affects these disclosures.

6. What segmental disclosures are required, if any, for interim reports?

7. What type of disclosure is required of a firm when the major portion of its operations takes place within a single reportable segment?

8. List the types of information that must be presented for each reportable segment of a company under the rules of *SFAS No. 131*.

9. Describe the methods that might be used to disclose reportable segment information.

10. What types of information must be disclosed about foreign operations under *SFAS No. 131*?

11. How are foreign operations defined under *SFAS No. 131*?

12. If the operations of a firm in some foreign countries are grouped into geographic areas, what factors should be considered in forming the groups?

13. When must a firm present segmental disclosures for major customers? What is the reason for this requirement?

14. How are common costs distinguished from general corporate expenses for segmental purposes?

15. What is the purpose of interim financial reporting?

16. Some accountants hold the view that each interim period should stand alone as a basic accounting period, whereas others view each interim period as essentially an integral part of the annual period. Distinguish between these views.

17. Describe the basic procedure for computing income tax provisions for interim financial statements.

18. Describe how changes in estimates should be treated in interim financial statements.

19. What are the minimum disclosure requirements established by the APB for interim financial reports?

20. What is the general rule regarding the treatment of costs and expenses associated directly with revenues for interim reporting purposes?

EXERCISES

EXERCISE 15-1 Operating Profit Test

Pong Industries' operations involve four operating segments, A, B, C, and D. During the past year, the operating profit (loss) of each segment was

Segment	Operating Profit (Loss)
A	$(600)
B	100
C	900
D	(700)

Required:

Applying the operating profit or loss test, determine which of the segments are reportable segments.

EXERCISE 15-2 Revenue Test

Mane Company operates in five identifiable segments, V, W, X, Y, and Z. During the past year, sales to unaffiliated customers and intersegment sales for each segment were as follows:

Segment	Sales to Nonaffiliates	Intersegment Sales	Total Sales
V	$2,000	$ 400	$2,400
W	280	20	300
X	100	600	700
Y	1,100	—0—	1,100
Z	350	25	375
Total	$3,830	$1,045	$4,875

Required:

Applying the revenue test, determine which of the segments are reportable segments.

EXERCISE 15-3 **Significance Tests**

Twodor Company is involved in four separate industries. Selected financial information concerning Twodor's involvement in each of the four industries is presented below:

	Industry Segment				
	A	B	C	D	Total
Sales to nonaffiliates	$ 80,000	$20,000	$24,000	$12,200	$136,200
Intersegment sales	130,000	84,000	12,000	3,800	229,800
Total revenue	210,000	104,000	36,000	16,000	366,000
Operating profit (loss)	(17,400)	12,000	1,500	(600)	(4,500)
Identifiable assets	222,000	110,500	28,000	26,000	386,500

Required:

Using all tests, determine which of the industry segments are reportable segments and explain how nonreportable segments (if any) should be reported.

EXERCISE 15-4 **Allocating Common Costs to Segments**

The following information concerns the operations of Blane Company for the year ended December 31, 2001.

	(In Thousands of Dollars)		
	General Office	Segment A	Segment B
Net sales (operating revenue)		$60,000	$99,000
Cost of goods sold		27,200	35,600
Allocable expenses		12,600	10,800
General corporate expenses	$15,000		
Payroll dollars	9,200	34,800	18,200
Average net book value of tangible capital assets and inventories	5,200	70,000	54,500

Required:

Determine the operating profit (loss) for each of Blane's two segments for 2001.

EXERCISE 15-5 **Provision for Taxes—Interim**

LAX Inc. has the following income before income tax and estimated effective annual income tax rates for the first three quarteres of 2001:

Quarter	Income Before Income Tax Provision	Estimated Effective Annual Tax Rate at End of Quarter
1st	$70,000	32%
2nd	50,000	32%
3rd	40,600	38%

Required:

What should be LAX's income tax provision in the third-quarter income statement?

(*AICPA adapted*)

EXERCISE 15-6 Amounts on Quarterly Reports

The following information is available for Bailey Company for 2001:

1. On January 2, 2001, Bailey paid property taxes amounting to $60,000 on its plant and equipment for the calendar year 2001. In late March 2001 Bailey made major repairs to its machinery amounting to $66,000. These repairs will benefit the remainder of the calendar year's operations.

2. An inventory loss of $150,000 from market decline occurred in August 2001. Bailey recorded this loss in August 2001 after its June 30 quarterly report was issued. None of this loss had been recovered by the end of 2001.

3. At the end of July 2001, Bailey sold some equipment with a book value of $22,000 for $32,500.

Required:

State the dollar amounts that should appear in Bailey Company's March 31, June 30, September 30, and December 31, 2001 quarterly financial statements to report:

A. Property taxes.

B. Major repairs to machinery.

C. Inventory loss from market decline.

D. The gain or loss on sale of equipment.

(*AICPA adapted*)

EXERCISE 15-7 Inventory and Quarterly Reports

Day Company, which uses the FIFO inventory method, had 254,000 units in inventory at the beginning of the year at a FIFO cost per unit of $30. No purchases were made during the year. Quarterly sales information and two sets of end-of-quarter replacement cost figures follow:

		End-of-Quarter Replacement Cost	
Quarter	*Unit Sales*	*Case A*	*Case B*
1	100,000	$29	$25
2	30,000	22	27
3	42,500	18	19
4	30,500	22	27

The market decline in the first quarter under Case A was expected to be temporary, whereas under Case B the decline was expected to be nontemporary. Declines in other quarters were expected to be permanent.

Required:

Determine cost of goods sold for the four quarters under each case and verify the amounts by computing cost of goods sold using the lower-of-cost-or-market method applied on an annual basis.

EXERCISE 15-8 Provision for Taxes—Quarterly Entries

Spur Company's actual earnings for the first two quarters of 2001 and its estimate during each quarter of its annual earnings are:

Actual first-quarter earnings	$ 400,000
Actual second-quarter earnings	510,000
First-quarter estimate of annual earnings	1,350,000
Second-quarter estimate of annual earnings	1,420,000

Spur Company estimated its permanent differences between accounting income and taxable income for 2001 as:

Goodwill amortization	$ 25,000
Dividend income exclusion	180,000

These estimates did not change during the second quarter. The combined state and federal tax rate for Spur Company for 2001 is 42%.

Required:

Prepare journal entries to record Spur Company's provisions for income taxes for each of the first two quarters of 2001.

EXERCISE 15-9 **Multiple Choice**

Select the best answer for each of the following.

1. Which of the following is *not* a consideration in segment reporting for diversified companies?
   (a) Consolidation policy.
   (b) Defining the segments.
   (c) Transfer pricing.
   (d) Allocation of joint costs.

2. Cream Company operates in three different industries, each of which is appropriately regarded as a reportable segment. Segment No. 1 contributed 60% of Cream Company's total sales. Sales for Segment No. 1 were $450,000 and traceable costs were $200,000. Total common costs for Cream were $300,000. Cream allocates common costs on the basis of the ratio of a segment's sales to total sales, an appropriate method of allocation. What should be the operating profit presented for Segment No. 1 for the year?
   (a) $270,000.
   (b) $70,000.
   (c) $180,000.
   (d) $250,000.

3. The profitability information that should be reported for each reportable segment of a business enterprise consists of
   (a) An operating profit or loss figure consisting of segment revenues less traceable costs but *not* allocated common costs.
   (b) An operating profit or loss figure consisting of segment revenues less allocated common costs but *not* traceable costs.
   (c) An operating profit or loss figure consisting of segment revenues less traceable costs and allocated common costs.
   (d) Segment revenues only.

4. In financial reporting for segments of a business enterprise, the operating profit or loss of a segment should include
   (a) Revenue from other segments.
   (b) Federal income taxes.
   (c) Interest expense even though the segment's operations are *not* principally of a financial nature.
   (d) Any of the above, *if* it is included in the measures reviewed by the chief operating decision maker.

5. A company that uses the LIFO method of inventory pricing finds at an interim reporting date that there has been a partial liquidation of the base period inventory level. The decline is considered temporary and the partial liquidation will be replaced before year-end. The amount shown as inventory at the interim reporting date should
   (a) Be shown at the actual level, and cost of sales for the interim reporting period should reflect the decrease in the LIFO base period inventory level.

(b) *Not* give effect to the LIFO liquidation, and cost of sales for the interim reporting period should reflect the decrease in the LIFO base period inventory level.

(c) *Not* give effect to the LIFO liquidation, and cost of sales for the interim reporting period should include the expected cost of replacement of the liquidated LIFO base.

(d) Be shown at the actual level, and the decrease in inventory level should *not* be reflected in the cost of sales for the interim reporting period.

6. Which of the following is an inherent difficulty in determination of the results of operations on an interim basis?

   (a) Costs expended in one interim period may benefit other periods.

   (b) Depreciation on an interim basis is a partial estimate of the actual annual amount.

   (c) Cost of sales reflects only the amount of product expense allocable to revenue recognized as of the interim date.

   (d) Revenues from long-term construction contracts accounted for by the percentage-of-completion method are based on annual completion, and interim estimates may be incorrect.

7. In considering interim financial reporting, how did the Accounting Principles Board conclude that such reporting should be viewed?

   (a) As useful only if activity is evenly spread throughout the year so that estimates are unnecessary.

   (b) As a "special" type of reporting that need *not* follow generally accepted accounting principles.

   (c) As reporting of an integral part of an annual period.

   (d) As reporting of a basic accounting period.

8. Which of the following methods of inventory valuation is allowable at interim dates but *not* at year-end?

   (a) Estimated gross profit rates.

   (b) Retail method.

   (c) Specific identification.

   (d) Weighted average.

(AICPA adapted)

PROBLEMS

PROBLEM 15-1 Significance Tests—Segmental Reporting

Bacon Industries operates in seven different segments. Information concerning the operations of these segments for the most recent fiscal period follows:

Operating Segment	Revenue Total	Revenue Intersegment	Operating Profit (Loss)	Identifiable Assets
1	$ 4,200	$ 800	$ (600)	$ 7,000
2	6,000	1,200	2,000	8,800
3	51,000	7,000	2,100	35,400
4	48,000	—0—	8,800	37,600
5	13,000	—0—	3,200	14,000
6	64,500	3,400	4,000	52,000
7	12,000	2,000	(3,000)	16,400

Required:

Determine which of the segments must be treated as reportable segments.

PROBLEM 15-2 Significance Tests—Segmental Reporting

Pacheco Industries is comprised of four separate profit centers, which are distributed throughout the United States. Relevant data for each profit center are summarized for 2001:

	Profit Center (in Thousands)				
	A	B	C	D	Total
Sales to nonaffiliates	$3,600	$ 8,700	$1,500	$1,200	$15,000
Intersegment sales	1,500	2,400	300	3,000	7,200
Operating profit (loss) before joint expense allocation	840	1,500	240	(60)	2,520
Identifiable assets	7,200	18,000	2,400	2,400	30,000
Labor hours worked	2,700	5,700	1,500	2,100	12,000

You determine that intersegment sales are distributed as follows:

	Buyer				
Seller	A	B	C	D	Total
A	$—0—	$1,200	$150	$150	$1,500
B	1,200	—0—	600	600	2,400
C	150	150	—0—	—0—	300
D	1,800	1,050	150	—0—	3,000
Total	$3,150	$2,400	$900	$750	$7,200

Common costs of $2,400,000 were incurred during 2001. Management believes that total labor hours worked during the year provides a reasonable basis for allocation of these costs.

In each situation described below, an operating segment is comprised of different combinations of profit centers. Thus, the "AB" operating segment consists of profit centers "A" and "B." Consider the following five combinations of operating segments:

1. AB, CD
2. AB, C, D
3. A, B, CD
4. A, B, C, D
5. A, BD, C

Required:

A. For each combination listed, determine which operating segments are reportable segments. Apply all required tests and indicate the results of each test separately.

B. For each combination given, indicate if the reportable segments determined in (A) above collectively represent a "substantial portion" of Pacheco Industries' total operations, applying the 75% revenue test.

PROBLEM 15-3 Issues in Segmental Reporting

Perez Industries, a publicly held corporation, consists of several companies, each of which provides an array of products and services to unaffiliated customers. In your opinion, each of these companies qualifies as a separate operating segment.

The corporation is in the process of completing its first-year financial statements. Although the directors of Perez Industries wish to comply with the provisions of *SFAS No. 131*, they believe that disclosing each individual segment would result in an unwieldy and cumbersome set of financial statements. For this reason, they request that when you prepare these statements, you keep the identified segments to the minimum number that would ensure compliance with *SFAS No. 131*.

Required:

A. To what extent does the management of Perez Industries have a choice in deciding whether an operating segment must be reported?

B. The directors of Perez Industries presumably feel that too much disclosure of financial information will impair the overall utility of the financial statements. What are the arguments against segmental disclosures? What flexibility, if any, does the FASB allow that could invalidate this criticism? Explain.

C. Explain the needs for segment reporting. Why do consolidated financial statements fail to meet these needs?

D. Relate the concept of comparability to the required accounting treatment for intersegment transactions. What arguments would favor *excluding* the effect of intersegment transfers?

PROBLEM 15-4 Comprehensive Segmental Reporting

Branson Industries conducts operations in five major industries, A, B, C, D, and E. Financial data relevant to each industry for the year ending December 31, 2001, are as follows:

(In Thousands)

	United States			Canada	
	A	B	C	D	E
Sales	$57,000	$120,000	$880,000	$50,000	$ 83,000
Cost of goods sold	20,000	75,000	400,000	9,400	49,000
Administrative expenses	18,000	26,000	152,000	12,000	8,000
Selling expenses	7,000	44,000	172,000	12,600	20,000
Total cost and expense	45,000	145,000	724,000	34,000	77,000
Operating profit	$12,000	$(25,000)	$156,000	$16,000	$ 6,000
Identifiable assets	$50,000	$95,000	$600,000	$98,000	$240,000
Depreciation and amortization expense	6,400	10,700	76,000	12,200	26,400
Capital expenditures	5,600	8,000	39,000	20,000	25,000

Included in the sales of segments C and E are intersegment sales of $120,000 and $40,000, respectively. Corporate offices have assets of $95,000 and incurred general corporate expenses of $76,000 and depreciation of $10,000. No single customer represents more than 10% of sales. There is no intercompany inventory in beginning or ending inventory. The intersegment sales are included in the measures reviewed by the chief operating decision maker, as are the capital expenditures and depreciation and amortization. Assume that all corporate assets are located in the U.S.

Required:

A. Which industry segments should be separately reported in the segment report, assuming that Branson defines its operating segments based on major industry (product/services)? Justify your answer.

B. Prepare a report to disclose required segment information under *SFAS No. 131*. Include the enterprisewide disclosures.

PROBLEM 15-5 Segmental Reconciliation

Bismac Industries is a diversified company whose operations are conducted in five product lines, L, M, N, O, and P. Segmented financial information is to be included with the December 31, 2001 annual report. Financial information pertaining to each segment for 2001 is as follows:

	L	M	N	O	P
Sales	$40,000	$ 85,000	$600,000	$50,000	$48,000
Cost of sales	15,000	45,000	275,000	22,000	29,000
Depreciation expense	5,000	8,000	54,000	6,000	5,000
Interest expense	4,000	11,000	50,000	4,000	1,000
Selling expense	8,000	32,000	140,000	9,000	10,000
Total cost and expense	32,000	96,000	519,000	41,000	45,000
Operating profit (loss)	$ 8,000	$(11,000)	$ 81,000	$ 9,000	$ 3,000
Identifiable assets	$30,000	$ 48,000	$320,000	$45,000	$95,000

Other information:

1. In addition to the identifiable assets listed, the general corporate office has assets of $90,000 on December 31, 2001, and incurred unallocated amounts related to corporate headquarters of: interest expense $1,000, depreciation expense $2,000.

2. Included in the sales of segment P are $15,000 of sales made to segment N during the year. None of these goods remains in the ending inventory of segment N on December 31, 2001. There were no capital expenditures during the year.

3. No single customer represented more than 10% of sales.

Required:

A. Determine which of the five segments must be treated as reportable segments and indicate the basis for your decision. Assume segments are defined based on product line.

B. Prepare a financial report by segments that is reconciled to consolidated data.

PROBLEM 15-6 Quarterly Income Tax Entries

Actual quarterly earnings and quarterly estimates of annual earnings for Sloan Company for the year ended December 31, 2001 are as follows:

Quarter	Actual Quarterly Earnings	Quarterly Estimates of Annual Earnings
1	$95,000	$400,000
2	85,000	370,000
3	92,000	370,000
4	96,000	N/A

The combined state and federal tax rate for 2001 is 30%. Sloan Company estimated it would have permanent differences between accounting income and taxable income during 2001. Each quarter's estimate of these annual differences is provided in the following table:

	Estimated Permanent Differences	
Estimate at End of Quarter	Goodwill Amortization	Dividend Exclusion
1	$14,000	$40,000
2	14,000	40,000
3	14,000	50,000

The actual amount of permanent differences for 2001 were goodwill amortization, $14,000 dividend exclusion, $55,000.

Required:

Prepare journal entries to record Sloan Company's 2001 quarterly income tax provisions.

PROBLEM 15-7 Various Interim Reporting Cases

The following statement is an excerpt from paragraphs 9 and 10 of *APB Opinion No. 28*, "Interim Financial Reporting":

> Interim financial information is essential to provide investors and others with timely information as to the progress of the enterprise. The usefulness of such information rests on the relationship that it has to the annual results of operations. Accordingly, the Board has concluded that each interim period should be viewed primarily as an integral part of an annual period.
>
> In general, the results for each interim period should be based on the accounting principles and practices used by an enterprise in the preparation of its latest annual financial statements unless a change in an accounting practice or policy has been adopted in the current year. The Board has

concluded, however, that certain accounting principles and practices followed for annual reporting purposes may require modification at interim reporting dates so that the reported results for the interim period may better relate to the results of operations for the annual period.

Required:

Listed below are six independent cases on how accounting facts might be reported on an individual company's interim financial reports. For each case, state whether the method proposed to be used for interim reporting would be acceptable under generally accepted accounting principles applicable to interim financial data. Support each answer with a brief explanation.

A. Reed Company wrote inventory down to reflect lower of cost or market in the first quarter of 2001. At year-end the market value exceeds the original acquisition cost of this inventory. Consequently, management plans to write the inventory back up to its original cost as a year-end adjustment.

B. Greenfield Company realized a large gain on the sale of investments at the beginning of the second quarter. The company wants to report one-third of the gain in each of the remaining quarters.

C. Dole Company has estimated its annual audit fee. They plan to prorate this expense equally over all four quarters.

D. Fur Company was reasonably certain they would have an employee strike in the third quarter. As a result, they shipped heavily during the second quarter but plan to defer the recognition of the sales in excess of the normal sales volume. The deferred sales will be recognized as sales in the third quarter when the strike is in progress. Fur Company management thinks this is more nearly representative of normal second- and third-quarter operations.

E. Rexx Company takes a physical inventory at year-end for annual financial statement purposes. Inventory and cost of sales reported in the interim quarterly statements are based on estimated gross profit rates, because a physical inventory would result in a cessation of operations. Rexx Company does have reliable perpetual inventory records.

F. Shelley Company is planning to report one-fourth of its pension expense in each quarter.

(*CMA adapted*)

16

PARTNERSHIPS: FORMATION, OPERATION, AND OWNERSHIP CHANGES

LEARNING OBJECTIVES

1. Describe the characteristics of a general partnership, a limited partnership, and a joint venture.

2. List some important items to be included in the partnership agreement.

3. Understand the differences between partnerships' and corporations' equity accounts in the balance sheet.

4. Explain the purpose of the partners' drawing accounts and capital accounts.

5. Prepare journal entries to form a partnership using the bonus and the goodwill methods.

6. Describe some common agreements used to allocate partnership net income or loss.

7. Explain why salary allowances and interest allowances are used in allocating partnership profits and losses.

8. Describe the methods used to record partnership changes when a new partner is admitted or when a partner withdraws from the partnership.

9. Describe the rationale behind the goodwill method in accounting for changes in partnership membership.

"Sustainability can be a 2 + 2 =5 (or even 50) game. To achieve outstanding triple bottom line performance, new types of economic, social, and environmental partnership are needed. Long-standing enemies must shift from mutual subversion to new forms of symbiosis. The resulting partnerships will help each partner perform traditional tasks more efficiently, while providing a platform from which to reach toward goals that none of the partners could hope to achieve on his own."[1]

The next two chapters deal exclusively with accounting and reporting problems associated with the partnership form of business organization. These chapters cover the complete life cycle of a partnership from its formation and operation to its

---

[1]*Environmental Quality Management*, "Partnerships from Cannibals with Forks: The Triple Bottom Line of 21st-Century Business," by John Elkington, Autumn 1998, p. 37.

liquidation. Partnerships are covered in this text because they are a common form of business organization. They are popular because they permit the pooling of limited resources, are easy to form (no special governmental approval is required), and may have certain tax advantages. Because partnerships are common, accountants are often called on to account for and serve in an advisory capacity to partnerships. Although many of the accounting concepts applicable to a sole proprietorship or a corporation are also applicable to partnerships, some aspects of partnership formation, operation, and liquidation require additional consideration. The unique aspects of accounting for a partnership are the focus of these chapters. Figure 16-1 presents a summary of statistics for partnerships in the United States from 1980 to 1995.

Accounting for a partnership is influenced by the agreement made among the partners and by the appropriate state statutes. Partnerships operate within the legal framework of the state in which they are organized and the statutes may vary from state to state. In order to illustrate statutory provisions, the Uniform Partnership

FIGURE 16-1

Partnerships—Selected Items by Industry: 1980 to 1995

| Year | Number of Partnerships | | | Number of Partners (000) | Total Assets (a) (millions) | Net Income (b) (millions) | Net Loss (b) (millions) |
	Total (000)	With Net Income (000)	With Net Loss (000)				
All industries:							
1980	1,380	774	605	8,420	$ 597,504	$ 45,062	$36,813
1985	1,714	876	838	13,245	1,269,434	77,045	85,928
1990	1,554	854	700	17,095	1,735,285	116,318	99,708
1992	1,485	856	629	15,735	1,907,345	121,834	78,918
1993	1,468	870	598	15,627	2,118,268	137,441	70,788
1994	1,494	890	604	14,990	2,295,212	150,928	68,745
1995	1,581	955	626	15,606	2,718,648	178,651	71,822
Wholesale and retail trade:							
1980	200	123	77	487	17,727	3,374	900
1985	201	113	88	493	20,568	3,467	1,490
1990	176	100	77	481	28,423	4,717	2,107
1992	162	86	76	425	32,777	4,758	2,205
1993	157	88	69	471	35,278	5,304	2,229
1994	153	87	66	443	44,367	6,344	2,043
Finance, insurance, and real estate:							
1980	637	313	325	5,566	454,531	15,169	19,418
1985	844	369	475	7,755	979,787	30,383	56,311
1990	822	401	422	10,846	1,329,452	47,577	66,790
1992	797	427	370	10,328	1,438,303	50,044	50,796
1993	793	443	350	9,944	1,612,142	59,062	43,802
1994	810	465	345	9,881	1,750,671	65,369	41,245
Services:							
1980	263	169	94	938	45,510	15,649	3,224
1985	341	207	134	1,713	106,597	26,942	10,400
1990	267	173	96	2,153	150,063	39,383	12,930
1992	253	169	84	2,167	178,577	42,748	9,744
1993	256	169	87	2,146	166,806	43,300	9,413
1994	261	170	91	2,060	177,992	46,048	9,730

Adapted from *Statistics of Income Bulletin, and Partnership Returns—1980–1995*, U.S. Internal Revenue Service.
(a) Total assets are understated because not all partnerships file complete balance sheets.
(b) Beginning in 1985, only net (not gross) income from farming, rents and royalties are included.

Act (UPA) is integrated throughout the partnership chapters because it, or some modification thereof, is the partnership law that has been adopted by the majority of the states. An in-depth study of the legal aspects of partnerships is generally contained in the typical business law course.

PARTNERSHIP DEFINED

A partnership is defined by the UPA as ''an association of two or more persons to carry on as co-owners a business for profit.''[2] Persons in this definition include individuals, partnerships, corporations, and other associations. Not only are corporations sometimes partners, but also partnerships can be shareholders in a corporation.

IN THE NEWS

EToys Inc. is betting that a lot of American parents want to buy Barbie, Arthur and other favorite playthings without visiting the mall, let alone chasing screaming children down toy store aisles. "We're benefiting from eToys' success and are happy to be their partner," says a Mattel spokesman. If the eToys' offering is completed as planned, it will mean big gains for the firm's top management and a small squad of venture capitalists. The company's biggest shareholders are various partnerships affiliated with Idealab!, a business incubator and venture-capital firm run by inventor Bill Gross.[3]

In some cases, it may be difficult to determine whether a partnership has been formed or whether an individual is a partner in a business arrangement. To determine the existence of a partnership, it may be helpful to look for the following three attributes: (1) there must be an agreement, either expressed or implied, between two or more persons; (2) the business must be operated for the purpose of making a profit; and (3) members of the firm must be co-owners of the business. Co-ownership involves the right of each partner to share in the profits of the business, to participate in the management of the business, and to hold an interest in properties conveyed to the partnership. These rights are shared equally unless agreed to otherwise in the partnership agreement.

REASONS FOR FORMING A PARTNERSHIP

The prospective owner(s) of a business should consider the various attributes of the different forms of business organizations before selecting the one that they believe best meets their organizational objectives and personal goals. A form suitable for one set of business objectives may not be appropriate for another. It is possible for a firm to start as a proprietorship and, as the business and personal environments change, to move to a partnership form, and ultimately, to incorporate.

One of the major advantages of a partnership is that it permits the pooling of capital and other resources without the complexities and formalities of a corporation. A partnership is easier and less costly to establish than a corporation and is

---

[2]UPA, Section 6.

[3]*WSJ*, ''EToys Plans to Join Web-Retailer Parade With Its Own IPO,'' by George Anders and Lisa Bannon, 4/6/99, p. B1.

generally not subject to as much governmental regulation. Furthermore, the partners may be able to operate with more flexibility because they are not subject to the control of a board of directors. There may also be certain tax advantages to a partnership, as discussed later.

Chip Bell, senior partner with Performance Research Associates in Dallas, compares partnering to dancing. He suggests six steps to great partnerships:
- **Focus**, or prepare to partner. There should be a clear commitment to some purpose.
- **Audition**, or pick great partners. Auditions are about discovery and disclosure. Be open for warning cues.
- **Rehearse**, or get the partnership in shape. Work the plan, ignoring opposition or objections.
- **Dance**, or keep the magic in motion. Great partnerships keep going and growing.
- **Hurt**, or manage the pain. Great dances are rarely flawless, and the capacity to bend and continue in the face of adversity makes for resilience.
- **Bow out**, or know when to call it curtains.[4]

CHARACTERISTICS OF A PARTNERSHIP

The principal types of partnerships are general partnerships, limited partnerships, and joint ventures. The characteristics of these types of business organization are discussed in this section. Some partnership characteristics may make it more difficult for a partnership to raise capital than for a corporation. Partnerships are thus most common in comparatively small businesses, professional organizations, such as medical clinics or an accounting practice, and some limited projects undertaken to accomplish a single goal, such as an oil and gas exploration project or the purchase of a parcel of real estate for investment purposes. However, there is no limit to the size or number of partners in a firm. For example, in the large international CPA firms, the number of partners is in the hundreds and revenue is in the millions of dollars.

General Partnership

In a general partnership, each member is a general partner within the firm. That is, there is no "limited partner" in the organization. The following are characteristics of a general partnership.

Mutual Agency Every general partner is an agent of both the partnership and every other partner. Thus, a partner can bind the other partners to a contract if he or she is acting within the apparent scope of the business. Outside parties transacting business with a partner can assume the partner has the power to bind the partnership unless they are informed otherwise. Outside parties should be aware, however, that for certain acts, such as the assignment of partnership property, unanimous consent of the partners is required.

Right to Dispose of a Partnership Interest A capital interest in a general partnership is a personal asset of the individual partner that can be sold or disposed of in

[4]Adapted from *Dance Lessons: Six Steps to Great Partnerships in Business and Life*, by Chip Bell and Heather Shea, Highbridge Company: St, Paul, MN, 1998. Also see *Executive Excellence*, "Steps to Great Partnerships," by Chip Bell and Heather Shea, March 1999, pp. 5–6.

any legal way. However, the UPA, recognizing the highly personal relationship of the partners, provides that a purchaser of another partner's interest does not have the right to participate in management unless he or she is accepted by all the partners. The new partner is entitled to the profit allocation acquired and, in the event of liquidation, to receive whatever assets the selling partner would have received had he or she continued in the partnership.

Unlimited Liability In a **general partnership**, each partner is jointly and severally liable for the debts and obligations of the partnership. This means that in the case of liquidation, the creditors of the partnership, if not satisfied from assets of the partnership, can look to each partner's personal resources for recovery of unsatisfied claims. Jointly and severally means that a creditor can seek recovery from all the partners or can proceed against one or more of them separately.

Limited or Uncertain Life A general partnership may be dissolved for a number of reasons, including the death of a partner, the bankruptcy of an individual partner, the withdrawal of a partner from the partnership, or a judgment by a court that a partner is unsound of mind and incapable of performing his or her partnership duties.

Tax Implications A general partnership is not subject to income tax, but it must file an information return. The income or loss of the partnership is allocated to the individual partners, and their respective share of the income or loss is reported on their individual income tax returns whether distributed by the partnership or not. Also, a partner's capital interest in a partnership for tax purposes is the amount of cash invested. If noncash assets are invested, his or her tax basis is the adjusted basis of the asset at the date of investment reduced by any related indebtedness assumed by the partnership, regardless of the fair value of the asset invested. For example, if a partner invests land with a tax basis of $50,000 and a fair value of $80,000, the partner's tax basis in the partnership is $50,000. Of course, for tax purposes, no gain or loss is recognized by the partner in the year the land was transferred to the partnership.

The characteristics just discussed underline the importance of careful selection of the individuals to be associated with in a general partnership. In particular, mutual agency and unlimited liability are distinctive features of a general partnership that could result in extensive personal liability resulting from the acts of other partners.

"Partnerships aren't for everyone. They require an investment of energy and demand vulnerability. And partnerships diminish the protection of anonymity. They are poor associations in which to hide. Partnership means working onstage, not backstage. Done well, partnerships work at amplifying disclosure and enhancing exposure."[5]

Limited Partnership

In a **limited partnership**, one or more of the partners are general partners and one or more are limited partners. General partners manage the firm and are personally

---

[5]*Executive Excellence*, "Steps to Great Partnerships," by Chip Bell and Heather Shea, March 1999, pp. 5–6.

liable for obligations of the partnership. Limited partners invest capital only and limit their liability for partnership obligations to the amount of investment they have agreed to make. In return, limited partners give up the right to participate in the management of the firm.

The limited partnership form of organization is selected when the general partners want to raise capital without giving up management control of the business. It is also an attractive form when the tax benefits associated with a partnership are desired, but the investors do not want to assume personal liability for the obligations of the partnership. For these reasons, the limited partnership form is often used for professional sports franchises and offerings of partnership interests made to the public for the purpose of carrying out a specific business plan, such as real estate ventures or oil and gas exploration projects.

Laws relating to a limited partnership are codified in the Uniform Limited Partnership Act (ULPA). The ULPA provides that in forming a limited partnership, a certificate required by state statute must be signed and filed with the appropriate government official. The certificate is generally drafted and filed by the general partners. Among other things, it should describe the nature of the business, state the firm's name, location, and term of its existence, and identify all partners and their capital contributions. Although the general partners must obtain the consent of the limited partners for certain actions, in general, partnership law applies to limited partnerships. The accounting procedures described in this and the following chapters are applicable to both general and limited partnerships.

IN THE NEWS

"Gene Phillips was at the helm when a now-defunct real estate partnership firm called Southmark sank into bankruptcy. His investors lost heavily. Phillips lived lavishly in Texas. . . . They say on Wall Street of limited partnerships: In the beginning, the limited partners have the money and the general partner has the experience. In the end the roles are reversed, especially if Gene Phillips is in the picture."[6]

Joint Ventures

A *joint venture* is an arrangement entered into by two or more parties to accomplish a single or limited purpose for the mutual benefit of the members of the group, often to earn a profit. For example, a firm in one country may enter into an agreement with the firm of another country to pool their resources to construct an automobile manufacturing plant, or two or more firms may enter into an arrangement to develop a new product that requires complementary technological knowledge. Thus, the life of the joint venture is limited to that of the undertaking, which may be of short- or long-term duration.

The relationship between the parties in the arrangement is generally governed by a written agreement. A distinguishing characteristic of the agreement is that each joint venturer participates directly or indirectly in the overall management of the resources. Accordingly, major decisions require the consent of the ownership group.

Joint ventures are commonly organized as corporations or partnerships. If organized as a corporation, the investment in the joint venture generally must be accounted for using the equity method in accordance with the provisions of Ac-

---

[6]*Forbes*, "The Old Double Dip," by Gretchen Morgenson, 7/7/97, pp. 54–56.

counting Principles Board Opinion No. 18.[7] As a corporation, a joint venture is governed by corporate law. If the arrangement is a partnership joint venture, interpretations of *Opinion No. 18* indicate that many of the provisions of that opinion are appropriate in accounting for the investment.[8] In general, partnership law applies to a partnership joint venture, but the authority of a joint venturer is limited to a greater extent than that of a general partner. For example, as a general rule, one party to the arrangement is not an agent of the other parties.

PARTNERSHIP AGREEMENT

A partnership is a voluntary association based on the contractual agreement between or among legally competent persons. The contract between the parties is called the *partnership agreement, partnership contract,* or *articles of partnership*. The partnership agreement generally contains provisions related to the nature of the business, operating policies, and the relations between the partners in operating and terminating the business. In the contract, the partners should clearly express their intention, and the document should cover all aspects of operating the partnership. If there are subsequent disputes and the partners are unable to reach a satisfactory agreement, it may be necessary to resort to litigation.

The partnership agreement should reflect fully the precise intentions of the parties and be as unambiguous as possible. The agreement should include the following important points:

1. The name of the firm and identity of the partners.
2. The nature, purpose, and scope of the business.
3. The effective date of organization.
4. The length of time the partnership is to operate.
5. Location of the place of business.
6. Provision for the allocation of profit and loss.
7. Provision for salaries and withdrawals of assets by partners.
8. The rights, duties, and obligations of each partner such as the amount of time each partner will spend on business activities, and whether each partner is a general or limited partner.
9. Authority of each partner in contract situations.
10. Procedures for admitting a new partner.
11. Provisions that specify how operations are to be conducted and how the various partners' interests are to be satisfied on the withdrawal or the death of a partner.
12. Procedures for the arbitration of disputes.
13. Fiscal period of the partnership.
14. Identification and valuation of initial asset investments and the specification of capital interest that each partner is to receive.
15. Situations that may cause the dissolution of the partnership and provisions for terminating or continuing the business.

---

[7] *Opinion of the Accounting Principles Board No. 18,* "The Equity Method of Accounting for Investments in Common Stock" (New York: AICPA, 1971).

[8] *Accounting Interpretations of APB Opinion No. 18* (New York: AICPA, 1972), par. 2.

16. Accounting practices to be followed, such as depreciation policies, the sequence of closing procedures, and whether the cash or accrual basis is to be used in measuring net income.

17. Whether or not an audit is to be performed.

Some of the items listed will be discussed in more detail in later sections.

The law does not specify the form of the agreement. Although it may be oral, it is good business practice to have the agreement in writing for the protection of the individual partners. A written agreement tends to reduce the number of disagreements resulting from misunderstandings and "loss of memory."

Legally, the partners have a great deal of flexibility in drafting an agreement among themselves, but they must recognize that the UPA specifies certain rights of and obligations to outside parties that may not be avoided by the individual partners. For example, as noted previously, the UPA (Section 15) imposes unlimited liability on each general partner for partnership debts and obligations. A provision in a partnership agreement that exempts a general partner from this obligation would be superseded by the provision in the UPA.

In drafting the agreement, the partners should seek both legal and accounting assistance to assure that their rights are protected and to help anticipate and avoid as many points of conflict as possible. If there are later disputes related to the relations between the partners, most provisions set out in the UPA control only if the partners have failed to make an express agreement, or if the partners are unable to reach a mutually satisfying agreement. For example, in the absence of an agreement concerning how to share profits, the UPA provides that profits are to be shared equally. Differences arising from ordinary matters may be decided by a majority vote of the partners [UPA, Section 18(H)].

The Greatest Show on Earth
William Cameron Coup organized a show in 1869 that staged simultaneous performances in two rings. He later formed a partnership with P. T. Barnum, and in 1871 they opened "The Greatest Show On Earth" in Brooklyn, N.Y. About ten years later, Barnum went into partnership with James Anthony Bailey, another American showman and one of the best organizers in the business, and with two other impresarios. Eventually, however, Barnum and Bailey became sole partners, with their circus giving simultaneous shows in three rings.[9]

Capital Interest versus Profit Interest

In preparing the partnership agreement, the partners must recognize that there is a distinction between a partner's capital interest and his or her interest in income and losses subsequently reported by the partnership. A partner's *capital interest* is a claim against the net assets of the partnership as shown by the balance in the partner's capital account; an *interest in income and loss* determines how the partner's capital interest will increase or decrease as a result of subsequent operations. The partners may agree that an individual partner is to receive a one-third capital interest in the partnership, but the same partner's interest in income and loss may be equal to, greater than, or less than one-third.

---

[9]From *Funk and Wagnalls' New Encyclopedia*, Funk and Wagnalls, Corp.: 1996. *Infopedia*, SoftKey Multimedia Inc., 1996.

ACCOUNTING FOR A PARTNERSHIP

For accounting purposes, a partnership is considered a separate economic and accounting entity. The assets, liabilities, and residual capital interest, as well as the transactions and events that affect the accounts of the partnership, are areas of interest that require a separate accounting to provide information to the partners and other interested parties. Separation of these activities from the personal transactions of the individual partners is necessary in order to evaluate the performance of the partnership. This does not mean that other forms of statements cannot be prepared for other purposes. For example, a general partner has unlimited liability to the creditors of the partnership. Accordingly, the creditors may require information concerning the personal assets and debt position of individual partners, as well as the financial statements of the firm.

Accounting for a partnership basically follows the same procedures and adheres to the same generally accepted accounting principles as accounting for a proprietorship or a corporation. The primary difference in accounting for the different forms of organization is in the recording and reporting of capital transactions. A corporation's equity section purports to report the different sources of capital (for example, the issue of capital stock, additional paid-in capital from various sources, and retained earnings). Because each share of common stock has the same proportional interest in net income, dividends, voting rights, and assets in liquidation as any other share of the same class of stock, a separate capital account for each shareholder is not needed. However, in the case of a partnership, the capital interest in assets of each partner can vary. In addition, the partners' interest in net income or loss can vary and may not be proportional to their respective capital interests. As a result, the relationship of the partners' capital interest will change over time. To report the interest of each partner, a partnership's equity section normally consists of one capital account and one drawing account for each partner.

Practice varies as to which of the two accounts is changed by capital transactions. Generally, investments and withdrawals of assets considered to be other than temporary are recorded in the capital account. The drawing account is typically debited to record withdrawals of assets in anticipation of profitable operations or payments of personal expenses of a partner from partnership assets. It is common practice to close the income summary account to either the drawing account or the capital account. The drawing account may be closed periodically to the capital account. The various sources of capital may thus be combined into one account. In this text, the income summary account and each partner's drawing account will be closed to the appropriate partners' capital accounts.

To illustrate the entries, assume that Ed Bell and Jane Peters operate a partnership in which they each originally contributed $25,000 cash. In the current year, income of $60,000 is to be allocated equally and each partner withdraws $1,000 per month or $12,000 a year. The entries follow:

At the beginning of the partnership:

Cash	50,000	
Bell, Capital		25,000
Peters, Capital		25,000
To form the partnership.		

Each month to record the withdrawals:

Bell, Drawing	1,000	
Peters, Drawing	1,000	
Cash		2,000
To record monthly withdrawals.		

At the end of the period:

Income Summary	60,000	
Bell, Capital		30,000
Peters, Capital		30,000
To close the income summary account.		
Bell, Capital	12,000	
Peters, Capital	12,000	
Bell, Drawing		12,000
Peters, Drawing		12,000
To close the partners' drawing accounts.		

Generally, the same accounting concepts are used to determine net income for proprietorships, partnerships, and corporations. There are, however, several differences. First, a partnership is not subject to income tax. Thus, no income tax expense is reported in the income statement of a partnership. Second, interest on capital investment and salaries to partners have traditionally been treated as allocations of net income, rather than as expenses of the business. This practice is considered appropriate under the proprietary theory view of the firm in which all transactions with the owners are viewed as capital transactions. In other words, no revenue or expense should be recognized in transactions with the partners. Also, since the partners are owners of the business, the interest and salaries may not represent objectively determined amounts.

In addition to the transactions discussed before that affect a partner's capital interest, an individual partner may also lend cash to the partnership that may be accounted for as a liability of the partnership. A partner may also borrow cash from the partnership with the intention of repaying the loan to the partnership. In contrast to capital transactions, such as the withdrawal of assets as part of a profit allocation, an advance to a partner is accounted for as a receivable of the partnership, provided that the receivable satisfies the normal tests of collectibility. Generally accepted accounting standards should also be followed in accounting for and disclosing receivables from officers or members of a firm.

Recording the Formation of a Partnership

Assets invested in the partnership, any debts assumed by the partnership, and the capital interest each partner is to receive should be specified in the partnership agreement. A listing of partnership assets is important, because creditors of the partnership must satisfy their claims from partnership assets before seeking recovery of unpaid claims from the personal assets of individual partners.

Assets invested in the partnership can be either cash or noncash assets, such as a patent, land, or equipment. Noncash assets invested in the partnership are properly recorded at fair values on the date of investment.[10] Liabilities assumed by the partnership should also be recorded at their fair values.

---

[10]*Accounting Principles Board Opinion No. 29*, "Accounting for Nonmonetary Transactions" (New York: AICPA, 1973), par. 18. Recall that the assets contributed retain their original *tax* basis.

Once the partners agree as to the identification and valuation of assets being invested, liabilities being assumed by the partnership, and the capital interest that each partner is to receive, the assets, liabilities, and equities are recorded on the books of the partnership. To illustrate, assume that the following items are being invested to form WY Partnership:

	Agreed Fair Values	
	Investment by Wright	Investment by Young
Cash	$10,000	$10,000
Inventory	10,000	—
Land	—	20,000
Building	—	40,000
Equipment	20,000	—0—
Totals	40,000	70,000
Mortgage on building assumed by the partnership	—0—	20,000
Net assets invested	$40,000	$50,000

The journal entry to record the initial investment, assuming that Wright and Young agree that each partner is to receive a capital credit equal to the fair value of the net assets each partner invested, is as follows:

Cash	20,000	
Inventory	10,000	
Land	20,000	
Building	40,000	
Equipment	20,000	
Mortgage Payable		20,000
Wright, Capital		40,000
Young, Capial		50,000

A problem results if the sum of the agreed net asset values does not equal the negotiated capital interest or if the agreement is unclear. For example, there are several possible interpretations of an agreement that each partner is to receive an equal capital interest. Two possible types of entries, the bonus method and the goodwill method, might be used to record the formation. Assuming the facts in the preceding paragraph, these entries are as follows:

	I Bonus Method		II Goodwill Method	
Cash	20,000		20,000	
Inventory	10,000		10,000	
Land	20,000		20,000	
Building	40,000		40,000	
Equipment	20,000		20,000	
Intangible Asset*	—		10,000	
Mortgage Payable		20,000		20,000
Wright, Capital		45,000		50,000
Young, Capital		45,000		50,000

*Generally referred to as partnership goodwill.

Under the **bonus** method, there is a capital interest transfer of $5,000 from Young to Wright to equalize the capital balances. Such an entry is made if Young recognizes that Wright is contributing something to the firm other than tangible assets, but the partners are reluctant to recognize an intangible asset, or a value for it cannot be determined objectively. Under the *goodwill* method, if equal capital interests are to be given to each partner, Wright's capital is increased by $10,000. This is accomplished by recognizing an intangible asset of $10,000 with a corresponding increase in the credit to the capital account of Wright. It is assumed that Wright is contributing something of value to the partnership that is intangible in nature, and which could not be specifically identified. The value assigned to the intangible asset could have been more than $10,000. Young may also be contributing an intangible asset to the partnership in addition to the tangible assets identified and valued. Unless the intangible is specifically identifiable, such as a patent, it should probably *not* be recognized. It is difficult to justify the recognition of an unspecified intangible such as goodwill on the books of a *new* partnership that does not have an established earnings record.

Allocation of Net Income or Net Loss

The partners should include in the articles of partnership a provision indicating how income and losses are to be allocated. The profit and loss agreement determines how much each partner's interest in the firm increases or decreases as a result of operations. Often one of the major problems of accounting for a partnership is to determine the intent of the partners as indicated in the partnership agreement. The partners have much flexibility in the area; however, if the intent of the partners is unclear, it may be necessary to settle the disagreement by litigation. To avoid disagreement and potential litigation, the profit and loss agreement should be explicitly stated, even to the extent of including examples of application of the allocation agreement in the articles of partnership. In the absence of an agreement, courts have generally concluded that the intent of the parties was to allocate profits and losses equally. If a provision for profits, but not losses, is included in the agreement, the courts have generally concluded that losses should be allocated in the same ratio that profits are allocated. Therefore, if losses are to be allocated differently than profits, the agreement should so state.

The objective of the profit and loss agreement should be to reward the individual partners for their contributions of resources to the partnership. Some of the more common agreements are based on some combination of the following:

1. A fixed ratio.
2. A ratio based on capital balances.
3. Interest on capital investment.
4. An allocation for time or managerial talent devoted to the partnership operation, either in the form of a fixed allocation or a bonus as a percentage of income.

There are a number of possibilities, some of which will be illustrated in the following sections. Unless otherwise stated, income for the period of $20,000 is assumed.

Fixed Ratio   One of the simplest agreements is for each partner to be allocated profit or loss on the basis of an equal percentage or some other specified ratio each period. For example, Adams and Brown may agree that profit and loss are to be allocated in the ratio 7:3. A profit of $20,000 would be allocated $14,000 to Adams and $6,000 to Brown. The entry to close the Income Summary account would take the following form:

Income Summary	20,000	
Adams, Capital		14,000
Brown, Capital		6,000

Note that the allocation determines the increase in each partner's interest in net assets resulting from operations. It has nothing to do with the withdrawals of assets by partners, which are recorded as debits to the capital or drawing accounts.

Unless stated otherwise, a loss of $20,000 would also be allocated using a 7:3 ratio. If this is not the intent of the partners, a separate loss agreement should be stipulated.

Capital Balances Assets invested in the partnership are important resources. The allocation of profits on the basis of the ratio of capital balances may result in an equitable allocation of profits where operation of the partnership requires little of the partners' time, for example, the operation of an apartment building in which there is a hired manager. To avoid conflicts, the capital ratio to be used should be clearly stated as, for example, original investment, beginning-of-year balances, average, or end-of-year balances. The partners should recognize that allocations based on beginning and ending balances could be inequitable. For example, if the allocation ratio is based on ending balances, a partner could make a large capital investment at the end of the year. To avoid such abuse, partners may want to provide for restrictions on investments and withdrawals.

Assuming that the ratio is based on beginning capital balances and that Adams and Brown had balances of $60,000 and $40,000, respectively, the net income of $20,000 would be allocated as follows:

	Capital Investment	*Net Income Allocation*
Adams	$ 60,000	($60,000/$100,000) × $20,000 = $12,000
Brown	40,000	($40,000/$100,000) × $20,000 = 8,000
	$100,000	$20,000

Sometimes net income allocation is based on a ratio of the weighted-average capital investment as computed in Illustration 16-1. The weighted average is computed by multiplying the various capital balances that each partner maintained during the year by the fraction of the year that a particular capital balance was maintained. The $20,000 net income is allocated on the basis of the ratio of the weighted-average capital investment.

The allocation of a loss on the basis of the ratio of capital balances would mean that Adams, who has invested the most capital, would absorb the greatest amount of the loss, which may be considered an unreasonable allocation. If this is the case, the partners may want to stipulate a different ratio for the allocation of losses.

Interest on Capital Investment Using the ratio of capital balances as the basis for allocation of profit assumes that invested capital is the most important resource of the partnership. However, in many profit-making organizations, it is only one resource, and other factors should be recognized. To recognize other factors and still provide an equitable allocation, the partners may want to provide for interest on

ILLUSTRATION 16-1

Computation of Weighted-Average Capital Balances

Adams, Capital	(A) Increase (Decrease) in Capital	(B) Cumulative Capital Balance	(C) Fraction of Year in Months	(D) Weighted Average (B) × (C)
January 1 Beginning Balance		$60,000	3/12	$15,000
April 1 Added $30,000 Investment	$ 30,000	90,000	3/12	22,500
July 1 Withdrew $10,000	(10,000)	80,000	6/12	40,000
Weighted-Average Capital Balance				$77,500

Brown, Capital				
January 1 Beginning Balance		40,000	9/12	$30,000
October 1 Withdrew $10,000	$(10,000)	30,000	3/12	7,500
Weighted-Average Capital Balance				$37,500

Weighted-Average Investment			
Adams	$ 77,500	*Net Income Allocation*	
Brown	37,500	($77,500/$115,000) × $20,000 =	$13,478
	$115,000	($37,500/$115,000) × $20,000 =	6,522
			$20,000

capital investment and allocate the remaining income on some other basis. Such a provision may also provide an incentive for capital to be invested, if the firm has a use for added investment. The agreement should specify at least:

1. The interest rate,
2. Which capital balance is to be used (beginning, ending, or average),
3. How remaining profits should be allocated, and
4. Whether or not interest should still be allocated in case of loss or in case profits are less than the agreed interest allocation.

It is easy to overlook provision 4 but, as will be shown, in the event of disagreement between the partners, the lack of such an express provision would result in an allocation of interest when there is a reported loss or when profits are insufficient to cover the interest allocation.

If interest is part of the profit allocation formula, the partners must be careful to distinguish between capital investments and loans made by a partner to the partnership. The UPA [Section 18(d)] provides that unless otherwise stated, a partner is entitled to receive interest on capital investment only from the date when repayment should be made. Then the partner is entitled to the legal rate in the absence of a specific provision. However, an advance made in excess of the agreed investment is considered a liability of the firm and subject to repayment with interest. Accountants also recognize this distinction and record accrued interest on a loan balance as an expense, whereas an interest allowance on capital is not an expense but rather is one element in the allocation of profit and loss. Thus, the manner in which a partner's investment is classified will affect the profit or loss allocation and the amount reported as net income.

Frequently, the interest allocation is based on weighted-average capital investment. To illustrate, assume the average investment in Illustration 16-1. Interest is then computed on this amount. Assuming a net income of $20,000, an 8% rate of interest, and that any remaining profit is to be divided equally, the profit (or loss, if negative) is allocated as follows:

Interest Allocation	*Adams*	*Brown*	*Total*
$77,500 × .08 =	$ 6,200		$ 6,200
37,500 × .08 =		$3,000	3,000
Total interest allocated	6,200	3,000	9,200
Remainder shared equally	5,400	5,400	10,800
Total to be allocated	$11,600	$8,400	$20,000

Salary The UPA [Section 18(f)] provides that a partner is not entitled to remuneration for services performed for the partnership unless such remuneration is provided for by the partners in their profit and loss agreement. The partners may provide, as part of the profit and loss formula, a salary allowance in recognition of personal services rendered by a partner. The amount by which net income exceeds the salary allowances may then be divided in any ratio agreed on by the partners. For example, if Adams devotes full time to the business activity and Brown spends a limited amount of time, the partnership agreement may provide that Adams is allowed a salary of $1,000 per month and that the remaining income is to be divided on the basis of the ratio of the beginning capital balances ($60,000 and $40,000, respectively). The allocation would be as follows:

	Adams	*Brown*	*Total*
Salary allowance	$12,000	$—0—	$12,000
Remainder			
($60,000/$100,000) × $8,000	4,800		
($40,000/$100,000) × $8,000		3,200	8,000
	$16,800	$3,200	$20,000

A salary agreement is considered part of the profit and loss allocation formula and may be made independent of the agreement between the partners as to the right to withdraw cash or other assets from the partnership. The withdrawal of cash reduces the partner's capital interest (debit to the drawing account) but plays no part in the allocation of net income. Since the term *salary* is normally understood to mean a cash payment for services received, it is important that the partners specify their intentions as to an allocation of profit or permission to withdraw assets.

Bonus Instead of basing the salary allocation on a fixed amount, the partners may provide for a bonus arrangement as a percentage of income or some other basis. Since a number of interpretations can result, the partners should explicitly state the basis to be used in calculating the bonus. Some possibilities based on net income are:

1. Net income before any allocation of income to partners (for example, before interest on capital, salaries to partners, and any bonus).
2. Net income after other income allocations, but before subtracting the bonus.
3. Net income after subtracting the bonus, but before subtracting the other allocations.
4. Net income after subtracting the bonus and other allocations from net income.

Calculation of the bonus in the first two alternatives is straightforward. To illustrate alternatives 3 and 4, assume that net income is $24,000, and a bonus of 20% is to be paid to Adams. Also, interest of $4,000 and $2,000 is to be allocated to Adams and Brown, respectively, and any remainder is to be allocated equally. The bonus and a proof of the calculation are as follows:

	Alternative 3		Alternative 4
Bonus	= .2($24,000 − Bonus)	Bonus	= .2($24,000 − $6,000 − Bonus)
Bonus	= $4,800 − .2Bonus	Bonus	= .2($18,000 − Bonus)
1.2 Bonus	= $4,800	Bonus	= $3,600 − .2Bonus
Bonus	= $4,000	1.2 Bonus	= $3,600
		Bonus	= $3,000

Proof:

	Alternative 3	Alternative 4
Net income	$24,000	$24,000
Bonus	4,000	3,000
Interest		6,000
Income subject to bonus	$20,000	$15,000
	Bonus = .2($20,000)	Bonus = .2($15,000)
	Bonus = $4,000	Bonus = $3,000

Insufficient Income to Cover Allocation

In some cases, the partnership net income may be less than the interest and/or salary provided for in the partnership agreement. If the partners fail to provide for such an occurrence in the profit and loss formula, the established practice is to allocate the interest and/or salary as if sufficient income had been earned. The amount by which the salary and/or interest exceeds the net income is allocated to the individual partners in their agreed ratio for allocating residual income. For example, assume that Adams and Brown agree to divide profits as follows:

1. Salary: Adams, $4,000; Brown, $2,000.
2. Interest: 8% on average capital balances (see Illustration 16-1).
3. Remainder: To be divided equally.

A net income of $11,000 would be allocated as follows:

	Adams	Brown	Total
Salary	$ 4,000	$ 2,000	$ 6,000
Interest	6,200	3,000	9,200
	10,200	5,000	15,200
Excess allocation ($11,000 − $15,200)	(2,100)	(2,100)	(4,200)
Income allocation	$ 8,100	$ 2,900	$11,000

The entry to close the Income Summary account is:

Income Summary	11,000	
Adams, Capital		8,100
Brown, Capital		2,900

As will be shown in the next section, this procedure produces the same results as if each partner's salary and interest had been treated as an expense in the determination of the partnership net income or loss.

In the case of a loss of $20,000, the allocation would be as follows:

	Adams	Brown	Total
Salary	$ 4,000	$ 2,000	$ 6,000
Interest	6,200	3,000	9,200
	10,200	5,000	15,200
Excess allocation (−$20,000 − $15,200)	(17,600)	(17,600)	(35,200)
Loss allocation	$ (7,400)	$(12,600)	$(20,000)

To avoid such an allocation, the partners may elect to state an alternative allocation in the articles of partnership. Once again, this situation indicates the need for careful planning in drafting the partnership agreement.

SPECIAL PROBLEMS IN ALLOCATION OF INCOME AND LOSS

Salaries and Interest as an Expense

In the foregoing illustrations, salaries and interest were accounted for as an allocation of net income, rather than as an expense in the determination of net income. However, the partners may find the income statement more useful for evaluating the operating performance of the partnership if either or both salary and interest allocations were treated as an expense in the determination of net income. If the salary levels and interest rates are reasonable for the resources provided, the income statement for the partnership may be more comparable to income statements of nonpartnership forms of organization. To illustrate, assume that the partnership reported net income of $11,000 before the interest and salaries of the partners. The partners are to be allocated salaries and interest as follows:

	Adams	Brown
Salary	$4,000	$2,000
Interest	6,200	3,000

The partners agree to allocate residual income and loss evenly. Journal entries to record the salaries and interest would be:

Salary Expense	6,000	
Adams, Capital		4,000
Brown, Capital		2,000
Interest Expense	9,200	
Adams, Capital		6,200
Brown, Capital		3,000

Net loss for the period after salaries and interest would be $4,200, computed as follows:

Net income before salaries and interest		$11,000
Less: Salary expense	$6,000	
Less: Interest expense	9,200	15,200
Net loss		$ 4,200

After the revenue and expense accounts are closed, Income Summary would have a debit balance of $4,200, which would be allocated evenly to the partners as agreed. The following entry would be recorded to close the income summary account:

Adams, Capital	2,100	
Brown, Capital	2,100	
Income Summary		4,200

Changes in the capital accounts are presented here:

Adams, Capital

From Income Summary	2,100	Salary entry	4,000
		Interest entry	6,200
		Net change in capital	8,100

Brown, Capital

From Income Summary	2,100	Salary entry	2,000
		Interest entry	3,000
		Net change in capital	2,900

This procedure results in the same change in the capital accounts as if the salaries and interest were considered an allocation of profit. (See the previous illustration where profits were insufficient to cover salary and interest allocations.) The method of reporting that is selected should be the one that provides the most useful information to the partners. Since the normal practice is to recognize salaries and interest as an allocation of profit, any such amounts treated as an expense should be adequately disclosed so the statement reader can properly evaluate the operating performance of the firm.

Adjustment of Income of Prior Years

Errors may occur in accounting for partnership operations, such as failure to accrue or defer expenses or revenue, errors in the inventory count or pricing, or errors in the calculation or amortization of fixed assets. Problems in the allocation of profit and loss can result if (1) errors are discovered that occurred in specific prior years, and (2) the partners have altered the profit and loss agreement since the period in which the error occurred. In a corporation, an error correction is accounted for as an adjustment to the beginning retained earnings balance. However, in a partnership the correction is allocated to the individual partners' capital accounts. The allocation should be based on the profit and loss agreement in effect during the period of the error.

Other allocation problems may arise, such as market changes in assets being held for investment purposes that occur before a change in the allocation formula, or an adjustment for bad debts that cannot be attributed to any specific period. There is no clear-cut answer to such problems. Litigation can be avoided by providing for the treatment of such potential problems in the partnership agreement.

FINANCIAL STATEMENT PRESENTATION

The income statement, balance sheet, and statement of cash flows for a partnership presented in conformity with GAAP are prepared in much the same manner as they

ILLUSTRATION 16-2   *Formal Financial Statement*

AB Partnership
Statement of Partners' Capital
For the Year Ended December 31, 2001

	Adams	*Brown*	*Total*
Capital Balance, January 1	$ 60,000	$40,000	$100,000
Add: Additional Investment	30,000	—0—	30,000
Net Income Allocation	16,800	3,200	20,000
	106,800	43,200	150,000
Less Withdrawals	10,000	10,000	20,000
Capital Balance, December 31	$96,800	$33,200	$130,000

are for a corporation. The following is a list of some of the differences in partnership reporting:

1. On the balance sheet or in a supplementary schedule, changes in partner's equity during the year should be disclosed.[11]
2. Partners' salary allowances are generally recognized as an allocation of net income, not as an expense in the determination of net income.
3. There is no income tax expense. The partners report their share of the partnership income or loss for the period on their individual income tax returns.
4. Interest paid to a partner on a loan balance is recognized as an expense. Interest allowance on capital investment is considered an allocation of profit.

A statement of changes in partners' capital is prepared to disclose changes in the interest of each partner during the year as shown in Illustration 16-2. For some external reporting purposes, such detail may not be considered necessary. The partnership capital, for example, may be reported as one amount, and the capital balance of each partner may be disclosed in a supplementary schedule or not disclosed at all.

CHANGES IN THE OWNERSHIP OF THE PARTNERSHIP

The UPA (Section 29) defines *dissolution* as "the change in the relation of the partners caused by any partner ceasing to be associated in the carrying on as distinguished from the winding up of the business." The partnership dissolution may be voluntary (for example, mutual agreement by the partners) or involuntary (for example, bankruptcy of an individual partner or the partnership itself). Although dissolution means the end of a specific relationship between the partners, it does not automatically result in the termination of business activity. For example, in some forms of dissolution, such as the bankruptcy of the partnership, the partnership operations are eventually terminated and the partnership ceases to exist. In other cases of dissolution the partnership may be dissolved, but the remaining partners may continue the normal operations of the partnership without any visible interruptions of the firm's operations.

---

[11]This disclosure is usually not made when the number of partners is very large. For example, some accounting firms have hundreds of partners.

In this chapter we consider the accounting problems associated with changes in the ownership of a continuing partnership. The changes that will be considered result from (1) admission of a new partner by the purchase of an interest directly from one or more current partners, which is frequently referred to as an assignment of a partnership interest, (2) admission of a new partner by investing assets in the partnership, and (3) withdrawal of a partner as a result of retirement or death. Unless precluded from doing so in the partnership agreement, generally a partner may insist on liquidation of the partnership in these forms of dissolutions. Because the going-concern value of the business is usually greater than its liquidation value, the partners may provide in the partnership agreement that such changes in the relations of the partners do not dissolve the partnership. Dissolution of the partnership in which operations are eventually terminated will be covered in the next chapter.

VALUATION—A CENTRAL ISSUE

When there is a change in the membership of the partnership, the problem of assigning a fair value to the firm arises. For example, if a partner withdraws from the partnership and there are no express provisions in the partnership agreement for determining the settlement, an equitable payment for his or her interest must be negotiated between the existing partners. Similarly, before admission, an incoming partner must negotiate with the existing partners an equitable purchase price for the interest he or she acquires. The settlement or purchase price is based on a number of factors, one of which is the fair values of the partnership assets. However, the fair values of the partnership assets are generally not reflected on the partnership books. In accordance with generally accepted accounting standards, partnership assets are recorded at cost, and subsequent increases in their market value are not recognized.

One approach is to first revalue assets and liabilities to their fair values and record any identifiable unrecorded assets and liabilities before recording the admission or withdrawal of a partner. In addition, the settlement price paid to a withdrawing partner or the purchase price paid by a new partner may be used to infer a value for the firm as a whole. Any difference between the value of the firm implied by the payment and the fair value of the net assets may be assigned to an intangible asset frequently referred to as partnership goodwill. An increase or decrease in net assets is allocated to the appropriate partners in their profit or loss ratio. Under this approach, the use of fair values provides an equitable measure of each partner's capital interest in the partnership. Furthermore, when a new partner is admitted, failure to recognize fair values will result in unrecorded value changes realized later being allocated in the profit- and loss-sharing ratio unless a separate provision is made. An unrecorded increase in value would benefit the new partner, whereas an unrecorded decrease would be a detriment. Revaluation of assets and liabilities is supported on the basis that, in dissolution, the old partnership is dissolved and a new entity is formed.

In practice, some accountants are reluctant to recognize a change in the value of an asset, even though there may be objective evidence that a specific asset is undervalued. They argue that recording an increase in fair value for external reporting purposes is not in accordance with generally accepted accounting practice and that economic substance should take precedence over legal form. That is, even though the partnership may be legally dissolved, the economic substance of some types of dissolution is that the business activity continues without interruption. Proponents of this method would retain the historical cost carrying value, and either prescribe in the agreement that unrecorded changes in value will not be shared with a new partner when realized, or will require a disproportionately high capital investment in relation to the new partner's income-sharing percentage. In this chapter, the revaluation of assets is shown as one of the approaches to recording changes in ownership because it is commonly advocated as an acceptable alternative and its use has some merit.

METHODS OF RECORDING CHANGES IN THE MEMBERSHIP OF THE PARTNERSHIP

Two methods are frequently used to record changes in partnership membership:

1. *The bonus method.* When this method is used, the assets of the partnership are increased by the amount of the assets invested by the partner being admitted. Any difference between the assets invested and the credit to the new partner's capital account is adjusted to the capital accounts of the other partners involved in the negotiations. If a partner withdraws from a partnership, the partners may agree to settle his or her capital interest by permitting the withdrawal of partnership assets. If the bonus method is used to record the withdrawal, the difference between the recorded value of the assets withdrawn and the debit to the withdrawing partner's capital account is adjusted to the capital accounts of the remaining partners.

2. *The goodwill method.* When this method is used, a new asset is recorded that is based on the difference between the value implied by the amount of consideration negotiated in the admission or withdrawal of a partner and the values reported in the partnership books.

Whether the bonus method or goodwill method is used, unrecorded changes in the value of existing assets and liabilities that are objectively determinable may be recorded before the change in membership is recorded.

As will be demonstrated, if certain limited conditions related to the profit and loss agreement are satisfied, the bonus and goodwill methods will produce the same result. If these conditions are met, the use of the bonus method precludes the problem of recording an intangible asset.

The bonus and goodwill methods are used for either *admission of a new partner* or the *withdrawal of a partner*, described in the following sections A and B.

SECTION A: ADMISSION OF A NEW PARTNER

An individual may acquire an interest in a partnership: (1) by purchasing all or part of an interest directly from one or more existing partners (this transaction occurs outside the partnership and represents a transfer of assets between individuals), or (2) by being admitted as an additional partner on the investment of assets in the firm. Generally, the individual invests cash and/or other assets (for example, land, patent rights, equipment, marketable securities). A new partner could be admitted, however, by contributing a resource such as managerial talent. Because accountants ordinarily do not record such assets, unless the partners agree to transfer capital to the new partner's account, he or she will begin with a zero capital balance.

Assignment of an Interest by an Existing Partner → *usually called purchase*

A partner is entitled to sell his or her interest in the firm, but no partner can be forced to accept a new member to the partnership. The UPA (Section 27) provides that the purchasing party acquires only the right to receive profits and assets in the event of liquidation to which the selling partner would otherwise be entitled. The purchaser does not acquire the right to participate in management unless all remaining partners agree to grant this right. The mere act of selling an interest does not dissolve the partnership, because the overall relation of the partners is not changed.

In the following illustrations, it is assumed that the partnership currently consists of two partners, Alan Adams and Bill Brown, with respective capital interests of $60,000 and $40,000. Adams and Brown share income and losses in the ratio of 6:4. Both partners agree to the admission of a new partner.

Acquisition of Interest by Payment to One Partner If an individual acquires an interest in a partnership by making payment directly to an existing partner, the interest acquired is recorded in a new capital account by transferring a corresponding amount equal to the percentage interest acquired from the selling partner's capital account. For example, assume that Adams sold one-half of his interest in the firm to Carol Call for $36,000. The only entry necessary on the partnership books is to record the transfer of capital interest from the selling partner to the capital account established for the new partner. The entry is:

Adams, Capital (.50 × $60,000)	30,000	
Call, Capital		30,000

The following should be noted:

1. Since this is a personal transaction between the two individuals, the entry is the same regardless of the amount paid by Call directly to Adams.
2. Net assets and equities of the firm are not changed as a direct result of the transaction, since the sale was negotiated outside the partnership. However, as noted earlier, the partners may choose to revalue assets and liabilities.
3. The amount of capital transferred to Call is equal to Adams' recorded capital multiplied by the percentage interest in Adams' capital acquired by Call.
4. Call now has a capital interest of 30% ($30,000 of total interest of $100,000), but her profit interest does not have to equal this percentage.

A simplified balance sheet after the admission of Call would be as follows:

Net assets	$100,000	Adams, Capital	$ 30,000
		Brown, Capital	40,000
		Call, Capial	30,000
Total	$100,000	Total	$100,000

Acquisition of an Interest by Payment to More Than One Partner If Call had purchased a 30% interest from each partner for $36,000, the entry would be:

Adams, Capital (.30 × $60,000)	18,000	
Brown, Capital (.30 × $40,000)	12,000	
Call, Capital (.30 × $100,000)		30,000

The observations outlined before when the purchase was made from one partner apply in this case as well. Furthermore, this entry has no effect on how the cash payment made by Call is to be distributed to Adams and Brown outside the partnership. The amount and distribution of cash is a negotiated transaction between individuals and does not affect the partnership accounts unless the amount is used as a basis for the revaluation of the firm.

Goodwill Implied by the Purchase Price In the foregoing examples, the amount paid by Call to gain admission to the firm was ignored in recording the transfer of interest. This procedure is often referred to as the bonus method. Some argue that the payment of $36,000 for a $30,000 interest in the partnership indicates that the firm has assets that are unrecorded or undervalued. The assumption is that the negotiated purchase price took into consideration such factors as the fair values of the firm's assets, the present value of the firm's liabilities, and the valuation of the firm on the basis of future prospects. Thus, the payment can be used to approximate the value of the firm. If Call is willing to pay $36,000 for a 30% interest in the firm, then the implied value of the partnership net assets is $120,000 ($36,000 .30). Net assets and capital should be increased $20,000 from the recorded amounts of $100,000. Since this represents an unrecorded increase in the value of the firm's assets, the increase in assets of $20,000 is allocated to Adams and Brown in their profit-sharing ratio. To the extent that the excess cannot be assigned to specific identifiable recorded assets, the remaining amount is recorded as partnership goodwill. Assuming that the book values of assets and liabilities equal their fair values, the entries to record the increase in assets and admission of Call are as follows:

Goodwill	20,000	
Adams, Capital (.60 × $20,000)		12,000
Brown, Capital (.40 × $20,000)		8,000
Adams, Capital (.30 × $72,000)	21,600	
Brown, Capital (.30 × $48,000)	14,400	
Call, Capital (.30 × $120,000, also equal to cash paid)		36,000

This results in account balances as presented in Illustration 16-3. The goodwill must be amortized over an appropriate period not to exceed 40 years, in accordance with *APB Opinion No. 17.*

Comparison of Bonus and Goodwill Methods In the illustration, Call is credited with a 30% interest in the firm under the bonus and the goodwill methods. To assist the partners in making a decision between the two methods, it may be helpful to demonstrate the effects of the two methods on their respective capital balances. To compare the two methods, the goodwill is initially recorded in the accounts and is amortized in future periods. If the firm were forced to liquidate, the unamortized goodwill would probably be of no value and, therefore, would represent a loss to

ILLUSTRATION 16-3

Schedule of Account Balances

	Net Assets	+	Goodwill	=	Capital Adams	+	Brown	+	Call
Book Values	$100,000	+	$—0—	=	$(60,000)	+	$(40,000)	+	$—0—
Record Goodwill			20,000		(12,000)		(8,000)		—0—
	100,000	+	20,000	=	(72,000)	+	(48,000)	+	—0—
Transfer of Capital					21,600		14,400		(36,000)
Balance After Admission of Call	$100,000	+	$20,000	=	$(50,400)	+	$(33,600)	+	$(36,000)

the partnership. In either case, the amortization of the goodwill reduces the partners' capital accounts by their agreed profit- and loss-sharing ratio.

In order to isolate the effect of the goodwill amortization, all other capital changes are ignored. The bonus and goodwill methods will yield the same result if two conditions related to the new profit and loss agreement are met. These are:

1. The new partner's profit-sharing percentage must be equal to his or her initial percentage interest in capital. In this illustration, Call received a capital interest of 30%. Her profit-sharing ratio must be 30%.

2. The old partner's profit-sharing ratio in the new partnership must be relatively the same as it was in the old partnership. Thus, if Call is to receive 30% of the profit in the new partnership, Adams and Brown must receive the remaining 70%. To be in the same relative ratio of 6:4, Adams must receive 42% (.6 × .70) of profits, and Brown must receive 28% (.4 × .70). The two methods are equivalent if, after amortizing goodwill, the account balances are the same as they would be under the bonus method. The balances for each method are presented in Illustration 16-4.

The two methods will also yield the same results if the bonus method is used and the unrecorded assets ($20,000) are ultimately realized and allocated to the partners in the ratio of 42:28:30.

Acquisition of an Interest by Investing Assets → *investment*

An individual may obtain a partnership interest in capital and future income by investing something of value in the firm. If assets are invested, the admission is recorded by debiting the assets invested and adjusting the net capital interest in the firm by a corresponding amount. It is important that the assets invested be fairly valued. Any gain or loss recognized on sales subsequent to recording the admission will be allocated on the basis of the new profit and loss formula.

Three situations can exist when an individual invests assets in a firm:

1. Book value of the capital interest acquired is equal to the fair value of the assets invested.

2. Book value of the capital interest acquired is less than the fair value of the assets invested.

3. Book value of the capital interest acquired is greater than the fair value of the assets invested.

ILLUSTRATION 16-4

Schedule of Account Balances

Goodwill Method	Net Assets	+	Goodwill	=	Capital Adams	+	Brown	+	Call
Balances after recording goodwill and admitting Call	$100,000	+	$ 20,000	=	$(50,400)	+	$(33,600)	+	$(36,000)
Amortize goodwill $20,000 × .42			(20,000)		8,400				
20,000 × .28							5,600		
20,000 × .30									6,000
Totals	$100,000	+	$—0—	=	$(42,000)	+	$(28,000)	+	$(30,000)

Bonus Method									
Balances after recording admission of Call	$100,000	+	$—0—	=	$(42,000)	+	$(28,000)	+	$(30,000)

The book value of the capital interest acquired is computed as follows:

$$\left(\begin{array}{c}\text{Capital balances of} \\ \text{existing partners}\end{array} + \begin{array}{c}\text{Investment of} \\ \text{new partner}\end{array}\right) \times \begin{array}{c}\text{Percentage} \\ \text{interest acquired} \\ \text{by new partner}\end{array} = \begin{array}{c}\text{Book value} \\ \text{of capital} \\ \text{interest acquired}\end{array}$$

To illustrate the three situations, assume that Adams and Brown have capital interests of $40,000 and $30,000, respectively. Assume further that, unless stated otherwise, the book values of the recorded assets and liabilities of the firm equal their fair values. Profits are shared in the ratio of 6:4. Call is to be admitted to the partnership, after which the profit ratio is to be 4:4:2. For simplicity, we will assume in all cases that Call invests cash.

Case 1: Book Value Acquired Is Equal to Assets Invested Assume that Adams, Brown, and Call agree that Call is to invest $35,000 for a one-third capital interest in the partnership. The book value of Call's interest is equal to the assets invested and is computed as follows:

$$(\$70,000 + \$35,000) = \$105,000 \times (1/3) = \$35,000$$

The entry to record the admission of Call is simply:

Cash	35,000	
Call, Capital		35,000

Adams' and Brown's capital accounts remain unchanged at $70,000, which represents the remaining two-thirds interest in the firm. Call's capital account properly reflects a one-third interest of $35,000. It should be noted that the ratio of the capital balance of 40:30:35 does not equal the agreed profit and loss ratio 4:4:2.

Case 2: Book Value Acquired Is Less Than Assets Invested Assume now that Call is to invest $50,000 for a one-third capital interest in the firm. Book value of the interest acquired is:

$$(\$70,000 + \$50,000) = \$120,000 \times (1/3) = \$40,000$$

In this case, the amount invested exceeds the book value interest acquired by $10,000. There could be a number of explanations for Call's willingness to pay this $10,000 excess. It could be that, as a result of a profitable and favorable outlook for the firm's operations, Adams and Brown are in a strong bargaining position.

The accounting problem is to record the admission of Call in accordance with the negotiated intentions of the parties involved. Obviously, if Call's capital account is credited with $50,000, her interest would exceed one-third of the partnership's total capital. Either the bonus method or the goodwill method can be used to record the admission so that Call will end up with a one-third capital interest.

Bonus Method When the bonus method is used, the excess of the amount invested over the book value interest received is considered a bonus to the existing partners. In this example, Call invested $10,000 more than the capital interest received. The $10,000 bonus is allocated to the old partners on the basis of their profit and loss ratio, since this is an increase in partnership assets. The entry to admit Call is:

Cash	50,000	
Adams, Capital (.6 × $10,000)		6,000
Brown, Capital (.4 × $10,000)		4,000
Call, Capital ((1/3) × $120,000)		40,000

Adams and Brown now have capital balances of $46,000 and $34,000 for a total capital interest of $80,000, which is a two-thirds interest in total capital of $120,000. Call has the remaining one-third interest of $40,000.

The assets of the partnership may have been revalued before the admission of a new partner was recorded. The bonus method is frequently used when the parties do not want to record an intangible asset. Notice in the entry to record the admission that the assets are increased only by the amount invested. Any difference between the capital credit for Call and the cash invested is an adjustment to the capital accounts of Adams and Brown.

Goodwill Method Call may negotiate that she is to receive a capital credit equal to her investment. If Call is to receive a capital credit of $50,000 for a one-third interest, the total capital interest implied by this contract is $150,000. Adams and Brown must have the remaining two-thirds interest, or $100,000. Since their current balances of $70,000 represent their interest in the net assets, assets and capital appear to be understated by $30,000.[12] Assuming that the specific assets and liabilities are fairly valued, this understatement is recognized as goodwill attributable to

---

[12]An alternate way to calculate goodwill is: Net value of firm implied by contract of $150,000 minus (capital balances of Adams and Brown plus Call's investment) of $120,000 equals goodwill of $30,000.

the old partners and is allocated to Adams and Brown on the basis of their current profit and loss ratios. The journal entry is:

Goodwill	30,000	
Adams, Capital (.60 × $30,000)		18,000
Brown, Capital (.40 × $30,000)		12,000

The entry to record the admission of Call is:

Cash	50,000	
Call, Capital		50,000

Net Assets Undervalued Had the net assets not been fairly valued as assumed here, the excess payment by Call could mean that specific assets of the firm are undervalued, or that partnership liabilities are overstated. If so, the specific assets (whether tangible or identifiable intangible assets) and liabilities of the partnership could be adjusted instead of creating a goodwill account. However, the specific accounts should not be adjusted in the absence of objective evidence that there are unrecorded changes in value.

Case 3: Book Value Acquired Is Greater Than Assets Invested Assume that Call is to invest $20,000 for a one-third capital interest in the firm. Book value of the interest acquired is:

$$($70,000 + $20,000) = $90,000 \times (1/3) = $30,000$$

In this case, the book value interest acquired exceeds the value of the assets invested by Call, which could imply that assets are overvalued ((1/3)(company value) = $20,000; or, company value = $60,000), or that for some reason, Adams and Brown are willing to grant Call a capital credit greater than the amount of assets she is investing. In some cases, for example, a partnership may be in need of operating capital and the partners may be willing to sacrifice their interest in existing assets to acquire the cash; or it could be that Call is bringing some particularly needed talent or reputation to the partnership.

In this case, as in Case 2, the admission could be recorded either by the bonus method or by the goodwill method. Under either method, Call will end up with a one-third interest in the net assets of the firm.

Bonus Method When the bonus method is used, assets are not increased above what the new partner is investing. If Call is to receive a $30,000 capital credit on investment of $20,000, then a bonus of $10,000 is being granted to Call. This bonus is allocated to reduce Adams' and Brown's capital in their agreed profit and loss ratio. The following entry reflects the bonus to Call and a resulting one-third interest in the total capital of $90,000:

Cash	20,000	
Adams, Capital (.60 × $10,000)	6,000	
Brown, Capital (.40 × $10,000)	4,000	
Call, Capital		30,000

Adams and Brown now have capital balances of $34,000 and $26,000, respectively, for a total of $60,000, or a two-thirds interest.

Goodwill Method If Adams and Brown are unwilling to reduce their capital accounts on the admission of Call, then an alternative to the bonus method is to compute and record the goodwill implicit in the agreement. Since Adams' and Brown's capital interests are to remain unchanged, the old partners' capital balances are used as the base to compute the value of the firm. If their interest represents a two-thirds interest in the net assets of the new partnership, then a three-thirds interest in the firm is $105,000 (or $70,000 ÷ 2/3), of which Call is to receive a capital credit of $35,000 ((1/3) × $105,000). The $15,000 difference between the capital credit of $35,000 and Call's investment of $20,000 is goodwill. The entry to record the admission of Call is:

Cash	20,000	
Goodwill	15,000	
Call, Capital		35,000

The entry recognizes that the new partner is investing cash and is bringing an intangible asset to the partnership. The amount recorded is based on the value implied by the partners' agreement.

Net Assets Overvalued The payment of $20,000 by Call for a larger capital interest may provide evidence that the recorded value of the firm's net assets does not reflect fair values and that the use of the bonus method or the creation of a goodwill account is an effort to avoid a reduction in net assets. The $20,000 invested by Call for a one-third interest could be used to impute a value for the partnership net assets after the admission of Call of only $60,000.[13] The journal entries to revalue the assets and admit Call are as follows:

Adams, Capital	18,000	
Brown, Capital	12,000	
Assets ($70,000 + $20,000 − $60,000)		30,000
Cash	20,000	
Call, Capital		20,000

Account balances that result from the admission of Call for the three alternatives discussed are given in Illustration 16-5. Subsequent events alone can indicate which method should have been used to record the admission. An examination of one of a number of events that could result will emphasize the importance of the initial asset valuation. Assume that the bonus method was used to record the admission of Call and that the assets were overvalued and subsequently sold at a loss of $30,000. The agreed profit and loss ratio is 4:4:2. After this transaction, the partners' capital balances are as follows:

	Adams	Brown	Call
Balance after admission of Call	$(34,000)	$(26,000)	$(30,000)
Share of $30,000 loss	12,000	12,000	6,000
	$(22,000)	$(14,000)	$(24,000)

[13]The implied value of $60,000 compared to the total *recorded* value of net assets of $90,000 ($40,000 + $30,000 + $20,000), including Call's investment, suggests that recorded assets are overvalued by $30,000.

ILLUSTRATION 16-5

Schedule of Account Balances

Debit	Bonus Method	Goodwill Method	Overvalued Net Assets
Net Assets	$90,000	$105,000	$60,000
Credits			
Adams, Capital	$34,000	$ 40,000	$22,000
Brown, Capital	26,000	30,000	18,000
Call, Capital	30,000	35,000	20,000
Totals	$90,000	$105,000	$60,000

The selection of the bonus method as opposed to reducing overvalued assets results in a gain in Call's capital relative to Brown's. Additional comparisons of the three methods assuming various other subsequent events could be developed.

SECTION B: WITHDRAWAL OF A PARTNER

A partner cannot be prevented from withdrawing from a partnership by the other partners. Although some complex legal issues are involved, the partnership agreement may specify conditions for withdrawal and provisions for computing the settlement. If a settlement is not specifically provided for in the partnership agreement, Section 42 of the UPA states that "he or his legal representative . . . may have the value of his interest ascertained and shall receive as an ordinary creditor an amount equal to the value of this interest."

A buy/sell agreement can mandate that the exiting partner or heirs, in the case of death, sell his or her interest to the remaining owners, who are legally bound to buy the interest according to an agreed-upon method of valuation. It can also designate which partner becomes the buyer and which the seller if it comes to that end.[14]

If a partner withdraws in violation of the partnership agreement and without approval of the remaining partners, he is entitled only to his interest in the firm without consideration of goodwill. In such a case, the withdrawing partner is liable for damages sustained by the remaining parties for his breach of the partnership agreement. A partner who is forced to withdraw from a partnership is entitled to compensation for his full interest including goodwill.

In the following examples, it is assumed that the partners mutually agree to the withdrawal: (1) the withdrawing partner may elect to sell his interest to an outside party; (2) the withdrawing partner may elect to sell his interest to one or more of the remaining partners; or (3) the partners may mutually agree to transfer partnership assets to the withdrawing partner for his interest in the firm. Case 1 has been discussed earlier and need not be reviewed again. The same considerations apply to Case 2, if negotiated outside the partnership. In Case 3 the partnership agreement may include requirements for determining the settlement price. In most cases the capital account does not reflect the current value of the partner's interest.

---

[14]*Forbes*, "Planning for Divorce," by Leigh Gallagher, 3/22/99, pp. 94–95.

To be equitable the fair values of the assets and liabilities need to be determined. It may be necessary to recognize unrecorded assets, correct the accounts for errors, or reflect changes in estimates such as the book value of depreciable assets. In the absence of a specific agreement, the partners may have to negotiate a settlement price at the date of withdrawal. Determination of an equitable value may be very difficult. The agreed settlement price may be equal to, greater than, or less than the book value interests of the withdrawing partner.

To illustrate the accounting for the withdrawal of a partner by transferring firm assets, assume a partnership consisting of three partners, Adams, Brown, and Call, with capital balances of $30,000, $40,000, $30,000, and a profit and loss ratio of 5:3:2. Any agreed asset and liability revaluations have already been recorded.

Bad things can happen if an outsider makes a bid for a piece of the company—the lead partner's share, say, but not everyone else's. You don't want to be forced to work alongside an incompetent heir or a crook. Solution: The buy/sell agreement dictates that an outsider cannot buy a majority interest without offering to buy out everyone else on the same terms. Alternatively, it might provide that the remaining partners have a right of first refusal on any shares being sold.[15]

Payment to a Retiring Partner

Payment in Excess of Book Value to a Withdrawing Partner Assume now that Adams is withdrawing from the partnership and the partners have mutually agreed that he is to receive payment of $40,000. The partners may agree to use the bonus method or the goodwill method to record the withdrawal.

Bonus Method If the bonus method is used, the remaining partners are charged with the amount of the payment that exceeds the book value of the retiring partner's capital balance. The amount of the bonus paid to the retiring partner is commonly allocated to the remaining partners on the basis of their relative profit and loss ratio (in this case the relative ratio of Brown to Call is 3:2). Support for this method is based on the cost principle. The bonus method may also be justified when the remaining partners are simply anxious to get rid of a partner for various reasons. Any recognition of goodwill is difficult to justify in the absence of an arm's-length transaction. The entry to record the withdrawal would be as follows:

Adams, Capital	30,000	
Brown, Capital	6,000	
Call, Capital	4,000	
Liability to Adams		40,000

Goodwill Method The goodwill method is used if (1) Brown and Call will not agree to a reduction in their capital balances; (2) the partners made specific provisions in the partnership agreement on how the withdrawal is to be recorded; or (3) the partners agree that an intangible asset should be recognized. If the partnership has been profitable, the firm as a whole may be worth more than the fair value of the net assets. Once again, the goodwill method is supported on the basis

---

[15]Ibid.

that a new entity is being formed and the accounts of the new entity should be based on fair values. One alternative is to calculate the implied goodwill from the price paid to the retiring partner. In our example, Adams receives a $10,000 excess payment over his capital balance. Since Adams' capital account is increased by 50% of any increase in assets, then a $10,000 excess payment implies a total goodwill of $20,000. The entries are:

Goodwill	20,000	
Adams, Capital		10,000
Brown, Capital		6,000
Call, Capital		4,000
Adams, Capital	40,000	
Liability to Adams		40,000

Some argue that, in accordance with the cost basis, only the goodwill of $10,000 that has been purchased should be recorded (called the partial goodwill method) and the entry should be:

Goodwill	10,000	
Adams, Capital		10,000
Adams, Capital	40,000	
Liability to Adams		40,000

Others would contend that the basis for recognizing goodwill should be "all or nothing at all."

It is probably difficult to justify recognition of any goodwill. If the goodwill is related to Adams, it will not exist if he withdraws. However, as discussed before, if the goodwill is based on past operations, the withdrawal may provide the objective evidence necessary to recognize it in the partnership accounts.

Payment of Less Than Book Value to a Withdrawing Partner A partner who is anxious to dispose of his or her interest in the partnership may agree to accept less than his or her book value interest in the partnership. The partner may do so for a number of reasons, such as (1) he or she may view the future of the company negatively, (2) he or she may need operating capital for personal reasons, or (3) the business association may no longer be acceptable to the partner and, in his or her opinion, a forced liquidation of the firm might be detrimental to his or her interest. In such cases, use of the bonus method is justified, since the settlement may not be based on the economic value of the firm.

To illustrate, assume that Adams withdraws from the ABC Partnership and agrees to settle his $30,000 interest for $25,000. A bonus of $5,000 accrues to the remaining partners. The common practice is to allocate the bonus on the basis of their relative profit and loss ratio of 3:2. The entry would be:

Adams, Capital	30,000	
Brown, Capital		3,000
Call, Capital		2,000
Liability to Adams		25,000

A payment to Adams that is less than his capital interest may be an indication that assets are overvalued. Assets should be written down to fair values if it is determined that they are overvalued and that the settlement price is based on the net assets' fair value. In particular, if goodwill was previously recorded, an agreement to accept a payment that is less than the partner's book value interest may provide evidence that the intangible is overstated. Accordingly, the intangible should be reduced by the difference between the settlement price and the capital interest being retired. Assuming that assets are overvalued by $10,000, the sequence of entries becomes:

Adams, Capital	5,000	
Brown, Capital	3,000	
Call, Capital	2,000	
Asset		10,000
Adams, Capital	25,000	
Liability to Adams		25,000

Reducing the assets to fair value provides an equitable starting point for the new partnership formed by Brown and Call. As long as Brown and Call share profits in the same relative ratio, they will be indifferent as to the method used. However, it is more informative and conceptually preferred for the recorded asset values to reflect fair values if such values can be determined.

Death of a Partner

Under the UPA [Section 31(4)], a partnership is dissolved by the death of a partner. Historically, if the surviving partners continued to operate the partnership, a new partnership was considered formed (that is, the old partnership was terminated), even though the partners may have provided for the continuation of the business in the partnership agreement. Under this interpretation, the surviving partners should enter into a new agreement. More recent court cases—and some state statutes—now permit the partnership to continue operating in accordance with terms provided for in the partnership agreement.

A deceased partner's estate is entitled to receive the partner's current equity in the partnership. Determining a partner's equity interest in the firm can result in disagreements between the surviving partners and the executor of the estate. To avoid litigation, the articles of partnership should contain procedures for determining a deceased partner's current equity in the partnership and the method of settlement. In the absence of specific provisions, the surviving partners and the executor of the estate must negotiate a settlement. To determine a partner's equity interest at the time of death, the assets and liabilities normally are adjusted to current values and the accounts are closed to determine the net income or loss earned since the end of the last fiscal period.

The partnership agreement may provide that the interest is to be settled by distributing partnership assets to the estate or the estate may receive payment by selling the interest to an outside party or to one or more of the surviving partners as individuals. Entries to record both types of settlements were presented in earlier sections of this chapter.

SUMMARY

1. *Describe the characteristics of a general partnership, a limited partnership, and a joint venture.* In a general partnership, the partners can bind the partnership into contracts, and the partnership interest is similar to a personal asset that can be sold. The primary difference between a general partnership and a limited partnership is that general partners are personally liable for the debts of the partnership, while a limited partner is only liable for the amount invested in the partnership. A joint venture occurs when two or more parties (agents) enter into an arrangement to pursue a specific purpose. When joint ventures are structured as partnerships, they follow the partnership laws. One exception is that one party cannot act (enter into a contract) on behalf of the joint venture without the consent of the other agents.

2. *List some important items to be included in the partnership agreement.* Important items to include in the partnership agreement are the name of the partnership, the identity of the partners, the effective date and the length of operations, the provision for allocating profits and losses, provisions for salaries and withdrawals, contracting authorities, procedures for admitting a new partner, and procedures for dissolution of the partnership.

3. *Understand the differences between partnerships' and corporations' equity accounts in the balance sheet.* In a corporation, amounts contributed by the owners (i.e., stockholders) are recorded in capital stock accounts. In addition, any income or loss earned by the corporation is reported in retained earnings. Dividends are considered a distribution of earnings and thus reduce retained earnings. In a partnership, amounts contributed by the owners (i.e., partners) are recorded in the partners' capital accounts. Any income or loss earned by the partnership is allocated to the partners' capital accounts. If a partner takes money out of the partnership, a drawing account is often used.

4. *Explain the purpose of the partners' drawing accounts and capital accounts.* In general, the partners' capital accounts are for permanent investments and should be updated periodically for withdrawals. Drawing accounts are often used in anticipation of earnings or to pay for personal expenses. Drawing accounts record withdrawals during the year and are closed to the partners' capital accounts at year-end.

5. *Prepare journal entries to form a partnership using the bonus and the goodwill methods.* A choice between the bonus and the goodwill methods for recording the formation of a partnership is needed if the amounts contributed by each partner do not agree with the amount of capital to be credited to each partner (for example, one partner contributes 40% of the assets but is to be given a 50% interest). For example, suppose that Bob and Ed enter into a partnership. Bob contributes $40 cash and Ed contributes $60. Yet each is to be given an equal interest. The journal entries under the bonus and goodwill methods are as follows:

Bonus Method		
Cash	$100	
Bob, Capital		$50
Ed, Capital		$50
Goodwill Method		
Cash	$100	
Intangible Asset	$ 20	
Bob, Capital		$60
Ed, Capital		$60

Under the bonus method, the total amount contributed is allocated to all partners in accordance with their agreed-upon capital share (equally in this illustration, resulting in a transfer of $10 from Ed to Bob). Under the goodwill method, Bob is assumed to be contributing an intangible asset to the firm. Since Ed contributed $60 and Bob only $40, an intangible asset of $20 is recorded to increase Bob's capital to $60.

6. *Describe some common agreements used to allocate partnership net income or loss.* Common agreements to allocate partnership net income or loss include using (1) fixed ratios, (2) a ratio based on the partners' capital balances, (3) an implicit interest rate based on the partners' capital accounts (such as 10% of the year-end capital balance), and (4) various amounts that represent salaries or bonuses. In addition, the agreement must specify how any excess or deficit after an original allocation is divided among the partners.

7. *Explain why salary allowances and interest allowances are used in allocating partnership profits and losses.* Interest allowances are often used as an incentive for capital to be invested and stay invested in the partnership. If a partner withdraws money from the partnership, that partner will receive a lower amount of interest and thus a smaller allocation of total profits. If the partner contributes more funds, that partner will receive a higher allocation. Similarly, a salary allowance

is a common method to reward partners providing services to the partnership for their efforts.

8. *Describe the methods used to record partnership changes when a new partner is admitted or when a partner withdraws from the partnership.* When a new partner is admitted, the new partner can purchase the interest from an existing partner or the new partner can contribute additional assets to the partnership. As when a partnership is formed, either the bonus or the goodwill method may be used if the amount contributed does not agree with the amount of capital to be credited to the new partner. Upon the withdrawal of a partner, the same procedures are applied. If the amount paid to the withdrawing partner is more or less than the partner's existing capital balance, either the bonus or the goodwill method can be used. In this case, the withdrawing partner's final capital balance must equal the amount paid. Under the bonus method, this is achieved by a transfer from (to) the remaining partners' capital accounts to (from) the withdrawing partner's capital balance. Under the goodwill method, the firm is revalued, using the amount paid to the withdrawing partner. All partners' capital accounts are adjusted.

9. *Describe the rationale behind the goodwill method in accounting for changes in partnership membership.* Under the goodwill method of accounting for changes in partnership membership, the capital interest assigned to the new or withdrawing partner implies a certain value for the firm. Since records are maintained on historical cost, differences in net asset values are likely. In addition, significant intangible assets may have been created by the partnership over time. The goodwill method assumes that the assigned capital interest provides a basis for total firm valuation.

QUESTIONS

1. Describe the tax treatment of partnership income.

2. Distinguish between a partner's interest in capital and his interest in the partnership's income and losses. Also, make a general distinction between a partner's capital account and his drawing account.

3. Explain why a partnership is viewed in accounting as a "separate economic entity."

4. What are some of the methods commonly used in allocating income and losses to the partners?

5. Explain the distinction between the terms "withdrawals" and "salaries."

6. List some of the alternative methods of calculating a bonus that may appear in a partnership agreement.

7. What is meant by dissolution and what are its causes?

8. Discuss the methods used to record changes in partnership membership.

9. Differentiate between the admission of a new partner through assignment of an interest and through investment in the partnership.

10. Under what two conditions will the bonus and goodwill methods of recording the admission of a partner yield the same result?

11. Describe the circumstances where neither the goodwill nor the bonus method should be used to record the admission of a new partner.

12. How might a partner withdrawing in violation of the partnership agreement and without the consent of the other partners be treated? What about a partner who is forced to withdraw?

EXERCISES

EXERCISE 16-1   Partnership Formation: Bonus and Goodwill Methods

John, Jeff, and Jane decided to engage in a real estate venture as a partnership. John invested $100,000 cash and Jeff provided office equipment that is carried on his books at $82,000. The partners agree that the equipment has a fair value of $110,000. There is a $30,000 note payable remaining on the equipment to be assumed by the partnership. Although Jane has no physical assets to invest in the partnership, both John and Jeff believe that her experience as a real estate appraiser is a valuable skill needed by the partnership and is a basis for granting her a capital interest in the partnership.

Required:

Assuming that each partner is to receive an equal capital interest in the partnership,

A. Record the partnership formation under the bonus method.

B. Record the partnership formation under the goodwill method, and assume a total goodwill of $90,000.

C. Discuss the appropriateness of using either the bonus or goodwill methods to record the formation of the partnership.

EXERCISE 16-2 **Partnership Transactions and Capital Statements**
Tom and Julie formed a management consulting partnership on January 1, 2001. The fair value of the net assets invested by each partner follows:

	Tom	*Julie*
Cash	$13,000	$12,000
Accounts receivable	8,000	6,000
Office supplies	2,000	800
Office equipment	30,000	—
Land	—	30,000
Accounts payable	2,000	5,000
Mortgage payable	—	18,800

During the year, Tom withdrew $15,000 and Julie withdrew $12,000 in anticipation of operating profits. Net profit for 2001 was $50,000, which is to be allocated based on the original net capital investment.

Required:

A. Prepare journal entries to:
  (1) Record the initial investment in the partnership.
  (2) Record the withdrawals.
  (3) Close the Income Summary and Drawing accounts.

B. Prepare a statement of changes in partners' capital for the year ended December 31, 2001.

EXERCISE 16-3 **Allocation of Income or Loss**
Jones, Silva, and Thompson form a partnership and agree to allocate income equally after recognition of 10% interest on beginning capital balances and monthly salary allowances of $2,000 to Jones and $1,500 to Thompson. Capital balances on January 1 were as follows:

Jones	$40,000
Silva	25,000
Thompson	30,000

Required:
Calculate the net income (loss) allocation to each partner under each of the following independent situations.

1. Net income for the year is $99,500.

2. Net income for the year is $38,300.

3. Net loss for the year is $15,100.

EXERCISE 16-4 **Allocation of Net Loss**
Mary and Nancy invested $80,000 each to form a partnership. Mary has been authorized a salary of $20,000, while Nancy's salary is $25,000. Each partner is to receive 10% on the original capital investment. The profit and loss agreement stipulates that any remaining income or loss is to be divided equally. The partnership had a net loss of $20,000 this year.

Required:
Prepare the journal entry to record the allocation of the net loss for the year. Show supporting computations.

EXERCISE 16-5 **Bonus Agreement**
On January 1, 2001, Tony and Jon formed T&J Personal Financial Planning with capital investments of $480,000 and $340,000, respectively. The partners wanted to draft a profit and

loss agreement that would reward each individual for the resources invested in the partnership. Accordingly, the partnership agreement provides that profits are to be allocated as follows:

1. Annual salaries of $42,000 and $66,000 are granted to Tony and Jon, respectively.
2. In addition to the salary, Jon is entitled to a bonus of 10% of net income after salaries and bonus but before interest on capital investments is subtracted.
3. Each partner is to receive an interest credit of 8% on the original capital investment.
4. Remaining profits are to be allocated 40% to Tony and 60% to Jon.

On December 31, 2001, the partnership reported net income before salaries, interest, and bonus of $188,000.

Required:
Calculate the 2001 allocation of partnership profit.

EXERCISE 16-6 **Profit Distribution and Capital Statements**
Hill, Jones, and Vose have been partners throughout 2001. Their average balances for the year and their balances at the end of the year before closing the nominal accounts are as follows:

Partner	Average Balances	Balances 12/31/01
Hill	$97,500	$70,000
Jones	27,300	21,800
Vose	14,250	11,700*

*Debit balance.

The income for 2001 is $108,000 before charging partners' salary allowances and before payment of interest on average balances at the agreed rate of 5% per annum. Annual salary allocations are $12,000 to Hill, $9,600 to Jones, and $8,800 to Vose. The balance of income is to be allocated at the rate of 60% to Hill, 10% to Jones, and 30% to Vose.

It is intended to distribute cash to the partners so that, after credits and allocations have been made as indicated in the preceding paragraph, the balances in the partners' accounts will be proportionate to their residual profit-sharing ratios. None of the partners is to invest additional cash, but they wish to distribute the lowest possible amount of cash.

Required:
Prepare a schedule of partners' accounts, showing balances at the end of 2001 before closing, the allocations of the net income for 2001, the cash distributed, and the closing balances.

(AICPA adapted)

EXERCISE 16-7 **Partner Admission**
Phil Phoenix and Tim Tucson are partners in an electrical repair business. Their respective capital balances are $90,000 and $50,000, and they share profits and losses equally. Because the partners are confronted with personal financial problems, they decided to admit a new partner to the partnership. After an extensive interviewing process they elect to admit Don Dallas into the partnership.

Required:
Prepare the journal entry to record the admission of Don Dallas into the partnership under each of the following conditions:

1. Don acquires one-fourth of Phil's capital interest by paying $30,000 directly to him.
2. Don acquires one-fifth of each of Phil's and Tim's capital interests. Phil receives $25,000 and Tim receives $15,000 directly from Don.

3. Don acquires a one-fifth capital interest for a $60,000 cash investment in the partnership. Total capital after the admission is to be $200,000.

4. Don invests $40,000 for a one-fifth interest in partnership capital. Implicit goodwill is to be recorded.

EXERCISE 16-8 Adjusting Entries for Partner Admission

Bill and Jane share profits and losses in a 70 : 30 ratio. Mike is to be admitted into a partnership upon the investment of $14,000 for a one-third capital interest. Account balances for Bill and Jane on June 30, 2001 just before the admission of Mike are as follows:

	Debit	Credit
Cash	$ 6,000	
Accounts Receivable	9,000	
Notes Receivable	2,000	
Merchandise Inventory	12,000	
Prepaid Insurance	500	
Accounts Payable		$ 9,500
Bill, Capital		12,000
Jane, Capital		8,000
	$29,500	$29,500

It is agreed that for purposes of establishing the interests of the former partners, the following adjustments shall be made:

1. An allowance for doubtful accounts of 2% of the accounts receivable is to be established.
2. The merchandise inventory is to be valued at $10,000.
3. Accrued expenses of $600 are to be recognized.
4. Prepaid insurance is to be valued at $300.
5. The goodwill method is to be used to record the admission of Mike.

Required:

Prepare the entries to adjust the account balances in establishing the interests of Bill and Jane and to record the investment by Mike.

EXERCISE 16-9 Partner Admission

Beth, Steph, and Linda have been operating a small gift shop for several years. After an extensive review of their past operating performance, the partners concluded that the business needed to expand in order to provide an adequate return to the partners. The following balance sheet is for the partnership prior to the admission of a new partner, Mary.

Cash	$160,000
Other Assets	640,000
	$800,000
Liabilities	$200,000
Beth, Capital (40%)	265,000
Steph, Capital (40%)	215,000
Linda, Capital (20%)	120,000
	$800,000

Figures shown parenthetically reflect agreed profit-and-loss sharing percentages.

Required:

Prepare the necessary journal entries to record the admission of Mary in each of the following independent situations. Some situations may be recorded in more than one way.

1. Mary is to invest sufficient cash to receive a one-sixth capital interest. The parties agree that the admission is to be recorded without recognizing goodwill or bonus.

2. Mary is to invest $160,000 for a one-fifth capital interest.

3. Mary is to invest $160,000 for a one-fourth capital interest.

4. Mary is to invest $160,000 for a 40% capital interest.

EXERCISE 16-10 **Multiple Choice**

Select the best answer for each of the following.

1. Jon and Joe formed a partnership on July 1, 2001, and invested the following assets:

	Jon	Joe
Cash	$65,000	$125,000
Realty		250,000

The realty was subject to a mortgage of $25,000, which was assumed by the partnership. The partnership agreement provides that Jon and Joe will share profits and losses in the ratio of one-third and two-thirds, respectively. Joe's capital account at July 1, 2001, should be

(a) $375,000
(b) $366,667
(c) $285,000
(d) $350,000

2. On July 1, 2001, Mary and Jane formed a partnership, agreeing to share profits and losses in the ratio of 4:6, respectively. Mary invested a parcel of land that cost her $40,000. Jane invested $50,000 cash. The land was sold for $60,000 on July 1, 2001, four hours after formation of the partnership. How much should be recorded in Mary's capital account on formation of the partnership?

(a) $8,000
(b) $24,000
(c) $60,000
(d) $20,000

3. The partnership agreement of Tami, Julie, and Kim provides for annual distribution of profit or loss in the following order:

Tami, the managing partner, receives a bonus of 15% of profit.
Each partner receives 10% interest on average capital investment.
Residual profit or loss is divided equally.

The average capital investments for 2001 were:

Tami	$100,000
Julie	200,000
Kim	300,000

How much of the $94,500 partnership profit for 2001 should be allocated to Tami?

(a) $10,000
(b) $20,000
(c) $30,950
(d) $14,175

4. Tom and Jim are partners who share profits and losses in the ratio of 3:2, respectively. On August 31, 2001, their capital accounts were as follows:

Tom	$ 80,000
Jim	50,000
	$130,000

On that date they agreed to admit John as a partner with a one-third interest in the capital and profits and losses, for an investment of $50,000. The new partnership will begin with a total capital of $180,000. Immediately after John's admission, what are the capital balances of the partners?

	Tom	*Jim*	*John*
(a)	$60,000	$60,000	$60,000
(b)	$73,333	$46,667	$60,000
(c)	$74,000	$46,000	$60,000
(d)	$80,000	$50,000	$50,000

5. On June 30, 2001, the balance sheet for the partnership of Al, Carl, and Paul, together with their respective profit and loss ratios, were as follows:

Assets, at Cost	$180,000
Al, Loan	$ 9,000
Al, Capital (20%)	42,000
Carl, Capital (20%)	39,000
Paul, Capital (60%)	90,000
Total	$180,000

Al has decided to retire from the partnership. By mutual agreement, the assets are to be adjusted to their fair value of $220,000 at June 30, 2001. It was agreed that the partnership would pay Al $61,200 cash for Al's partnership interest, including Al's loan, which is to be repaid in full. No goodwill is to be recorded. After Al's retirement, what is the balance of Carl's capital account?
   (a) $36,450.
   (b) $39,000.
   (c) $46,450.
   (d) $47,000.

(AICPA adapted)

EXERCISE 16-11 **Multiple Choice**
Select the best answer for each of the following.

1. Which of the following is *not* a characteristic of a partnership?
   (a) Limited life.
   (b) Mutual agency.
   (c) Limited liability.
   (d) Right to dispose of partnership interest.

2. The articles of partnership need not include which of the following?
   (a) Location of the place of business.
   (b) Allocation of profit/loss.
   (c) Procedures for admitting a new partner.
   (d) Fiscal period of the partnership.
   (e) All of the above should be included.

3. The High and Low partnership agreement provides special compensation to High for managing the business. High receives a bonus of 15% of partnership net income before salary and bonus, and also receives a salary of $45,000. Any remaining profit or loss is to be allocated equally. During 2001, the partnership had net income of $50,000 before the bonus and salary allowance. As a result of these distributions, Low's equity in the partnership would

   (a) Increase.
   (b) Not change.
   (c) Decrease the same as High's.
   (d) Decrease.

4. The allocation of an error correction should be based on the profit and loss agreement in effect when

   (a) The error was made.
   (b) The error was corrected.
   (c) The error was discovered.
   (d) The allocation should always be made equally.

5. If there is a provision for allocation of profits but not losses in the partnership agreement, courts have generally concluded that

   (a) Losses should not be allocated to the capital accounts, but matched against future earnings.
   (b) Losses should be allocated using the same approach as allocation of profits.
   (c) Losses should be allocated equally.
   (d) Losses should be allocated according to the ratio of balances in the capital accounts.

6. Partners E and F share profits and losses equally after each has been credited in all circumstances with annual salary allowances of $15,000 and $12,000, respectively. Under this agreement, E will benefit by $3,000 more than F in which of the following circumstances?

   (a) Only if the partnership has earnings of $27,000 or more for the year.
   (b) Only if the partnership does not incur a loss for the year.
   (c) In all earnings or loss situations.
   (d) Only if the partnership has earnings of at least $3,000 for the year.

EXERCISE 16-12 **Income Allocation with Bonus**

The partnership agreement of ABC Associates provides that income should be allocated in the following manner:

1. Each partner receives interest of 20% of beginning capital.
2. Sue receives a salary of $25,000 and Josh receives a salary of $21,000.
3. Josh also receives a bonus of 10%.
4. Residual—divided equally.

The partnership's net income for 2001 was $90,000. Beginning capital balances were Sue, $30,000; Josh, $40,000.

Required:
Prepare a schedule to allocate the net income under each of the following independent situations:

A. Bonus is to be based on income before any profit allocation to partners for interest and salary.
B. Bonus is to be based on income after subtracting the bonus, but before allocation to partners for interest and salary.
C. Bonus is to be based on income after subtracting the bonus, interest, and salary.

EXERCISE 16-13   **Partner Withdrawal**

Kazma, Folkert, and Tucker are partners with capital account balances of $30,000, $75,000, and $45,000, respectively. Income and losses are divided in a 4:4:2 ratio. When Tucker decided to withdraw, the partnership revalued its assets from $225,000 to $252,000, which represented an increase in the value of inventory of $8,000 and an increase in the value of land of $19,000. Tucker was then given $15,000 cash and a note for $40,000 for his withdrawal from the partnership.

Required:

A. Prepare the journal entry to record the revaluation of the partnership's assets.

B. Prepare the journal entry to record the withdrawal using the following independent methods.

  (1) Bonus.
  (2) Partial goodwill.
  (3) Full goodwill amount.

PROBLEMS

PROBLEM 16-1   **Profit Allocation**

Day and Night formed an accounting partnership in 2001. Capital transactions for Day and Night during 2001 are as follows:

Date	Transaction	Amount
Day		
1/1	Beginning balance	$75,000
4/1	Withdrawal	18,750
6/1	Investment	37,500
11/1	Investment	18,750
Night		
1/1	Beginning balance	$37,500
7/1	Investment	18,750
10/1	Withdrawal	9,375

Partnership net income for the year ended December 31, 2001, is $68,400 before considering salaries or interest.

Required:

Determine the amount of profit that is to be allocated to Day and Night in accordance with each of the following independent profit-sharing agreements:

1. Day and Night failed to provide a profit-sharing arrangement in the articles of partnership and fail to compromise on an agreement.

2. Net income is to be allocated 60% to Day and 40% to Night.

3. Net income is to be allocated in the ratio of ending capital balances.

4. Net income is to be allocated in the ratio of average capital balances.

5. Interest of 15% is to be granted on average capital balances, salaries of $15,000 and $8,250 are to be allocated to Day and Night, respectively, and the remainder is to be divided equally.

PROBLEM 16-2   **Income Allocation and Capital Statements**

Dave, Brian, and Paul are partners in a retail appliance store. The partnership was formed January 1, 2001, with each partner investing $45,000. They agreed that profits and losses are to be shared as follows:

1. Divided in the ratio of 40:30:30 if net income is not sufficient to cover salaries, bonus, and interest.

2. A net loss is to be allocated equally.

3. Net income is to be allocated as follows if net income is in excess of salaries, bonus, and interest.

(a) Monthly salary allowances are:

Dave	$3,500
Brian	2,500
Paul	1,500

(b) Brian is to receive a bonus of 8% of net income before subtracting salaries and interest, but after subtracting the bonus.

(c) Interest of 10% is allocated based on the beginning-of-year capital balances.

(d) Any remainder is to be allocated equally.

Operating performance and other capital transactions were as follows.

		Capital Transactions					
		Dave		Brian		Paul	
Year-End	Net Income (Loss)	Investment	Withdrawals	Investment	Withdrawals	Investment	Withdrawals
12/31/01	$ (5,400)	$15,000	$17,000	$15,000	$7,000	$6,000	$3,200
12/31/02	27,000	—0—	17,000	—0—	7,000	6,000	3,200
12/31/03	120,000	—0—	19,000	—0—	9,000	6,000	3,200

Required:

A. Prepare a schedule of changes in patners' capital accounts for each of the three years.

B. Prepare the journal entry to close the income summary account to the partners' capital accounts at the end of each year.

PROBLEM 16-3 **Conversion from Cash to Accrual Basis**

The partnership of Cain, Gallo, and Hamm engaged you to adjust its accounting records and convert them uniformly to the accrual basis in anticipation of admitting Kerns as a new partner. Some accounts are on the accrual basis and some are on the cash basis. The partnership's books were closed at December 31, 2001, by the bookkeeper, who prepared the general ledger trial balance that appears below.

Cain, Gallo, and Hamm
General Ledger Trial Balance
December 31, 2001

	Debit	Credit
Cash	$ 15,000	
Accounts Receivable	40,000	
Inventory	30,000	
Land	9,000	
Buildings	50,000	
Allowance for Depreciation of Buildings		$ 6,000
Equipment	56,000	
Allowance for Depreciation of Equipment		6,000
Goodwill	5,000	
Accounts Payable		56,000
Allowance for Future Inventory Losses		8,000
Cain, Capital		37,000
Gallo, Capital		60,000
Hamm, Capital		32,000
Totals	$205,000	$205,000

Your inquiries disclose the following:

1. The partnership was organized on January 1, 2000. No provision was made in the partnership agreement for the allocation of partnership profits and losses. During 2000, profits were allocated equally among the partners. The partnership agreement was amended, effective January 1, 2001, to provide for the following profit and loss ratio: Cain, 40%; Gallo, 40%; and Hamm, 20%. The amended partnership agreement also stated that the accounting records were to be maintained on the accrual basis and that any adjustments necessary for 2000 should be allocated according to the 2000 profit allocation agreement.

2. The following amounts were not recorded as prepayments or accruals.

| | December 31 | |
	2001	2000
Prepaid insurance	$700	$ 800
Advances from customers	900	1,500
Accrued interest expense	—	450

The advances from customers were recorded as sales in the year the cash was received.

3. In 2001, the partnership recorded a provision of $8,000 for anticipated declines in inventory prices. You convinced the partners that the provision was unnecessary and should be removed from the books.

4. The partnership charged equipment purchased for $4,400 on January 1, 2001, to expense. This equipment has an estimated life of 10 years and an estimated salvage value of $400. The partnership depreciates its capitalized equipment using the declining balance method at twice the straight-line depreciation rate.

5. The partners agreed to establish an allowance for doubtful accounts at 2% of current accounts receivable and 5% of past-due accounts. At December 31, 2000, the partnership had $54,000 of accounts receivable, of which only $4,000 was past due. At December 31, 2001, 20% of accounts receivable was past due, of which $4,000 represented sales made in 2000 and was considered collectible. The partnership had written off uncollectible accounts in the year the accounts became worthless as follows:

| | Accounts Written Off In | |
	2001	2000
2001 accounts	$ 800	—
2000 accounts	1,000	$250

6. Goodwill was recorded on the books in 2001 and credited to the partners' capital accounts in the profit and loss ratio in recognition of an increase in the value of the business resulting from improved sales volume. The partners agreed to write off the goodwill before admitting the new partner.

Required:
Prepare a worksheet showing the adjustments and the adjusted trial balance for the partnership on the accrual basis at December 31, 2001. All adjustments affecting income should be made directly to partners' capital accounts. Supporting computations should be in good form. (Do not prepare formal financial statements or formal journal entries.)

(*AICPA adapted*)

PROBLEM 16-4 **Partner Admission**
Brown and Coss have been operating a tax accounting service as a partnership for five years. Their current capital balances are $92,000 and $88,000, respectively, and they share profits

in a 60:40 ratio. Because of the growth in their tax business, they decide that they need a new partner. Moore is admitted to the partnership, after which the partners agree to share profits 40% to Brown, 35% to Coss, and 25% to Moore.

Required:

Prepare the necessary journal entries to admit Moore in each of the following independent conditions. If the information is such that both the bonus and goodwill methods are appropriate, record the admission using both methods.

1. Moore invests $90,000 in cash and receives a one-third capital interest.

2. Moore invests $120,000 cash for a 45% capital interest. Total capital after his admission is to be $300,000.

3. Moore agrees to invest $120,000 cash for a one-third capital interest, but will not accept a capital credit for less than his investment.

4. Moore invests $40,000 cash for a one-fourth capital interest. The partners agree that assets and the firm as a whole should not be revalued.

5. Moore invests $35,000 cash for a one-fifth capital interest. The partners agree that total capital after the admission of Moore should be $225,000.

6. Moore invests land in the partnership as a site for a new office building. The land, which originally cost Moore $90,000, now has a current market value of $150,000. Moore is admitted with a one-third capital interest.

7. Moore is admitted to the partnership by purchasing a 30% capital interest from each partner. A payment of $35,000 is made outside the partnership and is split between Brown and Coss.

PROBLEM 16-5 Adjusting Entries for Partner Admission

The CAB Partnership, although operating profitably, has had a cash flow problem. Unable to meet its current commitments, the firm borrowed $34,000 from a bank giving a long-term note. During a recent meeting, the partners decided to obtain additional cash by admitting a new partner to the firm. They feel that the firm is an attractive investment, but that proper management of their liquid assets will be required. Meyers agrees to invest cash in the firm if her chief accountant can review the accounting records of the partnership.

The balance sheet for CAB Partnership as of December 31, 2001, is as follows:

Assets	
Cash	$ 8,000
Accounts Receivable	33,600
Inventory (at cost)	35,750
Land	27,000
Building (net of depreciation)	41,600
Equipment (net of depreciation)	27,250
Total	$173,200

Liabilities and Capital	
Accounts Payable	$ 32,450
Other Current Liabilities	6,750
Long-Term Note (8% due 2005)	34,000
Cox, Capital	37,500
Andrews, Capital	25,000
Bennet, Capital	37,500
Total	$173,200

The review of the accounts resulted in the accumulation of the following information:

1. Approximately 5% of the accounts receivable are uncollectible. The old partnership had been using the direct write-off method of accounting for bad debts.

2. Current replacement cost of the inventory is $41,250.

3. The market value of the land based on a current appraisal is $65,000.

4. The partners had been using an unreasonably long estimated life in establishing a depreciation policy for the building. On the basis of sound value (current replacement cost adjusted for use), the value of the building is $32,750.

5. There are unrecorded accrued liabilities of $3,275.

The partners agree to recognize the foregoing adjustments to the accounts. Cox, Andrews, and Bennet share profits 40:30:30. After the admission of Meyers, the new profit agreement is to be 30:20:30:20. Meyers is to receive a 25% capital interest in the partnership after she invests sufficient cash to increase the total capital interest to $150,000. Because of the uncertainty of the business, no goodwill is to be recognized before or after Meyers is admitted.

Required:

A. Prepare the necessary journal entries on the books of the old partnership to adjust the accounts.

B. Record the admission of Meyers.

C. Prepare a new balance sheet giving effect to the foregoing requirements.

PROBLEM 16-6 Adjusting Entries for Partner Withdrawal

The December 31, 2001, balance sheet of the Datamation Partnership is shown below.

Datamation Partnership
Balance Sheet
December 31, 2001

Assets

Cash	$ 80,000
Accounts Receivable	80,000
Inventory	62,000
Equipment	290,000
Total Assets	$512,000

Liabilities and Partners' Equity

Accounts Payable	$ 60,000
Notes Payable to Dave, 8% dated September 1, 2001	22,000
Dave, Capital	220,000
Allen, Capital	110,000
Matt, Capital	100,000
Total Liabilities and Partners' Equity	$512,000

Dave, Allen, and Matt share profits and loses in the ratio of 50:30:20. The inventory on December 31 has a fair value of $68,000; accrued interest on the note payable to Dave is to be recognized as of December 31. The book values of all the other accounts are equal to their fair values. Allen withdrew from the partnership on December 31, 2001.

Required:

Prepare the journal entry or entries to record the withdrawal of Allen, given each of the following situations. Assume that the *bonus* method is used to account for the withdrawal.

1. Allen receives $36,624 cash and a $75,000 note from the partnership for his interest.

2. Matt purchases Allen's interest for $110,000.

3. The partnership gives Allen $35,000 cash and equipment with a book value and a fair value of $90,000 for his interest.

4. The partnership gives Allen $100,000 cash for his interest.

5. Allen sells one-fourth of his interest to Dave for $40,000 and three-fourths to Matt for $90,000.

PROBLEM 16-7 Partner Withdrawal and New Profit-Loss Ratio

Neal, Palmer, and Ruppe are partners in a real estate company. Their respective capital balances and profit-sharing ratios are as follows:

	As of December 31, 2001	
Partners	*Capital Balance*	*Profit-Sharing Ratio*
Neal	$250,000	4
Palmer	150,000	3
Ruppe	100,000	3

Neal wishes to withdraw from the partnership on January 1, 2002, Palmer and Ruppe have agreed to pay Neal $300,000 from the partnership assets for his 50% capital interest. This settlement price was based on such factors as capital investments, sales performance, and earning capacity.

Palmer and Ruppe must decide whether to use the bonus method or the goodwill method (recognize total goodwill implied by the payment) to record the withdrawal, and they wish to compare the results of using the two methods.

Required:

Prepare a comparison of capital balances using the bonus and goodwill methods (and amortizing goodwill implied from the payment to Neal), assuming that

1. The new profit and loss ratio is in the same relative ratio as that existing before Neal's withdrawal.

2. The profit and loss ratio is changed to 3:2. Palmer is particularly interested in these results, because he feels that his present contribution of time and capital is better reflected by this new profit and loss ratio.

PROBLEM 16-8 Comprehensive Partnership Problem

Brian Snow and Wendy Waite formed a partnership on July 1, 2000. Brian invested $20,000 cash, inventory valued at $15,000, and equipment valued at $67,000. Wendy invested $50,000 cash and land valued at $120,000. The partnership assumed the $40,000 mortgage on the land.

On June 30, 2001, the partnership reported a net loss of $24,000. The partnership contract specified that income and losses were to be allocated by allowing 10% interest on the original capital investment, salaries of $15,000 to Brian and $20,000 to Wendy, and the remainder to be divided in the ratio of 40:60.

On July 1, 2001, Alan Young was admitted into the partnership with a $70,000 cash investment. Alan was given a 30% interest in the partnership because of his special skills. The partners elect to use the bonus method to record the admission. Any bonus should be divided in the old ratio of 40:60.

On June 30, 2002, the partnership reported a net income of $150,000. The new partnership contract stipulated that income and losses were to be divided in a fixed ratio of 20:50:30.

On July 2, 2002, Brian withdrew from the partnership for personal reasons. Brian was given $40,000 cash and a $60,000 note for his capital interest.

Required:

Prepare journal entries for each of the following events. Show computations.

1. Formation of the partnership.
2. Distribution of the net loss for the first year.
3. Admission of Alan into the partnership.
4. Distribution of the net income for the second year.
5. Withdrawal of Brian from the partnership.

PROBLEM 16-9   Various Changes in Partnership Composition

The partnerships of Up & Down and Back & Forth started in business on July 1, 1998; each partnership owns one retail appliance store. It was agreed as of June 30, 2001, to combine the partnerships to form a new partnership to be known as Discount Partnership. Trial balances of the two original partnerships as of June 30, 2001 follow.

	Up & Down Trial Balance June 30, 2001		Back & Forth Trial Balance June 30, 2001	
Cash	$ 25,000		$ 20,000	
Accounts Receivable	90,000		140,000	
Allowance for Doubtful Accounts		$ 2,000		$ 6,000
Merchandise Inventory	180,000		115,000	
Land	25,000		35,000	
Buildings and Equipment	80,000		125,000	
Allowance for Depreciation		24,000		61,000
Prepaid Expenses	6,000		8,000	
Accounts Payable		42,000		54,000
Notes Payable		65,000		74,000
Accrued Expenses		34,000		44,000
Up, Capital		95,000		
Down, Capital		144,000		
Back, Capital				65,000
Forth, Capital				139,000
Totals	$406,000	$406,000	$443,000	$443,000

The following additional information is available.

1. The profit- and loss-sharing ratios for the former partnerships were 40% to Up and 60% to Down; 30% to Back and 70% to Forth. The profit- and loss-sharing ratio for the new partnersip will be Up, 20%; Down, 30%; Back, 15%; and Forth, 35%.
2. The opening capital ratios for the new partnership are to be the same as the profit- and loss-sharing ratios for the new partnership. The capital assigned to Up & Down will total $225,000. Any cash settlements among the partners arising from capital account adjustments will be a private matter and will not be recorded on the partnership books.
3. The partners agreed that the allowance for bad debts for the new partnership is to be 4% of the accounts receivable balances.
4. The opening inventory of the new partnership is to be valued by the FIFO method. The inventory of Up & Down was valued by the FIFO method and the Back & Forth inventory was valued by the LIFO method. The LIFO inventory represents 80% of its FIFO value.

5. Depreciation is to be computed by the double-declining balance method with a 10-year life for the depreciable assets. Depreciation for three years is to be accumulated in the opening balance of the Allowance for Depreciation account. Up & Down computed depreciation by the straight-line method, and Back & Forth used the double-declining balance method. All assets were obtained on July 1, 1998.

6. After the books were closed, an unrecorded merchandise purchase of $4,000 by Back & Forth was discovered. The merchandise had been sold by June 30, 2001.

7. The accounts of Up & Down include a vacation pay accrual. It was agreed that Back & Forth should make a similar accrual for their 10 employees, who will receive a two-week vacation of $200 per employee per week.

Required:

A. Prepare a worksheet to determine the opening balances of a new partnership after giving effect to the information above. Formal journal entries are not required. Supporting computations, including the computation of goodwill, should be in good form.

B. Prepare a schedule computing the cash to be exchanged between Up & Down and between Back & Forth, in settlement of the affairs of each original partnership.

(AICPA adapted)

17

PARTNERSHIP LIQUIDATION

LEARNING OBJECTIVES

1. Describe the steps used to distribute available partnership assets in liquidation under the Uniform Partnership Act (UPA).

2. List the order of priority for each class of creditors in partnership liquidation under the UPA.

3. Prepare a liquidation schedule to settle debts and allocate assets.

4. Prepare a "safe payment approach" liquidation schedule.

5. Describe the four steps in the preparation of an advance plan for the distribution of cash in a partnership liquidation.

6. Prepare the journal entries to incorporate a partnership.

IN THE NEWS

Hundreds of real-estate partnerships sold during the industry's heyday in the 1980s have either been liquidated or are in the process of liquidation. "By the time the year 2000 rolls around, at least 300 partnerships will have been liquidated between 1997 and 1999," says Spencer Jefferies, editor of *Partnership Spectrum*, a Dallas-based newsletter.[1]

In the preceding chapter, dissolution of a partnership in which the business affairs were continued without interruption was discussed. In this chapter, we will consider dissolutions in which the partnership is terminated. The phase of partnership operations that begins after dissolution and ends with the termination of partnership activities is referred to as "winding up the affairs." During this period the partnership's unfinished business is completed, some of the firm's noncash assets may be converted into cash (realization), liabilities are settled to the extent possible, and any remaining assets are distributed to the partners in settlement of their residual interest. These events may occur over a relatively short period of time (for example, there may be a lump-sum sale of the assets, and the liabilities may be assumed by the purchaser or discharged with the cash received), or over a period of several years if the assets are sold individually as the business affairs are gradually terminated.

In the first part of this chapter, we will assume that all noncash assets are converted into cash before any assets are distributed to creditors and partners; this

---

[1]*Barron's*, "The Ground Floor: Now's Not the Time to Sell Those Old Partnerships," by Barry Vinocur, 9/29/97, pp. 48–50.

737

procedure is referred to as a *simple liquidation*. In the second part of the chapter, we assume instead that noncash assets are sold in installments and cash is distributed to the various equity interests as it becomes available.

During the liquidation process, the accountant can provide service to the partners in a number of areas. He or she may assist in preparing financial statements and providing guidance to the partners to ensure that the liquidation proceeds in accordance with legal requirements and the partnership agreement. Much of the accounting for partnership liquidations depends on interpretation of the partnership agreement and the legal provisions governing partnership liquidation. The accountant needs to be familiar with pertinent statutory provisions, which may include the UPA and federal and state bankruptcy laws. In addition, for the protection of all parties concerned, it may be advisable to seek legal counsel.

"Long before your business partnership is dissolved, the handling of the breakup or transfer of ownership should be planned. Astonishingly, 80% of new businesses fail to spell out the mechanism for a divorce. Why? The very idea introduces a seed of suspicion into an otherwise happy union."[2]

STEPS IN THE LIQUIDATION PROCESS

The first step in the liquidation process is to compute any net income or loss up to the date of dissolution. The closing process should be completed and, as part of it, any net income or loss should be allocated to the partners in accordance with their profit and loss agreement.

In the next step of the liquidation process, assets that are not acceptable for distribution in their present form are converted into cash. If the sales price of an asset is greater than (less than) the recorded book value, there is a gain (loss) from the sale. Procedurally, gains and losses on the realization of assets may be collected in one account and then closed to the capital accounts of the individual partners. The allocation of realization gains or losses should be based on the residual profit and loss ratio, unless specific provisions for such allocation are made in the partnership agreement.[3] The rationale for this procedure is that since the changes in asset values are the result of risk assumed by the partnership, the gain or loss should be shared in the agreed profit and loss ratio. In addition, it may be difficult to separate gains and losses that result from liquidation from the under- or overstatement of book values that results from accounting policies followed in prior years. For example, a gain on the sale of an item of equipment could reflect the fact that the firm had used a conservative depreciation policy and recorded excessive depreciation in prior years. Other adjustments could result from the failure to recognize changes in market values in the appropriate year. Furthermore, any agreement as to interest and salaries in the income allocation formula is ignored when allocating realization gains and losses. The use of the residual ratio is justified,

---

[2]*Forbes*, "Planning for Divorce," by Leigh Gallagher, 3/22/99, pp. 94–95.

[3]Section 18 of the UPA provides a list of rights and duties of partners, "subject to any agreement between them." Section 18(a) provides that "each partner must contribute toward the losses, whether of capital or otherwise, sustained by the partnership according to his share in the profits."

since interest and salaries are income allocations for time and resources devoted to the normal operating activities of a going concern and are not directly associated with changes in fair values of assets.

The last step is to distribute the available assets to creditors and partners. Section 40(b) of the Uniform Partnership Act (UPA) provides that

The liabilities of the partnership shall rank in order of payment, as follows:

(I) Those owing to creditors other than partners,
(II) Those owing to partners other than for capital and profits, *→ for loans*
(III) Those owing to partners in respect of capital,
(IV) Those owing to partners in respect of profits.

According to this ranking, firm creditors are the first to be paid from partnership assets. In determining the rights of various creditors to payment, liabilities are classified as those that are secured, partially secured, and unsecured, with some unsecured having priority. Bankruptcy laws dictate which of the partnership creditors are to be paid as cash becomes available. However, since this decision would have no impact on the total unpaid claims of the partnership, we will view the pool of creditors as if it were one unsecured obligation and will treat any cash payment as a reduction in total liabilities.

The UPA then provides for an order of payment that ranks partnership obligations to a partner ahead of asset distribution to a partner for capital investment. However, if a partner has a debit balance in the partner's capital account and has lent money to the partnership, it is legally permissible to offset the loan balance against the debit capital balance. The courts have recognized that this "right of offset" is necessary in order to avoid the potential inequity of distributing cash to a partner to satisfy an outstanding loan balance when the partner has either a debit capital balance, or potential for a debit capital balance. A debit capital balance is considered an asset of the partnership.[4] If the partner is unable to honor this obligation to the partnership by contributing additional assets, and for some reason cannot be forced to do so, the debit capital balance is allocated as a realization loss to the remaining partners in their relative profit and loss ratio. The residual claims of the remaining partners are reduced, as is the amount of cash they will receive. Thus, without the right of offset, the order of payment established by the UPA may result in a payment to a partner who may eventually owe cash to the partnership as a result of a debit capital balance.

Items III and IV are generally combined into one balance because of the practical problem of separating them. In other words, after several years of operation, a partner's capital investments, withdrawals, and income and loss elements may become combined into one balance and difficult to separate if the income summary account is closed to the capital accounts of each partner. In settlement of a partner's claim against the partnership, the partners may agree to the distribution of noncash assets. If so, the carrying value of the asset should be adjusted to fair value and the amount of the adjustment allocated to all the partners in accordance with the part-

---

[4]Section 40(a) of the UPA defines the assets of a partnership as including not only the partnership property, but also the contributions of partners necessary for the payment of all liabilities specified in section 40(b). Section 40(b) specifies that amounts owing to creditors and to partners for loans, capital, and profits are liabilities of a partnership.

nership agreement. The fair value of the distributed asset is then charged against the proper capital account.

"If a farm family partnership is not salvageable, the best procedure may be to negotiate a business 'divorce' as quickly as possible. Dissolution will require a mediator or attorney and, unfortunately, it won't be cheap. Competent lawyers and mediators cost money. Still the family members' desire to save on professional fees shouldn't lock them into a waltz toward inevitable financial and emotional ruin."[5]

PRIORITIES OF PARTNERSHIP AND PERSONAL CREDITORS

The UPA (Section 15) provides that partners are jointly liable for all contracts and other obligations of the partnership. This means that creditors of a partnership that are not paid in full from distribution of partnership assets must bring legal action against all the partners together to enforce their unsettled claims. Partners are jointly and severally liable for obligations that arise out of a tort and breach of trust committed by a partner while acting within the scope of the partnership business. *Joint and several* means that legal action may be brought against all the partners together or against any one or more of the partners in separate suits. A number of states have enacted legislation eliminating the distinction, and in those jurisdictions both contract and tort actions are joint and several. This latter approach, which permits suits against all (joint) or less than all (several) of the partners, is followed in this chapter. Conversely, personal creditors of an individual partner can seek recovery of payment from personal assets of the respective partner, and under certain conditions from partnership assets. Recognition of the rights of these two groups of creditors and the classification of assets into personal and partnership categories is referred to as *marshaling of assets*. The order of priority concerning the availability of assets for each class of creditors in states that have adopted the UPA is as follows:

A. Partnership assets
  1. Partnership creditors.
  2. Personal creditors that did not recover their claims in full from personal assets. Recovery from partnership assets is limited to the extent that the partner has a credit interest in the partnership assets.
B. Personal assets
  1. Personal creditors.
  2. Partnership creditors who were not satisfied from partnership assets. Such claims may be made against an individual partner regardless of whether the partner has a debit or credit equity interest in the partnership.
  3. Claims of the partnership against the partner by nature of a deficit equity interest.

Because of the foregoing rules, the reader should recognize the importance of properly recording all partnership assets, liabilities, and capital interest of each partner.

---

[5]*Successful Farming*, Iowa edition, "Can Their Problem Be Solved?" by Donald Jonovic, May/June 1997, p. 65, copyright Meredith Corporation.

To illustrate the marshaling of assets rules, assume that ABCD Partnership reports the following balance sheet after the sale of all noncash assets:

Debits		Credits	
Cash	$ 50,000	Liabilities	$ 75,000
Bill Baker, Capital	15,000	Alice Amos, Capital	15,000
Carol Carter, Capital	35,000	Don Davis, Capital	10,000
Total	$100,000		$100,000

The partners share profits and losses equally. The personal and partnership status of each partner is as follows:

	Personal			Partnership
			Assets Greater Than (Less Than)	Capital Balance
Partner	Assets	Liabilities	Liabilities	(Cr.) Dr.
Alice Amos	$20,000	$50,000	$(30,000)	($15,000)
Bill Baker	33,000	30,000	3,000	(15,000)
Carol Carter	90,000	40,000	50,000	(35,000)
Don Davis	40,000	10,000	30,000	(10,000)

The personal assets of each partner must be applied to the settlement of his or her personal liabilities before personal assets can be used to satisfy any partnership claims. Thus, the maximum amount that the partnership creditors and other partners could recover from the personal assets is $83,000 ($3,000 + $50,000 + $30,000). Because the personal liabilities of Amos exceed her personal assets, partnership claims cannot be enforced against her personal assets even though she has a credit interest in the partnership. However, her unsettled personal creditors in the amount of $30,000 can look for full or partial settlement of their claims from final distribution of partnership assets in settlement of her capital interest. At this time, the partnership has a claim of $15,000 and $35,000 against Baker and Carter, respectively. Baker, however, will have only $3,000 left for investment in the partnership to reduce his capital deficit. Carter has sufficient personal assets to satisfy her personal liabilities and invest in the partnership to cover her share of partnership losses. Davis is personally solvent and has a credit capital interest in the partnership.

The liquidation of the partnership is summarized in Illustration 17-1. Although formal journal entries are not shown, they would be recorded in a journal in accordance with the tabular arrangement summarized in the liquidation schedule. The steps in the liquidation process may proceed in any order as long as the rights of the partners, partnership creditors, and personal creditors are recognized. In this example, the following sequence of events occurs.

1. Baker invests $3,000 in the partnership and his remaining deficit of $12,000 is a liquidation loss that is allocated to the remaining partners in their relative profit and loss ratio, one-third each. (Note that because Carter has sufficient assets to cover her share of additional losses, $4,000 loss is allocated to her, even though she currently has a deficit capital balance).
2. Cash of $53,000 is distributed to the creditors.

Marshaling of Assets

ILLUSTRATION 17–1

Schedule of Partnership Liquidation

			Capital and Loan Balances			
			Amos	*Baker*	*Carter*	*Davis*
	Cash	*Liabilities*	*1/4*	*1/4*	*1/4*	*1/4*
Balance before cash distributions	50,000	(75,000)*	(15,000)	15,000	35,000	(10,000)
Investment by Baker	3,000			(3,000)		
	53,000	(75,000)	(15,000)	12,000	35,000	(10,000)
Allocation of Baker's deficit			4,000	(12,000)	4,000	4,000
	53,000	(75,000)	(11,000)	—0—	39,000	(6,000)
Payment to creditors	(53,000)	53,000				
	—0—	(22,000)	(11,000)	—0—	39,000	(6,000)
Investment by Carter	39,000				(39,000)	
	39,000	(22,000)	(11,000)	—0—	—0—	(6,000)
Payment to creditors	(22,000)	22,000				
	17,000	—0—	(11,000)	—0—	—0—	(6,000)
Payment to partners	(17,000)		11,000			6,000
	—0—	—0—	—0—	—0—	—0—	—0—

*In this chapter ( ) means that an account has a credit balance or a credit posted to an account.

3. The partnership creditors obtain judgment against Carter. (The creditors could have proceeded to recover their claims from any solvent partner individually, including Davis, who has a credit capital interest, or from the partners jointly.) Since Carter has a personal net asset position of $50,000, she will invest an additional $39,000 in the partnership, $22,000 of which will go to partnership creditors and $17,000 to the other partners.

4. The cash is distributed first to liquidate partnership liabilities and then to satisfy partners' capital interests.

Observe that the cash distribution to partners is based on their capital balances, not their profit and loss ratio. The unpaid personal creditors of Amos have a claim against her $11,000 partnership distribution.

If, in the illustration above, Carter was able to invest only $20,000 from her personal assets and Davis was personally insolvent, then the creditors and partners Amos and Davis would have unrecoverable losses of $19,000 as shown next.

	Cash	*Liabilities*	*Amos*	*Baker*	*Carter*	*Davis*
From Illustration 17-1	—0—	(22,000)	(11,000)	—0—	39,000	(6,000)
Investment by Carter	20,000				(20,000)	
Payment to creditors	(20,000)	20,000				
	—0—	(2,000)	(11,000)	—0—	19,000	(6,000)

SIMPLE LIQUIDATION ILLUSTRATED

To illustrate the accounting for a simple liquidation, assume that the condensed balance sheet of ABC Partnership that follows was prepared just before the liquidation:

Assets, Liabilities, and Capital

Cash	$ 20,000	Liabilities	$ 70,000
Noncash Assets	180,000	Carter, Loan	10,000
		Alice Amos, Capital (50%)	80,000
		Bill Baker, Capital (30%)	30,000
		Carol Carter, Capital (20%)	10,000
Total	$200,000	Total	$200,000

The profit and loss ratio is in parentheses. Personal assets and liabilities of the partners are

	Assets	Liabilities	Net Assets
Amos	$50,000	$30,000	$20,000
Baker	40,000	12,000	28,000
Carter	20,000	25,000	(5,000)

The liquidation of the ABC Partnership is summarized in the schedule presented in Illustration 17-2. The following sequence of events recorded in Illustration 17-2 is based on the concepts that were discussed earlier:

1. Noncash assets of $180,000 are sold for $52,000 and the resulting realization loss of $128,000 is allocated to the partners according to their profit and loss ratio.

2. Partnership liabilities, other than to partners, are paid before assets are distributed to partners.

3. The right of offset is exercised where a partner with an outstanding loan has a debit capital balance.

4. In transactions (4) and (5), the principles concerning the marshaling of assets are applied to determine if additional investments can be expected. In this case,

Simple Liquidation

ILLUSTRATION 17–2

Schedule of Partnership Realization and Liquidation

					Capital Balances		
	Cash	Noncash Assets	Liabilities	Carter Loan	Amos .5	Baker .3	Carter .2
Account balances before realization	20,000	180,000	(70,000)	(10,000)	(80,000)	(30,000)	(10,000)
(1) Sale of assets and allocation of $128,000 loss	52,000	(180,000)			64,000	38,400	25,600
	72,000	—0—	(70,000)	(10,000)	(16,000)	8,400	15,600 Debit
(2) Payment to creditors	(70,000)		70,000				
	2,000	—0—	—0—	(10,000)	(16,000)	8,400	15,600 Debit
(3) Offset loan against debit capital balance				10,000			(10,000)
	2,000	—0—	—0—	—0—	(16,000)	8,400	5,600
(4) Allocate debit capital balance of insolvent partner					3,500	2,100	(5,600)
	2,000	—0—	—0—	—0—	(12,500)	10,500)	—0—
(5) Investment by Baker	10,500					(10,500)	
	12,500	—0—	—0—	—0—	(12,500)	—0—	—0—
(6) Payment to Amos	(12,500)				12,500		
	—0—	—0—	—0—	—0—	—0—	—0—	—0—

Carter with a deficit capital interest is also personally insolvent. Thus, her deficit is allocated to the other partners on the basis of their relative loss-sharing ratio: to Amos, to Baker.

5. Baker invests $10,500 in the partnership to eliminate his deficit after his personal assets were applied to the settlement of his personal liabilities.

6. Cash is distributed to Amos to satisfy her capital claim against the partnership assets.

INSTALLMENT LIQUIDATION → traditional (method)

In the preceding section, all the noncash assets were converted into cash and the resulting gain or loss allocated before any distribution was made to the creditors and to the partners. It could be an advantage to the partnership, however, if conversion of noncash assets into cash were extended over several months. For example, in certain types of businesses, such as land development, more cash may be generated if the company completes construction projects it has started, or, as is frequently the case, the partnership may receive a greater cash price for the noncash assets if they are not sold at a forced liquidation. If the liquidation extends over a period of time, the partners will probably prefer that cash be distributed as it becomes available. If partners are to receive cash in installments before the total liquidation losses and the total cash available are known, safeguards must be taken to protect the interests of the creditors and the respective interest of each partner. In addition, the individual in charge of the liquidation must use safeguards to avoid potential liability for wrongful distributions. The remainder of this chapter focuses on the problems associated with a liquidation in installments and the general rules governing such liquidations. Once again, many of the procedures followed are necessary to satisfy legal requirements and for the protection of the person in charge of the liquidation and the residual partners' interests.

Safe Payment Approach

In computing how cash is to be distributed to the partners before all assets are disposed of, care must be taken to ensure that the partners' remaining capital balances will be adequate to absorb any potential loss. However, at this point, the amount of cash to be generated from the sale of noncash assets and the resulting gain or loss is not known. Therefore, the partners should view each cash distribution as if it were the final distribution.

One approach used to calculate a safe cash distribution is based on three assumptions:

1. A loan to or from an individual partner will be combined with the respective partner's capital account to determine his or her net interest in the partnership assets.

2. The remaining noncash assets will not provide any additional cash. In other words, the maximum potential loss is equal to the book value of noncash assets. (This assumption will be modified later in the chapter.)

3. A partner with a debit balance in his or her capital account will be unable to pay amounts owed to the partnership (that is, each partner is personally insolvent).

The result of applying these assumptions is that cash will not be distributed to a partner whose capital account balance (including loan balance and drawing account) is insufficient to absorb his or her share of potential losses either from the write-off of assets or from the failure of a deficit partner to cover a debit capital balance. Of course, no partner should receive cash until the liabilities have been liquidated or provided for through the retention of adequate cash.

Computation of Safe Payment Before Each Distribution To illustrate the safe payment approach when a partnership is liquidated in installments, assume that the following condensed balance sheet was prepared before the partners' agreement to liquidate the partnership.

Cash	$ 10,000	Liabilities	$ 28,000
Noncash Assets	100,000	Alice Amos, Capital (30%)	34,000
		Bill Baker, Capital (50%)	30,000
		Carol Carter, Capital (20%)	18,000
Total	$110,000	Total	$110,000

The partners' income- and loss-sharing percentages are stated in parentheses. The noncash assets were converted into cash over a period of time as follows:

	Sales Price	Book Value	(Loss)
Sale No. 1	$20,000	$30,000	(10,000)
Sale No. 2	15,000	25,000	(10,000)
Sale No. 3	10,000	30,000	(20,000)
Sale No. 4	2,000	10,000	(8,000)
Sale No. 5	—0—	5,000	(5,000)

The realization of the partnership assets and liquidation of the partnership are summarized in Illustration 17-3. A safe payment schedule is prepared *each time cash is to be distributed.* After the first sale of assets and all creditors have been paid, $2,000 cash remains to be distributed to partners. Schedule I in Illustration 17-3 demonstrates how the $2,000 will be distributed. In this case, the assumption that the remaining noncash assets of $70,000 are worthless results in a debit balance in Baker's capital account. Another assumption is that all partners are personally insolvent. Therefore, the hypothetical deficit is allocated to the remaining partners with credit balances on the basis of their relative profit and loss ratio: 3/5 to Amos, 2/5 to Carter. This allocation results in a hypothetical debit balance in the capital account of Carter, which is assigned to Amos. Thus, if $2,000 is paid to Amos, this will leave her with a capital balance sufficient to absorb her share of the potential remaining losses. Amos will not be required to make an additional investment in the partnership unless significant amounts of unrecorded liabilities are discovered or significant amounts of liquidation expenses are incurred. But if it became necessary for Amos to make an additional investment, the other two partners would also be required to do so.

After the second sale of assets, $15,000 cash is available for distribution. The allocation of the $15,000 is shown in schedule II of Illustration 17-3. Note that, if the fair value of the remaining assets is zero, Baker's capital balance of $20,000 would be inadequate to absorb his share of the losses, which would be $22,500 ($45,000 × .50). Accordingly, at this time, Baker does not receive any of the cash to be distributed, since he could end up with a debit capital balance. After the third

ILLUSTRATION 17–3

Schedule of Partnership Realization and Liquidation
Installment Liquidation

	Cash	Other Assets	Liabilities	Capital and Loan Balances Amos .3	Baker .5	Carter .2
Balance before realization	10,000	100,000	(28,000)	(34,000)	(30,000)	(18,000)
Sale of assets	20,000	(30,000)		3,000	5,000	2,000
	30,000	70,000	(28,000)	(31,000)	(25,000)	(16,000)
Payment to creditors	(28,000)		28,000			
	2,000	70,000	—0—	(31,000)	(25,000)	(16,000)
Payment to partners						
Safe payment Schedule I (below)	(2,000)			2,000		
	—0—	70,000	—0—	(29,000)	(25,000)	(16,000)
Sale of assets	15,000	(25,000)		3,000	5,000	2,000
	15,000	45,000	—0—	(26,000)	(20,000)	(14,000)
Payment to partners						
Safe payment Schedule II (below)	(15,000)			11,000		4,000
	—0—	45,000	—0—	(15,000)	(20,000)	(10,000)
Sale of assets	10,000	(30,000)		6,000	10,000	4,000
	10,000	15,000	—0—	(9,000)	(10,000)	(6,000)
Payment to partners						
Safe payment Schedule III (below)	(10,000)			4,500	2,500	3,000
	—0—	15,000	—0—	(4,500)	(7,500)	(3,000)
Sale of assets	2,000	(10,000)		2,400	4,000	1,600
	2,000	5,000	—0—	(2,100)	(3,500)	(1,400)
Payment to partners	(2,000)			600	1,000	400
	—0—	5,000	—0—	(1,500)	(2,500)	(1,000)
Write-off of assets		(5,000)		1,500	2,500	1,000
	—0—	—0—	—0—	—0—	—0—	—0—

Schedule I
Computation of Safe Payments

[handwritten: It is done each month]

[handwritten: possible event]

	Amos .3	Baker .5	Carter .2
Capital and loan balances	(31,000)	(25,000)	(16,000)
Allocation of potential loss—$70,000	21,000	35,000	14,000
	(10,000)	10,000	(2,000)
Allocation of Baker's potential deficit	6,000	(10,000)	4,000
	(4,000)	—0—	2,000
Allocation of Carter's potential deficit	2,000		(2,000)
Safe payment	(2,000)	—0—	—0—

[handwritten: Credit balance is in brackets]

Schedule II
Computation of Safe Payments

	Amos .3	Baker .5	Carter .2
Capital and loan balances	(26,000)	(20,000)	(14,000)
Allocation of potential loss—$45,000	13,500	22,500	9,000
	(12,500)	2,500	(5,000)
Allocation of Baker's potential deficit	1,500	(2,500)	1,000
Safe payment	(11,000)	—0—	(4,000)

Schedule III
Computation of Safe Payments

	Amos .3	Baker .5	Carter .2
Capital and loan balances	(9,000)	(10,000)	(6,000)
Allocation of potential loss—$15,000	4,500	7,500	3,000
Safe payment	(4,500)	(2,500)	(3,000)

[handwritten: Credit balance]

cash distribution, the partners'/ capital balances are in their profit and loss ratio of $3:5:2$. Once their capital interests are in the profit and loss ratio, any subsequent distribution of assets will be based on the profit and loss ratio. Note that each partner's capital account is now sufficient to absorb the final potential loss of $5,000.

A safe payment schedule is prepared to compute the amount of cash to be distributed and to determine which partner(s) will receive cash. The series of computations is not recorded in the accounts, since they are based on certain assumed events that have not yet occurred. Only the actual transactions as they occur, such as the sale of assets and distribution of cash, are recorded in the accounts.

Additional Losses, Discovery of Liabilities, and Liquidation Expense Up to this point in this chapter, all available cash was distributed to (1) the partnership's creditors who were recorded on the partnership books or (2) the partners. In the calculation of a safe payment, it was assumed that the potential loss was equal to the book value of the remaining noncash assets. In addition, no liquidation expenses were incurred. As the liquidation proceeds, some liabilities that had not been recorded previously may be reported. These creditors have claims that must be satisfied from the available cash before payments are made to partners for their capital interest.

Certain expenses, such as the reasonable cost of carrying out the liquidation, have priority over payments to creditors. Furthermore, the disposal cost of assets may exceed the proceeds from the sale of the assets so that the resulting loss is greater than the assets' recorded book value. Such items can be considered in the safe payment schedule by adding the estimated liquidation expenses, disposal cost, and unrecorded liabilities to the book value of noncash assets. To illustrate, assume the facts presented in Illustration 17-3 except that it is estimated that added expenses of $1,000 will be incurred in completing the liquidation. The safe payment calculation for the first cash distribution would be modified as follows:

	Amos	*Baker*	*Carter*
Capital and loan balances	(31,000)	(25,000)	(16,000)
Allocation of potential losses ($70,000 + $1,000)	21,300	35,500	14,200
Balances	(9,700)	10,500	(1,800)
Allocation of Baker's potential deficit	6,300	(10,500)	4,200
Balances	(3,400)	—0—	2,400
Allocation of Carter's potential deficit	2,400		(2,400)
Safe payment	(1,000)	—0—	—0—

As can be seen, the effect of the adjustment is to hold back cash equal to the estimated expenses, which results in a corresponding reduction in the cash distributed to Amos.

Advance Plan for the Distribution of Cash

In the preceding illustration, a safe payment to each partner was calculated before each cash distribution. This process was necessary until the capital accounts were in the profit- and loss-sharing ratio. Although this method is feasible, it is more informative and efficient to prepare an advance schedule that specifies the order in which each partner will participate and the amount of cash each partner will receive as it becomes available for distribution. For example, from such a schedule, the personal creditors of an insolvent partner would be able to compute how much cash would have to be generated from the sale of the partnership assets before any cash is distributed to the insolvent partner.

To illustrate the procedures for the preparation of an advance cash distribution plan, assume the set of facts employed in Illustration 17-3. The objective of the procedure is to derive the order and the amount of cash that should be distributed to each partner such that no partner receiving a cash distribution will have to make an additional investment in the firm. Such a distribution plan will bring the balances of the partners' capital accounts into their profit and loss ratio as soon as possible. The rationale for this procedure is that once the capital balances are in the profit and loss ratio, no one partner is in any better position than any other partner to absorb losses.

ILLUSTRATION 17–4

Preparation of an Advance Plan for the Distribution of Cash

Step 1	Amos	Baker	Carter
Capital balances	$ 34,000	$ 30,000	$18,000
Loan balances	—	—	—
Net capital interest	$ 34,000	$ 30,000	$18,000
Profit and loss ratio	.30	.50	.20

Step 2			
Loss necessary to reduce net capital balance to zero	$113,333	$ 60,000	$90,000
Order of cash distribution	1	3	2

		Loss Absorption Potential			Asset Distribution		
Step 3		Amos	Baker	Carter	Amos	Baker	Carter
Profit and loss ratio		.30	.50	.20	.30	.50	.20
Loss absorption potential		$113,333	$60,000	$90,000			
Net capital interest					$34,000	$30,000	18,000
Distribution to Amos to reduce her capital interest so that her loss absorption potential is the same as Carter's ($111,333 − $90,000 = $23,333) × .30		23,333			7,000		
Balances after distribution to Amos		90,000	60,000	90,000	27,000	30,000	18,000
Distribution to Amos and Carter to reduce their capital interest so that their loss absorption potential is the same as Baker's ($90,000 − $60,000 = $30,000) × .30 ($90,000 − $60,000 = $30,000) × .20		30,000		30,000	9,000		6,000
Balances after distribution to Amos and Carter		60,000	60,000	60,000	18,000	30,000	12,000
Remainder of asset distributions					.30	.50	.20

Step 4				
	Cash Distribution Plan			
Order of Cash Distribution	Liabilities	Amos .3	Baker .5	Carter .2
1. First $28,000	100%			
2. Next $7,000		100%		
3. Next $15,000		60%		40%
4. Remainder		30%	50%	20%

Steps in the development of an advance cash distribution plan are presented in Illustration 17-4 and explained below.

Step 1 Determine the net capital interest of each partner by combining the balance in the partner's capital account with obligations to or receivables from the partner.

	Amos	Baker	Carter
Capital balance	$34,000	$30,000	$18,000
Loan balance	—0—	—0—	—0—
Net capital interest	$34,000	$30,000	$18,000

Step 2 Determine the order in which the partners are to participate in cash distributions. The objective of this step is to provide an order of cash distribution in which the ratio of the partners' capital interest will eventually be equal to their profit and loss ratio. Once this is accomplished, all partners will have an equal ability to absorb their share of partnership losses. Several approaches can be used to accomplish this objective. One systematic approach is to determine the loss absorption potential of each partner by dividing the net capital interest of each partner by his or her respective profit and loss ratio.

	Amos	Baker	Carter
Net capital interest	$ 34,000	$30,000	$18,000
Profit and loss ratio	.30	.50	.20
Loss absorption potential	$113,333	$60,000	$90,000
Order of cash distribution	1	3	2

This computation determines the maximum amount of loss each partner is capable of absorbing and provides a basis for ranking the partners in terms of each partner's capital interest relative to his or her loss ratio. The partner with the largest loss absorption potential has the ability to absorb a greater share of losses before his or her capital account would be reduced to a zero balance. Thus, Amos will receive the first distribution of assets after the creditors' claims have been satisfied. The partner with the lowest loss absorption potential (Baker) will be the last partner to participate in the distribution of assets from the partnership.

Step 3 In Step 2, the order in which each partner is to participate in cash distributions was determined. The next step is to compute the amount of cash each partner is to receive as it becomes available for distribution. The objective is to determine the *amount* of cash to distribute to each partner to bring the ratios of their capital interests in the partnership into alignment with their profit and loss ratios. One way to do this is to consider the loss absorption potential computed in Step 2. It was determined in Step 2 that Amos is in the strongest position relative to the other partners and is to receive the first cash distribution. Amos is capable of absorbing her share of $113,333 in losses, which is $23,333 greater than the loss potential of Carter ($113,333 − $90,000), who is the next partner to participate in cash distributions. However, Amos must absorb only 30% or $7,000 ($23,333 × .30) of such potential losses. Thus, a payment to Amos of $7,000 reduces her loss absorption potential to Carter's (the next closest loss potential) level ($34,000 − $7,000 = $27,000/.30 = $90,000). Amos and Carter now have the same absorption potential for future losses. Also, note that a payment of $7,000 to Amos brings her capital interest into a ratio of $3:2$ to that of Carter ($27,000:$18,000), which is the same as their relative profit and loss ratio.

The next step in the process is to bring the loss absorption potential of Amos and Carter into balance with that of Baker, who is the last partner to participate in the distribution of cash. Using the same rationale, Amos and Carter are now capable of absorbing losses of $30,000 ($90,000 − $60,000) greater than Baker. Since they must absorb 30% and 20% of the losses, respectively, the distribution to each partner is computed as follows:

$$\text{To Amos:}\quad \$30,000 \times .30 = \$9,000$$
$$\text{To Carter:}\quad \$30,000 \times .20 = \$6,000$$

Of the next $15,000, Amos is to receive $9,000 and Carter is to receive $6,000. Now all partners' capital balances are in the same ratio as their profit and loss sharing ratio.[6]

Step 4 A cash distribution plan is then prepared as follows:

Order of Cash Distribution	Liabilities	Amos	Baker	Carter
1. First $28,000	100%			
2. Next $7,000		100%		
3. Next $15,000		60%		40%
4. Remainder		30%	50%	20%

The first $28,000 available is, of course, paid to the creditors. Cash may be held back from distribution if it is anticipated that unrecorded liabilities will be discovered or if additional liquidation expenses will be incurred. The distribution of cash

------

[6]An alternative method of determining the amount to be distributed at each level is to compute the capital account balances needed by each partner so as to bring the partners' capital balances into their agreed profit- and loss-sharing ratio. This approach is simpler in certain cases, but the approach in the text is more systematic when there are numerous partners. The alternative works by bringing the ratio of the partners' capital account balances into their profit- and loss-sharing ratio in the order in which the partners are to participate in the distribution. In this case, the first step is to compute what the capital account balance of Amos should be so that her capital balance is in the profit- and loss-sharing ratio with that of Carter ($3:2$). This can be computed as follows:

$$\text{Let } X = \text{desired capital balance}$$
$$\frac{\text{Loss ratio of Amos}}{\text{Loss ratio of Carter}} = \frac{X}{\text{Capital balance of Carter}}$$
$$\frac{3}{2} = \frac{X}{\$18,000}$$
$$2X = \$54,000$$
$$X = \$27,000$$

Since Amos has a capital balance of $34,000, it would take a distribution of $7,000 to reduce the balance to $27,000. The next level of payments should reduce the capital balances of Amos and Carter in such a way that their capital balances will be in the loss ratio to that of Baker, which is $3:5$ and $2:5$, respectively.

$$\frac{3}{5} = \frac{X}{\$30,000} \qquad \frac{2}{5} = \frac{X}{\$30,000}$$
$$5X = \$90,000 \qquad 5X = \$60,000$$
$$X = \$18,000 \qquad X = \$12,000$$

A distribution of $9,000 to Amos ($27,000 − $18,000) and $6,000 to Carter ($18,000 − $12,000) will produce capital balances in the ratio of $3:5:2$ ($18,000: $30,0000: $12,000).

in excess of this reserve amount proceeds as determined. Amos will receive all of any additional cash up to $7,000. Additional cash in excess of $7,000 and up to $22,000 is distributed 60:40 to Amos and Carter. After $22,000 ($15,000 + $7,000) has been distributed to the partners, the capital accounts are in the desired profit and loss ratio of 3:5:2. Any further distributions to the partners are made in the profit and loss ratio.

The advance distribution plan developed before will yield the same cash distribution as the process of computing a safe payment each time cash is available. As proof, in Illustration 17-5, the advance plan for distributing cash as developed in Illustration 17-4 is applied to determine the cash distribution in Illustration 17-3. Even though both methods produce the same results, the advance plan is more informative to creditors, both personal and partnership, and to the partners, because the interested parties now know the order in which individual partners will receive cash and the amounts that each may receive at each stage of the distribution process.

One requirement that must be satisfied in the development of the advance plan is that the partners must share income in the same ratio that they share losses. If this were not the case, a new loss potential amount would need to be computed after every allocation to the partners' capital accounts. This occurs because the allocation of liquidation gains alters the order of cash distribution computed in the advance plan. To illustrate, assume that Amos, Baker, and Carter, with capital balances of $45,000, $24,000, and $20,000, respectively, share losses in the ratio of 5:3:2, but share income in the ratio of 3:5:2. The order of cash distribution based on the ratio of losses would be as follows:

	Amos	Baker	Carter
Net capital interest	$45,000	$24,000	$ 20,000
Loss ratios	.50	.30	.20
Loss absorption potential	$90,000	$80,000	$100,000
Order of cash distribution	2	3	1

ILLUSTRATION 17–5

Cash Distribution per Advance Plan

	Liabilities	Amos	Baker	Carter	Total
First Distribution: $30,000					
First—$28,000	$28,000				$28,000
Next—$2,000		$2,000			2,000
	$28,000	$2,000	—	—	$30,000
Second Distribution: $15,000					
First—$5,000					
(Remainder of $7,000 level)		$ 5,000			$ 5,000
Next—$10,000		6,000		$4,000	10,000
	—	$11,000	—	$4,000	$15,000
Third Distribution: $10,000					
First—$5,000					
(Remainder of $15,000 level)		$ 3,000		$2,000	$ 5,000
Next—$5,000		1,500	$2,500	1,000	5,000
	—	$ 4,500	$2,500	$3,000	$10,000
Last Distribution: $2,000					
First—$2,000	—	$ 600	$1,000	$ 400	$ 2,000

Now assume that the partnership realizes a $50,000 gain. The allocation of the gain in the ratio of $3:5:2$ and computation of the order of cash distribution follow:

	Amos	Baker	Carter
Net capital interest	$(45,000)	$(24,000)	$(20,000)
Allocation of $50,000 gain	(15,000)	(25,000)	(10,000)
Net capital interest	$(60,000)	$(49,000)	$(30,000)
Loss ratios	.50	.30	.20
New loss absorption potential	$120,000	$163,333	$150,000
New order of cash distribution	3	1	2

In this illustration an allocation of the $50,000 gain moved Baker from being the last partner to receive cash to being the first partner to receive cash.

It is also necessary to recompute an advance plan if a certain classification of losses is shared in a different ratio from the one used in preparing the advance plan, or if adjustments are made to the capital balances in other than the loss ratio. For example, assume that it has been discovered that a cash withdrawal by a partner had been expensed instead of debited to his drawing account. The correction of the error would modify the loss absorption potential of that partner. If such adjustments occur frequently, then the computation of a safe payment may be less time-consuming and easier to use than the development of an advance cash distribution plan.

INCORPORATION OF A PARTNERSHIP

After a partnership has been operating for a period of time, the partners may find that the partnership form of business is no longer satisfactory. The corporation, with its limited liability, continuity of existence, and ability to raise needed resources, may become more attractive. Upon incorporation, the assets and liabilities are transferred to the corporation and the partners receive capital stock in settlement of their interests. The partnership accounts should be restated to fair values to assure that the partners receive an equitable distribution of stock for their interests.

The partnership books may be retained for use by the corporation, or a new set of books may be established.

Retention of Partnership Books by Corporation

Assuming that the partnership books are used by the corporation, the steps to record the incorporation are as follows:

1. Assets and liabilities are adjusted to fair value. Frequently, a valuation adjustment account is created to accumulate the gains and losses.

2. The valuation adjustment account is closed to the partners' capital accounts in accordance with their profit and loss ratio.

3. The partners' capital accounts are closed upon the transfer of capital stock. Since the books are retained, offsetting credits are made to Capital Stock at par value for the number of shares issued. If the debit to partners' capital accounts exceeds the credit to Capital Stock, the difference is a credit to Additional Paid-in Capital.

To illustrate, assume that AB Partnership is to incorporate. The new corporation is authorized to issue 5,000 shares of $10 par value stock. Book values of the partnership accounts and fair values for the assets are determined to be:

| | Book Value | | Fair Values |
	Debit	Credit	
Cash	$ 5,000		$ 5,000
Accounts Receivable	4,000		3,600
Inventory	5,000		7,000
Land	10,000		15,000
Equipment (net of depreciation)	6,000		5,000
Accounts Payable		$ 7,000	
Notes Payable		10,000	
Art, Capital		8,000	
Beck, Capital		5,000	
Total	$30,000	$30,000	

Other facts are: (1) Liabilities are assumed to be fairly valued; (2) Art and Beck share profits equally; (3) Art and Beck are to receive par value stock equal to their adjusted ending capital balances. The journal entries to incorporate are:

(1)	Inventory	2,000	
	Land	5,000	
	Equipment		1,000
	Accounts Receivable		400
	Valuation Adjustment		5,600
(2)	Valuation Adjustment	5,600	
	Art, Capital		2,800
	Beck, Capital		2,800
(3)	Art, Capital	10,800	
	Beck, Capital	7,800	
	Capital Stock—$10 par		18,600

New Books Established by Corporation

If the corporation establishes a new set of books, then all accounts on the partnership books will end with a zero balance. The only difference as compared to the illustration above is that on receipt of the stock, asset and liability accounts are closed on the partnership books and transferred to the corporation. To balance the entry, an asset account is created for the capital stock received in the amount of $18,600. This balance should also equal the sum of the balances in the remaining capital accounts. The entry to record the distribution of the capital stock is:

Art, Capital	10,800	
Beck, Capital	7,800	
Capital Stock (from Corporation)		18,600

The corporation records the assets received and the liabilities assumed on the new books at the net cost of the stock issued ($18,600), which is also equal to the adjusted value of the net assets on the partnership books. A credit of $18,600 to balance the entry is made to capital stock issued.

SUMMARY

1. *Describe the steps used to distribute available partnership assets in liquidation under the Uniform Partnership Act (UPA).* The first step in the liquidation process is to compute any net income or loss up to the date of dissolution. The closing process should be completed and any net income or loss allocated to the partners in accordance with their profit and loss agreement. Next the assets that are not acceptable for distribution in their present form are converted into cash, and any gains or losses realized are allocated as specified in the partnership agreement (usually according to the profit and loss ratio). Finally, the available assets are distributed to creditors and partners.

2. *List the order of priority for each class of creditors in partnership liquidation under the UPA.* The liabilities are settled in the following order: (1) those owing to creditors other than partners, (2) those owing to partners other than for capital and profits, (3) those owing to partners in respect to capital, and (4) those owing to partners in respect to profits.

3. *Prepare a liquation schedule to settle debts and allocate assets.* The liquidation schedule begins with a listing, generally in columns, of the partnership's assets, liabilities, and partners' capital balances. Any additional investments made by individual partners are recorded first, including those made by partners with debit balances and those resulting from a judgment of partnership creditors against individual partners. Cash is distributed first to liquidate partnership liabilities and then to satisfy partners' capital interests. The cash distribution is based on the partners' capital balances, not their profit and loss ratios.

4. *Prepare a "safe payment approach" liquidation schedule.* To calculate a safe cash distribution, the following three assumptions may be made: (1) A loan to or from an individual partner is combined with the part-

ner's capital balance to determine his or her interest in the partnership assets. (2) The remaining noncash assets will not provide any additional cash (the worst-case scenario). (3) Any partner with a debit balance is assumed unable to pay the amounts owed to the partnership. The result of applying these assumptions is that cash will not be distributed to any partner whose capital balance is insufficient to absorb his or her share of potential losses.

5. *Describe the four steps in the preparation of an advance plan for the distribution of cash in a partnership liquidation.* Determine the net capital interest of each partner by combining the balance in the partner's capital account with any obligations to, or receivables from, that partner. Determine the order in which the partners are to participate in cash distributions. Compute the amount of cash each partner is to receive as it becomes available for distribution. Prepare a cash distribution plan. This plan will yield the same distribution as a safe payment plan computed each time cash becomes available, but it is more informative to both creditors and partners, as they know the plan in advance.

6. *Prepare the journal entries to incorporate a partnership.* Assets and liabilities are adjusted to fair values, often using a valuation adjustment account to accumulate gains and losses. The valuation adjustment account (or gains/losses) is closed to the partners' capital accounts in accordance with their profit and loss ratios. The partners' capital accounts are closed upon the transfer of capital stock. Since the books are retained, offsetting credits are made to the capital stock account at par for the number of shares issued. If the debit to partners' capital accounts is greater than the credit to the capital stock account, the difference is credited to additional paid-in capital.

QUESTIONS

1. Why are realization gains or losses allocated to partners in their profit and loss ratios?

2. In what manner should the final cash distribution be made in partnership liquidation?

3. Why does a debit balance in a partners' capital account create problems in the UPA order of payment for a partnership liquidation?

4. Is it important to maintain separate accounts for a partner's outstanding loan and capital accounts? Explain why or why not.

5. Discuss the possible outcomes in the situation

where the equity interest of one partner is inadequate to absorb realization losses.

6. During a liquidation, at which point may cash be distributed to any of the partners?

7. What is "marshaling of assets"?

8. To what extent can personal creditors seek recovery from partnership assets?

9. In an installment liquidation, why should the partners view each cash distribution as if it were the final distribution?

10. Discuss the three basic assumptions necessary for calculating a safe cash distribution. How is this safe cash distribution computed?

11. How are unexpected costs such as liquidation expenses, disposal costs, or unrecorded liabilities covered in the safe distribution schedule?

12. What is the objective of the procedures used for the preparation of an advance cash distribution plan?

13. What is the "loss absorption potential"?

14. In what order must partnership assets be distributed?

EXERCISES

EXERCISE 17-1 Simple Liquidation

The CPA Partnership operated by Cook, Parks, and Argo is being liquidated. A balance sheet prepared at this stage in their liquidation process is presented below.

Cash	$40,000	Liabilities	$25,000
Other Assets	50,000	Parks, Loan	10,000
		Cook, Capital	30,000
		Parks, Capital	10,000
		Argo, Capital	15,000
Total	$90,000	Total	$90,000

The partners share profits and losses 30% (Cook), 50% (Parks), and 20% (Argo). The partners are all personally insolvent.

Required:

A. The partners wish to distribute the $40,000 in cash. Record in journal entry form the distribution of the available cash.

B. Record in journal entry form the completion of the liquidation process, assuming that the other assets of $50,000 are sold for $15,000.

EXERCISE 17-2 Simple Liquidation

John, Jake, and Joe are partners with capital accounts of $90,000, $78,000, and $64,000 respectively. They share profits and loses in the ratio of 30:40:30. When the partners decide to liquidate, the business has $70,000 in cash, noncash assets totaling $260,000, and $98,000 in liabilities. The noncash assets are sold for $270,000, and the creditors are paid.

Required:

A. Prepare a schedule of partnership liquidation.

B. Prepare journal entries to record each of the following transactions.
   (1) The sale of the noncash assets.
   (2) The payment to the creditors.
   (3) The distribution of cash to the partners.

EXERCISE 17-3 Cash Distribution Schedule

The unsuccessful partnership of the Jones Brothers is about to undergo liquidation. They have asked you to estimate the amount of cash that each brother will receive. They share profits and losses equally.

Cash	$ 22,000	Liabilities	$ 35,000
Noncash Assets	110,000	Doug, Capital	55,000
		Dave, Capital	50,000
		Dan, Capital	(8,000)
	$132,000		$132,000

Both Doug and Dave are personally solvent, but Dan is not. They estimate that they will receive $65,000 from the sale of the noncash assets.

Required:
Prepare a schedule to estimate the amount of cash each brother will receive.

EXERCISE 17-4 Cash Distribution Schedule

The ABC Partnership is in the process of liquidation. The account balances prior to liquidation are given below:

Debits		Credits	
Cash	$ 72,000	Liabilities	$ 40,000
Amos, Drawing	10,000	Boone, Loan	8,000
Boone, Drawing	15,000	Childs, Loan	25,000
Childs, Drawing	20,000	Amos, Capital	49,000
Operating Loss	21,000	Boone, Capital	18,000
Liquidation Loss	12,000	Childs, Capital	10,000
	$150,000		$150,000

The partners share profits in the following ratio: Amos, 1/5; Boone, 2/5; Childs, 2/5.

Required:
Prepare a schedule showing the calculations of the distribution of cash under the Uniform Partnership Act, assuming that all three partners have personal liabilities in excess of their personal assets.

EXERCISE 17-5 Partnership Liquidation—Safe Payment Approach

Following is the balance sheet of the BDO Partnership:

Cash	$ 10,000	Liabilities	$ 18,000
Accounts Receivable	40,000	Brink, Capital	45,000
Inventory	30,000	Davis, Capital	27,000
Equipment	60,000	Olsen, Capital	50,000
	$140,000		$140,000

The partners share income 40:40:20, respectively. Assume that 70% of the receivables are collected and that inventory with a book value of $15,000 is sold for $10,000. All cash available at this time is to be distributed.

Required:
Determine the proper distribution of cash, using the safe payment approach.

EXERCISE 17-6 Partnership Liquidation with Personal Asset Information

Pete, Tom, and Zack have operated a laundromat for 10 years. The partners, who share profits 4:3:3, respectively, decide to liquidate the partnership. The firm's balance sheet just before the partners sell the other assets for $30,000 is as follows:

Assets		Liabilities and Capital	
Cash	$ 15,000	Liabilities	$ 42,000
Other Assets	110,000	Pete, Capital	55,000
		Tom, Capital	14,000
		Zack, Capital	14,000
	$125,000		$125,000

The personal status of each partner just before liquidation is as follows:

	Personal Assets	Personal Liabilities
Pete	$55,000	$80,000
Tom	30,000	10,000
Zack	30,000	50,000

The partnership operates in a state that has adopted the Uniform Partnership Act.

Required:
A. Determine the amount of cash each partner will receive in liquidation and how much cash each partner must invest in the firm, given their personal positions.
B. Determine the amounts that the personal creditors will receive from personal assets and any distribution from the partnership.

EXERCISE 17-7 **Multiple Choice**

Select the best answer for each of the following items:

1. In accordance with the marshaling of assets provision of the Uniform Partnership Act, rank the following liabilities of a partnership in order of payment.
   (1) $20,000 loan from B. Barry who is a partner.
   (2) $30,000 of profits from the last year of operations.
   (3) $3,000 payable to a supplier.
   (4) $100,000 in capital balances of the partners.
   (a) 2,3,4,1.
   (b) 4,2,1,3.
   (c) 3,1,4,2.
   (d) 3,1,2,4.

2. Personal assets are first allocated to partnership creditors and then to personal creditors.
   (a) This statement is true.
   (b) True if partner has debit balance in his/her capital account.
   (c) This statement is false.

3. The following condensed balance sheet is presented for the partnership of Lisa, Lori, and Lucy, who share profits and losses in the ratio of 5:3:2, respectively:

Cash	$ 80,000	Liabilities	$140,000
Other Assets	280,000	Lisa, Capital	100,000
		Lori, Capital	100,000
		Lucy, Capital	20,000
Total	$360,000	Total	$360,000

The partners agreed to liquidate the partnership after selling the other assets. If the other assets are sold for $160,000, how much should Lisa receive upon liquidation?
   (a) $37,500
   (b) $38,500
   (c) $40,000
   (d) $100,000.

Questions 4 and 5 are based on the following balance sheet for the partnership of Allen, Bob, and Cecil:

Cash	$ 20,000	Liabilities	$ 50,000
Other Assets	180,000	Allen, Capital (40%)	37,000
		Bob, Capital (30%)	65,000
		Cecil, Capital (30%)	48,000
	$200,000		$200,000

Figures shown parenthetically reflect agreed profit and loss sharing percentages.

4. If the firm, as shown on the original balance sheet, is dissolved and liquidated by selling assets in installments, the first sale of noncash assets having a book value of $90,000 realizes $50,000, and all cash available after settlement with creditors is distributed, the respective partners would receive (to the nearest dollar)
   (a) Allen, $8,000; Bob, $6,000; Cecil, $6,000.
   (b) Allen, $6,667; Bob, $6,667; Cecil, $6,666.
   (c) Allen, $0; Bob, $10,000; Cecil, $10,000.
   (d) Allen, $0; Bob, $18,500; Cecil, $1,500.

5. If the facts are as in item 4 above except that $3,000 cash is to be withheld, the respective partners would then receive (to the nearest dollar)
   (a) Allen, $6,800; Bob, $5,100, Cecil, $5,100.
   (b) Allen, $5,667; Bob, $5,667; Cecil, $5,666.
   (c) Allen, $0; Bob, $8,500; Cecil, $8,500.
   (d) Allen, $0; Bob, $17,000; Cecil, $0.

(AICPA adapted)

EXERCISE 17-8 Multiple Choice

Select the best answer for each of the following items. Questions 1 and 2 are based on the following condensed balance sheet for the partnership of Caine, Davis, and Jones.

Cash	$ 90,000	Accounts Payable	$220,000
Other Assets	820,000	Jones, Loan	40,000
Caine, Receivable	40,000	Caine, Capital	300,000
		Davis, Capital	200,000
		Jones, Capital	190,000
Total	$950,000	Total	$950,000

The partners share income and loss in the ratio of 5:3:2, respectively.

1. Assume that the assets and liabilities are fairly valued in the balance sheet and the partnership decides to admit Kuman as a new partner with a one-fourth capital interest. No goodwill or bonus is to be recorded. How much should Kuman invest in cash or other assets?
   (a) $172,500.
   (b) $175,000.
   (c) $230,000.
   (d) $233,333.

2. Assume that instead of admitting a new partner, the partners decide to liquidate the partnership. If the other assets are sold for $600,000, how much of the available cash should be distributed to Caine?
   (a) $170,000.
   (b) $150,000.
   (c) $190,000.
   (d) $300,000.

3. A, B, C, and D are partners sharing profits and losses equally. The partnership is insolvent and is to be liquidated. The status of the partnership and each partner is as follows:

	Partnership Capital Balance	Personal Assets (Exclusive of Partnership Interest)	Personal Liabilities (Exclusive of Partnership Interest)
A	$15,000 Credit	$100,000	$40,000
B	10,000 Credit	30,000	60,000
C	20,000 Debit	80,000	5,000
D	30,000 Debit	1,000	28,000

Assuming the Uniform Partnership Act applies, the partnership creditors
(a) Must first seek recovery against C because he is personally solvent and he has a negative capital balance.
(b) Will not be paid in full regardless of how they proceed legally because the partnership assets are less than the claims of the partnership creditors.
(c) Will have to share B's interest in the partnership on a pro-rata basis with B's personal creditors.
(d) Have first claim to the partnership assets before any partner's personal creditors have rights to the partnership assets.

4. If a partner with a debit capital balance during liquidation is insolvent, the following results:
(a) The partner must borrow money to invest in the partnership.
(b) The partnership will give the partner cash to the extent of the partners' debit balance.
(c) The partner's debit balance will be allocated to the other partners.
(d) None of the above.

5. If a partnership is undergoing a transformation to a corporation, which of the following is a result?
(a) Assets and liabilities are adjusted to fair value.
(b) The net assets are distributed to the partners in their profit and loss ratio.
(c) The partners receive stock in the new corporation.
(d) Both (a) and (c) are correct.

EXERCISE 17-9 **Multiple Choice**
Q, R, S, and T are partners, sharing profits and losses 40% : 20% : 20% : 20%, respectively. After sale of firm assets and payment of the available cash to the partnership creditors, a partnership trial balance and the personal status of each partner are as follows:

	Partnership Trial Balance		Personal Status Exclusive of Partnership Interest		
	Debit	Credit	Partner	Assets	Liabilities
Creditors		$ 2,000			
Q, Capital		500	Q	$15,000	$10,000
R, Capital		7,500	R	8,000	20,000
S, Capital	$ 6,000		S	15,000	4,000
T, Capital	4,000		T	6,000	8,000
	$10,000	$10,000			

The partnership operates in a state that has adopted the Uniform Partnership Act.

Required:
A. What are the rights of the partnership creditors on the unpaid balance of $2,000?
B. What are the rights of the individual creditors of each partner?

C. Assuming that Q pays the partnership creditors, prepare a schedule to show how the settlement by the partners will be completed.

D. Indicate the amount of assets that will be available to the personal creditors of R after the settlement by the partners.

E. Indicate the amount of assets that will be available to the personal creditors of T after the settlement by the partners.

EXERCISE 17-10 **Rights of Various Parties**

The trial balance for the MAD Partnership is as follows just before declaring bankruptcy.

Cash	Other Assets		Liabilities	Matt Loan	Matt Capital	Allen Capital	Dave Capital
$20,000	$100,000	=	$18,000	$10,000	$44,000	$30,000	$18,000

Partners share profits in the ratio 45:30:25.

Required:

A. Prepare a schedule to show how available cash would be distributed to the partners after creditors are paid in full. State which partner would receive the first cash available and at what point and to what degree each of the remaining partners would participate in cash distributions.

B. Cash of $30,000 is available to partners after the creditors have been paid in full. Prepare the general journal entry to record the distribution of $30,000.

PROBLEMS

PROBLEM 17-1 **Simple Liquidation**

The Discount Partnership is being liquidated. The current balance sheet is shown here.

Discount Partnership
Balance Sheet
January 14, 2001

Assets

Cash	$ 25,000
Other assets	120,000
Total assets	$145,000

Liabilities and Partners' Equity

Accounts payable	$ 40,000
Dawson, capital	31,000
Feeney, capital	65,000
Hardin, capital	9,000
Total liabilities and partners' equity	$145,000

Dawson, Feeney, and Hardin share profits and losses in a 30:40:30 ratio.

Required:

A. Prepare a schedule of partnership liquidation for each of the following three independent cases.

(1) The noncash assets are sold for $60,000, and any partner with a deficit is unable to eliminate any of the deficit.

(2) The noncash assets are sold for $60,000, and any partner with a deficit is able to invest cash equal to the amount of the deficit.

(3) The noncash assets are sold for $50,000, and any partner with a deficit is able to invest up to $8,000 cash in the partnership.

B. Prepare all necessary journal entries for case 2 above.

PROBLEM 17-2 Installment Liquidation

Nelson, Parker, and Rice are partners who share profits 4:3:3, respectively. Parker decides that it would be more profitable for him to operate as a sole proprietor. Nelson and Rice are in agreement that life would be more rewarding if Parker were to enter into direct competition with them. Nelson and Rice make repeated attempts to acquire Parker's interest in the partnership. Unable to reach an agreement, the partners mutually agree that their association should be dissolved. A condensed balance sheet before realization of assets shows the following balances:

Assets		Liabilities and Capital	
Cash	$ 5,000	Liabilities	$20,000
Other Assets	60,000	Nelson, Capital	20,000
		Parker, Capital	12,000
		Rice, Capital	13,000
Total	$65,000	Total	$65,000

Asset realization is accomplished in four stages as follows:

Stage	Sales Price	Book Value
1	$16,000	$12,000
2	12,000	10,000
3	10,000	20,000
4	2,000	18,000

The partners prefer that cash be distributed as soon as it is available.

Required:

Prepare a summary in columnar form of the partnership realization and liquidation. You should prepare supporting schedules of safe payments before each cash distribution.

PROBLEM 17-3 Installment Liquidation

Hann, Murphey, and Ryan have operated a retail furniture store for the past 30 years. Their business has been unprofitable for several years, since several large discount furniture stores opened in their sales territory. The partners recognize that they will be unable to compete with the larger chain stores and decide that since all the partners are near retirement, they should liquidate their business before it is necessary to declare bankruptcy. Account balances just before the liquidation process began were as follows:

Cash	$ 10,000	Liabilities	$110,000
Other Assets	218,000	Hann, Capital	50,000
		Murphey, Capital	42,000
		Ryan, Capital	26,000
	$228,000		$228,000

The partners share profits in the ratio of 5:3:2, respectively.

Rather than selling all the assets in a forced liquidation and incurring selling expenses, the partners agree that some of the noncash assets may be withdrawn in partial settlement of their capital interest. The partners agree that if the market value of a withdrawn asset is less than book value, the difference should be allocated to all partners in their loss ratio. If market value is greater than book value, the asset is to be adjusted to its market value before recording the withdrawal. All the partners are personally solvent and can make additional cash investment in the partnership up to $20,000 each. The following is a schedule of transactions that occurred in the liquidation process.

March 15, 2001	During liquidation sale, noncash assets with a book value of $90,000 were sold for $80,000.
March 16, 2001	Sold accounts receivable with a book value of $30,000 to a factor for $26,000.
March 16, 2001	Paid all recorded partnership creditors.
March 18, 2001	Distributed all but $1,000 of available cash to partners.
March 19, 2001	Murphey withdrew from inventory furniture with a book value of $10,000 and a market value of $13,000 to satisfy part of his capital interest.
March 21, 2001	Sold remainder of inventory with a book value of $50,000 to a discount furniture store for $30,000 cash.
March 25, 2001	Assigned for $12,000 cash the remaining term of the lease on the warehouse. The lease was accounted for as an operating lease.
March 25, 2001	Distributed all available cash to partners.
April 1, 2001	Hann agreed to accept two vehicles with a book value of $10,000 and a market value of $8,000 in partial settlement of his capital interest.
April 5, 2001	All remaining assets were sold for $4,000.
April 6, 2001	Received additional cash from partners with debit capital balances.
April 6, 2001	Distributed available cash to partners.

Required:
Prepare a schedule of partnership realization and liquidation in accordance with the sequence of the foregoing events. Compute a safe payment to support your cash distribution to partners.

PROBLEM 17-4   **Simple Liquidation with Personal Asset Information**

Mary, Paula, and Ray have operated a retail store for 20 years. The partners share profits and losses in the ratio of $4:3:3$, respectively. The partnership is unable to meet its obligations and the partners decide to liquidate the partnership. The firm's balance sheet just before the partners sell the other assets for $20,000 is as follows.

Assets		Liabilities and Partners' Equities	
Cash	$ 10,000	Liabilities	$ 40,000
Other Assets	100,000	Mary, Capital	50,000
		Paula, Capital	10,000
		Ray, Capital	10,000
	$110,000		$110,000

After the sale of the noncash assets, the personal assets and liabilities of each partner are determined to be the following:

	Personal Assets	Personal Liabilities
Mary	$50,000	$80,000
Paula	30,000	10,000
Ray	30,000	50,000

The partnership operates in a state that has adopted the Uniform Partnership Act.

Required:
A. Determine the amount of cash each partner will receive in liquidation and how much cash each partner must contribute to the firm, given their personal positions.
B. Determine the amounts that the personal creditors will receive from personal assets and any distribution from the partnership.

PROBLEM 17-5 **Advance Cash Distribution Plan**
Part A
Baker, Strong, and Weak have called on you to assist them in winding up the affairs of their partnership. You are able to gather the following information.

1. The trial balance of the partnership at June 30, 2001, is as follows.

	Debit	Credit
Cash	$ 6,000	
Accounts Receivable	22,000	
Inventory	14,000	
Plant and Equipment (net)	99,000	
Baker, Advance	12,000	
Weak, Advance	7,500	
Accounts Payable		$ 17,000
Baker, Capital		67,000
Strong, Capital		45,000
Weak, Capital		31,500
Total	$160,500	$160,500

2. The partners share profits and losses as follows: Baker, 40%; Strong, 40%; and Weak, 20%.

3. The partners are considering an offer of $100,000 for the accounts receivable, inventory, and plant and equipment as of June 30. The $100,000 would be paid to the partners in installments, the number and amounts of which are to be negotiated.

Required:
Prepare an advance cash distribution plan as of June 30, 2001. Prepare a schedule to show how the potential cash ($106,000) would be distributed as it becomes available.

Part B
Assume the facts in Part A except that the partners liquidate in stages instead of accepting the offer of $100,000. Cash is distributed to the partners at the end of each month.
 A summary of the liquidation transactions follows.

July
$16,500—collected on accounts receivable; balance is uncollectible.
$10,000—received for the entire inventory.
$ 1,000—liquidation expenses paid.
$ 8,000—cash retained in the business at the end of the month.

August
$ 1,500—liquidation expenses paid.
      As part payment of his capital interest, Weak accepted a piece of special equipment that he developed that had a book value of $4,000. The partners agreed that a value of $10,000 should be placed on the machine for liquidation purposes.
$ 2,500—cash retained in the business at the end of the month.

September
$75,000—received on sale of remaining plant and equipment.
$ 1,000—liquidation expenses paid.
      No cash retained in the business.

Required:
Prepare a schedule of cash payments as of September 30, 2001, showing how the cash was actually distributed. Use the advance cash distribution plan developed in Part A where appropriate.

(AICPA adapted)

PROBLEM 17-6 **Statement of Changes in Partners' Capital and Liquidation**
Mark Malone, Pete Patton, and Sally Spencer formed a partnership on January 1, 2001. Their original capital investments (all cash) were $140,000, $160,000, and $100,000, respectively. During the first year of operations, Mark withdrew $30,000, and the partnership reported a net income of $60,000. The partnership agreement stipulates that all income and losses are to be divided in the ratio of the original capital investments.

At the beginning of the second year, the partners decided to liquidate the business because of a disagreement. The assets and liabilities on January 2, 2002, were as follows: Cash, $37,000; Accounts Receivable, $129,000; Inventory, $188,000; Land, $85,000; Building (net), $180,000; Furniture and Fixtures (net), $30,000; Accounts Payable, $74,000; and Mortgage Payable, $145,000. The inventory was sold for three-quarters of its book value, the furniture and fixtures brought in $10,000, and $92,000 of the accounts receivable were collected. The remaining receivables were uncollectible. After the losses were allocated according to the partnership agreement and the accounts payable were paid in full, Pete accepted the land and building at book value and assumed the mortgage payable at book value as partial settlement of his capital interest. The cash balance was then distributed to the partners.

Required:
A. Prepare a statement of changes in partners' capital for the year ended December 31, 2001.
B. Prepare the journal entries to close the Drawing and Income Summary accounts for 2001.
C. Prepare a schedule of partnership liquidation.
D. Prepare the journal entries to record the liquidation activities.

PROBLEM 17-7 **Incorporation of a Partnership**
Jan and Sue have engaged successfully as partners in their law firm for a number of years. Soon after their state's incorporation laws are changed to allow professionals to incorporate, the partners decide to organize a corporation to take over the business of the partnership.
The after-closing trial balance for the partnership is as follows:

After-Closing Trial Balance
December 31, 2001

	Debit	Credit
Cash	$15,000	
Accounts Receivable	32,400	
Allowances for Uncollectibles		$ 2,000
Prepaid Insurance	800	
Office Equipment	30,200	
Accumulated Depreciation		12,600
Jan, Loan (outstanding since 1993, at 5%)		6,400
Jan, Capital (50%)		29,400
Sue, Capital (50%)		28,000
	$78,400	$78,400

Figures shown parenthetically reflect agreed profit- and loss-sharing ratios.
The partners have hired you as an accountant to adjust the recorded assets and liabilities to their market values and to close the partners' capital accounts to the new corporate capital

stock. The corporation is to retain the partnership's books, and the assets of the partnership should be taken over by the corporation in the following amounts:

Cash	$15,000
Accounts receivable	32,400
Allowance for uncollectibles	2,900
Office equipment	16,000
Prepaid insurance	800

Jan's loan is to be transferred to her capital account in the amount of $6,600.

Required:
A. Prepare the necessary journal entries to express the agreement described.
B. Prepare the entries to record the issuance of shares to Jan and Sue, assuming the issuance of 400 shares (par value $100) of stock to Jan and Sue.

PROBLEM 17-8 **Discussion Case with Ethical Issue**

Alan Norwood is currently a senior associate with the law firm of Butler, Starns, and Madden (BSM). His compensation currently includes a salary of $155,000, and benefits valued at $5,000. BSM is considered among the strongest of local firms, with assets of $10 million (cash $2,000,000, and accounts receivables $8,000,000), liabilities of $7.5 million, and 11 partners.

Alan anticipates admission to the partnership on July 1 of this year. The senior managing partner, Jane Butler, has had preliminary discussions with Alan in which the senior partner proposed the following:

1. A 5% interest in BSM capital and profits in recognition of Alan's commitment to the firm and in exchange for a capital investment by Alan of $150,000. This 5% interest would be acquired from the other partners.
2. Alan's compensation will consist of a monthly withdrawal of $18,000 and benefits valued at $5,000 annually. Monthly withdrawals approximate firm profits, but any unpaid profits will be distributed as a bonus to Alan after the end of each partnership year.

On March 1, only one month prior to Alan's final negotiation meeting for entry into the partnership, Mary, one of the junior associates, discreetly informed Alan that the firm was drawing up documents for Hugh Starns' retirement. Hugh has a 5% interest in the firm's capital and profits with a book value of $125,000. The partners have agreed upon a $75,000 cash settlement of the interest held by Mr. Starns. (Of the other 10 partners, numbers 1 through 9 hold 10% interests, and number 10 holds a 5% interest).

Required:
A. Assume Mr. Starns retires with his $75,000 settlement, and Alan is admitted to the partnership as proposed.
(1) Prepare journal entries to record the retirement and admission.
(2) Discuss the factors Alan needs to consider in evaluating whether he has improved his annual compensation from the firm. Although this is not a tax course, include a discussion of the various tax issues.
(3) Should Alan be concerned regarding the impending retirement and settlement of Mr. Starns' capital account assuming Alan is confident that he will be able to match the revenue-generating ability of Mr. Starns?
B. Assume instead that Alan is so disturbed by the impending departure of Mr. Starns that he decides to join Mary, the junior associate, in leaving the firm to form their own law partnership. Both Alan and Mary feel confident that during their tenures at BSM they

have developed such good working relationships with their clients that the majority of their clients will follow them to the new firm.

(1) Should Alan and Mary have any hesitation in quietly recruiting BSM clients to "follow them" to the new law firm?

(2) Can the partners of BSM prevent such recruiting of clients based on the claim that these clients are BSM "property"?

C. Assume instead that the firm encounters difficulties from which it is unable to recover, and in April, the decision is made to liquidate the firm. It is discovered that Mr. Starns has (in violation of the partnership agreement) taken draws which reduced firm cash and his capital account by $130,000. However, BSM owes Mr. Starns $10,000 for a separate loan made to the firm some 10 years ago. As of May 1, the firm had unallocated profits of $25,000, and cash had also increased by $25,000.

(1) Assuming that the provisions of UPA Section 40(b) are adhered to strictly, prepare entries to record the distributions. Assume that Mr. Starns is insolvent.

(2) If the other 10 partners are aware that Starns' capital account will take on a debit balance, can they rightfully hold repayment of the balance due to Starns for the $10,000 loan contingent on his reimbursement of his capital account's debit balance? Does this violate UPA Section 40(b)? On what basis can the partners justify their action (if challenged)?

18

INTRODUCTION TO FUND ACCOUNTING

LEARNING OBJECTIVES

1. Distinguish between a nonbusiness organization and a profit-oriented enterprise.

2. Explain the role of fund accounting.

3. Distinguish among the concepts of revenues, expenses, and expenditures as used in profit-oriented entities and as used for expendable fund entities.

4. Understand the classification of revenues and other resource inflows for fund accounting.

5. Understand the classification of expenditures and other resource outflows for fund accounting.

6. Describe the critical events in the use of financial resources of an expendable fund.

7. Explain how capital expenditures are recorded in an expendable fund.

8. Understand the role of a general fund.

9. Contrast the consumption and the purchases methods of accounting for inventories (and other prepaid items).

IN THE NEWS

In 1997 the federal government produced a consolidated, government-wide financial statement. It turned out that most of the financial data reported by the agencies was so unreliable the statement could not be audited by the GAO. Of the 24 major departments and agencies required to file financial statements with the Treasury for the consolidated statement, the GAO found that 19 were using financial systems that did not comply with federal law.[1]

Problems with the current state of *fund accounting*, or accounting for nonbusiness organizations, have been widely recognized, and efforts are being made to correct them. It is likely to take years of diligent work before many problems are fixed, however. "Significant financial systems weaknesses, problems with fundamental recordkeeping, incomplete documentation, and weak internal controls, including

---

[1] *Government Executive*, vol. 31:2, "Money Matters," by Katherine McIntire Peters, February 1999, pp. 31–34.

computer controls'' contributed to the GAO's inability to render an opinion on the consolidated statement, auditors wrote in their September 1998 report.[2]

Fund accounting concepts are generally associated with accounting for non-business organizations. Nonbusiness organizations are economic entities that are organized to provide a socially desirable service without regard to financial gain. In contrast to business enterprises, nonbusiness organizations are not operated for the *financial* benefit of any specific individual or group of individuals.

The purpose of this chapter is to introduce the reader to fund accounting concepts and procedures. In order to do this, however, it is necessary first to present a brief introduction to the types and characteristics of organizations that use fund accounting concepts.

CLASSIFICATIONS OF NONBUSINESS ORGANIZATIONS

Nonbusiness organizations may be separated into five major classifications, as follows:

1. *Governmental units.* Governmental units include federal, state, and local governmental entities. Local governmental units include counties, townships, municipalities, school districts, and special districts. Special districts include organizational units such as port authorities, industrial development districts, sanitation districts, and soil and water conservation districts.

2. *Hospitals and other health care providers.*

3. *Colleges and universities.*

4. *Voluntary health and welfare organizations.* Voluntary health and welfare organizations are organizations that derive their revenue from voluntary contributions of the general public to be used for purposes connected with health, welfare, or community services. Examples of such organizations include heart associations, family planning councils, mental health associations, and foundations for the blind.

5. *All other nonbusiness organizations.* Other nonbusiness organizations take a variety of forms. They include such organizations as trade associations (Electrical Contractors Association), professional associations (State Society of Certified Public Accountants), performing arts organizations (the Tennessee Performing Arts Center), museums, religious organizations, and research and scientific organizations.

DISTINCTIONS BETWEEN NONBUSINESS ORGANIZATIONS AND PROFIT-ORIENTED ENTERPRISES

The most obvious characteristic that distinguishes a *nonbusiness* organization from a *profit-oriented* enterprise is the absence of a primary goal to earn a profit. The services performed by nonbusiness organizations are based on social need rather than on the profit motive. Thus, their financial statements are sometimes referred

---

[2]Ibid.

to as *not-for-profit, or nonprofit, financial statements*. Other characteristics of nonbusiness organizations also distinguish them from profit-oriented enterprises. For example, persons who contribute resources to a nonbusiness organization receive no equity interest in the net assets of the organization. Nonbusiness organizations do not often finance their operations through charges to the individuals benefiting from the service. Thus, they must rely on political action (for example, tax levies) or fund-raising campaigns to sustain their activities and replenish their financial resources.

IN THE NEWS

"The Government is like a baby's alimentary canal, with a healthy appetite at one end and no responsibility at the other."[3] *Ronald Reagan*

In addition, tax levies and voluntary contributions cannot ordinarily be justified on the basis of the value of the nonbusiness organization's services to the individuals from whom such contributions come. Those who contribute resources to nonbusiness organizations do not necessarily benefit proportionately or at all from the services provided by such organizations. Because of these characteristics, the net income concept cannot be used to measure the effectiveness of the management of resources dedicated to nonbusiness objectives. Therefore, the income determination model of accounting is generally not applicable to such organizations.

In profit-oriented enterprises, net income functions as an implicit regulator in the sense that (1) in the long run, the organization must operate profitably to survive and (2) in the short run, failure to operate profitably will affect management's decisions and actions and perhaps the constituency of management itself. In the absence of this implicit regulator, stringent controls are often imposed to regulate the allocation and utilization of the financial resources of nonbusiness organizations. Such controls may be legally imposed (as in the case of governmental activities) or they may be imposed through formal action of the governing board.

Restrictions or limitations on the use of resources may also be directly imposed by the individuals or groups that contribute such resources. For example, most nonbusiness organizations receive gifts, grants, or endowments that are to be used only for specific purposes designated by the donor, such as construction of buildings, research activities, scholarships, operation of parks, recreation programs, or the acquisition of land. In addition, the donor may stipulate that the principal of the gift is to remain intact and that only the income on the invested principal is to be used for the purposes designated by the donor.

In order to account for these legally imposed, externally imposed, and self-imposed restrictions or limitations on the utilization of their resources, nonbusiness organizations have generally adopted the concepts of **fund accounting.** *In essence, an organization that uses fund accounting separates the assets, liabilities, and residual equity (known as a fund balance) into distinct funds organized for specific activities or objectives. In fund accounting, each fund consists of a self-balancing set of accounts and constitutes a* **separate accounting entity** *created and maintained for a specific purpose. The inflow and outflow of resources of each fund must be accounted for in such a way that they can be compared with the approved or stipulated resource flows for that fund.*

---

[3]Quoted in *New York Times Magazine*. From *The Merriam-Webster Dictionary of Quotations*, Merriam-Webster, Inc.: 1996. *Infopedia*, SoftKey Multimedia Inc., 1996.

FINANCIAL ACCOUNTING AND REPORTING STANDARDS FOR NONBUSINESS ORGANIZATIONS

The potential users of the financial reports of nonbusiness organizations include taxpayers, contributors, grantors, creditors, employees, managers, directors and trustees, service beneficiaries, financial analysts and advisers, brokers, underwriters, economists, taxing authorities, regulatory authorities, legislators, the financial press and reporting agencies, labor unions, trade associations, researchers, teachers, and students.

IN THE NEWS

"It was once said that the moral test of government is how that government treats those who are in the dawn of life, the children; those who are in the twilight of life, the elderly; and those who are in the shadows of life—the sick, the needy and the handicapped."[4] *Hubert H. Humphrey*

Until 1980, the Financial Accounting Standards Board (FASB) and its predecessor bodies gave little, if any, attention to standards of reporting for nonbusiness organizations. In 1980, however, the FASB issued *Statement of Financial Accounting Concepts No. 4*, "Objectives of Financial Reporting by Nonbusiness Organizations." In that statement, the Board identified providers such as members, taxpayers, contributors, and creditors as the most important users for purposes of establishing external financial reporting objectives for nonbusiness organizations.

In 1984, the Governmental Accounting Standards Board (GASB) was created. Like those of the FASB, the operations and financing of the GASB are overseen by the Financial Accounting Foundation. The GASB is responsible for establishing financial accounting standards for all state and local governmental bodies, and the FASB is responsible for establishing financial accounting standards for all other nonbusiness organizations. Accounting and reporting standards for governmental units are described and illustrated in this chapter and in Chapter 19. Accounting

ILLUSTRATION 18–1

Financial Accounting Standards for Nonbusiness Organizations

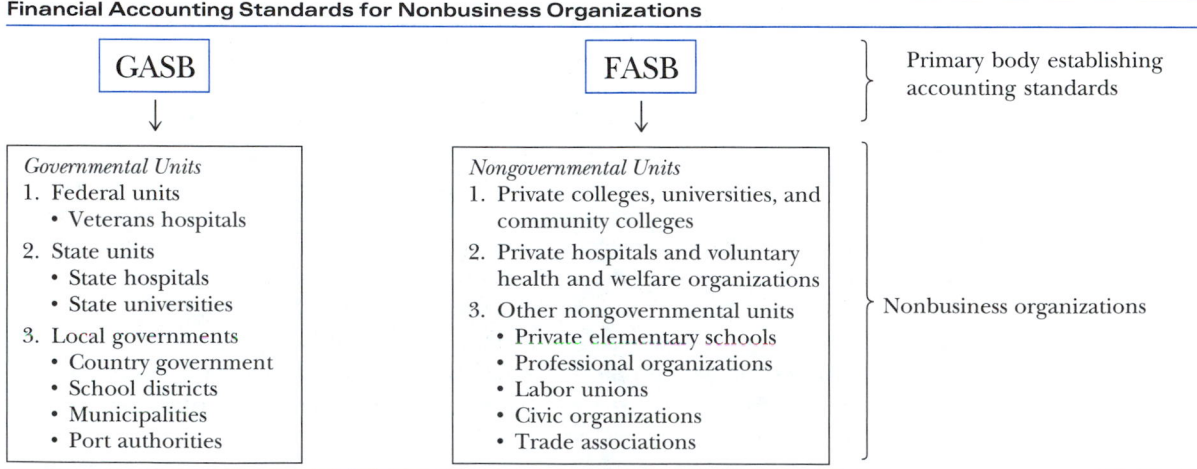

---

[4]Excerpt from a 1977 speech. From *The Merriam-Webster Dictionary of Quotations*, Merriam-Webster, Inc.: 1996. *Infopedia*, SoftKey Multimedia Inc., 1996.

and reporting standards for nongovernment nonbusiness organizations are described and illustrated in Chapter 20.

Illustration 18-1 indicates which standard-setting body (the GASB or the FASB) is primarily responsible for determining the accounting standards for various types of nonbusiness organizations. Having two separate bodies establishing accounting standards can be confusing for users of the financial statements. For instance, the financial statements of a state university, such as the University of Tennessee, are prepared using GASB rules, while a private university, such as Vanderbilt University, prepares its financial statements under the guidance of the FASB. Currently, there are significant accounting differences in rules between the FASB and the GASB. It is important for users of not-for-profit financial statements to have an understanding of the standards provided by both the GASB and the FASB. In this chapter and Chapter 19, the GASB rules are illustrated for governmental units; and in Chapter 20, the FASB's standards for other nonbusiness organizations are presented.

FUND ACCOUNTING

Fund accounting is designed primarily to meet internal reporting and control objectives; thus fund accounting may not be sufficient in itself to meet the objectives of financial reporting by nonbusiness organizations. Nevertheless, it does provide a basis for determining the fiscal responsibility and status of the organization and the compliance of administrators with the approved or stipulated receipt and utilization of financial resources. Therefore, fund accounting is an important means of meeting several of the accounting, control, and reporting objectives of most nonbusiness organizations.

Fund entities may be classified in a number of different ways. For example, they may be classified as expendable fund entities and proprietary fund entities. ***Expendable fund entities*** are the funds most closely associated with basic fund accounting concepts, while ***proprietary fund entities*** are the nonbusiness funds that are most similar to business entities.

Expendable Fund Entities

Expendable fund entities consist of net *financial resources* that are dedicated to a specified use. Thus, separate expendable fund entities are established based on the purpose for which financial resources may or must be used. Financial resources consist of cash and claims to cash such as receivables and investments in marketable securities. The difference between the financial resources of an expendable fund entity and claims against those resources is referred to as the fund balance. Thus, the statement of financial position, or balance sheet, for an expendable fund entity reflects the financial resources of the fund, the claims against those resources, and the fund balance. Typically, assets and liabilities are not subdivided into current and noncurrent portions. At a particular time the fund balance represents the net financial resources that are available for expenditure for the specified purposes or objectives for which the fund was created.

The financial resources of an expendable fund entity are not intended to be maintained intact. Ordinarily it is intended that they will be expended annually or over some other specified time period in order to carry out the objectives for which the fund was created. The measurement focus is on the flow of current financial resources in contrast to proprietary fund accounting, where the measurement focus is on the flow of economic resources.

The relevant measures of the operations of expendable fund entities are not, therefore, revenue, expense, and net income, but rather increases in fund resources, decreases in fund resources, and the change in the fund balance. The accounting model for the operating statement of an expendable fund entity is:

$$\begin{aligned} &\text{Financial resources inflows (by source)}\\ -\,&\underline{\text{Financial resource outflows (by function)}}\\ =\,&\text{Change in fund balance} \end{aligned}$$

Thus, increases in fund resources include not only revenues, but also items such as proceeds from debt issuances and transfers from other funds. Decreases in fund resources include expenses, other expenditures, and transfers to other funds. However, the term "expense" as defined under GAAP is typically not used with fund accounting. Instead the term "expenditure" includes expenses as well as other items giving rise to cash (or other resource) outlays, without regard to timing or the matching with revenue that is an integral part of income determination under GAAP. Conversely, expenses may include items that are not current expenditures because of the timing of the outlay. The operating results of expendable fund entities are thus measured in terms of inflow, outflow, and balances of net current financial resources assigned to the fund. The appropriate operating statement for such entities is essentially a statement of changes in net financial resources. To provide a basis for comparison, both budgeted and actual resource flows may be presented in the operating statement or in related schedules. Later in this chapter, we describe the modified accrual basis commonly used in fund accounting, and the need for accrual-based reporting under *GASB Statement No. 34.*

In summary, in accounting for expendable funds, the emphasis is changed from matching revenues and expenses to a comparison of the *actual* inflows and outflows of financial resources with *stipulated* or *approved* resource flows. The objective in accounting for expendable fund entities is to measure the extent to which management has *complied* with the regulations or restrictions that govern the use of expendable fund resources. A secondary objective is to assist management with such compliance.

Proprietary Fund Entities

Proprietary (nonexpendable) fund entities are used to account for the activities of nonbusiness organizations that are similar to those of business enterprises. Many nonbusiness organizations engage in quasi-commercial activities. The operation of an electric or water utility by a municipality and the rental of real estate by a religious organization are examples of such activities. Accordingly, even though these activities are accounted for in separate fund entities, relevant accounting measurements and reports are similar to those applicable to profit-oriented enterprises and focus on the determination of net income, financial position, and cash flows.

The accounting model for the statement of financial position of a proprietary fund entity is similar to a for-profit firm and is represented as follows:

$$\begin{array}{ccc} \underline{\text{Assets}} & = & \underline{\text{Liabilities}} & + & \underline{\text{Equity}}\\ \text{Current and Non-current} & & \text{Current and Non-current} & & \text{Net Assets} \end{array}$$

The accounting model for the statement of revenues, expenses, and changes in fund net assets of a proprietary fund entity is presented as follows using the all-inclusive format:

> Operating revenues
> <u>Less: operating expenses</u>
>
> = Operating income
> <u>Plus (minus): non-operating revenues and expenses</u>
>
> = Income before other revenue, expenses, gains and losses, and transfers
> Other revenue, expenses, etc.: capital contributions, additions to
> <u> permanent and term endowments, special and extraordinary items</u>
>
> = Increases (decreases) in net assets
> <u>Plus: net assets—beginning of period</u>
>
> = Net assets—end of period

Budgetary Fund Entities (Governmental Funds)

In the traditional compliance model of reporting on the operations of governmental units, actual resource inflows and outflows are compared with approved (or stipulated) inflows and outflows of resources. Approved resource flows are incorporated into annual budgets. In some instances the budget for an expendable fund entity is so important (often because of legal requirements) to management control of fund resources that entries for budgeted revenues and expenditures are recorded in the books. Fund entities in which the budget is formally incorporated into the accounting records are sometimes referred to as *budgetary funds*. (This is illustrated later in the chapter.)

The preparation, use, and importance of budgets for governmental units cannot be overemphasized. The annual budget for a governmental unit is usually prepared by the executive branch of the governmental unit. It is then presented to the legislative branch for consideration and enactment. In the case of annually levied taxes such as property taxes, adoption of budgeted revenue amounts may require the enactment of enabling legislation. In the case of continually levied taxes such as sales taxes and income taxes, no new legislation authorizing the tax is ordinarily required for the adoption of the budgeted amounts of revenue.

When budgeted expenditures are enacted into law, they are referred to as *appropriations*. Appropriations represent the maximum expenditures that are authorized by the legislature. As such, they represent (by budget category) amounts that cannot be legally exceeded unless subsequently amended by the legislative body. Accordingly, the accounting system must provide administrators of governmental units with timely information as to actual expenditures and allowable expenditures (appropriations) by budget category. In addition, financial reports must be prepared in such a way that the legislature or its representatives can determine that the spending limits authorized by it have not been exceeded. The approved budget may, therefore, be formally recorded in the accounting records of the appropriate fund(s). Such formal budgetary account integration is useful in assisting in the control and administration of fund resources.

Restricted and Unrestricted Fund Entities

Expendable fund entities may be further classified as *restricted* or *unrestricted*. This classification is usually applicable to nonbusiness organizations other than governmental units. The unrestricted expendable fund entity includes the net current financial resources of the nonbusiness organization that are available to carry out the primary or general activities of the organization at the discretion of the governing board. Current financial resources that are restricted by donors or other outside agencies for specific current operating purposes are included in restricted expendable fund entities. The term "restricted" refers to resources that bear a legal restriction as to use imposed by parties *outside* the organization. The primary purpose of this distinction is to assist in the determination of the current financial resources that are available for use at the discretion of the governing board and those over which the governing board has little, if any, discretion as to use because of **externally** imposed restrictions. As illustrated in Chapter 20, most nonbusiness organizations other than governmental units have one unrestricted fund and one or more restricted funds.

General Accounting and Reporting Considerations

Within the framework of expendable fund entities, **revenues** are defined as inflows of net current financial resources, and **expenditures** are defined as outflows of net current financial resources. Because different types of nonbusiness organizations have different sources of revenues and different purposes and objectives, the recognition and classification of fund entity revenues and expenditures vary among nonbusiness organizations. However, there is general agreement in the authoritative literature on the following points for financial reporting purposes:

1. Fund revenues should be classified by *source*, and transfers from other funds within the organization should be distinguished from, and classified separately from, revenue.
2. Fund expenditures should be classified by *function* or *activity*, and transfers to other funds within the organization should be distinguished from, and classified separately from, expenditures.
3. Fund revenues and expenditures should, where possible, be recognized using the *accrual basis* of accounting.

In the remainder of this chapter, fund accounting concepts are developed within the framework of state and local governmental units.

Basis of Accounting

To the extent practicable, the accrual method should be used in accounting for fund entities. The cash basis of accounting is not appropriate. There are, however, some special considerations in the application of accrual accounting to expendable fund entities.

Financial resources of an expendable fund entity include cash, receivables, and securities that can be converted into cash. If an increase in net financial resources (revenue) is recorded when a valid receivable is established, rather than when the cash is ultimately collected, and if a decrease in net financial resources (expenditure) is recorded when a liability is incurred, rather than when cash is ultimately disbursed, then the **accrual basis** rather than the cash basis of accounting is being applied to the fund entity. Because governments generally make no attempt to allocate costs to periods benefited and because some expenditures of the expendable fund entities of governmental units are not recognized in the period in which they are incurred, the term *modified accrual accounting* is used to describe the application of accrual accounting to expendable fund entities of governmental units. Under the modified accrual approach, it is not sufficient that an economic event has occurred for it to affect the operating statement. *Instead, the related cash flow must occur within a period short enough to have an effect on current spendable resources.* In other words, revenues must be both measurable and available to liquidate liabilities of the current period. Similarly, expenditures are recognizable when an event is expected to use current spendable resources (rather than future resources). Under *GASB Statement No. 34*, a *government-wide Statement of Activities* and a *government-wide Statement of Net Assets,* both prepared on an accrual basis, are required, in addition to the funds statements prepared on the modified accrual basis.[5]

Before proceeding further, it is useful to contrast the concepts of revenue, expense, and expenditure as they are used in relation to profit-oriented entities and to expendable fund entities.

Profit-Oriented Entities (Income Determination)

Revenue—increase in net assets resulting from the sale of goods or services.

Expense—cost of resources used to produce current period revenues.

Unusual, Infrequent, and Extraordinary Items—Extraordinary items are items that are *both* unusual in nature and infrequent of occurrence; they are reported net of taxes. Items that are either unusual or infrequent, but not both, are shown on a separate line, if material, but are not shown net of taxes.

Expendable Fund Entities

Revenue—any increase in (source of) net current financial resources *other than* increases from *other financing sources* (as defined below).

Expenditure—any decrease in (use of) net current financial resources *other than* decreases from *other financing uses* (as defined below); or the amount of financial resources expended during the period to carry out the operations and activities of the fund entity.

Other Financing Sources and Uses (and Transfers)—proceeds from debt issuances and transfers of financial resources to and from other funds.

Special and Extraordinary Items—Extraordinary items are both unusual in nature and infrequent of occurrence. Special items are significant transactions within the control of management that are either unusual or infrequent.

Classification of Revenues

Revenues are classified by fund and by major revenue source. Major sources of revenue for state and local governmental units are summarized in Illustration 18-2. As shown, the number of sources of revenue available to governmental units is impressive when compared with those available to business enterprises.

---

[5]Governmental Accounting Standards Board (GASB), *GASB Statement No. 34*, "Basic Financial Statements—and Management's Discussion and Analysis—For State and Local Governments" (Norwalk, CT), June 1999.

ILLUSTRATION 18–2

Major Sources of Revenue for State and Local Governmental Units

Property taxes	Grants from federal, state, or local government units
Income taxes	Shared revenues from federal, state, or local
Sales and excise taxes	government units
Gift and inheritance taxes	Payments in lieu of taxes from federal, state, or local
Fines and penalties	government units
Gifts and donations	Interest earned on loans and investments
Forfeits	
Licenses and permits	
Sales of property	
Charges for services	

Other Financing Sources

Debt Issue Proceeds Governmental units may finance their operations through the issuance of bonds or other debt instruments. Although debt issue proceeds are sometimes classified as revenue of a particular fund entity, they are *not revenue* from the point of view of the issuing governmental unit because of the offsetting debt. Accordingly, debt issue proceeds should be classified separately from revenue for purposes of financial reporting. Debt issue proceeds are accounted for as "other financing sources."

Transfers of Resources from Other Funds Transfers of resources from other fund entities within an organization do not represent an increase in the expendable financial resources of the organization as a whole. Accordingly, even though they represent an increase in the financial resources of the recipient fund entity, they should ordinarily *be classified separately from revenue* for financial reporting purposes. Interfund operating transfers are accounted for as "other financing sources," or "uses."

Recognition of Revenue

In accounting for profit-oriented enterprises, revenue is ordinarily not recognized until (1) a transaction has taken place (that is, the amount of revenue can be objectively measured) and (2) the earnings process is complete or substantially complete. Criterion 2 is not applicable to expendable fund entities. The revenue-recognition criteria for expendable fund entities can be stated as follows: *In accounting for expendable fund entities, revenue is ordinarily not recognized until (1) it can be objectively measured and (2) it is available to finance expenditures of the current period.*

Many sources of fund revenue do not meet the criteria of measurability and availability until they are received in cash. On the other hand, significant amounts of revenue (for example, property taxes, pledges, regularly billed charges for routine services, and some types of grants) meet both criteria and are recognized as revenue prior to the receipt of cash. The application of these criteria to several significant sources of revenue of governmental units may be illustrated as follows.

Property Taxes Property taxes usually meet both criteria when levied. The amount of property tax is precisely determinable when levied and the amount of uncollectible taxes ordinarily can be reasonably estimated on the basis of previous experience. Thus, the amount of property tax revenue is objectively determinable at the time the taxes are levied. Ordinarily, taxes are also considered to be *available* in the period levied, even though they are collectible in a period subsequent to the levy, because (1) they provide a basis for obtaining cash resources through the issuance of tax anticipation notes[6] and (2) they are usually collectible early in the subsequent period and thus are available to finance current period operations.

Income Tax and Sales Tax Self-assessed taxes such as the income tax and the sales tax usually are not objectively measurable or available until the tax returns are filed with payment. Where the tax returns have been filed but payment is delayed, revenue should be recognized when the returns are filed, assuming that a reasonable estimate can be made of noncollectible amounts, if any. In addition, sales taxes held by merchants may be recognized as revenue before they are received by the fund entity if the measurability and availability criteria are met.

Fines and Forfeits The amounts of fines, forfeits, inspection charges, parking meter receipts, and so on, are not objectively determinable or available until assessed or collected and are, therefore, not normally recognized as revenue until collected.

Sales of Property The entire amount of proceeds from the sale of property is treated as revenue at the time of sale because expendable assets are increased and are available to finance current expenditures in the same manner as any other revenues.

Pledges and Grants A pledge to contribute resources is considered revenue at the time it is made, so long as a reasonable estimate of uncollectible pledges can be made and there is no restriction on the time period in which the pledged resources can be expended. Grants may or may not be recognized as revenue at the time the grant is authorized. If the grant is dependent on the performance of services, or if the expenditure of funds is the prime factor for determining the eligibility for the grant funds, revenue should not be recognized until the time the services are performed or the expenditures are made. Grants that are not dependent on performance or expenditure of funds should be recognized in the period in which they are authorized.

The U.S. government has reached preliminary agreements with Chevron, Conoco, and BP Amoco on claims that they shortchanged the United States on royalty payments. In a 1996 lawsuit filed in Lufkin, Texas, two whistleblowers allege that several companies paid royalties based on a ''posted'' wellhead price rather than the fair market value. The government is seeking about five billion dollars from all the companies combined, which includes actual damages trebled plus civil penalties.[7]

Classification of Expenditures and Other Resource Outflows

As mentioned earlier, an expenditure is any decrease in net current financial resources other than transfers to other funds. Thus expenditures are not matched to

---

[6]Tax anticipation notes are notes or warrants issued in anticipation of the collection of taxes and are usually retirable only from the proceeds of the tax levy whose collection they anticipate.

[7]*WSJ*, ''Chevron to Pay About $95 Million to End Claim It Shortchanged U.S. on Royalties,'' by Alexei Barrionuevo, 9/10/99, p. A3.

the production of current revenues as are expenses for profit-seeking enterprises. Expenditures may be classified by fund, by function and/or activity, by organizational unit, by character (nature of the expenditure), or by object class. Since different classifications serve different purposes, multiple classification of expenditures is usually recommended. For example, the various classifications might be illustrated as follows:

> Function—Public Safety
> Organizational Unit—Fire Department or Police Department
> Activity—Drug Control
> Character—Current Operating
> Object Class—Supplies or Salaries

Classification by Function and Activity Typical functional classifications of expenditures for state and local governmental units are presented in Illustration 18-3. Classification by function refers to the broad purposes for which expenditures are made. Classification by activity refers to the specific types of work performed to accomplish such purposes. For example, public safety is a major function of a municipality. The *function* of public safety may be divided into *subfunctions* such as police protection, fire protection, and protective inspection. The subfunction of police protection can be classified into *activities* such as criminal investigation, vice control, patrol, custody of prisoners, and crime laboratory.

Functional and activity classifications are particularly important and are the classifications ordinarily recommended for published financial reports. In addition, as noted by the National Council on Governmental Accounting:

> *Activity* classification is particularly significant because it facilitates evaluation of the economy and efficiency of operations by providing data for calculating expenditures per unit of activity. That is, the expenditure requirements of performing a given unit of work can be determined by classifying expenditures by activities and providing for performance measurement where such techniques are practicable. These expenditure data, in turn, can be used in preparing future budgets and in setting standards against which future

ILLUSTRATION 18-3

Functional Classification of Expenditures for State and Local Governmental Units

General Government	*Health and Welfare*
Legislative	
Judicial	*Recreation—Cultural*
Executive	Playgrounds
Elections	Swimming pools
Financial administration	Golf courses
	Parks
Public Safety	Libraries
Police	
Fire	*Urban Redevelopment and Housing*
Inspection	
	Economic Development and Assistance
Public Works	
Highways and streets	
Sanitation	

expenditure levels can be evaluated. Further, activity expenditure data provide a convenient starting point for calculating total and/or unit expenses of activities where desired, e.g., for "make or buy" and "do or contract out" decisions. Current operating expenditures (total expenditures less those for capital outlay and debt service) may be adjusted by depreciation and amortization data . . . to determine activity expense.[8]

Classification by Organizational Unit Classification of expenditures by organizational unit is important for management, control, and internal reporting purposes including responsibility accounting. Classification of expenditures by organizational unit is based on the departments, divisions, bureaus, or other administrative units that make expenditures to carry out their designated functions. Examples include police department, attorney general's office, corporation commission, city planning, and the like. Each organizational unit may have responsibility for several functions or activities. In some instances a function or activity may cross organizational unit lines.

Classification by Object Class Classification of expenditures by object class identifies what is acquired in return for the expenditure (i.e., the types of items purchased or services obtained). Typical object classifications are presented in Illustration 18-4. Classification by object is useful primarily for internal management and may be omitted from published financial reports.

ILLUSTRATION 18–4

Classification of Expenditures by Object Class

Personal Services
   Salaries
   Employee health and retirement benefits
   Payroll taxes, etc.
Supplies
   Office supplies
   Operating supplies
   Small tools
Other
   Professional services
   Telephone and telegraph
   Travel
   Rental (equipment, buildings, machinery)
   Postage and shipping
   Printing and publications
   Repairs and maintenance
   Insurance
   Miscellaneous
Capital Expenditures
   Land
   Buildings
   Improvements
   Machinery and equipment
   Motor vehicles
   Furniture and furnishings
   Office machines

[8]National Council on Government Accounting, *Statement 1: Governmental Accounting and Financial Reporting Principles* (Chicago: Municipal Finance Officers Association of the United States and Canada, 1979), pp. 16 and 17.

It is generally recommended that excessively detailed object classifications be avoided, since they may unnecessarily complicate accounting procedures and reports and because the control and reporting emphasis of the organization should be on functions, activities, and organizational units, rather than on the object of expenditures per se.

With modern data-processing techniques, multiple classification of expenditures is easily accomplished. Multiple classification of expenditures by function, organizational unit, activity, character, and object class facilitates the aggregation and analysis of data in different ways for different purposes.

Transfers to Other Funds Transfers of resources to other fund entities within an organization do not represent decreases in the expendable financial resources of the organization as a whole. Accordingly, even though they represent a decrease in the financial resources of a particular fund, they ordinarily should be classified separately from expenditures for financial reporting purposes.

Recognition of Expenditures

An expenditure is one of four critical events in the use of the financial resources of an expendable fund entity. The sequence of events is as follows:

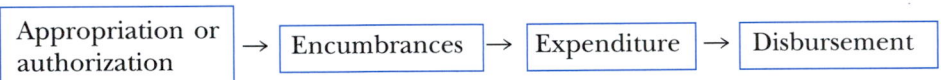

Appropriation Appropriations represent the maximum amount of expenditures that are authorized. The need for recognizing the next event, encumbrance, can be more clearly presented, however, by recalling that administrators are responsible for expending fund resources only in the amounts and for the purposes prescribed in the appropriations act. In the case of governmental units, administrators are held strictly accountable for the provisions of the appropriation act, and stiff penalties are provided by law for those who fail to adhere to them. Thus, it is crucial to administrators to know how they stand relative to their appropriation authority and to have accounting safeguards to prevent the misuse of fund resources.

Encumbrance Since the amount of an appropriation cannot be legally exceeded, the placing of purchase orders and the signing of contracts are critical events in controlling the expenditures of expendable fund entities. The financial resources of a fund are said to be encumbered when a transaction is entered into that requires performance on the part of another party before the governmental unit becomes liable to perform (by expending financial resources) its part of the transaction. An encumbrance reduces appropriation authority and is formally recorded in the accounting records. Thus, at any particular time the accounting records will reflect management's remaining available appropriation authority as follows:

Appropriations − (Encumbrances + Expenditures) = Unencumbered balance

The unencumbered balance is the amount of resources that can still be obligated or expended without exceeding the legal or authorized limit.

Encumbrances are recorded as follows:

Purchase Order (Encumbrance)

(1)   Encumbrance (appropriately classified)   10,000

       Reserve for Encumbrance   10,000

          To record an order for goods in the amount of $10,000.

Expenditures   When the vendor or supplier performs on a contract or purchase order and goods or services are received, an expenditure has taken place. Expenditures are recognized in the accounting period in which the fund liability is incurred, except for unmatured interest on long-term debt, which is recognized when due, and certain compensated absences and claims and judgments, which are recognized when obligations are expected to be liquidated with expendable available resources. Thus, an expenditure and a corresponding liability or cash disbursement is recorded at the time goods or services are received or at the time funds are granted to an authorized recipient. When the goods ordered in (1) above are received, the following entries are made:

Receipt of Goods (Expenditure)

(2)   Expenditures (appropriately classified)   12,000

       Vouchers Payable   12,000

          To record the receipt of goods invoiced at $12,000.

(3)   Reserve for Encumbrance   10,000

       Encumbrance   10,000

          To remove the encumbrance recorded in (1) for goods received and recorded as an expenditure in (2).

In this case, the goods cost $2,000 more than was estimated when the order was placed.

Disbursements   Disbursements represent the payment of cash for expenditures. Such payments may precede the expenditure (an advance), coincide with the expenditure (a direct payment), or follow the expenditure (the payment of a liability). The payment for the goods purchased in (2) above is recorded as follows:

Payment of Goods

(4)   Vouchers Payable   12,000

       Cash   12,000

          To record payment of vouchers payable.

Encumbrances and expenditures are classified on the same basis (by fund, function, organizational unit, activity, character, or object class) as appropriations. The effect on appropriation control of incorporating appropriations, encumbrances, and expenditures into the accounting records is demonstrated in Illustration 18-5. In Illustration 18-5, it is assumed that the appropriation for budget category 103 is $50,000 and that the amount of expenditures in this category prior to the entries illustrated above was $15,000. The effects of entries (1), (2), (3), and (4) above on the subsidiary ledger card for budget category 103 are as indicated. The most important thing to note is that at any particular time information is available to administrators as to their unexpended and uncommitted appropriation authority.

Capital Expenditures   In accounting for profit-oriented enterprises, capital expenditures are recorded as assets and are distinguished from expenses. The costs

ILLUSTRATION 18–5

Subsidiary Ledger Control Card for One Budget Category

Function: Sanitation; Activity: Sanitary Sewer Cleaning; Object: Operating Supplies

Budget Line 103	(A) Appropriation	(B) Encumbrance	(C) Expenditure	(D) Total (B) + (C)	(E) Unencumbered Balance (A) − (D)
Prior Balance	$50,000	$ —	$15,000	$15,000	$35,000
Purchase Order [entry (1)]		10,000		10,000	(10,000)
Balance	50,000	10,000	15,000	25,000	25,000
Expenditure [entries (2) & (3)]		(10,000)	12,000	2,000	(2,000)
Balance	$50,000	$ —	$27,000	$27,000	$23,000

of such assets are recognized in the operating statements (income statement) of such enterprises through depreciation.

In accounting for an expendable fund entity, capital expenditures, like other expenditures, are treated as an outflow of financial resources. The assets acquired do not represent expendable financial resources but rather reflect the purposes for which financial resources have been used. Thus, they are not recorded or reported as assets of the fund entity. This treatment is consistent with the primary purpose of fund accounting, which is to provide accounting control over the collection and expenditure of financial resources and to assure that no violations of authorized limits on expenditures occur. The operating statements of expendable fund entities are therefore designed to reflect **all** the sources and uses of its financial resources. The position statement of the expendable fund entity is designed to present the status of its *financial resources*, the related liabilities, and the *net financial resources* available for subsequent appropriation and expenditure. This emphasis on the status and flow of net financial resources requires that capital expenditures be treated the same as any other classification of expenditures and that they not be reflected as assets of the fund entity. This is not to say that controls are not maintained over fixed assets acquired by means of expendable fund resources. The organization establishes records and controls beyond the records of the expendable fund entity. Accounting for and reporting on fixed assets is illustrated in Chapter 19 for governmental units and in Chapter 20 for nongovernment nonbusiness organizations. General capital assets are assets associated with and arising from governmental activities. Although they are not reported as assets in government funds, they are reported as assets in government-wide statements required under *GASB Statement No. 34* (illustrated in the next chapter).

Depreciation is not accounted for in the records of an expendable fund entity for the same reason that fixed assets are excluded from the records of such entities. However, depreciation is recognized in the government-wide statement of assets and statement of activities. As stated previously, expenditures, not expenses, are generally measured in accounting for expendable fund entities. Acquisitions of fixed assets require the *use* of financial resources and are accounted for as expenditures. Proceeds from the sale of fixed assets *provide* financial resources and are accounted for as revenues. Depreciation expense is neither a source nor a use of the financial resources of an expendable fund entity, and thus is not properly recorded in the accounts of such entities. Inclusion of depreciation expense in the operating statement of an expendable fund entity would confuse two fundamentally different measurements—expenditures and expense—and would result in misleading inferences relative to the operating activities of the expendable fund entity. This does not mean that the concept or measurement of depreciation is not important from the point of view of the organization as a whole. Indeed, if meaningful cost/benefit analysis is to be attempted for a particular activity, the operating expenditures of the activity must be adjusted for depreciation to determine total activity cost. For this reason, depreciation expense is required on the government-wide statements (see Chapter 19). However, the primary objective of fund accounting is not to provide information relative to the costs and benefits of activities but to control the collection and expenditure of financial resources. Accounting for and reporting on depreciation are further discussed in Chapter 19 for state and local governmental units and in Chapter 20 for nongovernment nonbusiness organizations.

Recording Budgeted and Actual Revenue and Expenditures

Condensed financial statements for an expendable fund entity are presented in Illustration 18-6. Entries that were recorded in the records of the expendable fund entity during 2001 are presented in summary form as follows:

(1)	Estimated Revenue (classified)	800,000	
	Appropriations (classified)		780,000
	Unreserved Fund Balance		20,000
	To record budgeted revenues and expenditures adopted by legislative body or governing board.		

ILLUSTRATION 18–6

Condensed Financial Statements of Expendable Fund Entity

Balance Sheet—January 1, 2001

Net Financial Resources (Assets minus Liabilities)	$100,000
Fund Balance (Unreserved)	$100,000

Statement of Changes in Unreserved Fund Balance
For Period Ended December 31, 2001

	Budget	Actual	Actual Over (Under) Budget
Unreserved Fund Balance—1/1	$100,000	$100,000	$ 0
Revenue	800,000	850,000	50,000
Total Resources Available	$900,000	$950,000	$50,000
Appropriations	780,000		
Expenditures (current year)		600,000	
Encumbrances (outstanding at 12/31)		170,000	
Total Resources Expended or Committed	780,000	770,000	(10,000)
Unreserved Fund Balance—12/13	$120,000	$180,000	$60,000

Balance Sheet—December 31, 2001

Net Financial Resources (Assets minus Liabilities)		$350,000
Fund Balance		
Unreserved	$180,000	
Reserved for Encumbrances (Outstanding Commitments)	170,000	$350,000

The excess of budgeted revenue over (under) budgeted expenditures is recorded as an increase (decrease) in the unreserved fund balance. In addition to this entry, postings would be made to subsidiary accounts for each source of revenue and each appropriation expenditure category.

(2)	Receivables or Cash	850,000	
	Revenue (classified)		850,000
	To record revenues recognized during the year.		
(3)	Encumbrances (classified)	775,000	
	Reserve for Encumbrances		775,000
	To record commitments made against appropriations (*$775,000 is an* *assumed amount*).		

As encumbrances are recorded, they are also posted to the appropriate appropriation expenditure subsidiary account, thereby providing information as to the amount of each appropriation category that remains available for encumbrance or expenditure (see Illustration 18-5).

(4a)	Expenditures (classified)	600,000	
	Vouchers Payable or Cash		600,000
	To record receipt of encumbered goods and services.		
(4b)	Reserve for Encumbrances	605,000	
	Encumbrances		605,000
	To remove encumbrances on goods and services that have been recorded as expenditures (*$605,000 is an assumed figure*).		

Two entries are required to record expenditures for goods or services that have been previously encumbered. Since the amount expended will not necessarily equal the amount encumbered, the dollar amounts in the two entries may not be the same. The reversal of the encumbrance is for the amount of the original encumbrance, which is assumed to be $605,000 in this example. The amount of expenditure is for the approved invoice price of the goods or services received.

(5)	Revenue	850,000	
	Estimated Revenue		800,000
	Unreserved Fund Balance		50,000
	To close budgeted and actual revenue accounts.		

The excess of actual revenue over (under) budgeted revenue is recorded as an increase (decrease) in the unreserved fund balance. Postings would also be made to close out each subsidiary revenue account.

(6)	Appropriations	780,000	
	Expenditures		600,000
	Encumbrances ($775,000 − $605,000)		170,000
	Unreserved Fund Balance		10,000
	To close appropriations, expenditures, and encumbrances accounts.		

The excess of appropriations over (under) expenditures plus encumbrances is recorded as an increase (decrease) in the unreserved fund balance. The balance of encumbrances at year-end is matched against appropriations because, although they are not expenditures, encumbrances do represent commitments made against the current year's appropriations and therefore represent the use of the appropriation authority of the current year. Postings would also be made to close each subsidiary appropriation expenditure account.

After entries (5) and (6) are posted, all account balances except assets, liabilities, the unreserved fund balance, and the reserve for encumbrances have been closed. The balances in the unreserved fund balance and reserve for encumbrances accounts may be calculated as follows:

Reserve for encumbrances—January 1, 2001	$ —0—
Total amounts encumbered during 2001—entry (3)	775,000
Total encumbrances expended—entry (4)	(605,000)
Reserve for encumbrances—December 31, 2001	$ 170,000
Unreserved fund balance—January 1, 2001	$ 100,000
Excess of estimated revenue over appropriations—entry (1)	20,000
Excess of actual revenue over estimated revenue—entry (5)	50,000
Excess of appropriations over expenditures and encumbrances—entry (6)	10,000
Unreserved fund balance—December 31, 2001	$ 180,000

The balance in the reserve for encumbrances account at December 31, 2001, represents the estimated amount of the net financial resources of the fund entity that will be needed in the subsequent year to liquidate obligations entered into under the authority of the current year's appropriation. As such, it represents a restriction on the availability of fund resources for future appropriation rather than a liability and is properly considered as a portion (reserved) of the total fund balance. The concept that the year-end balance in the Reserve for Encumbrances account is in reality a reserved fund balance would perhaps be clearer if an analysis of the change in the total fund balance were presented in the following form:

Total fund balance—January 1	$ 100,000
Add actual revenue	850,000
Deduct actual expenditures	(600,000)
Total fund balance—December 31	350,000
Less amount reserved for commitments	(170,000)
Unreserved fund balance—December 31	$ 180,000

Note that the increase in the *total* fund balance ((\$100,000 to \$350,000, or \$250,000 in this example) is always equal to the excess of *actual* revenues (\$850,000; inflows of net financial resources) over *actual* expenditures (\$600,000; outflows of net financial resources).

In the next year, the balance of the reserve for encumbrances will be charged by means of a separate expenditures account with the actual expenditures arising from the year-end commitments that are incurred in the subsequent year. A difference between the amount encumbered at the end of the year and the actual amount of the related expenditures that are incurred in the subsequent year is debited or credited to the unreserved fund balance.

Comprehensive Illustration—General Fund

The General Fund of Model City is now used to illustrate the principles of fund accounting developed in this chapter.

The general fund of a municipality is used to account for all financial resources of the municipality other than those required to be accounted for in another fund. It is established at the inception of the municipality and is continued as long as the municipality exists. A government may never report more than one general fund. Most of the current operations of a municipality are financed by the resources of this fund. The general ledger trial balance of the General Fund of Model City on January 1, 2001, is as follows:

Model City
The General Fund
General Ledger Trial Balance
January 1, 2001

Cash	$ 45,000
Certificates of Deposit	100,000
Property Tax Receivable	190,000
Total Debits	$335,000
Estimated Uncollectible Taxes	$ 20,000
Vouchers Payable	65,000
Unreserved Fund Balance	95,000
Reserve for Encumbrances—2000	155,000
Total Credits	$335,000

The budget adopted by the City Council for the General Fund for the fiscal year ending December 31, 2001 is presented in summary form below.

Model City
The General Fund
2001 Fiscal-Year Budget

Estimated Revenue	
Licenses and Permits	$ 188,250
Property Tax	1,158,750
State Grant—education	300,000
Charges for Services	135,000
Proceeds from Sales of Equipment	78,000
Total	$1,860,000
Appropriations	
Public Safety	516,000
General Government	293,500
Highways and Streets	135,500
Sanitation	75,000
Health	148,500
Cultural—recreation	88,500
Education	687,000
Total	$1,944,000
Excess of appropriations over estimated revenue	($84,000)
Transfer from enterprise fund	150,000
Less transfers to: Debt service fund	(96,000)
Excess (deficiency) of revenue and transfers from other funds over appropriations and transfers to other funds	($30,000)

Summary entries to record the activities and transactions of the General Fund during 2001 are presented below. The assignment to specific subsidiary accounts of amounts credited to revenue or appropriations and of amounts debited to encumbrances, expenditures, or estimated revenue is not shown in these summary entries. Remember, however, that each entry to these general ledger control accounts also requires detailed postings by appropriate classifications to the related subsidiary accounts.

(1)	Estimated Revenue	1,860,000	
	Unreserved Fund Balance	84,000	
	Appropriations		1,944,000
	To record budgeted revenue and expenditures.		

(2)	Due from Enterprise Fund	150,000	
	Transfers from Other Funds		150,000
	To record authorization for transfer of resources from other fund entities incorporated in budget adopted by City Council.		

For financial reporting purposes, transfers of resources from other fund entities of the same organization are distinguished from revenue of the recipient fund entity. Interfund transfers are properly recognized (accrued) in the period in which they are authorized. Control over authorized transfers from other fund entities may be achieved by recording them as a receivable at the beginning of the year for which they are authorized (budgeted).

(3)	Transfer to Other Funds	96,000	
	Due to Debt Service Fund		96,000
	To record authorization for transfer of resources to another fund entity incorporated in budget adopted by city council.		

Although authorized transfers to other fund entities may be viewed as appropriation expenditures from the point of view of the General Fund entity, for purposes of financial reporting they are distinguished from expenditures. Control over authorized transfers to other fund entities may be achieved by recording them as liabilities at the beginning of the period for which they are authorized (budgeted).

(4)	Property Tax Receivable	1,287,500	
	Estimated Uncollectible Taxes		128,750
	Revenue		1,158,750
	To record property taxes at time they are levied.		

The estimate for uncollectible taxes is determined on the basis of collection policy and prior years' experience. It is recorded as a direct reduction of revenue, however, rather than as an expenditure, since the failure to collect taxes is not an outflow of net financial resources. Accordingly, there is no appropriation for the amount of estimated uncollectible taxes and it is, therefore, properly accounted for as a reduction of revenue rather than as an expenditure.

(5)	Other Receivables	80,000	
	Revenue		80,000
	To record billings for routine services.		

(6) Expenditures—2000	148,000	
Vouchers Payable		148,000

To record receipt of goods and services ordered in 2000 and originally
authorized for $155,000.

A separate expenditure control account (and subsidiary ledger) is used to record expenditures during the current year that were encumbered (authorized) in the prior year. At the end of the year, this expenditure account will be closed out against Reserve for Encumbrances—2000 and any difference taken to the unreserved fund balance [see entry (26) below].

(7) Encumbrances	1,291,000	
Reserve for Encumbrances—2001		1,291,000

To record encumbrances (commitments) on goods and services ordered
during current year.

(8) Cash	1,281,000	
Property Tax Receivable		1,201,000
Other Receivables		80,000

To record collection of $170,500 of property taxes levied in 2000 and
$1,030,500 of property taxes levied in 2001, and to record collection of
$80,000 in other receivables.

(9) Estimated Uncollectible Taxes	19,500	
Property Tax Receivable		19,500

To record write-off of uncollected 2000 property taxes authorized by City
Council ($190,000 − $170,500 = $19,500).

(10) Cash	221,000	
Revenue		221,000

To record collection of licenses, permits, fees, service charges, etc.

(11) Expenditures	1,050,000	
Vouchers Payable		1,050,000
Reserve for Encumbrances—2001	1,100,000	
Encumbrances		1,100,000

To record receipt of goods and services that had been previously
encumbered [entry (7) above] in amount of $1,100,000.

(12) Expenditures	210,000	
Vouchers Payable		210,000

To record receipt of goods and services that had *not* been previously
encumbered.

Not all expenditures go through the encumbrance process. Encumbrances are formally recognized in the accounts only when there is an extended period of time between the date the commitment is made and the date the expenditure is incurred. For example, routine payroll expenditures are not encumbered.

(13) Receivable from State Government	275,000	
Revenue		275,000

To record municipal education grant authorized by state legislature.

The amount of revenue recognized is based on an approved grant application filed with the Department of Education and is not dependent on the future performance of specific services or specified expenditures of financial resources.

(14) Encumbrances   250,000
          Reserve for Encumbrances—2001   250,000
              To record a contract to acquire office furnishings and equipment.

(15) Cash   100,000
          Due from Enterprise Fund   100,000
              To record receipt of a cash transfer from the Enterprise Fund.

(16) Expenditures   250,000
          Vouchers Payable   250,000
          Reserve for Encumbrances—2001   250,000
          Encumbrances   250,000
              To record receipt of office equipment and furnishings and to remove
              encumbrance.

Capital expenditures, like other expenditures, represent the approved utilization of the financial resources of the General Fund and therefore are recorded as expenditures and not as assets in the records of the General Fund. However, general capital assets (and related depreciation expense) are required to be reported in the government-wide financial statements.

(17) Vouchers Payable   1,650,000
          Cash   1,650,000
              To record payment of liabilities.

(18) Cash   87,250
          Revenue   87,250
              To record proceeds from sale of used furniture and equipment.

Since the proceeds from the sale of Model City assets constitute expendable financial resources, they are recorded as revenue by the recipient general fund.

Under *GASB Statement No. 34*, a government-wide Statement of Activities prepared on an accrual basis is now required, in addition to the funds statements prepared on the modified accrual basis. One entry that is affected is the sale of an asset such as entry (18) above. The proceeds from the sale of an asset are not reported as revenue; instead the difference between the carrying value of the asset (after considering depreciation) and the cash received is reported as a gain or loss on the government-wide statement of activities.[9]

(19) Cash   275,000
          Receivable from State Government   275,000
              To record collection of grant from state legislature.

(20) Due to Debt Service Fund   96,000
          Cash   96,000
              To record authorized transfers of cash to other Model City fund entities.

[9]Governmental Accounting Standards Board (GASB), *GASB Statement No. 34*, "Basic Financial Statements—and Management's Discussion and Analysis—For State and Local Governments" (Norwalk, CT), June 1999.

(21)	Certificates of Deposit	6,000	
	Revenue		6,000
	To record interest earned on certificates of deposit that has been reinvested in the certificates.		

(22)	Estimated Uncollectible Taxes	76,000	
	Property Tax Receivable		76,000
	To record write-off of 2001 property taxes authorized by City Council.		

(23)	Expenditures	200,000	
	Cash (to internal service fund)		200,000
	To record interfund services provided by the internal service fund.		

Summary of Expendable Fund Entries

1. At the beginning of the period, estimated revenues are debited against appropriations (estimated expenditures), with the difference recorded to Unreserved Fund Balance.

2. At the beginning of the period, transfers to and from other funds are recorded against ''due from or to other funds.''

3. During the period, revenues are recorded against an increase in assets (i.e., against receivables, cash, etc.).

4. During the period, when the firm makes a commitment for goods or services, the account encumbrances is debited and reserve for encumbrances is credited. (Encumbrances are future expenditures.)

5. During the period, when goods that have been ordered (and encumbered) are received or contracted services are performed, two entries are prepared:
   a. Expenditures are debited against a decrease in assets or an increase in liabilities. This may or may not equal the amount of the original encumbrance.
   b. When the expenditure is recorded, the entry to record the encumbrance (item 4 above) is reversed. (This may or may not be equal to the actual expenditure.) Therefore, the amount remaining in the reserve for encumbrances represents the amount of funds that have been committed in the current period, but that are expected to be paid in the next period.

6. Purchases of capital assets are recorded in the same manner as any expenditure. An expenditure is debited and either cash or a liability is credited.

7. Gross proceeds from the sale of capital assets are recorded as revenues.

Preclosing Trial Balance The transactions summarized in the journal entries above are reflected in the December 31, 2001, general ledger trial balance for the General Fund of Model City presented below.

Model City
The General Fund
General Ledger Trial Balance
December 31, 2001

	Dr.	Cr.
Cash	$ 63,250	
Certificates of Deposit	106,000	
Property Taxes Receivable	181,000	
Due from Enterprise Fund	50,000	

	Dr.	Cr.
Estimated Revenue	1,860,000	
Expenditures	1,710,000	
Encumbrances	191,000	
Transfers to Other Funds (debt service)	96,000	
Expenditures—2000	148,000	
Estimated Uncollectible Taxes		$ 53,250
Vouchers Payable		73,000
Unreserved Fund Balance		11,000
Reserve for Encumbrances		191,000
Reserve for Encumbrances—2000		155,000
Appropriations		1,944,000
Revenue		1,828,000
Transfer from Other Funds (enterprise fund)		150,000
Total	$4,405,250	$4,405,250

Closing Entries December 31, 2001, closing entries for the General Fund are as follows:

(24)	Unreserved Fund Balance	32,000	
	Revenue	1,828,000	
	Estimated Revenue		1,860,000
	To close out actual and budgeted revenue accounts.		

(25)	Appropriations	1,944,000	
	Expenditures (for 2001)		1,710,000
	Encumbrances		191,000
	Unreserved Fund Balance		43,000
	To close out appropriations and current year's expenditures and encumbrances accounts.		

Note that the reserve for encumbrances also has a credit balance of $191,000.

(26)	Reserve for Encumbrances—2000	155,000	
	Expenditures—2000		148,000
	Unreserved Fund Balance		7,000
	To close out expenditures for goods and services *ordered* and encumbered in prior year. See entry (6).		

(27)	Transfers from Other Funds	150,000	
	Unreserved Fund Balance		54,000
	Transfers to Other Funds		96,000
	To close out interfund transfers to the unreserved fund balance.		

Summary of Closing Entries for Expendable Funds

1. Revenues are closed against estimated revenues. The difference is recorded in unreserved fund balance.

2. Recall that appropriations are approved expenditures for the year. Appropriations are closed against expenditures (actual) and encumbrances (current year commitments). Any difference is reported in the unreserved fund balance.

3. Transfers to and from other funds are closed against the unreserved fund balance.

ILLUSTRATION 18–7

Model City
The General Fund
Balance Sheet
December 31, 2001 and 2000

Assets	*2001*	*2000*
Cash	$ 63,250	$ 45,000
Certificate of Deposit	106,000	100,000
Property Tax Receivable (less allowance for uncollectible		
amounts, 2001—$53,250; 2000—$20,000)	127,750	170,000
Due from Other Funds	50,000	—
Total	$347,000	$315,000
Liabilities and Fund Balance		
Vouchers Payable	$ 73,000	$ 65,000
Fund Balance		
Unreserved	83,000	95,000
Reserved for Encumbrances	191,000	155,000
Total Fund Balance	274,000	250,000
Total Liabilities and Fund Balances	$347,000	$315,000

ILLUSTRATION 18–8

Statement of Revenues, Expenditures, and Changes in Fund Balance
The General Fund
For Years Ended December 31, 2001 and December 31, 2000

	2001	*2000*
Revenues		
Property Taxes	1,158,750	1,105,000
Licenses and Permits	170,500	175,000
State Grant—education	275,000	250,000
Charges for Services	130,500	130,000
Interest	6,000	—
Total Revenue	1,740,750	1,660,000
Expenditures		
Public Safety	480,000	360,000
General Government	289,000	175,000
Highways and Streets	128,000	130,000
Sanitation	70,000	71,000
Health	141,000	132,000
Cultural—recreation	80,000	82,000
Education	670,000	640,000
Total Expenditures	1,858,000	1,590,000
Excess (deficiency) of revenues over expenditures	(117,250)	70,000
Other Financing Sources (Uses)		
Operating Transfers In—Enterprise Fund	150,000	—
Operating Transfers Out—Debt Service Fund	(96,000)	(60,000)
Total Other	54,000	(60,000)
Special Items		
Proceeds from sales of equipment	87,250	—
Net change in fund balance	24,000	10,000
Fund Balance—beginning	250,000	240,000
Fund Balance—ending	274,000	250,000

Financial Statements

The two basic statements prepared for expendable fund entities are (1) a balance sheet and (2) a statement of revenue, expenditures, and changes in fund balance. Revenue should be classified by major sources and expenditures by major functions in the statement of revenue, expenditures, and changes in fund balance. In addition, comparative information for the prior year should be presented both in that statement and in the balance sheet. For the general fund, these statements are presented in Illustrations 18-7 and 18-8.

For budgetary fund entities, a financial statement that compares budgeted and actual operating results should also be prepared. Budgeted comparison statements should be presented as required supplementary information (RSI). The purpose of budgetary comparison reporting is to show whether resources were obtained and used in accordance with the entity's legally adopted budget. Since amounts encumbered (encumbrances) against the current year's appropriation authority (budget) must be treated in the same manner as expenditures in budgeted statements, the "actual" data may be different from those presented in accordance with generally accepted accounting principles in the statement of revenue, expenditures, and other changes in fund balance. In that case, the difference between the budgetary basis and generally accepted accounting principles should be explained in the notes to the financial statements. An example of the Budgetary Comparison Schedule is shown in Illustration 18-9 and the Budget-to-GAAP Reconciliation schedule is shown in Illustration 18-10.

ILLUSTRATION 18–9

Model City
Budgetary Comparison Schedule
General Fund
For the Year Ended December 31, 2001

	Budgeted Amounts		Actual Amounts	Variance with Final Budget Favorable (Unfavorable)
	Original	Final		
Budgetary Fund Balance, January 1	$ 250,000	$ 250,000	$ 250,000	—
Resources				
Property Tax	1,158,750	1,158,750	1,158,750	—
Licenses and Permits	190,000	188,250	170,500	(17,750)
Grants	300,000	300,000	275,000	(25,000)
Charges for Services	131,000	135,000	130,500	(4,500)
Sale of Equipment	83,000	78,000	87,250	9,250
Interest	6,000	6,000	6,000	—
Transfers from Other Funds	150,000	150,000	150,000	—
Amounts Available for Appropriations	$2,268,750	$2,266,000	$2,228,000	$(38,000)
Charges to Appropriations				
Public Safety	510,000	516,000	480,000	36,000
General Government	290,000	293,500	289,000	4,500
Highways and Streets	135,000	135,500	128,000	7,500
Sanitation	73,000	75,000	70,000	5,000
Health	140,000	148,500	141,000	7,500
Cultural—recreation	90,000	88,500	80,000	8,500
Education	690,000	687,000	670,000	17,000
Transfers to Other Funds	96,000	96,000	96,000	—
Total Charges to Appropriations	2,024,000	2,040,000	1,954,000	86,000
Budgetary Fund Balance, December 31	$ 244,750	$ 226,000	$ 274,000	$ 48,000

ILLUSTRATION 18–10

Model City
Budgetary Comparison Schedule
Budget-to-GAAP Reconciliation

	General Fund
Sources/inflows of resources:	
Actual amounts (budgetary basis) "available for appropriation" from the Budget to Actual Comparison Statement (see Illustration 18–9)	$2,228,000
Differences—budget to GAAP	
The fund balance at the beginning of the year is a budgetary resource and is not a current year revenue for financial reporting purposes	(250,000)
Transfers from other funds are inflows of budgetary resources but are not revenues for financial reporting purposes	(150,000)
The proceeds from the sale of equipment are budgetary resources but are regarded as a special item, rather than revenue, for financial reporting purposes	(87,250)
Total revenues as reported on the Statement of Revenues, Expenditures, and Changes in Fund Balances—General Fund (see Illustration 18–8)	$1,740,750
Uses/outflows of resources:	
Actual amounts (budgetary basis) total charges to appropriation from the Budget to Actual Comparison Statement (see Illustration 18–9)	$1,954,000
Differences—budget to GAAP	
Transfers to other funds are outflows of budgetary resources but are not expenditures for financial reporting purposes	(96,000)
Total expenditures as reported on the Statement of Revenues, Expenditures, and Changes in Fund Balance—General Fund (See Illustration 18–8)	$1,858,000

REPORTING INVENTORY AND PREPAYMENTS IN THE FINANCIAL STATEMENTS

Inventory

There are two methods of accounting for and reporting inventory in the financial statements of expendable fund entities: the *consumption method* and the *purchases method*. Under *GASB Statement No. 34*, the consumption method is consistent with the government-wide approach, and the purchases method is not acceptable. Both are acceptable for fund purposes, however, and are illustrated here. Under the consumption method, inventory is considered to be a financial resource (asset), and expenditures for inventory are reported on the operating statement in the period in which the inventory is used. Under the purchases method, inventory is not considered to be a financial resource (asset) and expenditures are recognized in the period the inventory is purchased whether it is used or not.

To illustrate, assume that $20,000 in inventory is on hand at the beginning of the period, that $50,000 in inventory is purchased during the period, and that inventory at the end of the period is $24,000. Entries and balances under each method are as follows:

Consumption Method			Purchases Method		
Beginning inventory on the balance sheet		$20,000	No inventory on the balance sheet		
When Purchased:			*When Purchased:*		
Expenditures	50,000		Expenditures	50,000	
Cash		50,000	Cash		50,000
End of Year:			*End of Year:*		
Inventory	4,000		NO ENTRY		
Expenditures		4,000			
Ending inventory on the balance sheet		$24,000	No inventory on the balance sheet		

The entry at the end of the year under the consumption method adjusts the inventory account from its beginning of year balance, $20,000, to the correct ending inventory amount, $24,000. If inventory decreases, expenditures would be debited and inventory credited. Under the consumption method, inventories are automatically reported as an asset in the financial statements. As compared to the purchases method, financial statements prepared under the consumption method reflect $4,000 less expenditures and a similarly larger fund balance.

Reserve for Inventory

Purchases Method Some accountants believe that, even if the purchases method is used, material amounts of inventory should be disclosed in the financial statements either by footnote or by reporting an asset in the balance sheet with a contra account, Reserve for Inventory, reported as part of the total fund balance. To illustrate the reporting of inventory as both an asset and an expenditure under the purchases method, assume that the balance sheet at the beginning of the period was as shown here:

Inventory	$ 20,000
Other Financial Resources (net)	400,000
Net Assets	$420,000
Fund Balance	
Reserve for Inventory	$ 20,000
Unreserved Fund Balance	400,000
Total Fund Balance	$420,000

In addition to the purchases method entry illustrated above, another entry is necessary at the end of the year to record the $4,000 increase in inventory as follows:

Purchases Method		
End of Year		
Inventory	4,000	
Reserve for Inventory		4,000

If inventory decreases, Reserve for Inventory is debited and Inventory is credited. Assuming net financial resources (excluding inventory) increase by $100,000 during the period, the amounts that would be reported in the balance sheet at the end of the period are as follows:

Inventory	$ 24,000
Other Financial Resources (net)	500,000
Net Assets	$524,000
Fund Balance	
Reserve for Inventory	$ 24,000
Unreserved Fund Balance	500,000
Total Fund Balance	$520,000

When a reserve for inventory is created under the purchases method, the amounts reported for inventory and the *total* fund balance are the same as those reported under the consumption method. However, the amount of expenditures reported in the operating statement will still differ (in this case by $4,000).

Consumption Method In some cases it is considered desirable to both (1) use the consumption method and (2) report a reserve for inventory. If the consumption method is used, the reserve for inventory is created and adjusted by debiting or crediting the "unreserved fund balance." For example, using the above illustration and assuming the balance in Reserve for Inventory was $20,000 at the beginning of the year, another entry in addition to those illustrated under the consumption method above would be made at the end of the year as follows:

Consumption Method		
End of Year		
Unreserved Fund Balance	4,000	
Reserve for Inventory		4,000

Prepayments

Prepayments for items such as insurance or rent that cover more than one accounting period may also be reported using the consumption or purchase methods. Under the purchases method the cost is reported as an expenditure in the period when the insurance premium or rent is paid without regard to the period benefited (there is no allocation among accounting periods). Under the consumption method, a prepaid asset would be recorded and expenditures reduced to the extent that the premium or rent payment is for a subsequent period.

Lapsing of Appropriations

The treatment illustrated in this chapter for encumbrances outstanding at the end of the period was based on the assumption (and generally followed practice) that encumbered appropriations do not lapse at the end of the fiscal year. It is possible, however, for the legislative body or governing board to impose a provision that causes unexpended appropriations to lapse at the end of the year. In this case, the reserve for encumbrances must be closed out at the end of the year, and if the encumbered items are to be purchased in the next year, the appropriation for the next year must contain authority for such expenditures.

If appropriations lapse, the closing entry for appropriations at the end of the year takes the following form:

Reserve for Encumbrances	191,000	
Appropriations	1,744,000	
Expenditures		1,510,000
Encumbrances		191,000
Unreserved Fund Balance		234,000

The subsequent year's appropriation should include authorization for the purchase of the encumbered items. Therefore, the reserve for encumbrances would be reestablished at the beginning of the next year by a debit to encumbrances, and subsequent expenditures for the items would be accounted for the same as any other expenditures in that year.

According to a University of Tennessee study, the state of Tennessee lost $34 million in 1999 in tax revenue to e-commerce. The reason? Sales tax is not collected on most Internet sales, and Tennessee (currently with no state income tax) is among those states that rely heavily upon sales tax revenue. Although both Congress and President Clinton have been reluctant to take any steps toward inhibiting the growth of e-commerce, many believe that the Internet tax panel should recommend an approach to Congress that ensures that states get what they are entitled to in tax revenue.[10]

 ## SUMMARY

1. *Distinguish between a nonbusiness organization and a profit-oriented enterprise.* The primary goal of a profit-oriented enterprise is to earn a profit. Nonbusiness organizations provide services based on social need. Persons who contribute to nonbusiness organizations receive no equity in the organization and do not necessarily benefit proportionally or at all from the services provided.

2. *Explain the role of fund accounting.* Resources received by nonbusiness organizations typically have restrictions or are limited by use. In many cases, the nonbusiness organization has self-imposed restrictions on the use of resources. In order to account for these restrictions, nonbusiness organizations use fund accounting. In essence, the organization separates the assets, liabilities, and residual equity into distinct funds organized for specific objectives. Each fund is treated as a separate accounting entity consisting of a self-balancing set of books.

3. *Distinguish among the concepts of revenues, expenses, and expenditures as used in profit-oriented entities and as used for expendable fund entities.* Profit-oriented entities recognize revenues on an accrual basis and expenses using the matching principle. Expendable fund entities typically treat any increase in financial resources as revenues, such as from property taxes or sales of equipment (except debt issuances and trans-

fers from other funds). Also, expendable funds treat any decrease in resources as an expenditure (except transfers to other funds).

4. *Understand the classification of revenues and other resource inflows for fund accounting.* Revenues are classified by source, such as property taxes, fines and penalties, and licenses and permits.

5. *Understand the classification of expenditures and other resource outflows for fund accounting.* Expenditures are classified by function, by activity, by organizational unit, by object, or by character (nature of the item). For government-wide reporting, the statement of activities classifies expenses by function.

6. *Describe the critical events in the use of financial resources of an expendable fund.* Before resources can be spent, they must follow a series of events. First, the amount must be authorized (appropriated) by proper authorities. Second, since the amounts spent cannot exceed the appropriations, when a purchase order is placed (or a contract is signed), an encumbrance is recorded against a reserve for encumbrance. Any unencumbered balance indicates the amount of resources not yet committed. When a contract is performed or a service received, an expenditure is recorded and the encumbrance and the reserve for encumbrance are reduced. At year-end, appropriations, encumbrances, and expenditures are closed to

[10]The Leaf-Chronicle, "State is Losing Out On Revenue," by the editorial board of The Leaf-Chronicle, 2/12/00, p. A6.

fund balance. The reserve for encumbrances carries over to the next period.

7. *Explain how capital expenditures are recorded in an expendable fund.* In profit-oriented firms, capital expenditures are recorded as assets and depreciated over their useful lives. In an expendable fund, capital expenditures are treated as expenditures (as an outflow of resources), but are not depreciated. Funds are set up to properly account for the source and use of resources during a particular period and to ensure that the fund does not spend more than its limit (appropriation).

8. *Understand the role of a general fund.* The general fund is used to account for all externally *unrestricted* financial resources. In other words, the general fund is used to account for all resources that have not been set aside for specific activities. Funds typically divide governments into categories based on the restrictions of the resources.

9. *Contrast the consumption and the purchases methods of accounting for inventories (and other prepaid items).* The consumption method treats inventory as an asset until used, while the purchases method treats all inventory purchases as expenditures of the period. Therefore, inventory is not recorded on the balance sheet if the purchases method is used. Both methods are acceptable for fund purposes, but in the government-wide statements, only the consumption method is acceptable.

QUESTIONS

1. What characteristics distinguish nonbusiness organizations from profit-oriented enterprises?

2. Define a fund as the term is applied in accounting for the activities of governmental units and other nonbusiness organizations.

3. What is the significance of the ''unreserved fund balance'' of an expendable fund entity?

4. What are the major classifications of increases and decreases in expendable fund resources?

5. What are the revenue-recognition criteria for expendable fund entities? How do these criteria differ from revenue-recognition criteria for profit-oriented enterprises?

6. Expenditures may be classified by function, activity, object, or organizational unit. Give an example of each classification for a municipality. Which classification is the most appropriate for external financial reporting?

7. Distinguish between an appropriation, an encumbrance, an expenditure, and a disbursement.

8. Distinguish between an expense and an expenditure.

9. Explain and justify the difference between the treatment of estimated uncollectible taxes in fund accounting and the treatment of estimated bad debts in commercial accounting.

10. Explain the purposes of encumbrance accounting. Might encumbrance accounting be used by commercial enterprises?

11. Is the year-end balance in the Reserve for Encumbrances account a liability? Explain.

12. What columns would you suggest for a subsidiary ledger account in order that it might be a subsidiary not only to the ''appropriations'' control account but also the ''encumbrances'' and the ''expenditures'' control accounts?

13. Why is depreciation on fixed assets not recorded in the records of expendable fund entities?

14. How does the adoption of a budget for a general fund entity differ from the adoption of a budget by a commercial unit?

15. Describe the principal financial statements used to report on the activities and status of expendable fund entities.

16. Why may it be difficult or impossible for a governmental unit to determine the total cost of performing a particular activity or function?

EXERCISES

EXERCISE 18-1   General Fund Journal Entries
Several independent financial activities of a governmental unit are given below.

1. Revenue from the sale of licenses and permits for the first two months totaled $15,000.

2. Land that had been donated previously was sold for $100,000.

3. An order was placed for the purchase of a new fire engine at a price of $130,000.

4. Bonds with a face value of $500,000 were issued at par value to finance a new park.

5. A $250,000 grant was received from the federal government to help improve the local schools.

6. The new fire engine was received and accepted. The approved price, however, was $140,000 rather than $130,000.

Required:
Prepare the journal entries needed to account for each transaction in the General Fund.

EXERCISE 18-2 **General Fund Journal Entries**
Listed are typical financial activities of a local governmental unit.

1. The legislative unit approved the budget for the general operating fund. Estimated revenues are $4,000,000, and appropriations for expenditures are $3,800,000.

2. Statements of property tax assessments totaling $3,000,000 were mailed to property owners. It is estimated that 4% of the assessed taxes will be uncollectible.

3. Notification was received from the state that this unit's share of sales tax revenues from the fourth quarter of the previous year will be $500,000.

4. The manager signed a contract to purchase equipment costing $250,000.

5. The equipment ordered above was received and paid for.

6. Employees were paid their biweekly wages of $36,000.

7. Property taxes in the amount of $2,050,000 were collected.

Required:
Prepare the necessary journal entries to record the transactions listed above in the records of the General Fund.

EXERCISE 18-3 **General Fund Journal Entries**
Listed are transactions of the Town of Jackson.

1. A budget consisting of estimated revenues of $1,950,000 and appropriations for expenditures of $1,800,000 was passed by the town council.

2. Property taxes of $1,150,000 were assessed; $1,115,000 are expected to be collectible.

3. Property taxes in the amount of $1,080,000 were collected.

4. Equipment costing $200,000 was purchased, and the old equipment was sold at the end of its estimated useful life for $24,000.

5. A contract was signed with an independent company to do the trash collecting for the year. The contract price was $96,000.

6. The first monthly bill of $8,000 was received from the trash collector.

7. The $8,000 bill was paid.

Required:
Prepare the journal entries needed in the records of the General Fund to account for these transactions.

EXERCISE 18-4 **General Fund Closing Entries**
Following is the preclosing trial balance for the General Fund of the City of Doyle.

Doyle City
The General Fund
General Ledger Trial Balance
December 31, 2002

Cash	$ 400,000	
Certificates of Deposit	350,000	
Due from State Government	112,000	
Due from Other Funds	30,000	
Taxes Receivable	774,000	
Estimated Revenue	3,110,000	
Expenditures	1,960,000	
Encumbrances	734,000	
Transfers to Other Funds	90,000	
Expenditures—2001	55,000	
Estimated Uncollectible Taxes		$ 30,000
Vouchers Payable		64,000
Due to Other Funds		27,000
Unreserved Fund Balance		760,000
Reserve for Encumbrances		734,000
Reserve for Encumbrances—2001		50,000
Appropriations		2,700,000
Revenue		3,210,000
Transfers from Other Funds		40,000
	$7,615,000	$7,615,000

Required:
Prepare in general journal form the closing entries for the General Fund of Doyle City.

EXERCISE 18-5 General Fund Closing Entries

The preclosing trial balance for the General Fund of the City of Springfield is presented below.

City of Springfield
The General Fund
General Ledger Trial Balance
December 31, 2001

Cash	$ 90,000	
Certificates of Deposit	120,000	
Property Taxes Receivable	175,000	
Estimated Revenue	1,690,000	
Expenditures	1,310,000	
Expenditures—2000	32,000	
Encumbrances	165,000	
Estimated Uncollectible Taxes		$ 51,000
Vouchers Payable		65,000
Unreserved Fund Balance		41,000
Reserve for Encumbrances		165,000
Reserve for Encumbrances—2000		35,000
Appropriations		1,550,000
Revenue		1,675,000
	$3,582,000	$3,582,000

Required:
Prepare the closing entries for the General Fund.

EXERCISE 18-6 Accounting for Supplies

In 2001, Bay City purchased supplies valued at $350,000. At the end of the year, $65,000 of the supplies were still in the inventory. No supplies were on hand at the beginning of the year. The city uses the purchases method to account for supplies.

Required:

A. Prepare the journal entry necessary to report the supplies as an asset in the balance sheet of Bay City.

B. What amount of expenditures for supplies will be shown in the statement of revenues, expenditures, and changes in fund balance?

EXERCISE 18-7 **Purchases versus Consumption Methods**

At the beginning of 2001, the City of Fairview reported an Unreserved Fund Balance of $555,000 and a supplies inventory balance of $175,000. During the year, Fairview purchased $225,000 in supplies and used $220,000 worth. The city will report a reserve for supplies inventory.

Required:

A. Prepare the necessary journal entries under the purchases method.

B. Prepare the journal entries needed to account for the supplies under the consumption method.

C. What would the 13/31/01 balance in the Unreserved Fund Balance be under each method, assuming that the only transactions of the fund are those involving the supplies?

EXERCISE 18-8 **Journal Entries**

During 2001, the City of Greenfield engaged in the following financial activities:

1. The City Council approved the budget for the general operating fund. The budget shows estimated revenues of $1,900,000 and appropriations for expenditures of $1,850,000.

2. Property tax assessments for 2001 were compiled and statements mailed to property owners. Assessments total $955,000. Past collection experience indicates that approximately 5% of assessed property taxes are delinquent or uncollectible during the year of billing.

3. A low bid of $15,000 was accepted for a new vehicle for the fire chief. A purchase order was issued providing for additional costs for painting and ancillary equipment (negotiated after the bid) prior to delivery. The estimate of additional costs is $1,400.

4. Additional purchase orders placed during the year amount to $140,000.

5. City employees are issued paychecks for the month of April. The total payroll amounts to $90,000.

6. The City received a statement from the State Treasurer that the City's portion of the state sales tax for the first half-year is $375,000.

7. Vouchers for expenditures totaling $135,000 are approved for payment. Encumbrances against these vouchers were recorded at a total of $137,000.

8. The vehicle for the fire chief was delivered and accepted. The invoice in the amount of $16,200 was approved for payment.

9. Property tax collections for the month of June amounted to $450,000.

10. The City Treasurer issued checks in payment of the vouchers totaling $135,000 and for the invoice for the fire chief's vehicle.

11. A purchase order previously issued for an electric typewriter (estimated price $650) was canceled when the vendor indicated a three-month delay in delivery.

Required:

Prepare journal entries to record and account for the foregoing transactions.

EXERCISE 18-9 **General Fund Journal Entries**

The following events relate typical activities in a municipality that affect the General Fund.

1. The Meadville City Council passed an ordinance approving a general operating budget of $580,000 for fiscal year 2001. The city's only source of revenue is from property taxes. For 2001, these revenues are estimated at $565,000.

2. A property tax levy of $1 per $100 assessed valuation (total assessed valuation equals $60,000,000) is billed to property owners. Taxes are due in the current fiscal year. Experience indicates that 3% of taxes billed will be uncollectible.

3. A motorcycle for the Department of Public Safety is ordered by the purchasing department on the basis of a low bid of $4,200.

4. The motorcycle in (3) above is received and the invoice is approved for payment. Extra accessories not included in the bid price amount to $425.

5. Salaries and wages in the amount of $20,000 are paid by check to city employees for the two-week period ending on May 15.

6. The property division sold used typewriters and other office equipment at a public auction. Total receipts were $8,225.

7. Property taxes in the amount of $540,000 were collected.

Required:

Prepare the necessary journal entries to record each event in the accounts of the General Fund.

EXERCISE 18-10 **Multiple Choice**

Select the best answer for each of the following items:

1. When used in fund accounting, the term "fund" usually refers to
    (a) A sum of money designated for a special purpose.
    (b) A liability to other governmental units.
    (c) The equity of a municipality in its own assets.
    (d) A fiscal and accounting entity having a set of self-balancing accounts.

2. Authority granted by a legislative body to make expenditures and to incur obligations during a fiscal year is the definition of an
    (a) Appropriation.
    (b) Authorization.
    (c) Encumbrance.
    (d) Expenditure.

3. What type of account is used to earmark the fund balance to liquidate the contingent obligations of goods ordered but not yet received?
    (a) Appropriations.
    (b) Encumbrances.
    (c) Obligations.
    (d) Reserve for encumbrances.

4. A city's General Fund budget for the forthcoming fiscal year shows estimated revenues in excess of appropriations. The initial effect of recording this will result in an increase in
    (a) Taxes receivable.
    (b) Fund balance.
    (c) Reserve for encumbrances.
    (d) Encumbrances.

5. The Reserve for Encumbrances account is properly considered to be a
   (a) Current liability if payable within a year; otherwise, a long-term debt.
   (b) Fixed liability.
   (c) Floating debt.
   (d) Reservation of the fund's equity.

6. In preparing the General Fund budget of Dover City for the forthcoming fiscal year, the City Council appropriated a sum greater than expected revenues. This action of the Council will result in
   (a) A cash overdraft during that fiscal year.
   (b) An increase in encumbrances by the end of that fiscal year.
   (c) A decrease in the fund balance.
   (d) A necessity for compensatory offsetting action in the Debt Service Fund.

7. What would be the effect on the General Fund balance in the current fiscal year of recording a $150,000 purchase for a new fire truck out of General Fund resources, for which a $146,000 encumbrance had been recorded in the General Fund in the previous fiscal year?
   (a) Reduce the General Fund balance by $150,000.
   (b) Reduce the General Fund balance by $146,000.
   (c) Reduce the General Fund balance by $4,000.
   (d) Have no effect on the General Fund balance.

(*AICPA adapted*)

PROBLEMS

PROBLEM 18-1 **Journal Entries, Closing Entries, and Trial Balance**
The general ledger trial balance of the General Fund of the City of Bedford on January 1, 2001, shows the following:

	Dr.	Cr.
Cash	$100,000	
Taxes Receivable	75,000	
Allowance for Uncollectible Taxes		$ 35,000
Unreserved Fund Balance		110,000
Reserve for Encumbrances—2000		30,000
Total	$175,000	$175,000

A summary of activities and transactions for the General Fund during 2001 is presented here:

1. The City Council adopted a budget for the General Fund with estimated revenues of $1,560,000 and authorization for appropriated expenditures of $1,400,000. The budget authorized the transfer of $50,000 from the Water Fund to the General Fund for operating expenses as a payment in lieu of taxes. Cash for the payment of interest due for the year on the $1,000,000, 8% bond issue for the Civic Center is approved for transfer from the General Fund to the Debt Service Fund.

2. The annual property tax levy of 10% on assessed valuation ($11,000,000) is billed to property owners. Two percent is estimated to be uncollectible.

3. Goods and services amounting to $1,150,000 were ordered during the year.

4. Invoices for all goods ordered in 2000 amounting to $29,000 were approved for payment.

5. Funds for bond interest on Civic Center bonds were transferred to the Debt Service Fund.

6. Invoices for goods and services received during the year totaling $1,155,000 were recorded. These were encumbered previously [see (3) above].

7. Transfer of funds from the Water Company was received in lieu of taxes.

8. Taxes were collected from property owners in the amount of $1,050,000.

9. Past-due tax bills of $17,000 were charged off as uncollectible.

10. Checks in payment of invoices for goods and services ordered in 2000 and 2001 were issued [see items (4) and (6) above].

11. Revenues received from miscellaneous sources, other than property taxes, of $455,000 were recorded.

12. Purchase order for two trash collection vehicle systems complete with residence trash containers for automatic pickup of trash was issued. Bid price per system was $120,000.

Required:

A. Prepare journal entries to record the summary transactions. You may find it necessary or convenient to post journal entries to ledger T accounts before the preparation of the required trial balances.

B. Prepare a preclosing trial balance.

C. Prepare closing entries.

D. Prepare a postclosing trial balance.

PROBLEM 18-2 **Unreserved Fund Balance—Adjusting and Closing Entries**

The following account balances, among others, were included in the preclosing trial balance of the General Fund of the City of Lynchburg on December 31, 2002.

Estimated Revenue	$630,000
Expenditures	468,000
Encumbrances	120,000
Expenditures—2001	43,000
Reserve for encumbrances (Note 1)	162,000
Appropriations	672,000
Revenue	696,000
Reserve for Supplies Inventory (Note 2)	72,000
Supplies Inventory (Note 2)	72,000
Unreserved Fund Balance	24,000

Note 1: The balance in this account was $42,000 on January 1, 2002. Purchase orders outstanding on December 31, 2002, total $120,000.
Note 2: Supplies on hand on December 31, 2002, amount to $60,000.

Required:

A. What was the balance in the Unreserved Fund Balance account on December 31, 2001? What was the total Fund Balance on December 31, 2001?

B. Prepare the necessary adjusting and closing entries for the year ended December 31, 2002. Supplies inventory is accounted for using the purchases method.

C. Prepare a schedule to calculate the Unreserved Fund Balance and the total Fund Balance on December 31, 2002.

PROBLEM 18-3 **Computing Unreserved Fund Balance and Closing Entries**

The following account balances, among others, were included in the preclosing trial balance of the General Fund of the City of Madison on December 31, 2002.

Appropriations	$3,488,000
Cash	270,000
Due to Other Funds	100,000
Due from Other Funds	250,000
Encumbrances	382,000
Estimated Revenue	3,720,000

Expenditures	3,020,000
Expenditures—2001	296,000
Reserve for Encumbrances	382,000
Reserve for Encumbrances—2001	310,000
Revenue	3,656,000
Taxes Receivable	600,000
Transfers from Other Funds	300,000
Transfers to Other Funds	520,000
Unreserved Fund Balance	422,000
Vouchers Payable	400,000

Required:

A. Prepare the necessary closing entries on December 31, 2002.

B. Calculate the amount of both the unreserved fund balance and the total fund balance in the balance sheet (1) on December 31, 2001 and (2) on December 31, 2002.

C. Prepare a schedule reconciling the December 31, 2001, total fund balance with the December 31, 2002, total fund balance by reference to actual inflows and outflows of financial resources.

PROBLEM 18-4 **Entries, Balance Sheet, Statement of Revenues, Expenditures, and Changes in Fund Balance**

The trial balance for the General Fund of the City of Monte Vista as of December 31, 2001, is presented here:

	Debit	Credit
Cash	$300,000	
Supplies Inventory	75,000	
Unreserved Fund Balance		$300,000
Reserve for Supplies Inventory		75,000
	$375,000	$375,000

Transactions of the General Fund for the year ended December 31, 2002, are summarized as follows:

1. The City Council adopted the following budget for 2002:

Estimated revenue	$1,600,000
Transfer from trust fund	50,000
Appropriations	1,530,000
Transfer to debt service fund	80,000

2. Property taxes of $1,500,000 were levied, of which it is estimated that $30,000 will not be collected.

3. Purchase orders in the amount of $1,400,000 were placed with suppliers and other vendors.

4. Property taxes in the amount of $1,450,000 were collected.

5. Cash was received from the Trust Fund in the amount of $50,000.

6. Invoices in the amount of $1,380,000 were approved for payment. The amount originally encumbered for these invoices was $1,360,000. The invoices included $25,000 net of trade-in allowance for the purchase of a new minicomputer and $400,000 for supplies. The City received a trade-in allowance of $4,000 on its old minicomputer, which had been purchased three years earlier for $16,000. At the time the old minicomputer was pur-

chased, it was estimated that it would have a useful life of four years. The new minicomputer is expected to last at least six years. The City of Monte Vista uses the purchase method to account for supplies inventory.

7. Licenses and fees in the amount of $48,000 were collected.

8. Vouchers in the amount of $1,300,000 were paid.

9. Cash in the amount of $80,000 was transferred to the Debt Service Fund.

10. Supplies on hand at the end of the year amount to $100,000.

Required:

A. Prepare entries in general journal form to record the transactions of the General Fund for the year ended December 31, 2002.

B. Prepare a preclosing trial balance for the General Fund as of December 31, 2002.

C. Prepare the necessary closing entries for the General Fund for the year ended December 31, 2002.

D. Prepare a balance sheet and a statement of revenues, expenditures, and changes in fund balance for the General Fund for the year ended December 31, 2002.

PROBLEM 18-5 **Balance Sheet, Statement of Revenues, Expenditures, and Changes in Fund Balance**
The trial balance for the General Fund of the City of Fairfield as of December 31, 2001, is presented here:

City of Fairfield
The General Fund
Adjusted Trial Balance
December 31, 2001

	Debit	Credit
Cash	$430,000	
Property Tax Receivable	45,000	
Estimated Uncollectible Taxes		$ 20,000
Due from Trust Fund	50,000	
Vouchers Payable		60,000
Reserve for Encumbrances		30,000
Unreserved Fund Balance		415,000
	$525,000	$525,000

Transactions for the year ended December 31, 2002, are summarized as follows:

1. The City Council adopted a budget for the year with estimated revenue of $735,000 and appropriations of $700,000.

2. Property taxes in the amount of $590,000 were levied for the current year. It is estimated that $24,000 of the taxes levied will prove to be uncollectible.

3. Proceeds from the sale of equipment in the amount of $35,000 were received by the General Fund. The equipment was purchased 10 years ago with resources of the General Fund at a cost of $150,000. On the date of purchase, it was estimated that the equipment had a useful life of 15 years.

4. Licenses and fees in the amount of $110,000 were collected.

5. The total amount of encumbrances against fund resources for the year was $642,500.

6. Vouchers in the amount of $455,000 were authorized for payment. This was $15,000 less than the amount originally encumbered for these purchases.

7. An invoice in the amount of $28,000 was received for goods ordered in 2001. The invoice was approved for payment.

8. Property taxes in the amount of $570,000 were collected.

9. Vouchers in the amount of $475,000 were paid.

10. Fifty thousand dollars was transferred to the General Fund from the Trust Fund.

11. The City Council authorized the write-off of $30,000 in uncollected property taxes.

Required:

A. Prepare entries in general journal form to record the transactions for the year ended December 31, 2002.

B. Prepare a preclosing trial balance for the General Fund as of December 31, 2002.

C. Prepare the necessary closing entries for the year ended December 31, 2002.

D. Prepare a balance sheet and a statement of revenues, expenditures, and changes in fund balance for the General Fund for the year ended December 31, 2002.

PROBLEM 18-6 **Balance Sheet, Statement of Revenues, Expenditures, and Changes in Fund Balance**

Hunnington Township's adjusted trial balance for the General Fund at the close of its fiscal year ended June 30, 2002, is presented here:

Hunnington Township
General Fund Trial Balance
June 30, 2002

Cash	$ 11,000	
Property Tax Receivable—current (Note 1)	82,000	
Estimated Uncollectible Taxes—current		$ 1,500
Property Tax Receivable—delinquent	25,000	
Estimated Uncollectible Taxes—delinquent		16,500
Accounts Receivable (Note 1)	40,000	
Allowance for Uncollectible Accounts		4,000
Due from Internal Service Fund (Note 5)	50,000	
Expenditures (Note 2)	755,000	
Encumbrances	37,000	
Revenue (Note 3)		60,000
Due to Enterprise Fund (Note 5)		10,000
Vouchers Payable		20,000
Reserve for Encumbrances—prior year		44,000
Reserve for Encumbrances		37,000
Surplus Receipts (Note 4)		7,000
Appropriations		720,000
Unreserved Fund Balance		80,000
	$1,000,000	$1,000,000

Note 1: The current tax roll and accounts receivable, recorded on the accrual basis as sources of revenue, amounted to $500,000 and $200,000, respectively.

Note 2: Includes $42,500 paid during the fiscal year in settlement of all purchase orders outstanding at the beginning of the fiscal year.

Note 3: Represents the difference between the budgeted (estimated) revenue of $700,000 and the actual revenue realized during the fiscal year.

Note 4: Represents the proceeds from the sale of equipment damaged by fire. The equipment originally cost $40,000 and had been held for 80% of its useful life prior to the fire.

Note 5: The interfund payable and receivable resulted from cash advances (loans) to and from the respective funds.

Required:

A. Prepare a statement of revenues, expenditures, and changes in fund balance.

B. Prepare a balance sheet for the General Fund at June 30, 2002.

(AICPA adapted)

PROBLEM 18-7 **Complete Accounting Cycle—General Fund**

The January 1, 2001, trial balance, the calendar-year 2001 budget, and the 2001 transactions of the City of Roseburg are presented here:

City of Roseburg
Trial Balance
January 1, 2001

	Debit	Credit
Cash	$155,450	
Certificates of Deposit	200,000	
Accounts Receivable	28,675	
Supplied Inventory	37,600	
Due from Federal Government	58,000	
Property Taxes Receivable	75,600	
Allowance for Uncollectible Taxes		$ 32,150
Vouchers Payable		181,000
Unreserved Fund Balance		226,075
Reserve for Inventory		37,600
Reserve for Encumbrances		78,500
	$555,325	$555,325

City of Roseburg
Budget for General Fund
Calendar Year 2001

Estimated Revenue	
City Vehicle and Retail License Fees	$ 252,000
Property Taxes	1,448,000
City Sales Tax	327,000
Collections for Trash Service	153,000
Sale of City-Owned Property	88,000
Total Estimated Revenue	2,268,000
Appropriations	
General government	261,000
Public safety and security	875,000
Health and welfare	434,000
Recreation and parks	126,000
Street maintenance	367,000
Sanitation	162,000
Total appropriations	2,225,000
Excess of revenues over appropriations	43,000
Transfer from Water and Sewer Fund	118,000
Less payments (transfers) to Debt Service Funds	(55,000)
Excess of revenue and fund transfers to	
General Fund over appropriations and fund	
transfers out of General Fund	$ 106,000

Transactions of the City of Roseburg that affected the General Fund during the year are summarized below:

1. The City Council approved the budget and it was recorded.

2. Orders for goods and services were issued for a total of $1,202,000 during the year.

3. Goods and services were delivered against all orders placed with a total invoice amount of $1,165,600. Of this, $80,000 was for orders placed in the prior year.

4. The City accepted a low bid of $78,000 for a new street sweeper for the sanitation department. A purchase order was issued.

5. The City received $92,500 from the sale of an old street sweeper and one obsolete fire engine at public auction. The street sweeper cost $60,000 7 years ago, at which time it was estimated to have a useful life of 10 years. The fire engine cost $200,000 8 years ago, at which time it was estimated to have a useful life of 12 years.

6. Property tax statements were issued. The tax levy was 8% of the assessed valuation of $18,500,000. An estimated 2% of the tax levy will be uncollectible.

7. Payment was received from the federal government. This was a grant to be used for upgrading sanitation department equipment.

8. The amount of $55,000 was transferred to the Debt Service Fund for the payment of interest on the outstanding bond issue.

9. The city billed residents for trash service. Total billings amounted to $155,675.

10. Property taxes totaling $1,438,455 were collected, of which $34,200 was past-due collections from the prior year; $18,250 of past-due taxes was charged off as uncollectible.

11. Wages paid to employees during the year amounted to $998,765.

12. City retail establishments remitted a total of $333,650 in sales tax collections for the year.

13. Other cash receipts during the year were:

Vehicle license fees and parking fines	$ 98,682
Retail license fees	130,000
For trash services (including $28,675 due at end of prior year)	148,720
Transfer from Water and Sewer Fund	118,000

14. Cash purchases of printed forms and other office supplies for the year amounted to $57,680.

15. The street sweeper was delivered and an invoice for $78,000 plus freight charges of $1,280 was received. The invoice was approved for payment and a check issued.

16. Checks were issued in payment of outstanding vouchers totaling $1,207,100.

17. End-of-year activities: (adjustments)
    Supplies Inventory 12/31/01: $38,250
    Accrued interest on CDs at 5%

The city uses the purchases method to account for supplies expenditures.

Required:

A. Enter the opening trial balance data in T accounts.

B. Prepare journal entries for the year's transactions. Do not include entries for year-end adjustments. Post entries to T accounts.

C. Prepare a preclosing trial balance.

D. Prepare journal entries to adjust the Supplies Inventory and record the interest on the CDs.

E. Prepare journal entries to close the revenue, expenditures, and encumbrance accounts.

F. Prepare a comparative balance sheet for 2000–2001.

G. Prepare a statement of revenues, expenditures, and changes in fund balance for 2001.

PROBLEM 18-8   Reconstructing Journal Entries

The following summary of transactions was taken from the accounts of the Madras School District General Fund before the books were closed for the fiscal year ended June 30, 2002:

	Postclosing Balances *June 30, 2001*	*Preclosing Balances* *June 30, 2002*
Cash	$400,000	$ 700,000
Property tax receivable	150,000	170,000
Estimated uncollectible taxes	(40,000)	(70,000)
Estimated revenue		3,000,000
Expenditures		2,842,000
Expenditures—prior year		
Encumbrances		91,000
	$510,000	$6,733,000

	Postclosing Balances June 30, 2001	*Preclosing Balances June 30, 2002*
Vouchers payable	$ 80,000	$ 408,000
Due to other funds	210,000	142,000
Reserve for encumbrances	60,000	91,000
Unreserved fund balance	160,000	182,000
Revenue from taxes		2,800,000
Miscellaneous revenue		130,000
Appropriations		2,980,000
	$510,000	$6,733,000

Additional Information:

1. Property taxes in the amount of $2,870,000 were assessed for the year. Taxes collected during the year totaled $2,810,000.

2. An analysis of the transactions in the vouchers payable account for the year ended June 30, 2002, follows:

	Debit (Credit)
Current expenditures	$(2,700,000)
Expenditures for prior year	(58,000)
Vouchers for payment to other funds	(210,000)
Cash payments during year	2,640,000
Net change	$ (328,000)

3. During the year the General Fund was billed $142,000 for services performed on its behalf by other city funds.

4. On May 2, 2002, commitment documents were issued for the purchase of new textbooks at a cost of $91,000.

Required:

On the basis of the data presented, reconstruct the original detailed journal entries that were required to record all transactions for the fiscal year ended June 30, 2002, including the recording of the current year's budget. Do not prepare closing entries at June 30, 2002.

(*AICPA adapted*)

19

INTRODUCTION TO ACCOUNTING FOR STATE AND LOCAL GOVERNMENTAL UNITS

LEARNING OBJECTIVES

1. Identify the issues involved in developing standards for nonprofit organizations.
2. Describe the broad categories of government fund entities.
3. Distinguish between a general fund and a special revenue fund.
4. Explain the use of a capital projects fund.
5. Describe the purpose of a debt service fund.
6. Explain the use of a permanent fund.
7. Distinguish proprietary funds from government funds.
8. Understand the need for account group entities.
9. Describe the changes in reporting requirements under *GASB Statement No. 34.*
10. Explain the benefits of government-wide statements.
11. Describe the types of interfund activities.

IN THE NEWS

Annual financial reports of state and local governments will soon be a gold mine of information for those interested in evaluating a government's financial well-being. The reason is a whole new set of rules in the *Governmental Accounting Standards Board's* (GASB) *Statement No. 34*, "Basic Financial Statements—and Management's Discussion and Analysis—for State and Local Governments." They go into effect for larger governments (those with total annual revenue of $100 million or more) for fiscal years beginning after June 15, 2001. Other governments will get an extra one or two years to comply. The statement represents an immediate business opportunity for accountants as many governments will need help in complying with it.

GASB Chairman Tom L. Allen describes it as the "most significant change in the history of governmental accounting. It represents a dramatic shift in the way state and local governments present financial information to the public."[1]

---

[1] *Practical Accountant*, Vol. 32, "New Look for Government Statements," by Howard Wolosky, August 1999, pp. 47–50.

The lifestyles and well-being of all people are significantly affected by the activities of both profit-oriented enterprises and nonbusiness organizations. Of these, probably none is more important and pervasive in its impact on our daily lives than government. Today there are more than 70 thousand state and local governmental units, which employ more than 20 million people and collect annual revenues in excess of 500 billion dollars. The well-publicized problems of some city governments have attracted great interest and concern in the past. These problems focused attention on the need for (among other things) adequate accounting and financial reporting practices by cities and other governmental units as a basis for evaluating the extent of, and the suggested solutions for, such problems.

IN THE NEWS

In the 1991 annual report of Washington, D.C., the mayor announced that his campaign promise to balance the budget was met. The deficit was eliminated by issuing $336.6 million dollars in bonds. This transaction was reported as a source of financial resources and was used to offset the recorded deficit.[2]

As a consequence, the Governmental Accounting Standards Board (GASB) has reexamined the methods of accounting for state and local governments with significant changes to be implemented. The GASB's *Statement No. 34*, "Basic Financial Statements—and Management's Discussion and Analysis—for State and Local Governments,"[3] issued in June 1999, affects all governmental units and is considered to be one of the most important statements issued by a governing accounting body. The new rules require governments to provide basic financial statements using a government-wide (entity-wide) approach. This does not eliminate traditional fund accounting because governments are required to report statements emphasizing their major funds.[4] In addition, for the first time, financial managers are required to provide a management's discussion and analysis (MD&A) that gives readers an objective and easily readable analysis of the government's financial performance for the year. Thus, MD&A provides an analysis of the government's overall financial position and the results of the previous year's operations to assist users in assessing whether the government's finances have improved or deteriorated. Each analysis includes a comparison of the current year to the prior year based on the government-wide statements. In addition, the analysis explains significant variations in fund-based financial results and budgetary information, and describes capital assets and long-term debt activity during the year. The MD&A concludes with a description of currently known facts, decisions, or conditions that are expected to have a material impact on the government's future financial position and operations.

Generally, fund accounting rules follow a *flow of current financial resources* concept. Basically, this implies that each year is treated as a distinct event and the only measurement that is important is the source and use of funds (where funds are usually defined on a modified accrual basis). The simplicity of this concept, unfortunately, leaves room for inadequacies. For example, a city that borrows to balance a current period budget deficit, as in the Washington, DC, example above, must consider the future financial consequences of this decision. This example raises

---

[2]*Accounting Horizons*, Vol. 11, No. 3, "The New Governmental Reporting Model: Is it a 'Field of Dreams'?" by P. Copley, et al., September 1997, pp. 91–101.

[3]Governmental Accounting Standards Board, *Statement No. 34*, "Basic Financial Statements—and Management's Discussion and Analysis—for State and Local Governments," 1999, Norwalk, CT 06856.

[4]Major funds as defined by the GASB are discussed later in this chapter.

such questions as: Does fund accounting information alone provide users of governmental statements with sufficient information to evaluate the government? Therefore, *GASB Statement No. 34* requires "full accrual" accounting for all government-wide statements (i.e., *flow of economic resources approach*). Under this approach, governments would not be able to defer payment of expenses into the future and avoid recognition in the current year (e.g., avoiding payment of pension obligations). Under accrual accounting, the accountability of politicians for economic decisions made during the current period may be more readily assessed. The fund-based reports will still maintain the flow of current financial resources concept showing the short-term performance of the individual funds (as opposed to the long-term focus of the full accrual-based government-wide statements).

Until the mid-1990s, agencies' financial management systems were designed to keep track of how money was spent, much as consumers do with their checkbooks. But now, under a collection of new financial management laws, the requirements are much broader. Not only must agencies keep track of spending, but they must also account for the value and depreciation of assets, account for and justify inventory levels, plan for capital purchases, assess environmental liabilities, and estimate future costs such as postretirement health care benefits. In short, it is no longer enough to simply track spending. Agencies must manage their finances.[5]

It is indisputable that the accounting for governmental entities is changing. The new rules have their critics, however, as seen in the following quotation from an academic accounting journal. To what extent the changes will ultimately prove beneficial will be revealed only with the passage of time.

"It seems unlikely that the proposed financial statements will prove incrementally useful in evaluating the quality of services provided by the government. This is because accrual-based financial information, by itself, provides little indication of the effectiveness of government operations. To evaluate the quality of public services, users are more likely to need disaggregated information about the government's service efforts and accomplishments."[6]

THE HISTORY OF GENERALLY ACCEPTED GOVERNMENTAL ACCOUNTING STANDARDS

Like generally accepted accounting standards for profit-oriented enterprises, standards of accounting and reporting for governmental units are in a constant state of evolution and change. The pioneer organization in promulgating standards of accounting and reporting for state and local governmental units was the Municipal Finance Officers Association (MFOA). Such standards were formulated by its National Committee on Governmental Accounting, which in 1974 was reconstituted as the National Council on Governmental Accounting (NCGA). In 1979 the NCGA issued *Statement 1: Government and Financial Reporting Principles*. Until 1984 this and

---

[5] *Government Executive*, Vol. 31:2, "Money Matters," by Katherine McIntire Peters, February 1999, pp. 31–34.

[6] *Accounting Horizons*, Vol. 11, No. 3, "The New Governmental Reporting Model: Is it a 'Field of Dreams'?" by P. Copley, et al., September 1997, pp. 91–101.

subsequent statements and interpretations of the NCGA, along with the AICPA Industry Audit Guide: *Audits of State and Local Governmental Units* (1974) as amended by subsequently issued AICPA Statements of Position, constituted the primary sources of generally accepted governmental accounting standards.

In 1984 the GASB was established as a separate board under the oversight of the Financial Accounting Foundation (FAF), the same foundation that oversees the activities of the Financial Accounting Standards Board (FASB). The GASB is composed of two full-time and three part-time members supported by an administrative, technical, and research staff. Funding for the GASB is separate from that of the FASB.

The GASB is the body responsible for establishing financial accounting and reporting standards for governments. With its first pronouncement, *Authoritative Status of NCGA Pronouncements and AICPA Industry Audit Guide*, the GASB endorsed prior statements and interpretations of the NCGA, as well as the accounting and financial reporting standards embodied in the 1974 *AICPA Industry Audit Guide* as amended. Pronouncements of the GASB include GASB Statements (GASBS), GASB Interpretations (GASBI), GASB Concept Statements (GASBCS), and GASB Technical Bulletins (GASBTB). Pronouncements of the GASB are codified in the GASB's *Codification of Governmental Accounting and Financial Reporting Standards* (cited as *GASB Cod.*). This codification is updated annually.

Hierarchy of Generally Accepted Reporting Standards for Governmental Entities

The hierarchy used to establish generally accepted reporting standards for all state and local governmental-owned entities, including government-owned colleges and universities, health care providers, and utilities, is included in *Statement of Auditing Standards No. 69*, "The Meaning of 'Present Fairly in Conformity with Generally Accepted Accounting Principles' in the Independent Auditor's Report." The hierarchy lists the priority sequence of pronouncements that an entity should look to for accounting and reporting guidance and may be summarized as follows:

1. First level of priority
   A. GASB Statements and Interpretations.
   B. AICPA and FASB pronouncements that have *specifically been made applicable* to state and local governmental entities *by GASB Statements or Interpretations*.
2. Second level of priority
   A. GASB Technical Bulletins.
   B. AICPA Industry Audit and Accounting Guides and AICPA statements of position *made applicable* to state and local governmental entities by the AICPA *and cleared by the GASB*.
3. Third level of priority
   A. Consensus positions of the GASB Emerging Issues Task Force. (Note that no guidance is yet available in this category since the GASB has not yet established the task force.)
   B. AICPA AcSec Practice Bulletins if specifically *made applicable* to state and local governmental entities *and cleared by the GASB*.
4. Fourth level of priority
   A. Implementation Guides (Q&A's) published by the GASB staff.
   B. Practices widely prevalent in state and local government.

5. Fifth level of priority
   A. Other accounting literature including
   1. GASB Concepts Statements.
   2. AICPA and FASB pronouncements when not made specifically applicable to state and local governmental entities.

This hierarchy distinguishes the authority of the GASB and the FASB with regard to state and local governmental entities and implements the FAF trustees' jurisdictional determination of the respective roles of the GASB and the FASB. The GASB and the FASB each has primary responsibility for setting standards for entities under its jurisdiction, but pronouncements of one Board should not be mandatory for entities under the jurisdiction of the other Board *unless designated as such by the primary Board*.

THE STRUCTURE OF GOVERNMENTAL ACCOUNTING

A governmental unit, although a separate *legal* entity, consists of a number of separate fund and other *accounting* entities. There are eleven broad categories of fund entities and two account group entities. The eleven categories of fund entities fall under three subheadings: (I) governmental funds, (II) proprietary funds, and (III) fiduciary funds, as shown below.

Fund Entities

(I) Governmental Funds (expendable)—reporting focuses on the sources, use, and balances of current financial resources. The accounting and reporting emphasis for these types of funds is on the inflow, outflow, and unexpended balance of net financial resources and on compliance with detailed legal provisions that specify the types of revenue to be raised and the purposes for which financial resources may be expended (the flow of current financial resources measurement basis). The different types of governmental funds are distinguished by the sources of their financial resources or the types of activities financed by the resources of the fund.

   (1) *General Fund*—to account for all financial resources except those required to be accounted for in another fund.

   (2) *Special Revenue Funds*—to account for the proceeds of specific revenue sources (other than trusts for individuals, private organizations, or other governments or for major capital projects) that are legally restricted to expenditures for specified purposes. This category includes items reported as expendable trust funds under the former rules.

   (3) *Capital Projects Funds*—to account for financial resources to be used for the acquisition or construction of major capital facilities (other than those financed by proprietary funds or in trusts for individuals, private organizations, or other governments). Capital outlays financed by general obligation proceeds should be accounted for through a capital projects fund.

   (4) *Debt Service Funds*—to account for the accumulation of resources for, and the payment of, general long-term debt principal and interest. Debt service funds are required if they are legally mandated and/or if financial resources are being accumulated for principal and interest payments maturing in future years.

(5) *Permanent Funds*—to account for resources that are legally restricted to the extent that only earnings, and not principal, may be used for purposes that support the government's programs—that is, for the benefit of the government or its citizenry. An example is a cemetery perpetual-care fund, which provides resources for the ongoing maintenance of a public cemetery.

(II) Proprietary Funds (nonexpendable)—reporting focuses on the determination of operating income, changes in net assets, financial position, and cash flows. Government operations that are similar to commercial business operations such as a water utility, an electric utility, or a central garage or central computer facility are accounted for in the *proprietary fund* category. Financial accounting and reporting for these entities closely parallel accounting and reporting for profit-oriented enterprises. Thus both current and fixed assets and current and noncurrent liabilities are accounted for in the records of proprietary funds. In addition, revenue, expenses (including depreciation and amortization expense), and net income are determined and reported for these fund entities.

(6) *Enterprise Funds*—to account for any activity for which a fee is charged to external users for goods or services.

(7) *Internal Service Funds*—to report any activity that provides goods or services to other funds, departments, or agencies of the primary government and its component units, or to other governments, on a cost-reimbursement basis.

(III) Fiduciary Funds—reports assets held in a trustee or agency capacity for others and that cannot be used to support the government's own programs. Fiduciary fund reporting focuses on net assets and changes in net assets. These include:

(8) *Pension (and Other Employee Benefit) Trust Funds*—used to report resources that are required to be held in trust for the members and beneficiaries of defined benefit pension plans, defined contribution plans, other postemployment benefit plans, or other employee benefit plans.

(9) *Investment Trust Funds*—used to report the external portion of investment pools reported by the sponsoring government.

(10) *Private-Purpose Trust Funds*—used to report escheat property and to report all other trust agreements under which principal and income benefit individuals, private organizations, or other governments.

(11) *Agency Funds*—used to report resources held by the reporting government in a purely custodial capacity (assets equal liabilities). Agency funds typically involve only the receipt, temporary investment, and remittance of fiduciary resources to individuals, private organizations, or other governments.

There are several important changes for reporting funds from the rules in effect prior to the implementation of the *GASB Statement No. 34*. Expendable trust funds are generally reported as special revenue funds and included with governmental funds. Nonexpendable trust funds are generally accounted for in a new permanent fund category included with government funds. Initially, the GASB intended that these permanent funds be accounted for as proprietary funds, but ultimately concluded that the funds typically support government activities and thus should be accounted for with government funds rather than with proprietary funds. Nonexpendable trust funds are illustrated later in the chapter. We first provide a brief discussion of the role of account groups, followed by a detailed discussion of each fund type. Then we provide comprehensive examples of reporting, including the new government-wide statements, for both governmental activities and the business-like activities of the government.

Account Group Entities

Historically, governments have maintained two account groups: the general fixed assets account group and the general long-term obligation account group. Since capital assets and long-term debt are not reported in governmental funds, these account groups were formed to account for these assets and liabilities. In *GASB Statement No. 34*, separate reporting for the account group entities has been eliminated. This information is now reported on the government-wide statements discussed later in this chapter. Since the implementation of *GASB Statement No. 34* is a year away, most governments had not decided at the time of this writing how to account for these assets and liabilities (i.e., whether the account groups will be maintained or replaced with other subsidiary records). Therefore in this edition of the textbook, we assume that the account groups will continue to be maintained, at least in the short-run, to account for (1) fixed assets (including infrastructure assets) and (2) unmatured long-term obligations of the governmental unit. Adjustments must then be made to prepare the government-wide statements.

(1) *General Fixed Assets Account Group*—to account for all fixed assets of a governmental unit other than those fixed assets related to specific proprietary funds or trust funds. Fixed assets related to specific proprietary funds or trust funds should be accounted for through those funds. All other fixed assets of a governmental unit should be accounted for through the General Fixed Assets Account Group. This group now includes infrastructure assets (discussed in a later section of this chapter).

(2) *General Long-Term Obligation Account Group*—to account for all unmatured general obligation liabilities of a governmental unit other than long-term liabilities of proprietary funds and trust funds. Long-term liabilities of proprietary funds and trust funds should be accounted for through those funds. All other unmatured general obligation long-term liabilities of the governmental unit, including special assessment debt for which the government is obligated, should be accounted for through the General Long-Term Obligation Account Group.

"I don't make jokes—I just watch the government and report the facts."[7]
Will Rogers

---

[7]Quoted in *Saturday Review*. From *The Merriam-Webster Dictionary of Quotations*, Merriam-Webster, Inc., 1996; *Infopedia*, SoftKey Multimedia Inc., 1996.

GOVERNMENTAL FUND ENTITIES

General Fund

All revenues and expenditures of a governmental unit not accounted for in other governmental or proprietary funds are accounted for in the general fund. The variety of revenue sources available to the general fund and the variety of functions and activities financed by the resources of the general fund are ordinarily more numerous than are those for any other fund. Accounting entries and reports for the general fund of a governmental unit were illustrated in Chapter 18.

Special Revenue Funds

Special revenue funds are used to account for the proceeds of specific revenue sources that are required by statute, charter provisions, or local ordinance to be used to finance particular functions or activities of the governmental unit. Examples of special revenue funds are those established to finance the operations of special facilities, such as parks or museums, or of particular activities, such as the licensing and regulation of professions. Although the sources of revenue for special revenue funds in general are similar to those for the general fund, a typical special revenue fund will have only a single revenue source such as a single tax, or specified portion thereof, or a license fee, the proceeds of which are legally restricted to be expended for a specific purpose, function, or activity.

Accounting entries and financial reports for special revenue funds are analogous in all respects to the accounting entries and financial reports for the general fund illustrated in Chapter 18, and no further illustration is presented here beyond a brief summary. In special revenue funds, as in the general fund, the following steps are taken:

1. A budget is established and recorded in the accounts.
2. Encumbrances are used to control budgeted expenditures.
3. Fixed assets acquired by the expenditure of special revenue fund resources are not reported as assets of the special revenue fund but rather are recorded and reported in the General Fixed Assets Account Group.
4. Depreciation of fixed assets is not recorded or reported by the special revenue fund. (Depreciation expense on these assets is reported on the government-wide statements.)
5. The liability for long-term debt, the proceeds of which have been received and recorded by a special revenue fund, is not recorded or reported as a liability of the special revenue fund but is recorded and reported in the General Long-Term Obligation Account Group.

Under *GASB Statement No. 34*, expendable trust funds are reported with special revenue funds. Assume, for example, that Model City has an ordinance that requires all licensed contractors to deposit funds with the city to guarantee performance on their contracts. The deposits must be returned to the contractors when they relinquish their licenses. When a deposit is received, cash is debited and the fund balance is credited. When deposits are refunded, the fund balance is debited and cash is credited. Since the deposits may be held by the city for substantial periods of time, the resources of the trust fund are usually invested, and modest amounts of revenue may be earned.

Capital Projects Funds

Capital projects funds are established to account for the *resources* used by a governmental unit to acquire or construct major capital facilities (i.e., permanent assets with long lives). Major capital facilities include assets such as buildings, streets and highways, and storm drain systems. The primary purpose of accounting for the acquisition of major capital facilities in a separate capital projects fund is to show that the resources designated for such purposes were used for authorized purposes only and that any unexpended balances of such resources or resource deficits have been treated properly. *Resources* for the acquisition of major capital facilities include (1) proceeds of long-term debt issues, (2) grants or payments from other governmental units and agencies, (3) funds from private sources, (4) transfers of current revenues from other governmental funds, (5) special assessments (to be discussed later), and (6) other sources.

Not all major capital facilities acquisitions are accounted for in capital project funds. Construction and acquisition of capital facilities financed by enterprise funds are accounted for in the records of those funds. In addition, in some instances the resources of the general fund or a special revenue fund are appropriated for the acquisition of a major capital facility. So long as such acquisitions do not involve the issuance of general obligation long-term debt securities, they may be accounted for in the fund that appropriates the resources rather than in a separate capital projects fund.

The operations of a capital projects fund may extend over several accounting periods. Separate capital projects funds are ordinarily created for each major capital project. When the project is completed, the associated capital projects fund is closed out.

Capital Projects Fund Example To illustrate accounting and reporting procedures for a capital projects fund, assume that Model City authorizes the construction of a combination library and civic center that will be financed from the following sources (one from within the local government and one from the state):

General obligation bonds (par value)	$2,000,000
State government grant	1,000,000
Total authorized for construction	$3,000,000

Construction is to begin on September 1, 2001, and the bonds are to be issued on October 1, 2001.

Entries—2001 Entries to record the transactions of the capital projects fund during 2001 are summarized and explained as follows:

(1)	Due from State Government	1,000,000	
	Grant Revenue		1,000,000
	To open Capital Projects Fund.		

There is no budget entry to record estimated revenue and appropriations into the accounting records. Sources of estimated revenues for a capital project are few and predictable in amount. Thus, it serves no useful purpose to record them. Likewise, an appropriation account is not required as a formal control device, since the funds can be expended only for the single authorized project. Thus, the fund balance itself serves as an adequate measure of, and control over, unexpended appropriation authority.

(2) Cash	2,100,000	
Bond Issue Proceeds—Other Financing Sources		2,100,000

        To record receipt of proceeds from issuance of long-term debt securities.
        The bonds were issued at a market rate of 6.787%.

The Bond Issue Proceeds account is closed to the Fund Balance at the end of the year.

Effect of a Transaction on Different Funds

Each fund is a set of self-balancing accounts. The previous entry, to record the issuance of the bond, is a source of funds for the capital projects fund. Yet, the debt is not recorded as a liability of the fund. This transaction illustrates that one transaction can, and often does, affect several other funds at the same time. For example, as will be demonstrated later, at the time entry (2) is recorded, another entry is made in the General Long-Term Obligation Account Group to record the principal amount of the debt.

When bonds are issued at a premium, the difference between the bond issue proceeds and the par value of the bonds represents an interest adjustment and is usually transferred to the debt service fund that is used to service the principal and interest on the debt.

(3) Transfer to Debt Service Fund	100,000	
Cash		100,000

        To record transfer of cash in amount of bond premium to Debt Service Fund.

Transfers Between Funds

It is not unusual for resources to be transferred between funds. Most transfers, like the one in Entry (3), are recurring nonreciprocal transfers (also known as operating transfers) and are reported separately from revenues and expenditures on the statement of revenues, expenditures, and changes in fund balance as "other financing sources and uses." Transfers are discussed later in the chapter.

---

(4) Certificates of Deposit	1,000,000	
Cash		1,000,000

        To record investment of excess cash in temporary investments.

(5) Encumbrances	2,500,000	
Reserve for Encumbrances		2,500,000

        To record encumbrance created by signing construction contract with Lloyd-Jones Construction Company.

(6) Cash	750,000	
Due from State Government		750,000

        To record collection of part of grant from State Governmment

(7)	Expenditures	200,000	
	Vouchers Payable		200,000
	To record unencumbered expenditures for architect and legal fees.		
	Payment is recorded in entry (9).		
(8)	Reserve for Encumbrances	1,300,000	
	Encumbrances		1,300,000
	Expenditures	1,300,000	
	Contracts Payable		1,300,000
	To record approved contract billings on construction completed to date		
	and to remove encumbrance thereon.		
(9)	Vouchers Payable	150,000	
	Contracts Payable	1,300,000	
	Cash		1,450,000
	To record payment of liabilities (includes a portion of (7) and all of (8)).		
(10)	Interest Receivable	12,500	
	Interest Revenue		12,500
	To record interest earned on certificate of deposit to December 31, 2001.		

The treatment of interest earnings on temporary investments depends on legal provisions or established policy. One alternative is to transfer such earnings to the debt service fund. A second alternative is to treat such earnings as revenue of the capital projects fund. The latter treatment is justified on the grounds that resources allocated to the project are restricted exclusively to that project and, accordingly, any earnings on such resources are also restricted resources and should not be diverted to any other use.

December 31, 2001, Trial Balance The December 31, 2001, trial balance for the capital projects fund presented below reflects the transactions recorded in 2001.

	Debit	*Credit*
Cash	$ 300,000	
Interest Receivable	12,500	
Certificates of Deposit	1,000,000	
Due from State Government	250,000	
Encumbrances	1,200,000	
Expenditures	1,500,000	
Vouchers Payable		$ 50,000
Contracts Payable		—0—
Reserve for Encumbrances		1,200,000
Unreserved Fund Balance		—0—
Grant Revenue		1,000,000
Interest Revenue		12,500
Bond Issue Proceeds—Other Financing Sources		2,100,000
Transfer to Debt Service Fund—Other Financing Use	100,000	
	$4,362,500	$4,362,500

Closing Entries—December 31, 2001

(11)	Bond Issue Proceeds	2,100,000	
	Grant Revenue	1,000,000	
	Interest Revenue	12,500	
	Transfer to Debt Service Fund		100,000
	Unreserved Fund Balance		3,012,500
	To close revenue and related accounts to unreserved fund balance.		

(12)	Unreserved Fund Balance	2,700,000	
	Encumbrances		1,200,000
	Expenditures		1,500,000

To close expenditures and encumbrances accounts to unreserved fund balance.

Since no budget accounts were formally recorded in the accounting records, there are no budget accounts to be closed at year-end. Hence, the nominal accounts are closed directly to the unreserved fund balance. As was true in the general fund, the closing of the balance of the encumbrances account against the unreserved fund balance has the same effect as if an entry were made at year-end to reclassify an equal amount of the unreserved fund balance to a reserve for encumbrances.

At the end of each year, entries are also made in the General Fixed Asset Account Group to record the cost of construction in progress represented by expenditures incurred by the capital projects fund during the year.

Completion of Project Entries in 2002 to record the completion of the project are presented and explained below.

| (13) | Encumbrances | 1,200,000 | |
| | Unreserved Fund Balance | | 1,200,000 |

To reestablish the contract encumbrance closed out at end of previous year.

Since capital projects funds are project oriented rather than period oriented, there is no need, as there is in accounting for the general fund or a special revenue fund, to identify expenditures with appropriation authority of a particular year. Thus, expenditures for amounts encumbered in prior years are not segregated from other expenditures of the current year. Entry (13) reestablishes the encumbrance equal to the unencumbered amount remaining from the previous year (i.e., equal to the beginning of year balance in the reserve for encumbrances account).

| (14) | Expenditures | 225,000 | |
| | Vouchers Payable | | 225,000 |

To record unencumbered expenditures.

| (15) | Cash | 250,000 | |
| | Due from State Government | | 250,000 |

To record receipt of cash payment from State Government.

(16)	Cash	1,020,000	
	Certificate of Deposit		1,000,000
	Interest Receivable		12,500
	Interest Revenue		7,500

To record redemption of certificate of deposit.

(17)	Reserve for Encumbrances	1,200,000	
	Encumbrances		1,200,000
	Expenditures	1,200,000	
	Contracts Payable		1,200,000

To record approved final contract billings on completed construction and to remove remaining contract encumbrance.

(18)	Contracts Payable	1,200,000	
	Contracts Payable—Retained Percentage		125,000
	Cash		1,075,000

To record payment of contract except for retention of 5% of the contract price pending inspection of completed project.

(19)	Vouchers Payable	275,000	
	Cash		275,000

To record payment of liabilities.

December 31, 2002, Trial Balance The preclosing trial balance of the capital projects fund on December 31, 2002, is presented below:

	Debit	*Credit*
Cash	$ 220,000	
Expenditures	1,425,000	
Contracts Payable—Retained Percentage		$ 125,000
Unreserved Fund Balance		1,512,500
Interest Revenue		7,500
	$1,645,000	$1,645,000

Closing Entry—December 31, 2002

(20)	Unreserved Fund Balance	1,417,500	
	Interest Revenue	7,500	
	Expenditures		1,425,000

To close nominal accounts to unreserved fund balance.

Financial Statements A comparative balance sheet and a comparative statement of revenues, expenditures, and changes in fund balance for the years ended December 31, 2002, and December 31, 2001, are presented in Illustrations 19-1 and 19-2.

ILLUSTRATION 19–1

Library and Civic Center Capital Projects Fund
Balance Sheet at December 31, 2002 and December 31, 2002

Assets	*2002*	*2001*
Cash	$220,000	$ 300,000
Interest Receivable	—	12,500
Certificates of Deposit	—	1,000,000
Due from State Government	—	250,000
Total Assets	$220,000	$1,562,500
Liabilities and Fund Balance		
Vouchers Payable	$ —	$ 50,000
Contracts Payable—Retained Percentage	125,000	—
Total Liabilities	$125,000	$ 50,000
Fund Balance		
Unreserved	95,000	312,500
Reserve for Encumbrances	—	1,200,000
Total Fund Balance	95,000	1,512,500
Total	$220,000	$1,562,500

ILLUSTRATION 19–2

Library and Civic Center Capital Projects Fund
Statement of Revenues, Expenditures, and Other Changes
in Fund Balance for Years Ended December 31, 2002 and December 31, 2001

	2002	2001	Cumulative
Revenues			
Grant Revenue	$ —	1,000,000	1,000,000
Interest Revenue	7,500	12,500	20,000
Total Revenue	7,500	1,012,500	1,020,000
Expenditures			
Capital Asset/Construction	1,425,000	1,500,000	2,925,000
Total Expenditures	1,425,000	1,500,000	2,925,000
Excess (deficiency) of Revenues over Expenditures	(1,417,500)	(487,500)	(1,905,000)
Other Financing Sources (Uses)			
Proceeds of Long-Term Capital-related Debt	—	2,100,000	2,100,000
Operating Transfer Out	—	(100,000)	(100,000)
Total Other Financing Sources (Uses)	—	2,000,000	2,000,000
Net Change in Fund Balance	(1,417,500)	1,512,500	95,000
Fund Balance—January 1	1,512,500	—	—
Fund Balance—December 31	95,000	$1,512,500	$ 95,000

Closing Out a Capital Projects Fund Although the cost of a capital project should equal the resources provided for its acquisition, actual expenditures normally do not equal the project authorization. If an unexpended fund balance remains after the completion of the project, it should be distributed to the contributors of project resources in proportion to their contribution. For example, unless legal or policy decisions dictate otherwise, the capital projects fund of Model City illustrated above would be closed out as follows:

(21)	Contracts Payable—Retained Percentage	125,000	
	Cash		125,000
	To record final payment on contract.		

(22)	Transfer to Debt Service Fund—Other Financing Use		
	Use	(1) 63,333	
	Expenditures	(2) 31,667	
	Cash		95,000
	To record distribution of Fund Balance.		

(1) ($2,000,000/$3,000,000) × $95,000 = $63,333 to another governmental fund.
(2) ($1,000,000/$3,000,000) × $95,000 = $31,667 to the state government.

For financial reporting purposes, transfers to other funds within a governmental unit are distinguished from expenditures. The return of $31,667 to the state government is treated as an expenditure because it reduces the financial resources of Model City.

When construction is completed, the assets acquired with capital projects fund resources are recorded at cost in the government activities column in the government-wide statement of net assets. No assets are recorded in the capital projects fund.

Debt Service Funds

Debt issued by the government is separated into two categories: general obligation long-term debt that supports the activities of the government as a whole, and debt that is issued by proprietary funds to support specific activities of the fund. Long-term liabilities directly related to, and expected to be paid from, fiduciary funds should be reported in the statement of fiduciary net assets. General obligation long-term debt consists of bonds, notes, or warrants that are secured by the general credit and revenue-raising powers of the governmental unit as a whole, rather than by the resources of a specific fund. Two funds are involved in accounting for general obligation long-term debt. The debt is recorded in the General Long-Term Obligation Group while *the funds* used to meet the principal and interest payments are accumulated in the **debt service fund**. Since the principal is not reported as a liability of the debt service fund, payments of bond principal and interest are *expenditures* of (rather than reduction of liabilities of) the debt service fund.[8] On the other hand, long-term debt that is the specific obligation of an enterprise fund (a proprietary fund) is a liability of that fund, and the accumulation of resources for its payment will be accounted for in that fund, rather than in a debt service fund.

General obligation bonds may be serial bonds or term bonds. The principal of a term bond is repaid in one lump sum at a specified maturity date. The total principal of serial bonds is repaid in a specified number of annual (and usually equal) installments.

Debt service funds are usually financed by one or more of the following sources of revenue:

General property tax

Sales tax or other specified tax revenues

Transfers of other governmental fund revenues

Special assessments (to be discussed later)

Revenue from the investment of debt service fund resources

For purposes of illustrating the difference between the debt service for serial bonds and for term bonds, two debt service funds—Land Acquisition Serial Bonds Debt Service Fund and Library and Civic Center Term Bonds Debt Service Fund—are illustrated for Model City. In reality both these funds might be collapsed into a single debt service fund.

Serial Bonds Accounting for the accumulation of resources and payment of annual installments of principal and interest on serial bonds is relatively simple. To illustrate, assume that in 1998, Model City issued $1,800,000 in 8% serial bonds at par, $300,000 of which come due on July 1 of each year beginning July 1, 1999. On January 1, 2001, there is $1,200,000 in principal on these bonds outstanding, and $300,000 in principal and $96,000 in interest will come due on July 1, 2001. Annual installments of principal are financed from general property tax revenues, and

---

[8]Matured long-term debt that has not yet been redeemed with the resources of the debt service fund may be recorded as a liability of the debt service fund.

annual interest payments are financed by the appropriation of resources of the general fund. At the beginning of 2001, the debt service fund had cash and receivables of $5,000 available to make debt payments. The trial balance of the Land Acquisition Serial Bonds Debt Service Fund on January 1, 2001, is as follows:

Trial Balance—January 1, 2001

	Debit	Credit
Cash	$3,000	
Taxes Receivable	2,000	
Fund Balance		$5,000
Total	$5,000	$5,000

Transactions of the fund for 2001 are summarized in general journal form below.

A. Budgeting Revenue and Appropriations

(1)	Estimated Revenue	315,000	
	Authorized Transfer from the General Fund	96,000	
	Appropriations (300,000 + 96,000)		396,000
	Fund Balance		15,000

To record budgeted revenue, transfers, and appropriations for current year.

B. Revenue Generation and Fund Transfers

(2)	Property Tax Receivable	320,000	
	Allowance for Uncollectible Taxes		4,000
	Revenue (net)		316,000

To record general property tax levy earmarked for debt service on serial bonds.

(3)	Due from the General Fund	96,000	
	Transfer from General Fund—Other Financing Source		96,000

To record amount of resources authorized for transfer from General Fund during current period.

(4)	Cash	318,000	
	Property Tax Receivable		318,000

To record collection of property taxes.

(5)	Cash	96,000	
	Due from the General Fund		96,000

To record receipt of cash transfer from General Fund.

C. Debt Expenditure

(6)	Expenditures—Principal	300,000	
	Expenditures—Interest	96,000	
	Cash		396,000

To record payment of interest and principal on July 1.

D. Year-End Entries

(7)	Revenue	316,000	
	Estimated Revenue		315,000
	Fund Balance		1,000
	Transfer from General Fund—Other Financing Source	96,000	
	Authorized Transfer from General Fund		96,000
	Appropriations	396,000	
	Expenditures—Principal		300,000
	Expenditures—Interest		96,000

To close nominal and budget account balances at year-end.

(8)	Allowance for Uncollectible Taxes	4,000	
	Property Tax Receivable		4,000
	To record write-off of taxes authorized by City Council.		

The postclosing trial balance for this fund on December 31, 2001, is as follows:

Trial Balance—December 31, 2001

	Debit	Credit
Cash	$21,000	
Fund Balance		$21,000
Total	$21,000	$21,000

A statement of revenues, expenditures, and changes in fund balance is presented in Illustration 19-3 for the Land Acquisition Serial Bonds Debt Service Fund.

Term Bonds Accounting for the debt service of term bonds is more complicated than accounting for serial bonds. Debt service funds for term bonds require annual additions to fund resources that, with compound interest, will provide the total amount of bond principal by the maturity date of the bonds. In addition, the debt service fund for a term bond issue must provide for the payment of periodic interest on the bonds.

To illustrate, assume that the $2,000,000 in bonds issued on October 1, 2001, to finance the construction of the Library and Civic Center of Model City were 8% bonds that mature five years after their issue date. (These bonds were issued in the capital projects fund earlier in this chapter. The bonds have a stated interest rate of 8% and an original market rate of 6.787%.) The calculation of the required annual additions to the debt service fund is presented in Illustration 19-4. It is assumed that funds can be invested at an average annual return of 10%. The required annual principal addition of $327,595 is calculated by dividing the term bond principal of $2,000,000 by the amount of an ordinary annuity of $1.00 for five

---

ILLUSTRATION 19–3

Land Acquisition Serial Bonds Debt Service Fund
Statement of Revenues, Expenditure, and Changes in Fund Balance
for Year Ended December 31, 2001

Revenues	
General Property Taxes	$316,000
Expenditures	
Principal Payments on Serial Bonds	300,000
Interest on Bonds	96,000
Total Expenditures	396,000
Other Financing Sources (Uses)	
Transfers in (from General Fund)	96,000
Net Change in Fund Balance	$ 16,000
Fund Balance—January 1	5,000
Fund Balance—December 31	$ 21,000

ILLUSTRATION 19–4

Debt Service Fund—Term Bonds
Required Annual Additions and Required Earnings for
$2,000,000 Library and Civic Center Bond Issue

Year	Required Principal Additions (1)	Required Earnings (2)	Required Increase in Fund Balance (3)	Required Fund Balance (4)
2002	$ 327,595		$ 327,595	$ 327,595
2003	327,595	$ 32,760	360,355	687,950
2004	327,595	68,795	396,390	1,084,340
2005	327,595	108,434	436,029	1,520,369
2006	327,595	152,036	479,631	2,000,000
	$1,637,975	$362,025	$2,000,000	

Required Principal Addition (1)	$ 327,595
Required Interest Addition (0.08 × $2,000,000)	160,000
Required Annual Addition	$ 487,595

(1) The required principal addition equals $2,000,000/6.10510 or $327,595
(2) Required earnings equals 10% times the previous year's required fund balance (column (4))
(3) The required increase in fund balance equals the sum of column (1) and column (2)
(4) The required fund balance equals the cumulative sum of the required increase in fund balance, column (3)

periods at 10% ($2,000,000/6.1051 = $327,595). See Appendix Table A3 at the back of the textbook for the table factor. In addition, $160,000 is needed to cover the interest payments ($2,000,000 × .08).

These calculations do not take into account the $100,000 premium on the issue of the bonds that is transferred by the capital projects fund to the debt service fund in 2001. However, if the fund balance of a debt service fund exceeds actuarial requirements, the excess is ordinarily carried forward without adjustment until the final addition to the fund is made. It is assumed that annual additions to the Library and Civic Center Term Bonds Debt Service Fund are derived from an earmarked portion of the general property tax assessment.

Transactions—2001 Transactions of the fund in 2001 are summarized in general journal form as follows:

(1)	Cash	100,000	
	Transfer from Capital Projects Fund—Other Financing Use		100,000
	To record transfer of cash from Capital Projects Fund for the premium received on bond issue proceeds.		

Note that for fund accounting purposes, the premium on the bond issued is not amortized to expense over the life of the bond, but is considered an operating transfer-in that increases the fund balance. However, on the government-wide financial statements (illustrated later in the chapter), the premium needs to be amortized to expense.

Had there been no transfer of cash to the debt service fund by the capital projects fund, no entries would have been required in the debt service fund until the 2002 fiscal year.

(2)	Investments	100,000	
	Cash		100,000
	To record investment of cash in a certificate of deposit.		

(3) Interest Receivable   4,000

      Interest Income   4,000

        To accrue interest receivable from the certificate of deposit on December 31, 2001.

(4) Interest Income   4,000

      Transfer from Capital Projects Fund   100,000

            Fund Balance   104,000

        To close nominal accounts to Fund Balance.

The postclosing trial balance on December 31, 2001, is as follows:

Trial Balance—December 31, 2001

	Debit	Credit
Investments	$100,000	
Interest Receivable	4,000	
Fund Balance		$104,000
Total	$104,000	$104,000

Transactions—2002 Revenue and expenditure transactions for 2002 are summarized in Illustration 19-6. At the end of 2002, the postclosing trial balance for the fund is as follows:

Trial Balance—December 31, 2002

	Debit	Credit
Cash	$ 33,000	
Interest Receivable	4,000	
Property Tax Receivable	6,000	
Investments	400,000	
Allowance for Uncollectible Taxes		$ 1,000
Fund Balance		442,000
Total	$443,000	$443,000

Transactions—2003 Transactions for 2003 (also shown in Illustration 19-6) are summarized in general journal form as follows:

A. Budget Additions, Appropriations, and Estimated Revenues

(1) Required Additions ($327,595 + $160,000)   487,595

      Required Earnings   32,760

           Fund Balance   520,355

        To record budgeted additions and budgeted income on invested resources of fund for current year (see Illustration 19-4).

The amounts reported in the required additions and the required earnings accounts are determined (actuarially) to meet the current and future years' interest and principal payments. For example, $160,000 is needed to meet the current year's interest payment. An additional $327,595 is needed for the fund to accumulate to meet future payments. In addition, existing funds must earn some minimum rate to accumulate to the desired amount. The required earnings amount is $32,760 during the current year. If the actual amount of additions and earnings equals these budgeted amounts, the fund balance will equal the present value of the remaining interest and principal payments at the assumed interest rate.

(2) Fund Balance   160,000

      Appropriations   160,000

        To record budgeted expenditures for bond interest for current year.

(3)   Property Tax Receivable   503,000
         Allowance for Uncollectible Taxes   15,000
         Revenue (net of uncollectible accounts)   488,000
            To record property tax levy earmarked for debt service on Library and
            Civic Center term bonds.

B. Collection of Receivables, Investment Income, and Purchase of Investments

(4)   Cash   485,000
         Property Tax Receivable   485,000
            To record collection of property taxes.

(5)   Investments   360,000
      Premium on Investments   15,000
         Cash   375,000
            To record investment of fund resources.

Debt service fund investments are closely regulated by law and are usually restricted to quality government and municipal securities. When such investments are
expected to be held to maturity, they are recorded at their par value and premium
or discount is recorded in a *separate* account and amortized by reducing or increasing investment income over the remaining life of the investment.

(6)   Cash   26,000
         Interest Receivable   4,000
         Interest Income   22,000
            To record receipt of interest on investments.

(7)   Allowance for Uncollectible Taxes   13,000
         Property Tax Receivable   13,000
            To record write-off of property taxes authorized by City Council.

(8)   Interest Receivable   21,000
         Interest Income   21,000
            To record interest accrued on investments to December 31, 2003.

(9)   Interest Income   1,200
         Premium on Investments   1,200
            To record current year's amortization of premium on investments.

C. Expenditure for Interest

(10) Expenditures   160,000
         Interest Payable   160,000
            To record expenditures for current year's interest on bonds.

(11) Interest Payable   160,000
         Cash   160,000
            To record payment of interest.

D. Closing Entries

(12) Revenue   488,000
         Required Additions   487,595
         Fund Balance   405
      Interest Income   41,800
         Required Earnings   32,760
         Fund Balance   9,040
      Appropriations   160,000
         Expenditures   160,000
            To close budgeted and nominal account balances at year-end.

ILLUSTRATION 19–5

Model City
Library and Civic Center Term Bonds Debt Service Fund
Balance Sheet at December 31, 2003 and December 31, 2002

Assets	*2003*	*2002*	*2001*
Cash	$ 9,000	$ 33,000	$ —
Interest Receivable	21,000	4,000	4,000
Taxes Receivable (less allowance for uncollectible			
taxes, 2003—$3,000; 2002—$1,000)	8,000	5,000	
Investment (at maturity value)	760,000	400,000	100,000
Unamortized Premium on Investments	13,800	—	—
Total Assets	$811,800	$442,000	$104,000
Liabilities and Fund Balance			
Fund Balance:			
Reserved for Debt Service	$811,800	$442,000	$104,000

Disclosure:

The actuarial requirements in the fund balance are $687,950 in 2003 and $327,595 in 2002. See Illustration 19-4.

Comparative financial statements for the Library and Civic Center Term Bonds Debt Service Fund are presented in Illustrations 19-5 and 19-6. Two things should be noted about these statements, as follows:

(1) There is no interest payable accrual on general obligation long-term debt. For fund accounting, there are no entries to record the accrual of interest payable on the bonds from the last interest payment date (July 1 for the serial bonds and

ILLUSTRATION 19–6

Library and Civic Center Term Bonds Debt Service Fund
Statement of Revenues, Expenditures, and Changes
In Fund Balance for Years Ended December 31, 2003, 2002, and 2001

	2003	*2002*	*2001*
Revenues			
General Property Tax	$488,000	$488,000	$ —
Interest on Investments			
(net of amortization)	41,800	10,000	4,000
Total Revenues	529,800	498,000	4,000
Expenditures			
Redemption of Term Bonds	—	—	—
Interest on Bonds	160,000	160,000	—
Total Expenditures	160,000	160,000	—
Excess (Deficiency) of Revenues over			
Expenditures	369,800	338,000	4,000
Other Financing Sources (Uses)			
Transfers In	—	—	100,000
Net Change in Fund Balance	369,800	338,000	104,000
Fund Balance—January 1	442,000 ←	104,000 ←	—
Fund Balance—December 31	$811,800	$442,000	$104,000

Note: The actuarial requirements in the fund balance are $687,950 in 2003, $327,595 in 2002, and $—0— in 2001. See Illustration 19-4.

October 1 for the term bonds) to the end of the fiscal year. This action is justified because financial resources that are appropriated by the debt service fund are usually appropriated in the period the interest on the debt must be paid. To accrue the debt service fund expenditure and liability in one year, but record the transfer or collection of the financial resources appropriated for this purpose in a later year, would be confusing and would result in an overstatement of fund liabilities and expenditures and an understatement of the fund balance. Thus, for fund purposes it is considered appropriate and more informative to treat interest payable on general obligation long-term debt at the end of the year as an expenditure in the year of payment. *However, on the accrual-based government-wide statements, this interest must be accrued regardless of the period that the interest will be paid.* On the government-wide statement of net assets, accrued interest of $76,000 ($36,000 from the serial bond and $40,000 from the term bond) is included in liabilities, while no accrued interest is included on the governmental fund statements.

(2) Actuarial requirements must be disclosed. An essential disclosure in the financial statements of debt service funds for term bonds is the amount, actuarially determined, of resources that is necessary on the financial statement date for the accumulation of sufficient resources to redeem the debt on its maturity date. The actuarial requirements shown in Illustrations 19-5 and 19-6 are those determined in the "Required Fund Balance" column of Illustration 19-4.

Closing Out the Debt Service Fund Assume the following trial balance for the Library and Civic Center Term Bonds Debt Service Fund on September 15, 2006:

Trial Balance—September 15, 2006

	Debit	*Credit*
Cash	$2,220,000	
Fund Balance		$2,220,000
Total	$2,220,000	$2,220,000

Entries to close the fund are as follows:

(1)	Expenditures—Principal	2,000,000	
	Expenditures—Interest	160,000	
	Cash		2,160,000
	To record redemption of matured bonds and payment of interest.		

(2)	Transfer to X Fund—Other Financing Use	60,000	
	Cash		60,000
	To record transfer of unexpected fund resources to another governmental fund.		

The unexpended balance of the fund after the final payment of interest and principal on the matured bonds should be disposed of in accordance with legal or bond indenture requirements. Usually the unexpended balance is transferred to another debt service fund, but legal requirements may specify an alternative disposition. The accounts of the fund being terminated should be closed in such a way as to reflect compliance with applicable legal requirements.

(3)	Fund Balance	2,220,000	
	Expenditures—Principal		2,000,000
	Expenditures—Interest		160,000
	Transfer to X Fund—Other Financing Use		60,000
	To close out Debt Service Fund.		

After these entries are posted, the balance of all accounts would be zero and the Debt Service Fund would effectively cease to exist.

Permanent Funds

Nonexpendable Trust Funds Nonexpendable trust funds are generally reported as permanent funds. There are two types of nonexpendable trust funds: those in which the principal must be retained intact but earnings may be expended, and those in which both the principal and the earnings of the fund must be retained intact. An example of the latter type of nonexpendable trust funds is the *revolving loan fund*, in which interest collected on loans outstanding increases the funds available for subsequent loans.

Nonexpendable trust funds may be established as a result of a gift, a bequest, or some other action that requires the governmental unit to act in a fiduciary capacity and to maintain and conserve cash or other assets that it does not own. Trust funds must be accounted for in accordance with the terms of the trust agreement or the applicable provisions of statutory and common law. Accounting procedures must result in a clear distinction between nonexpendable fund resources and expendable resources resulting from the earnings of the fund. Appropriate procedures are also necessary to ensure that the expenditure of expendable resources is made in accordance with the trust agreement or other applicable legal provisions.

Where the earnings of a trust fund may be expended, they are generally transferred to a special revenue fund (expenditures restricted to specified use). To illustrate, assume that a private donor granted Model City $300,000 for the purpose of financing the purchase of rare editions of the classics for the public library. As a result of this grant, two funds were created:

1. The Classics Endowment Fund to account for the nonexpendable fund principal and the investment (this fund is classified as a permanent fund).
2. The Classics Acquisition Fund to account for the expenditure of the earnings of the endowment fund (this fund is classified as a special revenue fund).

The general ledger trial balances for each fund on January 1, 2001, are presented below.

Classics Endowment Fund
(Permanent Fund)

	Debit	Credit
Cash	$ 2,000	
Certificates of Deposit	300,000	
Interest Receivable (accrued)	7,500	
Due to Classics Acquisition Fund		$ 9,500
Fund Balance		300,000
Total	$309,500	$309,500

Classics Acquisition Fund
(Special Revenue Fund)

	Debit	Credit
Cash	$ 8,000	
Due from Classics Endowment Fund	9,500	
Fund Balance		$ 17,500
Total	$ 17,500	$ 17,500

Transactions for 2001 for each fund are summarized below in general journal form.

Classics Endowment Fund

(1)   Cash   30,000

        Interest Receivable   7,500

        Interest Income   22,500

            To record interest collected on certificate of deposit.

(2)   Interest Receivable   7,500

        Interest Income   7,500

            To accrue interest on certificate of deposit.

(3)   Transfer to Classic Acquisitions Fund   30,000

        Due to Classics Acquisition Fund   30,000

            To record amount of 2001 income transferable to Classics Acquisition Fund.

(4)   Due to Classics Acquisition Fund   32,000

        Cash   32,000

            To record cash payment to Classics Acquisition Fund.

For purposes of simplification, it is assumed that the trust agreement requires that the entire endowment principal be invested in a savings account earning 10%

ILLUSTRATION 19–7

Classics Endowment Fund
Balance Sheet
December 31, 2001 and December 31, 2000

Assets	*2001*	*2000*
Cash	$ —	$ 2,000
Interest Receivable	7,500	7,500
Investments	300,000	300,000
Total Assets	$307,500	$309,500

Liabilities and Fund Balance		
Due to Classics Acquisition Fund	$ 7,500	$ 9,500
Fund Balance	300,000	300,000
Total	$307,500	$309,500

Statement of Revenues, Expenditures, and Changes
In Fund Balances for Years Ended
December 31, 2001 and December 31, 2000

	2001	*2000*
Revenues		
Interest Income	$ 30,000	$ 30,000
Expenditures	—	—
Excess (Deficiency) of Revenues over Expenditures	30,000	30,000
Other Financing Sources (Uses)		
Transfers to Classics Acquisitions Fund	(30,000)	(30,000)
Net Change in Fund Balance:	—	—
Fund Balance—January 1	300,000	300,000
Fund Balance—December 31	$300,000	$300,000

interest. Usually, the principal of an endowment fund is invested in various securities. If the securities are purchased at a premium or discount, such amounts should ordinarily be amortized to interest income, and only the net amount of investment income would accrue to the recipient Classics Acquisition Fund. Accounting procedures for an endowment fund are complicated further if the endowment includes depreciable income-producing assets such as rental properties. In that case, earnings accruing to the recipient expendable fund must also be reduced by depreciation if the trust principal is to be maintained "intact."

Classics Acquisition Fund

(1)	Due from Classics Endowment Fund	30,000	
	Fund Balance		30,000
	To record expendable earnings due from endowment fund.		
(2)	Cash	32,000	
	Due from Classics Endowment Fund		32,000
	To record receipt of cash from endowment fund.		
(3)	Fund Balance	18,000	
	Cash		18,000
	To record acquisition of rare books.		

Financial statements for these funds are presented in Illustrations 19-7 and 19-8.

ILLUSTRATION 19–8

Classics Acquisition Fund
Balance Sheet
December 31, 2001 and December 31, 2000

Assets	2001	2000
Cash	$22,000	$ 8,000
Due From Classics Endowment Fund	7,500	9,500
Total Assets	$29,500	$17,500
Liabilities and Fund Balance		
Fund Balance	$29,500	$17,500

Statement of Revenues, Expenditures, and Changes
In Fund Balances for Years Ended
December 31, 2001 and December 31, 2000

	2001	2000
Revenues	$ —	$ —
Expenditures	18,000	20,000
Excess (Deficiency) of Revenues over Expenditures	(18,000)	(20,000)
Other Financing Sources (Uses)		
Transfers from Endowment Trust Fund	30,000	30,000
Excess (Deficiency) to Fund Balance	12,000	10,000
Fund Balance—January 1	17,500	7,500
Fund Balance—December 31	$29,500	$17,500

PROPRIETARY FUNDS

In *GASB Statement No. 34*, the proprietary fund operating statement requirements were changed from a capital maintenance approach to a change in net assets approach. Under a capital maintenance approach, certain resource flows such as contributions of capital assets and permanently restricted contributions of financial assets were excluded from the operating or income statement "bottom line" and were reported as direct charges to equity or net assets. In other words, they were not considered revenues or expenses, but "balance-sheet only" transactions. The board concluded that the change in net assets approach, which is already required in the government-wide statement of activities, is also appropriate for proprietary funds. Under the change in net assets approach, *all* changes in net assets are included somewhere in the "statement of activities" and are included in the "bottom-line" total in the change in net assets for the year. There are no "direct to equity" transactions and no mandatory reporting distinction between capital transactions and operating transactions. No additional change in net assets is reported between the beginning and ending net assets, as would be needed under the capital maintenance approach.

Proprietary fund reporting focuses on the determination of operating income, changes in net assets (or cost recovery), financial position, and cash flows. The cash flow statement is to be prepared using the direct basis. The proprietary category includes Enterprise and Internal Service Funds, illustrated in the following sections.

Enterprise Funds

Enterprise Funds may be used to report any activity for which a fee is charged to external users for goods and services. The most common examples of governmental enterprises are public utilities that provide such services as water or electricity. Other activities of governmental units that are accounted for in Enterprise Funds include airports, transportation systems, parking lots and garages, and recreational facilities such as swimming pools. Activities are required to be reported as Enterprise Funds if any one of the following is met:

- The activity is financed with debt that is secured solely by a pledge of the net revenues from fees and charges of the activity.
- Laws or regulations require that the activity's costs of providing services including capital costs (such as depreciation or debt service) be recovered with fees and charges, rather than with taxes or similar revenues.
- The pricing policies of the activity establish fees and charges designed to recover its costs, including capital costs (such as depreciation and debt service).

The resources to establish an enterprise fund may come from contributions or from the proceeds of long-term debt issues or both. Contributions may be obtained from other governmental units, resources of the General Fund of the same governmental unit, property owners, subdivision developers, or customers.

A balance sheet of the proprietary funds (both the Enterprise and the Internal Service Funds) is presented in Illustration 19-9, and several features of the enterprise fund are pointed out. Some assets are restricted in use by bond provisions or other arrangements and are classified on the balance sheet as *restricted assets*. Re-

ILLUSTRATION 19–9

Model City
Proprietary Funds
Balance Sheet at December 31, 2001*

	Business-Type Activities— Enterprise Fund	Governmental Activities
	Sewer Fund	Internal Service Fund
Assets		
Current Assets:		
Cash	$ 100,000	$ 22,500
Receivables	451,000	100,000
Total Current Assets	$ 551,000	$122,500
Noncurrent Assets:		
Restricted Assets	509,000	—
Capital Assets (net of accumulated depreciation)	10,000,000	420,000
Construction in Progress	40,000	—
Total Noncurrent Assets	10,549,000	420,000
Total Assets	$11,100,000	$542,500
Liabilities		
Current Liabilities:		
Current Liabilities (payable from current assets)	$ 361,000	$ 27,500
Current Liabilities (payable from restricted assets)	282,000	—
Total Current Liabilities	643,000	27,500
Revenue Bonds Payable	4,200,000	—
Total Liabilities	$ 4,843,000	$ 27,500
Net Assets		
Invested in capital assets, net of related debt	5,558,000	420,000
Restricted	500,000	
Unrestricted	199,000	95,000
Total Net Assets	$ 6,257,000	$515,000
Total Liabilities and Net Assets	$11,100,000	$542,500

*An alternative to the balance sheet format shown here is a Statement of Net Assets format.

stricted assets are generally reported between current assets and capital assets. In Illustration 19-9, the Restricted Assets consist of assets segregated in compliance with the sinking fund requirements of the revenue bonds,[9] and the Current Liabilities (Payable from Restricted Assets) consist of the current interest and principal installments due on the revenue bonds.

Under *GASB Statement No. 34*, proprietary funds will no longer report equity on the statement of net assets. Under the proposal, net assets will be reported externally as either (1) invested in capital assets, net of related debt, (2) unrestricted net assets, or (3) restricted net assets. Internally, the government may keep separate the sources of capital as in the past. In this case, contributions would be classified by source and segregated from retained earnings. Finally, both fixed assets and long-term debt are accounted for and reported as specific assets and liabilities of the Enterprise Fund.

---

[9]Revenue bonds are long-term obligations, where the principal and interest are paid from the earnings of self-supporting enterprises on which the bond proceeds were spent.

Internal Service Funds

Internal Service Funds are used to account for any activity that provides goods or services to *other funds, departments, or agencies of the primary governmental unit and its component units, or to other governments*, on a cost reimbursement basis. Internal service funds should be used only if the reporting government is the predominant participant in the activity. Otherwise, the activity should be reported as an Enterprise Fund.

Typical examples of activities accounted for in Internal Service Funds include the operations of central computer facilities, central garages and motor pools, central purchasing and stores departments, and central printing departments.

Internal Service Funds are established with resources obtained from contributions from other funds, proceeds from the sale of general obligation bonds, or long-term advances from other funds. If an Internal Service Fund obtains resources from the proceeds of the issuance of general obligation bonds, the bond liability is *not* accounted for in the records of the Internal Service Fund. Rather a Debt Service Fund is established, and the bond liability is accounted for in the General Long-Term Obligation Account Group. Upon the receipt of the bond issue proceeds, the entry in the records of the Internal Service Fund is a debit to Cash and a credit to Capital Contributions—General Obligation Bonds. A balance sheet and the statement of revenues, expenses, and changes in fund balance for an Internal Service Fund are included as part of the proprietary fund statements as shown in Illustrations 19-9 and 19-10. As indicated, fixed assets acquired with the resources of the

---

ILLUSTRATION 19–10

Model City
Proprietary Funds
Statement of Revenues, Expenses, and Changes in Fund Net Assets
For the Year Ended December 31, 2001

	Business-Type Activities— *Enterprise Fund*	Governmental Activities *Internal Service Fund*
	Sewer Fund	
Operating Revenues		
Charges for Services	$1,500,000	$200,000
Total Operating Revenues	1,500,000	200,000
Operating Expenses		
Personal Services	675,000	185,000
Utilities	105,000	20,000
Depreciation Expense	500,000	15,000
Total Operating Expenses	1,280,000	220,000
Operating Income (loss)	220,000	(20,000)
Nonoperating Revenue (Expenses)		
Interest Expense (10%)	(42,000)	—
Total Nonoperating Revenue (expenses)	(42,000)	—
Income Before Contributions and Transfers	178,000	(20,000)
Transfers Out—General Fund	(150,000)	—
Change in Net Assets	28,000	(20,000)
Total Net Assets—beginning of year	6,229,000	535,000
Total Net Assets—end of year	6,257,000	515,000

Internal Service Fund and depreciation thereon are recorded in the accounting records of that fund.

FIDUCIARY FUNDS

Trust and Agency Funds

As stated earlier, trust and agency funds focus on reporting net assets and changes in net assets. Fiduciary funds are used to report assets held in a trustee or agency capacity for others and therefore cannot be used to support the government's own programs. The fiduciary category includes pension trust funds, investment trust funds, private-purpose trust funds, and agency funds. The three types of trust funds should be used to report resources held and administered by the reporting government when it is acting in a fiduciary role. These funds are distinguished from agency funds generally by the existence of a trust agreement that affects the degree of management involvement and the length of time that the resources are held. Accounting procedures for agency funds and most trust funds are quite similar and are relatively simple. The disclosures under *GASB Statement No. 34* require a separate statement of fiduciary responsibilities with a statement of net assets and a statement of changes in net assets. The statement of net assets and the statement of changes in net assets may be presented in a "layered" approach or presented as separate statements.

Agency Funds For example, assume that Model City collects property taxes on behalf of a legally separate governmental unit such as a water improvement district. The following entries are made to record the amount of taxes to be collected and their remittance to the water improvement district.

(1)	Property Tax Receivable	250,000	
	Due to Water Improvement District		250,000
	To record levy of taxes ear-marked for Valley Water Improvement District.		
(2)	Cash	250,000	
	Property Tax Receivable		250,000
	To record collection of taxes ear-marked for Valley Water Improvement District.		
(3)	Due to Water Improvement District	250,000	
	Cash		250,000
	To record remittance to Valley Water Improvement District of taxes collected on its behalf.		

Agency funds are purely custodial, and assets always equal liabilities (no fund balance exists or if a fund balance is recorded, it is reported as a liability). These funds do not involve revenues or expenditures, nor do they require the preparation of a statement of revenues, expenditures, and changes in fund balance.

ACCOUNT GROUP ENTITIES

Under *GASB Statement No. 34*, governments report all capital assets, including infrastructure assets, and unmatured general long-term debt on a government-wide basis and report depreciation expense as a charge to operations in each period. Governments no longer report account groups such as the General Fixed Asset Account Group and the General Long-Term Obligation Account Group with the government funds. While account groups will no longer be *reported*, we assume that governments will still *maintain* the groups, at least in the short run, to account for general fixed assets and general obligation long-term debt.

General fixed assets of a governmental unit are the fixed assets owned by it that are not accounted for in its proprietary (enterprise, internal service, and nonexpendable trust) funds. These assets are accounted for in the General Fixed Asset Account Group, which is essentially an "inventory" of the general fixed assets owned by the governmental unit balanced by accounts listing the sources of the resources used to acquire them.

General long-term debt of a governmental unit is the unmatured principal of general obligation indebtedness that is not properly accounted for in a proprietary fund or trust fund. Such debt is accounted for in the General Long-Term Obligation Account Group, which lists the amounts of unmatured long-term debt principal balanced by accounts that reflect the amount of resources *available* in debt service funds for debt principal payments and the amount of resources that must be provided in *future years* for the payment of debt principal. While the information included in the general long-term obligation group will not be reported, *it will be imperative for governments to maintain amortization schedules for all debt issued since the effective interest expense is reported on the government-wide statement of activities and the amortized debt is reported on the statement of net assets.*

General Fixed Assets Account Group

General fixed assets may be acquired through gift or foreclosure, or they may be acquired through the expenditure of resources of the general fund, special revenue funds, or capital project funds.

Infrastructure Assets

How should a government account for streets, sidewalks, bridges and other immovable assets? Prior to the issuance of *GASB Statement No. 34* on reporting for state and local governments, most governments ignored accounting for these assets. Using the former rules, if the majority of a city's bridges needed repairs, there was no information provided in statements. Under the new rules, governments will be required to show the historical cost of these assets on the government-wide statement of net assets and include depreciation expense on the government-wide statement of activities. Although this topic is a controversial issue, the GASB felt that capitalization and depreciation of infrastructure assets is important to assist users in:

1. Determining whether current-year revenues are sufficient to pay for current-year services.
2. Assessing the service efforts and costs of programs.
3. Determining whether the government's financial position improved or deteriorated as a result of the year's operations.
4. Assessing the government's financial position and condition.

Governments are required to capitalize and report major general infrastructure assets that were acquired (purchased, constructed, or donated) in fiscal years ending after June 30, 1980. The initial capitalization amount should be based on historical cost. If determination of historical cost is not practical because of inadequate records, estimated historical cost may be used.

The valuation of constructed or purchased general fixed assets is determined using the cost basis. Donated assets are recorded at their estimated fair value at the time they are received. Since the account group is a set of self-balancing accounts, the offset (credit) to the asset account is generally to an "investment from government fund" account. Consider the following classifications of general fixed assets and the sources of the funds:

Classification of Assets	*Classification of Sources of Assets*
Land	Investments in general fixed asets from:
Buildings	Capital projects funds
Improvements other than buildings	General obligation bonds
Machinery and equipment	Special assessment debt with government
Construction in progress	commitment
Infrastructure assets	Federal grants
	State grants
	Local grants
	General fund revenues
	Special revenue fund revenues
	Contributions from property owners
	Private gifts

Accounting events in 2001 that affect the General Fixed Assets Account Group of Model City are summarized below in general journal form:

Purchase of a Fixed Asset
(1) Machinery and Equipment   250,000
     Investment from General Fund Revenues   250,000
       To record expenditure for office equipment made by General Fund in 2001 (see Chapter 18).

Sale of a Fixed Asset
(2) Investment from General Fund Revenues   225,000
    Accumulated Depreciation   140,000
     Machinery and Equipment   225,000
     Reduction in Investment from General   140,000
      Fund Revenue
      To record sale of used office equipment.

Equipment, which was purchased five years ago for $225,000, was sold for $87,250. Accumulated depreciation on the asset was $140,000. The proceeds of the sale were accounted for as revenue of the General Fund (see Chapter 18). When a general fixed asset is sold, both its original cost and accumulated depreciation are removed from the records of the General Fixed Asset Account Group. Under *GASB Statement No. 34,* the difference between the book value of the asset ($85,000) and the cash received ($87,500) is reported as a gain (loss) on sale and reported on the government-wide statement of activities. In this case, the gain is $2500.

Asset Being Constructed
(3) Construction in Progress   1,500,000
    Investment from General Obligation Bonds   1,000,000
    Investment from State Grant   500,000
     To record expenditures incurred during 2001 for construction of Model City Library and Civic Center.

The investment in general fixed assets is allocated between general obligation bonds and state grants in relation to the relative contribution of each to the authorized project (Bonds—$2,000,000, State Grant—$1,000,000; or a ratio of 2:1). When construction is completed in 2002, the following entry would be made in the records of the General Fixed Assets Account Group:

Constructed Asset Complete:

Land	200,000	
Buildings	2,725,000	
Construction in Progress		1,500,000
Investment from General Obligation Bonds		950,000
Investment from State Grant		475,000

Expenditures incurred in 2002 amount to $1,425,000 and are allocated to investment from general obligation bonds and state grants in the same manner as they were in 2001. The total cost of the completed project is $2,925,000 ($1,500,000 + $1,425,000); it is allocated to Land and Buildings in accordance with information supplied from the records of the capital projects fund.

Depreciation:

(4)	Reduction in Investment in General Fixed Assets Due to Accumulated Depreciation	306,000	
	Accumulated Depreciation—Buildings		120,000
	Accumulated Depreciation—Machinery and Equipment		55,000
	Accumulated Depreciation—Improvements		131,000
	To record accumulated depreciation on general fixed assets.		

As previously explained, depreciation of general fixed assets is not measured or reported in the accounts of governmental (expendable) funds. Since depreciation is now required on government-wide statements, accumulated depreciation is deducted from the related assets in the General Fixed Asset Account Group with a contra reduction from the total investments in general fixed assets balance. Notice that the recognition of accumulated depreciation does *not* result in the recording or reporting of depreciation expense in any governmental fund type. ***It is reported only on the government-wide statements.***

The new required disclosures about capital assets are presented in Illustration 19-11. The primary difference between past disclosures and the new disclosures is that the capital assets of the Internal Service Fund and infrastructure assets are now included in the new disclosures for *governmental activities.*

General Long-Term Obligation Account Group

General long-term obligations of a governmental unit include the unmatured principal on bonds, warrants, notes, and other long-term general obligations, including special assessment debt for which the government is obligated in some manner. It is not limited to liabilities arising from debt issues, but may include noncurrent liabilities arising from lease agreements and similar commitments. It does not include long-term debt that is the specific liability of proprietary funds. However, where the full faith and credit of the governmental unit is pledged as additional assurance that specific proprietary fund liabilities will be paid, the contingent lia-

ILLUSTRATION 19–11

Disclosure of Information About Capital Assets
For the Year Ending December 31, 2001

| | Primary Government | | | |
Governmental Activities	Beginning Balance	Additions	Retirements	Ending Balance
Land	$ 500,000			$ 500,000
Building*	4,760,000			4,760,000
Improvements	2,795,000			2,795,000
Machinery and Equipment*	950,000	250,000	(225,000)	975,000
Construction in Progress		1,500,000		1,500,000
Infrastructure	5,000,000			5,000,000
Total at historical cost	$14,005,000	1,750,000	(225,000)	$15,530,000
Less accumulated deprecation				
Building*	(1,490,000)	(130,000)		(1,620,000)
Improvements	(600,000)	(31,000)		(631,000)
Machinery and Equipment*	(235,000)	(60,000)	140,000	(155,000)
Infrastructure	(1,000,000)	(100,000)		$(1,100,000)
Total accumulated depreciation	$(3,325,000)	(321,000)	140,000	$(3,506,000)
Governmental activities capital assets, net	$10,680,000	1,429,000	(85,000)	$12,024,000
Business-Type Activities:				
Utility Plant	12,000,000			12,000,000
Construction in Progress	—	40,000		40,000
Totals at historical cost	12,000,000	40,000		12,040,000
Less accumulated depreciation				
Utility Plant	(1,800,000)	(200,000)		(2,000,000)
Business-type activities capital assets, net	$10,200,000	$(160,000)		$10,040,000

Depreciation expense *charged to governmental activities as follows:*	
Public Safety	$ 36,612
General Government	18,210
Highways and Streets	12,332
Sanitation	6,745
Health	13,585
Cultural—recreation	153,963
Education	64,553
In addition, depreciation held on capital assets held by the Internal Service Fund is charged to the various functions based on usage	15,000
	$ 321,000

*Includes, in ending balances, the capital assets of the Internal Service Fund ($360,000 and $200,000 in buildings and equipment respectively with $100,000 and $50,000 in accumulated depreciation).

bility should be disclosed in the notes to the Statement of General Long-Term Obligations.

Major credit account balances in the General Long-Term Obligation Account Group are Serial Bonds Payable, Term Bonds Payable, and Other General Long-Term Liabilities. The two major divisions of the offsetting debit account balances are "Resources to be Provided in Future Years for Payment of Long-Term Debt" and "Resources Available in Debt Service Funds for Payment of Long-Term Debt."

The use of these accounts can be illustrated by summarizing in general journal form the accounting events in 2001 that affect the General Long-Term Debt Obligation Group of Model City:

(1)   Resources to be Provided in Future Years
     for Payment of Term Bonds   2,000,000
     Term Bonds Payable   2,000,000
       To record issuance of $2,000,000 in par value of term bonds for
       construction of Model City Library and Civic Center.

(2)   Resources Available in Debt Service
     Fund—Term Bonds   104,000
     Resources to be Provided in Future Years
       for Payment of Term Bonds   104,000
       To record increase in balance of Library and Civic Center Term Bonds Debt
       Service Fund available for payment of principal.

(3)   Serial Bonds Payable   300,000
     Resources to be Provided in Future Years
       for Payment of Serial Bonds   300,000
       To record payment by Land Acquisition Serial Bonds Debt Service Fund of
       current year's installment of principal on Land Acquisition Serial Bonds.

(4)   Resources Available in Debt Service
     Fund—Serial Bonds   16,000
     Resources to be Provided in Future Years
       for Payment of Serial Bonds   16,000
       To record increase in balance of Land Acquisition Serial Bonds Debt
       Service Fund during 2001.

To meet the new reporting requirements, amortization schedules are needed. The following amortization schedules are prepared for the serial and the term bonds.

| | | | **Term Bond Amortization Schedule** | | |
| | | | *Effective interest rate = 6.787%. Coupon rate = 8%* | | |
Date	*Interest Expense*	*Cash*	*Premium Amortization*	*Unamortized Premium*	*Term Bond Balance*
				100,000	$2,100,000
10/1/02	142,537	160,000	17,463	82,537	2,082,537
10/1/03	141,352	160,000	18,648	63,889	2,063,889
10/1/04	140,086	160,000	19,914	43,975	2,043,975
10/1/05	138,734	160,000	21,266	22,709	2,022,709
10/1/06	137,291	160,000	22,709	0	2,000,000

| | | | **Serial Bond Amortization Schedule** | |
| | | | *Effective interest rate = 8%. Coupon rate = 8%* | |
Date	*Interest Expense*	*Cash*	*Principal Payment*	*Serial Bond Balance*
				1,200,000
7/1/01	96,000	396,000	300,000	900,000
7/1/02	72,000	372,000	300,000	600,000
7/1/03	48,000	348,000	300,000	300,000
7/1/04	24,000	324,000	300,000	—

ILLUSTRATION 19–12

Model City
Schedule of General Long-Term Obligations
December 31, 2001 and December 31, 2000

Governmental Activities	*Beginning Balance*	*Additions*	*Reductions*	*Ending Balance*	*Amounts Due Within One Year*
Term Bonds	$ —	$2,100,000	$ 4,366	$2,095,634	$ —
Serial Bonds	1,200,000	—	300,000	900,000	300,000
Governmental Activities Long-Term Liabilities	$1,200,000	$2,100,000	$304,366	$2,995,634	$300,000
Business-Type Activities					
Revenue Bonds Payable	$4,200,000	$ —	$ —	$4,200,000	$ —
Business-Type Activities Long-Term Liabilities	$4,200,000	$ —	$ —	$4,200,000	$ —

If the serial bonds were issued at a premium or discount, the amortization schedule would adjust interest expense to the historical market rate (effective interest rate), similar to the term bond illustrated above.

The total effective interest expense is $119,634 (or 50% of $96,000 plus 50% of $72,000 plus 25% of $142,537). Accrued interest payable is $76,000 (or 25% of $160,000 plus 50% of $72,000). An example of the new disclosure requirements concerning long-term liabilities is presented in Illustration 19-12.

"Certain economic events that have not been historically reported will also show up. Blossom gave two examples. (Andrew Blossom is a partner with KPMG Peat Marwick, Kansas City, MO, a member of the AICPA's Government Accounting and Auditing Committee, and chair of the AICPA's task force on rewriting its Government Audit Guide.) First under the old model, bonds weren't reported as a liability until they became due; under the new model, the full value of the bonds will be shown. The second involves litigation expenses, which have to be shown as an expense when the alleged incident is claimed to have occurred, rather than under the old system, when a payout was made."[10]

NEW EXTERNAL REPORTING REQUIREMENTS (GASB STATEMENT NO. 34)

The following statements and disclosures are required:[11]

Reporting governmental fund financial statements
1. Balance sheet (Illustration 19-13)
2. Statement of revenues, expenditures, and changes in fund balances (Illustration 19-14)
3. Reconciliation to the government-wide statements (Illustrations 19-15 and 19-16)

---

[10] *Practical Accountant*, Vol. 32, "New Look for Government Statements," by Howard Wolosky, August 1999, pp. 47–50.

[11] The focus of the governmental and proprietary fund statements is on major funds. Nonmajor funds are aggregated and displayed in a single column. Combining statements, showing the details of the nonmajor funds, are not required but may be presented as supplementary information.

Reporting proprietary fund financial statements

1. Balance sheet (Illustration 19-9) or a statement of net assets (not shown); either format is acceptable.

2. Statement of revenues, expenses, and changes in fund net assets (Illustration 19-10)

3. Statement of cash flows (not shown)—direct format

Reporting fiduciary funds (and similar component units) financial statements

1. Statement of fiduciary net assets (not shown)

2. Statement of changes in fiduciary net assets (not shown)

Reporting government-wide statements

1. Statement of net assets (Illustration 19-16)

2. Statement of activities (Illustration 19-17)

Combining statements for major component units

1. Statement of net assets (not shown)

2. Statement of activities (not shown)

Notes to the financial statements

1. Schedule of changes in capital assets (Illustration 19-11)

2. Schedule of changes in long-term liabilities (Illustration 19-12)

Required supplementary information (RSI)

1. Management's discussion and analysis (MD&A)

2. Budgetary comparison schedules (see Chapter 18, Illustration 18-9), accompanied by information reconciling the budget-to-GAAP (see Chapter 18, Illustration 18-10)

GOVERNMENT FUND-BASED REPORTING

Earlier in the chapter, several individual fund financial statements were illustrated. In this section, we discuss the reporting requirements for the governmental funds aggregated. See Illustrations 19-13 and 19-14 for the fund balance sheets and the statement of revenues, expenditures, and changes in fund balances for the governmental funds. Fund information is important because funds are created to account for financial resources and the activities that they support and to aid management in decision making. Because much of the government's activities is managed and accounted for in a limited number of funds, the governmental fund reporting is designed to report the government's **major funds**. For example, in Illustration 19-13, each of the funds is reported in separate columns. Governments are required only to report the **major funds** in separate columns, but have flexibility to report more funds separately if desired. *Individual governmental funds and proprietary funds are major funds if the total assets, liabilities, revenues, or expenditure/expenses of that individual fund are at least 10% of the corresponding total for the relevant fund category (governmental or enterprise funds) and at least 5% of the corresponding total for all governmental and enterprise funds combined.* In addition, any fund that may be important to financial statement users should be reported as a major fund also. Internal Service Funds are exempt from major fund reporting. Therefore to avoid double

ILLUSTRATION 19–13

Model City
Governmental Funds*
Fund Balance Sheets at December 31, 2001

Assets	General Fund	Capital Projects Fund — Library and Civic Center	Debt Service Funds — Library and Civic Center Term Bond	Debt Service Funds — Land Acquisition Serial Bond	Special Revenue Fund — Classics Acquisitions	Permanent Fund — Classics Endowment	Total Governmental Funds
Cash	$ 63,250	$ 300,000	$ —	$21,000	$22,000	$ —	$ 406,250
Interest Receivable		12,500	4,000			7,500	24,000
Investments	106,000	1,000,000	100,000			300,000	1,506,000
Property Tax Receivable	127,750						127,750
Due from Other Funds	50,000				7,500		57,500
Due from State Government		250,000					250,000
Total Assets	$347,000	$1,562,500	$104,000	$21,000	$29,500	$307,500	$2,371,500

Liabilities and Fund Balance

Vouchers Payable	$ 73,000	$ 50,000					$123,000
Due to Other Funds						7,500	7,500
Total Liabilities	$ 73,000	$ 50,000	$ —	$ —	$ —	$ 7,500	$ 130,500
Fund Balances:							
Unreserved	83,000	312,500					395,500
Reserved for							
Encumbrances	191,000	1,200,000					1,391,000
Debt Services			104,000	21,000			125,000
Other					29,500	300,000	329,500
Total Fund Balances	274,000	1,512,500	104,000	21,000	29,500	300,000	2,241,000
Total Liabilities and Fund Balances	$347,000	$1,562,500	$104,000	$21,000	$29,500	$307,500	$2,371,500

*Because Model City does not have very many funds, all of which were considered important to readers, the city reported on all funds rather than focusing on only the major funds, as defined by percentage cutoffs.

counting (revenue to the internal service fund is an expenditure of the government funds), the net effects of internal service transactions are eliminated.

Reconciliation Between Government Fund Balances and Government-wide Net Assets

The primary difference between the new disclosure requirement for capital assets (Illustration 19-11) and prior disclosures relates to the assets of the Internal Service Funds and infrastructure assets. On the statement of net assets, the Internal Service Fund's assets and liabilities are reported in governmental activities along with infrastructure assets. To assist the users of the financial statements, governments must reconcile the change in fund balances in the governmental funds (see Illustration 19-14) with the changes in fund balance reported on the government-wide statements (see Illustration 19-17). This reconciliation is reported in Illustration 19-15. In addition, governments must reconcile the fund balance in the governmental funds (see Illustration 19-13) with the fund balance reported in the statement of net assets prepared on a government-wide basis (from Illustration 19-16). This rec-

ILLUSTRATION 19–14

Model City
Governmental Funds*
Statement of Revenues, Expenditures, and Changes in Fund Balances for the Year Ended December 31, 2001

	General Fund	Capital Projects Fund — Library and Civic Center	Debt Service Funds — Library and Civic Center Term Bond	Debt Service Funds — Land Acquisition Serial Bond	Expendable Trust Fund — Classics Acquisitions	Permanent Fund — Classics Endowment	Total Governmental Funds
Revenues							
Property Taxes	$1,158,750		$316,000				$1,474,750
Licenses and Permits	170,500						170,500
State Grant—education	275,000						275,000
Intergovernmental		$1,000,000					1,000,000
Charges for Services	130,500						130,500
Interest	6,000	12,500		$ 4,000		$ 30,000	52,000
Total Revenue	$1,740,750	$1,012,500	$316,000	$ 4,000		$ 30,000	$3,103,250
Expenditures							
Public Safety	$ 480,000						$ 480,000
General Government	289,000						289,000
Highways and Streets	128,000						128,000
Sanitation	70,000						70,000
Health	141,000						141,000
Cultural—recreation	80,000				$ 18,000		98,000
Education	670,000						670,000
Debt service							
Principal			$300,000				300,000
Interest			96,000				96,000
Capital Outlay		$1,500,000					1,500,000
Total Expenditures	$1,858,000	$1,500,000	$396,000	—	$ 18,000	—	$3,772,000
Excess (deficiency) of revenues over expenditures	$ (117,250)	$ (487,500)	$(80,000)	$ 4,000	$(18,000)	$ 30,000	(668,750)
Other Financing Sources (Uses)							
Proceeds from long-term capital debt		$2,100,000					$2,100,000
Transfers in	$ 150,000		$ 96,000	$100,000	$ 30,000		376,000
Transfers out	(96,000)	(100,000)				$(30,000)	(226,000)
Total other	$ 54,000	$2,000,000	$ 96,000	$100,000	$ 30,000	$(30,000)	$2,250,000
Special Items							
Proceeds from sale of equipment	$ 87,250						$ 87,250
Net change in fund balance	24,000	$1,512,500	$ 16,000	$104,000	$ 12,000	$ —	**$1,668,600**
Fund balance—beginning	250,000	—	5,000	—	17,500	300,000	572,500
Fund balance—ending	$ 274,000	$1,512,500	$ 21,000	$104,000	$ 29,500	$300,000	**$2,241,000**

*Because Model City does not have very many funds, all of which were considered important to readers, the city reported on all funds rather than focusing on only the major funds, as defined by percentage cutoffs. In addition, $250,000 of capital expenditures made by the general fund are included in the following governmental activities: Public Safety, $100,000, Cultural–recreation, $50,000, and Education, $100,000.

ILLUSTRATION 19–15

Model City
Reconciliation of the Statement of Revenues,
Expenditures, and Changes in Fund Balances of Governmental
Funds to the Statement of Activities
For the Year Ended December 31, 2001

Net change in fund balances—total governmental funds (Illustration 19–14)	**$1,668,500**
Governmental funds report capital outlays as expenditures while governmental activities report depreciation expense to allocate those expenditures over the life of the asset. This is the amount by which capital outlays exceeded depreciation in the current period. (a)	1,444,000
In the statement of activities, only the gain on the sale of equipment is reported, while in the governmental funds, the proceeds from the sale increase financial resources. Thus, the change in net assets differs from the change in fund balance by the book value of the asset sold.	(85,000)
Bond proceeds provide current financial resources to governmental funds, but issuing debt increases long-term liabilities in the statement of net assets.	(2,100,000)
Repayment of bond principal is an expenditure in the government funds, but reduces long-term liabilities in the statement of net assets.	300,000
Some expenses reported on the statement of activities do not require the use of current financial resources and therefore are not reported as expenditures in government funds (in this case, accrued interest). (b)	(23,634)
Internal service funds are used by management to charge the cost of certain activities to individual funds. The net revenue (expense) of the internal service fund is reported with governmental activities. (c)	(20,000)
Change in Net Assets of Governmental Activities (see Illustration 19–17)	**$1,183,866**

(a) Total capital expenditures from the capital projects fund ($1,500,000) plus purchases by the General Fund ($250,000) less depreciation expense, excluding depreciation from the Internal Service Fund ($321,000 − $15,000).
(b) Total interest expense using the accrual basis is $119,634 but only $96,000 is recognized as an expenditure. (The $119,634 includes $84,000 from the serial bond and $35,634 from the term bond.)
(c) The $20,000 is charged equally to public safety and to the general government.

onciliation is reported at the bottom of Illustration 19-16. These reconciliations highlight the major differences between fund accounting and accrual accounting. For instance, in the governmental funds, amounts spent to acquire capital assets are expenditures; while under accrual accounting, these assets are capitalized on the balance sheet and depreciated on the statement of activities. Similarly, when bonds are issued, the total proceeds increase financial resources on the statement of revenues, expenditures, and changes in fund balance, whereas under accrual accounting, bond issues increase liabilities on the balance sheet. Total proceeds from the sale of an asset are also included on the statement of revenues, expenditures, and changes in fund balance, whereas under accrual accounting only the difference between the carrying value of the asset and the cash received is reported on the statement of activities. Similarly, in the governmental funds, only the amount of cash interest paid is treated as an expenditure; in the government-wide statements, the effective interest expense is recorded on the statement of activities with accrued interest payable reported on the balance sheet.

GOVERNMENT-WIDE REPORTING

As stated previously, the primary financial statements under *GASB Statement No. 34* are prepared on a government-wide basis. These statements are prepared on the accrual basis using the flow of economic resources concept. These primary statements include:

1. The statement of net assets.
2. The statement of activities.

Note that a governmental-wide statement of cash flows is *not* required. Cash flow statements are required for proprietary funds.

Statement of Net Assets

The statement of net assets reports both financial and capital resources. The statement of net assets is prepared using the accrual basis and a government-wide format (formerly called entity-wide basis). Under the prior rules, the balance sheet listed each fund's assets and liabilities with no overall government totals. Under the new format, governments are encouraged to present the statement that displays assets less liabilities equaling net assets, rather than the traditional balance sheet format. While permitted, no distinction between current and long-term is required under the proposal for government-wide assets and liabilities. However, if no distinction is made, the items should be listed in the order of liquidity. In Illustration 19-16, we show the "net asset format" with items listed in the order of liquidity rather than the classified version of the statement of net assets. If the classified format is used and there are liabilities with maturities longer than one year, the current portion should be listed separately from the amount due later than one year.

The statement of net assets is divided into two categories: the primary government and its discretely presented component units. The *primary government* columns include the governmental funds, the business-activities (proprietary) funds, and a total column.[12] *Component units* are governmental units that are legally independent of the reporting government, but within the reporting unit's control. Control means either appointing a majority of the unit's governing body members or being fiscally dependent (e.g., the budget is approved by the primary government). An example of a component unit is a school district that receives funding from the county. Because the school district is financially accountable to the county, it is considered a component unit. No component units are shown in Illustration 19-16.

At a minimum, assets, liabilities, and net assets should be disclosed for each of the following four categories:

A. Primary Government[13]
   1. Government activities
   2. Business-type activities
   3. Total primary government activities (total of 1 and 2)
B. Discretely Presented Component Units
   4. "Discretely presented" component units (discretely presented, as opposed to blended, means reporting the data in a separate column as if it were a separate fund).

---

[12]Fiduciary activities whose resources are not available to finance the government's programs should be excluded from the government-wide statements and should be reported only in the fund financial statements.

[13]Component units that meet the criteria for blending should be reported in the primary government columns (GASB Codification 2600.115).

ILLUSTRATION 19–16

Model City
Statement of Net Assets—Government-wide Basis At December 31, 2001

Assets	Primary Government		
	Total Government Activities	*Business-Type Activities*	*Total*
Cash	$ 428,750	$ 100,000	$ 528,750
Interest Receivable	24,000		24,000
Investments	1,506,000		1,506,000
Receivables	227,750	451,000	678,750
Internal Balances	50,000	(50,000)	—
Due from State Government	250,000		250,000
Restricted Assets		509,000	509,000
Capital Assets (net)	12,024,000	10,040,000	22,064,000
Total Assets	$14,510,500	$11,050,000	$25,560,500

Liabilities and Fund Balance			
Payables	$ 226,500	$ 593,000	$ 819,500
Long-Term Liabilities			
Due within one-year	300,000		300,000
Due in more than one year	2,695,634	4,200,000	6,895,634
Total Liabilities	3,222,134	4,793,000	$ 8,015,134

Net Assets			
Invested in Capital Assets, net of related debt	9,028,366	5,558,000	14,586,366
Unreserved	414,500	199,000	613,500
Reserved for			
Encumbrances	1,391,000		1,391,000
Debt Service	125,000	500,000	625,000
Other	329,500		329,500
Total Fund Balances	**11,288,366**	6,257,000	17,545,366
Total Liabilities and Fund Balances	$14,510,500	$11,050,000	$25,560,500

Reconciling the Statement of Net Assets with Governmental Fund Reporting

Fund balance for governmental activities (see Illustration 19–13)	**$ 2,241,000**
Capital assets used in governmental activities are not financial resources and are not reported in the funds ($12,024,000 less internal service fund assets of $420,000)	11,604,000
Internal service funds are used by management to charge the costs of certain activities to individual funds. The assets and liabilities of the internal service fund are included in the governmental activities in the statement of net assets. (Note: this line item includes capital assets.)	515,000
Some liabilities are not due in the current period and are not recognized in the funds ($40,000 and $36,000 accrued interest on the serial and term bonds)	(76,000)
Long-term liabilities (plus unamortized premium) are not due and payble in the current period and therefore are not reported in the funds.	(2,995,634)
Net assets in governmental activities (see Illustration 19–16)	**$11,288,366**

Under previous guidelines, long-term debt was reported as one amount. Under the new rules, the current portion of long-term debt must be listed separately from the noncurrent portion. In addition, a footnote is required for the governmental, business-type, and component units activities showing the additions and reductions to the long-term liability account for the year, including the current portion.

Similar to the requirements for long-term debt, a footnote is required showing the additions and reductions to the capital asset account. The amount of depreciation charged to governmental activities is required. This information is disclosed for the government, business-type, and component units activities.

Account Groups If a particular government does *not* use the accrual basis, long-term assets and liabilities are not recorded in the governmental funds. Therefore, account groups were established to provide a basis for recognizing these long-term items. Since the new rules require the accrual basis, these assets and liabilities will now be reported on the government-wide statement of net assets. Formal reporting of the account groups is no longer required since these assets and liabilities will now be reported on the statement of net assets.

Net Assets Net assets are displayed in three components as follows:

1. *Invested in capital assets, net of related debt.* This component consists of capital assets including restricted capital assets, net of accumulated depreciation and reduced by the outstanding balances of any bonds, mortgages, notes, or other borrowings attributable to the acquisition, construction, or improvement of those assets.
2. *Restricted* (listed by major categories of restrictions such as capital projects, debt service, etc.). Net assets are reported as restricted when constraints placed on net asset use are either: (a) externally imposed by creditors (such as through debt covenants), grantors, contributors, or laws and regulations of other governments, or (b) imposed by law. When permanent endowments or permanent fund principal amounts are included, ''restricted net assets'' should be displayed in two components—expendable and nonexpendable. Nonexpendable net assets are those that are required to be retained in perpetuity.
3. *Unrestricted.* Unrestricted net assets consist of net assets that do not meet the definition of *restricted* or *invested in capital assets, net of related debt.*

Infrastructure Asset Reporting Issues One of the more controversial rules of *GASB Statement No. 34* is that infrastructure assets such as roads, bridges, storm sewers, water systems, and so on will be reported as assets in the governmental-wide statements at historical cost (or estimated historical cost at transition). In addition, governments will be required to report depreciation on these assets.[14]

Statement of Activities

The statement of activities presented in Illustration 19-17 is prepared on a government-wide basis and is presented using a *net cost* format. This format separates

---

[14]Governments may elect not to report depreciation expense for infrastructure assets if two conditions are met. First, a government must use an asset management system that contains up-to-date inventories of the assets, be able to assess the condition of the assets, and be able to estimate the amounts needed to preserve the network at a level established by the government. Second, the government must be able to document that the network of infrastructure assets is being preserved at a level established and disclosed by the government.

revenues into program revenues and general revenues. Then expenses are reduced by program revenues resulting in "net (expense) revenue." General revenues, extraordinary items and special items, and transfers are reported separately. *Program revenues* include three categories: charges for services; program-operating grants and contributions; and capital grants and contributions. (In the illustration only two of the three categories are used.) Charges for services include revenues attributable to a specific program because they result from exchange transactions, such as charges to customers. Licenses and permits would generally be reported as charges for services under program revenues since the users benefit directly from the services provided. In illustration 19-17, the $170,500 of revenue from licenses and permits from Illustration 19-14 is included as charges for services: highways and streets ($94,000), cultural and recreation ($15,000), and general government ($61,500, along with an additional $130,500 from Illustration 19-14). "All" taxes are considered *general revenue*. In Illustration 19-17, columns are used to distinguish

ILLUSTRATION 19–17

Model City
Statement of Activities—Government-wide
For the Year Ended December 31, 2001

| Functions/Programs | Expenses | Program Revenues | | Net (Expense) Revenue and Changes in Net Assets | | |
| | | | | Primary Government | | |
		Charges for Services	Grants and Contributions	Governmental Activities	Business-Type Activities	Total
Primary Government						
Government Activities						
Public Safety	$426,612			$(426,612)		$(426,612)
General Government	317,210	$192,000	$1,000,000	874,790		874,790
Highways and Streets	140,332	94,000		(46,332)		(46,332)
Sanitation	76,745			(76,745)		(76,745)
Health	154,585			(154,585)		(154,585)
Cultural—recreation	201,963	15,000		(186,963)		(186,963)
Education	634,553		275,000	(359,553)		(359,553)
Interest on Long-Term Debt	119,634			(119,634)		(119,634)
Total Governmental Activities	2,071,634	301,000	1,275,000	(495,634)		(495,634)
Business-Type Activities						
Sewer	1,322,000	1,500,000			$ 178,000	178,000
Total Business-Type Activities	1,322,000	1,500,000			178,000	178,000
Total Primary Government	$3,393,634	$1,801,000	$1,275,000	$ (495,634)	$ 178,000	$ (317,634)
		General Revenues				
		Taxes:				
		Property taxes, levied for general purposes		$1,158,750		$1,158,750
		Property taxes, levied for debt service		316,000		316,000
		Interest and investment earnings		52,500		52,500
		Special item—gain on sale of equipment		2,250		2,250
		Transfers		150,000	(150,000)	—
		Total general revenues, special items, and transfers		1,679,500	(150,000)	1,529,500
		Change in Net Assets		**1,183,866**	**28,000**	**1,211,866**
		Net assets—beginning (assumed)		10,104,500	6,229,000	16,333,500
		Net assets—ending		**$11,288,366**	**$6,257,000**	**$17,545,366**

between governmental and business-type activities of the primary government. A total column for the primary government should be presented.[15]

IN THE NEWS

The statement of activities might actually change how governments do business, according to one expert, who claims that these net cost statements by departments and functions might give governments a lot of heartburn as the numbers for certain funds may look bad. Other funds, however, could look better. He gives the example of a police department being funded from an ad valorem tax collected for general purposes. Since the government specifically dedicates the revenue from the ad valorem tax for the police department, the net cost would no longer be as big a negative on the Statement of Activities since there would now be revenue directly associated with the function.[16]

MANAGEMENT'S DISCUSSION AND ANALYSIS (MD&A)

Management's Discussion and Analysis (MD&A) is an integral part of the annual reporting of a government entity, as required by *GASB Statement No. 34.* This discussion should provide an objective and easily readable analysis of the government's financial activities based on currently known facts, decisions, or conditions. It provides financial managers with the opportunity to present both a short-term and a long-term analysis of the government's activities. MD&A should discuss the current-year results in comparison with the prior year. This comparison should include a discussion of both the positive and the negative aspects of the current year changes. The focus of the MD&A is on the primary government (i.e., it should distinguish between the primary government and its component units). The MD&A requirements are general, rather than specific, to encourage financial managers to report effectively only the most relevant information. At a minimum, MD&A should include:

A. A brief discussion of the basic financial statements including interrelationships among the statements and significant differences in the information provided.
B. Condensed financial information derived from government-wide financial statements comparing the current year to the prior year.
C. An analysis of the government's overall financial position and results of operations to assist users in assessing whether financial position has improved or deteriorated as a result of the year's operations. The analysis should address both governmental and business-type activities as reported in the government-wide financial statements and the *reasons* for significant changes from the prior year.
D. An analysis of balances and transactions of individual funds. This analysis should address the reasons for significant changes in fund balances or fund net assets and whether restrictions, commitments, or other limitations significantly affect the availability of fund resources for future use.
E. An analysis of significant variations between original and final budget amounts and between final budget amounts and actual budget results for the general fund (or its equivalent).

---

[15]Discretely presented component units are shown in a separate column and not included in the totals for the primary government.

[16]*Practical Accountant*, Vol. 32, "New Look for Government Statements," by Howard Wolosky, August 1999, pp. 47–50.

    F. A description of significant capital asset and long-term debt activity during the year, including a discussion of commitments made for capital expenditures, changes in credit ratings, and debt limitations that may affect the financing of planned facilities or services.

    G. A discussion by governments that use the modified approach to report some or all of their infrastructure assets including significant changes in the assessed condition of eligible infrastructure assets from previous condition assessments, how the current assessed condition compares with the condition level the government has established, and any significant differences from the estimated annual amount to maintain/preserve eligible infrastructure assets compared with the actual amounts spent during the current year.

    H. A description of currently known facts, decisions, or conditions that are expected to have a significant effect on financial position (net assets) or results of operations (revenues, expenditures, and other changes in net assets).

SPECIAL ASSESSMENTS

Some capital improvements or services provided by a municipality are undertaken for the primary benefit of a particular property owner or groups of property owners rather than for the general public. In such cases, the costs of providing the capital improvements or services are often charged in whole or in part to the property owners who receive the benefit. In some cases, the municipality may share in the cost of an improvement in recognition of the public benefits that result from the project. Special assessments that are levied against the benefited property owners for services are referred to as *service-type special assessments*. Special assessments that are levied against the benefited property owners for capital improvements are referred to as *capital improvement special assessments*.

    Examples of service-type special assessment projects include street lighting, street cleaning, and snow plowing. Although financing for the routine provision of such services usually comes from general revenues, when such services are extended or provided at more frequent intervals, special assessments are sometimes levied. In such cases only the affected property owners are charged for the additional services.

    More frequently, special assessments are levied for capital improvement projects. Examples of such improvements include the paving or widening of residential streets or the construction of sidewalks or storm sewers. Although the affected property owners may be deemed the primary beneficiary of such projects, the projects often improve or add to the general fixed assets or infrastructure of the municipality as well. In some cases, such as the construction of water or sewer mains, such projects may provide capital assets that become an integral part of the government's enterprise activities.

    Unlike service-type special assessment projects, capital improvement special assessment projects have two distinct and functionally different phases. The first phase consists of financing and constructing the project. Generally, this phase is completed over a period of two months to two years depending on the nature of the project.

    The second phase consists of collecting the assessment principal and interest levied against the benefited properties and repaying the cost of financing the construction. Typically, capital improvement special assessment projects are financed by the issuance of long-term debt in the form of serial bonds, the principal and interest of which is repaid from the installment collection of special assessments. Thus, the collection of special assessment principal and interest and the repayment of the special assessment debt usually extend over a substantially longer period than the period it takes to complete the construction of the related project.

Reporting Service-type Special Assessments

Under *GASB Statements No. 6* and *No. 34*, transactions of a ***service-type special assessment*** are reported in the general fund, a special revenue fund, or an enterprise fund as best reflects the nature of the transactions. Service-type special assessments are recognized as revenue in the period the services are provided, regardless of when the assessment is billed or collected. Expenditures (or expenses) for which the assessments are levied are recognized on the same basis as other expenditures or expenses of the fund type used to account for the service assessment.

Reporting Capital Improvement Special Assessments

Where capital improvements are financed by special assessments, the transactions are recorded differently depending on whether the government is obligated in some way to assume the payment of related debt service in the event of default by property owners. The extent of the government's liability for debt related to a special assessment capital improvement can vary significantly. However, for purposes of financial reporting, a government is considered to be obligated in some manner for the repayment of special assessment debt unless (1) the government is prohibited by constitution, charter, statute, ordinance, or contract from assuming the debt in the event of default by the property owner, or (2) the government is not legally liable for assuming the debt and makes no statement, or gives no indication, that it will, or may, honor the debt in the event of default.

Where the government is obligated in some manner for the repayment of special assessment debt, all transactions related to capital improvements financed by special assessments are recorded like any other capital improvement and financing transactions. Transactions of the construction phase of the project are accounted for in a ***capital projects fund***. Transactions of the *debt service phase* are accounted for in a ***debt service fund***. The fixed assets constructed or acquired (other than those related to an enterprise fund) and the long-term debt are reported in the government-wide statement of net assets.

In capital improvement special assessment projects where special assessment debt is issued for which the government is not obligated in any manner, the debt is not reported in the general long-term obligations account group. Furthermore, the debt service transactions for such debt are reported in an ***agency fund*** rather than a debt service fund, to reflect the fact that the government's duties are limited to acting as an agent for the assessed property owners and the bondholders. The construction phase is still accounted for in a capital projects fund but the source of revenue is described as "contribution from property owners." The fixed assets constructed or acquired are recorded in the government-wide statement of net assets or an enterprise fund as appropriate. Recording this type of capital improvement special assessment project in this manner recognizes that the construction or acquisition is a governmental activity that results in the addition of a governmental asset but that the acquired asset is not financed by government debt.

To illustrate, assume that a municipality undertakes a street-widening project that will provide additional shop-front parking. Cash for the project will be provided by the proceeds of a $10 million issue of 8% special assessment debt and $2 million in general fund revenues. One-tenth of the debt plus interest is payable each July 1. A $10 million 8% special assessment levy against the benefiting property owners will provide most of the funds to service the debt and retire the bonds. However, since special assessments will be due on June 1, the city will make a one-time payment out of general fund revenues of one month's interest on the entire special assessment debt on June 1 of the first year.

Financed by Bonds for Which Government Is Obligated in Some Manner	*Financed by Bonds for Which Government Is Not Obligated in Any Manner*

Transactions

(1) $10 million in 8% special assessment serial bonds are issued and $2 million is transferred to the capital projects fund from the general fund:

Capital Projects Fund	*Capital Projects Fund*

Cash	10,000,000		Cash	10,000,000	
Bond Issue Proceeds		10,000,000	Contributions from		
To record proceeds from bond issue.			Property Owners		10,000,000

General Fund	*General Fund*

Transfer to Capital			Same entry as on left
Projects Fund	2,000,000		
Cash		2,000,000	

Capital Projects Fund	*Capital Projects Fund*

Cash	2,000,000		Same entry as on left
Transfer from General Fund		2,000,000	
To record transfer of funds from general fund to capital projects fund.			

General Long-Term Obligation Account Group	*General Long-Term Obligation Account Group*

Amount to be			No entry is made in the General Long-Term Obligation Account Group. The notes to the financial statements should show the amount of the debt and the fact that the government is in no way liable for repayment but is only acting as an agent.
Provided by Special			
Assessments	10,000,000		
Special Assessment			
Debt with			
Government			
Commitment		10,000,000	
To recognize the government's obligation for special assessment debt.			

(2) Construction is completed at a cost of $12 million:

Capital Projects Fund	*Capital Projects Fund*

Expenditures	12,000,000		Same entry as on left
Cash		12,000,000	
To record the cash outlay for capital projects.			

General Fixed Assets Account Group	*General Fixed Assets Account Group*

Improvements	12,000,000		Improvements	12,000,000	
Investment from Special			Contributed by Property		
Assessment Debt with			Owners		10,000,000
Government Commitment		10,000,000			
Investment from			Investment from General		
General Fund			Fund Revenues		2,000,000
Revenues		2,000,000			
To record completion of project.					

(3)   The first installment of the special assessment levy is billed and collected (11 months' interest is included in the billing) and an amount equal to one month's interest is transferred to the debt service fund or an agency fund from general fund revenues:

Debt Service Fund

Special Assessments		No entry
Receivable	1,733,333	
Special Assessment Revenue		1,733,333
To record billing of special assessment due June 1.		

General Fund			*General Fund*		
Transfer to Debt					
Service Fund	66,667		Expenditures	66,667	
Cash		66,667	Cash		66,667

Debt Service Fund			*Agency Fund*		
Cash	66,667		Cash	66,667	
Transfer from General Fund		66,667	Amount Held for Debt Service		66,667
Cash	1,733,333		Cash	1,733,333	
Special Assessments Receivable		1,733,333	Amount Held for Debt Service		1,733,333
To record cash collections from general fund revenues and from property owners.					

(4)   Twelve months' interest and principal is paid on the special assessment bonds on July 1:

Debt Service Fund			*Agency Fund*		
Expenditure—			Amount Held for		
Principal	1,000,000		Debt Service	1,800,000	
Expenditures—			Cash		1,800,000
Interest	800,000				
Cash		1,800,000			

General Long-Term Obligation Account Group			*General Long-Term Obligation Account Group*		
Special Assessment					
Debt with					
Government			No entry		
Commitment	1,000,000				
Amount to Be Provided by					
Special Assessments		1,000,000			
To record the payment of interest and principal on special assessment debt.					

Special assessment levies including interest are not recognized as revenue until the period in which payment is due from the assessed property owners. In particular, no revenue is recognized for unbilled but accrued interest on special assignments. Special assessment debt service expenditures for principal and interest are recognized in the period that the debt service payments are due. In particular, no expenditure is recognized for interest accrued, but not yet due, on special assessment debt. Nonrecognition of accrued interest receivable or payable on special assessments is based on the conclusion that the effect on the debt service fund balance would represent merely a timing difference rather than a true fund equity.

INTERFUND ACTIVITY

Interfund activity within and among the three fund categories (governmental, proprietary, and fiduciary) should be classified and reported as follows:

Interfund Activity

a. *Reciprocal interfund activity*—internal counterpart to exchange and exchange-like transactions. It includes:
   1. *Interfund loans*—Interfund loans should be reported as interfund receivables in the lender fund and as an interfund payable in the borrower fund.
   2. *Interfund services provided and used*—(previously known as quasi-external transactions) sales and purchases of goods and services between funds for a price approximating their external exchange value. Interfund services provided and used should be reported as revenues in seller funds and expenses or expenditures in the purchaser funds. Unpaid amounts should be reported as interfund receivables and payables in the fund balance sheet or the statement of net assets.
b. *Nonreciprocal interfund activity*—the internal counterpart to nonexchange transaction.
   1. *Interfund transfers*—(formerly known as either residual equity transfers or operating transfers) flows of assets without an equivalent flow of assets in return and without a requirement for repayment. In government funds, transfers should be reported as ''other financing uses'' in the funds and as ''other financing sources'' in the funds receiving the transfer. In proprietary funds, transfers should be reported after nonoperating revenues and expenses.
   2. *Interfund reimbursements*—repayments *from the funds* responsible for the particular expenditure or expense *to the funds* that initially paid for them. Reimbursements should not be displayed in the financial statements.

Illustration of Reciprocal Interfund Activity—Interfund Loans

Assume that the general fund advances $4,000 as a temporary loan to a special revenue fund. Corresponding entries to record the advance are

General Fund		
Due from Special Revenue Fund	4,000	
Cash		4,000

Special Revenue Fund		
Cash	4,000	
Due to General Fund		4,000

Interfund Services Provided and Used (Formerly Known as Quasi-External Transactions)

Interfund services provided and used are interfund transactions that would be treated as revenue, expense, or expenditures if they were entered into with organizations outside the governmental unit. Contributions in lieu of taxes from an enterprise fund to the general fund and internal service fund billings to government departments for services rendered are examples of interfund services provided and used. Interfund services provided and used are accounted for as revenue, expense, or expenditures of the funds involved. Accounting for interfund services provided and used in this manner is necessary for the determination of the operating results (net income) of proprietary funds.

To illustrate, assume that the internal service fund bills the Police Department for $3,000 for services rendered. The corresponding entries to record this billing are

	Internal Service Fund		
Due from General Fund		3,000	
Revenue			3,000

	General Fund		
Expenditures		3,000	
Due to Internal Service Fund			3,000

Illustration of Nonreciprocal Interfund Activity—Interfund Transfers

Some nonreciprocal interfund transfers represent nonrecurring transfers between funds. Examples include nonrecurring contributions from the general fund to proprietary funds, the return of part or all of such contributions to the general fund, and transfers of the residual balances of discontinued funds to the general fund or to debt service funds.

To illustrate, assume that an enterprise fund transfers $150,000 of excess resources to the general fund. Corresponding entries to record the transfer are

	Enterprise Fund		
Transfer to General Fund		150,000	
Cash			150,000

	General Fund		
Cash		150,000	
Transfer from Enterprise Fund			150,000

Nonreciprocal transfers should be reported as other financing sources or uses in the governmental funds. Nonreciprocal transfers to or from proprietary funds should be reported after nonoperating revenues and expenses.

In other cases, nonreciprocal transfers consist of recurring transfers between funds for the purpose of shifting resources from the fund legally required to record the revenue to the fund legally required to expend the revenue. An example of this type of transfer is the annual transfer of revenue from an endowment trust fund to an expendable trust fund. To illustrate, the net effect of the entries to record the transfer of revenue from the Classics Acquisition Endowment Trust Fund of Model City to the Classics Acquisition Expendable Trust Fund may be summarized as follows.

Endowment Trust Fund

Transfer to Expendable Trust Fund	30,000	
Cash		30,000

Expendable Trust Fund

Cash	30,000	
Transfer from Endowment Trust Fund		30,000

As stated earlier, nonreciprocal transfers should be reported as other financing sources or uses in the governmental funds. Nonreciprocal transfers to or from proprietary funds should be reported after nonoperating revenues and expenses.

Interfund Reimbursements

Interfund reimbursements are transactions that involve the transfer of resources from one fund to another in order to reimburse the recipient fund for expenditures made by it that are properly expenditures of the reimbursing fund. The recipient fund should record the transaction as a credit to expenditures, and the reimbursing fund should record the transaction as a debit to expenditures.

For example, assume that the general fund performs services in the amount of $10,000 for a special revenue fund. The corresponding entries to record the reimbursement are

Special Revenue Fund

Expenditures	10,000	
Due to General Fund (or cash)		10,000

General Fund

Due from Special Revenue Fund (or cash)	10,000	
Expenditures		10,000

REPORTING ON SERVICE EFFORTS AND ACCOMPLISHMENTS

One objective established by the GASB is that financial reporting should provide information to assist users in assessing the service efforts and accomplishments of the governmental entity. Recognizing that traditional governmental reports provide scant information or measurements relating to accomplishment, the Board undertook a research project to gather information on the measurement and reporting of *service efforts and accomplishment (SEA) indicators*. Based on that research the Board, in April 1994, issued a document that presented background information on the reporting of performance information as part of general purpose external financial reporting. The characteristics of SEA information and several different categories of SEA indicators are described in that document. In addition, the Board concluded that, although useful SEA indicators exist, additional experimentation with, and analysis of, SEA indicators should be undertaken before requiring their inclusion in financial reports. Such experimentation is ongoing, and it is likely that such measures will eventually become a commonplace component of reports by governmental entities.

ILLUSTRATION 19–18

Examples of SEA Indicators

	Activity		
Category of Indicator	*Secondary Education*	*Fire Suppression*	*Solid-Waste Collection*
Input	Number of personnel (by categories)	Total operating expenditures	Number of vehicles
Output	Number of student days	Number of fire calls answered	Tons of waste collected
Outcome	Standardized test score results	Response time	Percentage of collections missed
Efficiency	Cost per student graduated	Operating expenditure per $100,000 of property protected	Tons of solid waste collected per employee
Explanatory information	Percentage of students needing special remedial programs	Area served in square miles	Types of vehicle Crew size of vehicle Climatic conditions Terrain

SEA indicators are classified as follows:

Input indicators	Report the amount of resources that have been used for a specific service or program.
Output indicators	Report units produced or services provided by a service or program.
Outcome indicators	Report the results (including quality) of the service.
Efficiency (and cost-effectiveness) indicators	Measure the cost (whether in dollars or employee hours) per unit of output or outcome.
Explanatory information	Information about the environment or other factors that might affect an organization's performance on SEA indicators.

Examples of each type of indicator are presented in Illustration 19-18.

Illustration 19-18 presents a single SEA indicator for each SEA category. To be reasonably informative, several different SEA indicators in each category should be measured and reported. Indicators that relate inputs to outcomes also should be developed, because indicators that relate efforts to accomplishment help answer some of the fundamental questions of governments. How much better off might the public be as a result of a specific increase in resources for a specific activity? What are the trade-offs in terms of likely outcomes from cutting resources in one activity as compared to another? Designing and measuring such indicators is difficult and subjective. Examples might include cost per student achieving a prespecified test score gain or cost per mile of road maintained at some satisfactory level of condition.

SUMMARY

1. *Identify the issues involved in developing standards for nonprofit organizations.* Currently both the GASB and the FASB are responsible for setting standards for nonprofit organizations. The GASB is involved in establishing standards for governments, while the FASB has been responsible since 1979 for setting standards for all other nonbusiness organizations. Because of the dual nature of standard setting, public universities and hospitals follow different rules from private universities and hospitals. Therefore, it is important to the users of financial statements to understand the differences between the standards of public and private organizations.

2. *Describe the broad categories of government fund entities.* Government entities are composed of a set of separate self-balancing funds. The eight categories of funds fall under three primary groups. **Government funds** include the general fund, special revenue funds, capital projects funds, debt service funds, and permanent funds. Government funds report on current period resources and focus on inflows, outflows, and unexpended resources. In addition, they are designed to determine compliance with legal provisions specifying how revenues are raised and resources spent. The funds in this group are organized by the types of activities each fund is designed to carry out. The second primary group includes the **proprietary funds**, which in turn includes the enterprise funds and the internal service funds. These funds are used to account for the business-type activities of the government. Since these funds operate similarly to for-profit organizations, the accounting also parallels for-profit organizations. The statements issued by proprietary funds include cash flow statements, balance sheets, and accrual-based income statements. The last group includes **fiduciary funds**. These funds, which include trust and agency funds, account for assets held by the government for others, and these funds cannot be used to support the government's own programs.

3. *Distinguish between a general fund and a special revenue fund.* Special revenue funds are used to account for resources that are legally restricted for some specific expenditure (other than capital projects or debt service). If resources are unrestricted, then they will be accounted for in a general fund.

4. *Explain the use of a capital projects fund.* Capital projects funds are used to account for resources used to acquire permanent assets with long lives, such as buildings, streets and highways, and sewer systems. The purpose of this type of fund is to show that funds designated for capital projects are used for authorized purposes only and that any unexpended amounts are treated properly. Long-term assets acquired by proprietary funds are accounted for in the proprietary fund accounts.

5. *Describe the purpose of a debt service fund.* Governments issue two kinds of debt, general long-term debt that supports the activities of the government as a whole, and debt that is issued by a proprietary fund to support that fund's activities. The debt service fund accounts for the funds used to meet principal and interest payments for general long-term debt. The principal amounts of the general long-term debt are recorded in the General Long-Term Obligation Group. Therefore, payments of interest and principal are expenditures of the debt service fund. It should be noted that accrued interest is not recorded in the debt service fund (even though it is required on the government-wide statements).

6. *Explain the use of a permanent fund.* Permanent funds include nonexpendable trust funds. These are funds in which the principal must remain intact and the earnings either spent or retained also, as specified. The resources in these funds must be accounted for according to law or trust provisions.

7. *Distinguish proprietary funds from government funds.* Proprietary funds account for the activities of governments that are similar to for-profit enterprises. For example, cities often provide water to the public and recover all or most of the cost through charges to the public. These funds are accounted for using the accrual basis of accounting, and all assets (including fixed assets) and liabilities (including long-term debt) are accounted for. The cash flow statement is prepared using the direct format, and accrual-based revenues and expenses are reported on the income statement. Government funds operate using a flow of financial resources concept where each year is treated as a distinct event, and the important measurements are the current period's sources and uses of funds.

8. *Understand the need for account group entities.* Because government funds operate using a flow of financial resources, account groups were established to account for long-term assets and general long-term debt. Under the new rules, both long-term assets and long-term debt must be reported on the government-wide statements. In general, when long-term assets are acquired, the asset account is offset by the classification of the source of the asset (such as from general fund revenues or from capital projects' general obligation debt, etc.). In the General Long-Term Obligation Account Group, long-term debt is credited against the "resources to be provided" account. Then as resources become available in the debt service fund, an amount from the resources to be provided account is reclassified as a

resources available account. For the government-wide statements, both depreciation expense and accrued interest on debt must be reported.

9. *Describe the changes in reporting requirements under GASB Statement No. 34.* Two new statements are the statement of net assets and the statement of activities, both prepared on a government-wide basis using accrual accounting. Fund-based statements are still required, but only major funds are required to be shown separately (minor funds can be combined). New statements reconciling the differences between the government-wide statement and the fund statements are required. In addition, new disclosures relating to capital assets and long-term liabilities are added. Proprietary fund reports must include a direct-based statement of cash flows. Also, net assets are displayed by three categories: invested in capital assets, net of related debt; restricted; and unrestricted. Another important change is that infrastructure assets (i.e., roads, bridges, etc.) must be reported on the government-wide basis.

10. *Explain the benefits of government-wide statements.* The new government-wide statements help users assess the extent to which the government has invested in capital assets. Also, users can assess whether the public paid for services they received during the year or if the costs are shifted to other periods. The government-wide statement of activities focuses on the net cost of each of the government's functions. The expenses of the individual functions are compared to the revenues generated directly by that function. This helps users assess whether

each program provides a benefit or a burden to the public.

11. *Describe the types of interfund activities.* Reciprocal interfund activity is similar to exchanges or exchange-like transactions. It includes interfund loans and interfund services provided and used. Interfund loans should be reported as interfund receivables in the lender fund and as an interfund payable in the borrower fund. Interfund services provided and used are sales or purchases of goods and services between funds for a price approximating their external exchange value. Interfund services provided and used should be reported as revenues in the seller funds and expenses or expenditures in the purchaser funds. Unpaid amounts should be reported as interfund receivables and payables in the fund balance sheet or the statement of net assets.

Nonreciprocal interfund activity is similar to nonexchange transactions. This includes interfund transfers (e.g., outflows of assets without an equivalent inflow of assets in return and without a requirement for repayment) and interfund reimbursements (repayments from the funds responsible for a particular expenditure or expense to the funds that initially paid for them). In government funds, interfund transfers should be reported as "other financing uses" in the funds initiating the transfer and as "other financing sources" in the funds receiving the transfer. In proprietary funds, interfund transfers should be reported after non-operating revenues and expenses. Reimbursements should not be displayed in the financial statements.

QUESTIONS

1. Eleven funds are recommended to account for the various activities and resources of a governmental unit. Identify these funds by title and type and briefly state (in two sentences or less) the basic purpose of each fund.

2. In addition to fund entities, two nonfund "self-balancing" account group entities are recommended for use by governmental units. Identify these account groups and state the purpose of each. Prepare in general journal form an entry to record a typical "transaction" in the records of each.

3. Why are governments required to prepare financial statements on a government-wide basis using full accrual accounting?

4. What is the difference between a governmental fund and a proprietary fund?

5. Are fiduciary funds governmental funds or proprietary funds? Explain.

6. A disbursement by the general fund to another fund may be recorded as a receivable, an expenditure, or a fund transfer. Explain the circumstances that would result in each of these different treatments.

7. In what funds or account groups would you expect bonds payable to be included?

8. In what funds or account groups might property and other nonfinancial resources be recorded?

9. Why are budgeted revenues and expenditures formally recorded in the records of the general fund but not in the records of a capital projects fund?

10. Are all major capital facilities acquisitions accounted for in a capital projects fund? Explain.

11. Describe the reporting for service-type special assessments.

12. Describe the manner in which special assessment

debt for which the government is not obligated in any manner is reported in the financial statements.

13. What exception to the normal expenditure recognition criteria is associated with debt service funds and what is the justification for this exception?

14. Identify and describe four types of interfund activities.

15. The following funds and account groups are recommended for use in accounting for state and municipal governmental financial operations:
    A. General Fund.
    B. Special Revenue Fund.
    C. Debt Service Fund.
    D. Capital Projects Fund.
    E. Agency Fund.
    F. Enterprise Fund.
    G. Internal Service Fund.
    H. Trust Fund.

I. Government-wide Statement of Activities.
J. Government-wide Statement of Net Asets.
Identify, by the letters given above, the funds and account groups in which each of the account titles below might properly appear.
(1) Bonds Payable.
(2) Reserve for Encumbrances.
(3) Equipment.
(4) Appropriations.
(5) Estimated Revenue.
(6) Property Taxes Receivable.
(7) Construction Work in Progress.
(8) Accumulated Depreciation.
(9) Depreciation Expense.
(10) Required Earnings.

16. Describe some of the major reconciling items between a government fund and the government-wide financial statements.

EXERCISES

EXERCISE 19-1 Identify the Fund

The following transactions take place:

1. A cement mixer was purchased with resources of the general fund.
2. A contract was signed for the construction of a new civic center.
3. Bonds were issued to finance the construction of the new civic center.
4. Construction of the civic center was completed.

Required:
Indicate the name of the fund(s) and/or account group(s) in which each of the transactions or events should be recorded.

EXERCISE 19-2 Identify the Fund

The following transactions take place:

1. A commitment was made to transfer general revenues to the entity in charge of providing transportation for all government agencies.
2. Construction bonds were issued at a premium. The premium is to be included in funds accumulated to retire the debt.
3. Police salaries were paid.
4. Interest and principal were paid on general obligation serial bonds.

Required:
Indicate the name of the fund(s) and/or account group(s) in which each of the transactions or events should be recorded.

EXERCISE 19-3 Identify the Interfund Activity

The following events take place:

1. The Special Revenue Fund transfers $8,000 to the Internal Service Fund as a temporary loan.
2. The Internal Service Fund bills the Special Revenue Fund $20,000 for services performed.

3. Interest payments in the amount of $14,000 that are the responsibility of the Debt Service Fund are paid by the General Fund.

4. The unexpended balance of the Capital Projects Fund, which is $65,000, is transferred to the General Fund.

5. Current expendable revenues of the Trust Fund in the amount of $35,000 are transferred to the Special Revenue Fund.

6. The General Fund transfers $100,000 to start an Internal Service Fund.

Required:

A. Identify the interfund activity as a loan, services provided and used, interfund transfer, or interfund reimbursement and prepare entries in general journal form to record the transactions on the records of the funds involved.

B. Why is it important to distinguish residual equity transfers from operating transfers?

EXERCISE 19-4 Journal Entries

The following events take place:

1. Hector Madras died and left 100 acres of undeveloped land to the city for a future park. He acquired the land at $100 an acre, but at the date of his death the land was appraised at $8,000 an acre.

2. The city authorized the transfer of $100,000 of general revenues and the issuance of $1,000,000 in general obligation bonds to construct improvements on the donated land. The bonds were sold at par.

3. The improvements were completed at a cost of $1,100,000, and the operation of the park was turned over to the City Parks Department.

Required:

Prepare entries in general journal form to record these transactions in the proper fund(s) or account group(s). Designate the fund or account group in which each transaction is recorded.

EXERCISE 19-5 Journal Entries

The following transactions take place:

1. The General Fund repaid the Special Revenue Fund a loan of $10,000 plus $900 in interest on the loan.

2. On January 1, the city issued 9% general obligation bonds with a face value of $2,000,000 payable in 10 years to finance the construction of city offices. Total proceeds were $2,300,000.

3. On December 20, construction was completed and occupancy taken of the city offices. The full cost of $1,960,000 was paid to the contractor, and appropriate closing entries were made with regard to the project.

Required:

Prepare entries in general journal form to record these transactions in the proper fund(s) and/or account group(s). Designate the fund or account group in which each entry is recorded.

EXERCISE 19-6 Journal Entries

On January 1, 2001, Allentown issued $800,000 of 9% serial bonds at par. Semiannual interest is payable on January 1 and July 1 and principal of $80,000 matures each January 1 starting in 2002. The debt will be serviced through a special tax levy designed especially for this purpose. Therefore, transfers will be provided as needed from the Special Revenue Fund.

The following transactions occurred relating to the Debt Service Fund.

2001	
June 29	A transfer of $36,000 was received from the Special Revenue Fund.
July 1	The semiannual interest payment was made.
Dec. 18	A Special Revenue Fund transfer of $120,000 was received.

2002	
Jan. 1	A payment on bond principal and semiannual interest was made.

2011	
Jan. 2	Accumulations in the Debt Service Fund amounted to $55,000 in investments and $40,000 in cash. The investments were liquidated at face value and the final interest and principal payment was made.
Jan. 4	Having served its purpose, the Debt Service Fund's remaining assets were transferred to the Special Revenue Fund.

Required:

Prepare the journal entries necessary to record the foregoing transactions.

EXERCISE 19-7 **Multiple Choice**

Select the best answer for each of the following:

1. The City of Apache should use a Capital Projects Fund to account for
   (a) Structures and improvements constructed with the proceeds of a special assessment.
   (b) Special Revenue funds set aside to acquire land for city parks.
   (c) Construction in progress on the city-owned electric utility plant, financed by an issue of revenue bonds.
   (d) Assets to be used to retire bonds issued to finance an addition to the City Hall.

2. Activities of a central print shop offering printing services at cost to various city departments should be accounted for in
   (a) The General Fund.
   (b) An Internal Service Fund.
   (c) A Special Revenue Fund.
   (d) An Agency Fund.

3. Adams County collects property taxes for the benefit of the state government and the local school districts and periodically remits collections to these units. These activities should be accounted for in
   (a) An Agency Fund.
   (b) The General Fund.
   (c) An Internal Service Fund.
   (d) A Special Revenue Fund.

4. In order to provide for the retirement of general obligation bonds, the City of Globe invests a portion of its receipts from general property taxes in marketable securities. This investment activity should be accounted for in
   (a) A Capital Projects Fund.
   (b) A Debt Service Fund.
   (c) A Trust Fund.
   (d) The General Fund.

5. The transactions of a municipal police retirement system should be recorded in
   (a) The General Fund.
   (b) A Special Revenue Fund.
   (c) A Trust Fund.
   (d) An Internal Service Fund.

(AICPA adapted)

EXERCISE 19-8 Multiple Choice

Select the best answer for each of the following:

1. The Activities of a municipal golf course that receives three-fourths of its total revenue from a special tax levy should be accounted for in
   (a) An Enterprise Fund.
   (b) The General Fund.
   (c) A Trust Fund.
   (d) A Special Revenue Fund.

2. Equipment in general governmental service that had been constructed 10 years before with resources of a Capital Projects Fund was sold. The receipts were accounted for as unrestricted revenue. Entries are necessary in the
   (a) General Fund and Capital Projects Fund.
   (b) General Fund and General Fixed Assets Account Group.
   (c) General Fund, Capital Projects Fund, and Enterprise Fund.
   (d) General Fund, Capital Projects Fund, and General Fixed Assets Account Group.

3. An account for expenditures does not appear in which fund?
   (a) Capital Projects.
   (b) Enterprise.
   (c) General.
   (d) Special Revenue.

4. Part of the general obligation bond proceeds from a new issuance was used to pay for the cost of a new City Hall as soon as construction was completed. The remainder of the proceeds was transferred to repay the debt. Entries are needed to record these transactions in the
   (a) General Fund and General Long-Term Obligation Account Group.
   (b) General Fund, General Long-Term Obligation Account Group, and Debt Service Fund.
   (c) Trust Fund, Debt Service Fund, and General Fixed Assets Account Group.
   (d) General Long-term Obligation Account Group, Debt Service Fund, General Fixed Assets Account Group, and Capital Projects Fund.

5. Cash secured from property tax revenue was transferred for the eventual payment of principal and interest on general obligation bonds. The bonds had been issued when land was acquired several years ago for a city park. Upon the transfer, an entry would **not** be made in which of the following?
   (a) Debt Service Fund.
   (b) General Fixed Assets Account Group.
   (c) General Long-Term Obligation Account Group.
   (d) General Fund.

(AICPA adapted)

EXERCISE 19-9 Multiple Choice

Select the best answer for each of the following:

1. Premiums received on general obligation bonds are generally transferred to what fund or group of accounts?
   (a) Debt Service.
   (b) General Long-Term Obligation.

(c) General.

(d) Special Revenue.

2. Of the items listed below, those most likely to have parallel accounting procedures, account titles, and financial statements are
   (a) Special Revenue Funds and Internal Service Funds.
   (b) Internal Service Funds and Debt Service Funds.
   (c) The General Fixed Assets Account Group and the General Long-Term Obligation Account Group.
   (d) The General Fund and Special Revenue Funds.

3. Recreational facilities run by a governmental unit and financed on a user-charge basis would be accounted for in which fund?
   (a) General.
   (b) Trust.
   (c) Enterprise.
   (d) Capital Projects.

4. Taylor City should record depreciation as an expense in its
   (a) Enterprise Fund and Internal Service Fund.
   (b) Internal Service Fund and General Fixed Assets Account Group.
   (c) General Fund and Enterprise Fund.
   (d) Enterprise Fund and Capital Projects Fund.

5. A performance budget relates a governmental unit's expenditures to
   (a) Objects of Expenditure.
   (b) Expenditures of the preceding fiscal year.
   (c) Individual months within the fiscal year.
   (d) Activities and programs.

(*AICPA adapted*)

EXERCISE 19-10 **Multiple Choice**

Select the best answer for each of the following:

1. The City of Milford authorized the building of facilities through capital improvement special assessments. Bonds are issued that will be paid out of special assessments, and the municipality has no obligation whatsoever to the bondholders for the repayment of the debt. The proceeds from the bond issue will be reported in the special assessments capital project fund as
   (a) Transfer from Debt Service Fund.
   (b) Contributions from property owners.
   (c) Debt issue proceeds.
   (d) Special assessment revenue.

2. A fund of a municipality that rarely reports a fund balance is the
   (a) General Fund.
   (b) Agency Fund.
   (c) Special Revenue Fund.
   (d) Expendable Trust Fund.

3. When special assessment debt is issued for which the municipality is not obligated in any manner, the appropriate account to debit in the General Long-Term Obligation Account group is
   (a) Contributions from property owners.
   (b) Amount to be provided by special assessments.
   (c) Amounts available in debt service fund.
   (d) None of the above.

4. When the proceeds from special assessment debt for which the municipality is not obligated in any way is used to complete a special assessment capital project involving general

improvements, the appropriate account to debit in the General Fixed Asset Account Group on the completion of the project is

(a) Improvements.

(b) Investment from special assessment debt with government commitment.

(c) Contributions by property owners.

(d) Expenditures.

5. The payment of principal and interest on special assessment debt for which a municipality is not obligated in any way is accounted for in

(a) A special assessments debt service fund.

(b) The General Long-term Obligation Account Group.

(c) A capital projects fund.

(d) An agency fund.

EXERCISE 19-11 **Identify the Fund**

Write the name of the fund(s) and/or account group(s) in which each of the following transactions or events would be recorded.

1. Bonds, the proceeds of which were to be used for the construction of a new City Hall, were issued.

2. A sum of money was appropriated, to be advanced from monies on hand, to finance the establishment of a City Garage for servicing city-owned transportation equipment.

3. A contribution was received from a private source. The use of the income earned on the investment of this sum of money was specifically designated by the donor.

4. Proceeds received from a bond issue were used for the purchase of the privately owned water utility in the city.

5. Property taxes designated to be set aside for the eventual retirement of the City Hall building bonds were collected.

6. Real estate and personal property taxes, which had not been assessed or levied for any specific purpose, were collected.

7. Payment was made to the contractor for progress made in the construction of the new City Hall.

8. Interest was paid on the bonds issued for the purchase of the water utility.

9. Bonds, the proceeds of which are to be used to pay for the improvement of streets in the residential district, were issued. The debt is to be serviced by assessments on the property benefited. The government is obligated to the bondholders to assure the timely payment of principal and interest on the debt.

10. Salaries of personnel in the office of the mayor were paid.

11. Interest was paid on the City Hall building bonds.

12. Installment payments were received from the property owners assessed for the street improvement project.

13. Interest was paid on bonds issued for the payment of the improvement of streets in the residential district.

14. Interest was received on the investment of moneys set aside for the retirement of the City Hall building bonds.

15. Sums of money were received from employees by payroll deductions to be used for the purchase of United States government bonds for those employees individually.

16. City motor vehicle license fees, to be used for general street expenditures, were collected.

17. Materials to be used for the general repair of the streets were purchased.

18. The City Garage was reimbursed for services on the equipment of the fire and police departments.

19. Excess funds were transferred from the water utility to the General Fund.

(AICPA adapted)

EXERCISE 19-12 **Capital Projects Fund—Journal Entries**

On June 1, 2001, the City of Cape May authorized the construction of a police station at an expected cost of $250,000. Financing will be provided through transfers from a Special Revenue Fund.

The following transactions occurred during the fiscal year beginning June 1, 2001, relating to the Capital Project Fund.

1. The $250,000 receivable from the Special Revenue Fund was recorded.
2. The Special Revenue Fund transferred $125,000 to the Capital Project Fund to begin construction on the police station.
3. The Capital Project Fund invested the transfer of monies in a six-month certificate, at 5%.
4. A contract in the amount of $250,000 was let to the lowest bidder.
5. Architect and legal fees in the amount of $3,125 were approved for payment. There was no encumbrance for these expenditures.
6. Contract billings in the amount of $250,000 were approved for payment on the completion of the police station and the encumbrance was removed.
7. The six-month certificate was redeemed at maturity with interest revenue.
8. The Special Revenue Fund transferred the final amount of $125,000 to the Capital Projects Fund.
9. All liabilities except for the retention of 5% of the contract price were paid.
10. All requirements and obligations were completed; the final payment of the contract price was made and all nominal accounts were closed.

Required:

Prepare the journal entries necessary in the Capital Projects Fund to record the transactions and events described above.

EXERCISE 19-13 **Capital Projects Fund—Journal Entries**

The town of Aberdeen authorized a fire station to be built at an estimated cost of $150,000. On January 1, 2001, 6% bonds with a par value of $150,000 were authorized and issued. Any difference between the par value of the bonds and the proceeds from their sale is transferred to the Debt Service Fund.

The following transactions relating to the Capital Project Fund occurred during 2001.

1. Encumbrances were recorded on signing contracts in the amount of $150,000.
2. Proceeds from the bond issue were received in the amount of $155,000.
3. The premium on the bond issue was transferred to the Debt Service Fund.
4. Contract billings in the amount of $150,000 were approved for payment on the completion of the fire station.
5. The contractor was paid except for retention of 5% of the contract price.
6. The final contract price was paid on the completion of the requirements and obligations of the contract. The nominal accounts were closed.

Required:

Prepare the journal entries necessary in the Capital Projects Fund to record the transactions and events described above.

EXERCISE 19-14 **General Long-Term Obligation Account Group**

The Town of Aberdeen authorizes the construction of a Town Hall. The Town Hall is to be financed by a transfer from the General Fund in the amount of $15,000 and by the issuance of 6%, 10-year term bonds with a par value of $150,000.

The following transactions transpired relating to the General Long-Term Obligation Account Group:

1. On January 1, 2001, the 6%, 10-year term bonds were issued for $162,000. The premium was transferred to the Debt Service Fund.
2. The General Fund transferred $25,000 to the Debt Service Fund on December 20, 2010.
3. The $150,000 par value term bonds were redeemed when they matured on December 31, 2010.

Required:
Prepare the journal entries necessary in the General Long-Term Obligation Account Group to record the transactions and events described above.

EXERCISE 19-15   Determining a Government's Major Funds

Required:
Using Illustrations 19-9, 19-10, 19-13, and 19-14, determine which of Model City's funds qualify as major funds using the percentage cutoffs. Calculate aggregate amounts for all other nonmajor funds, and indicate how they would be presented.

EXERCISE 19-16   Determining Amounts to Report for Long-Term Liabilities
On January 1, 2001, Metropolis City issued a 7%, 5-year, $100,000 general obligation bond for $96,007. The bond pays interest annually (on December 31) and was issued to yield 8%. The bond was issued in the capital projects fund, and the proceeds are to be used to build a giant ball that will drop twenty stories on New Year's Eve. No construction has occurred. A debt service fund was created to meet the interest and principal payments. The city prepares financial statements on December 31 of each year.

Required:
Determine how the above information will be reflected on each of the following statements for the year 2001.

1. The governmental funds' statement of revenue, expenditures, and changes in fund balances. List the governmental fund and then list the dollar amount within the appropriate heading on the statement (such as Revenues, Expenditures, or Other Financing Sources (Uses)).
2. The government-wide statement of net assets.
3. The government-wide statement of activities.

EXERCISE 19-17   Determining Amounts to Report for Capital Assets
The following schedule of capital assets was prepared for Capital City.

Government Activities	Beginning Balance	Additions	Retirements	Ending Balance
Total Capital Assets (gross)	$ 500,000	100,000	(75,000)	$ 525,000
Less: Accumulated Depreciation	(200,000)	(30,000)	25,000	(205,000)
Net Capital Assets	$ 300,000	70,000	(50,000)	$ 320,000

All capital acquisitions were made in a capital projects fund (and paid for with cash). An asset was sold by the general fund for $65,000 cash.

Required:

Determine how the above information will be reflected on each of the following statements for the year 2001.

1. The governmental funds' statement of revenue, expenditures, and changes in fund balances. List the governmental fund and then list the dollar amount within the appropriate heading on the statement (such as Revenues, Expenditures, or Other Financing Sources (Uses)).

2. The government-wide statement of net assets.

3. The government-wide statement of activities.

EXERCISE 19-18 **Reconciliation Schedule—Statement of Activities**

The following information is available about items that differ between the governmental funds and the government-wide statements. Assume that there are no internal service funds. The schedule of capital assets prepared for the year ended December 31, 2001, includes the following items:

Government Activities	Beginning Balance	Additions	Retirements	Ending Balance
Total Capital Assets (at gross)	$ 700,000	$ 50,000	$(25,000)	$ 725,000
Less: Accumulated Depreciation	(170,000)	(30,000)	17,500	(182,500)
Net Capital Assets	$ 530,000	$ 20,000	$ (7,500)	$ 542,500

The bond was issued at the beginning of the year, and the following amortization schedule is available.

Date	Interest Expense	Cash Paid	Premium Amortization	Bond Balance
1/1/2001				$104,213
12/31/2001	6,253	7,000	747	$103,466

The net change in fund balances—total governmental funds was $1,100,000.

Required:

Prepare the reconciliation of the statement of revenues, expenditures, and changes in fund balances to the statement of activities on a government-wide basis for the year ended December 31, 2001.

EXERCISE 19-19 **Reconciliation Schedule—Statement of Net Assets**

The following information was available about items that differed between the governmental funds and the government-wide statements. Assume that there are no internal service funds. The schedule of capital assets prepared for the year ended December 31, 2001 included the following items:

Government Activities	Beginning Balance	Additions	Retirements	Ending Balance
Total Capital Assets (at gross)	$ 800,000	$ 60,000	$(30,000)	$ 830,000
Less: Accumulated Depreciation	(200,000)	(40,000)	22,500	(217,500)
Net Capital Assets	$ 600,000	$ 20,000	$ (7,500)	$ 612,500

The bond was issued at the beginning of the year and the following amortization schedule is available:

Date	Interest Expense	Cash Paid	Premium Amortization	Balance
1/1/2001				$104,213
12/31/2001	$6,253	$7,000	$747	$103,466

The total fund balances for governmental activities was $3,125,000 at the end of the year.

Required:
Prepare the reconciliation of the governmental fund balances to the net assets reported for governmental activities on the Statement of Net Assets as of December 31, 2001.

PROBLEMS

PROBLEM 19-1   **Debt Service Fund**
On January 1, 2001, the City of Cape May authorized and issued $200,000 of 5%, three-year term bonds. Interest is payable annually on December 31. A debt service fund is established to accumulate the necessary resources to pay the annual interest on the bonds and to redeem the bonds when they mature. The required annual addition for principal and interest will be transferred annually to the debt service fund from the general fund. It is assumed that amounts received by the debt service fund for the payment of principal can be invested at an annual return of 8%.

Required:
A. Prepare a schedule to calculate the annual required additions and annual required earnings to repay the principal on the bonds assuming that the first installment for principal and interest is transferred to the debt service fund from the general fund on December 30, 2001.

B. Prepare the entries to be recorded by the debt service fund as follows:
   (1) The 2002 budget entry.
   (2) The entry to record the annual transfer from the general fund.
   (3) The entry to record the annual payment of interest.
   (4) The entry to record $4,929 in interest income for 2002.
   (5) The entry(s) to close the accounts at the end of 2002.

PROBLEM 19-2   **Capital Projects Fund and Related Funds**
The Town of Green River authorized a municipal building to be constructed at a cost of $175,000. The construction will be financed from the proceeds from the issue of $175,000 of 6% bonds. Any difference between the par value of the bonds and the proceeds from their sale is transferred to the Debt Service Fund.
   Transactions and events relating to this project include the following:

1. The proceeds from the sale of the bonds were received and included a premium on the bond issue in the amount of $15,000. The premium was transferred to Debt Service Fund.
2. Encumbrances were recorded on signing of the construction contract in the amount of $175,000.
3. Contract billings in the amount of $85,000 were approved for payment.
4. Contract billings were paid in the amount of $85,000.

5. All nominal accounts were closed and construction in progress was recorded in the appropriate account group in anticipation of the preparation of financial statements.

6. Encumbrances that were closed in anticipation of the preparation of financial statements are reestablished in the Capital Projects Fund.

7. Contract billings in the amount of $90,000 were approved on the completion of the municipal building.

8. Contract billings of $90,000 less a retention of 5% were paid.

9. The building was accepted, all construction liabilities were paid, and the building was recorded as an asset in the appropriate account group.

Required:

Prepare the journal entries relating to the Capital Projects Fund and corresponding entries, if any, relating to the General Fixed Assets Account Group, the General Long-Term Obligation Account Group, and the Debt Service Fund for the transactions and events described above. Clearly identify the fund or account group in which each entry is recorded.

PROBLEM 19-3 **Special Assessment Debt**

The City of Dayville has undertaken a sidewalk construction project. The project is being financed by the proceeds from the issue on July 1, 2001, of $500,000 of 7% special assessment debt. One quarter of the principal plus interest is payable on June 30 of each year beginning June 30, 2002. Property owners are assessed to provide the funds to pay the principal and interest on the debt.

The following transactions occurred during the period July 1, 2001, through June 30, 2002.

1. The bonds for the construction of the sidewalks were issued at par value.

2. The sidewalks were completed at a cost of $500,000.

3. Property owners were assessed and billed for the first installment of principal and interest on the special assessment debt.

4. Assessments for the first installment of principal and interest on the special assessment debt were collected and the June 30, 2002, payment of principal and interest on the special assessment debt was made.

Required:

Prepare all journal entries for the above transactions that are necessary in the funds and account groups of City of Dayville assuming that

A. The City of Dayville has made a commitment to the holders of the special assessment debt to assure the timely and full payment of principal and interest on the appropriate due dates.

B. The City of Dayville has not obligated itself in any manner on the special assessment debt that was issued for the construction of the sidewalks.

PROBLEM 19-4 **Internal Service Fund**

The administrators of the City of Lyons have obtained approval from the City Council to centralize the computer facility as of January 1, 2001. An internal service fund is created to account for the activities of the computer facility. The City Council has approved a contribution of $25,000 from the General Fund for use as working capital and an advance from the Electric Utility Fund of $355,000 for the purchase of equipment and facilities. The $355,000 advance will be repaid by the internal service fund in 20 equal annual installments.

The following transactions relate to the establishment and operation of the Internal Service Fund.

January 1	The computer facility received the contribution from the General Fund and the advance from the Electric Utility Fund.
January 4	Land and a building were purchased for $175,000 of which $25,000 was assigned to land. Hardware was purchased for $125,000 and equipment to protect the hardware was purchased for $55,000.
April 10	The computer facility billed the Electric Utility Fund for service provided. The service cost $200,000 and was billed at a mark-up of 25% on cost. (Direct costs of providing computer services are accumulated in the ''Computer Service'' account. When services are billed to departments, this account is credited and the ''Cost of Service'' account is debited for the cost of services billed.)
April 29	Administrative expenses totaling $10,000 were approved for payment.
May 1	Payment of $37,750 was received from the Electric Utility in partial payment of the April 10 billing.
May 1	The administrative expense was paid.
December 2	The first of 20 equal annual installments to the Electric Utility Fund was paid.
December 30	Depreciation expense was recorded for the year as administration expense. The building was estimated to have a remaining useful life of 25 years; the hardware was estimated to have a useful life of 5 years; the equipment to protect the hardware was estimated to have a useful life of 10 years.
December 31	The nominal accounts of the internal service fund were closed through a closing account, ''Excess of Billings to Departments over Costs,'' which in turn was closed to unrestricted net assets.

Required:

Prepare the journal entries necessary in the Internal Service Fund to record the transactions and events described above. The chart of accounts presented below may be used as an aid.

Current Assets:	*Liabilities:*
Cash	Vouchers payable
Due from general fund	Advance from electric utility
Due from electric utility fund	
Computer service	*Net Assets:*
	Unrestricted net assets
Fixed Assets:	
Land	*Revenue:*
Building	Billing to departments
Equipment—hardware	Contribution from general fund
Equipment—protection	
Accumulated depreciation	*Costs and Expense:*
	Cost of computer service
	Administrative expense

The closing account, ''Excess of Billings to Departments over Costs,'' is similar to the ''Income Summary'' account of a corporation.

PROBLEM 19-5　**Tax Agency Fund**

An administrative section of the County Assessor's Office of Mecklenburg County serves as the billing and collection agency for all property taxes assessed in Mecklenburg County. A charge of 1% of taxes and penalties collected is apportioned among recipients of the taxes for this service. All property tax records—current and delinquent—are maintained in this administrative unit. The 1% charge is included as revenue in the General Fund budget of the county government.

Information relative to the collection of property taxes for fiscal year 2001 is as follows:

Assessed valuation	$5,826,300
Tax rates per $100 assessed:	
County government	$1.20
State government	.80
City of Midvale	2.80
Unified school district	3.20

Tax bills are issued on January 1; taxes are payable without penalty by April 30; taxes paid after April 30 are subject to a 5% penalty for late payment. Taxes not paid by June 30 are considered delinquent.

No delinquent taxes remain uncollected for years prior to 2001.

An estimated 3% of billed taxes for 2001 will be uncollectible.

A summary of the activities of the Tax Agency Fund for the period January 1, 2001, to June 30, 2001, includes the following:

January 1	Tax bills are mailed to property owners. Accounts are opened by the tax collection unit.
April 30	Taxes collected and deposited during first four months total $372,883.
	Distribution of taxes collected is made to the applicable governmental units.
June 30	Taxes collected and deposited during May and June including the 5% penalty total $73,412.
	Distribution of taxes and penalties collected is made to the applicable governmental units.

Required:

A. Prepare in general journal form entries to record the activities of the Tax Agency Fund from January 1 to June 30. Establish a Delinquent Account for taxes not collected.

B. Prepare a balance sheet for the Tax Agency Fund after adjusting the accounts on June 30.

PROBLEM 19-6 **Journal Entries—Identify the Fund**

The following activities and transactions are typical of those that may affect the various funds used by a typical municipal government.

Required:

Prepare journal entries to record each transaction and identify the fund or group of accounts in which each entry is recorded.

A. The Greenville City Council passed a resolution approving a general operating budget of $5,000,000 for the fiscal year 2001. Total revenues are estimated at $4,900,000.

B. The Greenville City Council Passed an ordinance providing a property tax levy of $6.25 per $100 of assessed valuation for the fiscal year 2001. Total property valuation in Greenville City is $204,800,000. Property is assessed at 25% of current property valuation. Property tax bills are mailed to property owners. An estimated 3% will be uncollectible.

C. Reed City sold a general obligation term bond issue for $1,000,000 at 105 to a major brokerage firm. The stated interest rate is 5%. Proceeds are to be used for construction of a new Central Law Enforcement Building. (*Note:* Entries are required in the Capital Project Fund and the General Long-Term Obligation Accounts.)

D. The premium on bond sale in (C) above is transferred to the Debt Service Fund.

E. At the end of fiscal year 2001, the Greenville City Council approves the write-off of $52,550 of uncollected 2000 taxes because of inability to locate the property owners. The tax bills have been referred to the legal department for further action.

F. The Reed City Central Law Enforcement Building [(C) above] is completed. Contracts and expenses total $989,000, and all have been paid and recorded in the Capital Project Fund. Prepare entries to close this project and record the completion of the project in all other funds or account groups affected. Any balance in the Capital Project Fund is to be applied to payment of interest and principal of the bond issue.

G. On May 1, 2001, Hopi City supervised the issue of 6% serial bonds at par to finance street curbing in an area recently incorporated in the city limits. The face amount of the bonds is $600,000; interest is payable annually, and bonds are to be retired in equal amounts over five years from collections from assessments against property owners. The City acts as a collection agent and has given assurances to the debt holders that it will guarantee payment of principal and interest even though it is not obligated to do so.

 (1) Record the issuance of the bonds on May 1, 2001.

 (2) Record the payment to bondholders on May 1, 2002.

H. The curbing project in (G) above was completed on November 30 at a total of $590,000. Record summary entries for expenditure transactions May 1–November 30, 2001, and on completion of the project.

PROBLEM 19-7 **Journal Entries—Identify the Fund**

The following transactions take place.

1. Bond proceeds of $1,000,000 were received to be used in constructing a firehouse. An equal amount is contributed from general revenues.

2. $800,000 of serial bonds matured. Interest of $120,000 was paid on these and other serial bonds outstanding.

3. $8,000 was received as insurance proceeds from the accidental destruction of a four-year-old police car costing $24,000.

4. $120,000 in expendable funds was transferred from the City Parks Endowment Fund to the City Parks Special Revenue Fund.

5. Equipment purchased from general revenues at a cost of $200,000 was sold for $40,000.

6. The City Water Company (an enterprise fund) issued a bill for $800 for water provided to the street department's street cleaner.

7. The City Water Company transferred $400,000 in excess funds to the General Fund.

8. A central motor pool was established by a contribution of $120,000 from the General Fund, a long-term loan of $80,000 from the City Parks Special Revenue Fund, and general obligation bond issue proceeds of $200,000.

9. The Motor Pool Fund billed the General Fund $10,000 and the City Parks Fund $4,000 for the use of motor vehicles.

10. Special Assessment Bonds in the amount of $400,000 were retired. The city has indicated a willingness to guarantee the payment of principal even though it was not obligated to do so.

11. Customers' deposits of $8,000 for water meters were received by the City Water Company during the year. The monies are to be held in trust until the customers request that their services be disconnected and the final bills are collected.

12. It is determined that the Debt Service Fund will require an annual contribution of $60,000 and earnings of $6,000 in the current year to accumulate the amounts necessary to retire general obligation term bonds.

Required:

Prepare entries in general journal form to record these transactions in the proper fund(s) or account group(s). Designate the fund or account group in which each entry is recorded.

PROBLEM 19-8 General Fund Journal Entries and Related Fund Adjustments

You have been engaged to examine the financial statements of the Town of Bridgeport for the year ended June 30, 2001. Your examination disclosed that, because of the inexperience of the town's bookkeeper, all transactions were recorded in the General Fund. The following General Fund trial balance as of June 30, 2001, was furnished to you.

General Fund Trial Balance
Town of Bridgeport
June 30, 2001

	Debit	Credit
Cash	$ 16,800	
Short-Term Investments	40,000	
Accounts Receivable	11,500	
Taxes Receivable—current year	30,000	
Tax Anticipation Notes Payable		$ 50,000
Appropriations		400,000
Expenditures	382,000	
Estimated Revenue	320,000	
Revenues		360,000
General Property	85,400	
Bonds Payable	52,000	
Fund Balance		127,700
	$937,700	$937,700

Your audit disclosed the following additional information:

1. The accounts receivable of $11,500 includes $1,500 due from the town's water utility for the sale of scrap sold on its behalf. Accounts for the municipal water utility are maintained in a separate fund.

2. The balance in Taxes Receivable—Current Year is now considered delinquent, and the town estimates that $24,000 will be uncollectible.

3. On June 30, 2001, the town retired, at par value, 6% general obligation serial bonds totaling $40,000. The bonds were issued on July 1, 1996, at a face value of $200,000. Interest paid during the year ended June 30, 2001, was charged to Bonds Payable.

4. Expenditures for the year ended June 30, 2001, included $11,200 applicable to purchase orders issued to the prior year. Outstanding purchase orders at June 30, 2001, not recorded in the accounts amounted to $17,500.

5. On June 28, 2001, the State Revenue Department informed the town that its share of a state-collected, locally shared tax would be $34,000.

6. During the year, equipment with a book value of $7,900 was removed from service and sold for $4,600. In addition, new equipment costing $90,000 was purchased. The transactions were recorded in General Property.

7. During the year, 100 acres of land were donated to the town for use as an industrial park. The land had a value of $400,000. This donation has not been recorded.

Required:

A. Prepare the formal reclassification, adjusting, and closing journal entries for the General Fund as of June 30, 2001.

B. Prepare the formal adjusting journal entries for any other fund or group of accounts as of June 30, 2001.

(*AICPA adapted*)

PROBLEM 19-9 Journal Entries—Various Funds

The Village of Oakridge, which was incorporated recently, began financial operations on July 1, 2001, the beginning of its fiscal year. The following transactions occurred during this first fiscal year, July 1, 2001, to June 30, 2002:

1. The Village Council adopted a budget for general operations during the fiscal year ended June 30, 2001. Revenues were estimated at $400,000. Legal authorizations for budgeted expenditures were $394,000.

2. Property taxes were levied in the amount of $390,000; it was estimated that 2% of this amount would prove to be uncollectible. These taxes are available as of the date of levy to finance current expenditures.

3. During the year, a resident of the village donated marketable securities valued at $50,000 to the village under the terms of a trust agreement. The terms of the trust agreement stipulated that the principal amount is to be kept intact; use of revenue generated by the securities is restricted to financing college scholarships for needy students. Revenue earned and received on these marketable securities amounted to $5,500 through June 30, 2002.

4. A General Fund transfer of $5,000 was made to establish an Internal Service Fund to provide for a permanent investment in inventory.

5. During the year the Internal Service Fund purchased various supplies at a cost of $1,900.

6. Cash collections recorded by the General Fund during the year were as follows:

Property taxes	$386,000
Licenses and permits	7,000

7. The Village Council decided to build a village hall at an estimated cost of $500,000 to replace space occupied in rented facilities. The village does not record project authorizations. It was decided that general obligation bonds bearing interest at 6.5% would be issued. On June 30, 2002, the bonds were issued at their face value of $500,000, payable June 30, 2019. No contracts have been signed for this project, and no expenditures have been made.

8. A fire truck was purchased for $150,000 and the voucher approved and paid by the General Fund. This expenditure was previously encumbered for $150,000.

Required:

Prepare journal entries to record each of the transactions above in the appropriate fund(s) or group of accounts of Oakridge Village for the fiscal year ended June 30, 2002. Use the following funds and account groups:

General Fund
Capital Projects Fund
Internal Service Fund
Permanent Fund
General Long-Term Obligation Group of Accounts
General Fixed Assets Group of Accounts
Special Revenue Fund

Each journal entry should be numbered to correspond with the transactions described above. Do *not* prepare closing entries for any fund. Present your answer in the following format:

Transaction Number	Fund or Group of Accounts	Account Title and Explanation	Amounts	
			Debit	Credit

(AICPA adapted)

PROBLEM 19-10 **Journal Entries—Various Funds**

The following transactions represent practical situations frequently encountered in accounting for municipal governments. Each transaction is independent of the others.

1. The City Council of Bernardville adopted a budget for the general operations of the government during the new fiscal year. Revenues were estimated at $695,000. Legal authorizations for budgeted expenditures were $650,000.

2. Taxes of $160,000 were levied for the special revenue fund of Millstown. One percent was estimated to be uncollectible.

3. (a) On July 25, 2002, office supplies estimated to cost $2,390 were ordered for the city manager's office of Bullersville. Bullersville, which operates on the calendar year, does not maintain an inventory of such supplies.
   (b) The supplies ordered July 25 were received on August 9, 2002, accompanied by an invoice for $2,500.

4. On October 10, 2002, the general fund of Washingtonville repaid to the utility fund a loan of $1,000 plus $40 interest. The loan had been made earlier in the fiscal year.

5. A prominent citizen died and left 10 acres of undeveloped land to Harper City for a future school site. The donor's cost of the land was $55,000. The fair value of the land was $85,000.

6. (a) On March 6, 2002, Dahlstrom City supervised the issue of 6% special assessment bonds payable March 6, 2007, at face value of $90,000. Interest is payable annually. Dahlstrom City, which operates on the calendar year, will supervise the use of the proceeds to finance a curbing project. The City has made no commitments and has not obligated itself in any manner with respect to the payment of principal and interest on the debt.
   (b) On October 26, 2002, the full $84,000 cost of the completed curbing project was recorded. Also, appropriate closing entries were made with regard to the project.

7. (a) Conrad Thamm, a citizen of Basking Knoll, donated common stock valued at $22,000 to the City under a trust agreement. Under the terms of the agreement, the principal amount is to be kept intact; use of revenue from the stock is restricted to financing college scholarships for needy students.
   (b) On December 14, 2002, dividends of $1,100 were received on the stock donated by Mr. Thamm.

8. (a) On February 23, 2002, the Town of Lincoln, which operates on the calendar year, issued 5% general obligation bonds with a face value of $300,000 payable February 23, 2012, to finance the construction of an addition to the City Hall. Total proceeds were $308,000.
   (b) On December 31, 2002, the addition to the City Hall was officially approved, the full cost of $297,000 was paid to the contractor, and appropriate closing entries were made with regard to the project. (Assume that no entries have been made with regard to the project since February 23, 2002.)

Required:

For each transaction, prepare the necessary journal entries for all the funds and groups of accounts involved. No explanation of the journal entries is required. Use the following headings for your workpaper.

Transaction Number	Journal Entries	Dr.	Cr.	Fund or Group of Accounts

In the far right column, indicate in which fund or group of accounts each entry is to be made, using the coding below:

Funds
- General — G
- Special revenue — SR
- Capital projects — CP
- Debt service — DS
- Enterprise — E
- Internal service — IS
- Permanent fund — P
- Trust or agency — TA

Groups of accounts
- General fixed assets — GFA
- General long-term obligation — LTO

(*AICPA adapted*)

PROBLEM 19-11 Capital Projects Fund

The City of Minden entered into the following transactions during the year 2002.

1. A bond issue was authorized by vote to provide funds for the construction of a new municipal building, which it was estimated would cost $1,000,000. The bonds are to be paid in 10 equal installments from a Debt Service Fund, and payments are due March 1 of each year. Any premium on the bond issue, as well as any balance of the Capital Projects Fund, is to be transferred directly to the Debt Service Fund.

2. An advance of $80,000 was received from the General Fund to underwrite a deposit on the land contract of $120,000. The deposit was made.

3. Bonds of $900,000 were sold for cash at 102. It was decided not to sell all the bonds because the cost of the land was less than expected.

4. Contracts amounting to $780,000 were let to Sandstone and Company, the low bidder, for construction of the municipal building.

5. The temporary advance from the General Fund was repaid and the balance on the land contract was paid.

6. On the basis of the architect's certificate, contract billings were approved for $640,000 for the work completed to date.

7. Contract billings paid in cash by the treasurer amounted to $620,000.

8. Because of changes in the plans, the contract with Sandstone and Company was revised to $880,000; the remainder of the bonds were sold at 101.

9. Before the end of the year, the building had been completed, and additional contract billings amounting to $230,000 approved. All contract billings were paid by the treasurer to the contractor in final payment for the work.

Required:

A. Prepare entries to record the foregoing transactions (excluding the entries necessary to close out the fund) of the Capital Projects Fund.

B. Prepare a preclosing trial balance for the Capital Projects Fund.

C. Prepare entries necessary to close out the Capital Projects Fund on the completion of construction.

D. Prepare a statement of revenues, expenditures, and changes in fund balance for the Capital Projects Fund.

E. Prepare preclosing trial balances at December 31, 2002, for the Debt Service Fund, General Fixed Assets Account Group, and General Long-Term Obligation Account Group, considering only the proceeds, expenditures, and transfers resulting from transactions of the Capital Projects Fund.

(AICPA adapted)

PROBLEM 19-12 Determining a Government's Major Funds

The following information is available about Gotham's City government funds.

Governmental Funds	Assets	Liabilities	Revenues	Expenditures
1 General Fund	$ 9,408	$ 7,753	$ 86,022	$ 88,717
2 HUD Programs	7,504	6,428	2,731	2,954
3 Community Development	13,616	440	549	2,664
4 Route 7 Construction	10,478	1,115	273	11,298
5 Impact Fees	371	61	35	755
6 Local Gas Tax	2,139	170	1,436	2,971
7 Historic District	194	4	60	47
8 Central City Development	1,618	151	4,783	6,804
9 Community Redevelopment	2,365	—	42	1,872
10 Culvert Project			1,471	1,974
11 Bridge	2,602	686	3	1,270
12 Cemetery Fund	1,405	—	72	—
	$51,700	$16,808	$ 97,477	$121,326
Proprietary Funds				
13 Water and Sewer	$12,149	$ 4,679	$11,329	$ 6,907
14 Parking Facilities	372	672	1,344	1,582
	12,521	5,351	12,673	8,489
Totals, All Funds	$64,221	$22,159	$110,150	$129,815

Required:

Using the information about the government's funds, determine which funds qualify as "major" funds using percentage cutoffs and would be required to be included in the governmental fund financial statements.

PROBLEM 19-13 Preparing Government-wide Financial Statements

Circus City issued an 8%, 10-year $2,000,000 bond to build a monorail mass transit system. The city received $1,754,217 cash from the bond issuance on January 1,2001. The bond yield is 10%. Interest is paid annually on December 31 of each year. Disclosure information about capital assets is reported below.

Disclosure of Information About Capital Assets
For the Year Ending December 31, 2001

Primary Government

Governmental Activities	Beginning Balance	Additions	Retirements	Ending Balance
Land	$ 500,000			$ 500,000
Building	760,000			760,000
Machinery and Equipment	950,000		$(225,000)	725,000
Construction in Progress		$1,500,000		1,500,000
Infrastructure	450,000			450,000
Totals at historical cost	$2,660,000	$1,500,000	$(225,000)	$3,935,000
Less accumulated depreciation				
Building	(190,000)	(59,150)		(249,150)
Machinery and Equipment	(235,000)	(76,050)	140,000	(171,050)
Infrastructure	(50,000)	(33,800)		(83,800)
Total accumulated depreciation	$ (475,000)	$ (169,000)	$ 140,000	$ (504,000)
Governmental activities capital assets, net	$2,185,000	$1,331,000	$ (85,000)	$3,431,000

Depreciation expense charged to governmental activities as follows:

Public Safety	$ 55,000
General Government	72,000
Highways and Streets	25,000
Sanitation	17,000
	$ 169,000

Circus City's governmental funds financial statements are as follows:

Circus City
Governmental Funds
Fund Balance Sheets at December 31, 2001

	General Fund	Capital Projects Fund — Monorail Fund	Debt Service Fund — Term Bond Fund	Total Governmental Funds
Assets				
Cash	$ 64,000	$ 300,000	$ —	$ 364,000
Interest Receivable		12,000	4,000	16,000
Investments	100,000	1,250,500	100,000	1,450,500
Property Tax Receivable	183,000			183,000
Total Assets	$347,000	$1,562,500	$104,000	$2,013,500
Liabilities and Fund Balance				
Vouchers Payable	$ 73,000	$ 50,000		$ 123,000
Total Liabilities	$ 73,000	$ 50,000	$ —	$ 123,000
Fund Balances:				
Unreserved	83,000	312,500		395,500
Reserved for				
Encumbrances	191,000	1,200,000		1,391,000
Debt Service			104,000	104,000
Total Fund Balance	274,000	1,512,500	104,000	1,890,500
Total Liabilities and Fund Balances	$347,000	$1,562,500	$104,000	$2,013,500

Circus City
Governmental Funds
Statement of Revenues, Expenditures, and Changes in Fund Balances
For the Year Ended December 31, 2001

	General Fund	Capital Projects Fund Monorail Fund	Debt Service Fund Term Bond	Total Governmental Funds
Revenues				
Property Taxes	$ 525,000		$ 50,000	$ 575,000
Licenses and Permits*	150,000			150,000
State Grant—highways and streets	250,000			250,000
Intergovernmental—state grant		$1,000,000		1,000,000
Charges for Services (general government)	130,000			130,000
Investment Earnings	75,000			75,000
Total Revenue	$1,130,000	$1,000,000	$ 50,000	$2,180,000
Expenditures				
Public Safety	$ 500,000			$ 500,000
General Government	300,000			300,000
Highways and Streets	130,000			130,000
Sanitation	70,000			70,000
Debt Service				
Interest			$ 160,000	160,000
Capital Outlay		$1,500,000		1,500,000
Total Expenditures	$1,000,000	$1,500,000	$ 160,000	$2,660,000
Excess (deficiency) of revenues over expenditures	$ 130,000	$ (500,000)	$(110,000)	$ (480,000)
Other Financing Sources (Uses)				
Proceeds from long-term capital debt		$1,754,217		$1,754,217
Transfers in			$ 160,000	160,000
Transfers out	$ (160,000)			(160,000)
Total other	$ (160,000)	$1,754,217	$ 160,000	$1,754,217
Special Items				
Proceeds from sales of equipment	$ 115,000			$ 115,000
Net change in fund balance	85,000	1,254,217	50,000	1,389,217
Fund balance—beginning	189,000	258,283	54,000	501,283
Fund balance—ending	$ 274,000	$1,512,500	$ 104,000	$1,890,500

*Revenues from licenses and permits are assigned to highways and streets ($100,000) and to the general government ($50,000).

Required:
Using the information above, prepare the statement of activities and the statement of net assets on a government-wide basis (using full accrual accounting). The beginning fund balance in the government-wide Statement of Net Assets is $2,686,283.

PROBLEM 19-14   **Reporting Information About Long-Term Liabilities**
On January 1, 1993, the city of Nashvegas issued an 8% annual, 10-year, $10,000 bond for $11,472 (an effective yield of 6%). The bonds become due on December 31, 2002. On June 30, 2001, the city of Nashvegas issued an 8% annual, 10-year, $10,000 bond to yield 10% (the proceeds are $8,771).

Required:

A. Assuming that both bonds are general obligation bonds, prepare the schedule of long-term liabilities at December 31, 2001 (see Illustration 19-12 for an example).

B. Determine the amount of interest reported on the government-wide statement of activities for the year ending December 31, 2001.

C. Determine the amount of long-term liabilities reported on the government-wide statement of net assets at December 31, 2001.

D. Determine the total amount of interest expenditures included in the governmental statement of revenues, expenditures, and changes in net assets for the year ending December 31, 2001.

E. Determine the amount of debt (if any) reported on the governmental funds balance sheet.

20

ACCOUNTING FOR NONGOVERNMENT NONBUSINESS ORGANIZATIONS: COLLEGES AND UNIVERSITIES, HOSPITALS, AND OTHER HEALTH CARE ORGANIZATIONS

LEARNING OBJECTIVES

1. Describe the source of accounting standards for nongovernment nonbusiness organizations (NNOs).

2. Identify the three basic statements for NNOs.

3. Describe the basic funds used by nongovernment nonbusiness organizations.

4. Distinguish between a current restricted fund and an unrestricted fund.

5. Explain the term "assets whose use is limited."

6. Distinguish between a mandatory and a nonmandatory transfer.

7. Explain how contributions are recorded by NNOs.

8. Understand how donated services are recorded.

9. Describe the funds used to account for property, plant and equipment.

10. Explain the basic accounting used by endowment funds.

11. Indicate how equity investments are reported in the financial statements.

12. Explain the change in accounting for loan funds brought about by new standards.

13. Understand the use of an annuity or life income fund.

14. Discuss the special reporting issues of hospitals.

revenues had made the hospital "look like" it had suddenly grown by $80 to $90 million.[1]

Nonbusiness organizations other than governmental units are referred to in this text as nongovernment nonbusiness organizations (NNOs). In this chapter, we describe the accounting for the following four major classifications of NNOs:

1. *Nonprofit institutions of higher education.* This category includes private colleges, universities, and community colleges.
2. *Hospitals and other health care providers.*
3. *Voluntary health and welfare organizations (VHWOs).* These are organizations that derive their revenue from voluntary contributions of the general public to be used for purposes connected with health, welfare, or community services. Examples of such organizations include heart associations, family planning councils, mental health associations, and foundations for the blind.
4. *Other nongovernment nonbusiness organizations (ONNOs).* ONNOs take a variety of forms and include a broad assortment of organizations such as cemetery organizations, civic organizations, fraternal organizations, labor unions, libraries, museums, other cultural institutions, performing arts organizations, political parties, private and community foundations, private elementary and secondary schools, professional associations, public broadcasting stations, religious organizations, social and country clubs, trade associations, and zoological and botanical societies.

SOURCES OF GENERALLY ACCEPTED ACCOUNTING STANDARDS FOR NONGOVERNMENT NONBUSINESS ORGANIZATIONS

Until the early 1970s, accounting and reporting practices for NNOs were developed under the auspices of various interested professional associations such as the American Hospital Association, the Hospital Financial Management Association, the American Council on Education, and the National Association of College and University Business Officers. In the early 1970s, the AICPA exhibited an interest in financial reporting problems in this area that resulted in the issuance of separate *Industry Audit Guides for Hospitals, Colleges and Universities,* and *Voluntary Health and Welfare Organizations.* These *Audit Guides* were developed by different committees over approximately the same time period.

Inevitably, there were differences in the practices and reporting standards recommended in the different *Audit Guides,* as well as differences between those recommended in the *Audit Guides* and those recommended in the publications of the professional associations. Later, several *Statements of Position* issued by the Accounting Standards Division of the AICPA resulted in amendments to each of the *Audit Guides.* In addition, a *Statement of Position* was issued containing the recommendations of the AICPA on accounting and reporting standards for NNOs not covered under the three *Industry Audit Guides.* By the late 1970s, all significant differences between the financial accounting and reporting standards recom-

---

[1]*Health Care Strategic Management,* Vol. 17:4, "Some on 'Fastest Fifty' List of Fast-growing Hospitals Say They Don't Belong There," by Ed Egger, April 1999, pp. 17–19.

mended in the *Audit Guides* and those recommended in the publications of the professional associations relating to hospitals and to colleges and universities had been resolved and the various professional association publications and *Audit Guides* had been amended accordingly. Unfortunately, there continue to be significant differences among the *Audit Guides* (as amended) themselves with regard to recommended accounting and reporting practices for different types of NNOs.

In 1979 the Financial Accounting Standards Board assumed responsibility for setting accounting and reporting standards for all nonbusiness organizations except governmental units. In preparation for addressing specific standards for NNOs, the Board first undertook to incorporate NNOs into its *Statements of Financial Accounting Concepts*. In 1980 the Board issued *FASB Concepts Statement No. 4*, "Objectives of Financial Reporting by Nonbusiness Organizations." In 1985, the Board amended *FASB Concepts Statement No. 2*, "Qualitative Characteristics of Accounting Information," to apply to NNOs as well as to business enterprises and issued *Concepts Statement No. 6*, "Elements of Financial Statements," which encompasses NNOs as well as business enterprises. The FASB has now issued four statements on nonprofit accounting, *SFAS Nos. 93, 116, 117, and 124*. These are discussed later in the chapter.

Hierarchy of Generally Accepted Reporting Standards for Nongovernment Nonbusiness Organizations

Not-for-profit organizations (such as colleges and universities and health care providers) that may be either government owned or privately owned are referred to herein as ***special entities***. Government-owned special entities come under the jurisdiction of the Government Accounting Standards Board (GASB). The hierarchy used to establish generally accepted reporting standards for all state and local governmental-owned entities was presented in Chapter 19. Government-owned special entities come under that hierarchy. The hierarchy used to establish generally accepted reporting standards for NNOs other than government-owned special entities is the same as that for business organizations and is summarized below.

1. First level of priority
   A. FASB Statements and Interpretations.
   B. APB Opinions (unless amended or superseded).
   C. AICPA Accounting Research Bulletins (unless amended or superseded).
2. Second level of priority
   A. FASB Technical Bulletins.
   B. AICPA Industry Audit and Accounting Guides and AICPA Statements of Position, *if cleared by the FASB*.
3. Third level of priority
   A. Consensus positions of the FASB Emerging Issues Task Force.
   B. AICPA AcSec Practice bulletins *if cleared by the FASB*.
4. Fourth level of priority
   A. AICPA Accounting Interpretations.
   B. Implementation Guides (Q&A's) published by the FASB staff.
   C. Widely recognized and prevalent industry practices.
5. Fifth level of priority
   A. FASB Concepts Statements.
   B. Pronouncements of other professional associations or regulatory agencies.
   C. Other accounting literature.

NNOs in the private sector should look to this hierarchy for accounting and reporting guidance.

With different hierarchies for entities under the jurisdiction of the FASB and entities under the jurisdiction of the GASB, different accounting standards may apply to special entities depending on whether they are privately owned or government owned. For example, *SFAS No. 93* requires that all privately owned not-for-profit organizations record depreciation. *GASB Statement No. 8* states that governmental entities including government-owned special entities need not record depreciation. As a result private-sector special entities (such as hospitals) will record depreciation, whereas many similar government-owned special entities will not report depreciation until the new rules under *GASB Statement No. 34* on state and local government reporting go into effect. This issue remains controversial.

Most of the guidance for NNOs other than government-owned special entities is found in *Audit and Accounting Guides* of the AICPA and in publications of industry associations.[2] Examples of industry association publications include:

Colleges and Universities
    Audits of Colleges and Universities, second edition (AICPA, 1975)
    Financial Accounting and Reporting Manual for Higher Education [National Association of College and University Business Officers (NACUBO), Loose Leaf]

Hospitals and Other Health Care Providers
    Audits of Providers of Health Care Services (AICPA, 1989)

Voluntary Health and Welfare Organizations (VHWOs)
    Audits of Voluntary Health and Welfare Organizations (AICPA, 1988)

Other Nongovernment Nonbusiness Organizations
    Audits of Certain Nonprofit Organizations, second edition (AICPA, 1987).

GASB Statement No. 15 allows public colleges and universities to use either the AICPA/NACUBO model (described in this chapter) or the government model (described in Chapter 19). In the discussion that follows, all illustrations, including those for colleges and universities, are based on the hierarchy described in this chapter for NNOs other than government-owned special entities.

"In a survey comparing the financial reporting of colleges and universities to publicly held corporations, a number of differences in styles and formats between the two groups were discovered. For example, 100% of the colleges responding to the survey listed the statement of financial position as the first statement that appeared in the annual report, while 69% of corporations listed the income statement first. In addition, 82% of colleges used the term 'statement of financial position' to describe the balance sheet, while 94% of the corporations surveyed used the term 'balance sheet.' All the income statements for publicly held corporations were single-column statements (for each year), unless they were part of some consolidating statement; in contrast, 84% of the national liberal arts colleges presented the statement of activities in multiple columns (with headings for different types of net assets), and only 10 out of 120 colleges used a single-column format, stacking the various categories of net assets."[3]

---

[2] Exceptions include *SFAS No. 93, No. 116, No. 117, and No. 124.*

[3] *NACUBO Business Officer*, "Corporate-Like," by Frederick M. Weis, June 1999, p. 28–33.

Financial Reporting for Not-for-Profit Organizations

In 1993, the FASB standardized much of the variability in reporting by issuing *SFAS No. 117*, "Financial Statements of Not-for-Profit Organizations." This statement requires far more aggregation of data than most organizations had previously reported. Three basic financial statements are required:

1. A statement of financial position (balance sheet).
2. A statement of activities.
3. A statement of cash flows.

Also, *SFAS No. 117* requires that net assets (assets less liabilities) be presented in three principal categories in the statement of financial position as follows:

1. *Unrestricted net assets.*
2. *Temporarily restricted net assets*—resources that must be used for a specific purpose or in a specific time period where the restriction is donor imposed.
3. *Permanently restricted net assets*—endowments, where the interest might be spent but the principal must not be used.

The categories of net assets under *SFAS No. 117* replace the fund balances used in previous reports. The term *restricted net assets* should not be confused with a restricted fund or assets whose use is limited. For example, a governing board of a hospital might designate certain resources to be used for a specific purpose; such items would still be classified on the statement of financial position as unrestricted net assets.

The FASB did not specify precise formats for the statements, but did require that information about liquidity be disclosed. Organizations can meet this requirement by classifying assets and liabilities as current or noncurrent, or they may choose to list the assets and liabilities in the order of liquidity. The FASB also expressed a strong preference for the term "statement of financial position" rather than balance sheet.

On the statement of activities, revenues may result in an increase in any one of the three categories of net assets. However, *all expenses must be reported as decreases in unrestricted net assets*. Thus, all expenses are listed in one column.

In the appendix to this chapter, the three financial statements are illustrated for a private educational institution (Illustrations 20-4A through 20-7A). Two formats are provided for the statement of financial position: one that displays a net asset desegregation (Illustration 20-4A) and one that displays a fund group desegregation (Illustration 20-5A). The statement of activities is shown in Illustration 20-6A and the statement of cash flows is presented in Illustration 20-7A.

GASB Project on Public Colleges and Universities

The Governmental Accounting Standards Board (GASB) announced in March 1999 that it would no longer recommend separate financial reporting standards for public colleges and universities. Rather, public colleges and universities would be required to follow standards established for all other state and local governmental entities (see Chapter 19). GASB argued that the complexities and disadvantages of separate reporting outweighed its benefits. In this chapter, the rules for *private* colleges and universities are illustrated.

FUND ACCOUNTING

Whereas in some instances the total resources of an NNO may be available to finance its functions and operating activities, in most cases restrictions are placed on certain of the organization's resources by donors, by law or contract, or by other external authorities. Donors, for example, often specify the specific purpose or program to which their contributions are to be applied, and sometimes the time period in which the resources contributed by them may be expended. To facilitate the observance of such restrictions, most NNOs use fund accounting for record-keeping and reporting purposes.

The fund structure of different nonbusiness organizations is summarized in Illustration 20-1. The fund structure and terminology differ among NNOs primarily because of the separate development of accounting and reporting standards for the different organizations. There are six funds commonly used, each of which will be discussed in turn. They are:

1. *Current Fund* (restricted and unrestricted). The unrestricted fund is often referred to by hospitals as the general fund, and the restricted fund as a special purpose fund.
2. *Plant Fund.* Several subfunds may be used to account for different aspects of plant and equipment, including the debt to acquire them.
3. *Endowment Fund.*
4. *Loan Fund.*
5. *Agency or Custodial Fund.*
6. *Annuity and Life Income Fund.*

ILLUSTRATION 20–1

Comparison of Fund Structures of Different Nonbusiness Organizations

Primary Purpose of Funds and Account Group	Names of the Funds Used by Different Nonbusiness Organizations			
	State and Local Governmental Units	Colleges and Universities	Hospitals	Voluntary Health and Welfare Organizations and ONNOs
Financing of Current Operations	General Fund Special Revenue Fund	Unrestricted Current Restricted Current	General Fund Specific Purpose	Unrestricted Current Restricted Current
Acquisition of and Accountability for Major Capital Assets and Related Long-Term Obligations	Capital Projects Debt Service General Fixed Assets Account Group General Long-Term Obligation Account Group	Plant: Unexpended For Renewals and Replacements For Retirement of Debt Investment in Plant	Plant Replacement and Expansion	Plant (Land, Building, and Equipment)
Fiduciary Responsibilities	Permanent Agency	Endowment Loan Agency Annuity Life Income	Endowment Agency	Endowment Loan Agency Annuity Life Income

ACCRUAL BASIS OF ACCOUNTING

Generally accepted accounting standards require that financial statements for NNOs be prepared using the accrual basis of accounting. Thus, revenues are reported when earned and realized or realizable, and expenditures are reported when materials or services are received. Expenses incurred before the reporting date are accrued, and expenses applicable to future periods are deferred. Although accrual accounting is used, the primary emphasis in reporting for NNOs is the disclosure of the sources of the entity's resources and how they were used to accomplish the objectives of the organization, rather than the determination of net income.

CLASSIFICATION OF REVENUE AND EXPENSE

IN THE NEWS

"Moody's Investors Service plans to make some changes in the way it rates the operating performance of colleges and universities, saying investors have been frustrated by accounting practices that can mask financial weaknesses. Most of the changes will be made in the ratings of private colleges and universities, which have widely divergent methods of reporting nonoperating revenues and expenses, rates of spending endowment funds, and participation in the private 'off-balance-sheet' financing of campus facilities, particularly dormitories."[4]

For external reporting purposes, revenues are classified by source (such as net patient service revenue), and expenses and expenditures are classified by function or activity (such as research). An example of major sources of revenue is presented in Illustration 20-2. As indicated, hospitals and colleges and universities distinguish

ILLUSTRATION 20–2

Major Sources of Revenue for Different Classifications of Nongovernment Nonbusiness Organizations

Colleges and Universities	*Hospitals*	*Voluntary Health and Welfare Organizations and ONNOs*
Tuition and Fees	***Operating Revenue***	***Public Support***
Federal, State, or Local Appropriations	Patient Service Revenue (Gross) Less Deductions (charity allowances, courtesy allowances, policy discounts, contractual adjustments, etc.)	Public Contributions
Federal, State, or Local Grants and Contracts		Special Events
		Legacies and Bequests
Private Gifts, Grants, and Contracts	Net Patient Service Revenue	Federated and Nonfederated Campaigns
Endowment Income	Other Operating Revenue (tuition from schools, specific-purpose grants, revenue from auxiliary enterprises, etc.)	
Sales and Services of Educational Activities (film rentals, testing services, etc.)		***Revenue***
		Membership Dues
Sales and Services of Auxiliary Enterprises (residence halls, food services, etc.)	***Nonoperating Revenue***	Investment Income
	Unrestricted Gifts and Grants	Realized Gains on Investment Activities
	Unrestricted Income from Endowment Funds	
	Donated Services	
	Income from Board Designated Funds	

---

[4]*Chronicle of Higher Education*, Vol. 45:22, "Investment Service Plans to Change the Way it Evaluates Colleges' Finances," by Martin van der Werf, Feb. 5, 1999, p. A40.

ILLUSTRATION 20–3

Functional Classification of Expenditures and Expenses for Different Types of Nongovernment Nonbusiness Organizations

Colleges and Universities	*Hospitals*	*Voluntary Health and Welfare Organizations and ONNOs*
Instruction	Professional Care of Patients	*Program Services*
Academic Instruction	Dietary Services	Research
Community Education	General Services	Public Education
Research	Administrative Services	Professional Education and Training
Institutes and Centers	Employee Health and Welfare	Community Service
Project Research	Medical Malpractice Costs	Other
Public Service	Depreciation and Amortization	*Support Services*
Community Service	Interest	Management and General Fund Raising
Conferences and Institutes	Provision for Bad Debts	
Extension Service		
Academic Support		
Computer Services		
Libraries		
Student Services		
Admissions		
Counseling		
Financial Aid		
Health and Infirmary		
Intramural Athletics		
Student Organizations		
Registrar		
Remedial Instruction		
Institutional Support		
Operation and Maintenance of Plant		
Scholarships and Fellowships		
Auxiliary Enterprises		

revenues between operating and nonoperating, while VHWOs and ONNOs classify revenues based on the source of the revenue, such as public support. Typical functional classifications of expenditures and expenses for different types of NNOs are presented in Illustration 20-3.

ACCOUNTING FOR CURRENT FUNDS

NNOs distinguish between unrestricted funds and restricted funds (or, for hospitals, between the general fund and specific purpose funds) in accounting for current operations. See Illustration 20-1.

Current Unrestricted Funds

Current unrestricted funds include financial resources of the organization that may be *expended at the discretion of the governing board* to carry out the operations of the organization and to accomplish its objectives. The resources and operations of current unrestricted funds of NNOs are similar in many ways to the resources and operations of the general fund of a municipality.

Current Restricted Funds

In a sense, all resources of an NNO that are not accounted for as current unrestricted funds are restricted because of *legal, contractual, or external restrictions on their use*. Current restricted funds are distinguished from other funds (such as plant or endowment funds) in that current restricted funds consist of financial resources that are **currently available** for use in **operations**, but which may be expended only for purposes specified by the donor, grantor, or other **external** party.

Thus, the resources of both current funds—restricted and unrestricted—may be used by the organization to carry out its current operations and activities. Current unrestricted resources may be expended at the discretion of the governing board, whereas current restricted resources may be expended only in accordance with externally imposed restrictions.

Accounting for Board Designated Funds

The governing board of an NNO may designate resources of the current unrestricted fund (general fund of hospitals) for specific purposes, projects, or investment. An example of a specific purpose might include research expenditures, while an addition to the plant would be an example of a specific project. Such designations are intended to aid in the planning and control of expenditures and to limit the discretion of management (as distinguished from the governing board) over expenditures of the designated resources. However, these designations do not constitute, and should not be confused with, donor or external restrictions on the use of resources. The governing board has the authority to reverse or modify such designations at will. Accordingly, board designated funds should be accounted for as unrestricted funds and the term "restricted" should **not** be used in connection with them. Such funds should never be included in the current restricted (specific purpose) funds.

Hospitals

Assets set aside by the governing board of a hospital for board-designated purposes are reported separately in the general funds portion of the statement of financial position as **assets whose use is limited**.

To illustrate, assume that the governing board designated $200,000 of current unrestricted funds for future research grants and $50,000 for financing an addition to plant and equipment. Hospitals would report these items separately from other assets in the assets section of the general fund statement of financial position as follows:

General Funds	
Assets whose use is limited:	
By board for research grants	$200,000
By board for acquisition of equipment	50,000
Total assets whose use is limited	$250,000

Assets whose use is limited under terms of debt indentures, trust agreements, third-party reimbursement arrangements, or other similar arrangements are also presented in the statement of financial position as "assets whose use is limited."

Other Nonbusiness Nongovernmental Organizations (ONNOs)

ONNOs report the amounts and purposes of board designated funds either in the *footnotes* to the financial statements *or by reclassification* of an equivalent portion of the Current Unrestricted Fund Balance similar to an appropriation of retained earnings. Using the information from the previous example and assuming reclassification of a portion of the Current Unrestricted Fund Balance, an entry is made as follows:

Current Unrestricted Fund

(1)	Fund Balance	250,000	
	Board Designated Reserve for Research Grants		200,000
	Board Designated Reserve for Plant Expansion		50,000
	To record designation of reserves by action of governing board.		

The reserves would be reported as part of the total Current Unrestricted Fund Balance as follows:

Current Unrestricted Fund Balance

Available for Current Expenditures	$1,500,000*
Board Designated Reserve for Research Grants	200,000
Board Designated Reserve for Plant Expansion	50,000
Total Current Unrestricted Fund Balance	$1,750,000

*This is an assumed amount.

Colleges and Universities

Unrestricted current funds of colleges and universities that are designated by the board for specific current operating purposes are accounted for in the same manner as board designated funds of ONNOs (by footnote or by reclassification of the Unrestricted Current Fund Balance). However, *some board-restricted current resources can be transferred to other funds.* The allowable transfers are resources designated by the governing boards for loans, investments, or plant expansion. These funds can be transferred to loan funds, endowment funds, or plant funds.

If in the preceding example, the governing board was the Board of Regents of a university, the entries recorded on the books of the university would be as follows:

Unrestricted Current Funds

(1)	Fund Balance—Unallocated	200,000	
	Fund Balance—Allocated for Research Grants		200,000
	To establish a reserve in Fund Balance for research grants.		
(2)	Nonmandatory Transfer to Plant Funds	50,000	
	Cash		50,000
	To record the transfer to Plant Funds for purposes of making additions to plant.		

Unexpended Plant Fund

(1)	Cash	50,000	
	Fund Balance—Unrestricted		50,000
	To record the receipt of cash from the Unrestricted Current Fund for the purpose of financing additions to plant.		

Mandatory and Nonmandatory Transfers

The terms *mandatory transfer* and *nonmandatory transfer*, which are unique to accounting and reporting for colleges and universities, are described in the *Industry Audit Guide* as follows:[5]

> *Mandatory Transfers.* This category includes *transfers* from the Current Funds group to other fund groups arising from (1) *binding legal agreements* related to the financing of educational plant, such as amounts for debt retirement, interest, and required provisions for renewals and replacements of plant not financed from other sources and (2) *grant agreements* with agencies of the federal government, donors, and other organizations to match gifts and grants to loan and other funds. Mandatory transfers may be specified to be made from unrestricted or from restricted current funds.
>
> *Nonmandatory Transfers.* This category includes those *transfers* from the Current Funds group to other fund groups made *at the discretion of the governing board* to serve a variety of objectives, such as additions to loan funds, additions to quasi-endowment funds, general or specific plant additions, voluntary renewals and replacements of plant, and prepayments on debt principal. It also may include the retransfer of resources back to current funds.

The recording of a nonmandatory (board designated) transfer was illustrated in the preceding section. To illustrate a mandatory transfer, assume that a university is required by the terms of a mortgage agreement to transfer $340,000 of tuition and fees that have been recorded as revenue in the unrestricted current funds to pay principal and interst on long-term debt that is carried as a liability in the plant fund accounts. The transfer of funds is recorded as follows:

Mandatory Transfer

Unrestricted Current Funds

Mandatory Transfer to Plant Funds	340,000	
Cash		340,000

To record transfer of funds for payment of principal and interest on mortgage note carried as a liability in Plant Fund.

Plant Fund (for Retirement of Indebtedness)

Cash	340,000	
Fund Balance—Restricted		340,000

To record receipt of mandatory transfer from Unrestricted Current Funds.

Mandatory and nonmandatory transfers are shown separately in both the statement of changes in fund balances and in the statement of current funds revenues, expenditures, and other changes.

Revenue and Support from Fund-Raising Events

The costs incurred by VHWOs and ONNOs in carrying out public support fund-raising events, such as dinners, dances, theater parties, auctions, and so on, are deducted from gross contributions received; and only the net funds provided by the event are reported as support in the financial statements.

---

[5] *Audits of Colleges and Universities*, second edition (New York: AICPA, 1975), p. 104.

CONTRIBUTIONS

In *SFAS No. 116*, "Accounting for Contributions Received and Contributions Made,"[6] the FASB adopted standards requiring all NNOs subject to its jurisdiction to recognize contributions, including unconditional promises to give, as *revenue* in the period received.[7] *SFAS No. 116* does not apply to tax exemptions, abatements, or incentives, or to transfers of assets from a government to a business enterprise. Contributions include gifts of cash, pledges (promises to give cash or other assets), donated services, and gifts of noncash assets. Conditional promises to give (where the contribution would be returned if the conditions are not met) are recognized when they become unconditional, that is, when the conditions are substantially met. Donors sometimes restrict unconditional contributions to be used for a specific purpose. Donor-restricted contributions are still reported as revenues and result in an increase in *restricted* net assets. Other contributions are reported as revenues resulting in increases in *unrestricted* net assets. Expiration of donor restrictions results in a transfer from restricted net assets to unrestricted net assets.

Pledges

Pledges are signed commitments to contribute specific amounts of money to an organization on a future date or in installments. Although resembling promissory notes, pledges generally are not enforceable contracts. Regardless, pledges are recorded as revenues when a promise to give is nonrevocable and unconditional, at the present value of the expected receipts.[8] All firms should establish an allowance for uncollectible pledges.

The recording of pledges may be illustrated by assuming that, as a result of a fund-raising campaign, an organization receives written and signed pledges to contribute $300,000 for unrestricted use by the organization in the current or future years. Experience indicates that about 15% of pledges from similar past campaigns were never collected. Entries to record the pledges using the accrual basis of accounting are as follows.

Current Unrestricted Fund

(1)	Pledges Receivable	300,000	
	Revenue—Contributions		300,000
	To record gross amount of campaign pledges.		
(2)	Expense—Provision for Uncollectible Pledges	45,000	
	Allowance for Uncollectible Pledges		45,000
	To record provision for estimated uncollectible pledges.		

Contributions are shown net of the Provision for Uncollectible Pledges in the operating statement, and Pledges Receivable are shown net of the Allowance for Uncollectible Pledges in the statement of financial position. If the amounts pledged

---

[6]FASB, *SFAS No. 116*, "Accounting for Contributions Received and Contributions Made" (Norwalk, CT), June 1993.

[7]*SFAS No. 116* defines a contribution as "an unconditional transfer of cash or other assets to an entity or a settlement or cancellation of its liabilities in a voluntary nonreciprocal transfer by another entity acting other than as an owner."

[8]Suppose an alumnus offered to give ten million dollars to the school *if* 90% of his fellow alumni contributed money to the school. This conditional promise would be disclosed in the footnotes and would not be recorded until the condition is met and the promise becomes unconditional.

contain restrictions on their use, entries similar to those made in the current unrestricted fund (above) would be made in the current restricted fund or in a loan, endowment, or plant fund as appropriate.

Donated Services

Some of the operations and activities of NNOs may be carried out by volunteers who donate their time and expertise. Donated services may range from the limited participation of large numbers of volunteers in fund-raising activities to active and sustained involvement in the organization by a few dedicated individuals.

Contributions of services are *recognized* only *if* the services received:

1. Create or enhance nonfinancial assets, *or*
2. a. Require specialized skills,
   b. Are provided by individuals possessing those skills, *and*
   c. Would need to be purchased if not provided by donation.

To illustrate the first alternative, consider an architect who contributes services to construct a building. Since the service helps create a fixed asset, the service would be recognized. For example, if a building valued at $1,500,000 included an estimated value of $400,000 assigned to the architectural services, then revenue from donated services of $400,000 would be recognized.

If the first alternative is not met, then all three conditions of the second alternative (2 above) must be satisfied in order for the contribution to be recognized. Suppose that a retired tax partner from a Big Five firm offers to teach a tax course at a local college. Since the school would need to hire a qualified person possessing specialized skills to teach the course, the service would be recorded. These conditions generally prohibit organizations from recording the value of the services of volunteer solicitors and from recording the value of donated services received on a casual or intermittent basis.

When these conditions are met, NNOs record and report the value of the services received, net of incidental expenses reimbursed to the contributing personnel, as revenue or support in the current unrestricted fund (or the general fund for hospitals). In the same entry, an amount equal to the revenue or support recognized is recorded as an expense in the appropriate expense account (e.g., professional fees expense).

Example of Donated Service Assume that the necessary conditions are met and that the services of a CPA who audited the records of a heart association at no charge were valued at $15,000, and those of an attorney who provided necessary legal services to the organization at no charge had a value of $6,000. The entry to record the revenue and expense resulting from the donated services is:

Current Unrestricted Fund

(1)	Management and General Expense	21,000	
	Donated Services Revenue		21,000
	To record value of donated services.		

Had the organization incurred any costs for incidental expenses of the CPA or attorney, the value of the services recorded would be reduced by the amount of those costs.

Donated Collection Items

Contributions of works of art, historical treasures, and similar assets are not capitalized if (a) the donated items are added to collections held for public exhibition, education, or research in furtherance of public service rather than financial gain; (b) the donated items are protected, cared for, and preserved; and (c) organizational policy requires proceeds from any future sale of the items to be used to acquire other items for collections.

Donor-imposed Restricted Contributions

Donor-imposed restrictions limit the use of assets that are received. Some restrictions limit the organization's ability to sell the asset. Restrictions may be permanent or temporary. For instance, temporary restrictions may stipulate that the resource can only be used after a specified date, for a particular program or service, or to acquire buildings or equipment. In any case, the organization needs to distinguish between contributions received that increase permanently restricted net assets, contributions that increase temporarily restricted net assets, and those that increase unrestricted net assets. This separation provides users with important information such as: Were aggregate net assets maintained only because permanently restricted net assets made up for a decline in unrestricted net assets? The primary difference between a donor-imposed restriction and a conditional contribution is that a donor-imposed restriction limits the use of donated assets while a conditional contribution creates a barrier that must be overcome before assets transferred or promised become contributions received. Therefore, donor-imposed restricted assets are recorded as contribution revenues (also known as restricted support) in the period received, thus increasing either temporarily or permanently restricted net assets. Then, as the expenditures are made, or the restriction expires, the net assets are released from temporarily restricted net assets or permanently restricted net assets and are reported as unrestricted net assets on the Statement of Activities.

For example, suppose a university received $120,000 in contributions that were restricted for specific operating purposes and spent $80,000 in the current year, with the remaining $40,000 spent in the second year. The following entries would be recorded:

Restricted Current Funds

(1)	Cash	120,000	
	Contribution Revenue (restricted support)		120,000
	To record restricted contributions.		
(2)	Net Assets Released from Restrictions	80,000	
	Cash		80,000
	To release funds from restricted into unrestricted assets.		

Unrestricted Current Funds

(1)	Cash	80,000	
	Net Assets Released from Restrictions		80,000
	To receive funds into unrestricted from restricted assets.		
(2)	Expenses—educational	80,000	
	Cash		80,000
	To record expenditures of restricted assets for specified purposes.		

The effect of these transactions is reported in the following condensed statement of activities.

	Unrestricted	Temporarily Restricted
Revenues and Support	$	$120,000
Net Assets Released from Restrictions	80,000	(80,000)
Total Revenues and Support	80,000	40,000
Expenses	(80,000)	
Changes in Net Assets	—0—	$ 40,000

In the next year, assuming that the money is spent as planned, the remaining $40,000 is released from restrictions and recorded as an expense.

ACCOUNTING FOR PLANT FUNDS

Most transactions involving property, plant and equipment are accounted for by NNOs other than hospitals in a plant fund. The plant fund is used to account for (1) the property, plant and equipment owned by the organization and the net investment, (2) the accumulation of financial resources for the acquisition or replacement of property, plant and equipment, (3) the acquisition and disposal of property, plant and equipment, (4) liabilities relating to the acquisition of property, plant and equipment, and (5) depreciation expense and accumulated depreciation.

Colleges and Universities

Colleges and universities also account for the accumulation of financial resources to service-related indebtedness in the plant fund. All types of NNOs are required by generally accepted accounting standards to record depreciation expense.

The combination of rapid change in technology and university capital budgeting procedures can result in what amounts to the university "capitalizing scrap." By the time the budgeting and purchasing procedures are implemented, and the equipment is delivered, it is not far from being obsolete, at which point the whole procedure has to start over. As an alternative, colleges can consider leasing equipment.[9]

The plant fund of colleges and universities is usually divided into four separate self-balancing subgroups:[10]

1. *Unexpended Plant Fund:* to account for resources used to purchase property, plant and equipment (similar to a capital projects fund of a municipality).
2. *Funds for Renewals and Replacements:* to account for resources used to renovate or replace existing property, plant and equipment (also similar to a capital projects fund of a municipality).
3. *Funds for Retirement of Indebtedness:* to account for resources to be used to retire or pay interest on debt incurred in the acquisition or replacement of property, plant and equipment (similar to the debt service fund of a municipality).

---

[9] *Tax Adviser*, Vol. 29: 11, "From Here to Technology in Less than an Eternity," by Corey Schou, K. Smith, and W. Stratton, November 1998, pp. 790–793.

[10] It is likely that most NNOs will reorganize the plant fund in the future to agree more readily with the new external reporting practices. For example, instead of using the four subfunds of the plant fund, they might collapse them all into one fund.

4. *Investment in Plant:* to account for the institution's property, plant and equipment, related debt, and net investment in plant (analogous to a combination of the General Fixed Assets and General Long-Term Obligation Account Groups of a municipality).

Both board-designated funds and externally restricted funds are accounted for in the plant fund of colleges and universities; therefore, a distinction is made between restricted and unrestricted fund balances.

To illustrate the funds and the procedures used to account for transactions relating to property, plant and equipment by different NNOs, assume the following example.

Plant Fund Example

1. During the year, resources are obtained for the acquisition of property, plant and equipment as follows:

Loan proceeds	$500,000
Contributions restricted by donor for plant	200,000
Board designation of unrestricted funds	50,000
	$750,000

2. Land is acquired for a building site for $750,000.
3. Principal and interest of $200,000 and $20,000, respectively, are paid on long-term obligations relating to property, plant and equipment.
4. The amount of depreciation expense on all fixed assets for the year is $235,000.

The transactions described above would be recorded by colleges and universities as follows (the journal entry numbers correspond to the information in the box above):

Unrestricted Current Fund

(1A)	Nonmandatory Transfer to Plant Funds (unexpended)	50,000	
	Cash		50,000
	To record transfer of board designated unrestricted funds to Plant Fund.		

Unexpended Plant Fund

(1B)	Cash	750,000	
	Notes Payable		500,000
	Revenue—Contributions—Restricted		200,000
	Fund Balance—Unrestricted		50,000
	To record receipt of resources to be used for additions to property, plant and equipment.		
(2A)	Land	750,000	
	Cash		750,000
	To record acquisition of land.		
(2B)	Fund Balance—Restricted	200,000	
	Fund Balance—Unrestricted	50,000	
	Notes Payable	500,000	
	Land		750,000
	To transfer assets and related liabilities to Investment in Plant Fund.		

Investment in Plant Fund

(2C)	Land		750,000	
	Notes Payable			500,000
	Net Investment in Plant			250,000
	To record acquisition of land and related indebtedness from the Unexpended Plant Fund.			

The construction of assets and related debt is accounted for in the *unexpended plant fund* until the construction is completed. On the completion of construction, the assets and related liabilities are transferred from the unexpended plant fund to the *investment in plant fund* using entries similar to those presented in (2B) and (2C) above.

Funds for Retirement of Indebtedness

(3A)	Fund Balance—Restricted		200,000	
	Cash (principal)			200,000
	Interest Expense		20,000	
	Cash			20,000
	To record payment of principal and interest on obligations related to property, plant and equipment.			

Investment in Plant Fund

(3B)	Notes Payable		200,000	
	Net Investment in Plant			200,000
	To record reduction in indebtedness related to property, plant and equipment.			

(4)	Depreciation Expense		235,000	
	Accumulated Depreciation			235,000
	To record annual depreciation on property, plant and equipment that is included in the assets of the Investment in Plant Fund.			

Prior to 1990, depreciation of assets was not required for colleges and universities (except in endowment funds and nonexpendable trust funds). *SFAS No. 93*, "Recognition of Depreciation by Not-for-Profit Organizations," as amended by *SFAS No. 99*, requires that all NNOs including colleges and universities measure and report depreciation and accumulated depreciation on all depreciable property, plant and equipment.

Hospitals

Most property, plant and equipment transactions of hospitals are accounted for in the General Fund and not in a Plant Fund. However, contributed resources that may be used only to acquire property, plant and equipment are accounted for in a *plant replacement and expansion (restricted) fund* until the expenditures that satisfy the donor's terms are made. At that time, the assets acquired and the related fund balance are recorded in (transferred to) the General Fund.

To illustrate, the transactions presented in the preceding example would be recorded by a hospital as follows:

Plant Replacement and Expansion Fund

(1A)	Cash		200,000	
	Revenue—Contributions—Restricted			200,000
	To record receipt of contributions that may be used only to acquire property, plant and equipment.			

General Fund

(1B)	Cash	500,000	
	Notes Payable		500,000
	To record proceeds from note authorized by governing board to be used for acquisition of property, plant and equipment.		

The hospital *may* also record a reclassification of the General Fund Balance and establish a Board Designated Reserve for Plant Expansion in an amount of unrestricted funds designated by the governing board for additions to property, plant and equipment. It is assumed here that such designations are not recorded but are simply disclosed in the footnotes to the financial statements.

Plant Replacement and Expansion Fund

| (2A) | Fund Balance | 200,000 | |
| | Cash | | 200,000 |

General Fund

(2B)	Land	750,000	
	Cash		550,000
	Fund Balance		200,000

Taken together, entries (2A) and (2B) record the acquisition of land with $200,000 in externally restricted funds and $550,000 in unrestricted board designated funds.

General Fund

(3)	Interest Expense	20,000	
	Notes Payable	200,000	
	Cash		220,000
	To record payment of principal and interest.		
(4)	Depreciation Expense	235,000	
	Accumulated Depreciation		235,000
	To record annual depreciation expense on property, plant and equipment that is included in assets of the General Fund.		

Voluntary Health and Welfare Organizations and Other Nongovernment Nonbusiness Organizations

Voluntary health and welfare organizations and ONNOs use a single Plant Fund and report the fund balance in two classifications as "expended" or "unexpended." The Expended Fund Balance is equal to the organization's net investment in property, plant and equipment (gross assets less related liabilities and accumulated depreciation). The Unexpended Fund Balance represents the amount of resources available to replace or acquire additional property, plant and equipment.

These same transactions illustrated previously would be accounted for by VHWOs or ONNOs as follows:

Current Unrestricted Fund

(1A)	Transfer to Plant Funds	50,000	
	Cash		50,000
	To record transfer of cash to Plant Fund.		

Plant Fund

(1B)	Cash	750,000	
	Notes Payable		500,000
	Contributions—Revenue—Restricted		200,000
	Transfer from Current Unrestricted Fund		50,000

To record receipt of resources to be used for additions to property, plant and equipment.

While VHWOs classify contributions that are restricted for the acquisition of plant assets as Support, ONNOs classify such contributions in a separate section of the operating statement entitled Capital Additions.

Plant Fund

(2)	Land	750,000	
	Cash		750,000

To record acquisition of land.

(3)	Notes Payable	200,000	
	Interest Expense	20,000	
	Cash		220,000

To record payment of principal and interest on obligations related to property, plant and equipment.

(4)	Depreciation Expense	235,000	
	Accumulated Depreciation		235,000

To record annual depreciation expense on property, plant and equipment included in assets of the Plant Fund.

As noted earlier, the Plant Fund Balance is classified as Expended Fund Balance and Unexpended Fund Balance. The Expended Fund Balance is analogous to the Net Investment in Plant recorded in the plant funds of a university. Before the financial statements are prepared, the Expended Fund Balance must be adjusted to reflect the change in the organization's net investment in plant resulting from the transactions above. The change in the net investment in plant is calculated as follows:

Increases:		
Purchase of Land	$ 750,000	
Reduction of Indebtedness	200,000	$ 950,000
Decreases:		
Issue Notes Payable	(500,000)	
Depreciation Expense	(235,000)	(735,000)
Net Increase in Investment in Plant		$ 215,000

Plant Fund

(5)	Unexpended Fund Balance	215,000	
	Expended Fund Balance		215,000

To recognize the effect on the Fund Balances of the increase in the organization's net investment in property, plant and equipment.

Nonexhaustible Assets of Other Nongovernment Nonbusiness Organizations

Prior to 1990, ONNOs were not required to recognize depreciation expense and accumulated depreciation on "nonexhaustible" assets such as landmarks, monuments, cathedrals, and historical treasures or on structures used primarily as houses of worship. In *SFAS No. 93*, the Board considered and rejected the assertions that such assets are nonexhaustible and that those assets and structures used primarily as houses of worship need not be depreciated. Thus depreciation concepts and measurement are applied to these as well as other depreciable assets of ONNOs. However, depreciation need not be recognized on historical treasures and works of art that have estimated useful lives that are extraordinarily long. To qualify, such assets must have cultural, historical, or esthetic value that is worth preserving perpetually, and the holder must have and exercise the financial and technological ability to protect and preserve the asset.

ACCOUNTING FOR ENDOWMENT FUNDS

Endowment funds are similar to the nonexpendable trust funds of governmental units described in Chapter 19. When the donated funds have been given in perpetuity, the endowment fund is referred to as a *pure endowment fund*. When the donor has specified a particular date or event after which the principal of the endowment fund may be expended, the endowment fund is referred to as a *term endowment fund*. Resources of an unrestricted fund that are designated by the governing board for endowment purposes are accounted for in the unrestricted fund by all NNOs except colleges and universities. Colleges and universities may transfer such resources from the unrestricted current fund to a separate fund referred to as a quasi-endowment fund. Since the establishment of a quasi-endowment fund may be rescinded at the discretion of the governing board, it is recorded as a nonmandatory transfer in the unrestricted current fund and as a credit to Fund Balance—Unrestricted in the quasi-endowment fund.

The income from endowment funds generally may be expended as earned either for specified purposes or at the discretion of the governing board. If there are no restrictions on the use of the endowment fund income, it is recognized as revenue in the organization's unrestricted or general fund. Otherwise, endowment fund income is recognized as a resource addition to current restricted (specific purpose) funds, loan funds, plant funds, or other funds as appropriate to the use of the endowment income specified by the donor.

To illustrate the recording of endowment fund income that may be used for restricted and unrestricted purposes, assume that dividends and interest on endowment fund investments amount to $400,000, of which $150,000 is restricted for research grants and the remainder is unrestricted. Suppose that $100,000 in research grants is awarded during the period. Entries to record the income on endowment fund investments are summarized here:

Endowment Fund

(1)	Cash	400,000	
	Due to Unrestricted Fund (General Fund of Hospital)		250,000
	Due to Restricted Fund (Specific Purpose Fund of Hospital)		150,000
	To record receipt of dividends and interest.		

Current Unrestricted Fund

(2)	Due from Endowment Fund	250,000	
	Unrestricted Income (Investment Income)		250,000
	To record unrestricted Endowment Fund income.		

Current Restricted Fund

(3)	Due from Endowment Fund	150,000	
	Restricted Income (Investment Income)		150,000
	To record restricted Endowment Fund income.		

(4)	Research Expense	100,000	
	Cash		100,000
	To record payment of research grants.		

Accounting for Public Nonprofit Organizations For *public* nonprofits (governmental nonprofits), accounting for endowment funds differs from the external reports of *private* NNOs. This section illustrates the differences in accounting between governmental nonprofits (under GASB rules) and private nonprofits (under FASB rules). For governmental nonprofits, restricted endowment fund income is not reported as revenue until it is expended for the restricted purposes. Entries (3) and (4) above would be replaced with entries (3a), (4a), and (4b) below:

Current Restricted Fund

(3a)	Due from Endowment Fund	150,000	
	Fund Balance (Deferred Income)		150,000
	To record availability of restricted income.		

(4a)	Expenditure	100,000	
	Cash		100,000
	To record payment of research grants.		

(4b)	Fund Balance (Deferred Income)	100,000	
	Income from Endowment Fund (Investment Income)		100,000
	To record revenue for restricted assets expended.		

Public hospitals would report the cash as a reduction of fund balance in the specific purpose fund, with the expenditure and the income offsetting each other in the General Fund.

ACCOUNTING FOR INVESTMENTS

SFAS No. 124, "Accounting for Certain Investments Held by Not-for-Profit Organizations," requires that all not-for-profit organizations report investments in equity securities with readily determinable fair values and all debt securities at fair value in the appropriate net asset category (unrestricted, temporarily restricted, or permanently restricted net assets). Unrealized gains and losses are to be recognized as well as realized gains and losses in the Statement of Activities. Investments accounted for using the equity method, as well as investments in consolidated subsidiaries, are excluded from this requirement.[11] Readily determined fair values are usually those quoted in a stock exchange.

To illustrate, suppose that Vanderbilt University receives an unrestricted cash gift of $800,000 and immediately purchases an equity investment with the same fair value. The following entries are made:

(1)	Cash	800,000	
	Revenue—Contributions—Unrestricted		800,000
	To record unrestricted contribution.		

---

[11]Real estate, mortgage notes, equity securities without a determinable fair value, and venture capital funds are also excluded.

(2)   Equity Investments   800,000
            Cash   800,000
                 To record the purchase of marketable equity investments.

There are no specific requirements for reporting investment income (such as dividends or interest) other than distinguishing among the net assets. Suppose that during the year, the investments earned dividend income of $30,000 and that at the end of the year, the investment was worth $820,000. The following entries would be made:

(1)   Cash   30,000
            Investment Income—Unrestricted   30,000
                 To record the receipt of dividends from investment.

(2)   Equity Investments   20,000
            Unrealized Gain on Investment—Unrestricted   20,000
                 To adjust the investment to market ($820,000 less $800,000).

If the investment income is restricted by donors, the income would be classified as either temporarily or permanently restricted.

Investment Pools

To improve effectiveness and flexibility in investing, NNOs often pool the investments of different funds into a single investment portfolio. Once placed in the pooled investment portfolio, individual securities are no longer identified with the contributing fund. Rather, they are pooled with all other investments. Gains, losses, and income of the investment portfolio pool are allocated by maintaining a record of the percentage interest (equity) of each fund in the investment pool. Investments that are nonmarketable should generally not be included in the pool but should be kept separate.

The initial equity interest of each fund in the investment pool is based on the *relative market value* of the investments contributed. Revised percentage (equity) interests in the investment pool must be calculated whenever additional resources are placed or removed from the investment pool. At the time securities are brought into, or removed from, the investment pool, the carrying values of the securities are usually adjusted to their fair market values on the records of the participating funds.

ACCOUNTING FOR LOAN FUNDS

Loan funds are used to account for loans to students and staff of colleges and universities, for loans to employees of hospitals, and for loans to beneficiaries of the interests of certain ONNOs (for example, loans to music students by symphony orchestra societies). Loan funds are generally revolving (repayments of loan balances and interest are in turn loaned to other individuals).

Historically, loan funds did not use any revenue or expense accounts, and all transactions were recorded directly to the fund balance. It was assumed that any income earned would offset the costs of operating the fund and was netted against the fund balance. For internal reporting purposes, these same procedures might be followed. Currently, for external reporting purposes, all revenues and expenses must be recognized on an accrual basis. Therefore, for external reporting purposes, the following entries would be made:

(1)	Cash	200,000	
	Revenue—Contributions—Restricted		200,000
	To record contribution received for establishment of a Loan Fund.		
(2)	Loans Receivable	125,000	
	Cash		125,000
	To record loans to students.		
(3)	Bad Debt Expense	2,500	
	Allowance for Uncollectible Loans		2,500
	To record estimated allowance for uncollectible loans.		
(4)	Investments	75,000	
	Cash		75,000
	To record investment of excess funds in money market account.		
(5)	Allowance for Uncollectible Loans	500	
	Loans Receivable		500
	To record write-off of a loan to student severely disabled in automobile accident.		
(6)	Investments	5,000	
	Investment Income—Restricted		5,000
	To record income on money market account.		

ACCOUNTING FOR AGENCY (CUSTODIAL) FUNDS

An agency (custodial) fund is the same as its counterpart in a governmental unit. It is used to account for the assets held by an NNO as a custodian for others. Unless significant amounts are involved, resources held by an NNO as an agent for others are often accounted for as assets and liabilities in the unrestricted or general fund rather than in a separate agency fund. When a separate agency fund is used, the balance in the fund is reported as a liability since the organization does not have any equity in the fund. To illustrate, assume that resources in the amount of $15,000 belonging to the Association of Volunteer Aids are deposited with an NNO. Entries to account for this agency relationship in the unrestricted fund are as follows:

Unrestricted Fund

(1)	Cash	15,000	
	Due to Volunteer Aids		15,000
	To record deposit of assets belonging to Association of Volunteer Aids.		
(2)	Due to Volunteer Aids	15,000	
	Cash		15,000
	To record distribution of assets to Association of Volunteer Aids.		

Similar entries are made in an agency fund if such a fund is used.

ACCOUNTING FOR ANNUITY AND LIFE INCOME FUNDS

An NNO may accept the contribution of assets to the organization on the condition that the organization make annuity payments to a specified recipient for a specified period of time (*annuity fund*) or that the organization pay the income earned on the contributed assets to a specified recipient during his or her lifetime (*life income fund*). The major distinction between the two funds is that the beneficiary of an annuity fund is assured of periodic payments of a ***stated amount***, whereas life income fund beneficiaries receive periodic payments of ***varying amounts*** depending on the earnings of the fund. At the end of the annuity or on the death of the life income beneficiary, the unexpended assets of the fund are transferred to the unrestricted fund or to an endowment fund, loan fund, plant fund, or other fund specified by the donor.

To illustrate transactions recorded in an Annuity Fund, assume that on January 1, 2001, an individual donated securities with a market value of $325,000 to an NNO on the condition that she be paid $40,000 a year for 10 years beginning December 31, 2001. At the end of the 10-year period, unexpended assets are to be placed in a permanent endowment fund. It is estimated that the investments in the Annuity Fund will yield at least 8% annually. Entries to account for the basic transactions of the Annuity Fund are presented here:

Annuity Fund

(1)	Investments	325,000	
	Annuity Payable		268,400
	Revenue—Contributions—Permanent Restriction		56,600
	To record establishment of an Annuity Fund with an Annuity Payable equal to the present value of an annuity of $40,000 discounted over 10 periods at 8% (6.71008 × $40,000 = $268,400).		
(2)	Cash	26,000	
	Annuity Payable		26,000
	To record investment income for year at 8%.		
(3)	Annuity Payable	40,000	
	Cash		40,000
	To record annual annuity payment.		

Each year the Annuity Payable balance is reduced by annuity payments and by losses on investments and is increased by investment income and gains on investments. The reasoning is that if actual investment earnings equal expected investment earnings, the net decrease in the Annuity Payable balance each year will be equal to the decrease in its present value. If the actuarial assumptions change, an entry to Annuity Payable would be made with an offset to a Change in Annuity Payable—Permanent Restriction account. This account is reported on the Statement of Activities.

ISSUES RELATING TO COLLEGES AND UNIVERSITIES

Recognition of Service Fee Revenue: The full amount of university tuition and fees is recorded as revenue at standard rates even though the university does not intend to collect the full amount because of remissions or waivers for scholarships and fellowships. Amounts of tuition and fees that are waived are recorded as expenditures for scholarships and fellowships.

Operating versus Nonoperating Income: The FASB does not require that organizations disclose a measure of operating income. Therefore, if an organization has a 5% spending rate, any investment income earned above or below this rate might be classified as nonoperating. It will be important to users to understand the institution's policies and any relevant state laws.

ISSUES RELATING TO HOSPITALS

Hospital patient service revenue is recorded at established rates, regardless of whether the hospital expects to collect the full amount. Some exceptions and several other issues relating to hospital revenues are addressed below:

Charity Care: Hospitals are required by some federal grant programs to provide healthcare services to individuals who cannot pay. Charity care revenues are not included in net revenues reported on the income statement. If the revenue was recorded, an entry to Debit Revenue and Credit Accounts Receivable should be made to reverse it out.

Contractual Allowances: Contractual allowances result from agreements made with third-party payors. Hospitals have standard rates that they charge for specific procedures. However, third-party payors, such as Blue Cross/Blue Shield, stipulate amounts that they are willing to pay. Therefore, contractual allowances are used to reduce the hospital's gross revenue to revenues net of contractual allowances.

Capitation Revenues: Health care organizations may contract with groups (or individuals) to provide health care services for some defined period of time. The health care firms generally receive a fixed amount each month to provide any necessary services needed for that month. Thus revenues are easily budgeted, and cost control becomes an important issue if a large percentage of revenues comes from capitation contracts.

Malpractice: Potential losses from malpractice claims are enormous. Health care organizations are constantly monitoring and altering the controls needed to help prevent such claims. Current rules for malpractice follow *SFAS No. 5*, "Accounting for Contingencies."

SUMMARY

1. *Describe the source of accounting standards for nongovernment nonbusiness organizations (NNOs).* Before 1970, there were several professional bodies that prescribed accounting practices for nongovernment nonbusiness organizations. During the 1970s, the AICPA developed audit guides for hospitals, colleges and universities, and voluntary health and welfare organizations. In 1979, the FASB assumed responsibility for setting accounting standards for all nonbusiness organizations except government units. Government units follow the direction of the GASB.

2. *Identify the three basic statements for NNOs.* The three basic financial statements include a statement of financial position (balance sheet), a statement of activities, and a statement of cash flows. Net assets are

presented in three categories in the statement of financial position. These categories are unrestricted net assets, temporarily restricted net assets, and permanently restricted net assets.

3. *Describe the basic funds used by nongovernment nonbusiness organizations.* Basic funds used by NNOs include the following six funds. (1) Current funds (both restricted and unrestricted): These funds account for financial resources used in current period operations. Hospitals typically call these special purpose funds and general funds respectively. (2) Plant funds: These funds are used to account for different aspects of property, plant, and equipment, including the debt to acquire them. (3) Endowment funds: These funds are used to account for donated

contributions that must be maintained permanently (pure endowment funds) or that must be maintained until a certain date (term endowment funds). (4) Loan funds: These funds are used to account for loans to students and staff of colleges and universities, for loans to employees of hospitals, and often to beneficiaries of other nongovernment nonbusiness organizations (ONNOs). (5) Agency or custodial funds: These funds are used to account for funds held for others. (6) Annuity or life income funds: Sometimes an NNO accepts a contribution on the condition that periodic payments be made to some recipient for a specific period of time (annuity fund) or that the earnings be paid to some recipient during his or her lifetime (life income fund).

4. *Distinguish between a current restricted fund and an unrestricted fund.* Current funds are used to account for current period resources. Current unrestricted funds include resources that may be expended at the discretion of the governing board, while current restricted funds account for resources that are restricted because of legal, contractual, or other external restrictions. Therefore, current restricted resources can only be expended in accordance with externally imposed restrictions.

5. *Explain the term "assets whose use is limited."* The governing board may designate resources of the current unrestricted fund for specific purposes, projects, or investments. Because the governing body can reverse such decisions, these funds should never be classified as restricted. These resources are typically reported separately on the statement of financial position.

6. *Distinguish between a mandatory and a nonmandatory transfer.* These terms are specific to accounting for colleges and universities. Mandatory transfers are interfund transfers made because of binding legal agreements or agreements made in receiving grants. For instance, if a debt agreement specifies that a portion of tuition revenues be used to meet interest payments, a university would transfer resources from a current unrestricted fund to the appropriate fund. A nonmandatory transfer would include any other transfer from the current funds to other funds made at the *discretion* of the governing board.

7. *Explain how contributions are recorded by NNOs.* Contributions, including unconditional promises to give, are recognized as revenue in the period received. Conditional promises are recognized when they become unconditional. Conditional promises should be distinguished from donor-restricted contributions. If the contributions are unconditional (cannot be returned if the condition is not met), donor-restricted contributions are still recognized as revenue. Pledges are recognized as revenues at the present value of the expected receipts when a promise is nonrevocable and unconditional.

8. *Understand how donated services are recorded.* If certain conditions are met, donated services are recognized as both revenue and expense. Contributions of services are recognized only if the services received create a nonfinancial asset (such as a building) or if the services received require specialized skills, are provided by someone possessing those skills, and would have to be purchased if not provided by the donation. Donated collections of art, historical treasures, or other similar assets are generally not capitalized.

9. *Describe the funds used to account for property, plant and equipment.* Plant funds may include an unexpended plant fund (to account for resources used to purchase plant and equipment), funds for renewals and replacement, funds for retirement of indebtedness, and investment in plant (to account for the assets and the related debt).

10. *Explain the basic accounting used by endowment funds.* When an endowment fund receives interest or dividends on endowment investments, the cash is recorded against a "due to fund" account. When the appropriate fund receives the cash, it is recognized as income for that fund. Also, any expenditures paid with the income of the endowment is recognized as an expense of the fund that incurred the expenditure.

11. *Indicate how equity investments are reported in the financial statements.* Equity investments (less than 20% ownership) and all debt investments are reported at fair value with any unrealized gains and losses reported on the Statement of Activities. Equity investments with ownership over 20% are excluded from this requirement. If the income from the investment is restricted by donors, then the income would be classified as either temporarily or permanently restricted.

12. *Explain the change in accounting for loan funds brought about by new standards.* Loan funds are typically revolving in that repayments of loan balances and interest are usually loaned to other individuals. Therefore, historically no revenues or expenses have been recorded. For external reporting purposes, since accrual accounting must be used, all revenues and expenses of the loan fund must now be recorded on the Statement of Activities.

13. *Understand the use of an annuity or life income fund.* Sometimes donors give institutions money with the condition that either a stated amount (annuity fund) or a part of the earnings (life income fund) be paid to some beneficiary. The organization rec-

ords the investment at market value. A payable is recorded at the present value of the estimated amount to be paid. Revenues are then recognized for the difference. As payments are made, the payable is reduced. As income is earned, no income is recorded but, instead, the Annuity Payable account is increased. Any adjustments to the actuarial assumptions result in an adjustment to the Payable account and to the statement of activities.

14. *Discuss the special reporting issues of hospitals.* Some of the issues related to hospitals include accounting for charity care, contractual allowances, and capitation revenues. Charity revenues should not be included in net revenues reported on the income statement. However, hospitals are free to disclose

the amount of charity care that they provide. Contractual allowances result from agreements that hospitals have made with third-party payors. Some third-party payors, such as Blue Cross/Blue Shield, stipulate amounts that they are willing to pay. The contractual allowance equals the hospital's billing rate and the amount the third-party payor actually pays. Health care organizations often contract with groups to provide health care services for a fixed fee. Therefore, the capitation revenues are the amount the health care organization receives from this contract. Under a capitation system, revenues are fixed and the costs of providing the service and cost control are key factors in measuring the organization's performance.

APPENDIX
Sample Financial Statements for Private Educational Institutions

ILLUSTRATION 20–4A

Private Educational Institution
Statement of Financial Position
Net Asset Class Desegregation

Assets	Unrestricted	Temporarily Restricted	Permanently Restricted	Total
Cash and Cash Equivalents	$ 22,368	$ 14,912	—	$ 37,280
Short-Term Investments	55,920	37,280	—	93,200
Accounts Receivable	55,920	—	—	55,920
Accrued Interest Receivable	11,184	7,456	—	18,640
Contributions Receivable	41,490	33,552	8,388	83,880
Prepaid Expenses and Other Assets	55,920	—	—	55,920
Loans to Students and Faculty	93,200	74,560	18,640	186,400
Deposits with Trustees	37,280	—	—	37,280
Long-Term Investments	97,860	78,288	19,572	195,720
Land, Buildings, and Equipment, less accumulated depreciation	83,880	67,104	16,776	167,760
Total Assets	$555,472	$313,152	$63,376	$932,000

Liabilities and Net Assets				
Accounts Payable and Accrued Liabilities	$ 34,500	—	—	$ 34,500
Deferred Revenues	13,800	—	—	13,800
Other Liabilities	11,500	—	—	11,500
Amounts Held on Behalf of Others	20,700	—	—	20,700
Annuities Payable	36,800	—	—	36,800
Long-Term Debt	82,800	—	—	82,800
U.S. Government Grants Refundable	29,900	—	—	29,900
Total Liabilities	$230,000	—	—	230,000
Net Assets:				
Unrestricted	325,472	—	—	325,472
Temporarily restricted	—	313,152	—	313,152
Permanently restricted	—	—	63,376	63,376
Total Net Assets	325,472	313,152	63,376	702,000
Total Liabilities and Net Assets	$555,472	$313,152	$63,376	$932,000

ILLUSTRATION 20–5A

Private Educational Institution
Statement of Financial Position
Fund Groups Desegregation

Assets	Current Funds	Loan Funds	Endowment & Similar Funds	Plant Funds	Total
Cash and Cash Equivalents	$ 22,368	$ 5,592	—	$ 9,320	$ 37,280
Short-Term Investments	55,920	13,980	—	23,300	93,200
Accounts Receivable	55,920	—	—	—	55,920
Accrued Interest Receivable	7,456	5,592	3,728	1,864	18,640
Contributions Receivable	50,328	—	12,582	20,970	83,880
Prepaid Expenses and Other Assets	55,920	—	—	—	55,920
Loans to Students and Faculty	—	186,400	—	—	186,400
Deposits with Trustees	—	—	—	37,280	37,280
Long-Term Investments	—	—	195,720	—	195,720
Land, Buildings, and Equipment, less accumulated depreciation	—	—	—	167,760	167,760
Total Assets	**$247,912**	**$211,564**	**$212,030**	**$260,494**	**$932,000**

Liabilities and Net Assets					
Accounts Payable and Accrued Liabilities	$ 20,700	—	—	$ 13,800	$ 34,500
Deferred Revenues	13,800	—	—	—	13,800
Other Liabilities	11,500	—	—	—	11,500
Amounts Held on Behalf of Others	20,700	—	—	—	20,700
Annuities Payable	—	—	36,800	—	36,800
Long-Term Debt	—	—	—	82,800	82,800
U.S. Government Grants Refundable	—	29,900	—	—	29,900
Total Liabilities	**$ 66,700**	**29,900**	**36,800**	**$ 96,600**	**$230,000**
Net Assets:					
Unrestricted	$163,091	$ 18,166	$ 35,046	$ 24,584	$325,472
Temporarily restricted	18,121	54,499	43,808	32,779	313,152
Permanently restricted	—	108,999	96,376	106,531	63,376
Total Net Assets	**$181,212**	**$181,664**	**$175,230**	**$163,894**	**$702,000**
Total Liabilities and Net Assets	**$247,912**	**$211,564**	**$212,030**	**$260,494**	**$932,000**

ILLUSTRATION 20–6A

Private Educational Institution
Statement of Activities
Multicolumn Format

	Unrestricted	Temporarily Restricted	Permanently Restricted	Total
Revenues and Gains:				
Tuition and Fees, net of scholarship allowances	$ 90,400	—	—	$ 90,400
Contributions	74,580	40,680	20,340	135,600
Contracts and Other Exchange Transactions	45,200	—	—	45,200
Investment Income on Endowment	10,576	8,407	8,137	27,120
Other Investment Income	10,848	7,232	—	18,080
Net Realized Gains on Investments	27,120	24,327	16,353	67,800
Net Unrealized Appreciation on Investments	18,080	18,080	9,040	45,200
Auxiliary Services	22,600	—	—	22,600
Total Revenues and Gains	$299,404	$ 98,726	$53,870	$452,000
Net Assets Released from Restrictions	91,450	(91,450)	—	—
Total Revenues, Gains and Other Support	$390,854	$ 7,276	$53,870	$452,000
Expenses and Losses:				
Educational and General:				
Instruction	$ 87,964	—	—	$ 87,964
Research	64,507	—	—	64,507
Public Service	29,321	—	—	29,321
Academic Support	32,253	—	—	32,253
Student Services	41,049	—	—	41,049
Institutional Support	8,796			8,796
Total Educational and General Expenses	263,890	—	—	$263,890
Auxiliary Enterprises	20,525	—	—	20,525
Total Expenses	284,415	—	—	$284,415
Fire Loss	8,796			8,796
Present Value Adjustment to Annuity Obligations	—	4,144	—	4,144
Total Expenses and Losses	$293,211	4,144	—	$297,355
Increase (Decrease) in Net Assets	**$ 97,643**	**$ 3,132**	**$53,870**	**$154,645**
Net assets at beginning of year	227,829	310,020	9,506	547,355
Net assets at end of year	$325,472	$313,152	$63,376	$702,000

ILLUSTRATION 20–7A

Private Educational Institution
Statement of Cash Flows
Indirect Method

Cash Flows from Operating Activities:

Changes in net assets	$154,643
Adjustments to reconcile change in net assets to net cash provided by (used for) operating activities:	
Depreciation	23,240
Amortization of discounts on investments	(10,315)
Amortization of discounts on indebtedness	9,860
Increase in accounts receivable	(7,680)
Decrease in contributions receivable	6,290
Increase in accounts payable and accrued expenses	4,513
Decrease in deferred revenues	(1,800)
Contributions restricted for long-term investment	(5,100)
Interest and dividends restricted for reinvestment	(1,400)
Net realized and unrealized gains from investments	(113,000)
Fire loss	8,796
Net cash provided by (used for) operating activities	$ 68,047

Cash Flows from Investing Activities:

Proceeds from sales and maturities of investments	5,678
Purchases of investments	(19,049)
Purchases of land, building, and equipment	(65,867)
Disbursements of loans to students and faculty	(23,156)
Repayments of loans from students and faculty	19,880
Net cash provided by (used for) investing activities	$(82,514)

Cash Flows from Financing Activities:

Proceeds from issuance of indebtedness	20,500
Repayments of principal of indebtedness	(10,500)
Receipts of interest and dividends restricted for reinvestment	4,200
Contributions received restricted for long-term investment	5,500
Payments to annuitants	(16,403)
Receipts of refundable governmental loan funds	12,600
Net cash provided by (used for) financing activities	$ 15,897
Net increase (decrease) in cash and cash equivalents	$ 1,430
Cash and cash equivalents at beginning of year	35,850
Cash and cash equivalents at end of year	$ 37,280

QUESTIONS

1. What authoritative body(s) is (are) responsible for establishing financial accounting standards for NNOs?

2. Why do most NNOs use fund accounting?

3. NNOs distinguish between restricted and unrestricted funds. Why is this distinction important?

4. What is the major difference in accounting for the general fund of a hospital and the unrestricted fund of other NNOs?

5. What is the major difference in accounting between conditional and unconditional pledges? Give an example of each.

6. What is the relationship (if any) between board designated funds and nonmandatory transfers?

7. May board designated funds ever be accounted for in the unrestricted current fund? Explain.

8. When should an NNO record donated services in its accounting records?

9. The donated services of volunteer workers on fundraising campaigns are usually not given accounting recognition. Why?

10. Universities and hospitals often reduce their standard service charge to students or patients. How are these reductions reflected in the statements

of revenue and expenses of these organizations? Explain.

11. What fund is used to account for the library books owned by a university? How should depreciation of the library books be reflected in the financial statements of the university?

12. In which fund of a hospital are medical equipment and related long-term obligations recorded? Would

your answer be the same for a voluntary health and welfare organization? Explain.

13. What capital assets (if any) of ONNOs need not be depreciated?

14. Identify three different types of endowment funds and explain how they differ.

15. Distinguish an annuity fund from a life income fund.

EXERCISES

EXERCISE 20-1 **Cash Gift to a College**

A $36,000 cash gift was received by a college during the year.

Required:
A. In which fund should the gift be recorded if there were no restrictions on the use of the cash?
B. In which fund should the gift be recorded if the donor specified that the cash was to be used to replace obsolete and damaged equipment?

EXERCISE 20-2 **Donated Services**

During 2001 volunteer pinstripers donated their services to General Hospital at no cost. The staff at General Hospital was in control of the pinstripers' duties. If regular employees had provided the services rendered by the volunteers, their salaries would have totaled $6,000.

While working for the hospital, the pinstripers received complimentary meals from the cafeteria, which normally would have cost $500.

Required:
Prepare the journal entry necessary in the General Fund to record the donated services on the books of General Hospital.

EXERCISE 20-3 **Journal Entries for a Library**

The Franklin Public Library received a restricted contribution of $300,000 in 2001. The donor specified that the money must be used to acquire books of poetry written in the sixteenth century. As of December 31, 2001, only $100,000 of the restricted resources had been expended.

Required:
Prepare the journal entries necessary to record these events during 2001. Indicate the fund in which each journal entry is recorded.

EXERCISE 20-4 **University Loan Fund**

The following events relate to Grearson University Loan Fund:

1. $100,000 is received from an estate to establish a faculty and student loan fund. Annual interest rates range from 8% for students to 10% for faculty.
2. Loans to students totaled $60,000, and $40,000 was disbursed to faculty members (of the total loans made, 10% are estimated to be uncollectible).
3. Grearson wrote off a $1,000 student loan as uncollectible.
4. The following loans were repaid.

	Principal	*Interest*
Faculty	$ 5,000	$500
Student	10,000	800

Required:

Prepare the journal entries necessary to record these transactions and indicate the fund(s) in which the transactions are recorded.

EXERCISE 20-5 Pooled Investment Fund

Hastings College pooled the individual investments of three of its funds on December 31, 2000. The recorded value and the fair market value of the investments on December 31, 2000, are presented here:

	Recorded Value	*Fair Value*
Loan fund	$121,000	$105,000
Quasi-endowment fund	128,000	147,000
Life income fund	151,000	168,000
Total	$400,000	$420,000

During 2001 the investment pool earned dividends of $12,000 and interest of $18,000 and distributed cash in these amounts to the respective funds. Realized gains on transactions of the investment pool amounted to $20,000 and were reinvested in securities held in the pool.

Required:

Prepare the journal entries that are necessary in the records of each of the funds to account for the earnings of the investment pool during 2001.

EXERCISE 20-6 Reporting Contributions

A well-known celebrity sponsored a telethon for the Help for the Blind Foundation on November 1, 2001. Pledges in the amount of $1,000,000 were called in. Using similar telethon campaigns as a basis, it is estimated that 25% of the pledges will be uncollectible.

During 2002, $700,000 of contributions from these pledges were collected. The remainder were uncollectible.

Required:

Identify the appropriate fund(s) and prepare the journal entries necessary in 2001 and 2002 to record these transactions.

EXERCISE 20-7 Endowment and Related Funds

Jefferson Hospital received money from a donor to set up an endowment fund. The following information pertains to this contribution:

2001

1. $2,000,000 was received to establish the fund. The requirements were
   (a) $100,000 of the endowment fund's income must be used for research grants each year.
   (b) The remainder of income is under the discretion of the governing board.
   (c) The principal is expendable after the donor's death. It shall be used to purchase equipment.

2. The cash received was invested in a number of securities.

2002

3. Dividends of $100,000 and interest of $300,000 were received.

4. The income was transferred to the appropriate funds.

5. Of the restricted income, only $80,000 was expended for its specified purpose during 2002.

6. The governing board specified that $200,000 of the income would be used for loans for deserving medical students.

2003

7. $180,000 was lent to medical students.

8. The donor died of cancer.

Required:

Set up headings for the following funds: Endowment, General, Specific Purpose, and Plant Replacement and Expansion. Prepare the entries necessary in each fund to record the events listed above.

EXERCISE 20-8   **Plant Fund**

After the election of a prominent political figure, the principal from a term endowment fund was expendable by Crandall University. The official was elected this year. The fund was restricted to the construction of a Political Science building annex. The following transactions occurred because of this event:

1. A transfer of $3,000,000 is made from the Endowment Fund (Term) to the Unexpended Plant Fund.

2. Construction is begun on the Political Science annex. Costs of construction during the year amounted to $1,000,000, of which $30,000 remained unpaid at the end of the year. (The financial controller does not record transfers to the Investment in Plant subgroup until a project has been completed.)

3. By the end of the following year, the annex is completed at an additional cost of $2,100,000. All costs have been paid.

4. The completed building is recorded in the Investment in Plant subgroup.

Required:

Record the journal entries for each transaction and identify the fund or fund subgroup in which each entry is recorded.

EXERCISE 20-9   **Multiple Choice**

Select the best answer for each of the following items:

1. Which of the following should be included in the current funds revenue of a not-for-profit private university?

	Tuition Waivers	*Unrestricted Bequests*
(a)	Yes	No
(b)	Yes	Yes
(c)	No	Yes
(d)	No	No

2. The current funds group of a not-for-profit private university includes which of the following subgroups?

	Term-Endowment Funds	Life-Income Funds
(a)	No	No
(b)	No	Yes
(c)	Yes	Yes
(d)	Yes	No

3. Tuition waivers for which there is *no* intention of collection from the student should be classified by a not-for-profit university as

	Revenue	Expenditures
(a)	No	No
(b)	No	Yes
(c)	Yes	Yes
(d)	Yes	No

4. Which of the following is utilized for current expenditures by a not-for-profit university?

	Unrestricted Current Funds	Restricted Current Funds
(a)	No	No
(b)	No	Yes
(c)	Yes	No
(d)	Yes	Yes

5. In the loan fund of a college or university, each of the following types of loans would be found except
   (a) Student.
   (b) Staff.
   (c) Building.
   (d) Faculty.

(*AICPA adapted*)

EXERCISE 20-10 **Multiple Choice**

Select the best answer choice for each of the following items:

1. Which of the following receipts is properly recorded as unrestricted current funds on the books of a university?
   (a) Tuition.
   (b) Student laboratory fees.
   (c) Housing fees.
   (d) Research grants.

2. The current funds group of a not-for-profit private university includes which of the following?

	Annuity Funds	Loan Funds
(a)	Yes	Yes
(b)	Yes	No
(c)	No	No
(d)	No	Yes

3. On January 2, 2001, John Reynolds established a $500,000 trust, the income from which is to be paid to Mansfield University for general operating purposes. The Wyndham National Bank was appointed by Reynolds as trustee of the fund. What journal entry is required on Mansfield's books?

(a) Memo entry only
(b) Cash 500,000
    Endowment Fund Balance 500,000
(c) Nonexpendable Endowment Fund 500,000
    Endowment Fund Balance 500,000
(d) Expendable Funds 500,000
    Endowment Fund Balance 500,000

4. For the fall semester of 2001, Cherry College assessed its students $2,300,000 for tuition and fees. The net amount realized was only $2,100,000 because of the following revenue reductions:

Refunds occasioned by class cancellations and student withdrawals	$ 50,000
Tuition remissions granted to faculty members' families	10,000
Scholarships and fellowships	140,000

How much should Cherry College report for the period for unrestricted current funds revenues from tuition and fees?

(a) $2,100,000.
(b) $2,150,000.
(c) $2,250,000.
(d) $2,300,000.

5. During the years ending June 30, 2000 and June 30, 2001, Schafer University conducted a cancer research project financed by a $2,000,000 gift from an alumnus. This entire amount was pledged by the donor on July 10, 1999, although he paid only $500,000 at that date. The gift was restricted to the financing of this particular research project. During the two-year research period, Schafer's related gift receipts and research expenditures were as follows:

	Year Ended June 30	
	2000	*2001*
Gift receipts	$700,000	$ 800,000
Cancer research restricted expenditures	900,000	1,100,000

How much gift revenue should Schafer University report in the temporarily restricted column of its statement of activities for the year ended June 30, 2001?

(a) $0.
(b) $800,000.
(c) $1,100,000.
(d) $2,000,000.

(AICPA adapted)

EXERCISE 20-11 **Multiple Choice**
Select the best answer for each of the following items:

1. Cura Foundation, a voluntary health and welfare organization, supported by contributions from the general public, included the following costs in its statement of functional expenses for the year ended December 31, 2002.

Fund raising	$500,000
Administrative	300,000
Research	100,000

Cura's functional expenses for 2002 program services included
(a) $900,000.
(b) $500,000.
(c) $300,000.
(d) $100,000.

2. Community Service Center is a voluntary welfare organization funded by contributions from the general public. During 2001 unrestricted pledges of $900,000 were received, half of which were payable in 2001 with the other half payable in 2002 for use in 2002. It was estimated that 10% of these pledges would be uncollectible. How much should Community report as net contribution revenue for 2001 with respect to the pledges?
(a) $0.
(b) $405,000.
(c) $810,000.
(d) $900,000.

3. Theresa Plato is a social worker on the staff of Community Service Center, a voluntary welfare organization. She earns $30,000 annually for a normal workload of 2,000 hours. During 2001 she contributed an additional 800 hours of her time to Community at no extra charge. How much should Community record in 2001 as contributed service expense?
(a) $12,000.
(b) $6,000.
(c) $1,200.
(d) $0.

4. The basis of accounting used by nonprofit organizations is the
(a) Cash basis.
(b) Modified accrual basis.
(c) Accrual basis.
(d) Modified cash basis.

(*AICPA adapted*)

EXERCISE 20-12   **Multiple Choice**
Select the best answer for each of the following items:

1. Which NNOs must record depreciation on exhaustible assets?
(a) Hospitals.
(b) VHWOs.
(c) ONNOs.
(d) All of the above.

2. Which statement relating to VHWOs is most nearly correct?
(a) Use modified accrual accounting practices.
(b) Report expenditures on a functional basis.
(c) Record pledges when they are received.
(d) Recognize donated services as revenue if measurable.

3. Which of the following funds of a VHWO does not have a counterpart fund in governmental accounting?
(a) Current Unrestricted Fund.
(b) Land, Building, and Equipment Fund.
(c) Agency Fund.
(d) Endowment Fund.

4. A voluntary health and welfare organization received a pledge in 2000 from a donor specifying that the amount pledged be used in 2002. The donor paid the pledge in cash in 2001. The pledge should be accounted for as
   (a) A deferred credit in the balance sheet at the end of 2000, and as support in 2001.
   (b) A deferred credit in the balance sheet at the end of 2000 and 2001, and as support in 2002.
   (c) Support in 2002.
   (d) Support in 2001, and no deferred credit in the balance sheet at the end of 2000.
   (e) None of the above.

5. Which of the following should be used in accounting for nonprofit health agencies?
   (a) Fund accounting and accrual accounting.
   (b) Fund accounting but not accrual accounting.
   (c) Accrual accounting but not fund accounting.
   (d) Neither accrual accounting nor fund accounting.

(AICPA adapted)

EXERCISE 20-13 Multiple Choice
Select the best answer for each of the following items:

1. Depreciation should be recognized in the financial statements of
   (a) Private sector proprietary (for profit) hospitals only.
   (b) Both private sector proprietary (for profit) hospitals and not-for-profit hospitals.
   (c) Both private sector proprietary (for profit) hospitals and not-for-profit hospitals, only when they are affiliated with a university.
   (d) All private sector hospitals, as a memorandum entry not affecting the statement of revenue and expenses.

2. Securities donated to a nonbusiness organization should be recorded at the
   (a) Donor's recorded amount.
   (b) Fair market value at the date of the gift.
   (c) Fair market value at the date of the gift or the donor's recorded value, whichever is lower.
   (d) Fair market value at the date of the gift or the donor's recorded value, whichever is higher.

3. The Charity Services ledger account of a nonprofit hospital is a(an)
   (a) Contra-asset account.
   (b) Expense account.
   (c) Contra-revenue account.
   (d) Loss account.

4. The restricted groupings recommended for hospitals do not include
   (a) Specific purpose funds.
   (b) Endowment funds.
   (c) Plant funds.
   (d) Plant replacement and expansion funds.

(AICPA adapted)

EXERCISE 20-14 Multiple Choice
Select the best answer for each of the following items:

1. An unrestricted pledge from an annual contributor to a not-for-profit hospital made in December 2000 and paid in cash in March 2001 would generally be credited to
   (a) Nonoperating revenue in 2000.
   (b) Nonoperating revenue in 2001.
   (c) Operating revenue in 2000.
   (d) Operating revenue in 2001.

2. A gift to a not-for-profit hospital that is not restricted by the donor should be credited directly to
   (a) Fund balance.
   (b) Deferred revenue.
   (c) Operating revenue.
   (d) Nonoperating revenue.

3. During the year ended December 31, 2001, Melford Hospital received the following donations, stated at their respective fair values:

Employee services from members of a religious group.	$100,000
Medical supplies from an association of physicians. These supplies were restricted for indigent care and were used for such purposes in 2001.	30,000

   How much revenue (both operating and nonoperating) from donations should Melford report in its 2001 statement activities?
   (a) $0.
   (b) $30,000.
   (c) $100,000.
   (d) $130,000.

4. On July 1, 2000, Lilydale Hospital's Board of Trustees designated $200,000 for expansion of outpatient facilities. The $200,000 is expected to be expended in the fiscal year ending June 30, 2003. In Lilydale's balance sheet at June 30, 2001, this cash should be classified as a $200,000
   (a) Restricted current asset.
   (b) Restricted noncurrent asset.
   (c) Unrestricted current asset.
   (d) Asset whose use is limited.

   (*AICPA adapted*)

PROBLEMS

PROBLEM 20-1 **Statement of Activities—Hospital**
The following events were recorded on the books of Mercy Hospital for the year ended December 31, 2001.

1. Revenue from patient services totaled $16,000,000. The allowance for uncollectibles was established at $3,400,000. Of the $16,000,000 revenue, $6,000,000 was recognized under cost reimbursement agreements. This revenue is subject to audit and retroactive adjustment by third-party payors (estimated adjustments are included in the allowance account).

2. Patient service revenue is accounted for at established rates on the accrual basis.

3. Other operating revenue totaled $346,000, of which $160,000 was from specific purpose funds.

4. Mercy received $410,000 in unrestricted gifts and bequests. They are recorded at fair market value when received.

5. Endowment funds earned $160,000 in unrestricted income.

6. Board designated funds earned $82,000 in income.

7. Mercy's operating expenses for the year amounted to $13,370,000. This included $500,000 in straight-line depreciation.

Required:
Prepare a statement of activities for Mercy Hospital for the year ended December 31, 2001.
(*AICPA adapted*)

PROBLEM 20-2 **Various Funds—Hospital**
On January 1, 2001, a new Board of Directors was elected for Bradley Hospital. The new board switched to a different accountant. After reviewing the hospital's books, the accountant

decided that the accounts should be adjusted. Effective January 1, 2001, the board decided that

1. Separate funds should be established for the General Fund, the Bradley Endowment Fund, and the Plant Replacement and Expansion Fund (the old balances will be reversed to eliminate them).

2. The accounts should be maintained in accordance with fund accounting principles. The balances in the general ledger at January 1, 2001, are presented here:

Cash	$ 50,000	
Investment in U.S. treasury bills	105,000	
Investment in common stock	417,000	
Interest receivable	4,000	
Accounts receivable	40,000	
Inventory	25,000	
Land	407,000	
Building	245,000	
Equipment	283,000	
Allowance for depreciation		$ 376,000
Accounts payable		70,000
Bank loan		150,000
Endowment fund balance		119,500
Other fund balances		860,500
Total	$1,576,000	$1,576,000

The following additional information is available:

1. Under the terms of the will of J. Ethington, founder of the hospital, "The principal of the bequest is to be fully invested in trust forevermore in mortgages secured by productive real estate in Central City and/or in U.S. Government securities . . . and the income therefrom is to be used to defray current expenses."

2. The Endowment Fund consists of the following:

Cash received in 1891 by bequest from Ethington	$ 81,500
Net gains realized from 1949 through 1982 from the sale of real estate acquired in mortgage foreclosures	23,500
Income received from 1983 through 2000 from 90-day U.S. treasury bill investments	14,500
Balance per general ledger on January 1, 2001	$119,500

3. The land account balance is composed of

1897 appraisal of land at $10,000 and building at $5,000, received by donation at that time. The building was demolished in 1927.	$ 15,000
Appraisal increase based on insured value in land title policies issued in 1947.	380,000
Landscaping costs for trees planted.	12,000
Balance per general ledger on January 1, 2001	$407,000

4. The building balance is composed of

Cost of present hospital building completed in January 1954, when the hospital commenced operations	$ 300,000
Adjustment to record appraised value of building in 1964.	(100,000)
Cost of elevator installed in hospital building in January 1980.	45,000
Balance per general ledger on January 1, 2001	$ 245,000

The estimated useful lives of the hospital building and the elevator when new were 50 years and 20 years, respectively.

5. The hospital's equipment was inventoried on January 1, 2001. The costs shown in the inventory agreed with the equipment account balance in the general ledger. The allowance for depreciation account at January 1, 2001, included $158,250 applicable to equipment, and that amount was determined to be accurate. All depreciation is computed on a straight-line basis.

6. A bank loan was obtained to finance the cost of new operating room equipment purchased in 1997. Interest was paid to December 31, 2000.

7. Common stock with a market value of $417,000 was donated to Bradley Hospital with the stipulation that the proceeds from the sale of the stock must be used for facilities expansion. The hospital plans to undertake expansion of its facilities next year and to sell these securities at that time.

Required:

Using the workpaper form below, prepare the entries necessary to establish the correct balances as of January 1, 2001.

Account Description	Trial Balance		Adjustments		General Fund		Endowment Fund		Plant Replacement Fund	
	Debit	Credit	Debit	Credit	Debit	Credit	Debit	Credit	Debit	Credit

(AICPA adapted)

PROBLEM 20-3   **Various Funds—University**

A partial statement of financial position of Century University is shown below.

Century University
Partial Statement of Financial Position
June 30, 2000

Assets

Current Funds	
Unrestricted	
Cash	$210,000
Accounts Receivable (less allowance for doubtful accounts, $9,000)	341,000
State Appropriations Receivable	75,000
Total Unrestricted	626,000
Restricted	
Cash	7,000
Investments	60,000
Total Restricted	67,000
Total Current	$693,000

Liabilities and Fund Balances

Current Funds	
Unrestricted	
Accounts Payable	$ 45,000
Deferred Revenues	66,000
Fund Balance	515,000
Total Unrestricted	626,000
Restricted	
Fund Balance	67,000
Total Restricted	67,000
Total Current	$693,000

During the fiscal year ended June 30, 2001, the following transactions occurred:

1. A gift of $100,000 was received from an alumnus on July 7, 2000. One-half of the gift was to be used for the purchase of books for the university's library and the rest was to be used to establish a scholarship fund per the alumnus's request. It was also requested that the income generated by the scholarship fund be awarded annually as a scholarship for a qualified disadvantaged student. The board decided that the funds for the new scholarship should be invested in savings certificates on July 20, 2000. These savings certificates were purchased on July 21, 2000.

2. Revenue for the fiscal period from student tuition and fees amounted to $1,900,000. During the fiscal year, $1,686,000 of this amount was collected; $66,000 had been collected in the prior year. The university had also received $158,000 by June 30, 2001, for fees for the session beginning July 1, 2001.

3. During the year ended June 30, 2001, the university collected $349,000 of the outstanding accounts receivable at the beginning of the year. The balance was determined to be uncollectible and was written off against the allowance account. At June 30, 2001, the allowance account was increased by $3,000.

4. Because of late student fee payments, $6,000 in interest charges were earned and collected.

5. The state appropriation was received. Another unrestricted appropriation of $50,000 was made by the state. This had not been paid to the university by the fiscal year-end.

6. An unrestricted gift of $25,000 cash was received from alumni of the university.

7. During the year, investments of $21,000 were sold for $26,000. Investment income amounting to $1,900 was received.

8. Unrestricted operating expenses were recorded at $1,777,000, $59,000 of which remains unpaid.

9. Restricted current funds of $13,000 were spent for authorized purposes during the year.

10. The accounts payable at June 30, 2000, were paid during the year.

11. During the year, $7,000 interest was earned and received on the savings certificates purchased in accordance with the board's resolution [in item (1)].

Required:

A. Prepare journal entries to record in summary form the transactions above for the year ended June 30, 2001. Each journal entry should be numbered to correspond with the transaction described above. Set up the following headings:

	Current Funds				Endowment Fund	
	Unrestricted		Restricted			
Accounts	Dr.	Cr.	Dr.	Cr.	Dr.	Cr.

B. Prepare a statement of activities for the year ended June 30, 2001.

C. Prepare a statement of activities for the current funds for the year ended June 30, 2001. Include more details about the revenues and expenses.

PROBLEM 20-4 Journal Entries—University

The following transactions of Beltville College transpired during 2001. The funds necessary are the Endowment Fund, the Annuity Fund, the Plant Fund—Unexpended, the Plant Fund—Investment in Plant, the Loan Fund, the Unrestricted Current Fund, and the Restricted Current Fund.

January 1

1. A gift of $10,000 was received from Carl Brown. The principal was to be held intact and the income to be used for any purpose designated by the governing board.

2. David Gross donated $20,000. The principal was to be held intact and the income to be used for scholarships for worthy students.

3. Roxanne Norton donated $30,000, of which the principal was to remain intact while the interest was to be used for student loans. All income is to be relent; all losses from loans are to be charged against income.

4. A gift of $205,000 was received from Brian Carr. Semiannual payments of $10,000 are to be made to the donor during his lifetime. On his death the fund is to be used to purchase or construct a students' residence. Mr. Carr has a life expectancy of five years and investments are expected to earn 8% annually.

5. Kathy Jackson donated 1,000 shares of BIM stock, which had a market value of $150 per share on that date. All income received from the shares is to be held intact and the shares cannot be held for more than five years. Once the board sells the shares, all the proceeds are to be used to build a student hospital.

6. The assets of the Brown and Gross funds were consolidated into a pooled investment account by the governing board (in proportion to the principal accounts). Electric Power Bonds worth $30,000 were purchased. The 12% interest was payable on January 1 and July 1.

7. The Norton Fund cash is used to purchase Cravit Company 10% bonds at par for $30,000. January 1 and July 1 are the interest dates.

8. With the cash from the Carr Fund, $200,000 of 8% U.S. Treasury notes was purchased at par. The interest dates are January 1 and July 1.

July 1

9. The interest has been received on all bonds and notes and has been transferred to the proper funds. Dividends of $4,000 were received from BIM stock.

10. The stipulated payment is made to Mr. Carr from the Endowment Fund.

11. Electric Power Company bonds bought at par value for $20,000 are sold at 102. The gain is added to the principal.

12. A $300 student loan was made from the Norton Fund.

October 1

13. A notice of Brian Carr's death is received. There is no liability to his estate.

14. The Gross Scholarship Fund awards a $200 scholarship.

15. $200,000 par of U.S. Treasury notes are sold for $206,000.

December 31

16. Interest on bonds is received.

17. $100 of principal and $5 of interest were repaid on the student loan.

18. A building was purchased for $250,000 using the funds available from the Carr gift. The residence hall will have a 20-year mortgage payable to account for the balance.

Required:

Using the following format, record the journal entries necessary for each event.

Event	Fund	Journal Entry

(*AICPA adapted*)

PROBLEM 20-5 **Journal Entries—Financial Statements—Library**
Preston Library, a nonprofit organization, presented the following statement of financial position and statement of activities for its fiscal year ended February 28, 2000.

Preston Library
Statement of Financial Position
February 28, 2000

Assets	Unrestricted	Temporarily Restricted
Current Assets		
Cash	$ 285,000	$80,000
Grants Receivable	80,000	
Prepaid Expenses	65,000	
Total	430,000	
Investments (at market)	1,020,000	
Land, Building, and Equipment		
(less accumulated depreciation of $50,000)	530,000	
Total Assets	$1,980,000	$80,000

Liabilities and Fund Balances		
Current Liabilities		
Accounts Payable and Accrued Expenses	$ 150,000	
Total	150,000	
Long-Term Debt	200,000	
Fund Balances	1,630,000	80,000
Total Liabilities and Fund Balances	$1,980,000	$80,000

Preston Library
Statement of Activities
For Year Ended February 28, 2000

Support and Revenue	Unrestricted	Temporarily Restricted
Support		
Grants	$ 70,000	$—0—
Gifts	300,000	80,000
Total	370,000	80,000
Revenue		
Service Fees	22,000	
Book Rentals and Fines	107,000	
Investment Income	71,000	—0—
Total	200,000	—0—
Total Support and Revenue	$ 570,000	$80,000

Expenses		
Program Services		
Circulating library	$ 212,000	
Research library	86,000	
Exhibits	20,000	
Community services	10,000	
Total	328,000	—0—
Supporting Services		
General and administrative	175,000	
Fund raising	111,000	
Total	286,000	—0—
Total Expenses	614,000	—0—
Increase (decrease) in net assets	(44,000)	80,000
Fund Balances—beginning of year	1,674,000	—0—
Fund Balances—end of year	$1,630,000	$80,000

The following transactions occurred during the fiscal year ended February 28, 2001.

1. Fees were billed as follows:

Service fees	$30,000
Book rentals	43,000
Book fines	78,000

2. $40,000 of the Grant Receivable was received. Another grant in the amount of $20,000 was promised.

3. Contributions in the amounts summarized below were received:

Unrestricted	$215,000
Restricted	108,000

4. Investment income totaled $75,000 for the year.

5. Vouchers for the year were approved as follows:

Circulating library	$189,000
Research library	74,000
Exhibits	15,000
Community services	12,000
General and administrative	166,000
Fund raising	103,000
Total	$559,000

6. During the year, $500,000 worth of vouchers were paid.

Adjustment Data

7. Accounts Payable and Accrued Expenses at February 28, 2001, should be $217,000. The difference should be allocated to the following expenses:

Research library	$5,000
General and administrative	3,000

8. Additions to the research library in the amount of $68,000 that were approved in (5) above were made in accordance with the terms of a contribution that had been received earlier and that was restricted for that purpose.

9. The current market value of the investments is $1,035,000 (no investment transactions occurred).

10. Depreciation amounted to $9,000 for the year. It should be allocated as follows:

Circulating library	$3,500
Research library	2,900
General and administrative	2,600

11. Prepaid Expenses should be $60,000. The difference should be allocated to:

Exhibits	$3,700
General and administrative	1,300

Required:

A. Prepare journal entries to record the transactions.

B. Prepare the statement of financial position and the statement of activities for the year ended February 28, 2001.

(AICPA adapted)

PROBLEM 20-6 **Statement of Financial Position**

The December 31, 2001, statement of financial position for the Blood Donors of America Foundation is presented below.

Statement of Financial Position
December 31, 2001

Assets

Cash	$ 470,000
Accounts Receivable	160,000
Allowance for Doubtful Accounts	(30,000)
Pledges Receivable	930,000
Allowance for Doubtful Pledges	(130,000)
Inventories	400,000
Investments	19,300,000
Land	1,300,000
Buildings and Improvements	46,500,000
Equipment	2,700,000
Accumulated Depreciation	(13,500,000)
Other Assets	200,000
Total Assets	$ 58,300,000

Liabilities

Accounts Payable	$ 700,000
Accrued Expenses	130,000
Deferred Revenue—Unrestricted	100,000
Deferred Capital Addition	1,600,000
Long-Term Debt	7,350,000
Total Liabilities	9,880,000

Fund Balances

Plant	29,000,000
Endowment	3,850,000
Restricted	7,300,000
Unrestricted	8,270,000
Total Fund Balances	48,420,000
Total Liabilities and Fund Balances	$ 58,300,000

Additional information concerning the statement of financial position is as follows:

1. Except for $70,000 of cash, the Endowment Fund is made up of investments only. There are no liabilities.

2. The Plant Fund has no current liabilities and includes some investments and $15,000 in cash.

3. In addition to investments, the Current Restricted Fund consists of the pledges receivable, $35,000 of accounts payable, and cash of $155,000.

Required:

Prepare a corrected statement of financial position for the Blood Donors of America Foundation at December 31, 2001, using the following columnar format:

	Current Unrestricted	Current Restricted	Plant	Endowment	Total
(Account Titles)	$	$	$	$	$

(AICPA adapted)

PROBLEM 20-7 **Investment Pool**

Three funds of the Leukemia Foundation, a nonprofit welfare organization, began an investment pool on January 1, 2002. The costs and fair market values on this date were as follows:

	Cost	Market Value
Restricted fund	$ 55,000	$ 70,000
Lambert endowment fund	215,000	210,000
Plant fund	200,000	220,000
Total	$470,000	$500,000

During 2002 the investment pool reinvested $20,000 in realized gains and received interest of $15,000 and dividends of $10,000. Interest and dividend income was distributed to the respective funds. The Plant Fund withdrew from the investment pool on December 31, 2002, when the total current market value was $540,000. It was distributed securities in the amount of its percentage share.

On January 3, 2003, the Fargot Annuity Fund entered the investment pool with investments costing $100,000 and having a current market value of $117,600. During 2003 the pool received interest of $25,000 and dividends of $15,000, which were distributed to the participating funds. Realized gains of $30,000 were reinvested in the pool.

Required:

A. Calculate the equity percentages of the contributing funds in the investment pool at January 1, 2002, and at January 3, 2003.

B. Using the format shown below, prepare entries necessary on the records of the funds that contributed securities to the investment pool to account for the earnings of the investment pool in 2002 and 2003.

Date	Fund	Journal Entry

GLOSSARY

Accretive Term applied to a business combination in which the acquirer's earnings per share increases as a result of the merger.

Accrual accounting The usual basis of accounting for profit-seeking enterprises under generally accepted accounting principles; revenues are recognized when earned, and expenses are matched against those revenues in the period of the benefit.

Adjusting entries Journal entries needed to correct any accounts of the affiliates that may be incorrect at the financial statement date, or to recognize the effects of a transaction made by one party (such as the parent), but not recorded by another party (such as a subsidiary).

Advance plan for the distribution of cash A schedule that specifies the order in which each partner will participate in sharing profit and losses and the amount of cash each partner will receive as it becomes available for distribution.

Affiliate An entity that controls, is controlled by, or is under common control with, another entity, either directly or indirectly through one or more intermediaries.

Agency funds Funds used to report resources held by the reporting government in a purely custodial capacity (assets equal liabilities). Agency funds typically involve only the receipt, temporary investment, and remittance of fiduciary resources to individuals, private organizations, or other governments.

Agency or custodial fund of an NNO Funds used to account for the assets held by an NNO (nongovernment nonbusiness organization) as a custodian for others.

American depository receipt (ADR) A depository receipt that is traded in the United States. ADRs may be sponsored or unsponsored.

Annuity and life income fund of an NNO An NNO may accept the contribution of assets to the organization on the condition that the organization make annuity payments to a specified recipient for a specified period of time (annuity fund) or that the organization pay the income earned on the contributed assets to a specified recipient during his or her lifetime (life income fund).

Appropriations The maximum expenditures that are authorized by the legislature when budgeted expenditures are enacted into law.

Articles of partnership Same as the partnership agreement.

Asset acquisition A business combination in which one corporation pays cash or issues stock or debt for the net assets of another company, and the acquired company no longer exists as a separate legal entity.

Bargain purchase A business combination in which the price paid to acquire another firm is lower than the fair value of identifiable net assets (assets minus liabilities).

Bonus method A method used when the composition of a partnership changes (such as admission of a new partner) to adjust the partners' capital accounts equitably to account for undervalued assets or the existence of implied goodwill. Under this method, the assets are not revalued (and goodwill is not recorded).

Book value method A method used to record an investment in a pooled subsidiary on the books of the parent company, analogous to the cost method under the purchase approach. The distinction is made because the investment is recorded initially at an amount equal to the book value of the subsidiary equity acquired rather than at cost.

Budgetary funds Fund entities in which the budget is formally incorporated into the accounting records.

Capital improvement special assessments Assessments levied against property owners for capital improvements that benefit them.

Capital maintenance approach An approach under which some changes in net assets are excluded from the Statement of Activities, such as capital contributions and permanently restricted contributions of financial assets.

Capital projects fund A fund used to account for financial resources to be used for the acquisition or construction of major capital facilities.

Change in net assets approach An approach, required on all governmentwide financial statements, under which all changes in net assets are reported on the Statement of Activities. There are no "balance sheet-only" transactions.

Chief operating decision maker A person whose general function (not specific title) is to allocate resources to, and assess the performance of, the segments of an enterprise.

Common costs Operating expenses incurred by the enterprise for the benefit of more than one segment.

Complete equity method A variation of the equity method, in which the reported income (loss) of the investee is adjusted for excess depreciation, goodwill amortization, and other differences implied by the investor's purchase price, in measuring the investor's income from investment.

Component units of a government Legally independent units that are within the government's control. (A school district is funded by the county, but is independent of the county; therefore, the county includes the school district as a component unit.)

Comprehensive income All changes in net assets (or equity) or an entity during the current period except those arising from investments by the owners and distributions to the owners.

Computation and Allocation Schedule A schedule used to show how the cost of an acquisition (the purchase price) is allocated to specific assets and liabilities of the subsidiary.

Conglomerate A business combination among firms in unrelated industries.

Connecting affiliates A type of indirect ownership where the parent and the parent's subsidiary both have ownership interests in a third company.

Consolidated entity (affiliated group) A group of firms consisting of a parent and all subsidiaries for which consolidated financial statements are prepared.

Consolidated financial statements The combined financial statements of a parent and its subsidiaries as one economic entity, as though the separate companies were a single company with one or more divisions or branches.

Consolidated net income A number equal to the parent company's income from its independent operations plus (minus) its share of reported subsidiary income (loss) plus or minus adjustments for the period relating to the amortization of the difference between cost and book value.

Consolidated retained earnings The retained earnings of the parent company, after reflecting any needed adjustments from the perspective of the consolidated entity. Under the complete equity method, the adjustments are already included in the books of the parent. Under the partial equity method, for example, the number is calculated as the parent company's recorded partial-equity basis retained earnings plus or minus the cumulative effect of the adjustments to date relating to the amortization of the difference between cost and book value.

Constructive retirement (of bond obligation) Extinguishment of debt from the perspective of the consolidated entity, occurring in situations such as when one affiliate purchases another affiliate's outstanding bonds from outsiders.

Consumption method for inventory Method of accounting for inventory in which the inventory is considered a financial resource (asset) and expenditures for inventory are reported on the operating statement in the period the inventory is used.

Control (effective control) The ability of an entity to direct the policies and management that guide the ongoing activities of another entity so as to increase its benefits and limit its losses from that other entity's activities. For purposes of consolidated financial statements, control involves decision-making ability not shared with others.

Controlling interest The interest of the parent company in a partially owned subsidiary. The term is also used to refer to the parent's interest in the combined profits of the parent and its subsidiary.

Corporate assets Assets maintained for general corporate purposes and not specifically used in the operations of any segment.

Cost method A method used to account for an investment in another company, in which the income from investment consists of dividends received. Under this method, the carrying value of the investment changes only when the percentage ownership changes, or when it is believed to be permanently impaired.

Current exchange rate The spot rate in effect at the end of the accounting period (i.e., the balance sheet date).

Current fund of an NNO (restricted and unrestricted). Current unrestricted funds include financial resources of an organization that may be expended at the discretion of the governing board. Current restricted funds consist of financial resources that are currently available for use in current operations, but which may be expended only for purposes specified by the donor, grantor, or other external party.

Current rate method A method of converting accounts from a foreign currency into the parent's reporting currency, in which all assets and liabilities are translated using the current exchange rate. This method is appropriate when the accounts are already measured in the functional currency (also called translation).

Debt service fund A fund used to account for the accumulation of resources for the payment of general long-term debt principal and interest.

Deferred taxes Taxes resulting from temporary differences between taxable income and income reported under generally accepted accounting principles; deferred tax liabilities represent an increase in taxes payable in future years as a result of these differences, while deferred tax assets represent a resulting decrease in taxes payable in future years.

Depository receipt (DR) A derivative instrument usually representing a certain fixed number of publicly traded shares of a non-U.S. corporation.

Derivative Financial product whose value depends on another *underlying* value of measure, but whose terms do not require the holder to own or deliver the underlying value of measure. Thus its value is *derived* from the underlying value of measure (examples include options, swaps, forwards, and futures).

Dilutive Term applied to an acquisition in which the acquirer's earnings per share decrease as a result of the combination.

Direct exchange quotation A quotation in which the exchange rate is quoted in terms of how many units of the domestic currency can be converted into one unit of foreign currency.

Direct expenses Expenses incurred in a business combination, such as accounting and consulting fees, that would not have been incurred in the absence of the combination. These types of expenses are capitalized (charged to an asset account) under purchase accounting rules.

Dissolution The change in the relation of the partners that occurs when a partner ceases to be associated with a partnership, as distinguished from the winding up of the business.

Downstream sales Sales by a parent company to one or more of its subsidiaries.

Economic unit concept A concept that emphasizes control of the whole by a single management, so that the consolidated financial statements are intended to provide information about a group of legal entities—a parent company and its subsidiaries—operating as a single unit.

Eliminating entries Journal entries that are made only on the consolidated workpaper (and not on the parent's or subsidiary's books) to cancel the effects of intercompany transactions and accounts.

Encumbrance Term applied to the financial resources of a fund when a transaction is entered into that requires the performance on the part of another party before the government becomes liable to perform its part of the transaction. (For example, placing a purchase order creates an encumbrance, but the government is not liable until the goods are received.)

Endowment fund of an NNO Category of funds that includes both pure endowment funds and term endowment funds. Pure endowment funds require that the principal be kept in perpetuity, while term endowment funds allow the principal to be spent after a particular date or event.

Enterprise fund A fund used to account for any activity for which a fee is charged to external users for goods and services.

Equity allocation rule When the par (or stated) value of the shares issued by the issuing firm in a pooling of interests exceeds the total par or stated value of the combining company's stock, the excess should be deducted first from the combined other contributed capital and then from combined retained earnings.

Equity method A method used to account for an investment in another company, in which the income from investment consists of the investor's share of the profits (losses) of the investee. Under this method, the carrying value of the investments is adjusted continually to reflect the investee's profits, losses, and dividends.

Exchange rate The ratio between a unit of one currency and the amount of another currency for which that unit can be exchanged at a particular time.

Expendable fund entity A fund entity established to account for net financial resources dedicated for specific use(s).

Expenditure Decrease in the financial resources of a fund or incurrence of a fund liability.

Father–son–grandson affiliation A type of indirect ownership where the parent has ownership interests in a subsidiary that owns a controlling interest in a third firm.

Fiduciary funds Funds that hold assets in a trustee or agency capacity for others and that cannot be used to support the government's own programs.

Financial synergy Financial advantages or benefits arising from a business combination; for example, the opportunity to file a consolidated tax return may allow profitable corporations' tax liability to be reduced by the losses of unprofitable affiliates. Also, when an acquisition is financed using debt, the interest payments are tax deductible, creating a financial synergy.

Floating rates The exchange rates between major currencies, largely determined by supply and demand factors.

Flow of current financial resources Concept under which each year is treated as a distinct event and the only measurement that is important is the source and use of funds (where funds are usually defined on a modified accrual basis). A charge to operations is generally made when goods and services are acquired rather than when the goods and services are consumed or used.

Flow of economic resources A concept or focus now required for governmentwide financial statements, which requires the accrual basis and thus recognizes economic transactions and other events when they occur, rather than only when the related inflows and outflows of cash or other financial resources occur. A charge is made to operations in the period when goods and services are used or consumed rather than when goods and services are acquired.

Forecasted transaction Expected future transaction that does not bear severe penalties for nonperformance or that is not under contract.

Foreign currency exposure The loss potential that exists as a result of uncertainty about future changes in exchange rates.

Foreign currency transaction A transaction that requires settlement in a foreign currency.

Forward exchange contract An agreement to exchange currencies of two different countries at a specified rate (the forward rate) on a stipulated future date. At the inception of the contract, the forward rate normally differs from the spot rate.

Forward rate An exchange rate quoted for future delivery of currencies exchanged.

Functional currency The currency in which a company primarily conducts its operations and generates and expends cash.

Fund accounting A system of accounting for nonbusiness organizations where the entities' resources are accounted for by individual funds.

GASB See Government Accounting Standards Board.

General corporate expense Any expense incurred for the benefit of the corporation as a whole, which cannot be reasonably allocated to any segment.

General Fixed Assets Account Group Account group used to account for all fixed assets of a governmental unit other than those fixed assets related to specific proprietary funds or trust funds. This group now includes infrastructure assets.

General fund A fund used to account for unrestricted financial resources, especially those required to be accounted for in another fund.

General Long-Term Obligation Account Group Account group used to account for all unmatured general obligation liabilities of a governmental unit other than long-term liabilities of proprietary funds and trust funds.

General partnership A partnership in which all partners are general (rather than limited). Characteristics of general partnerships include mutual agency, unlimited liability, limited life, and the right to dispose of a partnership interest.

Global depository receipt (GDR) A depository receipt that is traded globally.

Goodwill (or excess of cost over fair value) The excess of acquisition cost over the parent's equity in the fair value of the identifiable net assets of the subsidiary on the date of acquisition.

Goodwill method A method used when the composition of a partnership changes (such as admission of a new partner) to adjust the partners' capital accounts equitably to account for the existence of implied goodwill. Under this method, the goodwill is recorded, and the capital accounts of the partners responsible for creating the goodwill are credited.

Government Accounting Standards Board (GASB) The authoritative body responsible for establishing financial accounting standards for all state and local governmental bodies.

Governmentwide financial statements The Statement of Activities and the Statement of Net Assets now required to be prepared on an accrual basis listing the total activities of the government.

Hedge A purchase or sale transaction entered into to counterbalance potential losses (profits) arising from price fluctuations; a way of transferring the risk of price fluctuations from one group to another (for example, from seller to purchaser).

Historical exchange rate The spot rate in effect on the date a transaction takes place.

Horizontal combination (horizontal integration) A business combination among companies within the same industry operating at the same basic level (competitors).

Horizontal sales Sales from one subsidiary to another subsidiary.

Indirect expenses Expenses related to business combinations that are ongoing in nature, such as those incurred to maintain a mergers and acquisitions department, and that would have continued in the absence of a specific acquisition. These expenses, which also include managerial or secretarial time and overhead allocated to the merger, are expensed as incurred.

Indirect ownership A relationship created when a parent owns a subsidiary that owns an interest in another firm; i.e., the parent indirectly owns an interest in the third firm.

Infrastructure assets Immovable assets of a government such as streets, sidewalks, bridges, drains, street lights, etc.

Installment liquidation A liquidation that extends over a period of time, in which partners receive cash in installments before the total liquidation losses and total cash available are known.

Intercompany accounts (reciprocal accounts) Accounts that are maintained in the separate books of a parent and its subsidiaries that reflect a single transaction and should be eliminated in preparing the consolidated reports; for example, an ''account receivable from subsidiary'' on the books of a parent is reciprocal to an ''account payable to parent'' on the books of the subsidiary.

Interfund activity Activity between funds that includes reciprocal and nonreciprocal transactions. Reciprocal interfund activities include interfund loans and interfund services provided and used. Nonreciprocal interfund activities include interfund transfers and interfund reimbursements.

Interfund transfers See Interfund activity.

Internal service fund A fund used to account for any activity that provides goods or services to other funds, departments, or agencies of the primary government on a cost-reimbursement basis.

International Accounting Standards (IAS) Standards issued by the International Accounting Standards Committee (IASC) as part of a drive toward the global harmonization of accounting practices.

International Accounting Standards Committee (IASC) A committee whose missions are to formulate international accounting standards used in the presentation of financial statements and to promote their worldwide acceptance and observation. It consists of members from 142 accounting organizations in 103 countries.

International Federation of Accountants (IFAC) An organization of practicing international accountants that is responsible for appointing members to the IASC Board.

Investee A corporation that issues (sells) voting stock held by an investor (buyer).

Investment trust funds Funds used to report the external portion of investment pools reported by the sponsoring government.

Investor A business entity that holds an investment in voting stock of another company.

Joint and severally liable Legal action may be brought against all the partners together or against any one or more of the partners in separate suits.

Joint venture An arrangement entered into by two or more parties to accomplish a single or limited purpose for the mutual benefit of the members of the group, often to earn a profit.

Leveraged buyout (LBO) The creation by a group of employees (generally a management group) and third-party investors of a new company to acquire all the outstanding common shares of their employer company. The management group contributes whatever stock they hold to the new corporation and borrows sufficient funds to acquire the remainder of the common stock.

Limited partnership A partnership in which one or more of the partners are general and one or more are limited. Limited partners invest capital only and limit their liability for partnership obligations to the extent of the amount invested.

Liquidating dividend In the context of business combinations, dividends declared by a subsidiary in excess of its cumulative earnings since acquisition.

Loan funds of an NNO Funds used to account for loans to students and staff of colleges and universities, to hospitals, and to beneficiaries of the interests of certain ONNOs (e.g., loans to music students by symphony orchestra societies). Loan funds are generally revolving (repayments of loan balances and interest are in turn lent to other individuals).

Local currency The currency in which a foreign entity will generally measure and record its transactions, usually the currency of the country in which it is located.

Major funds of a government Funds of a government that are required to be displayed separately on the balance sheet and the statement of revenues, expenditures, and changes in fund balances. Size percentage cutoffs are used to determine the major funds.

Majority-owned subsidiary A subsidiary in which a parent or the parent's other majority-owned subsidiaries hold more than 50% of the outstanding voting stock.

Modified accrual accounting A variation of accrual accounting used by expendable fund entities. Revenues must be both measurable and available to liquidate liabilities of the current period before they are recognized. Expenditures are recognizable when an event is expected to use current spendable resources, rather than future resources.

Monetary accounts Cash and other assets and liability accounts that are to be settled in cash.

Mutual agency One of the characteristics of a general partnership; each general partner is an agent of both the partnership and every other partner. Thus a partner can bind the other partners to a contract.

Net assets An entity's assets minus liabilities.

Net assets (not-for-profit) Term replacing the label "fund balance" as historically used in not-for-profit organizations under the authority of the FASB. Net Assets are categorized into unrestricted, temporarily restricted, and permanently restricted categories.

Net monetary position Monetary assets minus monetary liabilities.

Noncontrolling interest (minority interest) The interest in the profits (losses) or net assets of a partially owned subsidiary of all shareholders other than the parent.

Nongovernment nonbusiness organizations (NNOs) NNOs include nonprofit institutions of higher education, hospitals and other healthcare providers, voluntary health and welfare organizations (VHWOs), and other nongovernment nonbusiness organizations (ONNOs).

Operating segment A component of an enterprise that may earn revenues and incur expenses, about which separate financial information is evaluated regularly by the chief operating decision maker in deciding how to allocate resources and in assessing performance.

Option A legal right to buy or sell something at a specified price, usually within a specified time period (for example, in a foreign currency option contract, the holder has the right to buy or sell a specified amount of currency according to stipulated terms).

Other financing sources Proceeds from debt issuances and transfers of financial resources to and from other funds.

Other nongovernment nonbusiness organizations (ONNOs) Wide variety of organizations taking assorted forms, ranging from cemetery organizations, civic organizations, and labor unions to performing arts organizations, political parties, private and community foundations, private elementary and secondary schools, and zoological and botanical societies.

Parent A company that controls another company, usually achieved by direct or indirect ownership of some or all of its voting stock.

Parent company concept A concept that emphasizes the interests of the parent's shareholders in such a way that the consolidated financial statements reflect those stockholder interests in the parent itself, plus their undivided interests in the net assets of the parent's subsidiaries.

"Parent only" financial statements The unconsolidated financial statements of a parent company, in which its subsidiaries are shown as investments.

Partial equity method A variation of the equity method, in which the reported income (loss) of the investee is used to measure the investor's income from investment, without adjustment.

Partnership agreement A contractual agreement between or among legally competent persons to form a voluntary partnership (may also be called a partnership contract or articles of partnership).

Pension (and other employee benefit) trust funds Funds used to report resources that are required to be held in trust for the members and beneficiaries of defined benefit pension plans, defined contribution plans, other postemployment benefit plans, or other employee benefit plans.

Permanent fund A fund used to account for resources that are legally restricted to the extent that the earnings, and not principal, can be used to support the activities of the government.

Permanently restricted net assets Endowments in which the interest may be spent but the principal must not be used.

Plant fund of an NNO Fund used to account for (1) the property and equipment owned by the organization and the net investment, (2) the accumulation of financial resources for the acquisition or replacement of property and equipment, (3) the acquisition and disposal of property and equipment, (4) liabilities relating to the acquisition of property and equipment, and (5) depreciation expense and accumulated depreciation.

Pooling of interests method A method of accounting for business combinations in which the assets and liabilities of the combining firm are carried forward at their historical book values. This method, which requires the use of stock as the medium of exchange, is sometimes justified as the uniting of two or more groups of shareholders into a single "pooled" entity, with no group being dominant.

Primary government Part of the government including the government funds and the proprietary funds, but not including component units of the government.

Private-purpose trust funds Funds used to report escheat property. These funds should be used to report all other trust agreements under which principal and income benefits individuals, private organizations, or other governments.

Pro forma statements Financial statements prepared to show the effect of planned or contemplated transactions as if they had occurred during the period covered by the financial statements; sometimes called "as if" statements.

Profit or loss agreement An agreement that indicates how a partnership's profits or losses should be allocated. Common agreements are based on a fixed ratio, a ratio based on capital balances, interest on capital balances, an allocation based on time or managerial talent, or some combination of these.

Proprietary (nonexpendable) fund entities The activities of nonbusiness organizations that operate similar to those of business enterprises, such as water utilities. Proprietary funds include enterprise and internal service funds.

Purchase method A method of accounting for business combinations in which the assets and liabilities of the acquired firm are valued at fair market values, including the recording of goodwill implied by any excess of purchase price over the net fair value.

Purchases method for inventory Method of accounting for inventory in which the inventory is not considered a financial resource (asset), and all inventory purchases are recognized as expenditures whether the inventory is used or not.

Push down accounting The establishment of a new accounting and reporting basis for a subsidiary company in its separate financial statements based on the purchase price paid by the parent company to acquire a controlling interest in the outstanding voting stock of the subsidiary company.

Reciprocal stockholdings A relationship created when two or more affiliates have ownership interests in each other; for example, the parent owns shares in a subsidiary that also owns shares in the parent.

Remeasurement gain or loss Gain or loss arising from the application of the temporal method to convert accounts from a nonfunctional foreign currency into U.S. dollars.

Remeasurement The process of translating the accounts of a foreign entity into its functional currency when they are stated in another currency (often used to refer to the temporal method).

Reportable segment A segment considered to be significant to an enterprise's operations; specifically one that has passed one of three 10% tests or has been identified as being reportable through other criteria (aggregation, for example).

Reporting currency The currency in which a company reporting entity prepares its financial statements, usually the domestic currency of the country in which the company is domiciled.

Reserve for inventory A fund balance account sometimes used under the purchases method for inventory to offset a debit to inventory.

Restricted fund entities An expendable fund whose current financial resources are limited as to use because of externally imposed restrictions.

Safe payment approach A schedule used in an installment liquidation that guarantees that before any cash is distributed to partners, the partners' remaining capital balances are sufficient to absorb any potential loss.

Segment assets Those tangible and intangible assets directly associated with, or used by, a segment, including any allocated portion of assets used jointly by more than one segment. If portions of assets are allocated internally and used by a chief operating decision maker, then those amounts should be allocated on a reasonable basis and disclosed for external reporting purposes as well.

Segment operating profit or loss All of a segment's revenue minus all operating expenses, including any allocated revenues or expenses (e.g., common costs).

Segment revenue The revenue from sales to unaffiliated customers and from intersegment sales or transfers.

Service-type special assessment An assessment levied against property owners for services that benefit them.

Settlement date Date at which a payable is paid or a receivable is collected.

Simple liquidation A procedure in which all noncash assets are converted into cash before any assets are distributed to creditors and partners.

Sound value The fair value of used assets in appraisal reports.

Special items Significant fund accounting transactions within the control of management that are either unusual or infrequent.

Special revenue fund A fund used to account for the proceeds of specific revenue sources that are legally restricted to expenditures for specified purposes.

Spot rate An exchange rate quoted for immediate delivery of a currency.

Statutory consolidation A consolidation resulting when a new corporation is formed to acquire two or more other corporations through an exchange of voting stock; the acquired corporations then cease to exist as separate legal entities.

Statutory merger A legal term referring to the loss of a subsidiary's corporate legal entity status by canceling its corporate charter. The parent takes title to the newly acquired subsidiary's assets and assumes responsibility for its liabilities, and the subsidiary ceases to exist as a separate legal entity, although it may be continued as a separate division of the acquiring company.

Stock acquisition A business combination in which one corporation pays cash or issues stock or debt for all or part of the voting stock of another company, and the acquired company remains intact as a separate legal entity.

Stock exchange ratio A ratio generally defined as the number of shares of the acquiring company to be exchanged for each share of the acquired company, thus constituting a negotiated price.

Subsidiary A company that is controlled by another company through direct or indirect ownership of some or all of its voting stock.

20-F statement A form filed annually with the Securities and Exchange Commission (SEC) by foreign firms that list in the U.S. stock exchanges.

Takeover premium The excess of the amount offered, or agreed upon, in an acquisition over the prior stock price of the acquired firm.

Temporal method A method of converting accounts from a foreign currency into the functional currency, in which monetary assets and liabilities are translated at the current exchange rate; assets and liabilities carried at historical cost are translated at historical exchange rates; and assets and liabilities carried at current values are translated at the current exchange rate (also called remeasurement).

Temporarily restricted net assets Resources that must be used for a specific purpose or in a specific time period where the restriction is donor imposed (rather than imposed by the governing board).

Tender offer An offer made directly to the shareholders of a company targeted by another company in a potential business combination. Usually published in a newspaper, a tender offer typically provides a price higher than the current market price for shares made available by a certain date.

Totally held subsidiary A subsidiary in which a parent or the parent's other majority-owned subsidiaries hold substantially all the subsidiary's outstanding equity securities and where the subsidiary is not materially indebted to any party other than the parent and/or the parent's other totally held subsidiaries.

Transaction gain or loss The gain or loss that arises from holding foreign currency receivables or payables and resulting from changes in exchange rates between the transaction date and the settlement date.

Transfer pricing The pricing of products or services between operating segments or geographic areas.

Translation Term is used in the two following ways: (1) as a generic term to apply to any restatement of foreign currency units into the reporting currency and (2) more specifically, to apply to the restatement of foreign currency units that are already measured in the functional currency into dollars (current rate method).

Translation adjustments Dual-meaning term referring either to: (1) any gains or losses resulting from the effects of converting financial statements from foreign currency into the parent's reporting currency;

or (2) those gains and losses arising from the application of the current method to convert from the functional currency into U.S. dollars.

Treasury stock method An accounting method under which a reciprocal stockholding is presented as treasury stock on the consolidated balance sheet from the perspective of the parent firm, and the noncontrolling shareholders' interest in the parent is essentially ignored.

Undistributed subsidiary income The difference between the parent's share of the subsidiary's income, which is included in consolidated net income, and the amount of dividends received from the subsidiary, which is included in its taxable income if the affiliates file separate tax returns.

Unlimited liability A feature of a general partnership, establishing that each partner is jointly and severally liable for the debts and obligations of the partnership. Thus creditors, in a liquidation, can proceed against the personal assets for recovery of claims.

Unrealized intercompany profit (loss) Profit (loss) that has not been realized from the point of view of the consolidated entity through subsequent sales to third parties and must be eliminated in the preparation of consolidated financial statements.

Unrestricted net assets Net Assets that do not meet the definition of temporarily or permanently restricted net assets and are designated to indicate their availability for general operations.

Upstream sales Sales by subsidiary companies to the parent company.

Vertical combination (vertical integration) A business combination among companies within the same industry operating at different levels (supplier and customer).

Voluntary health and welfare organizations (VHWOs) Organizations that derive their revenues from voluntary contributions of the general public to be used for purposes connected with health, welfare, or community services.

Wholly owned subsidiary A subsidiary in which all of the subsidiary's outstanding voting stock is owned by the parent and/or the parent's other wholly owned subsidiaries.

APPENDIX:
TABLES OF AMOUNTS
AND PRESENT VALUES

TABLE A1   Amount of 1

$$a = (1 + i)^n$$

(n) PERIODS	2%	2½%	3%	4%	5%	6%
1	1.02000	1.02500	1.03000	1.04000	1.05000	1.06000
2	1.04040	1.05063	1.06090	1.08160	1.10250	1.12360
3	1.06121	1.07689	1.09273	1.12486	1.15763	1.19102
4	1.08243	1.10381	1.12551	1.16986	1.21551	1.26248
5	1.10408	1.13141	1.15927	1.21665	1.27628	1.33823
6	1.12616	1.15969	1.19405	1.26532	1.34010	1.41852
7	1.14869	1.18869	1.22987	1.31593	1.40710	1.50363
8	1.17166	1.21840	1.26677	1.36857	1.47746	1.59385
9	1.19509	1.24886	1.30477	1.42331	1.55133	1.68948
10	1.21899	1.28008	1.34392	1.48024	1.62889	1.79085
11	1.24337	1.31209	1.38423	1.53945	1.71034	1.89830
12	1.26824	1.34489	1.42576	1.60103	1.79586	2.01220
13	1.29361	1.37851	1.46853	1.66507	1.88565	2.13293
14	1.31948	1.41297	1.51259	1.73168	1.97993	2.26090
15	1.34587	1.44830	1.55797	1.80094	2.07893	2.39656
16	1.37279	1.48451	1.60471	1.87298	2.18287	2.54035
17	1.40024	1.52162	1.65285	1.94790	2.29202	2.69277
18	1.42825	1.55966	1.70243	2.02582	2.40662	2.85434
19	1.45681	1.59865	1.75351	2.10685	2.52695	3.02560
20	1.48595	1.63862	1.80611	2.19112	2.65330	3.20714
21	1.51567	1.67958	1.86029	2.27877	2.78596	3.39956
22	1.54598	1.72157	1.91610	2.36992	2.92526	3.60354
23	1.57690	1.76461	1.97359	2.46472	3.07152	3.81975
24	1.60844	1.80873	2.03279	2.56330	3.22510	4.04893
25	1.64061	1.85394	2.09378	2.66584	3.38635	4.29187
26	1.67342	1.90029	2.15659	2.77247	3.55567	4.54938
27	1.70689	1.94780	2.22129	2.88337	3.73346	4.82235
28	1.74102	1.99650	2.28793	2.99870	3.92013	5.11169
29	1.77584	2.04641	2.35657	3.11865	4.11614	5.41839
30	1.81136	2.09757	2.42726	3.24340	4.32194	5.74349
31	1.84759	2.15001	2.50008	3.37313	4.53804	6.08810
32	1.88454	2.20376	2.57508	3.50806	4.76494	6.45339
33	1.92223	2.25885	2.65234	3.64838	5.00319	6.84059
34	1.96068	2.31532	2.73191	3.79432	5.25335	7.25103
35	1.99989	2.37321	2.81386	3.94609	5.51602	7.68609
36	2.03989	2.43254	2.89828	4.10393	5.79182	8.14725
37	2.08069	2.49335	2.98523	4.26809	6.08141	8.63609
38	2.12230	2.55568	3.07478	4.43881	6.38548	9.15425
39	2.16474	2.61957	3.16703	4.61637	6.70475	9.70351
40	2.20804	2.68506	3.26204	4.80102	7.03999	10.28572

8%	9%	10%	12%	15%	(n) PERIODS
1.08000	1.09000	1.10000	1.12000	1.15000	1
1.16640	1.18810	1.21000	1.25440	1.32250	2
1.25971	1.29503	1.33100	1.40493	1.52088	3
1.36049	1.41158	1.46410	1.57352	1.74901	4
1.46933	1.53862	1.61051	1.76234	2.01136	5
1.58687	1.67710	1.77156	1.97382	2.31306	6
1.71382	1.82804	1.94872	2.21068	2.66002	7
1.85093	1.99256	2.14359	2.47596	3.05902	8
1.99900	2.17189	2.35795	2.77308	3.51788	9
2.15892	2.36736	2.59374	3.10585	4.04556	10
2.33164	2.58043	2.85312	3.47855	4.65239	11
2.51817	2.81267	3.13843	3.89598	5.35025	12
2.71962	3.06581	3.45227	4.36349	6.15279	13
2.93719	3.34173	3.79750	4.88711	7.07571	14
3.17217	3.64248	4.17725	5.47357	8.13706	15
3.42594	3.97031	4.59497	6.13039	9.35762	16
3.70002	4.32763	5.05447	6.86604	10.76126	17
3.99602	4.71712	5.55992	7.68997	12.37545	18
4.31570	5.14166	6.11591	8.61276	14.23177	19
4.66096	5.60441	6.72750	9.64629	16.36654	20
5.03383	6.10881	7.40025	10.80385	18.82152	21
5.43654	6.65860	8.14028	12.10031	21.64475	22
5.87146	7.25787	8.95430	13.55235	24.89146	23
6.34118	7.91108	9.84973	15.17863	28.62518	24
6.84847	8.62308	10.83471	17.00000	32.91895	25
7.39635	9.39916	11.91818	19.04007	37.85680	26
7.98806	10.24508	13.10999	21.32488	43.53532	27
8.62711	11.16714	14.42099	23.88387	50.06561	28
9.31727	12.17218	15.86309	26.74993	57.57545	29
10.06266	13.26768	17.44940	29.95992	66.21177	30
10.86767	14.46177	19.19434	33.55511	76.14354	31
11.73708	15.76333	21.11378	37.58173	87.56507	32
12.67605	17.18203	23.22515	42.09153	100.69983	33
13.69013	18.72841	25.54767	47.14252	115.80480	34
14.78534	20.41397	28.10244	52.79962	133.17552	35
15.96817	22.25123	30.91268	59.13557	153.15185	36
17.24563	24.25384	34.00395	66.23184	176.12463	37
18.62528	26.43668	37.40434	74.17966	202.54332	38
20.11530	28.81598	41.14479	83.08122	232.92482	39
21.72452	31.40942	45.25926	93.05097	267.86355	40

TABLE A2   Present Value of 1

$$p^n = \frac{1}{(1 + i)^n} = (1 + i)^{-n}$$

(n) PERIODS	2%	2½%	3%	4%	5%	6%
1	.98039	.97561	.97087	.96154	.95238	.94340
2	.96117	.95181	.94260	.92456	.90703	.89000
3	.94232	.92860	.91514	.88900	.86384	.83962
4	.92385	.90595	.88849	.85480	.82270	.79209
5	.90573	.88385	.86261	.82193	.78353	.74726
6	.88797	.86230	.83748	.79031	.74622	.70496
7	.87056	.84127	.81309	.75992	.71068	.66506
8	.85349	.82075	.78941	.73069	.67684	.62741
9	.83676	.80073	.76642	.70259	.64461	.59190
10	.82035	.78120	.74409	.67556	.61391	.55839
11	.80426	.76214	.72242	.64958	.58468	.52679
12	.78849	.74356	.70138	.62460	.55684	.49697
13	.77303	.72542	.68095	.60057	.53032	.46884
14	.75788	.70773	.66112	.57748	.50507	.44230
15	.74301	.69047	.64186	.55526	.48102	.41727
16	.72845	.67362	.62317	.53391	.45811	.39365
17	.71416	.65720	.60502	.51337	.43630	.37136
18	.70016	.64117	.58739	.49363	.41552	.35034
19	.68643	.62553	.57029	.47464	.39573	.33051
20	.67297	.61027	.55368	.45639	.37689	.31180
21	.65978	.59539	.53755	.43883	.35894	.29416
22	.64684	.58086	.52189	.42196	.34185	.27751
23	.63416	.56670	.50669	.40573	.32557	.26180
24	.62172	.55288	.49193	.39012	.31007	.24698
25	.60953	.53939	.47761	.37512	.29530	.23300
26	.59758	.52623	.46369	.36069	.28124	.21981
27	.58586	.51340	.45019	.34682	.26785	.20737
28	.57437	.50088	.43708	.33348	.25509	.19563
29	.56311	.48866	.42435	.32065	.24295	.18456
30	.55207	.47674	.41199	.30832	.23138	.17411
31	.54125	.46511	.39999	.29646	.22036	.16425
32	.53063	.45377	.38834	.28506	.20987	.15496
33	.52023	.44270	.37703	.27409	.19987	.14619
34	.51003	.43191	.36604	.26355	.19035	.13791
35	.50003	.42137	.35538	.25342	.18129	.13011
36	.49022	.41109	.34503	.24367	.17266	.12274
37	.48061	.40107	.33498	.23430	.16444	.11579
38	.47119	.39128	.32523	.22529	.15661	.10924
39	.46195	.38174	.31575	.21662	.14915	.10306
40	.45289	.37243	.30656	.20829	.14205	.09722

8%	9%	10%	12%	15%	(n) PERIODS
.92593	.91743	.90909	.89286	.86957	1
.85734	.84168	.82645	.79719	.75614	2
.79383	.77218	.75132	.71178	.65752	3
.73503	.70843	.68301	.63552	.57175	4
.68058	.64993	.62092	.56743	.49718	5
.63017	.59627	.56447	.50663	.43233	6
.58349	.54703	.51316	.45235	.37594	7
.54027	.50187	.46651	.40388	.32690	8
.50025	.46043	.42410	.36061	.28426	9
.46319	.42241	.38554	.32197	.24719	10
.42888	.38753	.35049	.28748	.21494	11
.39711	.35554	.31863	.25668	.18691	12
.36770	.32618	.28966	.22917	.16253	13
.34046	.29925	.26333	.20462	.14133	14
.31524	.27454	.23939	.18270	.12289	15
.29189	.25187	.21763	.16312	.10687	16
.27027	.23107	.19785	.14564	.09293	17
.25025	.21199	.17986	.13004	.08081	18
.23171	.19449	.16351	.11611	.07027	19
.21455	.17843	.14864	.10367	.06110	20
.19866	.16370	.13513	.09256	.05313	21
.18394	.15018	.12285	.08264	.04620	22
.17032	.13778	.11168	.07379	.04017	23
.15770	.12641	.10153	.06588	.03493	24
.14602	.11597	.09230	.05882	.03038	25
.13520	.10639	.08391	.05252	.02642	26
.12519	.09761	.07628	.04689	.02297	27
.11591	.08955	.06934	.04187	.01997	28
.10733	.08216	.06304	.03738	.01737	29
.09938	.07537	.05731	.03338	.01510	30
.09202	.06915	.05210	.02980	.01313	31
.08520	.06344	.04736	.02661	.01142	32
.07889	.05820	.04306	.02376	.00993	33
.07305	.05340	.03914	.02121	.00864	34
.06763	.04899	.03558	.01894	.00751	35
.06262	.04494	.03235	.01691	.00653	36
.05799	.04123	.02941	.01510	.00568	37
.05369	.03783	.02674	.01348	.00494	38
.04971	.03470	.02430	.01204	.00429	39
.04603	.03184	.02210	.01075	.00373	40

TABLE A3   Amount of an Ordinary Annuity of 1

$$A_{\overline{n}|i} = \frac{(1 + i)^n - 1}{i}$$

(n) PERIODS	2%	2½%	3%	4%	5%	6%
1	1.00000	1.00000	1.00000	1.00000	1.00000	1.00000
2	2.02000	2.02500	2.03000	2.04000	2.05000	2.06000
3	3.06040	3.07563	3.09090	3.12160	3.15250	3.18360
4	4.12161	4.15252	4.18363	4.24646	4.31013	4.37462
5	5.20404	5.25633	5.30914	5.41632	5.52563	5.63709
6	6.30812	6.38774	6.46841	6.63298	6.80191	6.97532
7	7.43428	7.54743	7.66246	7.89829	8.14201	8.39384
8	8.58297	8.73612	8.89234	9.21423	9.54911	9.89747
9	9.75463	9.95452	10.15911	10.58280	11.02656	11.49132
10	10.94972	11.20338	11.46338	12.00611	12.57789	13.18079
11	12.16872	12.48347	12.80780	13.48635	14.20679	14.97164
12	13.41209	13.79555	14.19203	15.02581	15.91713	16.86994
13	14.68033	15.14044	15.61779	16.62684	17.71298	18.88214
14	15.97394	16.51895	17.08632	18.29191	19.59863	21.01507
15	17.29342	17.93193	18.59891	20.02359	21.57856	23.27597
16	18.63929	19.38022	20.15688	21.82453	23.65749	25.67253
17	20.01207	20.86473	21.76159	23.69751	25.84037	28.21288
18	21.41231	22.38635	23.41444	25.64541	28.13238	30.90565
19	22.84056	23.94601	25.11687	27.67123	30.53900	33.75999
20	24.29737	25.54466	26.87037	29.77808	33.06595	36.78559
21	25.78332	27.18327	28.67649	31.96920	35.71925	39.99273
22	27.29898	28.86286	30.53678	34.24797	38.50521	43.39229
23	28.84496	30.58443	32.45288	36.61789	41.43048	46.99583
24	30.42186	32.34904	34.42647	39.08260	44.50200	50.81558
25	32.03030	34.15776	36.45926	41.64591	47.72710	54.86451
26	33.67091	36.01171	38.55304	44.31174	51.11345	59.15638
27	35.34432	37.91200	40.70963	47.08421	54.66913	63.70577
28	37.05121	39.85980	42.93092	49.96758	58.40258	68.52811
29	38.79223	41.85630	45.21885	52.96629	62.32271	73.63980
30	40.56808	43.90270	47.57542	56.08494	66.43885	79.05819
31	42.37944	46.00027	50.00268	59.32834	70.76079	84.80168
32	44.22703	48.15028	52.50276	62.70147	75.29883	90.88978
33	46.11157	50.35403	55.07784	66.20953	80.06377	97.34316
34	48.03380	52.61289	57.73018	69.85791	85.06696	104.18376
35	49.99448	54.92821	60.46208	73.65222	90.32031	111.43478
36	51.99437	57.30141	63.27594	77.59831	95.83632	119.12087
37	54.03425	59.73395	66.17422	81.70225	101.62814	127.26812
38	56.11494	62.22730	69.15945	85.97034	107.70955	135.90421
39	58.23724	64.78298	72.23423	90.40915	114.09502	145.05846
40	60.40198	67.40255	75.40126	95.02552	120.79977	154.76197

8%	9%	10%	12%	15%	(n) PERIODS
1.00000	1.00000	1.00000	1.00000	1.00000	1
2.08000	2.09000	2.10000	2.12000	2.15000	2
3.24640	3.27810	3.31000	3.37440	3.47250	3
4.50611	4.57313	4.64100	4.77933	4.99338	4
5.86660	5.98471	6.10510	6.35285	6.74238	5
7.33592	7.52334	7.71561	8.11519	8.75374	6
8.92280	9.20044	9.48717	10.08901	11.06680	7
10.63663	11.02847	11.43589	12.29969	13.72682	8
12.48756	13.02104	13.57948	14.77566	16.78584	9
14.48656	15.19293	15.93743	17.54874	20.30372	10
16.64549	17.56029	18.53117	20.65458	24.34928	11
18.97713	20.14072	21.38428	24.13313	29.00167	12
21.49530	22.95339	24.52271	28.02911	34.35192	13
24.21492	26.01919	27.97498	32.39260	40.50471	14
27.15211	29.36092	31.77248	37.27972	47.58041	15
30.32428	33.00340	35.94973	42.75328	55.71747	16
33.75023	36.97371	40.54470	48.88367	65.07509	17
37.45024	41.30134	45.59917	55.74972	75.83636	18
41.44626	46.01846	51.15909	63.43968	88.21181	19
45.76196	51.16012	57.27500	72.05244	102.44358	20
50.42292	56.76453	64.00250	81.69874	118.81012	21
55.45676	62.87334	71.40275	92.50258	137.63164	22
60.89330	69.53194	79.54302	104.60289	159.27638	23
66.76476	76.78981	88.49733	118.15524	184.16784	24
73.10594	84.70090	98.34706	133.33387	212.79302	25
79.95442	93.32398	109.18177	150.33393	245.71197	26
87.35077	102.72314	121.09994	169.37401	283.56877	27
95.33883	112.96822	134.20994	190.69889	327.10408	28
103.96594	124.13536	148.63093	214.58275	377.16969	29
113.28321	136.30754	164.49402	241.33268	434.74515	30
123.34587	149.57522	181.94343	271.29261	500.95692	31
134.21354	164.03699	201.13777	304.84772	577.10046	32
145.95062	179.80032	222.25154	342.42945	644.66553	33
158.62667	196.98234	245.47670	384.52098	765.36535	34
172.31680	215.71076	271.02437	431.66350	881.17016	35
187.10215	236.12472	299.12681	484.46312	1014.34568	36
203.07032	258.37595	330.03949	543.59869	1167.49753	37
220.31595	282.62978	364.04343	609.83053	1343.62216	38
238.94122	309.06646	401.44778	684.01020	1546.16549	39
259.05652	337.88245	442.59256	767.09142	1779.09031	40

TABLE A4 Present Value of an Ordinary Annuity of 1

$$P_{\overline{n}|i} = \frac{1 - \dfrac{1}{(1+i)^n}}{i} = \frac{1 - v^n}{i}$$

(n) PERIODS	2%	2½%	3%	4%	5%	6%
1	.98039	.97561	.97087	.96154	.95238	.94340
2	1.94156	1.92742	1.91347	1.88609	1.85941	1.83339
3	2.88388	2.85602	2.82861	2.77509	2.72325	2.67301
4	3.80773	3.76197	3.71710	3.62990	3.54595	3.46511
5	4.71346	4.64583	4.57971	4.45182	4.32948	4.21236
6	5.60143	5.50813	5.41719	5.24214	5.07569	4.91732
7	6.47199	6.34939	6.23028	6.00205	5.78637	5.58238
8	7.32548	7.17014	7.01969	6.73274	6.46321	6.20979
9	8.16224	7.97087	7.78611	7.43533	7.10782	6.80169
10	8.98259	8.75206	8.53020	8.11090	7.72173	7.36009
11	9.78685	9.51421	9.25262	8.76048	8.30641	7.88687
12	10.57534	10.25776	9.95400	9.38507	8.86325	8.38384
13	11.34837	10.98319	10.63496	9.98565	9.39357	8.85268
14	12.10625	11.69091	11.29607	10.56312	9.89864	9.29498
15	12.84926	12.38138	11.93794	11.11839	10.37966	9.71225
16	13.57771	13.05500	12.56110	11.65230	10.83777	10.10590
17	14.29187	13.71220	13.16612	12.16567	11.27407	10.47726
18	14.99203	14.35336	13.75351	12.65930	11.68959	10.82760
19	15.67846	14.97889	14.32380	13.13394	12.08532	11.15812
20	16.35143	15.58916	14.87747	13.59033	12.46221	11.46992
21	17.01121	16.18455	15.41502	14.02916	12.82115	11.76408
22	17.65805	16.76541	15.93692	14.45112	13.16300	12.04158
23	18.29220	17.33211	16.44361	14.85684	13.48857	12.30338
24	18.91393	17.88499	16.93554	15.24696	13.79864	12.55036
25	19.52346	18.42438	17.41315	15.62208	14.09394	12.78336
26	20.12104	18.95061	17.87684	15.98277	14.37519	13.00317
27	20.70690	19.46401	18.32703	16.32959	14.64303	13.21053
28	21.28127	19.96489	18.76411	16.66306	14.89813	13.40616
29	21.84438	20.45355	19.18845	16.98371	15.14107	13.59072
30	22.39646	20.93029	19.60044	17.29203	15.37245	13.76483
31	22.93770	21.39541	20.00043	17.58849	15.59281	13.92909
32	23.46833	21.84918	20.38877	17.87355	15.80268	14.08404
33	23.98856	22.29188	20.76579	18.14765	16.00255	14.23023
34	24.49859	22.72379	21.13184	18.41120	16.19290	14.36814
35	24.99862	23.14516	21.48722	18.66461	16.37419	14.49825
36	25.48884	23.55625	21.83225	18.90828	16.54685	14.62099
37	25.96945	23.95732	22.16724	19.14258	16.71129	14.73678
38	26.44064	24.34860	22.49246	19.36786	16.86789	14.84602
39	26.90259	24.73034	22.80822	19.58448	17.01704	14.94907
40	27.35548	25.10278	23.11477	19.79277	17.15909	15.04630

8%	9%	10%	12%	15%	(n) PERIODS
.92593	.91743	.90909	.89286	.86957	1
1.78326	1.75911	1.73554	1.69005	1.62571	2
2.57710	2.53130	2.48685	2.40183	2.28323	3
3.31213	3.23972	3.16986	3.03735	2.85498	4
3.99271	3.88965	3.79079	3.60478	3.35216	5
4.62288	4.48592	4.35526	4.11141	3.78448	6
5.20637	5.03295	4.86842	4.56376	4.16042	7
5.74664	5.53482	5.33493	4.96764	4.48732	8
6.24689	5.99525	5.75902	5.32825	4.77158	9
6.71008	6.41766	6.14457	5.65022	5.01877	10
7.13896	6.80519	6.49506	5.93770	5.23371	11
7.53608	7.16073	6.81369	6.19437	5.42062	12
7.90378	7.48690	7.10336	6.42355	5.58315	13
8.24424	7.78615	7.36669	6.62817	5.72448	14
8.55948	8.06069	7.60608	6.81086	5.84737	15
8.85137	8.31256	7.82371	6.97399	5.95424	16
9.12164	8.54363	8.02155	7.11963	6.04716	17
9.37189	8.75563	8.20141	7.24967	6.12797	18
9.60360	8.95012	8.36492	7.36578	6.19823	19
9.81815	9.12855	8.51356	7.46944	6.25933	20
10.01680	9.29224	8.64869	7.56200	6.31246	21
10.20074	9.44243	8.77154	7.64465	6.35866	22
10.37106	9.58021	8.88322	7.71843	6.39884	23
10.52876	9.70661	8.98474	7.78432	6.43377	24
10.67478	9.82258	9.07704	7.84314	6.46415	25
10.80998	9.92897	9.16095	7.89566	6.49056	26
10.93516	10.02658	9.23722	7.94255	6.51353	27
11.05108	10.11613	9.30657	7.98442	6.53351	28
11.15841	10.19828	9.36961	8.02181	6.55088	29
11.25778	10.27365	9.42691	8.05518	6.56598	30
11.34980	10.34280	9.47901	8.08499	6.57911	31
11.43500	10.40624	9.52638	8.11159	6.59053	32
11.51389	10.46444	9.56943	8.13535	6.60046	33
11.58693	10.51784	9.60858	8.15656	6.60910	34
11.65457	10.56682	9.64416	8.17550	6.61661	35
11.71719	10.61176	9.67651	8.19241	6.62314	36
11.77518	10.65299	9.70592	8.20751	6.62882	37
11.82887	10.69082	9.73265	8.22099	6.63375	38
11.87858	10.72552	9.75697	8.23303	6.63805	39
11.92461	10.75736	9.77905	8.24378	6.64178	40

INDEX

ABOUT THE AUTHORS

Debra Jeter is an Associate Professor of Management in the Owen Graduate School of Management at Vanderbilt University. She received her Ph.D. in accounting from Vanderbilt University. Dr. Jeter has published articles in the *Accounting Review,* the *Journal of Accounting and Economics, Contemporary Accounting Research,* and *Accounting Horizons,* as well as in popular magazines including *Working Woman* and *Savvy.* She has co-authored one previous book, "Managerial Cost Accounting: Planning and Control," and has written chapters in others. She has taught at both the graduate and undergraduate levels, and is currently teaching financial accounting and accounting for mergers and acquisitions to MBA students.

Dr. Jeter has also taught financial accounting in the Executive International MBA program for the Vlerick School of Management in Ghent, and accounting for mergers and acquisitions in the Bank Administration Institute Conference at Vanderbilt. Debra Jeter is on the editorial board of the *Accounting Review* and *Accounting Enquiries.* She won a Dean's Award for Teaching Excellence in 1998 and was a finalist for the Webb Teaching Award in the same year. Her research interests extend to financial accounting and auditing, including earnings management, components of earnings, audit opinions, and the market for audit services. She practiced as a CPA in Columbus, Ohio, before entering academia in 1981.

Paul Chaney is an Associate Professor of Management in the Owen Graduate School of Management at Vanderbilt University. He has been at the Owen Graduate School since obtaining his Ph.D. from Indiana University in 1983. He has taught both undergraduate and graduate students, and currently teaches the core MBA accounting class and an elective financial accounting class. He has also taught extensively in executive programs, including courses in Accounting and Finance for the Non-Financial Executive and a Management Program for Physicians and Senior Health Care Administrators.

Dr. Chaney has published articles in the *Accounting Review,* the *Journal of Public Economics,* the *Journal of Business, Contemporary Accounting Research,* the *Journal of Accounting and Economics,* and *Accounting Horizons.* He has won two teaching awards, and has worked as a senior financial analyst for North American Van Lines before obtaining his doctorate.